Before You Begin

Please follow these instructions to download the book's examples and ensure you have a current web browser before you begin using this book.

Downloading the *Ajax, Rich Internet Applications and Web Development for Programmers* Source Code

The source code in *Ajax, Rich Internet Applications and Web Development for Programmers* can be downloaded as a ZIP archive file from www.deitel.com/books/ajaxfp/. After you register and log in, click the link for the examples under **Download Code Examples and Other Premium Content for Registered Users**. Extract the example files to your hard disk using a ZIP file extractor program, such as WinZip (www.winzip.com). On Windows, we suggest that you extract the files to a folder such as C:\ajaxfp_examples. On Mac OS X and Linux, we suggest that you extract the files to a folder named ajaxfp_examples in your home folder. [*Note:* If you are working in a computer lab, ask your instructor where you can save the example code.]

Web Browsers Used in This Book

We've tested every example in this book using Mozilla's Firefox 2 and Microsoft's Internet Explorer 7 web browsers. Before you begin, ensure that you have one or both of these browsers installed on your computer. Internet Explorer 7 is available only for Microsoft Windows operating systems. If you are a Windows user and do not have Internet Explorer 7, you can download it from www.update.microsoft.com using Microsoft's Windows Update service. Firefox 2 is available for most platforms. You can download Firefox 2 from www.firefox.com.

Many of the book's examples *will not work* in Internet Explorer 6. Though the examples in this book may run on other recent web browsers, such as Opera (www.opera.com) or Apple's Safari (www.apple.com/safari/), we have not tested the examples on these or any other browsers.

You are now ready to begin your web programming studies with *Ajax, Rich Internet Applications and Web Development for Programmers*. We hope you enjoy the book! If you have any questions, please feel free to email us at deitel@deitel.com. We'll respond promptly.

AJAX, Rich Internet Applications, and Web Development For Programmers

DEITEL® DEVELOPER SERIES

Deitel® Ser

How To Program Series

Internet & World Wide Web How to Program, 4/E

Java How to Program, 7/E

C++ How to Program, 6/E

C How to Program, 5/E

Visual Basic® 2005 How to Program, 3/E

Visual C#® 2005 How to Program, 2/E

Small Java™ How to Program, 6/E

Small C++ How to Program, 5/E

Advanced Java™ 2 Platform How to Program

XML How to Program

Visual C++® .NET How to Program

Perl How to Program

Python How to Program

Simply Series

Simply C++: An Application-Driven
   Tutorial Approach

Simply C#: An Application-Driven
   Tutorial Approach

Simply Java™ Programming: An
   Application-Driven Tutorial
   Approach

Simply Visual Basic® 2005: An
   Application-Driven Tutorial
   Approach, 2/E

Deitel Developer Series

AJAX, Rich Internet Applications and
   Web Development for Programmers

C# for Programmers, 2/E

Visual Basic 2005 for Programmers, 2/E

ies Page

SafariX Web Books

www.deitel.com/books/SafariX.html

C++ How to Program, 5/E & 6/E

Java How to Program, 6/E & 7/E

Simply C++: An Application-Driven
Tutorial Approach

Simply Visual Basic 2005: An Application-
Driven Tutorial Approach, 2/E

Small C++ How to Program, 5/E

Small Java How to Program, 6/E

Visual Basic 2005 How to Program, 3/E

Visual C# 2005 How to Program, 2/E

To follow the Deitel publishing program, please register for the free *Deitel® Buzz Online* e-mail newsletter at:

www.deitel.com/newsletter/subscribe.html

To communicate with the authors, send e-mail to:

deitel@deitel.com

For information on corporate on-site seminars offered by Deitel & Associates, Inc. worldwide, visit:

www.deitel.com/training/

or write to

deitel@deitel.com

For continuing updates on Prentice Hall/Deitel publications visit:

www.deitel.com
www.prenhall.com/deitel
www.InformIT.com/deitel

Check out our Resource Centers for valuable web resources that will help you master C++, other important programming languages, software and Web 2.0 topics:

www.deitel.com/ResourceCenters.html

This Book Is Safari Enabled

The Safari® Enabled icon on the cover of your favorite technology book means the book is available through Safari Bookshelf. When you buy this book, you get free access to the online edition for 45 days.

Safari Bookshelf is an electronic reference library that lets you easily search thousands of technical books, find code samples, download chapters, and access technical information whenever and wherever you need it.

To gain 45-day Safari Enabled access to this book:

- Go to http://www.prenhallprofessional.com/safarienabled
- Complete the brief registration form
- Enter the coupon code M8IP-VNEG-CZHV-DIG8-1652

If you have difficulty registering on Safari Bookshelf or accessing the online edition, please e-mail customer-service@safaribooksonline.com.

Library of Congress Cataloging-in-Publication Data

```
On file
```

© 2008 Pearson Education, Inc.

ISBN 0-13-158738-2

Text printed in the United States on recycled paper at R.R . Donnelley in Crawfordsville, Indiana.
First printing, January 2008

AJAX, Rich Internet Applications, and Web Development For Programmers

DEITEL® DEVELOPER SERIES

Paul J. Deitel
Deitel & Associates, Inc.

Harvey M. Deitel
Deitel & Associates, Inc.

PRENTICE
HALL

Upper Saddle River, NJ • Boston • Indianapolis • San Francisco
New York • Toronto • Montreal • London • Munich • Paris • Madrid
Capetown • Sydney • Tokyo • Singapore • Mexico City

Trademarks

DEITEL, the double-thumbs-up bug and DIVE INTO are registered trademarks of Deitel & Associates, Inc.

Adobe, Dreamweaver, Flex and Flash are either registered trademarks or trademarks of Adobe Systems, Inc.

Apache is a trademark of The Apache Software Foundation.

CSS, DOM, XHTML and XML are registered trademarks of the World Wide Web Consortium.

Del.icio.us and Flickr are trademarks of Yahoo! Inc.

Digg is a trademark of Digg Inc.

Firefox is a registered trademark of the Mozilla Foundation.

Google is a trademark of Google, Inc.

JavaScript, Java and all Java-based marks are trademarks or registered trademarks of Sun Microsystems, Inc. in the United States and other countries.

Microsoft, Internet Explorer, Silverlight and the Windows logo are either registered trademarks or trademarks of Microsoft Corporation in the United States and/or other countries.

MySpace is a registered trademark of MySpace.com.

UNIX is a registered trademark of The Open Group.

Ruby on Rails is a trademark of David Heinemeier Hansson.

MySQL is a registered trademark of MySQL AB.

Second Life is a registered trademark of Linden Research, Inc.

Skype is a trademark of eBay, Inc.

Web 2.0 is a service mark of CMP Media.

Wikipedia is a registered trademark of WikiMedia.

Throughout this book, trademarks are used. Rather than put a trademark symbol in every occurrence of a trademarked name, we state that we are using the names in an editorial fashion only and to the benefit of the trademark owner, with no intention of infringement of the trademark.

To Jesse James Garrett:

For recognizing that "something special was in the air" in web applications development; for coining the term "Ajax" (Asynchronous JavaScript and XML) to name that phenomenon; and for your tireless efforts in promoting Ajax— a key set of technologies defining Web 2.0.

Paul and Harvey Deitel

Deitel Resource Centers

Our Resource Centers focus on the vast amounts of free content available online. Find resources, downloads, tutorials, documentation, books, e-books, journals, articles, blogs, RSS feeds and more on many of today's hottest programming and technology topics. For the most up-to-date list of our Resource Centers, visit:

> www.deitel.com/ResourceCenters.html

Let us know what other Resource Centers you'd like to see! Also, please register for the free *Deitel® Buzz Online* e-mail newsletter at:

> www.deitel.com/newsletter/subscribe.html

Computer Science
Regular Expressions

Programming
ASP.NET 3.5
Adobe Flex
Ajax
Apex
ASP.NET Ajax
ASP.NET
C
C++
C++ Boost Libraries
C++ Game Programming
C#
Code Search Engines and Code Sites
Computer Game Programming
CSS 2.1
Dojo
Facebook Developer Platform
Flash 9
Java
Java Certification and Assessment Testing
Java Design Patterns
Java EE 5
Java SE 6
Java SE 7 (Dolphin) Resource Center
JavaFX
JavaScript
JSON
Microsoft LINQ
Microsoft Popfly
.NET
.NET 3.0
.NET 3.5
OpenGL
Perl
PHP
Programming Projects
Python
Regular Expressions
Ruby
Ruby on Rails
Silverlight

Visual Basic
Visual C++
Visual Studio Team System
Web 3D Technologies
Web Services
Windows Presentation Foundation
XHTML
XML

Games and Game Programming
Computer Game Programming
Computer Games
Mobile Gaming
Sudoku

Internet Business
Affiliate Programs
Competitive Analysis
Facebook Social Ads
Google AdSense
Google Analytics
Google Services
Internet Advertising
Internet Business Initiative
Internet Public Relations
Link Building
Location-Based Services
Online Lead Generation
Podcasting
Search Engine Optimization
Selling Digital Content
Sitemaps
Web Analytics
Website Monetization
YouTube and AdSense

Java
Java
Java Certification and Assessment Testing
Java Design Patterns
Java EE 5
Java SE 6

Java SE 7 (Dolphin) Resource Center
JavaFX

Microsoft
ASP.NET
ASP.NET 3.5
ASP.NET Ajax
C#
DotNetNuke (DNN)
Internet Explorer 7 (IE7)
Microsoft LINQ
.NET
.NET 3.0
.NET 3.5
SharePoint
Silverlight
Visual Basic
Visual C++
Visual Studio Team System
Windows Presentation Foundation
Windows Vista
Microsoft Popfly

Open Source & LAMP Stack
Apache
DotNetNuke (DNN)
Eclipse
Firefox
Linux
MySQL
Open Source
Perl
PHP
Python
Ruby

Software
Apache
DotNetNuke (DNN)
Eclipse
Firefox
Internet Explorer 7 (IE7)
Linux
MySQL
Open Source

Search Engines
SharePoint
Skype
Web Servers
Wikis
Windows Vista

Web 2.0
Alert Services
Attention Economy
Blogging
Building Web Communities
Community Generated Content
Facebook Developer Platform
Facebook Social Ads
Google Base
Google Video
Google Web Toolkit (GWT)
Internet Video
Joost
Location-Based Services
Mashups
Microformats
Recommender Systems
RSS
Social Graph
Social Media
Social Networking
Software as a Service (SaaS)
Virtural Worlds
Web 2.0
Web 3.0
Widgets

Dive Into Web 2.0 eBook
Web 2 eBook

Other Topics
Computer Games
Computing Jobs
Gadgets and Gizmos
Ring Tones
Sudoku

Contents

13 Ajax-Enabled Rich Internet Applications   411

Part 3: Rich Internet Application Client Technologies   451

14 Adobe® Flash® CS3   452

15 Adobe® Flash® CS3: Building an Interactive Game   492

16 Adobe® Flex™ 2 and Rich Internet Applications   517

Part 4: Rich Internet Application Server Technologies   568

17 Web Servers (IIS and Apache)   569

18 Database: SQL, MySQL, ADO.NET 2.0 and Java DB 585

19 PHP 606

23   Ajax-Enabled JavaServer™ Faces Web Applications   858

24   Web Services   891

Preface

... the challenges are for the designers of these applications: to forget what we think we know about the limitations of the Web, and begin to imagine a wider, richer range of possibilities. It's going to be fun.

   —Jesse James Garrett, Adaptive Path
     "Ajax: A New Approach to Web Applications"
     (adaptivepath.com/ideas/essays/archives/000385.php)

Introduction

Welcome to Internet and web programming and Web 2.0! And welcome to a walkthrough of the Web 2.0 phenomenon from the technical, business and social perspectives. We've worked hard to create what we hope you'll find to be an informative, entertaining and challenging learning experience. At Deitel & Associates, we write programming language professional books and textbooks for Prentice Hall, deliver corporate training worldwide and develop Web 2.0 Internet businesses. This book reflects today's Web 2.0, Ajax-based, Rich Internet Application-development methodologies.

The technologies you'll learn here are appropriate for experienced professionals who build substantial information systems. You'll find "industrial-strength" code examples. We have attempted to write in a clear and straightforward manner using best practices.

Perhaps most important, the book presents hundreds of working code examples and shows the outputs produced when these examples are rendered in browsers or run on computers. We present all concepts in the context of complete working programs. We call this the "live-code approach." All of the source code is available for download from

     www.deitel.com/books/ajaxfp/

under the heading "Download Code Examples and Other Premium Content for Registered Users," once you've registered and logged on to our site.

The early chapters present a carefully paced introduction to "client-side" web programming, using the popular JavaScript language and the closely related technologies of XHTML (Extensible HyperText Markup Language), CSS (Cascading Style Sheets) and the DOM (Document Object Model). The material in the JavaScript chapters presents a solid foundation for the deeper treatment of scripting in the Adobe Flash, Adobe Flex, PHP and Ruby on Rails chapters later in the book. Experienced programmers will read the early chapters quickly and find the treatment of scripting in the later chapters to be rigorous and challenging.

Today's users are accustomed to desktop applications with rich graphical user interfaces (GUIs), such as those used on Apple's Mac OS X systems, Microsoft Windows systems, various Linux systems and more. Users want applications that employ the multimedia capabilities of graphics, images, animation, audio and video. They want applications that can run on the Internet and the web and communicate with other applications. Users want to apply database technologies for storing and manipulating their business and personal data. They want applications that are not limited to the desktop or even to some local computer network, but that can integrate Internet and web components, and remote databases. Programmers want to use all these capabilities in a truly portable manner so that applications will run without modification on a variety of platforms.

In this book, we present a number of powerful software technologies that will enable you to build these kinds of systems. Early in the book we focus on building the portions of web-based applications that reside on the client side (i.e., the portions of applications that typically run in web browsers such as Mozilla's Firefox or Microsoft's Internet Explorer), using technologies such as the XHTML, JavaScript, CSS, Flash, Flex and Extensible Markup Language (XML). Later in the book we concentrate on using technologies such as web servers, databases, PHP, Ruby on Rails, ASP.NET, ASP.NET Ajax and JavaServer Faces (JSF) to build the server side of web-based applications. These portions of applications typically run on "heavy-duty" computer systems on which organizations' business-critical websites reside. By mastering the technologies in this book, you'll be able to build substantial web-based, client/server, database-intensive, "multitier" applications.

If you have questions as you read this book, send an e-mail to deitel@deitel.com—we'll respond promptly. For updates on the book and the status of all supporting software, and for the latest news on Deitel publications and services, visit www.deitel.com. Sign up at www.deitel.com/newsletter/subscribe.html for the free *Deitel® Buzz Online* e-mail newsletter and check out www.deitel.com/ResourceCenters.html for our growing list of Internet and web programming, Internet business, Web 2.0 and related Resource Centers. Each week we announce our latest Resource Centers in the newsletter.

Key Features

Here's some of the key features of *Ajax, Rich Internet Applications and Web Development for Programmers*:

- Reflects today's Web 2.0, Ajax-based, Rich Internet Application-development methodologies.

- Coverage of the two leading web browsers—Internet Explorer and Firefox. All client-side applications in the book run correctly on both browsers.

- Focus on Web 2.0 technologies and concepts.

- Chapter on Web 2.0 and Internet Business (reviewed by leaders in the Web 2.0 community).

- Focus on building Rich Internet Applications with the interactivity of desktop applications.

- Chapter on building Ajax-enabled web applications with "raw" Ajax and with the Dojo JavaScript libraries. Applications in this chapter demonstrate partial-page updates and type-ahead capabilities.

- Chapter on Adobe Flex—a Rich Internet Application framework for creating scalable, cross-platform, multimedia-rich applications for delivery within the enterprise or across the Internet.

- Chapter on rapid applications development of database-driven web applications with Ruby on Rails; also discusses developing Ajax applications with the Prototype and Script.aculo.us libraries.

- Two chapters on Adobe Flash CS3, including building a computer game.

- Significant treatment of client-side scripting with JavaScript.

- Significant treatments of XHTML DOM manipulation and JavaScript events.

- Significant treatment of XML DOM manipulation with JavaScript.

- Chapter on building SOAP-based web services with Java and REST-based web services with ASP.NET (using Visual Basic).

- Chapter on PHP 5.

- Coverage of ASP.NET, featuring ASP.NET Ajax.

- JavaServer Faces (JSF) coverage emphasizing building Ajax-enabled JSF applications.

- Client-side case studies that enable you to interact with preimplemented server-side applications and web services that we host at `test.deitel.com`.

- Case studies including Deitel Cover Viewer (JavaScript/DOM), Address Book (Ajax), Cannon Game (Flash), Weather/Yahoo! Maps Mashup (Flex), Mailing List (PHP/MySQL), Message Forum and Flickr Photo Viewer (Ruby on Rails), Guest Book and Secure Books Database (ASP.NET), Address Book with Google Maps (JavaServer Faces) and Blackjack (JAX-WS web services).

All of this has been carefully reviewed by a team of 38 distinguished industry developers and academics.

AJAX, Rich Internet Applications and Web Development for Programmers Architecture

This book focuses on Web 2.0 and Rich Internet Application (RIA) development. Our goal is to develop webtop applications that have the responsiveness, look and feel of traditional desktop applications. Deitel & Associates, Inc. has evolved into a development organization, while continuing its focus on programming languages textbook and professional book authoring, and corporate training. We're building the infrastructure for the Internet businesses we're designing and developing as part of our Web 2.0 Internet Business Initiative. This book includes discussions of many practical issues we've encountered in developing that infrastructure.

Figure 1 shows the architecture of *AJAX, Rich Internet Applications and Web Development for Programmers*. The book is divided into several parts. Chapter 1 introduces Web 2.0 from the technical, business and social perspectives, and provides a foundation for understanding Rich Internet Application development. If you are a serious web developer, you'll want to test your web applications across many browsers and platforms. The examples for the book execute correctly on both Microsoft's Internet Explorer 7 (IE7) and Mozilla's Firefox 2 (FF2) browsers. Most of the examples will also work in other browsers such as Opera and Safari, but may not work on earlier browsers. Microsoft Windows users should upgrade to IE7 and install Firefox; readers with other operating systems should install Firefox.

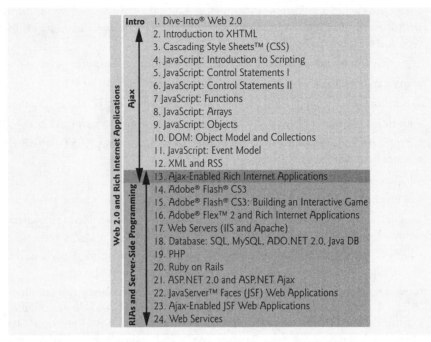

Fig. I | Architecture of *AJAX, Rich Internet Applications and Web Development for Programmers*.

The second part of the book, Chapters 2–13, presents a detailed treatment of Ajax component technologies, including a comprehensive treatment of JavaScript that spans nine chapters and concludes with Chapter 13's treatment of Ajax development. Ajax is not a new technology—we've been writing about all but one of its component technologies since 1999, and many of the technologies existed before that. However, Ajax is one of the key technologies of Web 2.0 and RIAs. Chapters 2–13 cover "raw" Ajax programming, where you'll handle the details yourself—several later chapters in the book demonstrate technologies that encapsulate Ajax functionality to help you easily build Ajax-based applications that operate across a wide variety of browsers and browser versions without your having to be concerned with the low-level details.

The third part of the book, Chapters 13–24, focuses on both the client and server sides of the GUI and the graphical part of RIA development. Here we cover client-side technologies such as Adobe Flash and Adobe Flex that use, or can be combined with, Ajax or Ajax-like capabilities to develop RIAs. Each of these technologies also can consume web services. Next, we present the server side of web application development with discussions of web servers (IIS and Apache), databases, server-side scripting languages such as PHP and Ruby on Rails, and several server-side frameworks such as ASP.NET 2.0 and Java-Server Faces. We complete our server-side discussion with a chapter on building both SOAP-based and REST-based web services.

You may have noticed that Chapter 13, Ajax-Enabled Rich Internet Applications, overlaps the second and third parts of the book. Chapter 13 serves as a bridge from "raw" Ajax development to "encapsulated" Ajax development with the Dojo libraries.

Dependency Chart

Figure 2 illustrates the dependencies that exist among chapters in the book. An arrow pointing into a chapter indicates that it depends on the content of the chapter from which the arrow points. For example, Chapter 24, Web Services, depends on both Chapters 21 and 23. We recommend that you read all of a given chapter's dependencies before reading that chapter, though other orders are possible. We've also commented on some additional dependencies in the diagram's footnotes.

Teaching Approach

AJAX, Rich Internet Applications and Web Development for Programmers contains a rich collection of examples. The book concentrates on the principles of good software engineering and stresses program clarity. We are educators who teach leading-edge topics in industry classrooms worldwide. Dr. Harvey M. Deitel has 20 years of college teaching experience and 18 years of industry teaching experience. Paul Deitel has 16 years of industry teaching experience. The Deitels have taught courses at all levels to government, industry, military and academic clients of Deitel & Associates.

Live-Code Approach. *AJAX, Rich Internet Applications and Web Development for Programmers* is loaded with "live-code" examples—each new concept is presented in the context of a complete working web application that is immediately followed by one or more screen captures showing the application's functionality. This style exemplifies the way we teach and write about programming; we call this the "live-code approach."

Syntax Shading. We syntax shade all the code, similar to the way most integrated-development environments and code editors syntax color code. This improves code readability—an important goal, given that this book contains about 18,000 lines of code in complete, working programs. Our syntax-shading conventions are as follows:

```
comments appear in italic
keywords appear in bold italic
PHP, Ruby, ASP.NET, JSP delimiters and errors appear in bold black
constants and literal values appear in bold gray
all other code appears in black
```

Code Highlighting. We place white rectangles around each program's key code segments.

Using Fonts for Emphasis. We place the key terms and the index's page reference for each defining occurrence in ***bold italic*** text for easier reference. We emphasize on-screen components in the **bold Helvetica** font (e.g., the **File** menu) and emphasize program text in the Lucida font (e.g., int x = 5).

Web Access. All of the source-code examples for *AJAX, Rich Internet Applications and Web Development for Programmers* are available for download from:

```
www.deitel.com/books/ajaxfp/
```

Site registration is quick, easy and free. Download all the examples, then run each program as you read the corresponding text discussions. Making changes to the examples and seeing the effects of those changes is a great way to enhance your Internet and web programming learning experience.

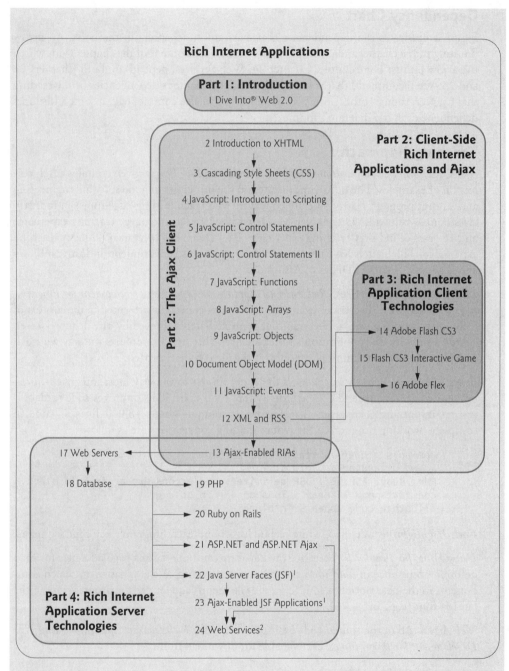

1. Chapters 22–23 require knowledge of Java Standard Edition 6.
2. Sections 24.2–24.8 require Chapters 22–22. Section 24.9 requires Chapter 21.

Fig. 2 | *AJAX, Rich Internet Applications and Web Development for Programmers* chapter dependency chart.

Objectives. Each chapter begins with a statement of objectives. This lets you know what to expect and gives you an opportunity to determine if you have met the objectives after reading the chapter.

Quotations. The learning objectives are followed by quotations. Some are humorous; some are philosophical; others offer interesting insights. We hope that you enjoy relating the quotations to the chapter material.

Outline. The chapter outline helps you approach the material in a top-down fashion, so you can anticipate what is to come and set a comfortable learning pace.

Illustrations/Figures. Abundant charts, tables, line drawings, programs and program output are included.

Programming Tips. We include programming tips to help you focus on important aspects of program development. These tips and practices represent the best we have gleaned from a combined six decades of programming and teaching experience. One of our readers told us that she feels this approach is like the highlighting of axioms, theorems and corollaries in mathematics books—it provides a basis on which to build good software.

Good Programming Practices

Good Programming Practices *call attention to techniques that will help you produce programs that are clearer, more understandable and more maintainable.*

Common Programming Errors

Programmers tend to make certain kinds of errors frequently. Pointing out these Common Programming Errors *reduces the likelihood that you'll make the same mistakes.*

Error-Prevention Tip

These tips contain suggestions for exposing bugs and removing them from your programs; many describe aspects of programming that prevent bugs from getting into programs in the first place.

Performance Tip

These tips highlight opportunities for making your programs run faster or minimizing the amount of memory that they occupy.

Portability Tip

We include Portability Tips *to help you write code that will run on a variety of platforms and to explain how to achieve a high degree of portability.*

Software Engineering Observation

The Software Engineering Observations *highlight architectural and design issues that affect the construction of software systems, especially large-scale systems.*

Thousands of Index Entries. We have included an extensive index which is especially useful when you use the book as a reference.

"Double Indexing" of Live-Code Examples. For every source-code program in the book, we index the figure caption both alphabetically and as a subindex item under "Examples." This makes it easier to find examples using particular features.

AJAX, Rich Internet Applications and Web Development for Programmers Software Downloads and Additional Resources

Many Internet and web development tools are available. We wrote *AJAX, Rich Internet Applications and Web Development for Programmers* using Internet Explorer 7, Firefox 2 and other free-for-download software. Links to additional resources and software downloads are available in our Internet and Web programming related Resource Centers:

> www.deitel.com/resourcecenters.html/

and at the website for this book:

> www.deitel.com/books/ajaxfp/

Deitel® Buzz Online Free E-mail Newsletter

Each week, the free *Deitel® Buzz Online* newsletter announces our latest Resource Center(s) and includes commentary on industry trends and developments, links to free articles and resources from our published books and upcoming publications, product-release schedules, errata, challenges, anecdotes, information on our corporate instructor-led training courses and more. It's also a good way for you to keep posted about issues related to *AJAX, Rich Internet Applications and Web Development for Programmers*. To subscribe, visit

> www.deitel.com/newsletter/subscribe.html

The Deitel Online Resource Centers

Our website, www.deitel.com, provides scores of Resource Centers on various topics including programming languages, software, Web 2.0, Internet business and open source projects (Fig. 3). The Resource Centers have evolved out of the research we do to support our books and business endeavors. We've found many exceptional resources including tutorials, documentation, software downloads, articles, blogs, podcasts, videos, code samples, books, e-books and more. Most of them are free. In the spirit of Web 2.0, we share these resources with the worldwide community. Each week we announce our latest Resource Centers in the *Deitel® Buzz Online* (www.deitel.com/newsletter/subscribe.html).

Acknowledgments

It is a great pleasure to acknowledge the efforts of many people whose names may not appear on the cover, but whose hard work, cooperation, friendship and understanding were crucial to the production of the book. Many people at Deitel & Associates, Inc. devoted long hours to this project—thanks especially to Abbey Deitel and Barbara Deitel.

We'd also like to thank the participants in our Honors Internship program who contributed to this publication—Ilana Segall, a mathematical and computational science major at Stanford University; Jennifer Fredholm, an English and computer science major at New York University; Scott Wehrwein, a computer science major at Middlebury College; Mark Kagan, a computer science, economics and math major at Brandeis University; Andrew Faden, a computer engineering major at Northeastern University; Jessica Henkel, a psychology major and business minor at Northeastern University; and Kyle Banks, a computer science and business major at Northeastern University.

Deitel Resource Centers

Programming
ASP.NET 3.5
Adobe Flex
Ajax
Apex
ASP.NET Ajax
ASP.NET
C
C++
C++ Boost Libraries
C++ Game
 Programming
C#
Code Search Engines
 and Code Sites
Computer Game
 Programming
CSS 2.1
Dojo
Facebook Developer
 Platform
Flash 9
Java
Java Certification and
 Assessment Testing
Java Design Patterns
Java EE 5
Java SE 6
Java SE 7 (Dolphin)
 Resource Center
JavaFX
JavaScript
JSON
Microsoft LINQ
Microsoft Popfly
.NET
.NET 3.0
.NET 3.5
OpenGL
Perl
PHP
Programming Projects
Python
Regular Expressions
Ruby
Ruby on Rails
Silverlight
Visual Basic
Visual C++

Visual Studio Team
 System
Web 3D Technologies
Web Services
Windows Presentation
 Foundation
XHTML
XML

Computer Science
Regular Expressions

**Games and Game
 Programming**
Computer Game
 Programming
Computer Games
Mobile Gaming
Sudoku

Internet Business
Affiliate Programs
Competitive Analysis
Facebook Social Ads
Google AdSense
Google Analytics
Google Services
Internet Advertising
Internet Business
 Initiative
Internet Public
 Relations
Link Building
Location-Based
 Services
Online Lead
 Generation
Podcasting
Search Engine
 Optimization
Selling Digital
 Content
Sitemaps
Web Analytics
Website Monetization
YouTube and AdSense

Java
Java
Java Certification and
 Assessment Testing
Java Design Patterns

Java EE 5
Java SE 6
Java SE 7 (Dolphin)
 Resource Center
JavaFX

Microsoft
ASP.NET
ASP.NET 3.5
ASP.NET Ajax
C#
DotNetNuke (DNN)
Internet Explorer 7
 (IE7)
Microsoft LINQ
.NET
.NET 3.0
.NET 3.5
SharePoint
Silverlight
Visual Basic
Visual C++
Visual Studio Team
 System
Windows Presentation
 Foundation
Windows Vista
Microsoft Popfly

**Open Source &
 LAMP Stack**
Apache
DotNetNuke (DNN)
Eclipse
Firefox
Linux
MySQL
Open Source
Perl
PHP
Python
Ruby

Software
Apache
DotNetNuke (DNN)
Eclipse
Firefox
Internet Explorer 7
 (IE7)
Linux

MySQL
Open Source
Search Engines
SharePoint
Skype
Web Servers
Wikis
Windows Vista

Web 2.0
Alert Services
Attention Economy
Blogging
Building Web
 Communities
Community
 Generated Content
Facebook Developer
 Platform
Facebook Social Ads
Google Base
Google Video
Google Web Toolkit
 (GWT)
Internet Video
Joost
Location-Based
 Services
Mashups
Microformats
Recommender
 Systems
RSS
Social Graph
Social Media
Social Networking
Software as a Service
 (SaaS)
Virtural Worlds
Web 2.0
Web 3.0
Widgets

**Dive Into Web 2.0
 eBook**

Other Topics
Computer Games
Computing Jobs
Gadgets and Gizmos
Ring Tones
Sudoku

Fig. 3 | Deitel Resource Centers at `www.deitel.com/resourcecenters.html`.

We are fortunate to have worked on this project with the talented and dedicated team of publishing professionals at Prentice Hall. We appreciate the extraordinary efforts of Marcia Horton, Editorial Director of Prentice Hall's Engineering and Computer Science Division, Mark Taub, Editor-in-Chief of Prentice Hall Professional, and John Fuller, Managing Editor of Prentice Hall Professional. Carole Snyder and Dolores Mars did a remarkable job recruiting the book's large review team and managing the review process. Sandra Schroeder and Chuti Prasertsith did a wonderful job designing the book's cover. Bob Engelhardt and Marta Samsel did a marvelous job managing the book's production.

This book was adapted from our book *Internet & World Wide Web How to Program, 4/e*. We wish to acknowledge the efforts of our reviewers on that book. Adhering to a tight time schedule, they scrutinized the text and the programs, providing countless suggestions for improving the accuracy and completeness of the presentation.

Reviewers

Roland Bouman (MySQL AB), Peter Brandano (KoolConnect Technologies, Inc.), Matt Chotin (Adobe), Chris Cornutt (PHPDeveloper.org), Phil Costa (Adobe), Umachitra Damodaran (Sun Microsystems), Vadiraj Deshpande (Sun Microsystems), Justin Erenkrantz (The Apache Software Foundation), Christopher Finke (Netscape), Jesse James Garrett (Adaptive Path), Kevin Henrikson (Zimbra.com), Tim Heuer (Microsoft), Molly E. Holtzschlag (W3C), Ralph Hooper (University of Alabama, Tuscaloosa), Johnvey Hwang (Splunk, Inc.), Joe Kromer (New Perspective and the Pittsburgh Adobe Flash Users Group), Eric Lawrence (Microsoft), Billy B. L. Lim (Illinois State University), Shobana Mahadevan (Sun Microsystems), Patrick Mineault (Freelance Flash Programmer), Anand Narayanaswamy (Microsoft), John Peterson (Insync and V.I.O., Inc.), Jennifer Powers (University of Albany), Robin Schumacher (MySQL AB), José Antonio González Seco (Parlamento de Andalucia), Dr. George Semeczko (Royal & SunAlliance Insurance Canada), Steven Shaffer (Penn State University), Tim Sneath (Microsoft), Karen Tegtmeyer (Model Technologies, Inc.), Paul Vencill (MITRE), Raymond Wen (Microsoft), Eric M. Wendelin (Auto-trol Technology Corporation), Raymond F. Wisman (Indiana University) and Daniel Zappala (Brigham Young University).

Well, there you have it! We hope you enjoy this look at the exciting world of Ajax, Rich Internet Applications and web development in a Web 2.0 world. As you read the book, we would sincerely appreciate your comments, criticisms, corrections and suggestions for improving the text. Please address all correspondence to:

deitel@deitel.com

We'll respond promptly, and post corrections and clarifications at:

www.deitel.com/books/ajaxfp/

We hope you enjoy reading *Ajax, Rich Internet Applications and Web Development for Programmers* as much as we enjoyed writing it!

Paul J. Deitel
Dr. Harvey M. Deitel
Maynard, Massachusetts

About the Authors

Paul J. Deitel, CEO and Chief Technical Officer of Deitel & Associates, Inc., is a graduate of MIT's Sloan School of Management, where he studied Information Technology. He holds the Java Certified Programmer and Java Certified Developer certifications, and has been designated by Sun Microsystems as a Java Champion. Through Deitel & Associates, Inc., he has delivered Internet and web programming, Java, C, C++, C# and Visual Basic courses to industry clients, including IBM, Sun Microsystems, Dell, Lucent Technologies, Fidelity, NASA at the Kennedy Space Center, the National Severe Storm Laboratory, White Sands Missile Range, Rogue Wave Software, Boeing, Stratus, Cambridge Technology Partners, Open Environment Corporation, One Wave, Hyperion Software, Adra Systems, Entergy, CableData Systems, Nortel Networks, Puma, iRobot, Invensys and many more. He has also lectured on Java and C++ for the Boston Chapter of the Association for Computing Machinery. He and his father, Dr. Harvey M. Deitel, are the world's best-selling programming language textbook authors.

Dr. Harvey M. Deitel, Chairman and Chief Strategy Officer of Deitel & Associates, Inc., has 46 years of experience in the computer field. Dr. Deitel earned B.S. and M.S. degrees from MIT and a Ph.D. from Boston University. He has 20 years of college teaching experience, including earning tenure and serving as the Chairman of the Computer Science Department at Boston College before founding Deitel & Associates, Inc., with his son, Paul J. Deitel. He and Paul are the co-authors of several dozen books and multimedia packages and they are writing many more. With translations published in Japanese, German, Russian, Spanish, Traditional Chinese, Simplified Chinese, Korean, French, Polish, Italian, Portuguese, Greek, Urdu and Turkish, the Deitels' texts have earned international recognition. Dr. Deitel has delivered hundreds of professional seminars to major corporations, academic institutions, government organizations and the military.

About Deitel & Associates, Inc.

Deitel & Associates, Inc., is an internationally recognized corporate training and content-creation organization specializing in computer programming languages, Internet and web software technology, object technology education and Internet business development through its Web 2.0 Internet Business Initiative. The company provides instructor-led courses on major programming languages and platforms, such as C++, Java, C, C#, Visual C++, Visual Basic, XML, object technology and Internet and web programming. The founders of Deitel & Associates, Inc. are Paul J. Deitel and Dr. Harvey M. Deitel. The company's clients include many of the world's largest companies, government agencies, branches of the military, and academic institutions. Through its 32-year publishing partnership with Prentice Hall, Deitel & Associates, Inc. publishes leading-edge programming professional books, textbooks, interactive multimedia *Cyber Classrooms, Complete Training Courses*, web-based training courses, online and offline *LiveLessons* video courses, and e-content for the popular course management systems WebCT, Blackboard and Pearson's CourseCompass. Deitel & Associates, Inc., and the authors can be reached via e-mail at:

> deitel@deitel.com

To learn more about Deitel & Associates, Inc., its publications and its worldwide *Dive Into*® Series Corporate Training curriculum, visit:

www.deitel.com

and subscribe to the free *Deitel® Buzz Online* e-mail newsletter at:

www.deitel.com/newsletter/subscribe.html

Check out the growing list of online Resource Centers at:

www.deitel.com/ResourceCenters.html

Individuals wishing to purchase Deitel publications can do so through:

www.deitel.com/books/index.html

The publisher offers excellent discounts on this book when ordered in quantity for bulk purchases or special sales, which may include electronic versions and/or custom covers and content particular to your business, training goals, marketing focus, and branding interests. For more information, please contact:

U. S. Corporate and Government Sales
(800) 382-3419
corpsales@pearsontechgroup.com

For sales outside the U. S., please contact:

International Sales
international@pearsoned.com

Visit the publisher on the Web at www.phptr.com.

1

Introduction

*The renaissance of interest in the web that we call
Web 2.0 has reached the mainstream.*

—Tim O'Reilly

1

Dive Into® Web 2.0

Network effects from user contributions are the key to market dominance in the Web 2.0 era.

—Tim O'Reilly

Link by link, click by click, search is building possibly the most lasting, ponderous, and significant cultural artifact in the history of humankind: the Database of Intentions.

—John Battelle, *The Search*

Web 2.0 is a massive social experiment...this is an opportunity to build a new kind of international understanding...citizen to citizen, person to person.

—Lev Grossman, *TIME*

One of the powerful things about networking technology like the Internet or the Web or the Semantic Web...is that the things we've just done with them far surpass the imagination of the people who invented them.

—Tim Berners-Lee, interviewed by Peter Moon, *IDG Now*

OBJECTIVES

In this chapter you will learn:

- The defining characteristics of Web 2.0.
- Why search is fundamental to Web 2.0.
- How Web 2.0 empowers the individual.
- The importance of collective intelligence and network effects.
- The significance and growth of blogging.
- Social networking, social media and social bookmarking.
- How tagging leads to folksonomies.
- How web services enable new applications to be quickly and easily "mashed up" from existing applications.
- Web 2.0 technologies.
- Web 2.0 Internet business and monetization models.
- The emerging Semantic Web (the "web of meaning").

[Note: *Chapter 1, Dive Into® Web 2.0, is also available as a free, frequently updated HTML-based e-book at* `http://www.deitel.com/freeWeb20ebook/`. *It is also available as a downloadable, fully-formatted PDF for a small fee. Check this site for the latest hyperlink-rich version. Many of the topics in this chapter are supplemented by extensive Resource Centers at* `http://www.deitel.com/ResourceCenters.html`. *The e-book and the PDF link to the Resource Centers and other web resources for further study.*]

1.1 Introduction

[*Note:* Please be sure to read the Preface for an introduction and an overview of the entire book.] We begin with the principles, applications, technologies, companies, business models and monetization strategies of Web 2.0. When the Mosaic browser was introduced in 1993, the web exploded in popularity. It continued to experience tremendous growth throughout the 1990s—a period referred to as the "dot-com bubble"; that bubble burst in 2001. In 2003 there was a noticeable shift in how people and businesses were using the web and developing web-based applications. The term *Web 2.0*—coined by *Dale Dougherty* of *O'Reilly® Media*[1] in 2003 to describe this trend—became a major media buzzword, but

---

1. O'Reilly, T. "What is Web 2.0: Design Patterns and Business Models for the Next Generation of Software." September 2005 <http://www.oreillynet.com/pub/a/oreilly/tim/news/2005/09/30/what-is-web-20.html>.

few people really know what it means. Generally, Web 2.0 companies use the web as a platform to create collaborative, community-based sites (e.g., social networking sites, blogs, wikis, etc.). Web 2.0 was popularized by the annual O'Reilly Media Web 2.0 Summit (launched in 2004), in Tim O'Reilly's defining article on Web 2.0 entitled, "What is Web 2.0: Design Patterns and Business Models for the Next Generation of Software,"[2] and in John Musser and Tim O'Reilly's for-sale report, "Web 2.0 Principles and Best Practices."[3]

The growth of Web 2.0 can be attributed to some key factors. First, hardware keeps getting cheaper and faster, with memory capacities and speeds increasing at a rapid rate. Moore's Law states that the power of hardware doubles every two years, while the price remains essentially the same.[4] This allows for development of applications with high demands that would have been previously unthinkable. Second, broadband Internet use has exploded—a Pew Internet study in March 2006 found 42% of American adults had high-speed Internet in their homes. Of the 35% of Internet users who had posted content online, 73% had broadband Internet.[5] The abundance of digital media online would never have been possible without high-speed Internet. Third, the availability of abundant open source software (see Section 1.11) has resulted in cheaper (and often free) customizable software options. This makes it easier to start new Web 2.0 companies and greatly decreases the cost of failure. Fourth, unlike in **Web 1.0** (the state of the web through the 1990s and early 2000s), there are many easy-to-employ models available to monetize Web 2.0 businesses—immediately generating (modest amounts of) revenue allows for more stable growth of new companies.

Our information on the companies in this chapter comes from common knowledge, the company websites and the footnoted books and articles.

1.2 What Is Web 2.0?

In a sense, this entire chapter defines Web 2.0, but let's begin with a brief, one-section discussion. Web 1.0 was focused on a relatively small number of companies and advertisers producing content for users to access—some people called the web at the time the "brochure web." Web 2.0 *involves* the user—not only is the content often created by users, but users help organize it, share it, remix it, critique it, update it, etc. One way to look at Web 1.0 is as a *lecture*, a small number of professors informing a large audience of students. In comparison, Web 2.0 is a *conversation*, with everyone having the opportunity to speak and share views.

Web 2.0 embraces an ***architecture of participation***—a design that encourages user interaction and community contributions.[6] You, the user, are the most important aspect

2. O'Reilly, T. "What is Web 2.0: Design Patterns and Business Models for the Next Generation of Software." September 2005 <http://www.oreillynet.com/pub/a/oreilly/tim/news/2005/09/30/what-is-web-20.html>.

3. Musser, J. and T. O'Reilly. *Web 2.0 Principles and Best Practices*. O'Reilly Media, Inc., 2006.

4. Moore, G. "Cramming More Components onto Integrated Circuits." *Electronics*, April 1965 <ftp://download.intel.com/museum/Moores_Law/Articles-Press_Releases/Gordon_Moore_1965_Article.pdf>.

5. Horrigan, J. B. "Home Broadband Adoption 2006." *Pew Internet & American Life Project*, May 2006 <http://www.pewinternet.org/pdfs/PIP_Broadband_trends2006.pdf>.

6. O'Reilly, T. "What is Web 2.0: Design Patterns and Business Models for the Next Generation of Software." September 2005 <http://www.oreillynet.com/pub/a/oreilly/tim/news/2005/09/30/what-is-web-20.html>.

of Web 2.0—so important, in fact, that in 2006, *TIME Magazine*'s "Person of the Year" was "you."[7] The article recognized the social phenomenon of Web 2.0—the shift away from a powerful few to an empowered many.

> *"We can't be device centric...we must be user centric."*
> —Bill Gates, MIX06 conference[8]

Many Web 2.0 companies are built almost entirely on user-generated content and *harnessing collective intelligence*. The significance is not just in having user-generated content, but in how it is used. Google—the leading search engine and Internet advertising company—sends its users to user-generated websites by considering what users collectively have valued in the past. For websites like MySpace®, Flickr™, YouTube and Wikipedia®, users create the content, while the sites provide the platforms. These companies *trust their users*—without such trust, users cannot make significant contributions to the sites.

> *"A platform beats an application every time."*
> —Tim O'Reilly[9]

The architecture of participation is seen in software development as well. Open source software is available for anyone to use and modify with few or no restrictions—this has played a major role in Web 2.0 development. Harnessing collective intelligence,[10] communities collaborate to develop software that many people believe is better than proprietary software.

You, the user, are not only contributing content and developing open source software, but you are also directing how media is delivered, and deciding which news and information outlets you trust. Many popular blogs now compete with traditional media powerhouses. Social bookmarking sites such as del.icio.us and Ma.gnolia allow users to recommend their favorite sites to others. Social media sites such as Digg™ or Reddit enable the community to decide which news articles are the most significant. You are also changing the way we find the information on these sites by *tagging* (i.e., labeling) web content by subject or keyword in a way that helps anyone locate information more effectively. This is just one of the ways Web 2.0 helps users identify new meaning in already existing content. RSS feeds (Chapter 12, XML and RSS) enable you to receive new information as it is updated—pushing the content right to your desktop.

The rise of *social networks* has changed the way we interact and network. MySpace—the largest social network—has rapidly become the world's most popular website. Other popular social networking sites include Facebook, Bebo, LinkedIn, and Second Life—a 3D virtual world where you interact with others via your online persona called an *avatar*.

7. Grossman, L. "TIME's Person of the Year: You." *TIME,* December 2006 <http://www.time.com/time/magazine/article/0,9171,1569514,00.html>.

8. "Bill Gates: Microsoft MIX06 Conference." *Microsoft,* March 2006 <http://www.microsoft.com/presspass/exec/billg/speeches/2006/03-20MIX.mspx>.

9. O'Reilly, T. "What is Web 2.0: Design Patterns and Business Models for the Next Generation of Software." September 2005 <http://www.oreillynet.com/pub/a/oreilly/tim/news/2005/09/30/what-is-web-20.html>.

10. O'Reilly, T. "What is Web 2.0: Design Patterns and Business Models for the Next Generation of Software." September 2005 <http://www.oreillynet.com/pub/a/oreilly/tim/news/2005/09/30/what-is-web-20.html>.

Many Web 2.0 businesses leverage the ***Long Tail***.[11] Coined by Chris Anderson in an article in the October 2004 *WIRED* magazine, the Long Tail refers to the economic model in which the market for non-hits (typically large numbers of low-volume items) could be significant and sometimes even greater than the market for big hits (typically small numbers of high-volume items).[12] So an online company like Netflix—which has a catalog of over 80,000 movie titles for rent—typically rents a large volume of less popular movies in addition to the substantial business it does renting hits. A local movie store has limited shelf space and serves a small, local population; it cannot afford the space to carry the Long Tail movies in every store. However, Netflix serves millions of people and does not have the physical constraints of stores; it can keep a small inventory of many Long Tail movies to serve its entire customer base. The opportunity to leverage the Long Tail is made possible by the relative ease of running a Web 2.0 Internet business and is fueled by the social effects of Web 2.0 that increase exposure for lesser-known products.

In this chapter, we introduce some of the key technologies used to create Web 2.0 applications. Many of these technologies are discussed in detail in the programming chapters of *Ajax, Rich Internet Applications and Web Development for Programmers*. You'll learn web development technologies, such as Ajax (Chapter 13); its component technologies, including XHTML (Chapter 2), Cascading Style Sheets (CSS, Chapter 3), JavaScript (Chapters 4–9), the Document Object Model (DOM, Chapter 10), XML (Chapter 12) and the XMLHttpRequest object (Chapter 13); and the popular Ajax toolkits—Dojo (Chapter 13) and Script.aculo.us (Chapter 20).

You'll learn how to build Rich Internet Applications (RIAs)—web applications that offer the responsiveness and rich GUI features of desktop applications. We discuss key tools for building RIAs, including Adobe's Flex (Chapter 16), ASP.NET Ajax (Chapter 21) and Sun's JavaServer Faces (Chapters 22–23). We also discuss other popular development technologies including JSON (Chapter 13), the web servers IIS and Apache (Chapter 17), MySQL (Chapter 18), PHP (Chapter 19), and ASP.NET (Chapter 21).

We discuss the emergence of web services (Chapter 24), which allow you to incorporate functionality from existing applications into your own applications quickly and easily. For example, using Amazon Web Services™, you can create a specialty bookstore and earn revenues through the Amazon Associates program; or using Google™ Maps web services with eBay web services, you can build location-based mashup applications to find auction items in certain geographical areas. Web services, inexpensive computers, abundant high-speed Internet access, open source software and many other elements have inspired new, exciting ***lightweight business models*** that people can launch with only a small investment. Some websites with robust functionality that might have required hundreds of thousands or even millions of dollars to build in the 1990s can now be built for nominal amounts of money.

Section 1.17 overviews key Web 2.0 business models, many of which are also explained in greater depth throughout the chapter. Fig. 1.1 includes a list of Web 2.0-related conferences. Some have a technology focus, while others have a business focus.

---

11. Anderson, C. *The Long Tail: Why the Future of Business Is Selling Less of More.* Hyperion, 2006.
12. Anderson, C. "The Long Tail." *WIRED*, October 2004 <http://www.wired.com/wired/archive/12.10/tail.html>.

Web 2.0 and related conferences	
AdTech	Microsoft MIX
Affiliate Marketing Summit	Microsoft Tech Ed
AjaxWorld Expo	MySQL Conference and Expo
All Things Digital	Open Source (OSCON)
Always On	RailsConf
Blog Business Summit	Search Engine Strategies
eBay Live	Tools of Change for Publishing
Emerging Technology	Ubuntu Live
Emerging Telephony	Web 2.0 Expo
Future of Online Advertising	Web 2.0 Summit
JavaOne	Where 2.0

Fig. 1.1 | Web 2.0 and related conferences.

1.3 Search

"Google's mission is to organize the world's information and make it universally accessible and useful."

—Google[13]

In Web 2.0, the saying "content is king" remains a prevailing theme. With seemingly endless content available online, the *findability* of content becomes key. *Search engines* are the primary tools people use to find information on the web. Today, you perform searches with keywords, but the future of web search will use natural language (see, for example, Powerset.com). Currently, when you enter a keyword or phrase, the search engine finds matching web pages and shows you a *search engine results page (SERP)* with recommended web pages listed and sorted by relevance. People-assisted search engines have also emerged, such as Mahalo, which pays people to develop search results.[14] The popularity of vertical search engines—ones that focus on a specific topic or industry—is on the rise, though traffic to these search engines is still far behind the major (more generalized) search engines.

Traffic to the major search engines is growing rapidly—according to a recent comScore (a web analytics company) report, Americans conducted 8 billion search queries in June 2007, up 26% from the previous year. In the same report, the comScore analysis of U.S. market share across the most popular search engines reported Google at the top with 49.5% of the U.S. search market, followed by Yahoo! with 25.1%, Microsoft with 13.2%, Ask with 5.0% and Time Warner Network with 4.2%.[15]

---

13. "Company Overview." *Google* <http://www.google.com/intl/en/corporate/index.html>.
14. "Mahalo Greenhouse FAQ." *Mahalo* <http://greenhouse.mahalo.com/Mahalo_Greenhouse_FAQ>.
15. "comScore Releases June U.S. Search Engine Rankings." *CNNMoney*, 16 July 2007 <http://money.cnn.com/news/newsfeeds/articles/prnewswire/AQM17916072007-1.htm>.

John Battelle's book *The Search: How Google and Its Rivals Rewrote the Rules of Business and Transformed Our Culture* provides an extensive history of search engines and presents strong arguments for the importance of search in almost every aspect of our personal and business lives. John Battelle's *Searchblog* discusses search and technology issues (`http://battellemedia.com`).

Attention Economy

> *"Telecommunications bandwidth is not a problem, but human bandwidth is."*
> —Thomas Davenport and John Beck, *The Attention Economy*[16]

The abundant amounts of information being produced and people's limited free time has led to an *attention economy*. More content is available than users can sort through on their own, especially given the demands on their time, such as responsibilities to children, parents, friends, employers, etc. *The Attention Economy*, by Thomas Davenport and John Beck, begins with the familiar story of a man whose attention is constantly demanded by work and family. The authors explain that the constant flow of information in today's world causes attention to continually be diverted.

Though it used to be difficult to obtain diverse content, there are now seemingly endless options competing for an audience's attention. As a result, search engines have gained popularity by helping users quickly find and filter the information they want.[17]

Google Search

Google is the leading search and online advertising company, founded by Larry Page and Sergey Brin while they were Ph.D. students at Stanford University. Google is so popular that its name has been added to the Oxford English Dictionary—the verb "Google" means to find something on the Internet using the Google search engine. ("google" with a lowercase "g" is a cricket term, whereas "googol" or 10^{100} is the mathematical term Google was named after.)[18]

Google's success in search is largely based on its *PageRank*™ algorithm (patented by Stanford University and Larry Page) and its unique infrastructure of servers that uses linked PCs to achieve faster responses and increased scalability at lower costs.[19] Estimates on the number of Google servers range from hundreds of thousands to over one million.[20] The PageRank algorithm considers the number of links into a web page and the quality of the linking sites (among other factors) to determine the importance of the page. Each inbound link is a vote saying that site is valuable to someone else; however, votes are given different weights depending on the "voter" site's own value. So, two pages could have the same PageRank even if one has numerous links in from other pages and the other has fewer links in but from pages with higher PageRank. Google search also considers all of the con-

16. Davenport, T. and J. Beck. *The Attention Economy: Understanding the New Currency of Business.* Harvard Business School Press, 2002, p.2.
17. Thompson, C. "Media in the Age of the Swarm." *cbc.ca* `<http://www.cbc.ca/10th/columns/media_thompson.html>`.
18. Brin, S. and L. Page. "The Anatomy of a Large-Scale Hypertextual Web Search Engine." `<http://infolab.stanford.edu/~backrub/google.html>`.
19. "Technology Overview." *Google* `<http://www.google.com/corporate/tech.html>`.
20. "Google: One Million and Counting." *Pandia Search Engine News*, 2 July 2007 `<http://www.pandia.com/sew/481-gartner.html>`.

tent on the page, its fonts, its headers and the content of neighboring pages.[21] Sites with the highest PageRank will appear at the top of the search results.

In addition to its regular search engine, Google offers specialty search engines for images, news, videos, blogs and more. Using Google web services, you can build Google Maps and other Google services into your applications (see Section 1.13, Web Services, Mashups, Widgets and Gadgets).

AdWords, Google's pay-per-click (PPC) contextual advertising program (launched in 2000), is the company's main source of revenue. AdWords ads appear next to search results on the Google site (and are related to the search query). Advertisers write their own ads, which are unobtrusive and uniform in appearance—each ad consists of a headline, limited text and a URL. Advertisers bid on search keywords related to their ads and pay based on the number of users who click on the ads.

AdSense is Google's advertising program for publishers (sites like `http://www.deitel.com` that offer content), inspired by Susan Wojcicki, the vice president of product management. (In 1998, Wojcicki rented a spare room in her house to Larry Page and Sergey Brin where they founded Google.)[22] AdSense is a fundamental and popular form of website monetization, particularly for Web 2.0 startup companies. Google text ads (as well as banner and rich-media ads) are placed on participating sites with related content. Click-through rates on contextual ads are often higher than on non-contextual ads because the ads reach people expressing interest in a related topic. As a result, contextual pay-per-click ads generally pay a higher eCPM (effective cost per thousand impressions).

Yahoo!

Yahoo! was started in 1994 by Jerry Yang and David Filo (also Stanford Ph.D. students) as a web directory rather than a search engine. The original site, "Jerry and David's Guide to the World Wide Web," consisted of their favorite websites manually added to a categorized directory.[23] As the web grew, maintaining the directory structure became increasingly difficult, and a search capability was created for better access to the data. Focusing more on search, Yahoo! also expanded into other areas, becoming a popular provider of e-mail, user groups and more. In 2003, Yahoo! acquired Overture (now Yahoo! Search Marketing), which was the first search engine to offer sponsored search results successfully.[24]

MSN

MSN search was created in 1998, a year after Google was launched.[25] Over the past few years, Microsoft has made search engine technology development a top priority.[26] Microsoft search query volume and its search market share grew rapidly in June 2007; analysis companies comScore and Compete attribute this boost largely to MSN's Live Search club, a program introduced in May 2007 to reward users of Live Search.[27, 28] MSN's Live

21. "Technology Overview." *Google* <http://www.google.com/corporate/tech.html>.
22. Graham, J. "The House that Helped Build Google." *USA TODAY,* 5 July 2007, 1B.
23. "Company History." *Yahoo!* <http://yhoo.client.shareholder.com/press/history.cfm>.
24. Mills, E. "Google Rises at Yahoo's Expense." *CNET,* 23 April 2007 <http://news.com.com/Google+rises+at+Yahoos+expense/2100-1038_3-6178164.html>.
25. Underwood, L. "A Brief History of Search Engines." *Web Ref* <http://www.webreference.com/authoring/search_history/>.
26. Olson, S. "MSN Launches Revamped Search Engine." *CNET,* 30 June 2004 <http://news.com.com/MSN+launches+revamped+search+engine/2100-1032_3-5254083.html>.

Search includes a new search engine, index and crawler.[29] It allows you to search the web, performing specialized searches (news, images, or local listings) or MSN content searches.[30] Another approach that Microsoft is taking to increase its search market share is buying vertical search sites such as MedStory, a health search engine.[31] Microsoft is also looking to gain market share in the contextual advertising market through Microsoft adCenter (similar to Google AdWords and Yahoo! Search Marketing).

Ask

Ask (formally known as AskJeeves.com) is owned by InterActiveCorp (IAC), which also owns Ticketmaster®, Match.com®, LendingTree.com®, RealEstate.com® and many other Internet properties. In June 2007, Ask launched a new search site, which includes a new design with a simple homepage default, customizable backgrounds, new video search (powered by Blinkx) and the ability to view video previews and listen to music clips. The search results are based on the searcher's location—Ask will report relevant local businesses and events. Searching for movies, for example, will show local show times.

Vertical Search

Vertical search engines are specialists (focusing on specific topics) in comparison to generalists (e.g., Google and Yahoo!).[32] Vertical search engines enable you to search for resources in a specific area, with the goal of providing you with a smaller number of more relevant results. Popular vertical search engines include travel sites (such as Kayak or Expedia), real-estate sites (such as Zillow or Trulia), job search sites (such as Indeed or Monster) and shopping search engines (such as Shopzilla and MySimon).

Location-Based Search

Location-based search (offered by most major search engines as well as some smaller specialized ones) uses geographic information about the searcher to provide more relevant search results. For example, search engines can ask the user for a ZIP code or estimate the user's general location based on IP address. The engine can then use this information to give higher priority to search results physically located near the user. This is particularly useful when searching for businesses such as restaurants or car services. (See Section 1.14 for more information on location-based services.)

Creating Customized Search Engines

Rollyo—a build-your-own customized search engine website—allows you to explore, create and personalize search engines ("searchrolls") created by others. This helps you narrow

---

27. "comScore Releases June U.S. Search Engine Rankings." *CNNMoney*, 16 July 2007 <http://money.cnn.com/news/newsfeeds/articles/prnewswire/AQM17916072007-1.htm>.
28. Sullivan, D. "Compete: Microsoft Gaining Searches; Live Search Club Giveaway Working?" *Search Engine Land*, 10 July 2007 <http://searchengineland.com/070710-105603.php>.
29. "MSN Live Search: About Us." *MSN* <http://search.msn.com/docs/default.aspx>.
30. "Web Search: How to use MSN Search." *MSN* <http://search.msn.com/docs/help.aspx?t=SEARCH_CONC_WhatsNewWithMSNSearch.htm>.
31. "Vertical Search-Engines: Know Your Subject." *Economist.com*, 12 July 2007 <http://www.economist.com/business/displaystory.cfm?story_id=9478224>.
32. "Vertical Search-Engines: Know Your Subject." *Economist.com*, 12 July 2007 <http://www.economist.com/business/displaystory.cfm?story_id=9478224>.

your search to sites you already trust.[33] Other custom search sites include Gigablast and Google Custom Search Engine.

Search Engine Optimization (SEO)

Search Engine Optimization (SEO) is the process of designing and tuning your website to maximize your findability and improve your rankings in organic (non-paid) search engine results. To maximize traffic, you need to take into consideration how search engines work when you design your website. There are two ways of employing SEO. The first, *white hat SEO*, refers to methods that are approved by search engines, do not attempt to deceive the search engines, and produce quality, long-term results. Top white hat techniques for SEO include: offering quality content, using proper metadata and effective keywords, and having inbound links from relevant high-quality pages.[34] *Black hat* methods are used to deceive search engines. Although they may result in temporary improvement in search engine results, these tactics could get your site banned by the search engines. A "Googlebomb" (or link bomb) is an example of a black hat method—it attempts to trick the Google algorithm into promoting a certain page (generally for humorous reasons).[35]

Link Building

Link building is the process of increasing search engine rankings and traffic by generating inbound links to a particular website. Search engine algorithms regard each link as a vote for the destination website's content, so sites with the greatest *link popularity* (or number of high-quality inbound links) appear highest on search engine result pages (SERPs). The three most practiced methods of building links include reciprocal linking, link baiting and natural linking. *Reciprocal linking* is an exchange in which two related websites link to each other, increasing the link popularity of both sites and adding value for site users. *Link baiting* involves creating attention-grabbing web content specifically for viral (exponentially increasing) exposure through social media and social bookmarking websites. *Natural linking* is the process of building one-way inbound links by optimizing website content and user experience without the explicit solicitation of a backlink. Search algorithms are continuously updated to prevent black hat SEOs from deceiving search engines with automated linking software and links from directories or other low-quality websites. One-way links from websites with strong, related pages are given greater weight than reciprocal links, links from sites with unrelated content or links from sites with low PageRank.

Search Engine Marketing (SEM)

Search Engine Marketing (SEM) is the method of promoting your website to increase traffic and search results by raising the site's visibility on search engine results pages. Danny Sullivan (founder of Search Engine Watch and, more recently, Search Engine Land) introduced the term "Search Engine Marketing" in 2001 to include SEO, managing paid listings, developing online marketing strategies and submitting sites to directories.[36] SEO is the most popular form of search engine marketing, which continues to take away business from other marketing channels (especially offline sources). According to the

---

33. "About Rollyo." *Rollyo* <http://www.rollyo.com/about.html>.
34. Wilding, R. "Top 5 Black Hat and White Hat Search Engines Optimisation Techniques."*PushON* <http://www.pushon.co.uk/articles/top5-black-hat-white-hat-seo.htm>.
35. Calore, M. "Remembering the First Google Bomb." *Compiler (WIRED blog)*, 26 January 2007 <http://blog.wired.com/monkeybites/2007/01/earlier_today_m.html>.

Search Engine Marketing Professional Organization's annual State of Search Engine Marketing survey, North American advertisers spent $9.4 billion on search engine marketing in 2006, a 62% increase over 2005 spending.[37]

Search Engine Watch and Search Engine Land

Search Engine Watch is a search engine marketing resource site. It includes articles, tutorials, conferences and more. The site, launched in 1997 by Danny Sullivan, was inspired by his 1996 release of "A Webmaster's Guide To Search Engines." Search Engine Watch incorporates Web 2.0 features (blogging and forums in addition to expert columnist articles). Other Search Engine Watch departments include search engine submission tips, web searching tips, popular search engines and search engine resources (numerous topics related to search engines). Danny Sullivan served as Search Engine Watch's editor-in-chief until November 2006, when he left the site and became the editor-in-chief for *Search Engine Land*. The site provides news and information on the major search engines—Google, Yahoo!, and Microsoft—as well as search engine marketing and searching issues. The site also informs users of upcoming related conferences and webcasts.

Search Engine Strategies Conferences

Search Engine Strategies is a global conference series focused on search engine advertising (including current SEO and SEM issues). Search Engine Strategies (hosted by Search Engine Watch) offers event information given by the top experts in the field as well as representatives from search engine companies.[38] Because traffic and advertising are so important to most Web 2.0 businesses, understanding the search process and making sure your site is easily found is vital.

Discovery

Rather than the traditional use of search engines (searching with a topic in mind), *discovery* refers to finding new content you would not have otherwise sought out. For example, Yahoo!'s original directory design allowed users to browse categories, and discover new interesting sites. StumbleUpon, a social bookmarking site, addresses discovery with its recommendation system that helps you discover and share websites based on your interests. Content networks also direct users to web content they would not necessarily have looked for otherwise.

1.4 Content Networks

Content networks are websites or collections of websites that provide information in various forms (such as articles, wikis, blogs, etc.). These provide another way of filtering the vast amounts of information on the Internet, by allowing users to go to a trusted site that has already sorted through many sources to find the best content or has provided its own content. Figure 1.2 shows some examples of content networks.

---

36. Sullivan, D. "Congratulations! You're a Search Engine Marketer!" *Search Engine Watch*, 5 November 2005 <http://searchenginewatch.com/showPage.html?page=2164351>.

37. Sherman, C. "The State of Search Engine Marketing 2006." *Search Engine Land*, 8 February 2007 <http://searchengineland.com/070208-095009.php>.

38. *Search Engine Strategies: Conference & Expos*, 2007 <http://www.searchenginestrategies.com>.

Content networks

About.com—Acquired by the *New York Times*, About is a collection of information on a wide variety of topics. About was founded in 1996 and provides over 500 guides written by topic experts. The guides include new content as well as links to other websites.

b5media—A blog network with over 200 blogs related to travel, entertainment, technology and more.

Corante—A blog network authored by leading commentators in technology, business, law, science, and culture.

Deitel—Deitel Resource Centers (currently about 80 sites and growing rapidly) include links to, and descriptions of, key tutorials, demos, free software tools, articles, e-books, whitepapers, videos, podcasts, blogs, RSS feeds and more. Resource Centers are grouped into major topic areas, including Web 2.0, Internet business, programming languages, software development and open source. See Fig. 3 in the Preface for a complete list of Resource Centers.

eHow—eHow claims over 35,000 articles explaining "how to do just about everything." The articles are written by members, and the site also features a section of "how to" videos.

Gawker Media—A blog network that includes 14 blogs, such as Gizmodo, Gawker, Valleywag and Lifehacker. The blogs cover a range of topics including technology, gossip and more.

HowStuffWorks—HowStuffWorks offers articles explaining "how the world actually works." Articles are written by freelance writers, and experts from *Consumer Guide* and *Mobil Travel Guide*.

LifeTips—LifeTips provides short articles on both work and general life issues from hundreds of writers. Tips are voted on by readers (who can also mark their favorites for easy access).

9rules—A blog network with a wide range of blog topics. The site also includes social networking aspects.

Suite101—Suite101 offers thousands of articles on a variety of topics written by freelance writers. In addition to the articles, the site also provides discussion areas and free courses.

Weblogs, Inc.—A blog network of 90 blogs, including Engadget, Autoblog and Joystiq. Users can apply to write for one of the blogs (and get paid) or suggest topics for potential new blogs.

Fig. 1.2 | Content networks.

1.5 User-Generated Content

User-generated content has been the key to success for many of today's leading Web 2.0 companies, such as Amazon, eBay and Monster. The community adds value to these sites, which, in many cases, are almost entirely built on user-generated content. For example, *eBay* (an online auction site) relies on the community to buy and sell auction items, and *Monster* (a job search engine) connects job seekers with employers and recruiters.

User-generated content includes explicitly generated content such as articles, home videos and photos. It can also include implicitly generated content—information that is gathered from the users' actions online. For example, every product you buy from Amazon and every video you watch on YouTube provides these sites with valuable information about your interests. Companies like Amazon have developed massive databases of anonymous user data to understand how users interact with their site. For example, Amazon uses your purchase history and compares it to purchases made by other users with similar interests to make personalized recommendations (e.g., "customers who bought this item also bought..."). Implicitly generated content is often considered hidden content. For example, web links and tags are hidden content; every site you link to from your own site or bookmark on a social bookmarking site could be considered a vote for that site's importance. Search engines such as Google (which uses the PageRank algorithm) use the number and quality of these links to a site to determine the importance of a site in search results.

Collective Intelligence

Collective intelligence is the concept that collaboration can result in smart ideas. Working together, users combine their knowledge for everyone's benefit.

The first chapter of *Wikinomics*, by Don Tapscott and Anthony D. Williams, tells the Goldcorp story. Inspired by the community efforts in Linux, the CEO of Goldcorp released to the public proprietary geological information about the company's land. Goldcorp offered cash rewards to people who could use this information to help the company locate gold on the land. The community helped his company find 8 million ounces of gold, catapulting Goldcorp from $100 million in stock equity to $9 billion.[39] Goldcorp reaped amazing benefits by sharing information and encouraging community participation.

User-generated content is significant to Web 2.0 companies because of the innovative ways companies are harnessing collective intelligence. We've already discussed Google's PageRank (Section 1.3), which is a product of collective intelligence. Amazon's and Last.fm's personalized recommendations also result from collective intelligence, as algorithms evaluate user preferences to provide you with a better experience by helping you discover new products or music preferred by other people with similar interests. Wesabe is a web community where members share their decisions about money and savings—the site uses the collective financial experiences of the community to create recommendations.[40] Reputation systems (used by companies like eBay) also use collective intelligence to build trust between buyers and sellers by sharing user feedback with the community. Social bookmarking sites (Section 1.10), and social media sites (like Digg and Flickr) use collective intelligence to promote popular material, making it easier for others to find.

Wikis

Wikis, websites that allow users to edit existing content and add new information, are prime examples of user-generated content and collective intelligence. The most popular wiki is *Wikipedia*, a community-generated encyclopedia with articles available in over 200 languages. Wikipedia trusts its users to follow certain rules, such as not deleting accurate information and not adding biased information, while allowing community members to enforce the rules. The result has been a wealth of information growing much faster than could otherwise be produced. In 2005, an experiment comparing 42 entries from Wikipedia and *Britannica* (a popular printed traditional encyclopedia) showed only slightly more inaccuracies in the Wikipedia articles.[41] The Wikipedia entries were promptly cor-

---

39. Tapscott, D. and A.D. Williams. *Wikinomics: How Mass Collaboration Changes Everything.* Portfolio Hardcover, 2006.
40. "FAQ." *Wesabe* <http://www.wesabe.com/page/faq>.
41. Cauchi, S. "Online Encyclopedias Put to the Test." *The Age*, 15 December 2005 <http://www.theage.com.au/news/national/online-encyclopedias-put-to-the-test/2005/12/14/1134500913345.html>.

rected, though, whereas errors in *Britannica* entries cannot be corrected until the book's next printing and will remain in already printed copies.

Wikipedia, *Wikia* (a site for specialized wiki communities about popular television shows, games, literature, shopping and more) and many other wikis use *MediaWiki* open source software (originally developed for Wikipedia). The software can be downloaded from MediaWiki's website (`www.mediawiki.org`), where you can also find descriptions, tutorials, suggestions and more to help navigate the software. Wikis are also used by many companies to provide product information, support and community resources. *Social-Text*, the first wiki company, provides corporate wiki services. Many companies have found that using wikis for project collaboration reduces e-mails and phone calls between employees, while allowing the ability to closely track a project's changes.[42]

Collaborative Filtering

Though collaboration can result in a wealth of knowledge, some users might submit false or faulty information. For example, Wikipedia has experienced instances of people deliberately adding false information to entries. While *moderation* (monitoring of content by staff) is sometimes necessary, it is time consuming and costly. Many Web 2.0 companies rely on the community to help police their sites. This *collaborative filtering* lets users promote valuable material and flag offensive or inappropriate material. Users have the power to choose for themselves what is important. Examples of sites using collaborative filtering include Digg, a news site where users rate the stories (see Section 1.8), and social bookmarking sites such as del.icio.us, where users can easily find popular sites (see Section 1.10). Customer reviews on Amazon products also employ collaborative filtering—readers vote on the usefulness of each review (helping other readers to find the best reviews).

Craigslist

Craigslist, founded by Craig Newmark, is a popular classified ads website that has radically changed the classified advertising market. Newspapers have experienced a decline in classified ad sales,[43] as revenues from help-wanted ads on Craigslist climbed to $50 million in 2006.[44] Most ad postings on Craigslist are free, and it's easy for anyone to post ads. The site has gained popularity because of its job and housing postings. In 2005, a documentary, "24 Hours on Craigslist," showed the diverse postings that occur on the site in a single day.[45] Craigslist is built on user content, leveraging the Long Tail by connecting the unique (often unusual) needs of its users. The site also uses collaborative filtering—users are encouraged to flag inappropriate postings.

Wisdom of Crowds

Wisdom of crowds (from the book of the same title written by James Surowiecki) is similar to collective intelligence—it suggests that a large diverse group of people (that does not necessarily include experts) can be smarter than a small group of specialists. The key difference between collective intelligence and the wisdom of crowds is that the latter is not meant to be a collaborative process—part of forming a reliable crowd is making sure peo-

---

42. "SocialText is the Enterprise Wiki Trusted Most by Global 2000 Corporations." *SocialText* <http://www.socialtext.com/products/overview>.

43. Steel, E. "Newspapers' Ad Sales Show Accelerating Drop." *The Wall Street Journal*, 18 July 2007, A4.

44. "Leading Indicators." *FORTUNE*, 13 November 2006, p.40.

45. "24 Hours on Craigslist." <http://24hoursoncraigslist.com/>.

ple don't influence each other.[46] For example, Surowiecki describes how calculating the average of all submissions in a guessing contest (e.g., guessing the number of jelly beans in a jar) often results in nearly the correct answer, even though most individual estimates are incorrect and vary considerably. When the U.S. submarine *Scorpion* sank in 1968, the Navy asked various experts to work individually assessing what might have happened; their collective answers were then analyzed to determine the accurate location of the submarine.[47] Practical everyday applications of the wisdom of crowds can be seen in sites employing collaborative filtering.

1.6 Blogging

> *"The blog is the best relationship generator you've ever seen."*
> —Robert Scoble, blogger[48]

History of Blogging

Blogs are websites consisting of entries listed in reverse chronological order. They have existed since the mid-1990s; however, interest in blogging has grown exponentially in recent years because of easy-to-use blogging software and increasingly economical Internet access. The term "blog" evolved from *weblog*, a regularly updated list of interesting websites. These blogs consisted of short postings, in reverse chronological order, that contained links to other web pages and short commentaries or reactions. Blogging has since taken on a looser structure—some blogs still follow the traditional format of links and small amounts of text, while others consist of essays, sometimes not containing any links. Blogs can also now incorporate media, such as music or videos. Many people are familiar with personal journal blogs, like those on *Xanga* or *LiveJournal*. These sites include social networking features and are particularly popular with teenage bloggers, who often write about their day-to-day lives for friends.

Blogging has become a major social phenomenon, empowering users to participate in, rather than just view, the web. In July 2006 most *bloggers*, or blog authors, had not had a personal website before starting their blog.[49] The increased availability of user-friendly blogging software has allowed blogging to become accessible to more mainstream Internet users.

Blog Components

Reader comments create an interactive experience, allowing readers to react to blog entries. According to a Pew Internet study, 87% of blogs allow reader comments.[50] Success-

---

46. Jenkins, H. "Collective Intelligence vs. The Wisdom of Crowds." *Confessions of an Aca-Fan*, 27 November 2006 <http://www.henryjenkins.org/2006/11/collective_intelligence_vs_the.html>.
47. Surowiecki, J. *The Wisdom of Crowds*. Anchor, 2005.
48. Kirkpatrick, D. "Why There's No Escaping the Blog." *FORTUNE*, 10 January 2005 <http://money.cnn.com/magazines/fortune/fortune_archive/2005/01/10/8230982/index.htm>.
49. Lenhart, A. and S. Fox. "Bloggers: A Portrait of the Internet's New Storytellers." *Pew Internet & American Life Project*, July 2006 <http://www.pewinternet.org/pdfs/PIP%20Bloggers%20Report%20July%2019%202006.pdf>.
50. Lenhart, A. and S. Fox. "Bloggers: A Portrait of the Internet's New Storytellers." *Pew Internet & American Life Project*, July 2006 <http://www.pewinternet.org/pdfs/PIP%20Bloggers%20Report%20July%2019%202006.pdf>.

ful bloggers pay attention to their readers and respond, often sparking interesting discussions and debates. However, allowing comments increases the possibility of spam (including irrelevant comments, inappropriate language and link spam—where a user tries to increase an irrelevant site's number of inbound links). By some estimates, over 90% of blog comments are spam.[51]

Permalinks provide blog readers with a way of linking to specific blog entries. Each blog post has a unique URL referring to that single post. Links stay relevant even after the blog entry moves off the homepage and into the archive.

Trackbacks tell bloggers who is linking to their posts. This enhances Internet content by making linking two-way. The blogger provides a trackback link, and sites that use the link are added to a list on the blog entry. For an example of a trackbacks section, visit `http://www.techcrunch.com/2006/08/08/web-20-the-24-minute-documentary/`. This is a permalink to a post on *TechCrunch*, a popular Internet technology blog, that features a Web 2.0 video from 2006.

A *blogroll* is a list of the blogger's favorite blogs. Though not all blogs feature a blogroll, it is common for the main page of a blog to contain links to several other blogs. For example, LiveJournal automatically incorporates a blogroll (consisting of users the blogger has marked as friends) into a user's profile page.

Blogging and Journalism

> *"Freedom of the press is guaranteed only to those who own one."*
> —A.J. Liebling[52]

Blogging has encouraged *citizen journalism*, allowing anyone to be a journalist. Blogs have become a significant news resource, drawing traffic away from the mainstream media. Some argue that this form of "participatory journalism" holds less biases than mainstream media, or at least makes these biases clear and provides many different views. This *democratization of media* allows a larger group to take part in journalism.[53] Traditional journalists had previously been able to create a representative democracy (much like the political system of the United States) by speaking for the masses. However, blogging gives a voice to everyone with a computer and Internet access, creating a more direct democracy.

Many bloggers are recognized as members of the media. Just as television and radio increased the speed of news delivery over that of newspapers, blogs have become a fast and in-depth (and often "unwashed") news medium. The mass media is embracing blogging; many TV news anchors suggest that viewers read their blogs after the show, and many newspaper websites feature blogs by reporters.

Though journalism is a large part of the blogging phenomenon, according to a Pew Internet study only one-third of bloggers consider their blogs a form of journalism. Eighty-four percent of bloggers consider it a hobby, and only 10% spend more than ten hours a week blogging.[54] Posting new content and responding to reader comments requires a substantial time commitment.

---

51. *Akismet*, 10 August 2007 <`http://akismet.com/stats/`>.
52. "A.J. Liebling Quotes." *ThinkExist.com Quotations* <`http://thinkexist.com/quotation/freedom_of_the_press_is_guaranteed_only_to_those/220714.html`>.
53. Bowman, S. and C. Willis. "We Media." July 2003 <`http://www.hypergene.net/wemedia/download/we_media.pdf`>.

Growth of Blogging

The number of blogs has been doubling about twice a year.[55] However, there is also a large number of abandoned blogs. A Caslon Analytics study found that "66.0% of surveyed blogs had not been updated in two months."[56]

Companies are reaching out to the *blogosphere*, or blogging community, to keep in touch with consumer opinions. Many CEOs and top executives from large companies such as Sun Microsystems, Marriott International and General Motors are now regular bloggers. This helps build consumer trust and loyalty. The NewPR Wiki lists over 250 CEOs and upper-management bloggers.[57]

Increased use of mobile devices has also lead to *moblogging*, or mobile blogging, as bloggers no longer need to be at their computer to update their blogs. Similarly, *vlogging*, or video blogging, has gained popularity. Rocketboom, for example, posts a three-minute video every day covering news and Internet stories.

Blogging and RSS Feeds

Many popular blogs provide RSS and Atom feeds to let readers know when new content is posted. Feeds, offered through blogging software or sites such as *Feedburner* (acquired by Google in 2007), help bloggers track and maintain a steady readership. The feeds (containing an entire post or just a selection with a link) can be automatically syndicated via the web and aggregated on a website or application designated by the user. Some sites (like Feedburner) provide an e-mail option, forwarding the day's posts to subscribers. While the use of feeds is certainly growing, a Pew Internet study in July 2006 reported that only 18% of bloggers provide RSS feeds.[58] (See RSS and Atom in Section 1.15.)

Blogging Software

Bloggers now have many options for building blogs. Online hosted blog software options include *WordPress* (which also offers server software), *TypePad* and *Blogger*. Blog server software programs include *Movable Type* and *Textpattern*. These require users to have their own web server; however, they also allow for more customization. Some word processors (such as Microsoft Word 2007) also offer blog publishing features or are compatible with blog posting extensions.

Blog Networks

Blog networks are collections of blogs, often with several editors. Popular blog networks include Corante, Weblogs, Inc., 9rules, b5media and Gawker Media. Many of these, with multiple bloggers and daily postings, draw significant traffic and a broad audience. Blog

---

54. Lenhart, A. and S. Fox. "Bloggers: A Portrait of the Internet's New Storytellers." *Pew Internet & American Life Project*, July 2006 <http://www.pewinternet.org/pdfs/PIP%20Bloggers%20Report%20July%2019%202006.pdf>.

55. Walsh, B. *Clear Blogging: How People Are Changing the World and How You Can Join Them*. Apress, 2007.

56. "Blog Statistics and Demographics." *Caslon Analytics*. March 2007 <http://www.caslon.com.au/weblogprofile1.htm>.

57. "CEO Blog List." *NewPR Wiki* <http://www.thenewpr.com/wiki/pmwiki.php/Resources/CEOBlogsList?pagename=Resources.CEOBlogsList>.

58. Lenhart, A. and S. Fox. "Bloggers: A Portrait of the Internet's New Storytellers." *Pew Internet & American Life Project*, July 2006 <http://www.pewinternet.org/pdfs/PIP%20Bloggers%20Report%20July%2019%202006.pdf>.

networks help bloggers build reputations and loyal readers. Some social networking sites like MySpace and Facebook also enable blogging to a private network of friends.

Blog Search Engines

Blog search engines, such as *Technorati* and *Google Blog Search*, monitor the blogosphere's constant changes. When dealing with blogs, search results cannot be based strictly on traditional factors such as reputations built over time (since the blogosphere is so dynamic). Technorati, which tracked over 93 million blogs in July 2007, addresses the unique needs of what they call the "World Live Web." Google Blog Search adjusts Google's search algorithms to specifically address the blogosphere. Other blog search engines include Feedster, IceRocket and Blogdigger.

1.7 Social Networking

Social networking sites, which allow users to keep track of their existing interpersonal relationships and form new ones, are experiencing extraordinary growth in Web 2.0. According to the "Hitwise US Consumer Generated Media Report," in September 2006 "one in every 20 Internet visits went to one of the top 20 social networks." A large portion of the traffic on shopping sites (and other Web 2.0 sites) comes from social networking websites such as MySpace.[59]

Network Effects

> *"What distinguished 2.0 is the design of systems that harness network effects—a broader way of saying community—to get better the more people use them."*
> —Tim O'Reilly[60]

The term *network effects* refers to the increased value of a network as its number of users grows. *Metcalfe's Law* states that the value of the network is proportional to the square of the number of users.[61] Consider, for example, eBay—the more buyers and sellers that use the site, the more valuable the site becomes to its users. Google's AdSense advertising program also increases in value as the number of participating advertisers and publishers grows and ads can be better matched to site content (see Section 1.3). Social networking sites also rely heavily on network effects, often attracting users only if their friends are on the site.

A key part of building a successful network and creating an architecture of participation is setting the user preferences to *default to share* content so users will automatically contribute to the value of the network.[62] Most users do not think about sharing capabilities, let alone care to alter their preferences. If companies do not enable sharing automatically, few users will take the time to share their data. *Providing the option to disable sharing is an important privacy feature.*

Network effects also make it difficult (though not impossible) to break into markets already claimed by successful companies. User content often loses value when moved into

---

59. Prescott, L. "Hitwise US Consumer Generated Media Report." *Hitwise,* February 2007.
60. Heiss, J. "Open Possibilities at the First CommunityOne Conference." *JavaOne,* 7 May 2007 <http://java.sun.com/javaone/sf/2007/articles/comm1_post.jsp>.
61. "Metcalf's Law." <http://www-ec.njit.edu/~robertso/infosci/metcalf.html>.
62. O'Reilly, T. "What is Web 2.0: Design Patterns and Business Models for the Next Generation of Software." September 2005 <http://www.oreillynet.com/pub/a/oreilly/tim/news/2005/09/30/what-is-web-20.html>.

a new network. For example, a photo's tags (created by the community) on Flickr are lost if the photo is taken to a different site. Competitors must then find a unique way of convincing users that it's worth the switch.

Friendster

Friendster was an early leader in social networking. Within a year of Friendster's founding in 2002, Google offered to buy the site (Friendster rejected the offer). Created as a dating site, Friendster experienced a boom in popularity that quickly overwhelmed its servers. Friendster's popularity declined as new sites like MySpace emerged.[63] Though Friendster has not been able to keep pace with competing social networking sites, it still claims over 45 million members worldwide. It was granted a patent in 2006 on a key part of social networking, specifically how networks of friends are developed (i.e., identifying mutual friends and degrees of separation).[64]

MySpace

MySpace is the most popular social networking site. Hitwise reported it as the top website in May 2007 based on market share (beating Google by 1.5%).[65] Self-defined as "an online community that lets you meet your friends' friends," MySpace allows you to build a network of friends and identify mutual friends. Each user's page can contain general info, pictures, blog entries, a message board and more. Customization options, such as changing the background or adding music, give users an easy way to create their own unique web page. The site also features a private messaging system and special sections for film, music, videos, classifieds, etc.

MySpace plays an important role in the music scene, and even companies and politicians are creating accounts. MySpace reaches a younger audience than most conventional media outlets. Some political candidates have used MySpace to reach out to young voters and find new volunteers. Though candidates risk embarrassing connections (to inappropriate accounts) on these sites, they have often found the benefits to be worth it.[66] Businesses can also create profiles, which then become a form of free advertising. News Corp, which acquired MySpace in 2005 for $580 million, recognizes its benefits for local businesses that want to gain exposure.[67] Though many consider social networking sites to be more popular with teenagers and young adults, the largest user group on MySpace (and other large social networking sites) consists of 35–54 year olds.[68]

---

63. Rivlin, G. "Wallflower at the Web Party." *New York Times*, 15 October 2006 <http://www.nytimes.com/2006/10/15/business/yourmoney/15friend.html>.

64. Kirkpatrick, M. "Friendster Awarded Patent on Social Networking." *TechCrunch*, 7 July 2006 <http://www.techcrunch.com/2006/07/07/friendster-awarded-patent-on-social-networking/>.

65. "Top 20 Websites." *Hitwise*, May 2007. <http://hitwise.com/datacenter/rankings.php>.

66. Jesdanun, A. "Candidates Seek Youths at MySpace." *ABC News*, 17 August 2006 <http://abcnews.go.com/Technology/wireStory?id=2325325&page=1>.

67. "Businesses Find MySpace is a Place to Reach Youth." *Trend Watching*, 11 July 2006 <http://www.trendwatching.com/about/inmedia/articles/youniversal_branding/businesses_find_myspace_is_a_p.html>.

68. Arrington, M. "Bear Stearns: Yahoo Must Form A Social Networking Strategy." *TechCrunch*, 3 August 2007 <http://www.techcrunch.com/2007/08/03/bear-stearns-yahoo-must-form-a-social-networking-strategy>.

Facebook

Hitwise named *Facebook* the "preferred network among college students. Because Facebook was closed to non-students, students felt safer than on MySpace, and Facebook became nearly a social necessity for students seeking to connect with peers."[69] In July 2007, Facebook held an 85% market share of four-year U.S. universities and had over 31 million users.[70] Though Facebook has since allowed users without an `.edu` e-mail address to join, this elitism and idea of increased privacy drew a large enough crowd to compete with MySpace. A user can set privacy levels for networks or even individuals, but Facebook users (as well as users of other social networking sites) are warned about possible repercussions from information they post.

> *"Remember, unless you're prepared to attach something in your profile to a resume or scholarship application, don't post it."*
> —Facebook[71]

The site has added many features over the past few years, including photo albums where you can tag your friends in pictures, recently updated profiles lists, events, groups, a marketplace for classified ads, and user status updates. In May 2007, the site introduced third-party applications that can be integrated directly into Facebook. Not all feature implementations have gone smoothly, though. In Fall 2006, Facebook experienced resistance from users concerned over privacy issues when it added a "News Feed" feature, which lists updates of friends' Facebook activities in real time.[72] Facebook increased privacy options in response, quieting most complaints.

LinkedIn

In June 2007, *LinkedIn* claimed a membership of "11 million experienced professionals." The business-oriented social networking site allows users to stay in touch with professional contacts, network with new contacts, check references, and find a job or a potential employee. Its low-key design and feature implementations keep the site unobtrusive.[73] Because of its older, more mature audience, privacy concerns are more prevalent—some users worry that their professional contacts will be abused by other users or even their employers for marketing reasons.[74] However, the site is popular as a convenient way of networking. Members can find other professionals through mutual acquaintances and get introductions.

LinkedIn monetizes the site through advertising, premium accounts for power users (mostly recruiters), and groups for companies and organizations. Because of the growing size of its network, LinkedIn maintains a strong hold on the professional market.[75]

69. Prescott, L. "Hitwise US Consumer Generated Media Report." *Hitwise,* February 2007.
70. "Facebook Statistics." *Facebook,* 17 July 2007 `<http://static.ak.facebook.com/press/facebook_statist ics.pdf?11:44617>`.
71. "Customer Support." *Facebook* `<http://www.facebook.com/help.php?tab=safety>`.
72. Schmidt, T. S. "Inside the Backlash Against Facebook." *TIME,* 6 September 2006 `<http://www.time.com/time/nation/article/0,8599,1532225,00.html>`.
73. Copeland, M. "The Missing Link." *CNNMoney.com,* 28 February 2007 `<http://money.cnn.com/magazines/business2/business2_archive/2006/12/01/8394967/index.htm>`.
74. "The CEO's Guide to Social Networks." *BusinessWeek,* 11 September 2006 `<http://businessweek.com/mediacenter/qt/podcasts/guide_to_tech/guidetotech_09_11_06.mp3>`.
75. Copeland, M. "The Missing Link." *CNNMoney.com,* 28 February 2007 `<http://money.cnn.com/magazines/business2/business2_archive/2006/12/01/8394967/index.htm>`.

Xing

Xing is a professional networking site based out of Germany. Xing is most popular in Europe and offers its services across many countries, industries, and languages—an important factor, given today's globalization of organizations. With its discovery capability and management tools, Xing helps members find professionals, search for job opportunities and locate other business prospects. In April 2007, Xing reached 2 million users.[76] Xing has also been acquiring other social networks in an attempt to increase its global reach.

Second Life

Second Life, developed by Linden Labs, is a ***3D virtual world*** with millions of inhabitants. Users create *avatars*, digital representations of themselves that they can use to meet other users with similar interests, conduct business, participate in group activities, take classes and more. Some users have created profitable businesses or continued their real-life professions in the virtual world. For example, lawyers have used Second Life to meet new clients (often software developers wanting to discuss patent laws).[77] Many large corporations, such as IBM and Hewlett-Packard, have created Second Life presences to connect with customers, hold meetings and even recruit and interview new hires.[78, 79]

Users can create objects and add scripts (to animate the objects) in the virtual world. Because Second Life allows users to maintain rights to whatever they create, a dynamic marketplace has emerged that does millions of dollars in transactions monthly—the site has its own exchange, the LindeX.[80] Not only does this create monetization opportunities for users (one woman claims to have earned over $1 million in Second Life assets[81]), but Second Life earns revenue from premium accounts, purchases of virtual land and more.

Gaia Online

Gaia Online is a popular teen virtual world. This online community allows teens to play games, make friends and express their creativity. Similar to Second Life, Gaia has its own marketplace where members can earn Gaia Gold for various actions they perform on the site (e.g., playing games or posting), and use their earnings at the virtual stores or for creating their own shops. Nearly 300,000 members login daily and about 2 million unique visitors login to Gaia every month.[82]

Mobile Social Networking

Many social networking sites have found innovative ways of connecting people through the Internet and their mobile devices (such as cell phones and PDAs). Mobile users can send instant messages, check e-mail, and post content to the web from Internet-enabled mobile devices. The new Apple iPhone further realizes the dream of having the *Internet*

---

76. "Xing Reaches 2 Million Users." Mashable, <http://mashable.com/2007/04/16/xing/>.
77. "Second Life Lawyer." *Business 2.0*, May 2007, p.86.
78. Athavely, A. "A Job Interview You Don't Have to Show Up For." *The Wall Street Journal Online*, 20 June 2007 <http://online.wsj.com/article/SB118229876637841321.html>.
79. Bulkeley, W. "Playing Well With Others." *The Wall Street Journal Online*, 18 June 2007 <http://online.wsj.com/article/SB118194536298737221.html>.
80. "What is Second Life." <http://secondlife.com/whatis>.
81. Lawson, S. "Second Life Creates a Millionaire." *IDG News*, 30 November 2006 <http://www.itworld.com/App/4201/061130secondlife/>.
82. "About Us." *Gaia Online*, <http://www.gaiaonline.com/info/about.php?>.

in your pocket by allowing the full Internet (not a simplified mobile one) to be accessed wherever wireless Internet access is available.

Google's *Dodgeball.com* provides users with mobile access to a network of friends in many cities. GPS chips in mobile devices allow Dodgeball users to update their location and be notified of nearby friends or "crushes." Dodgeball also provides an easy way of sending messages to groups of friends to plan get-togethers. (See Section 1.14, Location-Based Services.)

Other sites such as *Twitter* provide similar services, accessible by text message, IM or a web client. Twitter users can message groups of friends at once and automatically receive their friends' updates on a cell phone or through a chat window. The site is considered to be a *microblogging* service (since users are limited to a small number of characters for each update). Twitter offers a web services API, which allows developers to integrate Twitter into other applications. (See Section 1.13, Web Services, Mashups, Widgets and Gadgets, for more information on web services APIs.)

1.8 Social Media

Social media refers to any media shared online (e.g., videos, music, photos, news, etc.). Hitwise reported that "increased broadband penetration, combined with the rise of consumer generated content and the proliferation of webcams and cell phone and home video cameras have firmly entrenched online video viewing into the habits of entertainment seekers in the United States."[83]

YouTube

YouTube, launched in late 2005, is the leading Internet video site. In true Web 2.0 fashion, the entire site is based on user-generated content. Users upload videos, and rate and comment on videos posted by other users. YouTube's Quick Capture Flash software makes it easy to upload content directly from a webcam. Users can browse videos by category, tag, or by following "related video" links. Highly rated videos are featured on YouTube's homepage. While many professionals and film students post content on the site, the most popular submissions are often simple spoofs or home videos. Because of the viral network effects of YouTube, these amateur videos can quickly gain worldwide attention.

Users can subscribe to other users' content, share videos with friends by e-mail, or embed videos directly into their blogs or other websites. YouTube addresses privacy and spam concerns by allowing users to set videos as "public" or "private" and flag inappropriate material for review by YouTube's staff.

Less than a year after its official launch, YouTube was acquired by Google (which had its own less popular Google Video site) for $1.65 billion. Less than six months after the acquisition, Viacom sued YouTube for $1 billion for copyright infringement.[84] The Digital Millennium Copyright Act of 1998 protects companies from prosecution due to user actions if they work in "good faith" to remove offending content.[85] However, interpretations of this act vary, and it has become a point of contention for many companies. You-

83. Prescott, L. "Hitwise US Consumer Generated Media Report." *Hitwise,* February 2007.
84. Mills, E. "Copyright Quagmire for Google and YouTube." *ZDNet,* 14 March 2007 <http://news.zdnet.com/2100-9588_22-6167281.html>.
85. "Conference Report Filed in House." *Library of Congress,* 8 October 1998 <http://thomas.loc.gov/cgi-bin/bdquery/z?d105:HR02281:@@@D&summ2=m&>.

Tube is developing a mechanism that automatically detects copyrighted material. Currently, illegal content is removed from the site manually.

Internet TV

Many mass-media companies now offer full-length episodes of popular television shows on their websites to tap into the increasingly popular Internet television market. The average American watches 4.5 hours of television a day, not including Internet television.[86] Sites, such as *Joost*, Veoh and MobiTV, have emerged as a new way of watching television. Joost, for example, uses semantic technologies to help users find programs that interest them. (See Section 1.18, Future of the Web.)

Limited by copyright issues, Internet TV sites must make deals with mainstream networks to offer their content online. Viacom made a deal with Joost, allowing the site to include some shows from networks such as MTV, VH1 and Comedy Central.[87] As users take back the power to choose what they watch and when, networks may find themselves making more deals with Internet TV companies. As technologies continue to improve, Internet TV has the potential to radically change the television industry. Already, smaller content creators are able to gain access to worldwide audiences. In late June 2007, MySpace joined the market with its MySpaceTV. With MySpace's enormous membership, it could rapidly become a direct competitor to YouTube and Internet TV websites.

Internet TV allows advertisers to target their markets more precisely than with broadcast television. Advertisers can use demographic information, such as location, gender and age, to serve appropriate ads.

Digg

Digg features news, videos and podcasts, all posted and rated by users. It has gained popularity by allowing users to "digg" or "bury" posts and user comments. Valuable sites, marked by large numbers of diggs, are moved to the Digg front page where other users can easily find them. Formulas were adjusted to make sure the "wisdom of crowds" was not being hijacked by users trying to promote their own posts.[88] Sites that are "dugg" and featured on the homepage typically experience a traffic surge. Bloggers can add Digg buttons to their sites, making it easy for readers to "digg" their posts.

Digg uses collaborative filtering to help reduce spam by "burying" it (users can vote against posts they don't like). Users can also set the threshold of diggs to automatically filter out content with low ratings. The site was criticized for removing popular posts of HD DVD security cracks (on the advice of lawyers); however, Kevin Rose (Digg's founder) decided to support the crowds and "deal with whatever the consequences might be."[89] Digg has additional social networking capabilities; users can view their friends' Digg

---

86. Colvin, G. "TV Is Dying? Long Live TV!" *FORTUNE*, 5 February 2007, p.43.

87. O'Hear, S. "Viacom to Partner with Joost." *ZDNet*, 20 February 2007 <http://blogs.zdnet.com/social/?p=96>.

88. Maney, K. "Techies Hot on Concept of 'Wisdom of Crowds,' But It Has Some Pitfalls." *USA Today*, 12 September 2006 <http://www.usatoday.com/tech/columnist/kevinmaney/2006-09-12-wisdom-of-crowds_x.htm>.

89. Hefflinger, M. "Digg Users Revolt Over Deleted Posts of HD DVD Security Hack." *digitalmediawire*, 2 May 2007 <http://www.dmwmedia.com/news/2007/05/02/digg-users-revolt-over-deleted-posts-of-hd-dvd-security-hack>.

activities and the Diggs of other users with similar interests. Some Digg-like sites include Netscape, Reddit and Newsvine.

Last.fm

Last.fm is an Internet radio website that uses Web 2.0 concepts to make music recommendations and build communities. The site provides open source desktop software that can be integrated into most popular music players. Its *scrobbling* feature tracks the music users listen to so that Last.fm can provide users with personalized recommendations. A streamable radio with "discovery mode" and a network of like-minded listeners help users find new music. Groups and an events section add social value. The site also offers tagging and wiki pages for artists and record labels.

Digital Rights Management (DRM)

Digital Rights Management (DRM) systems add software to media files to prevent them from being misused, but these systems restrict compatibility with many media players. Companies want to protect their digital products from illegal distribution; however, users want unrestricted access to media they've purchased.

iTunes, Apple's music store, has been criticized for restricting users' access to their own music by allowing only up to five computers to be authorized to play any given file. However, Apple's Steve Jobs advocated a DRM-free music world in February 2007, arguing the greater risk for piracy is in DRM-free CDs, which make up the majority of music sales.[90] CDs remain DRM-free because many CD players are not compatible with DRM systems. In June 2007, Amazon offered DRM-free downloads from more than 12,000 record labels, and both iTunes and Amazon sell DRM-free music from EMI (one of the four major record companies).[91]

Podcasting

Podcasting was popularized by Apple's iPod portable media player. A *podcast* is a digital audio file (e.g., an .mp3) that often takes on the characteristics of a radio talk show (though without live callers).[92] Much as blogging has made journalism accessible to everyone, podcasting has introduced a more democratic form of radio broadcasting. Podcasts are easily created with audio software and can be played on a computer or portable media player. The files are posted online at individual websites or distributed via programs like Apple's iTunes. Listeners can often subscribe to podcasts via RSS feeds. Forrester Research predicted 12 million households will be regularly subscribing to podcasts by 2010.[93]

90. Jobs, S. "Thoughts on Music." 6 February 2007 <http://www.apple.com/hotnews/thoughtso nmusic/>.

91. "Amazon.com to Launch DRM-Free MP3 Music Download Store with Songs and Albums from EMI Music and More Than 12,000 Other Labels." 16 May 2007 <http://phx.corporate-ir .net/phoenix.zhtml?c=176060&p=irol-newsArticle&ID=1003003>.

92. Torrone, P. "What Is Podcasting?" *O'Reilly Media*, 20 July 2005 <http://digitalmedia.oreilly .com/2005/07/20/WhatIsPodcasting.html>.

93. D'Agostino, D. "Security in the World of Web 2.0." *Innovations*, Winter 2006, p.15.

1.9 Tagging

History of Tagging

Tagging, or labeling content, is part of the collaborative nature of Web 2.0. A tag is any user-generated word or phrase that helps organize web content and label it in a more human way. Though standard sets of labels allow users to mark content in a general way, tagging items with self-chosen labels creates a stronger identification of the content. In an interview by the Pew Internet & American Life Project, David Weinberger (author of *Everything is Miscellaneous*) said:

> *"Maybe the most interesting thing about tagging is that we now have millions and millions of people who are saying, in public, what they think pages and images are about."*
>
> —David Weinberger

As part of the same December 2006 report, 28% of Internet users had reportedly "tagged" content online.[94]

Tag Clouds

Tag Clouds are visual displays of tags weighted by popularity. Many Web 2.0 sites include a graphical representation of popular tags (the popularity of the tag marked by the size of its text). There are many ways of forming tag clouds—terms often appear in alphabetical order. However, tag clouds show only how the majority (or the crowd) thinks and disregard many individual unique points of view.[95] Figure 1.3 is an example of a "text cloud" that we created manually from the major terms in this chapter. (To build your own text cloud try ArtViper's TextTagCloud tool at `http://www.artviper.net/texttagcloud/`.)

Folksonomies

Folksonomies are classifications based on tags. The term is generally attributed to Thomas Vander Wal, who combined the words "taxonomy" and "folk" to create a new term for this Internet phenomenon.[96] Folksonomies are formed on sites such as Flickr, Technorati and del.icio.us. Users can search content by tags, which identify content in different (and sometimes more meaningful) ways than traditional keywords used by search engines.

An example of Web 2.0's reach outside of traditional technology fields can be seen in the *steve.museum project*, an experiment in tagging and folksonomies regarding museum collections. In 2005, The Metropolitan Museum of Art and the Guggenheim Museum organized a retreat to plan the project.[97] In 2007 they posted various collections of art online and asked the community for help tagging them.

---

94. Rainie, L. "Tagging." *Pew Internet & American Life Project*, 31 January 2007. <http://www.pewinternet.org/pdfs/PIP_Tagging.pdf>.

95. Rainie, L. "Tagging." *Pew Internet & American Life Project*, 31 January 2007. <http://www.pewinternet.org/pdfs/PIP_Tagging.pdf>.

96. Vander Wal, T. "Folksonomy Coinage and Definition." *Vanderwal.net*, 2 February 2007 <http://www.vanderwal.net/folksonomy.html>.

97. Chun, S., R. Cherry, D. Hiwiller, J. Trant and B. Wyman. "Steve.museum: An Ongoing Experiment in Social Tagging, Folksonomy, and Museums." *Archives & Museum Informatics*, 1 March 2006 <http://www.archimuse.com/mw2006/papers/wyman/wyman.html>.

37Signals℠ **AdSense™** **AdWords™** affiliate programs agile development

Ajax Amazon® Mechanical Turk **Amazon®** **Web** **Services™** **APIs**

architecture of participation **Attention Economy** blog

search engines **blogging** **blogosphere** **broadband Internet** citizen

journalism **collaborative filtering** **collective intelligence** contextual

advertising **Craigslist®** Creative Commons℠ default to share **Deitel®** **del.icio.us™**

democratization of media **Digg™** Digital Millenium Copyright Act Dojo DotNetNuke™ **DRM**

eBay® **Facebook®** Federated Media℠ Feedburner™ **findability** **Firefox® 2** Flash®

Flex™ **Flickr™** folksonomies *Getting Real* globalization **Google Maps™**

Google™ Google™ Gears GPS housingmaps.com **Internet advertising**

Internet business models Internet Explorer® 7 Internet TV **Internet video** iPhone™

iTunes® JavaServer™ Faces Joost™ JSON Last.fm® **lightweight business models** link popularity

LinkedIn® location-based services **mashups** Metcalf's Law microformats **Microsoft® adCenter**

moblogging **monetization** Moore's Law Mozilla® **MSN®** **MySpace®** MySQL®

network effects **O'Reilly® Media** ontologies **open source** outsourcing

permalinks **perpetual beta** PHPNuke **podcasting** premium content ProgrammableWeb.com℠ RDF

recommender systems **remixing** reputation systems REST **RIAs** RSS/Atom Ruby on Rails™

Salesforce.com® Script.aculo.us **search** Search Engine Marketing (SEM) **Search Engine**

Optimization (SEO) **Second Life®** Semantic Web Silverlight™ Skype™

social bookmarking **social media** **social networking**

Software as a Service (SaaS) tag clouds **tagging** TechCrunch

Technorati™ **The Long Tail** *TIME* Person of the Year trackbacks trust **Twitter**

user-generated content vertical search virtual worlds vlogging VoIP

Web 2.0 Web 2.0 Internet Business Initiative **Web 2.0 Summit** Web

3.0 web as a platform **web services** web-scale computing webtop widgets and gadgets

Wikinomics **Wikipedia®** wikis **wisdom of crowds** XML® **Yahoo!®**

Yahoo!® Publisher Network Yahoo!® Search Marketing **YouTube**

Fig. 1.3 | Text cloud of major Web 2.0 terms from this chapter.

Flickr

Flickr—a popular photo-sharing site—was launched in February 2004 and acquired by Yahoo! in 2005. The Flickr development team was originally working on "The Game Neverending"—a multiplayer Flash game based on IM (instant message) and chat interfaces.[98] However, the team listened to its users and developed real-time photo sharing (Flickr Live) and more traditional web pages where users could view uploaded pictures.

98. Schonfeld, E. "The Flickrization of Yahoo!" *CNN Money.com*, 1 December 2005 <http://money.cnn.com/magazines/business2/business2_archive/2005/12/01/8364623/>.

The Game Neverending and Flickr Live were later retired as the popularity of photo sharing and commenting on the web pages grew.[99]

Flickr is a key content-tagging site. Intended as a way of organizing personal photo collections, tagging on the site gained popularity as the community became interested in "a global view of the *tagscape*" (how other people are tagging photos).[100] Users can search for photos by meaningful tags. The tags also encourage loyalty to the site, since the tags are lost if photos are moved to another site.

Technorati

Technorati, a social media search engine, uses tags to find relevant blogs and other forms of social media. To become searchable by Technorati, bloggers can add tags to their posts with a simple line of HTML or use the automated category system offered by some blogging software packages.[101] Technorati tag searches return results from the blogosphere, YouTube videos and Flickr photos. Technorati features a tag cloud on its homepage and a "where's the fire" section to promote the most popular tags and search results.

1.10 Social Bookmarking

Social bookmarking sites let you share your Internet bookmarks (e.g., your favorite websites, blogs, and articles) through a website. Users can access these bookmarks from any computer and discover new sites by searching popular bookmarks and tags. Some of the most popular social bookmarking sites are del.icio.us, Ma.gnolia, Blue Dot, StumbleUpon, Simpy and Furl.

del.icio.us

del.icio.us, a self-described "collection of favorites," reported its two-millionth user registration in March 2007.[102] Users can add a bookmark by going to the site or by using the del.icio.us downloadable browser buttons. Some sites post clickable badges—a button provided by del.icio.us to "save this page"—that make it easy for users to bookmark the site using del.icio.us.

del.icio.us is a great example of a Web 2.0 company that uses tagging, social networking and user-generated content. When bookmarking a website, users can add notes and tags to describe the site. These tags are searchable and help organize sites, making it easier for users to find the content they want based on what other users have recommended (by bookmarking). Users can also add descriptions to tags, which can help clear up what a certain tag might mean to different people. Thus, searching for content on del.icio.us is based on collaborative filtering rather than search engine algorithms. The site also offers a fully searchable podcasting section.

Third parties can use the del.icio.us web services API to build tools and incorporate social bookmarking functionality into their applications (see Section 1.13, Web Services,

99. Garrett, J.J. "An Interview with Flickr's Eric Costello." *Adaptive Path*, 4 August 2005 <http://www.adaptivepath.com/publications/essays/archives/000519.php>.

100. Garrett, J.J. "An Interview with Flickr's Eric Costello." *Adaptive Path*, 4 August 2005 <http://www.adaptivepath.com/publications/essays/archives/000519.php>.

101. "Using Technorati Tags." *Technorati* <http://support.technorati.com/support/siteguide/tags>.

102. "That was Fast." del.icio.us blog, 29 March 2007 <http://blog.del.icio.us/blog/2007/03/that_was_fast.html>.

Mashups, Widgets and Gadgets). For example, Adobe Illustrator uses the del.icio.us technology to organize bookmarks in the program's documentation.[103]

Ma.gnolia

> *"If searching was the first day of the web, people helping each other find what they want must be the second."*
> —Ma.gnolia[104]

Ma.gnolia is another social bookmarking site offering tagging and convenient bookmark accessibility through the site. Bookmarked pages are saved (when possible) so users need not worry about losing content if a page goes offline. The site also provides browser buttons (bookmarklets) for posting sites to Ma.gnolia, and a "roots" feature, which lets you see what other users have said about a site while surfing the Internet. Ma.gnolia encourages social networking through user groups and a private messaging feature. To deal with spam, Ma.gnolia trusts handpicked moderators, called "gardeners."[105]

1.11 Software Development

A key to Web 2.0 software development is to KIS (keep it simple; keep it small). At the 2006 Emerging Technology Conference, Rael Dornfest (now CEO of the company "values of n" and former O'Reilly CTO) explained, "great businesses will be built on giving you less."[106] This is particularly important given the "attention economy" (too much information, too little time)—the theme of the 2006 conference.

The Webtop

The web has now become an application, development, delivery, and execution platform. The *webtop*, or web desktop, allows you to run web applications in a desktop-like environment in a web browser. Using the web as a platform is part of a movement toward operating-system–independent applications. The removal of OS barriers allows the potential audience for any single product to become larger. An example of a popular webtop is the Laszlo Webtop (built on the OpenLaszlo framework), which runs applications written in OpenLaszlo as well as those written in other frameworks using XML requests.[107] Examples of Laszlo Webtop applications can be seen at `http://www.laszlosystems.com/showcase/samples`. Other webtops include eyeOS and StartForce.

Software as a Service (SaaS)

Software as a Service (SaaS), application software that runs on a web server rather than being installed on the client computer, has gained popularity, particularly with businesses. It provides many benefits, including fewer demands on internal IT departments, increased

---

103. "Know How Adobe and del.icio.us Work Together?" del.icio.us blog, 30 May 2007 <http://blog.del.icio.us/blog/2007/05/knowhow_adobe_a.html>.

104. "About Ma.gnolia." <http://ma.gnolia.com/about>.

105. "Gardeners." Ma.gnolia Community Wiki, 29 March 2007 <http://wiki.ma.gnolia.com/Gardeners>.

106. Farber, D. "ETech: Attenuation, Web 2.0 and spimes." *ZDNet*, 7 March 2006 <http://blogs.zdnet.com/BTL/?p=2667>.

107. "The RIA Desktop in a Browser." *LaszloSystems* <http://www.laszlosystems.com/software/webtop>.

accessibility for out-of-the-office use, and an easy way to maintain software on a large scale.[108] Instead of being installed on the local machine, software is installed on the provider's web server and accessed by customers "as a service" over the Internet. Updates applied on the server impact every computer. This change from local to server machine makes it easier for large corporations to keep software updates uniform throughout the organization. Most Google software is offered as SaaS. Microsoft now offers SaaS products, Windows Live and Office Live.

Collaborating on projects with co-workers across the world is easier, since information is stored on a web server instead of on a single desktop. 37Signals has developed several SaaS products, including Basecamp (a product management and collaboration tool), Campfire (a group chat tool), Backpack (a personal organization tool), Ta-da (a "to-do" list tool), Highrise (a customer relations tool), and Writeboard (a collaborative word-processing tool). Salesforce.com, which specializes in Customer Relationship Management (CRM) software, is a key SaaS company—they provide popular business applications for sales, marketing, customer support, analytics and more.

Perpetual Beta and Agile Development

Due to the increased use of web applications there has been a shift away from the traditional software release cycle. Historically, companies would spend months or even years developing major new software releases. Because releases came so infrequently, each one had to go through extensive testing and beta periods to create a "final" release each time. There is now a greater focus on *agile software development*, which refers to development of fewer features at a time with more frequent releases. This "*perpetual beta*" of frequent smaller releases is made possible by using the web as a platform.[109] A new CD cannot be distributed to all customers every day; however, updates to web servers delivering the application can be easily made.

37Signals' *Getting Real*, an e-book that discusses agile techniques for building web applications, warns against the temptation to overuse "betas." The Internet is a dynamic medium—there will always be flaws and possible upgrades. Companies must decide how long it's really necessary to remain in a beta period, before it becomes just an excuse for a weak application. *Getting Real*, comprised of 91 short essays and numerous quotes and anecdotes, is a must read, providing an informative, insightful and entertaining walk through the software development process. The e-book can be read for free on their site or downloaded as a PDF for a fee.[110]

Open Source

The open source movement continues to gain momentum. The idea behind it is not new (it was popularized in 1998 with O'Reilly's Freeware Open Source Summit, now known as OSCON).[111] Historically, programs had been distributed by sharing the source code,

---

108. Peiris, M. "The Pros and Cons of Hosted Software." *SmartBiz*, March 2006 <http://www.smartbiz.com/article/articleview/1118/1/42>.

109. O'Reilly, T. "What is Web 2.0: Design Patterns and Business Models for the Next Generation of Software." September 2005 <http://www.oreillynet.com/pub/a/oreilly/tim/news/2005/09/30/what-is-web-20.html>.

110. 37Signals. *Getting Real*. 2006 <http://gettingreal.37signals.com>.

111. Van Rossum, G. "Open Source Summit Trip Report." *Linux Gazette*, 10 April 1998 <http://linuxgazette.net/issue28/rossum.html>.

before selling compiled programs became the norm. Though open source software is not always free, the source code is available (under license) to developers, who can customize it to meet their unique needs.

> *"Business-technology managers know all too well the adage about open source: It's free, as in a free puppy. The work and expense start once you get it home."*
> —Larry Greenemeier, *Information Week*[112]

Using open source projects, such as the popular Linux operating systems Red Hat or Ubuntu, may require more work and technical knowledge than using the Microsoft Windows or Apple Macintosh operating systems. However, advanced users are able to customize the software to fit their needs. Benefits to using an open source program include the possibility of reduced cost (if you have the skills to work with it) and the worldwide support networks where users help each other. Because the source code is available to everyone, users can look to the community for bug fixes and plug-ins (program extensions that add functionality), instead of waiting for the software vendor to address each issue. The Ubuntu forums, for example, contain a wealth of information created by users helping other users. In addition to the free support that springs up around open source projects, businesses have been built from developing project extensions and consulting. IBM invested $1 billion in Linux in 2001.

> *"Linux can do for business applications what the Internet did for networking and communications."*
> —Louis Gerstner, former CEO of IBM[113]

At `http://www.SourceForge.net` over 150,000 open source projects are under development. Other sites with open source downloads include freshmeat.net and Tucows. The popular *Firefox* web browser from the *Mozilla Foundation*, the Apache web server from the *Apache Software Foundation*, and the MySQL database system are all open source. DotNetNuke and PHPNuke offer open source frameworks for developing rich Internet portals, making it easy and economical to develop sophisticated websites. (`http://www.deitel.com` is a DotNetNuke site.)

Licensing: GNU Licenses and Creative Commons
Open source project licenses vary—many projects use the GNU General Public License (GPL), which allows redistribution of the project provided the source code is included and the copyright information is left intact. The Free Software Foundation provides other versions as well, including the GNU Lesser General Public License and the GNU Free Documentation License. The Open Source Initiative also lists over 50 licenses available to open source software developers, including the BSD license and the MIT license.[114]

Creative Commons (`creativecommons.org`) deals with licensing issues for all types of digital media. The organization offers a variety of options to support *remixing* (extending

---

112. Greenemeier, L. "Open-Source Exuberance." *Information Week*, 11 July 2005 <http://www.info rmationweek.com/story/showArticle.jhtml?articleID=165700923>.
113. Wilcox, J. "IBM to Spend $1 Billion on Linux in 2001." *CNET*, 12 December 2000 <http://news.com.com/IBM+to+spend+1+billion+on+Linux+in+2001/2100-1001_3-249750.html>.
114. Tiemann, M. "Licenses by Name." *Open Source Initiative*, 18 September 2006 <http://www.open source.org/licenses/alphabetical>.

existing content), commercial issues and attribution. By allowing users access to general licenses through Creative Commons or the Free Software Foundation, developers can worry less about the complicated issues of licensing and instead focus on developing.

1.12 Rich Internet Applications (RIAs)

Rich Internet Applications (RIAs) are web applications that offer the responsiveness, "rich" features and functionality approaching that of desktop applications. Early Internet applications supported only a basic HTML *graphical user interface (GUI)*. Though they could serve simple functions, these applications did not have the look or feel of a desktop application. The relatively slow Internet connections these applications relied on led to the term "World Wide Wait." RIAs are a result of today's more advanced technologies that allow greater responsiveness and advanced GUIs.

Ajax

The term *Ajax (Asynchronous JavaScript and XML)* was coined by Adaptive Path's Jesse James Garrett in February 2005. Ajax (see Chapter 13, Ajax-Enabled Rich Internet Applications) allows partial page updates—meaning updates of individual pieces of a web page without having to reload the entire page. This creates a more responsive GUI, allowing users to continue interacting with the page as the server processes requests.

The technologies that make up Ajax—XHTML, CSS, JavaScript, the DOM, XML, and the XMLHttpRequest object—are not new. In fact, in the 1990s, Netscape used asynchronous page updates in LiveScript, which evolved into JavaScript. However, the popularity of Ajax has dramatically increased since its naming. Ajax performs a vital role in Web 2.0, particularly in building webtop applications and enhancing the user's overall experience. The following toolkits and *frameworks* (environments with standard components that make development faster and easier) provide libraries and tools for convenient Ajax-enabled application development.

Dojo

Dojo is an open source JavaScript toolkit—it is a library, not a framework. Dojo development began in late 2004.[115] Dojo helps standardize JavaScript by providing a variety of packages for cross-browser compatibility, rich GUI controls, event handling and more. (See the Dojo section in Chapter 13.)

Flex

Adobe *Flex* (see Chapter 16) is an RIA framework that allows you to build scalable, cross-platform, multimedia-rich applications that can be delivered over the Internet. It uses the Flash Player 9 runtime environment, which is installed on over 97% of computers, allowing for almost universal compatibility.[116] Flash Player 9 is backed by ActionScript 3, Adobe's object-oriented scripting language—this uses an asynchronous programming model, which allows for partial page updates similar to Ajax. Flash CS3 (the development tool for creating Flash movies) is discussed in Chapters 14–15.

---

115. "History." *The Dojo Toolkit*, 10 April 2007 <http://dojotoolkit.org/book/dojo-book-0-9/
    introduction/history>.
116. "Adobe   Flex   2."   *Adobe*   <http://www.adobe.com/products/flex/whitepapers/pdfs/
    flex2wp_technicaloverview.pdf>.

JavaFX
JavaFX is Sun Microsystems' counterpart to Flex and Silverlight, also designed for building Rich Internet Applications. It consists of the JavaFX Script and JavaFX Mobile (for mobile devices). The JavaFX Script, which takes advantage of the fact Java is installed on most computers, will be available under open source licences (see `https://open jfx.dev.java.net/`).[117]

Ruby on Rails
Ruby on Rails (see Chapter 20), developed by 37Signals' David Heinemeier Hansson, is an open source framework based on the Ruby scripting language that allows you to build database-intensive applications quickly, easily, and with less code. Ruby on Rails was designed to build 37Signals' Basecamp (a project management and collaboration tool) and other SaaS products.

Script.aculo.us
The *Script.aculo.us* library for creating "eye candy" effects is built on the Prototype JavaScript framework. Prototype encapsulates the DOM (Document Object Model, Chapter 10) and provides cross-browser processing capabilities.[118] Script.aculo.us uses this framework and adds capabilities for rich user interfaces. Its core effects include opacity, scale, morph, move, highlight and parallel (for combining multiple effects).[119] Script.aculo.us is used on many popular websites and is incorporated into other frameworks (such as Ruby on Rails). We discuss Script.aculo.us and present examples in Chapter 20, Ruby on Rails.

JavaServer Faces
JavaServer Faces (JSF) is a Java-based web application framework. JSF separates design elements from business logic and provides a set of user-interface components (JSF components) that make developing RIAs simple. One of the *Java BluePrints* projects provides additional resources and libraries for building Ajax-enabled applications. We build RIAs with JSF in Chapters 22–23.

ASP.NET Ajax
ASP.NET Ajax (Chapter 21) is an extension of the .NET framework for creating Ajax-enabled applications. It includes an open source Ajax Control Toolkit for implementing asynchronous functionality. ASP.NET Ajax is easily used in Microsoft Visual Web Developer or Microsoft Visual Studio to quickly create Rich Internet Applications.

Adobe Integrated Runtime and Google Gears
Though web application use has been increasing, many feel these programs cannot truly compete with desktop applications until the "Offline Problem" (not being able to access web applications and data when not connected to the Internet) has been solved.[120] Busi-

---

117. "Sun Radically Simplifies Content Authoring—Previews JavaFX Script." *Sun Microsystems*, 8 May 2007 <http://www.sun.com/aboutsun/pr/2007-05/sunflash.20070508.2.xml>.
118. "Prototype Tips and Tutorials." *Prototype JavaScript* <http://prototypejs.org/learn>.
119. "Core Effects." *Script.aculo.us Wiki* <http://wiki.script.aculo.us/scriptaculous/show/CoreEffects>.

nesses can lose valuable time and money when Internet issues occur such as a slow or broken Internet connection.

Adobe released its **Adobe Integrated Runtime** (**AIR**; previously called Apollo) in beta form in June 2007. AIR allows users to run Flex web applications on their desktops even when they are *not* connected to the Internet, thus allowing users to remain efficient when they are unable to access the Internet or when an SaaS application server goes down. Users can continue their work and synchronize it with the servers again later.

Google Gears, also in beta, is a similar product, allowing use of web applications while offline. Google Gears was created out of a Google engineer's 20% project, inspired by wanting to use Google Reader on a bus with "flaky" Internet access.[121] (Google engineers devote 20% of their time to projects other than their usual work and 10% of their time to projects that are "truly new.")[122] **Dojo Offline** (using the Dojo library) is built on top of Google Gears, creating an easy-to-use interface for using web applications offline.[123]

1.13 Web Services, Mashups, Widgets and Gadgets

> *"Design for 'hackability' and remixability."*
> —Tim O'Reilly[124]

Instead of reinventing the wheel with every new project, developers can use existing companies' **web services** to create feature-rich applications. Incorporating web services into new programs allows people to develop new applications quickly.

APIs

APIs (Application Programming Interfaces) provide applications with access to external services and databases. For example, a traditional programming API, like the Sun's Java API, allows programmers to use already-written methods and functions in their programs. Web services APIs are now offered by some websites as ways of sharing some of their functionality and information across the Internet.

Unique databases are central to Web 2.0; "data is the next Intel Inside."[125] Whether data is obtained from a proprietary source or collected over time from users, much of a site's value is in its databases. Many major Web 2.0 companies (e.g., eBay, Amazon, Google, Yahoo! and Flickr) provide APIs to encourage use of their services and data in the development of mashups, widgets and gadgets.

---

120. Berlind, D. "Google Gears Vies to be De Facto Tech for Offline Web Apps." *ZDNet*, 31 May 2007 <http://blogs.zdnet.com/Berlind/?p=504>.

121. Mills, E. "Google Gears Churns Toward Microsoft." *CNET*, 31 May 2007 <http://news.com/2100-1012_3-6187942.html>.

122. "The 70 Percent Solution." *Business 2.0*, 28 November 2005 <http://money.cnn.com/2005/11/28/news/newsmakers/schmidt_biz20_1205/>.

123. "The Dojo Offline Toolkit." *The Dojo Toolkit* <http://dojotoolkit.org/offline>.

124. O'Reilly, T. "What is Web 2.0: Design Patterns and Business Models for the Next Generation of Software." September 2005 <http://www.oreillynet.com/pub/a/oreilly/tim/news/2005/09/30/what-is-web-20.html>.

125. O'Reilly, T. "What is Web 2.0: Design Patterns and Business Models for the Next Generation of Software." September 2005 <http://www.oreillynet.com/pub/a/oreilly/tim/news/2005/09/30/what-is-web-20.html>.

Mashups

Mashups combine content or functionality from existing web services, websites and RSS feeds to serve a new purpose. For example, *Housingmaps.com* is a mashup of Google Maps and real-estate listings from Craigslist. Mashups with maps are particularly popular, as are mashups using RSS feeds (see RSS and Atom in Section 1.15) created by using services such as Yahoo! Pipes™—a tool that enables you to aggregate and manipulate many data sources.

Using APIs can save time and money (some great mashups have been built in an afternoon); however, the mashup is then reliant on one or more third parties. If the API provider experiences downtime, the mashup will be unavailable as well (unless the mashup is programmed to avoid sites that are down). Always check the "terms of service" for using each company's web services. Many API providers charge usage fees based on the mashup's number of calls made to the server. Some sites require you to ask permission before using their APIs for commercial purposes, and others (e.g., Google) require that mashups based on their web services be free. Also, while mashups add value to data, there is always the question of who owns the data, and thus who should profit from the mashup.

Figure 1.4 lists some popular mashups. The site Programmable Web catalogs APIs and mashups and offers a "Mashup Matrix" (`http://www.programmableweb.com/matrix`) detailing which APIs have been combined to form each mashup. As more companies offer APIs, the only limitation on mashups (and the businesses built on them) is the developer's creativity. More complex mashups, using programs like Google Earth and Second Life, could be coming soon.[126]

Mashup	Combines
`http://www.housingmaps.com`	Google Maps and Craigslist real-estate listings to create a map marked with available housing listings.
`http://www.chicagocrime.org`	Google Maps and crime data from Citizen ICAM to create a map of Chicago marked with crime locations.
`http://www.feedmashr.com`	RSS feeds from Digg, ClipMarks, the *New York Times*, del.icio.us, Reddit and Slashdot to create a listing of the most popular stories from all sources.
`http://www.secretprices.com`	Amazon, Epinions.com and Shopping.com to create a comparison shopping site.
`http://paul.kedrosky.com/publicloos/`	Google Maps and Bathroom Diaries to create a map of San Francisco marked with the locations of public restrooms.

Fig. 1.4 | Mashup examples.

---

126. Roush, W. "Second Earth." *Technology Review*, July/August 2007, p.38.

Widgets and Gadgets

Widgets, also referred to as *gadgets*, are mini applications designed to run either as stand-alone applications or as add-on features in web pages. *Newsweek* called 2007 the "Year of the Widget" because of the huge increase in popularity of these applications.[127] Widgets can be used to personalize your Internet experience by displaying real-time weather conditions, aggregating RSS feeds, viewing maps, receiving event reminders, providing easy access to search engines and more. The availability of web services, APIs and various tools makes it easy even for beginner programmers to develop widgets. There are many catalogs of widgets online—one of the most all-inclusive is *Widgipedia*, which provides an extensive catalog of widgets and gadgets for a variety of platforms.

Amazon Web Services

Amazon is a leading provider of web services. The site provides historical pricing data and E-Commerce Services (ECS), which enable companies to use Amazon's systems to sell their own products. Amazon also offers hardware and communications infrastructure web services that are particularly popular with companies, providing economical *web-scale computing*. Amazon's Elastic Compute Cloud (EC2), Simple Storage Service (S3) and Simple Queue Service (SQS) enable businesses to pay for only the processing or storage space needed during any given period. This makes it possible for companies to save money (by not having to buy and maintain new hardware, software and communications equipment) while still being able to scale their storage and computing power to handle traffic surges (or reduce loss when the site's popularity declines). This is extremely significant in the Internet world, where a site's traffic can explode or crash overnight.

Amazon also provides "artificial artificial intelligence" with its unique *Mechanical Turk*. This web service allows applications to call on people to perform tasks (such as identifying pictures) that are easier for humans to do than computers. People can sign up to become part of Mechanical Turk and bid on jobs (called Human Intelligence Tasks or HITs). This creates a competitive market, driving down developer costs, creating opportunities for people worldwide and allowing more applications to become feasible.

REST (Representational State Transfer)-Based Web Services

Representational State Transfer (REST) (originally proposed in Roy Thomas Fielding's doctoral dissertation[128]) refers to an architectural style for implementing web services. Though REST is not a standard, RESTful web services are implemented using web standards. Each operation in a RESTful web service is easily identified by a unique URL. So, when the server receives a request, it immediately knows what operation to perform. Such web services can be used in a program or directly from a web browser. In some cases, the results of a particular operation may be cached locally by the browser. This can make subsequent requests for the same operation faster by loading the result directly from the browser's cache.[129] Amazon's S3 is RESTful, and many other Web 2.0 web services provide RESTful interfaces.[130]

---

127. Braiker, B. "Tech: Welcome, Year of the Widget." *Newsweek*, 30 December 2006 <http://www.msnbc.msn.com/id/16329739/site/newsweek/>.
128. Fielding, R. T. "Architectural Styles and the Design of Network-Based Software Architectures." <http://www.ics.uci.edu/~fielding/pubs/dissertation/top.htm>.
129. Costello, R. "REST Tutorial." *xFront*, 26 June 2002 <http://www.xfront.com/REST.html>.
130. Richardson, L. and S. Ruby. *RESTful Web Services*. O'Reilly, 2007.

RESTful web services are alternatives to those implemented with SOAP (Simple Object Access Protocol). (We discuss both REST-based and SOAP-based web services in Chapter 24, Web Services.) With SOAP-based web services, the request and response are hidden (in entities known as a SOAP "envelopes"). SOAP requests must be deciphered as they are received at the server to determine the operation to perform and the arguments required to perform that operation. Similarly, the responses are encoded and deciphered on the client to obtain the result of the operation. SOAP does not currently provide a mechanism for caching results.

1.14 Location-Based Services

Location-Based Services (LBS) are applications that take your geographic location (city, state, location of your mobile device, etc.) into consideration. While the term generally refers to services accessed on mobile devices using the Global Positioning System (GPS), it can also be used to describe web applications that take your location into account. Search engines including Yahoo! Local and Google Maps use *localization* to provide you with geographically relevant content. Local search is particularly useful when you want to find a nearby business (e.g., plumbers, taxis, etc.). Location-based services are becoming increasingly popular in Web 2.0 applications. Conferences related to LBS include O'Reilly's Where 2.0 and the Location Intelligence Conference.

Global Positioning System (GPS)

The *Global Positioning System (GPS)*, developed by the United States Department of Defense, uses numerous satellites that send signals to a GPS receiver to determine its exact location. (A Russian system called GLONASS also exists, and a new system named Galileo is under development in Europe.) In the 1980s, the US Department of Defense opened GPS for civilian use to encourage satellite technology development.[131] Numerous location-based services are now available using GPS technology, such as GPS mapping devices used in cars or on mobile devices. GPS is also being used for safety. The US Federal Communications Commission (FCC) now requires wireless carriers to provide the locations of wireless customers calling 911 so emergency services can find them faster. To meet this requirement, wireless carriers have developed GPS-enabled cell phones.[132] These phones also provide premium services, such as driving directions and local information. The Disney Family Locator service uses GPS-enabled phones to help parents keep track of their children (as long as the child is carrying the special cell phone).[133]

Mapping Services

Google Maps is one of the most popular mapping applications available online. You can use Google Maps to locate businesses in your area, get driving directions and live traffic information, create custom maps with images and more. You can even get the information by using your mobile device. Google's local search allows you to locate a business in a geographic area and get its address, phone number, driving directions and even user reviews. *Google Earth* provides satellite images of virtually any location on the planet. In some

---

131. Schiller, J. and A. Voisard. *Location-Based Services*. Morgan Kaufmann, 2004.
132. Malykhina, E. "Nokia Wants Your Cell Phone To Tell You Where You Are." *InformationWeek*, 9 October 2006 <http://www.informationweek.com/showArticle.jhtml?articleID=193105219>.
133. Magid, L. "Global Positioning by Cellphone." *New York Times*, 19 July 2007, C7.

areas, you can even get a panoramic view of a neighborhood at street level. You can use the Google Maps API to add mapping capabilities to your websites and web applications.

MapQuest, owned by AOL, provides similar mapping services. Use it to get directions and maps on your desktop or mobile device. The MapQuest OpenAPI allows you to add location-based services to your web applications. Additional mapping services include Yahoo! Local Maps and MSN Live Search. Both services offer maps, driving directions, traffic information and local search.

Companies such as *NAVTEQ* and *Tele Atlas* provide digital map data for in-vehicle and portable navigation devices, websites, location-based services and more. Developers building commercial location-based services can license the robust mapping products from these companies to build richly functional web applications.

GeoRSS and Geotagging

GeoRSS, based on the RSS standards, is a set of standards for representing geographical information in a feed. Location and geographical information in a GeoRSS feed can be used in GPS devices, mapping applications and other location-based services. For example, a blog post about a vacation could map the locations mentioned.[134]

Geotagging can be used to add location information (longitude, latitude, etc.) to websites, images, RSS feeds, videos and more. Websites can often determine a user's location by their IP address. Geotagging a website provides the user with location information about the site.[135] Geographic information can be used to add value to search results. Geotagging could also be mashed up with existing visualization systems, such as Google Earth or MSN Virtual Earth, which provide advanced satellite images for anywhere on the planet.

1.15 XML, RSS, Atom, JSON and VoIP

For more information on any of the following technologies, visit the corresponding Resource Centers at `http://www.deitel.com/resourcecenters.html` (see Fig. 3 in the Preface for a complete list of Deitel Resource Centers).

XML

XML (Extensible Markup Language, Chapter 12), developed in 1996 by the World Wide Web Consortium (W3C), is a markup language that allows you to label data based on its meaning. XML describes data in a way that is meaningful to both humans and computers.

XML documents are text files with a `.xml` extension; they can be created in text editors. These documents can reference a *Document Type Definition (DTD)* or a *schema*, which defines the structure for the document. This allows the information in the document to be verified by validating parsers, meaning they will check to make sure that no elements are missing (e.g., a last-name element in a document listing full names) and that the elements occur in the proper order. This makes XML data more reliable than data prepared with some other data-describing options. XML also can be used to create customized markup languages (e.g., XHTML for web content, CML for chemistry, MathML for mathematical content and formulas, and XBRL for financial data)—these are referred to as *XML vocab-*

---

134. "GeoRSS: Geographically Encoded Objects for RSS Feeds." *GeoRSS* `<http://georss.org/>`.
135. Turner, A. "Geotagging Web Pages and RSS Feeds." *Linux Journal*, 11 January 2005 `<http://in teractive.linuxjournal.com/node/8025>`.

ularies. XHTML is described in Chapter 2, Introduction to XHTML. Chapter 12, XML and RSS, presents several examples that use MathML to render mathematical expressions.

RSS and Atom

Sites that offer RSS (Chapter 12) and Atom feeds can maintain an "open connection" with their readers. Users no longer have to regularly visit sites for updates—by subscribing to a site's feed, users receive updates as new information is posted to the site. The difference between RSS and Atom is subtle and unimportant to most users—many tools support both formats. Versions of RSS (an XML-based web content syndication format) have existed since the late 1990s; Atom dates to 2003.

Most major web browsers support RSS and Atom feeds, and many *aggregators* (or feed readers) are available to help users organize their subscriptions. Feedburner (acquired by Google) is used by many blogs to provide their readers with new posts by e-mail. This service also helps bloggers get a better idea of the size of their audience (by allowing them to see the number of subscribers).

JSON

JavaScript Object Notation (JSON) was developed in 1999 as an alternative to XML. JSON (discussed in Chapter 13, Ajax-Enabled Rich Internet Applications) is a text-based data interchange format used to represent JavaScript objects as strings and transmit them over a network. It is commonly used in Ajax applications. JSON text is easy to produce and read—it is also faster to parse (or extract) than XML.

VoIP

Voice over Internet Protocol (VoIP) is the technology used to make free or inexpensive phone calls over the Internet. Some businesses and individuals have switched completely to VoIP and eliminated traditional phone lines to cut costs. There are many VoIP services, such as Vonage, Packet8 or Lingo; Skype is the most popular. Acquired by eBay to integrate buyer and seller voice communication into auctions,[136] Skype offers free and fee-based services (such as calling non-Skype phones). VoIP is an enabling technology that can be layered into Web 2.0 companies and websites.

1.16 Web 2.0 Monetization Models

> *"The advertising model has come along; we underestimated how big that would be."*
> —Bill Gates, MIX06

Many Web 1.0 businesses discovered that popularity ("eyeballs") was not the same as financial success. Web 2.0 companies are paying more attention to *monetizing* their traffic. Starting an Internet business is cheaper than ever, and the cost of failure is lower. Anyone can start earning modest amounts of money almost immediately, using the monetization models described in Fig. 1.5.

Web 2.0 monetization is heavily reliant on advertising. Using Google's AdSense contextual advertising program is one of the fastest and most popular ways of monetizing a new Internet business. For more information see Deitel's Google AdSense and Website Monetization Resource Centers at `http://www.deitel.com/resourcecenters.html`.

136.Broache, A. "eBay to Nab Skype for $2.6 Billion." *CNET*, 12 September 2005 <`http://news.com.com/eBay+to+nab+Skype+for+2.6+billion/2100-1030_3-5860055.html`>.

Web 2.0 monetization models

affiliate network—A business (such as Commission Junction and LinkShare) that connects web publishers with cost-per-action affiliate programs. See affiliate program.

affiliate program—A deal offered by a company to share a portion of the revenues earned from traffic coming from web publisher websites. Affiliates provide text and image ads to post on the publishers' sites. If a user clicks through to the affiliate site and takes a specified action (e.g., makes a purchase, fills out a registration form, etc.) the publisher is paid a portion of the revenue or a flat fee. Companies offering affiliate programs include Amazon (the Amazon Associates program), Indeed, ClickBank, eBay and thousands more.

banner ad—An ad that consists of an image, often placed at the top of a page.

blog advertising—Advertising specifically designed for display on blog sites. Companies include Federated Media and Blogads.

contextual advertising—Advertising that is targeted to the content on a web page. Contextual ad programs include Google AdSense, Yahoo! Publisher Network, Vibrant Media, Kontera and Tribal Fusion.

cost-per-action (CPA)—Advertising that is billed to the advertiser per user action (e.g., purchasing a product or filling out a mortgage application). Companies include Amazon and Indeed. See also performance-based advertising.

cost-per-click (CPC)—Advertising that is billed by user click. The web publisher receives revenue each time a user clicks an ad on the publisher's site, regardless of whether the user makes a subsequent purchase. Companies include Google AdSense and Yahoo! Publisher Network.

cost-per-thousand impressions (CPM)—Advertising (usually banner advertising) that is billed per thousand impressions, regardless of whether the user clicks on the ad.

Companies include DoubleClick, ValueClick and many more.

e-commerce—Selling products and/or services directly through a website. Companies include Amazon, Dell, CafePress.com and thousands more.

interstitial ad—An ad that plays between page loads. Companies include Tribal Fusion, DoubleClick, and many more.

in-text contextual advertising—Advertising that is marked by double-underlined keywords or phrases in the content of a web page. When a reader hovers the mouse cursor over a double-underlined word or phrase, a text ad pops up. By clicking on an ad, readers are taken to the advertiser's page. Companies providing in-text contextual advertising include Vibrant Media, Text Link Ads, Kontera and Tribal Fusion.

lead generation—Leads are generated when a visitor fills out an inquiry form so that a salesperson can follow through and potentially convert the lead to a sale. Lead generation is a subset of cost-per-action advertising. See cost-per-action (CPA).

paid blog post—A blog post (often a product review) that an advertiser pays a blogger to write. Some argue the ethics of this practice, and bloggers are encouraged to disclose that they are being paid for the posts. Companies that match bloggers and advertisers include PayPerPost, SponsoredReviews and ReviewMe.

performance-based advertising—Advertising that pays based on user action, such as making a purchase, filling out a registration form, etc. These are also often part of affiliate programs such as Amazon and ClickBank. See cost-per-action (CPA).

premium content—Content on a website that is available for an extra fee (e.g., e-books, articles, etc.). Companies that offer premium content include *The Wall Street Journal Online* and Search Engine Watch.

Fig. 1.5 | Web 2.0 monetization models. (Part 1 of 2.)

Web 2.0 monetization models	
RSS ad—An ad included in RSS feeds. Companies include Feedster, Feedburner and Yahoo! Search Marketing.	Search engines may lower the ranking of sites with paid links.] An example is 1000tags.com.
tagging for profit—A site that buys inbound links or tags from other sites to help increase traffic, and thus increase potential advertising revenue. High-traffic sites can sell tags or links to other websites for a profit. [*Caution:*	**virtual worlds monetization**—Selling products, premium services, virtual land and more in an online virtual world website. Virtual worlds include Second Life, IMVU, Habbo, Gaia Online and There.

Fig. 1.5 | Web 2.0 monetization models. (Part 2 of 2.)

1.17 Web 2.0 Business Models

The technologies and collaborative nature of Web 2.0 have opened up new business models. Some of these would not have been feasible even ten years ago, but because of Moore's Law they are not only possible but thriving. At the moment, there is no foreseeable end to the advancements attributed to Moore's Law, so fantastic ideas that are impossible today may become possible within just a few years. Figure 1.6 outlines many popular Internet business models and lists some companies that use each one. In just about every case, there are many more companies using that business model.

Web 2.0 business models	
advertising exchange—An online marketplace where web publishers can sell their advertising inventory (ad space) to advertisers. Companies include DoubleClick Advertising Exchange and Right Media Exchange.	**blog search engine**—A search engine devoted to the blogosphere. Companies include Technorati, Feedster, IceRocket and Google Blog Search.
affiliate network—A business that connects web publishers with cost-per-action affiliate programs, which are a form of cost-per-action advertising. Companies include Commission Junction and LinkShare. (See Fig. 1.5 for more information on affiliate programs.)	**blog network**—A collection of blogs with multiple editors. Popular blog networks include Corante, 9rules, Gawker Media and Weblogs, Inc.
blog—A website with a series of posts in reverse chronological order. Many blogs attract significant traffic and monetize with advertising and affiliate programs. Popular blogs include BoingBoing, Gizmodo, TechCrunch, John Battelle's Searchblog, Problogger and Scobleizer.	**buying and selling domain names**—A company purchases domain names with the intent of selling them in the future as Internet real estate becomes more valuable. Companies include Afternic.com and GreatDomains.
	competitive intelligence—A company that analyzes Internet usage for use by client websites. Companies include Hitwise and Compete, Inc.

Fig. 1.6 | Web 2.0 business models. (Part 1 of 4.)

Web 2.0 business models

content network—A site (or collection of sites) that provides content including articles, wikis, blogs and more. Companies include About.com, Deitel, LifeTips and Suite101.

discovery—A site that introduces users to valuable content they would not have looked for otherwise. Sites include StumbleUpon, Aggregate Knowledge, MOG and Deitel.

domain registrar—A site that sells domain names. Companies include Register.com, GoDaddy and Network Solutions.

encyclopedia and reference source—An online reference encyclopedia, dictionary, thesaurus, etc. Sites include Wikipedia, Reference.com and Citizendium.

feed aggregator—An application that combines RSS or Atom feeds so the user can view all subscriptions in a single location. Applications include NetNewsWire, Google Reader and Bloglines.

file sharing—An application where users can share files, music, software and more. Companies include BitTorrent, LimeWire, Kazaa, AllPeers and Shareaza.

infrastructure for distributing open source projects—A site that hosts collaborative open source software projects. Sites include SourceForge, freshmeat.net and Tucows.

Internet and web conference organizer—A company that organizes conferences on Internet and web topics. Companies include O'Reilly Media, CMP and Jupiter.

Internet radio—A site that distributes music and radio shows over the Internet. Companies include Last.fm and Pandora.

Internet TV—A site that distributes television shows (or allows you to distribute your own shows) over the Internet. Companies include Joost and Brightcove.

Internet video—A video sharing site where users upload and share content. Companies include YouTube and Yahoo! Video.

job boards and job search—A site that connects job seekers with employers and/or job search engines. Job boards include Monster, CareerBuilder and Dice. Job search engines include Indeed, Jobster and SimplyHired.

mashup—A combination of two or more existing web services and feeds to create a new application. For example, http://www.housingmaps.com combines real estate listings from Craigslist with Google Maps so you can view the listings on a map. For a list of popular mashups, see http://www.programmableweb.com/popular.

massively multiplayer online game—An online role playing or strategy game where Internet users interact with one another. Games include World of Warcraft, Guild Wars and Lineage.

mobile social networking—A social network oriented towards mobile devices (such as cell phones). Companies include Twitter, Dodgeball and MocoSpace.

music distribution site—An online music site where you can purchase electronic versions (e.g., .mp3) of single songs or entire albums. Companies include iTunes, Rhapsody and Amie Street.

online advertising—An online advertising company that offers contextual advertising, banner advertising, in-text contextual advertising and more. Companies include Google, Yahoo!, Microsoft, DoubleClick, Vibrant Media, Tribal Fusion, Kontera, Quigo, ValueClick, Federated Media and many more.

online auction—A marketplace where visitors bid for products (and services) over the Internet. Companies include eBay, Overstock.com and Amazon Auctions.

online classifieds—A classifieds "advertising" site where users can post jobs, real-estate listings, personal ads, etc. Companies include Craigslist, Yahoo! Classifieds and Google Base.

Fig. 1.6 | Web 2.0 business models. (Part 2 of 4.)

Web 2.0 business models

online survey site—A site that offers survey services to other companies. A popular example is Survey Monkey.

open source—Software that is available (under license) for anyone to use and modify with few or no restrictions. Many Web 2.0 companies use open source software to power their sites and offer open source products and content. Companies include the Free Software Foundation, Apache, Mozilla, Zend and many more.

outsourcing marketplaces—An online marketplace where contractors and freelancers can connect with potential clients for short-term work. Companies include Elance and Guru.com.

payments—A site that handles secure payments for e-commerce sites. Companies include PayPal and Google Checkout.

people-assisted search—A search engine or search-driven content site that is filtered and organized by people to provide users with more relevant search results. Companies include Mahalo and Deitel.

personalized start page—A site that allows you to customize a start page with weather, news, etc. Companies include Netvibes, iGoogle, Pageflakes and Protopage.

photo sharing site—A site where users can post and share their photos with other users. Companies include Flickr and Photobucket.

real estate—A site that offers online real estate listings and information. Companies include Redfin, Trulia and Zillow.

recommender system—A system that collects data using collaborative filtering systems to determine users' tastes and interests. Sites can gather information about your personal interests, compare you to other users with similar interests and make recommendations. Popular examples of sites using recommender systems include Pandora, Netflix, CleverSet, ChoiceStream, MyStrands, StumbleUpon, Last.fm, and MovieLens.

reputation system—A system used by businesses like eBay and Amazon to encourage trust. For example, after each eBay transaction, the buyer and the seller can each leave positive or negative comments about the other party.

search engine—The primary tool people use to find information on the web. Companies include Google, Yahoo!, MSN, Ask and many more.

selling digital content—An e-commerce site that sells digital media (e.g., e-books). Companies include ClickBank, Blish, Lulu and more.

social bookmarking site—A site that allows users to share their bookmarks with others. Users bookmark their favorites sites, articles, blogs and more, and tag them by keyword. Companies include del.icio.us, Ma.gnolia and Blue Dot.

social media site—A site that allows digital media (text, photos, videos, music, etc.) to be shared online. Companies include Digg, YouTube, Flickr, Reddit, Wikipedia and more.

social networking site—A site that helps users organize their existing relationships and establish new ones. Companies include MySpace, Facebook, Bebo, LinkedIn, Second Life, Gaia Online and more.

Software as a Service (SaaS)—Software that runs on a web server rather than being installed on a local client computer. By modifying the version of the software on the server, a company can simultaneously update all users to the latest version. SaaS applications include Salesforce.com, Microsoft Office Live, Microsoft Windows Live, Zoho Office Suite and many Google and 37Signals products.

subscription site—A site that offers member-only areas and premium content (additional content for a fee). Examples include Safari Books Online and the *Wall Street Journal*.

Fig. 1.6 | Web 2.0 business models. (Part 3 of 4.)

Web 2.0 business models

travel site—An online travel resource site that allows you to find and book hotels, air travel, rental cars and more. Companies include Expedia, Travelocity and Orbitz.

vertical search engine—A search engine that allows you to focus your search on a narrow topic. For example, travel search engines include Yahoo! Fare Finder, SideStep and Kayak; source-code search engines include Krugle and Koders.

virtual world—A social networking site (or program) where users create an avatar (their online image and persona) that they use to meet other users with similar interests, conduct business, participate in group activities, take classes and more. Companies include Second Life, Habbo, Gaia Online and There.

Voice over Internet Protocol (VoIP) site—A site that offers inexpensive or free telephone services over the Internet. Companies include Skype, Packet8, Lingo and Vonage.

Web 2.0 software—Software designed to build Web 2.0 sites and applications (e.g., blogging software). Companies include Six Apart, 37Signals, Adobe and Microsoft.

web analytics—Software (desktop and SaaS) and companies that analyze Internet traffic, demographics, navigation and more. Companies include Alexa, WebTrends, Click-Tracks, Google Analytics and WebSideStory.

web and mobile messaging—A service that allows you to chat with your contacts from various Internet messaging services (AIM, Yahoo! Messenger, MSN Messenger, Google Talk).·Companies include Meebo and eBuddy.

web conferencing—An application that enables users to collaborate remotely. This often includes chat, VoIP and desktop sharing. Companies include WebEx, GoToMeeting and DimDim (open source).

webmail—A web-based e-mail system that allows you to send and receive e-mail using a standard browser. Popular webmail services include Google gmail, .Mac, Yahoo! Mail and MSN Hotmail.

wiki—A site that offers collaborative, editable documents online. Companies include Wikipedia, Wikia and SocialText.

Fig. 1.6 | Web 2.0 business models. (Part 4 of 4.)

1.18 Future of the Web

"Web 2.0 will make the cover of Time *magazine, and thus its moment in the sun will have passed. However, the story that drives Web 2.0 will only strengthen, and folks will cast about for the next best name for the phenomenon."*
—John Battelle[137]

"We're a long way from the full realization of the potential of intelligent systems, and there will no doubt be a tipping point where the systems get smart enough that we'll be ready to say, 'this is qualitatively different. Let's call it Web 3.0.'"
—Tim O'Reilly[138]

---

137. Battelle, John. "2006 Predictions, How Did I Do?" *John Battelle Searchblog,* <http://battellemedia.com/archives/003216.php>.
138. O'Reilly, Tim. "Web 3.0 Maybe when we get there." *O'Reilly Radar,* 13 November 2006 <http://radar.oreilly.com/archives/2006/11/web_30_maybe_wh.html>.

The XHTML coding on websites defines their structure and layout, specifying colors, fonts, sizes, use of bold and italic, paragraphs, tables and the like, but *not* specifying the *meaning* of the data on the page. Web 1.0 servers sent mostly static web pages coded in HTML or XHTML to browsers that rendered the pages on the screen. Web 2.0 applications are more dynamic, generally enabling significant interaction between the user (the client) and the computer (the server), and among communities of users.

Computers have a hard time deciphering meaning from XHTML content. The web today involves *users'* interpretations of what pages and images mean, but the future entails a shift from XHTML to a more sophisticated system based on XML, enabling *computers* to better understand meaning.

Web 2.0 companies use "data mining" to extract as much meaning as they can from XHTML-encoded pages. For example, Google's AdSense contextual advertising program does a remarkable job placing relevant ads next to content based on some interpretation of the meaning of that content. XHTML-encoded content does not explicitly convey meaning, but XML-encoded content does. So if we can encode in XML (and derivative technologies) much or all of the content on the web, we'll take a great leap forward towards realizing the Semantic Web.

It is unlikely that web developers and users will directly encode all web content in XML—it's simply too tedious and probably too complex for most web designers. Rather, the XML encoding will occur naturally as a by-product of using various content creation tools. For example, to submit a resume on a website, there may be a tool that enables the user to fill out a form (with first name, last name, phone number, career goal, etc.). When the resume is submitted, the tool could create a computer readable microformat that could easily be found and read by applications that process resumes. Such tools might help a company find qualified potential employees, or help a job seeker who wants to write a resume find resumes of people with similar qualifications).

Tagging and Folksonomies

Tagging and folksonomies are early hints of a "web of meaning." Without tagging, searching for a picture on Flickr would be like searching for a needle in a giant haystack. Flickr's tagging system allows users to subjectively tag pictures with meaning, making photos findable by search engines. Tagging is a "loose" classification system, quite different, for example, from using the Dewey Decimal System for cataloging books, which follows a rigid taxonomy system, limiting your choices to a set of predetermined categories. Tagging is a more "democratic" labeling system that allows people, for example, to associate whatever meanings they choose with a picture (e.g. who is in the picture, where it was taken, what is going on, the colors, the mood, etc.).

Semantic Web

> *"People keep asking what Web 3.0 is. I think maybe when you've got an overlay of scalable vector graphics—everything rippling and folding and looking misty—on Web 2.0 and access to a semantic Web integrated across a huge space of data, you'll have access to an unbelievable data resource."*
>
> —Tim Berners-Lee[139]

139.Shannon, V. "A 'More Revolutionary' Web." May 2006 <http://www.iht.com/articles/2006/05/23/business/web.php>.

> *"The Holy Grail for developers of the semantic Web is to build a system that can give a reasonable and complete response to a simple question like: I'm looking for a warm place to vacation and I have a budget of $3,000. Oh, and I have an 11-year-old child...Under Web 3.0, the same search would ideally call up a complete vacation package that was planned as meticulously as if it had been assembled by a human travel agent."*
>
> —John Markoff[140]

Many people consider the **Semantic Web** to be the next generation in web development, one that helps to realize the full potential of the web. This is Tim Berners-Lee's original vision of the web, also known as the "**web of meaning**."[141] Though Web 2.0 applications are finding meaning in content, the Semantic Web will attempt to make those meanings clear to computers as well as humans. It will be a web able to answer complex and subtle questions.

Realization of the Semantic Web depends heavily on XML and XML-based technologies (see Chapter 12), which help make web content more understandable to computers. Currently, computers "understand" data on basic levels, but are progressing to find meaningful connections and links between data points. The emerging Semantic Web technologies highlight new relationships among web data. Some experiments that emphasize this are Flickr and FOAF (Friend of a Friend), a research project that "is creating a Web of machine-readable pages describing people, the links between them and the things they create and do."[142] Programming in both instances involves links between databases—ultimately allowing users to share, transfer, and use each other's information (photos, blogs, etc.).[143]

Preparations for the Semantic Web have been going on for years. XML is already widely used in both online and offline applications, but still only a minute portion of the web is coded in XML or derivative technologies. Many companies, including **Zepheira**, an information management company, and Joost, an Internet TV provider, already use semantic technologies in working with data. Deterring Semantic Web development are concerns about the consequences of false information and the abuse of data. Since the Semantic Web will rely on computers having greater access to information and will yield a deeper understanding of its significance, some people worry about the potentially increased consequences of security breaches. The **Policy Aware Web Project** is an early attempt at developing standards to encourage data sharing by providing access policies that can sufficiently protect individuals' privacy concerns.[144]

---

140. Markoff, John. "Entrepreneurs See a Web Guided by Common Sense." The New York Times, November 2006 <http://www.nytimes.com/2006/11/12/business/12web.html?ex=1320987600&en=254d697964cedc62&ei=5088>.
141. Berners-Lee, T. *Weaving the Web*. Harper-Collins, 2000.
142. Friend of a Friend Project homepage. <http://www.foaf-project.org/>.
143. Shannon, Victoria. "A 'More Revolutionary' Web." *International Herald Tribune*. May 24 2006 <http://www.iht.com/articles/2006/05/23/business/web.php>.
144. Weitzner, D., J. Hendler, T. Berners-Lee, and D. Connolly. "Creating a Policy-Aware Web: Discretionary, Rule-based Access for the World Wide Web." October 2004 <http://www.w3.org/2004/09/Policy-Aware-Web-acl.pdf>.

Microformats

> *"We need microformats that people agree on."*
> — Bill Gates, MIX06 conference[145]

Some people look at the web and see lots of "loose" information. Others see logical aggregates, such as business cards, resumes, events and so forth. *Microformats* are standard formats for representing information aggregates that can be understood by computers, enabling better search results and new types of applications. The key is for developers to use standard microformats, rather than developing customized, non-standard data aggregations. Microformat standards encourage sites to similarly organize their information, thus increasing interoperability. For example, if you want to create an event or an events calendar, you could use the hCalendar microformat. Some other microformats are adr for address information, hresume for resumes, and xfolk for collections of bookmarks.[146]

Resource Description Framework (RDF)

The *Resource Description Framework (RDF)*, developed by the World Wide Web Consortium (W3C), is based on XML and used to describe content in a way that is understood by computers. RDF helps connect isolated databases across the web with consistent semantics.[147] The structure of any expression in RDF is a collection of triples.[148] *RDF triples* consist of two pieces of information (subject and object) and a linking fact (predicate). Let's create a simple RDF triple. "Chapter 1, Dive Into® Web 2.0" is the title of this document and one property (the document's subject) that we'll use in our RDF triple. Another property of this chapter is "Deitel" as the author. So the sentence "Chapter 1, Dive Into® Web 2.0 is written by Deitel" is an RDF triple, containing two properties and a linking fact ("is written by").

DBpedia.org is currently transferring content into RDF from Wikipedia, one of the largest and most popular resources of online information. Using *SPARQL* (SPARQL Protocol and RDF Query Language), DBpedia.org is converting data from Wikipedia entries into RDF triples. In June 2007, they claimed to have over 91 million triples—this will allow the information (from Wikipedia) to be accessed by more advanced search queries.[149]

Ontologies

Ontologies are ways of organizing and describing related items, and are used to represent semantics. This is another means of cataloging Internet content in a way that can be understood by computers.[150] RDF is designed for formatting ontologies. *OWL (Web Ontology Language)*, also designed for formatting ontologies in XML, extends beyond the basic semantics of RDF ontologies to enable even deeper machine understanding of content.[151]

---

145. "Bill Gates: Microsoft MIX06 Conference." *Microsoft*, March 2006.

146. "Microformats Wiki." *microformats.org* <http://microformats.org/wiki/Main_Page>.

147. Miller, E. "An Introduction to the Resource Description Framework." *D-Lib Magazine*, May 1998 <http://dlib.org/dlib/may98/miller/05miller.html>.

148. "Resource Description Framework (RDF) Concepts and Abstract Sytax." *w3.org* <http://www.w3.org/TR/rdf-concepts/#section-Concepts>.

149. *DBPedia.org.* <http://dbpedia.org/docs/>.

150. Heflin, J. "OWL Web Ontology Language Use Cases and Requirements." *W3C*, 10 February 2004 <http://www.w3.org/TR/webont-req/>.

151. "Introduction to OWL." *W3Schools* <http://www.w3schools.com/rdf/rdf_owl.asp>.

Closing Comment

This book will get you up to speed on Web 2.0 applications development. Building a "web of meaning" will ultimately open a floodgate of opportunities for web developers and entrepreneurs to write new applications, create new kinds of businesses, etc. We don't know exactly what the "web of meaning" will look like, but it's starting to take shape. If it helps accomplish what many leaders in the web community believe is possible, the future of the web will be exciting indeed.

1.19 Where to Go for More Web 2.0 Information

Figure 1.7 lists some popular resources for Web 2.0 news and analysis.

Resource	Description
TechCrunch http://www.techcrunch.com/	Edited by Michael Arrington, this blog is the leading Web 2.0 news resource that profiles innovative and important Internet companies and products.
Mashable http://www.mashable.com/	A social networking news blog, edited by Pete Cashmore. The site includes sections devoted to MySpace, YouTube, Bebo, Facebook and Xanga.
ReadWriteWeb http://www.readwriteweb.com/	Edited by Richard MacManus, this blog provides web technology news, reviews and analysis.
GigaOM http://www.gigaom.com/	Technology news and analysis blog, edited by Om Malik—founder of GigaOmniMedia and a former writer for Business 2.0, Red Herring and Forbes.com.
Dion Hinchcliffe's Web 2.0 Blog http://web2.socialcomputingmagazine.com/	Web 2.0 news and analysis blog by Dion Hinchcliffe, Editor-in-Chief of *Social Computing* Magazine.
Matt Cutts' Blog http://www.mattcutts.com/blog/	Matt Cutts, a software engineer at Google, blogs about gadgets, Google and SEO.
O'Reilly Radar http://radar.oreilly.com/	O'Reilly Media's blog about Web 2.0, open source, emerging technology and more.
SearchEngineLand http://www.searchengineland.com/	Search engine news blog, edited by Danny Sullivan—a leading search engine expert.
SearchEngineWatch http://searchenginewatch.com/	News and analysis of the search engine industry. Includes blogs, tutorials, forums and more.
Deitel Resource Centers http://www.deitel.com/resourcecenters.html (See Fig. 3 in the Preface for a list of Resource Centers.)	Numerous Web 2.0 technology and Internet business Resource Centers that include links to, and descriptions of tutorials, demos, free software tools, articles, e-books, whitepapers, videos, podcasts, blogs, RSS feeds and more.

Fig. 1.7 | Web 2.0 news, analysis, technology and business resources.

1.20 Web 2.0 Bibliography

General Web 2.0
Anderson, C. *The Long Tail: Why the Future of Business Is Selling Less of More.* Hyperion, 2006.

Anderson, C. "The Long Tail." *WIRED*, October 2004 <http://www.wired.com/wired/archive/12.10/tail.html>.

Battelle, J. *The Search: How Google and Its Rivals Rewrote the Rules of Business and Transformed Our Culture.* Portfolio, 2005.

"Bill Gates: Microsoft MIX06 Conference." *Microsoft*, March 2006 <http://www.microsoft.com/presspass/exec/billg/speeches/2006/03-20MIX.mspx>.

Brin, S. and L. Page. "The Anatomy of a Large-Scale Hypertextual Web Search Engine." <http://infolab.stanford.edu/~backrub/google.html>.

Farber, D. "ETech: Attenuation, Web 2.0 and spimes." *ZDNet*, March 2006 <http://blogs.zdnet.com/BTL/?p=2667>.

Graham, P. "Web 2.0." November 2005 <http://www.paulgraham.com/web20.html>.

Grossman, L. "*TIME's* Person of the Year: You." *TIME*, December 2006 <http://www.time.com/time/magazine/article/0,9171,1569514,00.html>.

Hinchcliffe, D. "The State of Web 2.0." April 2006 <http://web2.socialcomputingmagazine.com/the_state_of_web_20.htm>.

Horrigan, J. B. "Home Broadband Adoption 2006." *Pew Internet & American Life Project*, May 2006 <http://www.pewinternet.org/pdfs/PIP_Broadband_trends2006.pdf>.

Madden, M. and S. Fox. "Riding the Waves of 'Web 2.0.'"*Pew Internet & American Life Project*, October 2006 <http://www.pewinternet.org/pdfs/PIP_Web_2.0.pdf>.

Miller, P. "Thinking About This Web 2.0 Thing." August 2005 <http://paulmiller.typepad.com/thinking_about_the_future/2005/08/thinking_about_.html>.

Moore, G. "Cramming More Components onto Integrated Circuits." *Electronics*, April 1965 <http://ftp://download.intel.com/museum/Moores_Law/Articles-Press_Releases/Gordon_Moore_1965_Article.pdf>.

Musser, J. and T. O'Reilly. *Web 2.0 Principles and Best Practices.* O'Reilly Media, Inc., 2006.

O'Reilly, T. "Web 2.0: Compact Definition?" October 2005 <http://radar.oreilly.com/archives/2005/10/web_20_compact_definition.html>.

O'Reilly, T. "What is Web 2.0: Design Patterns and Business Models for the Next Generation of Software." September 2005 <http://www.oreillynet.com/pub/a/oreilly/tim/news/2005/09/30/what-is-web-20.html>.

"Tim O'Reilly's seven principles of web 2.0 make a lot more sense if you change the order." *Open Gardens*, April 2006 <http://opengardensblog.futuretext.com/archives/2006/04/tim_o_reillys_s.html>.

Search
"About Rollyo." *Rollyo* <http://www.rollyo.com/about.html>.

"About Us."*Microsoft adCenter Labs* <http://adlab.msn.com/AboutUs.aspx>.

Brin, S. and L. Page. "The Anatomy of a Large-Scale Hypertextual Web Search Engine." <http://infolab.stanford.edu/~backrub/google.html>.

Calore, M. "Remembering the First Google Bomb." *Compiler (WIRED blog)*, 26 January 2007 <http://blog.wired.com/monkeybites/2007/01/earlier_today_m.html>.

"Company History." *Yahoo!* <http://yahoo.client.shareholder.com/press/history.cfm>.

"Company Overview." *Google* <http://www.google.com/intl/en/corporate/index.html>.

"comScore Search Rankings." *CNN,* 16 July 2007 <http://money.cnn.com/news/newsfeeds/articles/prnewswire/AQM17916072007-1.htm>.

Davenport, T. and J. Beck. *The Attention Economy: Understanding the New Currency of Business.* Harvard Business School Press, 2002.

"Google: One Million and Counting." *Pandia Search Engine News,* 2 July 2007 <http://www.pandia.com/sew/481-gartner.html>.

"Mahalo FAQ." *Mahalo* <http://www.mahalo.com/Mahalo_FAQ>.

"Microsoft Digital Advertising Solutions." *Microsoft.* <http://advertising.microsoft.com/advertising-online>.

Mills, E. "Google Rises at Yahoo's expense." *CNET,* 23 April 2007 <http://news.com.com/Google+rises+at+Yahoos+expense/2100-1038_3-6178164.html>.

Morville, P. *Ambient Findability: What We Find Changes Who We Become.* O'Reilly Media Inc., 2005.

"MSN Live Search: About Us." *MSN* <http://search.msn.com/docs/default.aspx?FORM=HLHP2>.

Olson, S. "MSN Launches Revamped Search Engine." *CNET,* 30 June 2004 <http://news.com.com/MSN+launches+revamped+search+engine/2100-1032_3-5254083.html>.

Search Engine Strategies: Conference & Expos, 2007 <http://www.searchenginestrategies.com>.

Sherman, C. "The State of Search Engine Marketing 2006." *Search Engine Land,* 8 February 2007 <http://searchengineland.com/070208-095009.php>.

Sullivan, D. "Congratulations! You're a Search Engine Marketer!" *Search Engine Watch,* 5 November 2005 <http://searchenginewatch.com/showPage.html?page=2164351>.

"Technology Overview." *Google* <http://www.google.com/corporate/tech.html>.

Thompson, C. "Media in the Age of the Swarm." *cbc.ca* <http://www.cbc.ca/10th/columns/media_thompson.html>.

Underwood, L. "A Brief History of Search Engines." *Web Ref.* <http://www.webreference.com/authoring/search_history/>.

"Vertical Search-Engines: Know Your Subject." *Economist.com,* 12 July 2007 <http://www.economist.com/business/displaystory.cfm?story_id=9478224>.

"Web Search: How to use MSN Search." *MSN* <http://search.msn.com/docs/help.aspx?t=SEARCH_CONC_WhatsNewWithMSNSearch.htm#2D>.

Wilding, R. "Top 5 Black Hat and White Hat Search Engines Optimisation Techniques." *PushON* <http://www.pushon.co.uk/articles/top5-black-hat-white-hat-seo.htm>.

User-Generated Content

Cauchi, S. "Online Encyclopedias Put to the Test." *The Age,* December 2005 <http://www.theage.com/au/news/national/online-encyclopedias-put-to-the-test/2005/12/14/1134500913345.html>.

"Leading Indicators." *FORTUNE,* 13 November 2006, p.40.

Maney, K. "Techies Hot on Concept of 'Wisdom of Crowds,' But It Has Some Pitfalls." *USA Today,* September 2006 <http://www.usatoday.com/tech/columnist/kevinmaney/2006-09-12-wisdom-of-crowds_x.htm>.

O'Reilly, T. "The Architecture of Participation." June 2004 <http://oreillynet.com/lpt/a/5994>.

Seigenthaler, J. "A False Wikipedia 'Biography.'" *USA Today*, November 2005 <http://www.usatoday.com/news/opinion/editorials/2005-11-29-wikipedia-edit_x.htm>.

"SocialText is the Enterprise Wiki Trusted Most by Global 2000 Corporations." *SocialText* <http://www.socialtext.com/products/overview>.

Steel, E. "Newspapers' Ad Sales Show Accelerating Drop." *The Wall Street Journal*, 18 July 2007, A4.

Surowiecki, J. *The Wisdom of Crowds*. Anchor, 2005.

Tapscott, D. and A. D. Williams. *Wikinomics: How Mass Collaboration Changes Everything*. Portfolio Hardcover, 2006.

Vara, V. "Wikis at Work." *The Wall Street Journal*, 18 June 2007, R11.

Blogging

Akismet <http://http://akismet.com/stats/>.

"Blog Statistics and Demographics." *Caslon Analytics*, March 2007 <http://www.caslon.comau/weblogprofile1.htm>.

Blood, R. "Weblogs: A History and Perspective." *Rebecca's Pocket*, September 2000 <http://www.rebeccablood.net/essays/weblog_history.html>.

Bowman, S. and C. Willis. "We Media." July 2003 <http://www.hypergene.net/wemedia/download/we_media.pdf>.

"CEO Blog List." *NewPR Wiki* <http://www.thenewpr.com/wiki/pmwiki.php/Resources/CEOBlogsList?pagename=Resources.CEOBlogsList>.

Kirkpatrick, D. "Why There's No Escaping the Blog." *FORTUNE*, 10 January 2005 <http://money.cnn.com/magazines/fortune/fortune_archive/2005/01/10/8230982/index.htm>.

Lenhart, A. and S. Fox. "Bloggers: A Portrait of the Internet's New Storytellers." *Pew Internet & American Life Project*, July 2006 <http://www.pewinternet.org/pdfs/PIP%20Bloggers%20Report%20July%2019%202006.pdf>.

Thompson, C. "A Timeline of the History of Blogging." *New York Magazine*, February 2006 <http://nymag.com/news/media/15971/>.

Walsh, B. *Clear Blogging: How People Are Changing the World and How You Can Join Them*. APress, 2007.

Social Networking

Arrington, M. "Bear Stearns: Yahoo Must Form A Social Networking Strategy." *TechCrunch*, 3 August 2007 <http://www.techcrunch.com/2007/08/03/bear-stearns-yahoo-must-form-a-social-networking-strategy>.

Athavely, A. "A Job Interview You Don't Have to Show Up For." *The Wall Street Journal Online*, June 2007 <http://online.wsj.com/article/SB118229876637841321.html?mod=tff_main_tff_top>.

Baker, S. "IBM on Second Life: More than PR." *BusinessWeek*, 15 November 2006 <http://www.businessweek.com/the_thread/blogspotting/archives/2006/11/ibm_on_second_1.html>.

Bulkeley, W. "Playing Well With Others." *The Wall Street Journal Online*, 18 June 2007 <http://online.wsj.com/article/SB118194536298737221.html>.

"Businesses Find MySpace is a Place to Reach Youth." *Trend Watching*, July 2006 <http://www.trendwatching.com/about/inmedia/articles/youniversal_branding/businesses_find_myspace_is_a_p.html>.

Copeland, M. "The Missing Link." *CNNMoney.com*, February 2007 <http://money.cnn.com/magazines/business2/business2_archive/2006/12/01/8394967/index.htm>.

"Customer Support." *Facebook* <http://www.facebook.com/help.php?tab=safety>.

"Facebook Statistics." *Facebook*, 17 July 2007 <http://static.ak.facebook.com/press/facebook_statistics.pdf?11:44617>.

Jesdanun, A. "Candidates Seek Youths at MySpace." *ABC News*, August 2006 <http://abcnews.go.com/Technology/wireStory?id=2325325&page=1>.

Kirkpatrick, M. "Friendster Awarded Patent on Social Networking." *TechCrunch*, July 2006 <http://www.techcrunch.com/2006/07/07/friendster-awarded-patent-on-social-networking/>.

Lawson, S. "Second Life Creates a Millionaire." *IDG News*, 30 November 2006 <http://www.itworld.com/App/4201/061130secondlife/>.

"Metcalf's Law." <http://www-ec.njit.edu/~robertso/infosci/metcalf.html>.

Prescott, L. "Hitwise US Consumer Generated Media Report." *Hitwise,* February 2007.

Rivlin, G. "Wallflower at the Web Party." *New York Times*, October 2006 <http://www.nytimes.com/2006/10/15/business/yourmoney/15friend.html>.

"Second Life Lawyer." *Business 2.0*, May 2007, p.86.

"The CEO's Guide to Social Networks." *BusinessWeek*, September 2006 <http://businessweek.com/mediacenter/qt/podcasts/guide_to_tech/guidetotech_09_11_06.mp3>.

"Top 20 Websites." *Hitwise*, May 2007 <http://hitwise.com/datacenter/rankings.php>.

"What is Second Life." <http://secondlife.com/whatis>.

Social Media

"Amazon.com to Launch DRM-Free MP3 Music Download Store with Songs and Albums from EMI Music and More Than 12,000 Other Labels." May 2007 <http://phx.corporate-ir.net/phoenix.zhtml?c=176060&p=irol-newsArticle&ID=1003003>.

Colvin, G. "TV Is Dying? Long Live TV!" *FORTUNE*, 5 February 2007, p.43.

"Conference Report Filed in House." *Library of Congress*, 8 October 1998 <http://thomas.loc.gov/cgi-bin/bdquery/z?d105:HR02281:@@@D&summ2=m&>.

D'Agostino, D. "Security in the World of Web 2.0." *Innovations*, Winter 2006, p.15.

Hefflinger, M. "Digg Users Revolt Over Deleted Posts of HD DVD Security Hack." *digitalmediawire*, 2 May 2007 <http://www.dmwmedia.com/news/2007/05/02/digg-users-revolt-over-deleted-posts-of-hd-dvd-security-hack>.

Jobs, S. "Thoughts on Music." February 2007 <http://www.apple.com/hotnews/thoughtsonmusic>.

"Leading Indicators." *FORTUNE*, 13 November 2006, p.40.

Maney, K. "Techies Hot on Concept of 'Wisdom of Crowds,' but it has some pitfalls." *USA Today*, September 2006 <http://www.usatoday.com/tech/columnist/kevinmaney/2006-09-12-wisdom-of-crowds_x.htm>.

Mills, E. "Copyright Quagmire for Google and YouTube." *ZDNet*, March 2007 <http://news.zdnet.com/2100-9588_22-6167281.html>.

O'Hear, S. "Viacom to Partner with Joost." *ZDNet*, 20 February 2007 <http://blogs.zdnet.com/social/?p=96>.

Prescott, L. "Hitwise US Consumer Generated Media Report." *Hitwise,* February 2007.

Steel, E. "Newspapers' Ad Sales Show Accelerating Drop." *The Wall Street Journal*, 18 July 2007, A4.

Smith E. and K. Delaney. "Vivendi's Universal Sues Two Web Sites Over Video Sharing." *The Wall Street Journal*, 18 October 2006, B3.

Torrone, P. "What Is Podcasting?" *O'Reilly Media*, 20 July 2005 <http://digitalmedia.oreilly.com/2005/07/20/WhatIsPodcasting.html>.

Tagging

Chun, S., R. Cherry, D. Hiwiller, J. Trant and B. Wyman. "Steve.museum: An Ongoing Experiment in Social Tagging, Folksonomy, and Museums." *Archives & Museum Informatics*, March 2006 <http://www.archimuse.com/mw2006/papers/wyman/wyman.html>.

Garrett, J. J. "An Interview with Flickr's Eric Costello." *Adaptive Path*, August 2005 <http://www.adaptivepath.com/publications/essays/archives/000519.php>.

Masters, C. "Programming Provocateurs." *TIME*, 19 March 2007, p. 84.

Mayfield, R. "Buy Side Publishing." *Ross Mayfield's Weblog*, April 2006 <http://ross.typepad.com/blog/2006/04/buy_side_publis.html>.

Rainie, L. "Tagging." *Pew Internet & American Life Project*, December 2006 <http://www.pewinternet.org/pdfs/PIP_Tagging.pdf>.

Schonfeld, E. "The Flickrization of Yahoo!" *CNN Money.com*, December 2005 <http://money.cnn.com/magazines/business2/business2_archive/2005/12/01/8364623/>.

"Using Technorati Tags." *Technorati* <http://support.technorati.com/support/siteguide/tags>.

Vander Wal, T. "Folksonomy Coinage and Definition." *Vanderwal.net*, February 2007 <http://www.vanderwal.net/folksonomy.html>.

Social Bookmarking

"About Ma.gnolia" <http://ma.gnolia.com/about>.

"Gardeners." *Ma.gnolia Community Wiki*, March 2007 <http://wiki.ma.gnolia.com/Gardeners>.

"Know How Adobe and del.icio.us Work Together?" *del.icio.us blog*, May 2007 <http://blog.del.icio.us/blog/2007/05/knowhow_adobe_a.html>.

"That was Fast." *del.icio.us blog*, March 2007 <http://blog.del.icio.us/blog/2007/03/that_was_fast.html>.

Software Development

37Signals. *Getting Real*, 2006 <http://gettingreal.37signals.com>.

Fallows, D. "China's Online Population Explosion." *Pew Internet & American Life Project*, July 2007 <http://www.pewinternet.org/pdfs/China_Internet_July_2007.pdf>.

Farber, D. "ETech: Attenuation, Web 2.0 and Spimes." *ZDNet*, March 2006 <http://blogs.zdnet.com/BTL/?p=2667>.

Greenemeier, L. "Open-Source Exuberance." *InformationWeek*, July 2005 <http://www.informationweek.com/story/showArticle.jhtml?articleID=165700923>.

Peiris, M. "The Pros and Cons of Hosted Software." *SmartBiz*, March 2006 <http://www.smartbiz.com/article/articleview/1118/1/42>.

Pink, D. H. "Why the World Is Flat." *Wired*, May 2005 <http://http://www.wired.com/wired/archive/13.05/friedman.html>.

Tapscott, D. and A. D. Williams. *Wikinomics: How Mass Collaboration Changes Everything*. Portfolio Hardcover, 2006.

"The RIA Desktop in a Browser." *LaszloSystems* <http://www.laszlosystems.com/software/webtop>.

Tiemann, M. "Licenses by Name." *Open Source Initiative*, 18 September 2006 <http://www.opensource.org/licenses/alphabetical>.

Van Rossum, G. "Open Source Summit Trip Report." *Linux Gazette*, 10 April 1998 <http://linuxgazette.net/issue28/rossum.html>.

Wilcox, J. "IBM to Spend $1 Billion on Linux in 2001." *CNET*, January 2002 <http://news.com.com/IBM+to+spend+1+billion+on+Linux+in+2001/2100-1001_3-249750.html>.

Rich Internet Applications

"Adobe Flex 2." *Adobe* <http://www.adobe.com/products/flex/whitepapers/pdfs/flex2wp_technicaloverview.pdf>.

Berlind, D. "Google Gears Vies to be De Facto Tech for Offline Web Apps." *ZDNet*, 31 May 2007 <http://blogs.zdnet.com/Berlind/?p=504>.

"Core Effects." *Script.aculo.us Wiki* <http://wiki.script.aculo.us/scriptaculous/show/Core Effects>.

Cubrilovic, N. "Silverlight: The Web Just Got Richer." *TechCrunch*, April 2007 <http://www.techcrunch.com/2007/04/30/silverlight-the-web-just-got-richer>.

Mills, E. "Google Gears Churns Toward Microsoft." *CNET*, 31 May 2007 <http://news.com.com/2100-1012_3-6187942.html>.

"Prototype Tips and Tutorials." *Prototype JavaScript* <http://prototypejs.org/learn>.

"Sun Radically Simplifies Content Authoring—Previews JavaFX Script." *Sun Microsystems*, 8 May 2007 <http://www.sun.com/aboutsun/pr/2007-05/sunflash.20070508.2.xml>.

Taft, E. "Google Gears Allows Offline Web Development." *eWeek*, 30 May 2007 <http://www.eweek.com/article2/0,1895,2139083,00.asp>.

"The 70 Percent Solution." *Business 2.0*, 28 November 2005 <http://money.cnn.com/2005/11/28/news/newsmakers/schmidt_biz20_1205/>.

"The Dojo Offline Toolkit." *The Dojo Toolkit* <http://dojotoolkit.org/offline>.

Web Services and Mashups

Amazon Web Services <http://aws.amazon.com>.

Braiker, B. "Tech: Welcome, Year of the Widget." *Newsweek*, December 2006 <http://www.msnbc.msn.com/id/16329739/site/newsweek/>.

Costello, R. "REST Tutorial." *xFront*, June 2002 <http://www.xfront.com/REST.html>.

Fielding, R. T. "Architectural Styles and the Design of Network-Based Software Architectures." <http://www.ics.uci.edu/~fielding/pubs/dissertation/top.htm>.

Richardson, L. and S. Ruby. *RESTful Web Services*. O'Reilly, 2007.

Roush, W. "Second Earth." *Technology Review*, July/August 2007, p.38.

Location-Based Services

Magid, L. "Global Positioning by Cellphone." *New York Times*, 19 July 2007, C7.

Malykhina, E. "Nokia Wants Your Cell Phone To Tell You Where You Are." *InformationWeek*, 9 October 2006 `<http://www.informationweek.com/showArticle.jhtml?articleID=1931 05219>`.

Schiller, J. and A. Voisard. *Location-Based Services*. Morgan Kaufmann, 2004.

XML, RSS, Atom, JSON and VoIP

Broache, A. "eBay to Nab Skype for $2.6 billion." *CNET*, 12 September 2005 `<http://news.com.com/eBay+to+nab+Skype+for+2.6+billion/2100-1030_3-5860055.html>`.

"Introducing JSON" `<http://www.json.org>`.

Internet Business

Anderson, C. *The Long Tail: Why the Future of Business Is Selling Less of More*. Hyperion, 2006.

Copeland, M. "The Missing Link." *CNNMoney.com*, February 2007 `<http://money.cnn.com/magazines/business2/business2_archive/2006/12/01/8394967/index.htm>`.

Deutschman, A. "Inside the Mind of Jeff Bezos." *Fast Company*, August 2004 `<http://www.fastcompany.com/magazine/85/bezos_1.html>`.

Graham, J. "The House that Helped Build Google." *USA TODAY*, 5 July 2007, 1B.

Helft, M. "eBay Spawns a Marketplace for the Bizarre." *CNN*, 20 September 1999 `<http://www.cnn.com/TECH/computing/9909/20/ebay.side.show.idg/>`.

Newman, A. A. "Google to Expand Program, Giving Newspapers a Lift." *New York Times*, 18 July 2007, C8.

O'Connell, P. "Pierre Omidyar on 'Connecting People.'" *BusinessWeek*, 20 June 2005 `<http://www.businessweek.com/magazine/content/05_25/b3938900.htm>`.

Second Life `<http://www.secondlife.com/whatis/economy.php>`.

Semantic Web

Berners-Lee, T. *Weaving the Web*. Harper-Collins, 2000.

"Bill Gates: Microsoft MIX06 Conference." *Microsoft*, March 2006 `<http://www.microsoft.com/presspass/exec/billg/speeches/2006/03-20MIX.mspx>`.

Copeland, M. V. "Weaving The [Semantic] Web." *Business 2.0*, July 2007, p.89-93.

Heflin, J. "OWL Web Ontology Language Use Cases and Requirements." *W3C*, 10 February 2004 `<http://www.w3.org/TR/webont-req/>`.

"Introduction to OWL." *W3Schools* `<http://www.w3schools.com/rdf/rdf_owl.asp>`.

"Microformats FAQs for RDF fans." *Microformat.org Wiki* `<http://microformats.org/wiki/faqs-for-RDF>`.

"Microformats Wiki." *microformats.org* `<http://microformats.org/wiki/Main_Page>`.

Miller, E. "An Introduction to the Resource Description Framework." *D-Lib Magazine*, May 1998 `<http://dlib.org/dlib/may98/miller/05miller.html>`.

Rapoza, J. "Semantic Web Technology Gains Steam." *eWEEK*, June 2007 `<http://etech.eweek.com/content/web_technology/semantic_web_technology_gains_steam.html>`.

Rapoza, J. "SPARQL Will Make the Web Shine." *eWEEK*, May 2006 `<http://www.eweek.com/article2/0,1759,1965980,00.asp>`.

Rapoza, J. "Weaving the Semantic Web." *eWEEK*, May 2007 `<http://etech.eweek.com/content/web_technology/spinning_the_semantic_web.html>`.

Tauberer, J. "What Is RDF?" *xml.com*, July 2006 <http://www.xml.com/pub/a/2001/01/24/rdf.html>.

Weitzner, D., J. Hendler, T. Berners-Lee, and D. Connolly. "Creating a Policy-Aware Web: Discretionary, Rule-based Access for the World Wide Web." October 2004 <http://www.w3.org/2004/09/Policy-Aware-Web-acl.pdf>.

1.21 Web 2.0 Glossary

Adaptive Path—A strategy and design consulting company that helps companies build products that improve the users' experiences. Founder Jesse James Garrett coined the term Ajax and is a major proponent of the technology.

Adobe Integrated Runtime (AIR)—Allows offline access to web applications (i.e., when an Internet connection is not available).

AdSense—Google's search advertising program for web publishers. This is a fundamental and popular form of monetization, particularly for Web 2.0 startup companies.

AdWords—Google's search advertising program for advertisers.

affiliate network—A company (see Commission Junction and LinkShare) that connects web publishers with cost-per-action affiliate programs. (See affiliate program.)

affiliate program—A program that allows publishers to post text and image ads on their sites. If a user clicks through to the affiliate site and takes a specified action (e.g., makes a purchase, fills out a registration form, etc.) the publisher is paid a portion of the sale or a flat fee.

agile software development—A process that focuses on developing small pieces and upgrades to a program quickly and continuously throughout the life cycle of the product.

Amazon—An online retailer and web services provider. The Amazon Associates affiliate program allows web publishers to monetize their sites by recommending Amazon products.

Apache—An open source software foundation, responsible for the Apache Web Server and many other open source products.

API (Application Programming Interface)—An interface called by a program. Web services are often referred to as APIs and are accessible over the Internet.

Apple—A leading computer company, responsible for Macintosh computers, the iPod, iTunes and the iPhone.

architecture of participation—A design that encourages user interaction, where the community contributes content and/or participates in the design and development process. Creating websites that encourage participation is a key part of Web 2.0.

Ajax (Asynchronous JavaScript and XML)—Allows pieces of a web page to be refreshed separately, while the user continues to work on the page. Ajax improves the user's experience by making webtop applications approach the responsiveness of desktop applications.

Atom—Used for web feeds; similar to RSS.

attention economy—The result of the abundant amounts of information being produced and people's limited free time. More content is available than users can sort through on their own.

avatar—A person's digital representation in a 3D world such as Second Life.

Basecamp—An SaaS project management and collaboration tool from 37Signals.

Blinkx—A video search engine with over 12 million hours of video indexed (which makes the content searchable).

blog—A website consisting of posts in reverse chronological order. For common blog components see: blogroll, permalink, reader comment, and trackback.

blog search engine—A search engine devoted to the blogosphere. Some of the top blog search engines include Technorati, Feedster, IceRocket and Google Blog Search.

Blogger—A popular blogging platform now owned by Google.

blogger—The author of a blog.

blogging—The act of writing a blog.

blog network—A collection of blogs with multiple editors. Popular blog networks include Corante, 9rules, Gawker and Weblogs, Inc.

blogosphere—The blogging community. In mid 2007 there were over 90 million blogs.

blogroll—A list of links to a blogger's favorite blogs.

broadband Internet—High-speed Internet, often offered by cable companies and satellite companies.

collaborative filtering—The act of working together to promote valuable content and remove spam or offensive content.

collective intelligence—The idea that collaboration and competition among large groups results in grand and intelligent ideas.

Commission Junction—A popular affiliate network with member advertisers including eBay, Best Buy, Hewlett-Packard and hundreds more.

community-generated content—Content (writing, videos, etc.) that is created by Internet users.

contextual advertising—Advertising that is targeted to web page content. Because these ads are relevant to the nearby content, contextual ads often enhance the value of that content and generate higher clickthrough rates.

Corante—A blog network whose blogs are written by leading commentators in their field. Categories include law, policy, business, management, media, the Internet, technology and science.

cost-per-action (CPA)—Advertising that is billed by user action (e.g., purchasing a product or filling out a form).

cost-per-click (CPC)—Advertising that is billed by user click. The publisher receives revenue each time the user clicks an ad on the publisher's site, regardless of whether the user makes a subsequent purchase.

cost-per-thousand impressions (CPM)—Advertising that is billed per thousand impressions, regardless of whether the user clicks the ad or makes a subsequent purchase.

Craigslist—A popular classifieds and social networking website that fits the Web 2.0 lightweight business model. The company has few employees and all of the content is user generated. Craigslist was originally free; however, it is now transitioning to charging for certain services such as real-estate and job postings. A portion of the company is owned by eBay.

DBPedia.org—A website working on converting Wikipedia articles into RDF triples. This is a step toward the Semantic Web.

Deitel—A content-creation, corporate training and Web 2.0 business development organization. Deitel has a rapidly growing content network (currently about 80 Resource Centers) specializing in topic categories, including Web 2.0, Internet business, programming languages, software development and more.

del.icio.us—A social bookmarking site.

Digg—A social media site where users submit news stories and the community votes on the stories. The most popular stories are featured on the site's front page.

Digital Rights Management (DRM)—Technology used to prevent piracy and misuse of digital media. Several high-profile executives, including Apple CEO Steve Jobs, have recently started an anti-DRM movement.

discovery—The future of search; the idea of introducing users to valuable content they might not have looked for otherwise. For example, social bookmarking sites and Deitel Resource Centers suggest valuable resources.

Dodgeball.com—A social networking site designed for use on mobile devices, owned by Google. Allows users to locate friends and "crushes" who are nearby so they can meet up.

DotNetNuke—An open source web application framework based on Microsoft's .NET framework. DotNetNuke allows users to build dynamic websites quickly and easily. For more information, visit the DotNetNuke Resource Center (`http://www.deitel.com/Resource Centers/Software/DotNetNukeDNN/tabid/1217/Default.aspx`).

DoubleClick—An Internet advertising company acquired by Google in 2007 for $3.1 billion. Their advertising exchange connects advertisers with online publishers.

Dougherty, Dale—Coined the term "Web 2.0."

eBay—The leading online auction site.

Extensible Markup Language (XML)—A widely supported open (i.e., nonproprietary) technology for electronic data exchange and storage, which is fundamental to Web 2.0 and the Semantic Web. It can be used to create other markup languages to describe data in a structured manner.

Facebook—A social networking site. Though it is now open to the public, Facebook was originally designed for and is especially popular with college students.

Federated Media—A company that connects bloggers with advertisers. Founded by John Battelle, the chair for the annual Web 2.0 Summit Conference, and the author of *The Search: How Google and Its Rivals Rewrote the Rules of Business and Transformed Our Culture*.

Feedburner—Provides RSS feeds for blogs, feed monetization, podcast tracking and more. Acquired by Google.

Firefox—Open source web browser (based on the Netscape Navigator browser introduced in 1994) developed by the Mozilla Foundation. For more information, visit the Firefox Resource Center (`http://www.deitel.com/ResourceCenters/Software/Firefox/tabid/1213/Default .aspx`).

Flex—A Rich Internet Application (RIA) framework developed by Adobe. For more information, visit the Flex Resource Center (`http://www.deitel.com/ResourceCenters/Programming/ AdobeFlex/tabid/1682/Default.aspx`).

Flickr—A photo-sharing website often credited as one of the best examples of tagging content.

folksonomy—A classification based on tagging content. Users tag the web content (web pages, photos, etc.), making it easier to find the content online. Folksonomies are formed on sites such as Flickr, Technorati and del.icio.us. Users can search tags for content that is identified in different (and sometimes more meaningful) ways than by traditional search engines.

Friendster—A social networking site; an early leader in the category of social networking. In 2006, Friendster was awarded a patent for a method and tool called the "Web of Friends," which gathers descriptive and relationship information for users in the network. The combined data is used to show all of the social relationships connecting two users in the social network. It also allows users to find people connected to their friends, their friends' friends, etc.

Garrett, Jesse James—Coined the term "Ajax" and founded Adaptive Path.

Gawker Media—A blog network that includes Gawker.com (New York City gossip), Gizmodo.com (technology and gadgets) and more.

Google—A Web 2.0 search and online advertising company founded by Larry Page and Sergey Brin when they were Ph.D. students at Stanford University. It is the most widely used search engine, commanding almost 50% market share. In addition to its regular search engine, Google offers specialty search engines for images, news, videos, blogs and more. Google provides web services that allow you to build Google Maps and other Google services into your applications.

Google Gears—An open source web browser extension that enables developers to provide offline usage of their web applications. The program can easily be resynchronized when an Internet connection becomes available.

Google Maps—Google's mapping web service, hugely popular in mashups.

Hitwise—An Internet competitive intelligence service provider. Hitwise collects and sells usage information from over one million websites in numerous industries. Clients use the information to find market share, keyword, web traffic flow and demographic data.

housingmaps.com—A mashup of Google Maps and Craigslist apartment and real-estate listings; often credited as being the first mashup.

IceRocket—A blog search engine.

Intel—The computer hardware company that creates the processors that power most of the world's computers.

interstitial ad—Ad that plays between page loads.

in-text contextual advertising—Advertising that is marked by double-underlined keywords in the content of a web page. When a reader hovers the mouse over a double-underlined word, a text ad pops up. By clicking on the ad, the reader is taken to the advertiser's page. Companies providing in-text contextual advertising include Vibrant Media, Kontera, Text Link Ads and Tribal Fusion.

iPhone—Apple's mobile phone, released June 2007. The iPhone is designed to run a full version of the Internet.

iPod—Apple's portable media player.

iTunes—Apple's online music and video store; designed to sync with the iPod.

John Battelle's Searchblog—A blog in which John Battelle discusses search, media, technology, and more. (See Federated Media.)

JSON (JavaScript Object Notation)—A text-based data interchange format used to represent data structures and objects, and transmit them over a network. JSON is most often used with JavaScript in Ajax applications, but it can also be used with other programming languages.

Joost—An Internet TV company using semantic technologies to provide high-quality video with time shifting (recording for later viewing) and social networking capabilities. Joost allows advertisers to target their markets precisely. Advertisers can use demographic information such as location, gender, age, and more, to serve appropriate ads and to get a better return on investment from their advertising campaigns.

Last.fm—A popular social music website that uses the wisdom of crowds to recommend music to its users. The Last.fm Audioscrobbler music engine automatically sends the name of every song the user plays to the server. It then uses the information to recommend songs and artists, connect users with similar tastes and more.

Laszlo Webtop—A desktop-like environment for running web applications built on the OpenLaszlo framework.

lead generation—A monetization model for many sites that send traffic to another site and typically collect a fee when the visitor fills out an inquiry form so a salesperson can follow through and potentially convert the lead into a sale.

lightweight business model—A plan that allows a company to start quickly and with little capital investment. This is facilitated by powerful yet economical computers, the wide availability of inexpensive broadband Internet, robust open source software offerings, and well-developed, easy-to-employ monetization models—especially advertising and affiliate programs.

link baiting—Attracting other sites to link to your site, but without specifically asking for links. Providing quality content is considered the best form of link baiting.

link building—Using various methods to encourage other sites to link to your site. It is widely believed that increasing the number of inbound links to your site will encourage search engines to send you more traffic.

LinkedIn—A social networking site for business professionals. It can be used to stay in touch with professional contacts or make new contacts in your extended network.

LinkShare—A popular affiliate network with over 600 member companies (including American Express, Office Depot and Walmart).

Livejournal—A website where you can create your own blog.

Long Tail—Coined by Chris Anderson in an article in the October 2004 *WIRED* magazine (`http://www.wired.com/wired/archive/12.10/tail.html`). Refers to the continuous sales of numerous items with low sales volume that can add up to a significant part of a company's total sales. Amazon and Netflix are classic Long Tail companies.

mashup—A combination of two or more existing web services, RSS feeds or other sources of data to create a new application. For example, `http://www.housingmaps.com` combines real estate listings from Craigslist with Google Maps so you can view the listings on a map. For a list of popular mashups, see `http://www.programmableweb.com/popular`.

Mechanical Turk—Amazon's "artificial artificial intelligence," which uses people in a web service to perform tasks that are difficult for computers to perform, such as identifying the subject of a picture and transcribing dictation recordings. Users can post a HIT (Human Intelligence Task). Anyone interested in completing the task can submit a response. If the response is approved by the person who posted the HIT, the responder is paid a predetermined fee for each task completed. The key is that the human task is interwoven with the execution of the web service, creating applications that mix computing power with human intelligence accessed worldwide.

MediaWiki—Open source software written originally for Wikipedia and now used by many popular wikis.

Metcalfe's Law—The value of a network is proportional to the square of the number of its users. Metcalfe's Law was authored by Robert Metcalfe, the creator of Ethernet. (See also network effects.)

microformat—A common standard for identifying information in a way that can be understood by computers. Some current microformats include adr (for address information), hresume (for resumes and CVs), and xfolk (for collections of bookmarks). See `http://microformats.org` for more information.

mobile technology—Devices such as cell phones and PDAs. An increasing number now offer web access, which has opened up new web application possibilities. (See also iPhone.)

moblogging—Blogging from mobile devices.

moderation—Monitoring and censoring inappropriate content and comments in blog or forum postings. The potential need for moderation is a drawback to allowing user-generated content.

monetization—Generating money through your website (e.g., using contextual advertising, affiliate programs, e-commerce and other revenue-generating models).

Moonlight—An open source version of Microsoft's Silverlight for Linux operating systems.

Movable Type—A blogging software package from the company Six Apart that is installed on the blogger's server.

Mozilla Foundation—Creates and maintains open source software including the Mozilla Firefox web browser and the Mozilla Thunderbird e-mail client.

MySpace—The most popular social networking site, and the most popular site on the Internet.

network effects—The increased value of a network as its number of users grows. For example, as the number of people with Internet connections grows worldwide, the value and benefit to all users of the Internet grows (individuals can communicate with more people, companies can reach more customers, etc.). (See Metcalfe's Law.)

9Rules—A blog network.

ontology—A way of organizing and relating things. Ontologies are a key technology in the Semantic Web.

open source software—Software that is available for anyone to use and modify with few or no restrictions. Users can modify source code to meet their unique needs, or collaborate with others to enhance the software. Many Web 2.0 companies use open source software to power their sites, and offer open source products and content.

O'Reilly Media—The company that introduced and promoted the term Web 2.0 (coined by company executive Dale Dougherty). O'Reilly Media publishes technology books and websites, and hosts several conferences, including the Web 2.0 Summit, Web 2.0 Expo, OSCON™ (the Open Source Convention), Emerging Technology, Emerging Telephony, Where 2.0, RailsConf, MySQL, Ubuntu Live and more. See the O'Reilly Radar (http://radar.oreilly.com/) to keep up-to-date on emerging technology trends.

outsourcing—A company's hiring of independent contractors or other companies to perform various tasks. Outsourcing is often cheaper for the company.

performance-based advertising—Advertising that pays based on user actions, such as making a purchase, filling out a registration form, etc. (See also cost-per-action.)

permalink—A URL that links to a specific blog entry instead of the blog's homepage. Links stay relevant even after the blog entry moves off the home page and into the archive.

perpetual beta—The idea of continually releasing new features even if they aren't "final." This allows software companies to constantly fix bugs and improve the software by getting continuous feedback from real users.

Pew Internet & American Life Project—A non-profit Internet research company. The project is funded by the Pew Charitable Trusts, which has also initiated other research and cultural projects.

PHPNuke—An open source content-management system and web publishing tool based on PHP and MySQL.

podcast—A media file designed for syndicated distribution online. It can be played on a personal computer or mobile media player (such as an iPod or MP3 player).

Policy Aware Web Project—A site devoted to developing policies regarding Internet data. This is an attempt to deal with Semantic Web security concerns.

premium content—Website content that is available for a fee (e.g., e-books, articles, etc.). It is a way for publishers to monetize their sites. Sites offering premium content typically offer free content as well.

Problogger—A blog about blogging. It teaches bloggers how to monetize their sites with Google AdSense and other programs.

Programmable Web—A website with extensive directories of web services APIs and mashups.

publisher—See "web publisher."

RDF (Resource Description Framework)—An XML-based language used to describe content attributes such as the page title, author, etc.

RDF triples—Composed of two pieces of information and a linking fact. They are used to help computers understand data, a vital part of the Semantic Web.

reader comment—Feedback left by readers on a blog.

recommender systems—Systems that collect data using collaborative filtering to determine users' tastes and interests as they search the Internet. For example, Amazon's "customers who bought this item also bought..."

Red Hat—A popular version of the Linux operating system. The company is a leader in the open source movement.

remixing—Combining existing applications and/or content into something new; this is fundamental to Web 2.0.

reputation systems—Systems used by businesses like eBay and Amazon to encourage trust. For example, after each eBay transaction, the buyer and the seller can each leave positive or negative comments about the other party.

REST (Representational State Transfer)—A simple alternative to SOAP for implementing web services. Many developers prefer REST-based web services to SOAP-based web services for their simplicity, their ability to be cached and more. Amazon offers some REST-based web services. (See also SOAP.)

Rich Internet Applications (RIAs)—Web applications that have the responsiveness and the rich GUI normally associated with desktop applications. Related technologies for building RIAs include Ajax, Dojo, Silverlight, Flex and more.

RSS—An XML-based web-content syndication format. Syndicated RSS feeds are used to publish frequently updated content such as news, blog entries, podcasts, and more. Some RSS feeds include the full text, but most contain only a portion of the document, encouraging the reader to visit the content site.

Ruby on Rails—An open source, web application development scripting language and framework that increases the speed at which you can create typical database-driven web applications.

Salesforce.com—An SaaS company that specializes in Customer Relationship Management (CRM) software; a leader in the SaaS movement.

scrobbling—Last.fm's music tracking and analysis feature that provides you with recommendations based on the music you listen to through the site or on your iPod. (See also recommender systems.)

search engine marketing (SEM)—Promoting your website to increase traffic and search results. This includes paid search, online advertising and more.

search engine optimization (SEO)—Designing your website to maximize your findability and improve your rankings in organic search engine results.

search engine result page (SERP)—The page shown to a user by a search engine with a listing of web pages matching the search query sorted by relevance.

SearchEngineLand.com—Danny Sullivan's search engine news blog.

SearchEngineWatch.com—A search engine marketing resource site. Includes articles, tutorials, conferences and more.

Second Life—A 3D virtual world social networking program developed by Linden Labs. Users create an avatar (their online image and persona) that they use to meet other users with similar interests, conduct business, participate in group activities, take classes and more.

Semantic Web—The "web of meaning." What some believe will be the next evolution of the web in which web content can be read and understood by software applications.

Silverlight—A Rich Internet Application (RIA) framework developed by Microsoft; competes with Adobe Flash and Flex.

Six Apart—The company responsible for several blogging software applications and websites, including Movable Type, TypePad and Vox.

Skype—The most popular VoIP company. Users can place free calls to other Skype users around the world over their Internet connection. They also offer fee-based services that allow you to call non-Skype phone numbers. Skype was purchased by eBay in 2005 for $2.6 billion. Its founders recently launched Joost (an Internet TV site).

SOAP (Simple Object Access Protocol)—A protocol for exchanging XML-based information over a network. SOAP is used as a messaging framework in web services.

social bookmarking—The act of sharing your bookmarks with others through a website such as del.icio.us or Ma.gnolia. Users bookmark their favorites sites, articles, blogs and more, and tag them by keyword.

social media—Any media (e.g., photos, videos, music, etc.) shared online. Social media sites, such as Digg, YouTube and Flickr, often include features for user comments, collaborative filtering and tagging.

social networking—Sites designed to organize users' existing relationships and help users establish new ones. Popular social networking sites include MySpace, Facebook, LinkedIn, Second Life and more.

SocialText—The first wiki company; provides wiki services to corporations. (See also wiki.)

Software as a Service (SaaS)—Software that runs on a web server. It does not need to be installed on your local computer, and companies can instantly update all users to the latest version. Salesforce.com, Google, 37Signals and Microsoft all have extensive SaaS offerings.

spam—Junk e-mail messages, blog comments and forum postings.

SPARQL Protocol and RDF Query Language (SPARQL)—An RDF query language for the Semantic Web.

tag—An author- and/or user-submitted label for web content used to classify it by subject or keyword. For example, a picture of the Statue of Liberty posted on Flickr might be tagged with "newyorkcity," "statueofliberty," "usa," etc. Users can search for content on a site by tags. For examples of tag usage, see Technorati and Flickr.

tag cloud—A weighted list of content tags on a website. A tag cloud is usually in alphabetical order, with the most popular tags often appearing in a larger or bold font. Each tag links to a page where you'll find all of the content on that site that has been "tagged" (by publishers and/or users) with that term. Tag clouds are used by many Web 2.0 companies, including Technorati, Flickr, del.icio.us and more.

tagging—The act of adding tags to content.

tagscape—The tagging "landscape"; the patterns and trends that are seen in tagging and tag clouds.

TechCrunch—A popular Internet technology blog that focuses on the companies, products, people and events of Web 2.0.

Technorati—A popular blog search engine that uses tagging.

37Signals—The company that developed Ruby on Rails (`http://www.deitel.com/Resource Centers/Programming/Ruby/tabid/715/Default.aspx`) and many SaaS applications, including Basecamp.

trackback—A method for web content authors to request notification when a website links to their content (articles, blog postings, etc.). It is a great way for authors to track links into their sites, measure the viral effects of their work, find related sites and more.

Twitter—A mobile web service that enables users to message groups of friends at once and automatically receive their friends' updates on a cell phone or through a chat window.

Ubuntu—A popular distribution of the Linux operating system.

user-generated content—Content that is created by users. User-generated content is central to Web 2.0.

ValueClick—An Internet advertising company.

vlogging—Video blogging.

VoIP (Voice over Internet Protocol)—Voice services over the Internet; used to build telephone services. The leading VoIP company is Skype, which offers free phone service among Skype users worldwide.

Vonage—A VoIP company. They provide broadband Internet telephone services that can be used with a standard phone (with adapter).

Web 1.0—The Internet experience previous to Web 2.0, focusing more on static content. Some people called it the "brochure web."

Web 2.0—A term coined by Dale Dougherty of O'Reilly Media in 2003. It refers to the current state of the web, which has a strong emphasis on user participation and community. Web 2.0 sites include social networking, wikis, blogging, social media, tagging, collaborative filtering, and more.

web as a platform—Instead of viewing the operating system as the application platform and building "Windows-based applications" or "Linux-based applications," developers now build "web-based applications."

web of meaning—Another name for the "Semantic Web."

Web Ontology Language (OWL)—A key Semantic Web technology, used for organizing data.

web publisher—A site that offers content. Advertisers place ads on web publisher sites.

web-scale computing—Refers to the ability to scale memory and processing power according to need, by using web-based processing power and memory, often provided by other companies. Amazon offers web-scale computing through web services such as Simple Storage Service (S3) and Elastic Compute Cloud (EC2).

web service—A service provided online that can be called by another program across the Internet.

Weblogsinc—A blog network.

webtop—A desktoplike environment (such as Laszlo Webtop) for running web applications in a web browser.

wiki—A collaborative, editable document online. The best known example of a wiki is Wikipedia, which has quickly become a leading web resource for virtually any topic.

Wikia—A site offering specialized wiki communities about popular television shows, games, literature, shopping and more.

Wikipedia—A community-generated encyclopedia using wiki technology.

wisdom of crowds—The concept that a large diverse group of individuals that does not necessarily include experts can provide more accurate answers than a small group of specialists working together.

WordPress—Popular blogging software.

World Wide Web Consortium (W3C)—An organization that develops web standards.

Xanga—A popular personal blogging site that includes community features.

XML (Extensible Markup Language)—A markup language developed in 1996 by the World Wide Web Consortium (W3C) that allows you to label data based on its meaning.

XML vocabularies—Customized XML-based markup languages, such as XHTML for web content, CML for chemistry, MathML for mathematical content and formulas, and XBRL for financial data.

Yahoo! Pipes—A mashup tool that enables you to aggregate and manipulate many data sources.

Yahoo! Publisher Network—Yahoo's contextual advertising program for publishers. This is a fundamental and popular form of monetization, particularly for Web 2.0 startup companies.

Yahoo! Search Marketing—Yahoo!'s advertising program for advertisers.

YouTube—An Internet video sharing site that has created a huge social phenomenon. Users upload and share videos. The company was bought by Google in 2006 for $1.65 billion.

Zepheira—A company that provides Semantic Web knowledge management and enterprise data integration products and services.

2

The Ajax Client

... the challenges are for the designers of these applications: to forget what we think we know about the limitations of the web, and begin to imagine a wider, richer range of possibilities. It's going to be fun.

—Jesse James Garrett

2

Introduction to XHTML

*To read between the lines
was easier than to follow the
text.*
—Henry James

*High thoughts must have
high language.*
—Aristophanes

*Yea, from the table of my
memory
I'll wipe away all trivial
fond records.*
—William Shakespeare

*He had a wonderful talent
for packing thought close,
and rendering it portable.*
—Thomas Babington
Macaulay

OBJECTIVES

In this chapter you will learn:

- To understand important components of XHTML documents.
- To use XHTML to create web pages.
- To add images to web pages.
- To create and use hyperlinks to navigate web pages.
- To mark up lists of information.
- To create tables with rows and columns of data and control table formatting.
- To create and use forms to get user input.
- To make web pages accessible to search engines using <meta> tags.

2.1 Introduction

Welcome to the world of opportunity created by the World Wide Web. The Internet is almost four decades old, but it wasn't until the web's growth in popularity in the 1990s and the recent start of the Web 2.0 era that the explosion of opportunity we are experiencing began. Exciting new developments occur almost daily—the pace of innovation is unprecedented. In this chapter, you'll develop your own web pages. As the book proceeds, you'll create increasingly appealing and powerful web pages. Later in the book, you'll learn how to create complete web-based applications with databases and user interfaces.

This chapter begins unlocking the power of web-based application development with *XHTML*—the *Extensible HyperText Markup Language*. Later in the chapter, we introduce more sophisticated XHTML techniques such as *internal linking* for easier page navigation, *forms* for collecting information from a web-page visitor and *tables*, which are particularly useful for structuring information from *databases* (i.e., software that stores structured sets of data). In the next chapter, we discuss a technology called *Cascading Style Sheets™* (*CSS*), a technology that makes web pages more visually appealing.

Unlike procedural programming languages such as C, C++, or Java, XHTML is a *markup language* that specifies the format of the text that is displayed in a web browser such as Microsoft's Internet Explorer or Mozilla Firefox.

One key issue when using XHTML is the separation of the *presentation* of a document (i.e., the document's appearance when rendered by a browser) from the *structure* of the document's information. XHTML is based on HTML (HyperText Markup Language)—a legacy technology of the World Wide Web Consortium (W3C). In HTML, it was common to specify both the document's structure and its formatting. Formatting might specify where the browser placed an element in a web page or the fonts and colors used to display an element. The *XHTML 1.0 Strict* recommendation (the version of XHTML that we use in this book) allows only a document's structure to appear in a valid XHTML document, and not its formatting. Normally, such formatting is specified with

Cascading Style Sheets (Chapter 3). All our examples in this chapter are based on the XHTML 1.0 Strict Recommendation.

2.2 Editing XHTML

In this chapter, we write XHTML in its *source-code form*. We create *XHTML documents* by typing them in a text editor (e.g., Notepad, TextEdit, vi, emacs) and saving them with either an `.html` or an `.htm` filename extension.

 Good Programming Practice 2.1

Assign filenames to documents that describe their functionality. This practice can help you identify documents faster. It also helps people who want to link to a page, by giving them an easy-to-remember name. For example, if you are writing an XHTML document that contains product information, you might want to call it products.html.

Computers called *web servers* running specialized software store XHTML documents. Clients (e.g., web browsers) request specific *resources* such as the XHTML documents from web servers. For example, typing `www.deitel.com/books/downloads.html` into a web browser's address field requests `downloads.html` from the `books` directory on the web server running at `www.deitel.com`. We discuss web servers in detail in Chapter 17. For now, we simply place the XHTML documents on our computer and render them by opening them locally with a web browser such as Internet Explorer or Firefox.

2.3 First XHTML Example

This chapter presents XHTML markup and provides screen captures that show how a browser renders (i.e., displays) the XHTML. You can download the examples from `www.deitel.com/books/ajaxfp`. Every XHTML document we show has line numbers for your convenience—these line numbers are not part of the XHTML documents. As you read this book, open each XHTML document in your web browser so you can view and interact with it as it was originally intended.

Figure 2.1 is an XHTML document named `main.html`. This first example displays the message "Welcome to XHTML!" in the browser. The key line in the program is line 13, which tells the browser to display "Welcome to XHTML!" Now let us consider each line of the program.

Lines 1–3 are required in XHTML documents to conform with proper XHTML syntax. For now, copy and paste these lines into each XHTML document you create. The meaning of these lines is discussed in detail in Chapter 12.

Lines 5–6 are *XHTML comments*. XHTML document creators insert comments to improve markup readability and describe the content of a document. Comments also help other people read and understand an XHTML document's markup and content. Comments do not cause the browser to perform any action when the user loads the XHTML document into the web browser to view it. XHTML comments always start with <!-- and end with -->. Each of our XHTML examples includes comments that specify the figure number and filename and provide a brief description of the example's purpose. Subsequent examples include comments in the markup, especially to highlight new features.

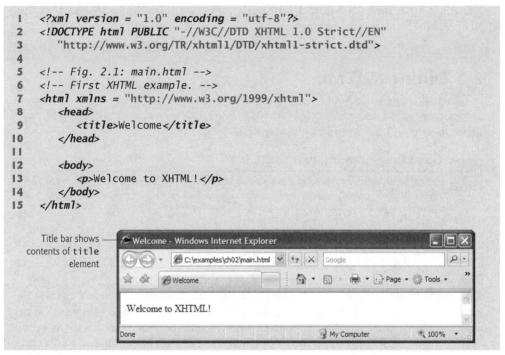

```
 1    <?xml version = "1.0" encoding = "utf-8"?>
 2    <!DOCTYPE html PUBLIC "-//W3C//DTD XHTML 1.0 Strict//EN"
 3       "http://www.w3.org/TR/xhtml1/DTD/xhtml1-strict.dtd">
 4
 5    <!-- Fig. 2.1: main.html -->
 6    <!-- First XHTML example. -->
 7    <html xmlns = "http://www.w3.org/1999/xhtml">
 8       <head>
 9          <title>Welcome</title>
10       </head>
11
12       <body>
13          <p>Welcome to XHTML!</p>
14       </body>
15    </html>
```

Title bar shows contents of `title` element

Fig. 2.1 | First XHTML example.

 Good Programming Practice 2.2

Place comments throughout your markup. Comments help other programmers understand the markup, assist in debugging and list useful information that you do not want the browser to render. Comments also help you understand your own markup when you revisit a document to modify or update it in the future.

XHTML markup contains text that represents the content of a document and *elements* that specify a document's structure. Some important elements of an XHTML document are the *html* element, the *head* element and the *body* element. The html element encloses the *head section* (represented by the head element) and the *body section* (represented by the body element). The head section contains information about the XHTML document, such as its *title*. The head section also can contain special document formatting instructions called *style sheets* and client-side programs called *scripts* for creating dynamic web pages. (We introduce style sheets in Chapter 3 and scripting with JavaScript in Chapter 4.) The body section contains the page's content that the browser displays when the user visits the web page.

XHTML documents delimit an element with *start* and *end* tags. A start tag consists of the element name in angle brackets (e.g., <html>). An end tag consists of the element name preceded by a forward slash (/) in angle brackets (e.g., </html>). In this example, lines 7 and 15 define the start and end of the html element. Note that the end tag in line 15 has the same name as the start tag, but is preceded by a / inside the angle brackets. Many start tags have *attributes* that provide additional information about an element. Browsers can use this additional information to determine how to process the element.

Each attribute has a *name* and a *value* separated by an equals sign (=). Line 7 specifies a required attribute (xmlns) and value (http://www.w3.org/1999/xhtml) for the html element in an XHTML document. For now, simply copy and paste the html element start tag in line 7 into your XHTML documents. We discuss the details of the xmlns attribute in Chapter 12.

Common Programming Error 2.1
Not enclosing attribute values in either single or double quotes is a syntax error. However, some web browsers may still render the element correctly.

Common Programming Error 2.2
Using uppercase letters in an XHTML element or attribute name is a syntax error. However, some web browsers may still render the element correctly.

An XHTML document divides the html element into two sections—head and body. Lines 8–10 define the web page's head section with a head element. Line 9 specifies a title element. This is called a *nested element* because it is enclosed in the head element's start and end tags. The head element is also a nested element because it is enclosed in the html element's start and end tags. The title element describes the web page. Titles usually appear in the *title bar* at the top of the browser window, in the browser tab that the page is displayed on, and also as the text identifying a page when users add the page to their list of **Favorites** or **Bookmarks** that enables them to return to their favorite sites. Search engines (i.e., sites that allow users to search the web) also use the title for indexing purposes.

Good Programming Practice 2.3
Indenting nested elements emphasizes a document's structure and promotes readability.

Common Programming Error 2.3
XHTML does not permit tags to overlap—a nested element's end tag must appear in the document before the enclosing element's end tag. For example, the nested XHTML tags <head><title>hello</head></title> cause a syntax error, because the enclosing head element's ending </head> tag appears before the nested title element's ending </title> tag.

Good Programming Practice 2.4
Use a consistent title-naming convention for all pages on a site. For example, if a site is named "Bailey's Website," then the title of the contact page might be "Bailey's Website—Contact." This practice can help users better understand the website's structure.

Line 12 begins the document's body element. The body section of an XHTML document specifies the document's content, which may include text and elements.

Some elements, such as the *paragraph element* (denoted with <p> and </p>) in line 13, mark up text for display in a browser. All the text placed between the <p> and </p> tags forms one paragraph. When the browser renders a paragraph, a blank line usually precedes and follows paragraph text.

This document ends with two end tags (lines 14–15). These tags close the body and html elements, respectively. The </html> tag in an XHTML document informs the browser that the XHTML markup is complete.

To open an XHTML example from this chapter, open the folder where you saved the book's examples, browse to the `ch04` folder and double click the file to open it in your default web browser. At this point your browser window should appear similar to the sample screen capture shown in Fig. 2.1. (Note that we resized the browser window to save space in the book.)

2.4 W3C XHTML Validation Service

Programming web-based applications can be complex, and XHTML documents must be written correctly to ensure that browsers process them properly. To promote correctly written documents, the World Wide Web Consortium (W3C) provides a *validation service* (`validator.w3.org`) for checking a document's syntax. Documents can be validated by providing a URL that specifies the file's location, by uploading a file to `validator.w3.org/file-upload.html` or by pasting code directly into a text area. Uploading a file copies the file from the user's computer to another computer on the Internet. The W3C's web page indicates that the service name is **MarkUp Validation Service** and that the validation service is able to validate the syntax of XHTML documents. All the XHTML examples in this book have been validated successfully using `validator.w3.org`.

By clicking **Choose...**, users can select files on their own computers for upload. After selecting a file, clicking the **Check** button uploads and validates the file. If a document contains syntax errors, the validation service displays error messages describing the errors.

Error-Prevention Tip 2.1

Most current browsers attempt to render XHTML documents even if they are invalid. This often leads to unexpected and possibly undesirable results. Use a validation service, such as the W3C **MarkUp Validation Service***, to confirm that an XHTML document is syntactically correct.*

2.5 Headings

Some text in an XHTML document may be more important than other text. For example, the text in this section is considered more important than a footnote. XHTML provides six *headings*, called *heading elements*, for specifying the relative importance of information. Figure 2.2 demonstrates these elements (`h1` through `h6`). Heading element `h1` (line 13) is considered the most significant heading and is typically rendered in a larger font than the other five headings (lines 14–18). Each successive heading element (i.e., `h2`, `h3`, etc.) is typically rendered in a progressively smaller font.

Portability Tip 2.1

The text size used to display each heading element can vary significantly between browsers. In Chapter 3, we discuss how to control the text size and other text properties.

Look-and-Feel Observation 2.1

Placing a heading at the top of every XHTML page helps viewers understand the purpose of each page.

Look-and-Feel Observation 2.2

Use larger headings to emphasize more important sections of a web page.

```
I    <?xml version = "1.0" encoding = "utf-8"?>
2    <!DOCTYPE html PUBLIC "-//W3C//DTD XHTML 1.0 Strict//EN"
3       "http://www.w3.org/TR/xhtml1/DTD/xhtml1-strict.dtd">
4
5    <!-- Fig. 2.2: heading.html -->
6    <!-- Heading elements h1 through h6. -->
7    <html xmlns = "http://www.w3.org/1999/xhtml">
8       <head>
9          <title>Headings</title>
10      </head>
11
12      <body>
13         <h1>Level 1 Heading</h1>
14         <h2>Level 2 heading</h2>
15         <h3>Level 3 heading</h3>
16         <h4>Level 4 heading</h4>
17         <h5>Level 5 heading</h5>
18         <h6>Level 6 heading</h6>
19      </body>
20   </html>
```

Fig. 2.2 | Heading elements h1 through h6.

2.6 Linking

One of the most important XHTML features is the *hyperlink*, which references (or *links* to) other resources, such as XHTML documents and images. When a user clicks a hyperlink, the browser tries to execute an action associated with it (e.g., navigate to a URL, open an e-mail client, etc.). In XHTML, both text and images can act as hyperlinks. Web browsers typically underline text hyperlinks and color their text blue by default, so that users can distinguish hyperlinks from plain text. In Fig. 2.3, we create text hyperlinks to four different websites.

Line 14 introduces the *strong element*, which indicates that its contents has high importance. Browsers typically display such text in a bold font.

Links are created using the *a* (*anchor*) element. Line 17 defines a hyperlink to the URL assigned to attribute *href*, which specifies the location of a linked resource, such as

```
 1   <?xml version = "1.0" encoding = "utf-8"?>
 2   <!DOCTYPE html PUBLIC "-//W3C//DTD XHTML 1.0 Strict//EN"
 3      "http://www.w3.org/TR/xhtml11/DTD/xhtml11-strict.dtd">
 4
 5   <!-- Fig. 2.3: links.html -->
 6   <!-- Linking to other web pages. -->
 7   <html xmlns = "http://www.w3.org/1999/xhtml">
 8      <head>
 9         <title>Links</title>
10      </head>
11
12      <body>
13         <h1>Here are my favorite sites</h1>
14         <p><strong>Click a name to go to that page.</strong></p>
15
16         <!-- Create four text hyperlinks -->
17         <p><a href = "http://www.deitel.com">Deitel</a></p>
18         <p><a href = "http://www.prenhall.com">Prentice Hall</a></p>
19         <p><a href = "http://www.yahoo.com">Yahoo!</a></p>
20         <p><a href = "http://www.usatoday.com">USA Today</a></p>
21      </body>
22   </html>
```

Fig. 2.3 | Linking to other web pages.

a web page, a file or an e-mail address. This particular anchor element links the text Deitel
to a web page located at http://www.deitel.com. When a URL does not indicate a specific document on the website, the web server returns a default web page. This page is often
called index.html; however, most web servers can be configured to use any file as the
default web page for the site. If the web server cannot locate a requested document, it
returns an error indication to the web browser, and the browser displays a web page containing an error message to the user.

Hyperlinking to an E-Mail Address

Anchors can link to e-mail addresses using a *mailto:* URL. When someone clicks this type of anchored link, most browsers launch the default e-mail program (e.g., Microsoft Outlook or Mozilla Thunderbird) to enable the user to write an e-mail message to the linked address. Figure 2.4 demonstrates this type of anchor. Lines 15–17 contain an e-mail link. The form of an e-mail anchor is `<a href = "mailto:`*emailAddress*`">...</a>`. In this case, we link to the e-mail address `deitel@deitel.com`.

```
 1   <?xml version = "1.0" encoding = "utf-8"?>
 2   <!DOCTYPE html PUBLIC "-//W3C//DTD XHTML 1.0 Strict//EN"
 3      "http://www.w3.org/TR/xhtml1/DTD/xhtml1-strict.dtd">
 4
 5   <!-- Fig. 2.4: contact.html -->
 6   <!-- Linking to an e-mail address. -->
 7   <html xmlns = "http://www.w3.org/1999/xhtml">
 8      <head>
 9         <title>Contact Page</title>
10      </head>
11
12      <body>
13         <p>
14            My email address is
15            <a href = "mailto:deitel@deitel.com">
16               deitel@deitel.com
17            </a>
18            . Click the address and your default email client
19             will open an e-mail message and address it to me.
20         </p>
21      </body>
22   </html>
```

Fig. 2.4 | Linking to an e-mail address.

2.7 Images

The examples discussed so far demonstrate how to mark up documents that contain only text. However, most web pages contain both text and images. In fact, images are an equally important, if not essential, part of web-page design. The three most popular image formats used by web developers are Graphics Interchange Format (GIF), Joint Photographic Experts Group (JPEG) and Portable Network Graphics (PNG) images. Users can create images using specialized software, such as Adobe Photoshop Elements (www.adobe.com), G.I.M.P. (http://www.gimp.org) and Inkscape (http://www.inkscape.org). Images may also be acquired from various websites. Figure 2.5 demonstrates how to incorporate images into web pages.

Lines 14–15 use an *img element* to insert an image in the document. The image file's location is specified with the img element's *src attribute*. This image is located in the same directory as the XHTML document, so only the image's filename is required. Optional attributes *width* and *height* specify the image's width and height, respectively. You can scale an image by increasing or decreasing the values of the image width and height attributes. If these attributes are omitted, the browser uses the image's actual width and height. Images are measured in *pixels* ("picture elements"), which represent dots of color on the screen. Any image-editing program will have a feature that displays the dimensions, in pixels, of an image. The image in Fig. 2.5 is 92 pixels wide and 120 pixels high.

Good Programming Practice 2.5

Always include the width and the height of an image inside the <img> tag. When the browser loads the XHTML file, it will know immediately from these attributes how much screen space to provide for the image and will lay out the page properly, even before it downloads the image.

Performance Tip 2.1

Including the width and height attributes in an <img> tag can help the browser load and render pages faster.

Common Programming Error 2.4

Entering new dimensions for an image that change its inherent width-to-height ratio distorts the appearance of the image. For example, if your image is 200 pixels wide and 100 pixels high, you should ensure that any new dimensions have a 2:1 width-to-height ratio.

```
 1    <?xml version = "1.0" encoding = "utf-8"?>
 2    <!DOCTYPE html PUBLIC "-//W3C//DTD XHTML 1.0 Strict//EN"
 3       "http://www.w3.org/TR/xhtml1/DTD/xhtml1-strict.dtd">
 4
 5    <!-- Fig. 2.5: picture.html -->
 6    <!-- Images in XHTML files. -->
 7    <html xmlns = "http://www.w3.org/1999/xhtml">
 8       <head>
 9          <title>Images</title>
10       </head>
11
```

Fig. 2.5 | Images in XHTML files. (Part 1 of 2.)

```
12      <body>
13        <p>
14          <img src = "cpphtp6.jpg" width = "92" height = "120"
15            alt = "C++ How to Program book cover" />
16          <img src = "jhtp.jpg" width = "92" height = "120"
17            alt = "Java How to Program book cover" />
18        </p>
19      </body>
20    </html>
```

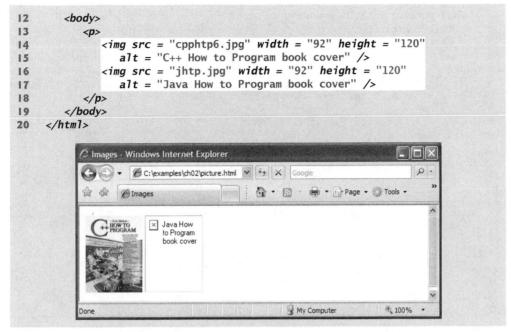

Fig. 2.5 | Images in XHTML files. (Part 2 of 2.)

Every img element in an XHTML document must have an **alt** *attribute*. If a browser cannot render an image, the browser displays the alt attribute's value. A browser may not be able to render an image for several reasons. It may not support images—as is the case with a *text-based browser* (i.e., a browser that can display only text)—or the client may have disabled image viewing to reduce download time. Figure 2.5 shows Internet Explorer 7 rendering a red x symbol and displaying the alt attribute's value, signifying that the image (jhtp.jpg) cannot be found.

The alt attribute helps you create *accessible* web pages for users with disabilities, especially those with vision impairments who use text-based browsers. Specialized software called a *speech synthesizer* can "speak" the alt attribute's value so that a user with a visual impairment knows what the browser is displaying.

Some XHTML elements (called *empty elements*) contain only attributes and do not mark up text (i.e., text is not placed between the start and end tags). Empty elements (e.g., img) must be terminated, either by using the *forward slash character* (/) inside the closing right angle bracket (>) of the start tag or by explicitly including the end tag. When using the forward slash character, we add a space before it to improve readability (as shown at the ends of lines 15 and 17). Rather than using the forward slash character, lines 16–17 could be written with a closing </img> tag as follows:

```
<img src = "jhtp.jpg" width = "92" height = "120"
  alt = "Java How to Program book cover"></img>
```

Using Images as Hyperlinks
By using images as hyperlinks, web developers can create graphical web pages that link to other resources. In Fig. 2.6, we create six different image hyperlinks.

```
1   <?xml version = "1.0" encoding = "utf-8"?>
2   <!DOCTYPE html PUBLIC "-//W3C//DTD XHTML 1.0 Strict//EN"
3      "http://www.w3.org/TR/xhtml1/DTD/xhtml1-strict.dtd">
4
5   <!-- Fig. 2.6: nav.html -->
6   <!-- Images as link anchors. -->
7   <html xmlns = "http://www.w3.org/1999/xhtml">
8      <head>
9         <title>Navigation Bar</title>
10     </head>
11
12     <body>
13        <p>
14           <a href = "links.html">
15              <img src = "buttons/links.jpg" width = "65"
16                 height = "50" alt = "Links Page" />
17           </a>
18
19           <a href = "list.html">
20              <img src = "buttons/list.jpg" width = "65"
21                 height = "50" alt = "List Example Page" />
22           </a>
23
24           <a href = "contact.html">
25              <img src = "buttons/contact.jpg" width = "65"
26                 height = "50" alt = "Contact Page" />
27           </a>
28
29           <a href = "table1.html">
30              <img src = "buttons/table.jpg" width = "65"
31                 height = "50" alt = "Table Page" />
32           </a>
33
34           <a href = "form.html">
35              <img src = "buttons/form.jpg" width = "65"
36                 height = "50" alt = "Feedback Form" />
37           </a>
38        </p>
39     </body>
40  </html>
```

Fig. 2.6 | Images as link anchors. (Part 1 of 2.)

Fig. 2.6 | Images as link anchors. (Part 2 of 2.)

Lines 14–17 create an *image hyperlink* by nesting an `img` element in an anchor (a) element. The value of the `img` element's `src` attribute value specifies that this image (`links.jpg`) resides in a directory named `buttons`. The `buttons` directory and the XHTML document are in the same directory. Images from other web documents also can be referenced by setting the `src` attribute to the name and location of the image. Note that if you're hosting a publicly available web page that uses an image from another site, you should get permission to use the image and host a copy of image on your own website. If you refer to an image on another website, the browser has to request the image resource from the other site's server. Clicking an image hyperlink takes a user to the web page specified by the surrounding anchor element's `href` attribute. Notice that when the mouse hovers over a link of any kind, the URL that the link points to is displayed in the status bar at the bottom of the browser window.

2.8 Special Characters and Horizontal Rules

When marking up text, certain characters or symbols (e.g., <) may be difficult to embed directly into an XHTML document. Some keyboards do not provide these symbols, or the presence of these symbols may cause syntax errors. For example, the markup

```
<p>if x < 10 then increment x by 1</p>
```

results in a syntax error because it uses the less-than character (<), which is reserved for start tags and end tags such as <p> and </p>. XHTML provides *character entity references* (in the form &*code*;) for representing special characters. We could correct the previous line by writing

```
<p>if x &lt; 10 then increment x by 1</p>
```

which uses the character entity reference *<* for the less-than symbol (<).

Figure 2.7 demonstrates how to use special characters in an XHTML document. Lines 24–25 contain other special characters, which can be expressed as either character entity references (coded using word abbreviations such as & for ampersand and © for copyright) or *numeric character references*—decimal or *hexadecimal* (*hex*) values representing special characters. For example, the & character is represented in decimal and hexadecimal notation as & and &, respectively. Hexadecimal numbers are base 16 numbers—digits in a hexadecimal number have values from 0 to 15 (a total of 16 different values). The letters A–F represent the hexadecimal digits corresponding to decimal values 10–15. Thus in hexadecimal notation we can have numbers like 876 consisting solely of decimal-like digits, numbers like DA19F consisting of digits and letters, and numbers like DCB consisting solely of letters.

```
 1  <?xml version = "1.0" encoding = "utf-8"?>
 2  <!DOCTYPE html PUBLIC "-//W3C//DTD XHTML 1.0 Strict//EN"
 3     "http://www.w3.org/TR/xhtml1/DTD/xhtml1-strict.dtd">
 4
 5  <!-- Fig. 2.7: contact2.html -->
 6  <!-- Inserting special characters. -->
 7  <html xmlns = "http://www.w3.org/1999/xhtml">
 8     <head>
 9        <title>Contact Page</title>
10     </head>
11
12     <body>
13        <p>
14           Click
15           <a href = "mailto:deitel@deitel.com">here</a>
16           to open an email message addressed to
17           deitel@deitel.com.
18        </p>
19
20        <hr /> <!-- inserts a horizontal rule -->
21
22        <!-- special characters are entered -->
23        <!-- using the form &code; -->
24        <p>All information on this site is <strong>&copy;
25           Deitel &amp; Associates, Inc. 2007.</strong></p>
26
27        <!-- to strike through text use <del> tags -->
28        <!-- to subscript text use <sub> tags -->
29        <!-- to superscript text use <sup> tags -->
30        <!-- these tags are nested inside other tags -->
31        <p><del>You may download 3.14 x 10<sup>2</sup>
32           characters worth of information from this site.</del>
33           Only <sub>one</sub> download per hour is permitted.</p>
34        <p><em>Note: &lt; &frac14; of the information
35           presented here is updated daily.</em></p>
36     </body>
37  </html>
```

Fig. 2.7 | Inserting special characters. (Part 1 of 2.)

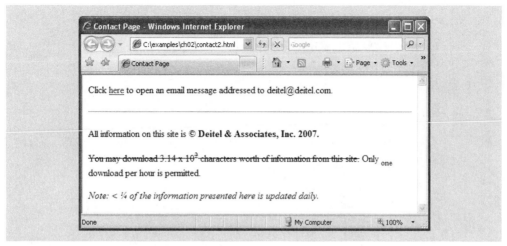

Fig. 2.7 | Inserting special characters. (Part 2 of 2.)

In lines 31–33, we introduce four new elements. Most browsers render the *del* element as strike-through text. With this format users can easily indicate document revisions. To *superscript* text (i.e., raise text above the baseline and decreased font size) or *subscript* text (i.e., lower text below the baseline and decreased font size), use the *sup* or *sub* element, respectively. The paragraph in lines 34–35 contains an *em element*, which indicates that its contents should be emphasized. Browsers usually render em elements in an italic font. We also use character entity reference < for a less-than sign and ¼ for the fraction 1/4 (line 34).

In addition to special characters, this document introduces a *horizontal rule*, indicated by the *<hr />* tag in line 22. Most browsers render a horizontal rule as a horizontal line with a blank line above and below it.

2.9 Lists

Up to this point, we have presented basic XHTML elements and attributes for linking to resources, creating headings, using special characters and incorporating images. In this section, we discuss how to organize information on a web page using lists. In the next section, we introduce another feature for organizing information, called a table. Figure 2.8 displays text in an *unordered list* (i.e., a list that does not order its items by letter or number). The unordered list element *ul* creates a list in which each item begins with a bullet symbol (called a disc). Each entry in an unordered list (element ul in line 17) is an *li* (*list item*) element (lines 19–22). Most web browsers render each li element on a new line with a bullet symbol indented from the beginning of the line.

```
1   <?xml version = "1.0" encoding = "utf-8"?>
2   <!DOCTYPE html PUBLIC "-//W3C//DTD XHTML 1.0 Strict//EN"
3      "http://www.w3.org/TR/xhtml1/DTD/xhtml1-strict.dtd">
4
```

Fig. 2.8 | Unordered list containing hyperlinks. (Part 1 of 2.)

```
 5    <!-- Fig. 2.8: links2.html -->
 6    <!-- Unordered list containing hyperlinks. -->
 7    <html xmlns = "http://www.w3.org/1999/xhtml">
 8       <head>
 9          <title>Links</title>
10       </head>
11
12       <body>
13          <h1>Here are my favorite sites</h1>
14          <p><strong>Click on a name to go to that page.</strong></p>
15
16          <!-- create an unordered list -->
17          <ul>
18             <!-- add four list items -->
19             <li><a href = "http://www.deitel.com">Deitel</a></li>
20             <li><a href = "http://www.w3.org">W3C</a></li>
21             <li><a href = "http://www.yahoo.com">Yahoo!</a></li>
22             <li><a href = "http://www.cnn.com">CNN</a></li>
23          </ul>
24       </body>
25    </html>
```

Fig. 2.8 | Unordered list containing hyperlinks. (Part 2 of 2.)

Nested Lists

Lists may be nested to represent hierarchical relationships, as in an outline format. Figure 2.9 demonstrates nested lists and *ordered lists*. The ordered list element *ol* creates a list in which each item begins with a number.

A web browser indents each nested list to indicate a hierarchical relationship. The first ordered list begins at line 30. Items in an ordered list are enumerated one, two, three and so on. Nested ordered lists are enumerated in the same manner. The items in the outermost unordered list (line 16) are preceded by discs. List items nested inside the unordered list of line 16 are preceded by circular bullets. Although not demonstrated in this example, subsequent nested list items are preceded by square bullets.

```
 1   <?xml version = "1.0" encoding = "utf-8"?>
 2   <!DOCTYPE html PUBLIC "-//W3C//DTD XHTML 1.0 Strict//EN"
 3      "http://www.w3.org/TR/xhtml1/DTD/xhtml1-strict.dtd">
 4
 5   <!-- Fig. 2.9: list.html -->
 6   <!-- Nested and ordered lists. -->
 7   <html xmlns = "http://www.w3.org/1999/xhtml">
 8      <head>
 9         <title>Lists</title>
10      </head>
11
12      <body>
13         <h1>The Best Features of the Internet</h1>
14
15         <!-- create an unordered list -->
16         <ul>
17            <li>You can meet new people from countries around
18               the world.</li>
19            <li>
20               You have access to new media as it becomes public:
21
22               <!-- this starts a nested list, which uses a -->
23               <!-- modified bullet. The list ends when you -->
24               <!-- close the <ul> tag. -->
25               <ul>
26                  <li>New games</li>
27                  <li>New applications
28
29                     <!-- nested ordered list -->
30                     <ol>
31                        <li>For business</li>
32                        <li>For pleasure</li>
33                     </ol>
34                  </li> <!-- ends line 27 new applications li -->
35
36                  <li>Around the clock news</li>
37                  <li>Search engines</li>
38                  <li>Shopping</li>
39                  <li>Programming
40
41                     <!-- another nested ordered list -->
42                     <ol>
43                        <li>XML</li>
44                        <li>Java</li>
45                        <li>XHTML</li>
46                        <li>Scripts</li>
47                        <li>New languages</li>
48                     </ol>
49                  </li> <!-- ends programming li of line 39 -->
50               </ul> <!-- ends the nested list of line 25 -->
51            </li>
52
```

Fig. 2.9 | Nested and ordered lists. (Part 1 of 2.)

```
53            <li>Links</li>
54            <li>Keeping in touch with old friends</li>
55            <li>It is the technology of the future!</li>
56        </ul> <!-- ends the unordered list of line 16 -->
57     </body>
58  </html>
```

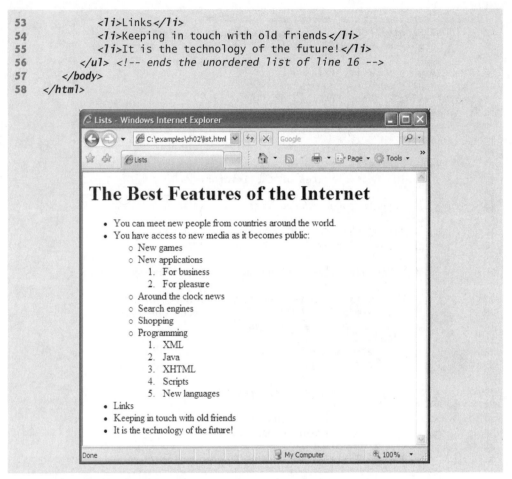

Fig. 2.9 | Nested and ordered lists. (Part 2 of 2.)

2.10 Tables

Tables are frequently used to organize data into rows and columns. Our first example (Fig. 2.10) creates a table with six rows and two columns to display price information for fruit.

Tables are defined with the *table* element (lines 15–62). Lines 15–17 specify the start tag for a table element that has several attributes. The *border* attribute specifies the table's border width in pixels. To create a table without a border, set border to "0". This example assigns attribute *width* the value "40%" to set the table's width to 40 percent of the browser's width. A developer can also set attribute width to a specified number of pixels. Try resizing the browser window to see how the width of the window affects the width of the table.

As its name implies, attribute *summary* (lines 16–17) describes the table's contents. Speech devices use this attribute to make the table more accessible to users with visual impairments. The *caption* element (line 21) describes the table's content and helps text-

```
 1   <?xml version = "1.0" encoding = "utf-8"?>
 2   <!DOCTYPE html PUBLIC "-//W3C//DTD XHTML 1.0 Strict//EN"
 3      "http://www.w3.org/TR/xhtml1/DTD/xhtml1-strict.dtd">
 4
 5   <!-- Fig. 2.10: table1.html -->
 6   <!-- Creating a basic table. -->
 7   <html xmlns = "http://www.w3.org/1999/xhtml">
 8      <head>
 9         <title>A simple XHTML table</title>
10      </head>
11
12      <body>
13
14         <!-- the <table> tag opens a table -->
15         <table border = "1" width = "40%"
16            summary = "This table provides information about
17               the price of fruit">
18
19            <!-- the <caption> tag summarizes the table's -->
20            <!-- contents (this helps the visually impaired) -->
21            <caption><strong>Price of Fruit</strong></caption>
22
23            <!-- the <thead> section appears first in the table -->
24            <!-- it formats the table header area -->
25            <thead>
26               <tr> <!-- <tr> inserts a table row -->
27                  <th>Fruit</th> <!-- insert a heading cell -->
28                  <th>Price</th>
29               </tr>
30            </thead>
31
32            <!-- the <tfoot> section appears last in the table -->
33            <!-- it formats the table footer -->
34            <tfoot>
35               <tr>
36                  <th>Total</th>
37                  <th>$3.75</th>
38               </tr>
39            </tfoot>
40
41            <!-- all table content is enclosed -->
42            <!-- within the <tbody> -->
43            <tbody>
44               <tr>
45                  <td>Apple</td> <!-- insert a data cell -->
46                  <td>$0.25</td>
47               </tr>
48               <tr>
49                  <td>Orange</td>
50                  <td>$0.50</td>
51               </tr>
52               <tr>
53                  <td>Banana</td>
```

Fig. 2.10 | Creating a basic table. (Part 1 of 2.)

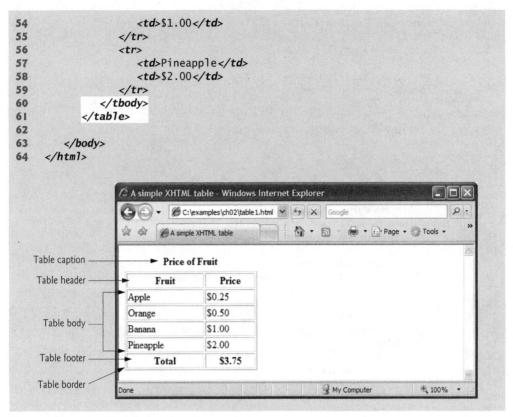

```
54                    <td>$1.00</td>
55                </tr>
56                <tr>
57                    <td>Pineapple</td>
58                    <td>$2.00</td>
59                </tr>
60            </tbody>
61        </table>
62
63      </body>
64  </html>
```

Table caption ——————▶ Price of Fruit

Table header ——————

Fruit	Price
Apple	$0.25
Orange	$0.50
Banana	$1.00
Pineapple	$2.00
Total	**$3.75**

Fig. 2.10 | Creating a basic table. (Part 2 of 2.)

based browsers interpret the table data. Text inside the <caption> tag is rendered above the table by most browsers. Attribute summary and element caption are two of the many XHTML features that make web pages more accessible to users with disabilities.

A table has three distinct sections—*head, body* and *foot*. The head section (or header cell) is defined with a ***thead*** element (lines 25–30), which contains header information such as column names. Each ***tr*** element (lines 26–29) defines an individual *table row*. The columns in the head section are defined with ***th*** elements. Most browsers center text formatted by th (table header column) elements and display them in bold. Table header elements are nested inside table row elements (lines 27–28).

The body section, or *table body*, contains the table's primary data. The table body (lines 43–60) is defined in a ***tbody*** element. In the body, each tr element specifies one row. *Data cells* contain individual pieces of data and are defined with ***td*** (*table data*) elements in each row.

The foot section (lines 34–39) is defined with a ***tfoot*** (table foot) element. The text placed in the footer commonly includes calculation results and footnotes. Like other sections, the foot section can contain table rows, and each row can contain cells. As in the head section, cells in the foot section are created using th elements, instead of the td elements used in the table body. Note that the table foot section must be above the body section in the code, but the table foot displays at the bottom of the table.

Using rowspan and colspan

Figure 2.10 explored a basic table's structure. Figure 2.11 presents another table example and introduces two new attributes that allow you to build more complex tables.

The table begins in line 15. Table cells are sized to fit the data they contain. Document authors can create larger data cells using the attributes *rowspan* and *colspan*. The values assigned to these attributes specify the number of rows or columns occupied by a cell. The th element at lines 23–26 uses the attribute rowspan = "2" to allow the cell containing the picture of the camel to use two vertically adjacent cells (thus the cell *spans* two rows). The th element in lines 29–32 uses the attribute colspan = "4" to widen the header cell (containing Camelid comparison and Approximate as of 6/2007) to span four cells.

```
 1   <?xml version = "1.0" encoding = "utf-8"?>
 2   <!DOCTYPE html PUBLIC "-//W3C//DTD XHTML 1.0 Strict//EN"
 3      "http://www.w3.org/TR/xhtml1/DTD/xhtml1-strict.dtd">
 4
 5   <!-- Fig. 2.11: table2.html -->
 6   <!-- Complex XHTML table. -->
 7   <html xmlns = "http://www.w3.org/1999/xhtml">
 8      <head>
 9         <title>Tables</title>
10      </head>
11
12      <body>
13         <h1>Table Example Page</h1>
14
15         <table border = "1">
16            <caption>Here is a more complex sample table.</caption>
17
18            <thead>
19               <!-- rowspans and colspans merge the specified -->
20               <!-- number of cells vertically or horizontally -->
21               <tr>
22                  <!-- merge two rows -->
23                  <th rowspan = "2">
24                     <img src = "camel.gif" width = "205"
25                        height = "167" alt = "Picture of a camel" />
26                  </th>
27
28                  <!-- merge four columns -->
29                  <th colspan = "4">
30                     <h1>Camelid comparison</h1>
31                     <p>Approximate as of 6/2007</p>
32                  </th>
33               </tr>
34               <tr>
35                  <th># of Humps</th>
36                  <th>Indigenous region</th>
37                  <th>Spits?</th>
38                  <th>Produces Wool?</th>
39               </tr>
40            </thead>
```

Fig. 2.11 | Complex XHTML table. (Part 1 of 2.)

```
41            <tbody>
42               <tr>
43                  <th>Camels (bactrian)</th>
44                  <td>2</td>
45                  <td>Africa/Asia</td>
46                  <td>Yes</td>
47                  <td>Yes</td>
48               </tr>
49               <tr>
50                  <th>Llamas</th>
51                  <td>1</td>
52                  <td>Andes Mountains</td>
53                  <td>Yes</td>
54                  <td>Yes</td>
55               </tr>
56            </tbody>
57         </table>
58      </body>
59   </html>
```

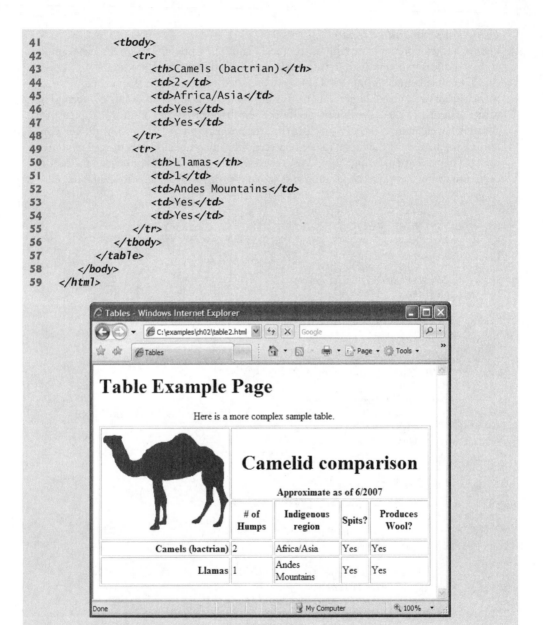

Fig. 2.11 | Complex XHTML table. (Part 2 of 2.)

2.11 Forms

When browsing websites, users often need to provide such information as search keywords, e-mail addresses and zip codes. XHTML provides a mechanism, called a form, for collecting data from a user.

Data that users enter on a web page is normally sent to a web server that provides access to a site's resources (e.g., XHTML documents, images). These resources are located either on the same machine as the web server or on a machine that the web server can access through the network. When a browser requests a web page or file that is located on a server, the server processes the request and returns the requested resource. A request contains the name and path of the desired resource and the method of communication (called a *protocol*). XHTML documents use the Hypertext Transfer Protocol (HTTP).

Figure 2.12 is a simple form that sends data to the web server, which passes the form data to a program. The program processes the data received from the web server and typically returns information to the web server. The web server then sends the information as an XHTML document to the web browser. We discuss web servers in Chapter 17. [*Note:* This example demonstrates client-side functionality. If the form is submitted (by clicking **Submit**), nothing will happen, because we don't yet know how to process the form data. In later chapters, we present the server-side programming (e.g., in Ruby on Rails, PHP, ASP.NET and JavaServer Faces) necessary to process information entered into a form.]

Forms can contain visual and nonvisual components. Visual components include clickable buttons and other graphical user interface components with which users interact. Nonvisual components, called *hidden inputs*, store any data that you specify, such as e-mail addresses and XHTML document filenames that act as links. The form is defined in lines 21–46 by a *form* element.

Attribute *method* (line 21) specifies how the form's data is sent to the web server. Using method = "*post*" appends form data to the browser request, which contains the protocol (HTTP) and the requested resource's URL. This method of passing data to the server is transparent—the user doesn't see the data after the form is submitted. The other possible value, method = "*get*", appends the form data directly to the end of the URL of the script, where it is visible in the browser's **Address** field. The *post* and *get* methods for sending form data are discussed in detail in Chapter 17.

```
 1   <?xml version = "1.0" encoding = "utf-8"?>
 2   <!DOCTYPE html PUBLIC "-//W3C//DTD XHTML 1.0 Strict//EN"
 3      "http://www.w3.org/TR/xhtml1/DTD/xhtml1-strict.dtd">
 4
 5   <!-- Fig. 2.12: form.html -->
 6   <!-- Form with hidden fields and a text box. -->
 7   <html xmlns = "http://www.w3.org/1999/xhtml">
 8      <head>
 9         <title>Forms</title>
10      </head>
11
12      <body>
13         <h1>Feedback Form</h1>
14
15         <p>Please fill out this form to help
16            us improve our site.</p>
17
18         <!-- this tag starts the form, gives the -->
19         <!-- method of sending information and the -->
20         <!-- location of form script -->
21         <form method = "post" action = "">
22            <p>
```

Fig. 2.12 | Form with hidden fields and a text box. (Part 1 of 2.)

```
23              <!-- hidden inputs contain non-visual -->
24              <!-- information -->
25              <input type = "hidden" name = "recipient"
26                 value = "deitel@deitel.com" />
27              <input type = "hidden" name = "subject"
28                 value = "Feedback Form" />
29              <input type = "hidden" name = "redirect"
30                 value = "main.html" />
31           </p>
32
33           <!-- <input type = "text"> inserts a text box -->
34           <p><label>Name:
35                 <input name = "name" type = "text" size = "25"
36                    maxlength = "30" />
37              </label></p>
38
39           <p>
40              <!-- input types "submit" and "reset" insert -->
41              <!-- buttons for submitting and clearing the -->
42              <!-- form's contents -->
43              <input type = "submit" value = "Submit" />
44              <input type = "reset" value = "Clear" />
45           </p>
46        </form>
47     </body>
48  </html>
```

Fig. 2.12 | Form with hidden fields and a text box. (Part 2 of 2.)

The *action* attribute in the <form> tag in line 21 specifies the URL of a script on the web server that will be invoked to process the form's data. Since we haven't introduced server-side programming yet, we leave this attribute empty for now.

Lines 25–44 define six *input* elements that specify data to provide to the script that processes the form (also called the *form handler*). There are several types of input elements. An input's type is determined by its *type attribute*. This form uses a text input, a submit input, a reset input and three hidden inputs.

The ***text*** input in lines 35–36 inserts a ***text box*** in the form. Users can type data in text boxes. The `label` element (lines 34–37) provides users with information about the `input` element's purpose. The `input` element's ***size*** attribute specifies the number of characters visible in the text box. Optional attribute ***maxlength*** limits the number of characters input into the text box—in this case, the user is not permitted to type more than 30 characters.

Look-and-Feel Observation 2.3

Include a `label` element for each form element to help users determine the purpose of each form element.

Two `input` elements in lines 43–44 create two buttons. The ***submit*** `input` element is a button. When the `submit` button is pressed, the user is sent to the location specified in the form's `action` attribute. The ***value*** attribute sets the text displayed on the button. The ***reset*** `input` element allows a user to reset all `form` elements to their default values. The `value` attribute of the `reset` `input` element sets the text displayed on the button (the default value is **Reset** if you omit the `value` attribute).

The three `input` elements in lines 25–30 have the `type` attribute `hidden`, which allows you to send form data that is not input by a user. The three hidden inputs are an e-mail address to which the data will be sent, the e-mail's subject line and a URL for the browser to open after submission of the form. Two other `input` attributes are ***name***, which identifies the `input` element, and ***value***, which provides the value that will be sent (or posted) to the web server.

Good Programming Practice 2.6

Place hidden `input` elements at the beginning of a form, immediately after the opening `<form>` tag. This placement allows document authors to locate hidden `input` elements quickly.

Additional Form Elements

In the previous example, you saw basic elements of XHTML forms. Now that you know the general structure of a form, we introduce elements and attributes for creating more complex forms. Figure 2.13 contains a form that solicits user feedback about a website.

```
1   <?xml version = "1.0" encoding = "utf-8"?>
2   <!DOCTYPE html PUBLIC "-//W3C//DTD XHTML 1.0 Strict//EN"
3      "http://www.w3.org/TR/xhtml1/DTD/xhtml1-strict.dtd">
4
5   <!-- Fig. 2.13: form2.html -->
6   <!-- Form using a variety of components. -->
7   <html xmlns = "http://www.w3.org/1999/xhtml">
8      <head>
9         <title>More Forms</title>
10     </head>
11
12     <body>
13        <h1>Feedback Form</h1>
```

Fig. 2.13 | Form using a variety of components. (Part 1 of 4.)

```
14    <p>Please fill out this form to help
15       us improve our site.</p>
16
17    <form method = "post" action = "">
18       <p>
19          <input type = "hidden" name = "recipient"
20             value = "deitel@deitel.com" />
21          <input type = "hidden" name = "subject"
22             value = "Feedback Form" />
23          <input type = "hidden" name = "redirect"
24             value = "main.html" />
25       </p>
26
27       <p><label>Name:
28          <input name = "name" type = "text" size = "25" />
29       </label></p>
30
31       <!-- <textarea> creates a multiline textbox -->
32       <p><label>Comments:<br />
33          <textarea name = "comments"
34             rows = "4" cols = "36">Enter comments here.</textarea>
35       </label></p>
36
37       <!-- <input type = "password"> inserts a -->
38       <!-- textbox whose display is masked with -->
39       <!-- asterisk characters -->
40       <p><label>E-mail Address:
41          <input name = "email" type = "password" size = "25" />
42       </label></p>
43
44       <p>
45          <strong>Things you liked:</strong><br />
46
47          <label>Site design
48             <input name = "thingsliked" type = "checkbox"
49                value = "Design" /></label>
50          <label>Links
51             <input name = "thingsliked" type = "checkbox"
52                value = "Links" /></label>
53          <label>Ease of use
54             <input name = "thingsliked" type = "checkbox"
55                value = "Ease" /></label>
56          <label>Images
57             <input name = "thingsliked" type = "checkbox"
58                value = "Images" /></label>
59          <label>Source code
60             <input name = "thingsliked" type = "checkbox"
61                value = "Code" /></label>
62       </p>
63
64       <!-- <input type = "radio" /> creates a radio -->
65       <!-- button. The difference between radio buttons -->
```

Fig. 2.13 | Form using a variety of components. (Part 2 of 4.)

```
66          <!-- and checkboxes is that only one radio button -->
67          <!-- in a group can be selected. -->
68          <p>
69              <strong>How did you get to our site?:</strong><br />
70
71              <label>Search engine
72                  <input name = "howtosite" type = "radio"
73                      value = "search engine" checked = "checked" /></label>
74              <label>Links from another site
75                  <input name = "howtosite" type = "radio"
76                      value = "link" /></label>
77              <label>Deitel.com Website
78                  <input name = "howtosite" type = "radio"
79                      value = "deitel.com" /></label>
80              <label>Reference in a book
81                  <input name = "howtosite" type = "radio"
82                      value = "book" /></label>
83              <label>Other
84                  <input name = "howtosite" type = "radio"
85                      value = "other" /></label>
86          </p>
87
88          <p>
89              <label>Rate our site:
90
91                  <!-- the <select> tag presents a drop-down -->
92                  <!-- list with choices indicated by the -->
93                  <!-- <option> tags -->
94                  <select name = "rating">
95                      <option selected = "selected">Amazing</option>
96                      <option>10</option>
97                      <option>9</option>
98                      <option>8</option>
99                      <option>7</option>
100                     <option>6</option>
101                     <option>5</option>
102                     <option>4</option>
103                     <option>3</option>
104                     <option>2</option>
105                     <option>1</option>
106                     <option>Awful</option>
107                 </select>
108             </label>
109         </p>
110
111         <p>
112             <input type = "submit" value = "Submit" />
113             <input type = "reset" value = "Clear" />
114         </p>
115     </form>
116 </body>
117 </html>
```

Fig. 2.13 | Form using a variety of components. (Part 3 of 4.)

Fig. 2.13 | Form using a variety of components. (Part 4 of 4.)

In line 32, we introduce the **br** element, which most browsers render as a =*line break*. Any markup or text following a br element is rendered on the next line. Like the img element, br is an example of an empty element terminated with a forward slash. We add a space before the forward slash to enhance readability.

The **textarea** element (lines 33–34) inserts a multiline text box, called a *text area*, into the form. The number of rows is specified with the **rows** attribute, and the number of columns (i.e., characters per line) is specified with the **cols** attribute. In this example, the textarea is four rows high and 36 characters wide. To display default text in the text area, place the text between the <textarea> and </textarea> tags. Default text can be specified in other input types, such as text boxes, by using the value attribute.

The **password** input in line 41 inserts a password box with the specified size (maximum number of characters allowed). A password box allows users to enter sensitive information, such as credit card numbers and passwords, by "masking" the information input with asterisks (*). The actual value input is sent to the web server, not the characters that mask the input.

Lines 47–61 introduce the *checkbox* form element. Checkboxes enable users to select from a set of options. When a user selects a checkbox, a check mark appears in the checkbox. Otherwise, the checkbox remains empty. Each **"checkbox"** input creates a new checkbox. Checkboxes can be used individually or in groups. Checkboxes that belong to a group are assigned the same name (in this case, "thingsliked").

Common Programming Error 2.5

When your form has several checkboxes with the same name, you must make sure that they have different values, or the scripts running on the web server will not be able to distinguish them.

After the checkboxes, we present two more ways to allow the user to make choices. In this example, we introduce two new input types. The first type is the *radio button* (lines 71–85) specified with type *"radio"*. Radio buttons are similar to checkboxes, except that only one radio button in a group of radio buttons may be selected at any time. The radio buttons in a group all have the same name attributes and are distinguished by their different value attributes. The attribute–value pair checked = "checked" (line 73) indicates which radio button, if any, is selected initially. The checked attribute also applies to checkboxes.

Common Programming Error 2.6

Not setting the name attributes of the radio buttons in a form to the same name is a logic error because it lets the user select all of them at the same time.

The *select* element (lines 94–107) provides a drop-down list from which the user can select an item. The name attribute identifies the drop-down list. The *option* elements (lines 95–106) add items to the drop-down list. The option element's *selected* attribute specifies which item initially is displayed as the selected item in the select element. If no option element is marked as selected, the browser selects the first option by default.

2.12 Internal Linking

Earlier in the chapter, we discussed how to hyperlink one web page to another. Figure 2.14 introduces *internal linking*—a mechanism that enables the user to jump between locations in the same document. Internal linking is useful for long documents that contain many sections. Clicking an internal link enables users to find a section without scrolling through the entire document.

Line 14 contains a tag with the id attribute (set to "features") for an internal hyperlink. To link to a tag with this attribute inside the same web page, the href attribute of an anchor element includes the id attribute value preceded by a pound sign (as in #features). Line 56 contains a hyperlink with the id features as its target. Selecting this hyperlink in a web browser scrolls the browser window to the h1 tag in line 14. Note that you may have to resize your browser to a small window and scroll down before clicking the link to see the browser scroll to the h1 element.

```
1   <?xml version = "1.0" encoding = "utf-8"?>
2   <!DOCTYPE html PUBLIC "-//W3C//DTD XHTML 1.0 Strict//EN"
3      "http://www.w3.org/TR/xhtml1/DTD/xhtml1-strict.dtd">
4
5   <!-- Fig. 2.14: internal.html -->
6   <!-- Internal hyperlinks to make pages more navigable. -->
7   <html xmlns = "http://www.w3.org/1999/xhtml">
```

Fig. 2.14 | Internal hyperlinks to make pages more navigable. (Part 1 of 3.)

```
 8    <head>
 9        <title>Internal Links</title>
10    </head>
11
12    <body>
13        <!-- id attribute creates an internal hyperlink destination -->
14        <h1 id = "features">The Best Features of the Internet</h1>
15
16        <!-- an internal link's address is "#id" -->
17        <p><a href = "#bugs">Go to <em>Favorite Bugs</em></a></p>
18
19        <ul>
20            <li>You can meet people from countries
21                around the world.</li>
22            <li>You have access to new media as it becomes public:
23                <ul>
24                    <li>New games</li>
25                    <li>New applications
26                        <ul>
27                            <li>For Business</li>
28                            <li>For Pleasure</li>
29                        </ul>
30                    </li>
31
32                    <li>Around the clock news</li>
33                    <li>Search Engines</li>
34                    <li>Shopping</li>
35                    <li>Programming
36                        <ul>
37                            <li>XHTML</li>
38                            <li>Java</li>
39                            <li>Dynamic HTML</li>
40                            <li>Scripts</li>
41                            <li>New languages</li>
42                        </ul>
43                    </li>
44                </ul>
45            </li>
46
47            <li>Links</li>
48            <li>Keeping in touch with old friends</li>
49            <li>It is the technology of the future!</li>
50        </ul>
51
52        <!-- id attribute creates an internal hyperlink destination -->
53        <h1 id = "bugs">My 3 Favorite Bugs</h1>
54        <p>
55            <!-- internal hyperlink to features -->
56            <a href = "#features">Go to <em>Favorite Features</em></a>
57        </p>
58        <ol>
59            <li>Fire Fly</li>
60            <li>Gal Ant</li>
```

Fig. 2.14 | Internal hyperlinks to make pages more navigable. (Part 2 of 3.)

```
61              <li>Roman Tic</li>
62          </ol>
63      </body>
64  </html>
```

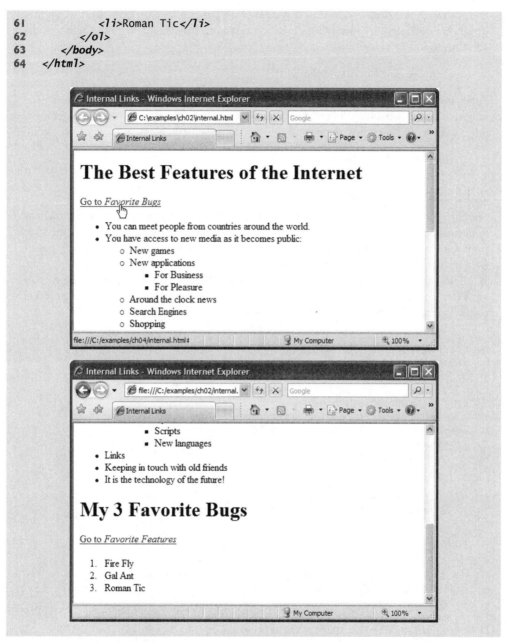

Fig. 2.14 | Internal hyperlinks to make pages more navigable. (Part 3 of 3.)

Look-and-Feel Observation 2.4

Internal hyperlinks are useful in XHTML documents that contain large amounts of information. Internal links to different parts of the page make it easier for users to navigate the page—they do not have to scroll to find the section they want.

Although not demonstrated in this example, a hyperlink can specify an internal link in another document by specifying the document name followed by a pound sign and the id value, as in:

```
href = "filename.html#id"
```

For example, to link to a tag with the id attribute called booklist in books.html, href is assigned "books.html#booklist". You can also send the browser to an internal link on another website by appending the pound sign and id value of an element to any URL, as in:

```
href = "URL/filename.html#id"
```

2.13 meta Elements

Search engines usually catalog sites by following links from page to page (often known as spidering or crawling) and saving identification and classification information for each page. One way that search engines catalog pages is by reading the content in each page's *meta* elements, which specify information about a document.

Two important attributes of the meta element are *name*, which identifies the type of meta element, and *content*, which provides the information search engines use to catalog pages. Figure 2.15 introduces the meta element.

```
 1   <?xml version = "1.0" encoding = "utf-8"?>
 2   <!DOCTYPE html PUBLIC "-//W3C//DTD XHTML 1.0 Strict//EN"
 3      "http://www.w3.org/TR/xhtml1/DTD/xhtml1-strict.dtd">
 4
 5   <!-- Fig. 2.15: meta.html -->
 6   <!-- meta elements provide keywords and a description of a page. -->
 7   <html xmlns = "http://www.w3.org/1999/xhtml">
 8      <head>
 9         <title>Welcome</title>
10
11         <!-- <meta> tags provide search engines with -->
12         <!-- information used to catalog a site -->
13         <meta name = "keywords" content = "web page, design,
14            XHTML, tutorial, personal, help, index, form,
15            contact, feedback, list, links, deitel" />
16         <meta name = "description" content = "This website will
17            help you learn the basics of XHTML and web page design
18            through the use of interactive examples and
19            instruction." />
20      </head>
21      <body>
22         <h1>Welcome to Our Website!</h1>
23
24         <p>We have designed this site to teach about the wonders
25         of <strong><em>XHTML</em></strong>. <em>XHTML</em> is
26         better equipped than <em>HTML</em> to represent complex
27         data on the Internet. <em>XHTML</em> takes advantage of
28         XML's strict syntax to ensure well-formedness. Soon you
```

Fig. 2.15 | meta elements provide keywords and a description of a page. (Part I of 2.)

```
29        will know about many of the great features of
30        <em>XHTML.</em></p>
31
32        <p>Have Fun With the Site!</p>
33     </body>
34 </html>
```

Fig. 2.15 | meta elements provide keywords and a description of a page. (Part 2 of 2.)

Lines 13–15 demonstrate a "keywords" meta element. The content attribute of such a meta element provides search engines with a list of words that describe a page. These words are compared with words in search requests. Thus, including meta elements and their content information can draw more viewers to your site.

Lines 16–19 demonstrate a "description" meta element. The content attribute of such a meta element provides a three- to four-line description of a site, written in sentence form. Search engines also use this description to catalog your site and sometimes display this information as part of the search results. Note that this use of the meta element is one of many methods of search engine optimization (SEO). For more information on SEO, visit Deitel's SEO Resource Center at www.deitel.com/searchengineoptimization.

Software Engineering Observation 2.1

meta elements are not visible to users and must be placed inside the head section of your XHTML document. If meta elements are not placed in this section, they will not be read by search engines.

2.14 Web Resources

www.deitel.com/xhtml

Visit our online XHTML Resource Center for links to some of the best XHTML information on the web. There you'll find categorized links to introductions, tutorials, books, blogs, forums, sample chapters, and more. Also check out links about XHTML 2, the upcoming version of the XHTML standard.

3

Cascading Style Sheets™ (CSS)

Fashions fade, style is eternal.
—Yves Saint Laurent

A style does not go out of style as long as it adapts itself to its period. When there is an incompatibility between the style and a certain state of mind, it is never the style that triumphs.
—Coco Chanel

How liberating to work in the margins, outside a central perception.
—Don DeLillo

I've gradually risen from lower-class background to lower-class foreground.
—Marvin Cohen

OBJECTIVES

In this chapter you will learn:

■ To control the appearance of a website by creating style sheets.

■ To use a style sheet to give all the pages of a website the same look and feel.

■ To use the class attribute to apply styles.

■ To specify the precise font, size, color and other properties of displayed text.

■ To specify element backgrounds and colors.

■ To understand the box model and how to control margins, borders and padding.

■ To use style sheets to separate presentation from content.

3.1 Introduction

In Chapter 2, we introduced the Extensible HyperText Markup Language (XHTML) for marking up information to be rendered in a browser. In this chapter, we shift our focus to formatting and presenting information. To do this, we use a W3C technology called *Cascading Style Sheets™* (*CSS*) that allows document authors to specify the presentation of elements on a web page (e.g., fonts, spacing, colors) separately from the structure of the document (section headers, body text, links, etc.). This *separation of structure from presentation* simplifies maintaining and modifying a web page.

XHTML was designed to specify the content and structure of a document. Though it has some attributes that control presentation, it is better not to mix presentation with content. If a website's presentation is determined entirely by a style sheet, a web designer can simply swap in a new style sheet to completely change the appearance of the site. CSS provides a way to apply style outside of XHTML, allowing the XHTML to dictate the content while the CSS dictates how it's presented.

As with XHTML, the W3C provides a CSS code validator located at jigsaw.w3.org/css-validator/. It is a good idea to validate all CSS code with this tool to make sure that your code is correct and works on as many browsers as possible.

CSS is a large topic. As such, we can introduce only the basic knowledge of CSS that you'll need to understand the examples in the rest of the book. For more CSS references and resources, check out our CSS Resource Center at www.deitel.com/css21.

The W3C's CSS specification is currently in its second major version, with a third in development. The current versions of most major browsers support much of the functionality in CSS 2. This allows programmers to make full use of its features. In this chapter, we introduce CSS, demonstrate some of the features introduced in CSS 2 and discuss some of the upcoming CSS 3 features. As you read this book, open each XHTML document in your web browser so you can view and interact with it in a web browser, as it was originally intended.

Remember that the examples in this book have been tested in Internet Explorer 7 and Firefox 2. The latest versions of many other browsers (e.g., Safari, Opera, Konqueror) should render this chapter's examples properly, but we have not tested them. Some examples in this chapter *will not work* in older browsers, such as Internet Explorer 6 and earlier. Make sure you have either Internet Explorer 7 (Windows only) or Firefox 2 (available for all major platforms) installed before running the examples in this chapter.

3.2 Inline Styles

You can declare document styles in several ways. This section presents *inline styles* that declare an individual element's format using the XHTML attribute **style**. Inline styles override any other styles applied using the techniques we discuss later in the chapter. Figure 3.1 applies inline styles to p elements to alter their font size and color.

Good Programming Practice 3.1

Inline styles do not truly separate presentation from content. To apply similar styles to multiple elements, use embedded stylesheets or external style sheets, introduced later in this chapter.

The first inline style declaration appears in line 17. Attribute style specifies an element's style. Each *CSS property* (**font-size** in this case) is followed by a colon and a value. In line 17, we declare this particular p element to use 20-point font size.

Line 21 specifies the two properties, font-size and **color**, separated by a semicolon. In this line, we set the given paragraph's color to light blue, using the hexadecimal code #6666ff. Color names may be used in place of hexadecimal codes.

```
 1   <?xml version = "1.0" encoding = "utf-8"?>
 2   <!DOCTYPE html PUBLIC "-//W3C//DTD XHTML 1.0 Strict//EN"
 3      "http://www.w3.org/TR/xhtml1/DTD/xhtml1-strict.dtd">
 4
 5   <!-- Fig. 3.1: inline.html -->
 6   <!-- Using inline styles -->
 7   <html xmlns = "http://www.w3.org/1999/xhtml">
 8      <head>
 9         <title>Inline Styles</title>
10      </head>
11      <body>
12         <p>This text does not have any style applied to it.</p>
13
14         <!-- The style attribute allows you to declare -->
15         <!-- inline styles. Separate multiple style properties -->
16         <!-- with a semicolon. -->
17         <p style = "font-size: 20pt">This text has the
18            <em>font-size</em> style applied to it, making it 20pt.
19         </p>
20
21         <p style = "font-size: 20pt; color: #6666ff">
22         This text has the <em>font-size</em> and
23         <em>color</em> styles applied to it, making it
24         20pt. and light blue.</p>
25      </body>
26   </html>
```

Fig. 3.1 | Using inline styles. (Part 1 of 2.)

Fig. 3.1 | Using inline styles. (Part 2 of 2.)

3.3 Embedded Style Sheets

A second technique for using style sheets is *embedded style sheets*. Embedded style sheets enable a you to embed an entire CSS document in an XHTML document's head section. To achieve this separation between the CSS code and the XHTML that it styles, we'll use *CSS selectors*. Figure 3.2 creates an embedded style sheet containing four styles.

```
1   <?xml version = "1.0" encoding = "utf-8"?>
2   <!DOCTYPE html PUBLIC "-//W3C//DTD XHTML 1.0 Strict//EN"
3      "http://www.w3.org/TR/xhtml1/DTD/xhtml1-strict.dtd">
4
5   <!-- Fig. 3.2: embedded.html -->
6   <!-- Embedded style sheets. -->
7   <html xmlns = "http://www.w3.org/1999/xhtml">
8      <head>
9         <title>Style Sheets</title>
10
11        <!-- this begins the style sheet section -->
12        <style type = "text/css">
13           em        { font-weight: bold;
14                       color: black }
15           h1        { font-family: tahoma, helvetica, sans-serif }
16           p         { font-size: 12pt;
17                       font-family: arial, sans-serif }
18           .special { color: #6666ff }
19        </style>
20     </head>
21     <body>
22        <!-- this class attribute applies the .special style -->
23        <h1 class = "special">Deitel &amp; Associates, Inc.</h1>
24
25        <p>Deitel &amp; Associates, Inc. is an internationally
26        recognized corporate training and publishing organization
```

Fig. 3.2 | Embedded style sheets. (Part 1 of 2.)

```
27              specializing in programming languages, Internet/World
28              Wide Web technology and object technology education.
29              The company provides courses on Java, C++, Visual Basic,
30              C#, C, Internet and World Wide Web programming, Object
31              Technology, and more.</p>
32
33          <h1>Clients</h1>
34          <p class = "special"> The company's clients include many
35          <em>Fortune 1000 companies</em>, government agencies,
36          branches of the military and business organizations.
37          Through its publishing partnership with Prentice Hall,
38          Deitel &amp; Associates, Inc. publishes leading-edge
39          programming textbooks, professional books, interactive
40          web-based multimedia Cyber Classrooms, satellite
41          courses and World Wide Web courses.</p>
42      </body>
43  </html>
```

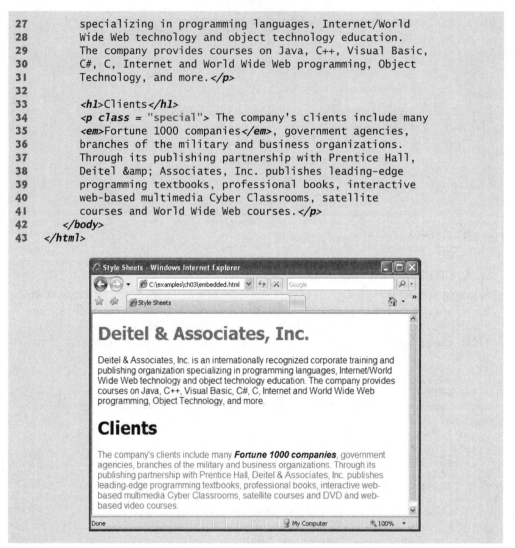

Fig. 3.2 | Embedded style sheets. (Part 2 of 2.)

The style element (lines 12–19) defines the embedded style sheet. Styles placed in the head apply to matching elements wherever they appear in the entire document. The style element's type attribute specifies the ***Multipurpose Internet Mail Extensions (MIME) type*** that describes a file's content. CSS documents use the MIME type text/css. Other MIME types include image/gif (for GIF images), text/javascript (for the JavaScript scripting language, which we discuss in Chapters 4–9), and more.

The body of the style sheet (lines 13–18) declares the ***CSS rules*** for the style sheet. A CSS selector determines which elements will be styled according to a rule. Our first rule begins with the selector em (line 13) to select all em elements in the document. The ***font-weight*** property in line 13 specifies the "boldness" of text. Possible values are bold, normal (the default), bolder (bolder than bold text) and lighter (lighter than normal text). Boldness also can be specified with multiples of 100, from 100 to 900 (e.g., 100, 200, ..., 900). Text specified as normal is equivalent to 400, and bold text is equivalent to 700. However, many systems do not have fonts that can scale with this level of precision, so using the values from 100 to 900 might not display the desired effect.

In this example, all em elements will be displayed in a bold font. We also apply styles to all h1 (line 15) and p (lines 16–17) elements. The body of each rule is enclosed in curly braces ({ and }).

Line 18 uses a new kind of selector to declare a *style class* named special. Style classes define styles that can be applied to any element. In this example, we declare class special, which sets color to blue. We can apply this style to any element type, whereas the other rules in this style sheet apply only to specific element types defined in the style sheet (i.e., em, h1 or p). Style-class declarations are preceded by a period. We'll discuss how to apply a style class momentarily.

CSS rules in embedded style sheets use the same syntax as inline styles; the property name is followed by a colon (:) and the value of the property. Multiple properties are separated by semicolons (;). In the rule for em elements, the color property specifies the color of the text, and property font-weight makes the font bold.

The *font-family* property (line 15) specifies the name of the font to use. Not all users have the same fonts installed on their computers, so CSS allows you to specify a comma-separated list of fonts to use for a particular style. The browser attempts to use the fonts in the order they appear in the list. It's advisable to end a font list with a *generic font family name* in case the other fonts are not installed on the user's computer. In this example, if the tahoma font is not found on the system, the browser will look for the helvetica font. If neither is found, the browser will display its default sans-serif font. Other generic font families include serif (e.g., times new roman, Georgia), cursive (e.g., script), fantasy (e.g., critter) and monospace (e.g., courier, fixedsys).

The *font-size* property (line 16) specifies a 12-point font. Other possible measurements in addition to pt (point) are introduced later in the chapter. Relative values— xx-small, x-small, small, smaller, medium, large, larger, x-large and xx-large—also can be used. Generally, relative values for font-size are preferred over point sizes because an author does not know the specific measurements of the display for each client. Relative font-size values permit more flexible viewing of web pages.

For example, a user may wish to view a web page on a handheld device with a small screen. Specifying an 18-point font size in a style sheet will prevent such a user from seeing more than one or two characters at a time. However, if a relative font size is specified, such as large or larger, the actual size is determined by the browser that displays the font. Using relative sizes also makes pages more accessible to users with disabilities. Users with impaired vision, for example, may configure their browser to use a larger default font, upon which all relative sizes are based. Text that the author specifies to be smaller than the main text still displays in a smaller size font, yet it is clearly visible to each user. Accessibility is an important consideration—in 1998, Congress passed the Section 508 Amendment to the Rehabilitation Act of 1973, mandating that websites of government agencies are required to be accessible to disabled users.

Line 23 uses the XHTML attribute *class* in an h1 element to apply a style class—in this case class special (declared with the .special selector in the style sheet in line 18). When the browser renders the h1 element, note that the text appears on screen with the properties of both an h1 element (arial or sans-serif font defined in line 17) and the .special style class applied (the color #6666ff defined in line 18). Also notice that the browser still applies its own default style to the h1 element—the header is still displayed in a large font size. Similarly, all em elements will still be italicized by the browser, but they will also be bold as a result of our style rule.

The formatting for the p element and the .special class is applied to the text in lines 34–41. In many cases, the styles applied to an element (the *parent* or *ancestor element*) also apply to the element's nested elements (*child* or *descendant elements*). The em element nested in the p element in line 35 *inherits* the style from the p element (namely, the 12-point font size in line 16) but retains its italic style. In other words, styles defined for the paragraph and not defined for the em element is applied to the em element. Because multiple values of one property can be set or inherited on the same element, they must be reduced to one style per element before being rendered. We discuss the rules for resolving these conflicts in the next section.

3.4 Conflicting Styles

Styles may be defined by a *user*, an *author* or a *user agent* (e.g., a web browser). A user is a person viewing your web page, you are the author—the person who writes the document—and the user agent is the program used to render and display the document. Styles "cascade," or flow together, such that the ultimate appearance of elements on a page results from combining styles defined in several ways. Styles defined by the user take precedence over styles defined by the user agent, and styles defined by authors take precedence over styles defined by the user.

Most styles defined for parent elements are also inherited by child (nested) elements. While it makes sense to inherit most styles, such as font properties, there are certain properties that we don't want to be inherited. Consider for example the background-image property, which allows the programmer to set an image as the background of an element. If the body element is assigned a background image, we don't want the same image to be in the background of every element in the body of our page. Instead, the background-image property of all child elements retains its default value of none. In this section, we discuss the rules for resolving conflicts between styles defined for elements and styles inherited from parent and ancestor elements.

Figure 3.2 presented an example of *inheritance* in which a child em element inherited the font-size property from its parent p element. However, in Fig. 3.2, the child em element had a color property that conflicted with (i.e., had a different value than) the color property of its parent p element. Properties defined for child and descendant elements have a greater *specificity* than properties defined for parent and ancestor elements. Conflicts are resolved in favor of properties with a higher specificity. In other words, the styles explicitly defined for a child element are more specific than the styles defined for the child's parent element; therefore, the child's styles take precedence. Figure 3.3 illustrates examples of inheritance and specificity.

Line 12 applies property text-decoration to all a elements whose class attribute is set to nodec. The text-decoration property applies *decorations* to text in an element. By default, browsers underline the text of an a (anchor) element. Here, we set the text-decoration property to none to indicate that the browser should not underline hyperlinks. Other possible values for text-decoration include overline, line-through, underline and `blink`. [*Note:* `blink` is not supported by Internet Explorer.] The `.nodec` appended to a is a more specific class selector; this style will apply only to a (anchor) elements that specify `nodec` in their `class` attribute.

 Portability Tip 3.1

To ensure that your style sheets work in various web browsers, test them on all the client web browsers that will render documents using your styles, as well as using the W3C CSS Validator.

```
 1   <?xml version = "1.0" encoding = "utf-8"?>
 2   <!DOCTYPE html PUBLIC "-//W3C//DTD XHTML 1.0 Strict//EN"
 3      "http://www.w3.org/TR/xhtml1/DTD/xhtml1-strict.dtd">
 4
 5   <!-- Fig. 3.3: advanced.html -->
 6   <!-- Inheritance in style sheets. -->
 7   <html xmlns = "http://www.w3.org/1999/xhtml">
 8      <head>
 9         <title>More Styles</title>
10         <style type = "text/css">
11            body      { font-family: arial, helvetica, sans-serif }
12            a.nodec   { text-decoration: none }
13            a:hover   { text-decoration: underline }
14            li em     { font-weight: bold }
15            h1, em    { text-decoration: underline }
16            ul        { margin-left: 20px }
17            ul ul     { font-size: .8em }
18         </style>
19      </head>
20      <body>
21         <h1>Shopping list for Monday:</h1>
22
23         <ul>
24            <li>Milk</li>
25            <li>Bread
26               <ul>
27                  <li>White bread</li>
28                  <li>Rye bread</li>
29                  <li>Whole wheat bread</li>
30               </ul>
31            </li>
32            <li>Rice</li>
33            <li>Potatoes</li>
34            <li>Pizza <em>with mushrooms</em></li>
35         </ul>
36
37         <p><em>Go to the</em>
38            <a class = "nodec" href = "http://www.deitel.com">
39               Grocery store</a>
40         </p>
41      </body>
42   </html>
```

Fig. 3.3 | Inheritance in style sheets. (Part 1 of 2.)

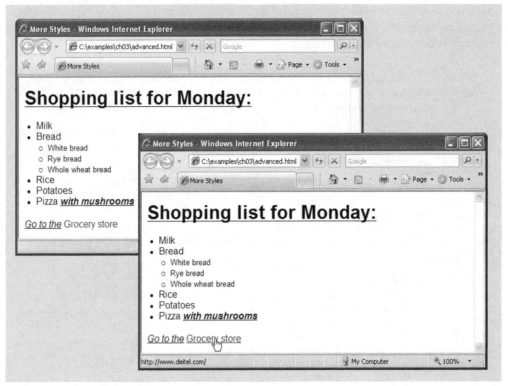

Fig. 3.3 | Inheritance in style sheets. (Part 2 of 2.)

Line 13 specifies a style for hover, which is a ***pseudoclass***. Pseudoclasses give the author access to content not specifically declared in the document. The ***hover pseudoclass*** is activated dynamically when the user moves the mouse cursor over an element. Note that pseudoclasses are separated by a colon (with no surrounding spaces) from the name of the element to which they are applied.

> ### Common Programming Error 3.1
> *Including a space before or after the colon separating a pseudoclass from the name of the element to which it is applied is an error that prevents the pseudoclass from being applied properly.*

Line 14 causes all em elements that are children of li elements to be bold. In the screen output of Fig. 3.3, note that **Go to the** (contained in an em element in line 37) does not appear bold, because the em element is not in an li element. However, the em element containing **with mushrooms** (line 34) is nested in an li element; therefore, it is formatted in bold. The syntax for applying rules to multiple elements is similar. In line 15, we separate the selectors with a comma to apply an underline style rule to all h1 and all em elements.

Line 16 assigns a left margin of 20 pixels to all ul elements. We'll discuss the margin properties in detail in Section 3.9. A pixel is a *relative-length measurement*—it varies in size, based on screen resolution. Other relative lengths include ***em*** (the *M*-height of the font, which is usually set to the height of an uppercase *M*), ***ex*** (the *x*-height of the font, which is usually set to the height of a lowercase *x*) and percentages (e.g., font-size: 50%).

To set an element to display text at 150 percent of its default text size, the author could use the syntax

> **font-size:** 1.5em

Alternatively, you could use

> **font-size:** 150%

Other units of measurement available in CSS are ***absolute-length measurements***—i.e., units that do not vary in size based on the system. These units are ***in*** (inches), ***cm*** (centimeters), ***mm*** (millimeters), ***pt*** (points; 1 pt = 1/72 in) and ***pc*** (picas; 1 pc = 12 pt). Line 17 specifies that all nested unordered lists (ul elements that are descendants of ul elements) are to have font size .8em. [*Note:* When setting a style property that takes a measurement (e.g. font-size, margin-left), no units are necessary if the value is zero.]

Good Programming Practice 3.2

Whenever possible, use relative-length measurements. If you use absolute-length measurements, your document may not be readable on some client browsers (e.g., wireless phones).

3.5 Linking External Style Sheets

Style sheets are a convenient way to create a document with a uniform theme. With ***external style sheets*** (i.e., separate documents that contain only CSS rules), you can provide a uniform look and feel to an entire website. Different pages on a site can all use the same style sheet. When changes to the styles are required, the author needs to modify only a single CSS file to make style changes across the entire website. Note that while embedded style sheets separate content from presentation, both are still contained in a single file, preventing a web designer and a content author from working in parallel. External style sheets solve this problem by separating the content and style into separate files.

Software Engineering Observation 3.1

Always use an external style sheet when developing a website with multiple pages. External style sheets separate content from presentation, allowing for more consistent look-and-feel, more efficient development, and better performance.

Figure 3.4 presents an external style sheet. Lines 1–2 are ***CSS comments***. Like XHTML comments, CSS comments describe the content of a CSS document. Comments may be placed in any type of CSS code (i.e., inline styles, embedded style sheets and external style sheets) and always start with /* and end with */. Text between these delimiters is ignored by the browser.

```
1   /* Fig. 3.4: styles.css */
2   /* External stylesheet */
3
4   body     { font-family: arial, helvetica, sans-serif }
5
6   a.nodec { text-decoration: none }
```

Fig. 3.4 | External style sheet. (Part 1 of 2.)

```
7
8   a:hover  { text-decoration: underline }
9
10  li em    { font-weight: bold }
11
12  h1, em   { text-decoration: underline }
13
14  ul       { margin-left: 20px }
15
16  ul ul    { font-size: .8em; }
```

Fig. 3.4 | External style sheet. (Part 2 of 2.)

Figure 3.5 contains an XHTML document that references the external style sheet in Fig. 3.4. Lines 10–11 (Fig. 3.5) show a *link* element that uses the *rel* attribute to specify a *relationship* between the current document and another document. In this case, we declare the linked document to be a *stylesheet* for this document. The type attribute specifies the MIME type of the related document as text/css. The href attribute provides the URL for the document containing the style sheet. In this case, styles.css is in the same directory as external.html.

```
1   <?xml version = "1.0" encoding = "utf-8"?>
2   <!DOCTYPE html PUBLIC "-//W3C//DTD XHTML 1.0 Strict//EN"
3      "http://www.w3.org/TR/xhtml11/DTD/xhtml11-strict.dtd">
4
5   <!-- Fig. 3.5: external.html -->
6   <!-- Linking an external style sheet. -->
7   <html xmlns = "http://www.w3.org/1999/xhtml">
8      <head>
9         <title>Linking External Style Sheets</title>
10        <link rel = "stylesheet" type = "text/css"
11           href = "styles.css" />
12     </head>
13     <body>
14        <h1>Shopping list for <em>Monday</em>:</h1>
15
16        <ul>
17           <li>Milk</li>
18           <li>Bread
19              <ul>
20                 <li>White bread</li>
21                 <li>Rye bread</li>
22                 <li>Whole wheat bread</li>
23              </ul>
24           </li>
25           <li>Rice</li>
26           <li>Potatoes</li>
27           <li>Pizza <em>with mushrooms</em></li>
28        </ul>
29
```

Fig. 3.5 | Linking an external style sheet. (Part 1 of 2.)

```
30        <p><em>Go to the</em>
31           <a class = "nodec" href = "http://www.deitel.com">
32              Grocery store</a>
33        </p>
34     </body>
35  </html>
```

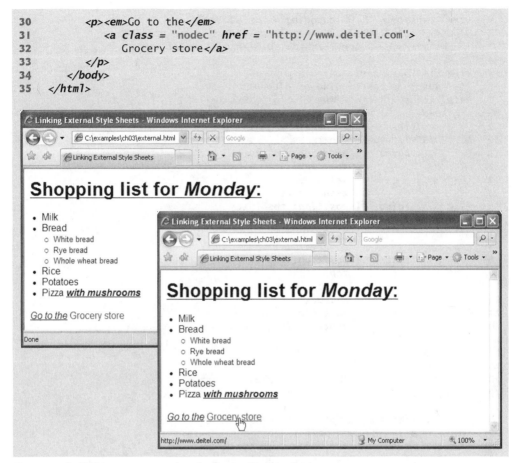

Fig. 3.5 | Linking an external style sheet. (Part 2 of 2.)

Software Engineering Observation 3.2

External style sheets are reusable. Creating them once and reusing them reduces programming effort.

Performance Tip 3.1

Reusing external style sheets reduces load time and bandwidth usage on a server, since the style sheet can be downloaded once, stored by the web browser, and applied to all pages on a website.

3.6 Positioning Elements

Before CSS, controlling the positioning of elements in an XHTML document was difficult—the browser determined positioning. CSS introduced the *position* property and a capability called *absolute positioning*, which gives authors greater control over how document elements are displayed. Figure 3.6 demonstrates absolute positioning.

Normally, elements are positioned on the page in the order that they appear in the XHTML document. Lines 11–14 define a style called bgimg for the first img element

```
1   <?xml version = "1.0" encoding = "utf-8"?>
2   <!DOCTYPE html PUBLIC "-//W3C//DTD XHTML 1.0 Strict//EN"
3       "http://www.w3.org/TR/xhtml1/DTD/xhtml1-strict.dtd">
4
5   <!-- Fig. 3.6: positioning.html -->
6   <!-- Absolute positioning of elements. -->
7   <html xmlns = "http://www.w3.org/1999/xhtml">
8      <head>
9         <title>Absolute Positioning</title>
10        <style type = "text/css">
11           .bgimg   { position: absolute;
12                      top: 0px;
13                      left: 0px;
14                      z-index: 1 }
15           .fgimg   { position: absolute;
16                      top: 25px;
17                      left: 100px;
18                      z-index: 2 }
19           .text    { position: absolute;
20                      top: 25px;
21                      left: 100px;
22                      z-index: 3;
23                      font-size: 20pt;
24                      font-family: tahoma, geneva, sans-serif }
25        </style>
26     </head>
27     <body>
28        <p><img src = "bgimg.gif" class = "bgimg"
29           alt = "First positioned image" /></p>
30
31        <p><img src = "fgimg.gif" class = "fgimg"
32           alt = "Second positioned image" /></p>
33
34        <p class = "text">Positioned Text</p>
35     </body>
36  </html>
```

Fig. 3.6 | Absolute positioning of elements.

(i.gif) on the page. Specifying an element's position as absolute removes the element from the normal flow of elements on the page, instead positioning it according to the distance from the top, left, right or bottom margins of its ***containing block-level element*** (i.e., an element such as body or p). Here, we position the element to be 0 pixels away from both the top and left margins of its containing element. In line 28, this style is applied to the image, which is contained in a p element.

The ***z-index*** property allows you to layer overlapping elements properly. Elements that have higher z-index values are displayed in front of elements with lower z-index values. In this example, i.gif has the lowest z-index (1), so it displays in the background. The .fgimg CSS rule in lines 15–18 gives the circle image (circle.gif, in lines 31–32) a z-index of 2, so it displays in front of i.gif. The p element in line 34 (Positioned Text) is given a z-index of 3 in line 22, so it displays in front of the other two. If you do not specify a z-index or if elements have the same z-index value, the elements are placed from background to foreground in the order they are encountered in the document.

Absolute positioning is not the only way to specify page layout. Figure 3.7 demonstrates ***relative positioning***, in which elements are positioned relative to other elements.

```
 1   <?xml version = "1.0" encoding = "utf-8"?>
 2   <!DOCTYPE html PUBLIC "-//W3C//DTD XHTML 1.0 Strict//EN"
 3      "http://www.w3.org/TR/xhtml1/DTD/xhtml1-strict.dtd">
 4
 5   <!-- Fig. 3.7: positioning2.html -->
 6   <!-- Relative positioning of elements. -->
 7   <html xmlns = "http://www.w3.org/1999/xhtml">
 8      <head>
 9         <title>Relative Positioning</title>
10         <style type = "text/css">
11            p          { font-size: 1.3em;
12                         font-family: verdana, arial, sans-serif }
13            span       { color: red;
14                         font-size: .6em;
15                         height: 1em }
16            .super     { position: relative;
17                         top: -1ex }
18            .sub       { position: relative;
19                         bottom: -1ex }
20            .shiftleft { position: relative;
21                         left: -1ex }
22            .shiftright { position: relative;
23                         right: -1ex }
24         </style>
25      </head>
26      <body>
27         <p>The text at the end of this sentence
28         <span class = "super">is in superscript</span>.</p>
29
30         <p>The text at the end of this sentence
31         <span class = "sub">is in subscript</span>.</p>
32
```

Fig. 3.7 | Relative positioning of elements. (Part 1 of 2.)

```
33          <p>The text at the end of this sentence
34          <span class = "shiftleft">is shifted left</span>.</p>
35
36          <p>The text at the end of this sentence
37          <span class = "shiftright">is shifted right</span>.</p>
38      </body>
39   </html>
```

Fig. 3.7 | Relative positioning of elements. (Part 2 of 2.)

Setting the position property to relative, as in class super (lines 16–17), lays out the element on the page and offsets it by the specified top, bottom, left or right value. Unlike absolute positioning, relative positioning keeps elements in the general flow of elements on the page, so positioning is relative to other elements in the flow. Recall that ex (line 17) is the *x*-height of a font, a relative-length measurement typically equal to the height of a lowercase *x*.

 Common Programming Error 3.2

Because relative positioning keeps elements in the flow of text in your documents, be careful to avoid unintentionally overlapping text.

Inline and Block-Level Elements

We introduce the **span** element in line 28. Lines 13–15 define the CSS rule for all span elements. The height of the span determines how much vertical space the span will occupy. The font-size determines the size of the text inside the span.

Element span is a ***grouping element***—it does not apply any inherent formatting to its contents. Its primary purpose is to apply CSS rules or id attributes to a section of text. Element span is an ***inline-level element***—it applies formatting to text without changing the flow of the document. Examples of inline elements include span, img, a, em and strong. The ***div*** element is also a grouping element, but it is a ***block-level element***. This means it is displayed on its own line and has a virtual box around it. Examples of block-level elements include div, p and heading elements (h1 through h6). We'll discuss inline and block-level elements in more detail in Section 3.9.

3.7 Backgrounds

CSS provides control over the background of block-level elements. CSS can set a background color or add background images to XHTML elements. Figure 3.8 adds a corporate logo to the bottom-right corner of the document. This logo stays fixed in the corner even when the user scrolls up or down the screen.

The **background-image** property (line 11) specifies the image URL for the image logo.gif in the format url(*fileLocation*). You can also set the **background-color** property in case the image is not found (and to fill in where the image does not cover).

The **background-position** property (line 12) places the image on the page. The keywords top, bottom, center, left and right are used individually or in combination for vertical and horizontal positioning. An image can be positioned using lengths by specifying the horizontal length followed by the vertical length. For example, to position the

```
1   <?xml version = "1.0" encoding = "utf-8"?>
2   <!DOCTYPE html PUBLIC "-//W3C//DTD XHTML 1.0 Strict//EN"
3      "http://www.w3.org/TR/xhtml1/DTD/xhtml1-strict.dtd">
4
5   <!-- Fig. 3.8: background.html -->
6   <!-- Adding background images and indentation. -->
7   <html xmlns = "http://www.w3.org/1999/xhtml">
8      <head>
9         <title>Background Images</title>
10        <style type = "text/css">
11           body  { background-image: url(logo.gif);
12                   background-position: bottom right;
13                   background-repeat: no-repeat;
14                   background-attachment: fixed;
15                   background-color: #eeeeee }
16           p     { font-size: 18pt;
17                   color: #1144AA;
18                   text-indent: 1em;
19                   font-family: arial, sans-serif; }
20           .dark { font-weight: bold }
21        </style>
22     </head>
23     <body>
24        <p>
25        This example uses the background-image,
26        background-position and background-attachment
27        styles to place the <span class = "dark">Deitel
28        &amp; Associates, Inc.</span> logo in the bottom,
29        right corner of the page. Notice how the logo
30        stays in the proper position when you resize the
31        browser window. The background-color fills in where
32        there is no image.
33        </p>
34     </body>
35  </html>
```

Fig. 3.8 | Adding background images and indentation. (Part 1 of 2.)

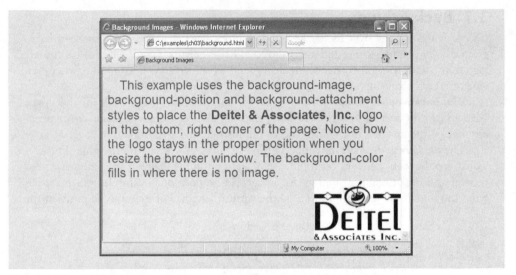

Fig. 3.8 | Adding background images and indentation. (Part 2 of 2.)

image as horizontally centered (positioned at 50 percent of the distance across the screen) and 30 pixels from the top, use

> *background-position:* 50% 30px;

The *background-repeat* property (line 13) controls background image *tiling*, which places multiple copies of the image next to each other to fill the background. Here, we set the tiling to no-repeat to display only one copy of the background image. Other values include repeat (the default) to tile the image vertically and horizontally, repeat-x to tile the image only horizontally or repeat-y to tile the image only vertically.

The final property setting, *background-attachment: fixed* (line 14), fixes the image in the position specified by *background-position*. Scrolling the browser window will not move the image from its position. The default value, scroll, moves the image as the user scrolls through the document.

Line 18 uses the *text-indent* property to indent the first line of text in the element by a specified amount, in this case 1em. An author might use this property to create a web page that reads more like a novel, in which the first line of every paragraph is indented.

The CSS property *font-style* property allows you to set the text style to none, italic or oblique (oblique is simply more slanted than italic—the browser will default to italic if the system or font does not support oblique text).

3.8 Element Dimensions

In addition to positioning elements, CSS rules can specify the actual dimensions of each page element. Figure 3.9 demonstrates how to set the dimensions of elements.

The inline style in line 17 illustrates how to set the *width* of an element on screen; here, we indicate that the div element should occupy 20 percent of the screen width. The height of an element can be set similarly, using the *height* property. The height and width values also can be specified as relative or absolute lengths. For example,

```
 I    <?xml version = "1.0" encoding = "utf-8"?>
 2    <!DOCTYPE html PUBLIC "-//W3C//DTD XHTML 1.0 Strict//EN"
 3       "http://www.w3.org/TR/xhtml1/DTD/xhtml1-strict.dtd">
 4
 5    <!-- Fig. 3.9: width.html -->
 6    <!-- Element dimensions and text alignment. -->
 7    <html xmlns = "http://www.w3.org/1999/xhtml">
 8       <head>
 9          <title>Box Dimensions</title>
10          <style type = "text/css">
11             div { background-color: #aaccff;
12                   margin-bottom: .5em;
13                   font-family: arial, helvetica, sans-serif }
14          </style>
15       </head>
16       <body>
17          <div style = "width: 20%">Here is some
18          text that goes in a box which is
19          set to stretch across twenty percent
20          of the width of the screen.</div>
21
22          <div style = "width: 80%; text-align: center">
23          Here is some CENTERED text that goes in a box
24          which is set to stretch across eighty percent of
25          the width of the screen.</div>
26
27          <div style = "width: 20%; height: 150px; overflow: scroll">
28          This box is only twenty percent of
29          the width and has a fixed height.
30          What do we do if it overflows? Set the
31          overflow property to scroll!</div>
32       </body>
33    </html>
```

Fig. 3.9 | Element dimensions and text alignment.

width: 10em

sets the element's width to 10 times the font size. Most elements are left aligned by default; however, this alignment can be altered to position the element elsewhere. Line 22 sets text in the element to be center aligned; other values for the **text-align** property include left and right.

In the third div, we specify a percentage height and a pixel width. One problem with setting both dimensions of an element is that the content inside the element can exceed the set boundaries, in which case the element is simply made large enough for all the content to fit. However, in line 27, we set the **overflow** property to scroll, a setting that adds scroll bars if the text overflows the boundaries.

3.9 Box Model and Text Flow

All block-level XHTML elements have a virtual box drawn around them based on what is known as the *box model*. When the browser renders elements using the box model, the content of each element is surrounded by *padding*, a *border* and a *margin* (Fig. 3.10).

CSS controls the border using three properties: **border-width**, **border-color** and **border-style**. We illustrate these three properties in Fig. 3.11.

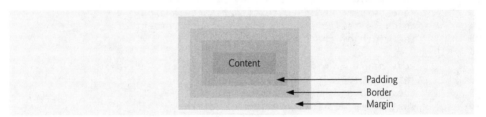

Fig. 3.10 | Box model for block-level elements.

```
1   <?xml version = "1.0" encoding = "utf-8"?>
2   <!DOCTYPE html PUBLIC "-//W3C//DTD XHTML 1.0 Strict//EN"
3      "http://www.w3.org/TR/xhtml11/DTD/xhtml11-strict.dtd">
4
5   <!-- Fig. 3.11: borders.html -->
6   <!-- Borders of block-level elements. -->
7   <html xmlns = "http://www.w3.org/1999/xhtml">
8      <head>
9         <title>Borders</title>
10        <style type = "text/css">
11           div     { text-align: center;
12                     width: 50%;
13                     position: relative;
14                     left: 25%;
15                     border-width: 4px }
16           .medium { border-width: medium }
17           .thin   { border-width: thin }
18           .solid  { border-style: solid }
19           .double { border-style: double }
```

Fig. 3.11 | Borders of block-level elements. (Part 1 of 2.)

```
20        .groove { border-style: groove }
21        .inset  { border-style: inset }
22        .outset { border-style: outset }
23        .dashed { border-style: dashed }
24        .red    { border-color: red }
25        .blue   { border-color: blue }
26     </style>
27  </head>
28  <body>
29     <div class = "solid">Solid border</div><hr />
30     <div class = "double">Double border</div><hr />
31     <div class = "groove">Groove border</div><hr />
32     <div class = "inset">Inset border</div><hr />
33     <div class = "dashed">Dashed border</div><hr />
34     <div class = "thin red solid">Thin Red Solid border</div><hr />
35     <div class = "medium blue outset">Medium Blue Outset border</div
36  </body>
37  </html>
```

Fig. 3.11 | Borders of block-level elements. (Part 2 of 2.)

Property border-width may be set to any valid CSS length (e.g., em, ex, px, etc.) or to the predefined value of thin, medium or thick. The **border-color property** sets the color. [*Note:* This property has different meanings for different style borders.] The border-style options are none, hidden, dotted, dashed, solid, double, groove, ridge, inset and outset. Borders groove and ridge have opposite effects, as do inset and outset. When border-style is set to none, no border is rendered.

Each border property may be set for an individual side of the box (e.g., border-top-style or border-left-color). Note that we assign more than one class to an XHTML element by separating multiple class names with spaces, as shown in lines 36–37.

As we have seen with absolute positioning, it is possible to remove elements from the normal flow of text. *Floating* allows you to move an element to one side of the screen; other content in the document then flows around the floated element. Figure 3.12 demonstrates how floats and the box model can be used to control the layout of an entire page.

```
 1   <?xml version = "1.0" encoding = "utf-8"?>
 2   <!DOCTYPE html PUBLIC "-//W3C//DTD XHTML 1.0 Strict//EN"
 3      "http://www.w3.org/TR/xhtml1/DTD/xhtml1-strict.dtd">
 4
 5   <!-- Fig. 3.12: floating.html -->
 6   <!-- Floating elements. -->
 7   <html xmlns = "http://www.w3.org/1999/xhtml">
 8      <head>
 9         <title>Flowing Text Around Floating Elements</title>
10         <style type = "text/css">
11            div.heading { background-color: #bbddff;
12                          text-align: center;
13                          font-family: arial, helvetica, sans-serif;
14                          padding: .2em }
15            p            { text-align: justify;
16                          font-family: verdana, geneva, sans-serif;
17                          margin: .5em }
18            div.floated { background-color: #eeeeee;
19                          font-size: 1.5em;
20                          font-family: arial, helvetica, sans-serif;
21                          padding: .2em;
22                          margin-left: .5em;
23                          margin-bottom: .5em;
24                          float: right;
25                          text-align: right;
26                          width: 50% }
27            div.section { border: 1px solid #bbddff }
28         </style>
29      </head>
30      <body>
31         <div class = "heading"><img src = "deitel.png" alt = "Deitel" />
32            </div>
33         <div class = "section">
34            <div class = "floated">Corporate Training and Publishing</div>
35            <p>Deitel &amp; Associates, Inc. is an internationally
36            recognized corporate training and publishing organization
37            specializing in programming languages, Internet/World
38            Wide Web technology and object technology education.
39            The company provides courses on Java, C++, Visual Basic, C#,
40            C, Internet and web programming, Object
41            Technology, and more.</p>
42         </div>
43         <div class = "section">
44            <div class = "floated">Leading-Edge Programming Textbooks</div>
45            <p>Through its publishing
46            partnership with Prentice Hall, Deitel &amp; Associates,
47            Inc. publishes leading-edge programming textbooks,
48            professional books, interactive CD-ROM-based multimedia
49            Cyber Classrooms, satellite courses and DVD and web-based
50            video courses.</p>
51         </div>
52      </body>
53   </html>
```

Fig. 3.12 | Floating elements. (Part 1 of 2.)

Fig. 3.12 | Floating elements. (Part 2 of 2.)

Looking at the XHTML code, we can see that the general structure of this document consists of a header and two main sections. Each section contains a subheading and a paragraph of text.

Block-level elements (such as divs) render with a line break before and after their content, so the header and two sections will render vertically one on top of another. In the absence of our styles, the subheading divs would also stack vertically on top of the text in the p tags. However, in line 24 we set the float property to right in the class floated, which is applied to the subheadings. This causes each subheading div to float to the right edge of its containing element, while the paragraph of text will flow around it.

Line 17 assigns a margin of .5em to all paragraph tags. The ***margin property*** sets the space between the outside of the border and all other content on the page. In line 21, we assign .2em of padding to the floated divs. The ***padding property*** determines the distance between the content inside an element and the inside of the element's border. Margins for individual sides of an element can be specified (lines 22–23) by using the properties ***margin-top***, ***margin-right***, ***margin-left*** and ***margin-bottom***. Padding can be specified in the same way, using ***padding-top***, ***padding-right***, ***padding-left*** and ***padding-bottom***. To see the effects of margins and padding, try putting the margin and padding properties inside comments and observing the difference.

In line 27, we assign a border to the section boxes using a shorthand declaration of the border properties. CSS allows shorthand assignments of borders to allow you to define all three border properties in one line. The syntax for this shorthand is border: <width> <style> <color>. Our border is one pixel thick, solid, and the same color as the background-color property of the heading div (line 11). This allows the border to blend with the header and makes the page appear as one box with a line dividing its sections.

3.10 Media Types

CSS *media types* allow a programmer to decide what a page should look like depending on the kind of media being used to display the page. The most common media type for a web page is the **screen media type**, which is a standard computer screen. Other media types in CSS 2 include **handheld**, **braille**, **aural** and **print**. The handheld medium is designed for mobile Internet devices, while braille is for machines that can read or print web pages in braille. aural styles allow the programmer to give a speech-synthesizing web browser more information about the content of the web page. This allows the browser to present a web page in a sensible manner to a visually impaired person. The print media type affects a web page's appearance when it is printed. For a complete list of CSS media types, see http://www.w3.org/TR/REC-CSS2/media.html#media-types.

Media types allow a programmer to decide how a page should be presented on any one of these media without affecting the others. Figure 3.13 gives a simple example that applies one set of styles when the document is viewed on the screen, and another when the document is printed. To see the difference, look at the screen captures below the paragraph or use the **Print Preview** feature in Internet Explorer or Firefox.

```
 1   <?xml version = "1.0" encoding = "utf-8"?>
 2   <!DOCTYPE html PUBLIC "-//W3C//DTD XHTML 1.0 Strict//EN"
 3      "http://www.w3.org/TR/xhtml1/DTD/xhtml1-strict.dtd">
 4
 5   <!-- Fig. 3.13: mediatypes.html -->
 6   <!-- CSS media types. -->
 7   <html xmlns = "http://www.w3.org/1999/xhtml">
 8      <head>
 9         <title>Media Types</title>
10         <style type = "text/css">
11            @media all
12            {
13               body  { background-color: #4488aa }
14               h1    { font-family: verdana, helvetica, sans-serif;
15                       color: #aaffcc }
16               p     { font-size: 12pt;
17                       color: white;
18                       font-family: arial, sans-serif }
19            } /* end @media all declaration. */
20            @media print
21            {
22               body  { background-color: white }
23               h1    { color: #008844}
24               p     { font-size: 14pt;
25                       color: #4488aa;
26                       font-family: "times new roman", times, serif }
27            } /* end @media print declaration. */
28         </style>
29      </head>
30      <body>
31         <h1>CSS Media Types Example</h1>
32
```

Fig. 3.13 | CSS media types. (Part 1 of 2.)

```
33        <p>
34        This example uses CSS media types to vary how the page
35        appears in print and how it appears on any other media.
36        This text will appear one font on the screen and a
37        different font on paper or in a print preview. To see
38        the difference in Internet Explorer, go to the Print
39        menu and select Print Preview. In Firefox, select Print
40        Preview from the File menu.
41        </p>
42     </body>
43  </html>
```

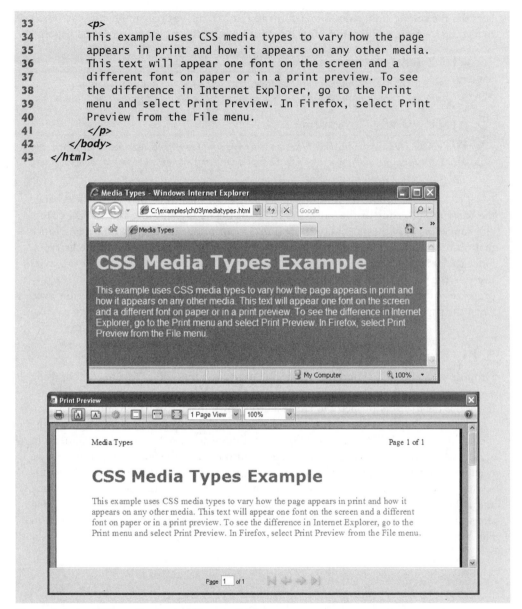

Fig. 3.13 | CSS media types. (Part 2 of 2.)

In line 11, we begin a block of styles that applies to all media types, declared by @media all and enclosed in curly braces ({ and }). In lines 13–18, we define some styles for all media types. Lines 20–27 set styles to be applied only when the page is printed, beginning with the declaration @media print and enclosed in curly braces.

The styles we applied for all media types look nice on a screen but would not look good on a printed page. A colored background would use a lot of ink, and a black-and-white printer may print a page that's hard to read because there isn't enough contrast between the colors. Also, `sans-serif` fonts like `arial`, `helvetica`, and `geneva` are easier to read on a screen, while `serif` fonts like `times new roman` are easier to read on paper.

Look-and-Feel Observation 3.1

Pages with dark background colors and light text use a lot of ink and may be difficult to read when printed, especially on a black-and white-printer. Use the `print` media type to avoid this.

Look-and-Feel Observation 3.2

In general, sans-serif fonts look better on a screen, while serif fonts look better on paper. The `print` media type allows your web page to display sans-serif font on a screen and change to a serif font when it is printed.

To solve these problems, we apply specific styles for the `print` media type. We change the `background-color` of the body, the `color` of the `h1` tag, and the `font-size`, `color`, and `font-family` of the p tag to be more suited for printing and viewing on paper. Notice that most of these styles conflict with the declarations in the section for all media types. Since the `print` media type has higher specificity than `all` media types, the `print` styles override the styles for all media types when the page is printed. Since the `font-family` property of the `h1` tag is not overridden in the `print` section, it retains its old value even when the page is printed.

3.11 Building a CSS Drop-Down Menu

Drop-down menus are a good way to provide navigation links on a website without using a lot of screen space. In this section, we take a second look at the `:hover` pseudoclass and introduce the `display` property to create a drop-down menu using CSS and XHTML.

We've already seen the `:hover` pseudoclass used to change a link's style when the mouse hovers over it. We'll use this feature in a more advanced way to cause a menu to appear when the mouse hovers over a menu button. The other important property we need is the ***display*** property. This allows a programmer to decide whether an element is rendered on the page or not. Possible values include `block`, `inline` and `none`. The `block` and `inline` values display the element as a block element or an inline element, while `none` stops the element from being rendered. The code for the drop-down menu is shown in Fig. 3.14.

```
1   <?xml version = "1.0" encoding = "utf-8"?>
2   <!DOCTYPE html PUBLIC "-//W3C//DTD XHTML 1.0 Strict//EN"
3      "http://www.w3.org/TR/xhtml1/DTD/xhtml1-strict.dtd">
4
5   <!-- Fig. 3.14: dropdown.html -->
6   <!-- CSS drop-down menu. -->
7   <html xmlns = "http://www.w3.org/1999/xhtml">
8      <head>
9         <title>
10           Drop-Down Menu
11        </title>
```

Fig. 3.14 | CSS drop-down menu. (Part 1 of 2.)

```
12        <style type = "text/css">
13          body                { font-family: arial, sans-serif }
14          div.menu            { font-weight: bold;
15                                color: white;
16                                border: 2px solid #225599;
17                                text-align: center;
18                                width: 10em;
19                                background-color: #225599 }
20          div.menu:hover a  { display: block }
21          div.menu a          { display: none;
22                                border-top: 2px solid #225599;
23                                background-color: white;
24                                width: 10em;
25                                text-decoration: none;
26                                color: black }
27          div.menu a:hover  { background-color: #dfeeff }
28        </style>
29     </head>
30     <body>
31        <div class = "menu">Menu
32           <a href = "#">Home</a>
33           <a href = "#">News</a>
34           <a href = "#">Articles</a>
35           <a href = "#">Blog</a>
36           <a href = "#">Contact</a>
37        </div>
38     </body>
39  </html>
```

Fig. 3.14 | CSS drop-down menu. (Part 2 of 2.)

First let's look at the XHTML code. In lines 31–37, a div of class menu has the text "Menu" and five links inside it. This is our drop-down menu. The behavior we want is as follows: the text that says "Menu" should be the only thing visible on the page, unless the mouse is over the menu div. When the mouse cursor hovers over the menu div, we want the links to appear below the menu for the user to choose from.

To see how we get this functionality, let's look at the CSS code. There are two lines that give us the drop-down functionality. Line 21 selects all the links inside the menu div and sets their display value to none. This instructs the browser not to render the links. The other important style is in line 20. The selectors in this line are similar to those in line 21, except that this line selects only the a (anchor) elements that are children of a menu div that has the mouse over it. The display: block in this line means that when the mouse is over the menu div, the links inside it will be displayed as block-level elements.

The selectors in line 27 are also similar to lines 20 and 21. This time, however, the style is applied only to any a element that is a child of the menu div when that child has the mouse cursor over it. This style changes the background-color of the currently highlighted menu option. The rest of the CSS simply adds aesthetic style to the components of our menu. Look at the screen captures or run the code example to see the menu in action.

This drop-down menu is just one example of more advanced CSS formatting. Many additional resources are available online for CSS navigation menus and lists. Specifically, check out List-o-Matic, an automatic CSS list generator located at www.accessify.com/ tools-and-wizards/developer-tools/list-o-matic/ and Dynamic Drive's library of vertical and horizontal CSS menus at www.dynamicdrive.com/style/.

3.12 User Style Sheets

Users can define their own *user style sheets* to format pages based on their preferences. For example, people with visual impairments may want to increase the page's text size. Web page authors need to be careful not to inadvertently override user preferences with defined styles. This section discusses possible conflicts between *author styles* and *user styles*.

Figure 3.15 contains an author style. The font-size is set to 9pt for all <p> tags that have class note applied to them.

User style sheets are external style sheets. Figure 3.16 shows a user style sheet that sets the body's font-size to 20pt, color to yellow and background-color to #000080.

```
1   <?xml version = "1.0" encoding = "utf-8"?>
2   <!DOCTYPE html PUBLIC "-//W3C//DTD XHTML 1.0 Strict//EN"
3      "http://www.w3.org/TR/xhtml1/DTD/xhtml1-strict.dtd">
4
5   <!-- Fig. 3.15: user_absolute.html -->
6   <!-- pt measurement for text size. -->
7   <html xmlns = "http://www.w3.org/1999/xhtml">
8      <head>
9         <title>User Styles</title>
10        <style type = "text/css">
11           .note { font-size: 9pt }
12        </style>
13     </head>
```

Fig. 3.15 | pt measurement for text size. (Part 1 of 2.)

```
14      <body>
15         <p>Thanks for visiting my website. I hope you enjoy it.
16         </p><p class = "note">Please Note: This site will be
17         moving soon. Please check periodically for updates.</p>
18      </body>
19   </html>
```

Fig. 3.15 | pt measurement for text size. (Part 2 of 2.)

```
1    /* Fig. 3.16: userstyles.css */
2    /* A user stylesheet */
3    body      { font-size: 20pt;
4                color: yellow;
5                background-color: #000080 }
```

Fig. 3.16 | User style sheet.

Fig. 3.17 | User style sheet in Internet Explorer 7. (Part 1 of 2.)

Fig. 3.17 | User style sheet in Internet Explorer 7. (Part 2 of 2.)

User style sheets are not linked to a document; rather, they are set in the browser's options. To add a user style sheet in IE7, select **Internet Options...**, located in the **Tools** menu. In the **Internet Options** dialog (Fig. 3.17) that appears, click **Accessibility...**, check the **Format documents using my style sheet** checkbox, and type the location of the user style sheet. Internet Explorer 7 applies the user style sheet to any document it loads. To add a user style sheet in Firefox, find your Firefox profile using the instructions at www.mozilla.org/support/firefox/profile#locate and place a style sheet called userContent.css in the chrome subdirectory.

The web page from Fig. 3.15 is displayed in Fig. 3.18, with the user style sheet from Fig. 3.16 applied.

In this example, if users define their own font-size in a user style sheet, the author style has a higher precedence and overrides the user style. The 9pt font specified in the author style sheet overrides the 20pt font specified in the user style sheet. This small font may make pages difficult to read, especially for individuals with visual impairments. You can avoid this problem by using relative measurements (e.g., em or ex) instead of absolute measurements, such as pt. Figure 3.19 changes the font-size property to use a relative measurement (line 11) that does not override the user style set in Fig. 3.16. Instead, the font size displayed is relative to the one specified in the user style sheet. In this case, text enclosed in the <p> tag displays as 20pt, and <p> tags that have class note applied to them are displayed in 15pt (.75 times 20pt).

Fig. 3.18 | User style sheet applied with pt measurement.

```
 1    <?xml version = "1.0" encoding = "utf-8"?>
 2    <!DOCTYPE html PUBLIC "-//W3C//DTD XHTML 1.0 Strict//EN"
 3       "http://www.w3.org/TR/xhtml1/DTD/xhtml1-strict.dtd"
 4
 5    <!-- Fig. 3.19: user_relative.html -->
 6    <!-- em measurement for text size. -->
 7                   "http://www.w3.org/1999/xhtml"
 8       <head>
 9          <title>User Styles</title>
10          <style type = "text/css">
             .note { font-size: .75em }
          </style>
       </head>
       <body>
          <p>Thanks for visiting my website. I hope you enjoy it.
          </p><p class = "note" Please Note: This site will be
          moving soon. Please check periodically for updates.
```

Fig. 3.19 | em measurement for text size.

Figure 3.20 displays the web page from Fig. 3.19 with the user style sheet from Fig. 3.16 applied. Note that the second line of text displayed is larger than the same line of text in Fig. 3.18.

Fig. 3.20   User style sheet applied with em measurement.

3.13 CSS 3

The W3C is currently developing CSS 3 and some browsers are beginning to implement some of the new features that will be in the *CSS 3* specification. We discuss a few of the upcoming features that will most likely be included in CSS 3.

CSS 3 will allow for more advanced control of borders. In addition to the border-style, border-color, and border-width properties, you will be able to set multiple border colors, use images for borders, add shadows to boxes, and create borders with rounded corners.

Background images will be more versatile in CSS 3, allowing you to set the size of a background image, specify an offset to determine where in the element the image should be positioned, and use multiple background images in one element. There will also be properties to set shadow effects on text and more options for text overflow when the text is too long to fit in its containing element.

Additional features will include resizable boxes, enhanced selectors, multicolumn layouts, and more developed speech (aural) styles. The Web Resources section points you to the Deitel CSS Resource Center, where you can find links to the latest information on the development and features of CSS 3.

3.14 Web Resources

http://www.deitel.com/css21

The Deitel CSS Resource Center contains links to some of the best CSS information on the web. There you'll find categorized links to tutorials, references, code examples, demos, videos, and more. Check out the demos section for more advanced examples of layouts, menus, and other web page components.

4

JavaScript: Introduction to Scripting

Comment is free, but facts are sacred.
—C. P. Scott

The creditor hath a better memory than the debtor.
—James Howell

When faced with a decision, I always ask, "What would be the most fun?"
—Peggy Walker

Equality, in a social sense, may be divided into that of condition and that of rights.
—James Fenimore Cooper

OBJECTIVES

In this chapter you will learn:

- To write simple JavaScript programs.
- To use input and output statements.
- Basic memory concepts.
- To use arithmetic operators.
- The precedence of arithmetic operators.
- To write decision-making statements.
- To use relational and equality operators.

4.1 Introduction

In the first three chapters, we introduced Web 2.0, XHTML and Cascading Style Sheets (CSS). In this chapter, we begin our introduction to the *JavaScript*[1] *scripting language,* which facilitates a disciplined approach to designing computer programs that enhance the functionality and appearance of web pages.[2]

Chapters 4–9 present a detailed discussion of JavaScript—the *de facto* standard client-side scripting language for web-based applications, due to its highly portable nature. Our treatment of JavaScript serves two purposes—it introduces client-side scripting (used in Chapters 4–11), which makes web pages more dynamic and interactive, and it provides the foundation for the server-side scripting presented later in the book.

We now introduce JavaScript programming and present examples that illustrate several important features of JavaScript. Each example is carefully analyzed one line at a time. In Chapters 5–6, we present a detailed treatment of program development and program control in JavaScript.

Before you can run code examples with JavaScript on your computer, you may need to change your browser's security settings. By default, Internet Explorer 7 prevents scripts on your local computer from running, displaying a yellow warning bar at the top of the window instead. To allow scripts to run in files on your computer, select **Internet Options** from the **Tools** menu. Click the **Advanced** tab and scroll down to the **Security** section of the **Settings** list. Check the box labeled **Allow active content to run in files on My Computer** (Fig. 4.1). Click **OK** and restart Internet Explorer. XHTML documents on your own computer that contain JavaScript code will now run properly. Firefox has JavaScript enabled by default.

---

1. Many people confuse the scripting language JavaScript with the programming language Java (from Sun Microsystems, Inc.). Java is a full-fledged object-oriented programming language. It can be used to develop applications that execute on a range of devices—from the smallest devices (such as cell phones and PDAs) to supercomputers. Java is popular for developing large-scale distributed enterprise applications and web applications. JavaScript is a browser-based scripting language developed by Netscape and implemented in all major browsers.

2. JavaScript was originally created by Netscape. Both Netscape and Microsoft have been instrumental in the standardization of JavaScript by ECMA International as ECMAScript. Detailed information about the current ECMAScript standard can be found at `www.ecma-international.org/publications/standards/ECMA-262.htm`.

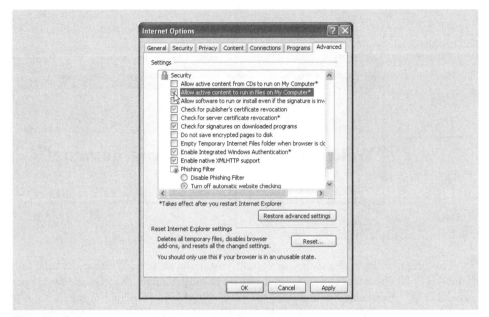

Fig. 4.1 | Enabling JavaScript in Internet Explorer 7

4.2 Simple Program: Displaying a Line of Text in a Web Page

JavaScript uses notations that are familiar to programmers. We begin by considering a simple *script* (or *program*) that displays the text "Welcome to JavaScript Programming!" in the body of an XHTML document. All major web browsers contain *JavaScript interpreters*, which process the commands written in JavaScript. The JavaScript code and its output in Internet Explorer are shown in Fig. 4.2.

```
1   <?xml version = "1.0" encoding = "utf-8"?>
2   <!DOCTYPE html PUBLIC "-//W3C//DTD XHTML 1.0 Strict//EN"
3      "http://www.w3.org/TR/xhtml1/DTD/xhtml1-strict.dtd">
4
5   <!-- Fig. 4.2: welcome.html -->
6   <!-- Displaying a line of text. -->
7   <html xmlns = "http://www.w3.org/1999/xhtml">
8      <head>
9         <title>A First Program in JavaScript</title>
10        <script type = "text/javascript">
11           <!--
12           document.writeln(
13              "<h1>Welcome to JavaScript Programming!</h1>" );
14           // -->
15        </script>
16     </head><body></body>
17  </html>
```

Fig. 4.2 | Displaying a line of text. (Part 1 of 2.)

Fig. 4.2 | Displaying a line of text. (Part 2 of 2.)

This program illustrates several important JavaScript features. We consider each line of the XHTML document and script in detail. As in the preceding chapters, we have given each XHTML document line numbers for your convenience; the line numbers are not part of the XHTML document or of the JavaScript programs. Lines 12–13 do the "real work" of the script, namely, displaying the phrase Welcome to JavaScript Programming! in the web page.

Line 8 indicates the beginning of the <head> section of the XHTML document. For the moment, the JavaScript code we write will appear in the <head> section. The browser interprets the contents of the <head> section first, so the JavaScript programs we write there execute before the <body> of the XHTML document displays. In later chapters on JavaScript and in the chapters on dynamic HTML, we illustrate *inline scripting*, in which JavaScript code is written in the <body> of an XHTML document.

Line 10 uses the *<script>* tag to indicate to the browser that the text which follows is part of a script. The *type* attribute specifies the type of file as well as the *scripting language* used in the script—in this case, a text file written in javascript. Both Internet Explorer and Firefox use JavaScript as the default scripting language.

Line 11 contains the XHTML opening comment tag <!--. Some older web browsers do not support scripting. In such browsers, the actual text of a script often will display in the web page. To prevent this from happening, many script programmers enclose the script code in an XHTML comment, so that browsers that do not support scripts will simply ignore the script. The syntax used is as follows:

```
<script type = "text/javascript">
   <!--
   script code here
   // -->
</script>
```

When a browser that does not support scripts encounters the preceding code, it ignores the <script> and </script> tags and the script code in the XHTML comment. Browsers that do support scripting will interpret the JavaScript code as expected. [*Note:* Some browsers require the *JavaScript single-line comment //* (see Section 4.4 for an explanation) before the ending XHTML comment delimiter (-->) to interpret the script properly. The opening HTML comment tag (<!--) also serves as a single-line comment delimiter in JavaScript, therefore it does not need to be commented.]

Portability Tip 4.1

Some browsers do not support the <script>...</script> tags. If your document is to be rendered with such browsers, enclose the script code between these tags in an XHTML comment, so that the script text does not get displayed as part of the web page. The closing comment tag of the XHTML comment (-->) is preceded by a JavaScript comment (//) to prevent the browser from trying to interpret the XHTML comment as a JavaScript statement.

Lines 12–13 instruct the browser's JavaScript interpreter to perform an ***action***, namely, to display in the web page the ***string*** of characters contained between the ***double quotation (") marks***. A string is sometimes called a ***character string***, a ***message*** or a ***string literal***. We refer to characters between double quotation marks as strings. Individual white-space characters between words in a string are not ignored by the browser. However, if consecutive spaces appear in a string, browsers condense them to a single space. Also, in most cases, browsers ignore leading white-space characters (i.e., white space at the beginning of a string).

Software Engineering Observation 4.1

Strings in JavaScript can be enclosed in either double quotation marks (") or single quotation marks (').

Lines 12–13 use the browser's ***document object***, which represents the XHTML document the browser is currently displaying. The document object allows you to specify text to display in the XHTML document. The browser contains a complete set of objects that allow script programmers to access and manipulate every element of an XHTML document. In later chapters, we overview some of these objects as we discuss the Document Object Model (DOM).

An object resides in the computer's memory and contains information used by the script. The term ***object*** normally implies that ***attributes*** (***data***) and ***behaviors*** (***methods***) are associated with the object. The object's methods use the attributes to perform useful actions for the ***client of the object*** (i.e., the script that calls the methods). A method may require additional information (***arguments***) to perform its action; this information is enclosed in parentheses after the name of the method in the script. In lines 12–13, we call the document object's ***writeln method*** to write a line of XHTML markup in the XHTML document. The parentheses following the method name writeln contain the one argument that method writeln requires (in this case, the string of XHTML that the browser is to display). Method writeln instructs the browser to display the argument string. If the string contains XHTML elements, the browser interprets these elements and renders them on the screen. In this example, the browser displays the phrase Welcome to JavaScript Programming! as an h1-level XHTML heading, because the phrase is enclosed in an h1 element.

The code elements in lines 12–13, including document.writeln, its argument in the parentheses (the string) and the ***semicolon*** (;), together are called a ***statement***. Every statement ends with a semicolon (also known as the ***statement terminator***), although this practice is not required by JavaScript. Line 15 indicates the end of the script.

Good Programming Practice 4.1

Always include a semicolon at the end of a statement to terminate the statement. This notation clarifies where one statement ends and the next statement begins.

Common Programming Error 4.1

Forgetting the ending </script> *tag for a script may prevent the browser from interpreting the script properly and may prevent the XHTML document from loading or rendering properly.*

The </head> tag in line 16 indicates the end of the <head> section. Also in line 16, the tags <body> and </body> specify that this XHTML document has an empty body. Line 17 indicates the end of this XHTML document.

We are now ready to view our XHTML document in a web browser—open it in Internet Explorer or Firefox. If the script contains no syntax errors, it should produce the output shown in Fig. 4.2.

Common Programming Error 4.2

JavaScript is case sensitive. Not using the proper uppercase and lowercase letters is a syntax error—a violation of the rules of writing correct statements in the programming language. The JavaScript interpreter in Internet Explorer reports all syntax errors by indicating in a separate popup window that a "runtime error" has occurred (i.e., a problem occurred while the interpreter was running the script). [Note: To enable this feature in IE7, select **Internet Options...** *from the* **Tools** *menu. In the* **Internet Options** *dialog that appears, select the* **Advanced** *tab and click the checkbox labelled* **Display a notification about every script error** *under the* **Browsing** *category. Firefox has an error console that reports JavaScript errors and warnings. It is accessible by choosing* **Error Console** *from the* **Tools** *menu.]*

4.3 Modifying Our First Program

This section continues our introduction to JavaScript programming with two examples that modify the example in Fig. 4.2.

Displaying a Line of Colored Text

A script can display Welcome to JavaScript Programming! several ways. Figure 4.3 uses two JavaScript statements to produce one line of text in the XHTML document. This example also displays the text in a different color, using the CSS color property.

```
1    <?xml version = "1.0" encoding = "utf-8"?>
2    <!DOCTYPE html PUBLIC "-//W3C//DTD XHTML 1.0 Strict//EN"
3       "http://www.w3.org/TR/xhtml1/DTD/xhtml1-strict.dtd">
4
5    <!-- Fig. 4.3: welcome2.html -->
6    <!-- Printing one line with multiple statements. -->
7    <html xmlns = "http://www.w3.org/1999/xhtml">
8       <head>
9          <title>Printing a Line with Multiple Statements</title>
10         <script type = "text/javascript">
11            <!--
12               document.write( "<h1 style = \"color: magenta\">" );
```

Fig. 4.3 | Printing one line with separate statements. (Part 1 of 2.)

```
13              document.write( "Welcome to JavaScript " +
14                 "Programming!</h1>" );
15             // -->
16           </script>
17         </head><body></body>
18      </html>
```

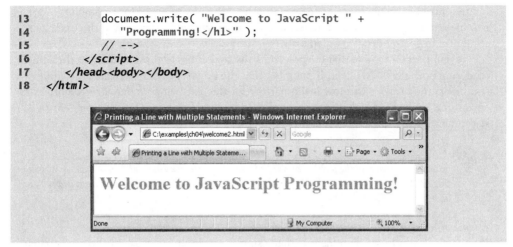

Fig. 4.3 | Printing one line with separate statements. (Part 2 of 2.)

Most of this XHTML document is identical to Fig. 4.2, so we concentrate only on lines 12–14 of Fig. 4.3, which display one line of text in the XHTML document. The first statement uses document method ***write*** to display a string. Unlike writeln, write does not position the output cursor in the XHTML document at the beginning of the next line after writing its argument. [*Note:* The output cursor keeps track of where the next character appears in the XHTML document, not where the next character appears in the web page as rendered by the browser.] The next character written in the XHTML document appears immediately after the last character written with write. Thus, when lines 13–14 execute, the first character written, "W," appears immediately after the last character displayed with write (the > character inside the right double quote in line 12). Each write or writeln statement resumes writing characters where the last write or writeln statement stopped writing characters. So, after a writeln statement, the next output appears on the beginning of the next line. In effect, the two statements in lines 12–14 result in one line of XHTML text. Remember that statements in JavaScript are separated by semicolons (;). Therefore, lines 13–14 represent only one complete statement. JavaScript allows large statements to be split over many lines. However, you cannot split a statement in the middle of a string. The + operator (called the "concatenation operator" when used in this manner) in line 13 joins two strings together and is explained in more detail later in this chapter.

 Common Programming Error 4.3

Splitting a statement in the middle of a string is a syntax error.

Note that the characters \" (in line 12) are not displayed in the browser. The ***backslash*** (\) in a string is an ***escape character***. It indicates that a "special" character is to be used in the string. When a backslash is encountered in a string of characters, the next character is combined with the backslash to form an ***escape sequence***. The escape sequence \" is the ***double-quote character***, which causes a double-quote character to be inserted into the string. We use this escape sequence to insert double quotes around the attribute value for style without terminating the string. Note that we could also have used single quotes for the attribute value, as in document.write("<h1 style = 'color: magenta'>");, because the single quotes do not terminate a double-quoted string. We discuss escape sequences in greater detail momentarily.

It is important to note that the preceding discussion has nothing to do with the actual rendering of the XHTML text. Remember that the browser does not create a new line of text unless the browser window is too narrow for the text being rendered or the browser encounters an XHTML element that explicitly starts a new line—for example, <br/> to start a new line or <p> to start a new paragraph.

Common Programming Error 4.4

Many people confuse the writing of XHTML text with the rendering of XHTML text. Writing XHTML text creates the XHTML that will be rendered by the browser for presentation to the user.

Displaying Multiple Lines of Text

In the next example, we demonstrate that a single statement can cause the browser to display multiple lines by using line-break XHTML tags (<br/>) throughout the string of XHTML text in a write or writeln method call. Figure 4.4 demonstrates the use of line-break XHTML tags. Lines 12–13 produce three separate lines of text when the browser renders the XHTML document.

```
1   <?xml version = "1.0" encoding = "utf-8"?>
2   <!DOCTYPE html PUBLIC "-//W3C//DTD XHTML 1.0 Strict//EN"
3       "http://www.w3.org/TR/xhtml1/DTD/xhtml1-strict.dtd">
4
5   <!-- Fig. 4.4: welcome3.html -->
6   <!-- Printing on multiple lines with a single statement. -->
7   <html xmlns = "http://www.w3.org/1999/xhtml">
8       <head>
9           <title>Printing Multiple Lines</title>
10          <script type = "text/javascript">
11              <!--
12              document.writeln( "<h1>Welcome to<br />JavaScript" +
13                  "<br />Programming!</h1>" );
14              // -->
15          </script>
16      </head><body></body>
17  </html>
```

Fig. 4.4 | Printing on multiple lines with a single statement.

Displaying Text in an Alert Dialog

The first several programs in this chapter display text in the XHTML document. Sometimes it is useful to display information in windows called *dialogs* (or *dialog boxes*) that "pop up" on the screen to grab the user's attention. Dialogs typically display important messages to users browsing the web page. JavaScript allows you easily to display a dialog box containing a message. The program in Fig. 4.5 displays Welcome to JavaScript Programming! as three lines in a predefined dialog called an *alert dialog*.

Line 12 in the script uses the browser's *window* object to display an alert dialog. The argument to the window object's *alert* method is the string to display. Executing the preceding statement displays the dialog shown in the first window of Fig. 4.5. The *title bar* of

```
1   <?xml version = "1.0" encoding = "utf-8"?>
2   <!DOCTYPE html PUBLIC "-//W3C//DTD XHTML 1.0 Strict//EN"
3       "http://www.w3.org/TR/xhtml1/DTD/xhtml1-strict.dtd">
4
5   <!-- Fig. 4.5: welcome4.html -->
6   <!-- Alert dialog displaying multiple lines. -->
7   <html xmlns = "http://www.w3.org/1999/xhtml">
8      <head>
9         <title>Printing Multiple Lines in a Dialog Box</title>
10        <script type = "text/javascript">
11           <!--
12              window.alert( "Welcome to\nJavaScript\nProgramming!" );
13           // -->
14        </script>
15     </head>
16     <body>
17        <p>Click Refresh (or Reload) to run this script again.</p>
18     </body>
19  </html>
```

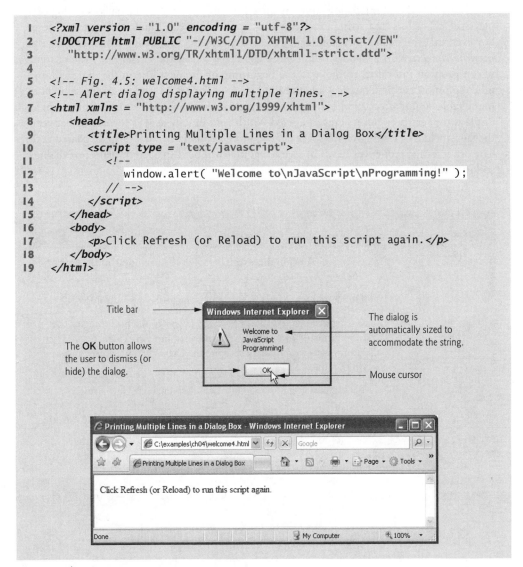

Fig. 4.5 | Alert dialog displaying multiple lines.

the dialog contains the string **Windows Internet Explorer** to indicate that the browser is presenting a message to the user. The dialog provides an **OK** button that allows the user to *dismiss* (i.e., *close*) the dialog by clicking the button. To dismiss the dialog, position the *mouse cursor* (also called the *mouse pointer*) over the **OK** button and click the mouse. Firefox's alert dialog looks similar, but the title bar contains the text **[JavaScript Application]**.

 Common Programming Error 4.5

Dialogs display plain text; they do not render XHTML. Therefore, specifying XHTML elements as part of a string to be displayed in a dialog results in the actual characters of the tags being displayed.

Note that the `alert` dialog contains three lines of plain text. Normally, a dialog displays the characters in a string exactly as they appear between the double quotes. Note, however, that the dialog does not display the characters \n. The escape sequence \n is the *newline character.* In a dialog, the newline character causes the *cursor* (i.e., the current screen position indicator) to move to the beginning of the next line in the dialog. Some other common escape sequences are listed in Fig. 4.6. The \n, \t and \r escape sequences in the table do not affect XHTML rendering unless they are in a *pre element* (this element displays the text between its tags in a fixed-width font exactly as it is formatted between the tags, including leading white-space characters and consecutive white-space characters). The other escape sequences result in characters that will be displayed in plain text dialogs and in XHTML.

Escape sequence	Description
\n	New line. Position the screen cursor at the beginning of the next line.
\t	Horizontal tab. Move the screen cursor to the next tab stop.
\r	Carriage return. Position the screen cursor to the beginning of the current line; do not advance to the next line. Any characters output after the carriage return overwrite the characters previously output on that line.
\\	Backslash. Used to represent a backslash character in a string.
\"	Double quote. Used to represent a double-quote character in a string contained in double quotes. For example, `window.alert( "\"in quotes\"" );` displays `"in quotes"` in an `alert` dialog.
\'	Single quote. Used to represent a single-quote character in a string. For example, `window.alert( '\'in quotes\'' );` displays `'in quotes'` in an `alert` dialog.

Fig. 4.6 | Some common escape sequences.

Common Programming Error 4.6

XHTML elements in an alert dialog's message are not interpreted as XHTML. This means that using <br />, for example, to create a line break in an alert box is an error. The string <br/> will simply be included in your message.

4.4 Obtaining User Input with prompt Dialogs

Scripting gives you the ability to generate part or all of a web page's content at the time it is shown to the user. A script can adapt the content based on input from the user or other variables, such as the time of day or the type of browser used by the client. Such web pages are said to be *dynamic*, as opposed to static, since their content has the ability to change. The next two subsections use scripts to demonstrate dynamic web pages.

4.4.1 Dynamic Welcome Page

Our next script builds on prior scripts to create a dynamic welcome page that obtains the user's name, then displays it on the page. The script uses another predefined dialog box from the window object—a *prompt* dialog—which allows the user to input a value that the script can use. The program asks the user to input a name, then displays the name in the XHTML document. Figure 4.7 presents the script and sample output. [*Note:* In later Java-Script chapters, we obtain input via GUI components in XHTML forms, as introduced in Chapter 2.]

```
1   <?xml version = "1.0" encoding = "utf-8"?>
2   <!DOCTYPE html PUBLIC "-//W3C//DTD XHTML 1.0 Strict//EN"
3      "http://www.w3.org/TR/xhtml1/DTD/xhtml1-strict.dtd">
4
5   <!-- Fig. 4.7: welcome5.html -->
6   <!-- Prompt box used on a welcome screen. -->
7   <html xmlns = "http://www.w3.org/1999/xhtml">
8      <head>
9         <title>Using Prompt and Alert Boxes</title>
10        <script type = "text/javascript">
11           <!--
12           var name; // string entered by the user
13
14           // read the name from the prompt box as a string
15           name = window.prompt( "Please enter your name" );
16
17           document.writeln( "<h1>Hello, " + name +
18              ", welcome to JavaScript programming!</h1>" );
19           // -->
20        </script>
21     </head>
22     <body>
23        <p>Click Refresh (or Reload) to run this script again.</p>
24     </body>
25  </html>
```

Fig. 4.7 | Prompt box used on a welcome screen. (Part 1 of 2.)

Fig. 4.7 | Prompt box used on a welcome screen. (Part 2 of 2.)

Line 12 is a ***declaration*** that contains the JavaScript ***keyword*** var. Keywords are words that have special meaning in JavaScript. The keyword ***var*** at the beginning of the statement indicates that the word name is a ***variable***. A variable is a location in the computer's memory where a value can be stored for use by a program. All variables have a name, type and value, and should be declared with a var statement before they are used in a program. Although using var to declare variables is not required, we'll see in Chapter 7, JavaScript: Functions, that var sometimes ensures proper behavior of a script.

The name of a variable can be any valid ***identifier***. An identifier is a series of characters consisting of letters, digits, underscores (_) and dollar signs ($) that does not begin with a digit and is not a reserved JavaScript keyword. [*Note:* A complete list of keywords can be found in Fig. 7.2.] Identifiers may not contain spaces. Some valid identifiers are Welcome, $value, _value, m_inputField1 and button7. The name 7button is not a valid identifier, because it begins with a digit, and the name input field is not valid, because it contains a space. Remember that JavaScript is ***case sensitive***—uppercase and lowercase letters are considered to be different characters, so name, Name and NAME are different identifiers.

Good Programming Practice 4.2

Choosing meaningful variable names helps a script to be "self-documenting" (i.e., easy to understand by simply reading the script, rather than having to read manuals or extended comments).

Good Programming Practice 4.3

By convention, variable-name identifiers begin with a lowercase first letter. Each subsequent word should begin with a capital first letter. For example, identifier itemPrice has a capital P in its second word, Price.

Common Programming Error 4.7

Splitting a statement in the middle of an identifier is a syntax error.

Declarations end with a semicolon (;) and can be split over several lines with each variable in the declaration separated by a comma—known as a *comma-separated list* of variable names. Several variables may be declared either in one declaration or in multiple declarations.

In line 12, a *single-line comment* that begins with the characters // states the purpose of the variable in the script. This form of comment is called a single-line comment because it terminates at the end of the line in which it appears. A // comment can begin at any position in a line of JavaScript code and continues until the end of the line.

Good Programming Practice 4.4

Declare each variable on a separate line. This format allows for easy insertion of a descriptive comment next to each declaration—a widely followed professional coding standard.

Another comment notation facilitates writing *multiline comments*. For example,

```
/* This is a multiline
   comment. It can be
   split over many lines. */
```

is a multiline comment spread over several lines. Such comments begin with the delimiter /* and end with the delimiter */. All text between the delimiters of the comment is ignored by the interpreter.

Common Programming Error 4.8

Forgetting one of the delimiters of a multiline comment is a syntax error.

Common Programming Error 4.9

Nesting multiline comments (i.e., placing a multiline comment between the delimiters of another multiline comment) is a syntax error.

JavaScript adopted comments delimited with /* and */ from the C programming language and single-line comments delimited with // from the C++ programming language. JavaScript programmers generally prefer C++-style single-line comments over C-style comments. Throughout this book, we use C++-style single-line comments.

Line 14 is a comment indicating the purpose of the statement in the next line. Line 15 calls the `window` object's `prompt` method, which displays the dialog in Fig. 4.8. The dialog allows the user to enter a string representing the user's name.

Fig. 4.8 | Prompt dialog displayed by the `window` object's `prompt` method.

The argument to `prompt` specifies a message telling the user what to type in the text field. An optional second argument, separated from the first by a comma, may specify the default string displayed in the text field; our code does not supply a second argument. In this case, Internet Explorer displays the default value `undefined`, while Firefox and most other browsers leave the text field empty. The user types characters in the text field, then clicks the **OK** button to submit the string to the program. We normally receive input from a user through a GUI component such as the `prompt` dialog, as in this program, or through an XHTML form GUI component, as we'll see in later chapters.

The user can type anything in the text field of the `prompt` dialog. For this program, whatever the user enters is considered the name. If the user clicks the **Cancel** button, no string value is sent to the program. Instead, the `prompt` dialog submits the value *null*, a JavaScript keyword signifying that a variable has no value. Note that `null` is not a string literal, but rather a predefined term indicating the absence of value. Writing a `null` value to the document, however, displays the word `null` in the web page.

The statement in line 15 *assigns* the value returned by the `window` object's `prompt` method (a string containing the characters typed by the user—or the default value or `null` if the **Cancel** button is clicked) to variable `name` by using the *assignment operator*, =. The statement is read as, "name gets the value returned by `window.prompt( "Please enter your name" )`." The = operator is called a *binary operator* because it has two *operands*— `name` and the result of the expression `window.prompt( "Please enter your name" )`. The expression to the right of the assignment operator is always evaluated first.

Good Programming Practice 4.5

Place spaces on either side of a binary operator. This format makes the operator stand out and makes the program more readable.

Lines 17–18 use `document.writeln` to display the new welcome message. The expression inside the parentheses uses the operator + to "add" a string (the literal `"<h1>Hello, "`), the variable `name` (the string that the user entered in line 15) and another string (the literal `", welcome to JavaScript programming!</h1>"`). JavaScript has a version of the + operator for *string concatenation* that enables a string and a value of another data type (including another string) to be combined. The result of this operation is a new (and normally longer) string. If we assume that `name` contains the string literal `"Jim"`, the expression evaluates as follows: JavaScript determines that the two operands of the first + operator (the string `"<h1>Hello, "` and the value of variable `name`) are both strings, then concatenates the two into one string. Next, JavaScript determines that the two operands of the second + operator (the result of the first concatenation operation, the string `"<h1>Hello, Jim"`, and the string `", welcome to JavaScript programming!</h1>"`) are both strings and concatenates the two. This results in the string `"<h1>Hello, Jim, welcome to JavaScript programming!</h1>"`. The browser renders this string as part of the XHTML document. Note that the space between `Hello,` and `Jim` is part of the string `"<h1>Hello, "`.

As we'll illustrate later, the + operator used for string concatenation can convert other variable types to strings if necessary. Because string concatenation occurs between two strings, JavaScript must convert other variable types to strings before it can proceed with the operation. For example, if a variable `age` has the integer value `21`, then the expression `"my age is " + age` evaluates to the string `"my age is 21"`. JavaScript converts the value of `age` to a string and concatenates it with the existing string literal `"my age is "`.

After the browser interprets the <head> section of the XHTML document (which contains the JavaScript), it then interprets the <body> of the XHTML document (lines 22–24) and renders the XHTML. Notice that the XHTML page is not rendered until the prompt is dismissed because the prompt pauses execution in the head, before the body is processed. If you click your browser's **Refresh** (Internet Explorer) or **Reload** (Firefox) button after entering a name, the browser will reload the XHTML document, so that you can execute the script again and change the name. [*Note:* In some cases, it may be necessary to hold down the *Shift* key while clicking the **Refresh** or **Reload** button, to ensure that the XHTML document reloads properly. Browsers often save a recent copy of a page in memory, and holding the *Shift* key forces the browser to download the most recent version of a page.]

4.4.2 Adding Integers

Our next script illustrates another use of prompt dialogs to obtain input from the user. Figure 4.9 inputs two *integers* (whole numbers, such as 7, –11, 0 and 31914) typed by a user at the keyboard, computes the sum of the values and displays the result.

Lines 12–16 declare the variables firstNumber, secondNumber, number1, number2 and sum. Single-line comments state the purpose of each of these variables. Line 19 employs a prompt dialog to allow the user to enter a string representing the first of the two integers that will be added. The script assigns the first value entered by the user to the

```xml
1   <?xml version = "1.0" encoding = "utf-8"?>
2   <!DOCTYPE html PUBLIC "-//W3C//DTD XHTML 1.0 Strict//EN"
3      "http://www.w3.org/TR/xhtml1/DTD/xhtml1-strict.dtd">
4
5   <!-- Fig. 4.9: addition.html -->
6   <!-- Addition script. -->
7   <html xmlns = "http://www.w3.org/1999/xhtml">
8      <head>
9         <title>An Addition Program</title>
10        <script type = "text/javascript">
11           <!--
12           var firstNumber; // first string entered by user
13           var secondNumber; // second string entered by user
14           var number1; // first number to add
15           var number2; // second number to add
16           var sum; // sum of number1 and number2
17
18           // read in first number from user as a string
19           firstNumber = window.prompt( "Enter first integer" );
20
21           // read in second number from user as a string
22           secondNumber = window.prompt( "Enter second integer" );
23
24           // convert numbers from strings to integers
25           number1 = parseInt( firstNumber );
26           number2 = parseInt( secondNumber );
27
28           sum = number1 + number2; // add the numbers
```

Fig. 4.9 | Addition script. (Part 1 of 2.)

```
29
30          // display the results
31          document.writeln( "<h1>The sum is " + sum + "</h1>" );
32          // -->
33       </script>
34    </head>
35    <body>
36       <p>Click Refresh (or Reload) to run the script again</p>
37    </body>
38 </html>
```

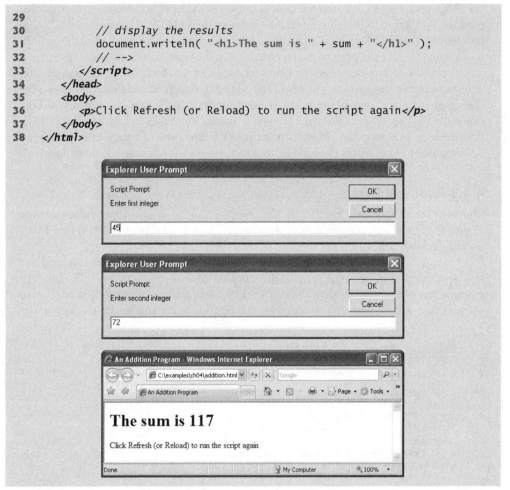

Fig. 4.9 | Addition script. (Part 2 of 2.)

variable firstNumber. Line 22 displays a prompt dialog to obtain the second number to add and assign this value to the variable secondNumber.

As in the preceding example, the user can type anything in the prompt dialog. For this program, if the user either types a noninteger value or clicks the **Cancel** button, a logic error will occur, and the sum of the two values will appear in the XHTML document as *NaN* (meaning *not a number*). A logic error is caused by syntactically correct code that produces an undesired result. In Chapter 9, JavaScript: Objects, we discuss the Number object and its methods that can determine whether a value is not a number.

Recall that a prompt dialog returns to the program as a string the value typed by the user. Lines 25–26 convert the two strings input by the user to integer values that can be used in a calculation. Function *parseInt* converts its string argument to an integer. Line 25 assigns to the variable number1 the integer that function parseInt returns. Line 26 assigns an integer value to variable number2 in a similar manner. Any subsequent references to number1 and number2 in the program use these integer values. [*Note:* We refer to `parseInt` as a *function* rather than a method because we do not precede the function call with an object name (such as `document` or `window`) and a dot (`.`). The term method means that the function belongs to a particular object. For example, method `writeln` belongs to the `document` object and method `prompt` belongs to the `window` object.]

Line 28 calculates the sum of the variables `number1` and `number2` using the ***addition operator***, +, and assigns the result to variable `sum` by using the assignment operator, =. Notice that the + operator can perform both addition and string concatenation. In this case, the + operator performs addition, because both operands contain integers. After line 28 performs this calculation, line 31 uses `document.writeln` to display the result of the addition on the web page. Lines 33 and 34 close the `script` and `head` elements, respectively. Lines 35–37 render the body of XHTML document. Use your browser's **Refresh** or **Reload** button to reload the XHTML document and run the script again.

Common Programming Error 4.10

Confusing the + operator used for string concatenation with the + operator used for addition often leads to undesired results. For example, if integer variable y has the value 5, the expression "y + 2 = " + y + 2 results in "y + 2 = 52", not "y + 2 = 7", because first the value of y (i.e., 5) is concatenated with the string "y + 2 = ", then the value 2 is concatenated with the new, larger string "y + 2 = 5". The expression "y + 2 = " + (y + 2) produces the string "y + 2 = 7" because the parentheses ensure that y + 2 is executed mathematically before it is conveted to a string.

4.5 Data Types in JavaScript

Unlike its predecessor languages C, C++ and Java, JavaScript does not require variables to have a declared type before they can be used in a program. A variable in JavaScript can contain a value of any data type, and in many situations JavaScript automatically converts between values of different types for you. For this reason, JavaScript is referred to as a ***loosely typed language***. When a variable is declared in JavaScript, but is not given a value, the variable has an ***undefined*** value. Attempting to use the value of such a variable is normally a logic error.

When variables are declared, they are not assigned values unless specified by you. Assigning the value `null` to a variable indicates that it does not contain a value.

4.6 Arithmetic

Many scripts perform arithmetic calculations. The ***arithmetic operators*** use various special symbols that are not used in algebra. The ***asterisk (*)*** indicates multiplication; the ***percent sign (%)*** is the ***remainder operator***, which will be discussed shortly. The arithmetic operators are binary operators, because each operates on two operands. For example, the expression `sum + value` contains the binary operator + and the two operands `sum` and `value`.

JavaScript provides the remainder operator, %, which yields the remainder after division. [*Note:* The % operator is known as the modulus operator in some programming languages.] The expression x % y yields the remainder after x is divided by y. Thus, 17 % 5 yields 2 (i.e., 17 divided by 5 is 3, with a remainder of 2), and 7.4 % 3.1 yields 1.2. In later chapters, we consider applications of the remainder operator, such as determining whether one number is a multiple of another. There is no arithmetic operator for exponentiation in JavaScript. (Chapter 6, JavaScript: Control Statements II, shows how to perform exponentiation in JavaScript using the Math object's pow method.)

4.7 Decision Making: Equality and Relational Operators

This section introduces a version of JavaScript's *if* statement that allows a program to make a decision based on the truth or falsity of a *condition*. If the condition is met (i.e., the condition is *true*), the statement in the body of the if statement is executed. If the condition is not met (i.e., the condition is *false*), the statement in the body of the if statement is not executed. We'll see an example shortly. [*Note:* Other versions of the if statement are introduced in Chapter 5, JavaScript: Control Statements I.]

Conditions in if statements can be formed by using the *equality operators* and *relational operators* summarized in Fig. 4.10. The relational operators all have the same level of precedence and associate from left to right. The equality operators both have the same level of precedence, which is lower than the precedence of the relational operators. The equality operators also associate from left to right.

Common Programming Error 4.11

It is a syntax error if the operators ==, !=, >= and <= contain spaces between their symbols, as in = =, ! =, > = and < =, respectively.

Common Programming Error 4.12

Reversing the operators !=, >= and <=, as in =!, => and =<, respectively, is a syntax error.

Common Programming Error 4.13

Confusing the equality operator, ==, with the assignment operator, =, is a logic error. The equality operator should be read as "is equal to," and the assignment operator should be read as "gets" or "gets the value of." Some people prefer to read the equality operator as "double equals" or "equals equals."

Standard algebraic equality operator or relational operator	JavaScript equality or relational operator	Sample JavaScript condition	Meaning of JavaScript condition
Equality operators			
=	==	x == y	x is equal to y
≠	!=	x != y	x is not equal to y
Relational operators			
>	>	x > y	x is greater than y
<	<	x < y	x is less than y
≥	>=	x >= y	x is greater than or equal to y
≤	<=	x <= y	x is less than or equal to y

Fig. 4.10 | Equality and relational operators.

The script in Fig. 4.11 uses four if statements to display a time-sensitive greeting on a welcome page. The script obtains the local time from the user's computer and converts it from 24-hour clock format (0–23) to a 12-hour clock format (0–11). Using this value, the script displays an appropriate greeting for the current time of day. The script and sample output are shown in Fig. 4.11.

```
 1   <?xml version = "1.0" encoding = "utf-8"?>
 2   <!DOCTYPE html PUBLIC "-//W3C//DTD XHTML 1.0 Strict//EN"
 3      "http://www.w3.org/TR/xhtml1/DTD/xhtml1-strict.dtd">
 4
 5   <!-- Fig. 4.11: welcome6.html -->
 6   <!-- Using equality and relational operators. -->
 7   <html xmlns = "http://www.w3.org/1999/xhtml">
 8      <head>
 9         <title>Using Relational Operators</title>
10         <script type = "text/javascript">
11            <!--
12            var name; // string entered by the user
13            var now = new Date();        // current date and time
14            var hour = now.getHours(); // current hour (0-23)
15
16            // read the name from the prompt box as a string
17            name = window.prompt( "Please enter your name" );
18
19            // determine whether it is morning
20            if ( hour < 12 )
21               document.write( "<h1>Good Morning, " );
22
23            // determine whether the time is PM
24            if ( hour >= 12 )
25            {
26               // convert to a 12-hour clock
27               hour = hour - 12;
28
29               // determine whether it is before 6 PM
30               if ( hour < 6 )
31                  document.write( "<h1>Good Afternoon, " );
32
33               // determine whether it is after 6 PM
34               if ( hour >= 6 )
35                  document.write( "<h1>Good Evening, " );
36            } // end if
37
38            document.writeln( name +
39               ", welcome to JavaScript programming!</h1>" );
40            // -->
41         </script>
42      </head>
43      <body>
44         <p>Click Refresh (or Reload) to run this script again.</p>
45      </body>
46   </html>
```

Fig. 4.11 | Using equality and relational operators. (Part 1 of 2.)

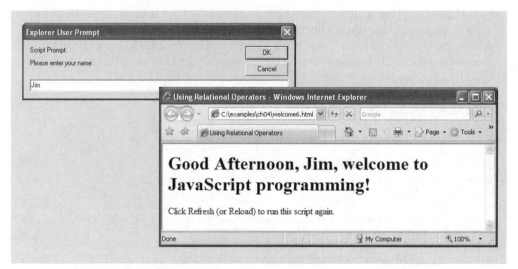

Fig. 4.11 | Using equality and relational operators. (Part 2 of 2.)

Lines 12–14 declare the variables used in the script. Remember that variables may be declared in one declaration or in multiple declarations. If more than one variable is declared in a single declaration (as in this example), the names are separated by commas (,). This list of names is referred to as a comma-separated list. Once again, note the comment at the end of each line, indicating the purpose of each variable in the program. Also note that some of the variables are assigned a value in the declaration—JavaScript allows you to assign a value to a variable when the variable is declared.

Line 13 sets the variable now to a new ***Date object***, which contains information about the current local time. In Section 4.2, we introduced the document object, an object that encapsulates data pertaining to the current web page. Programmers may choose to use other objects to perform specific tasks or obtain particular pieces of information. Here, we use JavaScript's built-in Date object to acquire the current local time. We create a new instance of an object by using the ***new*** operator followed by the type of the object, Date, and a pair of parentheses. Some objects require that arguments be placed in the parentheses to specify details about the object to be created. In this case, we leave the parentheses empty to create a default Date object containing information about the current date and time. After line 13 executes, the variable now refers to the new Date object. [*Note:* We did not need to use the new operator when we used the document and window objects because these objects always are created by the browser.] Line 14 sets the variable hour to an integer equal to the current hour (in a 24-hour clock format) returned by the Date object's getHours method. Chapter 9 presents a more detailed discussion of the Date object's attributes and methods, and of objects in general. As in the preceding example, the script uses window.prompt to allow the user to enter a name to display as part of the greeting (line 17).

To display the correct time-sensitive greeting, the script must determine whether the user is visiting the page during the morning, afternoon or evening. The first if statement (lines 20–21) compares the value of variable hour with 12. If hour is less than 12, then the user is visiting the page during the morning, and the statement at line 21 outputs the string "Good morning". If this condition is not met, line 21 is not executed. Line 24 determines whether hour is greater than or equal to 12. If hour is greater than or equal to 12, then the user is visiting the page in either the afternoon or the evening. Lines 25–36 execute to determine the appropriate greeting. If hour is less than 12, then the JavaScript interpreter does not execute these lines and continues to line 38.

The brace { in line 25 begins a block of statements (lines 27–35) that are executed if hour is greater than or equal to 12—to execute multiple statements inside an if construct, enclose them in curly braces. Line 27 subtracts 12 from hour, converting the current hour from a 24-hour clock format (0–23) to a 12-hour clock format (0–11). The if statement (line 30) determines whether hour is now less than 6. If it is, then the time is between noon and 6 PM, and line 31 outputs the beginning of an XHTML h1 element ("<h1>Good Afternoon, "). If hour is greater than or equal to 6, the time is between 6 PM and midnight, and the script outputs the greeting "Good Evening" (lines 34–35). The brace } in line 36 ends the block of statements associated with the if statement in line 24. Note that if statements can be **nested**, i.e., one if statement can be placed inside another if statement. The if statements that determine whether the user is visiting the page in the afternoon or the evening (lines 30–31 and lines 34–35) execute only if the script has already established that hour is greater than or equal to 12 (line 24). If the script has already determined the current time of day to be morning, these additional comparisons are not performed. (Chapter 5, presents a more in-depth discussion of blocks and nested if statements.) Finally, lines 38–39 output the rest of the XHTML h1 element (the remaining part of the greeting), which does not depend on the time of day.

Good Programming Practice 4.6

Include comments after the closing curly brace of control statements (such as if statements) to indicate where the statements end, as in line 36 of Fig. 4.11.

Note that there is no semicolon (;) at the end of the first line of each if statement. Including such a semicolon would result in a logic error at execution time. For example,

```
if ( hour < 12 ) ;
    document.write( "<h1>Good Morning, " );
```

would actually be interpreted by JavaScript erroneously as

```
if ( hour < 12 )
    ;
document.write( "<h1>Good Morning, " );
```

where the semicolon on the line by itself—called the **empty statement**—is the statement to execute if the condition in the if statement is true. When the empty statement executes, no task is performed in the program. The program then continues with the next statement, which executes regardless of whether the condition is true or false. In this example, "<h1>Good Morning, " would be printed regardless of the time of day.

Common Programming Error 4.14

Placing a semicolon immediately after the right parenthesis of the condition in an if statement is normally a logic error. The semicolon would cause the body of the if statement to be empty, so the if statement itself would perform no action, regardless of whether its condition was true. Worse yet, the intended body statement of the if statement would now become a statement in sequence after the if statement and would always be executed.

Common Programming Error 4.15

Leaving out a condition in a series of if *statements is normally a logic error. For instance, checking if* hour *is greater than 12 or less than 12, but not if* hour *is equal to 12, would mean that the script takes no action when* hour *is equal to 12. Always be sure to handle every possible condition.*

Note the use of spacing in lines 38–39 of Fig. 4.11. Remember that white-space characters, such as tabs, newlines and spaces, are normally ignored by the browser. So, statements may be split over several lines and may be spaced according to your preferences without affecting the meaning of a program. However, it is incorrect to split identifiers and string literals. Ideally, statements should be kept small, but it is not always possible to do so.

The chart in Fig. 4.12 shows the precedence of the operators introduced in this chapter. The operators are shown from top to bottom in decreasing order of precedence. Note that all of these operators, with the exception of the assignment operator, =, associate from left to right. Addition is left associative, so an expression like x + y + z is evaluated as if it had been written as (x + y) + z. The assignment operator, =, associates from right to left, so an expression like x = y = 0 is evaluated as if it had been written as x = (y = 0), which first assigns the value 0 to variable y, then assigns the result of that assignment, 0, to x.

Operators	Associativity	Type
* / %	left to right	multiplicative
+ -	left to right	additive
< <= > >=	left to right	relational
== !=	left to right	equality
=	right to left	assignment

Fig. 4.12 | Precedence and associativity of the operators discussed so far.

4.8 Web Resources

www.deitel.com/javascript

The Deitel JavaScript Resource Center contains links to some of the best JavaScript resources on the web. There you'll find categorized links to JavaScript tools, code generators, forums, books, libraries, frameworks and more. Also check out the tutorials for all skill levels, from introductory to advanced.

JavaScript: Control Statements I

Let's all move one place on.
—Lewis Carroll

The wheel is come full circle.
—William Shakespeare

How many apples fell on Newton's head before he took the hint!
—Robert Frost

OBJECTIVES

In this chapter you will learn:

- To use the if and if...else selection statements to choose among alternative actions.

- To use the while repetition statement to execute statements in a script repeatedly.

- Counter-controlled repetition and sentinel-controlled repetition.

- To use the increment, decrement and assignment operators.

5.1 Introduction

Before writing a script to solve a problem, it is essential to have a thorough understanding of the problem and a carefully planned approach to solving the problem. When writing a script, it is equally essential to understand the types of building blocks that are available and to employ proven program-construction principles. In this chapter and in Chapter 6, we discuss these issues in our presentation of the theory and principles of structured programming. The techniques you will learn here are applicable to most high-level languages, including JavaScript.

5.2 Control Statements

JavaScript provides three types of selection statements; we discuss each in this chapter and in Chapter 6. The if selection statement performs (selects) an action if a condition is true or skips the action if the condition is false. The if...else selection statement qperforms an action if a condition is true and performs a different action if the condition is false. The switch selection statement (Chapter 6) performs one of many different actions, depending on the value of an expression.

The *if* statement is called a *single-selection statement* because it selects or ignores a single action (or, as we'll soon see, a single group of actions). The if...else statement is a *double-selection statement* because it selects between two different actions (or groups of actions). The switch statement is a *multiple-selection statement* because it selects among many different actions (or groups of actions).

JavaScript provides four repetition statement types, namely *while*, do...while, for and for...in. (do...while and for are covered in Chapter 6; for...in is covered in Chapter 8.) Each of the words if, else, switch, while, do, for and in is a JavaScript *keyword*. These words are reserved by the language to implement various features, such as JavaScript's control statements. Keywords cannot be used as identifiers (e.g., for variable names). A complete list of JavaScript keywords is shown in Fig. 5.1.

 Common Programming Error 5.1

Using a keyword as an identifier is a syntax error.

JavaScript keywords				
break	case	catch	continue	default
delete	do	else	false	finally
for	function	if	in	instanceof
new	null	return	switch	this
throw	true	try	typeof	var
void	while	with		
Keywords that are reserved but not used by JavaScript				
abstract	boolean	byte	char	class
const	debugger	double	enum	export
extends	final	float	goto	implements
import	int	interface	long	native
package	private	protected	public	short
static	super	synchronized	throws	transient
volatile				

Fig. 5.1 | JavaScript keywords.

As we have shown, JavaScript has only eight control structures: sequence, three types of selection and four types of repetition. A program is formed by combining control statements as necessary to implement the program's algorithm.

Single-entry/single-exit control statements make it easy to build programs; the control statements are attached to one another by connecting the exit point of one to the entry point of the next. This process is called *control-statement stacking*. We'll learn that there is only one other way in which control statements may be connected—*control-statement nesting*. Thus JavaScript programs are constructed from only eight different types of control statements combined in only two ways.

5.3 if Selection Statement

A selection statement is used to choose among alternative courses of action in a program. For example, suppose that the passing grade on an examination is 60 (out of 100). Then the JavaScript statement

```
if ( studentGrade >= 60 )
    document.writeln( "Passed" );
```

determines whether the condition "student's grade is greater than or equal to 60" is true or false. If the condition is true, then "Passed" is output in the XHTML document, and the next JavaScript statement in order is performed. If the condition is false, the print statement is ignored, and the next JavaScript statement in order is performed.

Note that the second line of this selection statement is indented. The JavaScript interpreter ignores white-space characters—blanks, tabs and newlines used for indentation and vertical spacing.

The flowchart in Fig. 5.2 illustrates the single-selection if statement. This flowchart contains what is perhaps the most important flowcharting symbol—the diamond symbol (or decision symbol), which indicates that a decision is to be made. The decision symbol contains an expression, such as a condition, that can be either *true* or *false*. The decision symbol has two flowlines emerging from it. One indicates the path to follow in the program when the expression in the symbol is true; the other indicates the path to follow in the program when the expression is false. A decision can be made on any expression that evaluates to a value of JavaScript's boolean type (i.e., any expression that evaluates to true or false—also known as a *boolean expression*).

Software Engineering Observation 5.1

In JavaScript, any nonzero numeric value in a condition evaluates to true, and 0 evaluates to false. For strings, any string containing one or more characters evaluates to true, and the empty string (the string containing no characters, represented as "") evaluates to false. Also, a variable that has been declared with var but has not been assigned a value evaluates to false.

Note that the if statement is a single-entry/single-exit control statement. Flowcharts for the remaining control statements also contain (besides small circle symbols and flowlines) only rectangle symbols, to indicate the actions to be performed, and diamond symbols, to indicate decisions to be made. This type of flowchart represents the *action/decision model of programming*.

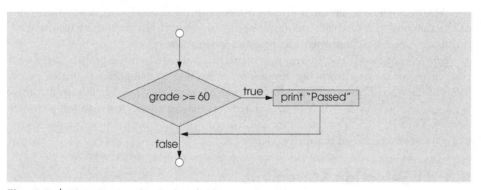

Fig. 5.2 | Flowcharting the single-selection if statement.

5.4 if...else Selection Statement

The if selection statement performs an indicated action only when the condition evaluates to true; otherwise, the action is skipped. The *if...else selection* statement allows you to specify that a different action is to be performed when the condition is true than when the condition is false. For example, the JavaScript statement

```
if ( studentGrade >= 60 )
    document.writeln( "Passed" );
else
    document.writeln( "Failed" );
```

outputs Passed in the XHTML document if the student's grade is greater than or equal to 60 and outputs Failed if the student's grade is less than 60. In either case, after printing occurs, the next JavaScript statement in sequence (i.e., the next statement after the whole if...else statement) is performed. Note that the body of the else part of the structure is also indented. The flowchart shown in Fig. 5.3 illustrates the if...else selection statement's flow of control.

JavaScript provides an operator, called the *conditional operator* (*?:*), that is closely related to the if...else statement. The operator ?: is JavaScript's only *ternary operator*—it takes three operands. The operands together with the ?: form a *conditional expression*. The first operand is a boolean expression, the second is the value for the conditional expression if the expression evaluates to true and the third is the value for the conditional expression if the expression evaluates to false. For example, consider the following statement

```
document.writeln( studentGrade >= 60 ? "Passed" : "Failed" );
```

contains a conditional expression that evaluates to the string "Passed" if the condition studentGrade >= 60 is true and evaluates to the string "Failed" if the condition is false. Thus, this statement with the conditional operator performs essentially the same operation as the preceding if...else statement. The precedence of the conditional operator is low, so the entire conditional expression is normally placed in parentheses to ensure that it evaluates correctly.

Nested if...else statements test for multiple cases by placing if...else statements inside if...else statements. For example, the following pseudocode statement indicates that the program should print A for exam grades greater than or equal to 90, B for grades in the range 80 to 89, C for grades in the range 70 to 79, D for grades in the range 60 to 69 and F for all other grades:

```
if ( studentGrade >= 90 )
   document.writeln( "A" );
else
   if ( studentGrade >= 80 )
      document.writeln( "B" );
   else
      if ( studentGrade >= 70 )
         document.writeln( "C" );
      else
         if ( studentGrade >= 60 )
            document.writeln( "D" );
         else
            document.writeln( "F" );
```

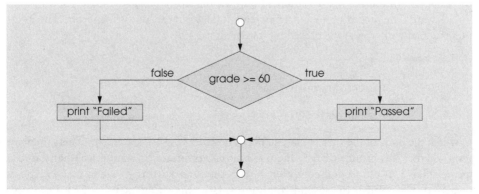

Fig. 5.3 | Flowcharting the double-selection if...else statement.

If studentGrade is greater than or equal to 90, all four conditions will be true, but only the document.writeln statement after the first test will execute. After that particular document.writeln executes, the else part of the outer if...else statements is skipped.

 Good Programming Practice 5.1

If there are several levels of indentation, each level should be indented the same additional amount of space.

Most JavaScript programmers prefer to write the preceding if statement as

```
if ( grade >= 90 )
   document.writeln( "A" );
else if ( grade >= 80 )
   document.writeln( "B" );
else if ( grade >= 70 )
   document.writeln( "C" );
else if ( grade >= 60 )
   document.writeln( "D" );
else
   document.writeln( "F" );
```

The two forms are equivalent. The latter form is popular because it avoids the deep indentation of the code to the right. Such deep indentation often leaves little room on a line, forcing lines to be split and decreasing program readability.

It is important to note that the JavaScript interpreter always associates an else with the previous if, unless told to do otherwise by the placement of braces ({}). This situation is referred to as the *dangling-else problem*. For example,

```
if ( x > 5 )
   if ( y > 5 )
      document.writeln( "x and y are > 5" );
else
   document.writeln( "x is <= 5" );
```

appears to indicate with its indentation that if x is greater than 5, the if statement in its body determines whether y is also greater than 5. If so, the body of the nested if statement outputs the string "x and y are > 5". Otherwise, it *appears* that if x is not greater than 5, the else part of the if...else statement outputs the string "x is <= 5".

Beware! The preceding nested if statement does not execute as it appears. The interpreter actually interprets the preceding statement as

```
if ( x > 5 )
   if ( y > 5 )
      document.writeln( "x and y are > 5" );
   else
      document.writeln( "x is <= 5" );
```

in which the body of the first if statement is a nested if...else statement. This statement tests whether x is greater than 5. If so, execution continues by testing whether y is also greater than 5. If the second condition is true, the proper string—"x and y are > 5"—is displayed. However, if the second condition is false, the string "x is <= 5" is displayed, even though we know that x is greater than 5.

To force the preceding nested if statement to execute as it was intended originally, it must be written as follows:

```
if ( x > 5 )
{
   if ( y > 5 )
      document.writeln( "x and y are > 5" );
}
else
   document.writeln( "x is <= 5" );
```

The braces ({}) indicate to the interpreter that the second if statement is in the body of the first if statement and that the else is matched with the first if statement.

The if selection statement expects only one statement in its body. To include several statements in an if statement's body, enclose the statements in braces ({ and }). This can also be done in the else section of an if...else statement. A set of statements contained within a pair of braces is called a *block*.

Software Engineering Observation 5.2

A block can be placed anywhere in a program that a single statement can be placed.

Software Engineering Observation 5.3

Unlike individual statements, a block does not end with a semicolon. However, each statement within the braces of a block should end with a semicolon.

The following example includes a block in the else part of an if...else statement:

```
if ( grade >= 60 )
   document.writeln( "Passed" );
else
{
   document.writeln( "Failed<br />" );
   document.writeln( "You must take this course again." );
}
```

In this case, if grade is less than 60, the program executes both statements in the body of the else and prints

```
Failed.
You must take this course again.
```

Note the braces surrounding the two statements in the else clause. These braces are important. Without them, the statement

```
document.writeln( "You must take this course again." );
```

would be outside the body of the else part of the if and would execute regardless of whether the grade is less than 60.

Common Programming Error 5.2

Forgetting one or both of the braces that delimit a block can lead to syntax errors or logic errors.

Good Programming Practice 5.2

Some programmers prefer to type the beginning and ending braces of blocks before typing the individual statements within the braces. This helps avoid omitting one or both of the braces.

Software Engineering Observation 5.4

Just as a block can be placed anywhere a single statement can be placed, it is also possible to have no statement at all (the empty statement) in such places. The empty statement is represented by placing a semicolon (;) where a statement would normally be.

Common Programming Error 5.3

Placing a semicolon after the condition in an if statement leads to a logic error in single-selection if statement and a syntax error in double-selection if statements (if the if part contains a non-empty body statement).

5.5 while Repetition Statement

A repetition statement allows you to specify that a script is to repeat an action while some condition remains true.

Common Programming Error 5.4

*If the body of a while statement never causes the while statement's condition to become true, a logic error occurs. Normally, such a repetition structure will never terminate—an error called an **infinite loop**. Both Internet Explorer and Firefox show a dialog allowing the user to terminate a script that contains an infinite loop.*

Common Programming Error 5.5

Remember that JavaScript is a case-sensitive language. In code, spelling the keyword while with an uppercase W, as in While, is a syntax error. All of JavaScript's reserved keywords, such as while, if and else, contain only lowercase letters.

As an example of a while statement, consider a program segment designed to find the first power of 2 larger than 1000. Variable product begins with the value 2:

```
var product = 2;

while ( product <= 1000 )
   product = 2 * product;
```

When the while statement finishes executing, product contains the result 1024. The flowchart in Fig. 5.4 illustrates the flow of control of the preceding while statement.

When the script enters the while statement, product is 2. The script repeatedly multiplies variable product by 2, so product takes on the values 4, 8, 16, 32, 64, 128, 256, 512 and 1024 successively. When product becomes 1024, the condition product <= 1000 in the while statement becomes false. This terminates the repetition, with 1024 as product's final value. Execution continues with the next statement after the while statement. [*Note:* If a while statement's condition is initially false, the body statement(s) will never execute.]

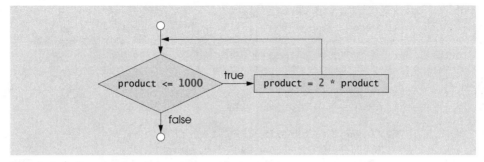

Fig. 5.4 | Flowcharting the `while` repetition statement.

5.6 Counter-Controlled Repetition

Consider the following problem statement:

> *A class of ten students took a quiz. The grades (integers in the range 0 to 100) for this quiz are available to you. Determine the class average on the quiz.*

The class average is equal to the sum of the grades divided by the number of students (10 in this case). The program for this problem (Fig. 5.5) must input each of the grades, perform the averaging calculation and display the result. We use *counter-controlled repetition* to input the grades one at a time. In this example, repetition terminates when the counter exceeds 10.

```
 1   <?xml version = "1.0" encoding = "utf-8"?>
 2   <!DOCTYPE html PUBLIC "-//W3C//DTD XHTML 1.0 Strict//EN"
 3      "http://www.w3.org/TR/xhtml1/DTD/xhtml1-strict.dtd">
 4
 5   <!-- Fig. 5.5: average.html -->
 6   <!-- Counter-controlled repetition to calculate a class average. -->
 7   <html xmlns = "http://www.w3.org/1999/xhtml">
 8      <head>
 9         <title>Class Average Program</title>
10         <script type = "text/javascript">
11            <!--
12            var total; // sum of grades
13            var gradeCounter; // number of grades entered
14            var grade; // grade typed by user (as a string)
15            var gradeValue; // grade value (converted to integer)
16            var average; // average of all grades
17
18            // Initialization Phase
19            total = 0; // clear total
20            gradeCounter = 1; // prepare to loop
21
22            // Processing Phase
23            while ( gradeCounter <= 10 ) // loop 10 times
24            {
25
```

Fig. 5.5 | Counter-controlled repetition to calculate a class average. (Part 1 of 2.)

```
26              // prompt for input and read grade from user
27              grade = window.prompt( "Enter integer grade:", "0" );
28
29              // convert grade from a string to an integer
30              gradeValue = parseInt( grade );
31
32              // add gradeValue to total
33              total = total + gradeValue;
34
35              // add 1 to gradeCounter
36              gradeCounter = gradeCounter + 1;
37           } // end while
38
39           // Termination Phase
40           average = total / 10; // calculate the average
41
42           // display average of exam grades
43           document.writeln(
44              "<h1>Class average is " + average + "</h1>" );
45           // -->
46        </script>
47     </head>
48     <body>
49        <p>Click Refresh (or Reload) to run the script again<p>
50     </body>
51  </html>
```

This dialog is displayed 10 times. User input is 100, 88, 93, 55, 68, 77, 83, 95, 73 and 62.

Explorer User Prompt

Script Prompt:

Enter integer grade:

OK

Cancel

100

Class Average Program - Windows Internet Explorer

C:\examples\ch05\average.html   Google

Class Average Program

Page · Tools ·

Class average is 79.4

Click Refresh (or Reload) to run the script again

Done   My Computer   100%

Fig. 5.5 | Counter-controlled repetition to calculate a class average. (Part 2 of 2.)

Lines 12–16 declare variables total, gradeCounter, grade, gradeValue, average. The variable grade will store the string the user types into the prompt dialog. The variable gradeValue will store the integer value of the grade the user enters into the prompt dialog.

Lines 19–20 are assignment statements that initialize total to 0 and gradeCounter to 1. Note that variables total and gradeCounter are initialized before they are used in a calculation.

Common Programming Error 5.6

Not initializing a variable that will be used in a calculation results in a logic error that produces the value NaN–Not a Number. You must initialize the variable before it is used in a calculation.

Line 23 indicates that the `while` statement continues iterating while the value of `gradeCounter` is less than or equal to 10. Line 27 corresponds to the pseudocode statement "*Input the next grade.*" The statement displays a `prompt` dialog with the prompt `"Enter integer grade:"` on the screen.

After the user enters the `grade`, line 30 converts it from a string to an integer. We must convert the string to an integer in this example; otherwise, the addition statement in line 33 will be a string-concatenation statement rather than a numeric sum.

The program now is ready to increment the variable `gradeCounter` to indicate that a grade has been processed and to read the next grade from the user. Line 36 adds 1 to `gradeCounter`, so the condition in the `while` statement will eventually become `false` and terminate the loop. After this statement executes, the program continues by testing the condition in the `while` statement in line 23. If the condition is still true, the statements in lines 27–36 repeat. Otherwise the program continues execution with the first statement in sequence after the body of the loop (i.e., line 40).

Line 40 assigns the results of the average calculation to variable `average`. Lines 43–44 write a line of XHTML text in the document that displays the string `"Class average is "` followed by the value of variable `average` as an `<h1>` element in the browser.

Execute the script in a web browser by double clicking the XHTML document (from Windows Explorer). This script parses any user input as an integer. In the sample program execution in Fig. 5.5, the sum of the values entered (100, 88, 93, 55, 68, 77, 83, 95, 73 and 62) is 794. Although the treats all input as integers, the averaging calculation in the program does not produce an integer. Rather, the calculation produces a *floating-point number* (i.e., a number containing a decimal point). The average of the 10 integers input by the user in this example is 79.4.

Software Engineering Observation 5.5

If the string passed to parseInt contains a floating-point numeric value, parseInt simply truncates the floating-point part. For example, the string "27.95" results in the integer 27, and the string "–123.45" results in the integer –123. If the string passed to parseInt is not a numeric value, parseInt returns NaN (not a number).

JavaScript actually represents all numbers as floating-point numbers in memory. Floating-point numbers often develop through division, as shown in this example. When we divide 10 by 3, the result is 3.3333333…, with the sequence of 3s repeating infinitely. The computer allocates only a fixed amount of space to hold such a value, so the stored floating-point value can be only an approximation.

5.7 Formulating Algorithms: Sentinel-Controlled Repetition

Let us generalize the class-average problem. Consider the following problem:

Develop a class-averaging program that will process an arbitrary number of grades each time the program is run.

In the first class-average example, the number of grades (10) was known in advance. In this example, no indication is given of how many grades the user will enter. The program must process an arbitrary number of grades. How can the program determine when to stop the input of grades? How will it know when to calculate and display the class average?

One way to solve this problem is to use a special value called a *sentinel value* (also called a *signal value*, a *dummy value* or a *flag value*) to indicate the end of data entry. The user types in grades until all legitimate grades have been entered. Then the user types the sentinel value to indicate that the last grade has been entered.

Clearly, one must choose a sentinel value that cannot be confused with an acceptable input value. −1 is an acceptable sentinel value for this problem because grades on a quiz are normally nonnegative integers from 0 to 100. Thus, an execution of the class-average program might process a stream of inputs such as 95, 96, 75, 74, 89 and −1. The program would compute and print the class average for the grades 95, 96, 75, 74 and 89 (−1 is the sentinel value, so it should not enter into the average calculation).

Figure 5.6 shows the JavaScript program and a sample execution. Although each grade is an integer, the averaging calculation is likely to produce a number with a decimal point (a real number).

```
 1    <?xml version = "1.0" encoding = "utf-8"?>
 2    <!DOCTYPE html PUBLIC "-//W3C//DTD XHTML 1.0 Strict//EN"
 3       "http://www.w3.org/TR/xhtml1/DTD/xhtml1-strict.dtd">
 4
 5    <!-- Fig. 5.6: average2.html -->
 6    <!-- Sentinel-controlled repetition to calculate a class average. -->
 7    <html xmlns = "http://www.w3.org/1999/xhtml">
 8       <head>
 9          <title>Class Average Program: Sentinel-controlled Repetition</title>
10
11          <script type = "text/javascript">
12             <!--
13             var total; // sum of grades
14             var gradeCounter; // number of grades entered
15             var grade; // grade typed by user (as a string)
16             var gradeValue; // grade value (converted to integer)
17             var average; // average of all grades
18
19             // Initialization phase
20             total = 0; // clear total
21             gradeCounter = 0;  // prepare to loop
22
23             // Processing phase
24             // prompt for input and read grade from user
25             grade = window.prompt(
26                "Enter Integer Grade, -1 to Quit:", "0" );
27
28             // convert grade from a string to an integer
29             gradeValue = parseInt( grade );
30
31             while ( gradeValue != -1 )
32             {
```

Fig. 5.6 | Sentinel-controlled repetition to calculate a class average. (Part 1 of 2.)

```
33              // add gradeValue to total
34              total = total + gradeValue;
35
36              // add 1 to gradeCounter
37              gradeCounter = gradeCounter + 1;
38
39              // prompt for input and read grade from user
40              grade = window.prompt(
41                 "Enter Integer Grade, -1 to Quit:", "0" );
42
43              // convert grade from a string to an integer
44              gradeValue = parseInt( grade );
45           } // end while
46
47           // Termination phase
48           if ( gradeCounter != 0 )
49           {
50              average = total / gradeCounter;
51
52              // display average of exam grades
53              document.writeln(
54                 "<h1>Class average is " + average + "</h1>" );
55           } // end if
56           else
57              document.writeln( "<p>No grades were entered</p>" );
58           // -->
59        </script>
60     </head>
61     <body>
62        <p>Click Refresh (or Reload) to run the script again</p>
63     </body>
64  </html>
```

This dialog is displayed four times. User input is 97, 88, 72 and –1.

Explorer User Prompt

Script Prompt:

Enter Integer Grade, -1 to Quit:

OK

Cancel

97

Class Average Program: Sentinel-controlled Repetition - Windows Internet Ex...

C:\examples\ch05\average2.html   Google

Class Average Program: Sentinel-co...   Page ▾   Tools ▾

Class average is 85.66666666666667

Click Refresh (or Reload) to run the script again

Done   My Computer   100%

Fig. 5.6 | Sentinel-controlled repetition to calculate a class average. (Part 2 of 2.)

In this example, we see that control statements may be stacked on top of one another (in sequence). The `while` statement (lines 31–45) is followed immediately by an `if...else` statement (lines 48–57) in sequence. Much of the code in this program is identical to the code in Fig. 5.5, so we concentrate in this example on the new features.

Line 21 initializes `gradeCounter` to 0, because no grades have been entered yet. Remember that the program uses sentinel-controlled repetition. To keep an accurate record of the number of grades entered, the script increments `gradeCounter` only after processing a valid grade value.

Note the block in the `while` loop in Fig. 5.6 (lines 32–45). Without the braces, the last three statements in the body of the loop would fall outside of the loop, causing the computer to interpret the code incorrectly, as follows:

```
while ( gradeValue != -1 )
   // add gradeValue to total
   total = total + gradeValue;

// add 1 to gradeCounter
gradeCounter = gradeCounter + 1;

// prompt for input and read grade from user
grade = window.prompt(
   "Enter Integer Grade, -1 to Quit:", "0" );

// convert grade from a string to an integer
gradeValue = parseInt( grade );
```

This interpretation would cause an infinite loop in the program if the user does not enter the sentinel -1 as the first input value in lines 25–26 (i.e., before the `while` statement).

Common Programming Error 5.7

Omitting the braces that delineate a block can lead to logic errors such as infinite loops.

5.8 Formulating Algorithms: Nested Control Statements

Consider the following problem statement:

A college offers a course that prepares students for the state licensing exam for real estate brokers. Last year, several of the students who completed this course took the licensing exam. Naturally, the college wants to know how well its students performed. You have been asked to write a program to summarize the results. You have been given a list of these 10 students. Next to each name is written a 1 if the student passed the exam and a 2 if the student failed.

Your program should analyze the results of the exam as follows:

1. *Input each test result (i.e., a 1 or a 2). Display the message "Enter result" on the screen each time the program requests another test result.*

2. *Count the number of test results of each type.*

3. *Display a summary of the test results indicating the number of students who passed and the number of students who failed.*

4. *If more than eight students passed the exam, print the message "Raise tuition."*

After reading the problem statement carefully, we make the following observations about the problem:

1. The program must process test results for 10 students. A counter-controlled loop will be used.

2. Each test result is a number—either a 1 or a 2. Each time the program reads a test result, the program must determine whether the number is a 1 or a 2. We test for a 1 in our algorithm. If the number is not a 1, we assume that it is a 2.

3. Two counters are used to keep track of the exam results—one to count the number of students who passed the exam and one to count the number of students who failed the exam.

After the program processes all the results, it must decide whether more than eight students passed the exam. The JavaScript program and two sample executions are shown in Fig. 5.7.

```
 1   <?xml version = "1.0" encoding = "utf-8"?>
 2   <!DOCTYPE html PUBLIC "-//W3C//DTD XHTML 1.0 Strict//EN"
 3      "http://www.w3.org/TR/xhtml1/DTD/xhtml1-strict.dtd">
 4
 5   <!-- Fig. 5.7: analysis.html -->
 6   <!-- Examination-results calculation. -->
 7   <html xmlns = "http://www.w3.org/1999/xhtml">
 8      <head>
 9         <title>Analysis of Examination Results</title>
10         <script type = "text/javascript">
11            <!--
12            // initializing variables in declarations
13            var passes = 0; // number of passes
14            var failures = 0; // number of failures
15            var student = 1; // student counter
16            var result; // one exam result
17
18            // process 10 students; counter-controlled loop
19            while ( student <= 10 )
20            {
21               result = window.prompt( "Enter result (1=pass,2=fail)", "0" );
22
23               if ( result == "1" )
24                  passes = passes + 1;
25               else
26                  failures = failures + 1;
27
28               student = student + 1;
29            } // end while
30
31            // termination phase
32            document.writeln( "<h1>Examination Results</h1>" );
```

Fig. 5.7 | Examination-results calculation. (Part 1 of 2.)

```
33              document.writeln(
34                 "Passed: " + passes + "<br />Failed: " + failures );
35
36              if ( passes > 8 )
37                 document.writeln( "<br />Raise Tuition" );
38              // -->
39           </script>
40        </head>
41        <body>
42           <p>Click Refresh (or Reload) to run the script again</p>
43        </body>
44     </html>
```

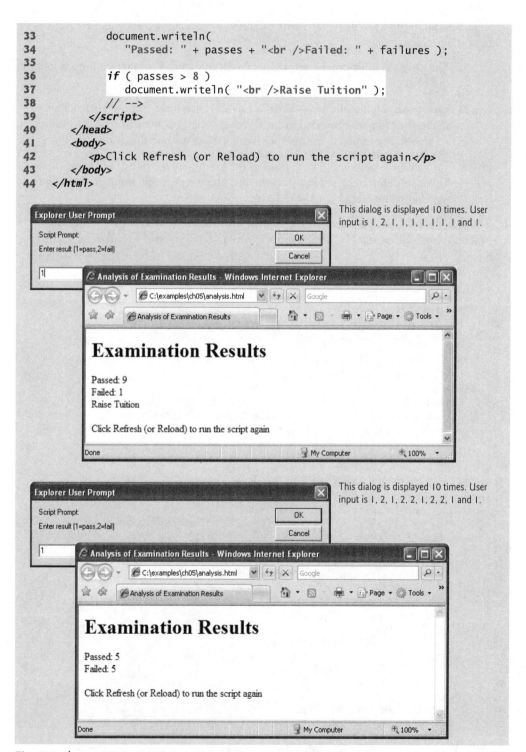

Fig. 5.7 | Examination-results calculation. (Part 2 of 2.)

Lines 13–16 declare the variables used to process the examination results. Note that JavaScript allows variable initialization to be incorporated into declarations (`passes` is assigned 0, `failures` is assigned 0 and `student` is assigned 1). Some programs may require reinitialization at the beginning of each repetition; such reinitialization would normally occur in assignment statements.

The processing of the exam results occurs in the `while` statement in lines 19–29. Note that the `if...else` statement in lines 23–26 in the loop tests only whether the exam result was 1; it assumes that all other exam results are 2. Normally, you should validate the values input by the user (i.e., determine whether the values are correct).

5.9 Assignment Operators

JavaScript provides several assignment operators (called *compound assignment operators*) for abbreviating assignment expressions. For example, the statement

```
c = c + 3;
```

can be abbreviated with the *addition assignment operator*, +=, as

```
c += 3;
```

The += operator adds the value of the expression on the right of the operator to the value of the variable on the left of the operator and stores the result in the variable on the left of the operator. Any statement of the form

variable = *variable operator expression*;

where *operator* is one of the binary operators +, -, *, / or % (or others we'll discuss later in the text), can be written in the form

variable operator = *expression*;

Thus, the assignment c += 3 adds 3 to c. Figure 5.8 shows the arithmetic assignment operators, sample expressions using these operators and explanations of the meaning of the operators.

Assignment operator	Initial value of variable	Sample expression	Explanation	Assigns
+=	c = 3	c += 7	c = c + 7	10 to c
-=	d = 5	d -= 4	d = d - 4	1 to d
*=	e = 4	e *= 5	e = e * 5	20 to e
/=	f = 6	f /= 3	f = f / 3	2 to f
%=	g = 12	g %= 9	g = g % 9	3 to g

Fig. 5.8 | Arithmetic assignment operators.

Performance Tip 5.1

Programmers can write programs that execute a bit faster when the arithmetic assignment operators are used, because the variable on the left side of the assignment does not have to be evaluated twice.

Performance Tip 5.2

Many of the performance tips we mention in this text result in only nominal improvements, so you may be tempted to ignore them. Significant performance improvement often is realized when a supposedly nominal improvement is placed in a loop that may repeat a large number of times.

5.10 Increment and Decrement Operators

JavaScript provides the unary *increment operator* (++) and *decrement operator* (--) (summarized in Fig. 5.9). If a variable c is incremented by 1, the increment operator, ++, can be used rather than the expression c = c + 1 or c += 1. If an increment or decrement operator is placed before a variable, it is referred to as the *preincrement* or *predecrement operator*, respectively. If an increment or decrement operator is placed after a variable, it is referred to as the *postincrement* or *postdecrement operator*, respectively.

Error-Prevention Tip 5.1

The predecrement and postdecrement JavaScript operators cause the W3C XHTML Validator to incorrectly report errors. The validator attempts to interpret the decrement operator as part of an XHTML comment tag (<!-- or -->). You can avoid this problem by using the subtraction assignment operator (-=) to subtract one from a variable. Note that the validator may report many more (nonexistent) errors once it improperly parses the decrement operator.

Preincrementing (or predecrementing) a variable causes the program to increment (decrement) the variable by 1, then use the new value of the variable in the expression in which it appears. Postincrementing (postdecrementing) the variable causes the program to use the current value of the variable in the expression in which it appears, then increment (decrement) the variable by 1.

Operator	Example	Called	Explanation
++	++a	preincrement	Increment a by 1, then use the new value of a in the expression in which a resides.
++	a++	postincrement	Use the current value of a in the expression in which a resides, then increment a by 1.
--	--b	predecrement	Decrement b by 1, then use the new value of b in the expression in which b resides.
--	b--	postdecrement	Use the current value of b in the expression in which b resides, then decrement b by 1.

Fig. 5.9 | Increment and decrement operators.

The script in Fig. 5.10 demonstrates the difference between the preincrementing version and the postincrementing version of the ++ increment operator. Postincrementing the variable c causes it to be incremented after it is used in the document.writeln method call (line 18). Preincrementing the variable c causes it to be incremented before it is used in the document.writeln method call (line 25). The program displays the value of c before and after the ++ operator is used. The decrement operator (--) works similarly.

 Good Programming Practice 5.3

For readability, unary operators should be placed next to their operands, with no intervening spaces.

The three assignment statements in Fig. 5.7 (lines 24, 26 and 28, respectively),

```
passes = passes + 1;
failures = failures + 1;
student = student + 1;
```

can be written more concisely with assignment operators as

```
passes += 1;
failures += 1;
student += 1;
```

```
1   <?xml version = "1.0" encoding = "utf-8"?>
2   <!DOCTYPE html PUBLIC "-//W3C//DTD XHTML 1.0 Strict//EN"
3      "http://www.w3.org/TR/xhtml1/DTD/xhtml1-strict.dtd">
4
5   <!-- Fig. 5.10: increment.html -->
6   <!-- Preincrementing and Postincrementing. -->
7   <html xmlns = "http://www.w3.org/1999/xhtml">
8      <head>
9         <title>Preincrementing and Postincrementing</title>
10        <script type = "text/javascript">
11           <!--
12           var c;
13
14           c = 5;
15           document.writeln( "<h3>Postincrementing</h3>" );
16           document.writeln( c ); // prints 5
17           // prints 5 then increments
18           document.writeln( "<br />" + c++ );
19           document.writeln( "<br />" + c ); // prints 6
20
21           c = 5;
22           document.writeln( "<h3>Preincrementing</h3>" );
23           document.writeln( c ); // prints 5
24           // increments then prints 6
25           document.writeln( "<br />" + ++c );
26           document.writeln( "<br />" + c ); // prints 6
27           // -->
28        </script>
29     </head><body></body>
30  </html>
```

Fig. 5.10 | Preincrementing and postincrementing. (Part 1 of 2.)

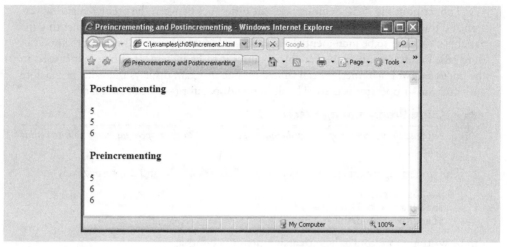

Fig. 5.10 | Preincrementing and postincrementing. (Part 2 of 2.)

with preincrement operators as

```
++passes;
++failures;
++student;
```

or with postincrement operators as

```
passes++;
failures++;
student++;
```

It is important to note here that when incrementing or decrementing a variable in a statement by itself, the preincrement and postincrement forms have the same effect, and the predecrement and postdecrement forms have the same effect. It is only when a variable appears in the context of a larger expression that preincrementing the variable and postincrementing the variable have different effects. Predecrementing and postdecrementing behave similarly.

Common Programming Error 5.8

*Attempting to use the increment or decrement operator on an expression other than a **left-hand-side expression**—commonly called an **lvalue**—is a syntax error. A left-hand-side expression is a variable or expression that can appear on the left side of an assignment operation. For example, writing ++(x + 1) is a syntax error, because (x + 1) is not a left-hand-side expression.*

Figure 5.11 lists the precedence and associativity of the operators introduced to this point. The operators are shown top to bottom in decreasing order of precedence. The second column describes the associativity of the operators at each level of precedence. Notice that the conditional operator (?:), the unary operators increment (++) and decrement (--) and the assignment operators =, +=, -=, *=, /= and %= associate from right to left. All other operators in the operator precedence table (Fig. 5.11) associate from left to right. The third column names the groups of operators.

Operator	Associativity	Type
++ --	right to left	unary
* / %	left to right	multiplicative
+ -	left to right	additive
< <= > >=	left to right	relational
== !=	left to right	equality
?:	right to left	conditional
= += -= *= /= %=	right to left	assignment

Fig. 5.11 | Precedence and associativity of the operators discussed so far.

5.11 Web Resources

www.deitel.com/javascript/

The Deitel JavaScript Resource Center contains links to some of the best JavaScript resources on the web. There you'll find categorized links to JavaScript tools, code generators, forums, books, libraries, frameworks and more. Also check out the tutorials for all skill levels, from introductory to advanced. Be sure to visit the related Resource Centers on XHTML (www.deitel.com/xhtml/) and CSS 2.1 (www.deitel.com/css21/).

6

JavaScript: Control Statements II

OBJECTIVES

In this chapter you will learn:

- The essentials of counter-controlled repetition

- To use the for and do...while repetition statements to execute statements in a program repeatedly.

- To perform multiple selection using the switch selection statement.

- To use the break and continue program-control statements

- To use the logical operators.

Not everything that can be counted counts, and not every thing that counts can be counted.
—Albert Einstein

Who can control his fate?
—William Shakespeare

The used key is always bright.
—Benjamin Franklin

Intelligence ... is the faculty of making artificial objects, especially tools to make tools.
—Henri Bergson

Every advantage in the past is judged in the light of the final issue.
—Demosthenes

6.1 Introduction

Chapter 5 began our introduction to the types of building blocks that are available for problem solving and used them to employ proven program-construction principles. In this chapter, we introduce JavaScript's remaining control statements (with the exception of for...in, which is presented in Chapter 8). As in Chapter 5, the JavaScript techniques you will learn here are applicable to most high-level languages. In later chapters, you'll see that control structures are helpful in manipulating objects.

6.2 Essentials of Counter-Controlled Repetition

Counter-controlled repetition requires:

1. The *name* of a control variable (or loop counter).

2. The *initial value* of the control variable.

3. The *increment* (or *decrement*) by which the control variable is modified each time through the loop (also known as *each iteration of the loop*).

4. The condition that tests for the *final value* of the control variable to determine whether looping should continue.

To see the four elements of counter-controlled repetition, consider the simple script shown in Fig. 6.1, which displays lines of XHTML text that illustrate the seven different font sizes supported by XHTML. The declaration in line 12 *names* the control variable (counter), reserves space for it in memory and sets it to an *initial value* of 1. The declaration and initialization of counter could also have been accomplished by the following declaration and assignment statement:

```
var counter; // declare counter
counter = 1; // initialize counter to 1
```

```
1  <?xml version = "1.0" encoding = "utf-8"?>
2  <!DOCTYPE html PUBLIC "-//W3C//DTD XHTML 1.0 Strict//EN"
3     "http://www.w3.org/TR/xhtml1/DTD/xhtml1-strict.dtd">
4
```

Fig. 6.1 | Counter-controlled repetition. (Part 1 of 2.)

```
5   <!-- Fig. 6.1: WhileCounter.html -->
6   <!-- Counter-controlled repetition. -->
7   <html xmlns = "http://www.w3.org/1999/xhtml">
8      <head>
9         <title>Counter-Controlled Repetition</title>
10        <script type = "text/javascript">
11           <!--
12           var counter = 1; // initialization
13
14           while ( counter <= 7 ) // repetition condition
15           {
16              document.writeln( "<p style = \"font-size: " +
17                 counter + "ex\">XHTML font size " + counter +
18                 "ex</p>" );
19              ++counter; // increment
20           } //end while
21           // -->
22        </script>
23     </head><body></body>
24  </html>
```

Fig. 6.1 | Counter-controlled repetition. (Part 2 of 2.)

Lines 16–18 in the while statement write a paragraph element consisting of the string "XHTML font size" concatenated with the control variable counter's value, which represents the font size. An inline CSS style attribute sets the font-size property to the value of counter concatenated to ex. Note the use of the escape sequence \", which is placed around attribute style's value. Because the double-quote character delimits the beginning and end of a string literal in JavaScript, it cannot be used in the contents of the string unless it is preceded by a \ to create the escape sequence \". For example, if counter is 5, the preceding statement produces the markup

```
<p style = "font-size: 5ex">XHTML font size 5ex</p>
```

XHTML allows either single quotes (') or double quotes (") to be placed around the value specified for an attribute. JavaScript allows single quotes to be placed in a string literal. Thus, we could have placed single quotes around the font-size property to produce equivalent XHTML output without the use of escape sequences.

Common Programming Error 6.1

Placing a double-quote (") character inside a string literal that is delimited by double quotes causes a runtime error when the script is interpreted. To be displayed as part of a string literal, a double-quote (") character must be preceded by a \ to form the escape sequence \".

Line 19 in the while statement *increments* the control variable by 1 for each iteration of the loop (i.e., each time the body of the loop is performed). The loop-continuation condition (line 14) in the while statement tests whether the value of the control variable is less than or equal to 7 (the *final value* for which the condition is true). Note that the body of this while statement executes even when the control variable is 7. The loop terminates when the control variable exceeds 7 (i.e., counter becomes 8).

Good Programming Practice 6.1

Indent the statements in the body of each control structure.

Good Programming Practice 6.2

Put a blank line before and after each control structure, to make it stand out in the program.

Good Programming Practice 6.3

Too many levels of nesting can make a program difficult to understand. As a general rule, try to avoid using more than three levels of nesting.

Good Programming Practice 6.4

Vertical spacing above and below control structures and indentation of the bodies of control structures in the headers of the control structure give programs a two-dimensional appearance that enhances readability.

6.3 for Repetition Statement

The *for repetition statement* handles all the details of counter-controlled repetition. Figure 6.2 illustrates the power of the for statement by reimplementing the script of Fig. 6.1.

```
1   <?xml version = "1.0" encoding = "utf-8"?>
2   <!DOCTYPE html PUBLIC "-//W3C//DTD XHTML 1.0 Strict//EN"
3      "http://www.w3.org/TR/xhtml1/DTD/xhtml1-strict.dtd">
4
5   <!-- Fig. 6.2: ForCounter.html -->
6   <!-- Counter-controlled repetition with the for statement. -->
7   <html xmlns = "http://www.w3.org/1999/xhtml">
8      <head>
```

Fig. 6.2 | Counter-controlled repetition with the for statement. (Part 1 of 2.)

```
 9          <title>Counter-Controlled Repetition</title>
10          <script type = "text/javascript">
11             <!--
12             // Initialization, repetition condition and
13             // incrementing are all included in the for
14             // statement header.
15             for ( var counter = 1; counter <= 7; ++counter )
16                document.writeln( "<p style = \"font-size: " +
17                   counter + "ex\">XHTML font size " + counter +
18                   "ex</p>" );
19             // -->
20          </script>
21       </head><body></body>
22    </html>
```

Fig. 6.2 | Counter-controlled repetition with the for statement. (Part 2 of 2.)

When the for statement begins executing (line 15), the control variable counter is declared and is initialized to 1 (i.e., the first statement of the for statement declares the control variable's *name* and provides the control variable's *initial value*). Next, the loop-continuation condition, counter <= 7, is checked. The condition contains the *final value* (7) of the control variable. The initial value of counter is 1. Therefore, the condition is satisfied (i.e., true), so the body statement (lines 16–18) writes a paragraph element in the XHTML document. Then, variable counter is incremented in the expression ++counter and the loop continues execution with the loop-continuation test. The control variable is now equal to 2, so the final value is not exceeded and the program performs the body statement again (i.e., performs the next iteration of the loop). This process continues until the control variable counter becomes 8, at which point the loop-continuation test fails and the repetition terminates.

The program continues by performing the first statement after the for statement. (In this case, the script terminates, because the interpreter reaches the end of the script.)

Figure 6.3 takes a closer look at the for statement at line 15 of Fig. 6.2. The for statement's first line (including the keyword for and everything in parentheses after for) is often called the ***for statement header***. Note that the for statement "does it all"—it specifies each of the items needed for counter-controlled repetition with a control variable.

Note that Fig. 6.3 uses the loop-continuation condition counter <= 7. If you incorrectly write counter < 7, the loop will execute only six times. This is an example of the common logic error called an *off-by-one error.*

Common Programming Error 6.2

Using an incorrect relational operator or an incorrect final value of a loop counter in the condition of a while, for or do...while statement can cause an off-by-one error or an infinite loop.

Error-Prevention Tip 6.1

*Using the final value in the condition of a while or for statement and using the <= relational operator will help avoid off-by-one errors. For a loop used to print the values 1 to 10, for example, the initial value of counter should be 1, and the loop-continuation condition should be counter <= 10 rather than counter < 10 (which is an off-by-one error) or counter < 11 (which is correct). Many programmers, however, prefer so-called **zero-based counting**, in which, to count 10 times through the loop, counter would be initialized to zero and the loop-continuation test would be counter < 10.*

The general format of the for statement is

> ***for*** (*initialization*; *loopContinuationTest*; *increment*)
>   *statements*

where the *initialization* expression names the loop's control variable and provides its initial value, *loopContinuationTest* is the expression that tests the loop-continuation condition (containing the final value of the control variable for which the condition is true), and *increment* is an expression that increments the control variable. The for statement can be represented by an equivalent while statement, with *initialization, loopContinuationTest* and *increment* placed as follows (Section 6.7 discusses an exception to this rule):

> *initialization*;
>
> ***while*** (*loopContinuationTest*)
> {
>   *statements*
>   *increment*;
> }

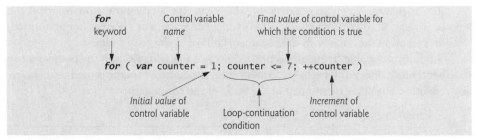

Fig. 6.3 | for statement header components.

If the *initialization* expression in the `for` statement's header is the first definition of the control variable, the control variable can still be used after the `for` statement in the script. The part of a script in which a variable name can be used is known as the variable's *scope*. Scope is discussed in detail in Chapter 7, JavaScript: Functions.

Good Programming Practice 6.5

Place only expressions involving the control variable in the initialization and increment sections of a `for` statement. Manipulations of other variables should appear either before the loop (if they execute only once, like initialization statements) or in the loop body (if they execute once per iteration of the loop, like incrementing or decrementing statements).

The three expressions in the `for` statement are optional. If *loopContinuationTest* is omitted, JavaScript assumes that the loop-continuation condition is `true`, thus creating an infinite loop. One might omit the *initialization* expression if the control variable is initialized before the loop. One might omit the *increment* expression if the increment is calculated by statements in the body of the `for` statement or if no increment is needed. The increment expression in the `for` statement acts like a stand-alone statement at the end of the body of the `for` statement. Therefore, the expressions

```
counter = counter + 1
counter += 1
++counter
counter++
```

are all equivalent in the incrementing portion of the `for` statement. Many programmers prefer the form `counter++`. This is because the incrementing of the control variable occurs after the body of the loop is executed, and therefore the postincrementing form seems more natural. Preincrementing and postincrementing both have the same effect in our example, because the variable being incremented does not appear in a larger expression. The two semicolons in the `for` statement header are required.

Common Programming Error 6.3

Using commas instead of the two required semicolons in the header of a `for` statement is a syntax error.

Common Programming Error 6.4

Placing a semicolon immediately to the right of the right parenthesis of the header of a `for` statement makes the body of that `for` statement an empty statement. This code is normally a logic error.

The "increment" may be negative, in which case the loop counts downward. If the loop-continuation condition initially is `false`, the `for` statement's body is not performed. Instead, execution proceeds with the statement following the `for` statement.

The control variable frequently is printed or used in calculations in the body of a `for` statement, but it does not have to be. Other times, the control variable is used for controlling repetition but never mentioned in the body of the `for` statement.

Error-Prevention Tip 6.2

Although the value of the control variable can be changed in the body of a `for` statement, avoid changing it, because doing so can lead to subtle errors.

The for statement is flowcharted much like the while statement. For example, Fig. 6.4 shows the flowchart of the for statement

```
for ( var counter = 1; counter <= 7; ++counter )
    document.writeln( "<p style = \"font-size: " +
        counter + "ex\">XHTML font size " + counter +
        "ex</p>" );
```

This flowchart makes it clear that the initialization occurs only once and that incrementing occurs *after* each execution of the body statement. Note that, besides small circles and arrows, the flowchart contains only rectangle symbols and a diamond symbol.

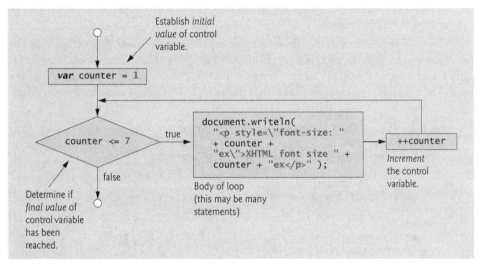

Fig. 6.4 | for repetition statement flowchart.

6.4 Examples Using the for Statement

The examples in this section show methods of varying the control variable in a for statement. In each case, we write the appropriate for header. Note the change in the relational operator for loops that decrement the control variable.

a) Vary the control variable from 1 to 100 in increments of 1.

```
for ( var i = 1; i <= 100; ++i )
```

b) Vary the control variable from 100 to 1 in increments of -1 (i.e., decrements of 1).

```
for ( var i = 100; i >= 1; --i )
```

c) Vary the control variable from 7 to 77 in steps of 7.

```
for ( var i = 7; i <= 77; i += 7 )
```

d) Vary the control variable from 20 to 2 in steps of -2.

```
for ( var i = 20; i >= 2; i -= 2 )
```

e) Vary the control variable over the following sequence of values: 2, 5, 8, 11, 14, 17, 20.

```
for ( var j = 2; j <= 20; j += 3 )
```

f) Vary the control variable over the following sequence of values: 99, 88, 77, 66, 55, 44, 33, 22, 11, 0.

```
for ( var j = 99; j >= 0; j -= 11 )
```

 Common Programming Error 6.5

Not using the proper relational operator in the loop-continuation condition of a loop that counts downward (e.g., using i <= 1 *in a loop that counts down to 1) is usually a logic error that will yield incorrect results when the program runs.*

The next two scripts demonstrate the for repetition statement. Figure 6.5 uses the for statement to sum the even integers from 2 to 100. Note that the increment expression adds 2 to the control variable number after the body executes during each iteration of the loop. The loop terminates when number has the value 102 (which is not added to the sum).

```xml
1   <?xml version = "1.0" encoding = "utf-8"?>
2   <!DOCTYPE html PUBLIC "-//W3C//DTD XHTML 1.0 Strict//EN"
3      "http://www.w3.org/TR/xhtml1/DTD/xhtml1-strict.dtd">
4
5   <!-- Fig. 6.5: Sum.html -->
6   <!-- Summation with the for repetition structure. -->
7   <html xmlns = "http://www.w3.org/1999/xhtml">
8      <head>
9         <title>Sum the Even Integers from 2 to 100</title>
10        <script type = "text/javascript">
11           <!--
12           var sum = 0;
13
14           for ( var number = 2; number <= 100; number += 2 )
15              sum += number;
16
17           document.writeln( "The sum of the even integers " +
18              "from 2 to 100 is " + sum );
19           // -->
20        </script>
21     </head><body></body>
22  </html>
```

Sum the Even Integers from 2 to 100 - Windows Internet Explorer

C:\examples\ch06\Sum.html   Google

Sum the Even Integers from 2 ...   Page ▾ Tools ▾

The sum of the even integers from 2 to 100 is 2550

My Computer   100%

Fig. 6.5 | Summation with the for repetition structure.

Note that the body of the for statement in Fig. 6.5 actually could be merged into the rightmost (increment) portion of the for header by using a comma, as follows:

```
for ( var number = 2; number <= 100; sum += number, number += 2)
   ;
```

Similarly, the initialization sum = 0 could be merged into the initialization section of the for statement.

Good Programming Practice 6.6

Although statements preceding a for statement and in the body of a for statement can often be merged into the for header, avoid doing so, because it makes the program more difficult to read.

Good Programming Practice 6.7

For clarity, limit the size of control-statement headers to a single line, if possible.

The next example computes compound interest (compounded yearly) using the for statement. Consider the following problem statement:

A person invests $1000.00 in a savings account yielding 5 percent interest. Assuming that all the interest is left on deposit, calculate and print the amount of money in the account at the end of each year for 10 years. Use the following formula to determine the amounts:

$$a = p (1 + r)^{n}$$

where

> *p is the original amount invested (i.e., the principal)*
> *r is the annual interest rate*
> *n is the number of years*
> *a is the amount on deposit at the end of the nth year.*

This problem involves a loop that performs the indicated calculation for each of the 10 years the money remains on deposit. Figure 6.6 presents the solution to this problem, displaying the results in a table.

```
1   <?xml version = "1.0" encoding = "utf-8"?>
2   <!DOCTYPE html PUBLIC "-//W3C//DTD XHTML 1.0 Strict//EN"
3      "http://www.w3.org/TR/xhtml1/DTD/xhtml1-strict.dtd">
4
5   <!-- Fig. 6.6: Interest.html -->
6   <!-- Compound interest calculation with a for loop. -->
7   <html xmlns = "http://www.w3.org/1999/xhtml">
8      <head>
9         <title>Calculating Compound Interest</title>
10        <style type = "text/css">
11           table { width: 100% }
12           th    { text-align: left }
13        </style>
```

Fig. 6.6 | Compound interest calculation with a for loop. (Part 1 of 2.)

```
14        <script type = "text/javascript">
15           <!--
16           var amount; // current amount of money
17           var principal = 1000.0; // principal amount
18           var rate = .05; // interest rate
19
20           document.writeln(
21              "<table border = \"1\">" ); // begin the table
22           document.writeln(
23              "<caption>Calculating Compound Interest</caption>" );
24           document.writeln(
25              "<thead><tr><th>Year</th>" ); // year column heading
26           document.writeln(
27              "<th>Amount on deposit</th>" ); // amount column heading
28           document.writeln( "</tr></thead><tbody>" );
29
30           // output a table row for each year
31           for ( var year = 1; year <= 10; ++year )
32           {
33              amount = principal * Math.pow( 1.0 + rate, year );
34              document.writeln( "<tr><td>" + year +
35                 "</td><td>" + amount.toFixed(2) +
36                 "</td></tr>" );
37           } //end for
38
39           document.writeln( "</tbody></table>" );
40           // -->
41        </script>
42     </head><body></body>
43  </html>
```

Fig. 6.6 | Compound interest calculation with a for loop. (Part 2 of 2.)

Lines 16–18 declare three variables and initialize principal to 1000.0 and rate to .05. Lines 20–21 write an XHTML <table> tag, and lines 22–23 write the caption that summarizes the table's content. Lines 24–25 create the table's header section (<thead>), a row (<tr>) and a column heading (<th>) containing "Year." Lines 26–28 create a table heading for "Amount on deposit" and write the closing </tr> and </thead> tags.

The for statement (lines 31–37) executes its body 10 times, incrementing control variable year from 1 to 10 (note that year represents *n* in the problem statement). Java-Script does not include an exponentiation operator. Instead, we use the Math object's pow method for this purpose. Math.pow(x, y) calculates the value of x raised to the yth power. Method Math.pow takes two numbers as arguments and returns the result.

Line 33 performs the calculation using the formula given in the problem statement. Lines 34–36 write a line of XHTML markup that creates another row in the table. The first column is the current year value. The second column displays the value of amount. Line 39 writes the closing </tbody> and </table> tags after the loop terminates.

Line 35 introduces the ***Number object*** and its ***toFixed method***. The variable amount contains a numerical value, so JavaScript represents it as a Number object. The toFixed method of a Number object formats the value by rounding it to the specified number of decimal places. In line 35, amount.toFixed(2) outputs the value of amount with two decimal places.

Variables amount, principal and rate represent numbers in this script. Remember that JavaScript represents all numbers as floating-point numbers. This feature is convenient in this example, because we are dealing with fractional parts of dollars and need a type that allows decimal points in its values.

Unfortunately, floating-point numbers can cause trouble. Here is a simple example of what can go wrong when using floating-point numbers to represent dollar amounts (assuming that dollar amounts are displayed with two digits to the right of the decimal point): Two dollar amounts stored in the machine could be 14.234 (which would normally be rounded to 14.23 for display purposes) and 18.673 (which would normally be rounded to 18.67 for display purposes). When these amounts are added, they produce the internal sum 32.907, which would normally be rounded to 32.91 for display purposes. Thus your printout could appear as

```
  14.23
+ 18.67
  ─────
  32.91
```

but a person adding the individual numbers as printed would expect the sum to be 32.90. You have been warned!

6.5 switch Multiple-Selection Statement

Occasionally, an algorithm will contain a series of decisions in which a variable or expression is tested separately for each of the values it may assume, and different actions are taken for each value. JavaScript provides the switch multiple-selection statement to handle such decision making. The script in Fig. 6.7 demonstrates three different CSS list formats determined by the value the user enters.

Line 12 in the script declares the variable choice. This variable stores the user's choice, which determines what type of XHTML list to display. Lines 13–14 declare variables `startTag` and `endTag`, which will store the XHTML tags that will be used to create the list element. Line 15 declares variable `validInput` and initializes it to `true`. The script uses this variable to determine whether the user made a valid choice (indicated by the value of `true`). If a choice is invalid, the script sets `validInput` to `false`. Line 16 declares variable `listType`, which will store an `h1` element indicating the list type. This heading appears before the list in the XHTML document.

```
1   <?xml version = "1.0" encoding = "utf-8"?>
2   <!DOCTYPE html PUBLIC "-//W3C//DTD XHTML 1.0 Strict//EN"
3       "http://www.w3.org/TR/xhtml1/DTD/xhtml1-strict.dtd">
4
5   <!-- Fig. 6.7: SwitchTest.html -->
6   <!-- Using the switch multiple-selection statement. -->
7   <html xmlns = "http://www.w3.org/1999/xhtml">
8       <head>
9           <title>Switching between XHTML List Formats</title>
10          <script type = "text/javascript">
11              <!--
12              var choice; // user's choice
13              var startTag; // starting list item tag
14              var endTag; // ending list item tag
15              var validInput = true; // indicates if input is valid
16              var listType; // type of list as a string
17
18              choice = window.prompt( "Select a list style:\n" +
19                  "1 (numbered), 2 (lettered), 3 (roman)", "1" );
20
21              switch ( choice )
22              {
23                  case "1":
24                      startTag = "<ol>";
25                      endTag = "</ol>";
26                      listType = "<h1>Numbered List</h1>";
27                      break;
28                  case "2":
29                      startTag = "<ol style = \"list-style-type: upper-alpha\">";
30                      endTag = "</ol>";
31                      listType = "<h1>Lettered List</h1>";
32                      break;
33                  case "3":
34                      startTag = "<ol style = \"list-style-type: upper-roman\">";
35                      endTag = "</ol>";
36                      listType = "<h1>Roman Numbered List</h1>";
37                      break;
38                  default:
39                      validInput = false;
40              } //end switch
41
42              if ( validInput == true )
43              {
44                  document.writeln( listType + startTag );
```

Fig. 6.7 | Using the `switch` multiple-selection statement. (Part 1 of 3.)

```
45
46              for ( var i = 1; i <= 3; ++i )
47                 document.writeln( "<li>List item " + i + "</li>" );
48
49              document.writeln( endTag );
50           } //end if
51           else
52              document.writeln( "Invalid choice: " + choice );
53           // -->
54        </script>
55     </head>
56     <body>
57        <p>Click Refresh (or Reload) to run the script again</p>
58     </body>
59  </html>
```

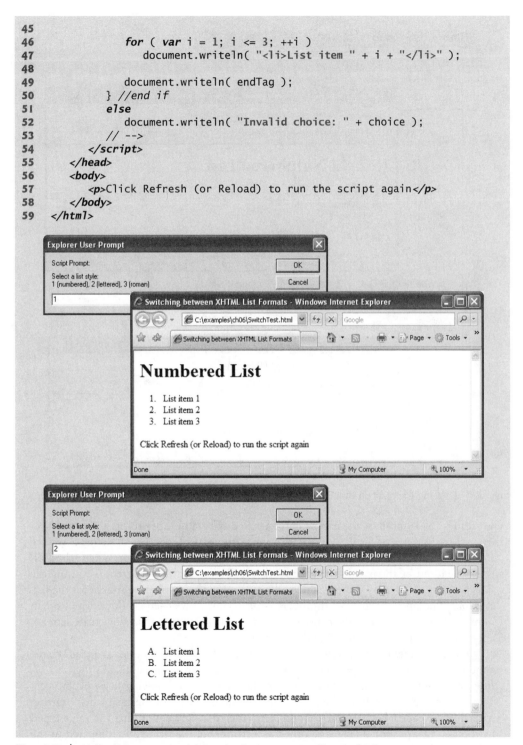

Fig. 6.7 | Using the switch multiple-selection statement. (Part 2 of 3.)

Fig. 6.7 | Using the switch multiple-selection statement. (Part 3 of 3.)

Lines 18–19 prompt the user to enter a 1 to display a numbered list, a 2 to display a lettered list and a 3 to display a list with roman numerals. Lines 21–40 define a *switch statement* that assigns to the variables startTag, endTag and listType values based on the value input by the user in the prompt dialog. We create these different lists using the CSS property *list-style-type*, which allows us to set the numbering system for the list. Possible values include decimal (numbers—the default), lower-roman (lowercase Roman numerals), upper-roman (uppercase Roman numerals), lower-alpha (lowercase letters), upper-alpha (uppercase letters), and several others.

The switch statement consists of a series of *case labels* and an optional *default case*. When the flow of control reaches the switch statement, the script evaluates the *controlling expression* (choice in this example) in the parentheses following keyword switch. The value of this expression is compared with the value in each of the case labels, starting with the first case label. Assume that the user entered 2. Remember that the value typed by the user in a prompt dialog is returned as a string. So, the string 2 is compared to the string in each case in the switch statement. If a match occurs (case "2":), the statements for that case execute. For the string 2 (lines 29–32), we set startTag to an opening ol tag with the style property list-style-type set to upper-alpha, set endTag to "</ol>" to indicate the end of an ordered list and set listType to "<h1>Lettered List</h1>". If no match occurs between the controlling expression's value and a case label, the default case executes and sets variable validInput to false.

The break statement in line 32 causes program control to proceed with the first statement after the switch statement. The break statement is used because the cases in a switch statement would otherwise run together. If break is not used anywhere in a switch statement, then each time a match occurs in the statement, the statements for all the remaining cases execute.

Next, the flow of control continues with the if statement in line 42, which tests variable validInput to determine whether its value is true. If so, lines 44–49 write the listType, the startTag, three list items (<li>) and the endTag. Otherwise, the script writes text in the XHTML document indicating that an invalid choice was made (line 52).

Each case can have multiple actions (statements). The switch statement is different from others in that braces are not required around multiple actions in a case of a switch. The general switch statement (i.e., using a break in each case) is flowcharted in Fig. 6.8. [*Note:* As an exercise, flowchart the general switch statement without break statements.]

The flowchart makes it clear that each break statement at the end of a case causes control to exit from the switch statement immediately. The break statement is not required for the last case in the switch statement (or the default case, when it appears last), because program control automatically continues with the next statement after the switch statement.

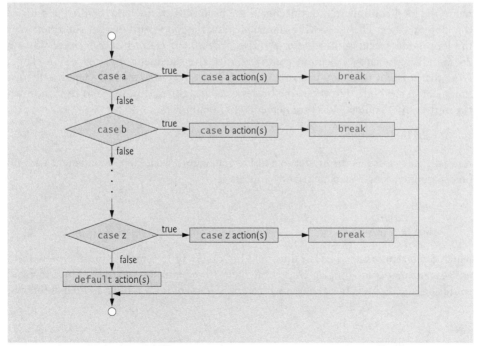

Fig. 6.8 | switch multiple-selection statement.

Common Programming Error 6.6

Forgetting a break statement when one is needed in a switch statement is a logic error.

Software Engineering Observation 6.1

Provide a default case in switch statements. Cases not explicitly tested in a switch statement without a default case are ignored. Including a default case focuses you on processing exceptional conditions. However, there are situations in which no default processing is needed.

Good Programming Practice 6.8

Although the case clauses and the default case clause in a switch statement can occur in any order, it is clearer (and more common) to place the default clause last.

Good Programming Practice 6.9

In a switch statement, when the default clause is listed last, the break for that case statement is not required. Some programmers include this break for clarity and for symmetry with other cases.

Note that having several case labels listed together (e.g., case 1: case 2: with no statements between the cases) simply means that the same set of actions is to occur for each case.

6.6 do...while Repetition Statement

The *do...while repetition statement* is similar to the while statement. In the while statement, the loop-continuation test occurs at the beginning of the loop, before the body of the loop executes. The do...while statement tests the loop-continuation condition *after* the loop body executes—therefore, *the loop body always executes at least once.* When a do...while terminates, execution continues with the statement after the while clause. Note that it is not necessary to use braces in a do...while statement if there is only one statement in the body. However, the braces usually are included, to avoid confusion between the while and do...while statements. For example,

> ***while*** (*condition*)

normally is regarded as the header to a while statement. A do...while statement with no braces around a single-statement body appears as

> ***do***
>   *statement*
> ***while*** (*condition*);

which can be confusing. The last line—while(*condition*);—may be misinterpreted as a while statement containing an empty statement (the semicolon by itself). Thus, to avoid confusion, the do...while statement with a one-statement body is often written as follows:

> ***do***
> {
>   *statement*
> } ***while*** (*condition*);

Good Programming Practice 6.10

Some programmers always include braces in a do...while statement even if they are not necessary. This helps eliminate ambiguity between the while statement and the do...while statement containing a one-statement body.

Error-Prevention Tip 6.3

Infinite loops are caused when the loop-continuation condition never becomes false *in a* while, *for or* do...while *statement. To prevent this, make sure that there is not a semicolon immediately after the header of a* while *or* for *statement. In a counter-controlled loop, make sure that the control variable is incremented (or decremented) in the body of the loop. In a sentinel-controlled loop, make sure that the sentinel value is eventually input.*

The script in Fig. 6.9 uses a do...while statement to display each of the six different XHTML heading types (h1 through h6). Line 12 declares control variable counter and initializes it to 1. Upon entering the do...while statement, lines 15–17 write a line of XHTML text in the document. The value of control variable counter is used to create the starting and ending header tags (e.g., <h1> and </h1>) and to create the line of text to display (e.g., This is an h1 level head). Line 18 increments the counter before the loop-continuation test occurs at the bottom of the loop.

The do...while flowchart in Fig. 6.10 makes it clear that the loop-continuation test does not occur until the action executes at least once.

```
1   <?xml version = "1.0" encoding = "utf-8"?>
2   <!DOCTYPE html PUBLIC "-//W3C//DTD XHTML 1.0 Strict//EN"
3       "http://www.w3.org/TR/xhtml1/DTD/xhtml1-strict.dtd">
4
5   <!-- Fig. 6.9: DoWhileTest.html -->
6   <!-- Using the do...while repetition statement. -->
7   <html xmlns = "http://www.w3.org/1999/xhtml">
8       <head>
9           <title>Using the do...while Repetition Statement</title>
10          <script type = "text/javascript">
11              <!--
12              var counter = 1;
13
14              do {
15                  document.writeln( "<h" + counter + ">This is " +
16                      "an h" + counter + " level head" + "</h" +
17                      counter + ">" );
18                  ++counter;
19              } while ( counter <= 6 );
20              // -->
21          </script>
22
23      </head><body></body>
24  </html>
```

Fig. 6.9 | Using the do...while repetition statement. (Part 1 of 2.)

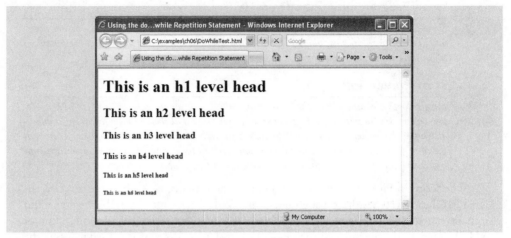

Fig. 6.9 | Using the do...while repetition statement. (Part 2 of 2.)

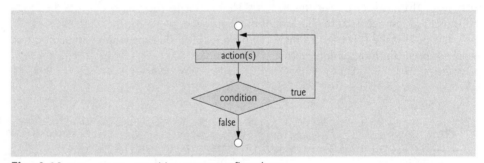

Fig. 6.10 | do...while repetition statement flowchart.

6.7 break and continue Statements

The *break* and *continue statements* alter the flow of control. The break statement, when executed in a while, for, do...while or switch statement, causes immediate exit from the statement. Execution continues with the first statement after the structure. The break statement is commonly used to escape early from a loop or to skip the remainder of a switch statement (as in Fig. 6.7). Figure 6.11 demonstrates the break statement in a for repetition statement.

During each iteration of the for statement in lines 14–20, the script writes the value of count in the XHTML document. When the if statement in line 16 detects that count is 5, the break in line 17 executes. This statement terminates the for statement, and the program proceeds to line 22 (the next statement in sequence immediately after the for statement), where the script writes the value of count when the loop terminated (i.e., 5). The loop executes line 19 only four times.

The continue statement, when executed in a while, for or do...while statement, skips the remaining statements in the body of the statement and proceeds with the next iteration of the loop. In while and do...while statements, the loop-continuation test evaluates immediately after the continue statement executes. In for statements, the increment expression executes, then the loop-continuation test evaluates. This is the one case in

```
 1  <?xml version = "1.0" encoding = "utf-8"?>
 2  <!DOCTYPE html PUBLIC "-//W3C//DTD XHTML 1.0 Strict//EN"
 3     "http://www.w3.org/TR/xhtml1/DTD/xhtml1-strict.dtd">
 4
 5  <!-- Fig. 6.11: BreakTest.html -->
 6  <!-- Using the break statement in a for statement. -->
 7  <html xmlns = "http://www.w3.org/1999/xhtml">
 8     <head>
 9        <title>
10           Using the break Statement in a for Statement
11        </title>
12        <script type = "text/javascript">
13           <!--
14           for ( var count = 1; count <= 10; ++count )
15           {
16              if ( count == 5 )
17                 break; // break loop only if count == 5
18
19              document.writeln( "Count is: " + count + "<br />" );
20           } //end for
21
22           document.writeln(
23              "Broke out of loop at count = " + count );
24           // -->
25        </script>
26     </head><body></body>
27  </html>
```

Using the break Statement in a for Statement - Windows Internet Explorer

C:\examples\ch06\BreakTest.html

Using the break Statement in a for S...

Count is: 1
Count is: 2
Count is: 3
Count is: 4
Broke out of loop at count = 5

My Computer   100%

Fig. 6.11 | Using the break statement in a for statement.

which for and while differ. Improper placement of continue before the increment in a while may result in an infinite loop.

Figure 6.12 uses continue in a for statement to skip the document.writeln statement in line 20 when the if statement in line 17 determines that the value of count is 5. When the continue statement executes, the script skips the remainder of the for statement's body. Program control continues with the increment of the for statement's control variable, followed by the loop-continuation test to determine whether the loop should continue executing.

```
1    <?xml version = "1.0" encoding = "utf-8"?>
2    <!DOCTYPE html PUBLIC "-//W3C//DTD XHTML 1.0 Strict//EN"
3       "http://www.w3.org/TR/xhtml1/DTD/xhtml1-strict.dtd">
4
5    <!-- Fig. 6.12: ContinueTest.html -->
6    <!-- Using the continue statement in a for statement. -->
7    <html xmlns = "http://www.w3.org/1999/xhtml">
8       <head>
9          <title>
10            Using the continue Statement in a for Statement
11         </title>
12
13         <script type = "text/javascript">
14            <!--
15            for ( var count = 1; count <= 10; ++count )
16            {
17               if ( count == 5 )
18                  continue; // skip remaining loop code only if count == 5
19
20               document.writeln( "Count is: " + count + "<br />" );
21            } //end for
22
23            document.writeln( "Used continue to skip printing 5" );
24            // -->
25         </script>
26
27      </head><body></body>
28   </html>
```

Count is: 1
Count is: 2
Count is: 3
Count is: 4
Count is: 6
Count is: 7
Count is: 8
Count is: 9
Count is: 10
Used continue to skip printing 5

Fig. 6.12 | Using the continue statement in a for statement.

Software Engineering Observation 6.2

Some programmers feel that break and continue violate structured programming. They do not use break and continue, because the effects of these statements can be achieved by structured programming techniques.

Performance Tip 6.1

The break and continue statements, when used properly, perform faster than the corresponding structured techniques.

Software Engineering Observation 6.3

There is a tension between achieving quality software engineering and achieving the best-performing software. Often, one of these goals is achieved at the expense of the other. For all but the most performance-intensive situations, the following rule of thumb should be followed: First make your code simple, readable and correct; then make it fast and small, but only if necessary.

6.8 Labeled break and continue Statements

The break statement can break out of an immediately enclosing while, for, do...while or switch statement. To break out of a nested set of structures, you can use the *labeled break statement*. This statement, when executed in a while, for, do...while or switch statement, causes immediate exit from that statement and any number of enclosing repetition statements; program execution resumes with the first statement after the enclosing *labeled statement* (a statement preceded by a label). The labeled statement can be a block (a set of statements enclosed in curly braces, {}). Labeled break statements commonly are used to terminate nested looping structures containing while, for, do...while or switch statements. Figure 6.13 demonstrates the labeled break statement in a nested for statement.

```
1    <?xml version = "1.0" encoding = "utf-8"?>
2    <!DOCTYPE html PUBLIC "-//W3C//DTD XHTML 1.0 Strict//EN"
3       "http://www.w3.org/TR/xhtml1/DTD/xhtml1-strict.dtd">
4
5    <!-- Fig. 6.13: BreakLabelTest.html -->
6    <!-- Labeled break statement in a nested for statement. -->
7    <html xmlns = "http://www.w3.org/1999/xhtml">
8       <head>
9          <title>Using the break Statement with a Label</title>
10         <script type = "text/javascript">
11            <!--
12            stop: { // labeled block
13               for ( var row = 1; row <= 10; ++row )
14               {
15                  for ( var column = 1; column <= 5 ; ++column )
16                  {
17                     if ( row == 5 )
18                        break stop; // jump to end of stop block
19
20                     document.write( "* " );
21                  } //end for
22
23                  document.writeln( "<br />" );
24               } //end for
25
26               // the following line is skipped
27               document.writeln( "This line should not print" );
28            } // end block labeled stop
```

Fig. 6.13 | Labeled break statement in a nested for statement. (Part 1 of 2.)

```
29
30          document.writeln( "End of script" );
31          // -->
32       </script>
33    </head><body></body>
34 </html>
```

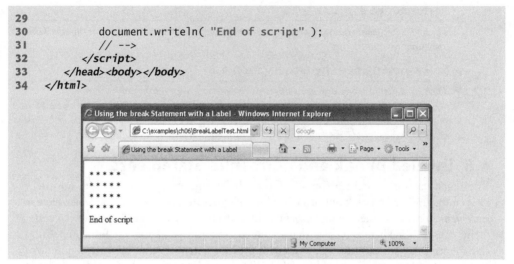

Fig. 6.13 | Labeled **break** statement in a nested **for** statement. (Part 2 of 2.)

The labeled block (lines 12–28) begins with a *label* (an identifier followed by a colon). Here, we use the label **stop:**. The block is enclosed between the braces at the end of line 12 and in line 28, and includes both the nested **for** statement starting in line 13 and the **document.writeln** statement in line 27. When the **if** statement in line 17 detects that row is equal to 5, the statement in line 18 executes. This statement terminates both the **for** statement in line 15 and its enclosing **for** statement in line 13, and the program proceeds to the statement in line 30 (the first statement in sequence after the labeled block). The inner **for** statement executes its body only four times. Note that the **document.writeln** statement in line 27 never executes, because it is included in the labeled block and the outer **for** statement never completes.

The **continue** statement proceeds with the next iteration (repetition) of the immediately enclosing **while**, **for** or **do...while** statement. The *labeled* **continue** *statement*, when executed in a repetition statement (**while**, **for** or **do...while**), skips the remaining statements in the structure's body and any number of enclosing repetition statements, then proceeds with the next iteration of the enclosing *labeled repetition statement* (a repetition statement preceded by a label). In labeled **while** and **do...while** statements, the loop-continuation test evaluates immediately after the **continue** statement executes. In a labeled **for** statement, the increment expression executes, then the loop-continuation test evaluates. Figure 6.14 uses the labeled **continue** statement in a nested **for** statement to cause execution to continue with the next iteration of the outer **for** statement.

```
1  <?xml version = "1.0" encoding = "utf-8"?>
2  <!DOCTYPE html PUBLIC "-//W3C//DTD XHTML 1.0 Strict//EN"
3     "http://www.w3.org/TR/xhtml1/DTD/xhtml1-strict.dtd">
4
5  <!-- Fig. 6.14: ContinueLabelTest.html -->
6  <!-- Labeled continue statement in a nested for statement. -->
```

Fig. 6.14 | Labeled **continue** statement in a nested **for** statement. (Part 1 of 2.)

```
7    <html xmlns = "http://www.w3.org/1999/xhtml">
8      <head>
9        <title>Using the continue Statement with a Label</title>
10       <script type = "text/javascript">
11         <!--
12           nextRow: // target label of continue statement
13             for ( var row = 1; row <= 5; ++row )
14             {
15                 document.writeln( "<br />" );
16
17                 for ( var column = 1; column <= 10; ++column )
18                 {
19                     if ( column > row )
20                         continue nextRow; // next iteration of labeled loop
21
22                     document.write( "* " );
23                 } //end for
24             } //end for
25           // -->
26       </script>
27     </head><body></body>
28 </html>
```

Fig. 6.14 | Labeled `continue` statement in a nested `for` statement. (Part 2 of 2.)

The labeled `for` statement (lines 13–24) starts with the `nextRow` label in line 12. When the `if` statement in line 19 in the inner `for` statement detects that `column` is greater than `row`, line 20 executes and program control continues with the increment of the control variable of the outer `for` statement. Even though the inner `for` statement counts from 1 to 10, the number of * characters output on a row never exceeds the value of `row`.

6.9 Logical Operators

So far, we have studied only such *simple conditions* as `count <= 10`, `total > 1000` and `number != sentinelValue`. These conditions were expressed in terms of the relational operators >, <, >= and <=, and in terms of the equality operators == and !=. Each decision tested one condition. To make a decision based on multiple conditions, we performed these tests in separate statements or in nested `if` or `if...else` statements.

JavaScript provides *logical operators* that can be used to form more complex conditions by combining simple conditions. The logical operators are **&&** (*logical AND*), **||**

(*logical OR*) and ! (*logical NOT*, also called *logical negation*). We consider examples of each of these operators.

Suppose that, at some point in a program, we wish to ensure that two conditions are *both* true before we choose a certain path of execution. In this case, we can use the logical && operator, as follows:

```
if ( gender == 1 && age >= 65 )
    ++seniorFemales;
```

This if statement contains two simple conditions. The condition gender == 1 might be evaluated to determine, for example, whether a person is a female. The condition age >= 65 is evaluated to determine whether a person is a senior citizen. The if statement then considers the combined condition

```
gender == 1 && age >= 65
```

This condition is true *if and only if* both of the simple conditions are true. Finally, if this combined condition is indeed true, the count of seniorFemales is incremented by 1. If either or both of the simple conditions are false, the program skips the incrementing and proceeds to the statement following the if statement. The preceding combined condition can be made more readable by adding redundant parentheses:

```
( gender == 1 ) && ( age >= 65 )
```

The table in Fig. 6.15 summarizes the && operator. The table shows all four possible combinations of false and true values for *expression1* and *expression2*. Such tables are often called *truth tables*. JavaScript evaluates to false or true all expressions that include relational operators, equality operators and/or logical operators.

Now let us consider the || (logical OR) operator. Suppose we wish to ensure that either *or* both of two conditions are true before we choose a certain path of execution. In this case, we use the || operator, as in the following program segment:

```
if ( semesterAverage >= 90 || finalExam >= 90 )
    document.writeln( "Student grade is A" );
```

This statement also contains two simple conditions. The condition semesterAverage >= 90 is evaluated to determine whether the student deserves an "A" in the course because of a solid performance throughout the semester. The condition finalExam >= 90 is evaluated to determine whether the student deserves an "A" in the course because of an outstanding performance on the final exam. The if statement then considers the combined condition

expression1	expression2	expression1 && expression2
false	false	false
false	true	false
true	false	false
true	true	true

Fig. 6.15 | Truth table for the && (logical AND) operator.

```
semesterAverage >= 90 || finalExam >= 90
```

and awards the student an "A" if either or both of the simple conditions are true. Note that the message "Student grade is A" is *not* printed only when both of the simple conditions are false. Figure 6.16 is a truth table for the logical OR operator (||).

The && operator has a higher precedence than the || operator. Both operators associate from left to right. An expression containing && or || operators is evaluated only until truth or falsity is known. Thus, evaluation of the expression

```
gender == 1 && age >= 65
```

stops immediately if gender is not equal to 1 (i.e., the entire expression is false) and continues if gender is equal to 1 (i.e., the entire expression could still be true if the condition age >= 65 is true). Similarly, the || operator immediately returns true if the first operand is true. This performance feature for evaluation of logical AND and logical OR expressions is called *short-circuit evaluation.*

JavaScript provides the ! (logical negation) operator to enable a programmer to "reverse" the meaning of a condition (i.e., a true value becomes false, and a false value becomes true). Unlike the logical operators && and ||, which combine two conditions (i.e., they are binary operators), the logical negation operator has only a single condition as an operand (i.e., it is a unary operator). The logical negation operator is placed before a condition to choose a path of execution if the original condition (without the logical negation operator) is false, as in the following program segment:

```
if ( ! ( grade == sentinelValue ) )
    document.writeln( "The next grade is " + grade );
```

The parentheses around the condition grade == sentinelValue are needed, because the logical negation operator has a higher precedence than the equality operator. Figure 6.17 is a truth table for the logical negation operator.

expression1	expression2	expression1 || expression2
false	false	false
false	true	true
true	false	true
true	true	true

Fig. 6.16 | Truth table for the || (logical OR) operator.

expression	!expression
false	true
true	false

Fig. 6.17 | Truth table for operator ! (logical negation).

In most cases, you can avoid using logical negation by expressing the condition differently with an appropriate relational or equality operator. For example, the preceding statement may also be written as follows:

```
if ( grade != sentinelValue )
    document.writeln( "The next grade is " + grade );
```

The script in Fig. 6.18 demonstrates all the logical operators by producing their truth tables. The script produces an XHTML table containing the results.

```
1  <?xml version = "1.0" encoding = "utf-8"?>
2  <!DOCTYPE html PUBLIC "-//W3C//DTD XHTML 1.0 Strict//EN"
3     "http://www.w3.org/TR/xhtml1/DTD/xhtml1-strict.dtd">
4
5  <!-- Fig. 6.18: LogicalOperators.html -->
6  <!-- Demonstrating logical operators. -->
7  <html xmlns = "http://www.w3.org/1999/xhtml">
8     <head>
9        <title>Demonstrating the Logical Operators</title>
10       <style type = "text/css">
11          table  { width: 100% }
12          td.left { width: 25% }
13       </style>
14       <script type = "text/javascript">
15          <!--
16          document.writeln(
17             "<table border = \"1\"" );
18          document.writeln(
19             "<caption>Demonstrating Logical " +
20                "Operators</caption>" );
21          document.writeln(
22             "<tr><td class = \"left\">Logical AND (&&)</td>" +
23             "<td>false && false: " + ( false && false ) +
24             "<br />false && true: " + ( false && true ) +
25             "<br />true && false: " + ( true && false ) +
26             "<br />true && true: " + ( true && true ) +
27             "</td></tr>" );
28          document.writeln(
29             "<tr><td class = \"left\">Logical OR (||)</td>" +
30             "<td>false || false: " + ( false || false ) +
31             "<br />false || true: " + ( false || true ) +
32             "<br />true || false: " + ( true || false ) +
33             "<br />true || true: " + ( true || true ) +
34             "</td></tr>" );
35          document.writeln(
36             "<tr><td class = \"left\">Logical NOT (!)</td>" +
37             "<td>!false: " + ( !false ) +
38             "<br />!true: " + ( !true ) + "</td></tr>" );
39          document.writeln( "</table>" );
40          // -->
41       </script>
42    </head><body></body>
43 </html>
```

Fig. 6.18 | Demonstrating logical operators. (Part 1 of 2.)

Fig. 6.18 | Demonstrating logical operators. (Part 2 of 2.)

In the output of Fig. 6.18, the strings "false" and "true" indicate false and true for the operands in each condition. The result of the condition is shown as true or false. Note that when you use the concatenation operator with a boolean value and a string, JavaScript automatically converts the boolean value to string "false" or "true". Lines 16–39 build an XHTML table containing the results.

An interesting feature of JavaScript is that most nonboolean values can be converted to a boolean true or false value. Nonzero numeric values are considered to be true. The numeric value zero is considered to be false. Any string that contains characters is considered to be true. The empty string (i.e., the string containing no characters) is considered to be false. The value null and variables that have been declared but not initialized are considered to be false. All objects (e.g., the browser's document and window objects and JavaScript's Math object) are considered to be true.

Figure 6.19 shows the precedence and associativity of the JavaScript operators introduced up to this point. The operators are shown top to bottom in decreasing order of precedence.

Operator	Associativity	Type
++ -- !	right to left	unary
* / %	left to right	multiplicative
+ -	left to right	additive
< <= > >=	left to right	relational
== !=	left to right	equality
&&	left to right	logical AND

Fig. 6.19 | Precedence and associativity of the operators discussed so far. (Part 1 of 2.)

Operator	Associativity	Type
||	left to right	logical OR
?:	right to left	conditional
= += -= *= /= %=	right to left	assignment

Fig. 6.19 | Precedence and associativity of the operators discussed so far. (Part 2 of 2.)

6.10 Web Resources

www.deitel.com/javascript/

The Deitel JavaScript Resource Center contains links to some of the best JavaScript resources on the web. There you'll find categorized links to JavaScript tools, code generators, forums, books, libraries, frameworks and more. Also check out the tutorials for all skill levels, from introductory to advanced. Be sure to visit the related Resource Centers on XHTML (www.deitel.com/xhtml/) and CSS 2.1 (www.deitel.com/css21/).

7

JavaScript: Functions

Form ever follows function.
—Louis Sullivan

E pluribus unum.
(One composed of many.)
—Virgil

O! call back yesterday, bid
time return.
—William Shakespeare

Call me Ishmael.
—Herman Melville

When you call me that,
smile.
—Owen Wister

OBJECTIVES

In this chapter you will learn:

- To construct programs modularly from small pieces called functions.

- How to create new functions.

- How to pass information between functions.

- Simulation techniques that use random number generation.

- How the visibility of identifiers is limited to specific regions of programs.

7.1 Introduction

Most computer programs that solve real-world problems are much larger than the programs presented in the first few chapters of this book. Experience has shown that the best way to develop and maintain a large program is to construct it from small, simple pieces, or *modules*. This technique is called *divide and conquer*. This chapter describes many key features of JavaScript that facilitate the design, implementation, operation and maintenance of large scripts.

7.2 Program Modules in JavaScript

Modules in JavaScript are called *functions*. JavaScript programs are written by combining new functions that you write with "prepackaged" functions and objects available in JavaScript. The prepackaged functions that belong to JavaScript objects (such as Math.pow and Math.round, introduced previously) are called *methods*. The term method implies that the function belongs to a particular object. We refer to functions that belong to a particular JavaScript object as methods; all others are referred to as functions.

JavaScript provides several objects that have a rich collection of methods for performing common mathematical calculations, string manipulations, date and time manipulations, and manipulations of collections of data called arrays. These objects make your job easier, because they provide many of the capabilities programmers frequently need. Some common predefined objects of JavaScript and their methods are discussed in Chapter 8, JavaScript: Arrays, and Chapter 9, JavaScript: Objects.

Good Programming Practice 7.1

Familiarize yourself with the rich collection of objects and methods provided by JavaScript.

Software Engineering Observation 7.1

Avoid reinventing the wheel. Use existing JavaScript objects, methods and functions instead of writing new ones. This reduces script-development time and helps avoid introducing errors.

Portability Tip 7.1

Using the methods built into JavaScript objects helps make scripts more portable.

You can write functions to define specific tasks that may be used at many points in a script. These functions are referred to as ***programmer-defined functions***. The actual statements defining the function are written only once and are hidden from other functions.

Functions are invoked by writing the name of the function, followed by a left parenthesis, followed by a comma-separated list of zero or more arguments, followed by a right parenthesis. For example, a programmer desiring to convert a string stored in variable inputValue to a floating-point number and add it to variable total might write

```
total += parseFloat( inputValue );
```

When this statement executes, JavaScript function ***parseFloat*** converts the string in the inputValue variable to a floating-point value and adds that value to total. Variable inputValue is function parseFloat's argument. Function parseFloat takes a string representation of a floating-point number as an argument and returns the corresponding floating-point numeric value. Function arguments may be constants, variables or expressions.

Methods are called in the same way, but require the name of the object to which the method belongs and a dot preceding the method name. For example, we've already seen the syntax document.writeln("Hi there.");. This statement calls the document object's writeln method to output the text.

7.3 Programmer-Defined Functions

Functions allow you to modularize a program. All variables declared in function definitions are *local variables*—they can be accessed only in the function in which they are defined. Most functions have a list of *parameters* that provide the means for communicating information between functions via function calls. A function's parameters are also considered to be local variables. When a function is called, the arguments in the function call are assigned to the corresponding parameters in the function definition.

Software Engineering Observation 7.2

If a function's task cannot be expressed concisely, perhaps the function is performing too many different tasks. It is usually best to break such a function into several smaller functions.

7.4 Function Definitions

Each script we have presented thus far in the text has consisted of a series of statements and control structures in sequence. These scripts have been executed as the browser loads the web page and evaluates the <head> section of the page. We now consider how you can write your own customized functions and call them in a script.

Programmer-Defined Function square

Consider a script (Fig. 7.1) that uses a function square to calculate the squares of the integers from 1 to 10. [*Note:* We continue to show many examples in which the body element of the XHTML document is empty and the document is created directly by

```
 1   <?xml version = "1.0" encoding = "utf-8"?>
 2   <!DOCTYPE html PUBLIC "-//W3C//DTD XHTML 1.0 Strict//EN"
 3      "http://www.w3.org/TR/xhtml1/DTD/xhtml1-strict.dtd">
 4
 5   <!-- Fig. 7.1: SquareInt.html -->
 6   <!-- Programmer-defined function square. -->
 7   <html xmlns = "http://www.w3.org/1999/xhtml">
 8      <head>
 9         <title>A Programmer-Defined square Function</title>
10         <script type = "text/javascript">
11            <!--
12            document.writeln( "<h1>Square the numbers from 1 to 10</h1>" );
13
14            // square the numbers from 1 to 10
15            for ( var x = 1; x <= 10; x++ )
16               document.writeln( "The square of " + x + " is " +
17                  square( x ) + "<br />" );
18
19            // The following square function definition is executed
20            // only when the function is explicitly called.
21
22            // square function definition
23            function square( y )
24            {
25               return y * y;
26            } // end function square
27            // -->
28         </script>
29      </head><body></body>
30   </html>
```

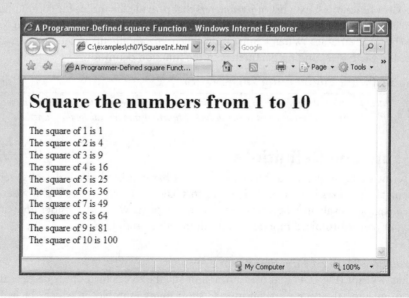

Fig. 7.1 | Programmer-defined function square.

JavaScript. In later chapters, we show many examples in which JavaScripts interact with the elements in the body of a document.]

The for statement in lines 15–17 outputs XHTML that displays the results of squaring the integers from 1 to 10. Each iteration of the loop calculates the square of the current value of control variable x and outputs the result by writing a line in the XHTML document. Function square is invoked, or called, in line 17 with the expression square(x). When program control reaches this expression, the program calls function square (defined in lines 23–26). The parentheses () represent the *function-call operator*, which has high precedence. At this point, the program makes a copy of the value of x (the argument) and program control transfers to the first line of function square. Function square receives the copy of the value of x and stores it in the parameter y. Then square calculates y * y. The result is passed back (returned) to the point in line 17 where square was invoked. Lines 16–17 concatenate "The square of ", the value of x, the string " is ", the value returned by function square and a <br /> tag and write that line of text in the XHTML document. This process is repeated 10 times.

The definition of function square (lines 23–26) shows that square expects a single parameter y. Function square uses this name in its body to manipulate the value passed to square from line 17. The **return statement** in square passes the result of the calculation y * y back to the calling function. Note that JavaScript keyword var is not used to declare variables in the parameter list of a function.

Common Programming Error 7.1

Using the JavaScript var keyword to declare a variable in a function parameter list results in a JavaScript runtime error.

In this example, function square follows the rest of the script. When the for statement terminates, program control does *not* flow sequentially into function square. A function must be called explicitly for the code in its body to execute. Thus, when the for statement terminates in this example, the script terminates.

Good Programming Practice 7.2

Place a blank line between function definitions to separate the functions and enhance program readability.

Software Engineering Observation 7.3

Statements that are enclosed in the body of a function definition are not executed by the JavaScript interpreter unless the function is invoked explicitly.

The format of a function definition is

```
function function-name( parameter-list )
{
    declarations and statements
}
```

The *function-name* is any valid identifier. The *parameter-list* is a comma-separated list containing the names of the parameters received by the function when it is called (remember that the arguments in the function call are assigned to the corresponding parameter in the function definition). There should be one argument in the function call for each parameter in the function definition. If a function does not receive any values, the *parameter-list* is empty (i.e., the function name is followed by an empty set of parentheses). The *declarations* and *statements* in braces form the ***function body***.

Common Programming Error 7.2

Forgetting to return a value from a function that is supposed to return a value is a logic error.

Common Programming Error 7.3

Placing a semicolon after the right parenthesis enclosing the parameter list of a function definition results in a JavaScript runtime error.

Common Programming Error 7.4

Redefining a function parameter as a local variable in the function is a logic error.

Common Programming Error 7.5

Passing to a function an argument that is not compatible with the corresponding parameter's expected type is a logic error and may result in a JavaScript runtime error.

Good Programming Practice 7.3

Although it is not incorrect to do so, do not use the same name for an argument passed to a function and the corresponding parameter in the function definition. Using different names avoids ambiguity.

Software Engineering Observation 7.4

To promote software reusability, every function should be limited to performing a single, well-defined task, and the name of the function should express that task effectively. Such functions make programs easier to write, debug, maintain and modify.

There are three ways to return control to the point at which a function was invoked. If the function does not return a result, control returns when the program reaches the function-ending right brace or by executing the statement

  `return`;

If the function does return a result, the statement

  `return` *expression*;

returns the value of *expression* to the caller. When a `return` statement is executed, control returns immediately to the point at which the function was invoked.

Programmer-Defined Function `maximum`

The script in our next example (Fig. 7.2) uses a programmer-defined function called `maximum` to determine and return the largest of three floating-point values.

The three floating-point values are input by the user via `prompt` dialogs (lines 12–14). Lines 16–18 use function `parseFloat` to convert the strings entered by the user to floating-point values. The statement in line 20 passes the three floating-point values to function `maximum` (defined in lines 28–31), which determines the largest floating-point value. This value is returned to line 20 by the `return` statement in function `maximum`. The

```
1   <?xml version = "1.0" encoding = "utf-8"?>
2   <!DOCTYPE html PUBLIC "-//W3C//DTD XHTML 1.0 Strict//EN"
3      "http://www.w3.org/TR/xhtml1/DTD/xhtml1-strict.dtd">
4
5   <!-- Fig. 7.2: maximum.html -->
6   <!-- Programmer-Defined maximum function. -->
7   <html xmlns = "http://www.w3.org/1999/xhtml">
8      <head>
9         <title>Finding the Maximum of Three Values</title>
10        <script type = "text/javascript">
11           <!--
12           var input1 = window.prompt( "Enter first number", "0" );
13           var input2 = window.prompt( "Enter second number", "0" );
14           var input3 = window.prompt( "Enter third number", "0" );
15
16           var value1 = parseFloat( input1 );
17           var value2 = parseFloat( input2 );
18           var value3 = parseFloat( input3 );
19
20           var maxValue = maximum( value1, value2, value3 );
21
22           document.writeln( "First number: " + value1 +
23              "<br />Second number: " + value2 +
24              "<br />Third number: " + value3 +
25              "<br />Maximum is: " + maxValue );
26
27           // maximum function definition (called from line 20)
28           function maximum( x, y, z )
29           {
30              return Math.max( x, Math.max( y, z ) );
31           } // end function maximum
32           // -->
33        </script>
34     </head>
35     <body>
36        <p>Click Refresh (or Reload) to run the script again</p>
37     </body>
38  </html>
```

Fig. 7.2 | Programmer-defined `maximum` function. (Part 1 of 2.)

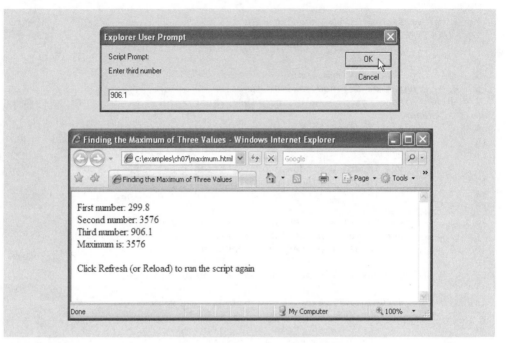

Fig. 7.2 | Programmer-defined `maximum` function. (Part 2 of 2.)

value returned is assigned to variable `maxValue`. Lines 22–25 display the three floating-point values input by the user and the calculated `maxValue`.

Note the implementation of the function `maximum` (lines 28–31). The first line indicates that the function's name is `maximum` and that the function takes three parameters (x, y and z) to accomplish its task. Also, the body of the function contains the statement which returns the largest of the three floating-point values, using two calls to the `Math` object's `max` method. First, method `Math.max` is invoked with the values of variables y and z to determine the larger of the two values. Next, the value of variable x and the result of the first call to `Math.max` are passed to method `Math.max`. Finally, the result of the second call to `Math.max` is returned to the point at which `maximum` was invoked (i.e., line 20). Note once again that the script terminates before sequentially reaching the definition of function `maximum`. The statement in the body of function `maximum` executes only when the function is invoked from line 20.

7.5 Random Number Generation

We now take a brief and, it is hoped, entertaining diversion into a popular programming application, namely simulation and game playing. In this section and the next, we develop a nicely structured game-playing program that includes multiple functions. The program uses most of the control statements we have studied.

There is something in the air of a gambling casino that invigorates people, from the high rollers at the plush mahogany-and-felt craps tables to the quarter poppers at the one-armed bandits. It is the *element of chance*, the possibility that luck will convert a pocketful of money into a mountain of wealth. The element of chance can be introduced through the Math object's ***random method***. (Remember, we are calling random a method because it belongs to the Math object.)

Consider the following statement:

```
var randomValue = Math.random();
```

Method random generates a floating-point value from 0.0 up to, but not including, 1.0. If random truly produces values at random, then every value from 0.0 up to, but not including, 1.0 has an equal ***chance*** (or ***probability***) of being chosen each time random is called.

The range of values produced directly by random is often different than what is needed in a specific application. For example, a program that simulates coin tossing might require only 0 for heads and 1 for tails. A program that simulates rolling a six-sided die would require random integers in the range from 1 to 6. A program that randomly predicts the next type of spaceship, out of four possibilities, that will fly across the horizon in a video game might require random integers in the range 0–3 or 1–4.

To demonstrate method random, let us develop a program (Fig. 7.3) that simulates 20 rolls of a six-sided die and displays the value of each roll. We use the multiplication operator (*) with random as follows:

```
Math.floor( 1 + Math.random() * 6 )
```

First, the preceding expression multiplies the result of a call to Math.random() by 6 to produce a number in the range 0.0 up to, but not including, 6.0. This is called scaling the range of the random numbers. Next, we add 1 to the result to shift the range of numbers to produce a number in the range 1.0 up to, but not including, 7.0. Finally, we use method ***Math.floor*** to *round* the result down to the closest integer not greater than the argument's value—for example, 1.75 is rounded to 1. Figure 7.3 confirms that the results are in the range 1 to 6.

```
1   <?xml version = "1.0" encoding = "utf-8"?>
2   <!DOCTYPE html PUBLIC "-//W3C//DTD XHTML 1.0 Strict//EN"
3      "http://www.w3.org/TR/xhtml1/DTD/xhtml1-strict.dtd">
4
5   <!-- Fig. 7.3: RandomInt.html -->
6   <!-- Random integers, shifting and scaling. -->
7   <html xmlns = "http://www.w3.org/1999/xhtml">
8      <head>
9         <title>Shifted and Scaled Random Integers</title>
10        <style type = "text/css">
11           table { width: 50%;
12                   border: 1px solid gray;
13                   text-align: center }
14        </style>
15        <script type = "text/javascript">
16           <!--
17           var value;
18
19           document.writeln( "<table>" );
20           document.writeln( "<caption>Random Numbers</caption><tr>" );
```

Fig. 7.3 | Random integers, shifting and scaling. (Part 1 of 2.)

```
21
22          for ( var i = 1; i <= 20; i++ )
23          {
24              value = Math.floor( 1 + Math.random() * 6 );
25              document.writeln( "<td>" + value + "</td>" );
26
27              // start a new table row every 5 entries
28              if ( i % 5 == 0 && i != 20 )
29                  document.writeln( "</tr><tr>" );
30          } // end for
31
32          document.writeln( "</tr></table>" );
33          // -->
34      </script>
35  </head>
36  <body>
37      <p>Click Refresh (or Reload) to run the script again</p>
38  </body>
39 </html>
```

Fig. 7.3 | Random integers, shifting and scaling. (Part 2 of 2.)

To show that these numbers occur with approximately equal likelihood, let us simulate 6000 rolls of a die with the program in Fig. 7.4. Each integer from 1 to 6 should appear approximately 1000 times. Use your browser's **Refresh** (or **Reload**) button to execute the script again.

```
1   <?xml version = "1.0" encoding = "utf-8"?>
2   <!DOCTYPE html PUBLIC "-//W3C//DTD XHTML 1.0 Strict//EN"
3      "http://www.w3.org/TR/xhtml1/DTD/xhtml1-strict.dtd">
4
5   <!-- Fig. 7.4: RollDie.html -->
6   <!-- Rolling a Six-Sided Die 6000 times. -->
7   <html xmlns = "http://www.w3.org/1999/xhtml">
8      <head>
9         <title>Roll a Six-Sided Die 6000 Times</title>
10        <script type = "text/javascript">
11           <!--
12           var frequency1 = 0;
13           var frequency2 = 0;
14           var frequency3 = 0;
15           var frequency4 = 0;
16           var frequency5 = 0;
17           var frequency6 = 0;
18           var face;
19
20           // roll die 6000 times and accumulate results
21           for ( var roll = 1; roll <= 6000; roll++ )
22           {
23              face = Math.floor( 1 + Math.random() * 6 );
24
25              switch ( face )
26              {
27                 case 1:
28                    ++frequency1;
29                    break;
30                 case 2:
31                    ++frequency2;
32                    break;
33                 case 3:
34                    ++frequency3;
35                    break;
36                 case 4:
37                    ++frequency4;
38                    break;
39                 case 5:
40                    ++frequency5;
41                    break;
42                 case 6:
43                    ++frequency6;
44                    break;
45              } // end switch
46           } // end for
47
48           document.writeln( "<table border = \"1\">" );
49           document.writeln( "<thead><th>Face</th>" +
50              "<th>Frequency</th></thead>" );
```

Fig. 7.4 | Rolling a six-sided die 6000 times. (Part 1 of 2.)

```
51          document.writeln( "<tbody><tr><td>1</td><td>" +
52             frequency1 + "</td></tr>" );
53          document.writeln( "<tr><td>2</td><td>" + frequency2 +
54             "</td></tr>" );
55          document.writeln( "<tr><td>3</td><td>" + frequency3 +
56             "</td></tr>" );
57          document.writeln( "<tr><td>4</td><td>" + frequency4 +
58             "</td></tr>" );
59          document.writeln( "<tr><td>5</td><td>" + frequency5 +
60             "</td></tr>" );
61          document.writeln( "<tr><td>6</td><td>" + frequency6 +
62             "</td></tr></tbody></table>" );
63          // -->
64       </script>
65    </head>
66    <body>
67       <p>Click Refresh (or Reload) to run the script again</p>
68    </body>
69 </html>
```

Face	Frequency
1	1016
2	980
3	1031
4	966
5	1016
6	991

Click Refresh (or Reload) to run the script again

Face	Frequency
1	979
2	1048
3	997
4	988
5	1011
6	977

Click Refresh (or Reload) to run the script again

Fig. 7.4 | Rolling a six-sided die 6000 times. (Part 2 of 2.)

As the output of the program shows, we used Math method random and the scaling and shifting techniques of the previous example to simulate the rolling of a six-sided die. Note that we used nested control statements to determine the number of times each side of the six-sided die occurred. Lines 12–17 declare and initialize counters to keep track of the number of times each of the six die values appears. Line 18 declares a variable to store the face value of the die. The for statement in lines 21–46 iterates 6000 times. During each iteration of the loop, line 23 produces a value from 1 to 6, which is stored in face. The nested switch statement in lines 25–45 uses the face value that was randomly chosen as its controlling expression. Based on the value of face, the program increments one of the six counter variables during each iteration of the loop. Note that no default case is provided in this switch statement, because the statement in line 23 produces only the values 1, 2, 3, 4, 5 and 6. In this example, the default case would never execute. After we study Arrays in Chapter 8, we discuss a way to replace the entire switch statement in this program with a single-line statement.

Run the program several times, and observe the results. Note that the program produces different random numbers each time the script executes, so the results should vary.

The values returned by random are always in the range

```
0.0 ≤Math.random() < 1.0
```

Previously, we demonstrated the statement

```
face = Math.floor( 1 + Math.random() * 6 );
```

which simulates the rolling of a six-sided die. This statement always assigns an integer (at random) to variable face, in the range 1 ≤face ≤6. Note that the width of this range (i.e., the number of consecutive integers in the range) is 6, and the starting number in the range is 1. Referring to the preceding statement, we see that the width of the range is determined by the number used to scale random with the multiplication operator (6 in the preceding statement) and that the starting number of the range is equal to the number (1 in the preceding statement) added to Math.random() * 6. We can generalize this result as

```
face = Math.floor( a + Math.random() * b );
```

where a is the *shifting value* (which is equal to the first number in the desired range of consecutive integers) and b is the *scaling factor* (which is equal to the width of the desired range of consecutive integers).

7.6 Example: Game of Chance

One of the most popular games of chance is a dice game known as craps, which is played in casinos and back alleys throughout the world. The rules of the game are straightforward:

A player rolls two dice. Each die has six faces. These faces contain one, two, three, four, five and six spots, respectively. After the dice have come to rest, the sum of the spots on the two upward faces is calculated. If the sum is 7 or 11 on the first throw, the player wins. If the sum is 2, 3 or 12 on the first throw (called "craps"), the player loses (i.e., the "house" wins). If the sum is 4, 5, 6, 8, 9 or 10 on the first throw, that sum becomes the player's "point." To win, you must continue rolling the dice until you "make your point" (i.e., roll your point value). You lose by rolling a 7 before making the point.

The script in Fig. 7.5 simulates the game of craps. Note that the player must roll two dice on the first and all subsequent rolls. When you execute the script, click the **Roll Dice** button to play the game. A message below the **Roll Dice** button displays the status of the game after each roll.

Until now, all user interactions with scripts have been through either a prompt dialog (in which the user types an input value for the program) or an alert dialog (in which a message is displayed to the user, and the user can click **OK** to dismiss the dialog). Although these dialogs are valid ways to receive input from a user and to display messages, they are fairly limited in their capabilities. A prompt dialog can obtain only one value at a time from the user, and a message dialog can display only one message.

```
1   <?xml version = "1.0" encoding = "utf-8"?>
2   <!DOCTYPE html PUBLIC "-//W3C//DTD XHTML 1.0 Strict//EN"
3      "http://www.w3.org/TR/xhtml1/DTD/xhtml1-strict.dtd">
4
5   <!-- Fig. 7.5: Craps.html -->
6   <!-- Craps game simulation. -->
7   <html xmlns = "http://www.w3.org/1999/xhtml">
8      <head>
9         <title>Program that Simulates the Game of Craps</title>
10        <style type = "text/css">
11           table  { text-align: right }
12           body   { font-family: arial, sans-serif }
13           div.red { color: red }
14        </style>
15        <script type = "text/javascript">
16           <!--
17           // variables used to test the state of the game
18           var WON = 0;
19           var LOST = 1;
20           var CONTINUE_ROLLING = 2;
21
22           // other variables used in program
23           var firstRoll = true; // true if current roll is first
24           var sumOfDice = 0; // sum of the dice
25           var myPoint = 0; // point if no win/loss on first roll
26           var gameStatus = CONTINUE_ROLLING; // game not over yet
27
28           // process one roll of the dice
29           function play()
30           {
31              // get the point field on the page
32              var point = document.getElementById( "pointfield" );
33
34              // get the status div on the page
35              var statusDiv = document.getElementById( "status" );
36              if ( firstRoll ) // first roll of the dice
37              {
38                 sumOfDice = rollDice();
39
```

Fig. 7.5 | Craps game simulation. (Part 1 of 4.)

```
40              switch ( sumOfDice )
41              {
42                  case 7: case 11: // win on first roll
43                      gameStatus = WON;
44                      // clear point field
45                      point.value = "";
46                      break;
47                  case 2: case 3: case 12: // lose on first roll
48                      gameStatus = LOST;
49                      // clear point field
50                      point.value = "";
51                      break;
52                  default:                        // remember point
53                      gameStatus = CONTINUE_ROLLING;
54                      myPoint = sumOfDice;
55                      point.value = myPoint;
56                      firstRoll = false;
57              } // end switch
58          } // end if
59          else
60          {
61              sumOfDice = rollDice();
62
63              if ( sumOfDice == myPoint ) // win by making point
64                  gameStatus = WON;
65              else
66                  if ( sumOfDice == 7 )       // lose by rolling 7
67                      gameStatus = LOST;
68          } // end else
69
70          if ( gameStatus == CONTINUE_ROLLING )
71              statusDiv.innerHTML = "Roll again";
72          else
73          {
74              if ( gameStatus == WON )
75                  statusDiv.innerHTML = "Player wins. " +
76                      "Click Roll Dice to play again.";
77              else
78                  statusDiv.innerHTML = "Player loses. " +
79                      "Click Roll Dice to play again.";
80
81              firstRoll = true;
82          } // end else
83      } // end function play
84
85      // roll the dice
86      function rollDice()
87      {
88          var die1;
89          var die2;
90          var workSum;
91
```

Fig. 7.5 | Craps game simulation. (Part 2 of 4.)

```
92              die1 = Math.floor( 1 + Math.random() * 6 );
93              die2 = Math.floor( 1 + Math.random() * 6 );
94              workSum = die1 + die2;
95
96              document.getElementById( "die1field" ).value = die1;
97              document.getElementById( "die2field" ).value = die2;
98              document.getElementById( "sumfield" ).value = workSum;
99
100             return workSum;
101          } // end function rollDice
102          // -->
103       </script>
104    </head>
105    <body>
106       <form action = "">
107          <table>
108          <caption>Craps</caption>
109          <tr><td>Die 1</td>
110             <td><input id = "die1field" type = "text" />
111             </td></tr>
112          <tr><td>Die 2</td>
113             <td><input id = "die2field" type = "text" />
114             </td></tr>
115          <tr><td>Sum</td>
116             <td><input id = "sumfield" type = "text" />
117             </td></tr>
118          <tr><td>Point</td>
119             <td><input id = "pointfield" type = "text" />
120             </td></tr>
121          <tr><td /><td><input type = "button" value = "Roll Dice"
122             onclick = "play()" /></td></tr>
123          </table>
124          <div id = "status" class = "red">
125             Click the Roll Dice button to play</div>
126       </form>
127    </body>
128 </html>
```

Fig. 7.5 | Craps game simulation. (Part 3 of 4.)

Fig. 7.5 | Craps game simulation. (Part 4 of 4.)

More frequently, multiple inputs are received from the user at once via an XHTML form (such as one in which the user enters name and address information) or to display many pieces of data at once (e.g., the values of the dice, the sum of the dice and the point in this example). To begin our introduction to more elaborate user interfaces, this program uses an XHTML form (discussed in Chapter 2) and a new graphical user interface concept—GUI *event handling*. This is our first example in which the JavaScript executes in response to the user's interaction with a GUI component in an XHTML form. This interaction causes an event. Scripts are often used to respond to events.

Before we discuss the script code, we discuss the XHTML document's body element (lines 105–126). The GUI components in this section are used extensively in the script.

Line 106 begins the definition of an XHTML form element. The XHTML standard requires that every form contain an action attribute, but because this form does not post its information to a web server, the empty string ("") is used.

In this example, we have decided to place the form's GUI components in an XHTML table element, so line 107 begins the definition of the XHTML table. Lines 109–120 create four table rows. Each row contains a left cell with a text label and an input element in the right cell.

Four input fields (lines 110, 113, 116 and 119) are created to display the value of the first die, the second die, the sum of the dice and the current point value, if any. Their id attributes are set to die1field, die2field, sumfield, and pointfield, respectively. The id attribute can be used to apply CSS styles and to enable script code to refer to an element in an XHTML document. Because the id attribute, if specified, must have a unique value, JavaScript can reliably refer to any single element via its id attribute. We see how this is done in a moment.

Lines 121–122 create a fifth row with an empty cell in the left column before the **Roll Dice** button. The button's *onclick attribute* indicates the action to take when the user of the XHTML document clicks the **Roll Dice** button. In this example, clicking the button causes a call to function play.

This style of programming is known as *event-driven programming*—the user interacts with a GUI component, the script is notified of the event and the script processes the event. The user's interaction with the GUI "drives" the program. The button click is known as the *event*. The function that is called when an event occurs is known as an *event-handling function* or *event handler*. When a GUI event occurs in a form, the browser calls the specified event-handling function. Before any event can be processed, each GUI component must know which event-handling function will be called when a particular event occurs. Most XHTML GUI components have several different event types. The event model is discussed in detail in Chapter 11, JavaScript: Events. By specifying onclick = "play()" for the **Roll Dice** button, we instruct the browser to *listen for events* (button-click events in particular). This *registers the event handler* for the GUI component, causing the browser to begin listening for the click event on the component. If no event handler is specified for the **Roll Dice** button, the script will not respond when the user presses the button.

Lines 123–125 end the table and form elements, respectively. After the table, a div element is created with an id attribute of "status". This element will be updated by the script to display the result of each roll to the user. A style declaration in line 13 colors the text contained in this div red.

The game is reasonably involved. The player may win or lose on the first roll, or may win or lose on any subsequent roll. Lines 18–20 create variables that define the three game states—game won, game lost and continue rolling the dice. Unlike many other programming languages, JavaScript does not provide a mechanism to define a *constant* (i.e., a variable whose value cannot be modified). For this reason, we use all capital letters for these variable names, to indicate that we do not intend to modify their values and to make them stand out in the code—a common industry practice for genuine constants.

Good Programming Practice 7.4

Use only uppercase letters (with underscores between words) in the names of variables that should be used as constants. This format makes such variables stand out in a program.

Good Programming Practice 7.5

Use meaningfully named variables rather than literal values (such as 2) to make programs more readable.

Lines 23–26 declare several variables that are used throughout the script. Variable firstRoll indicates whether the next roll of the dice is the first roll in the current game. Variable sumOfDice maintains the sum of the dice from the last roll. Variable myPoint stores the point if the player does not win or lose on the first roll. Variable gameStatus keeps track of the current state of the game (WON, LOST or CONTINUE_ROLLING).

We define a function rollDice (lines 86–101) to roll the dice and to compute and display their sum. Function rollDice is defined once, but is called from two places in the program (lines 38 and 61). Function rollDice takes no arguments, so it has an empty parameter list. Function rollDice returns the sum of the two dice.

The user clicks the **Roll Dice** button to roll the dice. This action invokes function play (lines 29–83) of the script. Lines 32 and 35 create two new variables with objects representing elements in the XHTML document using the document object's *getElementById method*. The getElementById method, given an id as an argument, finds the XHTML element with a matching id attribute and returns a JavaScript object representing the element. Line 32 stores an object representing the pointfield input element (line 119) in the variable point. Line 35 gets an object representing the status div from line 124. In a moment, we show how you can use these objects to manipulate the XHTML document.

Function play checks the variable firstRoll (line 36) to determine whether it is true or false. If true, the roll is the first roll of the game. Line 38 calls rollDice, which picks two random values from 1 to 6, displays the value of the first die, the value of the second die and the sum of the dice in the first three text fields and returns the sum of the dice. (We discuss function rollDice in detail shortly.) After the first roll (if firstRoll is false), the nested switch statement in lines 40–57 determines whether the game is won or lost, or whether it should continue with another roll. After the first roll, if the game is not over, sumOfDice is saved in myPoint and displayed in the text field point in the XHTML form.

Note how the text field's value is changed in lines 45, 50 and 55. The object stored in the variable point allows access to the pointfield text field's contents. The expression point.value accesses the *value property* of the text field referred to by point. The value property specifies the text to display in the text field. To access this property, we specify the object representing the text field (point), followed by a *dot* (.) and the name of the property to access (value). This technique for accessing properties of an object (also used to access methods as in Math.pow) is called *dot notation*. We discuss using scripts to access elements in an XHTML page in more detail in Chapter 10.

The program proceeds to the nested if...else statement in lines 70–82, which uses the statusDiv variable to update the div that displays the game status. Using the object's *innerHTML property*, we set the text inside the div to reflect the most recent status. In lines 71, 75–76 and 78–79, we set the div's innerHTML to

```
Roll again.
```

if gameStatus is equal to CONTINUE_ROLLING, to

   Player wins. Click Roll Dice to play again.

if gameStatus is equal to WON and to

   Player loses. Click Roll Dice to play again.

if gameStatus is equal to LOST. If the game is won or lost, line 81 sets firstRoll to true to indicate that the next roll of the dice begins the next game.

The program then waits for the user to click the button **Roll Dice** again. Each time the user clicks **Roll Dice**, the program calls function play, which, in turn, calls the rollDice function to produce a new value for sumOfDice. If sumOfDice matches myPoint, gameStatus is set to WON, the if...else statement in lines 70–82 executes and the game is complete. If sum is equal to 7, gameStatus is set to LOST, the if...else statement in lines 70–82 executes and the game is complete. Clicking the **Roll Dice** button starts a new game. The program updates the four text fields in the XHTML form with the new values of the dice and the sum on each roll, and updates the text field point each time a new game begins.

Function rollDice (lines 86–101) defines its own local variables die1, die2 and workSum (lines 88–90). Lines 92–93 pick two random values in the range 1 to 6 and assign them to variables die1 and die2, respectively. Lines 96–98 once again use the document's getElementById method to find and update the correct input elements with the values of die1, die2 and workSum. Note that the integer values are converted automatically to strings when they are assigned to each text field's value property. Line 100 returns the value of workSum for use in function play.

Error-Prevention Tip 7.1

Initializing variables when they are declared in functions helps avoid incorrect results and interpreter messages warning of uninitialized data.

7.7 Another Example: Random Image Generator

Web content that varies randomly adds dynamic, interesting effects to a page. In the next example, we build a *random image generator*, a script that displays a randomly selected image every time the page that contains the script is loaded.

For the script in Fig. 7.6 to function properly, the directory containing the file RandomPicture.html must also contain seven images with integer filenames (i.e., 1.gif, 2.gif, ..., 7.gif). The web page containing this script displays one of these seven images, selected at random, each time the page loads.

```
1   <?xml version = "1.0" encoding = "utf-8"?>
2   <!DOCTYPE html PUBLIC "-//W3C//DTD XHTML 1.0 Strict//EN"
3      "http://www.w3.org/TR/xhtml1/DTD/xhtml1-strict.dtd">
4
5   <!-- Fig. 7.6: RandomPicture.html -->
6   <!-- Random image generation using Math.random. -->
7   <html xmlns = "http://www.w3.org/1999/xhtml">
```

Fig. 7.6 | Random image generation using Math.random. (Part 1 of 2.)

```
 8      <head>
 9         <title>Random Image Generator</title>
10         <script type = "text/javascript">
11            <!--
12            document.write ( "<img src = \"" +
13               Math.floor( 1 + Math.random() * 7 ) + ".gif\" />" );
14            // -->
15         </script>
16      </head>
17      <body>
18         <p>Click Refresh (or Reload) to run the script again</p>
19      </body>
20   </html>
```

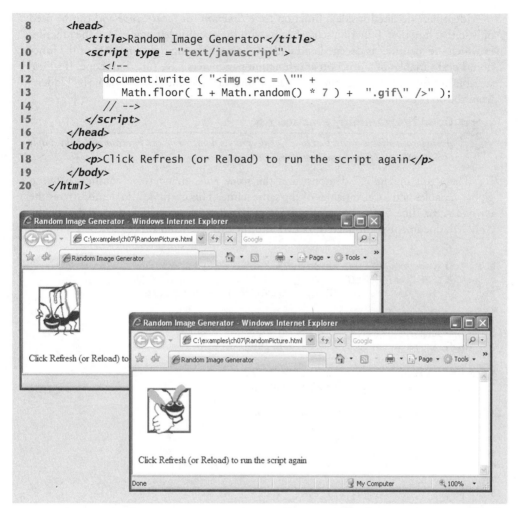

Fig. 7.6 | Random image generation using `Math.random`. (Part 2 of 2.)

Lines 12–13 randomly select an image to display on a web page. This `document.write` statement creates an image tag in the web page with the `src` attribute set to a random integer from 1 to 7, concatenated with `".gif"`. Thus, the script dynamically sets the source of the image tag to the name of one of the image files in the current directory.

7.8 Scope Rules

Chapters 4–6 used identifiers for variable names. The attributes of variables include name, value and data type (e.g., string, number or boolean). We also use identifiers as names for user-defined functions. Each identifier in a program also has a scope.

The *scope* of an identifier for a variable or function is the portion of the program in which the identifier can be referenced. *Global variables* or *script-level variables* that are declared in the `head` element are accessible in any part of a script and are said to have *global scope*. Thus every function in the script can potentially use the variables.

Identifiers declared inside a function have *function* (or *local*) *scope* and can be used only in that function. Function scope begins with the opening left brace ({) of the function in which the identifier is declared and ends at the terminating right brace (}) of the function. Local variables of a function and function parameters have function scope. If a local variable in a function has the same name as a global variable, the global variable is "hidden" from the body of the function.

Good Programming Practice 7.6

Avoid local-variable names that hide global-variable names. This can be accomplished by simply avoiding the use of duplicate identifiers in a script.

The script in Fig. 7.7 demonstrates the *scope rules* that resolve conflicts between global variables and local variables of the same name. This example also demonstrates the *onload event* (line 52), which calls an event handler (start) when the <body> of the XHTML document is completely loaded into the browser window.

```
1   <?xml version = "1.0" encoding = "utf-8"?>
2   <!DOCTYPE html PUBLIC "-//W3C//DTD XHTML 1.0 Strict//EN"
3      "http://www.w3.org/TR/xhtml1/DTD/xhtml1-strict.dtd">
4
5   <!-- Fig. 7.7: scoping.html -->
6   <!-- Scoping example. -->
7   <html xmlns = "http://www.w3.org/1999/xhtml">
8      <head>
9         <title>A Scoping Example</title>
10        <script type = "text/javascript">
11           <!--
12           var x = 1; // global variable
13
14           function start()
15           {
16              var x = 5; // variable local to function start
17
18              document.writeln( "local x in start is " + x );
19
20              functionA(); // functionA has local x
21              functionB(); // functionB uses global variable x
22              functionA(); // functionA reinitializes local x
23              functionB(); // global variable x retains its value
24
25              document.writeln(
26                 "<p>local x in start is " + x + "</p>" );
27           } // end function start
28
29           function functionA()
30           {
31              var x = 25; // initialized each time
32                          // functionA is called
33
34              document.writeln( "<p>local x in functionA is " +
35                                x + " after entering functionA" );
```

Fig. 7.7 | Scoping example. (Part 1 of 2.)

```
36              ++x;
37              document.writeln( "<br />local x in functionA is " +
38                  x + " before exiting functionA" + "</p>" );
39          } // end functionA
40
41          function functionB()
42          {
43              document.writeln( "<p>global variable x is " + x +
44                  " on entering functionB" );
45              x *= 10;
46              document.writeln( "<br />global variable x is " +
47                  x + " on exiting functionB"  + "</p>" );
48          } // end functionB
49          // -->
50       </script>
51    </head>
52    <body onload = "start()"></body>
53  </html>
```

Fig. 7.7 | Scoping example. (Part 2 of 2.)

Global variable x (line 12) is declared and initialized to 1. This global variable is hidden in any block (or function) that declares a variable named x. Function start (line 14–27) declares a local variable x (line 16) and initializes it to 5. This variable is output in a line of XHTML text to show that the global variable x is hidden in start. The script defines two other functions—functionA and functionB—that each take no arguments and return nothing. Each function is called twice from function start.

Function functionA defines local variable x (line 31) and initializes it to 25. When functionA is called, the variable is output in a line of XHTML text to show that the global variable x is hidden in functionA; then the variable is incremented and output in a line of XHTML text again before the function is exited. Each time this function is called, local variable x is re-created and initialized to 25.

Function functionB does not declare any variables. Therefore, when it refers to variable x, the global variable x is used. When functionB is called, the global variable is output in a line of XHTML text, multiplied by 10 and output in a line of XHTML text again before the function is exited. The next time function functionB is called, the global variable has its modified value, 10, which again gets multiplied by 10, and 100 is output. Finally, the program outputs local variable x in start in a line of XHTML text again, to show that none of the function calls modified the value of x in start, because the functions all referred to variables in other scopes.

7.9 JavaScript Global Functions

JavaScript provides seven global functions. We have already used two of these functions—parseInt and parseFloat. The global functions are summarized in Fig. 7.8.

Actually, the global functions in Fig. 7.8 are all part of JavaScript's *Global object*. The Global object contains all the global variables in the script, all the user-defined functions in the script and all the functions listed in Fig. 7.8. Because global functions and user-defined functions are part of the Global object, some JavaScript programmers refer to these functions as methods. We use the term method only when referring to a function that is called for a particular object (e.g., Math.random()). As a JavaScript programmer, you do not need to use the Global object directly; JavaScript references it for you.

Global function	Description
escape	Takes a string argument and returns a string in which all spaces, punctuation, accent characters and any other character that is not in the ASCII character set are encoded in a hexadecimal format that can be represented on all platforms.
eval	Takes a string argument representing JavaScript code to execute. The JavaScript interpreter evaluates the code and executes it when the eval function is called. This function allows JavaScript code to be stored as strings and executed dynamically. [*Caution:* It is considered a serious security risk to use eval to process any data entered by a user because a malicious user could exploit this to run dangerous code.]
isFinite	Takes a numeric argument and returns true if the value of the argument is not NaN, Number.POSITIVE_INFINITY or Number.NEGATIVE_INFINITY (values that are not numbers or numbers outside the range that JavaScript supports)—otherwise, the function returns false.
isNaN	Takes a numeric argument and returns true if the value of the argument is not a number; otherwise, it returns false. The function is commonly used with the return value of parseInt or parseFloat to determine whether the result is a proper numeric value.

Fig. 7.8 | JavaScript global functions. (Part 1 of 2.)

Global function	Description
parseFloat	Takes a string argument and attempts to convert the beginning of the string into a floating-point value. If the conversion is unsuccessful, the function returns NaN; otherwise, it returns the converted value (e.g., parse-Float("abc123.45") returns NaN, and parseFloat("123.45abc") returns the value 123.45).
parseInt	Takes a string argument and attempts to convert the beginning of the string into an integer value. If the conversion is unsuccessful, the function returns NaN; otherwise, it returns the converted value (e.g., parseInt("abc123") returns NaN, and parseInt("123abc") returns the integer value 123). This function takes an optional second argument, from 2 to 36, specifying the *radix* (or *base*) of the number. Base 2 indicates that the first argument string is in *binary* format, base 8 indicates that the first argument string is in *octal* format and base 16 indicates that the first argument string is in *hexadecimal* format.
unescape	Takes a string as its argument and returns a string in which all characters previously encoded with escape are decoded.

Fig. 7.8 | JavaScript global functions. (Part 2 of 2.)

7.10 Recursion

The programs we have discussed thus far are generally structured as functions that call one another in a disciplined, hierarchical manner. A *recursive function* is a function that calls *itself*, either directly, or indirectly through another function. In this section, we present a simple example of recursion.

We consider recursion conceptually first; then we examine several programs containing recursive functions. Recursive problem-solving approaches have a number of elements in common. A recursive function is called to solve a problem. The function actually knows how to solve only the simplest case(s), or *base case(s)*. If the function is called with a base case, the function returns a result. If the function is called with a more complex problem, it divides the problem into two conceptual pieces—a piece that the function knows how to process (the base case) and a piece that the function does not know how to process. To make recursion feasible, the latter piece must resemble the original problem, but be a simpler or smaller version of it. Because this new problem looks like the original problem, the function invokes (calls) a fresh copy of itself to go to work on the smaller problem; this invocation is referred to as a *recursive call*, or the *recursion step*. The recursion step also normally includes the keyword return, because its result will be combined with the portion of the problem the function knew how to solve to form a result that will be passed back to the original caller.

The recursion step executes while the original call to the function is still open (i.e., it has not finished executing). The recursion step can result in many more recursive calls as the function divides each new subproblem into two conceptual pieces. For the recursion eventually to terminate, each time the function calls itself with a simpler version of the original problem, the sequence of smaller and smaller problems must converge on the base case. At that point, the function recognizes the base case, returns a result to the previous copy of the function, and a sequence of returns ensues up the line until the original function call eventually returns the final result to the caller.

As an example of these concepts at work, let us write a recursive program to perform a popular mathematical calculation. The factorial of a nonnegative integer n, written $n!$ (and pronounced "n factorial"), is the product

$$n \cdot (n - 1) \cdot (n - 2) \cdot \ldots \cdot 1$$

where 1! is equal to 1 and 0! is defined as 1. For example, 5! is the product $5 \cdot 4 \cdot 3 \cdot 2 \cdot 1$, which is equal to 120.

The factorial of an integer (`number` in the following example) greater than or equal to zero can be calculated *iteratively* (nonrecursively) using a `for` statement, as follows:

```
var factorial = 1;

for ( var counter = number; counter >= 1; --counter )
   factorial *= counter;
```

A recursive definition of the factorial function is arrived at by observing the following relationship:

$$n! = n \cdot (n - 1)!$$

For example, *5!* is clearly equal to 5 * 4!, as is shown by the following equations:

$$5! = 5 \cdot 4 \cdot 3 \cdot 2 \cdot 1$$
$$5! = 5 \cdot (4 \cdot 3 \cdot 2 \cdot 1)$$
$$5! = 5 \cdot (4!)$$

The evaluation of 5! would proceed as shown in Fig. 7.9. Figure 7.9 (a) shows how the succession of recursive calls proceeds until 1! is evaluated to be 1, which terminates the

(a) Sequence of recursive calls.   (b) Values returned from each recursive call.

Fig. 7.9 | Recursive evaluation of 5!.

recursion. Figure 7.9 (b) shows the values returned from each recursive call to its caller until the final value is calculated and returned.

Figure 7.10 uses recursion to calculate and print the factorials of the integers 0 to 10. The recursive function `factorial` first tests (line 24) whether a terminating condition is true, i.e., whether number is less than or equal to 1. If so, `factorial` returns 1, no further recursion is necessary and the function returns. If number is greater than 1, line 27 expresses the problem as the product of number and the value returned by a recursive call to `factorial` evaluating the factorial of number - 1. Note that `factorial( number - 1 )` is a simpler problem than the original calculation, `factorial( number )`.

Function `factorial` (lines 22–28) receives as its argument the value for which to calculate the factorial. As can be seen in the screen capture in Fig. 7.10, factorial values become large quickly.

Common Programming Error 7.6

Forgetting to return a value from a recursive function when one is needed results in a logic error.

```
1   <?xml version = "1.0" encoding = "utf-8"?>
2   <!DOCTYPE html PUBLIC "-//W3C//DTD XHTML 1.0 Strict//EN"
3      "http://www.w3.org/TR/xhtml1/DTD/xhtml1-strict.dtd">
4
5   <!-- Fig. 7.10: FactorialTest.html -->
6   <!-- Factorial calculation with a recursive function. -->
7   <html xmlns = "http://www.w3.org/1999/xhtml">
8      <head>
9         <title>Recursive Factorial Function</title>
10        <script type = "text/javascript">
11        <!--
12           document.writeln( "<h1>Factorials of 1 to 10</h1>" );
13           document.writeln( "<table>" );
14
15           for ( var i = 0; i <= 10; i++ )
16              document.writeln( "<tr><td>" + i + "!</td><td>" +
17                 factorial( i ) + "</td></tr>" );
18
19           document.writeln( "</table>" );
20
21           // Recursive definition of function factorial
22           function factorial( number )
23           {
24              if ( number <= 1 )  // base case
25                 return 1;
26              else
27                 return number * factorial( number - 1 );
28           } // end function factorial
29        // -->
30        </script>
31     </head><body></body>
32  </html>
```

Fig. 7.10 | Factorial calculation with a recursive function. (Part 1 of 2.)

Fig. 7.10 | Factorial calculation with a recursive function. (Part 2 of 2.)

Common Programming Error 7.7

Omitting the base case and writing the recursion step incorrectly so that it does not converge on the base case are both errors that cause infinite recursion, eventually exhausting memory. This situation is analogous to the problem of an infinite loop in an iterative (nonrecursive) solution.

Error-Prevention Tip 7.2

Internet Explorer displays an error message when a script seems to be going into infinite recursion. Firefox simply terminates the script after detecting the problem. This allows the user of the web page to recover from a script that contains an infinite loop or infinite recursion.

7.11 Recursion vs. Iteration

In the preceding section, we studied a function that can easily be implemented either recursively or iteratively. In this section, we compare the two approaches and discuss why you might choose one approach over the other in a particular situation.

Both iteration and recursion are based on a control statement: Iteration uses a repetition statement (e.g., for, while or do...while); recursion uses a selection statement (e.g., if, if...else or switch). Both iteration and recursion involve repetition: Iteration explicitly uses a repetition statement; recursion achieves repetition through repeated function calls. Iteration and recursion each involve a termination test: Iteration terminates when the loop-continuation condition fails; recursion terminates when a base case is recognized. Iteration both with counter-controlled repetition and with recursion gradually approaches termination: Iteration keeps modifying a counter until the counter assumes a value that makes the loop-continuation condition fail; recursion keeps producing simpler versions of the original problem until the base case is reached. Both iteration and recursion can occur infinitely: An infinite loop occurs with iteration if the loop-continuation test never becomes false; infinite recursion occurs if the recursion step does not reduce the problem each time via a sequence that converges on the base case or if the base case is incorrect.

One negative aspect of recursion is that function calls require a certain amount of time and memory space not directly spent on executing program instructions. This is known as function-call overhead. Because recursion uses repeated function calls, this overhead greatly affects the performance of the operation. In many cases, using repetition statements in place of recursion is more efficient. However, some problems can be solved more elegantly (and more easily) with recursion.

Software Engineering Observation 7.5

Any problem that can be solved recursively can also be solved iteratively (nonrecursively). A recursive approach is normally chosen in preference to an iterative approach when the recursive approach more naturally mirrors the problem and results in a program that is easier to understand and debug. Another reason to choose a recursive solution is that an iterative solution may not be apparent.

Performance Tip 7.1

Avoid using recursion in performance-oriented situations. Recursive calls take time and consume additional memory.

Common Programming Error 7.8

Accidentally having a nonrecursive function call itself, either directly, or indirectly through another function, can cause infinite recursion.

In addition to the Factorial function example (Fig. 7.10), Fig. 12.26 uses recursion to traverse an XML document tree.

7.12 Web Resources

`www.deitel.com/javascript/`
The Deitel JavaScript Resource Center contains links to some of the best JavaScript resources on the web. There you'll find categorized links to JavaScript tools, code generators, forums, books, libraries, frameworks and more. Also check out the tutorials for all skill levels, from introductory to advanced. Be sure to visit the related Resource Centers on XHTML (`www.deitel.com/xhtml/`) and CSS 2.1 (`www.deitel.com/css21/`).

8

JavaScript: Arrays

OBJECTIVES

In this chapter you will learn:

- To use arrays to store lists and tables of values.
- To declare an array, initialize an array and refer to individual elements of an array.
- To pass arrays to functions.
- To sort an array.
- To declare and manipulate multidimensional arrays.

8.1 Introduction

Arrays are data structures consisting of related data items (sometimes called *collections* of data items). JavaScript arrays are "dynamic" entities in that they can change size after they are created. Many of the techniques demonstrated in this chapter are used frequently in Chapters 10–11 as we introduce the collections that allow a script programmer to manipulate every element of an XHTML document dynamically.

8.2 Arrays

An array is a group of memory locations that all have the same name and normally are of the same type (although this attribute is not required in JavaScript). To refer to a particular location or element in the array, we specify the name of the array and the position number of the particular element in the array.

Figure 8.1 shows an array of integer values named c. This array contains 12 *elements*. Any one of these elements may be referred to by giving the name of the array followed by the position number of the element in square brackets ([]). The first element in every array is the *zeroth element*. Thus, the first element of array c is referred to as c[0], the second element of array c is referred to as c[1], the seventh element of array c is referred to as c[6] and, in general, the ith element of array c is referred to as c[i-1]. Array names follow the same conventions as other identifiers.

The position number in square brackets is called a *subscript* (or an *index*). A subscript must be an integer or an integer expression. Note that a subscripted array name is a left-hand-side expression—it can be used on the left side of an assignment to place a new value into an array element. It can also be used on the right side of an assignment to assign its value to another left-hand side expression.

Let us examine array c in Fig. 8.1 more closely. The array's *name* is c. The *length* of array c is 12 and can be found using by the following expression:

```
c.length
```

Every array in JavaScript knows its own length. The array's 12 elements are referred to as c[0], c[1], c[2], …, c[11]. The *value* of c[0] is -45, the value of c[1] is 6, the value of c[2] is 0, the value of c[7] is 62 and the value of c[11] is 78.

Fig. 8.1 | Array with 12 elements.

The brackets that enclose the array subscript are a JavaScript operator. Brackets have the same level of precedence as parentheses. The chart in Fig. 8.2 shows the precedence and associativity of the operators introduced so far. They are shown from top to bottom in decreasing order of precedence, alongside their associativity and type.

Operators	Associativity	Type
() [] .	left to right	highest
++ -- !	right to left	unary
* / %	left to right	multiplicative
+ -	left to right	additive
< <= > >=	left to right	relational
== !=	left to right	equality
&&	left to right	logical AND
||	left to right	logical OR
?:	right to left	conditional
= += -= *= /= %=	right to left	assignment

Fig. 8.2 | Precedence and associativity of the operators discussed so far.

8.3 Declaring and Allocating Arrays

Arrays occupy space in memory. Actually, an array in JavaScript is an *Array object*. You use *operator new* to dynamically allocate (request memory for) the number of elements required by each array. Operator new creates an object as the program executes by obtaining enough memory to store an object of the type specified to the right of new. The process of creating new objects is also known as *creating an instance* or *instantiating an object,* and operator new is known as the *dynamic memory allocation operator.* Arrays are objects must be created with new. To allocate 12 elements for integer array c, use the statement

```
var c = new Array( 12 );
```

The preceding statement can also be performed in two steps, as follows:

```
var c; // declares the array
c = new Array( 12 ); // allocates the array
```

When arrays are allocated, the elements are not initialized—they have the value undefined.

Common Programming Error 8.1

Assuming that the elements of an array are initialized when the array is allocated may result in logic errors.

8.4 Examples Using Arrays

This section presents several examples of creating and manipulating arrays.

Creating and Initializing Arrays

The script in Fig. 8.3 uses operator new to allocate an Array of five elements and an empty array. The script demonstrates initializing an Array of existing elements and also shows that an Array can grow dynamically to accommodate new elements. The Array's values are displayed in XHTML tables.

```
 1  <?xml version = "1.0" encoding = "utf-8"?>
 2  <!DOCTYPE html PUBLIC "-//W3C//DTD XHTML 1.0 Strict//EN"
 3     "http://www.w3.org/TR/xhtml1/DTD/xhtml1-strict.dtd">
 4
 5  <!-- Fig. 8.3: InitArray.html -->
 6  <!-- Initializing the elements of an array. -->
 7  <html xmlns = "http://www.w3.org/1999/xhtml">
 8     <head>
 9        <title>Initializing an Array</title>
10        <style type = "text/css">
11           table { width: 10em }
12           th    { text-align: left }
13        </style>
14        <script type = "text/javascript">
15           <!--
16           // create (declare) two new arrays
17           var n1 = new Array( 5 ); // allocate five-element Array
18           var n2 = new Array(); // allocate empty Array
19
20           // assign values to each element of Array n1
21           for ( var i = 0; i < n1.length; ++i )
22              n1[ i ] = i;
```

Fig. 8.3 | Initializing the elements of an array. (Part 1 of 2.)

```
23
24            // create and initialize five elements in Array n2
25            for ( i = 0; i < 5; ++i )
26               n2[ i ] = i;
27
28         outputArray( "Array n1:", n1 );
29         outputArray( "Array n2:", n2 );
30
31         // output the heading followed by a two-column table
32         // containing subscripts and elements of "theArray"
33         function outputArray( heading, theArray )
34         {
35            document.writeln( "<h2>" + heading + "</h2>" );
36            document.writeln( "<table border = \"1\"" );
37            document.writeln( "<thead><th>Subscript</th>" +
38               "<th>Value</th></thead><tbody>" );
39
40            // output the subscript and value of each array element
41            for ( var i = 0; i < theArray.length; i++ )
42               document.writeln( "<tr><td>" + i + "</td><td>" +
43                  theArray[ i ] + "</td></tr>" );
44
45            document.writeln( "</tbody></table>" );
46         } // end function outputArray
47         // -->
48      </script>
49   </head><body></body>
50 </html>
```

Fig. 8.3 | Initializing the elements of an array. (Part 2 of 2.)

Line 17 creates Array n1 as an array of five elements. Line 18 creates Array n2 as an empty array. Lines 21–22 use a for statement to initialize the elements of n1 to their subscript numbers (0 to 4). Note the use of the expression n1.length in the condition for the for statement to determine the length of the array. In this example, the length of the array is 5, so the loop continues executing as long as the value of control variable i is less than 5. For a five-element array, the subscript values are 0 through 4, so using the less than operator, <, guarantees that the loop does not attempt to access an element beyond the end of the array. Zero-based counting is usually used to iterate through arrays.

Lines 25–26 use a for statement to add five elements to the Array n2 and initialize each element to its subscript number (0 to 4). Note that Array n2 grows dynamically to accommodate the values assigned to each element of the array.

Software Engineering Observation 8.1

JavaScript automatically reallocates an Array when a value is assigned to an element that is outside the bounds of the original Array. Elements between the last element of the original Array and the new element have undefined values.

Lines 28–29 invoke function outputArray (defined in lines 33–46) to display the contents of each array in an XHTML table. Function outputArray receives two arguments—a string to be output before the XHTML table that displays the contents of the array and the array to output. Lines 41–43 use a for statement to output XHTML text that defines each row of the table.

Common Programming Error 8.2

Referring to an element outside the Array bounds is normally a logic error.

If the values of an Array's elements are known in advance, the elements can be allocated and initialized in the declaration of the array. There are two ways in which the initial values can be specified. The statement

```
var n = [ 10, 20, 30, 40, 50 ];
```

uses a comma-separated *initializer list* enclosed in square brackets ([and]) to create a five-element Array with subscripts of 0, 1, 2, 3 and 4. The array size is determined by the number of values in the initializer list. Note that the preceding declaration does not require the new operator to create the Array object—this functionality is provided by the interpreter when it encounters an array declaration that includes an initializer list. The statement

```
var n = new Array( 10, 20, 30, 40, 50 );
```

also creates a five-element array with subscripts of 0, 1, 2, 3 and 4. In this case, the initial values of the array elements are specified as arguments in the parentheses following new Array. The size of the array is determined by the number of values in parentheses. It is also possible to reserve a space in an Array for a value to be specified later by using a comma as a place holder in the initializer list. For example, the statement

```
var n = [ 10, 20, , 40, 50 ];
```

creates a five-element array with no value specified for the third element (n[2]).

Initializing Arrays with Initializer Lists

The script in Fig. 8.4 creates three `Array` objects to demonstrate initializing arrays with initializer lists (lines 18–20) and displays each array in an XHTML table using the same function `outputArray` discussed in Fig. 8.3. Note that when `Array` `integers2` is displayed in the web page, the elements with subscripts 1 and 2 (the second and third elements of

```
1   <?xml version = "1.0" encoding = "utf-8"?>
2   <!DOCTYPE html PUBLIC "-//W3C//DTD XHTML 1.0 Strict//EN"
3      "http://www.w3.org/TR/xhtml1/DTD/xhtml1-strict.dtd">
4
5   <!-- Fig. 8.4: InitArray2.html -->
6   <!-- Declaring and initializing arrays. -->
7   <html xmlns = "http://www.w3.org/1999/xhtml">
8      <head>
9         <title>Initializing an Array with a Declaration</title>
10        <style type = "text/css">
11           table { width: 15em }
12           th    { text-align: left }
13        </style>
14        <script type = "text/javascript">
15           <!--
16           // Initializer list specifies the number of elements and
17           // a value for each element.
18           var colors = new Array( "cyan", "magenta","yellow", "black" );
19           var integers1 = [ 2, 4, 6, 8 ];
20           var integers2 = [ 2, , , 8 ];
21
22           outputArray( "Array colors contains", colors );
23           outputArray( "Array integers1 contains", integers1 );
24           outputArray( "Array integers2 contains", integers2 );
25
26           // output the heading followed by a two-column table
27           // containing the subscripts and elements of theArray
28           function outputArray( heading, theArray )
29           {
30              document.writeln( "<h2>" + heading + "</h2>" );
31              document.writeln( "<table border = \"1\"" );
32              document.writeln( "<thead><th>Subscript</th>" +
33                 "<th>Value</th></thead><tbody>" );
34
35              // output the subscript and value of each array element
36              for ( var i = 0; i < theArray.length; i++ )
37                 document.writeln( "<tr><td>" + i + "</td><td>" +
38                    theArray[ i ] + "</td></tr>" );
39
40              document.writeln( "</tbody></table>" );
41           } // end function outputArray
42           // -->
43        </script>
44     </head><body></body>
45  </html>
```

Fig. 8.4 | Declaring and initializing arrays. (Part 1 of 2.)

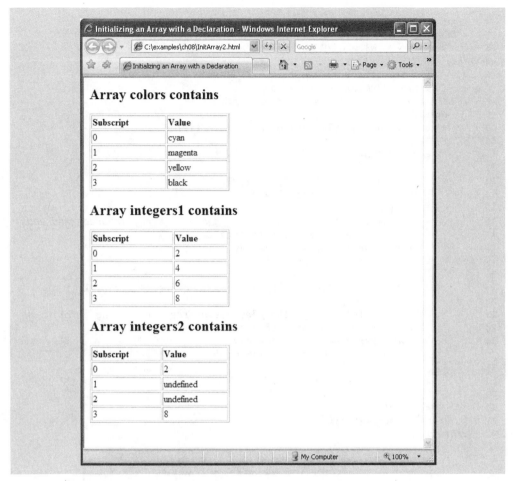

Fig. 8.4 | Declaring and initializing arrays. (Part 2 of 2.)

the array) appear in the web page as undefined. These are the two elements for which we did not supply values in the declaration in line 20 in the script.

Summing the Elements of an Array with for *and* for...in

The script in Fig. 8.5 sums the values contained in theArray, the 10-element integer array declared, allocated and initialized in line 13. The statement in line 19 in the body of the first for statement does the totaling. Note that the values supplied as initializers for array theArray could be read into the program using an XHTML form.

In this example, we introduce JavaScript's *for...in statement*, which enables a script to perform a task for each element in an array (or, as we'll see in Chapters 10–11, for each element in a collection). Lines 25-26 show the syntax of a for...in statement. Inside the parentheses, we declare the element variable used to select each element in the object to the right of keyword in (theArray in this case). When using for...in, JavaScript automatically determines the number of elements in the array. As the JavaScript interpreter iterates over theArray's elements, variable element is assigned a value that can be used as a sub-

```
1   <?xml version = "1.0" encoding = "utf-8"?>
2   <!DOCTYPE html PUBLIC "-//W3C//DTD XHTML 1.0 Strict//EN"
3      "http://www.w3.org/TR/xhtml1/DTD/xhtml1-strict.dtd">
4
5   <!-- Fig. 8.5: SumArray.html -->
6   <!-- Summing elements of an array. -->
7   <html xmlns = "http://www.w3.org/1999/xhtml">
8      <head>
9         <title>Sum the Elements of an Array</title>
10
11        <script type = "text/javascript">
12           <!--
13           var theArray = [ 1, 2, 3, 4, 5, 6, 7, 8, 9, 10 ];
14           var total1 = 0, total2 = 0;
15
16           // iterates through the elements of the array in order and adds
17           // each element's value to total1
18           for ( var i = 0; i < theArray.length; i++ )
19              total1 += theArray[ i ];
20
21           document.writeln( "Total using subscripts: " + total1 );
22
23           // iterates through the elements of the array using a for... in
24           // statement to add each element's value to total2
25           for ( var element in theArray )
26              total2 += theArray[ element ];
27
28           document.writeln( "<br />Total using for...in: " + total2 );
29           // -->
30        </script>
31     </head><body></body>
32  </html>
```

Sum the Elements of an Array - Windows Internet Explorer

C:\examples\ch08\SumArray.html   Google

Sum the Elements of an Array   Page ▾ Tools ▾

Total using subscripts: 55
Total using for...in: 55

My Computer   100%

Fig. 8.5 | Summing elements of an array.

script for theArray. In the case of an Array, the value assigned is a subscript in the range from 0 up to, but not including, theArray.length. Each value is added to total2 to produce the sum of the elements in the array.

Error-Prevention Tip 8.1

When iterating over all the elements of an Array, use a for... in statement to ensure that you manipulate only the existing elements of the Array. Note that a for... in statement skips any undefined elements in the array.

Using the Elements of an Array as Counters

In Chapter 7, we indicated that there is a more elegant way to implement the dice-rolling program in Fig. 7.4. The program rolled a single six-sided die 6000 times and used a `switch` statement to total the number of times each value was rolled. An array version of this script is shown in Fig. 8.6. The `switch` statement in Fig. 7.4 is replaced by line 24 of this program. This line uses the random `face` value as the subscript for the array `frequency` to determine which element to increment during each iteration of the loop. Because the random number calculation in line 23 produces numbers from 1 to 6 (the values for a six-sided die), the `frequency` array must be large enough to allow subscript values of 1 to 6. The smallest number of elements required for an array to have these subscript values is seven elements (subscript values from 0 to 6). In this program, we ignore element 0 of array `frequency` and use only the elements that correspond to values on the sides of a die. Also, lines 32–34 of this program use a loop to generate the table that was written one line at a time in Fig. 7.4. Because we can loop through array `frequency` to help produce the output, we do not have to enumerate each XHTML table row as we did in Fig. 7.4.

```
1   <?xml version = "1.0" encoding = "utf-8"?>
2   <!DOCTYPE html PUBLIC "-//W3C//DTD XHTML 1.0 Strict//EN"
3      "http://www.w3.org/TR/xhtml1/DTD/xhtml1-strict.dtd">
4
5   <!-- Fig. 8.6: RollDie.html -->
6   <!-- Dice-rolling program using an array instead of a switch. -->
7   <html xmlns = "http://www.w3.org/1999/xhtml">
8      <head>
9         <title>Roll a Six-Sided Die 6000 Times</title>
10        <style type = "text/css">
11           table { width: 15em }
12           th    { text-align: left }
13        </style>
14        <script type = "text/javascript">
15           <!--
16           var face;
17           var frequency = [ , 0, 0, 0, 0, 0, 0 ]; // leave frequency[0]
18                                                   // uninitialized
19
20           // summarize results
21           for ( var roll = 1; roll <= 6000; ++roll )
22           {
23              face = Math.floor( 1 + Math.random() * 6 );
24              ++frequency[ face ];
25           } // end for
26
27           document.writeln( "<table border = \"1\"><thead>" );
28           document.writeln( "<th>Face</th>" +
29              "<th>Frequency</th></thead><tbody>" );
30
31           // generate entire table of frequencies for each face
32           for ( face = 1; face < frequency.length; ++face )
33              document.writeln( "<tr><td>" + face + "</td><td>" +
34                 frequency[ face ] + "</td></tr>" );
```

Fig. 8.6 | Dice-rolling program using an array instead of a `switch`. (Part 1 of 2.)

```
35
36              document.writeln( "</tbody></table>" );
37              // -->
38          </script>
39      </head>
40      <body>
41          <p>Click Refresh (or Reload) to run the script again</p>
42      </body>
43  </html>
```

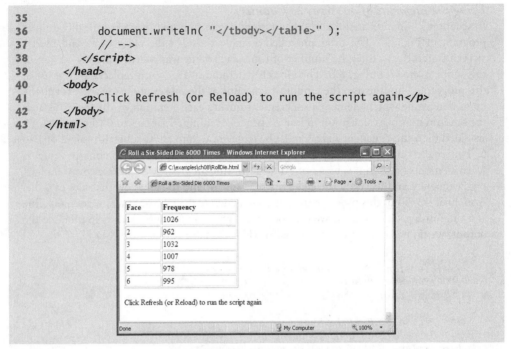

Fig. 8.6 | Dice-rolling program using an array instead of a `switch`. (Part 2 of 2.)

8.5 Random Image Generator Using Arrays

In Chapter 7, we created a random image generator that required image files to be named `1.gif`, `2.gif`, ..., `7.gif`. In this example (Fig. 8.7), we create a more elegant random image generator that does not require the image filenames to be integers. This version of the random image generator uses an array `pictures` to store the names of the image files as strings. The script generates a random integer and uses it as a subscript into the `pictures` array. The script outputs an XHTML `img` element whose `src` attribute contains the image filename located in the randomly selected position in the `pictures` array.

```
1   <?xml version = "1.0" encoding = "utf-8"?>
2   <!DOCTYPE html PUBLIC "-//W3C//DTD XHTML 1.0 Strict//EN"
3       "http://www.w3.org/TR/xhtml1/DTD/xhtml1-strict.dtd">
4
5   <!-- Fig. 8.7: RandomPicture2.html -->
6   <!-- Random image generation using arrays. -->
7   <html xmlns = "http://www.w3.org/1999/xhtml">
8       <head>
9           <title>Random Image Generator</title>
10          <style type = "text/css">
11              table { width: 15em }
12              th    { text-align: left }
13          </style>
```

Fig. 8.7 | Random image generation using arrays. (Part 1 of 2.)

```
14          <script type = "text/javascript">
15             <!--
16             var pictures =
17                [ "CPE", "EPT", "GPP", "GUI", "PERF", "PORT", "SEO" ];
18
19             // pick a random image from the pictures array and displays by
20             // creating an img tag and appending the src attribute to the
21             // filename
22             document.write ( "<img src = \"" +
23                pictures[ Math.floor( Math.random() * 7 ) ] + ".gif\" />" );
24             // -->
25          </script>
26       </head>
27       <body>
28          <p>Click Refresh (or Reload) to run the script again</p>
29       </body>
30    </html>
```

Fig. 8.7 | Random image generation using arrays. (Part 2 of 2.)

The script declares the array pictures in lines 16–17 and initializes it with the names of seven image files. Lines 22–23 create the img tag that displays the random image on the web page. Line 22 opens the img tag and begins the src attribute. Line 23 generates a random integer from 0 to 6 as an index into the pictures array, the result of which is a randomly selected image filename. The expression

```
pictures[ Math.floor( Math.random() * 7 ) ]
```

evaluates to a string from the pictures array, which then is written to the document (line 23). Line 23 completes the img tag with the extension of the image file (.gif).

8.6 References and Reference Parameters

Two ways to pass arguments to functions (or methods) in many programming languages are *pass-by-value* and *pass-by-reference*. When an argument is passed to a function by value, a *copy* of the argument's value is made and is passed to the called function. In JavaScript, numbers, boolean values and strings are passed to functions by value.

With pass-by-reference, the caller gives the called function direct access to the caller's data and allows it to modify the data if it so chooses. This procedure is accomplished by passing to the called function the address of the location in memory where the data resides. Pass-by-reference can improve performance because it can eliminate the overhead of copying large amounts of data, but it can weaken security because the called function can access the caller's data. In JavaScript, all objects (and thus all `Arrays`) are passed to functions by reference.

Error-Prevention Tip 8.2

With pass-by-value, changes to the copy of the called function do not affect the original variable's value in the calling function. This prevents the accidental side effects that so greatly hinder the development of correct and reliable software systems.

Software Engineering Observation 8.2

Unlike some other languages, JavaScript does not allow you to choose whether to pass each argument by value or by reference. Numbers, boolean values and strings are passed by value. Objects are passed to functions by reference. When a function receives a reference to an object, the function can manipulate the object directly.

Software Engineering Observation 8.3

When returning information from a function via a `return` statement, numbers and boolean values are always returned by value (i.e., a copy is returned), and objects are always returned by reference. Note that, in the pass-by-reference case, it is not necessary to return the new value, since the object is already modified.

To pass a reference to an object into a function, simply specify the reference name in the function call. Normally, the reference name is the identifier that the program uses to manipulate the object. Mentioning the reference by its parameter name in the body of the called function actually refers to the original object in memory, which can be accessed directly by the called function. In the next section, we demonstrate pass-by-value and pass-by-reference, using arrays.

8.7 Passing Arrays to Functions

To pass an array argument to a function (Fig. 8.8), specify the name of the array (a reference to the array) without brackets. For example, if array `hourlyTemperatures` has been declared as

```
var hourlyTemperatures = new Array( 24 );
```

then the function call

```
modifyArray( hourlyTemperatures );
```

passes array `hourlyTemperatures` to function `modifyArray`. As stated in Section 8.2, every array object in JavaScript knows its own size (via the `length` attribute). Thus, when we pass an array object into a function, we do not pass the size of the array separately as an argument. Figure 8.3 illustrated this concept when we passed `Arrays` n1 and n2 to function `outputArray` to display each `Array`'s contents.

```
 1  <?xml version = "1.0" encoding = "utf-8"?>
 2  <!DOCTYPE html PUBLIC "-//W3C//DTD XHTML 1.0 Strict//EN"
 3     "http://www.w3.org/TR/xhtml1/DTD/xhtml1-strict.dtd">
 4
 5  <!-- Fig. 8.8: PassArray.html -->
 6  <!-- Passing arrays and individual array elements to functions. -->
 7  <html xmlns = "http://www.w3.org/1999/xhtml">
 8     <head>
 9        <title>Passing arrays and individual array
10           elements to functions</title>
11        <script type = "text/javascript">
12           <!--
13           var a = [ 1, 2, 3, 4, 5 ];
14
15           document.writeln( "<h2>Effects of passing entire " +
16              "array by reference</h2>" );
17           outputArray( "Original array: ", a );
18
19           modifyArray( a );  // array a passed by reference
20
21           outputArray( "Modified array: ", a );
22
23           document.writeln( "<h2>Effects of passing array " +
24              "element by value</h2>" +
25              "a[3] before modifyElement: " + a[ 3 ] );
26
27           modifyElement( a[ 3 ] ); // array element a[3] passed by value
28
29           document.writeln( "<br />a[3] after modifyElement: " + a[ 3 ] );
30
31           // outputs heading followed by the contents of "theArray"
32           function outputArray( heading, theArray )
33           {
34              document.writeln(
35                 heading + theArray.join( " " ) + "<br />" );
36           } // end function outputArray
37
38           // function that modifies the elements of an array
39           function modifyArray( theArray )
40           {
41              for ( var j in theArray )
42                 theArray[ j ] *= 2;
43           } // end function modifyArray
44
45           // function that modifies the value passed
46           function modifyElement( e )
47           {
48              e *= 2; // scales element e only for the duration of the
49                      // function
50              document.writeln( "<br />value in modifyElement: " + e );
51           } // end function modifyElement
52           // -->
```

Fig. 8.8 | Passing arrays and individual array elements to functions. (Part 1 of 2.)

```
53          </script>
54        </head><body></body>
55      </html>
```

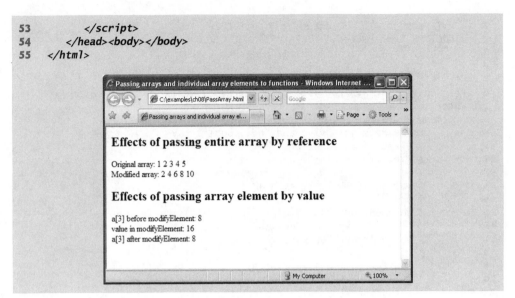

Fig. 8.8 | Passing arrays and individual array elements to functions. (Part 2 of 2.)

Although entire arrays are passed by reference, *individual numeric and boolean array elements* are passed *by value* exactly as simple numeric and boolean variables are passed (the objects referred to by individual elements of an Array of objects are still passed by reference). Such simple single pieces of data are called *scalars*. To pass an array element to a function, use the subscripted name of the element as an argument in the function call.

For a function to receive an Array through a function call, the function's parameter list must specify a parameter that will refer to the Array in the body of the function. Unlike other programming languages, JavaScript does not provide a special syntax for this purpose. JavaScript simply requires that the identifier for the Array be specified in the parameter list. For example, the function header for function modifyArray might be written as

```
function modifyArray( b )
```

indicating that modifyArray expects to receive a parameter named b (the argument supplied in the calling function must be an Array). Arrays are passed by reference, and therefore when the called function uses the array name b, it refers to the actual array in the caller (array hourlyTemperatures in the preceding call). The script in Fig. 8.8 demonstrates the difference between passing an entire array and passing an array element.

Software Engineering Observation 8.4

JavaScript does not check the number of arguments or types of arguments that are passed to a function. It is possible to pass any number of values to a function. JavaScript will attempt to perform conversions when the values are used.

The statement in line 17 invokes function outputArray to display the contents of array a before it is modified. Function outputArray (defined in lines 32–36) receives a string to output and the array to output. The statement in lines 34–35 uses Array method *join* to create a string containing all the elements in theArray. Method join takes as its argument a string containing the *separator* that should be used to separate the elements of the array in the string that is returned. If the argument is not specified, the empty string is used as the separator.

Line 19 invokes function modifyArray (lines 39–43) and passes it array a. The modifyArray function multiplies each element by 2. To illustrate that array a's elements were modified, the statement in line 21 invokes function outputArray again to display the contents of array a after it is modified. As the screen capture shows, the elements of a are indeed modified by modifyArray.

To show the value of a[3] before the call to modifyElement, line 25 outputs the value of a[3]. Line 27 invokes modifyElement (lines 46–51) and passes a[3] as the argument. Remember that a[3] actually is one integer value in the array a. Also remember that numeric values and boolean values are always passed to functions by value. Therefore, a copy of a[3] is passed. Function modifyElement multiplies its argument by 2 and stores the result in its parameter e. The parameter of function modifyElement is a local variable in that function, so when the function terminates, the local variable is no longer accessible. Thus, when control is returned to the main script, the unmodified value of a[3] is displayed by the statement in line 29.

8.8 Sorting Arrays

The Array object in JavaScript has a built-in method *sort* for sorting arrays. Figure 8.9 demonstrates the Array object's sort method.

```
1   <?xml version = "1.0" encoding = "utf-8"?>
2   <!DOCTYPE html PUBLIC "-//W3C//DTD XHTML 1.0 Strict//EN"
3      "http://www.w3.org/TR/xhtml1/DTD/xhtml1-strict.dtd">
4
5   <!-- Fig. 8.9: Sort.html -->
6   <!-- Sorting an array with sort. -->
7   <html xmlns = "http://www.w3.org/1999/xhtml">
8      <head>
9         <title>Sorting an Array with Array Method sort</title>
10        <script type = "text/javascript">
11           <!--
12           var a = [ 10, 1, 9, 2, 8, 3, 7, 4, 6, 5 ];
13
14           document.writeln( "<h1>Sorting an Array</h1>" );
15           outputArray( "Data items in original order: ", a );
16           a.sort( compareIntegers );  // sort the array
17           outputArray( "Data items in ascending order: ", a );
18
19           // output the heading followed by the contents of theArray
20           function outputArray( heading, theArray )
21           {
22              document.writeln( "<p>" + heading +
23                 theArray.join( " " ) + "</p>" );
24           } // end function outputArray
25
```

Fig. 8.9 | Sorting an array with Array method sort. (Part 1 of 2.)

```
26          // comparison function for use with sort
27          function compareIntegers( value1, value2 )
28          {
29             return parseInt( value1 ) - parseInt( value2 );
30          } // end function compareIntegers
31          // -->
32       </script>
33    </head><body></body>
34 </html>
```

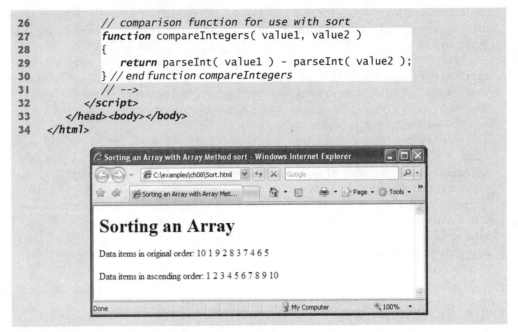

Fig. 8.9 | Sorting an array with `Array` method `sort`. (Part 2 of 2.)

By default, `Array` method `sort` (with no arguments) uses string comparisons to determine the sorting order of the `Array` elements. The strings are compared by the ASCII values of their characters. [*Note:* String comparison is discussed in more detail in Chapter 9, JavaScript: Objects.] In this example, we'd like to sort an array of integers.

Method `sort` takes as its optional argument the name of a function (called the *comparator function*) that compares its two arguments and returns one of the following:

- a negative value if the first argument is less than the second argument
- zero if the arguments are equal, or
- a positive value if the first argument is greater than the second argument

This example uses function `compareIntegers` (defined in lines 27–30) as the comparator function for method `sort`. It calculates the difference between the integer values of its two arguments (function `parseInt` ensures that the arguments are handled properly as integers). If the first argument is less than the second argument, the difference will be a negative value. If the arguments are equal, the difference will be zero. If the first argument is greater than the second argument, the difference will be a positive value.

Line 16 invokes `Array` object a's `sort` method and passes the name of function `compareIntegers` as an argument. Method `sort` receives function `compareIntegers` as an argument, then uses the function to compare elements of the `Array` a to determine their sorting order.

Software Engineering Observation 8.5

Functions in JavaScript are considered to be data. Therefore, functions can be assigned to variables, stored in Arrays and passed to functions just like other data types.

8.9 Multidimensional Arrays

Multidimensional arrays with two subscripts are often used to represent tables of values consisting of information arranged in *rows* and *columns*. To identify a particular table element, we must specify the two subscripts; by convention, the first identifies the element's row, and the second identifies the element's column. Arrays that require two subscripts to identify a particular element are called *two-dimensional arrays*.

Multidimensional arrays can have more than two dimensions. JavaScript does not support multidimensional arrays directly, but does allow you to specify arrays whose elements are also arrays, thus achieving the same effect. When an array contains one-dimensional arrays as its elements, we can imagine these one-dimensional arrays as rows of a table, and the positions in these arrays as columns. Figure 8.10 illustrates a two-dimensional array named a that contains three rows and four columns (i.e., a three-by-four array—three one-dimensional arrays, each with 4 elements). In general, an array with m rows and n columns is called an *m-by-n array*.

Every element in array a is identified in Fig. 8.10 by an element name of the form a[i][j]; a is the name of the array, and i and j are the subscripts that uniquely identify the row and column, respectively, of each element in a. Note that the names of the elements in the first row all have a first subscript of 0; the names of the elements in the fourth column all have a second subscript of 3.

Fig. 8.10 | Two-dimensional array with three rows and four columns.

Arrays of One-Dimensional Arrays

Multidimensional arrays can be initialized in declarations like a one-dimensional array. Array b with two rows and two columns could be declared and initialized with the statement

```
var b = [ [ 1, 2 ], [ 3, 4 ] ];
```

The values are grouped by row in square brackets. The array [1, 2] initializes element b[0], and the array [3, 4] initializes element b[1]. So 1 and 2 initialize b[0][0] and b[0][1], respectively. Similarly, 3 and 4 initialize b[1][0] and b[1][1], respectively. The interpreter determines the number of rows by counting the number of sub initializer lists—arrays nested within the outermost array. The interpreter determines the number of columns in each row by counting the number of values in the sub-array that initializes the row.

Two-Dimensional Arrays with Rows of Different Lengths

The rows of a two-dimensional array can vary in length. The declaration

```
var b = [ [ 1, 2 ], [ 3, 4, 5 ] ];
```

creates array b with row 0 containing two elements (1 and 2) and row 1 containing three elements (3, 4 and 5).

Creating Two-Dimensional Arrays with *new*

A multidimensional array in which each row has a different number of columns can be allocated dynamically, as follows:

```
var b;
b = new Array( 2 ); // allocate rows
b[ 0 ] = new Array( 5 ); // allocate columns for row 0
b[ 1 ] = new Array( 3 ); // allocate columns for row 1
```

The preceding code creates a two-dimensional array with two rows. Row 0 has five columns, and row 1 has three columns.

Two-Dimensional Array Example: Displaying Element Values

Figure 8.11 initializes two-dimensional arrays in declarations and uses nested for...in loops to *traverse the arrays* (i.e., manipulate every element of the array).

```
 1   <?xml version = "1.0" encoding = "utf-8"?>
 2   <!DOCTYPE html PUBLIC "-//W3C//DTD XHTML 1.0 Strict//EN"
 3      "http://www.w3.org/TR/xhtml1/DTD/xhtml1-strict.dtd">
 4
 5   <!-- Fig. 8.11: InitArray3.html -->
 6   <!-- Initializing multidimensional arrays. -->
 7   <html xmlns = "http://www.w3.org/1999/xhtml">
 8      <head>
 9         <title>Initializing Multidimensional Arrays</title>
10         <script type = "text/javascript">
11            <!--
12            var array1 = [ [ 1, 2, 3 ], // first row
13                           [ 4, 5, 6 ] ]; // second row
14            var array2 = [ [ 1, 2 ], // first row
15                           [ 3 ], // second row
16                           [ 4, 5, 6 ] ]; // third row
17
18            outputArray( "Values in array1 by row", array1 );
19            outputArray( "Values in array2 by row", array2 );
20
21            function outputArray( heading, theArray )
22            {
23               document.writeln( "<h2>" + heading + "</h2><pre>" );
24
25               // iterates through the set of one-dimensional arrays
26               for ( var i in theArray )
27               {
```

Fig. 8.11 | Initializing multidimensional arrays. (Part 1 of 2.)

```
28                  // iterates through the elements of each one-dimensional
29                  // array
30                  for ( var j in theArray[ i ] )
31                     document.write( theArray[ i ][ j ] + " " );
32
33                  document.writeln( "<br />" );
34              } // end for
35
36              document.writeln( "</pre>" );
37          } // end function outputArray
38          // -->
39       </script>
40    </head><body></body>
41 </html>
```

Values in array1 by row

1 2 3

4 5 6

Values in array2 by row

1 2

3

4 5 6

Fig. 8.11 | Initializing multidimensional arrays. (Part 2 of 2.)

The program declares two arrays in main script (in the XHTML head element). The declaration of array1 (lines 12–13 provides six initializers in two sublists. The first sublist initializes the first row of the array to the values 1, 2 and 3; the second sublist initializes the second row of the array to the values 4, 5 and 6. The declaration of array2 (lines 14–16) provides six initializers in three sublists. The sublist for the first row explicitly initializes the first row to have two elements, with values 1 and 2, respectively. The sublist for the second row initializes the second row to have one element, with value 3. The sublist for the third row initializes the third row to the values 4, 5 and 6.

The script calls function outputArray from lines 18–19 to display each array's elements in the web page. Function outputArray (lines 21–37) receives two arguments—a string heading to output before the array and the array to output (called theArray). Note the use of a nested for...in statement to output the rows of each two-dimensional array. The outer for...in statement iterates over the rows of the array. The inner for...in statement iterates over the columns of the current row being processed. The nested for...in statement in this example could have been written with for statements, as follows:

```
for ( var i = 0; i < theArray.length; ++i )
{
    for ( var j = 0; j < theArray[ i ].length; ++j )
        document.write( theArray[ i ][ j ] + " " );

    document.writeln( "<br />" );
}
```

In the outer `for` statement, the expression `theArray.length` determines the number of rows in the array. In the inner `for` statement, the expression `theArray[i].length` determines the number of columns in each row of the array. This condition enables the loop to determine, for each row, the exact number of columns.

Common Multidimensional-Array Manipulations with for and for… in Statements
Many common array manipulations use `for` or `for…in` statements. For example, the following `for` statement sets all the elements in the third row of array a in Fig. 8.10 to zero:

```
for ( var col = 0; col < a[ 2 ].length; ++col )
    a[ 2 ][ col ] = 0;
```

We specified the *third* row; therefore, we know that the first subscript is always 2 (0 is the first row and 1 is the second row). The `for` loop varies only the second subscript (i.e., the column subscript). The preceding `for` statement is equivalent to the statements

```
a[ 2 ][ 0 ] = 0;
a[ 2 ][ 1 ] = 0;
a[ 2 ][ 2 ] = 0;
a[ 2 ][ 3 ] = 0;
```

The following `for…in` statement is also equivalent to the preceding `for` statement:

```
for ( var col in a[ 2 ] )
    a[ 2 ][ col ] = 0;
```

The following nested `for` statement determines the total of all the elements in array a:

```
var total = 0;

for ( var row = 0; row < a.length; ++row )

    for ( var col = 0; col < a[ row ].length; ++col )
        total += a[ row ][ col ];
```

The `for` statement totals the elements of the array, one row at a time. The outer `for` statement begins by setting the row subscript to 0, so that the elements of the first row may be totaled by the inner `for` statement. The outer `for` statement then increments row to 1, so that the elements of the second row can be totaled. Then the outer `for` statement increments row to 2, so that the elements of the third row can be totaled. The result can be displayed when the nested `for` statement terminates. The preceding `for` statement is equivalent to the following `for…in` statement:

```
var total = 0;

for ( var row in a )

    for ( var col in a[ row ] )
        total += a[ row ][ col ];
```

8.10 Building an Online Quiz

Online quizzes and polls are popular web applications often used for educational purposes or just for fun. Web developers typically build quizzes using simple XHTML forms and process the results with JavaScript. Arrays allow a programmer to represent several possible answer choices in a single data structure. Figure 8.12 contains an online quiz consisting of one question. The quiz page contains one of the tip icons used throughout this book and an XHTML form in which the user identifies the type of tip the image represents by selecting one of four radio buttons. After the user selects one of the radio button choices and submits the form, the script determines whether the user selected the correct type of tip to match the mystery image. The JavaScript function that checks the user's answer combines several of the concepts from the current chapter and previous chapters in a concise and useful script.

```
1   <?xml version = "1.0" encoding = "utf-8"?>
2   <!DOCTYPE html PUBLIC "-//W3C//DTD XHTML 1.0 Strict//EN"
3      "http://www.w3.org/TR/xhtml1/DTD/xhtml1-strict.dtd">
4
5   <!-- Fig. 8.12: quiz.html -->
6   <!-- Online quiz graded with JavaScript. -->
7   <html xmlns = "http://www.w3.org/1999/xhtml">
8      <head>
9         <title>Online Quiz</title>
10        <script type = "text/JavaScript">
11           <!--
12           function checkAnswers()
13           {
14              var myQuiz = document.getElementById( "myQuiz" );
15
16              // determine whether the answer is correct
17              if ( myQuiz.elements[ 1 ].checked )
18                 alert( "Congratulations, your answer is correct" );
19              else // if the answer is incorrect
20                 alert( "Your answer is incorrect. Please try again" );
21           } // end function checkAnswers
22           -->
23        </script>
24     </head>
25     <body>
26        <form id = "myQuiz" onsubmit = "checkAnswers()" action = "">
27           <p>Select the name of the tip that goes with the
28              image shown:<br />
29              <img src="EPT.gif" alt="mystery tip"/>
30              <br />
31
32              <input type = "radio" name = "radiobutton" value = "CPE" />
33              <label>Common Programming Error</label>
34
35              <input type = "radio" name = "radiobutton" value = "EPT" />
36              <label>Error-Prevention Tip</label>
37
```

Fig. 8.12 | Online quiz graded with JavaScript. (Part 1 of 2.)

```
38              <input type = "radio" name = "radiobutton" value = "PERF" />
39              <label>Performance Tip</label>
40
41              <input type = "radio" name = "radiobutton" value = "PORT" />
42              <label>Portability Tip</label><br />
43
44              <input type = "submit" name = "submit" value = "Submit" />
45              <input type = "reset" name = "reset" value = "Reset" />
46          </p>
47      </form>
48   </body>
49 </html>
```

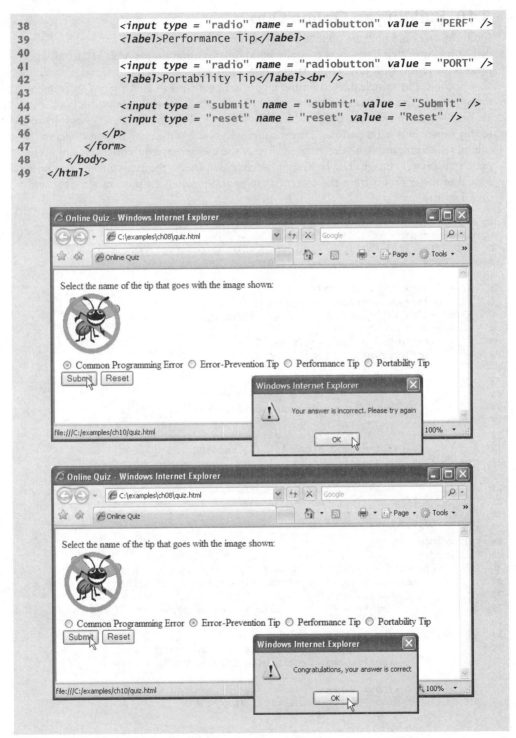

Fig. 8.12 | Online quiz graded with JavaScript. (Part 2 of 2.)

Before we discuss the script code, we first discuss the body element (lines 25–48) of the XHTML document. The body's GUI components play an important role in the script.

Lines 26–47 define the form that presents the quiz to users. Line 26 begins the form element and specifies the onsubmit attribute to "checkAnswers()", indicating that the interpreter should execute the JavaScript function checkAnswers (lines 12–21) when the user submits the form (i.e., clicks the **Submit** button or presses *Enter*).

Line 29 adds the tip image to the page. Lines 32–42 display the radio buttons and corresponding labels that display possible answer choices. Lines 44–45 add the submit and reset buttons to the page.

We now examine the script used to check the answer submitted by the user. Lines 12–21 declare the function checkAnswers that contains all the JavaScript required to grade the quiz. The if...else statement in lines 17–20 determines whether the user answered the question correctly. The image that the user is asked to identify is the Error-Prevention Tip icon. Thus the correct answer to the quiz corresponds to the second radio button.

An XHTML form's elements can be accessed individually using getElementById or through the *elements property* of the containing form object. The elements property contains an array of all the form's controls. The radio buttons are part of the XHTML form myQuiz, so we access the elements array in line 17 using dot notation (myQuiz.elements[1]). The array element myQuiz.elements[1] corresponds to the correct answer (i.e., the second radio button). Finally, line 17 determines whether the property *checked* of the second radio button is true. Property checked of a radio button is true when the radio button is selected, and it is false when the radio button is not selected. Recall that only one radio button may be selected at any given time. If property myQuiz.elements[1].checked is true, indicating that the correct answer is selected, the script alerts a congratulatory message. If property checked of the radio button is false, then the script alerts an alternate message (line 20).

8.11 Web Resources

www.deitel.com/javascript/
The Deitel JavaScript Resource Center contains links to some of the best JavaScript resources on the web. There you'll find categorized links to JavaScript tools, code generators, forums, books, libraries, frameworks and more. Also check out the tutorials for all skill levels, from introductory to advanced. Be sure to visit the related Resource Centers on XHTML (www.deitel.com/xhtml/) and CSS 2.1 (www.deitel.com/css21/).

9

JavaScript: Objects

OBJECTIVES

In this chapter you will learn:

- Object-based programming terminology and concepts.

- The concepts of encapsulation and data hiding.

- The value of object orientation.

- To use the JavaScript objects `Math`, `String`, `Date`, `Boolean` and `Number`.

- To use the browser's `document` and `window` objects.

- To use cookies.

- To represent objects simply using JSON.

My object all sublime
I shall achieve in time.
—W. S. Gilbert

Is it a world to hide virtues in?
—William Shakespeare

Good as it is to inherit a library, it is better to collect one.
—Augustine Birrell

9.1 Introduction

This chapter presents a more formal treatment of *objects*. We begin by briefly introducing the concepts of object orientation. The remainder of the chapter overviews several of Java-Script's built-in objects and demonstrates many of their capabilities. We also provide a brief introduction to JSON, a means for creating JavaScript objects. In the coming chapters on the Document Object Model and Events we discuss the objects provided by the browser that enable scripts to interact with the elements of an XHTML document.

9.2 Introduction to Object Technology

This section provides a general introduction to object orientation. The terminology and technologies discussed here support various chapters that come later in the book. Here, you'll learn that objects are a natural way of thinking about the world and about scripts that manipulate XHTML documents. In Chapters 4–8, we used built-in JavaScript objects—Math and Array—and objects provided by the web browser—document and window—to perform tasks in our scripts. JavaScript uses objects to perform many tasks and therefore is referred to as an *object-based programming language*. Our goal here is to help you develop an object-oriented way of thinking. Many technologies in this book, including CSS, JavaScript, Ajax, Ruby on Rails, ASP.NET, and JavaServer Faces are based on at least some of the concepts introduced in this section.

Basic Object-Technology Concepts

We begin our introduction to object technology with some key terminology. Everywhere you look in the real world you see objects—people, animals, plants, cars, planes, buildings, computers, monitors and so on. Humans think in terms of objects. Telephones, houses, traffic lights, microwave ovens and water coolers are just a few more common objects we see around us.

We sometimes divide objects into two categories: animate and inanimate. Animate objects are "alive" in some sense—they move around and do things. Inanimate objects do not move on their own. Objects of both types, however, have some things in common. They all have *attributes* (e.g., size, shape, color and weight), and they all exhibit *behaviors* (e.g., a ball rolls, bounces, inflates and deflates; a baby cries, sleeps, crawls, walks and blinks; a car accelerates, brakes and turns; a towel absorbs water). We'll study the kinds of attributes and behaviors that software objects have.

Humans learn about existing objects by studying their attributes and observing their behaviors. Different objects can have similar attributes and can exhibit similar behaviors. Comparisons can be made, for example, between babies and adults, and between humans and chimpanzees.

Object-oriented design (OOD) models software in terms similar to those that people use to describe real-world objects. It takes advantage of class relationships, where objects of a certain class, such as a class of vehicles, have the same characteristics—cars, trucks, little red wagons and roller skates have much in common. OOD takes advantage of *inheritance* relationships, where new classes of objects are derived by absorbing characteristics of existing classes and adding unique characteristics of their own. An object of class "convertible" certainly has the characteristics of the more general class "automobile," but more specifically, the roof goes up and down.

Object-oriented design provides a natural and intuitive way to view the software design process—namely, modeling objects by their attributes, behaviors and interrelationships, just as we describe real-world objects. OOD also models communication between objects. Just as people send messages to one another (e.g., a sergeant commands a soldier to stand at attention), objects also communicate via messages. A bank account object may receive a message to decrease its balance by a certain amount because the customer has withdrawn that amount of money.

OOD *encapsulates* (i.e., wraps) attributes and *operations* (behaviors) into objects—an object's attributes and operations are intimately tied together. Objects have the property of *information hiding*. This means that objects may know how to communicate with one another across well-defined *interfaces,* but normally they are not allowed to know how other objects are implemented—implementation details are hidden within the objects themselves. We can drive a car effectively, for instance, without knowing the details of how engines, transmissions, brakes and exhaust systems work internally—as long as we know how to use the accelerator pedal, the brake pedal, the steering wheel and so on. Information hiding, as we'll see, is crucial to good software engineering.

Like the designers of an automobile, the designers of web browsers have defined a set of objects that encapsulate an XHTML document's elements and expose to a JavaScript programmer the attributes and behaviors that enable a JavaScript program to interact with (or script) those elements (objects). You'll soon see that the browser's document object contains attributes and behaviors that provide access to every element of an XHTML document. Similarly, JavaScript provides objects that encapsulate various capabilities in a script. For example, the JavaScript Array object provides attributes and behaviors that enable a script to manipulate a collection of data. The Array object's length property (attribute) contains the number of elements in the `Array`. The `Array` object's `sort` method (behavior) orders the elements of the `Array`.

Some programming languages—like Java, Visual Basic, C# and C++—are *object oriented*. Programming in such a language is called *object-oriented programming (OOP)*, and it allows computer programmers to implement object-oriented designs as working software systems. Languages like C, on the other hand, are *procedural*, so programming tends to be *action oriented*. In procedural languages, the unit of programming is the *function*. In object-oriented languages, the unit of programming is the *class* from which objects are eventually *instantiated* (an OOP term for "created"). Classes contain functions that implement operations and data that comprises attributes.

Procedural programmers concentrate on writing functions. Programmers group actions that perform some common task into functions, and group functions to form programs. Data is certainly important in procedural languages, but the view is that data exists primarily in support of the actions that functions perform. The *verbs* in a system specification help a procedural programmer determine the set of functions that work together to implement the system.

Classes, Properties and Methods

Object-oriented programmers concentrate on creating their own *user-defined types* called *classes*. Each class contains data as well as the set of functions that manipulate that data and provide services to *clients* (i.e., other classes or functions that use the class). The data components of a class are called properties. For example, a bank account class might include an account number and a balance. The function components of a class are called methods. For example, a bank account class might include methods to make a deposit (increasing the balance), make a withdrawal (decreasing the balance) and inquire what the current balance is. You use built-in types (and other user-defined types) as the "building blocks" for constructing new user-defined types (classes). The *nouns* in a system specification help you determine the set of classes from which objects are created that work together to implement the system.

Classes are to objects as blueprints are to houses—a class is a "plan" for building an object of the class. Just as we can build many houses from one blueprint, we can instantiate (create) many objects from one class. You cannot cook meals in the kitchen of a blueprint; you can cook meals in the kitchen of a house. You cannot sleep in the bedroom of a blueprint; you can sleep in the bedroom of a house.

Classes can have relationships with other classes. For example, in an object-oriented design of a bank, the "bank teller" class needs to relate to other classes, such as the "customer" class, the "cash drawer" class, the "safe" class, and so on. These relationships are called *associations*.

Packaging software as classes makes it possible for future software systems to *reuse* the classes. Groups of related classes are often packaged as reusable *components*. Just as realtors often say that the three most important factors affecting the price of real estate are "location, location and location," some people in the software development community say that the three most important factors affecting the future of software development are "reuse, reuse and reuse."

Indeed, with object technology, you can build much of the new software you'll need by combining existing classes, just as automobile manufacturers combine interchangeable parts. Each new class you create will have the potential to become a valuable software asset that you and other programmers can reuse to speed and enhance the quality of future software development efforts.

9.3 Math Object

The Math object's methods allow you to perform many common mathematical calculations. As shown previously, an object's methods are called by writing the name of the object followed by a dot (.) and the name of the method. In parentheses following the method name is the argument (or a comma-separated list of arguments) to the method. For example, to calculate and display the square root of 900.0 you might write

```
document.writeln( Math.sqrt( 900.0 ) );
```

which calls method Math.sqrt to calculate the square root of the number contained in the parentheses (900.0), then outputs the result. The number 900.0 is the argument of the Math.sqrt method. The preceding statement would display 30.0. Some **Math** object methods are summarized in Fig. 9.1.

Method	Description	Examples
abs(x)	absolute value of x	abs(7.2) is 7.2 abs(0.0) is 0.0 abs(-5.6) is 5.6
ceil(x)	rounds x to the smallest integer not less than x	ceil(9.2) is 10.0 ceil(-9.8) is -9.0
cos(x)	trigonometric cosine of x (x in radians)	cos(0.0) is 1.0
exp(x)	exponential method e^x	exp(1.0) is 2.71828 exp(2.0) is 7.38906
floor(x)	rounds x to the largest integer not greater than x	floor(9.2) is 9.0 floor(-9.8) is -10.0
log(x)	natural logarithm of x (base e)	log(2.718282) is 1.0 log(7.389056) is 2.0
max(x, y)	larger value of x and y	max(2.3, 12.7) is 12.7 max(-2.3, -12.7) is -2.3
min(x, y)	smaller value of x and y	min(2.3, 12.7) is 2.3 min(-2.3, -12.7) is -12.7
pow(x, y)	x raised to power y (x^y)	pow(2.0, 7.0) is 128.0 pow(9.0, .5) is 3.0
round(x)	rounds x to the closest integer	round(9.75) is 10 round(9.25) is 9
sin(x)	trigonometric sine of x (x in radians)	sin(0.0) is 0.0
sqrt(x)	square root of x	sqrt(900.0) is 30.0 sqrt(9.0) is 3.0
tan(x)	trigonometric tangent of x (x in radians)	tan(0.0) is 0.0

Fig. 9.1 | Math object methods.

Common Programming Error 9.1

Forgetting to invoke a Math *method by preceding the method name with the object name* Math *and a dot (.) is an error.*

Software Engineering Observation 9.1

The primary difference between invoking a standalone function and invoking a method of an object is that an object name and a dot are not required to call a standalone function.

The Math object defines several commonly used mathematical constants, summarized in Fig. 9.2. [*Note:* By convention, the names of constants are written in all uppercase letters so they stand out in a program.]

Good Programming Practice 9.1

Use the mathematical constants of the Math *object rather than explicitly typing the numeric value of the constant.*

Constant	Description	Value
Math.E	Base of a natural logarithm (*e*).	Approximately 2.718
Math.LN2	Natural logarithm of 2	Approximately 0.693
Math.LN10	Natural logarithm of 10	Approximately 2.302
Math.LOG2E	Base 2 logarithm of *e*	Approximately 1.442
Math.LOG10E	Base 10 logarithm of *e*	Approximately 0.434
Math.PI	π—the ratio of a circle's circumference to its diameter	Approximately 3.141592653589793
Math.SQRT1_2	Square root of 0.5	Approximately 0.707
Math.SQRT2	Square root of 2.0	Approximately 1.414

Fig. 9.2 | Properties of the Math object.

9.4 String Object

In this section, we introduce JavaScript's string- and character-processing capabilities. The techniques discussed here are appropriate for processing names, addresses, telephone numbers, and similar items.

9.4.1 Fundamentals of Characters and Strings

Characters are the fundamental building blocks of JavaScript programs. Every program is composed of a sequence of characters grouped together meaningfully that is interpreted by the computer as a series of instructions used to accomplish a task.

A string is a series of characters treated as a single unit. A string may include letters, digits and various *special characters,* such as +, -, *, /, and $. JavaScript supports the set of characters called *Unicode*®, which represents a large portion of the world's languages. A string is an object of type **String**. *String literals* or *string constants* (often called *anonymous* **String** *objects*) are written as a sequence of characters in double quotation marks or single quotation marks, as follows:

```
"John Q. Doe"                    (a name)
'9999 Main Street'              (a street address)
"Waltham, Massachusetts"       (a city and state)
'(201) 555-1212'               (a telephone number)
```

A String may be assigned to a variable in a declaration. The declaration

```
var color = "blue";
```

initializes variable color with the String object containing the string "blue". Strings can be compared via the relational (<, <=, > and >=) and equality operators (== and !=). Strings are compared using the Unicode values of the corresponding characters. For example, the expression "hello" < "Hello" evaluates to false because lowercase letters have higher Unicode values.

9.4.2 Methods of the String Object

The String object encapsulates the attributes and behaviors of a string of characters. It provides many methods (behaviors) that accomplish useful tasks such as selecting characters from a string, combining strings (called *concatenation*), obtaining substrings of a string, searching for substrings within a string, tokenizing strings (i.e., splitting strings into individual words) and converting strings to all uppercase or lowercase letters. The String object also provides several methods that generate XHTML tags. Figure 9.3 summarizes many String methods. Figures 9.4–9.7 demonstrate some of these methods.

Method	Description
charAt(*index*)	Returns a string containing the character at the specified *index*. If there is no character at the *index*, charAt returns an empty string. The first character is located at *index* 0.
charCodeAt(*index*)	Returns the Unicode value of the character at the specified *index*, or NaN (not a number) if there is no character at that *index*.
concat(*string*)	Concatenates its argument to the end of the string that invokes the method. The string invoking this method is not modified; instead a new String is returned. This method is the same as adding two strings with the string-concatenation operator + (e.g., s1.concat(s2) is the same as s1 + s2).
fromCharCode(*value1*, *value2*, ...)	Converts a list of Unicode values into a string containing the corresponding characters.
indexOf(*substring*, *index*)	Searches for the first occurrence of *substring* starting from position *index* in the string that invokes the method. The method returns the starting index of *substring* in the source string or –1 if *substring* is not found. If the *index* argument is not provided, the method begins searching from index 0 in the source string.

Fig. 9.3 | Some String object methods. (Part 1 of 2.)

Method	Description
lastIndexOf(*substring*, *index*)	Searches for the last occurrence of *substring* starting from position *index* and searching toward the beginning of the string that invokes the method. The method returns the starting index of *substring* in the source string or –1 if *substring* is not found. If the *index* argument is not provided, the method begins searching from the end of the source string.
replace(*searchString*, *replaceString*)	Searches for the substring *searchString*, and replaces the first occurrence with *replaceString* and returns the modified string, or the original string if no replacement was made.
slice(*start*, *end*)	Returns a string containing the portion of the string from index *start* through index *end*. If the *end* index is not specified, the method returns a string from the *start* index to the end of the source string. A negative *end* index specifies an offset from the end of the string, starting from a position one past the end of the last character (so –1 indicates the last character position in the string).
split(*string*)	Splits the source string into an array of strings (tokens), where its *string* argument specifies the delimiter (i.e., the characters that indicate the end of each token in the source string).
substr(*start*, *length*)	Returns a string containing *length* characters starting from index *start* in the source string. If *length* is not specified, a string containing characters from *start* to the end of the source string is returned.
substring(*start*, *end*)	Returns a string containing the characters from index *start* up to but not including index *end* in the source string.
toLowerCase()	Returns a string in which all uppercase letters are converted to lowercase letters. Nonletter characters are not changed.
toUpperCase()	Returns a string in which all lowercase letters are converted to uppercase letters. Nonletter characters are not changed.
Methods that generate XHTML tags	
anchor(*name*)	Wraps the source string in an anchor element (`<a></a>`) with *name* as the anchor name.
fixed()	Wraps the source string in a `<tt></tt>` element.
link(*url*)	Wraps the source string in an anchor element (`<a></a>`) with *url* as the hyperlink location.
strike()	Wraps the source string in a `<strike></strike>` element.
sub()	Wraps the source string in a `<sub></sub>` element.
sup()	Wraps the source string in a `<sup></sup>` element.

Fig. 9.3 | Some String object methods. (Part 2 of 2.)

9.4.3 Character-Processing Methods

The script in Fig. 9.4 demonstrates some of the String object's character-processing methods, including **charAt** (returns the character at a specific position), **charCodeAt** (returns the Unicode value of the character at a specific position), **fromCharCode** (returns a string created from a series of Unicode values), **toLowerCase** (returns the lowercase version of a string) and **toUpperCase** (returns the uppercase version of a string).

Lines 16–17 display the first character in String s ("ZEBRA") using String method charAt. Method **charAt** returns a string containing the character at the specified index (0 in this example). Indices for the characters in a string start at 0 (the first character) and go up to (but do not include) the string's length (i.e., if the string contains five characters, the indices are 0 through 4). If the index is outside the bounds of the string, the method returns an empty string.

Lines 18–19 display the character code for the first character in String s ("ZEBRA") by calling String method charCodeAt. Method charCodeAt returns the Unicode value of

```
1   <?xml version = "1.0" encoding = "utf-8"?>
2   <!DOCTYPE html PUBLIC "-//W3C//DTD XHTML 1.0 Strict//EN"
3      "http://www.w3.org/TR/xhtml1/DTD/xhtml1-strict.dtd">
4
5   <!-- Fig. 9.4: CharacterProcessing.html -->
6   <!-- String methods charAt, charCodeAt, fromCharCode, toLowercase and
7      toUpperCase. -->
8   <html xmlns = "http://www.w3.org/1999/xhtml">
9      <head>
10        <title>Character Processing Methods</title>
11        <script type = "text/javascript">
12           <!--
13           var s = "ZEBRA";
14           var s2 = "AbCdEfG";
15
16           document.writeln( "<p>Character at index 0 in '" +
17              s + "' is " + s.charAt( 0 ) );
18           document.writeln( "<br />Character code at index 0 in '"
19              + s + "' is " + s.charCodeAt( 0 ) + "</p>" );
20
21           document.writeln( "<p>'" +
22              String.fromCharCode( 87, 79, 82, 68 ) +
23              "' contains character codes 87, 79, 82 and 68</p>" )
24
25           document.writeln( "<p>'" + s2 + "' in lowercase is '" +
26              s2.toLowerCase() + "'" );
27           document.writeln( "<br />'" + s2 + "' in uppercase is '"
28              + s2.toUpperCase() + "'</p>" );
29           // -->
30        </script>
31     </head><body></body>
32  </html>
```

Fig. 9.4 | String methods charAt, charCodeAt, fromCharCode, toLowercase and toUpperCase. (Part 1 of 2.)

Fig. 9.4 | String methods `charAt`, `charCodeAt`, `fromCharCode`, `toLowercase` and `toUpperCase`. (Part 2 of 2.)

the character at the specified index (0 in this example). If the index is outside the bounds of the string, the method returns `NaN`.

`String` method fromCharCode receives as its argument a comma-separated list of Unicode values and builds a string containing the character representation of those Unicode values. Lines 21–23 display the string `"WORD"`, which consists of the character codes 87, 79, 82 and 68. Note that the `String` object calls method `fromCharCode`, rather than a specific `String` variable.

The statements in lines 25–26 and 27–28 use `String` methods ***toLowerCase*** and ***toUpperCase*** to display versions of `String` s2 (`"AbCdEfG"`) in all lowercase letters and all uppercase letters, respectively.

9.4.4 Searching Methods

Being able to search for a character or a sequence of characters in a string is often useful. For example, if you are creating your own word processor, you may want to provide a capability for searching through the document. The script in Fig. 9.5 demonstrates the `String` object methods ***indexOf*** and ***lastIndexOf*** that search for a specified substring in a string. All the searches in this example are performed on the global string `letters` (initialized in line 14 with `"abcdefghijklmnopqrstuvwxyzabcdefghijklm"` in the script).

The user types a substring in the XHTML form searchForm's `inputVal` text field and presses the **Search** button to search for the substring in `letters`. Clicking the **Search** button calls function buttonPressed (defined in lines 16–29) to respond to the `onclick` event and perform the searches. The results of each search are displayed in the appropriate text field of searchForm.

Lines 21–22 use `String` method indexOf to determine the location of the first occurrence in string `letters` of the string `inputVal.value` (i.e., the string the user typed in the `inputVal` text field). If the substring is found, the index at which the first occurrence of the substring begins is returned; otherwise, −1 is returned.

Lines 23–24 use `String` method lastIndexOf to determine the location of the last occurrence in `letters` of the string in `inputVal`. If the substring is found, the index at which the last occurrence of the substring begins is returned; otherwise, −1 is returned.

```
 1   <?xml version = "1.0" encoding = "utf-8"?>
 2   <!DOCTYPE html PUBLIC "-//W3C//DTD XHTML 1.0 Strict//EN"
 3      "http://www.w3.org/TR/xhtml1/DTD/xhtml1-strict.dtd">
 4
 5   <!-- Fig. 9.5: SearchingStrings.html -->
 6   <!-- String searching with indexOf and lastIndexOf. -->
 7   <html xmlns = "http://www.w3.org/1999/xhtml">
 8      <head>
 9         <title>
10            Searching Strings with indexOf and lastIndexOf
11         </title>
12         <script type = "text/javascript">
13            <!--
14            var letters = "abcdefghijklmnopqrstuvwxyzabcdefghijklm";
15
16            function buttonPressed()
17            {
18               var searchForm = document.getElementById( "searchForm" );
19               var inputVal = document.getElementById( "inputVal" );
20
21               searchForm.elements[2].value =
22                  letters.indexOf( inputVal.value );
23               searchForm.elements[3].value =
24                  letters.lastIndexOf( inputVal.value );
25               searchForm.elements[4].value =
26                  letters.indexOf( inputVal.value, 12 );
27               searchForm.elements[5].value =
28                  letters.lastIndexOf( inputVal.value, 12 );
29            } // end function buttonPressed
30            // -->
31         </script>
32      </head>
33      <body>
34         <form id = "searchForm" action = "">
35            <h1>The string to search is:<br />
36               abcdefghijklmnopqrstuvwxyzabcdefghijklm</h1>
37            <p>Enter substring to search for
38            <input id = "inputVal" type = "text" />
39            <input id = "search" type = "button" value = "Search"
40               onclick = "buttonPressed()" /><br /></p>
41
42            <p>First occurrence located at index
43            <input id = "first" type = "text" size = "5" />
44            <br />Last occurrence located at index
45            <input id = "last" type = "text" size = "5" />
46            <br />First occurrence from index 12 located at index
47            <input id = "first12" type = "text" size = "5" />
48            <br />Last occurrence from index 12 located at index
49            <input id = "last12" type = "text" size = "5" /></p>
50         </form>
51      </body>
52   </html>
```

Fig. 9.5 | String searching with `indexOf` and `lastIndexOf`. (Part 1 of 2.)

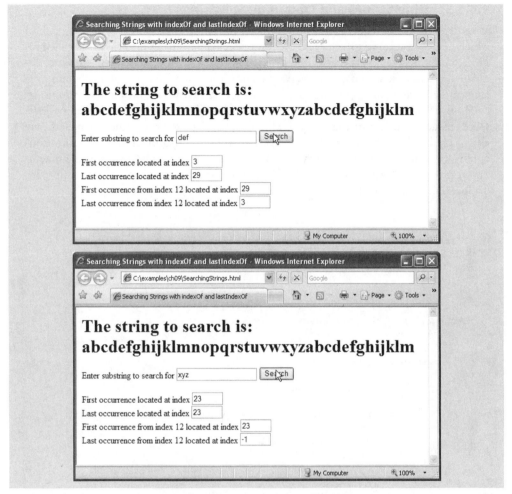

Fig. 9.5 | String searching with indexOf and lastIndexOf. (Part 2 of 2.)

Lines 25–26 use String method indexOf to determine the location of the first occurrence in string letters of the string in the inputVal text field, starting from index 12 in letters. If the substring is found, the index at which the first occurrence of the substring (starting from index 12) begins is returned; otherwise, –1 is returned.

Lines 27–28 use String method lastIndexOf to determine the location of the last occurrence in letters of the string in the inputVal text field, starting from index 12 in letters and moving toward the beginning of the input. If the substring is found, the index at which the first occurrence of the substring (if one appears before index 12) begins is returned; otherwise, –1 is returned.

Software Engineering Observation 9.2

String methods indexOf and lastIndexOf, with their optional second argument (the starting index from which to search), are particularly useful for continuing a search through a large amount of text.

9.4.5 Splitting Strings and Obtaining Substrings

When you read a sentence, your mind breaks it into individual words, or *tokens*, each of which conveys meaning to you. The process of breaking a string into tokens is called *tokenization*. Interpreters also perform tokenization. They break up statements into such individual pieces as keywords, identifiers, operators and other elements of a programming language. Figure 9.6 demonstrates `String` method *split*, which breaks a string into its component tokens. Tokens are separated from one another by *delimiters*, typically whitespace characters such as blanks, tabs, newlines and carriage returns. Other characters may also be used as delimiters to separate tokens. The XHTML document displays a form containing a text field where the user types a sentence to tokenize. The results of the tokenization process are displayed in an XHTML `textarea` GUI component. The script also demonstrates `String` method *substring*, which returns a portion of a string.

```
1   <?xml version = "1.0" encoding = "utf-8"?>
2   <!DOCTYPE html PUBLIC "-//W3C//DTD XHTML 1.0 Strict//EN"
3      "http://www.w3.org/TR/xhtml1/DTD/xhtml1-strict.dtd">
4
5   <!-- Fig. 9.6: SplitAndSubString.html -->
6   <!-- String object methods split and substring. -->
7   <html xmlns = "http://www.w3.org/1999/xhtml">
8      <head>
9         <title>String Methods split and substring</title>
10        <script type = "text/javascript">
11           <!--
12           function splitButtonPressed()
13           {
14              var inputString = document.getElementById( "inputVal" ).value;
15              var tokens = inputString.split( " " );
16              document.getElementById( "output" ).value =
17                 tokens.join( "\n" ) ;
18
19              document.getElementById( "outputSubstring" ).value =
20                 inputString.substring( 0, 10 );
21           } // end function splitButtonPressed
22           // -->
23        </script>
24     </head>
25     <body>
26        <form action = "">
27           <p>Enter a sentence to split into words<br />
28           <input id = "inputVal" type = "text" size = "40" />
29           <input type = "button" value = "Split"
30              onclick = "splitButtonPressed()" /></p>
31
32           <p>The sentence split into words is<br />
33           <textarea id = "output" rows = "8" cols = "34">
34           </textarea></p>
35
36           <p>The first 10 characters of the input string are
```

Fig. 9.6 | String object methods `split` and `substring`. (Part 1 of 2.)

```
37                <input id = "outputSubstring" type = "text"
38                   size = "15" /></p>
39          </form>
40       </body>
41    </html>
```

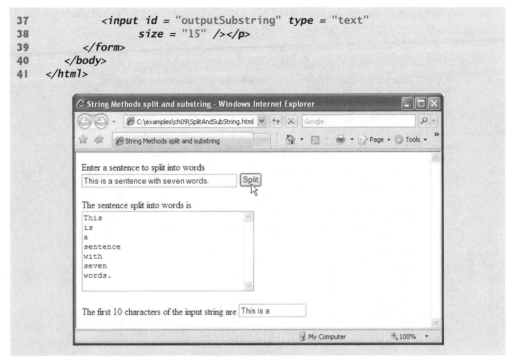

Fig. 9.6 | `String` object methods `split` and `substring`. (Part 2 of 2.)

The user types a sentence into the text field with id `inputVal` text field and presses the **Split** button to tokenize the string. Function `splitButtonPressed` (lines 12–21) handles the button's `onclick` event.

Line 14 gets the value of the input field and stores it in variable `inputString`. Line 15 calls `String` method `split` to tokenize `inputString`. The argument to method `split` is the *delimiter string*—the string that determines the end of each token in the original string. In this example, the space character delimits the tokens. The delimiter string can contain multiple characters that should be used as delimiters. Method `split` returns an array of strings containing the tokens. Line 17 uses `Array` method `join` to combine the tokens in array `tokens` and separate each token with a newline character (`\n`). The resulting string is assigned to the `value` property of the XHTML form's `output` GUI component (an XHTML `textarea`).

Lines 19–20 use `String` method `substring` to obtain a string containing the first 10 characters of the string the user entered (still stored in `inputString`). The method returns the substring from the *starting index* (`0` in this example) up to but not including the *ending index* (`10` in this example). If the ending index is greater than the length of the string, the substring returned includes the characters from the starting index to the end of the original string.

9.4.6 XHTML Markup Methods

The script in Fig. 9.7 demonstrates the `String` object's methods that generate XHTML markup tags. When a `String` object invokes a markup method, the method wraps the

String's contents in the appropriate XHTML tag. These methods are particularly useful for generating XHTML dynamically during script processing.

```
1   <?xml version = "1.0" encoding = "utf-8"?>
2   <!DOCTYPE html PUBLIC "-//W3C//DTD XHTML 1.0 Strict//EN"
3      "http://www.w3.org/TR/xhtml1/DTD/xhtml1-strict.dtd">
4
5   <!-- Fig. 9.7: MarkupMethods.html -->
6   <!-- String object XHTML markup methods. -->
7   <html xmlns = "http://www.w3.org/1999/xhtml">
8      <head>
9         <title>XHTML Markup Methods of the String Object</title>
10        <script type = "text/javascript">
11           <!--
12           var anchorText = "This is an anchor";
13           var fixedText = "This is monospaced text";
14           var linkText = "Click here to go to anchorText";
15           var strikeText = "This is strike out text";
16           var subText = "subscript";
17           var supText = "superscript";
18
19           document.writeln( anchorText.anchor( "top" ) );
20           document.writeln( "<br />" + fixedText.fixed() );
21           document.writeln( "<br />" + strikeText.strike() );
22           document.writeln(
23              "<br />This is text with a " + subText.sub() );
24           document.writeln(
25              "<br />This is text with a " + supText.sup() );
26           document.writeln( "<br />" + linkText.link( "#top" ) );
27           // -->
28        </script>
29     </head><body></body>
30  </html>
```

Fig. 9.7 | String object XHTML markup methods. (Part 1 of 2.)

Fig. 9.7 | String object XHTML markup methods. (Part 2 of 2.)

Lines 12–17 define the strings that call each of the XHTML markup methods of the String object. Line 19 uses String method **anchor** to format the string in variable anchorText ("This is an anchor") as

<a name = "top">This is an anchor</a>

The name of the anchor is the argument to the method. This anchor will be used later in the example as the target of a hyperlink.

Line 20 uses String method **fixed** to display text in a fixed-width font by formatting the string in variable fixedText ("This is monospaced text") as

<tt>This is monospaced text</tt>

Line 21 uses String method **strike** to display text with a line through it by formatting the string in variable strikeText ("This is strike out text") as

<strike>This is strike out text</strike>

Lines 22–23 use String method **sub** to display subscript text by formatting the string in variable subText ("subscript") as

_{subscript}

Note that the resulting line in the XHTML document displays the word subscript smaller than the rest of the line and slightly below the line.

Lines 24–25 call String method **sup** to display superscript text by formatting the string in variable supText ("superscript") as

^{superscript}

Note that the resulting line in the XHTML document displays the word superscript smaller than the rest of the line and slightly above the line.

Line 26 uses String method **link** to create a hyperlink by formatting the string in variable linkText ("Click here to go to anchorText") as

<a href = "#top">Click here to go to anchorText</a>

The target of the hyperlink (#top in this example) is the argument to the method and can be any URL. In this example, the hyperlink target is the anchor created in line 19. If you make your browser window short and scroll to the bottom of the web page, then click this link, the browser will reposition to the top of the web page.

9.5 Date Object

JavaScript's **Date** object provides methods for date and time manipulations. Date and time processing can be performed based on the computer's *local time zone* or based on World Time Standard's *Coordinated Universal Time* (abbreviated *UTC*)—formerly called *Greenwich Mean Time (GMT)*. Most methods of the Date object have a local time zone and a UTC version. The methods of the Date object are summarized in Fig. 9.8.

Method	Description
getDate() getUTCDate()	Returns a number from 1 to 31 representing the day of the month in local time or UTC.
getDay() getUTCDay()	Returns a number from 0 (Sunday) to 6 (Saturday) representing the day of the week in local time or UTC.
getFullYear() getUTCFullYear()	Returns the year as a four-digit number in local time or UTC.
getHours() getUTCHours()	Returns a number from 0 to 23 representing hours since midnight in local time or UTC.
getMilliseconds() getUTCMilliSeconds()	Returns a number from 0 to 999 representing the number of milliseconds in local time or UTC, respectively. The time is stored in hours, minutes, seconds and milliseconds.
getMinutes() getUTCMinutes()	Returns a number from 0 to 59 representing the minutes for the time in local time or UTC.
getMonth() getUTCMonth()	Returns a number from 0 (January) to 11 (December) representing the month in local time or UTC.
getSeconds() getUTCSeconds()	Returns a number from 0 to 59 representing the seconds for the time in local time or UTC.
getTime()	Returns the number of milliseconds between January 1, 1970, and the time in the Date object.
getTimezoneOffset()	Returns the difference in minutes between the current time on the local computer and UTC (Coordinated Universal Time).
setDate(*val*) setUTCDate(*val*)	Sets the day of the month (1 to 31) in local time or UTC.
setFullYear(*y*, *m*, *d*) setUTCFullYear(*y*, *m*, *d*)	Sets the year in local time or UTC. The second and third arguments representing the month and the date are optional. If an optional argument is not specified, the current value in the Date object is used.

Fig. 9.8 | Date object methods. (Part 1 of 2.)

Method	Description
setHours(*h*, *m*, *s*, *ms*) setUTCHours(*h*, *m*, *s*, *ms*)	Sets the hour in local time or UTC. The second, third and fourth arguments, representing the minutes, seconds and milliseconds, are optional. If an optional argument is not specified, the current value in the Date object is used.
setMilliSeconds(*ms*) setUTCMilliseconds(*ms*)	Sets the number of milliseconds in local time or UTC.
setMinutes(*m*, *s*, *ms*) setUTCMinutes(*m*, *s*, *ms*)	Sets the minute in local time or UTC. The second and third arguments, representing the seconds and milliseconds, are optional. If an optional argument is not specified, the current value in the Date object is used.
setMonth(*m*, *d*) setUTCMonth(*m*, *d*)	Sets the month in local time or UTC. The second argument, representing the date, is optional. If the optional argument is not specified, the current date value in the Date object is used.
setSeconds(*s*, *ms*) setUTCSeconds(*s*, *ms*)	Sets the second in local time or UTC. The second argument, representing the milliseconds, is optional. If this argument is not specified, the current millisecond value in the Date object is used.
setTime(*ms*)	Sets the time based on its argument—the number of elapsed milliseconds since January 1, 1970.
toLocaleString()	Returns a string representation of the date and time in a form specific to the computer's locale. For example, September 13, 2007, at 3:42:22 PM is represented as *09/13/07 15:47:22* in the United States and *13/09/07 15:47:22* in Europe.
toUTCString()	Returns a string representation of the date and time in the form: *15 Sep 2007 15:47:22 UTC*
toString()	Returns a string representation of the date and time in a form specific to the locale of the computer (*Mon Sep 17 15:47:22 EDT 2007* in the United States).
valueOf()	The time in number of milliseconds since midnight, January 1, 1970. (Same as getTime.)

Fig. 9.8 | Date object methods. (Part 2 of 2.)

The script of Fig. 9.9 demonstrates many of the local time zone methods in Fig. 9.8. Line 12 creates a new Date object. The new operator allocates the memory for the Date object. The empty parentheses indicate a call to the Date object's *constructor* with no arguments. A constructor is an initializer method for an object. Constructors are called automatically when an object is allocated with new. The Date constructor with no arguments initializes the Date object with the local computer's current date and time.

```
 1   <?xml version = "1.0" encoding = "utf-8"?>
 2   <!DOCTYPE html PUBLIC "-//W3C//DTD XHTML 1.0 Strict//EN"
 3      "http://www.w3.org/TR/xhtml1/DTD/xhtml1-strict.dtd">
 4
 5   <!-- Fig. 9.9: DateTime.html -->
 6   <!-- Date and time methods of the Date object. -->
 7   <html xmlns = "http://www.w3.org/1999/xhtml">
 8      <head>
 9         <title>Date and Time Methods</title>
10         <script type = "text/javascript">
11            <!--
12            var current = new Date();
13
14            document.writeln(
15               "<h1>String representations and valueOf</h1>" );
16            document.writeln( "toString: " + current.toString() +
17               "<br />toLocaleString: " + current.toLocaleString() +
18               "<br />toUTCString: " + current.toUTCString() +
19               "<br />valueOf: " + current.valueOf() );
20
21            document.writeln(
22               "<h1>Get methods for local time zone</h1>" );
23            document.writeln( "getDate: " + current.getDate() +
24               "<br />getDay: " + current.getDay() +
25               "<br />getMonth: " + current.getMonth() +
26               "<br />getFullYear: " + current.getFullYear() +
27               "<br />getTime: " + current.getTime() +
28               "<br />getHours: " + current.getHours() +
29               "<br />getMinutes: " + current.getMinutes() +
30               "<br />getSeconds: " + current.getSeconds() +
31               "<br />getMilliseconds: " + current.getMilliseconds() +
32               "<br />getTimezoneOffset: " + current.getTimezoneOffset() );
33
34            document.writeln(
35               "<h1>Specifying arguments for a new Date</h1>" );
36            var anotherDate = new Date( 2007, 2, 18, 1, 5, 0, 0 );
37            document.writeln( "Date: " + anotherDate );
38
39            document.writeln( "<h1>Set methods for local time zone</h1>" );
40            anotherDate.setDate( 31 );
41            anotherDate.setMonth( 11 );
42            anotherDate.setFullYear( 2007 );
43            anotherDate.setHours( 23 );
44            anotherDate.setMinutes( 59 );
45            anotherDate.setSeconds( 59 );
46            document.writeln( "Modified date: " + anotherDate );
47            // -->
48         </script>
49      </head><body></body>
50   </html>
```

Fig. 9.9 | Date and time methods of the Date object. (Part 1 of 2.)

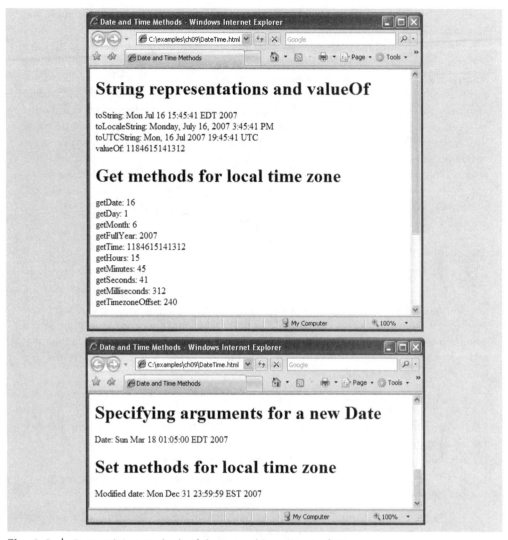

Fig. 9.9 | Date and time methods of the Date object. (Part 2 of 2.)

Software Engineering Observation 9.3

When an object is allocated with new, the object's constructor is called automatically to initialize the object before it is used in the program.

Lines 16–19 demonstrate the methods toString, toLocaleString, toUTCString and valueOf. Note that method valueOf returns a large integer value representing the total number of milliseconds between midnight, January 1, 1970, and the date and time stored in Date object current.

Lines 23–32 demonstrate the Date object's *get* methods for the local time zone. Note that method getFullYear returns the year as a four-digit number. Note as well that method getTimeZoneOffset returns the difference in minutes between the local time zone and UTC time (i.e., a difference of four hours in our time zone when this example was executed).

Line 36 demonstrates creating a new Date object and supplying arguments to the Date constructor for *year, month, date, hours, minutes, seconds* and *milliseconds*. Note that the *hours, minutes, seconds* and *milliseconds* arguments are all optional. If any one of these arguments is not specified, a zero is supplied in its place. For the *hours, minutes* and *seconds* arguments, if the argument to the right of any of these arguments is specified, it too must be specified (e.g., if the *minutes* argument is specified, the *hours* argument must be specified; if the *milliseconds* argument is specified, all the arguments must be specified).

Lines 40–45 demonstrate the Date object *set* methods for the local time zone. Date objects represent the month internally as an integer from 0 to 11. These values are off by one from what you might expect (i.e., 1 for January, 2 for February, ..., and 12 for December). When creating a Date object, you must specify 0 to indicate January, 1 to indicate February, ..., and 11 to indicate December.

Common Programming Error 9.2

Assuming that months are represented as numbers from 1 to 12 leads to off-by-one errors when you are processing Dates.

The Date object provides two other methods that can be called without creating a new Date object—***Date.parse*** and ***Date.UTC***. Method Date.parse receives as its argument a string representing a date and time, and returns the number of milliseconds between midnight, January 1, 1970, and the specified date and time. This value can be converted to a Date object with the statement

> ***var*** theDate = ***new*** Date(*numberOfMilliseconds*);

which passes to the Date constructor the number of milliseconds since midnight, January 1, 1970, for the Date object.

Method parse converts the string using the following rules:

- Short dates can be specified in the form MM-DD-YY, MM-DD-YYYY, MM/DD/YY or MM/DD/YYYY. The month and day are not required to be two digits.

- Long dates that specify the complete month name (e.g., "January"), date and year can specify the month, date and year in any order.

- Text in parentheses within the string is treated as a comment and ignored. Commas and white-space characters are treated as delimiters.

- All month and day names must have at least two characters. The names are not required to be unique. If the names are identical, the name is resolved as the last match (e.g., "Ju" represents "July" rather than "June").

- If the name of the day of the week is supplied, it is ignored.

- All standard time zones (e.g., EST for Eastern Standard Time), Coordinated Universal Time (UTC) and Greenwich Mean Time (GMT) are recognized.

- When specifying hours, minutes and seconds, separate each by colons.

- When using a 24-hour-clock format, "PM" should not be used for times after 12 noon.

Date method UTC returns the number of milliseconds between midnight, January 1, 1970, and the date and time specified as its arguments. The arguments to the UTC method include the required *year*, *month* and *date*, and the optional *hours*, *minutes*, *seconds* and *milliseconds*. If any of the *hours*, *minutes*, *seconds* or *milliseconds* arguments is not specified, a zero is supplied in its place. For the *hours*, *minutes* and *seconds* arguments, if the argument to the right of any of these arguments in the argument list is specified, that argument must also be specified (e.g., if the *minutes* argument is specified, the *hours* argument must be specified; if the *milliseconds* argument is specified, all the arguments must be specified). As with the result of Date.parse, the result of Date.UTC can be converted to a Date object by creating a new Date object with the result of Date.UTC as its argument.

9.6 Boolean and Number Objects

JavaScript provides the **Boolean** and **Number** objects as object *wrappers* for boolean true/false values and numbers, respectively. These wrappers define methods and properties useful in manipulating boolean values and numbers. Wrappers provide added functionality for working with simple data types.

When a JavaScript program requires a boolean value, JavaScript automatically creates a Boolean object to store the value. JavaScript programmers can create Boolean objects explicitly with the statement

> **var** b = **new** Boolean(*booleanValue*);

The constructor argument *booleanValue* specifies whether the value of the Boolean object should be true or false. If *booleanValue* is false, 0, null, Number.NaN or an empty string (""), or if no argument is supplied, the new Boolean object contains false. Otherwise, the new Boolean object contains true. Figure 9.10 summarizes the methods of the Boolean object.

JavaScript automatically creates Number objects to store numeric values in a JavaScript program. JavaScript programmers can create a Number object with the statement

> **var** n = **new** Number(*numericValue*);

The constructor argument *numericValue* is the number to store in the object. Although you can explicitly create Number objects, normally the JavaScript interpreter creates them as needed. Figure 9.11 summarizes the methods and properties of the Number object.

Method	Description
toString()	Returns the string "true" if the value of the Boolean object is true; otherwise, returns the string "false".
valueOf()	Returns the value true if the Boolean object is true; otherwise, returns false.

Fig. 9.10 | Boolean object methods.

Method or property	Description
toString(*radix*)	Returns the string representation of the number. The optional *radix* argument (a number from 2 to 36) specifies the number's base. For example, radix 2 results in the binary representation of the number, 8 results in the octal representation, 10 results in the decimal representation and 16 results in the hexadecimal representation.
valueOf()	Returns the numeric value.
Number.MAX_VALUE	This property represents the largest value that can be stored in a JavaScript program—approximately 1.79E+308.
Number.MIN_VALUE	This property represents the smallest value that can be stored in a JavaScript program—approximately 5.00E–324.
Number.NaN	This property represents *not a number*—a value returned from an arithmetic expression that does not result in a number (e.g., the expression parseInt("hello") cannot convert the string "hello" into a number, so parseInt would return Number.NaN. To determine whether a value is NaN, test the result with function isNaN, which returns true if the value is NaN; otherwise, it returns false.
Number.NEGATIVE_INFINITY	This property represents a value less than -Number.MAX_VALUE.
Number.POSITIVE_INFINITY	This property represents a value greater than Number.MAX_VALUE.

Fig. 9.11 | Number object methods and properties.

9.7 document Object

The *document* object is used to manipulate the document that is currently visible in the browser window. The document object has many properties and methods, such as methods document.write and document.writeln, which have both been used in prior JavaScript examples. Figure 9.12 shows the methods and properties of the document objects that are used in this chapter. You can learn more about the properties and methods of the document object in our JavaScript Resource Center (www.deitel.com/javascript).

Method or property	Description
getElementById(*id*)	Returns the DOM node representing the XHTML element whose id attribute matches *id*.

Fig. 9.12 | Important document object methods and properties. (Part 1 of 2.)

Method or property	Description
write(*string*)	Writes the string to the XHTML document as XHTML code.
writeln(*string*)	Writes the string to the XHTML document as XHTML code and adds a newline character at the end.
cookie	A string containing the values of all the cookies stored on the user's computer for the current document. See Section 9.9, Using Cookies.
lastModified	The date and time that this document was last modified.

Fig. 9.12 | Important **document** object methods and properties. (Part 2 of 2.)

9.8 window Object

The *window* object provides methods for manipulating browser windows. The following script shows many of the commonly used properties and methods of the window object and uses them to create a website that spans multiple browser windows. Figure 9.13 allows the user to create a new, fully customized browser window by completing an XHTML form and clicking the **Submit** button. The script also allows the user to add text to the new window and navigate the window to a different URL.

The script starts in line 10. Line 12 declares a variable to refer to the new window. We refer to the new window as the *child window* because it is created and controlled by the main, or *parent*, window in this script. Lines 14–50 define the createChildWindow function, which determines the features that have been selected by the user and creates a child window with those features (but does not add any content to the window). Lines 18–20 declare several variables to store the status of the checkboxes on the page. Lines 23–38 set each variable to "yes" or "no" based on whether the corresponding checkbox is checked or unchecked.

```
 1  <?xml version = "1.0" encoding = "utf-8"?>
 2  <!DOCTYPE html PUBLIC "-//W3C//DTD XHTML 1.0 Strict//EN"
 3      "http://www.w3.org/TR/xhtml1/DTD/xhtml1-strict.dtd">
 4
 5  <!-- Fig. 9.13: window.html -->
 6  <!-- Using the window object to create and modify child windows. -->
 7  <html xmlns = "http://www.w3.org/1999/xhtml">
 8  <head>
 9  <title>Using the Window Object</title>
10  <script type = "text/javascript">
11     <!--
12     var childWindow; // variable to control the child window
13
14     function createChildWindow()
15     {
```

Fig. 9.13 | Using the window object to create and modify child windows. (Part 1 of 4.)

```
16    // these variables all contain either "yes" or "no"
17    // to enable or disable a feature in the child window
18    var toolBar;
19    var menuBar;
20    var scrollBars;
21
22    // determine whether the Tool Bar checkbox is checked
23    if ( document.getElementById( "toolBarCheckBox" ).checked )
24       toolBar = "yes";
25    else
26       toolBar = "no";
27
28    // determine whether the Menu Bar checkbox is checked
29    if ( document.getElementById( "menuBarCheckBox" ).checked )
30       menuBar = "yes";
31    else
32       menuBar = "no";
33
34    // determine whether the Scroll Bar checkbox is checked
35    if ( document.getElementById( "scrollBarsCheckBox" ).checked )
36       scrollBars = "yes";
37    else
38       scrollBars = "no";
39
40    //display window with selected features
41    childWindow = window.open( "", "",
42       ",toolbar = " + toolBar +
43       ",menubar = " + menuBar +
44       ",scrollbars = " + scrollBars );
45
46    // disable buttons
47    document.getElementById( "closeButton" ).disabled = false;
48    document.getElementById( "modifyButton" ).disabled = false;
49    document.getElementById( "setURLButton" ).disabled = false;
50  } // end function createChildWindow
51
52  // insert text from the textbox in the child window
53  function modifyChildWindow()
54  {
55    if ( childWindow.closed )
56       alert( "You attempted to interact with a closed window" );
57    else
58       childWindow.document.write(
59          document.getElementById( "textForChild" ).value );
60  } // end function modifyChildWindow
61
62  // close the child window
63  function closeChildWindow()
64  {
65    if ( childWindow.closed )
66       alert( "You attempted to interact with a closed window" );
```

Fig. 9.13 | Using the `window` object to create and modify child windows. (Part 2 of 4.)

```
67         else
68             childWindow.close();
69
70         document.getElementById( "closeButton" ).disabled = true;
71         document.getElementById( "modifyButton" ).disabled = true;
72         document.getElementById( "setURLButton" ).disabled = true;
73     } // end function closeChildWindow
74
75     // set the URL of the child window to the URL
76     // in the parent window's myChildURL
77     function setChildWindowURL()
78     {
79         if ( childWindow.closed )
80             alert( "You attempted to interact with a closed window" );
81         else
82             childWindow.location =
83                 document.getElementById( "myChildURL" ).value;
84     } // end function setChildWindowURL
85     //-->
86 </script>
87 </head>
88 <body>
89     <h1>Hello, this is the main window</h1>
90     <p>Please check the features to enable for the child window<br/>
91     <input id = "toolBarCheckBox" type = "checkbox" value = ""
92         checked = "checked" />
93         <label>Tool Bar</label>
94     <input id = "menuBarCheckBox" type = "checkbox" value = ""
95         checked = "checked" />
96         <label>Menu Bar</label>
97     <input id = "scrollBarsCheckBox" type = "checkbox" value = ""
98         checked = "checked" />
99         <label>Scroll Bars</label></p>
100
101    <p>Please enter the text that you would like to display
102    in the child window<br/>
103    <input id = "textForChild" type = "text"
104        value = "<h1>Hello, I am a child window.</h1> " />
105    <input id = "createButton" type = "button"
106        value = "Create Child Window" onclick = "createChildWindow()" />
107    <input id= "modifyButton" type = "button" value = "Modify Child Window"
108        onclick = "modifyChildWindow()" disabled = "disabled" />
109    <input id = "closeButton" type = "button" value = "Close Child Window"
110        onclick = "closeChildWindow()" disabled = "disabled" /></p>
111
112    <p>The other window's URL is: <br/>
113    <input id = "myChildURL" type = "text" value = "./" />
114    <input id = "setURLButton" type = "button" value = "Set Child URL"
115        onclick = "setChildWindowURL()" disabled = "disabled" /></p>
116 </body>
117 </html>
```

Fig. 9.13 | Using the window object to create and modify child windows. (Part 3 of 4.)

Fig. 9.13 | Using the `window` object to create and modify child windows. (Part 4 of 4.)

Lines 41–44 use the `window` object's `open` method to create the child window. Method `open` has three parameters. The first parameter is the URL of the page to open in the new window, and the second parameter is the name of the window. If you specify the `target` attribute of an a (anchor) element to correspond to the name of a window, the href of the link will be opened in the window. In our example, we pass window.open empty strings as the first two parameter values because we want the new window to open a blank page, and we use a different method to manipulate the child window's URL.

The third parameter of the open method is a string of comma-separated, all-lowercase feature names, each followed by an = sign and either "yes" or "no" to determine whether that feature should be displayed in the new window. If these parameters are omitted, the browser defaults to a new window containing an empty page, no title and all features visible. [*Note:* If your menu bar is normally hidden in IE7, it will not appear in the child window. Press the *Alt* key to display it.] Lines 47–49 enable the buttons for manipulating the child window—these are initially disabled when the page loads.

Lines 53–60 define the function modifyChildWindow, which adds a line of text to the content of the child window. In line 55, the script determines whether the child window is closed. Function modifyChildWindow uses property childWindow.closed to obtain a boolean value that is true if childWindow is closed and false if the window is still open. If the window is closed, an alert box is displayed notifying the user that the window is currently closed and cannot be modified. If the child window is open, lines 58–59 obtain text from the textForChild input (lines 103–104) in the XHTML form in the parent window and uses the child's document.write method to write this text to the child window.

Function closeChildWindow (lines 63–73) also determines whether the child window is closed before proceeding. If the child window is closed, the script displays an alert box telling the user that the window is already closed. If the child window is open, line 68 closes it using the childWindow.close method. Lines 70–72 disable the buttons that interact with the child window.

Look-and-Feel Observation 9.1

Popup windows should be used sparingly. Many users dislike websites that open additional windows, or that resize or reposition the browser. Some users have popup blockers that will prevent new windows from opening.

Software Engineering Observation 9.4

window.location is a property that always contains a string representation of the URL displayed in the current window. Typically, web browsers will allow a script to retrieve the window.location property of another window only if the script belongs to the same website as the page in the other window.

Function setChildWindowURL (lines 77–84) copies the contents of the myChildURL text field to the location property of the child window. If the child window is open, lines 81–82 set property location of the child window to the string in the myChildURL textbox. This action changes the URL of the child window and is equivalent to typing a new URL into the window's address bar and clicking **Go** (or pressing *Enter*).

The script ends in line 86. Lines 88–116 contain the body of the XHTML document, comprising a form that contains checkboxes, buttons, textboxes and form field labels. The script uses the form elements defined in the body to obtain input from the user. Lines 106, 108, 110, and 115 specify the onclick attributes of XHTML buttons. Each button is set to call a corresponding JavaScript function when clicked.

Figure 9.14 contains a list of some commonly used methods and properties of the window object.

Method or property	Description
open(*url*, *name*, *options*)	Creates a new window with the URL of the window set to *url*, the name set to *name* to refer to it in the script, and the visible features set by the string passed in as *option*.
prompt(*prompt*, *default*)	Displays a dialog box asking the user for input. The text of the dialog is *prompt*, and the default value is set to *default*.
close()	Closes the current window and deletes its object from memory.
focus()	This method gives focus to the window (i.e., puts the window in the foreground, on top of any other open browser windows).
blur()	This method takes focus away from the window (i.e., puts the window in the background).
window.document	This property contains the document object representing the document currently inside the window.
window.closed	This property contains a boolean value that is set to true if the window is closed, and false if it is not.
window.opener	This property contains the window object of the window that opened the current window, if such a window exists.

Fig. 9.14 | Important window object methods and properties.

9.9 Using Cookies

Cookies provide web developers with a tool for personalizing web pages. A *cookie* is a piece of data that is stored on the user's computer to maintain information about the client during and between browser sessions. A website may store a cookie on the client's computer to record user preferences or other information that the website can retrieve during the client's subsequent visits. For example, a website can retrieve the user's name from a cookie and use it to display a personalized greeting.

Microsoft Internet Explorer and Mozilla Firefox store cookies as small text files on the client's hard drive. When a user visits a website, the browser locates any cookies written by scripts on that site and makes them available to any scripts located on the site. Note that cookies may be accessed only by scripts belonging to the same website from which they originated (i.e., a cookie set by a script on amazon.com can be read only by other scripts on amazon.com).

Cookies are accessible in JavaScript through the document object's **cookie** property. JavaScript treats a cookie as a string of text. Any standard string function or method can manipulate a cookie. A cookie has the syntax "*identifier=value*," where *identifier* is any valid JavaScript variable identifier, and *value* is the value of the cookie variable. When multiple cookies exist for one website, *identifier-value* pairs are separated by semicolons in the document.cookie string.

Cookies differ from ordinary strings in that each cookie has an expiration date, after which the web browser deletes it. This date can be defined by setting the **expires** property in the cookie string. If a cookie's expiration date is not set, then the cookie expires by default after the user closes the browser window. A cookie can be deleted immediately by setting the expires property to a date and time in the past.

The assignment operator does not overwrite the entire list of cookies, but appends a cookie to the end of it. Thus, if we set two cookies

```
document.cookie = "name1=value1;";
document.cookie = "name2=value2;";
```

document.cookie will contain "name1=value1; name2=value2".

Figure 9.15 uses a cookie to store the user's name and displays a personalized greeting. This example improves upon the functionality in the dynamic welcome page example of Fig. 4.11 by requiring the user to enter a name only during the first visit to the web page. On each subsequent visit, the script can display the user name that is stored in the cookie.

Line 10 begins the script. Lines 12–13 declare the variables needed to obtain the time, and line 14 declares the variable that stores the name of the user. Lines 16–27 contain the same if...else statement used in Fig. 4.11 to display a time-sensitive greeting.

Lines 30–66 contain the code used to manipulate the cookie. Line 30 determines whether a cookie exists on the client computer. The expression document.cookie evaluates to true if a cookie exists. If a cookie does not exist, then the script prompts the user to enter a name (line 45). The script creates a cookie containing the string "name=", followed by a copy of the user's name produced by the built-in JavaScript function *escape* (line 49). The function escape converts any non-alphanumeric characters, such as spaces and semicolons, in a string to their equivalent *hexadecimal escape sequences* of the form "%XX," where XX is the two-digit hexadecimal ASCII value of a special character. For example, if name contains the value "David Green", the statement escape(name) evaluates to "David%20Green", because the hexadecimal ASCII value of a blank space is 20. It

```
1    <?xml version = "1.0" encoding = "utf-8"?>
2    <!DOCTYPE html PUBLIC "-//W3C//DTD XHTML 1.0 Strict//EN"
3       "http://www.w3.org/TR/xhtml1/DTD/xhtml1-strict.dtd">
4
5    <!-- Fig. 9.15: cookie.html -->
6    <!-- Using cookies to store user identification data. -->
7    <html xmlns = "http://www.w3.org/1999/xhtml">
8       <head>
9          <title>Using Cookies</title>
10         <script type = "text/javascript">
11            <!--
12            var now = new Date(); // current date and time
13            var hour = now.getHours(); // current hour (0-23)
14            var name;
15
16            if ( hour < 12 ) // determine whether it is morning
17               document.write( "<h1>Good Morning, " );
18            else
19            {
20               hour = hour - 12; // convert from 24-hour clock to PM time
21
```

Fig. 9.15 | Using cookies to store user identification data. (Part 1 of 3.)

```
22              // determine whether it is afternoon or evening
23              if ( hour < 6 )
24                  document.write( "<h1>Good Afternoon, " );
25              else
26                  document.write( "<h1>Good Evening, " );
27          } // end else
28
29          // determine whether there is a cookie
30          if ( document.cookie )
31          {
32              // convert escape characters in the cookie string to their
33              // English notation
34              var myCookie = unescape( document.cookie );
35
36              // split the cookie into tokens using = as delimiter
37              var cookieTokens = myCookie.split( "=" );
38
39              // set name to the part of the cookie that follows the = sign
40              name = cookieTokens[ 1 ];
41          } // end if
42          else
43          {
44              // if there was no cookie, ask the user to input a name
45              name = window.prompt( "Please enter your name", "Paul" );
46
47              // escape special characters in the name string
48              // and add name to the cookie
49              document.cookie = "name=" + escape( name );
50          } // end else
51
52          document.writeln(
53              name + ", welcome to JavaScript programming!</h1>" );
54          document.writeln( "<a href = 'javascript:wrongPerson()'> " +
55              "Click here if you are not " + name + "</a>" );
56
57          // reset the document's cookie if wrong person
58          function wrongPerson()
59          {
60              // reset the cookie
61              document.cookie= "name=null;" +
62                  " expires=Thu, 01-Jan-95 00:00:01 GMT";
63
64              // reload the page to get a new name after removing the cookie
65              location.reload();
66          } // end function wrongPerson
67
68          // -->
69      </script>
70   </head>
71   <body>
72      <p>Click Refresh (or Reload) to run the script again</p>
73   </body>
74 </html>
```

Fig. 9.15 | Using cookies to store user identification data. (Part 2 of 3.)

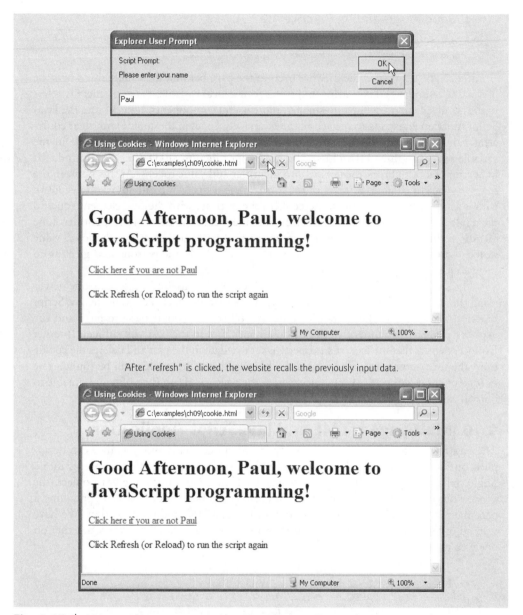

Fig. 9.15 | Using cookies to store user identification data. (Part 3 of 3.)

is a good idea to always escape cookie values before writing them to the client. This conversion prevents any special characters in the cookie from being misinterpreted as having a special meaning in the code, rather than being a character in a cookie value. For instance, a semicolon in a cookie value could be misinterpreted as a semicolon separating two adjacent *identifier-value* pairs. Applying the function **unescape** to cookies when they are read out of the document.cookie string converts the hexadecimal escape sequences back to English characters for display in a web page.

Good Programming Practice 9.2

Always store values in cookies with self-documenting identifiers. Do not forget to include the identifier followed by an = sign before the value being stored.

If a cookie exists (i.e., the user has been to the page before), then the script *parses* the user name out of the cookie string and stores it in a local variable. Parsing generally refers to the act of splitting a string into smaller, more useful components. Line 34 uses the Java-Script function unescape to replace all the escape sequences in the cookie with their equivalent English-language characters. The script stores the unescaped cookie value in the variable myCookie (line 34) and uses the JavaScript function split (line 37), introduced in Section 9.4.5, to break the cookie into identifier and value tokens. At this point in the script, myCookie contains a string of the form "name=*value*". We call split on myCookie with = as the delimiter to obtain the cookieTokens array, with the first element equal to the name of the identifier and the second element equal to the value of the identifier. Line 40 assigns the value of the second element in the cookieTokens array (i.e., the actual value stored in the cookie) to the variable name. Lines 52–53 add the personalized greeting to the web page, using the user's name stored in the cookie.

The script allows the user to reset the cookie, which is useful in case someone new is using the computer. Lines 54–55 create a hyperlink that, when clicked, calls the JavaScript function wrongPerson (lines 58–66). Lines 61–62 set the cookie name to null and the expires property to January 1, 1995 (though any date in the past will suffice). Internet Explorer detects that the expires property is set to a date in the past and deletes the cookie from the user's computer. The next time this page loads, no cookie will be found. The *reload* method of the location object forces the page to refresh (line 65), and, unable to find an existing cookie, the script prompts the user to enter a new name.

9.10 Multipage HTML and JavaScript Application

The past few chapters have explored many JavaScript concepts and how they can be applied on the web. The next JavaScript example combines many of these concepts into a single web page. Figure 9.16 uses functions, cookies, arrays, loops, the Date object, the window object and the document object to create a sample welcome screen containing a personalized greeting, a short quiz, a random image and a random quotation. We have seen all of these concepts before, but this example illustrates how they work together on one web page.

```
1   <?xml version = "1.0" encoding = "utf-8"?>
2   <!DOCTYPE html PUBLIC "-//W3C//DTD XHTML 1.0 Strict//EN"
3       "http://www.w3.org/TR/xhtml1/DTD/xhtml1-strict.dtd">
4
5   <!-- Fig. 9.16: final.html -->
6   <!-- Rich welcome page using several JavaScript concepts. -->
7   <html xmlns = "http://www.w3.org/1999/xhtml">
8      <head>
9         <title>Putting It All Together</title>
10        <script type = "text/javascript">
11           <!--
```

Fig. 9.16 | Rich welcome page using several JavaScript concepts. (Part 1 of 5.)

```
12        var now = new Date(); // current date and time
13        var hour = now.getHours(); // current hour
14
15        // array with names of the images that will be randomly selected
16        var pictures =
17           [ "CPE", "EPT", "GPP", "GUI", "PERF", "PORT", "SEO" ];
18
19        // array with the quotes that will be randomly selected
20        var quotes = [ "Form ever follows function.<br/>" +
21           " Louis Henri Sullivan", "E pluribus unum." +
22           " (One composed of many.) <br/> Virgil", "Is it a" +
23           " world to hide virtues in?<br/> William Shakespeare" ];
24
25        // write the current date and time to the web page
26        document.write( "<p>" + now.toLocaleString() + "<br/></p>" );
27
28        // determine whether it is morning
29        if ( hour < 12 )
30           document.write( "<h2>Good Morning, " );
31        else
32        {
33           hour = hour - 12; // convert from 24-hour clock to PM time
34
35           // determine whether it is afternoon or evening
36           if ( hour < 6 )
37              document.write( "<h2>Good Afternoon, " );
38           else
39              document.write( "<h2>Good Evening, " );
40        } // end else
41
42        // determine whether there is a cookie
43        if ( document.cookie )
44        {
45           // convert escape characters in the cookie string to their
46           // English notation
47           var myCookie = unescape( document.cookie );
48
49           // split the cookie into tokens using = as delimiter
50           var cookieTokens = myCookie.split( "=" );
51
52           // set name to the part of the cookie that follows the = sign
53           name = cookieTokens[ 1 ];
54        } // end if
55        else
56        {
57           // if there was no cookie, ask the user to input a name
58           name = window.prompt( "Please enter your name", "Paul" );
59
60           // escape special characters in the name string
61           // and add name to the cookie
62           document.cookie = "name =" + escape( name );
63        } // end else
```

Fig. 9.16 | Rich welcome page using several JavaScript concepts. (Part 2 of 5.)

```
64
65          // write the greeting to the page
66          document.writeln(
67            name + ", welcome to JavaScript programming!</h2>" );
68
69          // write the link for deleting the cookie to the page
70          document.writeln( "<a href = \"javascript:wrongPerson()\" > " +
71            "Click here if you are not " + name + "</a><br/>" );
72
73          // write the random image to the page
74          document.write ( "<img src = \"" +
75            pictures[ Math.floor( Math.random() * 7 ) ] +
76            ".gif\" /> <br/>" );
77
78          // write the random quote to the page
79          document.write ( quotes[ Math.floor( Math.random() * 3 ) ] );
80
81          // create a window with all the quotes in it
82          function allQuotes()
83          {
84            // create the child window for the quotes
85            var quoteWindow = window.open( "", "", "resizable=yes, " +
86              "toolbar=no, menubar=no, status=no, location=no," +
87              " scrollBars=yes" );
88            quoteWindow.document.write( "<p>" )
89
90            // loop through all quotes and write them in the new window
91            for ( var i = 0; i < quotes.length; i++ )
92              quoteWindow.document.write( ( i + 1 ) + ".) " +
93                quotes[ i ] + "<br/><br/>");
94
95            // write a close link to the new window
96            quoteWindow.document.write( "</p><br/><a href = " +
97              "\"javascript:window.close()\">Close this window</a>" );
98          } // end function allQuotes
99
100         // reset the document's cookie if wrong person
101         function wrongPerson()
102         {
103           // reset the cookie
104           document.cookie= "name=null;" +
105             " expires=Thu, 01-Jan-95 00:00:01 GMT";
106
107           // reload the page to get a new name after removing the cookie
108           location.reload();
109         } // end function wrongPerson
110
111         // open a new window with the quiz2.html file in it
112         function openQuiz()
113         {
114           window.open( "quiz2.html", "", "toolbar = no, " +
115             "menubar = no, scrollBars = no" );
116         } // end function openQuiz
```

Fig. 9.16 | Rich welcome page using several JavaScript concepts. (Part 3 of 5.)

```
117         // -->
118       </script>
119     </head>
120     <body>
121       <p><a href = "javascript:allQuotes()">View all quotes</a></p>
122
123       <p id = "quizSpot">
124         <a href = "javascript:openQuiz()">Please take our quiz</a></p>
125
126       <script type = "text/javascript">
127         // variable that gets the last modification date and time
128         var modDate = new Date( document.lastModified );
129
130         // write the last modified date and time to the page
131         document.write ( "This page was last modified " +
132           modDate.toLocaleString() );
133       </script>
134     </body>
135 </html>
```

Fig. 9.16 | Rich welcome page using several JavaScript concepts. (Part 4 of 5.)

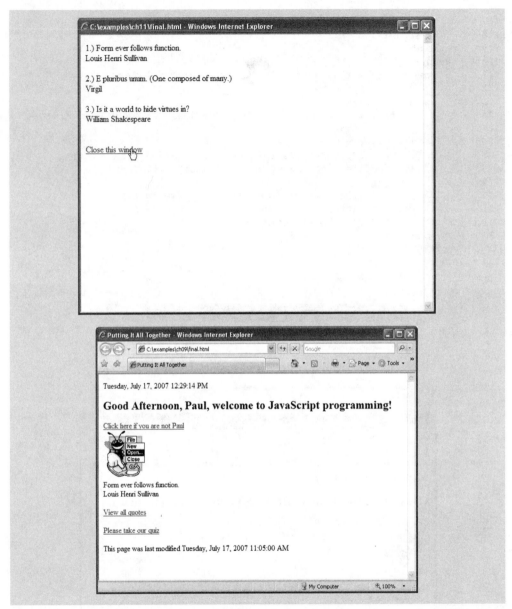

Fig. 9.16 | Rich welcome page using several JavaScript concepts. (Part 5 of 5.)

The script that builds most of this page starts in line 10. Lines 12–13 declare variables needed for determining the time of day. Lines 16–23 create two arrays from which content is randomly selected. This web page contains both an image (whose filename is randomly selected from the pictures array) and a quote (whose text is randomly selected from the quotes array). Line 26 writes the user's local date and time to the web page using the Date object's toLocaleString method. Lines 29–40 display a time-sensitive greeting using the same code as Fig. 4.11. The script either uses an existing cookie to obtain the user's name (lines 43–54) or prompts the user for a name, which the script then stores in a new cookie (lines 55–63). Lines 66–67 write the greeting to the web page, and lines 70–71 produce the link for resetting the cookie. This is the same code used in Fig. 9.15 to manipulate cookies. Lines 74–79 write the random image and random quote to the web page. The script chooses each by randomly selecting an index into each array. This code is similar to the code used in Fig. 10.7 to display a random image using an array.

Function allQuotes (lines 82–98) uses the window object and a for loop to open a new window containing all the quotes in the quotes array. Lines 85–87 create a new window called quoteWindow. The script does not assign a URL or a name to this window, but it does specify the window features to display. Line 88 opens a new paragraph in quoteWindow. A for loop (lines 91–93) traverses the quotes array and writes each quote to quoteWindow. Lines 96–97 close the paragraph in quoteWindow, insert a new line and add a link at the bottom of the page that allows the user to close the window. Note that allQuotes generates a web page and opens it in an entirely new window with JavaScript.

Function wrongPerson (lines 101–109) resets the cookie storing the user's name. This function is identical to function wrongPerson in Fig. 9.15.

Function openQuiz (lines 112–116) opens a new window to display a sample quiz. Using the window.open method, the script creates a new window containing quiz2.html (lines 114–115). We discuss quiz2.html later in this section.

The primary script ends in line 118, and the body of the XHTML document begins in line 120. Line 121 creates the link that calls function allQuotes when clicked. Lines 123–124 create a paragraph element containing the attribute id = "quizSpot". This paragraph contains a link that calls function openQuiz.

Lines 126–133 contain a second script. This script appears in the XHTML document's body because it adds a dynamic footer to the page, which must appear after the static XHTML content contained in the first part of the body. This script creates another instance of the Date object, but the date is set to the last modified date and time of the XHTML document, rather than the current date and time (line 128). The script obtains the last modified date and time using property document.lastModified. Lines 131–132 add this information to the web page. Note that the last modified date and time appear at the bottom of the page, after the rest of the body content. If this script were in the head element, this information would be displayed before the entire body of the XHTML document. Lines 133–135 close the script, the body and the XHTML document.

The Quiz Page
The quiz used in this example is in a separate XHTML document named quiz2.html (Fig. 9.17). This document is similar to quiz.html in Fig. 8.12. The quiz in this example differs from the quiz in Fig. 8.12 in that it shows the result in the main window in the example, whereas the earlier quiz example alerts the result. After the **Submit** button in the quiz window is clicked, the main window changes to reflect that the quiz was taken, and the quiz window closes.

Lines 15–22 of this script check the user's answer and output the result to the main window. Lines 16–17 use window.opener to write to the main window. The property *window.opener* always contains a reference to the window that opened the current window, if such a window exists. Lines 16–17 write to property window.opener.document.getElementById("quizSpot").innerHTML. Recall that quizSpot is the id of the paragraph in the main window that contains the link to open the quiz. Property **innerHTML** refers to the HTML code inside the quizSpot paragraph (i.e., the code between <p> and </p>). Modifying the innerHTML property dynamically changes the XHTML code in the paragraph. Thus, when lines 16–17 execute, the link in the main window disappears, and the string "Congratulations, your answer is correct." appears. Lines 19–22 modify window.opener.document.getElementById("quizSpot").innerHTML. Lines 19–22 use the same technique to display "Your answer is incorrect. Please try again", followed by a link to try the quiz again.

```
 1   <?xml version = "1.0" encoding = "utf-8"?>
 2   <!DOCTYPE html PUBLIC "-//W3C//DTD XHTML 1.0 Strict//EN"
 3      "http://www.w3.org/TR/xhtml1/DTD/xhtml1-strict.dtd">
 4
 5   <!-- Fig. 9.17: quiz2.html -->
 6   <!-- Online quiz in a child window. -->
 7   <html xmlns = "http://www.w3.org/1999/xhtml">
 8      <head>
 9         <title>Online Quiz</title>
10         <script type = "text/JavaScript">
11            <!--
12            function checkAnswers()
13            {
14               // determine whether the answer is correct
15               if ( document.getElementById( "myQuiz" ).elements[1].checked )
16                  window.opener.document.getElementById( "quizSpot" ).
17                     innerHTML = "Congratulations, your answer is correct";
18               else // if the answer is incorrect
19                  window.opener.document.getElementById( "quizSpot" ).
20                     innerHTML = "Your answer is incorrect. " +
21                     "Please try again <br /> <a href = " +
22                     \"javascript:openQuiz()\">Please take our quiz</a>";
23
24               window.opener.focus();
25               window.close();
26            } // end function checkAnswers
27            //-->
28         </script>
29      </head>
30      <body>
31         <form id = "myQuiz" action = "javascript:checkAnswers()">
32            <p>Select the name of the tip that goes with the
33               image shown:<br />
34               <img src = "EPT.gif" alt = "mystery tip"/>
35               <br />
36
37               <input type = "radio" name = "radiobutton" value = "CPE" />
38               <label>Common Programming Error</label>
39
40               <input type = "radio" name = "radiobutton" value = "EPT" />
41               <label>Error-Prevention Tip</label>
42
```

Fig. 9.17 | Online quiz in a child window. (Part 1 of 3.)

```
43              <input type = "radio" name = "radiobutton" value = "PERF" />
44              <label>Performance Tip</label>
45
46              <input type = "radio" name = "radiobutton" value = "PORT" />
47              <label>Portability Tip</label><br />
48
49              <input type = "submit" name = "Submit" value = "Submit" />
50              <input type = "reset" name = "reset" value = "Reset" />
51          </p>
52      </form>
53  </body>
54 </html>
```

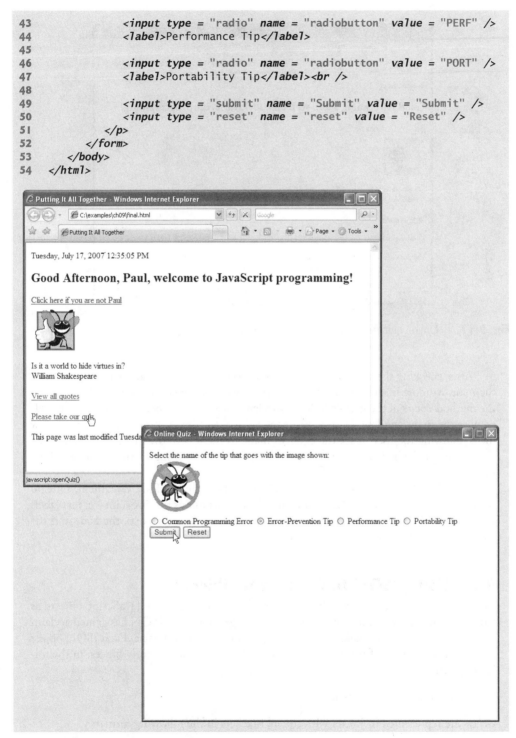

Fig. 9.17 | Online quiz in a child window. (Part 2 of 3.)

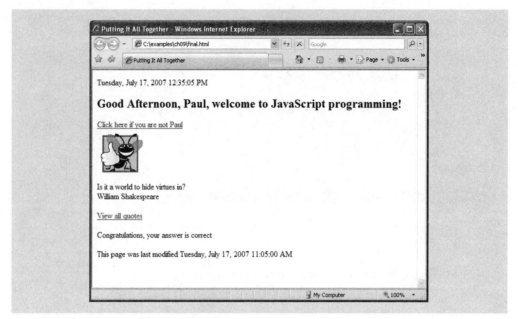

Fig. 9.17 | Online quiz in a child window. (Part 3 of 3.)

After checking the quiz answer, the script gives focus to the main window (i.e., puts the main window in the foreground, on top of any other open browser windows), using the method **focus** of the main window's window object. The property window.opener references the main window, so window.opener.focus() (line 24) gives the main window focus, allowing the user to see the changes made to the text of the main window's quizSpot paragraph. Finally, the script closes the quiz window, using method window.close (line 25).

Lines 28–29 close the script and head elements of the XHTML document. Line 30 opens the body of the XHTML document. The body contains the form, image, text labels and radio buttons that comprise the quiz. Lines 52–54 close the form, the body and the XHTML document.

9.11 Using JSON to Represent Objects

JSON (JavaScript Object Notation)—a simple way to represent JavaScript objects as strings—is an alternative to XML as a data-exchange technique. JSON has gained acclaim due to its simple format, making objects easy to read, create and parse. Each JSON object is represented as a list of property names and values contained in curly braces, in the following format:

{ *propertyName1* : *value1*, *propertyName2* : *value2* }

Arrays are represented in JSON with square brackets in the following format:

[*value1*, *value2*, *value3*]

Each value can be a string, a number, a JSON object, `true`, `false` or `null`. To appreciate the simplicity of JSON data, examine this representation of an array of address-book entries from Chapter 13:

```
[ { first: 'Cheryl', last: 'Black' },
  { first: 'James', last: 'Blue' },
  { first: 'Mike', last: 'Brown' },
  { first: 'Meg', last: 'Gold' } ]
```

JSON provides a straightforward way to manipulate objects in JavaScript, and many other programming languages now support this format. In addition to simplifying object creation, JSON allows programs to manipulate data easily and to efficiently transmit data across the Internet. JSON integrates well with Ajax applications—see Section 13.7 for a more detailed discussion of JSON and an Ajax-specific example. For more information on JSON, visit our JSON Resource Center at www.deitel.com/json.

9.12 Web Resources

www.deitel.com/javascript/
The Deitel JavaScript Resource Center contains links to some of the best JavaScript resources on the web. There you'll find categorized links to JavaScript tools, code generators, forums, books, libraries, frameworks and more. Also check out the tutorials for all skill levels, from introductory to advanced. Be sure to visit the related Resource Centers on XHTML (www.deitel.com/xhtml/) and CSS 2.1 (www.deitel.com/css21/).

10

Document Object Model (DOM): Objects and Collections

OBJECTIVES

In this chapter you will learn:

- How to use JavaScript and the W3C Document Object Model to create dynamic web pages.
- The concepts of DOM nodes and DOM trees.
- How to traverse, edit and modify elements in an XHTML document.
- How to change CSS styles dynamically.
- To create JavaScript animations.

Our children may learn about heroes of the past. Our task is to make ourselves architects of the future.
—Jomo Mzee Kenyatta

Though leaves are many, the root is one.
—William Butler Yeats

The thing that impresses me most about America is the way parents obey their children.
—Duke of Windsor

Most of us become parents long before we have stopped being children.
—Mignon McLaughlin

To write it, it took three months; to conceive it three minutes; to collect the data in it—all my life.
—F. Scott Fitzgerald

Sibling rivalry is inevitable. The only sure way to avoid it is to have one child.
—Nancy Samalin

10.1 Introduction

In this chapter we introduce the ***Document Object Model (DOM)***. The DOM gives you access to all the elements on a web page. Inside the browser, the whole web page—paragraphs, forms, tables, etc.—is represented in an ***object hierarchy***. Using JavaScript, you can create, modify and remove elements in the page dynamically.

Previously, both Internet Explorer and Netscape had different versions of Dynamic HTML, which provided similar functionality to the DOM. However, while they provided many of the same capabilities, these two models were incompatible with each other. In an effort to encourage cross-browser websites, the W3C created the standardized Document Object Model. Firefox 2, Internet Explorer 7, and many other major browsers implement *most* of the features of the W3C DOM.

This chapter begins by formally introducing the concept of DOM nodes and DOM trees. We then discuss properties and methods of DOM nodes and cover additional methods of the document object. We also discuss how to dynamically change style properties, which enables you to create many types of effects, such as user-defined background colors and animations. Then, we present a diagram of the extensive object hierarchy, with explanations of the various objects and properties, and we provide links to websites with further information on the topic.

> **Software Engineering Observation 10.1**
>
> *With the DOM, XHTML elements can be treated as objects, and many attributes of XHTML elements can be treated as properties of those objects. Then, objects can be scripted (through their* id *attributes) with JavaScript to achieve dynamic effects.*

10.2 Modeling a Document: DOM Nodes and Trees

As we saw in previous chapters, the document's getElementById method is the simplest way to access a specific element in a page. In this section and the next, we discuss more thoroughly the objects returned by this method.

The getElementById method returns objects called ***DOM nodes***. Every element in an XHTML page is modeled in the web browser by a DOM node. All the nodes in a document make up the page's ***DOM tree***, which describes the relationships among elements. Nodes are related to each other through child-parent relationships. An XHTML element inside another element is said to be a ***child*** of the containing element. The containing element is known as the ***parent***. A node may have multiple children, but only one parent. Nodes with the same parent node are referred to as ***siblings***.

Some browsers have tools that allow you to see a visual representation of the DOM tree of a document. When installing Firefox, you can choose to install a tool called the *DOM Inspector*, which allows you to view the DOM tree of an XHTML document. To inspect a document, Firefox users can access the **DOM Inspector** from the **Tools** menu of Firefox. If the DOM inspector is not in the menu, run the Firefox installer and choose **Custom** in the **Setup Type** screen, making sure the **DOM Inspector** box is checked in the **Optional Components** window.

Microsoft provides a *Developer Toolbar* for Internet Explorer that allows you to inspect the DOM tree of a document. The toolbar can be downloaded from Microsoft at go.microsoft.com/fwlink/?LinkId=92716. Once the toolbar is installed, restart the browser, then click the » icon at the right of the toolbar and choose **IE Developer Toolbar** from the menu. Figure 10.1 shows an XHTML document and its DOM tree displayed in Firefox's DOM Inspector and in IE's Web Developer Toolbar.

The XHTML document contains a few simple elements. We explain the example based on the Firefox DOM Inspector—the IE Toolbar displays the document with only minor differences. A node can be expanded and collapsed using the + and - buttons next to the node's name. Figure 10.1(b) shows all the nodes in the document fully expanded. The document node (shown as **#document**) at the top of the tree is called the *root node*, because it has no parent. Below the document node, the **HTML** node is indented from the document node to signify that the **HTML** node is a child of the **#document** node. The **HTML** node represents the html element (lines 7–24).

The **HEAD** and **BODY** nodes are siblings, since they are both children of the **HTML** node. The **HEAD** contains two **#comment** nodes, representing lines 5–6. The **TITLE** node

```
1   <?xml version = "1.0" encoding = "utf-8"?>
2   <!DOCTYPE html PUBLIC "-//W3C//DTD XHTML 1.0 Strict//EN"
3      "http://www.w3.org/TR/xhtml1/DTD/xhtml1-strict.dtd">
4
5   <!-- Fig. 10.1: domtree.html -->
6   <!-- Demonstration of a document's DOM tree. -->
7   <html xmlns = "http://www.w3.org/1999/xhtml">
8      <head>
9         <title>DOM Tree Demonstration</title>
10     </head>
11     <body>
12        <h1>An XHTML Page</h1>
13        <p>This page contains some basic XHTML elements. We use the Firefox
14           DOM Inspector and the IE Developer Toolbar to view the DOM tree
15           of the document, which contains a DOM node for every element in
16           the document.</p>
17        <p>Here's a list:</p>
18        <ul>
19           <li>One</li>
20           <li>Two</li>
21           <li>Three</li>
22        </ul>
23     </body>
24  </html>
```

Fig. 10.1 | Demonstration of a document's DOM tree. (Part 1 of 3.)

a) The XHTML document is rendered in Firefox.

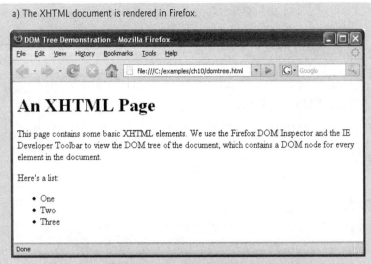

b) The Firefox DOM inspector displays the document tree in the left panel. The right panel shows information about the currently selected node.

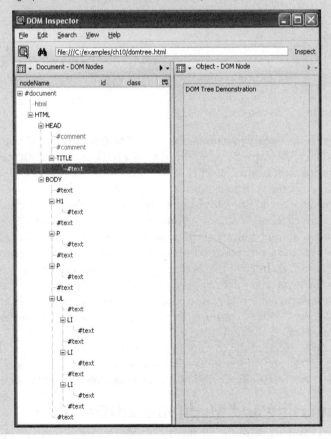

Fig. 10.1 | Demonstration of a document's DOM tree. (Part 2 of 3.)

c) The Internet Explorer Web Developer Toolbar displays much of the same information as the DOM inspector in Firefox in a panel at the bottom of the browser window.

Fig. 10.1 | Demonstration of a document's DOM tree. (Part 3 of 3.)

has a child text node (**#text**) containing the text **DOM Tree Demonstration**, visible in the right pane of the DOM inspector when the text node is selected. The **BODY** node contains nodes representing each of the elements in the page. Note that the **LI** nodes are children of the **UL** node, since they are nested inside it.

Also, notice that, in addition to the text nodes representing the text inside the body, paragraphs and list elements, a number of other text nodes appear in the document. These text nodes contain nothing but white space. When Firefox parses an XHTML document into a DOM tree, the white space between sibling elements is interpreted as text and placed inside text nodes. Internet Explorer ignores white space and does not convert it into empty text nodes. If you run this example on your own computer, you will notice that the **BODY** node has a **#comment** child node not present above in both the Firefox and Internet Explorer DOM trees. This is a result of the copyright line at the end of the example file that you downloaded.

This section introduced the concept of DOM nodes and DOM trees. The next section considers DOM nodes in more detail, discussing methods and properties of DOM nodes that allow you to modify the DOM tree of a document using JavaScript.

10.3 Traversing and Modifying a DOM Tree

The DOM gives you access to the elements of a document, allowing you to modify the contents of a page dynamically using event-driven JavaScript. This section introduces properties and methods of all DOM nodes that enable you to traverse the DOM tree, modify nodes and create or delete content dynamically.

Figure 10.2 shows some of the functionality of DOM nodes, as well as two additional methods of the document object. The program allows you to highlight, modify, insert and remove elements.

Lines 117–132 contain basic XHTML elements and content. Each element has an id attribute, which is also displayed at the beginning of the element in square brackets. For example, the id of the h1 element in lines 117–118 is set to bigheading, and the heading text begins with [bigheading]. This allows the user to see the id of each element in the page. The body also contains an h3 heading, several p elements, and an unordered list.

A div element (lines 133–162) contains the remainder of the XHTML body. Line 134 begins a form element, assigning the empty string to the required action attribute (because we're not submitting to a server) and returning false to the onsubmit attribute. When a form's onsubmit handler returns false, the navigation to the address specified in the action attribute is aborted. This allows us to modify the page using JavaScript event handlers without reloading the original, unmodified XHTML.

```
1   <?xml version = "1.0" encoding = "utf-8"?>
2   <!DOCTYPE html PUBLIC "-//W3C//DTD XHTML 1.0 Strict//EN"
3     "http://www.w3.org/TR/xhtml1/DTD/xhtml1-strict.dtd">
4
5   <!-- Fig. 10.2: dom.html -->
6   <!-- Basic DOM functionality. -->
7   <html xmlns = "http://www.w3.org/1999/xhtml">
8     <head>
9       <title>Basic DOM Functionality</title>
10      <style type = "text/css">
11        h1, h3      { text-align: center;
12                      font-family: tahoma, geneva, sans-serif }
13        p           { margin-left: 5%;
14                      margin-right: 5%;
15                      font-family: arial, helvetica, sans-serif }
16        ul          { margin-left: 10% }
17        a           { text-decoration: none }
18        a:hover     { text-decoration: underline }
19        .nav        { width: 100%;
20                      border-top: 3px dashed blue;
21                      padding-top: 10px }
22        .highlighted { background-color: yellow }
23        .submit     { width: 120px }
24      </style>
25      <script type = "text/javascript">
26        <!--
27        var currentNode; // stores the currently highlighted node
28        var idcount = 0; // used to assign a unique id to new elements
29
30        // get and highlight an element by its id attribute
31        function byId()
32        {
```

Fig. 10.2 | Basic DOM functionality. (Part 1 of 8.)

```
33          var id = document.getElementById( "gbi" ).value;
34          var target = document.getElementById( id );
35
36          if ( target )
37              switchTo( target );
38      } // end function byId
39
40      // insert a paragraph element before the current element
41      // using the insertBefore method
42      function insert()
43      {
44          var newNode = createNewNode(
45              document.getElementById( "ins" ).value );
46          currentNode.parentNode.insertBefore( newNode, currentNode );
47          switchTo( newNode );
48      } // end function insert
49
50      // append a paragraph node as the child of the current node
51      function appendNode()
52      {
53          var newNode = createNewNode(
54              document.getElementById( "append" ).value );
55          currentNode.appendChild( newNode );
56          switchTo( newNode );
57      } // end function appendNode
58
59      // replace the currently selected node with a paragraph node
60      function replaceCurrent()
61      {
62          var newNode = createNewNode(
63              document.getElementById( "replace" ).value );
64          currentNode.parentNode.replaceChild( newNode, currentNode );
65          switchTo( newNode );
66      } // end function replaceCurrent
67
68      // remove the current node
69      function remove()
70      {
71          if ( currentNode.parentNode == document.body )
72              alert( "Can't remove a top-level element." );
73          else
74          {
75              var oldNode = currentNode;
76              switchTo( oldNode.parentNode );
77              currentNode.removeChild( oldNode );
78          } // end else
79      } // end function remove
80
81      // get and highlight the parent of the current node
82      function parent()
83      {
84          var target = currentNode.parentNode;
85
```

Fig. 10.2 | Basic DOM functionality. (Part 2 of 8.)

```
 86              if ( target != document.body )
 87                 switchTo( target );
 88              else
 89                 alert( "No parent." );
 90           } // end function parent
 91
 92           // helper function that returns a new paragraph node containing
 93           // a unique id and the given text
 94           function createNewNode( text )
 95           {
 96              var newNode = document.createElement( "p" );
 97              nodeId = "new" + idcount;
 98              ++idcount;
 99              newNode.id = nodeId;
100              text = "[" + nodeId + "] " + text;
101              newNode.appendChild(document.createTextNode( text ) );
102              return newNode;
103           } // end function createNewNode
104
105           // helper function that switches to a new currentNode
106           function switchTo( newNode )
107           {
108              currentNode.className = ""; // remove old highlighting
109              currentNode = newNode;
110              currentNode.className = "highlighted"; // highlight new node
111              document.getElementById( "gbi" ).value = currentNode.id;
112           } // end function switchTo
113           // -->
114        </script>
115     </head>
116     <body onload = "currentNode = document.getElementById( 'bigheading' )">
117        <h1 id = "bigheading" class = "highlighted">
118           [bigheading] DHTML Object Model</h1>
119        <h3 id = "smallheading">[smallheading] Element Functionality</h3>
120        <p id = "para1">[para1] The Document Object Model (DOM) allows for
121           quick, dynamic access to all elements in an XHTML document for
122           manipulation with JavaScript.</p>
123        <p id = "para2">[para2] For more information, check out the
124           "JavaScript and the DOM" section of Deitel's
125           <a id = "link" href = "http://www.deitel.com/javascript">
126           [link] JavaScript Resource Center.</a></p>
127        <p id = "para3">[para3] The buttons below demonstrate:(list)</p>
128        <ul id = "list">
129           <li id = "item1">[item1] getElementById and parentNode</li>
130           <li id = "item2">[item2] insertBefore and appendChild</li>
131           <li id = "item3">[item3] replaceChild and removeChild </li>
132        </ul>
133        <div id = "nav" class = "nav">
134           <form onsubmit = "return false" action = "">
135              <table>
136                 <tr>
137                    <td><input type = "text" id = "gbi"
138                       value = "bigheading" /></td>
```

Fig. 10.2 | Basic DOM functionality. (Part 3 of 8.)

```
139              <td><input type = "submit" value = "Get By id"
140                  onclick = "byId()" class = "submit" /></td>
141          </tr><tr>
142              <td><input type = "text" id = "ins" /></td>
143              <td><input type = "submit" value = "Insert Before"
144                  onclick = "insert()" class = "submit" /></td>
145          </tr><tr>
146              <td><input type = "text" id = "append" /></td>
147              <td><input type = "submit" value = "Append Child"
148                  onclick = "appendNode()" class = "submit" /></td>
149          </tr><tr>
150              <td><input type = "text" id = "replace" /></td>
151              <td><input type = "submit" value = "Replace Current"
152                  onclick = "replaceCurrent()" class = "submit" /></td>
153          </tr><tr><td />
154              <td><input type = "submit" value = "Remove Current"
155                  onclick = "remove()" class = "submit" /></td>
156          </tr><tr><td />
157              <td><input type = "submit" value = "Get Parent"
158                  onclick = "parent()" class = "submit" /></td>
159          </tr>
160      </table>
161  </form>
162  </div>
163  </body>
164 </html>
```

a) This is the page when it first loads. It begins with the large heading highlighted.

Fig. 10.2 | Basic DOM functionality. (Part 4 of 8.)

b) This is the document after using the **Get By id** button to select para3.

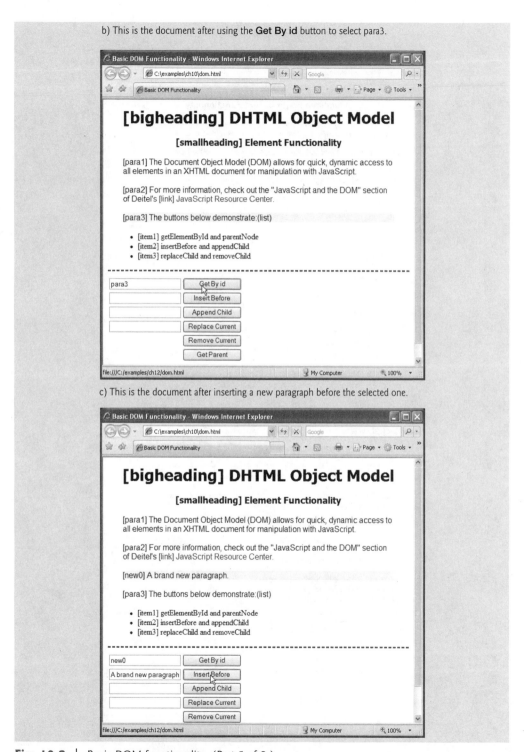

c) This is the document after inserting a new paragraph before the selected one.

Fig. 10.2 | Basic DOM functionality. (Part 5 of 8.)

d) Using the **Append Child** button, a child paragraph is created.

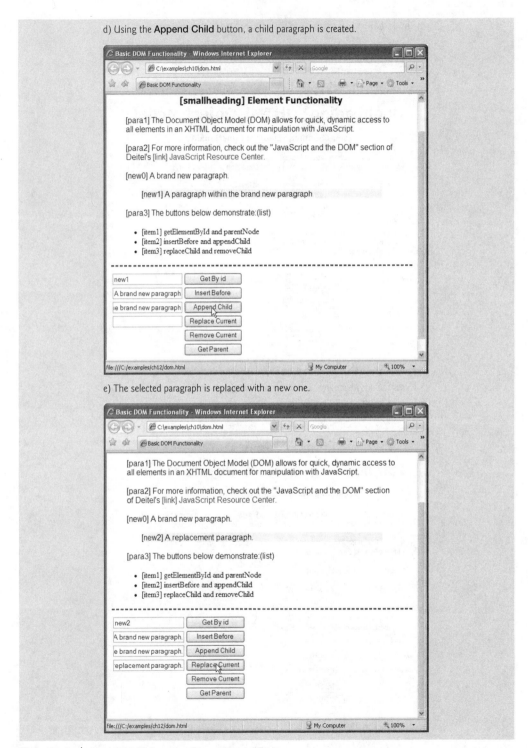

e) The selected paragraph is replaced with a new one.

Fig. 10.2 | Basic DOM functionality. (Part 6 of 8.)

f) The **Get Parent** button gets the parent of the selected node.

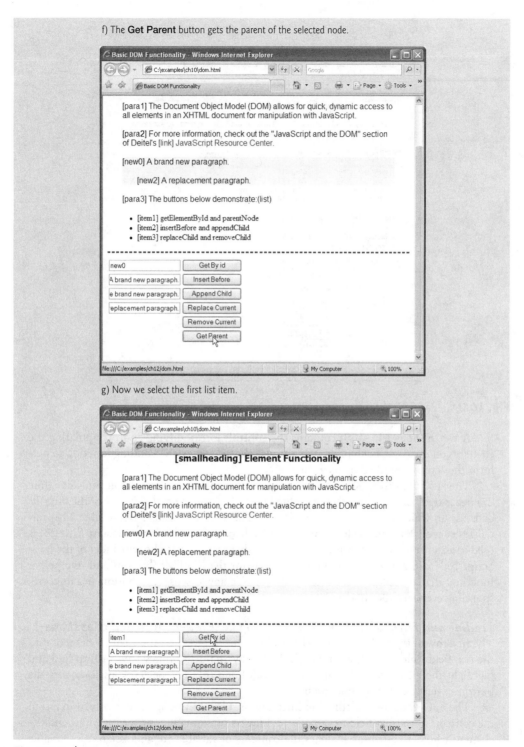

g) Now we select the first list item.

Fig. 10.2 | Basic DOM functionality. (Part 7 of 8.)

h) The **Remove Current** button removes the current node and selects its parent.

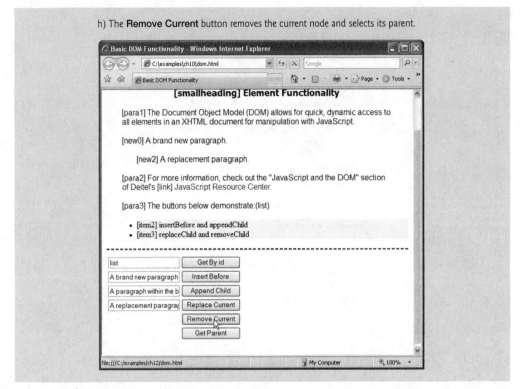

Fig. 10.2 | Basic DOM functionality. (Part 8 of 8.)

A `table` (lines 135–160) contains the controls for modifying and manipulating the elements on the page. Each of the six buttons calls its own event-handling function to perform the action described by its `value`.

The JavaScript code begins by declaring two variables. The variable `currentNode` (line 27) keeps track of the currently highlighted node, because the functionality of the buttons depends on which node is currently selected. The `body`'s `onload` attribute (line 116) initializes `currentNode` to the `h1` element with `id` `bigheading`. Variable `idcount` (line 28) is used to assign a unique `id` to any new elements that are created. The remainder of the Java-Script code contains event handling functions for the XHTML buttons and two helper functions that are called by the event handlers. We now discuss each button and its corresponding event handler in detail.

Finding and Highlighting an Element Using getElementById and className

The first row of the table (lines 136-141) allows the user to enter the `id` of an element into the text field (lines 137–138) and click the `Get By Id` button (lines 139–140) to find and highlight the element, as shown in Fig. 10.2(b) and (g). The `onclick` attribute sets the button's event handler to function `byId`.

The `byId` function is defined in lines 31–38. Line 33 uses `getElementById` to assign the contents of the text field to variable `id`. Line 34 uses `getElementById` again to find the element whose `id` attribute matches the contents of variable `id`, and assign it to variable `target`. If an element is found with the given `id`, `getElementById` returns an object representing that element. If no element is found, getElementById returns null. Line 36 checks whether target is an object—recall that any object used as a boolean expression is true, while null is false. If target evaluates to true, line 37 calls the switchTo function with target as its argument.

The switchTo function, defined in lines 106–112, is used throughout the program to highlight a new element in the page. The current element is given a yellow background using the style class highlighted, defined in line 22. Line 108 sets the current node's className property to the empty string. The *className property* allows you to change an XHTML element's class attribute. In this case, we clear the class attribute in order to remove the highlighted class from the currentNode before we highlight the new one.

Line 109 assigns the newNode object (passed into the function as a parameter) to variable currentNode. Line 110 adds the highlighted style class to the new currentNode using the className property.

Finally, line 111 uses the *id property* to assign the current node's id to the input field's value property. Just as className allows access to an element's class attribute, the id property controls an element's id attribute. While this isn't necessary when switchTo is called by byId, we will see shortly that other functions call switchTo. This line makes sure that the text field's value is consistent with the currently selected node's id. Having found the new element, removed the highlighting from the old element, updated the currentNode variable and highlighted the new element, the program has finished selecting a new node by a user-entered id.

Creating and Inserting Elements Using insertBefore *and* appendChild

The next two table rows allow the user to create a new element and insert it before the current node or as a child of the current node. The second row (lines 141–145) allows the user to enter text into the text field and click the Insert Before button. The text is placed in a new paragraph element, which is then inserted into the document before the currently selected element, as in Fig. 10.2(c). The button in lines 143–144 calls the insert function, defined in lines 42–48.

Lines 44–45 call the function createNewNode, passing it the value of the input field (whose id is ins) as an argument. Function createNewNode, defined in lines 94–103, creates a paragraph node containing the text passed to it. Line 96 creates a p element using the document object's *createElement method*. The createElement method creates a new DOM node, taking the tag name as an argument. Note that while createElement *creates* an element, it does not *insert* the element on the page.

Line 97 creates a unique id for the new element by concatenating "new" and the value of idcount before incrementing idcount in line 98. Line 99 assigns the id to the new element. Line 100 concatenates the element's id in square brackets to the beginning of text (the parameter containing the paragraph's text).

Line 101 introduces two new methods. The document's *createTextNode method* creates a node that can contain only text. Given a string argument, createTextNode inserts the string into the text node. In line 101, we create a new text node containing the contents of variable text. This new node is then used (still in line 101) as the argument to the *appendChild method*, which is called on the paragraph node. Method appendChild is called on a parent node to insert a child node (passed as an argument) after any existing children.

After the p element is created, line 102 returns the node to the calling function insert, where it is assigned to variable newNode in lines 44–45. Line 46 inserts the newly created node before the currently selected node. The **parentNode property** of any DOM node contains the node's parent. In line 46, we use the parentNode property of current-Node to get its parent.

We call the insertBefore method (line 46) on the parent with newNode and currentNode as its arguments to insert newNode as a child of the parent directly before currentNode. The general syntax of the **insertBefore method** is

> *parent*.insertBefore(*newChild, existingChild*);

The method is called on a parent with the new child and an existing child as arguments. The node *newChild* is inserted as a child of *parent* directly before *existingChild*. Line 47 uses the switchTo function (discussed earlier in this section) to update the currentNode to the newly inserted node and highlight it in the XHTML page.

The third table row (lines 145–149) allows the user to append a new paragraph node as a child of the current element, demonstrated in Fig. 10.2(d). This features uses a similar procedure to the insertBefore functionality. Lines 53–54 in function appendNode create a new node, line 55 inserts it as a child of the current node, and line 56 uses switchTo to update currentNode and highlight the new node.

Replacing and Removing Elements Using replaceChild and removeChild

The next two table rows (lines 149–156) allow the user to replace the current element with a new p element or simply remove the current element. Lines 150–152 contain a text field and a button that replaces the currently highlighted element with a new paragraph node containing the text in the text field. This feature is demonstrated in Fig. 10.2(e).

The button in lines 151–152 calls function replaceCurrent, defined in lines 60–66. Lines 62–63 call createNewNode, in the same way as in insert and appendNode, getting the text from the correct input field. Line 64 gets the parent of currentNode, then calls the replaceChild method on the parent. The **replaceChild method** works as follows:

> *parent*.replaceChild(*newChild, oldChild*);

The *parent*'s replaceChild method inserts *newChild* into its list of children in place of *old-Child*.

The Remove Current feature, shown in Fig. 10.2(h), removes the current element entirely and highlights the parent. No text field is required because a new element is not being created. The button in lines 154-155 calls the remove function, defined in lines 69–79. If the node's parent is the body element, line 72 alerts an error—the program does not allow the entire body element to be selected. Otherwise, lines 75–77 remove the current element. Line 75 stores the old currentNode in variable oldNode. We do this to maintain a reference to the node to be removed after we've changed the value of currentNode. Line 76 calls switchTo to highlight the parent node.

Line 77 uses the **removeChild method** to remove the oldNode (a child of the new currentNode) from its place in the XHTML document. In general,

> *parent*.removeChild(*child*);

looks in *parent*'s list of children for *child* and removes it.

The final button (lines 157–158) selects and highlights the parent element of the currently highlighted element by calling the `parent` function, defined in lines 82–90. Function `parent` simply gets the parent node (line 84), makes sure it is not the body element, (line 86) and calls `switchTo` to highlight it (line 87). Line 89 alerts an error if the parent node is the body element. This feature is shown in Fig. 10.2(f).

This section introduced the basics of DOM tree traversal and manipulation. Next, we introduce the concept of collections, which give you access to multiple elements in a page.

10.4 DOM Collections

Included in the Document Object Model is the notion of *collections*, which are groups of related objects on a page. DOM collections are accessed as properties of DOM objects such as the `document` object or a DOM node. The document object has properties containing the *images collection*, *links collection*, *forms collection* and *anchors collection*. These collections contain all the elements of the corresponding type on the page. Figure 10.3 gives an example that uses the `links` collection to extract all of the links on a page and display them together at the bottom of the page.

```
1   <?xml version = "1.0" encoding = "utf-8"?>
2   <!DOCTYPE html PUBLIC "-//W3C//DTD XHTML 1.0 Strict//EN"
3      "http://www.w3.org/TR/xhtml1/DTD/xhtml1-strict.dtd">
4
5   <!-- Fig. 10.3: collections.html -->
6   <!-- Using the links collection. -->
7   <html xmlns = "http://www.w3.org/1999/xhtml">
8      <head>
9         <title>Using Links Collection</title>
10        <style type = "text/css">
11           body         { font-family: arial, helvetica, sans-serif }
12           h1           { font-family: tahoma, geneva, sans-serif;
13                          text-align: center }
14           p          { margin: 5% }
15           p a          { color: #aa0000 }
16           .links       { font-size: 14px;
17                          text-align: justify;
18                          margin-left: 10%;
19                          margin-right: 10% }
20           .link a    { text-decoration: none }
21           .link a:hover { text-decoration: underline }
22        </style>
23        <script type = "text/javascript">
24           <!--
25           function processlinks()
26           {
27              var linkslist = document.links; // get the document's links
28              var contents = "Links in this page:\n<br />| ";
29
30              // concatenate each link to contents
31              for ( var i = 0; i < linkslist.length; i++ )
32              {
```

Fig. 10.3 | Using the `links` collection. (Part I of 2.)

```
33                  var currentLink = linkslist[ i ];
34                  contents += "<span class = 'link'>" +
35                      currentLink.innerHTML.link( currentLink.href ) +
36                      "</span> | ";
37              } // end for
38
39              document.getElementById( "links" ).innerHTML = contents;
40          } // end function processlinks
41          // -->
42      </script>
43  </head>
44  <body onload = "processlinks()">
45      <h1>Deitel Resource Centers</h1>
46      <p><a href = "http://www.deitel.com/">Deitel's website</a> contains
47          a rapidly growing
48          <a href = "http://www.deitel.com/ResourceCenters.html">list of
49          Resource Centers</a> on a wide range of topics. Many Resource
50          centers related to topics covered in this book,
51          <a href = "http://www.deitel.com/iw3htp4">Internet and World Wide
52          Web How to Program, 4th Edition</a>. We have Resouce Centers on
53          <a href = "http://www.deitel.com/Web2.0">Web 2.0</a>,
54          <a href = "http://www.deitel.com/Firefox">Firefox</a> and
55          <a href = "http://www.deitel.com/IE7">Internet Explorer 7</a>,
56          <a href = "http://www.deitel.com/XHTML">XHTML</a>, and
57          <a href = "http://www.deitel.com/JavaScript">JavaScript</a>.
58          Watch the list of Deitel Resource Centers for related new
59          Resource Centers.</p>
60      <div id = "links" class = "links"></div>
61  </body>
62  </html>
```

Fig. 10.3 | Using the `links` collection. (Part 2 of 2.)

The XHTML body contains a paragraph (lines 46–59) with links at various places in the text and an empty div (line 60) with id links. The body's onload attribute specifies that the processlinks method is called when the body finishes loading.

Method processlinks declares variable linkslist (line 27) to store the document's links collection, which is accessed as the links property of the document object. Line 28 creates the string (contents) that will contain all the document's links, to be inserted into the links div later. Line 31 begins a for statement to iterate through each link. To find the number of elements in the collection, we use the collection's *length property*.

Line 33 inside the for statement creates a variable (currentlink) that stores the current link. Note that we can access the collection stored in linkslist using indices in square brackets, just as we did with arrays. DOM collections are stored in objects which have only one property and two methods—the length property, the *item method* and the *namedItem method*. The item method—an alternative to the square bracketed indices—can be used to access specific elements in a collection by taking an index as an argument. The namedItem method takes a name as a parameter and finds the element in the collection, if any, whose id attribute or name attribute matches it.

Lines 34–36 add a span element to the contents string containing the current link. Recall that the link method of a string object returns the string as a link to the URL passed to the method. Line 35 uses the link method to create an a (anchor) element containing the proper text and href attribute.

Notice that variable currentLink (a DOM node representing an a element) has a specialized *href property* to refer to the link's href attribute. Many types of XHTML elements are represented by special types of nodes that extend the functionality of a basic DOM node. Line 39 inserts the contents into the empty div with id "links" (line 60) in order to show all the links on the page in one location.

Collections allow easy access to all elements of a single type in a page. This is useful for gathering elements into one place and for applying changes across an entire page. For example, the forms collection could be used to disable all form inputs after a submit button has been pressed to avoid multiple submissions while the next page loads. The next section discusses how to dynamically modify CSS styles using JavaScript and DOM nodes.

10.5 Dynamic Styles

An element's style can be changed dynamically. Often such a change is made in response to user events, which we discuss in Chapter 11. Such style changes can create many effects, including mouse hover effects, interactive menus, and animations. Figure 10.4 is a simple example that changes the background-color style property in response to user input.

```
 1   <?xml version = "1.0" encoding = "utf-8"?>
 2   <!DOCTYPE html PUBLIC "-//W3C//DTD XHTML 1.0 Strict//EN"
 3      "http://www.w3.org/TR/xhtml1/DTD/xhtml1-strict.dtd">
 4
 5   <!-- Fig. 10.4: dynamicstyle.html -->
 6   <!-- Dynamic styles. -->
 7   <html xmlns = "http://www.w3.org/1999/xhtml">
 8      <head>
```

Fig. 10.4 | Dynamic styles. (Part 1 of 2.)

```
9        <title>Dynamic Styles</title>
10       <script type = "text/javascript">
11          <!--
12          function start()
13          {
14             var inputColor = prompt( "Enter a color name for the " +
15                "background of this page", "" );
16             document.body.style.backgroundColor = inputColor;
17          } // end function start
18          // -->
19       </script>
20    </head>
21    <body id = "body" onload = "start()">
22       <p>Welcome to our website!</p>
23    </body>
24 </html>
```

a)

Explorer User Prompt

Script Prompt:

Enter a color name for the background of this page

OK

Cancel

cyan

b)

Dynamic Styles - Windows Internet Explorer

C:\examples\ch10\dynamicstyle.html   Google

Dynamic Styles   Page ▾ Tools ▾

Welcome to our website!

Done   My Computer   100%

Fig. 10.4 | Dynamic styles. (Part 2 of 2.)

Function `start` (lines 12–17) prompts the user to enter a color name, then sets the background color to that value. [*Note:* An error occurs if the value entered is not a valid color.] We refer to the background color as `document.body.style.backgroundColor`—the ***body property*** of the `document` object refers to the body element. We then use the `style` property (a property of most XHTML elements) to set the `background-color` CSS property. This is referred to as `backgroundColor` in JavaScript—the hyphen is removed to avoid confusion with the subtraction (-) operator. This naming convention is consistent for most CSS properties. For example, `borderWidth` correlates to the `border-width` CSS property, and `fontFamily` correlates to the `font-family` CSS property. In general, CSS properties are accessed in the format *node*.`style`.*styleproperty*.

Figure 10.5 introduces the `setInterval` and `clearInterval` methods of the `window` object, combining them with dynamic styles to create animated effects. This example is a basic image viewer that allows you to select a Deitel book cover and view it in a larger size. When one of the thumbnail images on the right is clicked, the larger version grows from the top-left corner of the main image area.

The body (lines 66–85) contains two `div` elements, both floated `left` using styles defined in lines 14 and 17 in order to present them side by side. The left `div` contains the full-size image `iw3htp4.jpg`, the cover of this book, which appears when the page loads.

The right `div` contains six thumbnail images which respond to the click event by calling the `display` method and passing it the filename of the corresponding full-size image.

The `display` function (lines 46–62) dynamically updates the image in the left `div` to the one corresponding to the user's click. Lines 48–49 prevent the rest of the function from executing if `interval` is defined (i.e., an animation is in progress.) Line 51 gets the left `div` by its `id`, imgCover. Line 52 creates a new `img` element. Lines 53–55 set its `id` to imgCover, set its `src` to the correct image file in the `fullsize` directory, and set its required `alt` attribute. Lines 56–59 do some additional initialization before beginning the animation in line 61. To create the growing animation effect, lines 57–58 set the image `width` and `height` to 0. Line 59 replaces the current `bigImage` node with `newNode` (created in line 52), and line 60 sets `count`, the variable that controls the animation, to 0.

Line 61 introduces the `window` object's ***setInterval*** *method*, which starts the animation. This method takes two parameters—a statement to execute repeatedly, and an integer specifying how often to execute it, in milliseconds. We use `setInterval` to call

```
 1   <?xml version = "1.0" encoding = "utf-8"?>
 2   <!DOCTYPE html PUBLIC "-//W3C//DTD XHTML 1.0 Strict//EN"
 3      "http://www.w3.org/TR/xhtml1/DTD/xhtml1-strict.dtd">
 4
 5   <!-- Fig. 10.5: coverviewer.html -->
 6   <!-- Dynamic styles used for animation. -->
 7   <html xmlns = "http://www.w3.org/1999/xhtml">
 8      <head>
 9         <title>Deitel Book Cover Viewer</title>
10         <style type = "text/css">
11            .thumbs   { width: 192px;
12                        height: 370px;
13                        padding: 5px;
14                        float: left }
15            .mainimg  { width: 289px;
16                        padding: 5px;
17                        float: left }
18            .imgCover { height: 373px }
19            img       { border: 1px solid black }
20         </style>
21         <script type = "text/javascript">
22            <!--
23            var interval = null; // keeps track of the interval
24            var speed = 6; // determines the speed of the animation
25            var count = 0; // size of the image during the animation
26
27            // called repeatedly to animate the book cover
28            function run()
29            {
30               count += speed;
31
32               // stop the animation when the image is large enough
33               if ( count >= 375 )
34               {
```

Fig. 10.5 | Dynamic styles used for animation. (Part 1 of 4.)

```
35              window.clearInterval( interval );
36              interval = null;
37           } // end if
38
39           var bigImage = document.getElementById( "imgCover" );
40           bigImage.style.width = .7656 * count + "px";
41           bigImage.style.height = count + "px";
42        } // end function run
43
44        // inserts the proper image into the main image area and
45        // begins the animation
46        function display( imgfile )
47        {
48           if ( interval )
49              return;
50
51           var bigImage = document.getElementById( "imgCover" );
52           var newNode = document.createElement( "img" );
53           newNode.id = "imgCover";
54           newNode.src = "fullsize/" + imgfile;
55           newNode.alt = "Large image";
56           newNode.className = "imgCover";
57           newNode.style.width = "0px";
58           newNode.style.height = "0px";
59           bigImage.parentNode.replaceChild( newNode, bigImage );
60           count = 0; // start the image at size 0
61           interval = window.setInterval( "run()", 10 ); // animate
62        } // end function display
63        // -->
64     </script>
65  </head>
66  <body>
67     <div id = "mainimg" class = "mainimg">
68        <img id = "imgCover" src = "fullsize/iw3htp4.jpg"
69           alt = "Full cover image" class = "imgCover" />
70     </div>
71     <div id = "thumbs" class = "thumbs" >
72        <img src = "thumbs/iw3htp4.jpg" alt = "iw3htp4"
73           onclick = "display( 'iw3htp4.jpg' )" />
74        <img src = "thumbs/chtp5.jpg" alt = "chtp5"
75           onclick = "display( 'chtp5.jpg' )" />
76        <img src = "thumbs/cpphtp6.jpg" alt = "cpphtp6"
77           onclick = "display( 'cpphtp6.jpg' )" />
78        <img src = "thumbs/jhtp7.jpg" alt = "jhtp7"
79           onclick = "display( 'jhtp7.jpg' )" />
80        <img src = "thumbs/vbhtp3.jpg" alt = "vbhtp3"
81           onclick = "display( 'vbhtp3.jpg' )" />
82        <img src = "thumbs/vcsharphtp2.jpg" alt = "vcsharphtp2"
83           onclick = "display( 'vcsharphtp2.jpg' )" />
84     </div>
85  </body>
86  </html>
```

Fig. 10.5 | Dynamic styles used for animation. (Part 2 of 4.)

a) The cover viewer page loads with the cover of this book.

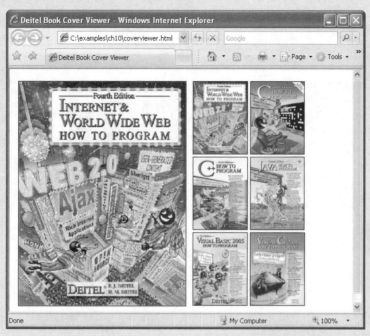

b) When the user clicks the thumbnail of *C How to Program*, the full-size image begins growing from the top-left corner of the window.

Fig. 10.5 | Dynamic styles used for animation. (Part 3 of 4.)

c) The cover continues to grow.

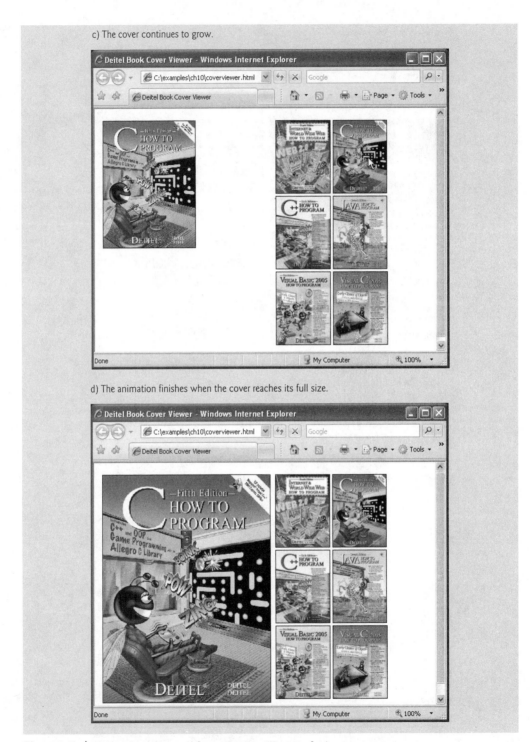

d) The animation finishes when the cover reaches its full size.

Fig. 10.5 | Dynamic styles used for animation. (Part 4 of 4.)

function run every 10 milliseconds. The setInterval method returns a unique identifier to keep track of that particular interval—we assign this identifier to the variable interval. We use this identifier to stop the animation when the image has finished growing.

The run function, defined in lines 28–42, increases the height of the image by the value of speed and updates its width accordingly to keep the aspect ratio consistent. Because the run function is called every 10 milliseconds, this increase happens repeatedly to create an animated growing effect. Line 30 adds the value of speed (declared and initialized to 6 in line 24) to count, which keeps track of the animation's progress and dictates the current size of the image. If the image has grown to its full height (375), line 35 uses the window's *clearInterval method* to stop the repetitive calls of the run method. We pass to clearInterval the interval identifier (stored in interval) that setInterval created in line 61. Although it seems unnecessary in this script, this identifier allows the script to keep track of multiple intervals running at the same time and to choose which interval to stop when calling clearInterval.

Line 39 gets the image and lines 40–41 set its width and height CSS properties. Note that line 40 multiplies count by a scaling factor of .7656 in order to keep the ratio of the image's dimensions consistent with the actual dimensions of the image. Run the code example and click on a thumbnail image to see the full animation effect.

This section demonstrated the concept of dynamically changing CSS styles using JavaScript and the DOM. We also discussed the basics of how to create scripted animations using setInterval and clearInterval.

10.6 Summary of the DOM Objects and Collections

As you've seen in the preceding sections, the objects and collections in the W3C DOM give you flexibility in manipulating the elements of a web page. We've shown how to access the objects in a page, how to access the objects in a collection, and how to change element styles dynamically.

The W3C DOM allows you to access every element in an XHTML document. Each element in a document is represented by a separate object. The diagram in Fig. 10.6 shows many of the important objects and collections provided by the W3C DOM. Figure 10.7 provides a brief description of each object and collection in Fig. 10.6.

Fig. 10.6 | W3C Document Object Model.

Object or collection	Description
Objects	
window	Represents the browser window and provides access to the window's document object. Also contains history and location objects.
document	Represents the XHTML document rendered in a window. Provides access to every element in the document and allows dynamic modification of it. Contains collections for accessing all elements of a given type.
body	Provides access to the body element of an XHTML document.
history	Keeps track of the sites visited by the browser user. The object provides a script programmer with the ability to move forward and backward through the visited sites.
location	Contains the URL of the rendered document. When this object is set to a new URL, the browser immediately navigates to the new location.
Collections	
anchors	Collection contains all the anchor elements (a) that have a name or id attribute. The elements appear in the collection in the order in which they were defined in the XHTML document.
forms	Contains all the form elements in the XHTML document. The elements appear in the collection in the order in which they were defined in the XHTML document.
images	Contains all the img elements in the XHTML document. The elements appear in the collection in the order in which they were defined in the XHTML document.
links	Contains all the anchor elements (a) with an href property. The elements appear in the collection in the order in which they were defined in the XHTML document.

Fig. 10.7 | Objects and collections in the W3C Document Object Model.

For a complete reference on the W3C Document Object Model, see the DOM Level 3 recommendation from the W3C at http://www.w3.org/TR/DOM-Level-3-Core/. The DOM Level 2 HTML Specification (the most recent HTML DOM standard), available at http://www.w3.org/TR/DOM-Level-2-HTML/, describes additional DOM functionality specific to HTML, such as objects for various types of XHTML elements. Keep in mind that not all web browsers implement all features included in the specification.

10.7 Web Resources

www.deitel.com/javascript/
The Deitel JavaScript Resource Center contains links to some of the best JavaScript resources on the web. There you'll find categorized links to JavaScript tools, code generators, forums, books, libraries, frameworks, tutorials and more. Check out the section specifically dedicated to the Document Object Model. Be sure to visit the related Resource Centers on XHTML (www.deitel.com/xhtml/) and CSS 2.1 (www.deitel.com/css21/).

JavaScript:
Events

OBJECTIVES

In this chapter you will learn:

- The concepts of events, event handlers and event bubbling.

- To create and register event handlers that respond to mouse and keyboard events.

- To use the event object to get information about an event.

- To recognize and respond to common events, including onload, onmousemove, onmouseover, onmouseout, onfocus, onblur, onsubmit and onreset.

11.1 Introduction

We've seen that XHTML pages can be controlled via scripting, and we've already used a few events to trigger scripts, such as the onclick and onsubmit events. This chapter goes into more detail on *JavaScript events*, which allow scripts to respond to user interactions and modify the page accordingly. Events allow scripts to respond to a user who is moving the mouse, entering form data or pressing keys. Events and event handling help make web applications more responsive, dynamic and interactive.

In this chapter, we discuss how to set up functions to react when an event *fires* (occurs). We give examples of event handling for nine common events, including mouse events and form-processing events. A the end of the chapter, we provide a table of the events covered in this chapter and other useful events.

11.2 Registering Event Handlers

Functions that handle events are called *event handlers*. Assigning an event handler to an event on a DOM node is called *registering an event handler*. Previously, we have registered event handlers using the *inline model*, treating events as attributes of XHTML elements (e.g., <p onclick = "myfunction()">). Another model, known as the *traditional model*, for registering event handlers is demonstrated alongside the inline model in Fig. 11.1.

In the earliest event-capable browsers, the inline model was the only way to handle events. Later, Netscape developed the traditional model and Internet Explorer adopted it. Since then, both Netscape and Microsoft have developed separate (incompatible) advanced event models with more functionality than either the inline or the traditional model. Netscape's advanced model was adapted by the W3C to create a DOM Events Specification. Most browsers support the W3C model, but Internet Explorer 7 does not.

```
1   <?xml version = "1.0" encoding = "utf-8"?>
2   <!DOCTYPE html PUBLIC "-//W3C//DTD XHTML 1.0 Strict//EN"
3       "http://www.w3.org/TR/xhtml1/DTD/xhtml1-strict.dtd">
4
5   <!-- Fig. 11.1: registering.html -->
6   <!-- Event registration models. -->
```

Fig. 11.1 | Event registration models. (Part 1 of 3.)

```
7   <html xmlns = "http://www.w3.org/1999/xhtml">
8     <head>
9       <title>Event Registration Models</title>
10      <style type = "text/css">
11        div { padding: 5px;
12               margin: 10px;
13               border: 3px solid #0000BB;
14               width: 12em }
15      </style>
16      <script type = "text/javascript">
17        <!--
18        // handle the onclick event regardless of how it was registered
19        function handleEvent()
20        {
21           alert( "The event was successfully handled." );
22        } // end function handleEvent
23
24        // register the handler using the traditional model
25        function registerHandler()
26        {
27           var traditional = document.getElementById( "traditional" );
28           traditional.onclick = handleEvent;
29        } // end function registerHandler
30        // -->
31      </script>
32    </head>
33    <body onload = "registerHandler()">
34      <!-- The event handler is registered inline -->
35      <div id = "inline" onclick = "handleEvent()">
36         Inline registration model</div>
37
38      <!-- The event handler is registered by function registerHandler -->
39      <div id = "traditional">Traditional registration model</div>
40    </body>
41  </html>
```

a) The user clicks the **div** for which the event handler was registered using the inline model.

Fig. 11.1 | Event registration models. (Part 2 of 3.)

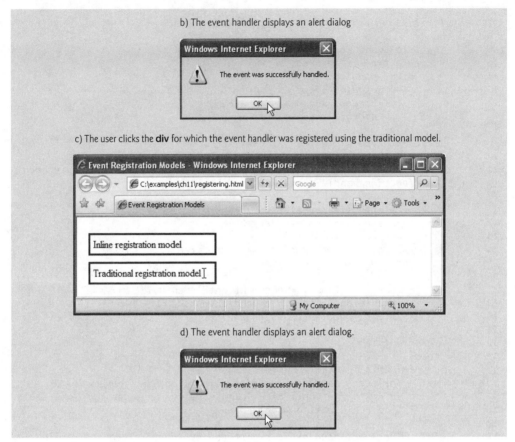

Fig. 11.1 | Event registration models. (Part 3 of 3.)

This means that to create cross-browser websites, we are mostly limited to the traditional and inline event models. While the advanced models provide more convenience and functionality, most of the features can be implemented with the traditional model.

Line 35 assigns "handleEvent()" to the onclick attribute of the div in lines 35–36. This is the inline model for event registration we've seen in previous examples. The div in line 39 is assigned an event handler using the traditional model. When the body element (lines 33–40) loads, the registerHandler function is called.

Function registerHandler (lines 25–29) uses JavaScript to register the function handleEvent as the event handler for the onclick event of the div with the id "traditional". Line 27 gets the div, and line 28 assigns the function handleEvent to the div's onclick property.

Notice that in line 28, we do not put handleEvent in quotes or include parentheses at the end of the function name, as we do in the inline model in line 35. In the inline model, the value of the XHTML attribute is a *JavaScript statement* to execute when the event occurs. The value of the onclick property of a DOM node is not an executable statement, but the name of a *function* to be called when the event occurs. Recall that JavaScript functions can be treated as data (i.e., passed into methods, assigned to variables, etc.).

Common Programming Error 11.1

Putting quotes around the function name when registering it using the inline model would assign a string to the onclick property of the node—a string cannot be called.

Common Programming Error 11.2

Putting parentheses after the function name when registering it using the inline model would call the function immediately and assign its return value to the onclick property.

Once the event handler is registered in line 28, the div in line 39 has the same behavior as the div in lines 35–36, because handleEvent (lines 19–22) is set to handle the onclick event for both divs. When either div is clicked, an alert will display "The event was successfully handled."

The traditional model allows us to register event handlers in JavaScript code. This has important implications for what we can do with JavaScript events. For example, traditional event-handler registration allows us to assign event handlers to many elements quickly and easily using repetition statements, instead of adding an inline event handler to each XHTML element. In the remaining examples in this chapter, we use both the inline and traditional registration models depending on which is more convenient.

11.3 Event onload

The onload event fires whenever an element finishes loading successfully (i.e., all its children are loaded). Frequently, this event is used in the body element to initiate a script after the page loads in the client's browser. Figure 11.2 uses the onload event for this purpose. The script called by the onload event updates a timer that indicates how many seconds have elapsed since the document was loaded.

```
1   <?xml version = "1.0" encoding = "utf-8"?>
2   <!DOCTYPE html PUBLIC "-//W3C//DTD XHTML 1.0 Strict//EN"
3      "http://www.w3.org/TR/xhtml1/DTD/xhtml1-strict.dtd">
4
5   <!-- Fig. 11.2: onload.html -->
6   <!-- Demonstrating the onload event. -->
7   <html xmlns = "http://www.w3.org/1999/xhtml">
8      <head>
9         <title>onload Event</title>
10        <script type = "text/javascript">
11           <!--
12           var seconds = 0;
13
14           // called when the page loads to begin the timer
15           function startTimer()
16           {
17              // 1000 milliseconds = 1 second
18              window.setInterval( "updateTime()", 1000 );
19           } // end function startTimer
20
```

Fig. 11.2 | Demonstrating the onload event. (Part 1 of 2.)

```
21                  // called every 1000 ms to update the timer
22                  function updateTime()
23                  {
24                      ++seconds;
25                      document.getElementById( "soFar" ).innerHTML = seconds;
26                  } // end function updateTime
27                  // -->
28              </script>
29          </head>
30          <body onload = "startTimer()">
31              <p>Seconds you have spent viewing this page so far:
32              <strong id = "soFar">0</strong></p>
33          </body>
34      </html>
```

Fig. 11.2 | Demonstrating the `onload` event. (Part 2 of 2.)

Our use of the `onload` event occurs in line 30. After the body section loads, the browser triggers the `onload` event. This calls function `startTimer` (lines 15–19), which in turn uses method `window.setInterval` to specify that function `updateTime` (lines 22–26) should be called every 1000 milliseconds. The `updateTime` function increments variable `seconds` and updates the counter on the page.

Note that we could not have created this program without the onload event, because elements in the XHTML page cannot be accessed until the page has loaded. If a script in the `head` attempts to get a DOM node for an XHTML element in the body, `getElement-ById` returns `null` because the body has not yet loaded. Other uses of the `onload` event include opening a pop-up window once a page has loaded and triggering a script when an image or Java applet loads.

Common Programming Error 11.3

Trying to get an element in a page before the page has loaded is a common error. Avoid this by putting your script in a function using the `onload` event to call the function.

11.4 Event onmousemove, the event Object and this

This section introduces the `onmousemove` event, which fires repeatedly whenever the user moves the mouse over the web page. We also discuss the `event` object and the keyword `this`, which permit more advanced event-handling capabilities. Figure 11.3 uses `onmousemove` and `this` to create a simple drawing program that allows the user to draw inside a box in red or blue by holding down the *Shift* or *Ctrl* keys.

The XHTML body has a table with a tbody containing one row that gives the user instructions on how to use the program. The body's onload attribute (line 61) calls function createCanvas, which initializes the program by filling in the table.

The createCanvas function (lines 23–41) fills in the table with a grid of cells. The CSS rule in lines 14–15 sets the width and height of every td element to 4px. Line 11

```
 1   <?xml version = "1.0" encoding = "utf-8"?>
 2   <!DOCTYPE html PUBLIC "-//W3C//DTD XHTML 1.0 Strict//EN"
 3      "http://www.w3.org/TR/xhtml1/DTD/xhtml1-strict.dtd">
 4
 5   <!-- Fig. 11.3: draw.html -->
 6   <!-- A simple drawing program. -->
 7   <html xmlns = "http://www.w3.org/1999/xhtml">
 8      <head>
 9         <title>Simple Drawing Program</title>
10         <style type = "text/css">
11            #canvas { width: 400px;
12                      border: 1px solid #999999;
13                      border-collapse: collapse }
14            td     { width: 4px;
15                     height: 4px }
16            th.key { font-family: arial, helvetica, sans-serif;
17                     font-size: 12px;
18                     border-bottom: 1px solid #999999 }
19         </style>
20         <script type = "text/javascript">
21            <!--
22            //initialization function to insert cells into the table
23            function createCanvas ()
24            {
25               var side = 100;
26               var tbody = document.getElementById( "tablebody" );
27
28               for ( var i = 0; i < side; i++ )
29               {
30                  var row = document.createElement( "tr" );
31
32                  for ( var j = 0; j < side; j++ )
33                  {
34                     var cell = document.createElement( "td" );
35                     cell.onmousemove = processMouseMove;
36                     row.appendChild( cell );
37                  } // end for
38
39                  tbody.appendChild( row );
40               } // end for
41            } // end function createCanvas
42
43            // processes the onmousemove event
44            function processMouseMove( e )
45            {
```

Fig. 11.3 | Simple drawing program. (Part 1 of 3.)

```
46              // get the event object from IE
47              if ( !e )
48                  var e = window.event;
49
50              // turn the cell blue if the Ctrl key is pressed
51              if ( e.ctrlKey )
52                  this.style.backgroundColor = "blue";
53
54              // turn the cell red if the Shift key is pressed
55              if ( e.shiftKey )
56                  this.style.backgroundColor = "red";
57          } // end function processMouseMove
58          // -->
59      </script>
60  </head>
61  <body onload = "createCanvas()">
62      <table id = "canvas" class = "canvas"><tbody id = "tablebody">
63      <tr><th class = "key" colspan = "100">Hold <tt>ctrl</tt>
64          to draw blue. Hold <tt>shift</tt> to draw red.</th></tr>
65      </tbody></table>
66  </body>
67 </html>
```

a) The page loads and fills with white cells. With no keys held down, moving the mouse does not draw anything.

Fig. 11.3 | Simple drawing program. (Part 2 of 3.)

b) The user holds the *Ctrl* key and moves the mouse to draw a blue line.

c) The user holds the *Shift* key and moves the mouse to draw a red line.

Fig. 11.3 | Simple drawing program. (Part 3 of 3.)

dictates that the table is 400px wide. Line 13 uses the `border-collapse` CSS property to eliminate space between the table cells.

Line 25 defines variable `side`, which determines the number of cells in each row and the number of rows created by the nested `for` statements in lines 28–40. We set `side` to 100 in order to fill the table with 10,000 4px cells. Line 26 stores the `tbody` element so that we can append rows to it as they are generated.

Common Programming Error 11.4

Although you can omit the `tbody` element in an XHTML table, without it you cannot append `tr` elements as children of a `table` using JavaScript. While Firefox treats appended rows as members of the table body, Internet Explorer will not render any table cells that are dynamically added to a table outside a `thead`, `tbody` or `tfoot` element.

The nested `for` statements in lines 28–40 fill the table with a 100×100 grid of cells. The outer loop creates each table row, while the inner loop creates each cell. The inner loop uses the `createElement` method to create a table cell, assigns function `process-MouseMove` as the event handler for the cell's onmousemove event and appends the cell as a child of the row. The ***onmousemove*** *event* of an element fires whenever the user moves the mouse over that element.

At this point, the program is initialized and simply calls `processMouseMove` whenever the mouse moves over any table cell. The function `processMouseMove` (lines 44–57) colors the cell the mouse moves over, depending on the key that is pressed when the event occurs. Lines 44–48 get the ***event object***, which stores information about the event that called the event-handling function.

Internet Explorer and Firefox do not implement the same event models, so we need to account for some differences in how the event object can be handled and used. Firefox and other W3C-compliant browsers (e.g., Safari, Opera) pass the event object as an argument to the event-handling function. Internet Explorer, on the other hand, stores the event object in the event property of the `window` object. To get the event object regardless of the browser, we use a two-step process. Function `processMouseMove` takes the parameter e in line 44 to get the event object from Firefox. Then, if e is undefined (i.e., if the client is Internet Explorer), we assign the object in `window.event` to e in line 48.

In addition to providing different ways to access the event object, Firefox and Internet Explorer also implement different functionality in the event object itself. However, there are several event properties that both browsers implement with the same name, and some that both browsers implement with different names. In this book, we use properties that are implemented in both event models, or we write our code to use the correct property depending on the browser—all of our code runs properly in IE7 and Firefox 2.

Once e contains the event object, we can use it to get information about the event. Lines 51–56 do the actual drawing. The event object's ***ctrlKey*** *property* contains a boolean which reflects whether the *Ctrl* key was pressed during the event. If ctrlKey is true, line 52 executes, changing the color of a table cell.

To determine which table cell to color, we introduce the ***this*** *keyword*. The meaning of this depends on its context. In an event-handling function, this refers to the DOM object on which the event occurred. Our function uses this to refer to the table cell over which the mouse moved. The this keyword allows us to use one event handler to apply a change to one of many DOM elements, depending on which one received the event.

Lines 51–52 change the background color of this table cell to blue if the *Ctrl* key is pressed during the event. Similarly, lines 55–56 color the cell red if the *Shift* key is pressed. To determine this, we use the **shiftKey** *property* of the event object. This simple function allows the user to draw inside the table on the page in red and blue.

This example demonstrated the ctrlKey and shiftKey properties of the event object. Figure 11.4 provides a table of some important cross-browser properties of the event object.

This section introduced the event onmousemove and the keyword this. We also discussed more advanced event handling using the event object to get information about the event. The next section continues our introduction of events with the onmouseover and onmouseout events.

Property	Description
altKey	This value is true if the *Alt* key was pressed when the event fired.
cancelBubble	Set to true to prevent the event from bubbling. Defaults to false. (See Section 11.8, Event Bubbling.)
clientX and clientY	The coordinates of the mouse cursor inside the client area (i.e., the active area where the web page is displayed, excluding scrollbars, navigation buttons, etc.).
ctrlKey	This value is true if the *Ctrl* key was pressed when the event fired.
keyCode	The ASCII code of the key pressed in a keyboard event.
screenX and screenY	The coordinates of the mouse cursor on the screen coordinate system.
shiftKey	This value is true if the *Shift* key was pressed when the event fired.
type	The name of the event that fired, without the prefix "on".

Fig. 11.4 | Some event object properties.

11.5 Rollovers with onmouseover and onmouseout

Two more events fired by mouse movements are onmouseover and onmouseout. When the mouse cursor moves into an element, an **onmouseover** *event* occurs for that element. When the cursor leaves the element, an **onmouseout** *event* occurs. Figure 11.5 uses these events to achieve a *rollover effect* that updates text when the mouse cursor moves over it. We also introduce a technique for creating rollover images.

```
1   <?xml version = "1.0" encoding = "utf-8"?>
2   <!DOCTYPE html PUBLIC "-//W3C//DTD XHTML 1.0 Strict//EN"
3      "http://www.w3.org/TR/xhtml1/DTD/xhtml1-strict.dtd">
4
```

Fig. 11.5 | Events onmouseover and onmouseout. (Part 1 of 5.)

```
5    <!-- Fig. 11.5: onmouseoverout.html -->
6    <!-- Events onmouseover and onmouseout. -->
7    <html xmlns = "http://www.w3.org/1999/xhtml">
8       <head>
9          <title>Events onmouseover and onmouseout</title>
10         <style type = "text/css">
11            body  { background-color: wheat }
12            table { border-style: groove;
13                    text-align: center;
14                    font-family: monospace;
15                    font-weight: bold }
16            td    { width: 6em }
17         </style>
18         <script type = "text/javascript">
19            <!--
20            image1 = new Image();
21            image1.src = "heading1.gif";
22            image2 = new Image();
23            image2.src = "heading2.gif";
24
25            function mouseOver( e )
26            {
27               if ( !e )
28                  var e = window.event;
29
30               var target = getTarget( e );
31
32               // swap the image when the mouse moves over it
33               if ( target.id == "heading" )
34               {
35                  target.src = image2.src;
36                  return;
37               } // end if
38
39               // if an element's id is defined, assign the id to its color
40               // to turn hex code's text the corresponding color
41               if ( target.id )
42                  target.style.color = target.id;
43            } // end function mouseOver
44
45            function mouseOut( e )
46            {
47               if ( !e )
48                  var e = window.event;
49
50               var target = getTarget( e );
51
52               // put the original image back when the mouse moves away
53               if ( target.id == "heading" )
54               {
55                  target.src = image1.src;
56                  return;
57               } // end if
```

Fig. 11.5 | Events onmouseover and onmouseout. (Part 2 of 5.)

```
58
59          // if an element's id is defined, assign id to innerHTML
60          // to display the color name
61          if ( target.id )
62              target.innerHTML = target.id;
63      } // end function mouseOut
64
65          // return either e.srcElement or e.target, whichever exists
66          function getTarget( e )
67          {
68              if ( e.srcElement )
69                  return e.srcElement;
70              else
71                  return e.target;
72          } // end function getTarget
73
74          document.onmouseover = mouseOver;
75          document.onmouseout = mouseOut;
76          // -->
77      </script>
78  </head>
79  <body>
80      <img src = "heading1.gif" id = "heading" alt = "Heading Image" />
81      <p>Can you tell a color from its hexadecimal RGB code
82      value? Look at the hex code, guess its color. To see
83      what color it corresponds to, move the mouse over the
84      hex code. Moving the mouse out of the hex code's table
85      cell will display the color name.</p>
86      <table>
87          <tr>
88              <td id = "Black">#000000</td>
89              <td id = "Blue">#0000FF</td>
90              <td id = "Magenta">#FF00FF</td>
91              <td id = "Gray">#808080</td>
92          </tr>
93          <tr>
94              <td id = "Green">#008000</td>
95              <td id = "Lime">#00FF00</td>
96              <td id = "Maroon">#800000</td>
97              <td id = "Navy">#000080</td>
98          </tr>
99          <tr>
100             <td id = "Olive">#808000</td>
101             <td id = "Purple">#800080</td>
102             <td id = "Red">#FF0000</td>
103             <td id = "Silver">#C0C0C0</td>
104         </tr>
105         <tr>
106             <td id = "Cyan">#00FFFF</td>
107             <td id = "Teal">#008080</td>
108             <td id = "Yellow">#FFFF00</td>
109             <td id = "White">#FFFFFF</td>
110         </tr>
```

Fig. 11.5 | Events onmouseover and onmouseout. (Part 3 of 5.)

```
111          </table>
112       </body>
113    </html>
```

a) The page loads with the blue heading image and all the hex codes in black.

b) The heading image switches to an image with green text when the mouse rolls over it.

Fig. 11.5 | Events **onmouseover** and **onmouseout**. (Part 4 of 5.)

c) When mouse rolls over a hex code, the text color changes to the color represented by the hex code. Notice that the heading image has become blue again because the mouse is no longer over it.

d) When the mouse leaves the hex code's table cell, the text changes to the name of the color.

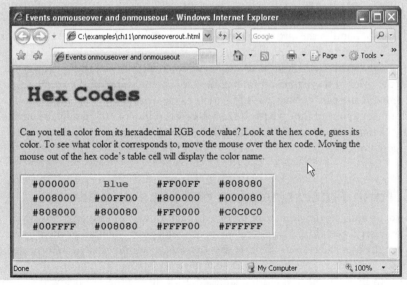

Fig. 11.5 | Events `onmouseover` and `onmouseout`. (Part 5 of 5.)

To create a rollover effect for the image in the heading, lines 20–23 create two new JavaScript `Image` objects—`image1` and `image2`. Image `image2` displays when the mouse hovers over the image. Image `image1` displays when the mouse is outside the image. The script sets the `src` properties of each `Image` in lines 21 and 23, respectively. Creating `Image` objects preloads the images (i.e., loads the images in advance), so the browser does not need to download the rollover image the first time the script displays the image. If the image is large or the connection is slow, downloading would cause a noticeable delay in the image update.

> **Performance Tip 11.1**
>
> *Preloading images used in rollover effects prevents a delay the first time an image is displayed.*

Functions `mouseOver` and `mouseOut` are set to process the `onmouseover` and `onmouseout` events, respectively, in lines 74–75. Both functions begin (lines 25–28 and 45–48) by getting the event object and using function `getTarget` to find the element that received the action. Because of browser event model differences, we need `getTarget` (defined in lines 66–72) to return the DOM node targeted by the action. In Internet Explorer, this node is stored in the event object's ***srcElement*** *property*. In Firefox, it is stored in the event object's ***target*** *property*. Lines 68–71 return the node using the correct property to hide the browser differences from the rest of our program. We must use function `getTarget` instead of `this` because we do not define an event handler for each specific element in the `document`. In this case, using `this` would return the entire document. In both `mouseOver` and `mouseOut`, we assign the return value of `getTarget` to variable `target` (lines 30 and 50).

Lines 33–37 in the `mouseOver` function handle the `onmouseover` event for the heading image by setting its `src` attribute (`target.src`) to the `src` property of the appropriate `Image` object (`image2.src`). The same task occurs with `image1` in the `mouseOut` function (lines 53–57).

The script handles the `onmouseover` event for the table cells in lines 41–42. This code tests whether an `id` is specified, which is true only for our hex code table cells and the heading image in this example. If the element receiving the action has an `id`, the code changes the color of the element to match the color name stored in the `id`. As you can see in the code for the `table` (lines 86–111), each `td` element containing a color code has an `id` attribute set to one of the 16 basic XHTML colors. Lines 61–62 handle the `onmouseout` event by changing the text in the table cell the mouse cursor just left to match the color that it represents.

11.6 Form Processing with onfocus and onblur

The `onfocus` and `onblur` events are particularly useful when dealing with form elements that allow user input (Fig. 11.6). The `onfocus` event fires when an element gains focus (i.e., when the user clicks a form field or uses the *Tab* key to move between form elements), and `onblur` fires when an element loses focus, which occurs when another control gains the focus. In lines 31–32, the script changes the text inside the `div` below the form (line 58) based on the `messageNum` passed to function `helpText` (lines 29–33). Each of the elements of the form, such as the `name` input in lines 40–41, passes a different value to the `helpText` function when it gains focus (and its `onfocus` event fires). These values are used as indices for `helpArray`, which is declared and initialized in lines 17–27 and stores help messages. When elements lose focus, they all pass the value 6 to `helpText` to clear the `tip` `div` (note that the empty string `""` is stored in the last element of the array).

```
 1   <?xml version = "1.0" encoding = "utf-8"?>
 2   <!DOCTYPE html PUBLIC "-//W3C//DTD XHTML 1.0 Strict//EN"
 3      "http://www.w3.org/TR/xhtml1/DTD/xhtml1-strict.dtd">
 4
 5   <!-- Fig. 11.6: onfocusblur.html -->
 6   <!-- Demonstrating the onfocus and onblur events. -->
 7   <html xmlns = "http://www.w3.org/1999/xhtml">
 8      <head>
 9         <title>A Form Using onfocus and onblur</title>
10         <style type = "text/css">
11            .tip { font-family: sans-serif;
12                   color: blue;
13                   font-size: 12px }
14         </style>
15         <script type = "text/javascript">
16            <!--
17            var helpArray =
18               [ "Enter your name in this input box.", // element 0
19                 "Enter your e-mail address in this input box, " +
20                 "in the format user@domain.", // element 1
21                 "Check this box if you liked our site.", // element 2
22                 "In this box, enter any comments you would " +
23                 "like us to read.", // element 3
24                 "This button submits the form to the " +
25                 "server-side script.", // element 4
26                 "This button clears the form.", // element 5
27                 "" ]; // element 6
28
29            function helpText( messageNum )
30            {
31               document.getElementById( "tip" ).innerHTML =
32                  helpArray[ messageNum ];
33            } // end function helpText
34            // -->
35         </script>
36      </head>
37      <body>
38         <form id = "myForm" action = "">
39            <div>
40            Name: <input type = "text" name = "name"
41               onfocus = "helpText(0)" onblur = "helpText(6)" /><br />
42            E-mail: <input type = "text" name = "e-mail"
43               onfocus = "helpText(1)" onblur = "helpText(6)" /><br />
44            Click here if you like this site
45            <input type = "checkbox" name = "like" onfocus =
46               "helpText(2)" onblur = "helpText(6)" /><br /><hr />
47
48            Any comments?<br />
49            <textarea name = "comments" rows = "5" cols = "45"
50               onfocus = "helpText(3)" onblur = "helpText(6)"></textarea>
51            <br />
52            <input type = "submit" value = "Submit" onfocus =
53               "helpText(4)" onblur = "helpText(6)" />
```

Fig. 11.6 | Demonstrating the onfocus and onblur events. (Part 1 of 2.)

```
54              <input type = "reset" value = "Reset" onfocus =
55                 "helpText(5)" onblur = "helpText(6)" />
56           </div>
57        </form>
58        <div id = "tip" class = "tip"></div>
59     </body>
60  </html>
```

a) The blue message at the bottom of the page instructs the user to enter an e-mail when the e-mail field has focus.

b) The message changes depending on which field has focus. Now it gives instructions for the comments box.

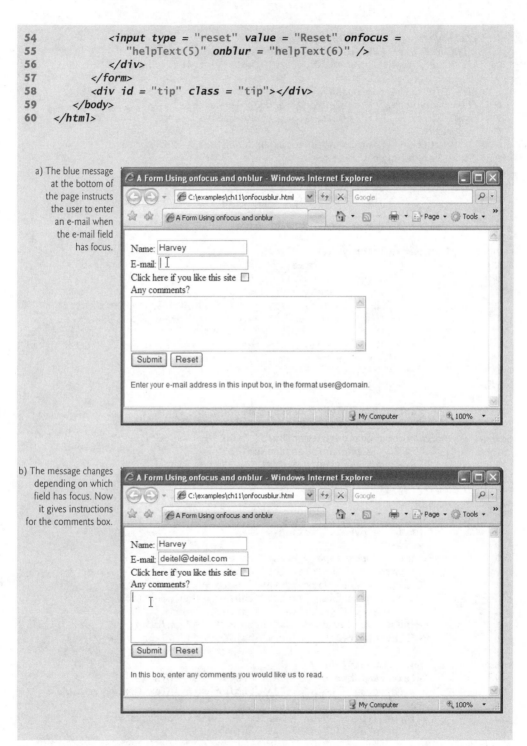

Fig. 11.6 | Demonstrating the onfocus and onblur events. (Part 2 of 2.)

11.7 Form Processing with onsubmit and onreset

Two more useful events for processing forms are onsubmit and onreset. These events fire when a form is submitted or reset, respectively (Fig. 11.7). Function registerEvents (lines 35–46) registers the event handlers for the form after the body has loaded.

```
 1  <?xml version = "1.0" encoding = "utf-8"?>
 2  <!DOCTYPE html PUBLIC "-//W3C//DTD XHTML 1.0 Strict//EN"
 3     "http://www.w3.org/TR/xhtml1/DTD/xhtml1-strict.dtd">
 4
 5  <!-- Fig. 11.7: onsubmitreset.html -->
 6  <!-- Demonstrating the onsubmit and onreset events. -->
 7  <html xmlns = "http://www.w3.org/1999/xhtml">
 8     <head>
 9        <title>A Form Using onsubmit and onreset</title>
10        <style type = "text/css">
11           .tip { font-family: sans-serif;
12                  color: blue;
13                  font-size: 12px }
14        </style>
15        <script type = "text/javascript">
16           <!--
17           var helpArray =
18              [ "Enter your name in this input box.",
19                "Enter your e-mail address in this input box, " +
20                "in the format user@domain.",
21                "Check this box if you liked our site.",
22                "In this box, enter any comments you would " +
23                "like us to read.",
24                "This button submits the form to the " +
25                "server-side script.",
26                "This button clears the form.",
27                "" ];
28
29           function helpText( messageNum )
30           {
31              document.getElementById( "tip" ).innerHTML =
32                 helpArray[ messageNum ];
33           } // end function helpText
34
35           function registerEvents()
36           {
37              document.getElementById( "myForm" ).onsubmit = function()
38              {
39                 return confirm( "Are you sure you want to submit?" );
40              } // end anonymous function
41
42              document.getElementById( "myForm" ).onreset = function()
43              {
44                 return confirm( "Are you sure you want to reset?" );
45              } // end anonymous function
46           } // end function registerEvents
```

Fig. 11.7 | Demonstrating the onsubmit and onreset events. (Part 1 of 2.)

```
47              // -->
48          </script>
49      </head>
50      <body onload = "registerEvents()">
51          <form id = "myForm" action = "">
52              <div>
53              Name: <input type = "text" name = "name"
54                  onfocus = "helpText(0)" onblur = "helpText(6)" /><br />
55              E-mail: <input type = "text" name = "e-mail"
56                  onfocus = "helpText(1)" onblur = "helpText(6)" /><br />
57              Click here if you like this site
58              <input type = "checkbox" name = "like" onfocus =
59                  "helpText(2)" onblur = "helpText(6)" /><br /><hr />
60
61              Any comments?<br />
62              <textarea name = "comments" rows = "5" cols = "45"
63                  onfocus = "helpText(3)" onblur = "helpText(6)"></textarea>
64              <br />
65              <input type = "submit" value = "Submit" onfocus =
66                  "helpText(4)" onblur = "helpText(6)" />
67              <input type = "reset" value = "Reset" onfocus =
68                  "helpText(5)" onblur = "helpText(6)" />
69              </div>
70          </form>
71          <div id = "tip" class = "tip"></div>
72      </body>
73  </html>
```

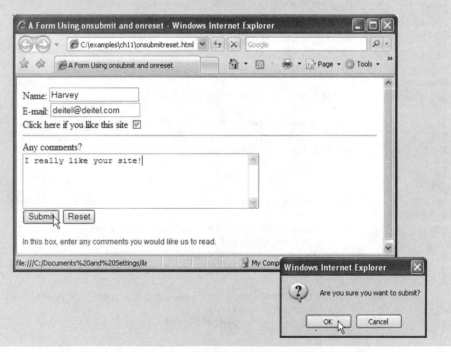

Fig. 11.7 | Demonstrating the onsubmit and onreset events. (Part 2 of 2.)

Lines 37–40 and 42–45 introduce several new concepts. Line 37 gets the form element ("myForm", lines 51–70), then lines 37–40 assign an *anonymous function* to its onsubmit property. An anonymous function is defined with no name—it is created in nearly the same way as any other function, but with no identifier after the keyword function. This notation is useful when creating a function for the sole purpose of assigning it to an event handler. We never call the function ourselves, so we don't need to give it a name, and it's more concise to create the function and register it as an event handler at the same time.

The anonymous function (lines 37–40) assigned to the onsubmit property of myForm executes in response to the user submitting the form (i.e., clicking the **Submit** button or pressing the *Enter* key). Line 39 introduces the *confirm method* of the window object. As with alert, we do not need to prefix the call with the object name window and the dot (.) operator. The confirm dialog asks the users a question, presenting them with an **OK** button and a **Cancel** button. If the user clicks **OK**, confirm returns true; otherwise, confirm returns false.

Our event handlers for the form's onsubmit and onreset events simply return the value of the confirm dialog, which asks the users if they are sure they want to submit or reset (lines 39 and 44, respectively). By returning either true or false, the event handlers dictate whether the default action for the event—in this case submitting or resetting the form—is taken. (Recall that we also returned false from some event-handling functions to prevent forms from submitting in Chapter 12.) Other default actions, such as following a hyperlink, can be prevented by returning false from an onclick event handler on the link. If an event handler returns true or does not return a value, the default action is taken once the event handler finishes executing.

11.8 Event Bubbling

Event bubbling is the process by which events fired in child elements "bubble" up to their parent elements. When an event is fired on an element, it is first delivered to the element's event handler (if any), then to the parent element's event handler (if any). This might result in event handling that was not intended. If you intend to handle an event in a child element alone, you should cancel the bubbling of the event in the child element's event-handling code by using the *cancelBubble property* of the event object, as shown in Fig. 11.8.

```
1   <?xml version = "1.0" encoding = "utf-8"?>
2   <!DOCTYPE html PUBLIC "-//W3C//DTD XHTML 1.0 Strict//EN"
3      "http://www.w3.org/TR/xhtml1/DTD/xhtml1-strict.dtd">
4
5   <!-- Fig. 11.8: bubbling.html -->
6   <!-- Canceling event bubbling. -->
7   <html xmlns = "http://www.w3.org/1999/xhtml">
8      <head>
9         <title>Event Bubbling</title>
10        <script type = "text/javascript">
11           <!--
```

Fig. 11.8 | Canceling event bubbling. (Part 1 of 3.)

```
12          function documentClick()
13          {
14              alert( "You clicked in the document." );
15          } // end function documentClick
16
17          function bubble( e )
18          {
19              if ( !e )
20                  var e = window.event;
21
22              alert( "This will bubble." );
23              e.cancelBubble = false;
24          } // end function bubble
25
26          function noBubble( e )
27          {
28              if ( !e )
29                  var e = window.event;
30
31              alert( "This will not bubble." );
32              e.cancelBubble = true;
33          } // end function noBubble
34
35          function registerEvents()
36          {
37              document.onclick = documentClick;
38              document.getElementById( "bubble" ).onclick = bubble;
39              document.getElementById( "noBubble" ).onclick = noBubble;
40          } // end function registerEvents
41          // -->
42      </script>
43   </head>
44   <body onload = "registerEvents()">
45      <p id = "bubble">Bubbling enabled.</p>
46      <p id = "noBubble">Bubbling disabled.</p>
47   </body>
48 </html>
```

a) The user clicks the first paragraph, for which bubbling is enabled.

Fig. 11.8 | Canceling event bubbling. (Part 2 of 3.)

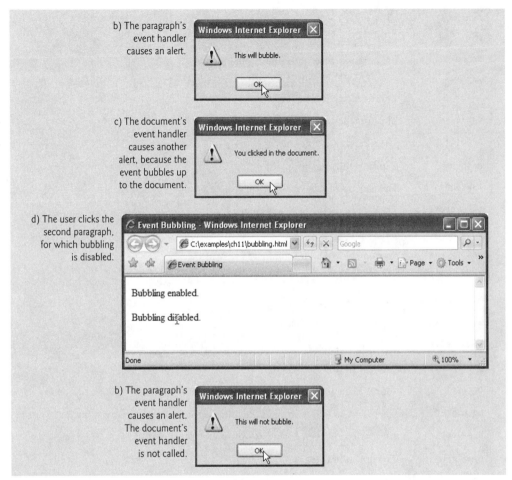

b) The paragraph's event handler causes an alert.

c) The document's event handler causes another alert, because the event bubbles up to the document.

d) The user clicks the second paragraph, for which bubbling is disabled.

b) The paragraph's event handler causes an alert. The document's event handler is not called.

Fig. 11.8 | Canceling event bubbling. (Part 3 of 3.)

Clicking the first p element (line 45) triggers a call to bubble. Then, because line 37 registers the document's onclick event, documentClick is also called. This occurs because the onclick event bubbles up to the document. This is probably not the desired result. Clicking the second p element (line 46) calls noBubble, which disables the event bubbling for this event by setting the cancelBubble property of the event object to true. [*Note:* The default value of cancelBubble is false, so the statement in line 23 is unnecessary.]

Common Programming Error 11.5

Forgetting to cancel event bubbling when necessary may cause unexpected results in your scripts.

11.9 More Events

The events we covered in this chapter are among the most commonly used. A list of some events supported by both Firefox and Internet Explorer is given with descriptions in Fig. 11.9.

Event	Fires when
onabort	Image transfer has been interrupted by user.
onchange	A new choice is made in a `select` element, or when a text input is changed and the element loses focus.
onclick	The user clicks using the mouse.
ondblclick	The mouse is double clicked.
onfocus	A form element gains focus.
onkeydown	The user pushes down a key.
onkeypress	The user presses then releases a key.
onkeyup	The user releases a key.
onload	An element and all its children have loaded.
onmousedown	A mouse button is pressed down.
onmousemove	The mouse moves.
onmouseout	The mouse leaves an element.
onmouseover	The mouse enters an element.
onmouseup	A mouse button is released.
onreset	A form resets (i.e., the user clicks a reset button).
onresize	The size of an object changes (i.e., the user resizes a window or frame).
onselect	A text selection begins (applies to `input` or `textarea`).
onsubmit	A form is submitted.
onunload	A page is about to unload.

Fig. 11.9 | Cross-browser events.

11.10 Web Resources

`http://www.quirksmode.org/js/introevents.html`
An introduction and reference site for JavaScript events. Includes comprehensive information on history of events, the different event models, and making events work across multiple browsers.

`wsabstract.com/dhtmltutors/domevent1.shtml`
This *JavaScript Kit* tutorial introduces event handling and discusses the W3C DOM advanced event model.

`http://www.w3schools.com/jsref/jsref_events.asp`
The W3 School's JavaScript Event Reference site has a comprehensive list of JavaScript events, a description of their usage and their browser compatibilities.

`http://www.brainjar.com/dhtml/events/`
BrainJar.com's DOM Event Model site provides a comprehensive introduction to the DOM event model, and has example code to demonstrate several different ways of assigning and using events.

XML and RSS

*Knowing trees, I understand
the meaning of patience.
Knowing grass, I can
appreciate persistence.*
—Hal Borland

*Like everything
metaphysical, the harmony
between thought and reality
is to be found in the
grammar of the language.*
—Ludwig Wittgenstein

*I played with an idea, and
grew willful; tossed it into
the air; transformed it; let it
escape and recaptured it;
made it iridescent with
fancy, and winged it with
paradox.*
—Oscar Wilde

OBJECTIVES

In this chapter you will learn:

■ To mark up data using XML.

■ How XML namespaces help provide unique XML element and attribute names.

■ To create DTDs and schemas for specifying and validating the structure of an XML document.

■ To create and use simple XSL style sheets to render XML document data.

■ To retrieve and manipulate XML data programmatically using JavaScript.

■ RSS and how to programmatically apply an XSL transformation to an RSS document using JavaScript.

12.1 Introduction

The *Extensible Markup Language (XML)* was developed in 1996 by the *World Wide Web Consortium's (W3C's)* XML Working Group. XML is a widely supported *open technology* (i.e., nonproprietary technology) for describing data that has become the standard format for data exchanged between applications over the Internet.

Web applications use XML extensively and web browsers provide many XML-related capabilities. Sections 12.2–12.7 introduce XML and XML-related technologies—XML namespaces for providing unique XML element and attribute names, and Document Type Definitions (DTDs) and XML Schemas for validating XML documents. These sections support the use of XML in many subsequent chapters. Sections 12.8–12.9 present additional XML technologies and key JavaScript capabilities for loading and manipulating XML documents programmatically—this material is optional but is recommended if you plan to use XML in your own applications. Finally, Section 12.10 introduces RSS—an XML format used to syndicate simple website content—and shows how to format RSS elements using JavaScript and other technologies presented in this chapter.

12.2 XML Basics

XML permits document authors to create *markup* (i.e., a text-based notation for describing data) for virtually any type of information. This enables document authors to create entirely new markup languages for describing any type of data, such as mathematical formulas, software-configuration instructions, chemical molecular structures, music, news, recipes and financial reports. XML describes data in a way that both human beings and computers can understand.

Figure 12.1 is a simple XML document that describes information for a baseball player. We focus on lines 5–9 to introduce basic XML syntax. You will learn about the other elements of this document in Section 12.3.

```
1   <?xml version = "1.0"?>
2
3   <!-- Fig. 12.1: player.xml -->
4   <!-- Baseball player structured with XML -->
5   <player>
6      <firstName>John</firstName>
7      <lastName>Doe</lastName>
8      <battingAverage>0.375</battingAverage>
9   </player>
```

Fig. 12.1 | XML that describes a baseball player's information.

XML documents contain text that represents content (i.e., data), such as John (line 6 of Fig. 12.1), and *elements* that specify the document's structure, such as firstName (line 6 of Fig. 12.1). XML documents delimit elements with *start tags* and *end tags*. A start tag consists of the element name in *angle brackets* (e.g., <player> and <firstName> in lines 5 and 6, respectively). An end tag consists of the element name preceded by a *forward slash (/)* in angle brackets (e.g., </firstName> and </player> in lines 6 and 9, respectively). An element's start and end tags enclose text that represents a piece of data (e.g., the player's firstName—John—in line 6, which is enclosed by the <firstName> start tag and </firstName> end tag). Every XML document must have exactly one *root element* that contains all the other elements. In Fig. 12.1, the root element is player (lines 5–9).

XML-based markup languages—called XML *vocabularies*—provide a means for describing particular types of data in standardized, structured ways. Some XML vocabularies include XHTML (Extensible HyperText Markup Language), MathML (for mathematics), VoiceXML™ (for speech), CML (Chemical Markup Language—for chemistry), XBRL (Extensible Business Reporting Language—for financial data exchange) and others that we discuss in Section 12.7.

Massive amounts of data are currently stored on the Internet in many formats (e.g., databases, web pages, text files). Much of this data, especially that which is passed between systems, will soon take the form of XML. Organizations see XML as the future of data encoding. Information technology groups are planning ways to integrate XML into their systems. Industry groups are developing custom XML vocabularies for most major industries that will allow business applications to communicate in common languages. For example, many web services allow web-based applications to exchange data seamlessly through standard protocols based on XML. We discuss web services in Chapter 24.

The next generation of the web is being built on an XML foundation, enabling you to develop more sophisticated web-based applications. XML allows you to assign meaning to what would otherwise be random pieces of data. As a result, programs can "understand" the data they manipulate. For example, a web browser might view a street address in a simple web page as a string of characters without any real meaning. In an XML document, however, this data can be clearly identified (i.e., marked up) as an address. A program that uses the document can recognize this data as an address and provide links to a map of that location, driving directions from that location or other location-specific information. Likewise, an application can recognize names of people, dates, ISBN numbers and any other type of XML-encoded data. The application can then present users with other related information, providing a richer, more meaningful user experience.

Viewing and Modifying XML Documents

XML documents are highly portable. Viewing or modifying an XML document—which is a text file that usually ends with the *.xml* filename extension—does not require special software, although many software tools exist, and new ones are frequently released that make it more convenient to develop XML-based applications. Any text editor that supports ASCII/Unicode characters can open XML documents for viewing and editing. Also, most web browsers can display XML documents in a formatted manner that shows the XML's structure. Section 12.3 demonstrates this in Internet Explorer and Firefox. An important characteristic of XML is that it is both human and machine readable.

Processing XML Documents

Processing an XML document requires software called an *XML parser* (or *XML processor*). A parser makes the document's data available to applications. While reading an XML document's contents, a parser checks that the document follows the syntax rules specified by the W3C's XML Recommendation (www.w3.org/XML). XML syntax requires a single root element, a start tag and end tag for each element, and properly nested tags (i.e., the end tag for a nested element must appear before the end tag of the enclosing element). Furthermore, XML is case sensitive, so the proper capitalization must be used in elements. A document that conforms to this syntax is a *well-formed XML document* and is syntactically correct. We present fundamental XML syntax in Section 12.3. If an XML parser can process an XML document successfully, that XML document is well-formed. Parsers can provide access to XML-encoded data in well-formed documents only.

Often, XML parsers are built into software or available for download over the Internet. Some popular parsers include *Microsoft XML Core Services (MSXML)*—which is included with Internet Explorer, the Apache Software Foundation's *Xerces* (xml.apache.org) and the open-source *Expat XML Parser* (expat.sourceforge.net).

Validating XML Documents

An XML document can reference a *Document Type Definition (DTD)* or a *schema* that defines the proper structure of the XML document. When an XML document references a DTD or a schema, some parsers (called *validating parsers*) can read the DTD/schema and check that the XML document follows the structure defined by the DTD/schema. If the XML document conforms to the DTD/schema (i.e., the document has the appropriate structure), the XML document is *valid*. For example, if in Fig. 12.1 we were referencing a DTD that specified that a player element must have firstName, lastName and battingAverage elements, then omitting the lastName element (line 7 in Fig. 12.1) would invalidate the XML document player.xml. However, the XML document would still be well-formed, because it follows proper XML syntax (i.e., it has one root element, each element has a start tag and an end tag, and the elements are nested properly). By definition, a valid XML document is well-formed. Parsers that cannot check for document conformity against DTDs/schemas are *nonvalidating parsers*—they determine only whether an XML document is well-formed, not whether it is valid.

We discuss validation, DTDs and schemas, as well as the key differences between these two types of structural specifications, in Sections 12.5–12.6. For now, note that schemas are XML documents themselves, whereas DTDs are not. As you will learn in Section 12.6, this difference presents several advantages in using schemas over DTDs.

Software Engineering Observation 12.1

DTDs and schemas are essential for business-to-business (B2B) transactions and mission-critical systems. Validating XML documents ensures that disparate systems can manipulate data structured in standardized ways and prevents errors caused by missing or malformed data.

Formatting and Manipulating XML Documents

Most XML documents contain only data, not formatting instructions, so applications that process XML documents must decide how to manipulate or display the data. For example, a PDA (personal digital assistant) may render an XML document differently than a wireless phone or a desktop computer. You can use *Extensible Stylesheet Language (XSL)* to specify rendering instructions for different platforms. We discuss XSL in Section 12.8.

XML-processing programs can also search, sort and manipulate XML data using XSL. Some other XML-related technologies are XPath (XML Path Language—a language for accessing parts of an XML document), XSL-FO (XSL Formatting Objects—an XML vocabulary used to describe document formatting) and XSLT (XSL Transformations—a language for transforming XML documents into other documents). We present XSLT and XPath in Section 12.8.

12.3 Structuring Data

In this section and throughout this chapter, we create our own XML markup. XML allows you to describe data precisely in a well-structured format.

XML Markup for an Article

In Fig. 12.2, we present an XML document that marks up a simple article using XML. The line numbers shown are for reference only and are not part of the XML document.

This document begins with an *XML declaration* (line 1), which identifies the document as an XML document. The *version attribute* specifies the XML version to which the document conforms. The current XML standard is version 1.0. Though the W3C released a version 1.1 specification in February 2004, this newer version is not yet widely supported. The W3C may continue to release new versions as XML evolves to meet the requirements of different fields.

```
 1   <?xml version = "1.0"?>
 2
 3   <!-- Fig. 12.2: article.xml -->
 4   <!-- Article structured with XML -->
 5   <article>
 6      <title>Simple XML</title>
 7      <date>July 4, 2007</date>
 8      <author>
 9         <firstName>John</firstName>
10         <lastName>Doe</lastName>
11      </author>
12      <summary>XML is pretty easy.</summary>
13      <content>This chapter presents examples that use XML.</content>
14   </article>
```

Fig. 12.2 | XML used to mark up an article.

Portability Tip 12.1

Documents should include the XML declaration to identify the version of XML used. A document that lacks an XML declaration might be assumed to conform to the latest version of XML—when it does not, errors could result.

As in most markup languages, blank lines (line 2), white spaces and indentation help improve readability. Blank lines are normally ignored by XML parsers. XML comments (lines 3–4), which begin with `<!--` and end with `-->`, can be placed almost anywhere in an XML document and can span multiple lines. There must be exactly one end marker (`-->`) for each begin marker (`<!--`).

Common Programming Error 12.1

Placing any characters, including white space, before the XML declaration is an error.

Common Programming Error 12.2

In an XML document, each start tag must have a matching end tag; omitting either tag is an error. Soon, you will learn how such errors are detected.

Common Programming Error 12.3

XML is case sensitive. Using different cases for the start tag and end tag names for the same element is a syntax error.

In Fig. 12.2, `article` (lines 5–14) is the root element. The lines that precede the root element (lines 1–4) are the XML *prolog*. In an XML prolog, the XML declaration must appear before the comments and any other markup.

The elements we use in the example do not come from any specific markup language. Instead, we chose the element names and markup structure that best describe our particular data. You can invent elements to mark up your data. For example, element `title` (line 6) contains text that describes the article's title (e.g., `Simple XML`). Similarly, `date` (line 7), `author` (lines 8–11), `firstName` (line 9), `lastName` (line 10), `summary` (line 12) and `content` (line 13) contain text that describes the date, author, the author's first name, the author's last name, a summary and the content of the document, respectively. XML element names can be of any length and may contain letters, digits, underscores, hyphens and periods. However, they must begin with either a letter or an underscore, and they should not begin with "xml" in any combination of uppercase and lowercase letters (e.g., `XML`, `Xml`, `xMl`), as this is reserved for use in the XML standards.

Common Programming Error 12.4

Using a white-space character in an XML element name is an error.

Good Programming Practice 12.1

XML element names should be meaningful to humans and should not use abbreviations.

XML elements are *nested* to form hierarchies—with the root element at the top of the hierarchy. This allows document authors to create parent/child relationships between data. For example, elements `title`, `date`, `author`, `summary` and `content` are nested within article. Elements `firstName` and `lastName` are nested within author. We discuss the hierarchy of Fig. 12.2 later in this chapter (Fig. 12.25).

 Common Programming Error 12.5

Nesting XML tags improperly is a syntax error. For example, <x><y>hello</x></y> is an error, because the </y> tag must precede the </x> tag.

Any element that contains other elements (e.g., `article` or author) is a *container element*. Container elements also are called *parent elements*. Elements nested inside a container element are *child elements* (or children) of that container element. If those child elements are at the same nesting level, they are *siblings* of one another.

Viewing an XML Document in Internet Explorer and Firefox
The XML document in Fig. 12.2 is simply a text file named `article.xml`. This document does not contain formatting information for the article. This is because XML is a technology for describing the structure of data. Formatting and displaying data from an XML document are application-specific issues. For example, when the user loads `article.xml` in Internet Explorer, MSXML (Microsoft XML Core Services) parses and displays the document's data. Firefox has a similar capability. Each browser has a built-in *style sheet* to format the data. Note that the resulting format of the data (Fig. 12.3) is similar to the format of the listing in Fig. 12.2. In Section 12.8, we show how to create style sheets to transform your XML data into various formats suitable for display.

Note the minus sign (–) and plus sign (+) in the screen shots of Fig. 12.3. Although these symbols are not part of the XML document, both browsers place them next to every container element. A minus sign indicates that the browser is displaying the container element's child elements. Clicking the minus sign next to an element collapses that element

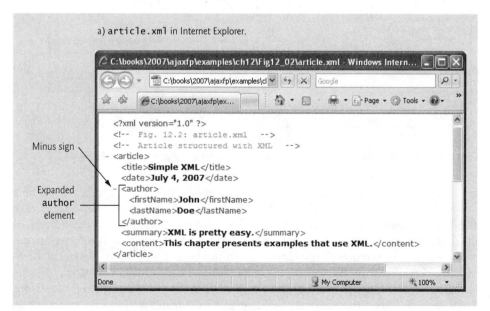

Fig. 12.3 | `article.xml` displayed by Internet Explorer 7 and Firefox 2. (Part 1 of 2.)

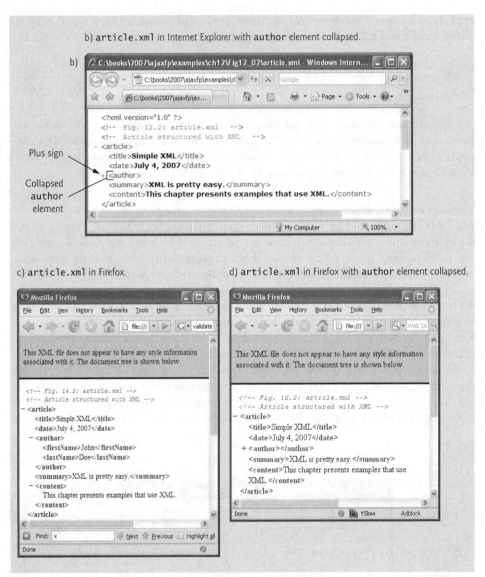

Fig. 12.3 | `article.xml` displayed by Internet Explorer 7 and Firefox 2. (Part 2 of 2.)

(i.e., causes the browser to hide the container element's children and replace the minus sign with a plus sign). Conversely, clicking the plus sign next to an element expands that element (i.e., causes the browser to display the container element's children and replace the plus sign with a minus sign). This behavior is similar to viewing the directory structure on your system in Windows Explorer or another similar directory viewer. In fact, a directory structure often is modeled as a series of tree structures, in which the *root* of a tree represents a disk drive (e.g., C:), and *nodes* in the tree represent directories. Parsers often store XML data as tree structures to facilitate efficient manipulation, as discussed in Section 12.9.

[*Note:* In Windows XP Service Pack 2 and Windows Vista, by default Internet Explorer displays all the XML elements in expanded view, and clicking the minus sign (Fig. 12.3(a)) does not do anything. To enable collapsing and expanding, right click the *Information Bar* that appears just below the **Address** field and select **Allow Blocked Content**.... Then click **Yes** in the pop-up window that appears.]

XML Markup for a Business Letter

Now that you've seen a simple XML document, let's examine a more complex XML document that marks up a business letter (Fig. 12.4). Again, we begin the document with the XML declaration (line 1) that states the XML version to which the document conforms.

```
 1   <?xml version = "1.0"?>
 2
 3   <!-- Fig. 12.4: letter.xml -->
 4   <!-- Business letter marked up as XML -->
 5   <!DOCTYPE letter SYSTEM "letter.dtd">
 6
 7   <letter>
 8      <contact type = "sender">
 9         <name>Jane Doe</name>
10         <address1>Box 12345</address1>
11         <address2>15 Any Ave.</address2>
12         <city>Othertown</city>
13         <state>Otherstate</state>
14         <zip>67890</zip>
15         <phone>555-4321</phone>
16         <flag gender = "F" />
17      </contact>
18
19      <contact type = "receiver">
20         <name>John Doe</name>
21         <address1>123 Main St.</address1>
22         <address2></address2>
23         <city>Anytown</city>
24         <state>Anystate</state>
25         <zip>12345</zip>
26         <phone>555-1234</phone>
27         <flag gender = "M" />
28      </contact>
29
30      <salutation>Dear Sir:</salutation>
31
32      <paragraph>It is our privilege to inform you about our new database
33         managed with XML. This new system allows you to reduce the
34         load on your inventory list server by having the client machine
35         perform the work of sorting and filtering the data.
36      </paragraph>
37
38      <paragraph>Please visit our website for availability and pricing.
39      </paragraph>
40
```

Fig. 12.4 | Business letter marked up as XML. (Part 1 of 2.)

```
41      <closing>Sincerely,</closing>
42      <signature>Ms. Jane Doe</signature>
43   </letter>
```

Fig. 12.4 | Business letter marked up as XML. (Part 2 of 2.)

Line 5 specifies that this XML document references a DTD. Recall from Section 12.2 that DTDs define the structure of the data for an XML document. For example, a DTD specifies the elements and parent/child relationships between elements permitted in an XML document.

Error-Prevention Tip 12.1

An XML document is not required to reference a DTD, but validating XML parsers can use a DTD to ensure that the document has the proper structure.

Portability Tip 12.2

Validating an XML document helps guarantee that independent developers will exchange data in a standardized form that conforms to the DTD.

The DOCTYPE reference (line 5) contains three items, the name of the root element that the DTD specifies (letter); the keyword *SYSTEM* (which denotes an *external DTD*—a DTD declared in a separate file, as opposed to a DTD declared locally in the same file); and the DTD's name and location (i.e., letter.dtd in the current directory; this could also be a fully qualified URL). DTD document filenames typically end with the *.dtd* extension. We discuss DTDs and letter.dtd in detail in Section 12.5.

Several tools (many of which are free) validate documents against DTDs (discussed in Section 12.5) and schemas (discussed in Section 12.6). Microsoft's *XML Validator* is available free of charge from the **Download sample** link at

```
msdn.microsoft.com/archive/en-us/samples/internet/
xml/xml_validator/default.asp
```

This validator can validate XML documents against both DTDs and schemas. To install it, run the downloaded executable file xml_validator.exe and follow the steps to complete the installation. Once the installation is successful, open the validate_js.htm file located in your XML Validator installation directory in IE to validate your XML documents. We installed the XML Validator at C:\XMLValidator (Fig. 12.5). The output (Fig. 12.6) shows the results of validating the document using Microsoft's XML Validator. You can click a node to expand it and see its contents. Visit www.w3.org/XML/Schema for a list of additional validation tools.

Root element letter (lines 7–43 of Fig. 12.4) contains the child elements contact, contact, salutation, paragraph, paragraph, closing and signature. Data can be placed between an elements' tags or as *attributes*—name/value pairs that appear within the angle brackets of an element's start tag. Elements can have any number of attributes (separated by spaces) in their start tags. The first contact element (lines 8–17) has an attribute named type with *attribute value* "sender", which indicates that this contact element identifies the letter's sender. The second contact element (lines 19–28) has attribute type with value "receiver", which indicates that this contact element identifies the letter's recipient. Like element names, attribute names are case sensitive, can be any

Fig. 12.5 | Validating an XML document with Microsoft's XML Validator.

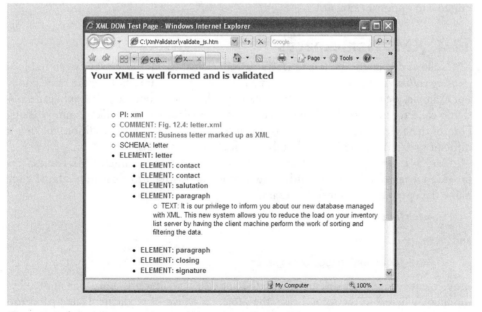

Fig. 12.6 | Validation result using Microsoft's XML Validator.

length, may contain letters, digits, underscores, hyphens and periods, and must begin with either a letter or an underscore character. A `contact` element stores various items of information about a contact, such as the contact's name (represented by element name), address (represented by elements address1, address2, city, state and zip), phone number (represented by element phone) and gender (represented by attribute gender of element flag). Element salutation (line 30) marks up the letter's salutation. Lines 32–39 mark up the letter's body using two paragraph elements. Elements closing (line 41) and signature (line 42) mark up the closing sentence and the author's "signature," respectively.

Common Programming Error 12.6

Failure to enclose attribute values in double ("") or single (' ') quotes is a syntax error.

Line 16 introduces the *empty element* flag. An empty element is one that does not have any content. Instead, an empty element sometimes places data in attributes. Empty element flag has one attribute that indicates the gender of the contact (represented by the parent contact element). Document authors can close an empty element either by placing a slash immediately preceding the right angle bracket, as shown in line 16, or by explicitly writing an end tag, as in line 22

> *<address2></address2>*

Note that the address2 element in line 22 is empty because there is no second part to this contact's address. However, we must include this element to conform to the structural rules specified in the XML document's DTD—letter.dtd (which we present in Section 12.5). This DTD specifies that each contact element must have an address2 child element (even if it is empty). In Section 12.5, you will learn how DTDs indicate required and optional elements.

12.4 XML Namespaces

XML allows document authors to create custom elements. This extensibility can result in *naming collisions* among elements in an XML document that each have the same name. For example, we may use the element book to mark up data about a Deitel publication. A stamp collector may use the element book to mark up data about a book of stamps. Using both of these elements in the same document could create a naming collision, making it difficult to determine which kind of data each element contains.

An XML *namespace* is a collection of element and attribute names. XML namespaces provide a means for document authors to unambiguously refer to elements with the same name (i.e., prevent collisions). For example,

> *<subject>*Geometry*</subject>*

and

> *<subject>*Cardiology*</subject>*

use element subject to mark up data. In the first case, the subject is something one studies in school, whereas in the second case, the subject is a field of medicine. Namespaces can differentiate these two subject elements—for example:

> *<highschool:subject>*Geometry*</highschool:subject>*

and

> *<medicalschool:subject>*Cardiology*</medicalschool:subject>*

Both highschool and medicalschool are *namespace prefixes*. A document author places a namespace prefix and colon (:) before an element name to specify the namespace to which that element belongs. Document authors can create their own namespace prefixes using virtually any name except the reserved namespace prefix xml. In the next subsections, we demonstrate how document authors ensure that namespaces are unique.

 Common Programming Error 12.7

Attempting to create a namespace prefix named xml in any mixture of uppercase and lowercase letters is a syntax error—the xml namespace prefix is reserved for internal use by XML itself.

Differentiating Elements with Namespaces

Figure 12.7 demonstrates namespaces. In this document, namespaces differentiate two distinct elements—the file element related to a text file and the file document related to an image file.

```
 1   <?xml version = "1.0"?>
 2
 3   <!-- Fig. 12.7: namespace.xml -->
 4   <!-- Demonstrating namespaces -->
 5   <text:directory
 6      xmlns:text = "urn:deitel:textInfo"
 7      xmlns:image = "urn:deitel:imageInfo">
 8
 9      <text:file filename = "book.xml">
10         <text:description>A book list</text:description>
11      </text:file>
12
13      <image:file filename = "funny.jpg">
14         <image:description>A funny picture</image:description>
15         <image:size width = "200" height = "100" />
16      </image:file>
17   </text:directory>
```

C:\books\2007\ajaxfp\examples\ch12\Fig12_07\namespace.xml - Windows Internet Explorer

C:\books\2007\ajaxfp\examples\ch12\Fig12_07\namespace   Google

C:\books\2007\ajaxfp\examples\...   Page ▾   Tools ▾

```
<?xml version="1.0" ?>
<!-- Fig. 12.7: namespace.xml    -->
<!-- Demonstrating namespaces    -->
- <text:directory xmlns:text="urn:deitel:textInfo" xmlns:image="urn:deitel:imageInfo">
- <text:file filename="book.xml">
    <text:description>A book list</text:description>
  </text:file>
- <image:file filename="funny.jpg">
    <image:description>A funny picture</image:description>
    <image:size width="200" height="100" />
  </image:file>
</text:directory>
```

Done   My Computer   100%

Fig. 12.7 | XML namespaces demonstration.

Lines 6–7 use the XML-namespace reserved attribute *xmlns* to create two namespace prefixes—text and image. Each namespace prefix is bound to a series of characters called a *Uniform Resource Identifier (URI)* that uniquely identifies the namespace. Document authors create their own namespace prefixes and URIs. A URI is a way to identifying a resource, typically on the Internet. Two popular types of URI are *Uniform Resource Name (URN)* and *Uniform Resource Locator (URL)*.

To ensure that namespaces are unique, document authors must provide unique URIs. In this example, we use the text urn:deitel:textInfo and urn:deitel:imageInfo as URIs. These URIs employ the URN scheme frequently used to identify namespaces. Under this naming scheme, a URI begins with "urn:", followed by a unique series of additional names separated by colons.

Another common practice is to use URLs, which specify the location of a file or a resource on the Internet. For example, www.deitel.com is the URL that identifies the home page of the Deitel & Associates website. Using URLs guarantees that the namespaces are unique because the domain names (e.g., www.deitel.com) are guaranteed to be unique. For example, lines 5–7 could be rewritten as

```
<text:directory
    xmlns:text = "http://www.deitel.com/xmlns-text"
    xmlns:image = "http://www.deitel.com/xmlns-image">
```

where URLs related to the deitel.com domain name serve as URIs to identify the text and image namespaces. The parser does not visit these URLs, nor do these URLs need to refer to actual web pages. They each simply represent a unique series of characters used to differentiate URI names. In fact, any string can represent a namespace. For example, our image namespace URI could be hgjfkdlsa4556, in which case our prefix assignment would be

```
    xmlns:image = "hgjfkdlsa4556"
```

Lines 9–11 use the text namespace prefix for elements file and description. Note that the end tags must also specify the namespace prefix text. Lines 13–16 apply namespace prefix image to the elements file, description and size. Note that attributes do not require namespace prefixes (although they can have them), because each attribute is already part of an element that specifies the namespace prefix. For example, attribute filename (line 9) is implicitly part of namespace text because its element (i.e., file) specifies the text namespace prefix.

Specifying a Default Namespace

To eliminate the need to place namespace prefixes in each element, document authors may specify a *default namespace* for an element and its children. Figure 12.8 demonstrates using a default namespace (urn:deitel:textInfo) for element directory.

Line 5 defines a default namespace using attribute xmlns with no prefix specified, but with a URI as its value. Once we define this default namespace, child elements belonging to the namespace need not be qualified by a namespace prefix. Thus, element file (lines 8–10) is in the default namespace urn:deitel:textInfo. Compare this to lines 9–10 of Fig. 12.7, where we had to prefix the file and description element names with the namespace prefix text.

The default namespace applies to the directory element and all elements that are not qualified with a namespace prefix. However, we can use a namespace prefix to specify a

```
 1   <?xml version = "1.0"?>
 2
 3   <!-- Fig. 12.8: defaultnamespace.xml -->
 4   <!-- Using default namespaces -->
 5   <directory xmlns = "urn:deitel:textInfo"
 6      xmlns:image = "urn:deitel:imageInfo">
 7
 8      <file filename = "book.xml">
 9         <description>A book list</description>
10      </file>
11
12      <image:file filename = "funny.jpg">
13         <image:description>A funny picture</image:description>
14         <image:size width = "200" height = "100" />
15      </image:file>
16   </directory>
```

Fig. 12.8 | Default namespace demonstration.

different namespace for a particular element. For example, the file element in lines 12–15 includes the image namespace prefix, indicating that this element is in the urn:deitel:imageInfo namespace, not the default namespace.

Namespaces in XML Vocabularies

XML-based languages, such as XML Schema (Section 12.6) and Extensible Stylesheet Language (XSL) (Section 12.8), often use namespaces to identify their elements. Each of these vocabularies defines special-purpose elements that are grouped in namespaces. These namespaces help prevent naming collisions between predefined elements and user-defined elements.

12.5 Document Type Definitions (DTDs)

Document Type Definitions (DTDs) are one of two main types of documents you can use to specify XML document structure. Section 12.6 presents W3C XML Schema documents, which provide an improved method of specifying XML document structure.

Software Engineering Observation 12.2

XML documents can have many different structures, and for this reason an application cannot be certain whether a particular document it receives is complete, ordered properly, and not missing data. DTDs and schemas (Section 12.6) solve this problem by providing an extensible way to describe XML document structure. Applications should use DTDs or schemas to confirm whether XML documents are valid.

Software Engineering Observation 12.3

*Many organizations and individuals are creating DTDs and schemas for a broad range of applications. These collections—called **repositories**—are available free for download from the web (e.g., www.xml.org, www.oasis-open.org).*

Creating a Document Type Definition

Figure 12.4 presented a simple business letter marked up with XML. Recall that line 5 of letter.xml references a DTD—letter.dtd (Fig. 12.9). This DTD specifies the business letter's element types and attributes, and their relationships to one another.

A DTD describes the structure of an XML document and enables an XML parser to verify whether an XML document is valid (i.e., whether its elements contain the proper attributes and appear in the proper sequence). DTDs allow users to check document structure and to exchange data in a standardized format. A DTD expresses the set of rules for document structure using an EBNF (Extended Backus-Naur Form) grammar. DTDs are not themselves XML documents. [*Note:* EBNF grammars are commonly used to define programming languages. To learn more about EBNF grammars, visit en.wikipedia.org/wiki/EBNF or www.garshol.priv.no/download/text/bnf.html.]

```
 1    <!-- Fig. 12.9: letter.dtd      -->
 2    <!-- DTD document for letter.xml -->
 3
 4    <!ELEMENT letter ( contact+, salutation, paragraph+,
 5       closing, signature )>
 6
 7    <!ELEMENT contact ( name, address1, address2, city, state,
 8       zip, phone, flag )>
 9    <!ATTLIST contact type CDATA #IMPLIED>
10
11    <!ELEMENT name ( #PCDATA )>
12    <!ELEMENT address1 ( #PCDATA )>
13    <!ELEMENT address2 ( #PCDATA )>
14    <!ELEMENT city ( #PCDATA )>
15    <!ELEMENT state ( #PCDATA )>
16    <!ELEMENT zip ( #PCDATA )>
17    <!ELEMENT phone ( #PCDATA )>
18    <!ELEMENT flag EMPTY>
19    <!ATTLIST flag gender (M | F) "M">
20
21    <!ELEMENT salutation ( #PCDATA )>
22    <!ELEMENT closing ( #PCDATA )>
23    <!ELEMENT paragraph ( #PCDATA )>
24    <!ELEMENT signature ( #PCDATA )>
```

Fig. 12.9 | Document Type Definition (DTD) for a business letter.

Common Programming Error 12.8

For documents validated with DTDs, any document that uses elements, attributes or nesting relationships not explicitly defined by a DTD is an invalid document.

Defining Elements in a DTD

The **ELEMENT** *element type declaration* in lines 4–5 defines the rules for element letter. In this case, letter contains one or more contact elements, one salutation element, one or more paragraph elements, one closing element and one signature element, in that sequence. The ***plus sign (+) occurrence indicator*** specifies that the DTD requires one or more occurrences of an element. Other occurence indicators include the ***asterisk*** (*), which indicates an optional element that can occur zero or more times, and the ***question mark (?)***, which indicates an optional element that can occur at most once (i.e., zero or one occurrence). If an element does not have an occurrence indicator, the DTD requires exactly one occurrence.

The contact element type declaration (lines 7–8) specifies that a contact element contains child elements name, address1, address2, city, state, zip, phone and flag—in that order. The DTD requires exactly one occurrence of each of these elements.

Defining Attributes in a DTD

Line 9 uses the **ATTLIST** *attribute-list declaration* to define an attribute named type for the contact element. Keyword ***#IMPLIED*** specifies that if the parser finds a contact element without a type attribute, the parser can choose an arbitrary value for the attribute or can ignore the attribute. Either way the document will still be valid (if the rest of the document is valid)—a missing type attribute will not invalidate the document. Other keywords that can be used in place of #IMPLIED in an ATTLIST declaration include ***#REQUIRED*** and ***#FIXED***. Keyword #REQUIRED specifies that the attribute must be present in the element, and keyword #FIXED specifies that the attribute (if present) must have the given fixed value. For example,

```
<!ATTLIST address zip CDATA #FIXED "01757">
```

indicates that attribute zip (if present in element address) must have the value 01757 for the document to be valid. If the attribute is not present, then the parser, by default, uses the fixed value that the ATTLIST declaration specifies.

Character Data vs. Parsed Character Data

Keyword ***CDATA*** (line 9) specifies that attribute type contains ***character data*** (i.e., a string). A parser will pass such data to an application without modification.

Software Engineering Observation 12.4

DTD syntax cannot describe an element's or attribute's data type. For example, a DTD cannot specify that a particular element or attribute can contain only integer data.

Keyword ***#PCDATA*** (line 11) specifies that an element (e.g., name) may contain ***parsed character data*** (i.e., data that is processed by an XML parser). Elements with parsed character data cannot contain markup characters, such as less than (<), greater than (>) or ampersand (&). The document author should replace any markup character in a #PCDATA element with the character's corresponding ***character entity reference***. For example, the character entity reference `&lt;` should be used in place of the less-than symbol (<), and the character entity reference `&gt;` should be used in place of the greater-than symbol (>). A document author who wishes to use a literal ampersand should use the entity reference `&amp;` instead—parsed character data can contain ampersands (&) only for inserting entities.

Common Programming Error 12.9

Using markup characters (e.g., <, > and &) in parsed character data is an error. Use character entity references (e.g., <, > and &) instead.

Defining Empty Elements in a DTD

Line 18 defines an empty element named `flag`. Keyword **EMPTY** specifies that the element does not contain any data between its start and end tags. Empty elements commonly describe data via attributes. For example, `flag`'s data appears in its `gender` attribute (line 19). Line 19 specifies that the `gender` attribute's value must be one of the enumerated values (`M` or `F`) enclosed in parentheses and delimited by a vertical bar (`|`) meaning "or." Note that line 19 also indicates that `gender` has a default value of `M`.

Well-Formed Documents vs. Valid Documents

In Section 12.3, we demonstrated how to use the Microsoft XML Validator to validate an XML document against its specified DTD. The validation revealed that the XML document `letter.xml` (Fig. 12.4) is well-formed and valid—it conforms to `letter.dtd` (Fig. 12.9). Recall that a well-formed document is syntactically correct (i.e., each start tag has a corresponding end tag, the document contains only one root element, etc.), and a valid document contains the proper elements with the proper attributes in the proper sequence. An XML document cannot be valid unless it is well-formed.

When a document fails to conform to a DTD or a schema, the Microsoft XML Validator displays an error message. For example, the DTD in Fig. 12.9 indicates that a `contact` element must contain the child element `name`. A document that omits this child element is still well-formed, but is not valid. In such a scenario, Microsoft XML Validator displays the error message shown in Fig. 12.10.

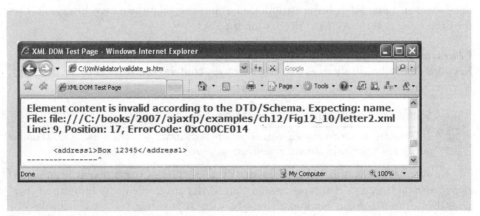

Fig. 12.10 | XML Validator displaying an error message.

12.6 W3C XML Schema Documents

In this section, we introduce schemas for specifying XML document structure and validating XML documents. Many developers in the XML community believe that DTDs are not flexible enough to meet today's programming needs. For example, DTDs lack a way of indicating what specific type of data (e.g., numeric, text) an element can contain, and DTDs are not themselves XML documents, forcing developers to learn multiple grammars and developers to create multiple types of parsers. These and other limitations have led to the development of schemas.

Unlike DTDs, schemas do not use EBNF grammar. Instead, schemas use XML syntax and are actually XML documents that programs can manipulate. Like DTDs, schemas are used by validating parsers to validate documents.

In this section, we focus on the W3C's *XML Schema* vocabulary (note the capital "S" in "Schema"). We use the term XML Schema in the rest of the chapter whenever we refer to W3C's XML Schema vocabulary. For the latest information on XML Schema, visit www.w3.org/XML/Schema. For tutorials on XML Schema concepts beyond what we present here, visit www.w3schools.com/schema/default.asp.

Recall that a DTD describes an XML document's structure, not the content of its elements. For example,

> *<quantity>*5*</quantity>*

contains character data. If the document that contains element `quantity` references a DTD, an XML parser can validate the document to confirm that this element indeed does contain PCDATA content. However, the parser cannot validate that the content is numeric; DTDs do not provide this capability. So, unfortunately, the parser also considers

> *<quantity>*hello*</quantity>*

to be valid. An application that uses the XML document containing this markup should test that the data in element `quantity` is numeric and take appropriate action if it is not.

XML Schema enables schema authors to specify that element `quantity`'s data must be numeric or, even more specifically, an integer. A parser validating the XML document against this schema can determine that 5 conforms and `hello` does not. An XML document that conforms to a schema document is *schema valid*, and one that does not conform is *schema invalid*. Schemas are XML documents and therefore must themselves be valid.

Validating Against an XML Schema Document

Figure 12.11 shows a schema-valid XML document named `book.xml`, and Fig. 12.12 shows the pertinent XML Schema document (`book.xsd`) that defines the structure for `book.xml`. By convention, schemas use the *.xsd* extension. We used an online XSD schema validator provided at

> www.xmlforasp.net/SchemaValidator.aspx

to ensure that the XML document in Fig. 12.11 conforms to the schema in Fig. 12.12. To validate the schema document itself (i.e., `book.xsd`) and produce the output shown in Fig. 12.12, we used an online XSV (XML Schema Validator) provided by the W3C at

> www.w3.org/2001/03/webdata/xsv

These tools are free and enforce the W3C's specifications regarding XML Schemas and schema validation.

```
1   <?xml version = "1.0"?>
2
3   <!-- Fig. 12.11: book.xml -->
4   <!-- Book list marked up as XML -->
5   <deitel:books xmlns:deitel = "http://www.deitel.com/booklist">
6      <book>
7         <title>Visual Basic 2005 How to Program, 3/e</title>
8      </book>
9      <book>
10        <title>Visual C# 2005 How to Program, 2/e</title>
11     </book>
12     <book>
13        <title>Java How to Program, 7/e</title>
14     </book>
15     <book>
16        <title>C++ How to Program, 6/e</title>
17     </book>
18     <book>
19        <title>Internet and World Wide Web How to Program, 4/e</title>
20     </book>
21  </deitel:books>
```

Fig. 12.11 | Schema-valid XML document describing a list of books.

```
1   <?xml version = "1.0"?>
2
3   <!-- Fig. 12.12: book.xsd          -->
4   <!-- Simple W3C XML Schema document -->
5   <schema xmlns = "http://www.w3.org/2001/XMLSchema"
6      xmlns:deitel = "http://www.deitel.com/booklist"
7      targetNamespace = "http://www.deitel.com/booklist">
8
9      <element name = "books" type = "deitel:BooksType"/>
10
11     <complexType name = "BooksType">
12        <sequence>
13           <element name = "book" type = "deitel:SingleBookType"
14              minOccurs = "1" maxOccurs = "unbounded"/>
15        </sequence>
16     </complexType>
17
18     <complexType name = "SingleBookType">
19        <sequence>
20           <element name = "title" type = "string"/>
21        </sequence>
22     </complexType>
23  </schema>
```

Fig. 12.12 | XML Schema document for book.xml. (Part 1 of 2.)

Fig. 12.12 | XML Schema document for `book.xml`. (Part 2 of 2.)

Figure 12.11 contains markup describing several Deitel books. The `books` element (line 5) has the namespace prefix `deitel`, indicating that the `books` element is a part of the `http://www.deitel.com/booklist` namespace.

Creating an XML Schema Document

Figure 12.12 presents the XML Schema document that specifies the structure of `book.xml` (Fig. 12.11). This document defines an XML-based language (i.e., a vocabulary) for writing XML documents about collections of books. The schema defines the elements, attributes and parent/child relationships that such a document can (or must) include. The schema also specifies the type of data that these elements and attributes may contain.

Root element *schema* (Fig. 12.12, lines 5–23) contains elements that define the structure of an XML document such as `book.xml`. Line 5 specifies as the default namespace the standard W3C XML Schema namespace URI—*http://www.w3.org/2001/XMLSchema*. This namespace contains predefined elements (e.g., root-element `schema`) that comprise the XML Schema vocabulary—the language used to write an XML Schema document.

 Portability Tip 12.3

W3C XML Schema authors specify URI `http://www.w3.org/2001/XMLSchema` *when referring to the XML Schema namespace. This namespace contains predefined elements that comprise the XML Schema vocabulary. Specifying this URI ensures that validation tools correctly identify XML Schema elements and do not confuse them with those defined by document authors.*

Line 6 binds the URI `http://www.deitel.com/booklist` to namespace prefix `deitel`. As we discuss momentarily, the schema uses this namespace to differentiate names created by us from names that are part of the XML Schema namespace. Line 7 also specifies `http://www.deitel.com/booklist` as the *targetNamespace* of the schema. This attribute identifies the namespace of the XML vocabulary that this schema defines. Note that the `targetNamespace` of `book.xsd` is the same as the namespace referenced in line 5 of `book.xml` (Fig. 12.11). This is what "connects" the XML document with the schema that defines its structure. When an XML schema validator examines `book.xml` and `book.xsd`, it will recognize that `book.xml` uses elements and attributes from the `http://www.deitel.com/booklist` namespace. The validator also will recognize that this namespace is the namespace defined in `book.xsd` (i.e., the schema's `targetNamespace`).

Thus the validator knows where to look for the structural rules for the elements and attributes used in book.xml.

Defining an Element in XML Schema

In XML Schema, the *element* tag (line 9) defines an element to be included in an XML document that conforms to the schema. In other words, element specifies the actual *elements* that can be used to mark up data. Line 9 defines the books element, which we use as the root element in book.xml (Fig. 12.11). Attributes *name* and *type* specify the element's name and type, respectively. An element's type indicates the data that the element may contain. Possible types include XML Schema-defined types (e.g., string, double) and user-defined types (e.g., BooksType, which is defined in lines 11–16). Figure 12.13 lists several of XML Schema's many built-in types. For a complete list of built-in types, see Section 3 of the specification found at www.w3.org/TR/xmlschema-2.

XML Schema type	Description	Ranges or structures	Examples
string	A character string		"hello"
boolean	True or false	true, false	true
decimal	A decimal numeral	$i * (10^n)$, where i is an integer and n is an integer that is less than or equal to zero.	5, -12, -45.78
float	A floating-point number	$m * (2^e)$, where m is an integer whose absolute value is less than 2^{24} and e is an integer in the range -149 to 104. Plus three additional numbers: positive infinity, negative infinity and not-a-number (NaN).	0, 12, -109.375, NaN
double	A floating-point number	$m * (2^e)$, where m is an integer whose absolute value is less than 2^{53} and e is an integer in the range -1075 to 970. Plus three additional numbers: positive infinity, negative infinity and not-a-number (NaN).	0, 12, -109.375, NaN
long	A whole number	-9223372036854775808 to 9223372036854775807, inclusive.	1234567890, -1234567890
int	A whole number	-2147483648 to 2147483647, inclusive.	1234567890, -1234567890

Fig. 12.13 | Some XML Schema types. (Part 1 of 2.)

XML Schema type	Description	Ranges or structures	Examples
`short`	A whole number	-32768 to 32767, inclusive.	12, -345
`date`	A date consisting of a year, month and day	yyyy-mm with an optional dd and an optional time zone, where yyyy is four digits long and mm and dd are two digits long.	2005-05-10
`time`	A time consisting of hours, minutes and seconds	hh:mm:ss with an optional time zone, where hh, mm and ss are two digits long.	16:30:25-05:00

Fig. 12.13 | Some XML Schema types. (Part 2 of 2.)

In this example, books is defined as an element of type deitel:BooksType (line 9). BooksType is a user-defined type (lines 11–16) in the http://www.deitel.com/booklist namespace and therefore must have the namespace prefix deitel. It is not an existing XML Schema type.

Two categories of type exist in XML Schema—*simple types* and *complex types*. Simple and complex types differ only in that simple types cannot contain attributes or child elements and complex types can.

A user-defined type that contains attributes or child elements must be defined as a complex type. Lines 11–16 use element ***complexType*** to define BooksType as a complex type that has a child element named book. The sequence element (lines 12–15) allows you to specify the sequential order in which child elements must appear. The element (lines 13–14) nested within the complexType element indicates that a BooksType element (e.g., books) can contain child elements named book of type deitel:SingleBookType (defined in lines 18–22). Attribute ***minOccurs*** (line 14), with value 1, specifies that elements of type BooksType must contain a minimum of one book element. Attribute ***maxOccurs*** (line 14), with value ***unbounded***, specifies that elements of type BooksType may have any number of book child elements.

Lines 18–22 define the complex type SingleBookType. An element of this type contains a child element named title. Line 20 defines element title to be of simple type string. Recall that elements of a simple type cannot contain attributes or child elements. The schema end tag (</schema>, line 23) declares the end of the XML Schema document.

A Closer Look at Types in XML Schema

Every element in XML Schema has a type. Types include the built-in types provided by XML Schema (Fig. 12.13) or user-defined types (e.g., SingleBookType in Fig. 12.12).

Every simple type defines a *restriction* on an XML Schema-defined type or a restriction on a user-defined type. Restrictions limit the possible values that an element can hold.

Complex types are divided into two groups—those with *simple content* and those with *complex content*. Both can contain attributes, but only complex content can contain child elements. Complex types with simple content must extend or restrict some other existing type. Complex types with complex content do not have this limitation. We demonstrate complex types with each kind of content in the next example.

The schema document in Fig. 12.14 creates both simple types and complex types. The XML document in Fig. 12.15 (laptop.xml) follows the structure defined in Fig. 12.14 to describe parts of a laptop computer. A document such as laptop.xml that conforms to a schema is known as an *XML instance document*—the document is an instance (i.e., example) of the schema.

Line 5 declares the default namespace to be the standard XML Schema namespace—any elements without a prefix are assumed to be in the XML Schema namespace. Line 6 binds the namespace prefix computer to the namespace http://www.deitel.com/computer. Line 7 identifies this namespace as the targetNamespace—the namespace being defined by the current XML Schema document.

To design the XML elements for describing laptop computers, we first create a simple type in lines 9–13 using the *simpleType* element. We name this simpleType gigahertz

```xml
1   <?xml version = "1.0"?>
2   <!-- Fig. 12.14: computer.xsd -->
3   <!-- W3C XML Schema document   -->
4
5   <schema xmlns = "http://www.w3.org/2001/XMLSchema"
6       xmlns:computer = "http://www.deitel.com/computer"
7       targetNamespace = "http://www.deitel.com/computer">
8
9       <simpleType name = "gigahertz">
10          <restriction base = "decimal">
11              <minInclusive value = "2.1"/>
12          </restriction>
13      </simpleType>
14
15      <complexType name = "CPU">
16          <simpleContent>
17              <extension base = "string">
18                  <attribute name = "model" type = "string"/>
19              </extension>
20          </simpleContent>
21      </complexType>
22
23      <complexType name = "portable">
24          <all>
25              <element name = "processor" type = "computer:CPU"/>
26              <element name = "monitor" type = "int"/>
27              <element name = "CPUSpeed" type = "computer:gigahertz"/>
28              <element name = "RAM" type = "int"/>
29          </all>
30          <attribute name = "manufacturer" type = "string"/>
31      </complexType>
32
33      <element name = "laptop" type = "computer:portable"/>
34  </schema>
```

Fig. 12.14 | XML Schema document defining simple and complex types.

because it will be used to describe the clock speed of the processor in gigahertz. Simple types are restrictions of a type typically called a ***base type***. For this `simpleType`, line 10 declares the base type as `decimal`, and we restrict the value to be at least `2.1` by using the ***minInclusive*** element in line 11.

Next, we declare a `complexType` named CPU that has ***simpleContent*** (lines 16–20). Remember that a complex type with simple content can have attributes but not child elements. Also recall that complex types with simple content must extend or restrict some XML Schema type or user-defined type. The ***extension*** element with attribute ***base*** (line 17) sets the base type to `string`. In this `complexType`, we extend the base type `string` with an attribute. The ***attribute*** element (line 18) gives the `complexType` an attribute of type `string` named `model`. Thus an element of type CPU must contain `string` text (because the base type is `string`) and may contain a `model` attribute that is also of type `string`.

Last, we define type `portable`, which is a `complexType` with complex content (lines 23–31). Such types are allowed to have child elements and attributes. The element ***all*** (lines 24–29) encloses elements that must each be included once in the corresponding XML instance document. These elements can be included in any order. This complex type holds four elements—`processor`, `monitor`, `CPUSpeed` and `RAM`. They are given types CPU, `int`, `gigahertz` and `int`, respectively. When using types CPU and `gigahertz`, we must include the namespace prefix `computer`, because these user-defined types are part of the `computer` namespace (`http://www.deitel.com/computer`)—the namespace defined in the current document (line 7). Also, `portable` contains an attribute defined in line 30. The `attribute` element indicates that elements of type `portable` contain an attribute of type `string` named `manufacturer`.

Line 33 declares the actual element that uses the three types defined in the schema. The element is called `laptop` and is of type `portable`. We must use the namespace prefix `computer` in front of `portable`.

We have now created an element named `laptop` that contains child elements `processor`, `monitor`, `CPUSpeed` and `RAM`, and an attribute `manufacturer`. Figure 12.15 uses the `laptop` element defined in the `computer.xsd` schema. Once again, we used an online XSD schema validator (`www.xmlforasp.net/SchemaValidator.aspx`) to ensure that this XML instance document adheres to the schema's structural rules.

Line 5 declares namespace prefix `computer`. The `laptop` element requires this prefix because it is part of the `http://www.deitel.com/computer` namespace. Line 6 sets the

```
1   <?xml version = "1.0"?>
2
3   <!-- Fig. 12.15: laptop.xml            -->
4   <!-- Laptop components marked up as XML -->
5   <computer:laptop xmlns:computer = "http://www.deitel.com/computer"
6      manufacturer = "IBM">
7
8      <processor model = "Centrino">Intel</processor>
9      <monitor>17</monitor>
10     <CPUSpeed>2.4</CPUSpeed>
11     <RAM>256</RAM>
12  </computer:laptop>
```

Fig. 12.15 │ XML document using the `laptop` element defined in `computer.xsd`.

laptop's `manufacturer` attribute, and lines 8–11 use the elements defined in the schema to describe the laptop's characteristics.

This section introduced W3C XML Schema documents for defining the structure of XML documents, and we validated XML instance documents against schemas using an online XSD schema validator. Section 12.7 discusses several XML vocabularies and demonstrates the MathML vocabulary. Section 12.10 demonstrates the RSS vocabulary.

12.7 XML Vocabularies

XML allows authors to create their own tags to describe data precisely. People and organizations in various fields of study have created many different kinds of XML for structuring data. Some of these markup languages are: *MathML (Mathematical Markup Language), Scalable Vector Graphics (SVG), Wireless Markup Language (WML), Extensible Business Reporting Language (XBRL), Extensible User Interface Language (XUL)* and *Product Data Markup Language (PDML).* Two other examples of XML vocabularies are W3C XML Schema and the Extensible Stylesheet Language (XSL), which we discuss in Section 12.8. The following subsections describe MathML and other custom markup languages.

12.7.1 MathML™

Until recently, computers typically required specialized software packages such as TeX and LaTeX for displaying complex mathematical expressions. This section introduces MathML, which the W3C developed for describing mathematical notations and expressions. One application that can parse, render and edit MathML is the W3C's *Amaya*™ browser/editor, which can be downloaded from

```
www.w3.org/Amaya/User/BinDist.html
```

This page contains download links for several platforms. Amaya documentation and installation notes also are available at the W3C website. Firefox also can render MathML, but it requires additional fonts. Instructions for downloading and installing these fonts are available at `www.mozilla.org/projects/mathml/fonts/`. You can download a plug-in (`www.dessci.com/en/products/mathplayer/`) to render MathML in Internet Explorer .

MathML markup describes mathematical expressions for display. MathML is divided into two types of markup—*content* markup and *presentation* markup. Content markup provides tags that embody mathematical concepts. Content MathML allows programmers to write mathematical notation specific to different areas of mathematics. For instance, the multiplication symbol has one meaning in set theory and another meaning in linear algebra. Content MathML distinguishes between different uses of the same symbol. Programmers can take content MathML markup, discern mathematical context and evaluate the marked-up mathematical operations. Presentation MathML is directed toward formatting and displaying mathematical notation. We focus on Presentation MathML in the MathML examples.

Simple Equation in MathML

Figure 12.16 uses MathML to mark up a simple expression. For this example, we show the expression rendered in Firefox.

```
 1    <?xml version="1.0" encoding="iso-8859-1"?>
 2    <!DOCTYPE math PUBLIC "-//W3C//DTD MathML 2.0//EN"
 3       "http://www.w3.org/TR/MathML2/dtd/mathml2.dtd">
 4
 5    <!-- Fig. 12.16: mathml1.mml -->
 6    <!-- MathML equation. -->
 7    <math xmlns="http://www.w3.org/1998/Math/MathML">
 8       <mn>2</mn>
 9       <mo>+</mo>
10       <mn>3</mn>
11       <mo>=</mo>
12       <mn>5</mn>
13    </math>
```

Fig. 12.16 | Expression marked up with MathML and displayed in the Firefox browser.

By convention, MathML files end with the `.mml` filename extension. A MathML document's root node is the `math` element, and its default namespace is `http://www.w3.org/1998/Math/MathML` (line 7). The *mn element* (line 8) marks up a number. The *mo element* (line 9) marks up an operator (e.g., +). Using this markup, we define the expression 2 + 3 = 5, which any MathML capable browser can display.

Algebraic Equation in MathML
Let's consider using MathML to mark up an algebraic equation containing exponents and arithmetic operators (Fig. 12.17). For this example, we again show the expression rendered in Firefox.

```
 1    <?xml version="1.0" encoding="iso-8859-1"?>
 2    <!DOCTYPE math PUBLIC "-//W3C//DTD MathML 2.0//EN"
 3       "http://www.w3.org/TR/MathML2/dtd/mathml2.dtd">
 4
 5    <!-- Fig. 12.17: mathml2.html -->
 6    <!-- MathML algebraic equation. -->
 7    <math xmlns="http://www.w3.org/1998/Math/MathML">
 8       <mn>3</mn>
 9       <mo>&InvisibleTimes;</mo>
10       <msup>
11          <mi>x</mi>
12          <mn>2</mn>
13       </msup>
```

Fig. 12.17 | Algebraic equation marked up with MathML and displayed in the Firefox browser. (Part 1 of 2.)

```
14      <mo>+</mo>
15      <mn>x</mn>
16      <mo>&minus;</mo>
17      <mfrac>
18          <mn>2</mn>
19          <mi>x</mi>
20      </mfrac>
21      <mo>=</mo>
22      <mn>0</mn>
23  </math>
```

Mozilla Firefox

File Edit View History Bookmarks Tools Help

examples/ch12/Fig12_17/mathml2.mml   G▼ Google

$3\,x^2 + x - \frac{2}{x} = 0$

Fig. 12.17 | Algebraic equation marked up with MathML and displayed in the Firefox browser. (Part 2 of 2.)

Line 9 uses *entity reference **⁢*** to indicate a multiplication operation without explicit *symbolic representation* (i.e., the multiplication symbol does not appear between the 3 and x). For exponentiation, lines 10–13 use the msup element, which represents a superscript. This *msup element* has two children—the expression to be superscripted (i.e., the base) and the superscript (i.e., the exponent). Correspondingly, the msub element represents a subscript. To display variables such as x, line 11 uses *identifier element mi*.

To display a fraction, lines 17–20 uses the *mfrac element*. Lines 18–19 specify the numerator and the denominator for the fraction. If either the numerator or the denominator contains more than one element, it must appear in an mrow element.

Calculus Expression in MathML

Figure 12.18 marks up a calculus expression that contains an integral symbol and a square-root symbol.

```
1   <?xml version="1.0" encoding="iso-8859-1"?>
2   <!DOCTYPE math PUBLIC "-//W3C//DTD MathML 2.0//EN"
3       "http://www.w3.org/TR/MathML2/dtd/mathml2.dtd">
4
5   <!-- Fig. 12.18 mathml3.html -->
6   <!-- Calculus example using MathML -->
7   <math xmlns="http://www.w3.org/1998/Math/MathML">
8       <mrow>
9           <msubsup>
10              <mo>&int;</mo>
```

Fig. 12.18 | Calculus expression marked up with MathML and displayed in the Amaya browser. [Courtesy of World Wide Web Consortium (W3C).] (Part 1 of 2.)

```
11              <mn>0</mn>
12              <mrow>
13                  <mn>1</mn>
14                  <mo>&minus;</mo>
15                  <mi>y</mi>
16              </mrow>
17          </msubsup>
18          <msqrt>
19              <mn>4</mn>
20              <mo>&InvisibleTimes;</mo>
21              <msup>
22                  <mi>x</mi>
23                  <mn>2</mn>
24              </msup>
25              <mo>+</mo>
26              <mi>y</mi>
27          </msqrt>
28          <mo>&delta;</mo>
29          <mi>x</mi>
30      </mrow>
31  </math>
```

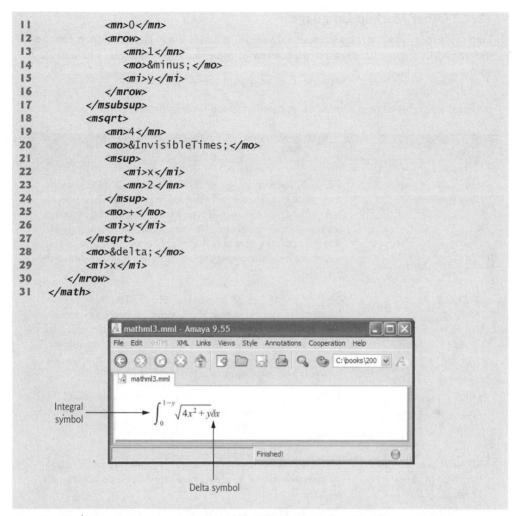

Fig. 12.18 | Calculus expression marked up with MathML and displayed in the Amaya browser. [Courtesy of World Wide Web Consortium (W3C).] (Part 2 of 2.)

Lines 8–30 group the entire expression in an *mrow element*, which is used to group elements that are positioned horizontally in an expression. The entity reference *∫* (line 10) represents the integral symbol, while the *msubsup element* (lines 9–17) specifies the subscript and superscript a base expression (e.g., the integral symbol). Element mo marks up the integral operator. The msubsup element requires three child elements—an operator (e.g., the integral entity, line 10), the subscript expression (line 11) and the superscript expression (lines 12–16). Element mn (line 11) marks up the number (i.e., 0) that represents the subscript. Element mrow (lines 12–16) marks up the superscript expression (i.e., 1-y).

Element *msqrt* (lines 18–27) represents a square-root expression. Line 28 introduces entity reference δ for representing a lowercase delta symbol. Delta is an operator, so line 28 places this entity in element mo. To see other operations and symbols in MathML, visit www.w3.org/Math.

12.7.2 Other Markup Languages

Literally hundreds of markup languages derive from XML. Every day developers find new uses for XML. Figure 12.20 summarizes a few of these markup languages. The website

```
www.service-architecture.com/xml/articles/index.html
```

provides a nice list of common XML vocabularies and descriptions.

Markup language	Description
Chemical Markup Language (CML)	Chemical Markup Language (CML) is an XML vocabulary for representing molecular and chemical information. Many previous methods for storing this type of information (e.g., special file types) inhibited document reuse. CML takes advantage of XML's portability to enable document authors to use and reuse molecular information without corrupting important data in the process.
VoiceXML™	The VoiceXML Forum founded by AT&T, IBM, Lucent and Motorola developed VoiceXML. It provides interactive voice communication between humans and computers through a telephone, PDA (personal digital assistant) or desktop computer. IBM's VoiceXML SDK can process VoiceXML documents. Visit www.voicexml.org for more information on VoiceXML.
Synchronous Multimedia Integration Language (SMIL™)	SMIL is an XML vocabulary for multimedia presentations. The W3C was the primary developer of SMIL, with contributions from some companies. Visit www.w3.org/AudioVideo for more on SMIL.
Research Information Exchange Markup Language (RIXML)	RIXML, developed by a consortium of brokerage firms, marks up investment data. Visit www.rixml.org for more information on RIXML.
Geography Markup Language (GML)	OpenGIS developed the Geography Markup Language to describe geographic information. Visit www.opengis.org for more information on GML.
Extensible User Interface Language (XUL)	The Mozilla Project created the Extensible User Interface Language for describing graphical user interfaces in a platform-independent way.

Fig. 12.19 | Various markup languages derived from XML.

12.8 Extensible Stylesheet Language and XSL Transformations

Extensible Stylesheet Language (XSL) documents specify how programs are to render XML document data. XSL is a group of three technologies—*XSL-FO (XSL Formatting Objects)*, *XPath (XML Path Language)* and *XSLT (XSL Transformations)*. XSL-FO is a vocabulary for specifying formatting, and XPath is a string-based language of expressions used by XML and many of its related technologies for effectively and efficiently locating structures and data (such as specific elements and attributes) in XML documents.

The third portion of XSL—XSL Transformations (XSLT)—is a technology for transforming XML documents into other documents—i.e., transforming the structure of the XML document data to another structure. XSLT provides elements that define rules for transforming one XML document to produce a different XML document. This is useful when you want to use data in multiple applications or on multiple platforms, each of which may be designed to work with documents written in a particular vocabulary. For example, XSLT allows you to convert a simple XML document to an XHTML document that presents the XML document's data (or a subset of the data) formatted for display in a web browser.

Transforming an XML document using XSLT involves two tree structures—the *source tree* (i.e., the XML document to be transformed) and the *result tree* (i.e., the XML document to be created). XPath is used to locate parts of the source-tree document that match *templates* defined in an *XSL style sheet*. When a match occurs (i.e., a node matches a template), the matching template executes and adds its result to the result tree. When there are no more matches, XSLT has transformed the source tree into the result tree. The XSLT does not analyze every node of the source tree; it selectively navigates the source tree using XPath's select and match attributes. For XSLT to function, the source tree must be properly structured. Schemas, DTDs and validating parsers can validate document structure before using XPath and XSLTs.

A Simple XSL Example

Figure 12.20 lists an XML document that describes various sports. The output shows the result of the transformation (specified in the XSLT template of Fig. 12.21) rendered by Internet Explorer.

To perform transformations, an XSLT processor is required. Popular XSLT processors include Microsoft's MSXML and the Apache Software Foundation's *Xalan 2* (xml.apache.org). The XML document in Fig. 12.20 is transformed into an XHTML document by MSXML when the document is loaded in Internet Explorer. MSXML is both an XML parser and an XSLT processor. Firefox also includes an XSLT processor.

```
 1   <?xml version = "1.0"?>
 2   <?xml-stylesheet type = "text/xsl" href = "sports.xsl"?>
 3
 4   <!-- Fig. 12.20: sports.xml -->
 5   <!-- Sports Database -->
 6
 7   <sports>
 8      <game id = "783">
 9         <name>Cricket</name>
10
11         <paragraph>
12            More popular among commonwealth nations.
13         </paragraph>
14      </game>
```

Fig. 12.20 | XML document that describes various sports. (Part 1 of 2.)

```
15
16      <game id = "239">
17          <name>Baseball</name>
18
19          <paragraph>
20              More popular in America.
21          </paragraph>
22      </game>
23
24      <game id = "418">
25          <name>Soccer (Futbol)</name>
26
27          <paragraph>
28              Most popular sport in the world.
29          </paragraph>
30      </game>
31  </sports>
```

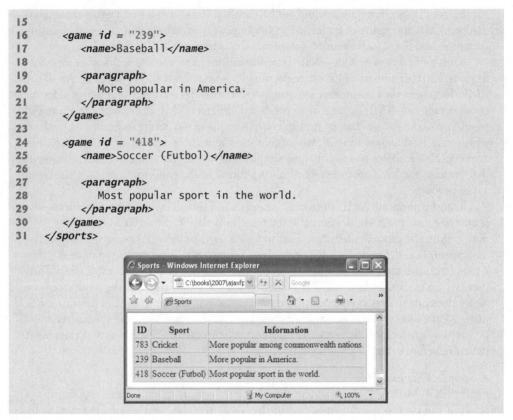

Fig. 12.20 | XML document that describes various sports. (Part 2 of 2.)

Line 2 (Fig. 12.20) is a *processing instruction* (*PI*) that references the XSL style sheet `sports.xsl` (Fig. 12.21). A processing instruction is embedded in an XML document and provides application-specific information to whichever XML processor the application uses. In this particular case, the processing instruction specifies the location of an XSLT document with which to transform the XML document. The **<?** and **?>** (line 2, Fig. 12.20) delimit a processing instruction, which consists of a *PI target* (e.g., `xml-stylesheet`) and a *PI value* (e.g., `type = "text/xsl" href = "sports.xsl"`). The PI value's `type` attribute specifies that `sports.xsl` is a `text/xsl` file (i.e., a text file containing XSL content). The `href` attribute specifies the name and location of the style sheet to apply—in this case, `sports.xsl` in the current directory.

Software Engineering Observation 12.5

XSL enables document authors to separate data presentation (specified in XSL documents) from data description (specified in XML documents).

Common Programming Error 12.10

You will sometimes see the XML processing instruction <?xml-stylesheet?> written as <?xml:stylesheet?> with a colon rather than a dash. The version with a colon results in an XML parsing error in Firefox.

Figure 12.21 shows the XSL document for transforming the structured data of the XML document of Fig. 12.20 into an XHTML document for presentation. By convention, XSL documents have the filename extension **.xsl**.

Lines 6–7 begin the XSL style sheet with the **stylesheet** start tag. Attribute **version** specifies the XSLT version to which this document conforms. Line 7 binds namespace prefix **xsl** to the W3C's XSLT URI (i.e., http://www.w3.org/1999/XSL/Transform).

```
 1   <?xml version = "1.0"?>
 2   <!-- Fig. 12.21: sports.xsl -->
 3   <!-- A simple XSLT transformation -->
 4
 5   <!-- reference XSL style sheet URI -->
 6   <xsl-stylesheet version = "1.0"
 7      xmlns:xsl = "http://www.w3.org/1999/XSL/Transform">
 8
 9      <xsl:output method = "html" omit-xml-declaration = "no"
10         doctype-system =
11            "http://www.w3c.org/TR/xhtml1/DTD/xhtml1-strict.dtd"
12         doctype-public = "-//W3C//DTD XHTML 1.0 Strict//EN"/>
13
14      <xsl:template match = "/"> <!-- match root element -->
15
16      <html xmlns = "http://www.w3.org/1999/xhtml">
17         <head>
18            <title>Sports</title>
19         </head>
20
21         <body>
22            <table border = "1" bgcolor = "wheat">
23               <thead>
24                  <tr>
25                     <th>ID</th>
26                     <th>Sport</th>
27                     <th>Information</th>
28                  </tr>
29               </thead>
30
31               <!-- insert each name and paragraph element value -->
32               <!-- into a table row. -->
33               <xsl:for-each select = "/sports/game">
34                  <tr>
35                     <td><xsl:value-of select = "@id"/></td>
36                     <td><xsl:value-of select = "name"/></td>
37                     <td><xsl:value-of select = "paragraph"/></td>
38                  </tr>
39               </xsl:for-each>
40            </table>
41         </body>
42      </html>
43
44      </xsl:template>
45   </xsl:stylesheet>
```

Fig. 12.21 | XSLT that creates elements and attributes in an XHTML document.

Lines 9–12 use element *xsl:output* to write an XHTML document type declaration (DOCTYPE) to the result tree (i.e., the XML document to be created). The DOCTYPE identifies XHTML as the type of the resulting document. Attribute method is assigned "html", which indicates that HTML is being output to the result tree. Attribute *omit-xml-declaration* specifies whether the transformation should write the XML declaration to the result tree. In this case, we do not want to omit the XML declaration, so we assign to this attribute the value "no". Attributes doctype-system and doctype-public write the DOCTYPE DTD information to the result tree.

XSLT uses *templates* (i.e., *xsl:template* elements) to describe how to transform particular nodes from the source tree to the result tree. A template is applied to nodes that are specified in the required match attribute. Line 14 uses the *match* attribute to select the *document root* (i.e., the conceptual part of the document that contains the root element and everything below it) of the XML source document (i.e., sports.xml). The XPath character / (a forward slash) always selects the document root. Recall that XPath is a string-based language used to locate parts of an XML document easily. In XPath, a leading forward slash specifies that we are using *absolute addressing* (i.e., we are starting from the root and defining paths down the source tree). In the XML document of Fig. 12.20, the child nodes of the document root are the two processing instruction nodes (lines 1–2), the two comment nodes (lines 4–5) and the sports element node (lines 7–31). The template in Fig. 12.21, line 14, matches a node (i.e., the root node), so the contents of the template are now added to the result tree.

The MSXML processor writes the XHTML in lines 16–29 (Fig. 12.21) to the result tree exactly as it appears in the XSL document. Now the result tree consists of the DOCTYPE definition and the XHTML code from lines 16–29. Lines 33–39 use element *xsl:for-each* to iterate through the source XML document, searching for game elements. Attribute *select* is an XPath expression that specifies the nodes (called the *node set*) on which the xsl:for-each operates. Again, the first forward slash means that we are using absolute addressing. The forward slash between sports and game indicates that game is a child node of sports. Thus, the xsl:for-each finds game nodes that are children of the sports node. The XML document sports.xml contains only one sports node, which is also the document root node. After finding the elements that match the selection criteria, the xsl:for-each processes each element with the code in lines 34–38 (these lines produce one row in a table each time they execute) and places the result of lines 34–38 in the result tree.

Line 35 uses element *value-of* to retrieve attribute id's value and place it in a td element in the result tree. The XPath symbol @ specifies that id is an attribute node of the context node game. Lines 36–37 place the name and paragraph element values in td elements and insert them in the result tree. When an XPath expression has no beginning forward slash, the expression uses *relative addressing*. Omitting the beginning forward slash tells the xsl:value-of select statements to search for name and paragraph elements that are children of the context node, not the root node. Due to the last XPath expression selection, the current context node is game, which indeed has an id attribute, a name child element and a paragraph child element.

Using XSLT to Sort and Format Data

Figure 12.22 presents an XML document (sorting.xml) that marks up information about a book. Note that several elements of the markup describing the book appear out of

```
 I   <?xml version = "1.0"?>
 2   <?xml-stylesheet type = "text/xsl" href = "sorting.xsl"?>
 3
 4   <!-- Fig. 12.22: sorting.xml -->
 5   <!-- XML document containing book information -->
 6   <book isbn = "999-99999-9-X">
 7      <title>Deitel&apos;s XML Primer</title>
 8
 9      <author>
10         <firstName>Jane</firstName>
11         <lastName>Blue</lastName>
12      </author>
13
14      <chapters>
15         <frontMatter>
16            <preface pages = "2" />
17            <contents pages = "5" />
18            <illustrations pages = "4" />
19         </frontMatter>
20
21         <chapter number = "3" pages = "44">Advanced XML</chapter>
22         <chapter number = "2" pages = "35">Intermediate XML</chapter>
23         <appendix number = "B" pages = "26">Parsers and Tools</appendix>
24         <appendix number = "A" pages = "7">Entities</appendix>
25         <chapter number = "1" pages = "28">XML Fundamentals</chapter>
26      </chapters>
27
28      <media type = "CD" />
29   </book>
```

Fig. 12.22 | XML document containing book information.

order (e.g., the element describing Chapter 3 appears before the element describing Chapter 2). We arranged them this way purposely to demonstrate that the XSL style sheet referenced in line 2 (sorting.xsl) can sort the XML file's data for presentation purposes.

Figure 12.23 presents an XSL document (sorting.xsl) for transforming sorting.xml (Fig. 12.22) to XHTML. Recall that an XSL document navigates a source tree and builds a result tree. In this example, the source tree is XML, and the output tree is XHTML. Line 14 of Fig. 12.23 matches the root element of the document in Fig. 12.22. Line 15 outputs an html start tag to the result tree. In line 16, the <xsl:apply-templates/> element specifies that the XSLT processor is to apply the xsl:templates defined in this XSL document to the current node's (i.e., the document root's) children. The content from the applied templates is output in the html element that ends at line 17.

Lines 21–84 specify a template that matches element book. The template indicates how to format the information contained in book elements of sorting.xml (Fig. 12.22) as XHTML.

Lines 23–24 create the title for the XHTML document. We use the book's ISBN (from attribute isbn) and the contents of element title to create the string that appears in the browser window's title bar (**ISBN 999-99999-9-X - Deitel's XML Primer**).

Line 28 creates a header element that contains the book's title. Lines 29–31 create a header element that contains the book's author. Because the context node (i.e., the current

```
1    <?xml version = "1.0"?>
2
3    <!-- Fig. 12.23: sorting.xsl -->
4    <!-- Transformation of book information into XHTML -->
5    <xsl:stylesheet version = "1.0"
6       xmlns:xsl = "http://www.w3.org/1999/XSL/Transform">
7
8       <!-- write XML declaration and DOCTYPE DTD information -->
9       <xsl:output method = "html" omit-xml-declaration = "no"
10         doctype-system = "http://www.w3.org/TR/xhtml11/DTD/xhtml11.dtd"
11         doctype-public = "-//W3C//DTD XHTML 1.1//EN"/>
12
13      <!-- match document root -->
14      <xsl:template match = "/">
15         <html xmlns = "http://www.w3.org/1999/xhtml">
16            <xsl:apply-templates/>
17         </html>
18      </xsl:template>
19
20      <!-- match book -->
21      <xsl:template match = "book">
22         <head>
23            <title>ISBN <xsl:value-of select = "@isbn"/> -
24               <xsl:value-of select = "title"/></title>
25         </head>
26
27         <body>
28            <h1 style = "color: blue"><xsl:value-of select = "title"/></h1>
29            <h2 style = "color: blue">by
30               <xsl:value-of select = "author/lastName"/>,
31               <xsl:value-of select = "author/firstName"/></h2>
32
33            <table style = "border-style: groove; background-color: wheat">
34
35               <xsl:for-each select = "chapters/frontMatter/*">
36                  <tr>
37                     <td style = "text-align: right">
38                        <xsl:value-of select = "name()"/>
39                     </td>
40
41                     <td>
42                        ( <xsl:value-of select = "@pages"/> pages )
43                     </td>
44                  </tr>
45               </xsl:for-each>
46
47               <xsl:for-each select = "chapters/chapter">
48                  <xsl:sort select = "@number" data-type = "number"
49                     order = "ascending"/>
50                  <tr>
51                     <td style = "text-align: right">
52                        Chapter <xsl:value-of select = "@number"/>
53                     </td>
```

Fig. 12.23 | XSL document that transforms sorting.xml into XHTML. (Part 1 of 2.)

```
54
55                           <td>
56                               <xsl:value-of select = "text()"/>
57                               ( <xsl:value-of select = "@pages"/> pages )
58                           </td>
59                       </tr>
60                   </xsl:for-each>
61
62                   <xsl:for-each select = "chapters/appendix">
63                       <xsl:sort select = "@number" data-type = "text"
64                           order = "ascending"/>
65                       <tr>
66                           <td style = "text-align: right">
67                               Appendix <xsl:value-of select = "@number"/>
68                           </td>
69
70                           <td>
71                               <xsl:value-of select = "text()"/>
72                               ( <xsl:value-of select = "@pages"/> pages )
73                           </td>
74                       </tr>
75                   </xsl:for-each>
76               </table>
77
78               <br /><p style = "color: blue">Pages:
79                   <xsl:variable name = "pagecount"
80                       select = "sum(chapters//*/@pages)"/>
81                   <xsl:value-of select = "$pagecount"/>
82               <br />Media Type: <xsl:value-of select = "media/@type"/></p>
83           </body>
84       </xsl:template>
85   </xsl:stylesheet>
```

Fig. 12.23 | XSL document that transforms `sorting.xml` into XHTML. (Part 2 of 2.)

node being processed) is book, the XPath expression author/lastName selects the author's last name, and the expression author/firstName selects the author's first name.

Line 35 selects each element (indicated by an asterisk) that is a child of element frontMatter. Line 38 calls *node-set function **name*** to retrieve the current node's element name (e.g., preface). The current node is the context node specified in the xsl:for-each (line 35). Line 42 retrieves the value of the pages attribute of the current node.

Line 47 selects each chapter element. Lines 48–49 use element ***xsl:sort*** to sort chapters by number in ascending order. Attribute ***select*** selects the value of attribute number in context node chapter. Attribute ***data-type***, with value "number", specifies a numeric sort, and attribute ***order***, with value "ascending", specifies ascending order. Attribute data-type also accepts the value "text" (line 63), and attribute order also accepts the value "descending". Line 56 uses *node-set function **text*** to obtain the text between the chapter start and end tags (i.e., the name of the chapter). Line 57 retrieves the value of the pages attribute of the current node. Lines 62–75 perform similar tasks for each appendix.

Lines 79–80 use an *XSL variable* to store the value of the book's total page count and output the page count to the result tree. Attribute ***name*** specifies the variable's name (i.e., pagecount), and attribute select assigns a value to the variable. Function ***sum*** (line 80) totals the values for all page attribute values. The two slashes between chapters and * indicate a *recursive descent*—the MSXML processor will search for elements that contain an attribute named pages in all descendant nodes of chapters. The XPath expression

    //*

selects all the nodes in an XML document. Line 81 retrieves the value of the newly created XSL variable pagecount by placing a dollar sign in front of its name.

Summary of XSL Style-Sheet Elements

This section's examples used several predefined XSL elements to perform various operations. Figure 12.24 lists these elements and several other commonly used XSL elements. For more information on these elements and XSL in general, see www.w3.org/Style/XSL.

Element	Description
`<xsl:apply-templates>`	Applies the templates of the XSL document to the children of the current node.
`<xsl:apply-templates match = "expression">`	Applies the templates of the XSL document to the children of *expression*. The value of the attribute match (i.e., *expression*) must be an XPath expression that specifies elements.
`<xsl:template>`	Contains rules to apply when a specified node is matched.
`<xsl:value-of select = "expression">`	Selects the value of an XML element and adds it to the output tree of the transformation. The required select attribute contains an XPath expression.

Fig. 12.24 | XSL style-sheet elements. (Part 1 of 2.)

Element	Description
`<xsl:for-each select = "expression">`	Applies a template to every node selected by the XPath specified by the `select` attribute.
`<xsl:sort select = "expression">`	Used as a child element of an `<xsl:apply-templates>` or `<xsl:for-each>` element. Sorts the nodes selected by the `<xsl:apply-template>` or `<xsl:for-each>` element so that the nodes are processed in sorted order.
`<xsl:output>`	Has various attributes to define the format (e.g., XML, XHTML), version (e.g., 1.0, 2.0), document type and media type of the output document. This tag is a top-level element—it can be used only as a child element of an `xml:stylesheet`.
`<xsl:copy>`	Adds the current node to the output tree.

Fig. 12.24 | XSL style-sheet elements. (Part 2 of 2.)

This section introduced Extensible Stylesheet Language (XSL) and showed how to create XSL transformations to convert XML documents from one format to another. We showed how to transform XML documents to XHTML documents for display in a web browser. Recall that these transformations are performed by MSXML, Internet Explorer's built-in XML parser and XSLT processor. In most business applications, XML documents are transferred between business partners and are transformed to other XML vocabularies programmatically. Section 12.9 discusses the XML Document Object Model (DOM) and demonstrates how to manupulate the DOM of an XML document using JavaScript.

12.9 Document Object Model (DOM)

Although an XML document is a text file, retrieving data from the document using traditional sequential file processing techniques is neither practical nor efficient, especially for adding and removing elements dynamically.

Upon successfully parsing a document, some XML parsers store document data as tree structures in memory. Figure 12.25 illustrates the tree structure for the root element of the document `article.xml` (Fig. 12.2). This hierarchical tree structure is called a *Document Object Model* (*DOM*) *tree*, and an XML parser that creates this type of structure is known as a *DOM parser*. Each element name (e.g., `article`, `date`, `firstName`) is represented by a node. A node that contains other nodes (called *child nodes* or children) is called a *parent node* (e.g., `author`). A parent node can have many children, but a child node can have only one parent node. Nodes that are peers (e.g., `firstName` and `lastName`) are called *sibling nodes*. A node's *descendant nodes* include its children, its children's children and so on. A node's *ancestor nodes* include its parent, its parent's parent and so on. Many of the XML DOM capabilities you'll see in this section are similar or identical to those of the XHTML DOM you learned in Chapter 10.

The DOM tree has a single *root node*, which contains all the other nodes in the document. For example, the root node of the DOM tree that represents `article.xml` contains a node for the XML declaration (line 1), two nodes for the comments (lines 3–4) and a node for the XML document's root element `article` (line 5).

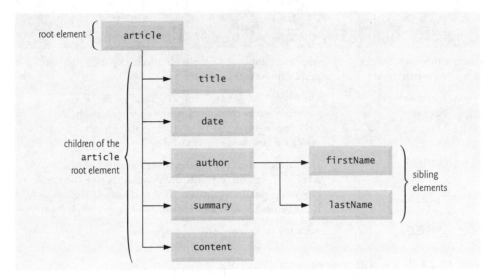

Fig. 12.25 | Tree structure for the document `article.xml` of Fig. 12.2.

To introduce document manipulation with the XML Document Object Model, we provide a scripting example (Fig. 12.26) that uses JavaScript and XML. This example loads the XML document `article.xml` (Fig. 12.2) and uses the XML DOM API to display the document's element names and values. The example also provides buttons that enable you to navigate the DOM structure. As you click each button, an appropriate part of the document is highlighted. All of this is done in a manner that enables the example to execute in both Internet Explorer 7 and Firefox 2. Figure 12.26 lists the JavaScript code that manipulates this XML document and displays its content in an XHTML page.

Overview of the body Element
Lines 203–217 create the XHTML document's `body`. When the body loads, its `onload` event calls our JavaScript function `loadXMLDocument` to load and display the contents of `article.xml` in the `div` at line 216 (`outputDiv`). Lines 204–215 define a form consisting of five buttons. When each button is pressed, it invokes one of our JavaScript functions to navigate `article.xml`'s DOM structure.

Global Script Variables
Lines 16–21 in the `script` element (lines 14–201) declare several variables used throughout the script. Variable `doc` references a DOM object representation of `article.xml`. Variable `outputHTML` stores the markup that will be placed in `outputDiv`. Variable `id-Counter` is used to track the unique `id` attributes that we assign to each element in the out-putHTML markup. These `id`s will be used to dynamically highlight parts of the document when the user clicks the buttons in the form. Variable `depth` determines the indentation level for the content in `article.xml`. We use this to structure the output using the nesting of the elements in `article.xml`. Variables `current` and `previous` track the current and previous nodes in `article.xml`'s DOM structure as the user navigates it.

```
1    <?xml version = "1.0" encoding = "utf-8"?>
2    <!DOCTYPE html PUBLIC "-//W3C//DTD XHTML 1.0 Strict//EN"
3       "http://www.w3.org/TR/xhtml1/DTD/xhtml1-strict.dtd">
4
5    <!-- Fig. 14.26: XMLDOMTraversal.html -->
6    <!-- Traversing an XML document using the XML DOM. -->
7    <html xmlns = "http://www.w3.org/1999/xhtml">
8    <head>
9       <title>Traversing an XML document using the XML DOM</title>
10      <style type = "text/css">
11         .highlighted { background-color: yellow }
12         #outputDiv { font: 10pt "Lucida Console", monospace; }
13      </style>
14      <script type="text/javascript">
15      <!--
16      var doc; // variable to reference the XML document
17      var outputHTML = ""; // stores text to output in outputDiv
18      var idCounter = 1; // used to create div IDs
19      var depth = -1; // tree depth is -1 to start
20      var current = null; // represents the current node for traversals
21      var previous = null; // represent prior node in traversals
22
23      // load XML document based on whether the browser is IE7 or Firefox 2
24      function loadXMLDocument( url )
25      {
26         if ( window.ActiveXObject ) // IE7
27         {
28            // create IE7-specific XML document object
29            doc = new ActiveXObject( "Msxml2.DOMDocument.6.0" );
30            doc.async = false; // specifies synchronous loading of XML doc
31            doc.load( url ); // load the XML document specified by url
32            buildHTML( doc.childNodes ); // display the nodes
33            displayDoc();
34         } // end if
35         else if ( document.implementation &&
36            document.implementation.createDocument ) // other browsers
37         {
38            // create XML document object
39            doc = document.implementation.createDocument( "", "", null );
40            doc.load( url ); // load the XML document specified by url
41            doc.onload = function() // function to execute when doc loads
42            {
43               buildHTML( doc.childNodes ); // called by XML doc onload event
44               displayDoc(); // display the HTML
45            } // end XML document's onload event handler
46         } // end else
47         else // not supported
48            alert( 'This script is not supported by your browser' );
49      } // end function loadXMLDocument
50
51      // traverse xmlDocument and build XHTML representation of its content
52      function buildHTML( childList )
53      {
```

Fig. 12.26 | Traversing an XML document using the XML DOM. (Part 1 of 8.)

```
54        ++depth; // increase tab depth
55
56        // display each node's content
57        for ( var i = 0; i < childList.length; i++ )
58        {
59           switch ( childList[ i ].nodeType )
60           {
61              case 1: // Node.ELEMENT_NODE; value used for portability
62                 outputHTML += "<div id=\"id" + idCounter + "\">";
63                 spaceOutput( depth ); // insert spaces
64                 outputHTML += childList[ i ].nodeName; // show node's name
65                 ++idCounter; // increment the id counter
66
67                 // if current node has children, call buildHTML recursively
68                 if ( childList[ i ].childNodes.length != 0 )
69                    buildHTML( childList[ i ].childNodes );
70
71                 outputHTML += "</div>";
72                 break;
73              case 3: // Node.TEXT_NODE; value used for portability
74              case 8: // Node.COMMENT_NODE; value used for portability
75                 // if nodeValue is not 3 or 6 spaces (Firefox issue),
76                 // include nodeValue in HTML
77                 if ( childList[ i ].nodeValue.indexOf( "   " ) == -1 &&
78                    childList[ i ].nodeValue.indexOf( "      " ) == -1 )
79                 {
80                    outputHTML += "<div id=\"id" + idCounter + "\">";
81                    spaceOutput( depth ); // insert spaces
82                    outputHTML += childList[ i ].nodeValue + "</div>";
83                    ++idCounter; // increment the id counter
84                 } // end if
85           } // end switch
86        } // end for
87
88        --depth; // decrease tab depth
89     } // end function buildHTML
90
91     // display the XML document and highlight the first child
92     function displayDoc()
93     {
94        document.getElementById( "outputDiv" ).innerHTML = outputHTML;
95        current = document.getElementById( 'id1' );
96        setCurrentNodeStyle( current.id, true );
97     } // end function displayDoc
98
99     // insert non-breaking spaces for indentation
100    function spaceOutput( number )
101    {
102       for ( var i = 0; i < number; i++ )
103       {
104          outputHTML += "   ";
105       } // end for
106    } // end function spaceOutput
```

Fig. 12.26 | Traversing an XML document using the XML DOM. (Part 2 of 8.)

```
107
108     // highlight first child of current node
109     function processFirstChild()
110     {
111        if ( current.childNodes.length == 1 && // only one child
112           current.firstChild.nodeType == 3 )  // and it's a text node
113        {
114           alert( "There is no child node" );
115        } // end if
116        else if ( current.childNodes.length > 1 )
117        {
118           previous = current; // save currently highlighted node
119
120           if ( current.firstChild.nodeType != 3 ) // if not text node
121              current = current.firstChild; // get new current node
122           else // if text node, use firstChild's nextSibling instead
123              current = current.firstChild.nextSibling; // get first sibling
124
125           setCurrentNodeStyle( previous.id, false ); // remove highlight
126           setCurrentNodeStyle( current.id, true ); // add highlight
127        } // end if
128        else
129           alert( "There is no child node" );
130     } // end function processFirstChild
131
132     // highlight next sibling of current node
133     function processNextSibling()
134     {
135        if ( current.id != "outputDiv" && current.nextSibling )
136        {
137           previous = current; // save currently highlighted node
138           current = current.nextSibling; // get new current node
139           setCurrentNodeStyle( previous.id, false ); // remove highlight
140           setCurrentNodeStyle( current.id, true ); // add highlight
141        } // end if
142        else
143           alert( "There is no next sibling" );
144     } // end function processNextSibling
145
146     // highlight previous sibling of current node if it is not a text node
147     function processPreviousSibling()
148     {
149        if ( current.id != "outputDiv" && current.previousSibling &&
150           current.previousSibling.nodeType != 3 )
151        {
152           previous = current; // save currently highlighted node
153           current = current.previousSibling; // get new current node
154           setCurrentNodeStyle( previous.id, false ); // remove highlight
155           setCurrentNodeStyle( current.id, true ); // add highlight
156        } // end if
157        else
158           alert( "There is no previous sibling" );
159     } // end function processPreviousSibling
```

Fig. 12.26 | Traversing an XML document using the XML DOM. (Part 3 of 8.)

```
160
161     // highlight last child of current node
162     function processLastChild()
163     {
164        if ( current.childNodes.length == 1 &&
165           current.lastChild.nodeType == 3 )
166        {
167           alert( "There is no child node" );
168        } // end if
169        else if ( current.childNodes.length != 0 )
170        {
171           previous = current; // save currently highlighted node
172           current = current.lastChild; // get new current node
173           setCurrentNodeStyle( previous.id, false ); // remove highlight
174           setCurrentNodeStyle( current.id, true ); // add highlight
175        } // end if
176        else
177           alert( "There is no child node" );
178     } // end function processLastChild
179
180     // highlight parent of current node
181     function processParentNode()
182     {
183        if ( current.parentNode.id != "body" )
184        {
185           previous = current; // save currently highlighted node
186           current = current.parentNode; // get new current node
187           setCurrentNodeStyle( previous.id, false ); // remove highlight
188           setCurrentNodeStyle( current.id, true ); // add highlight
189        } // end if
190        else
191           alert( "There is no parent node" );
192     } // end function processParentNode
193
194     // set style of node with specified id
195     function setCurrentNodeStyle( id, highlight )
196     {
197        document.getElementById( id ).className =
198           ( highlight ? "highlighted" : "" );
199     } // end function setCurrentNodeStyle
200     // -->
201     </script>
202  </head>
203  <body id = "body" onload = "loadXMLDocument( 'article.xml' );">
204     <form action = "" onsubmit = "return false;">
205        <input type = "submit" value = "firstChild"
206           onclick = "processFirstChild()"/>
207        <input type = "submit" value = "nextSibling"
208           onclick = "processNextSibling()"/>
209        <input type = "submit" value = "previousSibling"
210           onclick = "processPreviousSibling()"/>
211        <input type = "submit" value = "lastChild"
212           onclick = "processLastChild()"/>
```

Fig. 12.26 | Traversing an XML document using the XML DOM. (Part 4 of 8.)

```
213          <input type = "submit" value = "parentNode"
214              onclick = "processParentNode()"/>
215      </form><br/>
216      <div id = "outputDiv"></div>
217  </body>
218  </html>
```

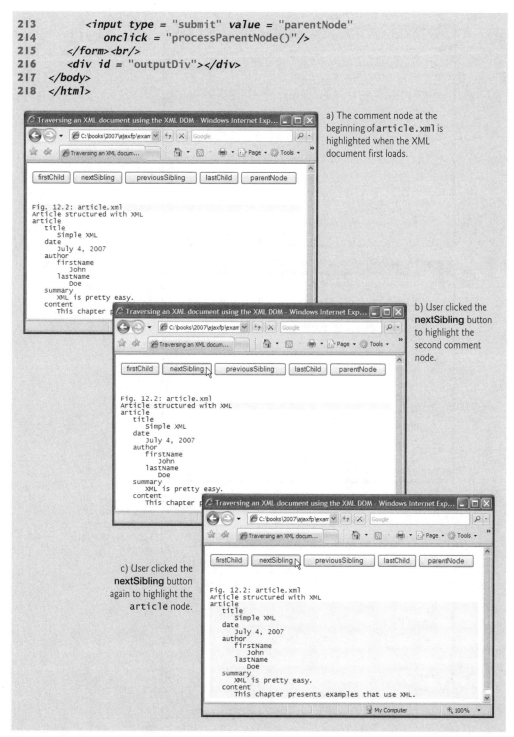

a) The comment node at the beginning of `article.xml` is highlighted when the XML document first loads.

b) User clicked the **nextSibling** button to highlight the second comment node.

c) User clicked the **nextSibling** button again to highlight the **article** node.

Fig. 12.26 | Traversing an XML document using the XML DOM. (Part 5 of 8.)

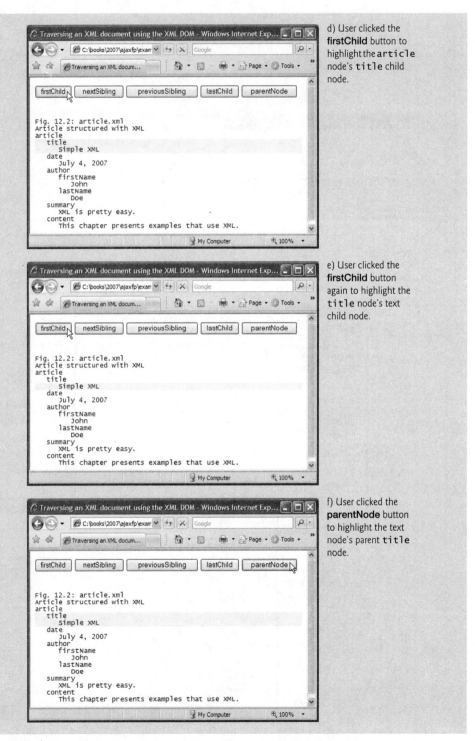

d) User clicked the **firstChild** button to highlight the `article` node's `title` child node.

e) User clicked the **firstChild** button again to highlight the `title` node's text child node.

f) User clicked the **parentNode** button to highlight the text node's parent `title` node.

Fig. 12.26 | Traversing an XML document using the XML DOM. (Part 6 of 8.)

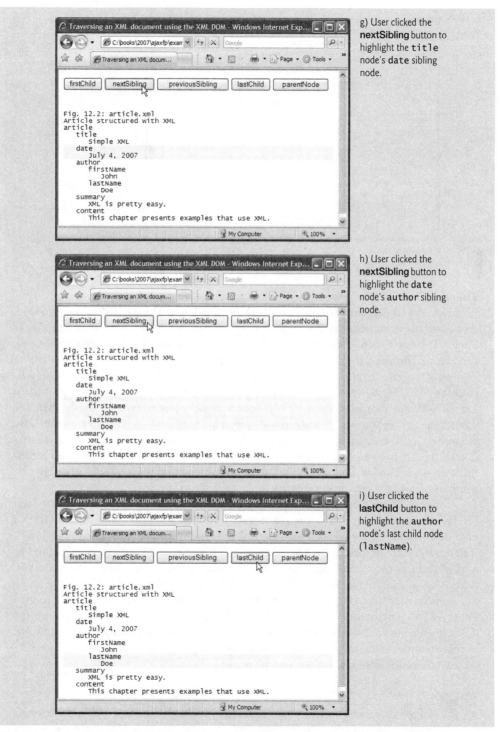

g) User clicked the **nextSibling** button to highlight the `title` node's `date` sibling node.

h) User clicked the **nextSibling** button to highlight the `date` node's `author` sibling node.

i) User clicked the **lastChild** button to highlight the `author` node's last child node (`lastName`).

Fig. 12.26 | Traversing an XML document using the XML DOM. (Part 7 of 8.)

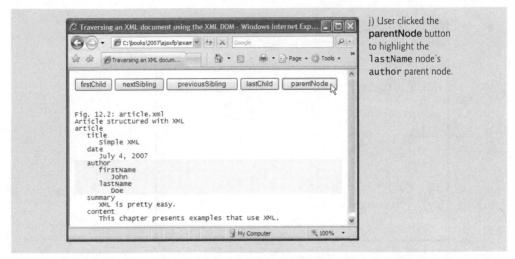

j) User clicked the
parentNode button
to highlight the
`lastName` node's
`author` parent node.

Fig. 12.26 | Traversing an XML document using the XML DOM. (Part 8 of 8.)

Function `loadXMLDocument`

Function `loadXMLDocument` (lines 24–49) receives the URL of an XML document to load, then loads the document based on whether the browser is Internet Explorer 7 (26–34) or Firefox 2 (lines 35–46)—the code for Firefox 2 works in several other browsers as well. Line 26 determines whether `window.`***ActiveXObject*** exists. If so, this indicates that the browser is Internet Explorer. Line 29 creates a Microsoft `ActiveXObject` that loads Microsoft's *MSXML parser*, which provides capabilities for manipulating XML documents. Line 30 indicates that we'd like the XML document to be loaded synchronously, then line 31 uses the `ActiveXObject`'s ***load* method** to load `article.xml`. When this completes, we call our `buildHTML` method (defined in lines 52–89) to construct an XHTML representation of the XML document. The expression `doc.childNodes` is a list of the XML document's top-level nodes. Line 33 calls our `displayDoc` function (lines 92–97) to display the contents of `article.xml` in `outputDiv`.

If the browser is Firefox 2, then the `document` object's ***implementation*** property and the `implementation` property's ***createDocument*** method will exist (lines 35–36). In this case, line 39 uses the `createDocument` method to create an empty XML document object. If necessary, you can specify the XML document's namespace as the first argument and its root element as the second argument. We used empty strings for both in this example. According to the site `www.w3schools.com/xml/xml_parser.asp`, the third argument is not implemented yet, so it should always be `null`. Line 40 calls its `load` method to load `article.xml`. Firefox loads the XML document asynchronously, so you must use the XML document's `onload` property to specify a function to call (an anonymous function in this example) when the document finishes loading. When this event occurs, lines 43–44 call `buildHTML` and `displayDoc` just as we did in lines 32–33.

Common Programming Error 12.11

Attempting to process the contents of a dynamically loaded XML document in Firefox before the document's `onload` event fires is a logic error. The document's contents are not available until the `onload` event fires.

Function *buildHTML*

Function buildHTML (lines 52–89) is a recursive function that receives a list of nodes as an argument. Line 54 increments the depth for indentation purposes. Lines 57–86 iterate through the nodes in the list. The switch statement (lines 59–85) uses the current node's *nodeType property* to determine whether the current node is an element (line 61), a text node (i.e., the text content of an element; line 73) or a comment node (line 74). If it is an element, then we begin a new div element in our XHTML (line 62) and give it a unique id. Then function spaceOutput (defined in lines 100–106) appends *nonbreaking spaces ( )*—i.e., spaces that the browser is not allowed to collapse or that can be used to keep words together—to indent the current element to the correct level. Line 64 appends the name of the current element using the node's *nodeName property*. If the current element has children, the length of the current node's childNodes list is nonzero and line 69 recursively calls buildHTML to append the current element's child nodes to the markup. When that recursive call completes, line 71 completes the div element that we started at line 62.

If the current element is a text node, lines 77–78 obtain the node's value with the *nodeValue property* and use the string method indexOf to determine whether the node's value starts with three or six spaces. Unfortunately, unlike MSMXL, Firefox's XML parser does not ignore the white space used for indentation in XML documents. Instead it creates text nodes containing just the space characters. The condition in lines 77–78 enables us to ignore these nodes in Firefox. If the node contains text, lines 80–82 append a new div to the markup and use the node's nodeValue property to insert that text in the div. Line 88 in buildHTML decrements the depth counter.

Portability Tip 12.4

Firefox's XML parser does not ignore white space used for indentation in XML documents. Instead, it creates text nodes containing the white-space characters.

Function *displayDoc*

In function displayDoc (lines 92–97), line 94 uses the DOM's getElementById method to obtain the outputDiv element and set its innerHTML property to the new markup generated by buildHTML. Then, line 95 sets variable current to refer to the div with id 'id1' in the new markup, and line 96 uses our setCurrentNodeStyle method (defined at lines 195–199) to highlight that div.

Functions *processFirstChild and processLastChild*

Function processFirstChild (lines 109–130) is invoked by the onclick event of the button at lines 205–206. If the current node has only one child and it's a text node (lines 111–112), line 114 displays an alert dialog indicating that there is no child node—we navigate only to nested XML elements in this example. If there are two or more children, line 118 stores the value of current in previous, and lines 120–123 set current to refer to its *firstChild* (if this child is not a text node) or its firstChild's *nextSibling* (if the firstChild is a text node)—again, this is to ensure that we navigate only to nodes that represent XML elements. Then lines 125–126 unhighlight the previous node and highlight the new current node. Function processLastChild (lines 162–178) works similarly, using the current node's *lastChild* property.

Functions processNextSibling *and* processPreviousSibling

Function processNextSibling (lines 133–144) first ensures that the current node is not the outputDiv and that nextSibling exists. If so, lines 137–140 adjust the previous and current nodes accordingly and update their highlighting. Function processPrevious-Sibling (lines 147–159) works similarly, ensuring first that the current node is not the outputDiv, that previousSibling exists and that previousSibling is not a text node.

Function processParentNode

Function processParentNode (lines 181–192) first checks whether the current node's **parentNode** is the XHTML page's body. If not, lines 185–188 adjust the previous and current nodes accordingly and update their highlighting.

Common DOM Properties

The tables in Figs. 12.27–12.32 describe many common DOM properties and methods. Some of the key DOM objects are **Node** (a node in the tree), **NodeList** (an ordered set of Nodes), **Document** (the document), **Element** (an element node), **Attr** (an attribute node) and **Text** (a text node). There are many more objects, properties and methods than we can possibly list here. Our XML Resource Center (www.deitel.com/XML/) includes links to various DOM reference websites.

Property/Method	Description
nodeType	An integer representing the node type.
nodeName	The name of the node.
nodeValue	A string or null depending on the node type.
parentNode	The parent node.
childNodes	A NodeList (Fig. 12.28) with all the children of the node.
firstChild	The first child in the Node's NodeList.
lastChild	The last child in the Node's NodeList.
previousSibling	The node preceding this node; null if there is no such node.
nextSibling	The node following this node; null if there is no such node.
attributes	A collection of Attr objects (Fig. 12.31) containing the attributes for this node.
insertBefore	Inserts the node (passed as the first argument) before the existing node (passed as the second argument). If the new node is already in the tree, it is removed before insertion. The same behavior is true for other methods that add nodes.
replaceChild	Replaces the second argument node with the first argument node.
removeChild	Removes the child node passed to it.
appendChild	Appends the node it receives to the list of child nodes.

Fig. 12.27 | Common Node properties and methods.

Property/Method	Description
item	Method that receives an index number and returns the element node at that index. Indices range from 0 to *length* − 1. You can also access the nodes in a NodeList via array indexing.
length	The total number of nodes in the list.

Fig. 12.28 | NodeList property and method.

Property/Method	Description
documentElement	The root node of the document.
createElement	Creates and returns an element node with the specified tag name.
createAttribute	Creates and returns an Attr node (Fig. 12.31) with the specified name and value.
createTextNode	Creates and returns a text node that contains the specified text.
getElementsByTagName	Returns a NodeList of all the nodes in the subtree with the name specified as the first argument, ordered as they would be encountered in a preorder traversal. An optional second argument specifies either the direct child nodes (0) or any descendant (1).

Fig. 12.29 | Document properties and methods.

Property/Method	Description
tagName	The name of the element.
getAttribute	Returns the value of the specified attribute.
setAttribute	Changes the value of the attribute passed as the first argument to the value passed as the second argument.
removeAttribute	Removes the specified attribute.
getAttributeNode	Returns the specified attribute node.
setAttributeNode	Adds a new attribute node with the specified name.

Fig. 12.30 | Element property and methods.

Property	Description
value	The specified attribute's value.
name	The name of the attribute.

Fig. 12.31 | Attr properties.

Property	Description
data	The text contained in the node.
length	The number of characters contained in the node.

Fig. 12.32 | Text methods.

Locating Data in XML Documents with XPath

Although you can use XML DOM capabilities to navigate through and manipulate nodes, this is not the most efficient means of locating data in an XML document's DOM tree. A simpler way to locate nodes is to search for lists of nodes matching search criteria that are written as XPath expressions. Recall that XPath (XML Path Language) provides a syntax for locating specific nodes in XML documents effectively and efficiently. XPath is a string-based language of expressions used by XML and many of its related technologies (such as XSLT, discussed in Section 12.8).

Figure 12.33 enables the user to enter XPath expressions in an XHTML form. When the user clicks the **Get Matches** button, the script applies the XPath expression to the XML DOM and displays the matching nodes. Figure 12.34 shows the XML document `sports.xml` that we use in this example. [*Note:* The versions of `sports.xml` presented in Fig. 12.34 and Fig. 12.20 are nearly identical. In the current example, we do not want to apply an XSLT, so we omit the processing instruction found in line 2 of Fig. 12.20. We also removed extra blank lines to save space.]

```
1    <?xml version = "1.0" encoding = "utf-8"?>
2    <!DOCTYPE html PUBLIC "-//W3C//DTD XHTML 1.0 Strict//EN"
3        "http://www.w3.org/TR/xhtml1/DTD/xhtml1-strict.dtd">
4
5    <!-- Fig. 12.33: xpath.html -->
6    <!-- Using XPath to locate nodes in an XML document. -->
7    <html xmlns = "http://www.w3.org/1999/xhtml">
8    <head>
9        <title>Using XPath to Locate Nodes in an XML Document</title>
10       <style type = "text/css">
11           #outputDiv { font: 10pt "Lucida Console", monospace; }
12       </style>
13       <script type = "text/javascript">
14       <!--
15       var doc; // variable to reference the XML document
16       var outputHTML = ""; // stores text to output in outputDiv
17       var browser = ""; // used to determine which browser is being used
18
19       // load XML document based on whether the browser is IE7 or Firefox 2
20       function loadXMLDocument( url )
21       {
22           if ( window.ActiveXObject ) // IE7
23           {
```

Fig. 12.33 | Using XPath to locate nodes in an XML document. (Part 1 of 3.)

```
24              // create IE7-specific XML document object
25              doc = new ActiveXObject( "Msxml2.DOMDocument.6.0" );
26              doc.async = false; // specifies synchronous loading of XML doc
27              doc.load( url ); // load the XML document specified by url
28              browser = "IE7"; // set browser
29           } // end if
30           else if ( document.implementation &&
31              document.implementation.createDocument ) // other browsers
32           {
33              // create XML document object
34              doc = document.implementation.createDocument( "", "", null );
35              doc.load( url ); // load the XML document specified by url
36              browser = "FF2"; // set browser
37           } // end else
38           else // not supported
39              alert( 'This script is not supported by your browser' );
40        } // end function loadXMLDocument
41
42        // display the XML document
43        function displayDoc()
44        {
45           document.getElementById( "outputDiv" ).innerHTML = outputHTML;
46        } // end function displayDoc
47
48        // obtain and apply XPath expression
49        function processXPathExpression()
50        {
51           var xpathExpression = document.getElementById( "inputField" ).value
52           outputHTML = "";
53
54           if ( browser == "IE7" )
55           {
56              var result = doc.selectNodes( xpathExpression );
57
58              for ( var i = 0; i < result.length; i++ )
59                 outputHTML += "<div style='clear: both'>" +
60                    result.item( i ).text + "</div>";
61           } // end if
62           else // browser == "FF2"
63           {
64              var result = document.evaluate( xpathExpression, doc, null,
65                 XPathResult.ANY_TYPE, null );
66              var current = result.iterateNext();
67
68              while ( current )
69              {
70                 outputHTML += "<div style='clear: both'>" +
71                    current.textContent + "</div>";
72                 current = result.iterateNext();
73              } // end while
74           } // end else
75
```

Fig. 12.33 | Using XPath to locate nodes in an XML document. (Part 2 of 3.)

```
76          displayDoc();
77      } // end function processXPathExpression
78      // -->
79      </script>
80   </head>
81   <body id = "body" onload = "loadXMLDocument( 'sports.xml' );">
82      <form action = "" onsubmit = "return false;">
83          <input id = "inputField" type = "text" style = "width: 200px"/>
84          <input type = "submit" value = "Get Matches"
85              onclick = "processXPathExpression()"/>
86      </form><br/>
87      <div id = "outputDiv"></div>
88   </body>
89   </html>
```

Fig. 12.33 | Using XPath to locate nodes in an XML document. (Part 3 of 3.)

```
 1   <?xml version = "1.0"?>
 2
 3   <!-- Fig. 12.34: sports.xml -->
 4   <!-- Sports Database       -->
 5   <sports>
 6     <game id = "783">
 7         <name>Cricket</name>
 8         <paragraph>
 9            More popular among commonwealth nations.
10         </paragraph>
11     </game>
12     <game id = "239">
13         <name>Baseball</name>
14         <paragraph>
15            More popular in America.
16         </paragraph>
17     </game>
18     <game id = "418">
19         <name>Soccer (Futbol)</name>
20         <paragraph>
21            Most popular sport in the world.
22         </paragraph>
23     </game>
24   </sports>
```

Fig. 12.34 | XML document that describes various sports.

The program of Fig. 12.33 loads the XML document sports.xml (Fig. 12.34) using the same techniques we presented in Fig. 12.26, so we focus on only the new features in this example. Internet Explorer 7 (MSXML) and Firefox 2 handle XPath processing differently, so this example declares the variable browser (line 17) to store the browser that loaded the page. In function loadDocument (lines 20–40), lines 28 and 36 assign a string to variable browser indicating the appropriate browser.

When the body of this XHTML document loads, its onload event calls loadDocument (line 81) to load the sports.xml file. The user specifies the XPath expression in the input element at line 83. When the user clicks the **Get Matches** button (lines 84–85), its onclick event handler invokes our processXPathExpression function to locate any matches and display the results in outputDiv (line 87).

Function processXPathExpression (lines 49–77) first obtains the XPath expression (line 51). The document object's getElementById method returns the element with the id "inputField"; then we use its value property to get the XPath expression. Lines 54–61 apply the XPath expression in Internet Explorer 7, and lines 62–74 apply the XPath expression in Firefox 2. In IE7, the XML document object's *selectNodes method* receives an XPath expression as an argument and returns a collection of elements that match the expression. Lines 58–60 iterate through the results and mark up each one in a separate div element. After this loop completes, line 76 displays the generated markup in outputDiv.

For Firefox 2, lines 64–65 invoke the XML document object's *evaluate method*, which receives five arguments—the XPath expression, the document to apply the expression to, a namespace resolver, a result type and an XPathResult object into which to place the results. If the last argument is null, the function simply returns a new *XPathResult object* containing the matches. The namespace resolver argument can be null if you are not using XML namespace prefixes in the XPath processing. Lines 66–73 iterate through the XPathResult and mark up the results. Line 66 invokes the XPathResult's iter-ateNext method to position to the first result. If there is a result, the condition in line 68 will be true, and lines 70–71 create a div for that result. Line 72 then positions to the next result. After this loop completes, line 76 displays the generated markup in outputDiv.

Figure 12.35 summarizes the XPath expressions that we demonstrate in Fig. 12.33's sample outputs. For more information on using XPath in Firefox, visit the site developer.mozilla.org/en/docs/XPath. For more information on using XPath in Internet Explorer, visit msdn.microsoft.com/msdnmag/issues/0900/xml/.

Expression	Description
/sports	Matches all sports nodes that are child nodes of the document root node.
/sports/game	Matches all game nodes that are child nodes of sports, which is a child of the document root.
/sports/game/name	Matches all name nodes that are child nodes of game. The game is a child of sports, which is a child of the document root.
/sports/game/paragraph	Matches all paragraph nodes that are child nodes of game. The game is a child of sports, which is a child of the document root.
/sports/game [@id='239']	Matches the game node with the id number 239. The game is a child of sports, which is a child of the document root.
/sports/game [name='Cricket']	Matches all game nodes that contain a child element whose name is Cricket. The game is a child of sports, which is a child of the document root.

Fig. 12.35 | XPath expressions and descriptions.

12.10 RSS

RSS stands for *RDF (Resource Description Framework) Site Summary* and is also known as *Rich Site Summary* and *Really Simple Syndication*. RSS is an XML format used to syndicate website content, such as news articles, blog entries, product reviews, podcasts, vodcasts and more for inclusion on other websites. An RSS feed contains an *rss root element* with a version attribute and a *channel child element* with *item subelements*. Depending on the RSS version, the channel and item elements have certain required and optional child elements. The item elements provide the feed subscriber with a link to a web page or file, a title and description of the page or file. The most commonly used RSS feed versions are 0.91, 1.0, and 2.0, with RSS 2.0 being the most popular version. We discuss only RSS version 2.0 in this section.

RSS version 2.0, introduced in 2002, builds upon the RSS 0.9x versions. Version 2.0 does not contain length limitations or item element limitations of earlier versions, makes some formerly required elements optional, and adds new channel and item subelements. Removing length limitations on item descriptions allows RSS feeds to contain entire articles, blog entries and other web content. You can also have partial feeds that provide only a summary of the syndicated content. Partial feeds require the RSS subscriber to visit a website to view the complete content. RSS 2.0 allows item elements to contain an enclosure element providing the location of a media file that is related to the item. Such enclosures enable syndication of audio and video (such as podcasts and vodcasts) via RSS feeds.

By providing up-to-date, linkable content for anyone to use, RSS enables website developers to draw more traffic. It also allows users to get news and information from many sources easily and reduces content development time. RSS simplifies importing information from portals, weblogs and news sites. Any piece of information can be syndicated via RSS, not just news. After putting information in RSS format, an RSS program, such as a feed reader or aggregator, can check the feed for changes and react to them. For more details on RSS and for links to many RSS sites, visit our RSS Resource Center at www.deitel.com/RSS.

RSS 2.0 channel *and* item *Elements*

In RSS 2.0, the required child elements of channel are description, link and title, and the required child element of an item is either title or description. Figures 12.36–12.37 overview the child elements of channels and items, respectively.

Element	Description
title	The name of the channel or feed.
link	The URL to the website of the channel or feed the RSS is coming from.
description	A description of the channel or feed.
language	The language the channel is in, using W3C language values.
copyright	The copyright material of the channel or feed.
managingEditor	The e-mail address of the editor of the channel or feed.
webMaster	The e-mail address for the webmaster of the channel or feed.
pubDate	The date of the channel or feed release, using the RFC 822 Date and Time Specification—e.g., Sun, 14 Jan 2007 8:00:00 EST.
lastBuildDate	The last date the channel or feed was changed, using the RFC 822 Date and Time Specification.
category	The category (or several categories) of the channel or feed. This element has an optional attribute tag.
generator	Indicates the program that was used to generate the channel or feed.

Fig. 12.36 | channel elements and descriptions. (Part 1 of 2.)

Element	Description
docs	The URL of the documentation for the format used in the RSS file.
cloud	Specifies a SOAP web service that supports the rssCloud interface (cyber.law.harvard.edu/rss/soapMeetsRss.html#rsscloudInterface).
ttl	(Time To Live) A number of minutes for how long the channel or feed can be cached before refreshing from the source.
image	The GIF, JPEG or PNG image that can be displayed with the channel or feed. This element contains the required children title, link and url, and the optional children description, height and width.
rating	The PICS (Platform for Internet Content Selection) rating for the channel or feed.
textInput	Specifies a text input box to display with the channel or feed. This element contains the required children title, name, link and description.
skipHours	Tells aggregators which hours they can skip checking for new content.
skipDays	Tells aggregators which days they can skip checking for new content.

Fig. 12.36 | channel elements and descriptions. (Part 2 of 2.)

Element	Description
title	The title of the item.
link	The URL of the item.
description	The description of the item.
author	The e-mail address of the author of the item.
category	The category (or several categories) of the item. This element has an optional attribute tag.
comments	The URL of a page for comments related to the item.
enclosure	The location of a media object attached to the item. This element has the required attributes type, url and length.
guid	(Globally Unique Identifier) A string that uniquely identifies the item.
pubDate	The date the item was published, using the RFC 822 Date and Time Specification—e.g., Sun, 14 Jan 2007 8:00:00 EST.
source	The RSS channel the item came from. This element has a required attribute url.

Fig. 12.37 | item elements and descriptions.

Browsers and RSS Feeds

Many of the latest web browsers can now view RSS feeds, determine whether a website offers feeds, allow you to subscribe to feeds and create feed lists. An *RSS aggregator* keeps tracks of many RSS feeds and brings together information from the separate feeds. There are many RSS aggregators available, including Bloglines, BottomFeeder, FeedDemon, Microsoft Internet Explorer 7, Mozilla Firefox 2.0, My Yahoo, NewsGator and Opera 9.

To allow browsers and search engines to determine whether a web page contains an RSS feed, a link element can be added to the head of a page as follows:

```
<link rel = "alternate" type = "application/rss+xml" title = "RSS"
href = "file">
```

Many sites provide RSS feed validators. Some examples of RSS feed validators are validator.w3.org/feed, feedvalidator.org, and www.validome.org/rss-atom/.

Creating a Feed Aggregator

The DOM and XSL can be used to create RSS aggregators. A simple RSS aggregator uses an XSL stylesheet to format RSS feeds as XHTML. Figure 12.38 loads two XML documents—an RSS feed (a small portion of which is shown in Fig. 12.39) and an XSL style sheet—then uses JavaScript to apply an XSL transformation to the RSS content and render it on the page. You'll notice as we discuss this program that there is little commonality between Internet Explorer 7 and Firefox with regard to programmatically applying XSL transformations. This is one of the reasons that JavaScript libraries have become popular in web development—they tend to hide such browser-specific issues from you. We discuss the Dojo toolkit—one of many popular JavaScript libraries—in Section 13.8. For more information on JavaScript libraries, see our JavaScript and Ajax Resource Centers (www.deitel.com/JavaScript/ and www.deitel.com/Ajax/, respectively).

Determining the Browser Type and Loading the Documents

When this page first loads, lines 19–23 (Fig. 12.38) determine whether the browser is Internet Explorer 7 or Firefox 2 and store the result in variable browser for use throughout the script. After the body of this XHTML document loads, its onload event calls function start (lines 26–48) to load RSS and XSL files as XML documents, and to transform the RSS. Since Internet Explorer 7 can download the files synchronously, lines 30–33 perform the loading, transformation and display steps sequentially. As mentioned previously, Firefox 2 loads the files asynchronously. For this reason, line 37 starts loading the rss.xsl document (included with this example's code), and lines 38–46 register an onload event handler for that document. When the document finishes loading, line 40 begins loading the deitel-20.xml RSS document. Lines 41–45 register an onload event handler for this second document. When it finishes loading, lines 43–44 perform the transformation and display the results.

Transforming the RSS to XHTML

Function applyTransform (Fig. 12.38, lines 75–96) performs the browser-specific XSL transformations using the RSS document and XSL document it receives as arguments. Line 81 uses the MSXML object's built-in XSLT capabilities to apply the transformations. Method *transformNode* is invoked on the rssDocument object and receives the xslDocument object as an argument.

```
1   <?xml version = "1.0" encoding = "utf-8"?>
2   <!DOCTYPE html PUBLIC "-//W3C//DTD XHTML 1.0 Strict//EN"
3      "http://www.w3.org/TR/xhtml1/DTD/xhtml1-strict.dtd">
4
5   <!-- Fig. 12.38: RssViewer.html -->
6   <!-- Simple RSS viewer. -->
7   <html xmlns = "http://www.w3.org/1999/xhtml">
8   <head>
9      <title>Simple RSS Viewer</title>
10     <style type = "text/css">
11        #outputDiv { font: 12px Verdana, Geneva, Arial,
12                     Helvetica, sans-serif; }
13     </style>
14     <script type = "text/javascript">
15     <!--
16     var browser = ""; // used to determine which browser is being used
17
18     // is the browser Internet Explorer 7 or Firefox 2?
19     if ( window.ActiveXObject ) // IE7
20        browser = "IE7";
21     else if ( document.implementation &&
22        document.implementation.createDocument ) // FF2 and other browsers
23        browser = "FF2";
24
25     // load both the RSS feed and the XSL file to process it
26     function start()
27     {
28        if ( browser == "IE7" )
29        {
30           var xsl = loadXMLDocument( 'rss.xsl' ); // load XSL file
31           var rss = loadXMLDocument( 'deitel-20.xml' ); // load RSS feed
32           var result = applyTransform( rss, xsl ); // apply transform
33           displayTransformedRss( result ); // display feed info
34        } // end if
35        else if ( browser == "FF2" )
36        {
37           var xsl = loadXMLDocument( 'rss.xsl' ); // load XSL file
38           xsl.onload = function() // function to execute when xsl loads
39           {
40              var rss = loadXMLDocument( 'deitel-20.xml' ); // load RSS fee
41              rss.onload = function() // function to execute when rss loads
42              {
43                 var result = applyTransform( rss, xsl ); // apply transfor
44                 displayTransformedRss( result ); // display feed info
45              } // end onload event handler for rss
46           } // end onload event handler for xsl
47        } // end else
48     } // end function start
49
50     // load XML document based on whether the browser is IE7 or Firefox 2
51     function loadXMLDocument( url )
52     {
53        var doc = ""; // variable to manage loading file
```

Fig. 12.38 | Rendering an RSS feed in a web page using XSLT and JavaScript. (Part 1 of 3.)

```
54
55         if ( browser == "IE7" ) // IE7
56         {
57             // create IE7-specific XML document object
58             doc = new ActiveXObject( "Msxml2.DOMDocument.6.0" );
59             doc.async = false; // specifies synchronous loading of XML doc
60             doc.load( url ); // load the XML document specified by url
61         } // end if
62         else if ( browser == "FF2" ) // other browsers
63         {
64             // create XML document object
65             doc = document.implementation.createDocument( "", "", null );
66             doc.load( url ); // load the XML document specified by url
67         } // end else
68         else // not supported
69             alert( 'This script is not supported by your browser' );
70
71         return doc; // return the loaded document
72     } // end function loadXMLDocument
73
74     // apply XSL transformation and show results
75     function applyTransform( rssDocument, xslDocument )
76     {
77         var result; // stores transformed RSS
78
79         // transform the RSS feed to XHTML
80         if ( browser == "IE7" )
81             result = rssDocument.transformNode( xslDocument );
82         else // browser == "FF2"
83         {
84             // create Firefox object to perform transformation
85             var xsltProcessor = new XSLTProcessor();
86
87             // specify XSL stylesheet to use in transformation
88             xsltProcessor.importStylesheet( xslDocument );
89
90             // apply the transformation
91             result =
92                 xsltProcessor.transformToFragment( rssDocument, document );
93         } // end else
94
95         return result; // return the transformed RSS
96     } // end function applyTransform
97
98     // display the XML document and highlight the first child
99     function displayTransformedRss( resultXHTML )
100    {
101        if ( browser == "IE7" )
102            document.getElementById( "outputDiv" ).innerHTML = resultXHTML;
103        else // browser == "FF2"
104            document.getElementById( "outputDiv" ).appendChild(
105                resultXHTML );
106    } // end function displayTransformedRss
```

Fig. 12.38 | Rendering an RSS feed in a web page using XSLT and JavaScript. (Part 2 of 3.)

```
107    // -->
108    </script>
109  </head>
110  <body id = "body" onload = "start();">
111    <div id = "outputDiv"></div>
112  </body>
113  </html>
```

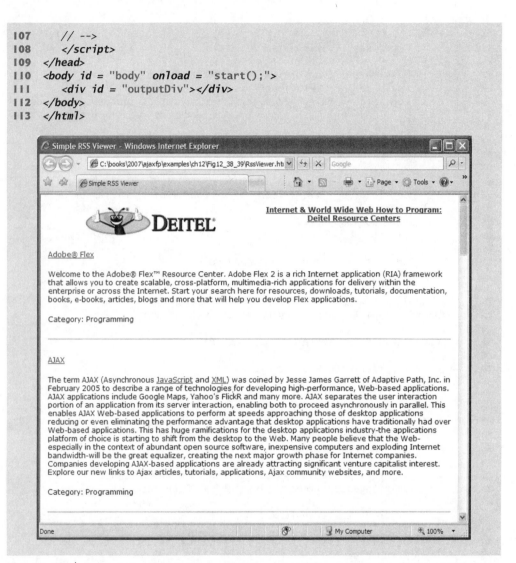

Fig. 12.38 | Rendering an RSS feed in a web page using XSLT and JavaScript. (Part 3 of 3.)

```
1    <?xml version="1.0" encoding="utf-8"?>
2
3    <!-- Fig. 12.39: deitel-20.xml -->
4    <!-- RSS 2.0 feed of Deitel Resource Centers -->
5    <rss version="2.0">
6      <channel>
7        <title>
8            Internet &#38; World Wide Web How to Program:
9            Deitel Resource Centers
10       </title>
```

Fig. 12.39 | RSS 2.0 sample feed. (Part 1 of 2.)

```
11        <link>http://www.deitel.com/ResourceCenters.html</link>
12        <description>
13           Check out our growing network of Resource Centers that focus on
14           many of today's hottest programming, Web 2.0 and technology
15           topics. Start your search here for downloads, tutorials,
16           documentation, books, e-books, blogs, RSS feeds, journals,
17           articles, training, webcasts, podcasts, videos and more.
18        </description>
19        <languague>en-us</languague>
20        <image>
21           <url>
22              http://www.deitel.com/Portals/0/deitel_transparent_smaller.png
23           </url>
24           <title>Deitel.com</title>
25           <link>http://www.deitel.com/</link>
26        </image>
27
28        <item>
29           <title>Adobe® Flex</title>
30           <link>http://www.deitel.com/Flex/</link>
31           <description>
32              <p>
33              Welcome to the Adobe® Flex™ Resource Center. Adobe Flex 2 is a
34              rich Internet application (RIA) framework that allows you to
35              create scalable, cross-platform, multimedia-rich applications
36              for delivery within the enterprise or across the Internet.
37              Start your search here for resources, downloads, tutorials,
38              documentation, books, e-books, articles, blogs and more that
39              will help you develop Flex applications.
40              </p>
41           </description>
42           <category>Programming</category>
43        </item>
44     </channel>
45  </rss>
```

Fig. 12.39 | RSS 2.0 sample feed. (Part 2 of 2.)

Firefox provides built-in XSLT processing in the form of the **XSLTProcessor** object (created at line 85). After creating this object, you use its **importStylesheet** method to specify the XSL stylesheet you'd like to apply (line 88). Finally, lines 91–92 apply the transformation by invoking the XSLTProcessor object's **transformToFragment** method, which returns a document fragment—i.e., a piece of a document. In our case, the rss.xsl document transforms the RSS into an XHTML table element that we'll append to the outputDiv element in our XHTML page. The arguments to transformToFragment are the document to transform and the document object to which the transformed fragment will belong. To learn more about XSLTProcessor, visit developer.mozilla.org/en/docs/The_XSLT/JavaScript_Interface_in_Gecko.

In each browser's case, after the transformation, the resulting XHTML markup is assigned to variable result and returned from function applyTransform. Then function displayTransformedRss is called.

Displaying the XHTML Markup

Function `displayTransformedRss` (lines 99–106) displays the transformed RSS in the `outputDiv` element (line 111 in the body). In both Internet Explorer 7 and Firefox 2, we use the DOM method `getElementById` to obtain the `outputDiv` element. In Internet Explorer 7, the node's `innerHTML` property is used to add the table as a child of the `outputDiv` element (line 102). In Firefox, the node's `appendChild` method must be used to append the table (a document fragment) to the `outputDiv` element.

12.11 Web Resources

www.deitel.com/XML/

The Deitel XML Resource Center focuses on the vast amount of free XML content available online, plus some for-sale items. Start your search here for tools, downloads, tutorials, podcasts, wikis, documentation, conferences, FAQs, books, e-books, sample chapters, articles, newsgroups, forums, downloads from CNET's download.com, jobs and contract opportunities, and more that will help you develop XML applications.

13

Ajax-Enabled Rich Internet Applications

OBJECTIVES

In this chapter you will learn:

- What Ajax is and why it is important for building Rich Internet Applications.

- What asynchronous requests are and how they help give web applications the feel of desktop applications.

- What the `XMLHttpRequest` object is and how it's used to create and manage asynchronous requests to servers and to receive asynchronous responses from servers.

- Methods and properties of the `XMLHttpRequest` object.

- How to use XHTML, JavaScript, CSS, XML, JSON and the DOM in Ajax applications.

- How to use Ajax frameworks and toolkits, specifically Dojo, to conveniently create robust Ajax-enabled Rich Internet Applications.

- About resources for studying Ajax-related issues such as security, performance, debugging, the "back-button problem" and more.

13.1 Introduction

Despite the tremendous technological growth of the Internet over the past decade, the usability of web applications has lagged behind compared to that of desktop applications. Every significant interaction in a web application results in a waiting period while the application communicates over the Internet with a server. *Rich Internet Applications (RIAs)* are web applications that approximate the look, feel and usability of desktop applications. RIAs have two key attributes—performance and a rich GUI.

RIA performance comes from *Ajax (Asynchronous JavaScript and XML)*, which uses client-side scripting to make web applications more responsive. Ajax applications separate client-side user interaction and server communication, and run them in parallel, reducing the delays of server-side processing normally experienced by the user.

There are many ways to implement Ajax functionality. *"Raw" Ajax* uses JavaScript to send asynchronous requests to the server, then updates the page using the DOM (see Section 13.5). "Raw" Ajax is best suited for creating small Ajax components that asynchronously update a section of the page. However, when writing "raw" Ajax you need to deal directly with cross-browser portability issues, making it impractical for developing large-scale applications. These portability issues are hidden by *Ajax toolkits*, such as *Dojo* (Section 13.8), *Prototype, Script.aculo.us* and ASP.NET Ajax, which provide powerful ready-to-use controls and functions that enrich web applications, and simplify JavaScript coding by making it cross-browser compatible.

Traditional web applications use XHTML forms (Chapter 2) to build simple and thin GUIs compared to the rich GUIs of Windows, Macintosh and desktop systems in general. We achieve rich GUI in RIAs with Ajax toolkits and with RIA environments such as Adobe Flex (Chapter 16) and JavaServer Faces (Chapters 22–23). Such toolkits and environments provide powerful ready-to-use controls and functions that enrich web applications.

Previous chapters discussed XHTML, CSS, JavaScript, dynamic HTML, the DOM and XML. This chapter uses these technologies to build Ajax-enabled web applications. The client-side of Ajax applications is written in XHTML and CSS, and uses JavaScript to add functionality to the user interface. XML is used to structure the data passed between the server and the client. We'll also use JSON (JavaScript Object Notation) for this purpose. The Ajax component that manages interaction with the server is usually implemented with JavaScript's *XMLHttpRequest object*—commonly abbreviated as XHR. The server processing can be implemented using any server-side technology, such as PHP, ASP. NET, JavaServer Faces and Ruby on Rails—each of which we cover in later chapters.

This chapter begins with several examples that build basic Ajax applications using JavaScript and the `XMLHttpRequest` object. We then build an Ajax application with a rich calendar GUI using the Dojo Ajax toolkit. In subsequent chapters, we use tools such as Adobe Flex, Microsoft Silverlight and JavaServer Faces to build RIAs using Ajax. In Chapter 20, we'll demonstrate features of the Prototype and Script.aculo.us Ajax libraries, which come with the Ruby on Rails framework (and can be downloaded separately). Prototype provides capabilities similar to Dojo. Script.aculo.us provides many "eye candy" effects that enable you to beautify your Ajax applications and create rich interfaces. In Chapter 23, we present Ajax-enabled JavaServer Faces (JSF) components. JSF uses Dojo to implement many of its client-side Ajax capabilities.

13.2 Traditional Web Applications vs. Ajax Applications

In this section, we consider the key differences between traditional web applications and Ajax-based web applications.

Traditional Web Applications

Figure 13.1 presents the typical interactions between the client and the server in a traditional web application, such as one that uses a user registration form. First, the user fills in the form's fields, then submits the form (Fig. 13.1, *Step 1*). The browser generates a request to the server, which receives the request and processes it (*Step 2*). The server generates and sends a response containing the exact page that the browser will render (*Step 3*), which causes the browser to load the new page (*Step 4*) and temporarily makes the browser window blank. Note that the client *waits* for the server to respond and *reloads the entire page* with the data from the response (*Step 4*). While such a *synchronous request* is being pro-

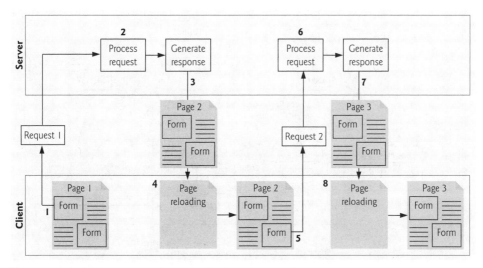

Fig. 13.1 | Classic web application reloading the page for every user interaction.

cessed on the server, the user cannot interact with the client web page. Frequent long periods of waiting, due perhaps to Internet congestion, have led some users to refer to the World Wide Web as the "World Wide Wait." If the user interacts with and submits another form, the process begins again (*Steps 5–8*).

This model was originally designed for a web of hypertext documents—what some people call the "brochure web." As the web evolved into a full-scale applications platform, the model shown in Fig. 13.1 yielded "choppy" application performance. Every full-page refresh required users to re-establish their understanding of the full-page contents. Users began to demand a model that would yield the responsive feel of desktop applications.

Ajax Web Applications

Ajax applications add a layer between the client and the server to manage communication between the two (Fig. 13.2). When the user interacts with the page, the client creates an XMLHttpRequest object to manage a request (*Step 1*). The XMLHttpRequest object sends the request to the server (*Step 2*) and awaits the response. The requests are ***asynchronous***, so the user can continue interacting with the application on the client-side while the server processes the earlier request concurrently. Other user interactions could result in additional requests to the server (*Steps 3* and *4*). Once the server responds to the original request (*Step 5*), the XMLHttpRequest object that issued the request calls a client-side function to process the data returned by the server. This function—known as a ***callback function***—uses ***partial page updates*** (*Step 6*) to display the data in the existing web page *without reloading the entire page*. At the same time, the server may be responding to the second request (*Step 7*) and the client-side may be starting to do another partial page update (*Step 8*). The callback function updates only a designated part of the page. Such partial page updates help make web applications more responsive, making them feel more like desktop applications. The web application does not load a new page while the user interacts with it.

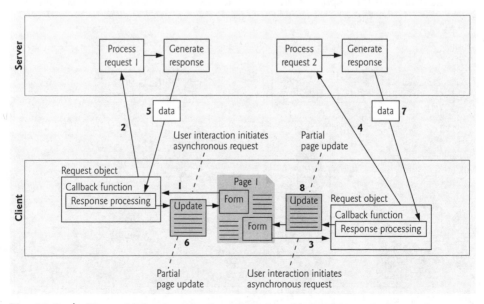

Fig. 13.2 | Ajax-enabled web application interacting with the server asynchronously.

13.3 Rich Internet Applications (RIAs) with Ajax

Ajax improves the user experience by making interactive web applications more responsive. Consider a registration form with a number of fields (e.g., first name, last name e-mail address, telephone number, etc.) and a **Register** (or **Submit**) button that sends the entered data to the server. Usually each field has rules that the user's entries have to follow (e.g., valid e-mail address, valid telephone number, etc.).

When the user clicks **Register**, a classic XHTML form sends the server all of the data to be validated (Fig. 13.3). While the server is validating the data, the user cannot interact with the page. The server finds invalid data, generates a new page identifying the errors in the form and sends it back to the client—which renders the page in the browser. Once the user fixes the errors and clicks the **Register** button, the cycle repeats until no errors are found, then the data is stored on the server. The entire page reloads every time the user submits invalid data.

Ajax-enabled forms are more interactive. Rather than sending the entire form to be validated, entries are validated dynamically as the user enters data into the fields. For example, consider a website registration form that requires a unique e-mail address. When the user enters an e-mail address into the appropriate field, then moves to the next form field to continue entering data, an asynchronous request is sent to the server to validate the e-mail address. If the e-mail address is not unique, the server sends an error message that is displayed on the page informing the user of the problem (Fig. 13.4). By sending each entry asynchronously, the user can address each invalid entry quickly, versus making edits and resubmitting the entire form repeatedly until all entries are valid. Asynchronous

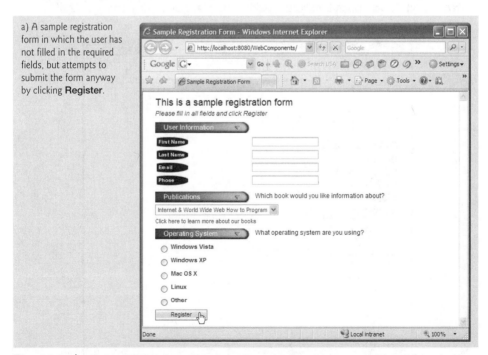

a) A sample registration form in which the user has not filled in the required fields, but attempts to submit the form anyway by clicking **Register**.

Fig. 13.3 | Classic XHTML form: User submits entire form to server, which validates the data entered (if any). Server responds indicating fields with invalid or missing data. (Part 1 of 2.)

b) The server responds by indicating all the form fields with missing or invalid data. The user must correct the problems and resubmit the entire form repeatedly until all errors are corrected.

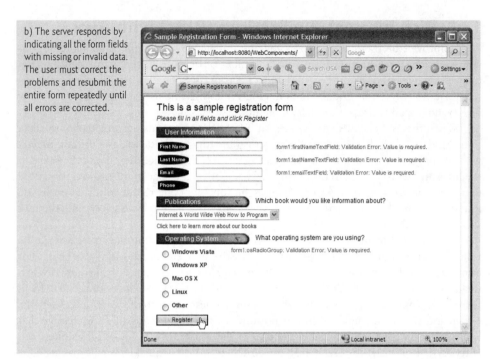

Fig. 13.3 | Classic XHTML form: User submits entire form to server, which validates the data entered (if any). Server responds indicating fields with invalid or missing data. (Part 2 of 2.)

Fig. 13.4 | Ajax-enabled form shows errors asynchronously when user moves to another field.

requests could also be used to fill some fields based on previous fields (e.g., automatically filling in the "city" and "state" fields based on the zip code entered by the user).

13.4 History of Ajax

The term Ajax was coined by Jesse James Garrett of Adaptive Path in February 2005, when he was presenting the previously unnamed technology to a client. The technologies of Ajax (XHTML, JavaScript, CSS, the DOM and XML) have all existed for many years.

Asynchronous page updates can be traced back to earlier browsers. In the 1990s, Netscape's LiveScript made it possible to include scripts in web pages (e.g., web forms) that could run on the client. LiveScript evolved into JavaScript. In 1998, Microsoft introduced the XMLHttpRequest object to create and manage asynchronous requests and responses. Popular applications like Flickr and Google's Gmail use the XMLHttpRequest object to update pages dynamically. For example, Flickr uses the technology for its text editing, tagging and organizational features; Gmail continuously checks the server for new e-mail; and Google Maps allows you to drag a map in any direction, downloading the new areas on the map without reloading the entire page.

The name Ajax immediately caught on and brought attention to its component technologies. Ajax has become one of the hottest web-development technologies, enabling webtop applications to challenge the dominance of established desktop applications.

13.5 "Raw" Ajax Example Using the XMLHttpRequest Object

In this section, we use the XMLHttpRequest object to create and manage asynchronous requests. The XMLHttpRequest object (which resides on the client) is the layer between the client and the server that manages asynchronous requests in Ajax applications. This object is supported on most browsers, though they may implement it differently—a common issue in JavaScript programming. To initiate an asynchronous request (shown in Fig. 13.5), you create an instance of the XMLHttpRequest object, then use its open method to set up the request and its send method to initiate the request. We summarize the XMLHttpRequest properties and methods in Figs. 13.6–13.7.

Figure 13.5 presents an Ajax application in which the user interacts with the page by moving the mouse over book-cover images. We use the onmouseover and onmouseout events (discussed in Chapter 11) to trigger events when the user moves the mouse over and out of an image, respectively. The onmouseover event calls function getContent with the URL of the document containing the book's description. The function makes this request asynchronously using an XMLHttpRequest object. When the XMLHttpRequest object receives the response, the book description is displayed below the book images. When the user moves the mouse out of the image, the onmouseout event calls function clearContent to clear the display box. These tasks are accomplished without reloading the page on the client. You can test-drive this example at test.deitel.com/examples/ajaxfp/ajax/fig13_05/SwitchContent.html.

Performance Tip 13.1

When an Ajax application requests a file from a server, such as an XHTML document or an image, the browser typically caches that file. Subsequent requests for the same file can load it from the browser's cache rather than making the round trip to the server again.

Software Engineering Observation 13.1

*For security purposes, the XMLHttpRequest object doesn't allow a web application to request resources from domain names other than the one that served the application. For this reason, the web application and its resources must reside on the same web server (this could be a web server on your local computer). This is commonly known as the **same origin policy (SOP)**. SOP aims to close a vulnerability called **cross-site scripting**, also known as **XSS**, which allows an attacker to compromise a website's security by injecting a malicious script onto the page from another domain. To learn more about XSS visit en.wikipedia.org/wiki/XSS. To get content from another domain securely, you can implement a server-side proxy—an application on the web application's web server—that can make requests to other servers on the web application's behalf.*

Asynchronous Requests

The function getContent (lines 19–35) sends the asynchronous request. Line 24 creates the XMLHttpRequest object, which manages the asynchronous request. We store the object in the global variable asyncRequest (declared at line 16) so that it can be accessed anywhere in the script.

```
1    <?xml version = "1.0" encoding = "utf-8"?>
2    <!DOCTYPE html PUBLIC "-//W3C//DTD XHTML 1.0 Strict//EN"
3       "http://www.w3.org/TR/xhtml1/DTD/xhtml1-strict.dtd">
4
5    <!-- Fig. 13.5: SwitchContent.html -->
6    <!-- Asynchronously display content without reloading the page. -->
7    <html xmlns = "http://www.w3.org/1999/xhtml">
8    <head>
9       <style type="text/css">
10         .box { border: 1px solid black;
11                padding: 10px }
12      </style>
13      <title>Switch Content Asynchronously</title>
14      <script type = "text/javascript" language = "JavaScript">
15         <!--
16         var asyncRequest; // variable to hold XMLHttpRequest object
17
18         // set up and send the asynchronous request
19         function getContent( url )
20         {
21            // attempt to create the XMLHttpRequest and make the request
22            try
23            {
24               asyncRequest = new XMLHttpRequest(); // create request object
25
26               // register event handler
27               asyncRequest.onreadystatechange = stateChange;
28               asyncRequest.open( 'GET', url, true ); // prepare the request
29               asyncRequest.send( null ); // send the request
30            } // end try
```

Fig. 13.5 | Asynchronously display content without reloading the page. (Part 1 of 3.)

```
31          catch ( exception )
32          {
33             alert( 'Request failed.' );
34          } // end catch
35       } // end function getContent
36
37       // displays the response data on the page
38       function stateChange()
39       {
40          if ( asyncRequest.readyState == 4 && asyncRequest.status == 200 )
41          {
42             document.getElementById( 'contentArea' ).innerHTML =
43                asyncRequest.responseText; // places text in contentArea
44          } // end if
45       } // end function stateChange
46
47       // clear the content of the box
48       function clearContent()
49       {
50          document.getElementById( 'contentArea' ).innerHTML = '';
51       } // end function clearContent
52       // -->
53    </script>
54 </head>
55 <body>
56    <h1>Mouse over a book for more information.</h1>
57    <img src =
58       "http://test.deitel.com/examples/iw3htp4/ajax/thumbs/cpphtp6.jpg"
59       onmouseover = 'getContent( "cpphtp6.html" )'
60       onmouseout = 'clearContent()'/>
61    <img src =
62       "http://test.deitel.com/examples/iw3htp4/ajax/thumbs/iw3htp4.jpg"
63       onmouseover = 'getContent( "iw3htp4.html" )'
64       onmouseout = 'clearContent()'/>
65    <img src =
66       "http://test.deitel.com/examples/iw3htp4/ajax/thumbs/jhtp7.jpg"
67       onmouseover = 'getContent( "jhtp7.html" )'
68       onmouseout = 'clearContent()'/>
69    <img src =
70       "http://test.deitel.com/examples/iw3htp4/ajax/thumbs/vbhtp3.jpg"
71       onmouseover = 'getContent( "vbhtp3.html" )'
72       onmouseout = 'clearContent()'/>
73    <img src =
74       "http://test.deitel.com/examples/iw3htp4/ajax/thumbs/vcsharphtp2.jpg"
75       onmouseover = 'getContent( "vcsharphtp2.html" )'
76       onmouseout = 'clearContent()'/>
77    <img src =
78       "http://test.deitel.com/examples/iw3htp4/ajax/thumbs/chtp5.jpg"
79       onmouseover = 'getContent( "chtp5.html" )'
80       onmouseout = 'clearContent()'/>
81    <div class = "box" id = "contentArea"> </div>
82 </body>
83 </html>
```

Fig. 13.5 | Asynchronously display content without reloading the page. (Part 2 of 3.)

a) User hovers over *C++ How to Program* book cover image, causing an asynchronous request to the server to obtain the book's description. When the response is received, the application performs a partial page update to display the description.

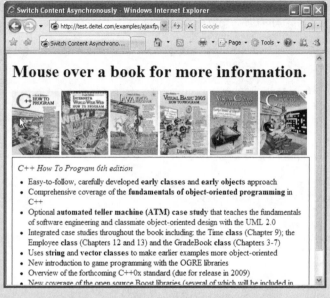

b) User hovers over *Java How to Program* book cover image, causing the process to repeat.

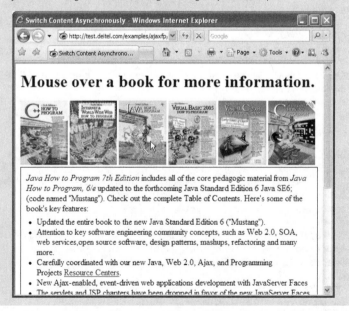

Fig. 13.5 | Asynchronously display content without reloading the page. (Part 3 of 3.)

Line 28 calls the XMLHttpRequest open method to prepare an asynchronous GET request. In this example, the url parameter specifies the address of an HTML document containing the description of a particular book. When the third argument is true, the request is asynchronous. The URL is passed to function getContent in response to the onmouseover event for each image. Line 29 sends the asynchronous request to the server by calling XMLHttpRequest send method. The argument null indicates that this request is not submitting data in the body of the request.

Exception Handling

Lines 22–34 introduce *exception handling*. An *exception* is an indication of a problem that occurs during a program's execution. The name "exception" implies that the problem occurs infrequently—if the "rule" is that a statement normally executes correctly, then the "exception to the rule" is that a problem occurs. Exception handling enables you to create applications that can resolve (or handle) exceptions—in some cases allowing a program to continue executing as if no problem had been encountered.

Lines 22–30 contain a *try block*, which encloses the code that might cause an exception and the code that should not execute if an exception occurs (i.e., if an exception occurs in a statement of the try block, the remaining code in the try block is skipped). A try block consists of the keyword try followed by a block of code enclosed in curly braces ({}). If there is a problem sending the request—e.g., if a user tries to access the page using an older browser that does not support XMLHttpRequest—the try block terminates immediately and a *catch block* (also called a *catch clause* or *exception handler*) catches (i.e., receives) and handles an exception. The catch block (lines 31–34) begins with the keyword catch and is followed by a parameter in parentheses (called the exception parameter) and a block of code enclosed in curly braces. The exception parameter's name (exception in this example) enables the catch block to interact with a caught exception object (for example, to obtain the name of the exception or an exception-specific error message via the exception object's name and message properties). In this case, we simply display our own error message 'Request Failed' and terminate the getContent function. The request can fail because a user accesses the web page with an older browser or the content that is being requested is located on a different domain.

Callback Functions

The stateChange function (lines 38–45) is the callback function that is called when the client receives the response data. Line 27 registers function stateChange as the event handler for the XMLHttpRequest object's onreadystatechange event. Whenever the request makes progress, the XMLHttpRequest calls the onreadystatechange event handler. This progress is monitored by the readyState property, which has a value from 0 to 4. The value 0 indicates that the request is not initialized and the value 4 indicates that the request is complete—all the values for this property are summarized in Fig. 13.6. If the request completes successfully (line 40), lines 42–43 use the XMLHttpRequest object's responseText property to obtain the response data and place it in the div element named contentArea (defined at line 81). We use the DOM's getElementById method to get this div element, and use the element's innerHTML property to place the content in the div.

XMLHttpRequest Object Properties and Methods

Figures 13.6 and 13.7 summarize some of the XMLHttpRequest object's properties and methods, respectively. The properties are crucial to interacting with asynchronous requests. The methods initialize, configure and send asynchronous requests.

Property	Description
onreadystatechange	Stores the callback function—the event handler that gets called when the server responds.
readyState	Keeps track of the request's progress. It is usually used in the callback function to determine when the code that processes the response should be launched. The readyState value 0 signifies that the request is uninitialized; 1 signifies that the request is loading; 2 signifies that the request has been loaded; 3 signifies that data is actively being sent from the server; and 4 signifies that the request has been completed.
responseText	Text that is returned to the client by the server.
responseXML	If the server's response is in XML format, this property contains the XML document; otherwise, it is empty. It can be used like a document object in JavaScript, which makes it useful for receiving complex data (e.g. populating a table).
status	HTTP status code of the request. A status of 200 means that request was successful. A status of 404 means that the requested resource was not found. A status of 500 denotes that there was an error while the server was proccessing the request.
statusText	Additional information on the request's status. It is often used to display the error to the user when the request fails.

Fig. 13.6 | XMLHttpRequest object properties.

Method	Description
open	Initializes the request and has two mandatory parameters—method and URL. The method parameter specifies the purpose of the request—typically GET if the request is to take data from the server or POST if the request will contain a body in addition to the headers. The URL parameter specifies the address of the file on the server that will generate the response. A third optional boolean parameter specifies whether the request is asynchronous—it's set to true by default.
send	Sends the request to the sever. It has one optional parameter, data, which specifies the data to be POSTed to the server—it's set to null by default.
setRequestHeader	Alters the header of the request. The two parameters specify the header and its new value. It is often used to set the content-type field.

Fig. 13.7 | XMLHttpRequest object methods. (Part 1 of 2.)

Method	Description
getResponseHeader	Returns the header data that precedes the response body. It takes one parameter, the name of the header to retrieve. This call is often used to determine the response's type, to parse the response correctly.
getAllResponseHeaders	Returns an array that contains all the headers that precede the response body.
abort	Cancels the current request.

Fig. 13.7 | XMLHttpRequest object methods. (Part 2 of 2.)

13.6 Using XML and the DOM

When passing structured data between the server and the client, Ajax applications often use XML because it is easy to generate and parse. When the XMLHttpRequest object receives XML data, it parses and stores the data as an XML DOM object in the responseXML property. The example in Fig. 13.8 asynchronously requests from a server XML documents containing URLs of book-cover images, then displays the images in an HTML table. The code that configures the asynchronous request is the same as in Fig. 13.5. You can test-drive this application at test.deitel.com/examples/ajaxfp/ajax/fig13_08/ PullImagesOntoPage.html (the book-cover images will be easier to see on the screen).

```
1  <?xml version = "1.0" encoding = "utf-8"?>
2  <!DOCTYPE html PUBLIC "-//W3C//DTD XHTML 1.0 Strict//EN"
3     "http://www.w3.org/TR/xhtml1/DTD/xhtml1-strict.dtd">
4
5  <!-- Fig. 13.8: PullImagesOntoPage.html -->
6  <!-- Image catalog that uses Ajax to request XML data asynchronously. -->
7  <html xmlns = "http://www.w3.org/1999/xhtml">
8  <head>
9  <title> Pulling Images onto the Page </title>
10 <style type = "text/css">
11    td { padding: 4px }
12    img { border: 1px solid black }
13 </style>
14 <script type = "text/javascript" language = "Javascript">
15    var asyncRequest; // variable to hold XMLHttpRequest object
16
17    // set up and send the asynchronous request to the XML file
18    function getImages( url )
19    {
20       // attempt to create the XMLHttpRequest and make the request
21       try
22       {
23          asyncRequest = new XMLHttpRequest(); // create request object
24
```

Fig. 13.8 | Image catalog that uses Ajax to request XML data asynchronously. (Part 1 of 4.)

```
25          // register event handler
26          asyncRequest.onreadystatechange = processResponse;
27          asyncRequest.open( 'GET', url, true ); // prepare the request
28          asyncRequest.send( null ); // send the request
29       } // end try
30       catch ( exception )
31       {
32          alert( 'Request Failed' );
33       } // end catch
34    } // end function getImages
35
36    // parses the XML response; dynamically creates a table using DOM and
37    // populates it with the response data; displays the table on the page
38    function processResponse()
39    {
40       // if request completed successfully and responseXML is non-null
41       if ( asyncRequest.readyState == 4 && asyncRequest.status == 200 &&
42          asyncRequest.responseXML )
43       {
44          clearTable(); // prepare to display a new set of images
45
46          // get the covers from the responseXML
47          var covers = asyncRequest.responseXML.getElementsByTagName(
48             "cover" )
49
50          // get base URL for the images
51          var baseUrl = asyncRequest.responseXML.getElementsByTagName(
52             "baseurl" ).item( 0 ).firstChild.nodeValue;
53
54          // get the placeholder div element named covers
55          var output = document.getElementById( "covers" );
56
57          // create a table to display the images
58          var imageTable = document.createElement( 'table' );
59
60          // create the table's body
61          var tableBody = document.createElement( 'tbody' );
62
63          var rowCount = 0; // tracks number of images in current row
64          var imageRow = document.createElement( "tr" ); // create row
65
66          // place images in row
67          for ( var i = 0; i < covers.length; i++ )
68          {
69             var cover = covers.item( i ); // get a cover from covers array
70
71             // get the image filename
72             var image = cover.getElementsByTagName( "image" ).
73                item( 0 ).firstChild.nodeValue;
74
75             // create table cell and img element to display the image
76             var imageCell = document.createElement( "td" );
```

Fig. 13.8 | Image catalog that uses Ajax to request XML data asynchronously. (Part 2 of 4.)

```
77                  var imageTag = document.createElement( "img" );
78
79                  // set img element's src attribute
80                  imageTag.setAttribute( "src", baseUrl + escape( image ) );
81                  imageCell.appendChild( imageTag ); // place img in cell
82                  imageRow.appendChild( imageCell ); // place cell in row
83                  rowCount++; // increment number of images in row
84
85                  // if there are 6 images in the row, append the row to
86                  // table and start a new row
87                  if ( rowCount == 6 && i + 1 < covers.length )
88                  {
89                     tableBody.appendChild( imageRow );
90                     imageRow = document.createElement( "tr" );
91                     rowCount = 0;
92                  } // end if statement
93               } // end for statement
94
95               tableBody.appendChild( imageRow ); // append row to table body
96               imageTable.appendChild( tableBody ); // append body to table
97               output.appendChild( imageTable ); // append table to covers div
98            } // end if
99         } // end function processResponse
100
101        // deletes the data in the table.
102        function clearTable()
103        {
104           document.getElementById( "covers" ).innerHTML = '';
105        }// end function clearTable
106     </script>
107  </head>
108  <body>
109     <input type = "radio" checked = "unchecked" name ="Books" value = "all"
110        onclick = 'getImages( "all.xml" )'/> All Books
111     <input type = "radio" checked = "unchecked"
112        name = "Books" value = "simply"
113        onclick = 'getImages( "simply.xml" )'/>  Simply Books
114     <input type = "radio" checked = "unchecked"
115        name = "Books" value = "howto"
116        onclick = 'getImages( "howto.xml" )'/> How to Program Books
117     <input type = "radio" checked = "unchecked"
118        name = "Books" value = "dotnet"
119        onclick = 'getImages( "dotnet.xml" )'/> .NET Books
120     <input type = "radio" checked = "unchecked"
121        name = "Books" value = "javaccpp"
122        onclick = 'getImages( "javaccpp.xml" )'/> Java, C, C++ Books
123     <input type = "radio" checked = "checked" name = "Books" value = "none"
124        onclick = 'clearTable()'/> None
125     <br/>
126     <div id = "covers"></div>
127  </body>
128  </html>
```

Fig. 13.8 | Image catalog that uses Ajax to request XML data asynchronously. (Part 3 of 4.)

a) User clicks the **All Books** radio button to display all the book covers. The application sends an asynchronous request to the server to obtain an XML document containing the list of book-cover filenames. When the response is received, the application performs a partial page update to display the set of book covers.

b) User clicks the **How to Program Books** radio button to select a subset of book covers to display. Application sends an asynchronous request to the server to obtain an XML document containing the appropriate subset of book-cover filenames. When the response is received, the application performs a partial page update to display the subset of book covers.

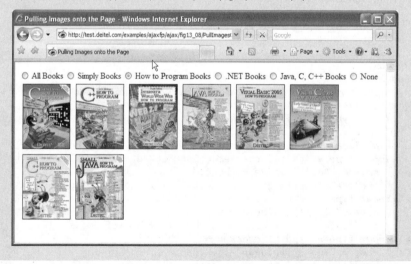

Fig. 13.8 | Image catalog that uses Ajax to request XML data asynchronously. (Part 4 of 4.)

When the XMLHttpRequest object receives the response, it invokes the callback function processResponse (lines 38–99). We use XMLHttpRequest object's responseXML property to access the XML returned by the server. Lines 41–42 check that the request was successful, and that the responseXML property is not empty. The XML file that we requested includes a baseURL node that contains the address of the image directory and a collection of cover nodes that contain image filenames. responseXML is a document object, so we can extract data from it using the XML DOM functions. Lines 47–52 use the DOM's method **getElementsByTagName** to extract all the image filenames from cover nodes and the URL of the directory from the baseURL node. Since the baseURL has no child nodes, we use item(0).firstChild.nodeValue to obtain the directory's address and store it in variable baseURL. The image filenames are stored in the covers array.

As in Fig. 13.5 we have a placeholder div element (line 126) to specify where the image table will be displayed on the page. Line 55 stores the div in variable output, so we can fill it with content later in the program.

Lines 58–93 generate an XHTML table dynamically, using the createElement, setAttribute and appendChild DOM methods. Method createElement creates an XHTML element of the specified type. Method **setAttribute** adds or changes an attribute of an XHTML element. Method appendChild inserts one XHTML element into another. Lines 58 and 61 create the table and tbody elements, respectively. We restrict each row to no more than six images, which we track with variable rowCount variable. Each iteration of the for statement (lines 67–93) obtains the filename of the image to be inserted (lines 69–73), creates a table cell element where the image will be inserted (line 76) and creates an <img> element (line 77). Line 80 sets the image's src attribute to the image's URL, which we build by concatenating the filename to the base URL of the XHTML document. Lines 81–82 insert the <img> element into the cell and the cell into the table row. When the row has six cells, it is inserted into the table and a new row is created (lines 87–92). Once all the rows have been inserted into the table, the table is inserted into the placeholder element covers that is referenced by variable output (line 97). This element is located on the bottom of the web page.

Function clearTable (lines 102–105) is called to clear images when the user switches radio buttons. The text is cleared by setting the innerHTML property of the placeholder element to the empty string.

13.7 Creating a Full-Scale Ajax-Enabled Application

Our next example demonstrates additional Ajax capabilities. The web application interacts with a web service to obtain data and to modify data in a server-side database. The web application and server communicate with a data format called JSON (JavaScript Object Notation). In addition, the application demonstrates server-side validation that occurs in parallel with the user interacting with the web application. You can test the application at test.deitel.com/examples/ajaxfp/ajax/fig13_09_10/AddressBook.html.

Using JSON
JSON (JavaScript Object Notation)—a simple way to represent JavaScript objects as strings—is an alternative way (to XML) for passing data between the client and the server. Each object in JSON is represented as a list of property names and values contained in curly braces, in the following format:

> { *"propertyName1"* : *value1*, *"propertyName2"*: *value2* }

Arrays are represented in JSON with square brackets in the following format:

> [*value1*, *value2*, *value3*]

Each value can be a string, a number, a JSON representation of an object, true, false or null. You can convert JSON strings into JavaScript objects with JavaScript's eval function. To evaluate a JSON string properly, a left parenthesis should be placed at the beginning of the string and a right parenthesis at the end of the string before the string is passed to the eval function.

The eval function creates a potential security risk—it executes any embedded JavaScript code in its string argument, possibly allowing a harmful script to be injected into JSON. A more secure way to process JSON is to use a JSON parser. In our examples, we use the open source parser from www.json.org/js.html. When you download its JavaScript file, place it in the same folder as your application. Then, link the json.js file into your XHTML file with the following statement in the head section:

```
<script type = "text/javascript" src = "json.js">
```

You can now call function parseJSON on a JSON string to convert it to a JavaScript object.

JSON strings are easier to create and parse than XML, and require fewer bytes. For these reasons, JSON is commonly used to communicate in client/server interaction. For more information on JSON, visit our JSON Resource Center at www.deitel.com/json.

Rich Functionality

The previous examples in this chapter requested data from static files on the server. The example in Fig. 13.9 is an address-book application that communicates with a server-side application. The application uses server-side processing to give the page the functionality and usability of a desktop application. We use JSON to encode server-side responses and to create objects on the fly.

Initially the address book loads a list of entries, each containing a first and last name (Fig. 13.9(a)). Each time the user clicks a name, the address book uses Ajax functionality to load the person's address from the server and expand the entry *without reloading the page* (Fig. 13.9(b))—and it does this *in parallel* with allowing the user to click other names. The application allows the user to search the address book by typing a last name. As the user enters each keystroke, the application asynchronously displays the list of names in which the last name starts with the characters the user has entered so far (Fig. 13.9(c), Fig. 13.9 (d) and Fig. 13.9(e))—a popular feature called *type ahead*.

```
1   <?xml version = "1.0" encoding = "utf-8"?>
2   <!DOCTYPE html PUBLIC "-//W3C//DTD XHTML 1.0 Strict//EN"
3      "http://www.w3.org/TR/xhtml1/DTD/xhtml1-strict.dtd">
4
5   <!-- Fig. 13.9 addressbook.html -->
6   <!-- Ajax enabled address book application. -->
7   <html xmlns = "http://www.w3.org/1999/xhtml">
8   <head>
9      <title>Address Book</title>
10     <link rel = "stylesheet" type = "text/css" href = "address.css" />
11     <script type = "text/javascript" src = "json.js"></script>
12     <script type = "text/javascript">
13        <!--
14        // URL of the web service
15        var webServiceUrl = '/AddressBookWebService/AddressService.asmx';
```

Fig. 13.9 | Ajax-enabled address-book application. (Part 1 of 10.)

```
16
17    var phoneValid = false; // indicates if the telephone is valid
18    var zipValid = false; //indicates if the zip code is valid
19
20    // get a list of names from the server and display them
21    function showAddressBook()
22    {
23       // hide the "addEntry" form and show the address book
24       document.getElementById( 'addEntry' ).style.display = 'none';
25       document.getElementById( 'addressBook' ).style.display = 'block';
26
27       var params = "[]"; // create an empty object
28       callWebService( 'getAllNames', params, parseData );
29    } // end function showAddressBook
30
31    // send the asynchronous request to the web service
32    function callWebService( method, paramString, callBack )
33    {
34       // build request URL string
35       var requestUrl = webServiceUrl + "/" + method;
36       var params = paramString.parseJSON();
37
38       // build the parameter string to add to the url
39       for ( var i = 0; i < params.length; i++ )
40       {
41          // checks whether it is the first parameter and builds
42          // the parameter string accordingly
43          if ( i == 0 )
44             requestUrl = requestUrl + "?" + params[ i ].param +
45                "=" + params[ i ].value; // add first parameter to url
46          else
47             requestUrl = requestUrl + "&" + params[ i ].param +
48                "=" + params[ i ].value; // add other parameters to url
49       } // end for
50
51       // attempt to send the asynchronous request
52       try
53       {
54          var asyncRequest = new XMLHttpRequest(); // create request
55
56          // set up callback function and store it
57          asyncRequest.onreadystatechange = function()
58          {
59             callBack( asyncRequest );
60          }; // end anonymous function
61
62          // send the asynchronous request
63          asyncRequest.open( 'GET', requestUrl, true );
64          asyncRequest.setRequestHeader("Accept",
65             "application/json; charset=utf-8" );
66          asyncRequest.send(); // send request
67       } // end try
```

Fig. 13.9 | Ajax-enabled address-book application. (Part 2 of 10.)

```
68              catch ( exception )
69              {
70                 alert ( 'Request Failed' );
71              } // end catch
72           } // end function callWebService
73
74           // parse JSON data and display it on the page
75           function parseData( asyncRequest )
76           {
77              // if request has completed successfully process the response
78              if ( asyncRequest.readyState == 4 && asyncRequest.status == 200 )
79              {
80                 // convert the JSON string to an Object
81                 var data = asyncRequest.responseText.parseJSON();
82                 displayNames( data ); // display data on the page
83              } // end if
84           } // end function parseData
85
86           // use the DOM to display the retrieved address book entries
87           function displayNames( data )
88           {
89              // get the placeholder element from the page
90              var listBox = document.getElementById( 'Names' );
91              listBox.innerHTML = ''; // clear the names on the page
92
93              // iterate over retrieved entries and display them on the page
94              for ( var i = 0; i < data.length; i++ )
95              {
96                 // dynamically create a div element for each entry
97                 // and a fieldset element to place it in
98                 var entry = document.createElement( 'div' );
99                 var field = document.createElement( 'fieldset' );
100                entry.onclick = handleOnClick; // set onclick event handler
101                entry.id = i; // set the id
102                entry.innerHTML = data[ i ].First + ' ' + data[ i ].Last;
103                field.appendChild( entry ); // insert entry into the field
104                listBox.appendChild( field ); // display the field
105             } // end for
106          } // end function displayAll
107
108          // event handler for entry's onclick event
109          function handleOnClick()
110          {
111             // call getAddress with the element's content as a parameter
112             getAddress( eval( 'this' ), eval( 'this.innerHTML' ) );
113          } // end function handleOnClick
114
115          // search the address book for input
116          // and display the results on the page
117          function search( input )
118          {
119             // get the placeholder element and delete its content
120             var listBox = document.getElementById( 'Names' );
```

Fig. 13.9 | Ajax-enabled address-book application. (Part 3 of 10.)

```
121        listBox.innerHTML = ''; // clear the display box
122
123        // if no search string is specified all the names are displayed
124        if ( input == "" ) // if no search value specified
125        {
126           showAddressBook(); // Load the entire address book
127        } // end if
128        else
129        {
130           var params = '[{"param": "input", "value": "' + input + '"}]';
131           callWebService( "search",  params , parseData );
132        } // end else
133     } // end function search
134
135     // Get address data for a specific entry
136     function getAddress( entry, name )
137     {
138        // find the address in the JSON data using the element's id
139        // and display it on the page
140        var firstLast = name.split(" "); // convert string to array
141        var requestUrl = webServiceUrl + "/getAddress?first="
142           + firstLast[ 0 ] + "&last=" + firstLast[ 1 ];
143
144        // attempt to send an asynchronous request
145        try
146        {
147           // create request object
148           var asyncRequest = new XMLHttpRequest();
149
150           // create a callback function with 2 parameters
151           asyncRequest.onreadystatechange = function()
152           {
153              displayAddress( entry, asyncRequest );
154           }; // end anonymous function
155
156           asyncRequest.open( 'GET', requestUrl, true );
157           asyncRequest.setRequestHeader("Accept",
158           "application/json; charset=utf-8"); // set response datatype
159           asyncRequest.send(); // send request
160        } // end try
161        catch ( exception )
162        {
163           alert ( 'Request Failed.' );
164        } // end catch
165     } // end function getAddress
166
167     // clear the entry's data.
168     function displayAddress( entry, asyncRequest )
169     {
170        // if request has completed successfully, process the response
171        if ( asyncRequest.readyState == 4 && asyncRequest.status == 200 )
172        {
```

Fig. 13.9 | Ajax-enabled address-book application. (Part 4 of 10.)

```
173             // convert the JSON string to an object
174             var data = asyncRequest.responseText.parseJSON();
175             var name = entry.innerHTML // save the name string
176             entry.innerHTML = name + '<br/>' + data.Street +
177                 '<br/>' + data.City + ', ' + data.State
178                 + ', ' + data.Zip + '<br/>' + data.Telephone;
179
180             // clicking on the entry removes the address
181             entry.onclick = function()
182             {
183                 clearField( entry, name );
184             }; // end anonymous function
185
186         } // end if
187     } // end function displayAddress
188
189     // clear the entry's data
190     function clearField( entry, name )
191     {
192         entry.innerHTML = name; // set the entry to display only the name
193         entry.onclick = function() // set onclick event
194         {
195             getAddress( entry, name ); // retrieve address and display it
196         }; // end function
197     } // end function clearField
198
199     // display the form that allows the user to enter more data
200     function addEntry()
201     {
202         document.getElementById( 'addressBook' ).style.display = 'none';
203         document.getElementById( 'addEntry' ).style.display = 'block';
204     } // end function addEntry
205
206     // send the zip code to be validated and to generate city and state
207     function validateZip( zip )
208     {
209         // build parameter array
210         var params = '[{"param": "zip", "value": "' + zip + '"}]';
211         callWebService ( "validateZip", params, showCityState );
212     } // end function validateZip
213
214     // get city and state that were generated using the zip code
215     // and display them on the page
216     function showCityState( asyncRequest )
217     {
218         // display message while request is being processed
219         document.getElementById( 'validateZip' ).
220             innerHTML = "Checking zip...";
221
222         // if request has completed successfully, process the response
223         if ( asyncRequest.readyState == 4 )
224         {
```

Fig. 13.9 | Ajax-enabled address-book application. (Part 5 of 10.)

```
225                        if ( asyncRequest.status == 200 )
226                        {
227                           // convert the JSON string to an object
228                           var data = asyncRequest.responseText.parseJSON();
229
230                           // update zip code validity tracker and show city and state
231                           if ( data.Validity == 'Valid' )
232                           {
233                              zipValid = true; // update validity tracker
234
235                              // display city and state
236                              document.getElementById( 'validateZip' ).innerHTML = '';
237                              document.getElementById( 'city' ).innerHTML = data.City;
238                              document.getElementById( 'state' ).
239                                 innerHTML = data.State;
240                           } // end if
241                           else
242                           {
243                              zipValid = false; // update validity tracker
244                              document.getElementById( 'validateZip' ).
245                                 innerHTML = data.ErrorText; // display the error
246
247                              // clear city and state values if they exist
248                              document.getElementById( 'city' ).innerHTML = '';
249                              document.getElementById( 'state' ).innerHTML = '';
250                           } // end else
251                        } // end if
252                        else if ( asyncRequest.status == 500 )
253                        {
254                           document.getElementById( 'validateZip' ).
255                              innerHTML = 'Zip validation service not avaliable';
256                        } // end else if
257                     } // end if
258                  } // end function showCityState
259
260                  // send the telephone number to the server to validate format
261                  function validatePhone( phone )
262                  {
263                     var params = '[{ "param": "tel", "value": "' + phone + '"}]';
264                     callWebService( "validateTel", params, showPhoneError );
265                  } // end function validatePhone
266
267                  // show whether the telephone number has correct format
268                  function showPhoneError( asyncRequest )
269                  {
270                     // if request has completed successfully, process the response
271                     if ( asyncRequest.readyState == 4 && asyncRequest.status == 200 )
272                     {
273                        // convert the JSON string to an object
274                        var data = asyncRequest.responseText.parseJSON();
275
276                        if ( data.ErrorText != "Valid Telephone Format" )
277                        {
```

Fig. 13.9 | Ajax-enabled address-book application. (Part 6 of 10.)

```
278                 phoneValid = false; // update validity tracker
279              } // end if
280              else
281              {
282                 phoneValid = true; // update validity tracker
283              } // end else
284
285              document.getElementById( 'validatePhone' ).
286                 innerHTML = data.ErrorText; // display the error
287           } // end if
288        } // end function showPhoneError
289
290        // enter the user's data into the database
291        function saveForm()
292        {
293           // retrieve the data from the form
294           var first = document.getElementById( 'first' ).value;
295           var last = document.getElementById( 'last' ).value;
296           var street = document.getElementById( 'street' ).value;
297           var city = document.getElementById( 'city' ).innerHTML;
298           var state = document.getElementById( 'state' ).innerHTML;
299           var zip = document.getElementById( 'zip' ).value;
300           var phone = document.getElementById( 'phone' ).value;
301
302           // check if data is valid
303           if ( !zipValid || !phoneValid  )
304           {
305              // display error message
306              document.getElementById( 'success' ).innerHTML =
307                 'Invalid data entered. Check form for more information';
308           } // end if
309           else if ( ( first == "" ) || ( last == "" ) )
310           {
311              // display error message
312              document.getElementById( 'success').innerHTML =
313                 'First Name and Last Name must have a value.';
314           } // end if
315           else
316           {
317              // hide the form and show the addressbook
318              document.getElementById( 'addEntry' )
319                 .style.display = 'none';
320              document.getElementById( 'addressBook' ).
321                 style.display = 'block';
322
323              // build the parameter to include in the web service URL
324              params = '[{"param": "first", "value": "' + first +
325                 '"}, { "param": "last", "value": "' + last +
326                 '"}, { "param": "street", "value": "'+ street +
327                 '"}, { "param": "city", "value": "' +  city +
328                 '"}, { "param":  "state", "value:": "' + state +
329                 '"}, { "param": "zip", "value": "' + zip +
330                 '"}, { "param": "tel", "value": "' + phone + '"}]';
```

Fig. 13.9 | Ajax-enabled address-book application. (Part 7 of 10.)

```
331
332                    // call the web service to insert data into the database
333                    callWebService( "addEntry", params, parseData );
334              } // end else
335         } // end function saveForm
336         //-->
337      </script>
338   </head>
339   <body onload = "showAddressBook()">
340      <div>
341         <input type = "button" value = "Address Book"
342            onclick = "showAddressBook()"/>
343         <input type = "button" value = "Add an Entry"
344            onclick = "addEntry()"/>
345      </div>
346      <div id = "addressBook" style = "display : block;">
347          Search By Last Name:
348         <input onkeyup = "search( this.value )"/>
349         <br/>
350         <div id = "Names">
351         </div>
352      </div>
353      <div id = "addEntry" style = "display : none">
354         First Name: <input id = 'first'/>
355         <br/>
356         Last Name: <input id = 'last'/>
357         <br/>
358         <strong> Address: </strong>
359         <br/>
360         Street: <input id = 'street'/>
361         <br/>
362         City: <span id = "city" class = "validator"></span>
363         <br/>
364         State: <span id = "state" class = "validator"></span>
365         <br/>
366         Zip: <input id = 'zip' onblur = 'validateZip( this.value )'/>
367         <span id = "validateZip" class = "validator">
368         </span>
369         <br/>
370         Telephone:<input id = 'phone'
371            onblur = 'validatePhone( this.value )'/>
372         <span id = "validatePhone" class = "validator">
373         </span>
374         <br/>
375         <input type = "button" value = "Submit"
376            onclick = "saveForm()" />
377         <br/>
378         <div id = "success" class = "validator">
379         </div>
380      </div>
381   </body>
382   </html>
```

Fig. 13.9 | Ajax-enabled address-book application. (Part 8 of 10.)

a) Page is loaded. All the entries are displayed.

b) User clicks on an entry. The entry expands, showing the address and the telephone.

c) User types "B" in the search field. Application loads the entries whose last names start with "B".

d) User types "Bl" in the search field. Application loads the entries whose last names start with "Bl".

e) User types "Bla" in the search field. Application loads the entries whose last names start with "Bla".

f) User clicks **Add an Entry** button. The form allowing user to add an entry is displayed.

Fig. 13.9 | Ajax-enabled address-book application. (Part 9 of 10.)

g) User types in a nonexistent zip code. An error is displayed.

h) User enters a valid zip code. While the server processes it, **Checking Zip...** is displayed on the page.

i) The server finds the city and state associated with the zip code entered and displays them on the page.

j) The user enters a telephone number and tries to submit the data. The application does not allow this, because the First Name and Last Name are empty.

k) The user enters the last name and the first name and clicks the Submit button.

l) The address book is redisplayed with the new name added in.

Fig. 13.9 | Ajax-enabled address-book application. (Part 10 of 10.)

The application also enables the user to add another entry to the address book by clicking the **addEntry** button (Fig. 13.9(f)). The application displays a form that enables live field validation. As the user fills out the form, the zip-code value is validated and used to generate the city and state (Fig. 13.9(g), Fig. 13.9(h) and Fig. 13.9(i)). The telephone number is validated for correct format (Fig. 13.9(j)). When the Submit button is clicked, the application checks for invalid data and stores the values in a database on the server (Fig. 13.9(k) and Fig. 13.9(l)). You can test-drive this application at test.deitel.com/ examples/ajaxfp/ajax/fig13_09_10/AddressBook.html.

Interacting with a Web Service on the Server

When the page loads, the onload event (line 339) calls the showAddressBook function to load the address book onto the page. Function showAddressBook (lines 21–29) shows the addressBook element and hides the addEntry element using the HTML DOM (lines 24–25). Then it calls function callWebService to make an asynchronous request to the server (line 28). Function callWebService requires an array of parameter objects to be sent to the server. In this case, the function we are invoking on the server requires no arguments, so line 27 creates an empty array to be passed to callWebService. Our program uses an ASP.NET web service that we created for this example to do the server-side processing. The web service contains a collection of methods that can be called from a web application.

Function callWebService (lines 32–72) contains the code to call our web service, given a method name, an array of parameter bindings (i.e., the method's parameter names and argument values) and the name of a callback function. The web-service application and the method that is being called are specified in the request URL (line 35). When sending the request using the GET method, the parameters are concatenated URL starting with a ? symbol and followed by a list of *parameter=value* bindings, each separated by an &. Lines 39–49 iterate over the array of parameter bindings that was passed as an argument, and add them to the request URL. In this first call, we do not pass any parameters because the web method that returns all the entries requires none. However, future web method calls will send multiple parameter bindings to the web service. Lines 52–71 prepare and send the request, using similar functionality to the previous two examples. There are many types of user interaction in this application, each requiring a separate asynchronous request. For this reason, we pass the appropriate asyncRequest object as an argument to the function specified by the callBack parameter. However, event handlers cannot receive arguments, so lines 57–60 assign an anonymous function to asyncRequest's onreadystatechange property. When this anonymous function gets called, it calls function callBack and passes the asyncRequest object as an argument. Lines 64–65 set an Accept request header to receive JSON formatted data.

Parsing JSON Data

Each of our web service's methods in this example returns a JSON representation of an object or array of objects. For example, when the web application requests the list of names in the address book, the list is returned as a JSON array, as shown in Fig. 13.10. Each object in Fig. 13.10 has the attributes first and last.

Line 11 links the json.js script to the XHTML file so we can parse JSON data. When the XMLHttpRequest object receives the response, it calls function parseData (lines 75–84). Line 81 calls the string's parseJSON function, which converts the JSON string into a JavaScript object. Then line 82 calls function displayNames (lines 87–106), which

```
1   [ { "first": "Cheryl", "last": "Black" },
2       { "first": "James", "last": "Blue" },
3       { "first": "Mike", "last": "Brown" },
4       { "first": "Meg", "last": "Gold" } ]
```

Fig. 13.10 | Address-book data formatted in JSON.

displays the first and last name of each address-book entry passed to it. Lines 90–91 use the DOM to store the placeholder div element Names in the variable listbox, and clear its content. Once parsed, the JSON string of address-book entries becomes an array, which this function traverses (lines 94–105).

Creating XHTML Elements and Setting Event Handlers on the Fly
Line 99 uses an XHTML fieldset element to create a box in which the entry will be placed. Line 100 registers function handleOnClick as the onclick event handler for the div created in line 98. This enables the user to expand each address-book entry by clicking it. Function handleOnClick (lines 109–113) calls the getAddress function whenever the user clicks an entry. The parameters are generated dynamically and not evaluated until the getAddress function is called. This enables each function to receive arguments that are specific to the entry the user clicked. Line 102 displays the names on the page by accessing the first (first name) and last (last name) fields of each element of the data array.

Function getAddress (lines 136–166) is called when the user clicks an entry. This request must keep track of the entry where the address is to be displayed on the page. Lines 151–154 set the displayAddress function (lines 168–187) as the callback function, and pass it the entry element as a parameter. Once the request completes successfully, lines 174–178 parse the response and display the addresses. Lines 181–184 update the div's onclick event handler to hide the address data when that div is clicked again by the user. When the user clicks an expanded entry, function clearField (lines 190–197) is called. Lines 192–196 reset the entry's content and its onclick event handler to the values they had before the entry was expanded.

Implementing Type-Ahead
The input element declared in line 348 enables the user to search the address book by last name. As soon as the user starts typing in the input box, the onkeyup event handler calls the search function (lines 117–133), passing the input element's value as an argument. The search function performs an asynchronous request to locate entries with last names that start with its argument value. When the response is received, the application displays the matching list of names. Each time the user changes the text in the input box, function search is called again to make another asynchronous request.

The search function (lines 117–133) first clears the address-book entries from the page (lines 120–121). If the input argument is the empty string, line 126 displays the entire address book by calling function showAddressBook. Otherwise lines 130–131 send a request to the server to search the data. Line 130 creates a JSON string to represent the parameter object to be sent as an argument to the callWebServices function. Line 131 converts the string to an object and calls the callWebServices function. When the server responds, callback function parseData is invoked, which calls function displayNames to display the results on the page.

Implementing a Form with Asynchronous Validation

When the **Add an Entry** button (lines 343–344) is clicked, the addEntry function (lines 200–204) is called, which hides the addressBook element and shows the addEntry element that allows the user to add a person to the address book. The addEntry element (lines 353–380) contains a set of entry fields, some of which have event handlers that enable validation that occurs asynchronously as the user continues to interact with the page. When a user enters a zip code, the validateZip function (lines 207–212) is called. This function calls an external web service to validate the zip code. If it is valid, that external web service returns the corresponding city and state. Line 210 builds a parameter object containing validateZip's parameter name and argument value in JSON format. Line 211 calls the callWebService function with the appropriate method, the parameter object created in line 210 and showCityState (lines 216–258) as the callback function.

Zip-code validation can take a long time due to network delays. The showCityState function is called every time the request object's readyState property changes. Until the request completes, lines 219–220 display "Checking zip code..." on the page. After the request completes, line 228 converts the JSON response text to an object. The response object has four properties—Validity, ErrorText, City and State. If the request is valid, line 233 updates the zipValid variable that keeps track of zip-code validity (declared at line 18), and lines 237–239 show the city and state that the server generated using the zip code. Otherwise lines 243–245 update the zipValid variable and show the error code. Lines 248–249 clear the city and state elements. If our web service fails to connect to the zip-code validator web service, lines 252–256 display an appropriate error message.

Similarly, when the user enters the telephone number, the function validatePhone (lines 261–265) sends the phone number to the server. Once the server responds, the showPhoneError function (lines 268–288) updates the validatePhone variable (declared at line 17) and shows the message that the web service returned.

When the **Submit** button is clicked, the saveForm function is called (lines 291–335). Lines 294–300 retrieve the data from the form. Lines 303–308 check if the zip code and telephone number are valid, and display the appropriate error message in the Success element on the bottom of the page. Before the data can be entered into a database on the server, both the first-name and last-name fields must have a value. Lines 309–314 check that these fields are not empty and, if they are empty, display the appropriate error message. Once all the data entered is valid, lines 318–321 hide the entry form and show the address book. Lines 324–333 build the parameter object using JSON and send the data to the server using the callWebService function. Once the server saves the data, it queries the database for an updated list of entries and returns them; then function parseData displays the entries on the page.

13.8 Dojo Toolkit

Developing web applications in general, and Ajax applications in particular, involves a certain amount of painstaking and tedious work. Cross-browser compatibility, DOM manipulation and event handling can get cumbersome, particularly as an application's size increases. Dojo is a free, open source JavaScript library that takes care of these issues. Dojo reduces asynchronous request handling to a single function call. Dojo also provides cross-browser DOM functions that simplify partial page updates. It covers many more areas of web development, from simple event handling to fully functional rich GUI controls.

To install Dojo, download the Dojo version 0.4.3 from www.Dojotoolkit.org/downloads to your hard drive. Extract the files from the archive file you downloaded to your web development directory or web server. Including the dojo.js script file in your web application will give you access to all the Dojo functions. To do this, place the following script in the head element of your XHTML document:

<script type = "text/javascript" src = "*path*/Dojo.js">

where *path* is the relative or complete path to the Dojo toolkit's files. Quick installation instructions for Dojo are provided at Dojotoolkit.org/book/Dojo-book-0-9/part-1-life-Dojo/quick-installation.

Figure 13.11 is a calendar application that uses Dojo to create the user interface, communicate with the server asynchronously, handle events and manipulate the DOM. The application contains a calendar control that shows the user six weeks of dates (see the screen captures in Fig. 13.11). Various arrow buttons allow the user to traverse the calendar. When the user selects a date, an asynchronous request obtains from the server a list of the scheduled events for that date. There is an **Edit** button next to each scheduled event. When the **Edit** button is clicked, the item is replaced by a text box with the item's content, a **Save** button and a **Cancel** button. When the user presses **Save**, an asynchronous request saves the new value to the server and displays it on the page. This feature, often referred to as *edit-in-place*, is common in Ajax applications. You can test-drive this application at test.deitel.com/examples/ajaxfp/ajax/fig13_11/calendar.html.

```
1   <?xml version = "1.0" encoding = "utf-8"?>
2   <!DOCTYPE html PUBLIC "-//W3C//DTD XHTML 1.0 Strict//EN"
3      "http://www.w3.org/TR/xhtml1/DTD/xhtml1-strict.dtd">
4
5   <!-- Fig. 13.11 Calendar.html -->
6   <!-- Calendar application built with dojo. -->
7   <html xmlns = "http://www.w3.org/1999/xhtml">
8   <head>
9      <script type = "text/javascript" src = "/dojo043/dojo.js"></script>
10     <script type = "text/javascript" src = "json.js"></script>
11     <script type = "text/javascript">
12        <!--
13        // specify all the required dojo scripts
14        dojo.require( "dojo.event.*" ); // use scripts from event package
15        dojo.require( "dojo.widget.*" ); // use scripts from widget package
16        dojo.require( "dojo.dom.*" ); // use scripts from dom package
17        dojo.require( "dojo.io.*" ); // use scripts from the io package
18
19        // configure calendar event handler
20        function connectEventHandler()
21        {
22           var calendar = dojo.widget.byId( "calendar" ); // get calendar
23           calendar.setDate( "2007-07-04" );
24           dojo.event.connect(
25              calendar, "onValueChanged", "retrieveItems" );
26        } // end function connectEventHandler
27
```

Fig. 13.11 | Calendar application built with Dojo. (Part 1 of 7.)

```
28    // location of CalendarService web service
29    var webServiceUrl = "/CalendarService/CalendarService.asmx";
30
31    // obtain scheduled events for the specified date
32    function retrieveItems( eventDate )
33    {
34       // convert date object to string in yyyy-mm-dd format
35       var date = dojo.date.toRfc3339( eventDate ).substring( 0, 10 );
36
37       // build parameters and call web service
38       var params = '[{ "param":"eventDate", "value":"' +
39          date + "'}]";
40       callWebService( 'getItemsByDate', params, displayItems );
41    } // end function retrieveItems
42
43    // call a specific web service asynchronously to get server data
44    function callWebService( method, params, callback )
45    {
46       // url for the asynchronous request
47       var requestUrl = webServiceUrl + "/" + method;
48       var params = paramString.parseJSON();
49
50       // build the parameter string to append to the url
51       for ( var i = 0; i < params.length; i++ )
52       {
53          // check if it is the first parameter and build
54          // the parameter string accordingly
55          if ( i == 0 )
56             requestUrl = requestUrl + "?" + params[ i ].param +
57                "=" + params[ i ].value; // add first parameter to url
58          else
59             requestUrl = requestUrl + "&" + params[ i ].param +
60                "=" + params[ i ].value; // add other parameters to url
61       } // end for
62
63       // call asynchronous request using dojo.io.bind
64       dojo.io.bind( { url: requestUrl, handler: callback,
65          accept: "application/json; charset=utf-8" } );
66    } // end function callWebService
67
68    // display the list of scheduled events on the page
69    function displayItems( type, data, event )
70    {
71       if ( type == 'error' ) // if the request has failed
72       {
73          alert( 'Could not retrieve the event' ); // display error
74       } // end if
75       else
76       {
77          var placeholder = dojo.byId( "itemList" ); // get placeholder
78          placeholder.innerHTML = ''; // clear placeholder
79          var items = data.parseJSON(); // parse server data
80
```

Fig. 13.11 | Calendar application built with Dojo. (Part 2 of 7.)

```
 81                    // check whether there are events;
 82                    // if none then display message
 83                    if ( items == "" )
 84                    {
 85                        placeholder.innerHTML = 'No events for this date.';
 86                    }
 87
 88                    for ( var  i = 0; i < items.length; i++ )
 89                    {
 90                        // initialize item's container
 91                        var item = document.createElement( "div" );
 92                        item.id = items[ i ].id; // set DOM id to database id
 93
 94                        // obtain and paste the item's description
 95                        var text = document.createElement( "div" );
 96                        text.innerHTML =  items[i].description;
 97                        text.id = 'description' + item.id;
 98                        dojo.dom.insertAtIndex( text, item, 0 );
 99
100                        // create and insert the placeholder for the edit button
101                        var buttonPlaceHolder = document.createElement( "div" );
102                        dojo.dom.insertAtIndex( buttonPlaceHolder, item, 1 );
103
104                        // create the edit button and paste it into the container
105                        var editButton = dojo.widget.
106                            createWidget( "Button", {}, buttonPlaceHolder );
107                        editButton.setCaption( "Edit" );
108                        dojo.event.connect(
109                            editButton, 'buttonClick', handleEdit );
110
111                        // insert item container in the list of items container
112                        dojo.dom.insertAtIndex( item, placeholder, i );
113                    } // end for
114                } // end else
115            } // end function displayItems
116
117            // send the asynchronous request to get content for editing and
118            // run the edit-in-place UI
119            function handleEdit( event )
120            {
121                var id = event.currentTarget.parentNode.id; // retrieve id
122                var params = '[{ "param":"id", "value":"' + id +  '"}]';
123                callWebService( 'getItemById', params, displayForEdit );
124            } // end function handleEdit
125
126            // set up the interface for editing an item
127            function displayForEdit(type, data, event)
128            {
129                if ( type == 'error' ) // if the request has failed
130                {
131                    alert( 'Could not retrieve the event' ); // display error
132                }
```

Fig. 13.11 | Calendar application built with Dojo. (Part 3 of 7.)

```
133        else
134        {
135            var item = data.parseJSON(); // parse the item
136            var id = item.id; // set the id
137
138            // create div elements to insert content
139            var editElement = document.createElement( 'div' );
140            var buttonElement = document.createElement( 'div' );
141
142            // hide the unedited content
143            var oldItem = dojo.byId( id ); // get the original element
144            oldItem.id = 'old' + oldItem.id; // change element's id
145            oldItem.style.display = 'none'; // hide old element
146            editElement.id = id; // change the "edit" container's id
147
148            // create a textbox and insert it on the page
149            var editArea = document.createElement( 'textarea' );
150            editArea.id = 'edit' + id; // set textbox id
151            editArea.innerHTML = item.description; // insert description
152            dojo.dom.insertAtIndex( editArea, editElement, 0 );
153
154            // create button placeholders and insert on the page
155            // these will be transformed into dojo widgets
156            var saveElement = document.createElement( 'div' );
157            var cancelElement = document.createElement( 'div' );
158            dojo.dom.insertAtIndex( saveElement, buttonElement, 0 );
159            dojo.dom.insertAtIndex( cancelElement, buttonElement, 1 );
160            dojo.dom.insertAtIndex( buttonElement, editElement, 1 );
161
162            // create "save" and "cancel" buttons
163            var saveButton =
164                dojo.widget.createWidget( "Button", {}, saveElement );
165            var cancelButton =
166                dojo.widget.createWidget( "Button", {}, cancelElement );
167            saveButton.setCaption( "Save" ); // set saveButton label
168            cancelButton.setCaption( "Cancel" ); // set cancelButton text
169
170            // set up the event handlers for cancel and save buttons
171            dojo.event.connect( saveButton, 'buttonClick', handleSave );
172            dojo.event.connect(
173                cancelButton, 'buttonClick', handleCancel );
174
175            // paste the edit UI on the page
176            dojo.dom.insertAfter( editElement, oldItem );
177        } // end else
178    } // end function displayForEdit
179
180    // sends the changed content to the server to be saved
181    function handleSave( event )
182    {
183        // grab user entered data
184        var id = event.currentTarget.parentNode.parentNode.id;
185        var descr = dojo.byId( 'edit' + id ).value;
```

Fig. 13.11 | Calendar application built with Dojo. (Part 4 of 7.)

```
186
187            // build parameter string and call the web service
188            var params = '[{ "param":"id", "value":"' + id +
189               '"}, {"param": "descr", "value":"' + descr + '"}]';
190            callWebService( 'Save', params, displayEdited );
191         } // end function handleSave
192
193         // restores the original content of the item
194         function handleCancel( event )
195         {
196            var voidEdit = event.currentTarget.parentNode.parentNode;
197            var id = voidEdit.id; // retrieve the id of the item
198            dojo.dom.removeNode( voidEdit, true ); // remove the edit UI
199            var old = dojo.byId( 'old' + id ); // retrieve pre-edit version
200            old.style.display = 'block'; // show pre-edit version
201            old.id = id; // reset the id
202         } // end function handleCancel
203
204         // displays the updated event information after an edit is saved
205         function displayEdited( type, data, event )
206         {
207            if ( type == 'error' )
208            {
209               alert( 'Could not retrieve the event' );
210            }
211            else
212            {
213               editedItem = data.parseJSON(); // obtain updated description
214               var id = editedItem.id; // obtain the id
215               var editElement = dojo.byId( id ); // get the edit UI
216               dojo.dom.removeNode( editElement, true ); // delete edit UI
217               var old = dojo.byId( 'old' + id ); // get item container
218
219               // get pre-edit element and update its description
220               var oldText = dojo.byId( 'description' + id );
221               oldText.innerHTML = editedItem.description;
222
223               old.id = id; // reset id
224               old.style.display = 'block'; // show the updated item
225            } // end else
226         } // end function displayEdited
227
228         // when the page is loaded, set up the calendar event handler
229         dojo.addOnLoad( connectEventHandler );
230         // -->
231      </script>
232      <title> Calendar built with dojo </title>
233   </head>
234   <body>
235      Calendar
236      <div dojoType = "datePicker" style = "float: left"
237         widgetID = "calendar"></div>
238      <div id = "itemList" style = "float: left"></div>
```

Fig. 13.11 | Calendar application built with Dojo. (Part 5 of 7.)

```
239   </body>
240   </html>
```

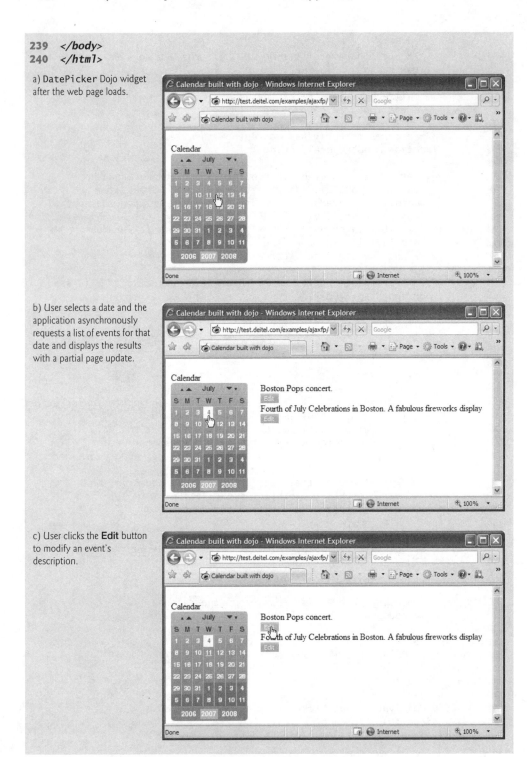

a) `DatePicker` Dojo widget after the web page loads.

b) User selects a date and the application asynchronously requests a list of events for that date and displays the results with a partial page update.

c) User clicks the **Edit** button to modify an event's description.

Fig. 13.11 | Calendar application built with Dojo. (Part 6 of 7.)

d) Application performs a partial page update, replacing the original description and the **Edit** button with a text box, **Save** button and **Cancel** button. User modifies the event description and clicks the **Save** button.

d) The **Save** button's event handler uses an asynchronous request to update the server and uses the server's response to perform a partial page update, replacing the editing GUI components with the updated description and an **Edit** button.

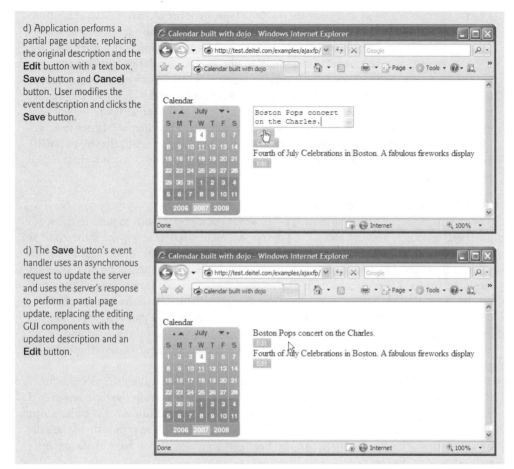

Fig. 13.11 | Calendar application built with Dojo. (Part 7 of 7.)

Loading Dojo Packages

Lines 9–17 load the Dojo framework. Line 9 links the dojo.js script file to the page, giving the script access to all the functions in the Dojo toolkit. Dojo is organized in packages of related functionality. Lines 14–17 use the dojo.require call, provided by the dojo.js script to include the packages we need. The dojo.io package functions communicate with the server, the dojo.event package simplifies event handling, the dojo.widget package provides rich GUI controls, and the dojo.dom package contains additional DOM functions that are portable across many different browsers.

The application cannot use any of this functionality until all the packages have been loaded. Line 229 uses the dojo.addOnLoad method to set up the event handling after the page loads. Once all the packages have been loaded, the connectEventHandler function (lines 20–26) is called.

Using an Existing Dojo Widget

A *Dojo widget* is any predefined user interface element that is part of the Dojo toolkit. The calendar control on the page is the DatePicker widget. To incorporate an existing

Dojo widget onto a page, you must set the `DojoType` attribute of any HTML element to the type of widget that you want it to be (line 236). Dojo widgets also have their own `widgetID` property (line 237). Line 22 uses the `dojo.widget.byId` method, rather than the DOM's `document.getElementById` method, to obtain the calendar widget element. The `dojo.events.connect` method links functions together. Lines 24–25 use it to connect the calendar's `onValueChanged` event handler to the `retrieveItems` function. When the user picks a date, a special `onValueChanged` event that is part of the `DatePicker` widget calls `retrieveItems`, passing the selected date as an argument. The `retrieveItems` function (lines 32–41) builds the parameters for the request to the server, and calls the `callWebService` function. Line 35 uses the `dojo.date.toRfc3339` method to convert the date passed by the calendar control to *yyyy-mm-dd* format.

Asynchronous Requests in Dojo
The `callWebService` function (lines 44–66) sends the asynchronous request to the specified web-service method. Lines 47–61 build the request URL using the same code as Fig. 13.9. Dojo reduces the asynchronous request to a single call to the `dojo.io.bind` method (lines 64–65), which works on all the popular browsers such as Firefox, Internet Explorer, Opera, Mozilla and Safari. The method takes an array of parameters, formatted as a JavaScript object. The `url` parameter specifies the destination of the request, the `handler` parameter specifies the callback function, and the `mimetype` parameter specifies the format of the response. The `handler` parameter can be replaced by the `load` and `error` parameters. The function passed as `load` handles successful requests and the function passed as `error` handles unsuccessful requests.

Response handling is done differently in Dojo. Rather than calling the callback function every time the request's `readyState` property changes, Dojo calls the function passed as the "handler" parameter when the request completes. In addition, in Dojo the script does not have access to the request object. All the response data is sent directly to the callback function The function sent as the `handler` argument must have three parameters—type, data and event.

In the first request, the function `displayItems` (lines 69–115) is set as the callback function. Lines 71–74 check if the request is successful, and display an error message if it isn't. Lines 77–78 obtain the place-holder element (`itemList`), where the items will be displayed, and clear its content. Line 79 converts the JSON response text to a JavaScript object, using the same code as the example in Fig. 13.9.

Partial Page Updates Using Dojo's Cross-Browser DOM Manipulation Capabilities
The Dojo toolkit (like most other Ajax libraries) provides functionality that enables you to manipulate the DOM in a cross-browser portable manner. Lines 83–86 check if the server-side returned any items, and display an appropriate message if it didn't. For each item object returned from the server, lines 91–92 create a `div` element and set its `id` to the item's `id` in the database. Lines 95–97 create a container element for the item's description. Line 98 uses Dojo's `dojo.dom.insertAtIndex` method to insert the description element as the first element in the item's element.

For each entry, the application creates an **Edit** button that enables the user to edit the event's content on the page. Lines 101–109 create a Dojo `Button` widget programmatically. Lines 101–102 create a `buttonPlaceHolder` `div` element for the button and paste it on the page. Lines 105–106 convert the `buttonPlaceHolder` element to a Dojo `Button` widget by calling the `dojo.widget.createWidget` function. This function takes three parameters—the type of widget to be created, a list of additional widget parameters and the element which is to be converted to a Dojo widget. Line 107 uses the button's `set-Caption` method to set the text that appears on the button. Line 112 uses the `insertAtIndex` method to insert the items into the `itemList` placeholder, in the order in which they were returned from the server.

Adding Edit-In-Place Functionality

Dojo `Button` widgets use their own `buttonClick` event instead of the DOM `onclick` event to store the event handler. Lines 108–109 use the `dojo.event.connect` method to connect the `buttonClick` event of the Dojo `Button` widget and the `handleEdit` event handler (lines 119–124). When the user clicks the **Edit** button, the `Event` object gets passed to the event handler as an argument. The `Event` object's `currentTarget` property contains the element that initiated the event. Line 121 uses the `currentTarget` property to obtain the `id` of the item. This `id` is the same as the item's `id` in the server database. Line 123 calls the web service's `getItemById` method, using the `callWebService` function to obtain the item that needs to be edited.

Once the server responds, function `displayForEdit` (lines 127–178) replaces the item on the screen with the user interface for editing the item's content. The code for this is similar to the code in the `displayItems` function. Lines 129–132 make sure the request was successful and parse the data from the server. Lines 139–140 create the container elements into which we insert the new user-interface elements. Lines 143–146 hide the element that displays the item and change its `id`. Now the `id` of the user-interface element is the same as the `id` of the item that it's editing stored in the database. Lines 149–152 create the text-box element that will be used to edit the item's description, paste it into the text box, and paste the resulting text box on the page. Lines 156–173 use the same syntax that was used to create the **Edit** button widget to create **Save** and **Cancel** button widgets. Line 176 pastes the resulting element, containing the text box and two buttons, on the page.

When the user edits the content and clicks the **Cancel** button, the `handleCancel` function (lines 194–202) restores the item element to what it looked like before the button was clicked. Line 198 deletes the edit UI that was created earlier, using Dojo's `removeNode` function. Lines 200–201 show the item with the original element that was used to display the item, and change its `id` back to the item's `id` on the server database.

When the user clicks the **Save** button, the `handleSave` function (lines 181–191) sends the text entered by the user to the server. Line 185 obtains the text that the user entered in the text box. Lines 188–190 send to the server the `id` of the item that needs to be updated and the new description.

Once the server responds, `displayEdited` (lines 205–226) displays the new item on the page. Lines 214–217 contain the same code that was used in `handleCancel` to remove the user interface used to edit the item and redisplay the element that contains the item. Line 221 changes the item's description to its new value.

13.9 Web Resources

www.deitel.com/ajax

Our *Ajax Resource Center* contains links to some of the best Ajax resources on the web from which you can learn more about Ajax and its component technologies. Find categorized links to Ajax tools, code, forums, books, libraries, frameworks, conferences, podcasts and more. Check out the tutorials for all skill levels, from introductory to advanced. See our comprehensive list of developer toolkits and libraries. Visit the most popular Ajax community websites and blogs. Explore many popular commercial and free open-source Ajax applications. Download code snippets and complete scripts that you can use on your own website. Also, be sure to visit our Resource Centers with information on Ajax's component technologies, including XHTML (www.deitel.com/xhtml/), CSS 2.1 (www.deitel.com/css21/), XML (www.deitel.com/XML/) and JavaScript (www.deitel.com/javascript/). For a complete Resource Center list, visit www.deitel.com/ResourceCenters.html.

3 PART

Rich Internet Application Client Technologies

The user should feel in control of the computer; not the other way around. This is achieved in applications that embody three qualities: responsiveness, permissiveness, and consistency.

—*Inside Macintosh*, Volume 1,
Apple Computer, Inc., 1985

14

Adobe®
Flash® CS3

OBJECTIVES

In this chapter you will learn:

- Flash CS3 multimedia development.
- To develop Flash movies.
- Flash animation techniques.
- ActionScript 3.0, Flash's object-oriented programming language.
- To create a preloading animation for a Flash movie.
- To add sound to Flash movies.
- To publish a Flash movie.
- To create special effects with Flash.
- To create a Splash Screen.

Science and technology and the various forms of art, all unite humanity in a single and interconnected system.
—Zhores Aleksandrovich Medvede

All the world's a stage, and all the men and women merely players; they have their exits and their entrances; and one man in his time plays many parts. . .
—William Shakespeare

Music has charms to soothe a savage breast,
To soften rocks, or bend a knotted oak.
—William Congreve

A flash and where previously the brain held a dead fact, the soul grasps a living truth! At moments we are all artists.
—Arnold Bennett

14.1 **Introduction**

Adobe *Flash CS3* (Creative Suite 3) is a commercial application that you can use to produce interactive, animated *movies*. Flash can be used to create web-based banner advertisements, interactive websites, games and web-based applications with stunning graphics and multimedia effects. It provides tools for drawing graphics, generating animations, and adding sound and video. Flash movies can be embedded in web pages, distributed on CDs and DVDs as independent applications, or converted into stand-alone, executable programs. Flash includes tools for coding in its scripting language—*ActionScript 3.0*—which is similar to JavaScript and enables interactive applications. A fully functional, 30-day trial version of Flash CS3 is available for download from:

> www.adobe.com/products/flash/

To follow along with the examples in this chapter, please install this software before continuing. Follow the on-screen instructions to install the trial version of the Flash software.

To play Flash movies, the *Flash Player plug-in* must be installed in your web browser. The most recent version of the plug-in (at the time of this writing) is version 9. You can download the latest version from:

> www.adobe.com/go/getflashplayer

According to Adobe's statistics, approximately 98.7 percent of web users have Flash Player version 6 or greater installed, and 83.4 percent of web users have Flash Player version 9 installed.[1] There are ways to detect whether a user has the appropriate plug-in to view Flash content. Adobe provides a tool called the Flash Player Detection Kit which contains files that work together to detect whether a suitable version of Adobe Flash Player is installed in a user's web browser. This kit can be downloaded from:

www.adobe.com/products/flashplayer/download/detection_kit/

This chapter introduces building Flash movies. You'll create interactive buttons, add sound to movies, create special graphic effects and integrate ActionScript in movies.

14.2 Flash Movie Development

Once Flash CS3 is installed, open the program. Flash's **Welcome Screen** appears by default. The **Welcome Screen** contains options such as **Open a Recent Item**, **Create New** and **Create from Template**. The bottom of the page contains links to useful help topics and tutorials. [*Note:* For additional help, refer to Flash's **Help** menu.]

To create a blank Flash document, click **Flash File (ActionScript 3.0)** under the **Create New** heading. Flash opens a new file called **Untitled-1** in the Flash development environment (Fig. 14.1).

At the center of the development environment is the movie *stage*—the white area in which you place graphic elements during movie development. Above the stage is the *timeline*, which represents the time period over which a movie runs. The timeline is divided into increments called *frames*, represented by gray and white rectangles. Each frame depicts a moment in time during the movie, into which you can insert movie elements. The *playhead* indicates the current frame.

 Common Programming Error 14.1

Elements placed off stage can still appear if the user changes the aspect ratio of the movie. If an element should not be visible, use an alpha of 0% to hide the element.

The development environment contains several windows that provide options and tools for creating Flash movies. Many of these tools are located in the ***Tools bar***, the vertical window located at the left side of the development environment. The **Tools** bar (Fig. 14.2) is divided into multiple sections, each containing tools and functions that help you create Flash movies. The tools near the top of the **Tools** bar select, add and remove graphics from Flash movies. The **Hand** and **Zoom** tools allow you to pan and zoom in the stage. Another section of tools provides colors for shapes, lines and filled areas. The last section contains settings for the ***active tool*** (i.e., the tool that is highlighted and in use). You can make a tool behave differently by selecting a new mode from the options section of the **Tools** bar.

Application windows called ***panels*** organize frequently used movie options. Panel options modify the size, shape, color, alignment and effects associated with a movie's graphic elements. By default, panels line the right and bottom edges of the window. Panels

---

1. Flash Player statistics from Adobe's Flash Player Penetration Survey website at www.adobe.com/products/player_census/flashplayer/version_penetration.html.

Tools   Timeline   Playhead   Menu bar   Frames   Stage   Panel windows

Fig. 14.1 | Flash CS3 development environment.

Fig. 14.2 | CS3 **Tools** bar.

may be placed anywhere in the development environment by dragging the tab at the left edge of their bars.

The context-sensitive **Properties** panel (frequently referred to as the **Properties** window) is located at the bottom of the screen by default. This panel displays various information about the currently selected object. It is Flash's most useful tool for viewing and altering an object's properties.

The **Color, Swatches, Properties, Filters** and **Parameters** panels also appear in the development environment by default. You can access different panels by selecting them from the **Window** menu. To save and manage customized panel layouts, select **Window > Workspace**, then use the **Save Current...** and **Manage...** options to save a layout or load an existing layout, respectively.

14.3 Learning Flash with Hands-On Examples

Now you'll create several complete Flash movies. The first example demonstrates how to create an interactive, animated button. ActionScript code will produce a random text string each time the button is clicked. To begin, create a new Flash movie. First, select **File > New**. In the **New Document** dialog (Fig. 14.3), select **Flash File (ActionScript 3.0)** under the **General** tab and click **OK**. Next, choose **File > Save As...** and save the movie as Ceo-Assistant.fla. The **.fla** file extension is a Flash-specific extension for editable movies.

Good Programming Practice 14.1

Save each project with a meaningful name in its own folder. Creating a new folder for each movie helps keep projects organized.

Right click the stage to open a menu containing different movie options. Select **Document Properties...** to display the **Document Properties** dialog (Fig. 14.4). This dialog can also be accessed by selecting **Document...** from the **Modify** menu. Settings such as the **Frame rate, Dimensions** and **Background color** are configured in this dialog.

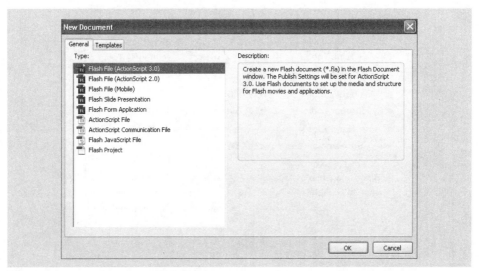

Fig. 14.3 | **New Document** dialog.

Fig. 14.4 | **Document Properties** dialog.

The **Frame rate** sets the speed at which movie frames display. A higher frame rate causes more frames to be displayed in a given unit of time (the standard measurement is seconds), thus creating a faster movie. The frame rate for Flash movies on the web is generally between 12 and 60 frames per second (**fps**). Flash's default frame rate is 12 fps. For this example, set the **Frame Rate** to 10 frames per second.

Performance Tip 14.1

Higher frame rates increase the amount of information to process, and thus increase the movie's processor usage and file size. Be especially aware of file sizes when catering to low bandwidth web users.

The background color determines the color of the stage. Click the background-color box (called a *swatch*) to select the background color. A new panel opens, presenting a web-safe palette. Web-safe palettes and color selection are discussed in detail in Chapter 3. Note that the mouse pointer changes into an eyedropper, which indicates that you may select a color. Choose a light blue color (Fig. 14.5).

The box in the upper-left corner of the dialog displays the new background color. The *hexadecimal notation* for the selected color appears to the right of this box. The hexadecimal notation is the color code that a web browser uses to render color.

Fig. 14.5 | Selecting a background color.

Dimensions define the size of the movie as it displays on the screen. For this example, set the movie **width** to **200** pixels and the movie **height** to **180** pixels. Click **OK** to apply the changes in the movie settings.

Software Engineering Observation 14.1

A movie's contents are not resized when you change the size of the movie stage.

With the new dimensions, the stage appears smaller. Select the ***Zoom Tool*** from the toolbox (Fig. 14.2) and click the stage once to enlarge it to 200 percent of its size (i.e., zoom in). The current zoom percentage appears in the upper-right above the stage editing area. Editing a movie with small dimensions is easier when the stage is enlarged. Press the *Alt* key while clicking the zoom tool to reduce the size of the work area (i.e., zoom out). Select the ***Hand Tool*** from the toolbox, and drag the stage to the center of the editing area. The hand tool may be accessed at any time by holding down the *spacebar* key.

14.3.1 Creating a Shape with the Oval Tool

Flash provides several editing tools and options for creating graphics. Flash creates shapes using *vectors*—mathematical equations that Flash uses to define size, shape and color. Some other graphics applications create raster graphics or bitmapped graphics. When vector graphics are saved, they are stored using equations. ***Raster graphics*** are defined by areas of colored *pixels*—the unit of measurement for most computer monitors. Raster graphics typically have larger file sizes because the computer saves the information for every pixel. Vector and raster graphics also differ in their ability to be resized. Vector graphics can be resized without losing clarity, whereas raster graphics lose clarity as they are enlarged or reduced.

We'll now create an interactive button out of a circular shape. You can create shapes by dragging with the shape tools. Select the Oval tool from the toolbox. If the Oval tool is not already displayed, click and hold the Rectangle/Oval tool to display the list of rectangle and oval tools. We use this tool to specify the button area. Every shape has a ***Stroke color*** and a ***Fill color***. The stroke color is the color of a shape's outline, and the fill color is the color that fills the shape. Click the swatches in the **Colors** section of the toolbox (Fig. 14.6) to set the fill color to red and the stroke color to black. Select the colors from the web-safe palette or enter their hexadecimal values.

Clicking the **Black and white** button resets the stroke color to black and the fill color to white. Selecting the *Swap colors* option switches the stroke and fill colors. A shape can be created without a fill or stroke color by selecting the *No color* option (☒|) when you select either the stroke or fill swatch.

Create the oval anywhere on the stage by dragging with the Oval tool while pressing the *Shift* key. The *Shift* key constrains the oval's proportions to have equal height and

Fig. 14.6 | Setting the fill and stroke colors.

width (i.e., a circle). The same technique creates a square with the Rectangle tool or draws a straight line with the Pencil tool. Drag the mouse until the circle is approximately the size of a dime, then release the mouse button.

After you draw the oval, a dot appears in frame 1, the first frame of the timeline for **Layer 1**. This dot signifies a *keyframe* (Fig. 14.7), which indicates a point of change in a timeline. Whenever you draw a shape in an empty frame, Flash creates a keyframe.

The shape's fill and stroke may be edited individually. Click the red area with the *Selection* tool (black arrow) to select the circle fill. A grid of white dots appears over an object when it is selected (Fig. 14.8). Click the black stroke around the circle while pressing the *Shift* key to add to this selection. You can also make multiple selections by dragging with the selection tool to draw a selection box around specific items.

A shape's size can be modified with the **Properties** panel when the shape is selected (Fig. 14.9). If the panel is not open, open it by selecting **Properties** from the **Window** menu or pressing *<Ctrl>-F3*.

Set the width and height of the circle by typing **30** into the **W:** text field and **30** into the **H:** text field. Entering an equal width and height maintains a *constrained aspect ratio* while changing the circle's size. A constrained aspect ratio maintains an object's proportions as it is resized. Press *Enter* to apply these values.

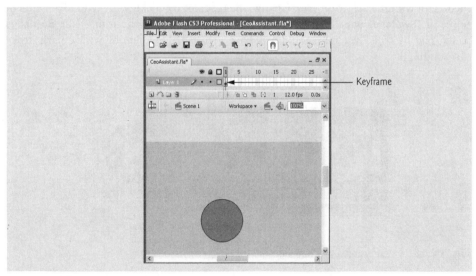

Fig. 14.7 | Keyframe added to the timeline.

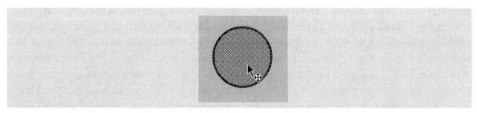

Fig. 14.8 | Making multiple selections with the Selection tool.

Fig. 14.9 | Modifying the size of a shape with the **Properties window.**

The next step is to modify the shape's color. We'll apply a *gradient fill*—a gradual progression of color that fills the shape. Open the **Swatches** panel (Fig. 14.10), either by selecting **Swatches** from the **Window** menu or by pressing *<Ctrl>-F9*. The **Swatches** panel provides four *radial gradients* and three *linear gradients*, although you also can create and edit gradients with the **Color** panel.

Click outside the circle with the Selection tool to deselect the circle. Now, select only the red fill with the Selection tool. Change the fill color by clicking the red radial gradient fill in the **Swatches** panel. The gradient fills are located at the bottom of the **Swatches** panel (Fig. 14.10). The circle should now have a red radial gradient fill with a black stroke surrounding it.

Fig. 14.10 | Choosing a gradient fill.

14.3.2 Adding Text to a Button

Button titles communicate a button's function to the user. The easiest way to create a title is with the *Text* tool. Create a button title by selecting the Text tool and clicking the center of the button. Next, type GO in capital letters. Highlight the text with the Text tool. Once text is selected, you can change the font, text size and font color with the **Properties** window (Fig. 14.11). Select a sans-serif font, such as **Arial** or **Verdana**, from the font drop-down list. Set the font size to **14** pt either by typing the size into the font size field or by pressing the arrow button next to it, revealing the *size selection slider*—a vertical slider that, when moved, changes the font size. Set the font weight to bold by clicking the bold

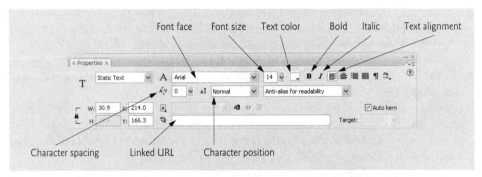

Fig. 14.11 │ Setting the font face, size, weight and color with the **Properties window**.

button (**B**). Finally, change the font color by clicking the text color swatch and selecting white from the palette.

Look-and-Feel Observation 14.1

Sans-serif fonts, such as Arial, Helvetica and Verdana, are easier to read on a computer monitor, and therefore ensure better usability.

If the text does not appear in the correct location, drag it to the center of the button with the Selection tool. The button is almost complete and should look similar to Fig. 14.12.

Fig. 14.12 │ Adding text to the button.

14.3.3 Converting a Shape into a Symbol

A Flash movie consists of *scenes* and *symbols*. Each scene contains all graphics and symbols. The parent movie may contain several symbols that are reusable movie elements, such as *graphics*, *buttons* and *movie clips*. A scene timeline can contain numerous symbols, each with its own timeline and properties. A scene may have several *instances* of any given symbol (i.e., the same symbol can appear multiple times in one scene). You can edit symbols independently of the scene by using the symbol's *editing stage*. The editing stage is separate from the scene stage and contains only one symbol.

Good Programming Practice 14.2

Reusing symbols can drastically reduce file size, thereby allowing faster downloads.

To make our button interactive, we must first convert the button into a button symbol. The button consists of distinct text, color fill and stroke elements on the parent stage. These items are combined and treated as one object when the button is converted into a symbol. Use the Selection tool to drag a *selection box* around the button, selecting the button fill, the button stroke and the text all at one time (Fig. 14.13).

Now, select **Convert to Symbol…** from the **Modify** menu or use the shortcut *F8* on the keyboard. This opens the **Convert to Symbol** dialog, in which you can set the properties of a new symbol (Fig. 14.14).

Every symbol in a Flash movie must have a unique name. It is a good idea to name symbols by their contents or function, because this makes them easier to identify and reuse. Enter the name **go button** into the **Name** field of the **Convert to Symbol** dialog. The **Behavior** option determines the symbol's function in the movie.

You can create three different types of symbols—movie clips, buttons and graphics. A *movie clip symbol's* behavior is similar to that of a scene and thus it is ideal for recurring animations. *Graphic symbols* are ideal for static images and basic animations. *Button symbols* are objects that perform button actions, such as *rollovers* and hyperlinking. A rollover is an action that changes the appearance of a button when the mouse passes over it. For this example, select **Button** as the type of symbol and click **OK**. The button should now be surrounded by a blue box with crosshairs in the upper-left corner, indicating that the button is a symbol. Also, in the **Properties** window panel, name this instance of the **go button** symbol **goButton** in the field containing **<Instance Name>**. Use the selection tool to drag the button to the lower-right corner of the stage.

The **Library** panel (Fig. 14.15) stores every symbol present in a movie and is accessed through the **Window** menu or by the shortcuts *<Ctrl>-L* or *F11*. Multiple instances of a symbol can be placed in a movie by dragging and dropping the symbol from the **Library** panel onto the stage.

The **Movie Explorer** displays the movie structure and is accessed by selecting **Movie Explorer** from the **Window** menu or by pressing *<Alt>-F3* (Fig. 14.16). The **Movie Explorer** panel illustrates the relationship between the current scene (**Scene 1**) and its symbols.

Fig. 14.13 | Selecting an object with the selection tool.

Fig. 14.14 | Creating a new symbol with the **Convert to Symbol** dialog.

Fig. 14.15 | **Library** panel.

Fig. 14.16 | **Movie Explorer** for CeoAssistant.fla.

14.3.4 Editing Button Symbols

The next step in this example is to make the button symbol interactive. The different components of a button symbol, such as its text, color fill and stroke, may be edited in the symbol's editing stage, which you can access by double clicking the icon next to the symbol in the **Library**. A button symbol's timeline contains four frames, one for each of the button states (up, over and down) and one for the hit area.

The *up state* (indicated by the **Up** frame on screen) is the default state before the user presses the button or rolls over it with the mouse. Control shifts to the *over state* (i.e., the **Over** frame) when the user rolls over the button with the mouse cursor. The button's *down state* (i.e., the **Down** frame) plays when a user presses a button. You can create interactive, user-responsive buttons by customizing the appearance of a button in each of these states. Graphic elements in the *hit state* (i.e., the **Hit** frame) are not visible to a viewer of the movie; they exist simply to define the active area of the button (i.e., the area that can be clicked). The hit state will be discussed further in Section 14.6.

By default, buttons have only the up state activated when they are created. You may activate other states by adding keyframes to the other three frames. Keyframes for a button, discussed in the next section, determine how a button reacts when it is rolled over or clicked with the mouse.

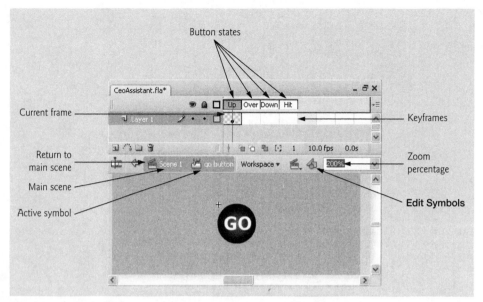

Fig. 14.17 | Modifying button states with a button's editing stage.

14.3.5 Adding Keyframes

Keyframes are points of change in a Flash movie and appear in the timeline with a dot. By adding keyframes to a button symbol's timeline, you can control how the button reacts to user interactions. The following step shows how to create a button rollover effect, which is accomplished by inserting a keyframe in the button's **Over** frame, then changing the button's appearance in that frame. Right click the **Over** frame and select **Insert Keyframe** from the resulting menu or press *F6* (Fig. 14.18).

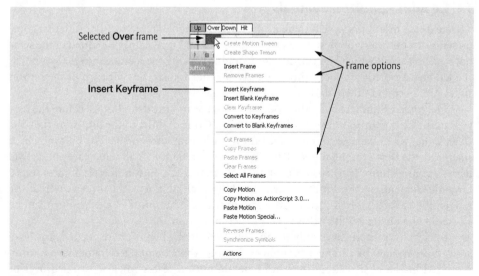

Fig. 14.18 | Inserting a keyframe.

Select the **Over** frame and click outside the button area with the selection tool to deselect the button's components. Change the color of the button in the **Over** state from red gradient fill to green gradient fill by selecting only the fill portion of the button with the Selection tool. Select the green gradient fill in the **Swatches** panel to change the color of the button in the **Over** state. Changing the color of the button in the over state does not affect the color of the button in the up state. Now, when the user moves the cursor over the button (in the up state) the button animation is replaced by the animation in the **Over** state. Here, we change only the button's color, but we could have created an entirely new animation in the **Over** state. The button will now change from red to green when the user rolls over the button with the mouse. The button will return to red when the mouse is no longer positioned over the button.

14.3.6 Adding Sound to a Button

The next step is to add a sound effect that plays when a user clicks the button. Flash imports sounds in the WAV (Windows), AIFF (Macintosh) or MP3 formats. Several button sounds are available free for download from sites such as Flashkit (`www.flashkit.com`) and Muinar (`www.sounds.muinar.com`). For this example, download the *cash register* sound in WAV format from

> `www.flashkit.com/soundfx/Industrial_Commercial/Cash`

Click the **Download** link to download the sound from this site. This link opens a new web page from which the user chooses the sound format. Choose MP3 as the file format by clicking the **mp3** link. Save the file to the same folder as `CeoAssistant.fla`. Extract the sound file and save it in the same folder as `CeoAssistant.fla`.

Once the sound file is extracted, it can be imported into Flash. Import the sound into the **Library** by choosing **Import to Library...** from the **Import** submenu of the **File** menu. Select **All Formats** in the **Files of type** field of the **Import** dialog so that all available files are displayed. Select the sound file and press **Open**. This imports the sound file and places it in the movie's **Library**, making it available to use in the movie.

You can add sound to a movie by placing the sound clip in a keyframe or over a series of frames. For this example, we add the sound to the button's down state so that the sound plays when the user presses the button. Select the button's **Down** frame and press *F6* to add a keyframe.

Add the sound to the **Down** keyframe by dragging it from the **Library** to the stage. Open the **Properties** window (Fig. 14.19) and select the **Down** frame in the timeline to define the sound's properties in the movie. To ensure the desired sound has been added to the keyframe, choose the sound filename from the **Sound** drop-down list. This list contains all the sounds that have been added to the movie. Make sure the **Sync** field is set to **Event** so that the sound plays when the user clicks the button. If the **Down** frame has a blue wave or line through it, the sound effect has been added to the button.

Next, optimize the sound for the web. Double click the sound icon in the **Library** panel to open the **Sound Properties** dialog (Fig. 14.20). The settings in this dialog change the way that the sound is saved in the final movie. Different settings are optimal for different sounds and different audiences. For this example, set the **Compression** type to **MP3**, which reduces file size. Ensure that **Use imported MP3 quality** is selected. If the sound clip

Fig. 14.19 | Adding sound to a button.

Fig. 14.20 | Optimizing sound with the **Sound Properties** dialog.

is long, or if the source MP3 was encoded with a high bitrate, you may want to deselect this and specify your own bitrate to save space.

The sound clip is now optimized for use on the web. Return to the scene by pressing the **Edit Scene** button (🔳) and selecting **Scene 1** or by clicking **Scene 1** at the top of the movie window.

14.3.7 Verifying Changes with Test Movie

It is a good idea to ensure that movie components function correctly before proceeding further with development. Movies can be viewed in their *published state* with the Flash Player. The published state of a movie is how it would appear if viewed over the web or with the Flash Player. Published Flash movies have the Shockwave Flash extension *.swf* (pronounced "swiff"). SWF files can be viewed but not edited.

Select **Test Movie** from the **Control** menu (or press *<Ctrl>-Enter*) to *export* the movie into the Flash Player. A window opens with the movie in its published state. Move the cursor over the **GO** button to view the color change (Fig. 14.21), then click the button to play the sound. Close the test window to return to the stage. If the button's color does not change, return to the button's editing stage and check that you followed the steps correctly.

Fig. 14.21 | **GO** button in its up and over states.

14.3.8 Adding Layers to a Movie

The next step in this example is to create the movie's title animation. It's a good idea for you to create a new *layer* for new movie items. A movie can be composed of many layers, each having its own attributes and effects. Layers organize movie elements so that they can be animated and edited separately, making the composition of complex movies easier. Graphics in higher layers appear over the graphics in lower layers.

Before creating a new title layer, double click the text **Layer 1** in the timeline. Rename the layer by entering the text `Button` into the name field (Fig. 14.22).

Create a new layer for the title animation by clicking the Insert a new layer button or by selecting **Layer** from the **Timeline** submenu of the **Insert** menu. The Insert a new layer button places a layer named **Layer 2** above the selected layer. Change the name of **Layer 2** to **Title**. Activate the new layer by clicking its name.

 Good Programming Practice 14.3

Always give movie layers descriptive names. Descriptive names are especially helpful when working with many layers.

Select the Text tool to create the title text. Click with the Text tool in the center of the stage toward the top. Use the **Property** window to set the font to **Arial**, the text color to navy blue (hexadecimal value #000099) and the font size to **20** pt (Fig. 14.23). Set the text alignment to center by clicking the center justify button.

Type the title **CEO Assistant 1.0** (Fig. 14.24), then click the selection tool. A blue box appears around the text, indicating that it is a *grouped object*. This text is a grouped object because each letter is a part of a text string and cannot be edited independently. Text can be broken apart for color editing, shape modification or animation (shown in a later example). Once text has been broken apart, it may not be edited with the Text tool.

Fig. 14.22 | Renaming a layer.

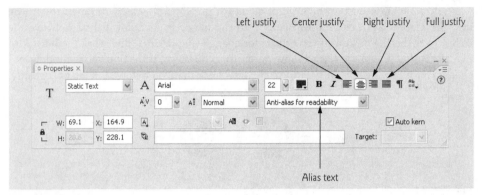

Fig. 14.23 | Setting text alignment with the **Properties window**.

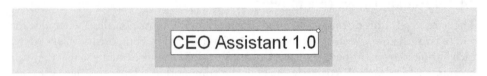

Fig. 14.24 | Creating a title with the Text tool.

14.3.9 Animating Text with Tweening

Animations in Flash are created by inserting keyframes into the timeline. Each keyframe represents a significant change in the position or appearance of the animated object.

You may use several methods to animate objects in Flash. One is to create a series of successive keyframes in the timeline. Modifying the animated object in each keyframe creates an animation as the movie plays. Another method is to insert a keyframe later in the timeline representing the final appearance and position of the object, then create a tween between the two keyframes. *Tweening* is an automated process in which Flash creates the intermediate steps of the animation between two keyframes.

Flash provides two tweening methods. *Shape tweening* morphs an object from one shape to another. For instance, the word "star" could morph into the shape of a star. Shape tweening can be applied only to ungrouped objects, not symbols or grouped objects. Be sure to break apart text before attempting to create a shape tween. *Motion tweening* moves objects around the stage. Motion tweening can be applied to symbols or grouped objects.

You can only have one symbol per layer if you intend to tween the symbol. At this point in the development of the example movie, only frame 1 is occupied in each layer. Keyframes must be designated in the timeline before adding the motion tween. Click frame 15 in the **Title** layer and press *F6* to add a new keyframe. All the intermediate frames in the timeline should turn gray, indicating that they are active (Fig. 14.25). Until the motion tween is added, each active frame contains the same image as the first frame.

The button disappears from the movie after the first frame because only the first frame is active in the button layer. Before the movie is completed, we'll move the button to frame 15 of its layer so that the button appears once the animation stops.

We now create a motion tween by modifying the position of the title text. Select frame 1 of the **Title** layer and select the title text with the Selection tool. Drag the title text directly above the stage. When the motion tween is added, the title will move onto the stage. Add

Fig. 14.25 | Adding a keyframe to create an animation.

the motion tween by right clicking frame 1 in the **Title** layer. Then select **Create Motion Tween** from the **Insert > Timeline** menu. Tweens also can be added using the **Tween type** drop down menu in the **Properties** window. Frames 2–14 should turn light blue, with an arrow pointing from the keyframe in frame 1 to the keyframe in frame 15 (Fig. 14.26).

Test the movie again with the Flash Player by pressing *<Ctrl>-Enter* to view the new animation. Note that the animation continues to loop—all Flash movies loop by default. Adding the ActionScript function ***stop*** to the last frame in the movie stops the movie from looping. For this example, click frame 15 of the **Title** layer, and open the **Actions** panel by selecting **Window > Actions** or by pressing *F9* (Fig. 14.27). The **Actions** panel is used to add

Fig. 14.26 | Creating a motion tween.

Fig. 14.27 | Adding ActionScript to a frame with the **Actions** panel.

actions (i.e., scripted behaviors) to symbols and frames. Here, add `stop();` so that the movie does not loop back to the first frame.

Minimize the **Actions** panel by clicking the down arrow in its title bar. The small letter a in frame 15 of the **Title** layer indicates the new action. Test the movie again in Flash Player. Now, the animation should play only once.

The next step is to move the button to frame 15 so that it appears only at the end of the movie. Add a keyframe to frame 15 of the **Button** layer. A copy of the button should appear in the new keyframe. Select the button in the first frame and delete it by pressing the *Delete* key. The button will now appear only in the keyframe at the end of the movie.

14.3.10 Adding a Text Field

The final component of our movie is a *text field*, which contains a string of text that changes every time the user presses the button. An instance name is given to the text field so that ActionScript added to the button can control its contents.

Create a layer named **Advice** for the new text field, and add a keyframe to frame 15 of the **Advice** layer. Select the Text tool and create the text field by dragging with the mouse in the stage (Fig. 14.28). Place the text field directly below the title. Set the text font to **Courier New, 12 pt** and the style to bold in the **Properties** window. You can alter the size of the text field by dragging the *anchor* that appears in its upper-right corner.

You'll now assign an instance name to the text field. Select the text field and open the **Properties** window (Fig. 14.29). The **Properties** window contains several options for modifying text fields. The top-left field contains the different types of text fields. **Static Text**, the default setting for this panel, creates text that does not change. The second option,

Fig. 14.28 | Creating a text field.

Fig. 14.29 | Creating a dynamic text field with the **Properties** window.

Dynamic Text, creates text that can be changed or determined by outside variables through ActionScript. When you select this text type, new options appear below this field. The **Line type** drop-down list specifies the text field size as either a single line or multiple lines of text. The **Instance Name** field allows you to give the text field an instance name by which it can be referenced in script. For example, if the text field instance name is newText, you could write a script setting newText.text equal to a string or a function output. The third text type, **Input Text**, creates a text field into which the viewers of the movie can input their own text. For this example, select **Dynamic Text** as the text type. Set the line type to **Single Line** and enter advice as the instance name. This instance name will be used in Action-Script later in this example.

14.3.11 Adding ActionScript

All the movie objects are now in place, so CEO Assistant 1.0 is almost complete. The final step is to add ActionScript to the button, enabling the script to change the contents of the text field every time a user clicks the button. Our script calls a built-in Flash function to generate a random number. This random number corresponds to a message in a list of possible messages to display. [*Note:* The ActionScript in this chapter has been formatted to conform with the code-layout conventions of this book. The Flash application may produce code that is formatted differently.]

Select frame 15 of the **Button** layer and open the **Actions** panel. We want the action to occur when the user clicks the button. To achieve this, insert the statement:

```
goButton.addEventListener( MouseEvent.MOUSE_DOWN, goFunction );
```

This statement uses the button object's instance name (**goButton**) to call the ***addEventListener*** function, which registers an event handler (goFunction in this example) that will be called when the event takes place (i.e., when you click the button). The first argument, MouseEvent.MOUSE_DOWN, specifies that an action is performed when the user presses the button with the mouse.

The next step is to add the function that handles this event. Create a new function named goFunction by using the code

```
function goFunction( event : MouseEvent ) : void
{
} // end function goFunction
```

The function's one parameter is a MouseEvent, implying that the function has to be provided with a mouse action to be accessed. The function does not return anything, hence the void return value. Inside this function, add the following statement:

```
var randomNumber : int = Math.floor( ( Math.random() * 5 ) );
```

which creates an integer variable called randomNumber and assigns it a random value. For this example, we use the Math.random function to choose a random number from 0 to 1. Math.random returns a random floating-point number from 0.0 up to, but not including, 1.0. Then, it is scaled accordingly, depending on what the range should be. Since we want all the numbers between 0 and 4, inclusive, the value returned by the Math.random should be multiplied by 5 to produce a number in the range 0.0 up to, but not including, 5.0.

Finally, this new number should be rounded down to the largest integer smaller than itself, using the Math.floor function.

 Error-Prevention Tip 14.1

ActionScript is case sensitive. Be aware of the case when entering arguments or variable names.

The value of randomNumber determines the text string that appears in the text field. A switch statement sets the text field's value based on the value of randomNumber. [*Note:* For more on switch statements, refer to Chapter 6.] On a new line in the goFunction function, insert the following switch statement:

```
switch ( randomNumber )
{
   case 0:
      advice.text = "Hire Someone!";
      break;
   case 1:
      advice.text = "Buy a Yacht!";
      break;
   case 2:
      advice.text = "Buy stock!";
      break;
   case 3:
      advice.text = "Go Golfing!";
      break;
   case 4:
      advice.text = "Hold a meeting!";
      break;
} // end switch
```

This statement displays different text in the advice text field based on the value of the variable randomNumber. The text field's text property specifies the text to display. If you feel ambitious, increase the number of advice statements by producing a larger range of random values and adding more cases to the switch statement. Minimize the **Actions** panel to continue.

Congratulations! You have now completed building CEO Assistant 1.0. Test the movie by pressing <*Ctrl*>-*Enter* and clicking the **GO** button. After testing the movie with the Flash Player, return to the main window and save the file.

14.4 Publishing Your Flash Movie

Flash movies must be *published* for users to view them outside the Flash CS3 environment and Flash Player. This section discusses the more common methods of publishing Flash movies. For this example, we want to publish in two formats, Flash and *Windows Projector*, which creates a standard Windows-executable file that works even if the user hasn't installed Flash. Select **Publish Settings...** from the **File** menu to open the **Publish Settings** dialog.

Select the **Flash**, **HTML** and **Windows Projector** checkboxes and uncheck all the others. Then click the **Flash** tab at the top of the dialog. This section of the dialog allows you to choose the Flash settings. Flash movies may be published in an older Flash version if you wish to support older Flash Players. Note that ActionScript 3.0 is not supported by older players, so choose a version with care. Publish the movie by clicking **Publish** in the **Publish Settings** dialog or by selecting **Publish** from the **File** menu. After you've published the movie, the directory in which you saved the movie will have several new files (Fig. 14.30). If you wish to place your movie on a website, be sure to copy the HTML, JavaScript and SWF files to your server.

Good Programming Practice 14.4

It is not necessary to transfer the .fla *version of your Flash movie to a web server unless you want other users to be able to download the editable version of the movie.*

As we can see in the Ceo Assistant 1.0 example, Flash is a feature-rich program. We have only begun to use Flash to its full potential. ActionScript can create sophisticated programs and interactive movies. It also enables Flash to interact with ASP.NET (Chapter 21), PHP (Chapter 19), and JavaScript (Chapters 4–9), making it a program that integrates smoothly into a web environment.

Fig. 14.30 | Published Flash files.

14.5 Creating Special Effects with Flash

The following sections introduce several Flash special effects. The preceding example familiarized you with basic movie development. The next sections cover many additional topics, from importing bitmaps to creating splash screens that display before a web page loads.

14.5.1 Importing and Manipulating Bitmaps

Some of the examples in this chapter require importing bitmapped images and other media into a Flash movie. The importing process is similar for all types of media, including images, sound and video. The following example shows how to import an image into a Flash movie.

Begin by creating a new Flash document. The image we are going to import is located in the Chapter 14 examples folder. Select **File > Import > Import to Stage...** (or press <*Ctrl*>-*R*) to display the **Import** dialog. Browse to the folder on your system containing this chapter's examples and open the folder labeled images. Select bug.bmp and click **OK** to continue. A bug image should appear on the stage. The **Library** panel stores imported images. You can convert imported images into editable shapes by selecting the image and pressing <*Ctrl*>-*B* or by choosing **Break Apart** from the **Modify** menu. Once an imported image is broken apart, it may be shape tweened or edited with *editing tools*, such as the

Lasso, Paint bucket, Eraser and Paintbrush. The editing tools are found in the toolbox and apply changes to a shape.

Dragging with the **Lasso tool** selects areas of shapes. The color of a selected area may be changed or the selected area may be moved. Click and drag with the Lasso tool to draw the boundaries of the selection. As with the button in the last example, when you select a shape area, a mesh of white dots covers the selection. Once an area is selected, you may change its color by selecting a new fill color with the fill swatch or by clicking the selection with the Paint bucket tool. The Lasso tool has different options (located in the **Options** section of the toolbox) including **Magic wand** and **Polygon mode**. The Magic wand option changes the Lasso tool into the Magic wand tool, which selects areas of similar colors. The polygonal lasso selects straight-edged areas.

The **Eraser tool** removes shape areas when you click and drag the tool across an area. You can change the eraser size using the tool options. Other options include settings that make the tool erase only fills or strokes.

The **Brush tool** applies color in the same way that the eraser removes color. The paintbrush color is selected with the fill swatch. The paintbrush tool options include a **Brush mode** option. These modes are **Paint behind**, which sets the tool to paint only in areas with no color information; **Paint selection**, which paints only areas that have been selected; and **Paint inside**, which paints inside a line boundary.

Each of these tools can create original graphics. Experiment with the different tools to change the shape and color of the imported bug graphic.

Portability Tip 14.1

When building Flash movies, use the smallest possible file size and web-safe colors to ensure that most people can view the movie regardless of bandwidth, processor speed or monitor resolution.

14.5.2 Creating an Advertisement Banner with Masking

Masking hides portions of layers. A *masking layer* hides objects in the layers beneath it, revealing only the areas that can be seen through the shape of the mask. Items drawn on a masking layer define the mask's shape and cannot be seen in the final movie. The next example, which builds a website banner, shows how to use masking frames to add animation and color effects to text.

Create a new Flash document and set the size of the stage to **470** pixels wide by **60** pixels high. Create three layers named **top**, **middle** and **bottom** according to their positions in the layer hierarchy. These names help track the masked layer and the visible layers. The **top** layer contains the mask, the **middle** layer becomes the masked animation and the **bottom** layer contains an imported bitmapped logo. Import the graphic bug_apple.bmp (from the images folder in this chapter's examples folder) into the first frame of the **top** layer, using the method described in the preceding section. This image will appear too large to fit in the stage area. Select the image with the selection tool and align it with the upper-left corner of the stage. Then select the *Free transform* tool in the toolbox (Fig. 14.31).

The Free transform tool allows us to resize an image. When an object is selected with this tool, anchors appear around its corners and sides. Click and drag an anchor to resize the image in any direction. Holding the *Shift* key while dragging a corner anchor ensures

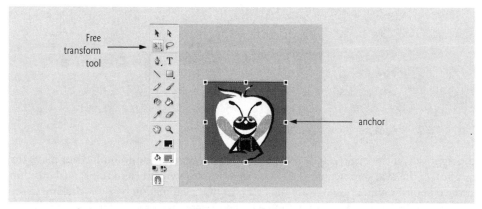

Fig. 14.31 | Resizing an image with the Free transform tool.

that the image maintains the original height and width ratio. Hold down the *Shift* key while dragging the lower-right anchor upward until the image fits on the stage.

Use the text tool to add text to frame 1 of the **top** layer. Use **Verdana**, **28** pt bold, as the font. Select a blue text color, and make sure that **Static Text** is selected in the **Properties** window. Type the banner text "Deitel and Associates", making sure that the text fits inside the stage area, and use the Selection tool to position the text next to the image. This text becomes the object that masks an animation.

We must convert the text into a shape before using it as a mask. Click the text field with the Selection tool to ensure that it is active and select **Break Apart** twice from the **Modify** menu. Breaking the text apart once converts each letter into its own text field. Breaking it apart again converts the letters into shapes that cannot be edited with the text tool, but can be manipulated as regular graphics.

Copy the contents of the **top** layer to the **bottom** layer before creating the mask, so that the text remains visible when the mask is added. Right click frame 1 of the **top** layer, and select **Copy Frames** from the resulting menu. Paste the contents of the **top** layer into frame 1 of the **bottom** layer by right clicking frame 1 of the **bottom** layer and selecting **Paste Frames** from the menu. This shortcut pastes the frame's contents in the same positions as the original frame. Delete the extra copy of the bug image by selecting the bug image in the **top** layer with the selection tool and pressing the *Delete* key.

Next, you'll create the animated graphic that the banner text in the **top** layer masks. Click in the first frame of the **middle** layer and use the Oval tool to draw a circle to the left of the image that is taller than the text. The oval does not need to fit inside the banner area. Set the oval stroke to *no color* by clicking the stroke swatch and selecting the **No color** option. Set the fill color to the rainbow gradient (Fig. 14.32), found at the bottom of the **Swatches** panel.

Select the oval by clicking it with the Selection tool, and convert the oval to a symbol by pressing *F8*. Name the symbol **oval** and set the behavior to **Graphic**. When the banner is complete, the oval will move across the stage; however, it will be visible only through the text mask in the **top** layer. Move the oval just outside the left edge of the stage, indicating the point at which the oval begins its animation. Create a keyframe in frame 20 of the **middle** layer and another in frame 40. These keyframes indicate the different locations of the **oval** symbol during the animation. Click frame 20 and move the oval just outside

Fig. 14.32 | Creating the oval graphic.

the right side of the stage to indicate the animation's next key position. Do not move the position of the **oval** graphic in frame 40, so that the oval will return to its original position at the end of the animation. Create the first part of the animation by right clicking frame 1 of the **middle** layer and choosing **Create Motion Tween** from the menu. Repeat this step for frame 20 of the **middle** layer, making the **oval** symbol move from left to right and back. Add keyframes to frame 40 of both the **top** and **bottom** layers so that the other movie elements appear throughout the movie.

Now that all the supporting movie elements are in place, the next step is to apply the masking effect. To do so, right click the **top** layer and select **Mask** (Fig. 14.33). Adding a mask to the **top** layer masks only the items in the layer directly below it (the **middle** layer), so the bug logo in the **bottom** layer remains visible at all times. Adding a mask also locks the **top** and **middle** layers to prevent further editing.

Now that the movie is complete, save it as `banner.fla` and test it with the Flash Player. The rainbow oval is visible through the text as it animates from left to right. The text in the bottom layer is visible in the portions not containing the rainbow (Fig. 14.34).

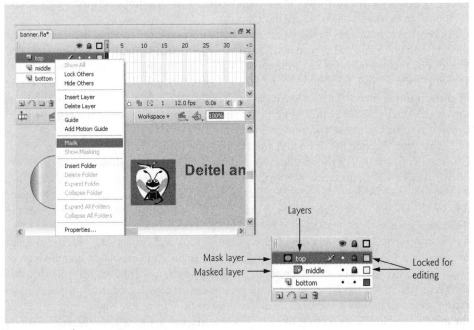

Fig. 14.33 | Creating a mask layer.

Fig. 14.34 | Completed banner.

14.5.3 Adding Online Help to Forms

In this section, we build on Flash techniques introduced earlier in this chapter, including tweening, masking, importing sound and bitmapped images, and writing ActionScript. In the following example, we apply these various techniques to create an online form that offers interactive help. The interactive help consists of animations that appear when a user presses buttons located next to the form fields. Each button contains a script that triggers an animation, and each animation provides the user with information regarding the form field that corresponds to the pressed button.

Each animation is a movie-clip symbol that is placed in a separate frame and layer of the scene. Adding a stop action to frame 1 pauses the movie until the user presses a button.

Begin by creating a new movie, using default movie size settings. Set the frame rate to 24 fps. The first layer will contain the site name, form title and form captions. Change the name of **Layer 1** to text. Add a stop action to frame 1 of the text layer. Create the site name Bug2Bug.com as static text in the **text** layer using a large, bold font, and place the title at the top of the page. Next, place the form name Registration Form as static text beneath the site name, using the same font, but in a smaller size and different color. The final text element added to this layer is the text box containing the form labels. Create a text box using the **Text Tool**, and enter the text: Name:, Member #: and Password:, pressing *Enter* after entering each label to put it on a different line. Next, adjust the value of the **Line Spacing** field (the amount of space between lines of text) found by clicking the **Edit Format Options** button (¶) in the **Properties** window. Change the form field caption line spacing to **22** in the **Format Options** dialog (Fig. 14.35) and set the text alignment (found in the **Properties** window) to right justify.

Now we'll create the form fields for our help form. The first step in the production of these form fields is to create a new layer named **form**. In the **form** layer, draw a rectangle that is roughly the same height as the caption text. This rectangle will serve as a background for the form text fields (Fig. 14.36). We set a **Rectangle corner radius** of 6 px in the **Properties** panel. Feel free to experiment with other shapes and colors.

The next step is to convert the rectangle into a symbol so that it may be reused in the movie. Select the rectangle fill and stroke with the selection tool and press *F8* to convert the selection to a symbol. Set the symbol behavior to **Graphic** and name the symbol **form**

Fig. 14.35 | Adjusting the line spacing with the **Format Options** dialog.

Fig. 14.36 | Creating a rectangle with rounded corners.

field. This symbol should be positioned next to the **Name:** caption. When the symbol is in place, open the **Library** panel by pressing *<Ctrl>-L*, select the **form** layer and drag two copies of the **form field** symbol from the **Library** onto the stage. This will create two new instances of this symbol. Use the Selection tool to align the fields with their corresponding captions. For more precise alignment, select the desired object with the Selection tool and press the arrow key on the keyboard in the direction you want to move the object. After alignment of the **form field** symbols, the movie should resemble Fig. 14.37.

We now add *input text fields* to our movie. An input text field is a text field into which the user can enter text. Select the Text tool and, using the **Properties** window, set the font to **Verdana, 16** pt, with dark blue as the color. In the **Text type** pull-down menu in the **Properties** window, select **Input Text** (Fig. 14.38). Then, click and drag in the stage to create a text field slightly smaller than the **form field** symbol we just created. With the Selection tool, position the text field over the instance of the **form field** symbol associated with the name. Create a similar text field for member number and password. Select the Password text field, and select **Password** in the Line type pull-down menu in the **Properties** window. Selecting **Password** causes any text entered into the field by the user to appear as an asterisk (*). We have now created all the input text fields for our help form. In this

Bug2Bug.com

Registration Form

Name:

Member#:

Password:

Fig. 14.37 | Creating multiple instances of a symbol with the **Library** panel.

Fig. 14.38 | Input and password text-field creation.

example, we won't actually process the text entered into these fields. Using ActionScript, we could give each input text field a variable name, and send the values of these variables to a server-side script for processing.

Now that the form fields are in place, we can create the help associated with each field. Add two new layers. Name one layer **button** and the other **labels**. The **labels** layer will hold the *frame label* for each keyframe. A frame label is a text string that corresponds to a specific frame or series of frames. In the **labels** layer, create keyframes in frames 2, 3 and 4. Select frame 2 and enter name into the **Frame** field in the **Properties** window (Fig. 14.39).

Fig. 14.39 | Adding **Frame Labels** using the **Properties window**.

Name frame 3 and frame 4 memberNumber and password, respectively. These frames can now be accessed either by number or by name. We use the labels again later in this example.

In frame 1 of the **button** layer, create a small circular button containing a question mark. [*Note:* the **Text type** property of the **Text Tool** will still be **Input Text**, so you must change it back to **Static Text**]. Position it next to the **name** field. When the button is complete, select all of its pieces with the selection tool, and press *F8* to convert the shape into a button symbol named **helpButton**. Drag two more instances of the **helpButton** symbol from the **Library** panel onto the stage next to each of the form fields.

These buttons will trigger animations that provide information about their corresponding form fields. A script will be added to each button so that the movie jumps to a particular frame when a user presses the button. Click the **helpButton** symbol associated with the **name** field and give it the instance name nameHelp. As in Section 14.3.11, we'll now add event-handling code. Open the **Actions** for the first frame of the **buttons** layer and invoke the nameHelp button's addEventListener function to register the function name-Function as the handler of the mouse-click event. In nameFunction, add a gotoAndStop action, causing the movie play to skip to a particular frame and stop playing. Enter "name" between the function's parentheses. The script should now read as follows:

```
nameHelp.addEventListener( MouseEvent.MOUSE_DOWN, nameFunction );

function nameFunction( event : MouseEvent ) : void
{
    gotoAndStop( "name" );
}
```

When the user presses the nameHelp button, this script advances to the frame labeled name and stops. [*Note:* We could also have entered gotoAndStop(2), referenced by frame number, in place of gotoAndStop("name").] Add similar code for the memberHelp and passwordHelp buttons, changing the frame labels to memberNumber and password, the button instance names to memberHelp and passwordHelp and the function names to memberFunction and passwordFunction, respectively. Each button now has an action that points to a distinct frame in the timeline. We next add the interactive help animations to these frames.

The animation associated with each button is created as a movie-clip symbol that is inserted into the scene at the correct frame. For instance, the animation associated with the **Password** field is placed in frame 4, so that when the button is pressed, the gotoAndStop action skips to the frame containing the correct animation. When the user clicks the button, a help rectangle will open and display the purpose of the associated field.

Each movie clip should be created as a *new symbol* so that it can be edited without affecting the scene. Select **New Symbol...** from the **Insert** menu (or use the shortcut *<Ctrl>-F8*), name the symbol **nameWindow** and set the behavior to **Movie Clip**. Press **OK** to open the symbol's stage and timeline.

Next, you'll create the interactive help animation. This animation contains text that describes the form field. Before adding the text, we are going to create a small background animation that we'll position behind the text. Begin by changing the name of **Layer 1** to **background**. Draw a dark blue rectangle with no border. This rectangle can be of any size, because we'll customize its proportions with the **Properties** window. Select the rectangle with the Selection tool, then open the **Properties** window. Set the **W:** field to **200** and the **H:** field to **120**, to define the rectangle's size. Next, center the rectangle by entering **–100** and **–60** into the **X:** and **Y:** fields, respectively (Fig. 14.40).

Now that the rectangle is correctly positioned, we can begin to create its animation. Add keyframes to frames 5 and 10 of the **background** layer. Use the **Properties** window to change the size of the rectangle in frame 5, setting its height to **5.0**. Next, right click frame 5 and select **Copy Frames**. Then right click frame 1 and select **Paste Frames**. While in frame 1, change the width of the rectangle to **5.0**.

The animation is created by applying shape tweening to frames 1 and 5. Recall that shape tweening morphs one shape into another. The shape tween causes the dot in frame 1 to grow into a line by frame 5, then into a rectangle in frame 10. Select frame 1 and apply the shape tween by right clicking frame 1 and selecting **Create Shape Tween**. Do the same for frame 5. Shape tweens appear green in the timeline (Fig. 14.41). Follow the same procedure for frame 5.

Now that this portion of the animation is complete, it may be tested on the stage by pressing *Enter*. The animation should appear as the dot from frame 1 growing into a line by frame 5 and into a rectangle by frame 10.

The next step is to add a mock form field to this animation which demonstrates what the user would type in the actual field. Add two new layers above the **background** layer, named **field** and **text**. The **field** layer contains a mock form field, and the **text** layer contains the help information.

First, create an animation similar to the growing rectangle we just created for the mock form field. Add a keyframe to frame 10 in both the **field** and **text** layers. Fortunately, we have a form field already created as a symbol. Select frame 10 of the **field** layer, and drag

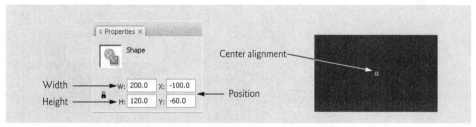

Fig. 14.40 | Centering an image on the stage with the **Properties** window.

Fig. 14.41 | Creating a shape tween.

the **form field** symbol from the **Library** panel onto the stage, placing it within the current movie clip. Symbols may be embedded in one another; however, they cannot be placed within themselves (i.e., an instance of the **form field** symbol cannot be dragged onto the **form field** symbol editing stage). Align the **form field** symbol with the upper-left corner of the background rectangle, as shown in Fig. 14.42.

Next, set the end of this movie clip by adding keyframes to the **background** and **field** layers in frame 40. Also add keyframes to frames 20 and 25 of the **field** layer. These keyframes define intermediate points in the animation. Refer to Fig. 14.43 for correct keyframe positioning.

The next step in creating the animation is to make the **form field** symbol grow in size. Select frame 20 of the **field** layer, which contains only the **form field** symbol. Next open the **Transform** panel from the **Window** menu. The **Transform** panel can be used to change an object's size. Check the **Constrain** checkbox to constrain the object's proportions as it is resized. Selecting this option causes the *scale factor* to be equal in the width and height fields. The scale factor measures the change in proportion. Set the scale factor for the width and height to **150%**, and press *Enter* to apply the changes. Repeat the previous step for frame 10 of the **field** layer, but scale the **form field** symbol down to **0%**.

The symbol's animation is created by adding a motion tween. Adding the motion tween to **field** layer frames 10 and 20 will cause the **form field** symbol to grow from 0% of the original size to 150%, then to 100%. Figure 14.43 illustrates this portion of the animation.

Next, you'll add text to the movie clip to help the user understand the purpose of the corresponding text field. You'll set text to appear over the **form field** symbol as an example to the user. The text that appears below the **form field** symbol tells the user what should be typed in the text field.

Fig. 14.42 | Adding the **field** symbol to the **nameWindow** movie clip.

Fig. 14.43 | Creating an animation with the **form field** symbol.

To add the descriptive text, first insert a keyframe in frame 25 of the **text** layer. Use the Text tool (white, **Arial**, **16** pt text and **3** pt line spacing) to type the help information for the **Name** field. Make sure the text type is **Static Text**. This text will appear in the help window. For instance, our example gives the following directions for the **Name** field: **Enter your name in this field. First name, Last name.** Align this text with the left side of the rectangle. Next, add a keyframe to frame 40 of this layer, causing the text to appear throughout the animation.

Next, duplicate this movie clip so that it may be customized and reused for the other two help button animations. Open the **Library** panel and right click the **nameWindow** movie clip. Select **Duplicate** from the resulting menu, and name the new clip **passwordWindow**. Repeat this step once more, and name the third clip **memberWindow** (Fig. 14.44).

You must customize the duplicated movie clips so their text reflects the corresponding form fields. To begin, open the **memberWindow** editing stage by pressing the **Edit Symbols** button, which is found in the upper-right corner of the editing environment, and selecting **memberWindow** from the list of available symbols (Fig. 14.44). Select frame 25 of the **text** layer and change the form field description with the Text tool so that the box contains the directions **Enter your member number here in the form: 556677**. Copy the text in frame 25 by selecting it with the Text tool and using the shortcut *<Ctrl>-C*. Click frame 40 of the **text** layer, which contains the old text. Highlight the old text with the Text tool, and use the shortcut *<Ctrl>-V* to paste the copied text into this frame. Repeat these steps for the **passwordWindow** movie clip using the directions **Enter your secret password in this field**. [*Note:* Changing a symbol's function or appearance in its editing stage updates the symbol in the scene.]

The following steps further customize the help boxes for each form field. Open the **nameWindow** symbol's editing stage by clicking the **Edit Symbols** button (Fig. 14.44) and selecting **nameWindow**. Add a new layer to this symbol called **typedText** above the **text** layer. This layer contains an animation that simulates the typing of text into the form field.

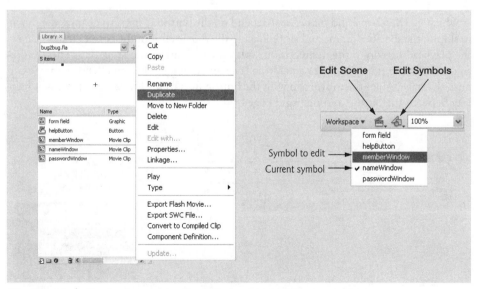

Fig. 14.44 | Duplicating movie-clip symbols with the **Library** panel.

Insert a keyframe in frame 25. Select this frame and use the Text tool to create a text box on top of the **form field** symbol. Type the name **John Doe** in the text box, then change the text color to black.

The following frame-by-frame animation creates the appearance of the name being typed into the field. Add a keyframe to frame 40 to indicate the end of the animation. Then add new keyframes to frames 26–31. Each keyframe contains a new letter being typed in the sequence, so when the playhead advances, new letters appear. Select the **John Doe** text in frame 25 and delete everything except the first **J** with the Text tool. Next, select frame 26 and delete all of the characters except the **J** and the **o**. This step must be repeated for all subsequent keyframes up to frame 31, each keyframe containing one more letter than the last (Fig. 14.45). Frame 31 should show the entire name. When this process is complete, press *Enter* to preview the frame-by-frame typing animation.

Create the same type of animation for both the **passwordWindow** and the **member-Window** movie clips, using suitable words. For example, we use six asterisks for the **passwordWindow** movie clip and six numbers for the **memberWindow** movie clip. Add a `stop` action to frame 40 of all three movie clips so that the animations play only once.

The movie clips are now ready to be added to the scene. Click the **Edit Scene** button next to the **Edit Symbols** button, and select **Scene 1** to return to the scene. Before inserting the movie clips, add the following layers to the timeline: **nameMovie**, **memberMovie** and **passwordMovie**, one layer for each of the movie clips. Add a keyframe in frame 2 of the **nameMovie** layer. Also, add keyframes to frame 4 of the **form**, **text** and **button** layers, ensuring that the form and text appear throughout the movie.

Now you'll place the movie clips in the correct position in the scene. Recall that the ActionScript for each help button contains the script

```
function functionName( event : MouseEvent ) : void
{
    gotoAndStop( frameLabel );
}
```

in which *functionName* and *frameLabel* depend on the button. This script causes the movie to skip to the specified frame and stop. Placing the movie clips in the correct frames causes the playhead to skip to the desired frame, play the animation and stop. This effect is created by selecting frame 2 of the **nameMovie** layer and dragging the **nameWindow** movie clip onto the stage. Align the movie clip with the button next to the **Name** field, placing it halfway between the button and the right edge of the stage.

Deleting a letter from each subsequent frame

Frames for text animation

Fig. 14.45 | Creating a frame-by-frame animation.

The preceding step is repeated twice for the other two movie clips so that they appear in the correct frames. Add a keyframe to frame 3 of the **memberMovie** layer and drag the **memberWindow** movie clip onto the stage. Position this clip in the same manner as the previous clip. Repeat this step for the **passwordWindow** movie clip, dragging it into frame 4 of the **passwordMovie** layer.

The movie is now complete. Press *<Ctrl>-Enter* to preview it with the Flash Player. If the triggered animations do not appear in the correct locations, return to the scene and adjust their position. The final movie is displayed in Fig. 14.46.

In our example, we have added a picture beneath the text layer. Movies can be enhanced in many ways, such as by changing colors and fonts or by adding pictures. Our movie (bug2bug.fla) can be found in the this chapter's examples directory. If you want to use our symbols to recreate the movie, select **Open External Library...** from the **Import** submenu of the **File** menu and open bug2bug.fla. The **Open External Library...** option allows you to reuse symbols from another movie.

Fig. 14.46 | **Bug2Bug.com** help form.

14.6 Creating a Website Splash Screen

Flash is becoming an important tool for e-businesses. Many organizations use Flash to create website splash screens (i.e., introductions), product demos and web applications. Others use Flash to build games and interactive entertainment in an effort to attract new visitors. However, these types of applications can take a long time to load, causing visitors—especially those with slow connections—to leave the site. One way to alleviate this problem is to provide visitors with an animated Flash introduction that draws and keeps their attention. Flash animations are ideal for amusing visitors while conveying information as the rest of a page downloads "behind the scenes."

A *preloader* or *splash screen* is a simple animation that plays while the rest of the web page is loading. Several techniques are used to create animation preloaders. The following example creates an animation preloader that uses ActionScript to pause the movie at a particular frame until all the movie elements have loaded.

To start building the animation preloader, create a new Flash document. Use the default size, and set the background color to a light blue. First, you'll create the movie pieces that will be loaded later in the process. Create five new layers, and rename **Layer 2** to **C++**, **Layer 3** to **Java** and **Layer 4** to **IW3**. **Layer 5** will contain the movie's ActionScript, so rename it **actions**. Because **Layer 1** contains the introductory animation, rename this layer **animation**.

The preloaded objects we use in this example are animated movie clip symbols. Create the first symbol by clicking frame 2 of the **C++** layer, inserting a keyframe, and creating a new movie-clip symbol named **cppbook**. When the symbol's editing stage opens, import the image `cpphtp.gif` (found in the `images` folder with this chapter's examples). Place a keyframe in frame 20 of **Layer 1** and add a `stop` action to this frame. The animation in this example is produced with the motion tween *Rotate* option, which causes an object to spin on its axis. Create a motion tween in frame 1 with the **Properties** window, setting the **Rotate** option to **CCW** (counterclockwise) and the **times** field to **2** (Fig. 14.47). This causes the image `cpphtp.gif` to spin two times counterclockwise over a period of 20 frames.

After returning to the scene, drag and drop a copy of the **cppbook** symbol onto the stage in frame 2 of the **C++** layer. Move this symbol to the left side of the stage. Insert a frame in frame 25 of the **C++** layer.

Build a similar movie clip for the **Java** and **IW3** layers, using the files `java.gif` and `iw3.gif` to create the symbols. Name the symbol for the **Java** layer **jbook** and the **IW3** symbol **ibook** to identify the symbols with their contents. In the main scene, create a keyframe in frame 8 of the **Java** layer, and place the **jbook** symbol in the center of the stage. Insert a frame in frame 25 of the **Java** layer. Insert the **ibook** symbol in a keyframe in frame 14 of the **IW3** layer, and position it to the right of the **jbook** symbol. Insert a frame in frame 25 of the **IW3** layer. Make sure to leave some space between these symbols so that they will not overlap when they spin (Fig. 14.48). Add a keyframe to the 25th frame of the actions layer, then add a `stop` to the **Actions** panel of that frame.

Now that the loading objects have been placed, it is time to create the preloading animation. By placing the preloading animation in the frame preceding the frame that contains the objects, we can use ActionScript to pause the movie until the objects have loaded. Begin by adding a stop action to frame 1 of the **actions** layer. Select frame 1 of the **animation** layer and create another new movie-clip symbol named **loader**. Use the text tool with a medium-sized sans-serif font, and place the word **Loading** in the center of the symbol's

Fig. 14.47 | Creating a rotating object with the motion tween **Rotate** option.

Fig. 14.48 | Inserted movie clips.

editing stage. This title indicates to the user that objects are loading. Insert a keyframe into frame 14 and rename this layer **load**.

Create a new layer called **orb** to contain the animation. Draw a circle with no stroke about the size of a quarter above the word **Loading**. Give the circle a green-to-white radial gradient fill color. The colors of this gradient can be edited in the **Color** panel (Fig. 14.49).

The block farthest to the left on the *gradient range* indicates the innermost color of the radial gradient, whereas the block farthest to the right indicates the outermost color of the radial gradient. Click the left block to reveal the *gradient color* swatch. Click the swatch and select a medium green as the inner color of the gradient. Select the right, outer color box and change its color to white. Deselect the circle by clicking on a blank portion of the stage. Note that a white ring appears around the circle due to the colored background. To make the circle fade into the background, we adjust its *alpha* value. Alpha is a value between 0 and 100% that corresponds to a color's transparency or opacity. An alpha value of 0% appears transparent, whereas a value of 100% appears completely opaque. Select the circle again and click the right gradient box (white). Adjust the value of the **Alpha** field in the **Color Mixer** panel to 0%. Deselect the circle. It should now appear to fade into the background.

The rate of progression in a gradient can also be changed by sliding the color boxes. Select the circle again. Slide the left color box to the middle so that the gradient contains more green than transparent white, then return the slider to the far left. Intermediate colors may be added to the gradient range by clicking beneath the bar, next to one of the existing

Fig. 14.49 | Changing gradient colors with the **Color** panel.

color boxes. Click to the right of the inner color box to add a new color box (Fig. 14.50). Slide the new color box to the right and change its color to a darker green. Any color box may be removed from a gradient by dragging it downward off the gradient range.

Insert keyframes into frame 7 and 14 of the **orb** layer. Select the circle in frame 7 with the selection tool. In the **Color** panel change the alpha of every color box to 0%. Select frame 1 in the **Timeline** and add shape tween. Change the value of the **Ease** field in the **Properties** window to **–100**. **Ease** controls the rate of change during tween animation. Negative values cause the animated change to be gradual at the beginning and become increasingly drastic. Positive values cause the animation to change quickly in the first frames, becoming less drastic as the animation progresses. Add shape tween to frame 7 and set the **Ease** value to 100. In frame 14, add the action gotoAndPlay(1); to repeat the animation. You can preview the animation by pressing *Enter*. The circle should now appear to pulse.

Before inserting the movie clip into the scene, we are going to create a ***hypertext linked button*** that will enable the user to skip over the animations to the final destination. Add a new layer called **link** to the **loader** symbol with keyframes in frames 1 and 14. Using the text tool, place the words **skip directly to Deitel website** below **Loading** in a smaller font size. Select the words with the selection tool and convert them into a button symbol named **skip**. Converting the text into a button simulates a text hyperlink created with XHTML. Double click the words to open the **skip** button's editing stage. For this example, we are going to edit only the hit state. When a button is created from a shape, the button's hit area is, by default, the area of the shape. It is important to change the hit state of a button created from text so that it includes the spaces between the letters; otherwise, the link will work only when the user hovers over a letter's area. Insert a keyframe in the hit state. Use the rectangle tool to draw the hit area of the button, covering the entire length and height of the text. This rectangle is not visible in the final movie, because it defines only the hit area (Fig. 14.51).

The button is activated by giving it an action that links it to another web page. After returning to the **loader** movie-clip editing stage, give the **skip** button the instance name **skipButton** and open the **Actions** panel for the first frame of the **link** layer. Invoke the add-EventListener function using the **skipButton** instance to call function onClick whenever

Click and drag to add or remove a color

Intermediate color

Resulting gradient

Fig. 14.50 | Adding an intermediate color to a gradient.

Up state   Hit state

Fig. 14.51 │ Defining the hit area of a button.

the button is clicked. Then, create an object of type URLRequest and give the constructor a parameter value of "http://www.deitel.com". The function onClick employs Flash's navigateToURL function to access the website given to it. Thus, the code now reads

```
skipButton.addEventListener( MouseEvent.CLICK, onClick );
var url : URLRequest = new URLRequest( "http://www.deitel.com" );

function onClick( e : MouseEvent ) : void
{
    navigateToURL( url, "_blank" );
} // end function onClick
```

The "_blank" parameter signifies that a new browser window displaying the Deitel website should open when the user presses the button.

Return to the scene by clicking **Scene 1** directly below the timeline, next to the name of the current symbol. Drag and drop a copy of the **loader** movie clip from the **Library** panel into frame 1 of the **animation** layer, center it on the stage, and set its **Instance name** to **loadingClip**.

The process is nearly complete. Open the **Actions** panel for the **actions** layer. The following actions direct the movie clip to play until all the scene's objects are loaded. First, add a stop to the frame so that it doesn't go to the second frame until we tell it to. Using the **loadingClip** movie instance, use the addEventListener function to invoke the function onBegin whenever the event Event.ENTER_FRAME is triggered. The ENTER_FRAME event occurs every time the playhead enters a new frame. Since this movie's frame rate is 12 fps (frames per second), the ENTER_FRAME event will occur 12 times each second.

```
loadingClip.addEventListener( Event.ENTER_FRAME, onBegin );
```

The next action added to this sequence is the function onBegin. The condition of the if statement will be used to determine how many frames of the movie are loaded. Flash movies load frame by frame. Frames that contain complex images take longer to load. Flash will continue playing the current frame until the next frame has loaded. For our movie, if the number of frames loaded (frameLoaded) is equal to the total number of frames (totalFrames), then the movie is finished loading, so it will play frame 2. It also invokes the removeEventListener function to ensure that onBegin is not called for the remainder of the movie. If the number of frames loaded is less than the total number of frames, then the current movie clip continues to play. The code now reads:

```
stop();

loadingClip.addEventListener( Event.ENTER_FRAME, onBegin );

// check if all frames have been loaded
function onBegin( event : Event ) : void
{
    if ( framesLoaded == totalFrames )
    {
```

```
        loadingClip.removeEventListener( Event.ENTER_FRAME, onBegin );
        gotoAndPlay( 2 );
    } // end if
} // end function onBegin
```

Create one more layer in the scene, and name the layer **title**. Add a keyframe to frame 2 of this layer, and use the Text tool to create a title that reads **Recent Deitel Publications**. Below the title, create another text hyperlink button to the Deitel website. The simplest way to do this is to duplicate the existing **skip** button and modify the text. Right click the **skip** symbol in the **Library** panel, and select **Duplicate**. Name the new button **visit**, and place it in frame 2 of the **title** layer. Label the instance **visitButton**, then create a keyframe in the second frame of the **actions** layer. Duplicate the code from the **Actions** panel of the first frame of the **link** layer in the **loader** symbol, and replace `skipButton` with `visitButton`. Double click the **visit** button and edit the text to say **visit the Deitel website**. Add keyframes to each frame of the **title** layer and manipulate the text to create a typing effect similar to the one we created in the `bug2bug` example.

The movie is now complete. Test the movie with the Flash Player (Fig. 14.52). When viewed in the testing window, the loading sequence will play for only one frame because your processor loads all the frames almost instantly. Flash can simulate how a movie would appear to an online user, though. While still in the testing window, select **56K** from the **Download Settings** submenu of the **View** menu. Also, select *Bandwidth Profiler* from the **View** menu. Then select *Simulate Download* from the **View** menu or press *<Ctrl>-Enter*. The graph at the top of the window displays the amount of bandwidth required to load each frame.

Fig. 14.52 | Creating an animation to preload images.

14.7 ActionScript

Figure 14.53 lists common Flash ActionScript 3.0 functions. By attaching these functions to frames and symbols, you can build some fairly complex Flash movies.

Function	Description
gotoAndPlay	Jump to a frame or scene in another part of the movie and start playing the movie.
gotoAndStop	Jump to a frame or scene in another part of the movie and stop the movie.
play	Start playing a movie from the beginning, or from wherever it has been stopped.
stop	Stop a movie.
SoundMixer.stopAll	Stop the sound track without affecting the movie.
navigateToUrl	Load a URL into a new or existing browser window.
fscommand	Insert JavaScript or other scripting languages into a Flash movie.
Loader class	Load a SWF or JPEG file into the Flash Player from the current movie. Can also load another SWF into a particular movie.
framesLoaded	Check whether certain frames have been loaded.
addEventListener	Assign functions to a movie clip based on specific events. The events include load, unload, enterFrame, mouseUp, mouseDown, mouseMove, keyUp, keyDown and data.
if	Set up condition statements that run only when the condition is true.
while/do while	Run a collection of statements while a condition statement is true.
trace	Display programming notes or variable values while testing a movie.
Math.random	Returns a random number less than or equal to 0 and less than 1.

Fig. 14.53 | Common ActionScript functions.

14.8 Web Resources

www.deitel.com/flash9/

The Deitel Flash 9 Resource Center contains links to some of the best Flash 9 and Flash CS3 resources on the web. There you'll find categorized links to forums, conferences, blogs, books, open source projects, videos, podcasts, webcasts and more. Also check out the tutorials for all skill levels, from introductory to advanced. Be sure to visit the related Resource Centers on Microsoft Silverlight (www.deitel.com/silverlight/) and Adobe Flex (www.deitel.com/flex/).

15

Adobe® Flash® CS3: Building an Interactive Game

Knowledge must come through action.
—Sophocles

It is circumstance and proper timing that give an action its character and make it either good or bad.
—Agesilaus

Life's but a walking shadow, a poor player that struts and frets his hour upon the stage and then is heard no more: it is a tale told by an idiot, full of sound and fury, signifying nothing.
—William Shakespeare

Come, Watson, come! The game is afoot.
—Sir Arthur Conan Doyle

Cannon to right of them, Cannon to left of them, Cannon in front of them Volley'd and thunder'd.
—Alfred, Lord Tennyson

OBJECTIVES

In this chapter you'll learn:

- Advanced ActionScript 3 in Flash CS3.
- How to build on Flash CS3 skills learned in Chapter 14.
- The basics of object-oriented programming in Flash CS3.
- How to create a functional, interactive Flash game.
- How to make objects move in Flash.
- How to embed sound and text objects into a Flash movie.
- How to detect collisions between objects in Flash.

15.1 Introduction

While Adobe Flash CS3 is useful for creating short animations, it is also capable of building large, interactive applications. In this chapter, we build a fully functional interactive video game. First, download the Chapter 15 examples from www.deitel.com/books/ ajaxfp. Then, open FullCannon.swf and run the completed game. In the cannon game, the player has a limited amount of time to hit every part of a moving target. Hitting the target increases the remaining time, and missing the target or hitting the blocker decreases it. Some elements of the FullCannon.swf game are not discussed in the body of the chapter. This case study will sharpen the Flash skills you acquired in Chapter 14 and introduce you to more advanced ActionScript. For this case study, we assume that you are comfortable with the material on Flash in Chapter 14. The completed game should run similar to what is shown in Fig. 15.1. Notice how in Fig. 15.1(c), before the ball collides with the

Fig. 15.1 | Ball fired from the cannon and hitting the target. (Part 1 of 3.)

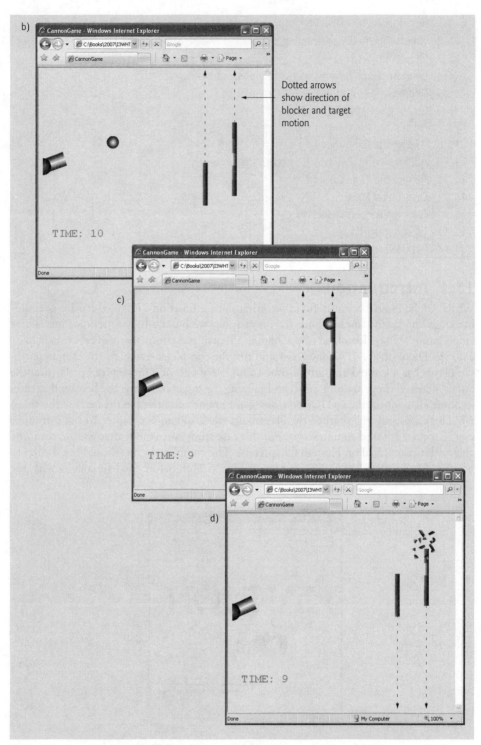

Fig. 15.1 | Ball fired from the cannon and hitting the target. (Part 2 of 3.)

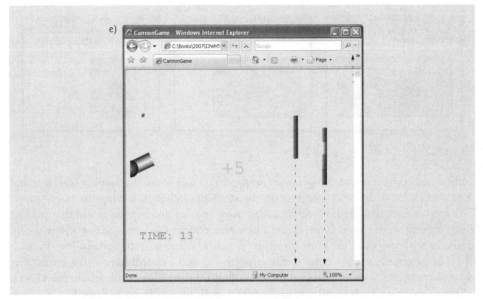

Fig. 15.1 | Ball fired from the cannon and hitting the target. (Part 3 of 3.)

target, the timer displays 9 seconds on the clock. Once the topmost part of the target is hit, 5 seconds are added onto the clock but the clock displays only 13 seconds in Fig. 15.1(d). This is because one second has already passed in this duration, causing the timer to decrease from 14 to 13.

15.2 Object-Oriented Programming

ActionScript 3.0 is an object-oriented scripting language that closely resembles JavaScript. The knowledge you gained from the JavaScript treatment in Chapters 4–9 will help you understand the ActionScript used in this case study.

An ActionScript class is a collection of characteristics known as ***properties*** and behaviors known as ***functions***. You can create your own classes or use any of Flash's predefined classes. A symbol stored in the **Library** is a class. A class can be used to create many objects. Dragging a symbol from the **Library** onto the stage created an instance (object) of the class. Multiple instances of one class can exist on the stage at the same time. Any changes made to an individual instance (resizing, rotating, etc.) affect only that one instance. Changes made to a class (accessed through the **Library**), however, affect every instance of the class.

15.3 Objects in Flash

In this section, we introduce object-oriented programming in Flash. We also demonstrate dynamic positioning (i.e., moving an object). We create two boxes. Each time you click on the left box, the right box will move to the left (Fig. 15.2).

Start by creating a new Flash document named Box.fla. Set the movie's dimensions to 230 px wide and 140 px high. On the stage, draw a 100-px-wide blue box with a black

Fig. 15.2 | Dynamic positioning.

outline and convert it into a movie-clip symbol. You can name this symbol **box**, but that is not necessary. Next, select the box on the stage and delete it, leaving the stage empty. This step ensures that the box will be added using the ActionScript code and that the box is not already on the stage. Now, create a new **ActionScript File** from the **File > New** menu, save it as BoxCode.as in the same directory as Box.fla, and add the code in Fig. 15.3.

The properties x and y refer to the respective *x*- and *y*-coordinates of the boxes. The two imports (lines 5–6) at the top of the code allow for the code to utilize those two classes, which in this case are MouseEvent and Sprite, both of which are built-in Flash classes. Inside the class, the two Box instances are declared. By declaration of the two Box objects at the beginning of the class (lines 11–12), they become instance variables and have scope through the entire class. Once the boxes have been allocated positions (lines 18–21), they must be placed on the stage using the addChild function (lines 23–24). The function handleClick is called every time the user clicks box1. The addEventListener function, which is invoked by box1, specifies that handleClick will be called whenever box1 is clicked (line 27).

```
1   // Fig. 15.2: BoxCode.as
2   // Object animation in ActionScript.
3   package
4   {
5      import flash.events.MouseEvent; // import MouseEvent class
6      import flash.display.Sprite; // import Sprite class
7
8      public class BoxCode extends Sprite
9      {
10        // create two new box objects
11        public var box1 = new Box();
12        public var box2 = new Box();
13
14        // initialize Box coordinates, add Boxes
15        // to the stage and register MOUSE_DOWN event handler
16        public function BoxCode() : void
17        {
18           box1.x = 15; // set box1's x-coordinate
19           box1.y = 20; // set box1's y-coordinate
20           box2.x = 115; // set box2's x-coordinate
21           box2.y = 20; // set box2's y-coordinate
```

Fig. 15.3 | Object animation in ActionScript. (Part 1 of 2.)

```
22
23            addChild( box1 ); // add box1 to the stage
24            addChild( box2 ); // add box2 to the stage
25
26            // handleClick is called when box1 is clicked
27            box1.addEventListener( MouseEvent.MOUSE_DOWN, handleClick );
28         } // end BoxCode constructor
29
30         // move box2 5 pixels to the left whenever box1 is clicked
31         private function handleClick( args : MouseEvent )
32         {
33            box2.x -= 5;
34         } // end function handleClick
35      } // end class BoxCode
36   } // end package
```

Fig. 15.3 | Object animation in ActionScript. (Part 2 of 2.)

To test the code, return to Box.fla. In the **Library** panel, right click the Box symbol and select **Linkage**. In the pop-up box, check off the box next to **Export for ActionScript** and type Box in the space provided next to **Class**. Ignore Flash's warning that a definition for this class doesn't exist in the classpath. Once you return to the stage, go to the **Property Inspector** panel and in the space next to **Document Class**, type BoxCode and press *Enter*. Now, the BoxCode ActionScript file has been linked to this specific Flash document. Type *<Ctrl>-Enter* to test the movie.

15.4 Cannon Game: Preliminary Instructions and Notes

Open the template file named CannonTemplate.fla from Chapter 15's examples folder. We'll build our game from this template. For this case study, the graphics have already been created so that we can focus on the ActionScript. We created all the images using Flash. Chapter 14 provides a detailed coverage of Flash's graphical capabilities. Take a minute to familiarize yourself with the symbols in the **Library**. Note that the **target** movie clip has movie clips within it. Also, the **ball**, **sound**, **text** and **scoreText** movie clips have stop actions and labels already in place. Throughout the game, we play different sections of these movie clips by referencing their frame labels. The stop action at the end of each section ensures that only the desired animation will be played.

Labeling Frames
Before writing any ActionScript to build the game, we must label each frame in the main timeline to represent its purpose in the game. First, add a keyframe to frames 2 and 3 of the **Labels** layer. Select the first frame of the **Labels** layer and enter **intro** into the **Frame Label** field in the **Property Inspector**. A flag should appear in the corresponding box in the timeline. Label the second frame **game** and the third frame **end**. These labels will provide useful references as we create the game.

Using the Actions Layer
In our game, we use an **Actions** layer to hold any ActionScript attached to a specific frame. ActionScript programmers often create an **Actions** layer to better organize Flash movies.

Add keyframes in the second and third frame of the **Actions** layer, and place a stop function in all three frames.

15.5 Adding a Start Button

Most games start with an introductory animation. In this section, we create a simple starting frame for our game (Fig. 15.1(a)).

Select the first frame of the **Intro/End** layer. From the **Library**, drag the **introText** movie clip and the **Play** button onto the stage. Resize and position both objects any way you like. Set the **Play** button's instance name to **playButton**. Don't worry that **introText** is invisible when deselected; it will fade in when the movie is viewed.

Test the movie. The text effects were created by manipulating alpha and gradient values with shape tweening. Explore the different symbols in the **Library** to see how they were created. Now, in the first frame of the **Actions** layer, add the code shown in Fig. 15.4 in the **Actions** panel. When the **Play** button is clicked, the movie will now play the second frame, labeled **game**.

```
1   // Fig. 15.4: Handle playButton click event.
2
3   // call function playFunction when playButton is clicked
4   playButton.addEventListener( MouseEvent.MOUSE_DOWN, playFunction );
5
6   // go to game frame
7   function playFunction( event : MouseEvent ) : void
8   {
9      gotoAndPlay( "game" );
10  } // end function playFunction
```

Fig. 15.4 | Handle playButton click event.

15.6 Creating Moving Objects

Adding the Target

In our game, the player's goal is to hit a moving target, which we create in this section. Create a keyframe in the second frame of the **Target** layer, then drag an instance of the **target** movie clip from the **Library** onto the stage. Using the **Property Inspector**, position the target at the x- and y-coordinates 490 and 302, respectively. The position (0, 0) is located in the upper-left corner of the screen, so the target should appear near the lower-right corner of the stage. Give the **target** symbol the instance name **target**. Right click the **target** symbol in the **Library** and select **Linkage**. In the box that pops up, select **Export for Action-Script** and enter **Target** in the **Class** field.

The **target** symbol is now linked with a class named **Target**. Create a new **ActionScript File** from the **File > New** menu. Save this file immediately and give it the name **Target.as**. This will serve as the **Target** class definition. In this file, add the code in Fig. 15.5.

The **Target** class has four instance variables—the speed of the **Target** (**speed**), the direction of the **Target** (**upDown**), the number of times the **Target** has been hit by the ball (**hitCounter**), and the **Timer** variable (**moveTargetTimer**). We specify that **moveTarget-Timer** is a **Timer** using the colon syntax in line 18. The first parameter of the **Timer** constructor is the delay between timer events in milliseconds. The second parameter is the

```
 1   // Fig. 15.5: Target.as
 2   // Move target, set direction and speed,
 3   // and keep track of number of blocks hit.
 4   package
 5   {
 6      // import relevant classes
 7      import flash.display.MovieClip;
 8      import flash.events.TimerEvent;
 9      import flash.utils.Timer;
10
11      public class Target extends MovieClip
12      {
13         var speed; // speed of Target
14         var upDown; // direction of Target
15         var hitCounter; // number of times Target has been hit
16
17         // timer runs indefinitely every 33 ms
18         var moveTargetTimer : Timer = new Timer ( 33, 0 );
19
20         // register function moveTarget as moveTargetTimer's
21         // event handler, start timer
22         public function Target() : void
23         {
24            moveTargetTimer.addEventListener (
25               TimerEvent.TIMER, moveTarget );
26            moveTargetTimer.start(); // start timer
27         } // end Target constructor
28
29         // move the Target
30         private function moveTarget( t : TimerEvent )
31         {
32            // if Target is at the top or bottom of the stage,
33            // change its direction
34            if ( y > 310 )
35            {
36               upDown = -1; // change direction to up
37            } // end if
38
39            else if ( y < 90 )
40            {
41               upDown = 1; // change direction to down
42            } // end else
43
44            y += (speed * upDown); // move target
45         } // end function moveTarget
46
47         // set direction of the Target
48         public function setUpDown( newUpDown : int )
49         {
50            upDown = newUpDown;
51         } // end function setUpDown
52
```

Fig. 15.5 | Move target, set direction and speed, and track number of blocks hit. (Part 1 of 2.)

```
53          // get direction of the Target
54          public function getUpDown() : int
55          {
56              return upDown;
57          } // end function getUpDown
58
59          // set speed of the Target
60          public function setSpeed ( newSpeed : int )
61          {
62              speed = newSpeed;
63          } // end function setSpeed
64
65          // get speed of the Target
66          public function getSpeed() : int
67          {
68              return speed;
69          } // end function getSpeed
70
71          // set the number of times the Target has been hit
72          public function setHitCounter( newCount : int )
73          {
74              hitCounter = newCount;
75          } // end setHitCounter function
76
77          // return the number of times the Target has been hit
78          public function getHitCounter () : int
79          {
80              return hitCounter;
81          } // end function getHitCounter
82
83          // stop moveTargetTimer
84          public function stopTimers() : void
85          {
86              moveTargetTimer.stop();
87          }
88      } // end class Target
89  } // end package
```

Fig. 15.5 | Move target, set direction and speed, and track number of blocks hit. (Part 2 of 2.)

number of times the Timer should repeat. A value of 0 means that the Timer will run inde-finately. The constructor function (lines 22–27) activates moveTargetTimer, which in turn calls the moveTarget function (lines 30–45) to move the Target every 33 millisec-onds. The moveTarget function contains a nested if...else statement (lines 34–42) that sets upDown to -1 (up) when the target reaches the bottom of the screen and sets upDown to 1 (down) when it reaches the top of the screen. It does this by testing if the target's *y*-coor-dinate is greater than 310 or less than 90. [*Note:* The property y refers specifically to the *y*-coordinate of the small white circle that appears on the main stage.] Since the stage is 400 pixels high and the target is 180 pixels high (half of which is below its *y*-coordinate), when the target's *y*-coordinate is equal to 310, the bottom end of the target is even with bottom of the stage. Similar logic applies when the target is at the top of the stage.

Line 44 moves the target by incrementing its *y*-coordinate by the result of getSpeed() * upDown. The remaining functions in this class are the public *get* and *set* functions for the upDown, speed and hitCounter variables. These allow us to retrieve and set the values outside of the class. The stopTimers function allows us to stop the moveTargetTimer from outside of the class.

Now, we can enable the target on stage, **target**, to move vertically simply by adding the calling methods setSpeed, setUpDown and setHitCounter in the second frame of the **Actions** layer:

```
target.setSpeed( 8 );
target.setUpDown( -1 );
target.setHitCounter( 0 );
```

Now, test the movie to see the target oscillate between the top and bottom of the stage.

Adding the Blocker

An additional moving object is used to block the ball, increasing the game's difficulty. Insert a keyframe in the second frame of the Blocker layer and drag an instance of the **blocker** object from the **Library** onto the stage. Give this **blocker** instance the name **blocker**. Set the blocker instance's *x*- and *y*-coordinates to 415 and 348, respectively. Create a Blocker.as file and class and link it to the **blocker** symbol. In this file, add the code in Fig. 15.6.

```
1   // Fig. 15.6: Blocker.as
2   // Set position and speed of Blocker.
3   package
4   {
5      // import relevant classes
6      import flash.display.MovieClip;
7      import flash.events.TimerEvent;
8      import flash.utils.Timer;
9
10     public class Blocker extends MovieClip
11     {
12        var speed : int; // speed of Blocker
13        var upDown : int; // direction of Blocker
14        var moveBlockerTimer : Timer = new Timer ( 33, 0 );
15
16        // call function moveBlocker as moveBlockerTimer event handler
17        public function Blocker() : void
18        {
19           moveBlockerTimer.addEventListener (
20              TimerEvent.TIMER, moveBlocker );
21           moveBlockerTimer.start();
22        } // end Blocker constructor
23
24        // move the Blocker
25        private function moveBlocker( t : TimerEvent )
26        {
27           // if Blocker is at the top or bottom of the stage,
28           // change its direction
```

Fig. 15.6 | Set position and speed of Blocker. (Part 1 of 2.)

```
29              if ( y > 347.5 )
30              {
31                 upDown = -1;
32              } // end if
33
34              else if ( y < 52.5 )
35              {
36                 upDown = 1;
37              } // end else
38
39              y += getSpeed() * upDown;
40           } // end function moveBlocker
41
42           // set speed for the Blocker
43           public function setSpeed ( v : int )
44           {
45              speed = v;
46           } // end function setSpeed
47
48           // get speed of the Blocker
49           public function getSpeed() : int
50           {
51              return speed;
52           } // end function getSpeed
53
54           // set direction for the Blocker
55           public function setUpDown( newUpDown : int )
56           {
57              upDown = newUpDown;
58           } // end function setUpDown
59
60           // get direction of the Blocker
61           public function getUpDown() : int
62           {
63              return upDown;
64           } // end function getUpDown
65
66           // stop moveBlockerTimer
67           public function stopTimers() : void
68           {
69              moveBlockerTimer.stop();
70           }
71        } // end class Blocker
72     } // end package
```

Fig. 15.6 | Set position and speed of Blocker. (Part 2 of 2.)

This code is very similar to that of the Target.as. Add the following code in the second frame of the **Actions** layer to set the speed and direction of the blocker:

```
blocker.setSpeed( 5 );
blocker.setUpDown( 1 );
```

Test the movie. The blocker and target should both oscillate at different speeds (Fig. 15.7).

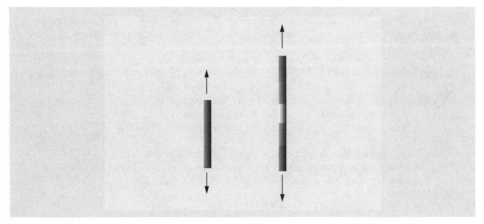

Fig. 15.7 | Oscillating blocker and target.

15.7 Adding the Rotating Cannon

Many Flash applications include animation that responds to mouse-cursor motions. In this section, we discuss how to make the cannon's barrel follow the cursor, allowing the player to aim at the moving target. The skills you learn here can be used to create many effects that respond to cursor movements.

Add a keyframe to the second frame of the **Cannon** layer and drag the **cannon** object from the **Library** onto the stage. Set its *x*- and *y*-coordinates to 0 and 200. Give this cannon instance the name **cannon**. The cannon should appear in the middle of the stage's left edge (Fig. 15.8).

Fig. 15.8 | Cannon position.

Coding the Cannon's Rotation

Now, add the code from Fig. 15.9 to the second frame of the **Actions** layer. This code rotates the cannon barrel to point toward the cursor. The *x*- and *y*-coordinates of the cursor are directly accessed using the `stage.mouseX` and `stage.mouseY` properties. The code ex-

```
1    // Fig. 15.9: Register mouseInHandler as MOUSE_MOVE event handler.
2    stage.addEventListener( MouseEvent.MOUSE_MOVE, mouseInHandler );
3
4    // rotate cannon when mouse is moved
5    function mouseInHandler( args : MouseEvent ) : void
6    {
7       // rotates cannon if cursor is within stage
8       if ( ( stage.mouseX > 0 ) && ( stage.mouseY > 0 ) &&
9          ( stage.mouseX < 550 ) && ( stage.mouseY < 400 ) )
10      {
11         // adjust cannon rotation based on cursor position
12         var angle = Math.atan2( ( stage.mouseY - 200 ), stage.mouseX );
13         cannon.rotation = angle * ( 180 / Math.PI );
14      } // end if
15   } // end function mouseInHandler
```

Fig. 15.9 | Register mouseInHandler as MOUSE_MOVE event handler.

ecutes any time the player moves the cursor, so the cannon always points toward the mouse cursor. The addEventListener function of the stage object registers the mouseInHandler function as the event handler of the MOUSE_MOVE event (line 2). Inside the mouseInHandler function, an if statement (lines 8–9) checks whether the cursor is within the stage. If it is, the code adjusts the cannon's rotation so that it points toward the cursor (line 13). The *rotation property* (line 13) controls an object's rotation, assuming its natural orientation to be 0 degrees.

ActionScript's *Math class* contains various mathematical functions and values that are useful when performing complex operations. For a full list of the Math class's functions and values, refer to the **Flash Help** in the **Help** menu. We use the Math class to help us compute the rotation angle required to point the cannon toward the cursor.

First, we need to find the cursor's coordinates relative to the cannon. Subtracting 200 from the cursor's *y*-coordinate gives us the cursor's vertical position, assuming (0, 0) lies at the cannon's center (Fig. 15.10). We then determine the desired angle of rotation. Note the

Fig. 15.10 | Trigonometry of the **cannon** object.

right triangle created by the cannon and the cursor in Fig. 15.10. From trigonometry, we know that the tangent of angle α equals the length of side y divided by side x: $\tan(\alpha) = y/x$. We want the value of α, though, not the value of $\tan(\alpha)$. Since the arc tangent is the inverse of the tangent, we can rewrite this equation as $\alpha = \arctan(y/x)$. The Math object provides us with an arc tangent function: `Math.atan2(y, x)`. This function returns a value, in radians, equal to the angle opposite side y and adjacent to side x (line 12). Radians are a type of angle measurement similar to degrees that range from 0 to 2π instead of 0 to 360. To convert from radians to degrees, we multiply by $180/\pi$ (line 13). The constant `Math.PI` provides the value of π. Since this rotation adjustment is performed every time the mouse moves within the stage, the cannon barrel appears to constantly point at the cursor. Test the movie to observe this effect.

Error-Prevention Tip 15.1

If your code is not working and no error message displays, ensure that every variable points to the correct object. One incorrect reference can prevent an entire function from operating correctly.

Hiding the Cannon Layer

We won't make any other changes to the **Cannon** layer. Hide the **Cannon** layer by selecting the *show/hide* selector (dot) in the portion of the **Timeline** to the right of the layer name (Fig. 15.11). A red **x** should appear in place of the dot to indicate that the layer is hidden while editing the movie. The layer will still be visible when the movie is viewed. Clicking the show/hide **x** again makes the **Cannon** layer visible.

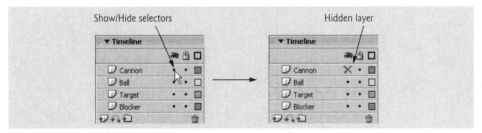

Fig. 15.11 | Using selectors to show/hide layers.

15.8 Adding the Cannonball

In this section, we add the cannonball to our game. Create a keyframe in frame 2 of the **Ball** layer, then drag the **ball** symbol from the **Library** onto the stage. Give the **ball** object the instance name **ball**. Notice that the ball instance appears as a small white circle on the stage. This circle is Flash's default appearance for a movie clip that has no graphic in its first frame. The ball will appear hidden beneath the cannon when the movie is viewed, because it is on a lower layer. Provide the Ball object with the x- and y-coordinates 0 and 200, respectively. This places the ball right under the cannon, so that when the ball is fired, it appears to have been fired from inside the cannon.

Initializing the Ball's Motion Variables

Link the **ball** symbol to a Ball class, as we did previously with the Target and Blocker classes. Next, create a new ActionScript 3.0 file named Ball.as and add the code shown in Fig. 15.12 to the file.

This code defines the Ball class. It has three properties—the speed in the *x*-direction, speedX (line 12), the speed in the *y*-direction, speedY (line 13), and a timer that moves the ball, moveBallTimer (line 16). Since the speed in the *x*-direction will be only integer values, it is of type int. However, the speed in the *y*-direction is also dependent on fireRatio, which can be a decimal value, and thus, speedY is of type Number, which is Action-Script 3's floating-point variable type. The class definition also creates the *get* and *set* functions for these properties. When the Ball object is created, the Ball constructor function starts the moveBallTimer, which calls the moveBall function every 33 ms. Function moveBall (lines 28–32) increments the *x*- and *y*-coordinates by speedX and speedY. The stopTimers function allows us to stop the moveBallTimer from outside of the class.

```
1   // Fig. 15.12: Ball.as
2   // Move ball and set speed.
3   package
4   {
5      // import relevant classes
6      import flash.display.MovieClip;
7      import flash.events.TimerEvent;
8      import flash.utils.Timer;
9
10     public class Ball extends MovieClip
11     {
12        var speedX : int; // speed in x-direction
13        var speedY : Number; // speed in y-direction
14
15        // Create Timer object to move ball
16        var moveBallTimer : Timer = new Timer( 33, 0 );
17
18        // Ball constructor starts moveBallTimer
19        public function Ball() : void
20        {
21           // call function moveBall as moveBallTimer event handler
22           moveBallTimer.addEventListener(
23              TimerEvent.TIMER, moveBall );
24           moveBallTimer.start();
25        } // end Ball constructor
26
27        // update the x and y coordinates using the specific speeds
28        private function moveBall( t : TimerEvent )
29        {
30           x += speedX;
31           y += speedY;
32        } // end function moveBall
33
34        // set speed in x direction
35        public function setSpeedX( v : int )
36        {
37           speedX = v;
38        } // end function setSpeedX
39
```

Fig. 15.12 | Move ball and set speed. (Part 1 of 2.)

```
40        // get speed in x direction
41        public function getSpeedX() : int
42        {
43            return speedX;
44        } // end function getSpeedX
45
46        // set speed in y direction
47        public function setSpeedY( v : int, fireRatio : Number )
48        {
49            speedY = v * fireRatio;
50        } // end function setSpeedY
51
52        // get speed in y direction
53        public function getSpeedY() : Number
54        {
55            return speedY;
56        } // end function getSpeedY
57
58        public function stopTimers() : void
59        {
60            moveBallTimer.stop();
61        } // end function stopTimer
62    } // end class Ball
63 } // end package
```

Fig. 15.12 | Move ball and set speed. (Part 2 of 2.)

Scripting the Ball's Motion

In the second frame of the **Actions** layer, add the code in Fig. 15.13. The new code moves the ball along a straight line in the direction the cannon was pointing when the mouse was clicked.

```
1  // Fig. 15.13: Fire ball on click event.
2  var firing : Boolean = false; // is ball firing?
3  var exploding : Boolean = false; // is ball exploding?
4  var fireRatio : Number = 0; // firing direction of ball
5  var speed : int = 30; // speed of ball
6  ball.setSpeedX( 0 );
7  ball.setSpeedY( 0, 0 );
8
9  // register function mouseDownHandler as MOUSE_DOWN event handler
10 stage.addEventListener( MouseEvent.MOUSE_DOWN, mouseDownHandler );
11
12 function mouseDownHandler( args : MouseEvent ) : void
13 {
14    // if the mouse is within the stage and the ball has not been fired or
15    // exploded yet, fire ball toward mouse cursor
16    if ( ( !firing ) && ( !exploding ) && ( stage.mouseX > 0 ) &&
17       ( stage.mouseY > 0 ) && ( stage.mouseX < 550 ) &&
18       ( stage.mouseY < 400 ) )
19    {
```

Fig. 15.13 | Fire ball on click event. (Part 1 of 2.)

```
20        firing = true;
21        fireRatio = ( stage.mouseY - 200 ) / stage.mouseX;
22        ball.setSpeedX( speed );
23        ball.setSpeedY( speed, fireRatio );
24     } // end if
25  } // end function mouseDownHandler
```

Fig. 15.13 | Fire ball on click event. (Part 2 of 2.)

This code initializes four variables—`firing`, `exploding`, `fireRatio` and `speed` (lines 2–5). Variables `firing` and `exploding` are set to `false` to signify that the ball is not moving or exploding. Later, we'll set `exploding` to `true` and play a brief explosion animation upon collision with the target or the blocker. Variables `fireRatio` and `speed` specify the ball's firing direction and speed, respectively. The function `addEventListener` (line 10) registers the function `mouseDownHandler` (lines 12–25) as the event handler for the stage's `MOUSE_DOWN` event. The `if` statement in the `mouseDownHandler` function (lines 16–24) checks that the ball is not currently in flight (`!firing`) or exploding (`!exploding`), and the mouse is within the stage (lines 16–18). If the condition evaluates to true, `firing` is set to `true` (line 20), and `fireRatio` is set to the mouse's *y*-coordinate (relative to the cannon) divided by its *x*-coordinate (line 21). This `fireRatio` will move the ball toward the cursor's position when it is fired. Lines 22–23 set the ball's speed in the *x*-direction to `speed`, and the ball's speed in the *y*-direction to `speed * fireRatio`. The expression `speed * fireRatio` returns the appropriate change in y based on the given change in x (`speed`).

15.9 Adding Sound and Text Objects to the Movie

Next, we add sound and text to our movie. Add a keyframe to frame 2 of the **Text** layer and drag the **text** symbol from the **Library** onto the stage. Note that the **text** object, like the ball, is represented by a small white dot. This dot will not appear when the movie is viewed. Position the **text** symbol in the center of the `stage` at coordinate (275, 200), and name the instance **text**. Then, add a keyframe to the second frame of the **Sounds** and **ScoreText** layers, and add an instance of the **sound** and **scoreText** objects, respectively. Center both objects on the stage and give them instance names matching their symbol names—**sound** and **scoreText**. Lock these three layers by clicking the *lock/unlock* selector (dot) to the right of the layer name in the timeline (Fig. 15.14). When a layer is locked,

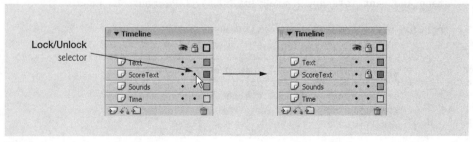

Fig. 15.14 | **Lock/Unlock** layers.

its elements are visible, but they cannot be edited. This allows you to use one layer's elements as visual references for designing another layer, while ensuring that no elements are moved unintentionally. To unlock a layer, click the lock symbol to the right of the layer name in the **Timeline**.

All the necessary sound and text capabilities have now been added to the game. In the next section, we add the time counter to the game.

15.10 Adding the Time Counter

What makes the cannon game challenging is the limited amount of time the player has to completely destroy the **target**. Time, whether increasing or decreasing, is an important aspect of many games and applications. In this section, we discuss adding a time counter that decreases as the game progresses.

Adding the Time Box

In the cannon game, the player has a limited amount of time to destroy every section of the target. The amount of time remaining appears in a dynamic text box in the bottom-left corner of the screen. To create this dynamic text box, first add a keyframe to frame 2 of the **Time** layer and add an instance of the **time** symbol to the stage. Position it at coordinate (100, 365), which should be in the lower-left corner of the stage. Name the instance **time**. Open the **time** symbol from the **Library** and select the text field. In the **Property Inspector**, change the text type to **Dynamic Text** and name the instance **timeText**. Return to the main scene, and add the code in Fig. 15.15 to the **Actions** panel in the second frame.

The variable **timer** is initialized to 10 (line 2). This variable will hold the amount of time remaining. The **countTimer** (lines 3–7) calls the **countDown** function (lines 9–18) each second. The **countDown** function decrements the **timer** by 1, and also sets the **text** of the **time** symbol's **timeText** element to "TIME: ", followed by the current value of **timer**.

```
 1    // Fig. 15.15: Timer countdown.
 2    var timer = 10; // set initial timer value to 10 seconds
 3    var countTimer : Timer = new Timer( 1000, 0 );
 4
 5    // call function countDown as countTimer event handler
 6    countTimer.addEventListener( TimerEvent.TIMER, countDown );
 7    countTimer.start(); // start Timer
 8
 9    function countDown( t : TimerEvent )
10    {
11       --timer;   // decrement timer by 1 every second
12       time.timeText.text = "TIME: " + timer;
13       // player loses game if he/she runs out of time
14       if( ( !firing ) && timer <= 0 )
15       {
16          gotoAndPlay( "end" ); // call end frame sequence
17       } // end if
18    } // end function countDown
```

Fig. 15.15 | Timer countdown.

Lines 14–17 test whether time has run out and the ball is not firing. If the condition is true, the movie will skip to the (empty) end frame.

Test the movie. The time should decrease from 10 to 0. When the time reaches 0, the end frame should play. Because none of the functions or objects in the second frame currently exist in the third frame, the timers that are still active will try to call those functions and fail, returning an error message. To fix this, we must first include all of the objects on the stage in the second frame in the third frame. You can do this by inserting a new frame (not keyframe) in the third frame of the **Text**, **ScoreText**, **Sounds**, **Time**, **Cannon**, **Ball**, **Target**, and **Blocker** layers. Next, we must stop all timers and hide most of the elements at the beginning of the third frame. Add the code in Fig. 15.16 to the third frame of the Actions layer.

Lines 2–3 remove the event listeners for the stage's MOUSE_MOVE and MOUSE_DOWN events, which are no longer needed. Lines 4–7 stop all of the timers that we have used, either by accessing the timer's stop method directly (line 4), or by accessing the class's stopTimers method (lines 5–7). Lines 8–13 hide every element on the stage by playing the hidden frame of each element, which is an empty frame.

```
 1  // Fig. 15.16: Stops all timers and sends objects into hidden frame.
 2  stage.removeEventListener( MouseEvent.MOUSE_MOVE, mouseInHandler );
 3  stage.removeEventListener( MouseEvent.MOUSE_DOWN, mouseDownHandler );
 4  countTimer.stop();
 5  blocker.stopTimers();
 6  ball.stopTimers();
 7  target.stopTimers();
 8  blocker.gotoAndPlay( "hidden" );
 9  cannon.gotoAndPlay( "hidden" );
10  ball.gotoAndPlay( "hidden" );
11  target.gotoAndPlay( "hidden" );
12  time.gotoAndPlay( "hidden" );
13  scoreText.gotoAndPlay( "hidden" );
```

Fig. 15.16 | Stops all timers and sends objects into hidden frame.

Creating a Final Animation Sequence

Games generally have a final animation sequence that informs the player of the outcome of the game. In this section, we create a final animation sequence for the game.

First, we must create a winner boolean to keep track of whether the player has won or lost the game. To do this, add the following code to the second frame of the Actions layer.

```
var winner : Boolean = false; // Keep track of who won
```

Next, add the code in Fig. 15.17 to the third frame of the Actions layer. This if...else statement checks the winner variable. If winner is true, the **text** movie clip goes to the **win** frame. Otherwise **text** goes to the **lose** frame. Test the movie again. When the time runs out, the **lose** frame, containing the text **Game Over**, should appear on an otherwise blank stage.

```
1   // Fig. 15.17: Check winner and show "Winner" or "Game Over".
2   if (winner == true)
3   {
4      text.gotoAndPlay( "win" );
5   }
6
7   else
8   {
9      text.gotoAndPlay( "lose" );
10  }
```

Fig. 15.17 | Check winner and show **Winner** or **Game Over**.

15.11 Detecting a Miss

We now add code to the **ball** instance that detects when the ball has moved outside of the stage. First, add the checkBall function in Fig. 15.18 to the second frame of the **Actions** panel.

Lines 5–6 test whether the ball is outside the bounds of the stage. If it is, the checkBallTimer is stopped (line 8), because the ball is no longer in motion and does not need to be checked until it has been fired again. Boolean firing is set to false (line 9). Then, lines 10–12 play the text movie clip's miss frame, the scoreText movie clip's minusTwo frame and the sound movie clip's miss frame. This will display **MISS** and **-2** on the stage, and play the miss sound. Also, the timer variable is decreased by 2 (line 13). Finally, the Ball object is reset to its starting position and speed (lines 14–17).

In order to check the ball at regular intervals, we create a timer that calls checkBall every 33 ms. First, add the following code to the second frame of the **Actions** layer:

```
// Check ball at 33-ms intervals
var checkBallTimer : Timer = new Timer( 33, 0 );
```

```
1   // Fig. 15.18: Detecting a miss.
2   function checkBall ( e : TimerEvent )
3   {
4      // if ball is not inside stage, go through miss sequence
5      if ( ( ball.x < 0 ) || ( ball.y  < 0 ) || ( ball.x > 550 ) ||
6         ( ball.y > 400 ) )
7      {
8            checkBallTimer.stop(); // stop checkBallTimer
9            firing = false; // ball is no longer being fired
10           text.gotoAndPlay( "miss" ); // display miss on the stage
11           scoreText.gotoAndPlay ( "minusTwo" ); // display "-2"
12           sound.gotoAndPlay ( "miss" ); // miss sound is played
13           timer -= 2; // deduct 2 seconds from timer
14           ball.x = 0; // set ball back to initial x-coordinate
15           ball.y = 200; // set ball back to initial y-coordinate
16           ball.setSpeedX( 0 ); // set ball speed in x-direction to 0
17           ball.setSpeedY( 0, 0 ); // set ball speed in y-direction to 0
18      } // end if
19  } // end function checkBall
```

Fig. 15.18 | Detecting a miss.

Next, we must start the timer. Since this timer needs to run only after the ball has been fired, we'll start the timer in the `mouseDownHandler`. Insert the following code between lines 13 and 14 of Fig. 15.13.

```
// call function checkBall as checkBallTimer event handler
checkBallTimer.addEventListener( TimerEvent.TIMER, checkBall );
checkBallTimer.start(); // start Timer
```

We must also stop this timer at the end of the game by adding the following code to the third frame of the `Actions` layer.

```
checkBallTimer.stop();
```

Test the movie with your computer's sound turned on. At this point, every fired ball should travel off the stage and count as a miss. In the next few sections, we discuss how to add features that allow the player to gain time and win the game.

15.12 Adding Collision Detection

Before we add collision detection to the target and blocker, we add a function that handles the actions common to all of our collisions. Add the `onBallContact` function (Fig. 15.19) to the second frame of the `Actions` layer.

```
1   // Fig. 15.19: Common actions after collision.
2   function onBallContact( timeChange : int )
3   {
4      // adjust variables to play exploding sequence
5      exploding = true;
6      firing = false;
7      timer += timeChange; // add the amount of time passed as parameter
8      ball.gotoAndPlay( "explode" ); // explode the Ball object
9      ball.setSpeedX( 0 ); // set ball speed in x-direction to 0
10     ball.setSpeedY( 0, 0 ); // set ball speed in y-direction to 0
11
12     // give explode animation time to finish, then call resetBall
13     explodeTimer.addEventListener( TimerEvent.TIMER, resetBall );
14     explodeTimer.start();
15
16     // play appropriate sound and text based on timeChange
17     if ( timeChange < 0 )
18     {
19        sound.gotoAndPlay( "blocked" );
20        text.gotoAndPlay( "blocked" );
21        if ( timeChange == -5 )
22        {
23           scoreText.gotoAndPlay( "minusFive" );
24        } // end if
25     } // end if
26
27     else if ( timeChange >= 0 )
28     {
```

Fig. 15.19 | Common actions after collision. (Part 1 of 2.)

```
29          sound.gotoAndPlay( "hit" );
30          text.gotoAndPlay( "hit" );
31
32          // increment the hitCounter by 1
33          target.setHitCounter( target.getHitCounter() + 1 );
34
35          if ( target.getHitCounter() >= 5 )
36          {
37              // if target has been hit 5 times, then declare player winner
38              winner = true;
39              gotoAndPlay( "end" ); // go to third frame
40          } // end if
41
42          if ( timeChange == 5 )
43          {
44              scoreText.gotoAndPlay( "plusFive" );
45          } // end if
46
47          else if ( timeChange == 10 )
48          {
49              scoreText.gotoAndPlay( "plusTen" );
50          } // end else
51
52          else if ( timeChange == 20 )
53          {
54              scoreText.gotoAndPlay( "plus20" );
55          } // end else
56      }   // end else
57  } // end function onBallContact
```

Fig. 15.19 | Common actions after collision. (Part 2 of 2.)

The onBallContact function takes a timeChange parameter that specifies how many seconds to add or remove from the time remaining. Line 7 adds timeChange to the timer. Lines 8–10 tell the ball to explode and stop. Lines 13–14 start a timer that calls the reset-Ball function after completion. We must create this timer by adding the following code to the second frame of the **Actions** layer:

```
// Delay for ball explosion
var explodeTimer : Timer = new Timer( 266, 1 );
```

This timer gives the ball's explode animation time to complete before it calls reset-Ball. We must stop this timer at the end of the game, by adding the following code to the third frame of the **Actions** layer.

```
explodeTimer.stop();
```

The resetBall function (Fig. 15.20) sets exploding to false (line 4), then resets the ball to the starting frame and position (lines 5–7). Add the resetBall function to the second frame of the Actions layer.

The onBallContact function (Fig. 15.19) also plays a frame from the sound, text and scoreText movie clips, depending on the timeChange, to notify the player whether

```
1    // Fig. 15.20: Reset the ball to its original position.
2    function resetBall( t : TimerEvent )
3    {
4       exploding = false; // set the ball explosion status to false
5       ball.gotoAndPlay( "normal" );
6       ball.x = 0; // set x-coordinate to original position
7       ball.y = 200; // set y-coordinate to original position
8    } // end function resetBall
```

Fig. 15.20 | Reset the ball to its original position.

they hit a target or a blocker, and to show the player how many points they gained or lost (lines 17–56). Lines 35–40 test whether the target has been hit 5 times. If it has, winner is set to true and the end frame is played.

Adding Collision Detection to the Target and Blocker

Flash has a built-in *collision detection* function that determines whether two objects are touching. The function *object1*.**hitTestObject**(*object2*) returns true if any part of *object1* touches *object2*. Many games must detect collisions between moving objects to control game play or add realistic effects. In this game, we rely on collision detection to determine if the ball hits either the blocker or the target.

In this section, we add code to **target** and **blocker** that increases or decreases your remaining time, depending on what you hit. Note that the **target** object comprises five instances of three different symbols: one **targetCenter** (white), two **targetMiddles** (gray) and two **targetOuts** (red). The closer to the center the **target** is hit, the more seconds get added to the total time.

Add the collision detection function shown in Fig. 15.21 to the second frame of the **Actions** layer.

```
1    // Fig. 15.21: Detect collision using hitTestObject.
2    function collisionDetection()
3    {
4       if ( target.out1.hitTestObject( ball ) && ( !exploding ) )
5       {
6          onBallContact ( 5 ); // hit upper outer part of target
7          target.out1.gotoAndPlay( "hit" );
8       } // end if
9
10      else if ( target.mid1.hitTestObject( ball ) && ( !exploding ) )
11      {
12         onBallContact ( 10 ); // hit upper middle part of target
13         target.mid1.gotoAndPlay( "hit" );
14      } // end else
15
16      else if ( target.center.hitTestObject( ball ) && ( !exploding ) )
17      {
18         onBallContact ( 20 ); // hit center of target
19         target.center.gotoAndPlay( "hit" );
20      } // end else
```

Fig. 15.21 | Detect collision using hitTestObject. (Part 1 of 2.)

```
21
22      else if ( target.mid2.hitTestObject( ball ) && ( !exploding ) )
23      {
24        onBallContact ( 10 ); // hit lower middle part of target
25        target.mid2.gotoAndPlay( "hit" );
26      } // end else
27
28      else if ( target.out2.hitTestObject( ball ) && ( !exploding ) )
29      {
30        onBallContact ( 5 ); // hit lower outer part of target
31        target.out2.gotoAndPlay( "hit" );
32      } // end else
33
34      else if ( blocker.hitTestObject( ball ) && ( !exploding ) )
35      {
36        onBallContact ( -5 );
37
38        // if timer runs out, player loses
39        if ( timer < 0 )
40        {
41          winner = false;
42          gotoAndPlay( "end" );
43        } // end if
44      } // end else
45    } // end function collisionDetection
```

Fig. 15.21 | Detect collision using `hitTestObject`. (Part 2 of 2.)

Function `collisionDetection` consists of an `if...else` statement that tests whether the ball has hit the blocker or one of the parts of the target. It ensures that the ball is not currently exploding, to prevent the ball from hitting more than one part of the target at a time. If these conditions return true, the `onBallContact` function is called with the appropriate number of seconds to add to or subtract from the timer as the parameter. For each of the parts of the target, that part's `hit` animation is played upon being hit. For the blocker, an `if` statement (lines 39–43) checks whether time has run out (line 39). If it has, the `winner` is set to `false` and the movie moves to the `end` frame.

To run the `collisionDetection` function at a regular interval, we'll call it from the `checkBall` function. Add the following at the beginning of the `checkBall` function.

```
collisionDetection();
```

Now test the movie. The target pieces should disappear when hit by the ball, as shown in Fig. 15.1. The player can now gain time by hitting the target and lose time by hitting the blocker. The ball should explode in the position where it hit the blocker, then reset to under the cannon, allowing the player to fire again.

15.13 Finishing the Game

Open the **text** symbol's editing stage from the **Library**. An action that plays the frame labeled **intro** in the main scene has already been attached to the last frame of the sections labeled **win** and **lose**. These actions, which were included in the original CannonTemplate.fla file, cause the game to restart after the final text animation is played.

To change the game's difficulty, adjust speed in the **blocker** and/or the **target**. Adjusting the time change in the `timeText` instance also changes the difficulty (a smaller decrement gives more time).

Congratulations! You have created an interactive Flash game. Now you can play the completed version.

15.14 ActionScript 3.0 Elements Introduced in This Chapter

Figure 15.22 lists the Flash ActionScript 3.0 elements introduced in this chapter, which are useful in building complex Flash movies.

Element	Description
object.x	Property that refers to *object*'s x-coordinate.
object.y	Property that refers to *object*'s y-coordinate.
addChild(*object*)	Function that adds the object to the stage.
addEventListener(*event*, *function*)	Function that invokes another function in response to an event.
mouseX	Mouse's x-coordinate property.
mouseY	Mouse's y-coordinate property.
object.rotation	Property that rotates the *object*.
stage	Manipulates objects on the stage.
object1.hitTestObject(*object2*)	Built-in function that determines when two objects collide.
Math	Built-in object that contains useful functions and properties (refer to Flash's ActionScript Dictionary for a full list).

Fig. 15.22 | ActionScript 3.0 elements.

Adobe® Flex™ 2 and Rich Internet Applications

Becoming more flexible, open-minded, having a capacity to deal with change is a good thing.
—Eda Le Shan

We wove a web in childhood, a web of sunny air.
—Charlotte Brontë

Genius is the ability to put into effect what is on your mind.
—F. Scott Fitzgerald

A fair request should be followed by the deed in silence.
—Dante

The transition from cause to effect, from event to event, is often carried on by secret steps, which our foresight cannot divine, and our sagacity is unable to trace.
—Joseph Addison

OBJECTIVES

In this chapter you will learn:

- What Flex is and what it's used for.
- How to design user interfaces in Flex's user interface markup language, MXML.
- How to embed multimedia in a Flex application.
- How to use data binding to create responsive user interfaces.
- How to access XML data from a Flex application.
- Client-side scripting in ActionScript 3.0, Flex's object-oriented scripting language.
- How to interact with a web service.
- How to create an advanced user interface.
- How the Adobe Integrated Runtime allows Flex applications to run on the desktop without an Internet connection.

16.1 Introduction

In Chapter 13, we introduced Ajax, which uses a combination of XHTML, JavaScript and XML to produce a web application with a desktop-like feel through client-side processing. In this chapter, we introduce *Adobe Flex*, another means of achieving that same goal. Flex uses Adobe's ubiquitous Flash platform to deliver a rich graphical user interface backed by *ActionScript 3*, Adobe's implementation of *ECMAScript 4* (better known as JavaScript 2). The relationship between Flex and ActionScript is similar to that between Ajax libraries and JavaScript. The powerful graphical capabilities and cross-platform nature of Flash allow web developers to deliver Rich Internet Applications (RIAs) to a large user base. The term RIA was coined in 2001 by Macromedia, the creator of Flash and Flex; Adobe acquired Macromedia in 2005.

Flex provides user interface library elements that can easily be accessed and customized. You can see these user interface elements in action using Adobe's Flex 2 Component Explorer at examples.adobe.com/flex2/inproduct/sdk/explorer/explorer.html. The user interface library helps you present a consistent user experience in all applications, a quality that various Ajax and Flash applications lack. Additionally, Flash has the advantage of a large installed base—98.6% penetration for Flash 6 and up, and 84.0% penetration for Flash 9 in the United States as of March 2007.[1] This allows applications developed in Flex to be used on most Windows, Mac and Linux computers. Since the Flash engine is virtually equivalent across browsers and platforms, Flex developers can avoid the cross-platform conflicts of Ajax and even Java. This significantly reduces development time.

The Flex framework enables a wide variety of web applications, from simple image viewers to RSS feed readers to complex data analysis tools. This flexibility is partly derived from Flex's separation of the user interface from the data. Visually appealing and consistent user interfaces are easily described using the *MXML markup language*, which is converted to Flash's executable *SWF (Shockwave Flash)* format when the application is compiled.

---

1. Adobe Flash Player Version Penetration, March 2007, www.adobe.com/products/player_census/flashplayer/version_penetration.html.

Flex is appropriate for online stores, where Flex's versatile user interface library allows for drag-and-drop, dynamic content, multimedia, visual feedback and more. Applications that require real-time streaming data benefit from Flex's ability to accept data "pushed" from the server and instantly update content, without constantly polling the server as some Ajax applications do. Applications that require data visualization benefit from Flex's Charting library which can create interactive and customized charts and graphs. Action-Script adds to the power of the Flex user interface library by allowing you to code powerful logic into your Flex applications.

In this chapter, you'll learn how to implement these elements in real-world applications. You'll run the examples from your local computer as well as from deitel.com. A comprehensive list of Flex resources is available in our Flex Resource Center at www.deitel.com/flex. Another helpful resource is Adobe's Flex 2 Language Reference at www.adobe.com/go/flex2_apiref.

16.2 Flex Platform Overview

The Flex platform requires the Flash Player 9 runtime environment. Flash Player 9 provides the *ActionScript Virtual Machine* and graphical capabilities that execute Flex applications. Flash Player 9, as described in Chapters 14–15, is a multimedia-rich application environment that runs on most platforms. Flash Player installation is detailed in those chapters, but for end users, only the *Flash Player 9* browser plug-in is required. The plug-in, including a debug version, is included as part of the *Flex SDK (Software Development Kit)* installation. Flex applications are essentially Flash programs that use the Flex framework of user interface elements, web services, animations and more. The Flex development environment is programming-centric in contrast to the animation-centric Flash authoring tool.

In addition to describing user interfaces, MXML can describe web services, data objects, visual effects and more. Flex's user interface elements are much richer and more consistent than those of HTML and AJAX because they're rendered the same way on all platforms by the Flash player. The root element of every MXML application is the *Application element* (<mx:Application>), inside which all Flex elements reside.

The Flex SDK is a free download, which you can get from www.adobe.com/products/flex/downloads. It includes an MXML compiler and debugger, the Flex framework, the user interface components, and some templates and examples. You can extract the zip file anywhere on your computer. The compiler and debugger included with the Flex SDK are command-line utilities. They're written in Java, so you must have Java Runtime Edition 1.4.2_06 (or later) installed. To check your current version, run java -version in your command line.

ActionScript 3 is Adobe's object-oriented scripting language. Flash Player 9 uses version 2 of the ActionScript Virtual Machine (AVM2), which adds support for ActionScript 3 and provides many performance improvements over the previous version. This virtual machine is being submitted as open source to the Mozilla Firefox project to provide support for ActionScript 3 and JavaScript 2. This engine, called Tamarin, is slated to be included in Firefox 4.

ActionScript 3 supports such object-oriented capabilities as inheritance, encapsulation and polymorphism. Also, it uses an *asynchronous programming model.* This means that the program will continue to execute while another operation is being completed, such as a call to a web service. This ensures that the user interface is responsive even while the application is busy processing data, an important feature of RIAs. In many cases, you'll need to take advantage of event handling and data binding to handle asynchronous operations.

Flex Builder is Adobe's graphical IDE for Flex applications. A 30-day free trial is available at www.adobe.com/go/tryflex. It is based on Eclipse, a popular open source IDE. Because Flex Builder costs money, and because you can develop Flex applications without it, we won't use Flex Builder in this book.

Adobe LiveCycle Data Services ES extends Flex's built-in data connectivity, allowing for such features as data push and synchronization. It also enables Flex applications to handle disconnection from the server, synchronizing data upon reconnection. The Express edition of Adobe LiveCycle Data Services ES is available for free at www.adobe.com/go/trylivecycle_dataservices/. This version is limited to use on a single server with a single CPU (the license agreement is included with the download).

Flex Charting provides an extensible library of plotting and graphing elements, including pie charts, line graphs, bar graphs, bubble charts and plots. Flex Charting also provides appealing animations for dynamic data representations. Flex Charting is available for purchase from Adobe, and a 30-day free trial is available at www.adobe.com/go/tryflex. An excellent demonstration of Flex Charting is the **Flex Charting Sampler** available at demo.quietlyscheming.com/ChartSampler/app.html.

16.3 Creating a Simple User Interface

Our first example application is a simple image viewer (Fig. 16.1) that displays thumbnail (i.e., small) images of several Deitel book covers. In this example, we specify the images with a static array within the MXML, but you could load this type of data dynamically from a web service. You can select a thumbnail to view a larger cover image, or use the horizontal slider to select an image. These two elements are bound to each other, meaning that when the user changes one, the other is updated. The image viewer also allows you to zoom the image. You can try this application at test.deitel.com/examples/ajaxfp/flex/coverViewer/ (Fig. 16.2).

```
 1   <?xml version = "1.0" encoding = "utf-8"?>
 2   <!-- Fig. 16.1: coverViewer.mxml -->
 3   <!-- Creating a simple book cover viewer in Flex 2 -->
 4   <mx:Application xmlns:mx = "http://www.adobe.com/2006/mxml">
 5      <!-- an array of images -->
 6      <mx:ArrayCollection id = "bookCovers">
 7         <!-- each image has a name and source attribute -->
 8         <mx:Object name = "C How to Program" source = "chtp5.jpg" />
 9         <mx:Object name = "C++ How to Program" source = "cpphtp6.jpg" />
10         <mx:Object name = "Internet How to Program"
11            source = "iw3htp4.jpg" />
12         <mx:Object name = "Java How to Program" source = "jhtp7.jpg" />
13         <mx:Object name = "VB How to Program" source = "vbhtp3.jpg" />
14         <mx:Object name = "Visual C# How to Program"
15            source = "vcsharphtp2.jpg" />
16         <mx:Object name = "Simply C++" source = "simplycpp.jpg" />
17         <mx:Object name = "Simply VB 2005" source = "simplyvb2005.jpg" />
```

Fig. 16.1 | Creating a simple book cover viewer in Flex 2. (Part 1 of 3.)

```
18          <mx:Object name = "Simply Java" source = "simplyjava.jpg" />
19          <mx:Object name = "Small C++ How to Program"
20             source = "smallcpphtp5.jpg" />
21          <mx:Object name = "Small Java" source = "smalljavahtp6.jpg" />
22       </mx:ArrayCollection>
23
24       <!-- bind largeImage's source to the slider and selected thumbnail -->
25       <mx:Binding
26          source = "'fullsize/' +
27            bookCovers.getItemAt( selectCoverSlider.value ).source"
28          destination = "largeImage.source" />
29       <mx:Binding source = "'fullsize/' + thumbnailList.selectedItem.source"
30          destination = "largeImage.source" />
31
32       <!-- user interface begins here -->
33       <mx:Panel id = "viewPanel" title = "Deitel Book Cover Viewer"
34          width = "100%" height = "100%" horizontalAlign = "center">
35
36          <mx:HBox height = "100%" width = "100%">
37             <mx:VSlider id = "zoomSlider" value = "100" minimum = "0"
38                maximum = "100" liveDragging = "true"
39                change = "largeImage.percentWidth = zoomSlider.value;
40                   largeImage.percentHeight = zoomSlider.value;"
41                height = "100%" width = "0%"
42                labels = "[ '0%', 'Zoom', '100%' ]" />
43             <mx:VBox width = "100%" height = "100%"
44                horizontalAlign = "center">
45
46                <!-- We bind the source of this image to the source of -->
47                <!-- the selected thumbnail, and center it in the VBox. -->
48                <!-- completeEffect tells Flex to fade the image in -->
49                <mx:Image id = "largeImage"
50                   source = ""
51                   horizontalAlign = "center"
52                   verticalAlign = "middle"
53                   width = "100%" height = "100%"
54                   completeEffect = "Fade" />
55
56                <!-- bind this Label to the name of the selected thumbnail -->
57                <mx:Label text = "{ thumbnailList.selectedItem.name }" />
58             </mx:VBox>
59          </mx:HBox>
60
61          <!-- slider can switch between images -->
62          <mx:HSlider id = "selectCoverSlider" height = "0%"
63             minimum = "0" maximum = "{ bookCovers.length - 1 }"
64             showDataTip = "false" snapInterval = "1" tickInterval = "1"
65             liveDragging = "true"
66             change = "thumbnailList.selectedIndex =
67                selectCoverSlider.value;
68                thumbnailList.scrollToIndex( selectCoverSlider.value )" />
69
```

Fig. 16.1 | Creating a simple book cover viewer in Flex 2. (Part 2 of 3.)

```
70            <!-- display thumbnails of the images in bookCovers horizontally -->
71            <mx:HorizontalList id = "thumbnailList"
72               dataProvider = "{ bookCovers }" width = "100%" height = "160"
73               selectedIndex = "0"
74               change = "selectCoverSlider.value = thumbnailList.selectedIndex">
75
76               <!-- define how each item is displayed -->
77               <mx:itemRenderer>
78                  <mx:Component>
79                     <mx:VBox width = "140" height = "160"
80                        horizontalAlign = "center" verticalAlign = "middle"
81                        verticalScrollPolicy = "off"
82                        horizontalScrollPolicy = "off" paddingBottom = "20">
83
84                        <!-- display a thumbnail of each image -->
85                        <mx:Image source = "{ 'thumbs/' + data.source }"
86                           verticalAlign = "middle" />
87
88                        <!-- display the name of each image -->
89                        <mx:Label text = "{ data.name }" />
90                     </mx:VBox>
91                  </mx:Component>
92               </mx:itemRenderer>
93            </mx:HorizontalList>
94         </mx:Panel>
95      </mx:Application>
```

Fig. 16.1 | Creating a simple book cover viewer in Flex 2. (Part 3 of 3.)

Line 1 of Fig. 16.1 declares the document to be an XML document, because MXML is a type of XML. The *mx prefix*, defined in line 4, is commonly associated with the *"http://www.adobe.com/2006/mxml" namespace*, which is used for the Flex elements in an MXML document. The *Panel element* (lines 33–94 is a container, and is generally the outermost container of a Flex application. This element has many attributes, including title, width, height, horizontalAlign and verticalAlign. The id = "viewPanel" attribute allows us to reference this item in ActionScript using the identifier viewPanel. Flex elements can contain an *id attribute*, so that their properties can be accessed programatically. The value of the title attribute is displayed at the top of the Panel, in the border. Inside the Panel element, there is an *HBox element* (lines 36–59), which is a container that organizes its enclosed elements horizontally. There is also a *VBox element* available for organizing elements vertically, which we'll use later.

In the HBox, we have a VSlider (lines 37–42) and a VBox (lines 43–58) containing an *Image element* (lines 49–54) and a *Label element* (line 57). The *VSlider element* provides a vertically oriented slider user interface element. The VSlider controls the zoom level of the image. The value attribute sets the slider's initial value (100 in this example). The minimum and maximum attributes set the range of values you can select with the slider. The change attribute (lines 39–40) allows ActionScript to execute whenever the user changes the slider's value. Lines 39–40 scale the image by setting its percentWidth and percentHeight properties to the slider's value. The liveDragging attribute with the value "true" indicates that the ActionScript in the change attribute executes immediately

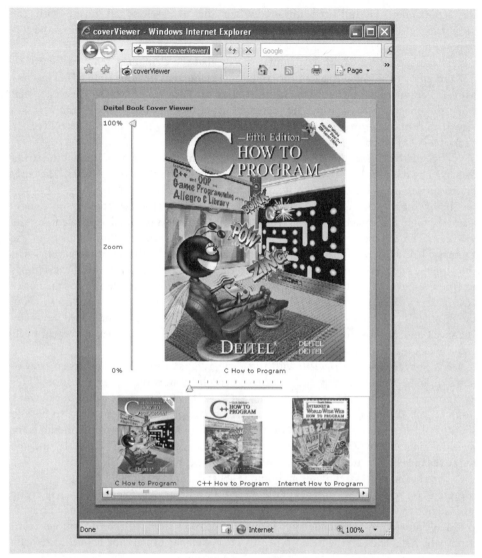

Fig. 16.2 | Deitel cover Viewer displaying *C How to Program* cover.

when the user changes the slider value, even if the user is still clicking it. The `labels` attribute places text next to the slider. You can give it any number of labels, and it will equidistantly space them.

The `Image` element has the attribute `source = ""` (line 50). This is because in lines 25–28, we use a **Binding element** to bind the value of `largeImage`'s source attribute (line 50) to the value of the `source` attribute of an element in the `bookCovers` `ArrayCollection` (defined in lines 6–22). In line 27, we use the horizontal slider's value to select an element from `bookCovers` and set the `largeImage`'s source. Lines 29–30 set up a second `Binding` element that binds the image's `source` to the `source` of the selected item in `thumb-nailList` (defined in lines 71–74). For each binding, we prepend `'fullsize/'`, the directory containing the full-sized images. When the user selects an image with the selectCoverSlider or thumbnailList, largeImage shows the full-size version of the corresponding image.

The Image element's other attributes specify that the element is centered (lines 51–52) and takes up as much space in the containing element as possible (line 53). The completeEffect attribute of the Image element is set to "Fade" (line 54), which means that when the image is loaded, it will be presented using Flex's built-in Fade effect. You can view the list of built-in effects at livedocs.adobe.com/flex/201/langref/mx/effects/package-detail.html.

The *Label* *element* (line 57) has a text attribute, in which we indicate that the string displayed by the Label is bound to the name of thumbnailList's selectedItem. The curly braces surrounding this ActionScript are another way to indicate data binding.

Following the HBox is an HSlider (lines 62–68) that gives the user another way to navigate through the images. The *HSlider* *element* is the horizontal equivalent of the VSlider. The change attribute (lines 66–68) changes the selected thumbnail from the thumbnailList based on the value of the HSlider and ensures that the thumbnailList is showing the selected thumbnail by scrolling to the HSlider's value. We set the HSlider's maximum value to { bookCovers.length - 1 }, the index of the last element of the bookCovers array. We set showDataTip to "false" (line 64) to turn off the tool tip showing the HSlider's current value while the user is dragging the slider. Finally, we set snapInterval and tickInterval to "1" (line 64), so that the slider's values increment by 1, and the tick marks are displayed at intervals of 1.

The *HorizontalList* *element* with id thumbnailList (lines 71–93) takes an array of items from a *dataProvider* and displays them in a horizontal configuration. This HorizontalList's dataProvider is the ArrayCollection of Objects called bookCovers (lines 6–22). *Object* is the root class of the ActionScript hierarchy, and is used here to simply hold attributes. An *ArrayCollection* is a type of Array that provides methods for manipulating an Array. Each of the items in the HorizontalList is selectable, and the selectedIndex attribute dictates that the first array element is selected initially.

The thumbnailList contains an inline itemRenderer (lines 77–92), which gives you complete control over the contents of the list. At runtime, the HorizontalList will create an instance of the itemRenderer for each of the elements in the dataProvider array. If you don't provide an itemRenderer, Flex will render each item with the default item renderer, which depends on the item's type. An itemRenderer can also be defined externally by giving the HorizontalList an itemRenderer attribute equal to the filename (without the extension) of an external MXML file containing the elements you want.

This itemRenderer contains a *Component* *element* (lines 78–91), which encloses the item to render. Inside the Component element, there is a VBox containing an Image (lines 85–86) and a Label (line 89). The verticalScrollPolicy and horizontalScrollPolicy attributes (lines 81–82) are set to off so that even if the Image or Label elements don't fit in the VBox, they won't show scroll bars. The paddingBottom attribute (line 82) ensures that there is 20 pixels of space for the HorizontalList's horizontal scroll bar. The Image element's source attribute has the specifies the location of the image file. The thumbs/ directory contains the thumbnails we want to display, and data refers to the corresponding item from the list's dataProvider, in this case the bookCovers ArrayCollection. We must use the keyword data because everything inside the Component element is located in a new, separate scope, meaning that it cannot access the variables of the enclosing program. The Label element displays the name element of the corresponding item in the ArrayCollection. The *Spacer element* ensures that there will be enough room for a horizontal scroll bar at the bottom of the thumbnailList in case the window is not wide enough to display all of the thumbnails.

Compiling an Application

Flex applications are converted from MXML into ActionScript, which is then compiled and output as SWF files. We'll compile our applications using the *mxmlc* command-line compiler, included in the Flex SDK. If you do not want to specify the compiler's path every time you run it, you can add the directory to your Path system variable. To do this in Windows XP, first right click **My Computer**, click **Properties**, select the **Advanced** tab, click **Environment Variables**, select **Path** in the list of **System variables**, and append your path to the flex_sdk_2\bin directory (e.g. C:\flex_sdk_2\bin if you extracted it into the C:\ directory). For Mac OS X and Linux, visit www.linuxheadquarters.com/howto/basic/path.shtml for instructions. The simplest syntax of the mxmlc command is mxmlc *filename*. You can see a full list of the compiler's parameters by executing mxmlc -help. For instance, if we're in the directory containing coverViewer.mxml, and we have added the bin directory to the **Path** system variable, the command for compiling coverViewer.mxml would be mxmlc coverViewer.mxml (Fig. 16.3).

This command creates coverViewer.swf in the current directory. If you'd like, you can test coverViewer.swf in the standalone Flash 9 Player by double clicking the file coverViewer.swf. If this does not work, you can locate the Flash 9 Player at flex_sdk_2\player\debug\SAFlashPlayer.exe for Windows or flex_sdk_2/player/debug/SAFlashPlayer.dmg for Mac OS X.

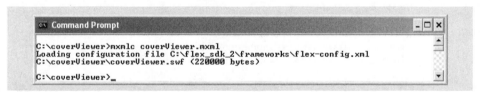

Fig. 16.3 | mxmlc running in Windows XP **Command Prompt**.

Running a Flex Application in the Browser

Because Flex applications run using the Flash Player, they can be embedded into a web page, then run with the Flash Player browser plug-in. The Flex SDK install includes a folder of HTML templates for embedding your application. You can copy a template and edit it to point to your SWF file. These templates are located in the folder flex_sdk_2/resources/html-templates/. The six templates give you different combinations of Flash installation and version detection (checks the user's Flash Player version) as well as browser history support. For our examples, we use the no-player-detection template. If you would like to implement the install and history features, more information is available at livedocs.adobe.com/flex/201/html/wrapper_131_05.html.

To create an HTML wrapper for the application, first copy the files AC_OETags.js and index.template.html from flex_sdk_2/resources/html-templates/no-player-detection to your Flex application's base directory. Rename index.template.html to index.html if you want it to be the default HTML file of the directory on a web server. Now, open the HTML file in your text editor, and replace the variables ${title}, ${swf}, and ${application} with your application's filename without .swf (in this case, cov‑erViewer). For ${height} and ${width}, use 100%. For ${bgcolor}, use #869ca7 (this is Flex's default color). The modified HTML wrapper for coverViewer is shown in Fig. 16.4.

```
1   <!-- Fig. 16.4: index.html -->
2   <!-- HTML wrapper for coverViewer.swf -->
3   <!-- saved from url=(0014)about:internet -->
4   <html lang="en">
5   <head>
6   <meta http-equiv="Content-Type" content="text/html; charset=utf-8" />
7   <title>coverViewer</title>
8   <script src="AC_OETags.js" language="javascript"></script>
9   <style>
10     body { margin: 0px; overflow: hidden; }
11  </style>
12  </head>
13
14  <body scroll='no'>
15  <script language="JavaScript" type="text/javascript">
16  <!--
17     AC_FL_RunContent(
18        "src", "coverViewer",
19        "width", "100%",
20        "height", "100%",
21        "align", "middle",
22        "id", "coverViewer",
23        "quality", "high",
24        "bgcolor", "#869ca7",
25        "name", "coverViewer",
26        "allowScriptAccess","sameDomain",
27        "type", "application/x-shockwave-flash",
28        "pluginspage", "http://www.adobe.com/go/getflashplayer"
29     );
30  // -->
31  </script>
32  <noscript>
33     <object classid="clsid:D27CDB6E-AE6D-11cf-96B8-444553540000"
34        id="coverViewer" width="100%" height="100%"
35        codebase="http://fpdownload.macromedia.com/get/
36           flashplayer/current/swflash.cab">
37        <param name="movie" value="coverViewer.swf" />
38        <param name="quality" value="high" />
39        <param name="bgcolor" value="#869ca7" />
40        <param name="allowScriptAccess" value="sameDomain" />
41        <embed src="coverViewer.swf" quality="high" bgcolor="#869ca7"
42           width="100%" height="100%" name="coverViewer" align="middle"
43           play="true"
44           loop="false"
45           quality="high"
46           allowScriptAccess="sameDomain"
```

Fig. 16.4 | HTML wrapper for coverViewer.swf. (Part 1 of 2.)

```
47                  type="application/x-shockwave-flash"
48                  pluginspage="http://www.adobe.com/go/getflashplayer">
49          </embed>
50      </object>
51   </noscript>
52   </body>
53   </html>
```

Fig. 16.4 | HTML wrapper for `coverViewer.swf`. (Part 2 of 2.)

Embedding Images

Instead of referencing external images, we could embed the images into the SWF file to make it more portable. We specify that an image is embedded by enclosing the source attribute inside an @Embed directive, as in `source = "@Embed( 'image.jpg' )"`. This tells the compiler to include the image in the SWF file, which results in a program that not only loads faster, but also is less dependent on external resources, since the SWF includes all resources it needs. In this case, embedding images would significantly increase the size of the SWF. Also, we may later want to update or change the images.

Using View States

Next, we'll add the ability to hide the thumbnail `HorizontalList` and to increase the size of the current image. We'll accomplish this using *view states* (Fig. 16.5), which enable us to change an application's layout on the fly, allowing for more usable interfaces. You can test this application at `test.deitel.com/examples/ajaxfp/flex/coverViewerStates/` (Fig. 16.6).

```
1    <?xml version = "1.0" encoding = "utf-8"?>
2    <!-- Fig. 16.5: coverViewerStates.mxml -->
3    <!-- Using States to dynamically modify a user interface -->
4    <mx:Application xmlns:mx = "http://www.adobe.com/2006/mxml">
5
6        <!-- ActionScript goes in this section -->
7        <mx:Script>
8            // import the Cubic easing function for state transitions
9            import mx.effects.easing.Cubic;
10       </mx:Script>
11
12       <!-- an array of images -->
13       <mx:ArrayCollection id = "bookCovers">
14           <!-- each image has a name and source attribute -->
15           <mx:Object name = "C How to Program" source = "chtp5.jpg" />
16           <mx:Object name = "C++ How to Program" source = "cpphtp6.jpg" />
17           <mx:Object name = "Internet How to Program"
18               source = "iw3htp4.jpg" />
19           <mx:Object name = "Java How to Program" source = "jhtp7.jpg" />
20           <mx:Object name = "VB How to Program" source = "vbhtp3.jpg" />
21           <mx:Object name = "Visual C# How to Program"
22               source = "vcsharphtp2.jpg" />
23           <mx:Object name = "Simply C++" source = "simplycpp.jpg" />
```

Fig. 16.5 | Using States to dynamically modify a user interface. (Part 1 of 3.)

```
24        <mx:Object name = "Simply VB 2005" source = "simplyvb2005.jpg" />
25        <mx:Object name = "Simply Java" source = "simplyjava.jpg" />
26        <mx:Object name = "Small C++ How to Program"
27           source = "smallcpphtp5.jpg" />
28        <mx:Object name = "Small Java" source = "smalljavahtp6.jpg" />
29     </mx:ArrayCollection>
30
31     <!-- define the application's states -->
32     <mx:states>
33        <mx:State name = "HideThumbnails">
34           <mx:RemoveChild target = "{ thumbnailList }" />
35
36           <!-- switch the showHideButton to hide -->.
37           <mx:SetEventHandler target = "{ showHideButton }" name = "click"
38              handler = "currentState = ''" />
39        </mx:State>
40     </mx:states>
41
42     <!-- define the transition effect for application state changes -->
43     <mx:transitions>
44        <mx:Transition>
45           <mx:Resize
46              target = "{ largeImage }"
47              duration = "750" easingFunction = "Cubic.easeOut" />
48        </mx:Transition>
49     </mx:transitions>
50
51     <!-- bind the source of largeImage to the selected thumbnail -->
52     <mx:Binding
53        source = "'fullsize/' +
54           bookCovers.getItemAt( selectCoverSlider.value ).source"
55        destination = "largeImage.source" />
56     <mx:Binding source = "'fullsize/' + thumbnailList.selectedItem.source"
57        destination = "largeImage.source" />
58
59     <!-- user interface begins here -->
60     <mx:Panel id = "viewPanel" title = "Deitel Book Cover Viewer"
61        width = "100%" height = "100%" horizontalAlign = "center">
62
63        <mx:HBox height = "100%" width = "100%">
64           <mx:VSlider id = "zoomSlider" value = "100" minimum = "0"
65              maximum = "100" liveDragging = "true"
66              change = "largeImage.percentWidth = zoomSlider.value;
67                 largeImage.percentHeight = zoomSlider.value;"
68              height = "100%" width = "0%"
69              labels = "[ '0%', 'Zoom', '100%' ]" />
70           <mx:VBox width = "100%" height = "100%"
71              horizontalAlign = "center">
72
73              <!-- We bind the source of this image to the source of -->
74              <!-- the selected thumbnail, and center it in the VBox. -->
75              <!-- completeEffect tells Flex to fade the image in -->
76              <mx:Image id = "largeImage"
```

Fig. 16.5 | Using States to dynamically modify a user interface. (Part 2 of 3.)

```
77                    source = ""
78                    horizontalAlign = "center"
79                    verticalAlign = "middle"
80                    width = "100%" height = "100%"
81                    completeEffect = "Fade" />
82
83               <!-- bind this Label to the name of the selected thumbnail -->
84               <mx:Label text = "{ thumbnailList.selectedItem.name }" />
85            </mx:VBox>
86         </mx:HBox>
87
88         <!-- slider can switch between images -->
89         <mx:HSlider id = "selectCoverSlider" height = "0%"
90              minimum = "0" maximum = "{ bookCovers.length - 1 }"
91              showDataTip = "false" snapInterval = "1" tickInterval = "1"
92              liveDragging = "true"
93              change = "thumbnailList.selectedIndex =
94                  selectCoverSlider.value;
95                  thumbnailList.scrollToIndex( selectCoverSlider.value )" />
96
97         <!-- display thumbnails of the images in bookCovers horizontally -->
98         <mx:HorizontalList id = "thumbnailList"
99              dataProvider = "{ bookCovers }" width = "100%" height = "160"
100             selectedIndex = "0"
101             change = "selectCoverSlider.value = thumbnailList.selectedIndex">
102
103             <!-- define how each item is displayed -->
104             <mx:itemRenderer>
105                 <mx:Component>
106                     <mx:VBox width = "140" height = "160"
107                         horizontalAlign = "center" verticalAlign = "middle"
108                         verticalScrollPolicy = "off"
109                         horizontalScrollPolicy = "off" paddingBottom = "20">
110
111                         <!-- display a thumbnail of each image -->
112                         <mx:Image source = "{ 'thumbs/' + data.source }"
113                             verticalAlign = "middle" />
114
115                         <!-- display the name of each image -->
116                         <mx:Label text = "{ data.name }" />
117                     </mx:VBox>
118                 </mx:Component>
119             </mx:itemRenderer>
120         </mx:HorizontalList>
121
122         <!-- this will exist in the bottom border of the Panel -->
123         <mx:ControlBar>
124             <mx:LinkButton label = "Show/Hide Thumbnails"
125                 click = "currentState = 'HideThumbnails';"
126                 id = "showHideButton" />
127         </mx:ControlBar>
128      </mx:Panel>
129 </mx:Application>
```

Fig. 16.5 | Using States to dynamically modify a user interface. (Part 3 of 3.)

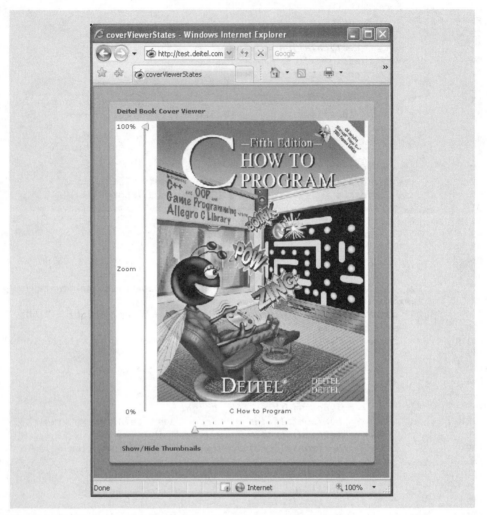

Fig. 16.6 | Deitel Cover Viewer using States to hide thumbnails.

We define an application's states in a **states** *element* (lines 32–40). An application has a *default state* that contains its initial elements, layout and properties. Each additional state is enclosed in a **State** *element*, with a name attribute, which is the identifier for the State. View states allow you to add elements via the **AddChild** *element*, remove elements via the **RemoveChild** *element*, modify elements' properties via the **SetProperty** *element*, set style via the **SetStyle** *element*, and set event handlers via the **SetEventHandler** *element*. The RemoveChild element in line 34 removes the thumbnailList. After the RemoveChild element, there is a **SetEventHandler** *element* (lines 39–38). Whenever the State is activated, this event handler will be registered. In this case, we change the click event handler of the showHideButton LinkButton (lines 124–126) to set the current-State to an empty string, signifying the application's default state (with the thumbnail viewer displayed). This LinkButton is enclosed in a **ControlBar** *element* (lines 123–127)—this embeds the elements it encloses into the bottom border of the Panel. The showHideButton element initially has a click attribute set to "currentState = 'Hide-Thumbnails';".

After we define the application's states, we define a transition effect for the State change. Any State transition effects are enclosed in the ***transitions element*** (lines 43–49). For each ***Transition***, you can specify a fromState and toState, using the State's name. In this case, we leave out these attributes so that the transition effect applies to all State changes. Inside the Transition, we have a Resize effect (lines 45–47). This effect has a targets attribute that specifies which elements it applies to. It also has a duration attribute, which defines how long the effect lasts in milliseconds. Finally, we define the optional easingFunction attribute. Normally, the Resize effect would go at a linear speed. Instead, we have specified that it should use the Cubic.easeOut function[2] (line 47), which controls the acceleration of the Resize animation. We import this function from the Flex library using ActionScript. A ***Script element*** (lines 7–10) encapsulates the application's ActionScript code. Line 9 allows the Cubic function to be used anywhere in the program.

16.4 Accessing XML Data from Your Application

Flex has the ability to access XML natively, using the *E4X (ECMAScript for XML)* standard. In this example, we use this capability to create an address book application. Figure 16.7 loads an XML file containing names and addresses into the application and displays its contents in a DataGrid (Fig. 16.8). The application also displays the selected contact's location in an embedded Yahoo! Map (Fig. 16.9). Finally, the application allows you to edit any of the selected contact's data (Fig. 16.10). You can test a live version of this application at test.deitel.com/examples/ajaxfp/flex/addressBook/. Note that because this application makes requests over HTTP, it must be run from a web server. To learn how to set up your own web server, see Chapter 17.

```
1   <?xml version = "1.0" encoding = "utf-8"?>
2   <!-- Fig. 16.7: addressBook.mxml -->
3   <!-- HTTPService, Validators, and new UI elements -->
4   <mx:Application xmlns:mx = "http://www.adobe.com/2006/mxml"
5      layout = "vertical"
6      xmlns:yahoo = "com.yahoo.webapis.maps.*"
7      creationComplete = "getContacts.send(); initMap();">
8
9      <!-- import XML file -->
10     <mx:HTTPService
11        id = "getContacts"
12        url = "contacts.xml"
13        showBusyCursor = "true"
14        resultFormat = "object"
15        result = "addressCollection = ArrayCollection(
16           getContacts.lastResult.contacts.contact )"
17        fault = "Alert.show( event.fault.message )" />
```

Fig. 16.7 | HTTPService, validators and new UI elements. (Part 1 of 5.)

---

2. A list of the available easing functions is available at livedocs.adobe.com/flex/201/langref/mx/effects/easing/package-detail.html.

```
18
19      <!-- validators for "Edit Contact" fields -->
20      <mx:StringValidator id = "firstnameValidator" source = "{ firstName }"
21        property = "text" required = "true" trigger = "{ save }"
22        triggerEvent = "click" valid = "saveContact()" />
23      <mx:StringValidator id = "lastnameValidator" source = "{ lastName }"
24        property = "text" required = "false" />
25      <mx:ZipCodeValidator id = "zipValidator" source = "{ zipCode }"
26        property = "text" required = "false" />
27      <mx:EmailValidator id = "emailValidator" source = "{ eMail }"
28        property = "text" required = "false" />
29      <mx:PhoneNumberValidator id = "phoneValidator" source = "{ phone }"
30        property = "text" required = "false" />
31
32      <mx:Script>
33        import mx.collections.ArrayCollection;
34
35        // tell compiler to register an event for the addressCollection
36        // variable, allowing it to be bound to another object
37        [Bindable]
38        private var addressCollection : ArrayCollection;
39      </mx:Script>
40
41      <!-- include ActionScript to implement search filter -->
42      <mx:Script source = "search.as" />
43
44      <!-- include ActionScript to implement Yahoo! Maps component -->
45      <mx:Script source = "map.as" />
46
47      <!-- include ActionScript to implement button actions -->
48      <mx:Script source = "buttonActions.as" />
49
50      <mx:Panel
51        layout = "vertical" width = "100%" height = "100%"
52        title = "Address Book">
53        <mx:Accordion id = "accordion" width = "100%" height = "100%"
54          creationPolicy = "all">
55          <mx:VBox label = "View Contacts">
56            <!-- search box, calls filter function on any change -->
57            <mx:ApplicationControlBar>
58              <mx:Label text = "Search:" />
59              <mx:TextInput id = "textFilter"
60                width = "100%"
61                change = "filter();"/>
62            </mx:ApplicationControlBar> <!-- End Search Box -->
63
64            <!-- contacts data grid, populated with addressCollection -->
65            <!-- call setMarkerByAddress on change of selection -->
66            <mx:DataGrid id = "contactsView"
67              dataProvider = "{ addressCollection }"
68              width = "100%" height = "100%"
69              change = "setMarkerByAddress();">
70              <mx:columns>
```

Fig. 16.7 | HTTPService, validators and new UI elements. (Part 2 of 5.)

```
71          <mx:DataGridColumn dataField = "firstname"
72              headerText = "First Name" />
73          <mx:DataGridColumn dataField = "lastname"
74              headerText = "Last Name" />
75          <mx:DataGridColumn dataField = "street"
76              headerText = "Street" />
77          <mx:DataGridColumn dataField = "city"
78              headerText = "City" />
79          <mx:DataGridColumn dataField = "state"
80              headerText = "State" />
81          <mx:DataGridColumn dataField = "zip"
82              headerText = "Zip" />
83          <mx:DataGridColumn dataField = "email"
84              headerText = "E-Mail" />
85          <mx:DataGridColumn dataField = "phone"
86              headerText = "Phone Number" />
87      </mx:columns>
88  </mx:DataGrid>
89
90  <mx:ControlBar>
91      <!-- start contact action buttons -->
92      <mx:Button label = "New"
93          click = "newContact()" />
94      <mx:Button label = "Delete"
95          click = "Alert.show( 'Are you sure?',
96          'Delete Contact',
97          mx.controls.Alert.YES | mx.controls.Alert.CANCEL,
98          this, deleteContact );" />
99      <mx:Button label = "Get Directions"
100         click = "getDirections();" />
101     <mx:Button label = "Edit"
102         click = "accordion.selectedIndex = 2;" />
103     <mx:Button label = "View on Map"
104         click = "accordion.selectedIndex = 1;" />
105     <mx:Button label = "E-Mail"
106         click = "emailContact();" />
107     <!-- end contact action buttons -->
108 </mx:ControlBar>
109 </mx:VBox> <!-- end "View Contacts" Section -->
110
111 <mx:VBox label = "Map View">
112     <!-- create Yahoo! Map -->
113     <yahoo:YahooMapService id = "yahooMap" UUID = "{ UUID }"
114         swfDomId = "{ swfDomID }"
115         apiId = "{ YahooAPIKey }"
116         mapURL = "{ mapURL }" width = "600" height = "400" />
117     <mx:Button label = "Back to Contacts"
118         click = "accordion.selectedIndex = 0;" />
119 </mx:VBox> <!-- end "Map View" Section -->
120
121 <mx:VBox label = "Edit Contact">
122     <!-- begin edit contact form, set default button to "save" -->
```

Fig. 16.7 | HTTPService, validators and new UI elements. (Part 3 of 5.)

```
123        <mx:Form width = "100%" backgroundColor = "#ffffff"
124           defaultButton = "{ save }">
125           <!-- edit contact text fields, bound to data -->
126           <mx:FormItem label = "First Name:" required = "true">
127              <mx:TextInput id = "firstName"
128                 text = "{ contactsView.selectedItem.firstname }" />
129           </mx:FormItem>
130           <mx:FormItem label = "Last Name:">
131              <mx:TextInput id = "lastName"
132                 text = "{ contactsView.selectedItem.lastname }" />
133           </mx:FormItem>
134           <mx:FormItem label = "Street Address:">
135              <mx:TextInput id = "streetAddress"
136                 text = "{ contactsView.selectedItem.street }" />
137           </mx:FormItem>
138           <mx:FormItem label = "City:">
139              <mx:TextInput id = "city"
140                 text = "{ contactsView.selectedItem.city }" />
141           </mx:FormItem>
142           <mx:FormItem label = "State:">
143              <mx:TextInput id = "state"
144                 text = "{ contactsView.selectedItem.state }" />
145           </mx:FormItem>
146           <mx:FormItem label = "Zip Code:">
147              <mx:TextInput id = "zipCode"
148                 text = "{ contactsView.selectedItem.zip }" />
149           </mx:FormItem>
150           <mx:FormItem label = "E-Mail Address:">
151              <mx:TextInput id = "eMail"
152                 text = "{ contactsView.selectedItem.email }" />
153           </mx:FormItem>
154           <mx:FormItem label = "Phone Number:">
155              <mx:TextInput id = "phone"
156                 text = "{ contactsView.selectedItem.phone }" />
157           </mx:FormItem>
158           <!-- end contact text fields -->
159
160           <!-- edit contact action buttons -->
161           <mx:FormItem>
162              <mx:Button id = "save" label = "Save" />
163           </mx:FormItem>
164           <mx:FormItem>
165              <!-- cancel button reverts fields to previous values -->
166              <!-- return user to "View Contacts" section -->
167              <mx:Button id = "cancel" label = "Cancel"
168                 click = "cancelContact()" />
169           </mx:FormItem>
170           <mx:FormItem>
171              <!-- pull up "Delete Contact" dialog box -->
172              <mx:Button label = "Delete"
173                 click = "Alert.show( 'Are you sure?',
174                    'Delete Contact',
```

Fig. 16.7 | HTTPService, validators and new UI elements. (Part 4 of 5.)

```
175                              mx.controls.Alert.YES | mx.controls.Alert.CANCEL,
176                              this, deleteContact );" />
177                      </mx:FormItem>
178                  </mx:Form> <!-- end edit contact form -->
179              </mx:VBox> <!-- end "Edit Contact" Section -->
180          </mx:Accordion> <!-- end Accordion navigation element -->
181      </mx:Panel> <!-- end UI layout -->
182  </mx:Application>
```

Fig. 16.7 | HTTPService, validators and new UI elements. (Part 5 of 5.)

Fig. 16.8 | Address book's **View Contacts** mode.

We begin by looking at the user interface code in the Panel element (lines 50–181, Fig. 16.7). An ***Accordion element*** (lines 53–180) allows the user to easily navigate between multiple VBoxes. As you click the title of one VBox, it slides on top of the previously active VBox. This Accordion contains three VBoxes, **View Contacts**, **Map View**, and **Edit Contact** (lines 55–109, 111–119, and 121–179, respectively). The Accordion attribute creationPolicy with the value "all" (line 54) forces the Flash player to load all components, even those that are not initially visible to the user. This is necessary to allow the Yahoo! Map to load before we create the map navigation elements.

Inside the **View Contacts** VBox (as seen in Fig. 16.8), we first define an ***Application-ControlBar*** container for the search field (line 57–62). An ApplicationControlBar is a type of ControlBar that can be placed anywhere or docked at the top of an application.

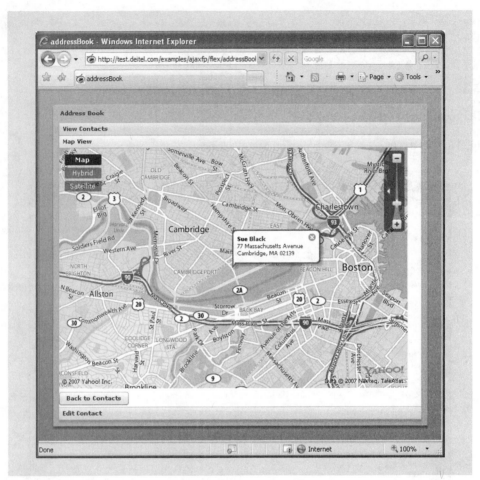

Fig. 16.9 | Address book's **Map View** mode.

This ApplicationControlBar contains a Label explaining to the user what the text field is for, followed by the TextInput element itself (lines 59–61). This element's change attribute indicates that the filter function (located in the search.as file) should be called whenever a change is made to the field, such as adding or removing characters. We'll discuss the filter function in detail when we review the ActionScript code.

Lines 66–88 create a **DataGrid element** with a dataProvider attribute that specifies what data will fill the rows and columns. The dataProvider addressCollection is placed in curly braces (line 67) to indicate that the dataProvider is being bound to the Data-Grid—any changes to the addressCollection will be displayed in the DataGrid. This DataGrid also has a change attribute. This is set to call the setMarkerByAddress function located in the map.as file whenever the user selects a different contact, so that the map will update to display that contact's location. In the DataGrid, we define each column using **DataGridColumn elements** inside a parent columns element. Each DataGridColumn (e.g., lines 71–72) has a dataField attribute that tells the element which data it should display, and a headerText attribute that defines the text in the column header.

Fig. 16.10 | Address book's **Edit Contact** mode.

Following the DataGrid are a series of Buttons that perform actions. These Buttons reside in a ControlBar container (lines 90–108), and each has a click attribute that defines the ActionScript code that will be executed when the user clicks the Button. For the **New** (lines 92–93), **Get Directions** (lines 99–100), and **E-Mail** (lines 105–106) Buttons, the code executed by click calls a function specific to that Button, located in button-Actions.as. For the **Delete** Button (94–98), the code executed by click calls the *Alert.show function* to display a dialog box confirming the user's action. This specific call to the Alert.show function sends five parameters—text, title, flags (specifies which buttons should appear), parent, and closeHandler. For the **Edit** (lines 101–102) and **View on Map** (lines 103–104) Buttons, the click attribute sets the selectedIndex of the Accordion to the index of the appropriate VBox.

The next VBox is **Map View** (lines 111–119 in Fig. 16.7, as seen in Fig. 16.9), which contains two items. The first is the YahooMapService element (lines 113–116). Note that the namespace of this element is yahoo—line 6 defines the yahoo namespace, which directs the compiler to the com/yahoo/webapis/maps directory located in the base directory of your application. This directory contains the YahooMapService.as file, which defines the YahooMapService element. This element has seven attributes. After the id, the next four are constants that we set in the ActionScript file for the Yahoo! Map, map.as.

The last two define the width and height of the map element. We discuss using the Yahoo! Maps API when we describe the map.as file. Following the map is a Button (lines 117–118) that when clicked switches to the **View Contacts** VBox.

The final VBox is **Edit Contact** (lines 121–179 in Fig. 16.7, as seen in Fig. 16.10). This element contains a *Form element* (lines 123–178) that groups the *TextInput elements* and the Button elements into a single entity. This aligns the elements and also allows us to specify such things as defaultButton (line 124), which is set to the **Save** Button. Each TextInput resides in a *FormItem element*, which can specify whether or not the item must be filled in via the required attribute. If this attribute is set to true, Flex will display a red asterisk next to the item. In the addressBook program, only the firstName field is required. When a user leaves this field blank and clicks the **Save** Button, the action is ignored and the firstName field is highlighted. This is an improvement over HTML forms, with which the user is notified of invalid data only after the form is sent to the server (though client-side validation can be performed with JavaScript).

Lines 20–30 create validator elements that check the contents of the TextInput elements to ensure that the user entered data correctly. Flex provides preconfigured validators for Strings, zip codes, e-mail addresses, phone numbers and more. There are several attributes for a validator element. The source attribute specifies which object to validate. The required attribute specifies whether the user is required to fill in data. The trigger attribute determines which button to listen to. The triggerEvent attribute specifies which event from the trigger initiates validation. The valid attribute specifies what ActionScript to execute if the triggerEvent is triggered and the data is valid.

Lines 10–17 create an *HTTPService* named getContacts. An HTTPService downloads a URL using the HTTP protocol. The *send method* of an HTTPService executes a request to the service, and can include parameters if the service requires them. We specify the url attribute to be contacts.xml (Fig. 16.11). We set the showBusyCursor attribute to true (line 13) so that the application displays a busy cursor while a request is being processed. We set the resultFormat to object (line 14), so that the XML is parsed as a tree of ActionScript objects. Some other valid resultFormats are array (which parses the tree as an array object), text (which returns the raw XML) and e4x (which allows you to use E4X expressions, explained in Section 16.4). The expression in the result attribute is executed when the HTTP request is complete. It stores each contact node from the HTTPService's lastResult property into an ArrayCollection called addressCollection. We create this ArrayCollection in lines 37–38. The *[Bindable] metadata tag* allows the variable that follows to be bound. It does this by registering an event to keep track of changes to the variable. The fault attribute (line 17) of an HTTPService specifies what to do in the event of a failed request. In this example, a failed request triggers an Alert displaying the error message. Finally, we call the send method at line 7, using the Application's *creationComplete attribute*. This attribute registers an event handler that is triggered after the Flash Player creates all of the interface elements.

```
1    <?xml version = "1.0" encoding = "utf-8" ?>
2    <!-- Fig. 16.11: contacts.xml -->
3    <!-- XML file containing contacts -->
```

Fig. 16.11 | XML file containing contacts. (Part 1 of 2.)

```
 4   <contacts>
 5       <contact id = "1">
 6           <firstname>Sue</firstname>
 7           <lastname>Black</lastname>
 8           <street>77 Massachusetts Avenue</street>
 9           <city>Cambridge</city>
10           <state>MA</state>
11           <zip>02139</zip>
12           <email>sue.black@email.com</email>
13           <phone>555-555-5555</phone>
14       </contact>
15       <contact id = "2">
16           <firstname>James</firstname>
17           <lastname>Blue</lastname>
18           <street>219 4th Avenue</street>
19           <city>Seattle</city>
20           <state>WA</state>
21           <zip>98109</zip>
22           <email>james.blue@email.com</email>
23           <phone>555-555-5555</phone>
24       </contact>
25       <contact id = "3">
26           <firstname>Mike</firstname>
27           <lastname>Brown</lastname>
28           <street>1315 Cestnut Street</street>
29           <city>St. Louis</city>
30           <state>MO</state>
31           <zip>63103</zip>
32           <email>mike.brown@email.com</email>
33           <phone>555-555-5555</phone>
34       </contact>
35       <contact id = "4">
36           <firstname>Meg</firstname>
37           <lastname>Gold</lastname>
38           <street>700 14th Street</street>
39           <city>Denver</city>
40           <state>CO</state>
41           <zip>80206</zip>
42           <email>meg.gold@email.com</email>
43           <phone>555-555-5555</phone>
44       </contact>
45       <contact id = "5">
46           <firstname>John</firstname>
47           <lastname>Gray</lastname>
48           <street>525 Arch Street</street>
49           <city>Philadelphia</city>
50           <state>PA</state>
51           <zip>19106</zip>
52           <email>john.gray@email.com</email>
53           <phone>555-555-5555</phone>
54       </contact>
55   </contacts>
```

Fig. 16.11 | XML file containing contacts. (Part 2 of 2.)

You can embed ActionScript in MXML through use of the Script tag (lines 32–39). To better organize the code, we also place ActionScript in separate .as files. The address-Book.mxml file includes these files using a Script element with a source attribute (lines 42–48). There are three script files—search.as, map.as and buttonActions.as. We now explain each of these ActionScript files.

Search Function ActionScript

The search.as ActionScript file (Fig. 16.12) contains the function filter (lines 3–8), which is called any time a change is made in the textFilter TextInput—as specified by the change attribute in line 61 of Fig. 16.7. This function defines addressCollection's filterFunction (line 6) to be testMatch (lines 10–31). An ArrayCollection's *filterFunction* is passed each item of the collection and returns true if the item matches the search criteria, and false otherwise. Function testMatch tests whether the searchTerm matches the text in any of the data fields of each item.

```
1   // Fig. 16.12: search.as
2   // Using a filterFunction for a live search feature
3   private function filter() : void
4   {
5      // define filter function
6      addressCollection.filterFunction = testMatch;
7      addressCollection.refresh(); // refresh data to only display matches
8   } // end function filter
9
10  private function testMatch( item : Object ) : Boolean
11  {
12     // save search term to variable
13     var searchTerm:String = textFilter.text.toLowerCase();
14
15     // return whether search parameter matches any field for each item
16     return( item.firstname.toLowerCase().search( searchTerm ) != -1 ||
17        item.lastname.toLowerCase().search( searchTerm ) != -1 ||
18        item.street.toLowerCase().search( searchTerm ) != -1 ||
19        item.city.toLowerCase().search( searchTerm ) != -1 ||
20        item.state.toLowerCase().search( searchTerm ) != -1 ||
21        String( item.zip ).search( searchTerm ) != -1 ||
22        item.email.toLowerCase().search( searchTerm ) != -1 ||
23        item.phone.toLowerCase().search( searchTerm ) != -1 )
24  } // end function testMatch
```

Fig. 16.12 | Using a filterFunction for a live search feature.

Yahoo! Map ActionScript

The map.as ActionScript file (Fig. 16.13) handles the addressBook application's map functionality. We use the *Yahoo! Maps API*, because Yahoo! provides the ability to embed maps in Flex 2 applications[3] (the map itself is a Flash application). The first step in using the Yahoo! Maps API is to get a Yahoo! account and Application ID. These are available at developer.yahoo.com. You then need to download the Yahoo! AS3 API Libraries at developer.yahoo.com/flash/as3_api_libraries.html. Move the source/as3/com/

---

3. For more information see developer.yahoo.com/flash/howto-maps-as3.html.

folder and the source/as2/as2map.swf file into the base directory of your application. This allows you to use the as2map.swf file, which contains the ActionScript 2-based map, as well as use the ActionScript 3 functions Yahoo! provides to control the map.

```
 1   // Fig. 16.13: map.as
 2   // Handle the map functions for the Address Book application
 3   import mx.managers.CursorManager;
 4   import com.yahoo.webapis.maps.methodgroups.*;
 5   import mx.controls.Alert;
 6
 7   // define constants
 8   private const swfDomID : String = "addressBook";
 9   private const UUID : int = Math.random() * 10000;
10
11   // YahooAPIKey string must be your own from developer.yahoo.com
12   private const YahooAPIKey : String = "Your Yahoo API Key Here";
13   private const mapURL : String = "as2map.swf";
14   private var mapController : MapController;
15
16   private function initMap() : void
17   {
18      CursorManager.setBusyCursor(); // turn on busy cursor
19
20      // wait for map to load, then call onMapLoaded method
21      yahooMap.addEventListener( 'onMapLoad', onMapLoaded );
22      yahooMap.addEventListener( 'onMapError', onMapError );
23   } // end function initMap
24
25   // handle map after it has loaded
26   public function onMapLoaded( event : Object ) : void
27   {
28      // instantiate map controller
29      mapController = new MapController( yahooMap );
30
31      // instantiate panTool method
32      var panTools : PanTool = new PanTool( yahooMap );
33
34      // allow user to pan across the map
35      panTools.setPanTool( true );
36
37      // instantiate the maps widget class
38      var widgets : Widgets = new Widgets( yahooMap );
39
40      // activate Navigator widget
41      widgets.showNavigatorWidget();
42
43      // activate map-type selection widget
44      widgets.showSatelliteControlWidget();
45
46      // turn off busy cursor
47      CursorManager.removeBusyCursor();
48   } // end function onMapLoaded
```

Fig. 16.13 | Handle the map functions for the Address Book application. (Part 1 of 2.)

```
49
50   public function onMapError( errorCode:String, httpStatus:String ) : void
51   {
52      Alert.show( errorCode + '\n' + httpStatus, 'Map Load Error' );
53   } // end function onMapError
54
55   // place a labeled marker at the currently selected address
56   public function setMarkerByAddress() : void
57   {
58      mapController.removeAllMarkers(); // clear previous markers
59
60      // add marker at specified address,
61      // labeled with contact's name and address
62      mapController.addCustomPOIMarker(
63         ( contactsView.selectedItem.street + " " +
64         contactsView.selectedItem.city + " " +
65         contactsView.selectedItem.state ),
66         contactsView.selectedItem.firstname,
67         contactsView.selectedItem.lastname,
68         (contactsView.selectedItem.street + "\n" +
69         contactsView.selectedItem.city + ", " +
70         contactsView.selectedItem.state + " " +
71         contactsView.selectedItem.zip ),
72         0x990099, 0xFFFFFF );
73
74      // instantly center on address and zoom in
75      mapController.setCenterByAddressAndZoom(
76         contactsView.selectedItem.street + " " +
77         contactsView.selectedItem.city + " " +
78         contactsView.selectedItem.state, 5, 0 );
79   } // end function setMarkerByAddress
```

Fig. 16.13 | Handle the map functions for the Address Book application. (Part 2 of 2.)

We first import the classes that we use in this ActionScript file (lines 3–5). The CursorManager class allows us to set and remove the busy cursor. We also import all of the classes located in the com/yahoo/webapis/maps/methodgroups directory, which provide us with the ability to control the map and to create the map's user interface widgets. We set the constants necessary for using a Yahoo! Map in lines 8–13. swfDomID (line 8) is a string that must be equal to the object id used in the .html file containing the application. UUID (line 9) is the unique ID of the map element and is set to Math.random()*10000 so that it is a random integer from 0 up to 9999. YahooAPIKey (lines 12) should be set to the Yahoo Application ID you obtained from developer.yahoo.com. Constant mapURL (line 13) is the path to the as2map.swf file. Because we placed that file in the base directory of the application, we can simply specify the file's name. Line 14 creates the mapController variable that we'll instantiate at line 29.

The function initMap (lines 16–23) is called when the application has finished creating the user interface elements, as specified by addressBook's creationComplete attribute (line 7 in Fig. 16.7). This function sets the busy cursor, then registers event handlers for the onMapLoad and onMapError events for the map. The onMapError event handler (lines 50–53) triggers an Alert displaying the error. The onMapLoaded event handler (lines 26–48) adds MapController, PanTool and Widgets objects to the map.

MapController enables programmatic control of the map's location and zoom and the placing of markers on the map at a specified address.[4] *PanTool* (line 32) enables the user to click and drag the map, as well as double click a location to center on it. *Widgets* (line 38) add the ability to show a navigator widget (line 41), which provides zoom controls and an overview map, and a satellite control widget (line 44), which provides the user with a selection of the regular map view, the satellite view, or the hybrid view. After loading all of the map's functions, initMap removes the busy cursor (line 47).

Function setMarkerByAddress (lines 56–79) provides the ability to place a marker at the location of the selected contact's location. It uses the mapController's addCustom-POIMarker function (lines 62–72) to place a marker at the contact's address that contains the contact's first and last name as well as the address. It also uses the mapController's setCenterByAddressAndZoom function (lines 75–78) to center the map on that contact's location and zoom down to the street level (zoom level 5). The final parameter of the set-CenterByAddressAndZoom function is the amount of time in milliseconds the map should take to pan to the new location. We set this to 0, because the map will not be visible when this function is called.

Button Event-Handling ActionScript

The buttonActions.as ActionScript file (Fig. 16.14) handles the functionality of most of the addressBook application's Buttons. Each Button has a corresponding function. The first Button it handles is the **Cancel** Button (lines 167–168 of Fig. 16.7). The cancelContact function (lines 6–19 of Fig. 16.14) reverts **Edit Contact**'s fields back to the previous value of the selected contact, then switches the Accordion to **View Contacts**. The delete-Contact function (lines 22–35) handles when the user clicks a **Delete** Button (lines 94–98 or 172–176 of Fig. 16.7), then clicks **Yes** in the confirmation dialog box. It switches the Accordion to **View Contacts** if the user was not already there, and removes the currently selected contact. The emailContact function (lines 38–46 of Fig. 16.14) creates a new URLRequest object that contains a mailto URL for the current contact's e-mail address. The call to navigateToURL opens that URL in _self, which refers to the current browser window. Since the URL is a mailto URL, however, the browser tells the user's default e-mail client to open and to compose a new message addressed to the specified e-mail address. The getDirections function (lines 49–60) uses the same method to open a URL; however, instead of forming a mailto URL, it forms a URL pointing to the Yahoo! Maps page, specifying that we want directions ending at the currently selected contact's address. It opens this URL in _blank, which creates a new browser window with the specified URL. The saveContact function (lines 63–82) sets the data in the addressCollection item corresponding to the currently selected contact to be equal to that of the text in **Edit Contact**'s TextInputs. It then refreshes addressCollection in case the contactsView DataGrid is being filtered (the refresh ensures that the filter results are current). The newContact function (lines 85–93) creates a new item in addressCollection whose firstname is set to "New" and whose lastname is set to "Contact". It then sets the selectedIndex of the contactsView DataGrid to be the new item, and switches to the **Edit Contacts** view.

---

4. The full list of functions this enables is available at developer.yahoo.com/flash/as3webapis/docs/com/yahoo/webapis/maps/methodgroups/MapController.html.

```
 1    // Fig. 16.14: buttonActions.as
 2    // Implement the actions of each button
 3    import mx.events.CloseEvent;
 4
 5    // "Cancel" button
 6    private function cancelContact() : void
 7    {
 8       // revert edit fields to original value
 9       firstName.text = contactsView.selectedItem.firstname;
10       lastName.text = contactsView.selectedItem.lastname;
11       streetAddress.text = contactsView.selectedItem.street;
12       city.text = contactsView.selectedItem.city;
13       state.text = contactsView.selectedItem.state;
14       zipCode.text = contactsView.selectedItem.zip;
15       eMail.text = contactsView.selectedItem.email;
16       phone.text = contactsView.selectedItem.phone;
17       // return user to "View Contacts" section
18       accordion.selectedIndex = 0;
19    } // end function cancelContact
20
21    // "Delete" button
22    private function deleteContact( event : CloseEvent ) : void
23    {
24       // handle if user clicked "Yes" in "Delete Contact" dialog box
25       if ( event.detail == Alert.YES )
26       {
27          // return user to "View Contacts" section if
28          // the user was in "Edit Contacts" section
29          if ( accordion.selectedIndex == 2 )
30             accordion.selectedIndex = 0;
31
32          // remove selected contact
33          addressCollection.removeItemAt( contactsView.selectedIndex );
34       } // end if
35    } // end function deleteContact
36
37    // "E-Mail" button
38    public function emailContact() : void
39    {
40       // form "mailto" URL given the selected e-mail address
41       var mailURL : URLRequest = new URLRequest( 'mailto:' +
42          contactsView.selectedItem.email );
43
44       // open the URL without opening new window
45       navigateToURL( mailURL, "_self" );
46    } // end function emailContact
47
48    // "Directions" button
49    public function getDirections() : void
50    {
51       // form directions URL given the selected address
52       var directionsURL : URLRequest = new URLRequest(
53          'http://maps.yahoo.com/broadband#mvt=m&q2=' +
```

Fig. 16.14 | Implement the actions of each button. (Part 1 of 2.)

```
54        contactsView.selectedItem.street + ' ' +
55        contactsView.selectedItem.city + ' ' +
56        contactsView.selectedItem.state +  ' ' +
57        contactsView.selectedItem.zip );
58     // open URL in a new window
59     navigateToURL( directionsURL, "_blank" );
60  } // end function getDirections
61
62  // "Save" button
63  private function saveContact() : void
64  {
65     // write changes to data array
66     addressCollection.setItemAt( {
67        firstname : firstName.text,
68        lastname : lastName.text,
69        street : streetAddress.text,
70        city : city.text,
71        state : state.text,
72        zip : zipCode.text,
73        email : eMail.text,
74        phone : phone.text },
75        contactsView.selectedIndex );
76
77     // refresh data collection so that search will still work
78     addressCollection.refresh();
79
80     // return user to "View Contacts" section
81     accordion.selectedIndex = 0;
82  } // end function saveContact
83
84  // "New" button
85  private function newContact() : void
86  {
87     addressCollection.addItem( {
88        firstname : 'New', lastname : 'Contact',
89        street : null, city : null, state : null,
90        zip : null, email : null, phone : null } );
91     contactsView.selectedIndex = addressCollection.length;
92     accordion.selectedIndex = 2;
93  } // end function newContact
```

Fig. 16.14 | Implement the actions of each button. (Part 2 of 2.)

16.5 Interacting with Server-Side Applications

Flex makes it easy to consume web services. In this example (Fig. 16.15), we use a web service from WebServiceX.net to obtain weather data based on a zip code. The user inputs the zip code, clicks a button and a five-day forecast is displayed on the screen (Fig. 16.16). Additionally, a marker is placed on a Yahoo! Map at the zip code's location, and the forecast information is displayed in the marker's tool tip (Fig. 16.17). You can test a live version of this application at test.deitel.com/examples/ajaxfp/flex/weather/. More information on web services is available in Chapter 24, Web Services, and at our Web Services Resource Center at www.deitel.com/webservices.

```
 1   <?xml version = "1.0" encoding = "utf-8" ?>
 2   <!-- Fig. 16.15: weather.mxml -->
 3   <!-- Weather Forecast application in Flex 2 -->
 4   <mx:Application xmlns:mx = "http://www.adobe.com/2006/mxml"
 5      layout = "absolute" xmlns:yahoo = "com.yahoo.webapis.maps.*"
 6      creationComplete = "initMap();" >
 7
 8      <mx:Script source = "map.as" />
 9
10      <mx:Script>
11      <![CDATA[
12         import mx.controls.dataGridClasses.DataGridColumn;
13         import mx.rpc.events.ResultEvent;
14         import mx.managers.CursorManager;
15         import mx.controls.Alert;
16         import mx.collections.ArrayCollection;
17         import flash.events.MouseEvent;
18
19         // define default namespace
20         default xml namespace = "http://www.webservicex.net";
21
22         [Bindable]
23         private var xmlData : XML;
24         [Bindable]
25         private var highLowTemp : String;
26         [Bindable]
27         private var fiveDayForecast : String = "";
28         [Bindable]
29         private var placeName : String;
30
31         // handle getWeatherButton click action
32         private function getWeather() : void
33         {
34            // disable button while request is pending
35            getWeatherButton.enabled = false;
36
37            // hide the old forecast data before displaying new data
38            forecastBox.visible = false;
39
40            // reset place name while loading new data
41            placeNameText.text = "";
42
43            // show the loading progress bar
44            loadingBar.visible = true;
45
46            // request the new data
47            weatherService.GetWeatherByZipCode.send();
48         } // end function getWeather
49
50         private function weatherResultHandler(event : ResultEvent) : void
51         {
52            // save the result of the web service as XML
53            xmlData = XML( event.result );
```

Fig. 16.15 | Weather Forecast application in Flex 2. (Part 1 of 5.)

```
54
55      // check that result is valid by checking length of StateCode
56      if ( xmlData.GetWeatherByZipCodeResult[ 0 ].
57        StateCode.text().length() != 0 )
58      {
59        // set placeNameText to the city and state of the zip code
60        placeName = xmlData.GetWeatherByZipCodeResult[ 0 ].
61          PlaceName.text() + ", " +
62          xmlData.GetWeatherByZipCodeResult[ 0 ].StateCode.text();
63        placeNameText.text = "5 Day Forecast for " + placeName;
64
65        // set image, temperature and date for each day
66        setData( weatherImage0, weatherTemp0, weatherDay0, 0 );
67        setData( weatherImage1, weatherTemp1, weatherDay1, 1 );
68        setData( weatherImage2, weatherTemp2, weatherDay2, 2 );
69        setData( weatherImage3, weatherTemp3, weatherDay3, 3 );
70        setData( weatherImage4, weatherTemp4, weatherDay4, 4 );
71
72        forecastBox.visible = true;
73
74        // save today's high/low as a string
75        highLowTemp = xmlData.GetWeatherByZipCodeResult.
76          Details.WeatherData.MaxTemperatureF[ 0 ].text() +
77          "/" + xmlData.GetWeatherByZipCodeResult.Details.
78          WeatherData.MinTemperatureF[ 0 ].text();
79
80        // save the five-day forecast as a string
81        fiveDayForecast = highLowTemp;
82
83        for ( var i : int = 1; i < 5; i++ )
84        {
85          fiveDayForecast += ", " + xmlData.
86            GetWeatherByZipCodeResult.Details.WeatherData.
87              MaxTemperatureF[ i ].text() + "/" + xmlData.
88              GetWeatherByZipCodeResult.Details.
89              WeatherData.MinTemperatureF[ i ].text();
90        } // end for
91
92        // place a marker on the map with the forecast
93        mapController.addCustomPOIMarker(
94          zipcode.text, placeName, highLowTemp, fiveDayForecast,
95          0x990099, 0xFFFFFF);
96
97        mapController.setCenterByAddressAndZoom(
98          zipcode.text, 7, 0 );
99      }
100     else
101     {
102       Alert.show( "Invalid zip code" );
103     }
104     // hide the loading progress bar
105     loadingBar.visible = false;
106
```

Fig. 16.15 | Weather Forecast application in Flex 2. (Part 2 of 5.)

```
107          // enable getWeatherButton
108          getWeatherButton.enabled = true;
109       } // end function weatherResultHandler
110
111       private function setData( forecastImage : Image,
112          tempText : Text, dateText : Text, i : int ) : void
113       {
114          // set the image for each day
115          forecastImage.source = xmlData.GetWeatherByZipCodeResult.
116             Details.WeatherData.WeatherImage[ i ].text();
117
118          // set the temperature for each day
119          tempText.text = xmlData.GetWeatherByZipCodeResult.
120             Details.WeatherData.MaxTemperatureF[ i ].text() +
121             "\n" + xmlData.GetWeatherByZipCodeResult.Details.
122             WeatherData.MinTemperatureF[ i ].text();
123
124          // set the date for each day
125          dateText.text = xmlData.GetWeatherByZipCodeResult.
126             Details.WeatherData.Day[ i ].text();
127       }
128    ]]>
129    </mx:Script>
130
131    <!-- show/hide animations for forecast boxes -->
132    <mx:Parallel id = "forecastAnimationIn">
133       <mx:Fade duration = "1000" alphaFrom = "0.0" alphaTo = "1.0" />
134       <mx:Zoom zoomWidthTo = "1" zoomHeightTo = "1" zoomWidthFrom = "0
135          zoomHeightFrom = "0" />
136    </mx:Parallel>
137
138    <mx:Parallel id = "forecastAnimationOut">
139       <mx:Fade duration = "500" alphaFrom = "1.0" alphaTo = "0.0" />
140       <mx:Zoom zoomWidthTo = "0" zoomHeightTo = "0" zoomWidthFrom = "1"
141          zoomHeightFrom = "1" />
142    </mx:Parallel>
143
144    <!-- WebService description -->
145    <mx:WebService id = "weatherService"
146       wsdl = "http://www.webservicex.net/WeatherForecast.asmx?WSDL"
147       fault = "Alert.show( event.fault.faultString )"
148       result = "weatherResultHandler( event )"
149       showBusyCursor = "true">
150       <mx:operation name = "GetWeatherByZipCode" resultFormat = "e4x">
151          <mx:request>
152             <ZipCode>{ zipcode.text }</ZipCode>
153          </mx:request>
154       </mx:operation>
155    </mx:WebService>
156
157    <!-- user interface begins here -->
158    <mx:Panel title = "Weather" width = "100%" height = "100%">
159       <mx:Accordion id = "accordion" width = "100%" height = "100%"
```

Fig. 16.15 | Weather Forecast application in Flex 2. (Part 3 of 5.)

```
160            creationPolicy = "all">
161            <mx:VBox label = "Forecast View" width = "100%" height = "100%">
162              <mx:ApplicationControlBar
163                defaultButton = "{ getWeatherButton }">
164                <mx:Label width = "100%"
165                  text = "Enter a zip code:" />
166                <mx:TextInput id = "zipcode" left = "10" />
167                <mx:Button id = "getWeatherButton" label = "Get Weather"
168                  click = "getWeather()" left = "10" />
169              </mx:ApplicationControlBar>
170
171              <mx:Text fontWeight = "bold" id = "placeNameText" />
172              <mx:ProgressBar id = "loadingBar" indeterminate = "true"
173                labelPlacement = "bottom" visible = "false" minimum = "0"
174                maximum = "100" label = "Loading Weather Data"
175                direction = "right" width = "75%" />
176
177              <!-- forecastBox holds the five-day forecast -->
178              <!-- start off as hidden, define show and hide effects -->
179              <mx:HBox id = "forecastBox" width = "100%" height = "100%"
180                visible = "false" showEffect = "{ forecastAnimationIn }"
181                hideEffect = "{ forecastAnimationOut }">
182                <mx:VBox id = "forecastBox0" horizontalAlign = "center"
183                  borderStyle = "solid" width = "20%" height = "0%">
184                  <mx:Text id = "weatherDay0" />
185                  <mx:Image id = "weatherImage0" />
186                  <mx:Text id = "weatherTemp0" />
187                </mx:VBox>
188
189                <mx:VBox horizontalAlign = "center"
190                  borderStyle = "solid" width = "20%">
191                  <mx:Text id = "weatherDay1" />
192                  <mx:Image id = "weatherImage1" />
193                  <mx:Text id = "weatherTemp1" />
194                </mx:VBox>
195
196                <mx:VBox horizontalAlign = "center"
197                  borderStyle = "solid" width = "20%">
198                  <mx:Text id = "weatherDay2" />
199                  <mx:Image id = "weatherImage2" />
200                  <mx:Text id = "weatherTemp2" />
201                </mx:VBox>
202
203                <mx:VBox horizontalAlign = "center"
204                  borderStyle = "solid" width = "20%">
205                  <mx:Text id = "weatherDay3" />
206                  <mx:Image id = "weatherImage3" />
207                  <mx:Text id = "weatherTemp3" />
208                </mx:VBox>
209
210                <mx:VBox horizontalAlign = "center"
211                  borderStyle = "solid" width = "20%">
212                  <mx:Text id = "weatherDay4" />
```

Fig. 16.15 | Weather Forecast application in Flex 2. (Part 4 of 5.)

```
213                        <mx:Image id = "weatherImage4" />
214                        <mx:Text id = "weatherTemp4" />
215                     </mx:VBox>
216                  </mx:HBox>
217               </mx:VBox>
218               <mx:VBox label = "Map View" width = "100%" height = "100%">
219                  <!-- create Yahoo! Map -->
220                  <yahoo:YahooMapService id = "yahooMap" UUID = "{ UUID }"
221                     swfDomId = "{ swfDomID }"
222                     apiId = "{ YahooAPIKey }"
223                     mapURL = "{ mapURL }" width = "600" height = "400" />
224                  <mx:HBox>
225                     <mx:Button label = "Back"
226                        click = "accordion.selectedIndex=0;" />
227                     <mx:Button label = "Clear"
228                        click = "mapController.removeAllMarkers();" />
229                  </mx:HBox>
230               </mx:VBox> <!-- end "Map View" Section -->
231            </mx:Accordion>
232         </mx:Panel>
233      </mx:Application>
```

Fig. 16.15 | Weather Forecast application in Flex 2. (Part 5 of 5.)

Fig. 16.16 | **Forecast View** of five-day weather forecast for Boston, MA.

We first look at the user interface part of weather.mxml (lines 158–232). Line 158 begins the user interface definition with a Panel, which holds an Accordion. In the Accordion (lines 159–231), there are two VBoxes, one for the **Forecast View** section (lines 161–217) and one for the **Map View** section (lines 218–230). The **Forecast View** VBox holds a ApplicationControlBar (lines 162–169) that contains the zipcode TextInput box, the **Get Weather** Button and a ProgressBar that notifies the user that the web service call is

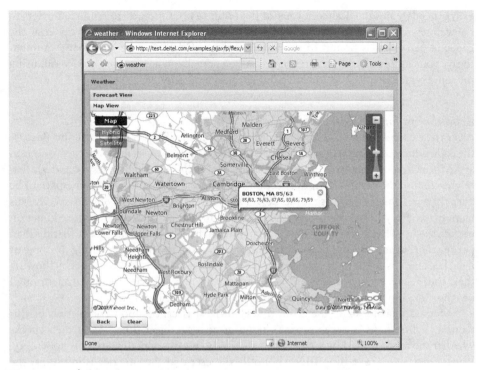

Fig. 16.17 | **Map View** of 5-Day Weather Forecast for Boston, MA.

being processed. The ***ProgressBar*** element allows you to give the user an idea of an operation's state. We set the indeterminate attribute of this ProgressBar to true because the application doesn't know when the web service call will complete.

The VBox also holds an HBox (lines 179–216) that contains the five-day forecast. Each day's forecast is held in a VBox that displays the date, an image representing the weather, and the high and low temperature in Fahrenheit. The HBox containing the forecast is not initially visible (line 180) because we do not want to see the borders of its VBoxes before there is any content. It also has the attributes showEffect and hideEffect (lines 180–181). These tell Flex which animation to use when the element is shown or hidden. These animations (lines 132–142) use the ***Parallel*** *element* to play effects simultaneously. Each Parallel element contains two effects, Fade and Zoom. The **Map View** VBox (lines 218–230) contains the ***YahooMapService*** element, as well as two Buttons. The first Button simply returns the user to the **Forecast View**, and the second Button tells the YahooMapService object to remove any markers from the map.

The weatherService WebService element (lines 145–155) specifies the URL of the ***Web Services Description Language (WSDL)*** file for the web service. A WSDL file is an XML file describing what services are available on a server, how to consume those services, what parameters they accept and what they return. Flex uses this WSDL file to make it easy to access the services without further configuration. We specify the fault event handler for the web service (line 147) to show an Alert dialog, and the result event handler to be weatherResultHandler (line 148). We then describe a specific method using the ***operation*** *element* (lines 150–154), which specifies the name of the method (GetWeatherByZipCode), and the desired format of the result (e4x). One way to send parameters to the web service is to enclose request elements in the operation element. In this case, the ZipCode parameter is bound to the text property of the zipcode TextInput. Alternatively, you can specify the parameters when you actually make the web service call using the same syntax that is used to send parameters to a function.

ActionScript for Weather Application

A Script element (lines 10–129) contains most of this application's ActionScript. Because the code is located in a CDATA section, the MXML compiler knows not to parse this section as XML in case it contains any reserved characters, such as angle brackets (< and >), that might confuse the compiler. In this section, we define the default XML namespace to be http://www.webservicex.net (line 20). This prevents us from having to specify this namespace every time we access the XML returned by the web service. Function getWeather (lines 32–48) is invoked when getWeatherButton is clicked. It first disables getWeatherButton and sets the busy cursor. It then hides the HBox containing the forecast data, because it is about to be changed, and resets placeNameText. It continues by showing the loadingBar ProgressBar (line 44) and finally requests the weather data through weatherService.GetWeatherByZipCode's send method (line 47).

Method weatherResultHandler (lines 50–109) is called upon completion of this request. It first saves the web service's result as an XML object (line 53). It then checks whether the result is valid by seeing if the StateCode returned by the service is not empty. If it is empty, an Alert (line 102) will notify the user that the zip code is invalid. If the StateCode exists, that indicates that the zip code was valid, and that we have received weather data. In this case, the program continues to set placeNameText (line 63) based on the city and state returned by the service, traversing the XML's tree down to the PlaceName and StateCode items using dot operators (lines 60–62). Next, it displays the data for each data with multiple calls to the setData function (lines 66–70).

This function (lines 111–127) sets the source URL of the forecast image for a given day to the URL in the XML's corresponding WeatherImage element (lines 115–116). The first WeatherImage in the XML has an index of 0. We apply a similar technique to populate the high and low temperature (lines 119–122) and the date for a given day (lines 125–126). Lines 75–78 save today's high and low temperature, as well as the five-day forecast, as strings for use in the map marker.

Finally, we place a marker on the map using mapController's addCustomPOIMarker function (lines 93–95). We specify the location of the marker to be the zip code we obtained data for, and title of the marker to be the name of that town or city, as well as today's high and low temperature. The body of the marker is set to display the five-day forecast. The setCenterByAddressAndZoom function (lines 97–98) zooms in and centers the map on the zip code's location. The function finally hides the ProgressBar, removes the busy cursor, and enables getWeatherButton.

The map.as ActionScript file (Fig. 16.18) handles the map functionality of the weather application. You need to copy the Yahoo! Map com folder and as2map.swf file into the application's base directory, just as we did for the addressBook application. This version of map.as contains the same initMap, onMapLoaded and onMapError functions as addressBook's version of map.as, but doesn't include the function setMarkerByAddress. The only other change is the swfDomID, which is set to weather (line 10).

```
 1    // Fig. 16.18: map.as
 2    // Handle the map functions for the Weather application
 3    import mx.managers.CursorManager;
 4    import com.yahoo.webapis.maps.methodgroups.*;
 5    import mx.controls.Alert;
 6
 7    // define constants
 8    private const swfDomID : String = "weather";
 9    private const UUID : int = Math.random() * 10000;
10
11    // YahooAPIKey string must be your own from developer.yahoo.com
12    private const YahooAPIKey : String = "Your Yahoo API Key Here";
13    private const mapURL : String = "as2map.swf";
14    private var mapController : MapController;
15
16    private function initMap() : void
17    {
18       CursorManager.setBusyCursor(); // turn on busy cursor
19
20       // wait for map to load, then call onMapLoaded method
21       yahooMap.addEventListener( 'onMapLoad', onMapLoaded );
22       yahooMap.addEventListener( 'onMapError', onMapError );
23    } // end function initMap
24
25    // handle map after it has loaded
26    public function onMapLoaded( event : Object ) : void
27    {
28       // instantiate map controller
29       mapController = new MapController( yahooMap );
30
31       // instantiate panTool method
32       var panTools : PanTool = new PanTool( yahooMap );
33
34       // allow user to pan across the map
35       panTools.setPanTool( true );
36
37       // instantiate the maps widget class
38       var widgets : Widgets = new Widgets( yahooMap );
39
40       // activate Navigator widget
41       widgets.showNavigatorWidget();
42
43       // activate map-type selection widget
44       widgets.showSatelliteControlWidget();
45
46       // turn off busy cursor
47       CursorManager.removeBusyCursor();
48    } // end function onMapLoaded
49
50    public function onMapError( errorCode:String, httpStatus:String ) : void
51    {
52       Alert.show(errorCode + '\n' + httpStatus, 'Map Load Error');
53    } // end function onMapError
```

Fig. 16.18 | Handle the map functions for the Weather application.

16.6 Customizing Your User Interface

Flex allows you to customize the style of your user interface. Just as in XHTML, you can include the styles inline, put them in a separate style section, or place them in a separate style-sheet file. The syntax is similar to that of CSS, but the names of the properties are different when used inline. Here, we add a style section and an inline style to our coverViewer application (Fig. 16.19). You can try this application at test.deitel.com/examples/ajaxfp/flex/coverViewerStyles/.

The first change we make is to add a *Style* *element* (lines 7–15). Inside the Style element is a format virtually identical to CSS (Chapter 3). We first give all LinkButton and HorizontalList elements custom styles, by setting the font family, size and color. We specify a custom style by using a dot before the style name, customStyle. We can then apply that style to any eligible element by adding a styleName = "customStyle" attribute, as we do in line 101. Finally, we can specify a style inline as we do for the Panel element (lines 74–76). Some of the names of the inline style attributes are different from those in the Style element and in CSS, using a camel-case naming convention instead of hyphenation (e.g. font-family becomes fontFamily).

```
1   <?xml version = "1.0" encoding = "utf-8" ?>
2   <!-- Fig. 16.19: coverViewerStyles.mxml -->
3   <!-- Using a Style element and inline styles -->
4   <mx:Application xmlns:mx = "http://www.adobe.com/2006/mxml">
5
6       <!-- define styles for application -->
7       <mx:Style>
8          LinkButton      { font-family: "Helvetica, sans-serif";
9                            font-size: 14 }
10         HorizontalList { font-size: 12;
11                          color: black }
12         .customStyle    { font-size: 16;
13                            font-weight: bold;
14                            color: black }
15      </mx:Style>
16
17      <!-- ActionScript goes in this section -->
18      <mx:Script>
19         <![CDATA[
20            // import the Cubic easing function for state transitions
21            import mx.effects.easing.Cubic;
22         ]]>
23      </mx:Script>
24
25      <!-- an array of images -->
26      <mx:ArrayCollection id = "bookCovers">
27         <!-- each image has a name and source attribute -->
28         <mx:Object name = "C How to Program" source = "chtp5.jpg" />
29         <mx:Object name = "C++ How to Program" source = "cpphtp6.jpg" />
30         <mx:Object name = "Internet How to Program"
31            source = "iw3htp4.jpg" />
32         <mx:Object name = "Java How to Program" source = "jhtp7.jpg" />
```

Fig. 16.19 | Using a Style element and inline styles. (Part 1 of 4.)

```
33        <mx:Object name = "VB How to Program" source = "vbhtp3.jpg" />
34        <mx:Object name = "Visual C# How to Program"
35           source = "vcsharphtp2.jpg" />
36        <mx:Object name = "Simply C++" source = "simplycpp.jpg" />
37        <mx:Object name = "Simply VB 2005" source = "simplyvb2005.jpg" />
38        <mx:Object name = "Simply Java" source = "simplyjava.jpg" />
39        <mx:Object name = "Small C++ How to Program"
40           source = "smallcpphtp5.jpg" />
41        <mx:Object name = "Small Java" source = "smalljavahtp6.jpg" />
42     </mx:ArrayCollection>
43
44     <!-- define the application's states -->
45     <mx:states>
46        <mx:State name = "HideThumbnails">
47           <mx:RemoveChild target = "{ thumbnailList }" />
48
49           <!-- switch the showHideButton to hide -->
50           <mx:SetEventHandler target = "{ showHideButton }" name = "click"
51              handler = "currentState = ''" />
52        </mx:State>
53     </mx:states>
54
55     <!-- define the transition effect for application state changes -->
56     <mx:transitions>
57        <mx:Transition>
58           <mx:Resize
59              targets = "{ [ thumbnailList, viewPanel, largeImage ] }"
60              duration = "750" easingFunction = "Cubic.easeOut" />
61        </mx:Transition>
62     </mx:transitions>
63
64     <!-- bind the source of largeImage to the selected thumbnail -->
65     <mx:Binding
66        source = "'fullsize/' +
67           bookCovers.getItemAt( selectCoverSlider.value ).source"
68        destination = "largeImage.source" />
69     <mx:Binding source = "'fullsize/' + thumbnailList.selectedItem.source"
70        destination = "largeImage.source" />
71
72     <!-- user interface begins here -->
73     <mx:Panel id = "viewPanel" title = "Deitel Book Cover Viewer"
74        width = "100%" height = "100%" horizontalAlign = "center"
75        color = "blue" fontSize = "18" fontFamily = "Helvetica"
76        textAlign = "center">
77
78        <mx:HBox height = "100%" width = "100%">
79           <mx:VSlider id = "zoomSlider" value = "100" minimum = "0"
80              maximum = "100" liveDragging = "true"
81              change = "largeImage.percentWidth = zoomSlider.value;
82                 largeImage.percentHeight = zoomSlider.value;"
83              height = "100%" width = "0%"
84              labels = "[ '0%', 'Zoom', '100%' ]" />
```

Fig. 16.19 | Using a Style element and inline styles. (Part 2 of 4.)

```
85      <mx:VBox width = "100%" height = "100%"
86          horizontalAlign = "center">
87
88          <!-- We bind the source of this image to the source of -->
89          <!-- the selected thumbnail, and center it in the VBox. -->
90          <!-- completeEffect tells Flex to fade the image in -->
91          <mx:Image id = "largeImage"
92              source = ""
93              horizontalAlign = "center"
94              verticalAlign = "middle"
95              width = "100%" height = "100%"
96              completeEffect = "Fade" />
97
98          <!-- bind this Label to the name of the selected thumbnail -->
99          <!-- also specify a styleName to use the customStyle style -->
100         <mx:Label text = "{ thumbnailList.selectedItem.name }"
101             styleName = "customStyle" />
102     </mx:VBox>
103 </mx:HBox>
104
105 <!-- slider can switch between images -->
106 <mx:HSlider id = "selectCoverSlider" height = "0%"
107     minimum = "0" maximum = "{ bookCovers.length - 1 }"
108     showDataTip = "false" snapInterval = "1" tickInterval = "1"
109     liveDragging = "true"
110     change = "thumbnailList.selectedIndex =
111         selectCoverSlider.value;
112         thumbnailList.scrollToIndex( selectCoverSlider.value )" />
113
114 <!-- display thumbnails of the images in bookCovers horizontally -->
115 <mx:HorizontalList id = "thumbnailList"
116     dataProvider = "{ bookCovers }" width = "100%" height = "160"
117     selectedIndex = "0"
118     change = "selectCoverSlider.value = thumbnailList.selectedIndex">
119
120     <!-- define how each item is displayed -->
121     <mx:itemRenderer>
122         <mx:Component>
123             <mx:VBox width = "140" height = "160"
124                 horizontalAlign = "center" verticalAlign = "middle"
125                 verticalScrollPolicy = "off"
126                 horizontalScrollPolicy = "off" paddingBottom = "20">
127
128                 <!-- display a thumbnail of each image -->
129                 <mx:Image source = "{ 'thumbs/' + data.source }"
130                     verticalAlign = "middle" />
131
132                 <!-- display the name of each image -->
133                 <mx:Label text = "{ data.name }" />
134             </mx:VBox>
135         </mx:Component>
136     </mx:itemRenderer>
137 </mx:HorizontalList>
```

Fig. 16.19 | Using a Style element and inline styles. (Part 3 of 4.)

```
138
139         <!-- this will exist in the bottom border of the Panel -->
140         <mx:ControlBar>
141             <mx:LinkButton label = "Show/Hide Thumbnails"
142                 click = "currentState = 'HideThumbnails';"
143                 id = "showHideButton" />
144         </mx:ControlBar>
145     </mx:Panel>
146 </mx:Application>
```

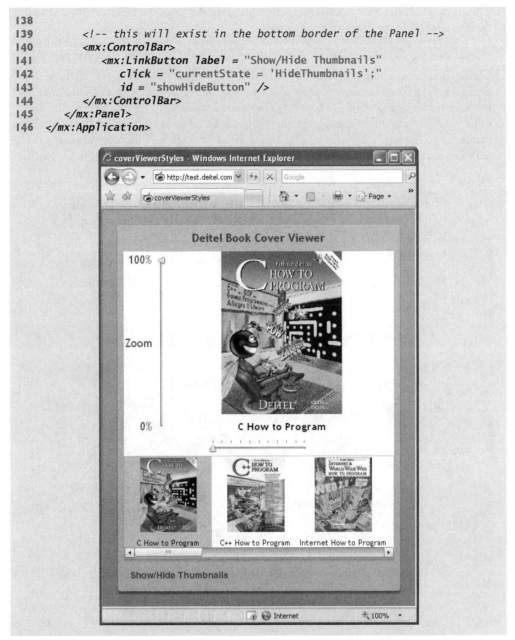

Fig. 16.19 │ Using a Style element and inline styles. (Part 4 of 4.)

To specify an external style-sheet, which uses syntax identical to the contents of a Style element, you simply add a Style element with a source attribute pointing to the style-sheet file, as in <mx:Style source = "styles.css" />.

A great way to try out different styles is Adobe's Flex Style Explorer, which you can find at weblogs.macromedia.com/mc/archives/FlexStyleExplorer.html. This allows you to visually create styles for most Flex user interface elements and generate the CSS you need to apply that style to your application.

Another way to customize the look of your application is through themes. The default theme of Flex applications is Halo. Other themes available with the Flex 2 SDK are Halo Classic (the former default), Ice, Institutional, Smoke and Wooden. All of these are defined in CSS files, but some of them also reference outside images and SWF files. These theme files can be found in `flex_sdk_2/frameworks/themes/`. You can specify that you want your application to use any of these themes at compile time by adding a `theme` parameter to the `mxmlc` command. Fig. 16.20 shows how to compile `coverViewer.mxml` with the `ice.css` theme. You can see how it looks in Fig. 16.21.

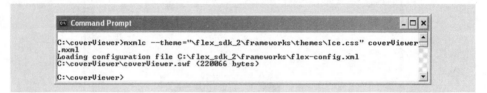

Fig. 16.20 | Running `mxmlc` with the `theme` parameter in Windows XP **Command Prompt**.

Fig. 16.21 | Deitel Cover Viewer compiled with the Ice theme.

16.7 Creating Charts and Graphs

To use Flex's charting components, first install Flex Charting. A trial version is available at `www.adobe.com/go/tryflex`. Installation instructions are available at `www.adobe.com/support/documentation/en/flex/2/install.html#installingcharts`.

To demonstrate Flex's charting capabilities, we've added a **Chart View** section to our weather application (Fig. 16.22) and populated it with two charts. The first is a *Line-Chart* that separately plots the high and low temperatures against the date. The user can mouse over any point of data and a data tip will tell the user whether it is a high or low temperature, the date and the temperature. The second chart is a *CandlestickChart*, displaying the range of temperatures for each day. This element also uses data tips to show greater detail. You can test a live version of this application at `test.deitel.com/examples/ajaxfp/flex/weatherChart/`.

A chart is just another type of user interface element. In addition to the chart types mentioned in Section 16.2, a full list of charting components is available from Adobe at `livedocs.adobe.com/flex/201/html/charts_intro_108_03.html`.

Figure 16.23 is a listing of the weather application with charting capabilities added. The first change we make in the code is to create an `ArrayCollection` to make our weather data available to a chart. To do this, we add the code `[Bindable] public var weatherArray : ArrayCollection;` in lines 31–32. We want it to be `Bindable` so that whenever the `ArrayCollection` is changed, the chart updates automatically. Next, we add lines 47 and 70 to create text showing the place name in the **Chart View** that acts just like the text in our **Forecast View**. We also add line 182 to animate changes in a chart's data.

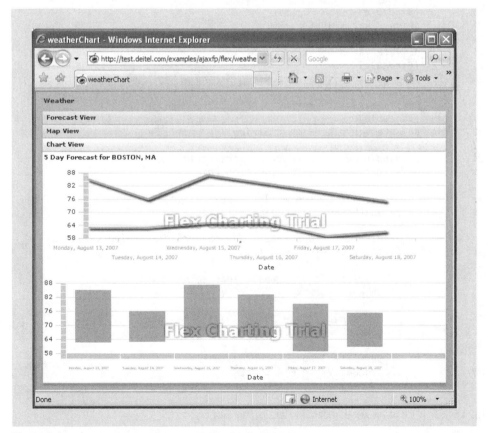

Fig. 16.22 | **Chart View** showing Boston, MA, forecast.

```
 1   <?xml version = "1.0" encoding = "utf-8" ?>
 2   <!-- Fig. 16.23: weatherChart.mxml -->
 3   <!-- Charting weather data in Flex 2 -->
 4   <mx:Application xmlns:mx = "http://www.adobe.com/2006/mxml"
 5      layout = "absolute"
 6      xmlns = "*" xmlns:yahoo = "com.yahoo.webapis.maps.*"
 7      creationComplete = "initMap();" >
 8
 9      <mx:Script source = "map.as" />
10
11      <mx:Script>
12      <![CDATA[
13         import mx.controls.dataGridClasses.DataGridColumn;
14         import mx.rpc.events.ResultEvent;
15         import mx.managers.CursorManager;
16         import mx.controls.Alert;
17         import mx.collections.ArrayCollection;
18         import flash.events.MouseEvent;
19
20         // define default namespace so we don't have to write it every time
21         default xml namespace = "http://www.webservicex.net";
22
23         [Bindable]
24         private var xmlData : XML;
25         [Bindable]
26         private var highLowTemp : String;
27         [Bindable]
28         private var fiveDayForecast : String = "";
29         [Bindable]
30         public var weatherArray : ArrayCollection;
31         [Bindable]
32         private var placeName : String;
33
34         // handle getWeatherButton click action
35         private function getWeather() : void
36         {
37            // disable button while request is pending
38            getWeatherButton.enabled = false;
39
40            // hide the old forecast data before displaying new data
41            forecastBox.visible = false;
42
43            // reset place name while loading new data
44            placeNameText.text = "";
45
46            // reset place name while loading new data
47            placeNameChartText.text = "";
48
49            // show the loading progress bar
50            loadingBar.visible = true;
51
```

Fig. 16.23 | Charting weather data in Flex 2. (Part 1 of 6.)

```
52        // request the new data
53        weatherService.GetWeatherByZipCode.send();
54    } // end function getWeather
55
56    private function weatherResultHandler(event : ResultEvent) : void
57    {
58        // save the result of the web service as XML
59        xmlData = XML( event.result );
60
61        // check that result is valid by checking length of StateCode
62        if ( xmlData.GetWeatherByZipCodeResult[ 0 ].
63            StateCode.text().length() != 0 )
64        {
65            // set placeNameText to the city and state of the zip code
66            placeName = xmlData.GetWeatherByZipCodeResult[ 0 ].
67                PlaceName.text() + ", " +
68                xmlData.GetWeatherByZipCodeResult[ 0 ].StateCode.text();
69            placeNameText.text = "5 Day Forecast for " + placeName;
70            placeNameChartText.text = "5 Day Forecast for " + placeName;
71
72            // set image, temperature and date for each day
73            setData( weatherImage0, weatherTemp0, weatherDay0, 0 );
74            setData( weatherImage1, weatherTemp1, weatherDay1, 1 );
75            setData( weatherImage2, weatherTemp2, weatherDay2, 2 );
76            setData( weatherImage3, weatherTemp3, weatherDay3, 3 );
77            setData( weatherImage4, weatherTemp4, weatherDay4, 4 );
78
79            forecastBox.visible = true;
80
81            // save today's high/low as a string
82            highLowTemp =  xmlData.GetWeatherByZipCodeResult.
83                Details.WeatherData.MaxTemperatureF[ 0 ].text() +
84                "/" + xmlData.GetWeatherByZipCodeResult.Details.
85                WeatherData.MinTemperatureF[ 0 ].text();
86
87            // save the five-day forecast as a string
88            fiveDayForecast = highLowTemp;
89
90            for ( var i : int = 1; i < 5; i++ )
91            {
92                fiveDayForecast += ", " + xmlData.
93                    GetWeatherByZipCodeResult.Details.WeatherData.
94                        MaxTemperatureF[ i ].text() + "/" + xmlData.
95                        GetWeatherByZipCodeResult.Details.
96                        WeatherData.MinTemperatureF[ i ].text();
97            } // end for
98
99            // place a marker on the map with the forecast
100           mapController.addCustomPOIMarker(
101               zipcode.text, placeName, highLowTemp, fiveDayForecast,
102               0x990099, 0xFFFFFF);
103
```

Fig. 16.23 | Charting weather data in Flex 2. (Part 2 of 6.)

```
104            mapController.setCenterByAddressAndZoom(
105               zipcode.text, 7, 0 );
106
107            // begin charting functionality
108
109            // saves date, high and low temp into an ArrayCollection
110            // so it can act as a chart's dataProvider
111            weatherArray = new ArrayCollection( );
112
113            for ( var j : int = 0; j < weatherService.GetWeatherByZipCode.
114               lastResult.GetWeatherByZipCodeResult.Details.
115               WeatherData.length(); j++ )
116            {
117               // create the object to be added to the array
118               var weatherDataObject : Object = new Object();
119
120               // extract the data from the e4x-formatted result
121               weatherDataObject.Date =  weatherService.
122                  GetWeatherByZipCode.lastResult.
123                  GetWeatherByZipCodeResult.Details.WeatherData[ j ].Day;
124               weatherDataObject.HighTemp = weatherService.
125                  GetWeatherByZipCode.lastResult.
126                  GetWeatherByZipCodeResult.Details.
127                  WeatherData[ j ].MaxTemperatureF;
128               weatherDataObject.LowTemp = weatherService.
129                  GetWeatherByZipCode.lastResult.
130                  GetWeatherByZipCodeResult.Details.
131                  WeatherData[ j ].MinTemperatureF;
132
133               // add the object to the array
134               weatherArray.addItem( weatherDataObject );
135            } //end for
136         // end charting functionality
137         }
138         else
139         {
140            Alert.show( "Invalid zip code" );
141         }
142         // hide the loading progress bar
143         loadingBar.visible = false;
144
145         // enable getWeatherButton
146         getWeatherButton.enabled = true;
147      } // end function weatherResultHandler
148
149      private function setData( forecastImage : Image,
150         tempText : Text, dateText : Text, i : int ) : void
151      {
152         // set the image for each day
153         forecastImage.source = xmlData.GetWeatherByZipCodeResult.
154            Details.WeatherData.WeatherImage[ i ].text();
155
```

Fig. 16.23 | Charting weather data in Flex 2. (Part 3 of 6.)

```
156          // set the temperature for each day
157          tempText.text = xmlData.GetWeatherByZipCodeResult.
158             Details.WeatherData.MaxTemperatureF[ i ].text() +
159             "\n" + xmlData.GetWeatherByZipCodeResult.Details.
160             WeatherData.MinTemperatureF[ i ].text();
161
162          // set the date for each day
163          dateText.text = xmlData.GetWeatherByZipCodeResult.
164             Details.WeatherData.Day[ i ].text();
165       }
166    ]]>
167    </mx:Script>
168
169    <!-- show/hide animations for forecast boxes -->
170    <mx:Parallel id = "forecastAnimationIn">
171       <mx:Fade duration = "1000" alphaFrom = "0.0" alphaTo = "1.0" />
172       <mx:Zoom zoomWidthTo = "1" zoomHeightTo = "1" zoomWidthFrom = "0"
173          zoomHeightFrom = "0" />
174    </mx:Parallel>
175
176    <mx:Parallel id = "forecastAnimationOut">
177       <mx:Fade duration = "500" alphaFrom = "1.0" alphaTo = "0.0" />
178       <mx:Zoom zoomWidthTo = "0" zoomHeightTo = "0" zoomWidthFrom = "1"
179          zoomHeightFrom = "1" />
180    </mx:Parallel>
181
182    <mx:SeriesInterpolate id = "interpolateEffect" duration = "1000" />
183
184    <!-- WebService description -->
185    <mx:WebService id = "weatherService"
186       wsdl = "http://www.webservicex.net/WeatherForecast.asmx?WSDL"
187       fault = "Alert.show( event.fault.faultString )"
188       result = "weatherResultHandler( event )"
189       showBusyCursor = "true">
190       <mx:operation name = "GetWeatherByZipCode" resultFormat = "e4x">
191          <mx:request>
192             <ZipCode>{ zipcode.text }</ZipCode>
193          </mx:request>
194       </mx:operation>
195    </mx:WebService>
196
197    <!-- user interface begins here -->
198    <mx:Panel title = "Weather" width = "100%" height = "100%">
199       <mx:Accordion id = "accordion" width = "100%" height = "100%"
200          creationPolicy = "all">
201          <mx:VBox label = "Forecast View" width = "100%" height = "100%">
202             <mx:ApplicationControlBar
203                defaultButton = "{ getWeatherButton }">
204                <mx:Label width = "100%"
205                   text = "Enter a zip code:" />
206                <mx:TextInput id = "zipcode" left = "10" />
207                <mx:Button id = "getWeatherButton" label = "Get Weather"
208                   click = "getWeather()" left = "10" />
```

Fig. 16.23 | Charting weather data in Flex 2. (Part 4 of 6.)

```
209            </mx:ApplicationControlBar>
210
211            <mx:Text fontWeight = "bold" id = "placeNameText" />
212            <mx:ProgressBar id = "loadingBar" indeterminate = "true"
213              labelPlacement = "bottom" visible = "false" minimum = "0"
214              maximum = "100" label = "Loading Weather Data"
215              direction = "right" width = "75%" />
216
217            <!-- forecastBox holds the five-day forecast -->
218            <!-- start off as hidden, define show and hide effects -->
219            <mx:HBox id = "forecastBox" width = "100%" height = "100%"
220              visible = "false" showEffect = "{ forecastAnimationIn }"
221              hideEffect = "{ forecastAnimationOut }">
222              <mx:VBox id = "forecastBox0" horizontalAlign = "center"
223                borderStyle = "solid" width = "20%" height = "0%">
224                <mx:Text id = "weatherDay0" />
225                <mx:Image id = "weatherImage0" />
226                <mx:Text id = "weatherTemp0" />
227              </mx:VBox>
228
229              <mx:VBox horizontalAlign = "center"
230                borderStyle = "solid" width = "20%">
231                <mx:Text id = "weatherDay1" />
232                <mx:Image id = "weatherImage1" />
233                <mx:Text id = "weatherTemp1" />
234              </mx:VBox>
235
236              <mx:VBox horizontalAlign = "center"
237                borderStyle = "solid" width = "20%">
238                <mx:Text id = "weatherDay2" />
239                <mx:Image id = "weatherImage2" />
240                <mx:Text id = "weatherTemp2" />
241              </mx:VBox>
242
243              <mx:VBox horizontalAlign = "center"
244                borderStyle = "solid" width = "20%">
245                <mx:Text id = "weatherDay3" />
246                <mx:Image id = "weatherImage3" />
247                <mx:Text id = "weatherTemp3" />
248              </mx:VBox>
249
250              <mx:VBox horizontalAlign = "center"
251                borderStyle = "solid" width = "20%">
252                <mx:Text id = "weatherDay4" />
253                <mx:Image id = "weatherImage4" />
254                <mx:Text id = "weatherTemp4" />
255              </mx:VBox>
256            </mx:HBox>
257          </mx:VBox>
258          <mx:VBox label = "Map View" width = "100%" height = "100%">
259            <!-- create Yahoo! Map -->
260            <yahoo:YahooMapService id = "yahooMap" UUID = "{ UUID }"
261              swfDomId = "{ swfDomID }"
```

Fig. 16.23 | Charting weather data in Flex 2. (Part 5 of 6.)

```
262                      apiId = "{ YahooAPIKey }"
263                      mapURL = "{ mapURL }" width = "600" height = "400" />
264              <mx:HBox>
265                  <mx:Button label = "Back"
266                      click = "accordion.selectedIndex=0;" />
267                  <mx:Button label = "Clear"
268                      click = "mapController.removeAllMarkers();" />
269              </mx:HBox>
270          </mx:VBox> <!-- end "Map View" Section -->
271
272          <!-- begin "Chart View" pane -->
273          <mx:VBox label = "Chart View" width = "100%" height = "100%">
274              <mx:Text fontWeight = "bold" id = "placeNameChartText" />
275              <mx:LineChart id = "lineChart" width = "100%" height = "100%"
276                  dataProvider = "{ weatherArray }" showDataTips = "true">
277                  <mx:verticalAxis>
278                      <mx:LinearAxis baseAtZero = "false" />
279                  </mx:verticalAxis>
280                  <mx:horizontalAxis>
281                      <mx:CategoryAxis categoryField = "Date"
282                          title = "Date" />
283                  </mx:horizontalAxis>
284                  <mx:series>
285                      <mx:LineSeries yField = "HighTemp"
286                          displayName = "High Temp"
287                          showDataEffect = "{ interpolateEffect }" />
288                      <mx:LineSeries yField = "LowTemp"
289                          displayName = "Low Temp"
290                          showDataEffect = "{ interpolateEffect }" />
291                  </mx:series>
292              </mx:LineChart>
293              <mx:CandlestickChart id = "candlestickChart" width = "100%"
294                  height = "100%" showDataTips = "true"
295                  dataProvider = "{ weatherArray }">
296                  <mx:verticalAxis>
297                      <mx:LinearAxis baseAtZero = "false" />
298                  </mx:verticalAxis>
299                  <mx:horizontalAxis>
300                      <mx:CategoryAxis categoryField = "Date"
301                          title = "Date"/>
302                  </mx:horizontalAxis>
303                  <mx:series>
304                      <mx:CandlestickSeries openField = "HighTemp"
305                          highField = "HighTemp" lowField = "LowTemp"
306                          closeField = "LowTemp"
307                          showDataEffect = "{ interpolateEffect }" />
308                  </mx:series>
309              </mx:CandlestickChart>
310          </mx:VBox> <!-- end "Chart View" section -->
311      </mx:Accordion>
312   </mx:Panel>
313 </mx:Application>
```

Fig. 16.23 | Charting weather data in Flex 2. (Part 6 of 6.)

Lines 113–135 declare a for statement that iterates over the WeatherData objects returned by the weatherService WebService. Inside the for statement, we create a weatherDataObject and give it the attributes Date, HighTemp, and LowTemp (lines 121–131). We give these attributes values from the XML returned by the web service. Finally, we add each weatherDataObject to weatherArray (line 134).

We also add a new pane in the Accordion for our chart, a VBox called **Chart View** (lines 273–310). This contains a Text element called placeNameChartText (line 274). This element serves an identical purpose to placeNameText (line 211). Next, we add a LineChart element (lines 275–292). This LineChart has the dataProvider attribute set to { weatherArray } to indicate that the data presented in the chart is bound to weatherArray. We also specify that showDataTips is true (line 276), meaning that when the user mouses over a data point on the graph, a data tip will pop up, giving the user more detailed information about that point. Line 278 specifies that the baseAtZero attribute of the verticalAxis' LinearAxis is false. This way, the graph displays the range of temperatures only from lowest to highest, rather than starting at zero. Inside the horizontalAxis element (lines 280–283), we specify one CategoryAxis named Date. The CategoryAxis' category-Field attribute is set to "Date", meaning that the axis receives data from the Date field of weatherArray. Next, we specify LineSeries elements, located in the series element (lines 284–291). The first LineSeries' yField attribute is set to "HighTemp", which means that the LineSeries gets its data from the HighTemp field of weatherArray. We also set showDataEffect to "{ interpolateEffect }". This calls the interpolateEffect SeriesEffect that we created every time the data is updated. We also create a second LineSeries displaying LowTemp from weatherArray, using the same effect.

The second chart is a CandlestickChart (lines 293–309). This chart also sets show-DataTips to "true" and uses the same dataProvider (weatherArray). It also sets the ver-ticalAxis' baseAtZero attribute to "false" and has a horizontalAxis that displays the Date. In the CandlestickChart's series element (lines 303–307) is a Candlestick-Series with several attributes. The four attributes that define the data it displays are open-Field, highField, lowField and closeField. A CandlestickChart is designed to display financial data, such as stock prices. Therefore, it requires a start value and end value in addition to a high and low value. Since we have only high and low data for the weather, we place HighTemp in both openField and highField. Similarly, we place LowTemp in both closeField and lowField. We use interpolateEffect as the showDataEffect. Finally, the swfDomID constant in map.as must point to the filename of our application without .swf (in this case, weatherChart).

16.8 Connection-Independent RIAs on the Desktop: Adobe Integrated Runtime (AIR)

The *Adobe Integrated Runtime (AIR)* allows developers to deploy Ajax, Flash and Flex web applications to the desktop. It requires the user to download and install the runtime (planned to be between 5 and 9 MB). Once installed, the user can download and run AIR applications as if they were native desktop applications, including running them while disconnected from the server. This ability to function while disconnected is similar to that of Google's Gears.[5]

---

5. Information on Google Gears can be found at code.google.com/apis/gears/.

AIR (as of the Beta version) supports Mac OS X 10.4.8 and up, Windows XP with Service Pack 2 (SP2) and Windows Vista. Adobe plans to add Linux support "shortly after the 1.0. release."[6] AIR uses Flash Player 9 as well as the the open source WebKit HTML rendering and JavaScript engine (also found in Apple's Safari and KDE's Konqueror browsers).

AIR provides an API for file input and output, a SQLite embedded database, windowing support, and file-type association (so that you can make it the operating system's default application for a type of document). It is also planned to support native menus (the Beta version supports this for Mac OS X), and contextual (right click) menus.

Adobe's AIR web page is currently located at `labs.adobe.com/technologies/air/`. From there, you will find links to learn more about AIR, download the runtime environment, download the SDK, and try sample applications.

16.9 Flex 3 Beta

At the time of publication, Flex 3 was in beta. The Flex 3 beta homepage is `labs.adobe.com/technologies/flex/`. The final version of Flex 3 is planned to be released in Q4 2007[7]. You can download the Flex SDK beta from `labs.adobe.com/technologies/flex/sdk/flex3sdk.html`. Install instructions are available at `labs.adobe.com/wiki/index.php/Flex_3:Release_Notes#Installation_Instructions`.

An introduction to the features planned for Flex 3 is available at `labs.adobe.com/wiki/index.php/Flex_3:Feature_Introductions`. Flex Builder 3, for instance, will add a wizard to easily consume web services, improve the user interface designer, and also add support for AIR development. Some of the new features are discussed at `www.adobe.com/devnet/flex/articles/flex3_whatsnew.html`.

16.10 Web Resources

`www.deitel.com/flex`

The Deitel Flex Resource Center contains many resources, downloads, tutorials, documentation, books, e-books, articles, blogs and more that will help you develop Flex applications. The Deitel Flex Resource Center will provide you resources to allow you to pursue more advanced Flex programming.

---

6.   From `labs.adobe.com/wiki/index.php/AIR:Developer_FAQ`.
7.   From `flexwiki.adobe.com/confluence/display/ADOBE/Flex+3+Planning`.

PART 4

Rich Internet Application Server Technologies

One of the powerful things about networking technology like the Internet or the Web or the Semantic Web...is that the things we've just done with them far surpass the imagination of the people who invented them.

—Tim Berners-Lee, interviewed
by Peter Moon, *IDG Now*

17

Web Servers (IIS and Apache)

Stop abusing my verses, or publish some of your own.
—Martial

There are three difficulties in authorship: to write anything worth the publishing, to find honest men to publish it, and to get sensible men to read it.
—Charles Caleb Colton

When your Daemon is in charge, do not try to think consciously. Drift, wait and obey.
—Rudyard Kipling

OBJECTIVES

In this chapter you will learn:

- To understand a web server's functionality.
- To introduce Microsoft Internet Information Services (IIS) and Apache HTTP Server.
- To set up virtual directories from which content can be served.
- To test whether you set up the virtual directory properly.

17.1 Introduction

In this chapter, we discuss the specialized software—called a *web server*—that responds to client requests (typically from a web browser) by providing resources such as XHTML documents. For example, when users enter a Uniform Resource Locator (URL) address, such as www.deitel.com, into a web browser, they are requesting a specific document from a web server. The web server maps the URL to a resource on the server (or to a file on the server's network) and returns the requested resource to the client. During this interaction, the web server and the client communicate using the platform-independent Hypertext Transfer Protocol (HTTP), a protocol for transferring requests and files over the Internet or a local intranet.

Our web server discussion introduces *Microsoft Internet Information Services (IIS)* and the open source *Apache HTTP Server*. Sections 17.6 and 17.7 discuss IIS and Apache, respectively.

17.2 HTTP Transactions

In this section, we discuss what occurs behind the scenes when a user requests a web page in a browser. The HTTP protocol allows clients and servers to interact and exchange information in a uniform and reliable manner.

In its simplest form, a web page is nothing more than an XHTML document that describes to a web browser how to display and format the document's information. XHTML documents normally contain hyperlinks that link to different pages or to other parts of the same page. When the user clicks a hyperlink, the requested web page loads into the user's web browser. Similarly, the user can type the address of a page into the browser's address field.

URIs

HTTP uses URIs (Uniform Resource Identifiers) to identify data on the Internet. URIs that specify document locations are called URLs (Uniform Resource Locators). Common URLs refer to files, directories or objects that perform complex tasks, such as database lookups and Internet searches. If you know the URL of a publicly available resource or file anywhere on the web, you can access it through HTTP.

Parts of a URL

A URL contains information that directs a browser to the resource that the user wishes to access. Computers that run *web server* software make such resources available. Let's examine the components of the URL

```
http://www.deitel.com/books/downloads.html
```

The `http://` indicates that the resource is to be obtained using the HTTP protocol. The middle portion, `www.deitel.com`, is the server's fully qualified *hostname*—the name of the server on which the resource resides. This computer usually is referred to as the *host*, because it houses and maintains resources. The hostname `www.deitel.com` is translated into an *IP address*—a unique numerical value that identifies the server much as a telephone number uniquely defines a particular phone line. More information on IP addresses is available at `en.wikipedia.org/wiki/IP_address`. This translation is performed by a *domain name system (DNS) server*—a computer that maintains a database of hostnames and their corresponding IP addresses—and the process is called a *DNS lookup*.

The remainder of the URL (i.e., `/books/downloads.html`) specifies both the name of the requested resource (the XHTML document `downloads.html`) and its path, or location (`/books`), on the web server. The path could specify the location of an actual directory on the web server's file system. For security reasons, however, the path normally specifies the location of a *virtual directory*. The server translates the virtual directory into a real location on the server (or on another computer on the server's network), thus hiding the true location of the resource. Some resources are created dynamically using other information stored on the server computer, such as a database. The hostname in the URL for such a resource specifies the correct server; the path and resource information identify the resource with which to interact to respond to the client's request.

Making a Request and Receiving a Response

When given a URL, a web browser performs a simple HTTP transaction to retrieve and display the web page found at that address. Figure 17.1 illustrates the transaction, showing the interaction between the web browser (the client side) and the web server application (the server side).

In Fig. 17.1, the web browser sends an HTTP request to the server. The request (in its simplest form) is

```
GET /books/downloads.html HTTP/1.1
```

The word *GET* is an *HTTP method* indicating that the client wishes to obtain a resource from the server. The remainder of the request provides the path name of the resource (e.g., an XHTML document) and the protocol's name and version number (`HTTP/1.1`). The client's request also contains some required and optional headers.

Any server that understands HTTP (version 1.1) can translate this request and respond appropriately. Figure 17.2 depicts the server responding to a request. The server first responds by sending a line of text that indicates the HTTP version, followed by a numeric code and a phrase describing the status of the transaction. For example,

```
HTTP/1.1 200 OK
```

Fig. 17.1 | Client interacting with web server. *Step 1:* The GET request.

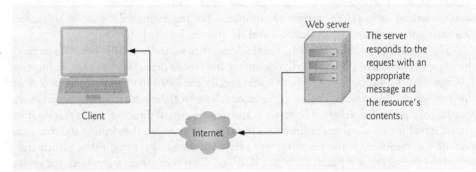

Fig. 17.2 | Client interacting with web server. *Step 2:* The HTTP response.

indicates success, whereas

```
HTTP/1.1 404 Not found
```

informs the client that the web server could not locate the requested resource. A complete list of numeric codes indicating the status of an HTTP transaction can be found at www.w3.org/Protocols/rfc2616/rfc2616-sec10.html.

HTTP Headers
The server then sends one or more *HTTP headers*, which provide additional information about the data that will be sent. In this case, the server is sending an XHTML text document, so one HTTP header for this example would read:

```
Content-type: text/html
```

The information provided in this header specifies the *Multipurpose Internet Mail Extensions (MIME)* type of the content that the server is transmitting to the browser. MIME is an Internet standard that specifies data formats so that programs can interpret data correctly. For example, the MIME type text/plain indicates that the sent information is text that can be displayed directly, without any interpretation of the content as XHTML mark-up. Similarly, the MIME type image/jpeg indicates that the content is a JPEG image. When the browser receives this MIME type, it attempts to display the image.

The header or set of headers is followed by a blank line, which indicates to the client browser that the server is finished sending HTTP headers. The server then sends the contents of the requested XHTML document (downloads.html). The client-side browser parses the XHTML markup it receives and renders (or displays) the results. The server normally keeps the connection open to process other requests from the client.

HTTP get and post Requests

The two most common *HTTP request types* (also known as *request methods*) are get and post. A get request typically gets (or retrieves) information from a server. Common uses of get requests are to retrieve an XHTML document or an image, or to fetch search results based on a user-submitted search term. A post request typically posts (or sends) data to a server. Common uses of post requests are to send form data or documents to a server.

An HTTP request often posts data to a *server-side form handler* that processes the data. For example, when a user performs a search or participates in a web-based survey, the web server receives the information specified in the XHTML form as part of the request. Get requests and post requests can both be used to send form data to a web server, yet each request type sends the information differently.

A get request sends information to the server as part of the URL, e.g., www.google.com/search?q=deitel. In this case search is the name of Google's server-side form handler, q is the name of a variable in Google's search form and deitel is the search term. Notice the ? in the preceding URL. A ? separates the *query string* from the rest of the URL in a request. A *name/value* pair is passed to the server with the *name* and the *value* separated by an equals sign (=). If more than one *name/value* pair is submitted, each pair is separated by an ampersand (&). The server uses data passed in a query string to retrieve an appropriate resource from the server. The server then sends a *response* to the client. A get request may be initiated by submitting an XHTML form whose method attribute is set to "get", or by typing the URL (possibly containing a query string) directly into the browser's address bar.

A post request is specified in an XHTML form by the method "post". The post method sends form data as part of the HTTP message, not as part of the URL. A get request typically limits the query string (i.e., everything to the right of the ?) to a specific number of characters (2083 in IE; more in other browsers), so it is often necessary to send large pieces of information using the post method. The post method is also sometimes preferred because it hides the submitted data from the user by embedding it in an HTTP message. If a form submits several hidden input values along with user-submitted data, the post method might generate a URL like www.searchengine.com/search. The form data still reaches the server and is processed in a similar fashion to a get request, but the user does not see the exact information sent.

> ### Software Engineering Observation 17.1
>
> *The data sent in a post request is not part of the URL and the user can't see the data by default. However there are tools available that expose this data, so you should not assume that the data is secure just because a post request is used.*

Client-Side Caching

Browsers often *cache* (save on disk) web pages for quick reloading. If there are no changes between the version stored in the cache and the current version on the web, this speeds up your browsing experience. An HTTP response can indicate the length of time for which the content remains "fresh." If this amount of time has not been reached, the browser can avoid another request to the server. If not, the browser loads the document from the cache. Thus, the browser minimizes the amount of data that must be downloaded for you to view a web page. Browsers typically do not cache the server's response to a post request, because the next post might not return the same result. For example, in a survey, many users could visit the same web page and answer to a question. The survey results could then be displayed for the user. Each new answer changes the overall results of the survey.

When you use a web-based search engine, the browser normally supplies the information you specify in an HTML form to the search engine with a get request. The search engine performs the search, then returns the results to you as a web page. Such pages are sometimes cached by the browser in case you perform the same search again.

17.3 Multitier Application Architecture

Web-based applications are *multitier applications* (sometimes referred to as *n-tier applications*) that divide functionality into separate *tiers* (i.e., logical groupings of functionality). Although tiers can be located on the same computer, the tiers of web-based applications often reside on separate computers. Figure 17.3 presents the basic structure of a *three-tier web-based application*.

The *bottom tier* (also called the data tier or the information tier) maintains the application's data. This tier typically stores data in a relational database management system (RDBMS). We discuss RDBMSs in Chapter 18. For example, a retail store might have an inventory information database containing product descriptions, prices and quantities in stock. Another database might contain customer information, such as user names, billing addresses and credit card numbers. These may reside on one or more computers, which together comprise the application's data.

The *middle tier* implements business logic, controller logic and presentation logic to control interactions between the application's clients and its data. The middle tier acts as an intermediary between data in the information tier and the application's clients. The middle-tier *controller logic* processes client requests (such as requests to view a product

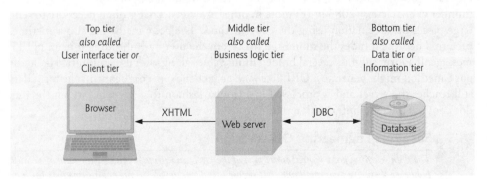

Fig. 17.3 | Three-tier architecture.

catalog) and retrieves data from the database. The middle-tier *presentation logic* then processes data from the information tier and presents the content to the client. Web applications typically present data to clients as XHTML documents.

Business logic in the middle tier enforces **business rules** and ensures that data is reliable before the application updates a database or presents data to users. Business rules dictate how clients access data, and how applications process data. For example, a business rule in the middle tier of a retail store's web-based application might ensure that all product quantities remain positive. A client request to set a negative quantity in the bottom tier's product information database would be rejected by the middle tier's business logic.

The *top tier*, or client tier, is the application's user interface, which gathers input and displays output. Users interact directly with the application through the user interface, which is typically a web browser, keyboard and mouse, or a mobile device. In response to user actions (e.g., clicking a hyperlink), the client tier interacts with the middle tier to make requests and to retrieve data from the information tier. The client tier then displays the data retrieved for the user. The client tier never directly interacts with the information tier.

17.4 Client-Side Scripting versus Server-Side Scripting

In earlier chapters, we focused on client-side scripting with JavaScript. Client-side scripting can be used to validate user input, to interact with the browser, to enhance web pages by manipulating the DOM of a page, and to add Ajax functionality.

Client-side scripting does have limitations, such as browser dependency; the browser or *scripting host* must support the scripting language and capabilities. Scripts are restricted from accessing the local hardware and filesystem for security reasons. Another issue is that client-side scripts can be viewed by the client by using the browser's source-viewing capability. Sensitive information, such as passwords or other personally identifiable data, should not be on the client. All client-side data validation should be mirrored on the server. Also, placing certain operations in JavaScript on the client can open web applications to attack and other security issues.

Programmers have more flexibility with *server-side scripts*, which often generate custom responses for clients. For example, a client might connect to an airline's web server and request a list of flights from Boston to San Antonio between April 19th and May 5th. The server queries the database, dynamically generates XHTML content containing the flight list and sends the XHTML to the client. This technology allows clients to obtain the most current flight information from the database by connecting to an airline's web server.

Server-side scripting languages have a wider range of programmatic capabilities than their client-side equivalents. For example, server-side scripts often can access the server's file directory structure, whereas client-side scripts cannot access the client's directories.

Server-side scripts also have access to server-side software that extends server functionality—Microsoft web servers use *ISAPI (Internet Server Application Program Interface) extensions* and Apache HTTP Servers use *modules*. Components and modules range from programming language support to counting the number of web-page hits. We discuss some of these components and modules in the remaining chapters of the book.

Software Engineering Observation 17.2

Properly configured server-side script source code is not visible to the client; only XHTML and any client-side scripts are visible to the client.

17.5 Accessing Web Servers

To request documents from web servers, users must know the hostnames on which the web server software resides. Users can request documents from *local web servers* (i.e., ones residing on users' machines) or *remote web servers* (i.e., ones residing on different machines).

Local web servers can be accessed through your computer's name or through the name `localhost`—a hostname that references the local machine and normally translates to the IP address `127.0.0.1` (known as the *loopback address*). We sometimes use `localhost` in this book for demonstration purposes. To display the machine name in Windows XP, Windows Server 2003, Windows Vista, Mac OS X or Linux, run the `hostname` command in a command prompt or terminal window.

A remote web server referenced by a fully qualified hostname or an IP address can also serve documents. In the URL `http://www.deitel.com/books/downloads.html`, the middle portion, `www.deitel.com`, is the server's fully qualified hostname.

Windows Firewall Settings

If you'd like to test your web server over a network, you may need to change your Windows Firewall settings. For security reasons, Windows Firewall does not allow remote access to a web server on your local computer by default. To change this, open the Windows Firewall utility in the Windows Control Panel. Click the **Advanced** tab and select your network connection from the **Network Connection Settings** list, then click **Settings....** On the **Services** tab of the **Advanced Settings** dialog, ensure that **Web Server (HTTP)** is checked.

17.6 Microsoft Internet Information Services (IIS)

Microsoft Internet Information Services (IIS) is a web server that is included with several versions of Windows. Installing IIS enables a computer to serve documents. To install IIS 5.1 on Windows XP Professional, open the **Add or Remove Programs** control panel, click **Add/Remove Windows Components**, check the checkbox next to **Internet Information Services (IIS)**, and click **Next >**. You may need the original operating system disk to complete the installation. For IIS 6.0 on Windows Server 2003 and IIS 7.0 on Windows Vista, the software should already be installed (but is also on your installation disk). The remainder of this section assumes that either IIS 5.1, IIS 6.0 or IIS 7.0 is installed on your system. In Windows Server 2003, you'll need to use the **Manager Your Server** window to add the **Application Server** role. In Windows Vista, go to the **Control Panel**, select **Programs**, then select **Turn Windows Features On or Off**.

The following subsections explain how to configure IIS 5.1, IIS 6.0 and IIS 7.0 to serve documents via HTTP. If you are using Windows XP or Windows Server 2003, see Section 17.6.1. If you are using Windows Vista, skip to Section 17.6.2.

17.6.1 Microsoft Internet Information Services (IIS) 5.1 and 6.0

Start the Internet services manager by clicking the **Start** button and opening the **Control Panel**. If the **Control Panel** is currently in **Category View**, click **Switch to Classic View**. Then, double click the **Administrative Tools** icon and double click the **Internet Services Manager** icon (**Internet Information Services (IIS) Manager** in Windows Server 2003). For Windows XP, this opens the **Internet Information Services** window (Fig. 17.4)—the administration

Fig. 17.4 | Internet Information Services window of IIS 5.1.

program for IIS 5.1. For Windows Server 2003, this opens the (**Internet Information Services (IIS) Manager**, which provides the same capabilities. Alternatively, you can type inetmgr at the **Start** menu's **Run...** command prompt to open this window. You place documents that will be requested from IIS either in the website's *default directory* (i.e., C:\Inetpub\wwwroot) or in a *virtual directory*. A virtual directory is an alias for an existing directory that resides on the local machine (e.g., C:\) or on the network. When a server is accessed from a web browser, content in the default directory and virtual directories is visible to the client.

In the window, the left pane contains the web server's directory structure. The name of the machine running IIS (e.g., **RESILIANT**) is listed under **Internet Information Services**. Clicking the + symbol to the left of the machine name displays **Default Web Site** (and possibly several other nodes).

Expand the **Default Web Site** directory by clicking the + to the left of it. In this directory, we'll create a virtual directory for the website. Most web documents are placed in the web server's wwwroot directory or one of its subdirectories. For this example, we create a directory in the wwwroot directory and have our virtual directory point to it. To create a virtual directory in this directory, right click **Default Web Site** and select **New > Virtual Directory....** This starts the **Virtual Directory Creation Wizard** (Fig. 17.5), which guides you through creating a virtual directory.

Fig. 17.5 | Virtual Directory Creation Wizard welcome page.

To begin, click **Next >** in the **Virtual Directory Creation Wizard** welcome page. In the **Virtual Directory Alias** page (Fig. 17.6), enter a name for the virtual directory and click **Next >**. We use the name `Chapter17Test`, although the virtual directory may have any name, provided that it does not conflict with an existing virtual directory name.

In the **Web Site Content Directory** page (Fig. 17.7), enter the path for the directory containing the documents that clients will view. We created a directory named `C:\Chapter17Examples` that serves our documents. You can select the **Browse** button to navigate to the desired directory or to create a new one. Click **Next >**.

The **Access Permissions** page (Fig. 17.8) presents the virtual directory *security level* choices. Choose the access level appropriate for a web document. The **Read** option allows users to read and download files located in the directory. The **Run scripts (such as ASP)**

Fig. 17.6 | Virtual Directory Alias page of the Virtual Directory Creation Wizard.

Fig. 17.7 | Web Site Content Directory page of the Virtual Directory Creation Wizard.

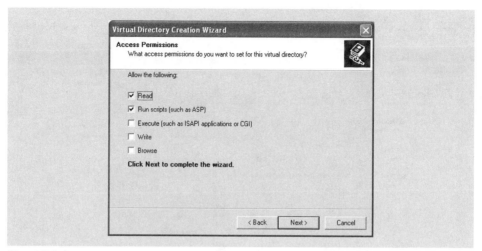

Fig. 17.8 | Access Permissions page of the **Virtual Directory Creation Wizard**.

option allows scripts to run in the directory. The **Execute (such as ISAPI applications or CGI)** option allows applications to run in the directory. The **Write** option allows a web page to write to files on the server, which could be a security risk. The **Browse** option allows users to see a full list of the folder's files through a web browser. By default, **Read** and **Run scripts** are enabled. Click **Next >**.

Click **Finish** to complete the creation of the virtual directory and exit the **Virtual Directory Creation Wizard**. The newly created virtual directory, Chapter17Test, is now part of the **Default Web Site**. The IIS server is configured to serve documents through the Chapter17Test virtual directory. The URL http://localhost/Chapter17Test now references the C:\Chapter17Examples directory.

To start IIS so it can serve content, right click **Default Web Site** and select **Start**. If you need to stop IIS, right click **Default Web Site** and select **Stop**. The web server is not available to serve content if it is stopped.

17.6.2 Microsoft Internet Information Services (IIS) 7.0

To start the *Internet Information Services (IIS) Manager*, click the start ( ) button, select the **Control Panel**, click **Classic View**, double click the **Administrative Tools** icon and double click the **Internet Information Services (IIS) Manager** icon. Click **Continue** in the dialog that appears to display the **Internet Information Services (IIS) Manager** window (Fig. 17.9)—the administration program for IIS 7.0. You place documents that will be requested from IIS either in the *default directory* (i.e., C:\Inetpub\wwwroot) or in a *virtual directory*. A virtual directory is an alias for an existing directory that resides on the local machine (e.g., C:\) or on the network. When a server is accessed from a browser, only the default directory and virtual directories are visible to the client.

In the **Internet Information Services (IIS) Manager** window, the left pane contains the web server's directory structure. The name of the machine running IIS (e.g., **QUALIFLY**) is listed at the top of the **Connections** column. Clicking the arrow (▷) symbol to the left of the machine name displays **Application Pools** and **Web Sites**. The **Application Pools** folder contains tools for configuring advanced features of IIS 7.0.

Fig. 17.9 | Internet Information (IIS) Services Manager window (IIS 7.0).

Expand **Web Sites** by clicking the arrow (▷) to the left of it. This should display **Default Web Site**. Expand **Default Web Site** by clicking the arrow (▷) to the left of it. These are the folders and virtual directories in the default website. For this example, we create a virtual directory from which we request our documents. To create a virtual directory, right click **Default Web Site** and select **Add Virtual Directory...**. This displays the **Add Virtual Directory** dialog (Fig. 17.10). In the **Alias:** field, enter a name for the virtual directory. We use the name Chapter17Test, although the virtual directory may have any name, provided that it does not conflict with an existing virtual directory. In the **Physical path:** field, enter the path for the directory containing the documents that clients will view. We created a directory named C:\Chapter17Examples for our documents. If necessary, select the ... button to navigate to the desired directory or to create a new one. Click **OK** to create the new virtual directory.

In Windows Vista, before you can use IIS, you must enable the World Wide Web Publishing Service (W3SVC). To do so, go to the start (🔲) button, select **Control Panel**, select **Classic View**, double click **Administrative Tools** and double click **Services**. This displays the **Services** window. Locate **World Wide Web Publishing Service** in the list of services, then right click it and select **Properties**. In the window that appears, change the **Startup type:** option to **Automatic**, then click **OK**. Next, right click **World Wide Web Publishing Service** again and select **Start** to run IIS so that it can accept requests.

Fig. 17.10 | **Add Virtual Directory** dialog.

17.7 Apache HTTP Server

The Apache HTTP Server, maintained by the Apache Software Foundation, is currently the most popular web server because of its stability, efficiency, portability, security and small size. It is open source software that runs on UNIX, Linux, Mac OS X, Windows and numerous other platforms.

Mac OS X and many versions of Linux come preinstalled with Apache. If your system does not have Apache preinstalled, you can obtain the Apache HTTP Server for a variety of platforms from `httpd.apache.org/download.cgi`. For instructions on installing version 2.2 of the Apache HTTP Server on Windows, please visit

`http://httpd.apache.org/docs-2.2/platform/windows.html`

After installing the Apache HTTP Server, start the application. For Windows, open the **Start** menu, select **Programs > Apache HTTP Server** [*version number*] **> Control Apache Server > Monitor Apache Servers**. Double click on the **Apache Service Monitor** that appears in your **Taskbar**, select **Apache2**, and click **Start** (Fig. 17.11). For Mac OS X, you can start Apache from the **System Preferences** by opening the **Sharing** preference pane and checking the checkbox next to **Web Sharing**. To stop Apache in Windows, open the **Apache Service Monitor**, select your server, and click **Stop**. For Mac OS X, open the **Sharing** preference pane and uncheck the checkbox next to **Web Sharing**.

All documents that will be requested from an Apache HTTP Server must either be in the default directory (i.e., `C:\Program Files\Apache Software Foundation\Apache2.2\htdocs` for Windows, `/Library/WebServer/Documents` for Mac OS X, and `/var/www/html` or `/var/www` for most Linux distros) or in a directory for which an Apache HTTP Server *alias* is configured. An alias is Apache's equivalent to Microsoft IIS's virtual directory. It is a pointer to an existing directory that resides on the local machine or on the network. We'll create an alias for the examples in this chapter.

Instead of using an administrative utility or set of wizards, we configure the Apache HTTP Server by editing the `httpd.conf` file. This file contains all the information that

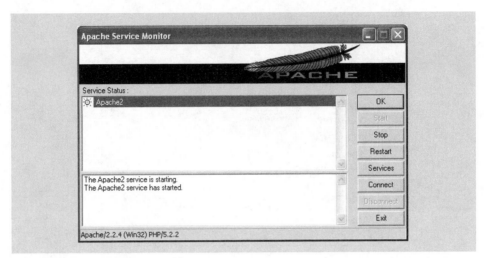

Fig. 17.11 | **Apache Service Monitor**. (Courtesy of The Apache Software Foundation, <http://www.apache.org/>.)

the Apache HTTP Server needs to run correctly and serve web documents. For Windows, the httpd.conf file is located in the conf subdirectory of Apache's installation directory. For Mac OS X and most Linux distros, it is located in the /etc/apache2/ directory. To edit this file, either open the httpd.conf in a text editor, or in Windows go to the **Start** menu and select **Programs > Apache HTTP Server** [*version number*] **> Configure Apache Server > Edit the Apache httpd.conf Configuration File**. httpd.conf is a large text file containing all of Apache HTTP Server's configuration information. In this file, any line that starts with a # is a comment that explains the various configuration options.

Good Programming Practice 17.1

Place a small comment near any changes you make to the Apache httpd.conf file.

An introductory comment at the top of the httpd.conf file explains how the file is organized. After this comment, the configuration information starts with the most important, global settings. These should have been configured correctly by the Apache installer. Scroll down in the file until you have reached the section titled DocumentRoot (using your text editor's search function will save time). The DocumentRoot setting specifies Apache's default directory. In Windows, the default setting is:

```
DocumentRoot "C:/Program Files/Apache Software Foundation/Apache2.2/
htdocs"
```

Now, find the section starting with <IfModule alias_module> and ending with </IfModule>. To create an alias, we add the following lines below the comment.

```
# This alias is for the examples used in Chapter 21
Alias /Chapter17Test "C:/Chapter17Examples"
```

This creates an alias called Chapter17Test that points to the physical directory C:\Chapter17Examples. We use the name Chapter17Test, but any name that does not conflict with an existing alias is allowed. We created a directory named C:\Chapter17Examples that contains our documents (you should specify an appropriate path on Linux or Mac OS X). Note that in both the name of the alias and the path of the directory to which the alias points we must use forward slashes (/), not backslashes (\).

Error-Prevention Tip 17.1

If you place a forward slash (/) at the end of the alias name, Apache will require this slash when a document is requested from the server. For example, if your alias is /myExamples/, then a user request for http://localhost/myExamples *will not work as expected. The user will need to request* http://localhost/myExamples/ *to access the alias. If the forward slash (/) is not placed at the end of the alias name, Apache will not require this slash, and will work as expected whether or not it is present in the request.*

Once we have created the alias, we must set the access settings of that directory so that users have permission to access it. The default access settings for every directory are to deny access to everybody. In order to override those settings for our new directory, C:\Chapter17Examples, we must create a new Directory entry. We append this new Directory entry to the end of the file:

```
# Begin Chapter17Examples directory access settings
<Directory "C:/Chapter17Examples">

    Options Indexes
    Order allow,deny
    Allow from all

</Directory>
# End Chapter17Examples directory access settings
```

We begin by specifying the location of the directory, then proceed to configure that directory. Indexes on the Options line specifies that if an index file, such as index.html, does not exist, Apache will generate one for you that contains the filenames of every document in the directory. Order allow,deny specifies that users are permitted access by default, and are denied only if they are specifically blocked. Allow from all specifies that all users are permitted access.

Now, the Apache HTTP Server is configured to serve our web document from the C:\Chapter17Examples directory. We need to restart the server so that our changes to httpd.conf file will take effect. Then we'll be ready to request documents from the Apache HTTP Server. To restart the server, we must first stop it and start it again. Please refer to the beginning of this section for instructions on how to stop and start the Apache HTTP Server.

17.8 Requesting Documents

This section demonstrates how an HTTP server responds to requests for XHTML documents. Requesting other types of documents is similar. We discuss serving these documents using the IIS and Apache HTTP Servers. The server sends XHTML documents to the client as *static web pages*. The server response for a given XHTML document is always the same. For other types of documents, such as PHP, Ruby on Rails, ASP.NET and Java-Server Faces, the appropriate language interpreter or scripting engine first generates XHTML content, then transmits it to the client over HTTP. These are often referred to as *dynamic web pages*, because the results of these requests might vary based on numerous factors, such as user input, the time of day and current database content.

Copy `test.html` from the Chapter 21 examples directory into the directory `C:\Chapter17Examples` (or to the directory you created in Section 17.6 or 17.7). This is the directory that is referenced by our virtual directory (`Chapter17Test`). [*Note*: A file cannot be copied directly to a virtual directory, because a virtual directory is only a name referring to a physical local directory.] To request the document from IIS or Apache, start the server, launch a web browser and enter the XHTML document's URL (i.e., `http://localhost/Chapter17Test/test.html`) in the **Address** field. Figure 17.12 displays the result of requesting `test.html` in Internet Explorer 7.

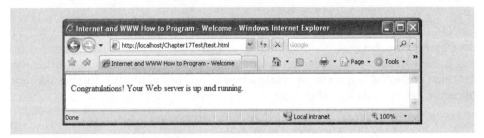

Fig. 17.12 | Requesting `test.html`.

17.9 Web Resources

www.deitel.com/WebServers/

The Web Servers Resource Center guides you through learning the basics behind web servers, deciding which server is best suited to you, and configuring and maintaining your own web server. Start your search here for resources, downloads, tutorials, documentation, books, e-books, articles, blogs and more that will help you run your own web server.

www.fiddlertool.com/fiddler/

Fiddler is a freeware web debugging proxy that logs all HTTP traffic between your computer and the Internet. Fiddler allows you to inspect traffic, set breakpoints, and "fiddle" with incoming or outgoing data. The tool includes a JavaScript-based scripting system, and can be extended using any .NET language.

addons.mozilla.org/en-US/firefox/addon/3829

An add-on for Firefox that enables you to view HTTP traffic as you browse the web. This can help you learn more about HTTP.

18

Database: SQL, MySQL, ADO.NET 2.0 and Java DB

It is a capital mistake to theorize before one has data.
—Arthur Conan Doyle

Now go, write it before them in a table, and note it in a book, that it may be for the time to come for ever and ever.
—The Holy Bible, Isaiah 30:8

Get your facts first, and then you can distort them as much as you please.
—Mark Twain

I like two kinds of men: domestic and foreign.
—Mae West

OBJECTIVES

In this chapter you will learn:

- Relational database concepts.
- To use Structured Query Language (SQL) to retrieve data from and manipulate data in a database.
- To install and configure MySQL.
- To create a MySQL database.
- The ADO.NET 2.0 object model.

18.1 Introduction

A *database* is an organized collection of data. There are many different strategies for organizing data to facilitate easy access and manipulation. A *database management system* (*DBMS*) provides mechanisms for storing, organizing, retrieving and modifying data. Database management systems allow for the access and storage of data without concern for the internal representation of the data in the database.

Today's most popular database systems are relational databases, where the data is stored without consideration of its physical structure (Section 18.2). A language called *SQL*—pronounced "sequel," or as its individual letters—is the international standard language used almost universally with relational databases to perform *queries* (i.e., to request information that satisfies given criteria) and to manipulate data. [*Note:* As you learn about SQL, you will see some authors writing "a SQL statement" (which assumes the pronunciation "sequel") and others writing "an SQL statement" (which assumes that the individual letters are pronounced). In this book we pronounce SQL as "sequel."] Some popular *relational database management systems* (*RDBMSs*) are Microsoft SQL Server, Oracle, Sybase, IBM DB2, Informix, PostgreSQL and MySQL.

Programs connect to, and interact with, a relational database via an *interface*—software that facilitates communication between a database management system and a program. For example, Java developers can use the JDBC interface to interact with databases. Similarly, ASP.NET programmers communicate with databases and manipulate their data through the interface provided by ADO.NET.

18.2 Relational Databases

A *relational database* is a logical representation of data that allows the data to be accessed without consideration of its physical structure. A relational database stores data in *tables*. Figure 18.1 illustrates a sample table that might be used in a personnel system. The table name is Employee, and its primary purpose is to store the attributes of an employee. Tables are composed of *rows*, and rows are composed of *columns* in which values are stored. This table consists of six rows. The Number column of each row in this table is the table's *primary key*—a column (or group of columns) in a table with a unique value that cannot be duplicated in other rows. This guarantees that each row can be identified by its primary key. Good examples of primary key columns are a social security number, an employee ID number and a part number in an inventory system, as values in each of these columns are guaranteed to be unique. The rows in Fig. 18.1 are displayed in order by primary key. In this case, the rows are listed in increasing order, but we could also use decreasing order.

Rows in tables are not guaranteed to be stored in any particular order. As we'll demonstrate in an upcoming example, programs can specify ordering criteria when requesting data from a database.

Each column represents a data attribute. Rows are normally unique (by primary key) within a table, but particular column values may be duplicated between rows—e.g., three different rows in the Employee table's Department column contain number 413.

Different users of a database are often interested in different data and different relationships among the data. Most users require only subsets of the rows and columns. To obtain these subsets, we use queries to specify which data to select from a table. We use SQL to define complex queries that select data from a table. For example, we might select data from the Employee table to create a result that shows where each department is located, and present the data sorted in increasing order by department number. This result is shown in Fig. 18.2. SQL queries are discussed in Section 18.4.

	Number	Name	Department	Salary	Location
	23603	Jones	413	1100	New Jersey
	24568	Kerwin	413	2000	New Jersey
Row	34589	Larson	642	1800	Los Angeles
	35761	Myers	611	1400	Orlando
	47132	Neumann	413	9000	New Jersey
	78321	Stephens	611	8500	Orlando
	Primary key		Column		

Fig. 18.1 | Employee table sample data.

Department	Location
413	New Jersey
611	Orlando
642	Los Angeles

Fig. 18.2 | Result of selecting distinct Department and Location data from table Employee.

18.3 Relational Database Overview: A books Database

We now overview relational databases in the context of a sample books database we created for this chapter. Before we discuss SQL, we overview the tables of the books database. We use this database to introduce various database concepts, including how to use SQL to obtain information from the database and to manipulate the data. We provide a script to create the database. You can find the script in the examples directory for this chapter. Section 18.8 explains how to use this script.

The database consists of three tables—authors, authorISBN and titles. The authors table (described in Fig. 18.3) consists of three columns that maintain each author's unique ID number, first name and last name. Figure 18.4 contains sample data from the authors table of the books database.

The authorISBN table (described in Fig. 18.5) has two columns that maintain each ISBN and the corresponding author's ID number. This table associates authors with their books. The columns represent the relationship between the authors and titles tables—

Column	Description
authorID	Author's ID number in the database. In the books database, this integer column is defined as *autoincremented*—for each row inserted in this table, the authorID value is increased by 1 automatically to ensure that each row has a unique authorID. This column represents the table's primary key.
firstName	Author's first name (a string).
lastName	Author's last name (a string).

Fig. 18.3 | authors table from the books database.

authorID	firstName	lastName
1	Harvey	Deitel
2	Paul	Deitel
3	Andrew	Goldberg
4	David	Choffnes

Fig. 18.4 | Sample data from the authors table.

Column	Description
authorID	The author's ID number, a foreign key to the authors table.
isbn	The ISBN for a book, a foreign key to the titles table.

Fig. 18.5 | authorISBN table from the books database.

one row in authors may be associated with many rows in titles, and vice versa. Figure 18.6 contains sample data from the authorISBN table. [*Note:* To save space, we split the table's contents into two columns, each containing the authorID and isbn columns.] The authorID column (and similarly, the isbn column) is a *foreign key*—a column in this table that matches the primary-key column in another table (i.e., authorID in the authors table). Foreign keys are specified when creating a table. The foreign key helps maintain the *Rule of Referential Integrity*—every foreign-key value must appear as another table's primary-key value. This enables the DBMS to determine whether the authorID value for a particular book is valid. Foreign keys also allow related data in multiple tables to be selected from those tables for analytic purposes—this is known as *joining* the data. If you were to remove an author from the authors table, you'd also want to remove the corresponding rows in the authorISBN table.

The titles table described in Fig. 18.7 consists of four columns that stand for each book's ISBN, the title, the edition number and the copyright year. The table is in Fig. 18.8.

authorID	isbn	authorID	isbn
1	0131869000	2	0131450913
2	0131869000	1	0131828274
1	0131483986	2	0131828274
2	0131483986	3	0131450913
1	0131450913	4	0131828274

Fig. 18.6 | Sample data from the authorISBN table of books.

Column	Description
isbn	ISBN of the book (a string). The table's primary key. ISBN is an abbreviation for "International Standard Book Number"—a numbering scheme that publishers use to give every book a unique identification number.
title	Title of the book (a string).
editionNumber	Edition number of the book (an integer).
copyright	Copyright year of the book (a string).

Fig. 18.7 | titles table from the books database.

isbn	title	editionNumber	copyright
0131869000	Visual Basic How to Program	3	2006
0131525239	Visual C# How to Program	2	2006

Fig. 18.8 | Sample data from the titles table of the books database. (Part 1 of 2.)

isbn	title	editionNumber	copyright
0132222205	Java How to Program	7	2007
0131857576	C++ How to Program	5	2005
0132404168	C How to Program	5	2007
0131450913	Internet and World Wide Web How to Program	3	2004

Fig. 18.8 | Sample data from the `titles` table of the `books` database. (Part 2 of 2.)

There is a one-to-many relationship between a primary key and a corresponding foreign key (e.g., one author can write many books). A foreign key creates a relationship between two tables in which the record with a given primary key can be referenced many times in the foreign key's table. Figure 18.9 is an *entity-relationship* (*ER*) *diagram* for the books database. This diagram shows the database tables and the relationships among them. The first compartment in each box contains the table's name. The names in italic are primary keys. A table's primary key uniquely identifies each row in the table. Every row must have a primary-key value, and that value must be unique in the table. This is known as the *Rule of Entity Integrity*.

Common Programming Error 18.1

Not providing a value for every column in a primary key breaks the Rule of Entity Integrity and causes the DBMS to report an error.

Common Programming Error 18.2

Providing the same value for the primary key in multiple rows causes the DBMS to report an error.

The lines connecting the tables in Fig. 18.9 represent the relationships between the tables. Consider the line between the `authorISBN` and `authors` tables. On the `authors` end of the line, there is a 1, and on the `authorISBN` end, there is an infinity symbol (∞), indicating a *one-to-many relationship* in which every author in the `authors` table can have an arbitrary number of ISBNs in the `authorISBN` table. Note that the relationship line links the `authorID` column in the table `authors` (i.e., its primary key) to the `authorID` column in table `authorISBN` (i.e., its foreign key). The `authorID` column in the `authorISBN` table is a foreign key.

Fig. 18.9 | Table relationships in the `books` database.

Common Programming Error 18.3

Providing a foreign-key value that does not appear as a primary-key value in another table breaks the Rule of Referential Integrity and causes the DBMS to report an error.

The line between the `titles` and `authorISBN` tables illustrates another one-to-many relationship; a title can be written by any number of authors. In fact, the sole purpose of the `authorISBN` table is to provide a many-to-many relationship between the `authors` and `titles` tables—an author can write any number of books and a book can have any number of authors. The primary key for `authorISBN` is the combination of `authorID` and `ISBN`.

18.4 SQL

We now provide an overview of SQL in the context of our `books` database. You will be able to use the SQL discussed here in the examples later in the chapter and in examples in Chapters 19–24.

The next several subsections discuss most of the SQL keywords listed in Fig. 18.10 in the context of SQL queries and statements. Other SQL keywords are beyond this text's scope. To learn other keywords, refer to the SQL reference guide supplied by the vendor of the RDBMS you are using. [*Note:* For more information on SQL, refer to the web resources in Section 18.11.]

SQL keyword	Description
SELECT	Retrieves data from one or more tables.
FROM	Tables involved in the query. Required in every SELECT.
WHERE	Criteria for selection that determine the rows to be retrieved, deleted or updated. Optional in a SQL query or a SQL statement.
GROUP BY	Criteria for grouping rows. Optional in a SELECT query.
ORDER BY	Criteria for ordering rows. Optional in a SELECT query.
INNER JOIN	Combine rows from multiple tables.
INSERT	Insert rows into a specified table.
UPDATE	Update rows in a specified table.
DELETE	Delete rows from a specified table.

Fig. 18.10 | SQL query keywords.

18.4.1 Basic SELECT Query

Let us consider several SQL queries that extract information from database `books`. A SQL query "selects" rows and columns from one or more tables in a database. Such selections are performed by queries with the SELECT keyword. The basic form of a SELECT query is

SELECT * FROM *tableName*

in which the **asterisk (*)** indicates that all rows and columns from the *tableName* table should be retrieved. For example, to retrieve all the data in the authors table, use

>   **SELECT * FROM** authors

Most programs do not require all the data in a table. To retrieve only specific columns from a table, replace the asterisk (*) with a comma-separated list of the column names. For example, to retrieve only the columns authorID and lastName for all rows in the authors table, use the query

>   **SELECT** authorID, lastName **FROM** authors

This query returns the data listed in Fig. 18.11.

Software Engineering Observation 18.1

For most queries, the asterisk (*) should not be used to specify column names. In general, you process results by knowing in advance the order of the columns in the result—for example, selecting authorID and lastName from table authors ensures that the columns will appear in the result with authorID as the first column and lastName as the second column. Programs typically process result columns by specifying the column number in the result (starting from number 1 for the first column). Selecting columns by name also avoids returning unneeded columns and protects against changes in the actual order of the columns in the table(s).

Common Programming Error 18.4

If you assume that the columns are always returned in the same order from a query that uses the asterisk (*), the program may process the results incorrectly. If the column order in the table(s) changes or if additional columns are added at a later time, the order of the columns in the result changes accordingly.

authorID	lastName
1	Deitel
2	Deitel
3	Goldberg
4	Choffnes

Fig. 18.11 | Sample authorID and lastName data from the authors table.

18.4.2 WHERE Clause

In most cases, it is necessary to retrieve rows in a database that satisfy certain *selection criteria*. Only rows that satisfy the selection criteria (formally called *predicates*) are selected. SQL uses the optional WHERE *clause* in a query to specify the selection criteria for the query. The basic form of a query with selection criteria is

>   **SELECT** *columnName1*, *columnName2*, ... **FROM** *tableName* **WHERE** *criteria*

For example, to select the title, editionNumber and copyright columns from table titles for which the copyright year is greater than 2005, use the query

```
SELECT title, editionNumber, copyright
   FROM titles
   WHERE copyright > '2005'
```

Figure 18.12 shows the result of the preceding query. The WHERE clause criteria can contain the operators <, >, <=, >=, =, <> and LIKE. Operator **LIKE** is used for *pattern matching* with wildcard characters *percent (%)* and *underscore (_)*. Pattern matching allows SQL to search for strings that match a given pattern.

A pattern that contains a percent character (%) searches for strings that have zero or more characters at the percent character's position in the pattern. For example, the next query locates the rows of all the authors whose last name starts with the letter D:

```
SELECT authorID, firstName, lastName
   FROM authors
   WHERE lastName LIKE 'D%'
```

This query selects the two rows shown in Fig. 18.13—two of the four authors have a last name starting with the letter D (followed by zero or more characters). The % in the WHERE clause's LIKE pattern indicates that any number of characters can appear after the letter D in the lastName. Note that the pattern string is surrounded by single-quote characters.

 Portability Tip 18.1

See the documentation for your database system to determine whether SQL is case sensitive on your system and to determine the syntax for SQL keywords (i.e., should they be all uppercase letters, all lowercase letters or some combination of the two?).

An underscore (_) in the pattern string indicates a single wildcard character at that position in the pattern. For example, the following query locates the rows of all the authors

title	editionNumber	copyright
Visual C# How to Program	2	2006
Visual Basic 2005 How to Program	3	2006
Java How to Program	7	2007
C How to Program	5	2007

Fig. 18.12 | Sampling of titles with copyrights after 2005 from table titles.

authorID	firstName	lastName
1	Harvey	Deitel
2	Paul	Deitel

Fig. 18.13 | Authors whose last name starts with D from the authors table.

whose last names start with any character (specified by _), followed by the letter o, followed by any number of additional characters (specified by %):

```
SELECT authorID, firstName, lastName
    FROM authors
    WHERE lastName LIKE '_o%'
```

The preceding query produces the row shown in Fig. 18.14, because only one author in our database has a last name that contains the letter o as its second letter.

authorID	firstName	lastName
3	Andrew	Goldberg

Fig. 18.14 | The only author from the `authors` table whose last name contains o as the second letter.

18.4.3 ORDER BY Clause

The rows in the result of a query can be sorted into ascending or descending order by using the optional *ORDER BY clause*. The basic form of a query with an ORDER BY clause is

```
SELECT columnName1, columnName2, ... FROM tableName ORDER BY column ASC
SELECT columnName1, columnName2, ... FROM tableName ORDER BY column DESC
```

where ASC specifies ascending order (lowest to highest), DESC specifies descending order (highest to lowest) and *column* specifies the column on which the sort is based. For example, to obtain the list of authors in ascending order by last name (Fig. 18.15), use the query

```
SELECT authorID, firstName, lastName
    FROM authors
    ORDER BY lastName ASC
```

Note that the default sorting order is ascending, so ASC is optional. To obtain the same list of authors in descending order by last name (Fig. 18.16), use the query

authorID	firstName	lastName
4	David	Choffnes
1	Harvey	Deitel
2	Paul	Deitel
3	Andrew	Goldberg

Fig. 18.15 | `authors` sample data in ascending order by `lastName`.

authorID	firstName	lastName
3	Andrew	Goldberg
1	Harvey	Deitel
2	Paul	Deitel
4	David	Choffnes

Fig. 18.16 | authors sample data in descending order by lastName.

```
SELECT authorID, firstName, lastName
    FROM authors
    ORDER BY lastName DESC
```

Multiple columns can be used for sorting with an ORDER BY clause of the form

> **ORDER BY** *column1 sortingOrder*, *column2 sortingOrder*, ...

where *sortingOrder* is either ASC or DESC. Note that the *sortingOrder* does not have to be identical for each column. The query

```
SELECT authorID, firstName, lastName
    FROM authors
    ORDER BY lastName, firstName
```

sorts all the rows in ascending order by last name, then by first name. If any rows have the same value in the lastName column, they are returned sorted by firstName (Fig. 18.17).

The WHERE and ORDER BY clauses can be combined in one query, as in

```
SELECT isbn, title, editionNumber, copyright
    FROM titles
    WHERE title LIKE '%How to Program'
    ORDER BY title ASC
```

which returns the isbn, title, editionNumber and copyright of each book in the titles table that has a title ending with "How to Program" and sorts them in ascending order by title. The query results are shown in Fig. 18.18.

authorID	firstName	lastName
4	David	Choffnes
1	Harvey	Deitel
2	Paul	Deitel
3	Andrew	Goldberg

Fig. 18.17 | authors sample data in ascending order by lastName and firstName.

isbn	title	edition-Number	copy-right
0132404168	C How to Program	5	2007
0131857576	C++ How to Program	5	2005
0131450913	Internet and World Wide Web How to Program	3	2004
0132222205	Java How to Program	7	2007
0131869000	Visual Basic 2005 How to Program	3	2006
0131525239	Visual C# How to Program	2	2006

Fig. 18.18 | Sampling of books from table `titles` whose titles end with `How to Program` in ascending order by `title`.

18.4.4 Combining Data from Multiple Tables: INNER JOIN

Database designers often split related data into separate tables to ensure that a database does not store data redundantly. For example, the `books` database has tables `authors` and `titles`. We use an `authorISBN` table to store the relationship data between authors and their corresponding titles. If we did not separate this information into individual tables, we would need to include author information with each entry in the `titles` table. Then the database would store duplicate author information for authors who wrote multiple books. Often, it is necessary to combine data from multiple tables into a single result. Referred to as joining the tables, this is specified by an `INNER JOIN` operator in the query. An `INNER JOIN` combines rows from two tables by matching values in columns that are common to the tables. The basic form of an `INNER JOIN` is:

```
SELECT columnName1, columnName2, ...
FROM table1
INNER JOIN table2
    ON table1.columnName = table2.columnName
```

The **ON** *clause* of the `INNER JOIN` specifies a condition (often comparing columns from each table) that determines which rows are combined. For example, the following query produces a list of authors accompanied by the ISBNs for books written by each author:

```
SELECT firstName, lastName, isbn
FROM authors
INNER JOIN authorISBN
    ON authors.authorID = authorISBN.authorID
ORDER BY lastName, firstName
```

The query combines the `firstName` and `lastName` columns from table `authors` with the `isbn` column from table `authorISBN`, sorting the result in ascending order by `lastName` and `firstName`. Only rows in which the `authorID`s match are combined. Note the use of the syntax *tableName.columnName* in the `ON` clause. This syntax, called a *qualified name*, specifies the columns from each table that should be compared to join the tables. The "*tableName.*" syntax is required if the columns have the same name in both tables. The same syntax can be used in any query to distinguish columns in different tables that have the same name. In some systems, table names qualified with the database name can be used to perform cross-database queries. As always, the query can contain an ORDER BY clause. Figure 18.19 depicts a portion of the results of the preceding query, ordered by lastName and firstName. [*Note:* To save space, we split the result of the query into two columns, each containing the firstName, lastName and isbn columns.]

Software Engineering Observation 18.2

If a SQL statement includes columns with the same name from multiple tables, the statement must precede those column names with their table names and a dot (e.g., authors.authorID).

Common Programming Error 18.5

Failure to qualify names for columns that have the same name in two or more tables is an error.

firstName	lastName	isbn	firstName	lastName	isbn
David	Choffnes	0131828274	Paul	Deitel	0131869000
Harvey	Deitel	0131869000	Paul	Deitel	0131525239
Harvey	Deitel	0131525239	Paul	Deitel	0132222205
Harvey	Deitel	0132222205	Paul	Deitel	0131857576
Harvey	Deitel	0131857576	Paul	Deitel	0132404168
Harvey	Deitel	0132404168	Paul	Deitel	0131450913
Harvey	Deitel	0131450913	Paul	Deitel	0131869000
Harvey	Deitel	0131869000	Paul	Deitel	0131828274
Harvey	Deitel	0131828274	Andrew	Goldberg	0131450913

Fig. 18.19 | Sampling of authors and ISBNs for the books they have written in ascending order by lastName and firstName.

18.4.5 INSERT Statement

The INSERT statement inserts a row into a table. The basic form of this statement is

> **INSERT INTO** *tableName* (*columnName1*, *columnName2*, ..., *columnNameN*)
> **VALUES** (*value1*, *value2*, ..., *valueN*)

where *tableName* is the table in which to insert the row. The *tableName* is followed by a comma-separated list of column names in parentheses (this list is not required if the IN-SERT operation specifies a value for every column of the table in the correct order). The list of column names is followed by the SQL keyword VALUES and a comma-separated list of values in parentheses. The values specified here must match the columns specified after the table name in both order and type (e.g., if *columnName1* is supposed to be the firstName column, then *value1* should be a string in single quotes representing the first name).

Good Programming Practice 18.1

Always explicitly list the columns when inserting rows. If the table's column order changes or a new column is added, omitting the columns list may cause an error.

The INSERT statement

```
INSERT INTO authors ( firstName, lastName )
    VALUES ( 'Sue', 'Smith' )
```

inserts a row into the authors table. The statement indicates that values are provided for the firstName and lastName columns. The corresponding values are 'Sue' and 'Smith'. We do not specify an authorID in this example because authorID is an autoincremented column in the authors table. For every row added to this table, the database assigns a unique authorID value that is the next value in the autoincremented sequence (i.e., 1, 2, 3 and so on). In this case, Sue Smith would be assigned authorID number 5. Figure 18.20 shows the authors table after the INSERT operation. [*Note:* Not every database management system supports autoincremented columns. Check the documentation for your DBMS for alternatives to autoincremented columns.]

Common Programming Error 18.6

It is normally an error to specify a value for an autoincrement column.

Common Programming Error 18.7

SQL uses the single-quote (') character as a delimiter for strings. To specify a string containing a single quote (e.g., O'Malley) in a SQL statement, the string must have two single quotes in the position where the single-quote character appears in the string (e.g., 'O''Malley'). The first of the two single-quote characters acts as an escape character for the second. Not escaping single-quote characters in a string that is part of a SQL statement is a SQL syntax error.

authorID	firstName	lastName
1	Harvey	Deitel
2	Paul	Deitel
3	Andrew	Goldberg
4	David	Choffnes
5	Sue	Smith

Fig. 18.20 | Sample data from table Authors after an INSERT operation.

18.4.6 UPDATE Statement

An UPDATE statement modifies data in a table. The basic form of the UPDATE statement is

```
UPDATE tableName
    SET columnName1 = value1, columnName2 = value2, ..., columnNameN = valueN
    WHERE criteria
```

where *tableName* is the table to update. The *tableName* is followed by keyword SET and a comma-separated list of column name/value pairs in the format *columnName* = *value*. The *value* can be an expression that yields a value. The optional WHERE clause provides criteria that determine which rows to update. Though not required, the WHERE clause is typically used, unless a change is to be made to every row. The UPDATE statement

```
UPDATE authors
    SET lastName = 'Jones'
    WHERE lastName = 'Smith' AND firstName = 'Sue'
```

updates a row in the authors table. The statement indicates that lastName will be assigned the value Jones for the row in which lastName is equal to Smith and firstName is equal to Sue. [*Note:* If there are multiple rows with the first name "Sue" and the last name "Smith," this statement will modify all such rows to have the last name "Jones."] If we know the authorID in advance of the UPDATE operation (possibly because we searched for it previously), the WHERE clause can be simplified as follows:

```
WHERE authorID = 5
```

Figure 18.21 shows the authors table after the UPDATE operation has taken place.

authorID	firstName	lastName
1	Harvey	Deitel
2	Paul	Deitel
3	Andrew	Goldberg
4	David	Choffnes
5	Sue	Jones

Fig. 18.21 | Sample data from table authors after an UPDATE operation.

18.4.7 DELETE Statement

A SQL DELETE statement removes rows from a table. The basic form of a DELETE is

```
DELETE FROM tableName WHERE criteria
```

where *tableName* is the table from which to delete. The optional WHERE clause specifies the criteria used to determine which rows to delete. If this clause is omitted, all the table's rows are deleted. The DELETE statement

```
DELETE FROM authors
    WHERE lastName = 'Jones' AND firstName = 'Sue'
```

deletes the row (or rows) for Sue Jones in the authors table. If we know the authorID in advance of the DELETE operation, the WHERE clause can be simplified as follows:

```
WHERE authorID = 5
```

Figure 18.22 shows the authors table after the DELETE operation has taken place.

authorID	firstName	lastName
1	Harvey	Deitel
2	Paul	Deitel
3	Andrew	Goldberg
4	David	Choffnes

Fig. 18.22 | Sample data from table `authors` after a `DELETE` operation.

18.5 MySQL

In 1994, TcX, a Swedish consulting firm, needed a fast and flexible way to access its tables. Unable to find a database server that could accomplish the required task adequately, Michael Widenius, the principal developer at TcX, decided to create his own database server. The resulting product was called *MySQL* (pronounced "my sequel"), a robust and scalable relational database management system (RDBMS).

MySQL is a multiuser, multithreaded (i.e., allows multiple simultaneous connections) RDBMS server that uses SQL to interact with and manipulate data. The MySQL Manual (www.mysql.com/why-mysql/topreasons.html) lists numerous benefits of MySQL. A few important benefits include:

1. Scalability. You can embed it in an application or use it in massive data warehousing environments.

2. Performance. You can optimize performance based on the purpose of the database in your application.

3. Support for many programming languages. Later chapters demonstrate how to access a MySQL database from PHP (Chapter 19) and Ruby on Rails (Chapter 20).

4. Implementations of MySQL for Windows, Mac OS X, Linux and UNIX.

5. Handling large databases (e.g., tens of thousands of tables with millions of rows).

For these reasons and more, MySQL is the database of choice for many businesses, universities and individuals. MySQL is an open source software product. [*Note:* Under certain situations, a commercial license is required for MySQL. See www.mysql.com/company/legal/licensing/ for details.]

18.6 Instructions for Installing MySQL

MySQL 5.0 Community Edition is an open source database management system that executes on many platforms, including Windows, Solaris, Linux, and Macintosh. Complete information about MySQL is available from www.mysql.com.

Installing MySQL
To install MySQL Community Edition:

1. To learn about the installation requirements for your platform, visit the site dev.mysql.com/doc/refman/5.0/en/general-installation-issues.html.

2. Visit `dev.mysql.com/downloads/mysql/5.0.html` and download the installer for your platform. For our MySQL examples, you need only the Windows Essentials package on Microsoft Windows, or the Standard package on most other platforms. [*Note:* For these instructions, we assume you are running Microsoft Windows. Complete installation instructions for other platforms are available at `dev.mysql.com/doc/refman/5.0/en/installing.html`.]

3. Double click `mysql-essential-5.0.45-win32.msi` to start the installer. [*Note:* This filename may differ, based on the current version of MySQL 5.0.]

4. Choose **Typical** for the **Setup Type** and click **Next >**. Then click **Install**.

When the installation completes, you will be asked to set up an account on MySQL.com. If you do not wish to do this, select **Skip Sign-up** and click **Next >**. After completing the sign-up process or skipping it, you can configure the MySQL Server. Click **Finish** to start the **MySQL Server Instance Configuration Wizard**. To configure the server:

1. Click **Next >**, then select **Standard Configuration** and click **Next >** again.

2. You have the option of installing MySQL as a Windows service, which enables the MySQL server to begin executing automatically each time your system starts. For our examples, this is unnecessary, so uncheck **Install as a Windows Service**, then check **Include Bin Directory in Windows PATH**. This will enable you to use the MySQL commands in the Windows Command Prompt.

3. Click **Next >**, then click **Execute** to perform the server configuration.

4. Click **Finish** to close the wizard.

18.7 Instructions for Setting Up a MySQL User Account

For the MySQL examples to execute correctly, you need to set up a user account that allows users to create, delete and modify a database. After MySQL is installed, follow the steps below to set up a user account (these steps assume MySQL is installed in its default installation directory):

1. Open a Command Prompt and start the database server by executing the command `mysqld-nt.exe`. (On Linux, execute `mysqld start` from a shell or terminal window.) Note that this command has no output—it simply starts the MySQL server. Do not close this window—doing so terminates the server.

2. Next, you'll start the *MySQL command-line client tool* so you can set up a user account, open another Command Prompt and execute the command

   ```
   mysql -h localhost -u root
   ```

   The `-h` option indicates the host (i.e., computer) on which the MySQL server is running—in this case your local computer (`localhost`). The `-u` option indicates the user account that will be used to log in to the server—`root` is the default user account that is created during installation to allow you to configure the server. Once you've logged in, you'll see a `mysql>` prompt at which you can type commands to interact with the MySQL server.

3. Next, you'll add the iw3htp4 user account to the mysql built-in database. To create the iw3htp4 user account with the password iw3htp4, execute the following commands from the mysql> prompt:

   ```
   create user 'iw3htp4'@'localhost' identified by 'iw3htp4';

   grant select, insert, update, delete, create, drop, references,
       execute on *.* to 'iw3htp4'@'localhost';
   ```

   This creates the iw3htp4 user with the privileges needed to create the databases used in this chapter and manipulate those databases.

4. Type the command

   ```
   exit;
   ```

   to terminate the MySQL monitor.

18.8 Creating a Database in MySQL

For each MySQL database we discuss in this book, we provide a SQL script in a file with the .sql extension that sets up the database and its tables. You can execute these scripts in the MySQL command-line client tool. In the examples directory for this chapter, you'll find the SQL script books.sql to create the books database. For the following steps, we assume that the MySQL server (mysqld-nt.exe) is still running. To execute the books.sql script:

1. Open a command prompt and use the cd command to change directories to the location that contains the books.sql script.

2. Start the MySQL monitor by typing

   ```
   mysql -h localhost -u iw3htp4 -p
   ```

   The -p option prompts you for the password for the iw3htp4 user account. When prompted, enter the password iw3htp4.

3. Execute the script by typing

   ```
   source books.sql;
   ```

   This creates a books database in the server's data directory—located on Windows at C:\Program Files\MySQL\MySQL Server 5.0\data by default.

4. Type the command

   ```
   exit;
   ```

   to terminate the MySQL command-line client tool. You are now ready to use your MySQL database.

18.9 ADO.NET Object Model

Several examples in Chapter 21, ASP.NET 2.0 and ASP.NET Ajax, use ADO.NET 2.0 to access and manipulate SQL Server 2005 Express databases. The *ADO.NET object model* provides an API for accessing database management systems programmatically. ADO.NET was created for the .NET framework to replace Microsoft's ActiveX Data Objects™ (ADO) technology. Microsoft's Visual Studio IDE features visual programming tools that simplify the process of using a database in your projects. While you may not need to work directly with many ADO.NET objects to develop simple applications, basic knowledge of how the ADO.NET object model works is important for understanding data access in Visual Basic (the programming language we use in Chapter 21).

Namespaces *System.Data, System.Data.OleDb* and *System.Data.SqlClient*

Namespace *System.Data* is the root namespace for the ADO.NET API. The other important ADO.NET namespaces, *System.Data.OleDb* and *System.Data.SqlClient*, contain classes that enable programs to connect with and manipulate *data sources*—locations that contain data, such as a database or an XML file. Namespace System.Data.OleDb contains classes that are designed to work with any data source that supports the OLE DB API, whereas System.Data.SqlClient contains classes that are optimized to work with Microsoft SQL Server databases. The Chapter 21 examples manipulate SQL Server 2005 Express databases, so we use the classes of namespace System.Data.SqlClient. SQL Server 2005 Express is available at msdn.microsoft.com/vstudio/express/sql/default.aspx.

An object of class *SqlConnection* (namespace System.Data.SqlClient) represents a connection to a data source—specifically a Microsoft SQL Server database. A SqlConnection object keeps track of the location of the data source and any settings that specify how the data source is to be accessed. A connection is either *active* (i.e., open and permitting data to be sent to and retrieved from the data source) or *closed*.

An object of class *SqlCommand* (namespace System.Data.SqlClient) represents a SQL command that a DBMS can execute on a database. A program can use SqlCommand objects to manipulate a data source through a SqlConnection. The program must open the connection to the data source before executing one or more SqlCommands and close the connection once no further access to the data source is required. A connection that remains active for some length of time to permit multiple data operations is known as a *persistent connection*.

Class *DataTable* (namespace System.Data) represents a table of data. A DataTable contains a collection of *DataRows* that represent the table's data. A DataTable also has a collection of *DataColumns* that describe the columns in a table. DataRow and DataColumn are both located in namespace System.Data. An object of class *System.Data.DataSet*, which consists of a set of DataTables and the relationships among them, represents a *cache* of data—data that a program stores temporarily in local memory. The structure of a DataSet mimics the structure of a relational database.

ADO.NET's Disconnected Model

An advantage of using class DataSet is that it is *disconnected*—the program does not need a persistent connection to the data source to work with data in a DataSet. Instead, the program connects to the data source to *populate the DataSet* (i.e., fill the DataSet's DataTables with data), but disconnects from the data source immediately after retrieving the desired data. The program then accesses and potentially manipulates the data stored in the DataSet. The program operates on this local cache of data, rather than the original data in the data source. If the program makes changes to the data in the DataSet that need to be permanently saved in the data source, the program reconnects to the data source to perform an update, then disconnects promptly. Thus the program does not require any active, persistent connection to the data source.

An object of class *SqlDataAdapter* (namespace System.Data.SqlClient) connects to a SQL Server data source and executes SQL statements to both populate a DataSet and update the data source based on the current contents of a DataSet. A SqlDataAdapter maintains a SqlConnection object that it opens and closes as needed to perform these operations, using SqlCommands.

18.10 Java DB/Apache Derby

As of the Java SE 6 Development Kit (JDK), Sun Microsystems now bundles the open source, pure Java database *Java DB* (the Sun branded version of Apache Derby) with the JDK. Chapters 23–24 use Java DB in data-driven web applications. Similar to MySQL, Java DB has both an embedded version and a network (client/server) version. The tools we use in Chapters 23–24 come with Java DB. For those examples, we use Java DB's network version, and we provide all the information you need to configure each example's database. You can learn more about Apache Derby at db.apache.org/derby. You can learn more about Java DB at developers.sun.com/javadb/.

18.11 Web Resources

Many database-related resources are available on the web. This section lists several database resources.

www.sql.org
The sql.org site is an online resource that provides a tutorial on the SQL programming language. It offers links to news groups, discussion forums, free software and various database vendors.

www.deitel.com/mysql/
The Deitel MySQL Resource Center focuses on the vast amount of free MySQL content available online, plus some for-sale items. Start your search here for tools, downloads, tutorials, podcasts, wikis, documentation, conferences, FAQs, books, sample chapters, articles, newsgroups, forums, jobs, contract opportunities, and more that will help you develop MySQL database applications.

www.mysql.com
This site is the MySQL database home page. You can download the latest version of MySQL and access its online documentation.

www.mysql.com/products/enterprise/server.html
Introduction to the MySQL database server and links to its documentation and download sites.

dev.mysql.com/doc/mysql/en/index.html
MySQL reference manual.

developers.sun.com/prodtech/javadb/reference/docs/10.2.1.6/devguide/index.html
The *Java DB Developer's Guide*.

www.microsoft.com/sql
The *Microsoft SQL Server* website contains product information, technical support, SQL news and tips on using the SQL Server to solve business problems.

msdn.microsoft.com/vstudio/express/sql/
The *Microsoft SQL Server Express* website.

www.w3schools.com/sql
The *SQL School* website provides a tutorial on basic to advanced SQL commands. The site contains a short quiz that reinforces SQL concepts.

`www.sqlmag.com`

SQL Server Magazine is an excellent SQL Server resource. Subscribers receive monthly issues filled with articles on SQL design and information on current developments involving SQL. Certain articles are available for free at the website.

`db.apache.org/derby/`

The Apache Derby website provides downloads and resources for Apache Derby.

19

PHP

OBJECTIVES

In this chapter you will learn:

- To manipulate data of various types.

- To use operators, arrays and control statements.

- To use regular expressions to search for patterns.

- To construct programs that process form data.

- To store data on the client using cookies.

- To create programs that interact with MySQL databases.

Conversion for me was not a
Damascus Road experience.
I slowly moved into an
intellectual acceptance of
what my intuition had
always known.
—Madeleine L'Engle

Be careful when reading
health books; you may die of
a misprint.
—Mark Twain

Reckoners without their host
must reckon twice.
—John Heywood

There was a door to which I
found no key;
There was the veil through
which I might not see.
—Omar Khayyam

19.1 Introduction

PHP, or *PHP: Hypertext Preprocessor*, has become one of the most popular server-side scripting languages for creating dynamic web pages. PHP was created by Rasmus Lerdorf to track users at his website. In 1995, Lerdorf released it as a package called the "Personal Home Page Tools." Two years later, PHP 2 featured built-in database support and form handling. In 1997, PHP 3 was released with a rewritten parser, which substantially increased performance and led to an explosion of PHP use. The release of PHP 4 featured the new *Zend Engine* from Zend, a PHP software company. This version was considerably faster and more powerful than its predecessor, further increasing PHP's popularity. It is estimated that over 15 million domains now use PHP, accounting for more than 20 percent of web pages.[1] Currently, PHP 5 features the *Zend Engine 2*, which provides further speed increases, exception handling and a new object-oriented programming model.[2] More information about the Zend Engine can be found at www.zend.com.

PHP is an open-source technology that is supported by a large community of users and developers. PHP is platform independent—implementations exist for all major UNIX, Linux, Mac and Windows operating systems. PHP also supports many databases, including MySQL.

After introducing the basics of the PHP scripting language, we discuss form processing and business logic, which are vital to e-commerce applications. Next, we build a three-tier web application that queries a MySQL database. We also show how PHP can use cookies to store information on the client that can be retrieved during future visits to the website. Finally, we revisit the form-processing example to demonstrate some of PHP's more dynamic capabilities.

---

1. "History of PHP," 30 June 2007, *PHP* <us.php.net/history>.
2. Suraski, Z., "The OO Evolution of PHP," 16 March 2004, *Zend* <devzone.zend.com/node/view/id/1717>.

19.2 PHP Basics

The power of the web resides not only in serving content to users, but also in responding to requests from users and generating web pages with dynamic content. Interactivity between the user and the server has become a crucial part of web functionality, making PHP—a language written specifically for interacting with the web—a valuable tool.

Installing PHP

PHP code is embedded directly into XHTML documents, though these script segments are interpreted by the server before being delivered to the client. This allows the document author to write XHTML in a clear, concise manner. PHP script file names end with .php.

To run a PHP script, PHP must first be installed on your system. All examples in this chapter have been verified using PHP 5.2.3, the most current release at the time of publication. The most recent version of PHP can be downloaded from www.php.net/downloads.php, and installation instructions are available at www.php.net/manual/en/installation.php. Be sure to check for specific instructions that pertain to the server you want to use. During setup, when the **Choose Items to Install** window is displayed, expand the **Extensions** menu by clicking the small plus sign to its left. Then click the down arrow to the left of the MySQL option, and select the **Will be installed on local hard drive** option. This will ensure that your PHP script will be able to access your MySQL database server for examples later in this chapter.

Although PHP can be used from the command line, a web server is necessary to take full advantage of the scripting language. Before continuing, load files from the Chapter 19 examples directory to the web server's root directory (e.g., C:\Inetpub\wwwroot for IIS or C:\Program Files\Apache Software Foundation\Apache2\htdocs for Apache on Windows or /var/www/html or similar on Linux).

Simple PHP Program

Figure 19.1 presents a simple PHP program that displays a welcome message. In PHP, code is inserted between the scripting delimiters *<?php* and *?>*. PHP code can be placed anywhere in XHTML markup, as long as the code is enclosed in these delimiters. Line 1 uses function print to output the XML declaration. This avoids the <? in the XML dec-

```
 1   <?php print( '<?xml version = "1.0" encoding = "utf-8"?>' ) ?>
 2   <!DOCTYPE html PUBLIC "-//W3C//DTD XHTML 1.0 Strict//EN"
 3      "http://www.w3.org/TR/xhtml1/DTD/xhtml1-strict.dtd">
 4
 5   <!-- Fig. 19.1: first.php -->
 6   <!-- Simple PHP program. -->
 7   <html xmlns = "http://www.w3.org/1999/xhtml">
 8   <?php
 9      $name = "Harvey"; // declaration and initialization
10   ?><!-- end PHP script -->
11      <head>
12         <title>Using PHP document</title>
13      </head>
14      <body style = "font-size: 2em">
```

Fig. 19.1 | Simple PHP program. (Part 1 of 2.)

```
15          <p>
16            <strong>
17              <!-- print variable name's value -->
18              Welcome to PHP, <?php print( "$name" ); ?>!
19            </strong>
20          </p>
21        </body>
22      </html>
```

Welcome to PHP, Harvey!

Fig. 19.1 | Simple PHP program. (Part 2 of 2.)

laration getting interpreted as an incorrect PHP scripting delimiter. Line 9 declares variable $name and assigns it the string "Harvey". All variables are preceded by a $ and are created the first time they are encountered by the PHP interpreter. PHP statements terminate with a *semicolon (;)*.

Common Programming Error 19.1

Failing to precede a variable name with a $ is a syntax error.

Common Programming Error 19.2

Variable names in PHP are case sensitive. Failure to use the proper mixture of cases to refer to a variable will result in a logic error, since the script will create a new variable for any name it doesn't recognize as a previously used variable.

Common Programming Error 19.3

Forgetting to terminate a statement with a semicolon (;) is a syntax error.

Line 9 also contains a *single-line comment*, which begins with two forward slashes (//). Text to the right of the slashes is ignored by the interpreter. Single-line comments can also begin with the pound sign (#). Multiline comments begin with delimiter /* and end with delimiter */.

Line 18 outputs the value of variable $name by calling function **print**. The actual value of $name is printed, not the string "$name". When a variable is encountered inside a double-quoted ("") string, PHP *interpolates* the variable. In other words, PHP inserts the variable's value where the variable name appears in the string. Thus, variable $name is replaced by Harvey for printing purposes. All operations of this type execute on the server before the XHTML document is sent to the client. You can see by viewing the source of a PHP document that the code sent to the client does not contain any PHP code.

PHP variables are loosely typed—they can contain different types of data (e.g., *integers*, *doubles* or *strings*) at different times. Figure 19.2 introduces these data types.

Type	Description
int, integer	Whole numbers (i.e., numbers without a decimal point).
float, double, real	Real numbers (i.e., numbers containing a decimal point).
string	Text enclosed in either single (' ') or double ("") quotes. [*Note:* Using double quotes allows PHP to recognize more escape sequences.]
bool, boolean	True or false.
array	Group of elements.
object	Group of associated data and methods.
resource	An external source—usually information from a database.
NULL	No value.

Fig. 19.2 | PHP types.

Converting Between Data Types

Converting between different data types may be necessary when performing arithmetic operations with variables. Type conversions can be performed using function settype. Figure 19.3 demonstrates type conversion of some types introduced in Fig. 19.2.

```php
1  <?php print( '<?xml version = "1.0" encoding = "utf-8"?>' ) ?>
2  <!DOCTYPE html PUBLIC "-//W3C//DTD XHTML 1.0 Strict//EN"
3     "http://www.w3.org/TR/xhtml1/DTD/xhtml1-strict.dtd">
4
5  <!-- Fig. 19.3: data.php -->
6  <!-- Data type conversion. -->
7  <html xmlns = "http://www.w3.org/1999/xhtml">
8     <head>
9        <title>Data type conversion</title>
10    </head>
11    <body>
12       <?php
13          // declare a string, double and integer
14          $testString = "3.5 seconds";
15          $testDouble = 79.2;
16          $testInteger = 12;
17       ?><!-- end PHP script -->
18
19       <!-- print each variable's value and type -->
20       <?php
21          print( "$testString is a(n) " . gettype( $testString )
22             . "<br />" );
```

Fig. 19.3 | Data type conversion. (Part 1 of 2.)

```
23          print( "$testDouble is a(n) " . gettype( $testDouble )
24             . "<br />" );
25          print( "$testInteger is a(n) " . gettype( $testInteger)
26             . "<br />" );
27       ?><!-- end PHP script -->
28       <br />
29       converting to other data types:<br />
30       <?php
31          // call function settype to convert variable
32          // testString to different data types
33          print( "$testString" );
34          settype( $testString, "double" );
35          print( " as a double is $testString <br />" );
36          print( "$testString" );
37          settype( $testString, "integer" );
38          print( " as an integer is $testString <br />" );
39          settype( $testString, "string" );
40          print( "converting back to a string results in
41             $testString <br /><br />" );
42
43          // use type casting to cast variables to a different type
44          $data = "98.6 degrees";
45          print( "before casting, $data is a " .
46             gettype( $data ) . "<br /><br />" );
47          print( "using type casting instead: <br />
48             as a double: " . (double) $data .
49             "<br />as an integer: " . (integer) $data );
50          print( "<br /><br />after casting, $data is a " .
51             gettype( $data ) );
52       ?><!-- end PHP script -->
53    </body>
54 </html>
```

Fig. 19.3 | Data type conversion. (Part 2 of 2.)

Lines 14–16 of Fig. 19.3 assign a string to variable `$testString`, a floating-point number to variable `$testDouble` and an integer to variable `$testInteger`. Variables are automatically converted to the type of the value they are assigned. For example, variable `$testString` becomes a string when assigned the value `"3.5 seconds"`. Lines 22–27 print the value of each variable and their types using function ***gettype***, which returns the current type of its argument. Note that when a variable is in a `print` statement but not part of a string, enclosing the variable name in double quotes is unnecessary. Lines 35, 38 and 40 call ***settype*** to modify the type of each variable. Function `settype` takes two arguments—the variable whose type is to be changed and the variable's new type.

Calling function `settype` can result in loss of data. For example, doubles are truncated when they are converted to integers. When converting from a string to a number, PHP uses the value of the number that appears at the beginning of the string. If no number appears at the beginning, the string evaluates to 0. In line 35, the string `"3.5 seconds"` is converted to a double, storing `3.5` in variable `$testString`. In line 38, double `3.5` is converted to integer 3. When we convert this variable to a string (line 40), the variable's value becomes `"3"`—much of the original content from the variable's declaration in line 14 is lost.

Another option for conversion between types is *casting* (or *type casting*). Unlike `settype`, casting does not change a variable's content—it creates a temporary copy of a variable's value in memory. Lines 48–49 cast variable `$data`'s value (declared in line 17) from a `string` to a `double` and an `integer`. Casting is useful when a different type is required in a specific operation but you would like to retain the variable's original value and type. Lines 45–51 show that the type and value of `$data` remain unchanged even after it has been cast several times.

The *concatenation operator (.)* combines multiple strings in the same `print` statement, as demonstrated in lines 45–51. A `print` statement may be split over multiple lines—all data that is enclosed in the parentheses and terminated by a semicolon is printed to the XHTML document.

Error-Prevention Tip 19.1

Function `print` can be used to display the value of a variable at a particular point during a program's execution. This is often helpful in debugging a script.

Arithmetic Operators

PHP provides several arithmetic operators, which we demonstrate in Fig. 19.4. Line 13 declares variable `$a` and assigns to it the value 5. Line 17 calls function `define` to create a ***named constant***. Function `define` takes two arguments—the name and value of the constant. An optional third argument accepts a `bool` value that specifies whether the constant is case insensitive—constants are case sensitive by default.

Common Programming Error 19.4

Assigning a value to a constant after it is declared is a syntax error.

Line 20 adds constant `VALUE` to variable `$a`. Line 25 uses the *multiplication assignment operator* `*=` to yield an expression equivalent to `$a = $a * 2` (thus assigning `$a` the value 20). Arithmetic assignment operators—like the ones described in Chapter 4—are syntactical shortcuts. Line 33 adds 40 to the value of variable `$a`.

```
 1    <?php print( '<?xml version = "1.0" encoding = "utf-8"?>' ) ?>
 2    <!DOCTYPE html PUBLIC "-//W3C//DTD XHTML 1.0 Strict//EN"
 3       "http://www.w3.org/TR/xhtml1/DTD/xhtml1-strict.dtd">
 4
 5    <!-- Fig. 19.4: operators.php -->
 6    <!-- Using arithmetic operators. -->
 7    <html xmlns = "http://www.w3.org/1999/xhtml">
 8       <head>
 9          <title>Using arithmetic operators</title>
10       </head>
11       <body>
12          <?php
13             $a = 5;
14             print( "The value of variable a is $a <br />" );
15
16             // define constant VALUE
17             define( "VALUE", 5 );
18
19             // add constant VALUE to variable $a
20             $a = $a + VALUE;
21             print( "Variable a after adding constant VALUE
22                is $a <br />" );
23
24             // multiply variable $a by 2
25             $a *= 2;
26             print( "Multiplying variable a by 2 yields $a <br />" );
27
28             // test if variable $a is less than 50
29             if ( $a < 50 )
30                print( "Variable a is less than 50 <br />" );
31
32             // add 40 to variable $a
33             $a += 40;
34             print( "Variable a after adding 40 is $a <br />" );
35
36             // test if variable $a is 50 or less
37             if ( $a < 51 )
38                print( "Variable a is still 50 or less<br />" );
39
40             // test if variable $a is between 50 and 100, inclusive
41             elseif ( $a < 101 )
42                print( "Variable a is now between 50 and 100,
43                   inclusive<br />" );
44             else
45                print( "Variable a is now greater than 100 <br />" );
46
47             // print an uninitialized variable
48             print( "Using a variable before initializing:
49                $nothing <br />" ); // nothing evaluates to ""
50
51             // add constant VALUE to an uninitialized variable
52             $test = $num + VALUE; // num evaluates to 0
```

Fig. 19.4 | Using arithmetic operators. (Part 1 of 2.)

```
53          print( "An uninitialized variable plus constant
54              VALUE yields $test <br />" );
55
56          // add a string to an integer
57          $str = "3 dollars";
58          $a += $str;
59          print( "Adding a string to variable a yields $a <br />" );
60      ?><!-- end PHP script -->
61  </body>
62 </html>
```

Fig. 19.4 | Using arithmetic operators. (Part 2 of 2.)

Uninitialized variables have the value ***undef***, which evaluates to different values, depending on its context. For example, when undef is used in a numeric context (e.g., $num in line 52), it evaluates to 0. In contrast, when undef is interpreted in a string context (e.g., $nothing in line 49), it evaluates to an empty string ("").

Error-Prevention Tip 19.2

Initialize variables before they are used to avoid subtle errors. For example, multiplying a number by an uninitialized variable results in 0.

Strings are automatically converted to integers or doubles when they are used in arithmetic operations. In line 58, a copy of the value of variable str, "3 dollars", is converted to the integer 3 for use in the calculation. The type and value of variable $str are left unchanged.

Keywords (examples from Fig. 19.4 include if, elseif and else) may not be used as identifiers. Figure 19.5 lists all keywords.

Initializing and Manipulating Arrays

PHP provides the capability to store data in arrays. Arrays are divided into elements that behave as individual variables. Array names, like other variables, begin with the $ symbol. Figure 19.6 demonstrates initializing and manipulating arrays. Individual array elements

PHP keywords				
abstract	die	exit	interface	require
and	do	extends	isset	require_once
array	echo	__FILE__	__LINE__	return
as	else	file	line	static
break	elseif	final	list	switch
case	empty	for	__METHOD__	throw
catch	enddeclare	foreach	method	try
__CLASS__	endfor	__FUNCTION__	new	unset
class	endforeach	function	or	use
clone	endif	global	php_user_filter	var
const	endswitch	if	print	while
continue	endwhile	implements	private	xor
declare	eval	include	protected	
default	exception	include_once	public	

Fig. 19.5 | PHP keywords.

are accessed by following the array's variable name with an index enclosed in square brackets ([]). If a value is assigned to an array that does not exist, then the array is created (line 15). Likewise, assigning a value to an element where the index is omitted appends a new element to the end of the array (line 18). The for statement (lines 21–22) prints each element's value. Function **count** returns the total number of elements in the array. In this example, the for statement terminates when the counter ($i) is equal to the number of array elements.

Line 28 demonstrates a second method of initializing arrays. Function **array** creates an array that contains the arguments passed to it. The first item in the argument list is stored as the first array element (recall that the first element's index is 0), the second item is stored as the second array element and so on. Lines 30–31 display the array's contents.

```
 1   <?php print( '<?xml version = "1.0" encoding = "utf-8"?>' ) ?>
 2   <!DOCTYPE html PUBLIC "-//W3C//DTD XHTML 1.0 Strict//EN"
 3      "http://www.w3.org/TR/xhtml1/DTD/xhtml1-strict.dtd">
 4
 5   <!-- Fig. 19.6: arrays.php -->
 6   <!-- Array manipulation. -->
 7   <html xmlns = "http://www.w3.org/1999/xhtml">
 8      <head>
 9         <title>Array manipulation</title>
10      </head>
11      <body>
12         <?php
```

Fig. 19.6 | Array manipulation. (Part 1 of 3.)

```
13          // create array first
14          print( "<strong>Creating the first array</strong><br />" );
15          $first[ 0 ] = "zero";
16          $first[ 1 ] = "one";
17          $first[ 2 ] = "two";
18          $first[] = "three";
19
20          // print each element's index and value
21          for ( $i = 0; $i < count( $first ); $i++ )
22             print( "Element $i is $first[$i] <br />" );
23
24          print( "<br /><strong>Creating the second array
25             </strong><br />" );
26
27          // call function array to create array second
28          $second = array( "zero", "one", "two", "three" );
29
30          for ( $i = 0; $i < count( $second ); $i++ )
31             print( "Element $i is $second[$i] <br />" );
32
33          print( "<br /><strong>Creating the third array
34             </strong><br />" );
35
36          // assign values to entries using nonnumeric indices
37          $third[ "Amy" ] = 21;
38          $third[ "Bob" ] = 18;
39          $third[ "Carol" ] = 23;
40
41          // iterate through the array elements and print each
42          // element's name and value
43          for ( reset( $third ); $element = key( $third ); next( $third ) )
44             print( "$element is $third[$element] <br />" );
45
46          print( "<br /><strong>Creating the fourth array
47             </strong><br />" );
48
49          // call function array to create array fourth using
50          // string indices
51          $fourth = array(
52             "January"   => "first",    "February" => "second",
53             "March"     => "third",    "April"    => "fourth",
54             "May"       => "fifth",    "June"     => "sixth",
55             "July"      => "seventh",  "August"   => "eighth",
56             "September" => "ninth",    "October"  => "tenth",
57             "November"  => "eleventh", "December" => "twelfth"
58             );
59
60          // print each element's name and value
61          foreach ( $fourth as $element => $value )
62             print( "$element is the $value month <br />" );
63       ?><!-- end PHP script -->
64    </body>
65 </html>
```

Fig. 19.6 | Array manipulation. (Part 2 of 3.)

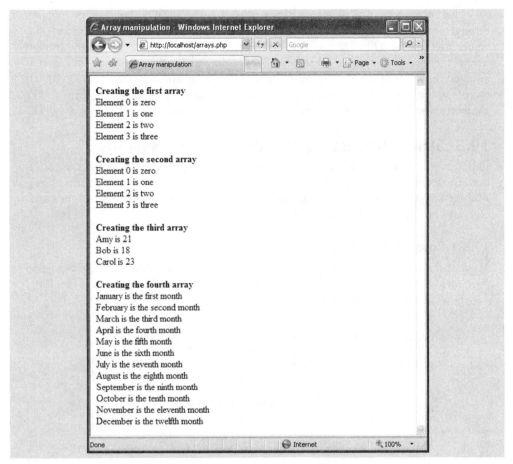

Fig. 19.6 | Array manipulation. (Part 3 of 3.)

In addition to integer indices, arrays can have float or nonnumeric indices (lines 37–39). An array with noninteger indices is called an *associative array*. For example, indices Amy, Bob and Carol are assigned the values 21, 18 and 23, respectively.

PHP provides functions for *iterating* through the elements of an array (line 43). Each array has a built-in *internal pointer*, which points to the array element currently being referenced. Function *reset* sets the internal pointer to the first array element. Function *key* returns the index of the element currently referenced by the internal pointer, and function *next* moves the internal pointer to the next element and returns the element. In our script, the for statement continues to execute as long as function key returns an index. Function next returns false when there are no more elements in the array. When this occurs, function key cannot return an index, $element is set to false and the for statement terminates. Line 44 prints the index and value of each element.

The array $fourth is also associative. To override the automatic numeric indexing performed by function array, you can use operator =>, as demonstrated in lines 51–58. The value to the left of the operator is the array index and the value to the right is the element's value.

The ***foreach*** control statement (lines 61–62) is specifically designed for iterating through arrays, especially associative arrays, because it does not assume that the array has consecutive integer indices that start at 0. The foreach statement starts with the array to iterate through, followed by the keyword ***as***, followed by two variables—the first is assigned the index of the element, and the second is assigned the value of that index. (If there is only one variable listed after as, it is assigned the value of the array element.) We use the foreach statement to print the index and value of each element in array $fourth.

19.3 String Processing and Regular Expressions

PHP can process text easily and efficiently, enabling straightforward searching, substitution, extraction and concatenation of strings. Text manipulation is usually done with ***regular expressions***—a series of characters that serve as pattern-matching templates (or search criteria) in strings, text files and databases.

19.3.1 Comparing Strings

Many string-processing tasks can be accomplished by using the ***equality*** and ***comparison*** operators, demonstrated in Fig. 19.7. Line 14 declares and initializes array $fruits. Lines 17–36 iterate through each element in the $fruits array.

```
1    <?php print( '<?xml version = "1.0" encoding = "utf-8"?>' ) ?>
2    <!DOCTYPE html PUBLIC "-//W3C//DTD XHTML 1.0 Strict//EN"
3       "http://www.w3.org/TR/xhtml1/DTD/xhtml1-strict.dtd">
4
5    <!-- Fig. 19.7: compare.php -->
6    <!-- Using the string-comparison operators. -->
7    <html xmlns = "http://www.w3.org/1999/xhtml">
8       <head>
9          <title>String Comparison</title>
10      </head>
11      <body>
12         <?php
13            // create array fruits
14            $fruits = array( "apple", "orange", "banana" );
15
16            // iterate through each array element
17            for ( $i = 0; $i < count( $fruits ); $i++ )
18            {
19               // call function strcmp to compare the array element
20               // to string "banana"
21               if ( strcmp( $fruits[ $i ], "banana" ) < 0 )
22                  print( $fruits[ $i ] . " is less than banana " );
23               elseif ( strcmp( $fruits[ $i ], "banana" ) > 0 )
24                  print( $fruits[ $i ] . " is greater than banana " );
25               else
26                  print( $fruits[ $i ] . " is equal to banana " );
27
28               // use relational operators to compare each element
29               // to string "apple"
```

Fig. 19.7 | Using the string-comparison operators. (Part 1 of 2.)

```
30          if ( $fruits[ $i ] < "apple" )
31              print( "and less than apple! <br />" );
32          elseif ( $fruits[ $i ] > "apple" )
33              print( "and greater than apple! <br />" );
34          elseif ( $fruits[ $i ] == "apple" )
35              print( "and equal to apple! <br />" );
36      } // end for
37    ?><!-- end PHP script -->
38  </body>
39  </html>
```

Fig. 19.7 | Using the string-comparison operators. (Part 2 of 2.)

Lines 21 and 23 call function **strcmp** to compare two strings. The function returns
-1 if the first string alphabetically precedes the second string, 0 if the strings are equal, and
1 if the first string alphabetically follows the second. Lines 21–26 compare each element
in the $fruits array to the string "banana", printing whether each is greater than, less than
or equal to the string.

Relational operators (==, !=, <, <=, > and >=) can also be used to compare strings. Lines
30–35 use relational operators to compare each element of the array to the string "apple".

19.3.2 Regular Expressions

Functions **ereg** and **preg_match** use regular expressions to search a string for a specified
pattern. Function ereg recognizes *Portable Operating System Interface (POSIX) extended regular expressions*, while function preg_match provides *Perl-compatible regular expressions (PCRE)*. To use preg_match, you must install the PCRE library on your web
server and add support for the library to PHP. More information on PCRE can be found
at www.pcre.org. PHP 5 supports POSIX regular expressions, so we use function ereg in
this section. Figure 19.8 demonstrates regular expressions.

```
1   <?php print( '<?xml version = "1.0" encoding = "utf-8"?>' ) ?>
2   <!DOCTYPE html PUBLIC "-//W3C//DTD XHTML 1.0 Strict//EN"
3      "http://www.w3.org/TR/xhtml1/DTD/xhtml1-strict.dtd">
4
5   <!-- Fig. 19.8: expression.php -->
6   <!-- Regular expressions. -->
7   <html xmlns = "http://www.w3.org/1999/xhtml">
8      <head>
```

Fig. 19.8 | Regular expressions. (Part 1 of 2.)

```
 9       <title>Regular expressions</title>
10    </head>
11    <body>
12      <?php
13        $search = "Now is the time";
14        print( "Test string is: '$search'<br /><br />" );
15
16        // call ereg to search for pattern 'Now' in variable search
17        if ( ereg( "Now", $search ) )
18          print( "String 'Now' was found.<br />" );
19
20        // search for pattern 'Now' in the beginning of the string
21        if ( ereg( "^Now", $search ) )
22          print( "String 'Now' found at beginning
23             of the line.<br />" );
24
25        // search for pattern 'Now' at the end of the string
26        if ( ereg( "Now$", $search ) )
27          print( "String 'Now' was found at the end
28             of the line.<br />" );
29
30        // search for any word ending in 'ow'
31        if ( ereg( "[[:<:]]([a-zA-Z]*ow)[[:>:]]", $search, $match ) )
32          print( "Word found ending in 'ow': " .
33             $match[ 1 ] . "<br />" );
34
35        // search for any words beginning with 't'
36        print( "Words beginning with 't' found: " );
37
38        while ( eregi( "[[:<:]](t[[:alpha:]]+)[[:>:]]",
39           $search, $match ) )
40        {
41          print( $match[ 1 ] . " " );
42
43          // remove the first occurrence of a word beginning
44          // with 't' to find other instances in the string
45          $search = ereg_replace( $match[ 1 ], "", $search );
46        } // end while
47      ?><!-- end PHP script -->
48    </body>
49 </html>
```

Fig. 19.8 | Regular expressions. (Part 2 of 2.)

Searching for Expressions

Line 13 assigns the string "Now is the time" to variable $search. The condition in line 17 calls function ereg to search for the *literal characters* "Now" inside variable $search. If the pattern is found, ereg returns the length of the matched string—which evaluates to true in a boolean context—and line 18 prints a message indicating that the pattern was found. We use single quotes (' ') inside the string in the print statement to emphasize the search pattern. Anything enclosed in single quotes is not interpolated (unless the single quotes are nested in a double-quoted string literal, as in line 14). For example, '$name' in a print statement would output $name, not variable $name's value.

Function ereg takes two arguments—a regular expression pattern to search for and the string to search. Although case mixture is often significant in patterns, PHP provides function *eregi* for specifying case-insensitive pattern matches.

Representing Patterns

In addition to literal characters, regular expressions can include *metacharacters* that specify patterns. Examples of metacharacters include the ∧, $ and . characters. The *caret (∧)* metacharacter matches the beginning of a string (line 21), while the *dollar sign ($)* matches the end of a string (line 26). The *period (.)* metacharacter matches any single character. Line 21 searches for the pattern "Now" at the beginning of $search. Line 26 searches for "Now" at the end of the string. Since the pattern is not found in this case, the body of the if statement (lines 27–28) does not execute. Note that Now$ is not a variable—it is a pattern that uses $ to search for the characters "Now" at the end of a string.

Line 31 searches (from left to right) for the first word ending with the letters ow. *Bracket expressions* are lists of characters enclosed in square brackets ([]) that match any single character from the list. Ranges can be specified by supplying the beginning and the end of the range separated by a *dash (-)*. For instance, the bracket expression [a-z] matches any lowercase letter and [A-Z] matches any uppercase letter. In this example, we combine the two to create an expression that matches any letter. The special bracket expressions [[:<:]] and [[:>:]] match the beginning and end of a word, respectively.

The expression [a-zA-Z]*ow inside the parentheses represents any word ending in ow. The *quantifier* * matches the preceding pattern zero or more times. Thus, [a-zA-Z]*ow matches any number of letters followed by the literal characters ow. Quantifiers are used in regular expressions to denote how often a particular character or set of characters can appear in a match. Some PHP quantifiers are listed in Fig. 19.9.

Quantifier	Matches
{n}	Exactly n times.
{m,n}	Between m and n times, inclusive.
{$n,$}	n or more times.
+	One or more times (same as {1,}).
*	Zero or more times (same as {0,}).
?	Zero or one time (same as {0,1}).

Fig. 19.9 | Some PHP quantifiers.

Finding Matches

The optional third argument to function ereg is an array that stores matches to the regular expression. When the expression is broken down into parenthetical sub-expressions, function ereg stores the first encountered instance of each expression in this array, starting from the leftmost parenthesis. The first element (i.e., index 0) stores the string matched for the entire pattern. The match to the first parenthetical pattern is stored in the second array element, the second in the third array element and so on. If the parenthetical pattern is not encountered, the value of the array element remains uninitialized. Because the statement in line 31 is the first parenthetical pattern, Now is stored in variable $match[1] (and, because it is the *only* parenthetical statement in this case, it is also stored in $match[0]).

Searching for multiple instances of a single pattern in a string is slightly more complicated, because the ereg function returns only the first instance it encounters. To find multiple instances of a given pattern, we must make multiple calls to ereg, and remove any matched instances before calling the function again. Lines 38–46 use a *while* statement and the *ereg_replace* function to find all the words in the string that begin with t. We'll say more about this function momentarily.

Character Classes

The pattern in line 38, [[:<:]](t[[:alpha:]]+)[[:>:]], matches any word beginning with the character t followed by one or more letters. The pattern uses the *character class* [[:alpha:]] to recognize any letter—this is equivalent to the [a-zA-Z]. Figure 19.10 lists some character classes that can be matched with regular expressions.

Character classes are enclosed by the delimiters [: and :]. When this expression is placed in another set of brackets, such as [[:alpha:]] in line 38, it is a regular expression matching a single character that is a member of the class. A bracketed expression containing two or more adjacent character classes in the class delimiters represents those character sets combined. For example, the expression [[:upper:][:lower:]]* represents all strings of uppercase and lowercase letters in any order, while [[:upper:]][[:lower:]]* matches strings with a single uppercase letter followed by any number of lowercase characters. Also, note that ([[:upper:]][[:lower:]])* is an expression for all strings that alternate between uppercase and lowercase characters (starting with uppercase and ending with lowercase).

Character class	Description
alnum	Alphanumeric characters (i.e., letters [a-zA-Z] or digits [0-9]).
alpha	Word characters (i.e., letters [a-zA-Z]).
digit	Digits.
space	White space.
lower	Lowercase letters.
upper	Uppercase letters.

Fig. 19.10 | Some PHP character classes.

Finding Multiple Instances of a Pattern

The quantifier + matches one or more consecutive instances of the preceding expression. The result of the match is stored in $match[1]. Once a match is found, we print it in line 41. We then remove it from the string in line 45, using function ereg_replace. This function takes three arguments—the pattern to match, a string to replace the matched string and the string to search. The modified string is returned. Here, we search for the word that we matched with the regular expression, replace the word with an empty string, then assign the result back to $search. This allows us to match any other words beginning with the character t in the string and print them to the screen.

19.4 Form Processing and Business Logic

Superglobal Arrays

Knowledge of a client's execution environment is useful to system administrators who want to access client-specific information such as the client's web browser, the server name or the data sent to the server by the client. One way to obtain this data is by using a ***superglobal array***. Superglobal arrays are associative arrays predefined by PHP that hold variables acquired from user input, the environment or the web server, and are accessible in any variable scope. Some of PHP's superglobal arrays are listed in Fig. 19.11.

Superglobal arrays are useful for verifying user input. The arrays $_GET and $_POST retrieve information sent to the server by HTTP get and post requests, respectively, making it possible for a script to have access to this data when it loads another page. For example, if data entered by a user into a form is posted to a script, the $_POST array will contain all of this information in the new script. Thus, any information entered into the form can be accessed easily from a confirmation page, or a page that verifies whether fields have been entered correctly.

Variable name	Description
$_SERVER	Data about the currently running server.
$_ENV	Data about the client's environment.
$_GET	Data sent to the server by a get request.
$_POST	Data sent to the server by a post request.
$_COOKIE	Data contained in cookies on the client's computer.
$GLOBALS	Array containing all global variables.

Fig. 19.11 | Some useful superglobal arrays.

Using PHP to Process XHTML Forms

XHTML forms enable web pages to collect data from users and send it to a web server for processing. Such capabilities allow users to purchase products, request information, send and receive web-based e-mail, create profiles in online networking services and take advantage of various other online services. The XHTML form in Fig. 19.12 gathers information to add a user to a mailing list.

```
 1    <?xml version = "1.0" encoding = "utf-8"?>
 2    <!DOCTYPE html PUBLIC "-//W3C//DTD XHTML 1.0 Strict//EN"
 3       "http://www.w3.org/TR/xhtml1/DTD/xhtml1-strict.dtd">
 4
 5    <!-- Fig. 19.12: form.html -->
 6    <!-- XHTML form for gathering user input. -->
 7    <html xmlns = "http://www.w3.org/1999/xhtml">
 8       <head>
 9          <title>Sample form to take user input in XHTML</title>
10          <style type = "text/css">
11             .prompt { color: blue;
12                       font-family: sans-serif;
13                       font-size: smaller }
14          </style>
15       </head>
16       <body>
17          <h1>Sample Registration Form</h1>
18          <p>Please fill in all fields and click Register.</p>
19
20          <!-- post form data to form.php -->
21          <form method = "post" action = "form.php">
22             <div>
23                <img src = "images/user.gif" alt = "User" /><br />
24                <span class = "prompt">
25                   Please fill out the fields below.<br />
26                </span>
27
28                <!-- create four text boxes for user input -->
29                <img src = "images/fname.gif" alt = "First Name" />
30                <input type = "text" name = "fname" /><br />
31
32                <img src = "images/lname.gif" alt = "Last Name" />
33                <input type = "text" name = "lname" /><br />
34
35                <img src = "images/email.gif" alt = "Email" />
36                <input type = "text" name = "email" /><br />
37
38                <img src = "images/phone.gif" alt = "Phone" />
39                <input type = "text" name = "phone" /><br />
40
41                <span style = "font-size: 10pt">
42                   Must be in the form (555)555-5555</span>
43                <br /><br />
44
45                <img src = "images/downloads.gif"
46                alt = "Publications" /><br />
47
48                <span class = "prompt">
49                   Which book would you like information about?
50                </span><br />
51
52                <!-- create drop-down list containing book names -->
53                <select name = "book">
```

Fig. 19.12 | XHTML form for gathering user input. (Part I of 2.)

```
54              <option>Internet and WWW How to Program 4e</option>
55              <option>C++ How to Program 6e</option>
56              <option>Java How to Program 7e</option>
57              <option>Visual Basic 2005 How to Program 3e</option>
58           </select>
59           <br /><br />
60
61           <img src = "images/os.gif" alt = "Operating System" />
62           <br /><span class = "prompt">
63              Which operating system are you currently using?
64           <br /></span>
65
66           <!-- create five radio buttons -->
67           <input type = "radio" name = "os" value = "Windows XP"
68              checked = "checked" /> Windows XP
69           <input type = "radio" name = "os" value =
70              "Windows Vista" /> Windows Vista<br />
71           <input type = "radio" name = "os" value =
72              "Mac OS X" /> Mac OS X
73           <input type = "radio" name = "os" value = "Linux" /> Linux
74           <input type = "radio" name = "os" value = "Other" />
75              Other<br />
76
77           <!-- create a submit button -->
78           <input type = "submit" value = "Register" />
79        </div>
80     </form>
81  </body>
82 </html>
```

Fig. 19.12 | XHTML form for gathering user input. (Part 2 of 2.)

The form's `action` attribute (line 21) indicates that when the user clicks the **Register** button, the `form` data will be `post`ed to `form.php` (Fig. 19.13) for processing. Using `method = "post"` appends form data to the browser request that contains the protocol (i.e., HTTP) and the URL of the requested resource (specified by the `action` attribute). Scripts located on the web server's machine can access the form data sent as part of the request.

We assign a unique `name` (e.g., `email`) to each of the `form`'s controls. When **Register** is clicked, each field's `name` and `value` are sent to the web server. Script `form.php` accesses the value for each field through the superglobal array *$_POST*, which contains key/value pairs corresponding to name/value pairs for variables submitted through the form. [*Note:* The superglobal array *$_GET* would contain these key/value pairs if the form had been submitted using the HTTP *get* method. In general, `get` is not as secure as `post`, because it appends the information directly to the URL, which is visible to the user.] Figure 19.13 processes the data `post`ed by `form.html` and sends XHTML back to the client.

Good Programming Practice 19.1

Use meaningful XHTML object names for `input` fields. This makes PHP scripts that retrieve form data easier to understand.

Function ***extract*** (line 29 in Fig. 19.13) creates a variable/value pair corresponding to each key/value pair in the associative array passed as an argument (i.e., `$_POST`). This creates variables whose respective names and values correspond to the names and values of each posted form field. For example, line 36 in Fig. 19.12 creates an XHTML text box with the name `email`. In line 70 of our PHP script (Fig. 19.13), after having called function `extract`, we access the field's value by using variable `$email`. Elements in `$_POST` can also be accessed using standard array notation. For example, we could have accessed the form field `email`'s value by referring to `$_POST[ 'email' ]`.

```
 1    <?php print( '<?xml version = "1.0" encoding = "utf-8"?>' ) ?>
 2    <!DOCTYPE html PUBLIC "-//W3C//DTD XHTML 1.0 Strict//EN"
 3       "http://www.w3.org/TR/xhtml1/DTD/xhtml1-strict.dtd">
 4
 5    <!-- Fig. 19.13: form.php -->
 6    <!-- Process information sent from form.html. -->
 7    <html xmlns = "http://www.w3.org/1999/xhtml">
 8       <head>
 9          <title>Form Validation</title>
10          <style type = "text/css">
11             body        { font-family: arial, sans-serif }
12             div         { font-size: 10pt;
13                           text-align: center }
14             table       { border: 0 }
15             td          { padding-top: 2px;
16                           padding-bottom: 2px;
17                           padding-left: 10px;
18                           padding-right: 10px }
19             .error      { color: red }
20             .distinct   { color: blue }
21             .name       { background-color: #ffffaa }
```

Fig. 19.13 | Process information sent from `form.html`. (Part 1 of 4.)

```
22            .email    { background-color: #ffffbb }
23            .phone    { background-color: #ffffcc }
24            .os       { background-color: #ffffdd }
25        </style>
26    </head>
27    <body>
28        <?php
29            extract( $_POST );
30
31            // determine whether phone number is valid and print
32            // an error message if not
33            if ( !ereg( "^\([0-9]{3}\)[0-9]{3}-[0-9]{4}$", $phone ) )
34            {
35                print( "<p><span class = 'error'>
36                    Invalid phone number</span><br />
37                    A valid phone number must be in the form
38                    <strong>(555)555-5555</strong><br />
39                    <span class = 'distinct'>
40                    Click the Back button, enter a valid phone
41                    number and resubmit.<br /><br />
42                    Thank You.</span></p>" );
43                die( "</body></html>" ); // terminate script execution
44            }
45        ?><!-- end PHP script -->
46        <p>Hi
47            <span class = "distinct">
48                <strong><?php print( "$fname" ); ?></strong>
49            </span>.
50            Thank you for completing the survey.<br />
51            You have been added to the
52            <span class = "distinct">
53                <strong><?php print( "$book " ); ?></strong>
54            </span>
55            mailing list.
56        </p>
57        <p><strong>The following information has been saved
58            in our database:</strong></p>
59        <table>
60            <tr>
61                <td class = "name">Name </td>
62                <td class = "email">Email</td>
63                <td class = "phone">Phone</td>
64                <td class = "os">OS</td>
65            </tr>
66            <tr>
67                <?php
68                    // print each form field's value
69                    print( "<td>$fname $lname</td>
70                        <td>$email</td>
71                        <td>$phone</td>
72                        <td>$os</td>" );
73                ?><!-- end PHP script -->
74            </tr>
```

Fig. 19.13 | Process information sent from form.html. (Part 2 of 4.)

```
75          </table>
76          <br /><br /><br />
77          <div>This is only a sample form.
78             You have not been added to a mailing list.</div>
79       </body>
80    </html>
```

a) The form in `form.html` is filled out with an incorrect phone number.

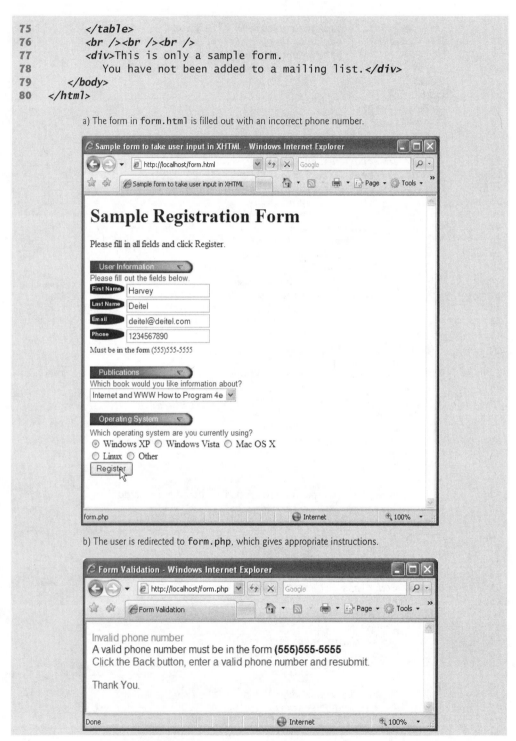

b) The user is redirected to `form.php`, which gives appropriate instructions.

Fig. 19.13 | Process information sent from `form.html`. (Part 3 of 4.)

c) The form is now filled out correctly.

d) The user is directed to an acceptance page, which displays the entered information.

Fig. 19.13 | Process information sent from `form.html`. (Part 4 of 4.)

Line 33 determines whether the phone number entered by the user is valid. In this case, the phone number must begin with an opening parenthesis, followed by an area code, a closing parenthesis, an exchange, a hyphen and a line number. It is crucial to validate information that will be entered into databases or used in mailing lists. For example, validation can be used to ensure that credit card numbers contain the proper number of digits before the numbers are encrypted and sent to a merchant. This script implements the *business logic*, or *business rules*, of our application.

Software Engineering Observation 19.1

Use business logic to ensure that invalid information is not stored in databases. When possible, validate important or sensitive form data on the server, since JavaScript may be disabled by the client. Some data, such as passwords, must always be validated on the server side.

The expression \(matches the opening parenthesis of the phone number. We want to match the literal character (, so we *escape* its normal meaning by preceding it with the backslash character (\). This parenthesis in the expression must be followed by three digits ([0-9]{3}), a closing parenthesis, three more digits, a literal hyphen and four additional digits. Note that we use the ∧ and $ symbols to ensure that no extra characters appear at either end of the string.

If the regular expression is matched, the phone number has a valid format, and an XHTML document is sent to the client that thanks the user for completing the form. Otherwise, the body of the if statement executes and displays an error message.

Function *die* (line 43) terminates script execution. This function is called if the user did not enter a correct telephone number, since we do not want to continue executing the rest of the script. The function's optional argument is a string, which is printed as the script exits.

Error-Prevention Tip 19.3

Be sure to close any open XHTML tags when calling function die. Not doing so can produce invalid XHTML output that will not display properly in the client browser. Function die has an optional parameter that specifies a message to output when exiting, so one technique for closing tags is to close all open tags using die, as in die("</body></html>").

19.5 Connecting to a Database

Databases enable companies to enter the world of e-commerce by maintaining crucial data. Database connectivity allows system administrators to maintain and update such information as user accounts, passwords, credit card numbers, mailing lists and product inventories. PHP offers built-in support for many databases. In this example, we use MySQL. Install MySQL using the instructions in Sections 18.6–18.7. Then execute the Products script (refer to Section 18.8) from the Script Examples folder of the Chapter 19 examples directory at www.deitel.com/books/ajaxfp.

In this example, the client selects the name of a column in the database. The PHP script then executes—it builds a SELECT query, queries the database to obtain the column's data and sends a record set in the form of XHTML to the client. Chapter 18 discusses how to build SQL queries.

Figure 19.14 is a web page that posts form data consisting of a selected database column to the server. The script in Fig. 19.15 processes the form data.

```
1   <?xml version = "1.0" encoding = "utf-8"?>
2   <!DOCTYPE html PUBLIC "-//W3C//DTD XHTML 1.0 Strict//EN"
3      "http://www.w3.org/TR/xhtml1/DTD/xhtml1-strict.dtd">
4
5   <!-- Fig. 19.14: data.html -->
6   <!-- Form to query a MySQL database. -->
7   <html xmlns = "http://www.w3.org/1999/xhtml">
8      <head>
9         <title>Sample Database Query</title>
10        <style type = "text/css">
11           body  { background-color: #F0E68C }
12           h2    { font-family: arial, sans-serif;
13                   color: blue }
14           input { background-color: blue;
15                   color: yellow;
16                   font-weight: bold }
17        </style>
18     </head>
19     <body>
20        <h2> Querying a MySQL database.</h2>
21        <form method = "post" action = "database.php">
22           <div>
23              <p>Select a field to display:
24                 <!-- add a select box containing options -->
25                 <!-- for SELECT query -->
26                 <select name = "select">
27                    <option selected = "selected">*</option>
28                    <option>ID</option>
29                    <option>Title</option>
30                    <option>Category</option>
31                    <option>ISBN</option>
32                 </select></p>
33              <input type = "submit" value = "Send Query" />
34           </div>
35        </form>
36     </body>
37  </html>
```

Fig. 19.14 | Form to query a MySQL database.

```
1   <?php print( '<?xml version = "1.0" encoding = "utf-8"?>' ) ?>
2   <!DOCTYPE html PUBLIC "-//W3C//DTD XHTML 1.0 Strict//EN"
3      "http://www.w3.org/TR/xhtml1/DTD/xhtml1-strict.dtd">
4
5   <!-- Fig. 19.15: database.php -->
6   <!-- Querying a database and displaying the results. -->
7   <html xmlns = "http://www.w3.org/1999/xhtml">
8      <head>
9         <title>Search Results</title>
10     <style type = "text/css">
11        body  { font-family: arial, sans-serif;
12               background-color: #F0E68C }
13        table { background-color: #ADD8E6 }
14        td    { padding-top: 2px;
15               padding-bottom: 2px;
16               padding-left: 4px;
17               padding-right: 4px;
18               border-width: 1px;
19               border-style: inset }
20     </style>
21     </head>
22     <body>
23        <?php
24           extract( $_POST );
25
26           // build SELECT query
27           $query = "SELECT " . $select . " FROM books";
28
29           // Connect to MySQL
30           if ( !( $database = mysql_connect( "localhost",
31              "iw3htp4", "iw3htp4" ) ) )
32              die( "Could not connect to database </body></html>" );
33
34           // open Products database
35           if ( !mysql_select_db( "products", $database ) )
36              die( "Could not open products database </body></html>" );
37
38           // query Products database
39           if ( !( $result = mysql_query( $query, $database ) ) )
40           {
41              print( "Could not execute query! <br />" );
42              die( mysql_error() . "</body></html>" );
43           } // end if
44
45           mysql_close( $database );
46        ?><!-- end PHP script -->
47        <h3>Search Results</h3>
48        <table>
49           <?php
50              // fetch each record in result set
51              for ( $counter = 0; $row = mysql_fetch_row( $result );
52                 $counter++ )
53              {
```

Fig. 19.15 | Querying a database and displaying the results. (Part 1 of 2.)

```
54                      // build table to display results
55                      print( "<tr>" );
56
57                      foreach ( $row as $key => $value )
58                          print( "<td>$value</td>" );
59
60                      print( "</tr>" );
61                  } // end for
62              ?><!-- end PHP script -->
63          </table>
64          <br />Your search yielded <strong>
65          <?php print( "$counter" ) ?> results.<br /><br /></strong>
66          <h5>Please email comments to
67              <a href = "mailto:deitel@deitel.com">
68                  Deitel and Associates, Inc.</a>
69          </h5>
70      </body>
71  </html>
```

Fig. 19.15 | Querying a database and displaying the results. (Part 2 of 2.)

Line 21 of Fig. 19.14 creates an XHTML form, specifying that the data submitted from the form will be sent to script database.php (Fig. 19.15) in a post request. Lines 26–32 add a select box to the form, set the name of the select box to select and set its default selection to *. This value specifies that all rows and columns are to be retrieved from the database. Each database column is set as an option in the select box.

Script database.php (Fig. 19.15) builds a SQL query with the specified field name and sends it to the database management system. Line 27 concatenates the posted field name to a SELECT query. Line 30 calls function **mysql_connect** to connect to the MySQL database. We pass three arguments to function mysql_connect—the server's hostname, a username and a password (in this case, both our username and password are iw3htp4, based on the account we set up in Chapter 18). This function returns a *database handle*—

a representation of PHP's connection to the database—which we assign to variable $data-base. If the connection to MySQL fails, the function returns `false` and function `die` is called to output an error message and terminate the script. Line 35 calls function **_mysql_select_db_** to specify the database to be queried (in this case, `products`), which returns `true` on success or `false` on failure. Function `die` is called if the database cannot be opened.

To query the database, line 39 calls function **_mysql_query_**, specifying the query string and the database to query. If the query fails, the function returns `false`. Function `die` is then called with a call to function **_mysql_error_** as an argument. Function `mysql_error` returns any error strings from the database. If the query succeeds, `mysql_query` returns a `resource` containing the query result, which we assign to variable $result. Once we have stored the data in $result, we call **_mysql_close_** in line 45 to close the connection to the database. Function `mysql_query` can also execute SQL statements such as `INSERT` or `DELETE` that do not return results.

Lines 51–61 iterate through each record in the result set and construct an XHTML table from the results. The `for` statement's condition calls function **_mysql_fetch_row_** to return an array containing the values for each column of the current row in the query result ($result). The array is stored in variable $row. Lines 57–58 construct individual cells for each column in the row. The `foreach` statement takes the name of the array ($row), iterates through each index value of the array ($key) and stores the value in variable $value. Each element of the array is then printed as an individual cell. When the result has no more rows, `false` is returned by function `mysql_fetch_row`, which terminates the `for` statement.

After all the rows in the result have been displayed, the table's closing tag is written (line 63). The number of rows contained in $counter is printed in line 65. Alternatively, calling function **_mysql_num_rows_**($result) would return the number of rows in the result.

19.6 Using Cookies

A *cookie* is a piece of information stored in a text file on a client's computer to maintain information about the client during and between browsing sessions. A website can store a cookie on a client's computer to record user preferences and other information that the website can retrieve during the client's subsequent visits. For example, a website can use cookies to store clients' zip codes, so that it can provide weather reports and news updates tailored to the user's region. Websites also can use cookies to track information about client activity. Analysis of information collected via cookies can reveal the popularity of websites or products. In addition, marketers can use cookies to determine the effects of advertising campaigns.

Websites store cookies on users' hard drives, which raises issues regarding security and privacy. Websites should not store critical information, such as credit card numbers or passwords, in cookies, because cookies are typically stored in text files that any program can read. Several cookie features address security and privacy concerns. A server can access only the cookies that it has placed on the client. For example, a web application running on www.deitel.com cannot access cookies that the website www.prenhall.com has placed on the client's computer. A cookie also has an expiration date, after which the web browser deletes it. Users who are concerned about the privacy and security implications of cookies can disable cookies in their web browsers. However, disabling cookies can make it impossible for the user to interact with websites that rely on cookies to function properly.

The information stored in a cookie is sent back to the web server from which it originated whenever the user requests a web page from that particular server. The web server can send the client XHTML output that reflects the preferences or information that is stored in the cookie.

Writing Cookies

Figure 19.16 uses a script to write a cookie to the client's machine. The cookies.html file displays an XHTML form that allows a user to enter a name, height and favorite color. When the user clicks the **Write Cookie** button, the cookies.php script (Fig. 19.17) executes.

```
1   <?xml version = "1.0" encoding = "utf-8"?>
2   <!DOCTYPE html PUBLIC "-//W3C//DTD XHTML 1.0 Strict//EN"
3      "http://www.w3.org/TR/xhtml1/DTD/xhtml1-strict.dtd">
4
5   <!-- Fig. 19.16: cookies.html -->
6   <!-- Gathering data to be written as a cookie. -->
7   <html xmlns = "http://www.w3.org/1999/xhtml">
8      <head>
9         <title>Writing a cookie to the client computer</title>
10        <style type = "text/css">
11           body    { font-family: arial, sans-serif;
12                     background-color: #99CCFF }
13           form    { font-size: 10pt }
14           .submit { background-color: #F0E86C;
15                     color: navy;
16                     font-weight: bold }
17        </style>
18     </head>
19     <body>
20        <h2>Click Write Cookie to save your cookie data.</h2>
21        <form method = "post" action = "cookies.php">
22           <div>
23              <strong>Name:</strong><br />
24              <input type = "text" name = "Name" /><br />
25
26              <strong>Height:</strong><br />
27              <input type = "text" name = "Height" /><br />
28
29              <strong>Favorite Color:</strong><br />
30              <input type = "text" name = "Color" /><br />
31
32              <input type = "submit" value = "Write Cookie"
33                 class = "submit" />
34           </div>
35        </form>
36     </body>
37  </html>
```

Fig. 19.16 | Gathering data to be written as a cookie. (Part 1 of 2.)

Fig. 19.16 | Gathering data to be written as a cookie. (Part 2 of 2.)

```php
1   <?php
2      // Fig. 19.17: cookies.php
3      // Writing a cookie to the client.
4      extract( $_POST );
5
6      // write each form field's value to a cookie and set the
7      // cookie's expiration date
8      setcookie( "Name", $Name, time() + 60 * 60 * 24 * 5 );
9      setcookie( "Height", $Height, time() + 60 * 60 * 24 * 5 );
10     setcookie( "Color", $Color, time() + 60 * 60 * 24 * 5 );
11  ?><!-- end PHP script -->
12
13  <?php print( '<?xml version = "1.0" encoding = "utf-8"?>' ) ?>
14  <!DOCTYPE html PUBLIC "-//W3C//DTD XHTML 1.0 Strict//EN"
15     "http://www.w3.org/TR/xhtml1/DTD/xhtml1-strict.dtd">
16
17  <html xmlns = "http://www.w3.org/1999/xhtml">
18     <head>
19        <title>Cookie Saved</title>
20        <style type = "text/css">
21           body { font-family: arial, sans-serif }
22           span { color: blue }
23        </style>
24     </head>
25     <body>
26        <p>The cookie has been set with the following data:</p>
27
28        <!-- print each form field's value -->
29        <br /><span>Name:</span><?php print( $Name ) ?><br />
```

Fig. 19.17 | Writing a cookie to the client. (Part 1 of 2.)

```
30          <span>Height: </span><?php print( $Height ) ?><br />
31          <span>Favorite Color: </span>
32          <span style = "color: <?php print( "$Color\">$Color" ) ?>
33          </span><br />
34          <p>Click <a href = "readCookies.php">here</a>
35              to read the saved cookie.</p>
36      </body>
37  </html>
```

Cookie Saved - Windows Internet Explorer

http://localhost/cookies.php

Cookie Saved

The cookie has been set with the following data:

Name:Harvey
Height:5 Feet 7 Inches
Favorite Color: Blue

Click here to read the saved cookie.

Fig. 19.17 | Writing a cookie to the client. (Part 2 of 2.)

 Software Engineering Observation 19.2

Some clients do not accept cookies. When a client declines a cookie, the browser application normally informs the user that the site may not function correctly without cookies enabled.

 Software Engineering Observation 19.3

Cookies should not be used to store e-mail addresses or private data on a client's computer.

Script `cookies.php` (Fig. 19.17) calls function ***setcookie*** (lines 8–10) to set the cookies to the values passed from `cookies.html`. The cookies defined in function `setcookie` are sent to the client at the same time as the information in the HTTP header; therefore, `setcookie` needs to be called before any XHTML (including comments) is printed.

Function `setcookie` takes the name of the cookie to be set as the first argument, followed by the value to be stored in the cookie. For example, line 8 sets the name of the cookie to "Name" and the value to variable `$Name`, which is passed to the script from `cookies.html`. The optional third argument indicates the expiration date of the cookie. In this example, we set the cookies to expire in five days by taking the current time, which is returned by function ***time***, and adding the number of seconds after which the cookie is to expire (60 seconds/minute * 60 minutes/hour * 24 hours/day * 5 = 5 days). If no expiration date is specified, the cookie lasts only until the end of the current session, which is the total time until the user closes the browser. This type of cookie is known as a ***session cookie***, while one with an expiration date is a ***persistent cookie***. If only the name argument is passed to function `setcookie`, the cookie is deleted from the client's computer. Lines 13–37 send a web page to the client indicating that the cookie has been written and listing the values that are stored in the cookie.

When using Internet Explorer, cookies are stored in a **Cookies** directory on the client's machine, while Firefox stores them in a single file called `cookies.txt`. Figure 19.18 shows the contents of this directory (for a Windows XP and IE7 user `harvey`) prior to the execution of `cookies.php`. After the cookie is written, a text file is added to the directory. In Fig. 19.19, the file `harvey@localhost[1].txt` appears in the **Cookies** directory. [*Note:* The name of the file created will vary from user to user.]

Fig. 19.18 | IE7's `Cookies` directory before a cookie is written.

Fig. 19.19 | IE7's `Cookies` directory after a cookie is written.

Reading an Existing Cookie
Figure 19.20 reads the cookie that was written in Fig. 19.17 and displays the cookie's information in a table. PHP creates the superglobal array *$_COOKIE*, which contains all the cookie values indexed by their names, similar to the values stored in array $_POST when an XHTML form is posted (see Section 19.4).

```
 1  <?php print( '<?xml version = "1.0" encoding = "utf-8"?>' ) ?>
 2  <!DOCTYPE html PUBLIC "-//W3C//DTD XHTML 1.0 Strict//EN"
 3     "http://www.w3.org/TR/xhtml1/DTD/xhtml1-strict.dtd">
 4
 5  <!-- Fig. 19.20: readCookies.php -->
 6  <!-- Displaying the cookie's contents. -->
 7  <html xmlns = "http://www.w3.org/1999/xhtml">
 8     <head>
 9        <title>Read Cookies</title>
10        <style type = "text/css">
11           body    { font-family: arial, sans-serif }
12           table   { border-width: 5px;
13                     border-style: outset }
14           td      { padding: 10px }
15           .key    { background-color: #F0E68C }
16           .value  { background-color: #FFA500 }
17        </style>
18     </head>
19     <body>
20        <p>
21           <strong>The following data is saved in a cookie on your
22              computer.</strong>
23        </p>
24        <table>
25           <?php
26              // iterate through array $_COOKIE and print
27              // name and value of each cookie
28              foreach ( $_COOKIE as $key => $value )
29                 print( "<tr><td class = 'key' >$key</td>
30                    <td class = 'value' >$value</td></tr>" );
31           ?><!-- end PHP script -->
32        </table>
33     </body>
34  </html>
```

Fig. 19.20 | Displaying the cookie's contents.

Lines 28–30 iterate through the $_COOKIE array using a foreach statement, printing out the name and value of each cookie in an XHTML table. The foreach statement takes the name of the array ($_COOKIE) and iterates through each index value of the array ($key). In this case, the index values are the names of the cookies. Each element is then stored in variable $value, and these values become the individual cells of the table.

We could have also used the function extract to create individual variables out of the key-value pairs in $_COOKIE, just as we did with $_POST. For example, after the function extract($_COOKIE) is called, the value of a cookie set with the name "Color" is assigned to variable $Color. Try closing your browser and revisiting readCookies.php to confirm that the cookie has persisted.

19.7 Dynamic Content

PHP can dynamically change the XHTML it outputs based on a user's input. We now build on Section 19.4's example by combining the XHTML form of Fig. 19.12 and the PHP script of Fig. 19.13 into one dynamic document. The form in Fig. 19.21 is created using a series of loops, arrays and conditionals. We add error checking to each of the text input fields and inform the user of invalid entries on the form itself, rather than on an error page. If an error exists, the script maintains the previously submitted values in each form element. Finally, after the form has been successfully completed, we store the input from the user in a MySQL database. Before running the following example, make sure MySQL is installed, then execute the MailingList script (refer to Section 18.8) from the Script Examples folder of the Chapter 19 examples directory at www.deitel.com/books/ajaxfp.

Lines 36–47 create three arrays, $booklist, $systemlist and $inputlist, that are used to dynamically create the form's input fields. We specify that the form created in this document is self-submitting (i.e., it posts to itself) by setting the action to 'dynamicForm.php' in line 148. [*Note:* We enclose XHTML attribute values in the string argument of a print statement in single quotes so that they do not interfere with the double quotes that delimit the string. We could alternatively have used the escape sequence \" to print double quotes instead of single quotes.] Line 50 uses function *isset* to determine whether the **Register** button has been pressed. If it has, each of the text input fields' values is validated. If an error is detected (e.g., a text field is blank or the phone number is improperly formatted), an entry is added to array $formerrors containing a key corresponding to the field name with the error and a value of true. Also, variable $iserror is set to true. If the **Register** button has not been pressed, we skip ahead to line 138.

```
1    <?php print( '<?xml version = "1.0" encoding = "utf-8"?>' ) ?>
2    <!DOCTYPE html PUBLIC "-//W3C//DTD XHTML 1.0 Strict//EN"
3        "http://www.w3.org/TR/xhtml1/DTD/xhtml1-strict.dtd">
4
5    <!-- Fig. 19.21: dynamicForm.php -->
6    <!-- Dynamic form. -->
7    <html xmlns = "http://www.w3.org/1999/xhtml">
8        <head>
9            <title>Sample form to take user input in XHTML</title>
10           <style type = "text/css">
```

Fig. 19.21 | Dynamic form. (Part 1 of 7.)

```
11          td            { padding-top: 2px;
12                          padding-bottom: 2px;
13                          padding-left: 10px;
14                          padding-right: 10px }
15          div           { text-align: center }
16          div div       { font-size: larger }
17          .name         { background-color: #ffffaa }
18          .email        { background-color: #ffffbb }
19          .phone        { background-color: #ffffcc }
20          .os           { background-color: #ffffdd }
21          .smalltext    { font-size: smaller }
22          .prompt       { color: blue;
23                          font-family: sans-serif;
24                          font-size: smaller }
25          .largeerror { color: red }
26          .error        { color: red;
27                          font-size: smaller }
28       </style>
29    </head>
30    <body>
31       <?php
32          extract( $_POST );
33          $iserror = false;
34
35          // array of book titles
36          $booklist = array( "Internet and WWW How to Program 4e",
37             "C++ How to Program 6e", "Java How to Program 7e",
38             "Visual Basic 2005 How to Program 3e" );
39
40          // array of possible operating systems
41          $systemlist = array( "Windows XP", "Windows Vista",
42             "Mac OS X", "Linux", "Other");
43
44          // array of name values for the text input fields
45          $inputlist = array( "fname" => "First Name",
46             "lname" => "Last Name", "email" => "Email",
47             "phone" => "Phone" );
48
49          // ensure that all fields have been filled in correctly
50          if ( isset ( $submit ) )
51          {
52             if ( $fname == "" )
53             {
54                $formerrors[ "fnameerror" ] = true;
55                $iserror = true;
56             } // end if
57
58             if ( $lname == "" )
59             {
60                $formerrors[ "lnameerror" ] = true;
61                $iserror = true;
62             } // end if
63
```

Fig. 19.21 | Dynamic form. (Part 2 of 7.)

```
64          if ( $email == "" )
65          {
66             $formerrors[ "emailerror" ] = true;
67             $iserror = true;
68          } // end if
69
70          if ( !ereg( "^\([0-9]{3}\)[0-9]{3}-[0-9]{4}$", $phone ) )
71          {
72             $formerrors[ "phoneerror" ] = true;
73             $iserror = true;
74          } // end if
75
76          if ( !$iserror )
77          {
78             // build INSERT query
79             $query = "INSERT INTO contacts " .
80                "( LastName, FirstName, Email, Phone, Book, OS ) " .
81                "VALUES ( '$lname', '$fname', '$email', " .
82                "'" . quotemeta( $phone ) . "', '$book', '$os' )";
83
84             // Connect to MySQL
85             if ( !( $database = mysql_connect( "localhost",
86                "iw3htp4", "iw3htp4" ) ) )
87                die( "Could not connect to database" );
88
89             // open MailingList database
90             if ( !mysql_select_db( "MailingList", $database ) )
91                die( "Could not open MailingList database" );
92
93             // execute query in MailingList database
94             if ( !( $result = mysql_query( $query, $database ) ) )
95             {
96                print( "Could not execute query! <br />" );
97                die( mysql_error() );
98             } // end if
99
100            mysql_close( $database );
101
102            print( "<p>Hi<span class = 'prompt'>
103               <strong>$fname</strong></span>.
104               Thank you for completing the survey.<br />
105
106               You have been added to the
107               <span class = 'prompt'>
108               <strong>$book</strong></span>
109               mailing list.</p>
110               <strong>The following information has been saved
111               in our database:</strong><br />
112
113               <table><tr>
114               <td class = 'name'>Name </td>
115               <td class = 'email'>Email</td>
116               <td class = 'phone'>Phone</td>
```

Fig. 19.21 | Dynamic form. (Part 3 of 7.)

```
117                    <td class = 'os'>OS</td>
118                    </tr><tr>
119
120                    <!-- print each form field's value -->
121                    <td>$fname $lname</td>
122                    <td>$email</td>
123                    <td>$phone</td>
124                    <td>$os</td>
125                    </tr></table>
126
127                    <br /><br /><br />
128                    <div><div>
129                    <a href = 'formDatabase.php'>
130                    Click here to view entire database.</a>
131                    </div>This is only a sample form.
132                    You have not been added to a mailing list.
133                    </div></body></html>" );
134               die();
135           } // end if
136       } // end if
137
138       print( "<h1>Sample Registration Form.</h1>
139          Please fill in all fields and click Register." );
140
141       if ( $iserror )
142       {
143          print( "<br /><span class = 'largeerror'>
144             Fields with * need to be filled in properly.</span>" );
145       } // end if
146
147       print( "<!-- post form data to form.php -->
148          <form method = 'post' action = 'dynamicForm.php'>
149          <img src = 'images/user.gif' alt = 'User' /><br />
150          <span class = 'prompt'>
151          Please fill out the fields below.<br /> </span>
152
153          <!-- create four text boxes for user input -->" );
154       foreach ( $inputlist as $inputname => $inputalt )
155       {
156          $inputtext = $inputvalues[ $inputname ];
157
158          print( "<img src = 'images/$inputname.gif'
159             alt = '$inputalt' /><input type = 'text'
160             name = '$inputname' value = '" . $$inputname . "' />" );
161
162          if ( $formerrors[ ( $inputname )."error" ] == true )
163             print( "<span class = 'error'>*</span>" );
164
165          print( "<br />" );
166       } // end foreach
167
168       if ( $formerrors[ "phoneerror" ] )
169          print( "<span class = 'error'>" );
```

Fig. 19.21 | Dynamic form. (Part 4 of 7.)

```
170        else
171           print("<span class = 'smalltext'>");
172
173        print( "Must be in the form (555)555-5555
174           </span><br /><br />
175
176           <img src = 'images/downloads.gif'
177              alt = 'Publications' /><br />
178
179           <span class = 'prompt'>
180           Which book would you like information about?
181           </span><br />
182
183           <!-- create drop-down list containing book names -->
184           <select name = 'book'>" );
185
186        foreach ( $booklist as $currbook )
187        {
188           print( "<option" );
189
190           if ( ( $currbook == $book ) )
191              print( " selected = 'true'" );
192
193           print( ">$currbook</option>" );
194        } // end foreach
195
196        print( "</select><br /><br />
197           <img src = 'images/os.gif' alt = 'Operating System' />
198           <br /><span class = 'prompt'>
199           Which operating system are you currently using?
200           <br /></span>
201
202           <!-- create five radio buttons -->" );
203
204        $counter = 0;
205
206        foreach ( $systemlist as $currsystem )
207        {
208           print( "<input type = 'radio' name = 'os'
209              value = '$currsystem'" );
210
211           if ( $currsystem == $os )
212              print( "checked = 'checked'" );
213           elseif ( !$os && $counter == 0 )
214              print( "checked = 'checked'" );
215
216           print( " />$currsystem" );
217
218           // put a line break in list of operating systems
219           if ( $counter == 1 ) print( "<br />" );
220           ++$counter;
221        } // end foreach
222
```

Fig. 19.21 | Dynamic form. (Part 5 of 7.)

```
223                print( "<!-- create a submit button -->
224                   <br /><input type = 'submit' name = 'submit'
225                   value = 'Register' /></form></body></html>" );
226       ?><!-- end PHP script -->
```

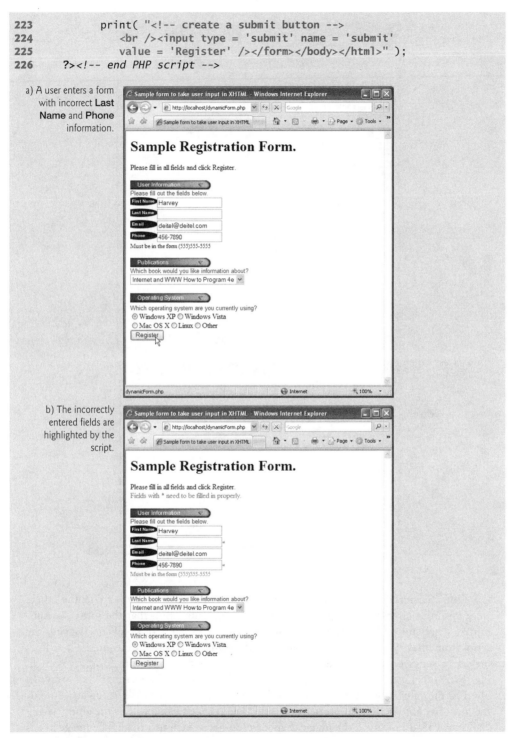

a) A user enters a form with incorrect **Last Name** and **Phone** information.

b) The incorrectly entered fields are highlighted by the script.

Fig. 19.21 | Dynamic form. (Part 6 of 7.)

c) The user fills in these fields correctly.

d) The information is submitted to the database and displayed on the screen.

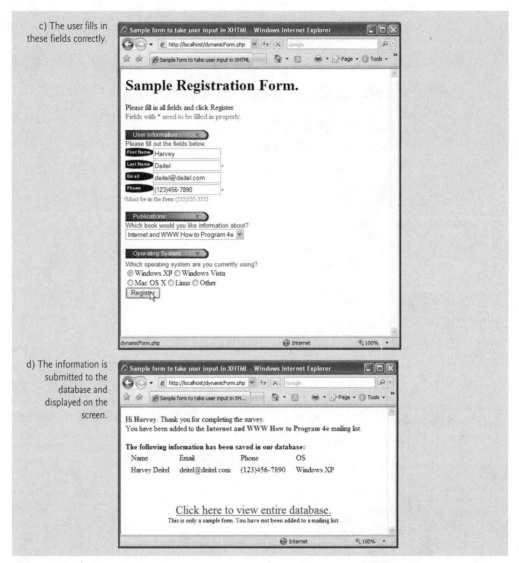

Fig. 19.21 | Dynamic form. (Part 7 of 7.)

Line 76 determines whether any errors were detected. If $iserror is false (i.e., there were no input errors), lines 79–133 display the page indicating that the form was submitted successfully. We'll say more about lines 79–133 later. If $iserror is true, the script from lines 79–133 is skipped, and the code from lines 138–224 executes. These lines include a series of print statements and conditionals to output the form, as seen in Fig. 19.21(a). Lines 154–166 iterate through each element in the $inputlist array. In line 156 the value of variable $inputtext is assigned to the text field's value attribute. If the form has not yet been submitted, variable $inputtext's value will be the empty string "". Lines 158–159 output the image that corresponds to each text field. The image src is set to 'images/$inputname.gif' because the images are stored in the images directory, and each image shares the name of its corresponding text field and ends with the .gif extension. Lines 159–160 initialize the input text field. The text field's name attribute is set to variable $inputname.

In line 160 we encounter the **$$variable** notation for specifying a *variable variable*. A variable variable allows the code to reference variables dynamically. You can use this expression to obtain the value of the variable whose name is equal to the value of $*variable*. PHP first determines the value of $*variable*, then appends this value to the leading $ to form the identifier of the variable you wish to reference dynamically. (The expression $$*variable* can also be written as ${$*variable*} to convey this procedure.) For example, in lines 154–166, we write $$inputname to reference the value of each form-field variable. During the iteration of the loop, $inputname contains the value "email". Therefore, PHP replaces $inputname in the expression $$inputname with the string "email", forming the expression ${"email"}. The entire expression then evaluates to the value of the variable $email. Thus, the variable $email, which stores the value of the e-mail text field after the form has been submitted, is dynamically referenced. This dynamic variable reference is added to the string as the value of the input field (using the concatenation operator) to maintain data over multiple submissions of the form.

Lines 162–163 add a red asterisk next to the text input fields that were filled out incorrectly. Lines 168–169 color the phone instructions red if the user entered an invalid phone number by assigning the class error to the span tag surrounding the text.

Lines 186–194 and 206–221 generate options for the book drop-down list and operating-system radio buttons, respectively. Lines 190–191 and 211–214 ensure that the previously selected or checked element (if one exists) remains selected or checked over multiple attempts to correctly fill out the form. If any book was previously selected, lines 190–191 add the string selected = 'true' to its option tag. Lines 211–214 select an operating system radio button under two conditions. First, lines 211–212 select the button if it was previously selected, before an unsuccessful submit operation. Lines 213–214 select the first radio button only if the form has not yet been submitted ($os is not set) and it is the first radio button. This ensures that the form cannot be submitted without a radio button selected.

If the form has been filled out correctly, lines 79–98 place the form information in the MySQL database MailingList using an INSERT statement. Line 82 uses the **quote-meta** function to insert a backslash (\) before any special characters in the passed string. We must use this function so that MySQL does not interpret the parentheses in the phone number as having a special meaning aside from being part of a value to insert into the database. Lines 102–133 generate the web page indicating a successful form submission, which also provides a link to formDatabase.php (Fig. 19.22). This script displays the contents of the MailingList database.

```
1   <?php print( '<?xml version = "1.0" encoding = "utf-8"?>' ) ?>
2   <!DOCTYPE html PUBLIC "-//W3C//DTD XHTML 1.0 Strict//EN"
3      "http://www.w3.org/TR/xhtml1/DTD/xhtml1-strict.dtd">
4
5   <!-- Fig. 19.22: formDatabase.php -->
6   <!-- Displaying the MailingList database. -->
```

Fig. 19.22 | Displaying the MailingList database. (Part 1 of 3.)

```
7    <html xmlns = "http://www.w3.org/1999/xhtml">
8       <head>
9          <title>Search Results</title>
10         <style type = "text/css">
11            body  { font-family: arial, sans-serif;
12                    background-color: #F0E68C }
13            h3    { color: blue }
14            table { background-color: #ADD8E6 }
15            td    { padding-top: 2px;
16                    padding-bottom: 2px;
17                    padding-left: 4px;
18                    padding-right: 4px;
19                    border-width: 1px;
20                    border-style: inset }
21         </style>
22      </head>
23      <body>
24         <?php
25            extract( $_POST );
26
27            // build SELECT query
28            $query = "SELECT * FROM contacts";
29
30            // Connect to MySQL
31            if ( !( $database = mysql_connect( "localhost",
32               "iw3htp4", "iw3htp4" ) ) )
33               die( "Could not connect to database </body></html>" );
34
35            // open MailingList database
36            if ( !mysql_select_db( "MailingList", $database ) )
37               die( "Could not open MailingList database </body></html>" );
38
39            // query MailingList database
40            if ( !( $result = mysql_query( $query, $database ) ) )
41            {
42               print( "Could not execute query! <br />" );
43               die( mysql_error() . "</body></html>" );
44            } // end if
45         ?><!-- end PHP script -->
46
47         <h3>Mailing List Contacts</h3>
48         <table>
49            <tr>
50               <td>ID</td>
51               <td>Last Name</td>
52               <td>First Name</td>
53               <td>E-mail Address</td>
54               <td>Phone Number</td>
55               <td>Book</td>
56               <td>Operating System</td>
57            </tr>
58            <?php
```

Fig. 19.22 | Displaying the MailingList database. (Part 2 of 3.)

```
59          // fetch each record in result set
60          for ( $counter = 0; $row = mysql_fetch_row( $result );
61             $counter++ )
62          {
63             // build table to display results
64             print( "<tr>" );
65
66             foreach ( $row as $key => $value )
67                print( "<td>$value</td>" );
68
69             print( "</tr>" );
70          } // end for
71
72          mysql_close( $database );
73       ?><!-- end PHP script -->
74    </table>
75  </body>
76 </html>
```

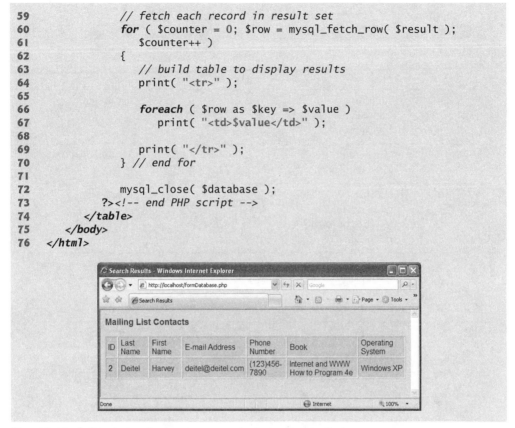

Fig. 19.22 | Displaying the MailingList database. (Part 3 of 3.)

19.8 Operator Precedence Chart

This section contains the operator precedence chart for PHP. In Fig. 19.23, the operators are shown from top to bottom in decreasing order of precedence.

Operator	Type	Associativity
new	constructor	none
[]	subscript	right to left
~ ! ++ -- - @	bitwise not not increment decrement unary negative error control	right to left

Fig. 19.23 | PHP operator precedence and associativity. (Part I of 2.)

Operator	Type	Associativity
* / %	multiplication division modulus	left to right
+ - .	addition subtraction concatenation	left to right
<< >>	bitwise shift left bitwise shift right	left to right
< > <= >=	less than greater than less than or equal greater than or equal	none
== != === !==	equal not equal identical not identical	none
&	bitwise AND	left to right
^	bitwise XOR	left to right
|	bitwise OR	left to right
&&	logical AND	left to right
||	logical OR	left to right
= += -= *= /= &= |= ^= .= <<= >>=	assignment addition assignment subtraction assignment multiplication assignment division assignment bitwise AND assignment bitwise OR assignment bitwise exclusive OR assignment concatenation assignment bitwise shift left assignment bitwise shift right assignment	left to right
and	logical AND	left to right
xor	exclusive OR	left to right
or	logical OR	left to right
,	list	left to right

Fig. 19.23 | PHP operator precedence and associativity. (Part 2 of 2.)

19.9 Web Resources

www.deitel.com/PHP/

The Deitel PHP Resource Center contains links to some of the best PHP information on the web. There you'll find categorized links to PHP tools, code generators, forums, books, libraries, frameworks and more. Also check out the tutorials for all skill levels, from introductory to advanced. Be sure to visit the related Resource Centers on XHTML (www.deitel.com/xhtml/) and CSS 2.1 (www.deitel.com/css21/).

20

Ruby on Rails

OBJECTIVES

In this chapter you will learn:

- Basic Ruby programming.
- How to use the Rails framework.
- The Model-View-Controller paradigm.
- How to use `ActiveRecord` to model a database.
- How to construct web applications that interact with a database.
- How to create a web-based message forum.
- How to develop Ajax-enabled applications in Ruby on Rails.
- How to use the built-in Script.aculo.us library to add visual effects to your programs.

Convention is the ruler of all.
—Pindar

Where the telescope ends, the microscope begins. Which of the two has the grander view?
—Victor Hugo

… We grow more partial for the observer's sake.
—Alexander Pope

Those who cannot remember the past are condemned to repeat it.
—George Santayana

Let's look at the record.
—Alfred Emanuel Smith

All that matters is that the miraculous become the norm.
—Henry Miller

20.1 Introduction

Ruby on Rails (also known as *RoR* or just *Rails*) is a framework for developing data-driven web applications using the *Ruby* scripting language. A *web framework* is a set of libraries and useful tools that can be used to build dynamic web applications. Ruby on Rails is different from most other programming languages because it takes advantage of many conventions to reduce development time. If you follow these conventions, the Rails framework generates substantial functionality and perform many tasks for you. Ruby on Rails has built-in libraries for performing common web development tasks, such as interacting with a database, sending mass e-mails to clients or generating web services. In addition, Rails has built-in libraries that provide Ajax functionality (discussed in Chapter 13), to improve the user experience. Rails is quickly becoming a popular web development environment.

Ruby on Rails was created by David Heinemeier Hansson of the company 37Signals. After developing Basecamp, a web application written in Ruby that allows a business to organize multiple projects. Hansson extracted the reusable components to create the Rails framework. Since then, many developers have enhanced the Rails framework. For more information, visit our Ruby on Rails Resource Center at `www.deitel.com/RubyOnRails`. Full documentation of the Rails Framework can be found at `api.rubyonrails.org`.

20.2 Ruby

The first several examples are simple command-line programs that demonstrate fundamental Ruby programming concepts. The Ruby scripting language was developed by Yukihiro "Matz" Matsumoto in 1995 to be a flexible, object-oriented scripting language. Ruby's syntax and conventions are intuitive—they attempt to mimic the way a developer thinks. Ruby is an interpreted language.

Installing Instant Rails

To run the Ruby scripts in this chapter, Ruby must first be installed on your system. In this chapter we use the *Instant Rails* package to run our applications. Instant Rails includes Ruby, Rails, MySQL, Apache, PHP and other components necessary to create and run Rails applications. PHP is used specifically for **phpMyAdmin**, a web interface to MySQL. Instant Rails is a stand-alone Rails development and testing environment.

To install Instant Rails, download Instant Rails 1.7 from //rubyforge.org/frs/ ?group_id=904. Once the zip file is downloaded, extract its contents to a folder on your hard drive.

After installing Instant Rails, make sure that you stop any existing web servers on your computer such as IIS or Apache— Instant Rails needs port 80 to be available for using **phpMyAdmin** to administer MySQL. If you are not using this tool then you don't need to stop other web servers on your computer. To run Instant Rails, navigate to the folder where you extracted the contents of the zip file and run **InstantRails.exe**. You should see a window similar to Fig. 20.1.

If you are using Mac OS X, there is an application similar to Instant Rails called Locomotive. You can download Locomotive from locomotive.raaum.org. Linux users might want to try LinRails (available from linrails.thembid.com). Another program useful for Rails development is Aptana Radrails—a free, open-source IDE. Radrails can be downloaded from www.aptana.com/download_rails_rdt.php.

Fig. 20.1 | Instant Rails application running.

Printing a Line of Text

Figure 20.2 presents a simple Ruby program that prints the text "Welcome to Ruby!". Lines 1–2 are single-line comments that instruct the interpreter to ignore everything on the current line following the # symbol. Line 3 uses the method *puts* that takes a single parameter (a string) and prints the text to the terminal, followed by a newline. A method can have parentheses surrounding its parameters, but this is not typical in Ruby unless they are used to avoid ambiguity. A line of Ruby code does not have to end with a semicolon, although one can be placed there. The puts method automatically adds a newline escape sequence (\n) at the end of the string if one is not explicitly added.

```
1   # Fig. 20.2: welcome.rb
2   # Simple Ruby program.
3   puts "Welcome to Ruby!"
```

Fig. 20.2 | Simple Ruby program. (Part 1 of 2.)

```
Welcome to Ruby!
```

Fig. 20.2 | Simple Ruby program. (Part 2 of 2.)

Running a Ruby Script

A Ruby script can be run several ways. One is to use the *Ruby interpreter*. To do so, launch Instant Rails, click the **I** button in the top-left corner and select **Rails Applications > Open Ruby Console Window** from the drop-down menu (see Fig. 20.3).

In the console, use the cd command to navigate to the directory where welcome.rb is located, then enter ruby welcome.rb. Figure 20.4 shows the Ruby interpreter executing the Ruby file from Fig. 20.2 in the **Ruby Console** window.

Ruby can also execute interactively, using *IRB (Interactive Ruby)*. IRB interprets Ruby code statement by statement. This is useful for debugging code and for experimenting with Ruby functionality. IRB can be run through Instant Rails by typing IRB in the Ruby Console. Figure 20.5 shows simple Ruby statements interpreted in IRB.

The code after the prompt (irb(main):001:0>) shows the statement that was executed using the Ruby interpreter in Fig. 20.4. It sends the same string to the output, then returns the value of method puts, which is nil, an object that represents nothing in Ruby.

Fig. 20.3 | Launching the Ruby Interpreter in Instant Rails.

Fig. 20.4 | Using the Ruby interpreter to run a simple Ruby script.

Fig. 20.5 | Using Interactive Ruby to execute Ruby statements.

The code after the second IRB prompt sends the arithmetic expression 2+2 to the interpreter, which evaluates the expression and returns 4. The code after the third prompt requests the class type of the number 4. The interpreter returns *Fixnum*—a class that represents integers in Ruby. Last, the code after the fourth prompt calls the ceil method of 4.5 to round the number up to the next whole-number value. The IRB returns 5. Type exit to quit IRB.

Variables and Data Types in Ruby

Like most scripting languages, Ruby uses *dynamic typing*, which allows changes to a variable's type during runtime. There are several variable types in Ruby, including String and Fixnum. Everything is an object in Ruby, so you can call methods on any piece of data. Figure 20.6 invokes methods on numeric and string data.

Line 3 initializes the variable myvar. Setting myvar to 7.5 temporarily makes it a Float object. The highlighted portion of line 4 is an example of *interpolation* in Ruby. It inserts the object value of the variable inside the braces into the string. Lines 6 and 12 invoke the

```ruby
 1  # Fig. 20.6: types.rb
 2  # Method calls on numeric and string data
 3  myvar = 5.7 # binds the value 5.7 to myvar
 4  puts "The value of myvar is #{myvar}"
 5
 6  myvar = myvar.round # return a rounded value Fixnum
 7  puts "The rounded value of myvar is #{myvar}"
 8
 9  myvar = 5.4 # bind the value 5.4 to myvar
10  puts "The value of myvar is #{myvar}"
11
12  myvar = myvar.round # return a rounded value Fixnum
13  puts "The rounded value of myvar is #{myvar}"
14
15  myvar = "mystring" # bind the value 'mystring' to myvar
16  puts "The value of myvar is '#{myvar}'"
17
18  myvar = myvar.capitalize # capitalize the value of myvar
19  puts "The capitalized form of myvar is '#{myvar}'"
20
21  myvar = "my string" # bind the value 'my string' to myvar
22  puts "The value of myvar is '#{myvar}'"
23
24  myvar = myvar.capitalize # capitalize the value of myvar
25  puts "The capitalized form of myvar is '#{myvar}'"
```

```
The value of myvar is 5.7
The rounded value of myvar is 6
The value of myvar is 5.4
The rounded value of myvar is 5
The value of myvar is 'mystring'
The capitalized form of myvar is 'Mystring'
The value of myvar is 'my string'
The capitalized form of myvar is 'My string'
```

Fig. 20.6 | Method calls on numeric and string data.

round method on the Float object to demonstrate rounding a value up or down, respectively. The type of myvar changes to String in line 15. Lines 18 and 24 changes the first letter of the first word of this String by calling its capitalize method. A list of the available methods for the Ruby types can be found at www.ruby-doc.org/core/.

Using Arrays and Hashes

Ruby provides both **Arrays** and **Hashes** to store data. Each stores a list of objects. In an Array, indices of type Fixnum are used to select an Object from the Array. In a Hash, Objects are mapped to other Objects in key/value pairs. Figure 20.7 shows an example of using both an Array and a Hash to store information.

Line 3 instantiates a Ruby Array. Array elements can be accessed by their index number in square brackets (line 5). You may also traverse Arrays backward by using negative number indices. For example line 6 outputs the last array element. Line 8 reverses the elements in the Array with method **reverse!**. The exclamation point after the method name is a Ruby convention indicating that the object on which the method is called will be modified. Method reverse without an exclamation point returns a copy of the original array with its elements reversed. Many Ruby methods follow this convention.

Line 14 is an example of a Hash. The key/value pairs are separated by commas, and each key points to its corresponding value using the => operator. The value of a hash element can be found by passing in the key in square brackets, as shown in lines 16–17.

```
1   # Fig. 20.7: arraysAndHashes.rb
2   # Arrays and hashes in Ruby.
3   fruits = [ "mango", "orange",  "apple", "pear" ] # create an array
4   puts "The length of the fruits array is #{fruits.length}" # output length
5   puts "The first fruit is #{fruits[0]}" # output first element
6   puts "The last fruit is #{fruits[-1]}\n\n" # output last element
7
8   fruits.reverse! # reverse the order of the elements in the fruits array
9   puts "The length of the fruits array is #{fruits.length}" # output length
10  puts "The first fruit is #{fruits[0]}" # output first element
11  puts "The last fruit is #{fruits[-1]}\n\n" # output last element
12
13  # a simple hash
14  food = { "mango" => "fruit", "banana" => "fruit", "onion" => "vegetable" }
15  puts "The length of the food hash is #{food.length}" # output length
16  puts "A mango is a #{food["mango"]}" # output value of key mango
17  puts "An onion is a #{food["onion"]}" # output value of key onion
```

```
The length of the fruits array is 4
The first fruit is mango
the last fruit is pear

The length of the fruits array is 4
The first fruit is pear
the last fruit is mango

The length of the food hash is 3
A mango is a fruit
An onion is a vegetable
```

Fig. 20.7 | Arrays and hashes in Ruby.

Conditionals, Loops and Code Blocks

Like any other programming language, Ruby provides selection and repetition statements. In addition, Ruby has support for *code blocks*—groupings of Ruby statements that can be passed to a method as an argument. Figure 20.8 shows a program that returns a student's letter grade based on a numerical grade.

Lines 3–15 of Fig. 20.8 contain a Ruby method definition. Methods must be defined in a program before they are used. All methods start with *def* and end with *end*. Methods do not have to specify parameter types, but they must specify the name of each parameter. Lines 4–14 show a nested if...elsif...else statement that returns an appropriate letter grade based on the numeric value the method receives as an argument. If a method does not include an explicit return statement Ruby returns the last value or variable it encounters when executing the function.

Line 17 defines a Hash of students and their numeric grades. Lines 19–21 show an example of a code block. A method may have a parameter containing a block of code, such as the each method. The block of code appears in brackets directly after the method call. A code block is similar to a method, in that parameters can be passed into it. The parameters for a code block are given between pipe characters (|) and are separated by commas. The parameters are followed immediately by the code block's statements. The code block in lines 19–21 outputs a line of text based on the key/value pair of every key in the Hash.

```ruby
1   # Fig. 20.8: controlStatements.rb
2   # Conditionals, loops, and codeblocks.
3   def letter_grade( x ) # define method letterGrade
4      if x >= 90 # if x is greater than or equal to 90
5         "A" # grade is A
6      elsif x >= 80 # if x is greater than or equal to 80
7         "B" # grade is B
8      elsif x >= 70 # if x is greater than or equal to 70
9         "C" # grade is C
10     elsif x >= 60 # if x is greater than or equal to 60
11        "D" # grade is D
12     else # grade is less than 60
13        "F" # grade is F
14     end # if
15  end # method letterGrade
16
17  students = { "John" => 100, "Sue" => 92, "Tom" => 56, "Jill" => 80 }
18
19  students.each() { |key, value| # display the letter grade for each student
20     puts "#{key} received a #{letter_grade(value)}"
21  } # end codeblock
```

```
Jill received a B
Sue received a A
John received a A
Tom received a F
```

Fig. 20.8 | Conditionals, loops and codeblocks.

Classes

You can create your own classes and instantiate objects. Classes enable you to encapsulate methods and data. Figure 20.9 shows a class named Point that stores *x-y* coordinates.

Line 3 begins the class definition with the keyword class followed by the class name. The initialize method (lines 7–11), like constructors in other object-oriented languages, is used to declare and initialize an object's data. When each instance of a class maintains its own copy of a variable, the variable is known as an ***instance variable***. Lines 8–9 use the @ symbol to define the instance variables x and y. Classes can also have ***class variables*** that are shared by all copies of a class. Class variables always begin with @@ (line 4) and are visible to all instances of the class in which they are defined. Line 10 increments @@num_points every time a new Point is defined.

You can create new classes by inheriting from existing ones and providing your own additional or enhanced functionality. Lines 14–16 override the inherited ***to_s method***, which is a method of all Ruby objects. When an object is concatenated with a string, the to_s method is implicitly called to convert the object to its string representation. Class Point's to_s method for the Point class returns a string containing the *x-y* coordinates.

```ruby
1   # Fig. 20.9: Classes.rb
2   # A Ruby class.
3   class Point
4      @@num_points = 0 # initialize numPoints
5
6      # create a new Point object
7      def initialize(x, y)
8         @x = x # initialize x-coordinate
9         @y = y # initialize y-coordinate
10        @@num_points +=1  # increment numPoints counter
11     end # method initialize
12
13     # return a string containing the x-y values
14     def to_s
15        return "x: #{@x}; y: #{@y}"
16     end # method to_s
17
18     # return how many Points have been instantiated
19     def num_points
20        return @@num_points
21     end # method numPoints
22  end # class Point
23
24  p = Point.new( 8, 9 ) # instantiate a Point
25  q = Point.new( 1, 1 ) # instantiate another Point
26  puts "the value of p is '#{p}'"
27  puts "the value of q is '#{q}'"
28  puts "the number of points created is #{p.num_points}"
```

```
the value of p is 'x: 8; y: 9'
the value of q is 'x: 1; y: 1'
the number of points created is 2
```

Fig. 20.9 | A Ruby class.

20.3 Rails Framework

While users have benefitted from the rise of database-driven web applications, web developers have had to implement rich functionality with technology that was not designed for this purpose. The Rails framework combines the simplicity of Ruby with the ability to rapidly develop database-driven web applications.

Model-View-Controller

Ruby on Rails is built on the philosophies of *Convention over Configuration* and *Don't Repeat Yourself (DRY)*. If you follow certain programming idioms, your applications will require minimal configuration, and Rails will generate substantial portions of your web applications for you. One of these conventions is using the *Model-View-Controller (MVC)* design pattern, which splits the application into the business logic aspects handled by the model and the design aspects handled by the view. The controller handles client requests by obtaining information from the model and rendering it to the view.

The MVC architectural pattern separates application data (contained in the *model*) from graphical presentation components (the *view*) and input-processing logic (the *controller*). Figure 20.10 shows the relationships between components in MVC.

The controller implements logic for processing user input. The model contains application data, and the view presents the data from the model. When a user provides input, the controller modifies the model with the given input. When the model changes, the controller notifies the view so that it can update its presentation with the changed data.

MVC does not restrict an application to a single view and a single controller. In a more sophisticated program, there might be two views of a document model. One view might display an outline of the document and the other might display the complete document. An application also might implement multiple controllers—one for handling keyboard input and another for handling mouse selections. If either controller makes a change in the model, both the outline view and the print-preview window will show the change immediately when the controller notifies all views of changes.

The primary benefit to the MVC architectural pattern is that developers can modify each component individually without having to modify the others. For example, developers could modify the view that displays the document outline without having to modify either the model or other views or controllers.

Fig. 20.10 | Model-View-Controller architecture.

Overview

In the following examples, we show how to create a Ruby on Rails application. We show how a controller can be used to send information to the client directly, and how a controller can render a view for a cleaner and more organized design. We then show how to set up a database in a Ruby on Rails application. Finally, we show how to generate a model to be the front end of a database in a dynamic web application.

Creating a Rails Application

The Instant Rails package comes with a full install of Rails that includes ActiveRecord, ActionView, and ActionController. *ActiveRecord* is used to map a database table to an Object. *ActionView* is a set of helper methods to modify user interfaces. *ActionController* is a set of helper methods to create controllers. To generate an empty Rails application in Instant Rails, click the **I** button and select **Rails Applications > Manage Rails Applications...** from the drop-down menu to display the **Rails Applications** window. In that window click the **Create New Rails App...** button. In the console that appears, type rails *Application Name* at the command line to create a directory named *Application Name* with a prebuilt directory structure inside. For the first example, use Welcome as the application name. Figure 20.11 shows the directory structure that is automatically generated by Rails. The directories that we'll be primarily concerned with are app\controllers, app\models, and app\views.

Fig. 20.11 | Rails directory structure for a new Rails application.

20.4 **ActionController** and **ActionView**

Ruby on Rails has two classes that work together to process a client request and render a view. These classes are `ActionController` and `ActionView`.

Rails Controller

To generate a controller in Rails, you can use the built-in `Controller` generator. To do that, open the **Ruby Console** window and navigate to the application directory by typing in:

> cd *pathToInstantRails*\rails_apps*applicationName*

To generate a controller for the welcome application type:

> ruby script/generate controller Welcome

This creates several files including `welcome_controller.rb`, which contains a class named `WelcomeController`. Figure 20.12 shows a controller for our Welcome example containing only one method.

Line 3 defines a class `WelcomeController` that inherits from `ApplicationController`. `ApplicationController` inherits from `ActionController::Base`, which provides all of the default functionality for a controller. The method in lines 5–7 renders text in XHTML format to the browser using the `render` method

Line 6 specifies the `text` parameter of the render variable using a *ruby symbol*. Symbols are identifiers preceded by a colon that have a particular value or variable associated with them. When specifying a parameter in a method the notation is as follows:

> *parameter_symbol* => *parameter_value*

```
1   # Fig. 20.12: app/controllers/welcome_controller.rb
2   # Simple controller that renders a message on a web page.
3   class WelcomeController < ApplicationController
4      # render text in page
5      def index
6         render :text => "Welcome to Ruby on Rails!"
7      end # method index
8   end # class WelcomeController
```

Fig. 20.12 | Simple controller that renders a message on the web page.

Running Ruby on Rails

A Ruby on Rails application must be run from a web server. In addition to Apache, Instant Rails comes with a built-in web server named Mongrel, which is easy to use to test Rails applications on the local machine. You can start the Mongrel server through Instant Rails by going to the **Rails Application** window, selecting the **Welcome** application from the list and clicking the **Start with Mongrel** button (Fig. 20.13).

One important feature of Rails is its URL mapping ability. Rails automatically sets up your web application in a tree structure, where the controller's name in lowercase is the directory, and the method name is the subdirectory. Since the controller name is Welcome and the method name is index, the URL to display the text in Figure 20.12 is http://localhost:3000/welcome/index. Notice in the screen capture of Figure 20.12 that the URL is simply http://localhost:3000/welcome. The default action called on any controller is the one specified by the method index. So, you do not need to explicitly invoke the index in the URL to render the text in line 6.

Fig. 20.13 | Starting the Mongrel web server.

Rendering a View

When generating output, a controller usually renders a *template*—an XHTML document with embedded Ruby that has the .rhtml filename extension. [*Note:* The next version of Rails will use the extension .html.erb rather than .rhtml.] The embedded Ruby comes from a library named erb. A method in a controller will automatically render a view with the same name by default. For example, an empty hello method would look for a hello.rhtml view to render. Fig. 20.14 is the Welcome controller with a hello method added. The index method has been removed for simplicity.

The server_software method (line 6) is called on the *request object*—an object that contains all of the environment variables and other information for that web page. The method *server_software* returns the name of the server that is running the web application. This name is stored in an instance variable that will be used by the view. Our hello method looks for a hello.rhtml file in the web application's app/views/welcome directory. Figure 20.15 shows a sample hello.rhtml file.

The view consists mostly of XHTML. The erb is shown in line 14, surrounded by <%= and %> tags. Everything between these tags is parsed as Ruby code and formatted as text. Ruby delimiters without an equals sign—<% %>—represents statements to execute as Ruby code but not formatted as text. The @server_name variable is passed in directly from the controller in the view. To run this application, modify the welcome.rb controller file to look like Figure 20.14. Then go to the /app/views/welcome directory, create the hello.rhtml file in Fig. 20.15. Run the welcome application on the Mongrel server (if it is not already running) and direct your browser to the URL http://localhost:3000/welcome/hello.

```
1   # Fig. 20.14: app/controllers/welcome_controller.rb
2   # Simple controller that passes a parameter to the view.
3   class WelcomeController < ApplicationController
4      # set server_name to server information
5      def hello
6         @server_name = request.server_software # retrieve software of server
7      end # method hello
8   end # class WelcomeController
```

Fig. 20.14 | Simple controller that passes a parameter to the view.

```
1   <?xml version = "1.0" encoding = "utf-8"?>
2   <!DOCTYPE html PUBLIC "-//W3C//DTD XHTML 1.0 Strict//EN"
3      "http://www.w3.org/TR/xhtml1/DTD/xhtml1-strict.dtd">
4
5   <!-- Fig. 20.15: app/views/welcome/hello.rhtml -->
6   <!-- View that displays the server name. -->
7   <html xmlns = "http://www.w3.org/1999/xhtml">
8   <head>
9      <title>hello</title>
10  </head>
11  <body style = "background-color: lightyellow">
12     <strong>Hello from the view!</strong><br />
13     The server you are coming from is
14     <em><%= @server_name %></em>
15  </body>
16  </html>
```

Fig. 20.15 | View that displays the name of the server.

Using a Layout

Often, information spans multiple web pages that could be viewed as a header or footer. Rails allows you to add headers and footers with a *layout*—a master view that is displayed by every method in a controller. A layout can refer to a template of the method that is being called, using *yield*. A layout has the same name as the controller, and is placed in the app/views/layouts directory. Figure 20.16 is a layout for the Welcome controller. To add a layout to the application create a welcome.rhtml file in the apps/views/layouts directory. To run this application, re-load the page from Fig. 20.15.

Line 9 invokes the **action_name** method on the controller object. This displays the name of the method that is currently being called in the controller. Instance variables defined in the controller are copied to both the layout and the view that the layout renders. Line 14 is a placeholder for the view content (hello.rhtml in this example) that is specific to the action called in the controller.

```
1    <?xml version = "1.0" encoding = "utf-8"?>
2    <!DOCTYPE html PUBLIC "-//W3C//DTD XHTML 1.0 Strict//EN"
3       "http://www.w3.org/TR/xhtml1/DTD/xhtml1-strict.dtd">
4
5    <!-- Fig. 20.16: app/views/layouts/welcome.rhtml -->
6    <!-- Layout that displays a greeting. -->
7    <html xmlns = "http://www.w3.org/1999/xhtml">
8    <head>
9       <title><%= controller.action_name %></title>
10   </head>
11   <body style = "background-color: lightyellow">
12      Hello from the Layout!<br />
13      <hr />
14      <%= yield %> <!-- render template -->
15   </body>
16   </html>
```

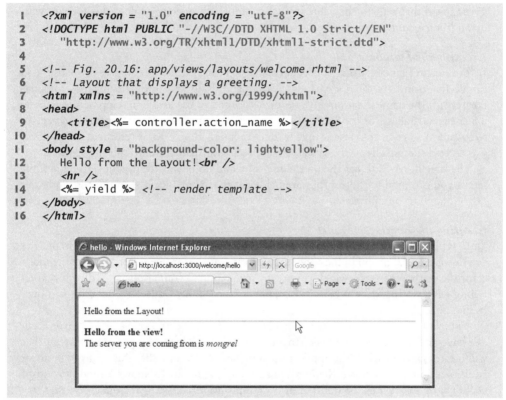

Fig. 20.16 | Layout that displays a greeting.

20.5 A Database-Driven Web Application

The third tier of a typical Rails application—the model—manages the data used in the application. In this section, we set up a database and build a fully functional web application using the ActionView and ActionController classes that we introduced in Section 20.4. We create an application that allows the user to browse and edit an employee list. To create this application's structure, type rails Employees in the **Ruby Console** window.

Object Relational Mapping

Rails makes extensive use of *Object-Relational Mapping (ORM)* in its web framework. ORM maps a table to application objects. The objects that Rails uses to encapsulate a database inherit from *ActiveRecord*. By using ActiveRecord and Rails conventions, you can avoid a lot of explicit configuration.

One ActiveRecord convention is that every model that extends ActiveRecord::Base in an application represents a table in a database. The table that the model represents is, by convention, the lowercase, pluralized form of the model. For example, if there were a messages table in your database, Message would be the name of the model representing it. ActiveRecord follows many standard English pluralization rules as well, which means that a Person model would automatically correspond to a people table. Furthermore, if a people table has a first_name column, the Person model would have a method named first_name that returns the value in that column. ActiveRecord does this for you with no additional configuration.

Creating the Database
Before creating a model using ActiveRecord, we need to create the database it will use. You can do that using MySQL's mysqladmin command. Rails will automatically look for a database with the name *applicationName*_development to use as the development database. To create a database for the Employees application, launch the **Ruby Console** and type in mysqladmin -u root create employees_development. If no error is returned, the database was created successfully in the mysql/data directory of your InstantRails installation.

By default MySQL has the user name root and no password. If your settings are different you can modify the appropriate fields database.yml, located in the config folder in your application directory.

Creating the Employee Model
Since Rails separates the model from the rest of the application, we simply need to put the Employee class definition in the models directory. Rails uses a generator to create the model for the employees table, which you use by navigating to your application directory then typing ruby script/generate model employee in the **Ruby Console**. The result is shown in Fig. 20.17.

The last line the console returns is create db/migrate/001_create_employees.rb. We have not yet created a table employees, so Ruby automatically generates a script that will create this table when the application launches. We can modify this script to perform additional initial changes to the employees table. Figure 20.18 shows a modification of 001_create_employees.rb (located in your application's db/migrate directory) that creates the table and adds three records to it.

ActiveRecord has a special feature called Migration, which allows you to preform database operations within Rails. Each object that inherits from ActiveRecord::Migra-

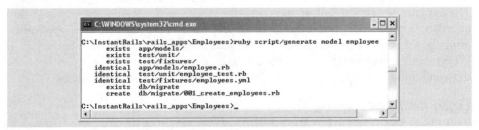

Fig. 20.17 | Creating a model in the Ruby Console.

```
 1   # Fig. 20.18: db/migrate/001_create_employees.rb
 2   # Database migration script modified to add data to the table
 3   class CreateEmployees < ActiveRecord::Migration
 4      # create the table with three columns and insert some rows.
 5      def self.up
 6         create_table  :employees do |t|
 7            t.column :first_name, :string
 8            t.column :last_name, :string
 9            t.column :job_title, :string
10         end # do block
11
12         Employee.create :first_name => "Sue", :last_name => "Green",
13            :job_title => "Programmer"
14         Employee.create :first_name => "Meg", :last_name => "Gold",
15            :job_title => "Programmer"
16         Employee.create :first_name => "John", :last_name => "Gray",
17            :job_title => "Programmer"
18      end # method self.up
19
20      # reverse the migration, delete the table that was created
21      def self.down
22         drop_table :employees
23      end # method self.down
24   end # class CreateEmployees
```

Fig. 20.18 | Database migration script modified to add data to the table.

tion must implement two methods—self.up (lines 5–18), which preforms a set of database operations, and self.down (lines 21–23), which reverses the database operations performed in self.up. In this case self.up creates the table with three columns and adds data to it, and self.down deletes the table. Line 6 calls the create_table function passing as a parameter a code block, inside the do, containing the table's column names and types. Lines 12–17 use ActiveRecord's built in create method to add data to the Employees table. ActiveRecord has built-in functionality for many create, retrieve, update, and destroy methods—known in Rails as *CRUD*. These methods represent the trivial operations that you would want to do with a database.

We can execute the migration using Ruby's rake command. To do so open up the **Ruby Console**, navigate to your application's directory and type rake db:migrate. This command will call the self.up method of all the migrations located in your db/migrate directory. If you ever want to roll back the migrations you can type in rake db:migrate VERSION=0, which calls each migration's self.down method. Specifying a version number other than 0 will call the self.down method of all the migrations whose number is greater then the version number.

Common Programming Error 20.1

If the code that comes after the creation of the table in the self.up is erroneous, the migration will fail, and will not be able to execute again because the table will already exist. Also, Rails will not have marked the migration as successfully completed, so the version will still be 0 and the migration cannot be rolled back. One way to prevent this problem is to force the table to be dropped every time before creating it. Another solution is splitting up the migration into smaller discrete migrations, one to create the table and another to insert data in the table.

Because our model will never be modified by the application, we do not need to add any functionality to it. Figure 20.19, which represents the employee.rb file located in the app/Models directory, contains all the code that is needed to integrate the employees database table into the application.

```
1   # Fig. 20.19: employee.rb
2   # Generated code for an Employee Model.
3   class Employee < ActiveRecord::Base
4   end # class Employee
```

Fig. 20.19 | Generated code for an Employee model.

Employee Controller

Next, create the controller with the ruby script/generate controller employees command as shown in Section 20.4. Figure 20.20 shows the example controller for the Employee application. Line 4 calls the *scaffold method*. This is a powerful tool that automatically creates CRUD functionality. It creates methods such as new, edit and list so you don't have to create them yourself. It also defines default views for these methods that are rendered when each method is called. You can override the default functionality by defining your own methods. If you override all the CRUD methods you can delete the scaffold method. When you override a method, you must also create the corresponding view. Since we will not modify the new method created by the scaffold you can see the new method's view with the URL http://localhost:3000/employee/new (Figure 20.21). Line 7–9 override the list method. Line 8 queries the database and returns a list of all of the Employee objects, which gets stored in an @employees instance array. This data will be passed to the view.

The list View

The list template is rendered by the list method from the EmployeeController. Code for the list template is shown in Fig. 20.22. This file should be placed in your application's app/views/employee directory. While most of it is just standard XHTML, lines 14–17 contain Ruby code that iterates through all the employees in the @employees array instance variable, and outputs each employee's first and last name (line 16). A for statement like this in a list view is common in database-driven web applications.

```
1    # Fig. 20.20: app/controllers/employees_controller.rb
2    # Provides all of the functionality for the application.
3    class EmployeesController < ApplicationController
4        scaffold :employee  # create scaffold code for controller
5
6        # override scaffold list method
7        def list
8            @employees = Employee.find( :all )  # return an array of Employees
9        end # method list
10   end # class EmployeeController
```

Fig. 20.20 | Employee controller provides all of the functionality for the application.

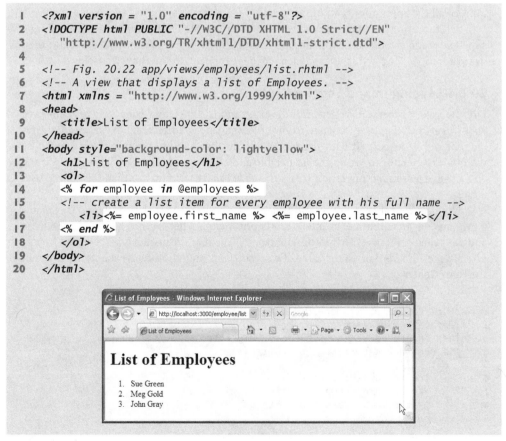

Fig. 20.21 | View of the new action when generated by the scaffold.

```
 1   <?xml version = "1.0" encoding = "utf-8"?>
 2   <!DOCTYPE html PUBLIC "-//W3C//DTD XHTML 1.0 Strict//EN"
 3      "http://www.w3.org/TR/xhtml1/DTD/xhtml1-strict.dtd">
 4
 5   <!-- Fig. 20.22 app/views/employees/list.rhtml -->
 6   <!-- A view that displays a list of Employees. -->
 7   <html xmlns = "http://www.w3.org/1999/xhtml">
 8   <head>
 9      <title>List of Employees</title>
10   </head>
11   <body style="background-color: lightyellow">
12      <h1>List of Employees</h1>
13      <ol>
14   <% for employee in @employees %>
15      <!-- create a list item for every employee with his full name -->
16         <li><%= employee.first_name %> <%= employee.last_name %></li>
17   <% end %>
18      </ol>
19   </body>
20   </html>
```

Fig. 20.22 | A view that displays a list of employees.

20.6 Case Study: Message Forum

Our next example uses Ruby on Rails to create a *message forum* website. Message forums enable users to discuss various topics. Common features of message forums include discussion groups, questions and answers and general comments. To see some popular message forums, visit messages.yahoo.com, web.eesite.com/forums and groups.google.com. In this example, users can post messages to several different forums, and administrators of the message forum site can create and delete forums.

Design

For our message forum application, we need a table containing all of the messages. This table will be called messages and will contain attributes such as id, title, author, e-mail, created_on (the date the message was created) and forum_id (the id of the forum to which the message belongs). In addition, we need a table of all the available forums. This table, called forums, will contain attributes such as id, name, administrator and created_on (the date the forum was created).

In our message forum application, we want to have the functionality to create and delete forums, but we don't want everyone who uses our application to be able to do this. Therefore, we'll also have a users table, which contains the username/password combinations of all the application's administrators.

Before we implement this design we must create the empty application called messageboard and the database for this application. Type in rails Messageboard and then mysqladmin -u root create messageboard_development in the **Ruby Console**.

20.6.1 Logging In and Logging Out

Use the model generator to generate the User model by typing ruby script/generate model User into the **Ruby Console** (from the Messageboard directory). Next, create the table that will be associated with the model. To do that, modify the migration created by the model generator to set up the users table and add some data to it. Figure 20.23 is the 001_create_users.rb migration (from the db/migrate directory) which sets up the user table.

The create_table function call (lines 6–9) specifies the table's columns. By default a primary key id column is created, so it is not included here. Lines 7–8 create the name and password columns with appropriate types. Note that the name has a limit of 11 characters. Line 11 adds data to the table. To execute this migration type rake db:migrate in the **Ruby Console**.

```ruby
1   # Fig. 20.23: db/migrate/001_create_users.rb
2   # Database migration script modified to add data to the table.
3   class CreateUsers < ActiveRecord::Migration
4      # create and configure users table
5      def self.up
6         create_table :users do |t|
7            t.column :name, :string, :limit => 11
8            t.column :password, :string
9         end # do block
```

Fig. 20.23 | Database migration script modified to add data to the table. (Part 1 of 2.)

```
10
11          User.create :name => "user1", :password => "54321"
12      end # method self.up
13
14      # remove users table
15      def self.down
16          drop_table :users
17      end # method self.down
18  end # class CreateUsers
```

Fig. 20.23 | Database migration script modified to add data to the table. (Part 2 of 2.)

 Common Programming Error 20.2

Creating a column without explicitly specifying a limit on length will cause Rails to truncate the data entered into the database with database-defined limits.

Since the users table never changes, nothing needs to be specified in the User model, but one still needs to exist. This will allow the controller to access a User as an ActiveRecord. Figure 20.24 shows the empty model for the users table.

Next, we need to provide user creation, field validation and user logout functionality through the use of a controller (Fig. 20.25). Create this controller by typing ruby script/generate controller user. When a user logs in, we'll keep track of that User object in a *session variable*—a variable that maintains information across multiple pages of a web application. The purpose of the admin method (lines 5–7) is to pass a blank user object into the admin page, which will get filled with information, then render the admin.rhtml template. The validate method (lines 10–21) checks the user model to determine

```
1   # Fig. 20.24: app/models/user.rb
2   # Generated code for the User model.
3   class User < ActiveRecord::Base
4   end # method User
```

Fig. 20.24 | Generated code for the User model.

```
1   # Fig. 20.25: app/controllers/users_controller.rb
2   # UsersController provides validation functionality for the table.
3   class UsersController < ApplicationController
4       # create a new User object
5       def admin
6           @user = User.new # create a new User object
7       end # method admin
8
9       # validate that user exists
10      def validate
11          # find a user with the correct name and password
12          @user = User.find_by_name_and_password( params[ :user ][ :name ],
13              params[ :user ][ :password ] )
14
```

Fig. 20.25 | UsersController provides validation functionality for the table. (Part 1 of 2.)

```
15        if ( @user == nil )   # if the user doesn't exist
16            redirect_to :action => "admin" # redirect to admin action
17        else # user does exist
18            session[ :user ] = @user # store the user in a session variable
19            redirect_to :controller => "forums", :action => "index"
20        end # if
21    end # method validate
22
23    # log user out
24    def logout
25        reset_session # delete all session variables
26        redirect_to :controller => "forums", :action => "index" # redirect
27    end # method logout
28 end # class UserController
```

Fig. 20.25 | UsersController provides validation functionality for the table. (Part 2 of 2.)

whether the username exists, then redirects the application to the next action based on the result of that check.

Rails allows us to generate methods dynamically to serve a specific purpose. Lines 12–13 call the find_by_name_and_password method, which searches the model with the name and password, passed as a parameter.

The validate method assigns to an instance variable named @user (line 12) the value of the User that was returned by the find_by_name_and_password method. If no such User exists, the client is redirected to the admin page and asked to log in again (line 16). If the User does exist, a session variable is created (line 18), and line 19 redirects the client to the index of the forums controller, which we create in Section 20.6.4. The logout method (lines 24–27) uses the reset_session method to delete all the user's session variables, forcing the user to sign in again to use administrative options.

Performance Tip 20.1

Storing full objects in the session is inefficient. The user object is one of the rare exceptions, because it doesn't change very often and is frequently needed in web applications that manage the state information for unique clients.

Method admin's view is a simple login form. The template is shown in Fig. 20.26. It asks the user for a name and password using the ***text_field*** (line 6) and ***password_field*** (line 9) helpers, then sends the information to the validate method when the user clicks **Sign In**.

```
1  <!-- Fig. 20.26: app/views/users/admin.rhtml -->
2  <!-- Login form used to send data to the user controller. -->
3  <h1>Please Log In</h1>
4  <% form_tag :action => 'validate' do %> <!-- create form tag -->
5      <p><label for="user_name">Name</label><br/>
6      <%= text_field 'user', 'name' %></p> <!-- create input tag -->
7
```

Fig. 20.26 | Login form used to send data to the user controller. (Part 1 of 2.)

```
8      <p><label for="user_password">Password</label><br/>
9      <%= password_field 'user', 'password' %></p> <!-- create input tag -->
10     <%= submit_tag "Sign In" %> <!-- create submit tag -->
11  <% end %> <!-- create an end form tag -->
```

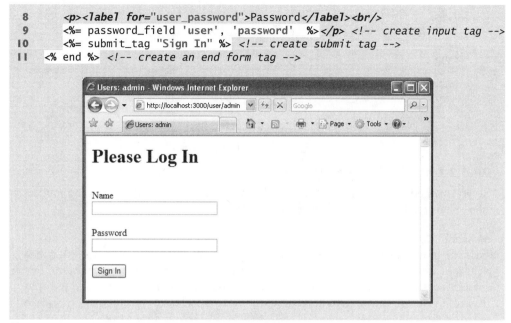

Fig. 20.26 | Login form used to send data to the `user` controller. (Part 2 of 2.)

Rails *helpers* are methods that generate XHTML content for the view. The `password_field` helper method generates a text field that masks the text inside it. Both `text_field` and `password_field` specify a model and the column. This information is used to determine the validation properties for each column when validating the text typed into these fields. When the user clicks the submit button defined in line 10, the **`form_tag`** method (line 4) automatically generates a `Hash`, where the keys are the names of the input fields and the values are what the user entered, and sends it to the `validate` action. The link to the `validate` action is specified by the `action` option. To display this action, run the Mongrel server and navigate your browser to `http://localhost:3000/user/admin`.

We define the `user` controller's template in Fig. 20.27. Because the `user` controller has only a single view to render, we could have simply include this XHTML in the view. The benefit of a template is that it allows us to easily add more views in the future that are all based on the same template and adhere to Ruby on Rails' DRY (Don't Repeat Yourself) philosophy. Line 9 displays the current action in the title bar. Line 12 is the placeholder for the content of the action's view.

```
1   <?xml version = "1.0" encoding = "utf-8"?>
2   <!DOCTYPE html PUBLIC "-//W3C//DTD XHTML 1.0 Strict//EN"
3       "http://www.w3.org/TR/xhtml1/DTD/xhtml1-strict.dtd">
4
5   <!-- Fig. 20.27: app/views/layouts/users.rhtml-->
6   <!-- Display the name of the current action in the title bar -->
7   <html xmlns = "http://www.w3.org/1999/xhtml">
```

Fig. 20.27 | Display the name of the current action in the title bar. (Part 1 of 2.)

```
 8    <head>
 9       <title>Users: <%= controller.action_name %></title>
10    </head>
11    <body>
12       <%= yield %>
13    </body>
14    </html>
```

Fig. 20.27 | Display the name of the current action in the title bar. (Part 2 of 2.)

20.6.2 Embellishing the Models

Several methods must be added to the model so that it can be modified from the application. These methods are all defined by ActiveRecord.

Message *Model*

First, we must create an empty Message model by typing ruby script/generate model Message in the **Ruby Console**. Before we make any change to the model we must create the messages table. Figure 20.28 is the migration that creates the messages table and adds data to it. To run this migration, navigate to the messageboard directory and type rake db:migrate.

```
 1    # Fig. 20.28: db/migrate/002_create_messages.rb
 2    # Database migration script modified to add data to the table.
 3    class CreateMessages < ActiveRecord::Migration
 4       # create and configure messages table
 5       def self.up
 6          create_table :messages, do |t|
 7             t.column :title, :string, :limit => 64
 8             t.column :author, :string, :limit => 20
 9             t.column :created_on, :timestamp
10             t.column :email, :string, :limit => 40
11             t.column :message, :text
12             t.column :forum_id, :integer
13          end # do block
14
15          Message.create :title => "Welcome to the Fourth Edition",
16             :author => "Bob Green",
17             :email => "noone@deitel.com",
18             :message => "We hope you enjoy the book.",
19             :forum_id => 2
20       end # method self.up
21
22       # remove messages table
23       def self.down
24          drop_table :messages
25       end # method self.down
26    end # class CreateForums
```

Fig. 20.28 | Database migration script modified to add data to the table.

The create_table function call (lines 6–13) specifies the columns of the table. Lines 7–12 create the title, author, created_on, email, message and forum_id columns with appropriate variable types and length limits. Lines 15–20 add data to the table. Rails fills the created_on column value automatically when a new row is created. To apply the migration, type rake db:migrate in the console window.

Figure 20.29 shows the Message model that encapsulates the messages table in the database. Line 4 invokes the belongs_to method, which defines an association with the forums table that can be used to access elements of the forums table. This method will allow the Message to access the forum to which the given Message belongs simply by calling a method named forum on the Message. This is known as an *association method*.

Lines 7–9 are examples of *validators* that can be applied to an object that inherits from ActiveRecord. These validations occur when the save method is called on a message object in an attempt to store it in the database. If the validations are successful, then the object is saved to the database and the method returns true. If the validations fail, an Errors object associated with the Message object is updated and the method returns false. The method *validates_presence_of* ensures that all of the fields specified by its parameters are not empty. The method *validates_format_of* matches all of the fields specified by its parameters with a regular expression. The regular expression in line 9 represents a valid e-mail address. This regular expression can be found in the Rails framework documentation at api.rubyonrails.org.

```ruby
1   # Fig. 20.29: app/models/message.rb
2   # Message Model containing validation and initialization functionality.
3   class Message < ActiveRecord::Base
4      belongs_to :forum # adds a forum method to Message
5
6      # validators (validates automatically before ActiveRecord.save)
7      validates_presence_of :title, :author, :email, :message
8      validates_format_of :email,
9         :with => /^([^@\s]+)@((?:[-a-z0-9]+\.)+[a-z]{2,})$/i
10  end # class Message
```

Fig. 20.29 | Message model containing validation and initialization functionality.

Forum Model

Next, create an empty forum model by typing in ruby script/generate model forum. Then create the forums table in a similar fashion to messages and users. Figure 20.30 is the Migration that sets up the messages table.

The create_table function call (lines 6–10) specifies the columns of the table. Lines 7–9 create the name, administrator and created_on columns with appropriate variable types and length limits. Lines 12–16 add data to the table. To apply the migration, type in rake db:migrate.

The model for the forums table (Fig. 20.31) looks similar to the model for the messages table. We can create an association method that allows a Forum to access every Message that is associated with it. Line 4 shows the *has_many* method, which will create a method called messages for every Forum object. The messages method will return an array of all the messages in the Forum.

```
1   # Fig. 20.30 db/migrate/003_create_forums.rb
2   # Database migration script modified to add data to the table.
3   class CreateForums < ActiveRecord::Migration
4      # Create and configure forums table
5      def self.up
6         create_table :forums do |t|
7            t.column :name, :string, :limit => 64
8            t.column :administrator, :string, :limit => 20
9            t.column :created_on, :timestamp
10        end # do block
11
12        Forum.create :name => "Ruby On Rails",
13           :administrator => "user1"
14        Forum.create :name => "Internet and World Wide Web: 4th Edition",
15           :administrator => "user1"
16     end # method self.up
17
18     # remove forums table
19     def self.down
20        drop_table :forums
21     end # method self.down
22  end # class CreateForums
```

Fig. 20.30 | Database migration script modified to add data to the table.

```
1   # Fig. 20.31: app/models/forum.rb
2   # Forum model that includes validation and initialization functionality.
3   class Forum < ActiveRecord::Base
4      has_many :messages, :dependent => :destroy
5      validates_presence_of :name
6   end # class Forum
```

Fig. 20.31 | Forum model that includes validation and initialization functionality.

When a forum is deleted, all of that forum's messages should also be deleted. Line 4 sets the dependent parameter of the has_many method to :destroy to ensure that when a forum is destroyed all the messages that are associated with it are destroyed as well.

20.6.3 Generating Scaffold Code

Now that the user can log in and out of our application, we need to create the messages and forums views and controllers. Since much of this code is standard CRUD, we can use the Rails scaffold generator by typing ruby script/generate scaffold message and ruby script/generate scaffold forum in the **Ruby Console**. The scaffold generator creates the scaffold code that would be generated using the scaffold method in the controller. When using the scaffold method, notice that the controller name and the view directory are both pluralized forms of the name, rather than the singular form that the model generator and controller generator would create.

20.6.4 Forum Controller and Forum Views

The ForumsController (Fig. 20.32), which was initially generated as part of the scaffolding, handles all incoming requests from the client. The index, list, new, and delete methods are all responsible for rendering a view, while the create and destroy methods are responsible for processing incoming data and then redirecting to another action. We will not use the edit or show methods so you may delete the .rhtml view files associated with them.

The verify method call in lines 4–5 is edited scaffold code, which ensures a post request is used to send data to the server for each request that modifies the database. Whenever a method modifies a database, the arguments should be from a post so that they don't show up in the URL. The :only argument specifies which actions this verification should be applied (create and destroy in this case). If a call to create or destroy is not made via a post request, line 5 redirects the request to the list action.

```ruby
 1   # Fig. 20.32: app/controllers/forums_controller.rb
 2   # ForumsController implements CRUD functionality.
 3   class ForumsController < ApplicationController
 4      verify :method => :post, :only => [ :destroy, :create ],
 5         :redirect_to => { :action => :list }
 6
 7      # shortcut to the list method
 8      def index
 9         list
10         render :action => 'list'
11      end # method index
12
13      # set up the list web page that lists all forums
14      def list
15         @forums = Forum.find( :all )
16      end # method list
17
18      # set up the new web page that adds a new forum
19      def new
20         if ( session[ :user ] == nil ) # if user is not logged in
21            flash[ :error ] = 'you must be logged in to complete this action'
22            redirect_to :action => "index" and return
23         end # if
24
25         @forum = Forum.new
26      end # method new
27
28      # attempt to create a new forum with the parameters passed in
29      def create
30         @forum = Forum.new( params[ :forum ] )
31         @forum.administrator = session[ :user ].name
32
33         if @forum.save # if save method was successful
34            flash[ :notice ] = 'Forum was successfully created.'
35            redirect_to :action => 'list'
```

Fig. 20.32 | ForumsController implements CRUD functionality. (Part 1 of 2.)

```
36            else # save was unsuccessful
37                render :action => 'new' # go to new
38            end # if...else
39        end # method create
40
41        # set up the delete web page
42        def delete
43            if ( session[ :user ] == nil ) # if user is not logged in
44                flash[ :error ] = 'you must be logged in to complete this action'
45                redirect_to :action => "index" and return
46            else
47                @forums = Forum.find( :all,
48                    :conditions => "administrator = '#{ session[:user].name }'" )
49            end # if else
50        end # method delete
51
52        # delete a forum with a specified parameter
53        def destroy
54            # find the forum and delete it
55            Forum.destroy( params[ :forum ][ :id ] ) # delete the forum
56            redirect_to :action => 'list' # redirect to list
57        end # method destroy
58    end # class ForumsController
```

Fig. 20.32 | ForumsController implements CRUD functionality. (Part 2 of 2.)

Method index (line 8–11) redirects the client to the list method (lines 14–16), which obtains a list of forums from the database to be displayed on the page. The new method (lines 19–26) checks whether the user has privileges to create a new forum. If not, lines 21–22 display an error and redirect the user to the index action. The hash called flash in line 21 is used to display messages in the view. Flash is a special type of session storage that is always automatically cleared after every request to the controller. If the user has privileges, line 25 creates a new instance of the forum object which is initialized with data from the user input.

The create method (lines 29–39) is similar to the scaffold code, but differs in that the administrator attribute of the forum being saved must be the name of the user who is logged in. Line 33 attempts to save the forum, and either renders a template if the method returns false (line 37), or redirects to the list method and updates the flash object if the method returns true (lines 34–35). The delete method (lines 42–50) sets up the deletion operation by finding all the forums created by the user currently logged in. Once the user picks a forum to delete in the view, the destroy method (lines 53–58) destroys the forum specified by the user (line 55) and re-displays the list (line 56).

List View

Figure 20.33 is the template that is rendered by the list method from the Forum controller. [*Note:* We replaced the auto-generated list.rhtml from the scaffolding]. This is also the template rendered by the index method. Line 10 uses the *link_to* method to create a link with the name of the forum and the list action of its messages, which we build in Section 20.6.5. Lines 12–13 contain a conditional statement which make the forum italicized for five minutes after it has been created by using the minutes.ago method of the

```
I    <!-- Fig. 20.33: app/views/forums/list.rhtml -->
2    <!-- Template for the list action that displays a list of forums. -->
3    <h1>Deitel Message Forums</h1>
4    <h2>Available Forums</h2>
5    <ul>
6        <% for forum in @forums %>
7        <!-- create a list item for every forum -->
8            <li>
9                <!-- link to list action in messages -->
10               <%= link_to ( forum.name, {:controller => 'messages',
11                   :action => 'list', :forum_id => forum.id},
12                   { :class => (forum.created_on < 5.minutes.ago ?
13                   'recent': nil ) } ) %>
14           </li>
15       <% end %> <!-- end for -->
16   </ul>
17   <% if ( session[ :user ] ) then %>
18       <!-- a user is logged in -->
19       <h2>Forum Management</h2>
20       <ul>
21           <li><%= link_to 'Add a Forum', :action => 'new' %></li>
22           <li><%= link_to 'Delete a Forum', :action => 'delete' %></li>
23       </ul>
24   <% end %>  <!-- end if -->
```

Fig. 20.33 | Template for the list action that displays a list of forums.

Fixnum class. The if statement in lines 17–24 displays the XHTML in lines 19–23 only if there is a user logged in.

New View

Figure 20.34 shows the template for the Forum controller's new method. This is code generated by the scaffold. Lines 4–7 create a form that is rendered to the page, and indicate

```
I   <!-- Fig. 20.34 app/views/forums/new.rhtml -->
2   <!-- Template for a new action that adds a forum to the forums table. -->
3   <h1>New forum</h1>
4   <% form_tag :action => 'create' do %>
5      <%= render :partial => 'form' %>
6      <%= submit_tag "Create" %>
7   <% end %>
8
9   <%= link_to 'Back', :action => 'list' %>
```

Fig. 20.34 | Template for a new action that adds a forum to the forums table.

that the action create will be called when the **Create** button is pressed. This template renders a *partial*—a block of HTML and embedded Ruby code stored in another file and inserted directly into the document. A partial allows the same block of code to be used across multiple documents. In this example, line 5 renders the partial named form, which inserts the file _form.rhtml at that line of code. A partial filename always begins with an underscore.

Line 6 uses the submit_tag method to create a submit button that when clicked will create a Hash with the form's fields as keys and the user's input as values. Line 9 uses the link_to function to allow the user to go back to the forums list by redirecting the client to the list action of the forum controller.

The partial in Fig. 20.35 renders the input text field for the form. The administrator and created_on fields will be generated on the server, so they've been deleted from the scaffold's code. The created_on field will be automatically set to the time when the forum is created. The administrator field will be set by the controller.

```
I   <!-- Fig. 20.35: app/views/forums/_form.rhtml -->
2   <!-- Partial that contains a form used to add a new forum. -->
3   <%= error_messages_for 'forum' %>
4   <p><label for="forum_name">Name</label><br/>
5   <%= text_field 'forum', 'name'  %></p>
```

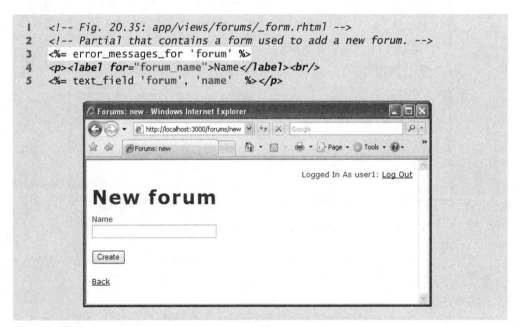

Fig. 20.35 | Partial that contains a form used to add a new forum.

Delete View

The delete view (Fig. 20.36) is not generated by the scaffold, so we create it ourselves. It is similar to create in that it renders a form, but uses the collection_select method to display for that administrator the list of available forums to delete. The **collection_select** takes five parameters—the type of object to be selected, the field which the options are to be grouped by, the collection from that to obtain the list of objects, the field that will be sent once an option is selected and the field that is to be displayed on the screen for each option.

```
1    <!-- Fig. 20.36: app/views/forums/delete.rhtml -->
2    <!-- Template for delete action used to delete a Forum. -->
3    <h1>Delete a Forum</h1><br />
4
5    <% form_tag  :action => :destroy do %> <!-- create from tag -->
6       <p><label for="forum_id">Forum Name</label><br />
7       <%= collection_select "forum", "id", @forums, "id", "name" %></p>
8       <%= submit_tag "Delete" %> <!-- create submit tag -->
9    <% end %> <!-- create end form tag -->
10
11   <%= link_to 'Back', :action => 'list' %> <!-- link back to list method -->
```

Fig. 20.36 | Template for Delete action used to delete a forum.

Forum Layout

Figure 20.37 is the layout that renders every template for the ForumsController. It has all the necessary XHTML, and contains the login/logout text (lines 13–25). Line 29 automatically renders the template of any action that uses the template.

```
1    <?xml version = "1.0" encoding = "utf-8"?>
2    <!DOCTYPE html PUBLIC "-//W3C//DTD XHTML 1.0 Strict//EN"
3       "http://www.w3.org/TR/xhtml1/DTD/xhtml1-strict.dtd">
4
5    <!-- Fig. 20.37: app/views/layouts/forums.rhtml -->
6    <!-- Layout that displays the logged-in user for every Forums action. -->
```

Fig. 20.37 | Layout that displays the logged-in user for every Forums action. (Part 1 of 2.)

```
 7   <html xmlns = "http://www.w3.org/1999/xhtml">
 8   <head>
 9     <title>Forums: <%= controller.action_name %></title>
10     <%= stylesheet_link_tag 'scaffold' %> <!-- link to a stylesheet -->
11   </head>
12   <body>
13     <div style = "text-align: right">
14       <% if ( session[ :user ] ) then %> <!-- if user is logged on -->
15         <!-- code to display if user is logged on -->
16         <%= "Logged In As #{ session[ :user ].name }: " %>
17         <%= link_to 'Log Out',
18           :controller => 'users', :action => 'logout' %>
19       <% else %> <!-- user is not logged on -->
20         <!-- code to display if user is not logged on -->
21         <%= "Not Currently Logged In:" %>
22         <%= link_to 'Log In',
23           :controller => 'users', :action => 'admin' %>
24       <% end %> <!-- end if -->
25     </div>
26     <p style="color: green"><%= flash[ :notice ] %></p>
27     <p style="color: red"><%= flash[ :error ] %></p>
28
29     <%= yield %> <!-- displays template -->
30   </body>
31   </html>
```

Fig. 20.37 | Layout that displays the logged-in user for every `Forums` action. (Part 2 of 2.)

If the user is logged in (line 14), lines 16–18 display the username on the page and use the `link_to` method to enable the user to log out by redirecting to the `logout` action. Otherwise, lines 21–23 allow the user to log in, using the `link_to` helper method to redirect the user to the `admin` action. Lines 26–27 display any error messages or success messages that result from user interactions.

20.6.5 Message Controller and Message Views

The `MessagesController` (Fig. 20.38) is similar to the `ForumsController`, except that its `list` method (lines 8–22) doesn't list all of the `messages`—it lists only the ones with the specified `forum_id` that is passed in as a URL parameter from the `Forum list` view. Line 10 updates the `session` variable to match the URL parameter. If no parameter value is specified, the `forum_id` session variable is used. If neither of these exists, line 14 displays an error and line 15 redirects the client to the `list` action of the forum `controller`. The `find` method which is called on `Message` (line 18–19) specifies that the messages should be ordered by their `created_on` dates in descending order. Line 20 also calls the `find` method to obtain the `forum` object, which we'll need to add messages to the `forum`.

The `create` method (lines 30–40) replaces the method generated by the scaffold. Line 31 obtains the `id` of the forum to which the message should be added and line 32 obtains the new message entered by the user. If the message is added to the database successfully, lines 35–36 set the appropriate message to be displayed in the view using the `flash` object and redirect the client to the `list` action. Otherwise, line 38 redirects the client to the `new` action, prompting the user to enter the message again.

```
 1   # Fig. 20.38: app/controllers/messages_controller.rb
 2   # MessagesController that implements CRUD functionality.
 3   class MessagesController < ApplicationController
 4      verify :method => :post, :only => [ :destroy, :create ],
 5         :redirect_to => { :action => :list }
 6
 7      # sets up the list web page that lists all messages
 8      def list
 9         if ( params[ :forum_id ] )  # if parameter forum_id is provided
10            session[ :forum_id ] = params[ :forum_id ]
11         end # if
12
13         if ( session[ :forum_id ] == nil ) # if no forum_id is provided
14            flash[ :notice ]  = 'there has been an error.'
15            redirect_to :controller => "forums", :action => "list" and return
16         end # if
17
18         @messages = Message.find( :all, :order => "created_on desc",
19            :conditions => "forum_id = #{ session[:forum_id ] }" )
20         @forum = Forum.find( :first,
21            :conditions => "id = #{ session[ :forum_id ] }" )
22      end # method list
23
24      # sets up the new web page that creates a message
25      def new
26         @message = Message.new
27      end # method new
28
29      # attempts to create a new message with the parameters passed in
30      def create
31         @message = Message.new( params[ :message ] )
32         @message.forum_id = session[ :forum_id ]
33
34         if @message.save  # if save method was successful
35            flash[ :notice ] = 'Message was successfully created.'
36            redirect_to :action => 'list'
37         else # save was unsuccessful
38            render :action => 'new'
39         end # if
40      end # method create
41   end # class MessagesController
```

Fig. 20.38 | `MessagesController` that implements CRUD functionality.

List *View*

The list view (Fig. 20.39) for the Message controller is similar to the list view for the Forum controller, except that more information is displayed in the messages list view. It uses CSS to format the output. In this view, every message object acts like a Hash—passing a column name as a key returns the corresponding value in the message object. To obtain an a column's value, include the attribute method's name in square brackets after the name of the object. For each message in the forum, line 12 displays the title, line 13 displays the author and line 19 displays the message's text. At line 14, the Ruby Time object that is returned by the message['created on'] is formatted using the Ruby Time class formatting

```
1   <!-- Fig. 20.39: app/views/messages/list.rhtml -->
2   <!-- Template for the list action that displays a list of Forums. -->
3   <div style = "text-align: center">
4      <table style = "width: 600px; margin: 0 auto 0 auto">
5         <tr class="msgHeader">
6            <td><%= @forum.name %></td>
7         </tr>
8         <% for message in @messages %>
9            <!-- create two table rows for every message -->
10           <tr class="msgTitle">
11              <td>
12              <strong><%= message[ 'title' ] %></strong><br />
13              by <em><%= message[ 'author' ] %></em> at
14              <%= message[ 'created_on' ].strftime("%m/%d/%Y at %I:%M%p") %>
15              </td>
16           </tr>
17           <tr class="msgPost">
18              <!-- message content -->
19              <td><%= message[ 'message' ] %></td>
20           </tr>
21        <% end %>
22     </table>
23
24     <%= link_to 'New message', :action => 'new' %> |
25     <%= link_to 'list forums',
26        :controller => 'forums', :action => 'index' %>
27  </div>
```

Fig. 20.39 | Template for the list action that displays a list of messages.

options. Lines 24–26 use the link_to method to allow the user to create a message in the current forum or to go back to the list of the forums.

New View
The new template for the Message controller is omitted here because it is scaffold code that is nearly identical to the new template for the Forum controller. The partial shown in Fig. 20.40 for the messages form is also similar. Lines 8, 12 and 16 use the text_field helper method to create fields for specifying the title, author and email. Line 20 uses the text_area helper method to create an input area of a certain size, to be used to input the message. These fields are validated when the Message model's save method is called. If the model does not deem the data valid, line 3 displays the error messages.

```
1   <!-- Fig. 20.40: app/views/messages/_form.rhtml -->
2   <!-- A form that allows the user to enter a new message. -->
3   <%= error_messages_for 'message' %>
4
5   <table>
6      <tr class = "alignRight">
7         <td>Title</td>
8         <td><%= text_field 'message', 'title'  %></td>
9      </tr>
10     <tr class = "alignRight">
11        <td>Author</td>
12        <td><%= text_field 'message', 'author' %></td>
13     </tr>
14     <tr class = "alignRight">
15        <td>Email</td>
16        <td><%= text_field 'message', 'email'  %></td>
17     </tr>
18     <tr><td colspan = "2">Message</td></tr>
19     <tr><td colspan = "2">
20        <%= text_area 'message', 'message', :cols => "30", :rows => "4"%>
21     </td></tr>
22   </table>
```

Fig. 20.40 | Form that allows the user to enter a new message.

Message Layout

Figure 20.41 shows the layout used to render all Message templates. Line 10 invokes the scaffold.css style sheet, which we changed slightly to improve our page's presentation. To make the style sheet available for import it must be placed in the public/stylesheets directory of the application. When a forum has been modified, line 14 displays the appropriate message.

```
I    <?xml version = "1.0" encoding = "utf-8"?>
2    <!DOCTYPE html PUBLIC "-//W3C//DTD XHTML 1.0 Strict//EN"
3       "http://www.w3.org/TR/xhtml1/DTD/xhtml1-strict.dtd">
4
5    <!-- Fig. 20.41: app/views/layouts/messages.rhtml -->
6    <!-- Message layout that links a style sheet and displays a message. -->
7    <html xmlns = "http://www.w3.org/1999/xhtml">
8    <head>
9       <title>Messages: <%= controller.action_name %></title>
10      <%= stylesheet_link_tag 'scaffold' %>
11   </head>
12   <body>
13      <% if ( flash[ :notice ] ) then %>
14         <p style="color: green"><%= flash[ :notice ] %></p>
15      <% end %>
16      <%= yield %>
17   </body>
18   </html>
```

Fig. 20.41 | Message layout that links a style sheet and displays a message.

We have now implemented the basic functionality of the forum application. To test this application execute it on Mongrel and browse to http://localhost:3000/forums. To test the administrative privileges of the forum go to http://localhost:3000/user/admin and login with the username user1 and password 54321. In the next section we'll add Ajax capabilities to make our forum more responsive.

20.6.6 Ajax-Enabled Rails Applications

Adding Ajax functionality to Rails applications is straightforward. Rails includes a JavaScript library called Prototype that contains easy-to-use cross-browser Ajax functions. Figure 20.42 is the modified layout for the forum file, which now links the prototype library to the application. For the application to have the correct look, make sure you insert the modified style sheet, which can be found in our examples folder, into the public/stylesheets directory of the application.

```
I    <?xml version = "1.0" encoding = "utf-8"?>
2    <!DOCTYPE html PUBLIC "-//W3C//DTD XHTML 1.0 Strict//EN"
3       "http://www.w3.org/TR/xhtml1/DTD/xhtml1-strict.dtd">
4
5    <!-- Fig. 20.42: app/views/layouts/forums.rhtml -->
6    <!-- Forums layout that uses the default JavaScript libraries. -->
7    <html xmlns = "http://www.w3.org/1999/xhtml">
8    <head>
9       <title>Forums: <%= controller.action_name %></title>
10      <%= stylesheet_link_tag 'scaffold' %> <!-- link to a stylesheet -->
11      <%= javascript_include_tag :defaults %>
12   </head>
13   <body>
```

Fig. 20.42 | Forums layout that uses the default JavaScript libraries. (Part 1 of 2.)

```
14      <div style = "text-align: right">
15        <% if ( session[ :user ] ) then %> <!-- if user is logged on -->
16          <!-- code to display if user is logged on -->
17          <%= "Logged In As #{ session[ :user ].name }: " %>
18          <%= link_to 'Log Out',
19              :controller => 'users', :action => 'logout' %>
20        <% else %> <!-- user is not logged on -->
21          <!-- code to display if user is not logged on -->
22          <%= "Not Currently Logged In:" %>
23          <%= link_to 'Log In',
24              :controller => 'users', :action => 'admin' %>
25        <% end %> <!-- end if -->
26      </div>
27      <p style="color: green"><%= flash[ :notice ] %></p>
28      <p style="color: red"><%= flash[ :error ] %></p>
29
30      <%= yield %> <!-- displays template -->
31    </body>
32  </html>
```

Fig. 20.42 | Forums layout that uses the default JavaScript libraries. (Part 2 of 2.)

Line 11 links in the JavaScript library using the ***javascript_include_tag*** helper method. The defaults parameter tells javascript_include_tag to link all the defaults JavaScript Rails libraries including Prototype and Script.aculo.us. The rest of the layout file is the same as in the non-Ajax version.

Figure 20.43 changes the Forum object's list view to perform Ajax requests rather than load a new page. Now, whenever the user clicks a forum's name, the page loads the forum's messages to the right of the forums list with a partial page update.

```
1   <!-- Fig. 20.43: app/views/forums/list.rhtml -->
2   <!-- Displaying a list of messages without reloading the page. -->
3   <h1>Deitel Message Forums</h1>
4   <div class = "forumList">
5     <h2>Available Forums</h2>
6     <ul>
7       <% for forum in @forums %>
8         <li>
9           <%= link_to_remote ( forum.name,
10              { :url => { :controller => 'messages',
11              :action => 'list', :forum_id => forum.id },
12              :update => 'currentForum' },
13              { :class => ( forum.created_on < 5.minutes.ago ?
14              'recent': nil ) } ) %>
15        </li>
16      <% end %>
17    </ul>
18    <% if ( session[ :user ] ) then %>
19      <h2>Forum Management</h2>
20      <ul>
```

Fig. 20.43 | Displaying a list of messages without reloading the page. (Part 1 of 2.)

```
21                <li><%= link_to 'Add a Forum', :action => 'new' %></li>
22                <li><%= link_to 'Delete a Forum', :action => 'delete' %></li>
23          </ul>
24       <% end %>
25    </div>
26    <div id = 'currentForum' class = "ajaxComponent">
27    </div>
```

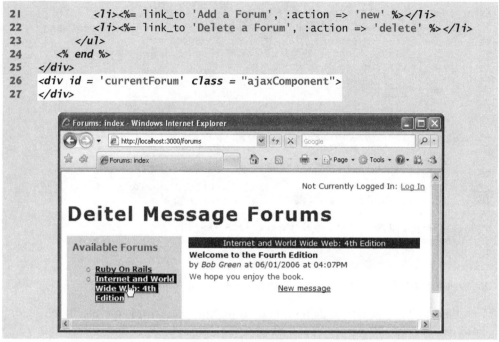

Fig. 20.43 | Displaying a list of messages without reloading the page. (Part 2 of 2.)

The key change is lines 9–12, which have been changed to call the `link_to_remote` helper method instead of the `link_to` helper method. The `link_to_remote` method allows us to link to JavaScript that we included in the layout file. By specifying the `url` and `update` parameters inside the `link_to_remote` method we are telling Rails to convert these tags into *prototype **Ajax.Updater** objects* that will update the page asynchronously. The `url` argument (line 10) specifies the `controller` in which to look for the action. The `action` parameter (line 11) specifies the action to invoke. The `forum_id` parameter (line 11) specifies the id to pass to the action. Line 12 specifies `currentForum` as the `id` of the placeholder `div` in the page that needs to be updated. Lines 26–27 define the placeholder `div` element where the list of messages will be inserted. The rest of the code is the same as in the non-Ajax version of this application.

In similar fashion, we modify the `list` and `new` views of the `message` object, to be able to add a message to a forum without reloading the page. First we include all the default JavaScript libraries in the `message.rhtml` layout file (not shown here), ensuring all the views in the message object have access to Prototype. After that we modify all the calls to other actions to be asynchronous. Figure 20.44 is the updated `list.rhtml`.

```
1    <!-- Fig. 20.44: app/views/messages/list.rhtml -->
2    <!-- Forum that allows the user to add a message on the same page. -->
3    <div class = "messageList">
4    <table style = "width: 400">
5       <tr class="msgHeader">
```

Fig. 20.44 | Forum that allows the user to add a message on the same page. (Part 1 of 2.)

```
 6          <td><%= @forum.name %></td>
 7       </tr>
 8       <% for message in @messages %>
 9          <tr class="msgTitle">
10             <td>
11                <strong><%= message.title %></strong><br/>
12                by <em><%= message.author %></em> at
13                <%= message.created_on.strftime( "%m/%d/%Y at %I:%M%p" ) %>
14             </td>
15          </tr>
16          <tr class="msgPost">
17             <td><%= message.message %></td>
18          </tr>
19       <% end %>
20    </table>
21
22    <%= link_to_remote 'New message',
23       :url => { :action => 'new' },
24       :update => 'currentForum'%>
25    </div>
```

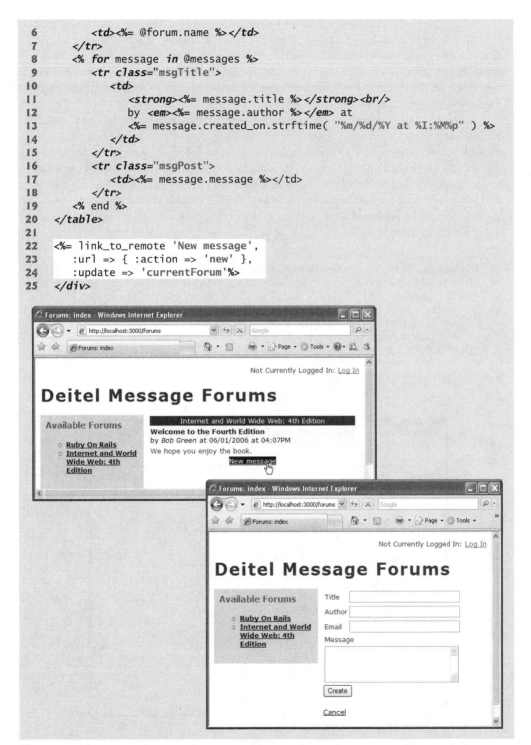

Fig. 20.44 | Forum that allows the user to add a message on the same page. (Part 2 of 2.)

Lines 22–24 use the `link_to_remote` helper method to allow the user to add new messages without reloading the page. The `url` is the `new` action, which returns the form and the placeholder to update is `currentForum`, defined in the `list.rhtml` view of the forum object (Fig. 20.43). The `new` view is also modified, so that once the user submits the new message, the updated `div` named `currentForum` is shown without reloading the page. Figure 20.45 shows the modified `new.rhtml`.

Lines 3–7 have been changed to use the ***form_remote_tag*** helper method, which redirects the client to the next action without reloading the page. Once the user clicks the **Submit** button, generated by `submit_tag` (line 6), the form will generate a Prototype `Ajax.Updater` object that will send the data to the action specified and display the result in the specified placeholder. This placeholder is set to `currentForum`, the same element inside which this forum will be displayed. When the user finishes adding the new message, a new forum will replace this form, without reloading the page. Lines 8–9 provide the user a way to cancel the new-message operation, in which case the original forum displays.

```
1   <!-- Fig. 20.45: app/views/messages/new.rhtml -->
2   <!-- Allows the user to add a new message without reloading the page. -->
3   <%= form_remote_tag :url=> { :action => 'create' },
4      :update => 'currentForum' %>
5     <%= render :partial => 'form' %>
6     <%= submit_tag "Create" %>
7   <%= end_form_tag %>
8   <%= link_to_remote 'Cancel', :url=> { :action => 'list' },
9      :update => 'currentForum' %>
```

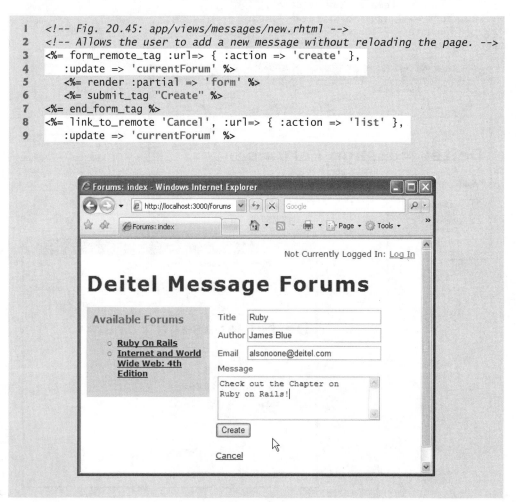

Fig. 20.45 | Adding a new message without reloading the page. (Part 1 of 2.)

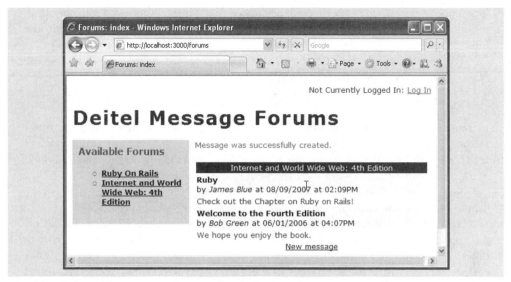

Fig. 20.45 | Adding a new message without reloading the page. (Part 2 of 2.)

20.7 Script.aculo.us

Visual Effects

Rails includes the *Script.aculo.us JavaScript library*, which allows you to easily create visual effects similar to those in Adobe Flash and Microsoft Silverlight. The library provides many pre-defined effects, as well as the ability to create your own effects from the pre-defined ones. The following example demonstrates many of the effects provided by this library. Figure 20.46 demonstrates the Fade effect. When the user clicks the link above the

Fig. 20.46 | Script.aculo.us's Fade effect.

image, the effect named in the link will be applied to the image. Once you start the application with Mongrel, open `http://localhost:3000/scriptaculous_demo/` in your web browser.

To create this application, first type `rails scriptaculous_demo` in the Ruby console. Next, create the controller by executing

```
ruby script/generate controller ScriptaculousDemo
```

In `app/controllers/scriptaculous_demo_controller.rb` (Fig. 20.47), add the `index` method. This method sets to 0 the `currentEffect` instance variable, which keeps track of which effect the application is currently playing. Next, add the `PlayEffect` method (lines 4–6), which will be called when the user clicks to show the next effect.

Now, create `application.rhtml` (Fig. 20.48) in `app/view/layouts`. This acts as the default layout. Content from `render :partial` commands replaces line 13.

Next, create `index.rhtml` (Fig. 20.49) in `app/views/scriptaculous_demo`. This is the application's default view. The `"link"` div (lines 3–8) contains a `link_to_remote` (lines 4–7) that initially is labeled `'Shrink'`, calls `playEffect` with a `effect_index` parameter of 0, updates itself and plays an effect on the `before` event. The effect is created using the `visual_effect` method (lines 6–7). The parameters of this method call are the effect name, the name of the element the effect should apply to, the `duration` and the loca-

```
1  <!-- Fig. 20.47: app/views/scriptaculous_demo/index.rhtml -->
2  <!-- Default view for Script.aculo.us demo. -->
3  <div id = "link">
4     <%= link_to_remote 'Shrink', :url => {:action => 'playEffect',
5        :effect_index => 0}, :update => "link",
6        :before => visual_effect(
7           :Shrink, 'image', :duration => 1.0, :queue => 'end') %>
8  </div>
9
10 <div id = "image" style = "width: 244px; height: 320px;">
11    <%= image_tag "jhtp7medium.jpg" %>
12 </div>
```

Fig. 20.47 | Default view for Script.aculo.us demo.

```
1  # Fig. 20.48: app/controllers/scriptaculous_demo_controller.rb
2  # Script.aculo.us Demo controller
3  class ScriptaculousDemoController < ApplicationController
4     def index
5        @currentEffect = 0
6     end
7     def playEffect
8        @currentEffect = params[ :effect_index ]
9        render :partial => "link"
10    end # method playEffect
11 end # class ScriptaculousDemoController
```

Fig. 20.48 | Script.aculo.us Demo controller.

```
 1   <?xml version = "1.0" encoding = "utf-8"?>
 2   <!DOCTYPE html PUBLIC "-//W3C//DTD XHTML 1.0 Strict//EN"
 3      "http://www.w3.org/TR/xhtml1/DTD/xhtml1-strict.dtd">
 4
 5   <!-- Fig. 20.49: app/views/layouts/application.rhtml -->
 6   <!-- Default layout of Script.aculo.us demo. -->
 7   <html xmlns = "http://www.w3.org/1999/xhtml">
 8      <head>
 9         <title>Script.aculo.us Effects Demo</title>
10         <%= javascript_include_tag :defaults %>
11      </head>
12      <body>
13         <%= yield %>
14      </body>
15   </html>
```

Fig. 20.49 | Default layout of Script.aculo.us demo.

tion in the queue. The queue is set to end so that any new effects will be played after all the others are complete. The image in line 11 must be in the `public/images` directory.

The `playEffect` method (lines 7–10, Fig. 20.47) sets the `currentEffect` instance variable to the `effect_index` parameter, then renders the `link` view in the `link` div. In `app/views/scriptaculous_demo/_link.rhtml` (Fig. 20.50), the application demonstrates several Script.aculo.us effects by using nested `if` statements to check the `currentEffect`, apply it, then increment `currentEffect` after each effect with the `effect_index` parameter. The link text corresponds to the name of the effect the link activates.

```
 1   <!-- Fig. 20.50: app/views/scriptaculous_demo/_link.rhtml -->
 2   <!-- link partial view for Script.aculo.us demo -->
 3   <!-- Grow effect -->
 4   <% if @currentEffect == '0' %>
 5      <%= link_to_remote 'Grow', :url => { :action => 'playEffect',
 6      :effect_index => 1 }, :update => "link",
 7         :before => ( visual_effect(
 8            :Grow, 'image', :duration => 1.0, :queue => 'end' ) ) %>
 9
10   <!-- Fade effect -->
11   <% elsif @currentEffect == '1' %>
12      <%= link_to_remote 'Fade', :url => { :action => 'playEffect',
13         :effect_index => 2 }, :update => "link",
14         :before => ( visual_effect(
15            :Fade, 'image', :duration => 1.0, :queue => 'end' ) ) %>
16
17   <!-- Appear effect -->
18   <% elsif @currentEffect == '2' %>
19      <%= link_to_remote 'Appear', :url => {:action => 'playEffect',
20         :effect_index => 3 }, :update => "link",
21         :before => ( visual_effect(
22            :Appear, 'image', :duration => 1.0, :queue => 'end' ) ) %>
```

Fig. 20.50 | link partial view for Script.aculo.us demo. (Part 1 of 3.)

```
23
24   <!-- BlindUp effect -->
25   <% elsif @currentEffect == '3' %>
26      <%= link_to_remote 'BlindUp', :url => { :action => 'playEffect',
27         :effect_index => 4 }, :update => "link",
28         :before => ( visual_effect(
29            :BlindUp, 'image', :duration => 1.0, :queue => 'end' ) ) %>
30
31   <!-- BlindDown effect -->
32   <% elsif @currentEffect == '4' %>
33      <%= link_to_remote 'BlindDown', :url => { :action => 'playEffect',
34         :effect_index => 5 }, :update => "link",
35         :before => ( visual_effect(
36            :BlindDown, 'image', :duration => 1.0, :queue => 'end' ) ) %>
37
38   <!-- Puff effect -->
39   <% elsif @currentEffect == '5' %>
40      <%= link_to_remote 'Puff', :url => { :action => 'playEffect',
41         :effect_index => 6 }, :update => "link",
42         :before => ( visual_effect(
43            :Puff, 'image', :duration => 1.0, :queue => 'end' ) ) %>
44
45   <!-- SwitchOff effect -->
46   <% elsif @currentEffect == '6' %>
47      <%= link_to_remote 'SwitchOff', :url => { :action => 'playEffect',
48         :effect_index => 7 }, :update => "link",
49         :before => ( visual_effect(
50            :SwitchOff, 'image', :duration => 1.0, :queue => 'end' ) ) %>
51
52   <!-- SlideUp effect -->
53   <% elsif @currentEffect == '7' %>
54      <%= link_to_remote 'SlideUp', :url => { :action => 'playEffect',
55         :effect_index => 8 }, :update => "link",
56         :before => ( visual_effect(
57            :SlideUp, 'image', :duration => 1.0, :queue => 'end' ) ) %>
58
59   <!-- SlideDown effect -->
60   <% elsif @currentEffect == '8' %>
61      <%= link_to_remote 'SlideDown', :url => { :action => 'playEffect',
62         :effect_index => 9 }, :update => "link",
63         :before => ( visual_effect(
64            :SlideDown, 'image', :duration => 1.0, :queue => 'end' ) ) %>
65
66   <!-- Shake effect -->
67   <% elsif @currentEffect == '9' %>
68      <%= link_to_remote 'Shake', :url => { :action => 'playEffect',
69         :effect_index => 10 }, :update => "link",
70         :before => ( visual_effect(
71            :Shake, 'image', :duration => 1.0, :queue => 'end' ) ) %>
72
73   <!-- Pulsate effect -->
74   <% elsif @currentEffect == '10' %>
75      <%= link_to_remote 'Pulsate', :url => { :action => 'playEffect',
```

Fig. 20.50 | link partial view for Script.aculo.us demo. (Part 2 of 3.)

```
76        :effect_index => 11 }, :update => "link",
77        :before => ( visual_effect(
78          :Pulsate, 'image', :duration => 1.0, :queue => 'end' ) ) %>
79
80   <!-- Squish effect -->
81   <% elsif @currentEffect == '11' %>
82     <%= link_to_remote 'Squish', :url => { :action => 'playEffect',
83        :effect_index => 12 }, :update => "link",
84        :before => ( visual_effect(
85          :Squish, 'image', :duration => 1.0, :queue => 'end' ) ) %>
86
87   <!-- Grow effect -->
88   <% elsif @currentEffect == '12' %>
89     <%= link_to_remote 'Grow', :url => { :action => 'playEffect',
90        :effect_index => 13 }, :update => "link",
91        :before => ( visual_effect(
92          :Grow, 'image', :duration => 1.0, :queue => 'end' ) ) %>
93
94   <!-- Fold effect -->
95   <% elsif @currentEffect == '13' %>
96     <%= link_to_remote 'Fold', :url => { :action => 'playEffect',
97        :effect_index => 14 }, :update => "link",
98        :before => ( visual_effect(
99          :Fold, 'image', :duration => 1.0, :queue => 'end' ) ) %>
100
101  <!-- Grow effect -->
102  <% elsif @currentEffect == '14' %>
103    <%= link_to_remote 'Grow', :url => { :action => 'playEffect',
104       :effect_index => 15 }, :update => "link",
105       :before => ( visual_effect(
106         :Grow, 'image', :duration => 1.0, :queue => 'end' ) ) %>
107
108  <!-- DropOut effect -->
109  <% elsif @currentEffect == '15' %>
110    <%= link_to_remote 'DropOut', :url => { :action => 'playEffect',
111       :effect_index => 16 }, :update => "link",
112       :before => ( visual_effect(
113         :DropOut, 'image', :duration => 1.0, :queue => 'end' ) ) %>
114
115  <!-- Grow effect -->
116  <% elsif @currentEffect == '16' %>
117    <%= link_to_remote 'Grow', :url => { :action => 'playEffect',
118       :effect_index => 17 }, :update => "link",
119       :before => ( visual_effect(
120         :Grow, 'image', :duration => 1.0, :queue => 'end' ) ) %>
121
122  <!-- Shrink effect -->
123  <% elsif @currentEffect == '17' %>
124    <%= link_to_remote 'Shrink', :url => { :action => 'playEffect',
125       :effect_index => 0 }, :update => "link",
126       :before => ( visual_effect(
127         :Shrink, 'image', :duration => 1.0, :queue => 'end' ) ) %>
128  <% end %>
```

Fig. 20.50 | link partial view for Script.aculo.us demo. (Part 3 of 3.)

Other Script.aculo.us Features

The Script.aculo.us library also brings other features to Rails. It provides drag-and-drop capability through the `draggable_element` and `drop_receiving_element` methods. A live example of this can be found at `demo.script.aculo.us/shop`.

Script.aculo.us also provides the `sortable_element` method which allows you to describe a list that allows the user to drag and drop list items to reorder them. A live example of this can be found at `demo.script.aculo.us/ajax/sortable_elements`.

Another interereresting capability is the `text_field_with_auto_complete` method, which enables server-side auto completion of a text field. A live example of this can be found at `demo.script.aculo.us/ajax/autocompleter`.

Flickr Photo Viewer with Effects

The Script.aculo.us library's effects are useful for adding a desktop-like feel to a web page. In the following example (Fig. 20.51), the user can search for photos with specific tags and can specify the number of images for each search to return. The application uses the Script.aculo.us sliding effect to show when the thumbnails for the specified tags have finished loading from Flickr. The application also uses the grow effect when the user clicks an image to display the full-size version of the image.

After creating the `FlickrPhotoViewer` application, you must install the Flickr library for Ruby. This library can be installed by executing `gem install flickr` in the Ruby console. More information about this library is available at `redgreenblu.com/flickr/`. Once

Fig. 20.51 | Flickr Photo Viewer showing search results for **bugs**.

installed, you must configure the library to use your own Flickr API key. You can sign up for a free API key at www.flickr.com/services/api/misc.api_keys.html. Once you receive your API key, you *must* replace the key in flickr.rb with your own. If you are using Instant Rails, flickr.rb will be located in the Instant Rails directory, in the folder. If you are running Mac OS X, or otherwise have installed Ruby system-wide, this file will be harder to find. If you cannot locate it with a normal search in Mac OS X, open **Terminal** and use find / -name flickr.rb to locate it. The API key to replace should be located at line 57, in the initialize method. Finally, you must tell the application to include the Flickr library by adding require 'flickr' to the end of config/environment.rb.

Create the controller with ruby script/generate controller flickr. In app/views/flickr/index.rhtml (Fig. 20.52), we create the application's main view. Be sure to copy the flickrPhotoViewer.css file from this chapter's folder into the public/stylesheets/ directory. Lines 15–31 contain a form_remote_tag element that implements the application's photo tag search functionality. Line 17 creates a BlindDown visual_effect for the thumbs div (line 32) when the search action is complete. Lines 18–19 create the corresponding BlindUp visual_effect for the loading div (lines 28–29). Lines 20–21 hide the loading div on failure and success events, respectively. The fullsizeImage div (line 33) will be populated later with an img element.

```
1   <?xml version = "1.0" encoding = "utf-8"?>
2   <!DOCTYPE html PUBLIC "-//W3C//DTD XHTML 1.0 Strict//EN"
3      "http://www.w3.org/TR/xhtml1/DTD/xhtml1-strict.dtd">
4
5   <!-- Fig. 20.52: app/view/flickr/index.rhtml -->
6   <!-- Main view for Flickr Photo Viewer. -->
7   <html xmlns = "http://www.w3.org/1999/xhtml">
8      <head>
9         <title>Flickr Photo Viewer</title>
10        <%= javascript_include_tag :defaults %>
11        <%= stylesheet_link_tag 'flickrPhotoViewer' %>
12     </head>
13     <body>
14        <!-- Form to search for tags -->
15        <%= form_remote_tag :url => { :action => 'search' },
16           :update => 'thumbs',
17           :complete => visual_effect( :BlindDown, 'thumbs' ),
18           :before => { visual_effect( :BlindUp, 'thumbs' ),
19              %( Element.show( 'loading' ) ) },
20           :failure => %( Element.hide( 'loading' ) ),
21           :success => %( Element.hide( 'loading' ) ) %>
22              <div id = "search">
23                 Tags:
24                 <%= text_field_tag "tags" %>
25                 #:
26                 <%= text_field_tag "numImages", "8", :size => "3" %>
27                 <%= submit_tag "Search" %>
28                 <div id = "loading"
29                    style = "display: none">Loading...</div>
30              </div>
```

Fig. 20.52 | Main view for Flickr Photo Viewer. (Part 1 of 2.)

```
31        <%= end_form_tag %>
32        <div id = "thumbs"></div>
33        <div id = "fullsizeImage"></div>
34    </body>
35 </html>
```

Fig. 20.52 | Main view for Flickr Photo Viewer. (Part 2 of 2.)

The controller located at app/controllers/flickr_controller.rb (Fig. 20.53) handles the search action called by the form in line 15 of Fig. 20.52 and the fullsizeImage action called by the link_to_remote in lines 3–9 of Fig. 20.54. In the search method, line 6 creates the flickr object using the Flickr class we installed previously. Lines 7–9 use the flickr object to populate thumbs with photos, supplying as arguments the tags and numImages values from the corresponding text_field_tags in lines 24 and 26 of Fig. 20.52. The fullsizeImage method (lines 13–15) takes the imageURL parameter's value and uses it to set the currentURL variable.

The thumbs view (Fig. 20.54) defines each thumbnail as a link_to_remote with an image_tag as the link's contents. The source of the image is retrieved from the thumbs collection that was passed by line 8 of Fig. 20.53. The first index, 0, specifies the image size to be the smallest provided by Flickr. In lines 5–6 of Fig. 20.54, we specify that the url should

```
1  # Fig. 20.53: app/controllers/flickr_controller.rb
2  # Controller for Flickr Photo Viewer.
3  class FlickrController < ApplicationController
4     # handle the search request
5     def search
6        flickr = Flickr.new
7        render :partial => "thumbs",
8           :collection => flickr.photos( :tags => params[ :tags ],
9           :per_page => params[ :numImages ] )
10    end # method search
11
12    # handle the thumbnail click, sets the currentURL variable
13    def fullsizeImage
14       @currentURL = params[ :imageURL ]
15    end # method fullsizeImage
16 end # class FlickrController
```

Fig. 20.53 | Controller for Flickr Photo Viewer.

```
1  <!-- Fig. 20.54: app/views/flickr/_thumbs.rhtml -->
2  <!-- thumbs view of Flickr Photo Viewer. -->
3  <%= link_to_remote image_tag( thumbs.sizes[ 0 ][ 'source' ],
4        :class => "image" ),
5     :url => { :action => 'fullsizeImage',
6        :imageURL => thumbs.sizes[ 3 ][ 'source' ] },
7     :update => "fullsizeImage",
8     :success => visual_effect( :grow, 'fullsizeImage',
9        :queue => 'last' ) %>
```

Fig. 20.54 | thumbs view of Flickr photo viewer.

activate the `fullsizeImage` action and pass an `imageURL` parameter. This parameter is set to the source of the image's large version. Lines 8–9 apply the `grow` `visual_effect` to `fullsizeImage`.

The `fullsizeImage` view (Fig. 20.55) fills the `fullsizeImage` div in line 33 of Fig. 20.52 with an `image_tag`. The source of this image is set to the `currentURL` variable. Try the program out with different tag searches and numbers of images.

```
1  <!-- Fig. 20.55: app/views/flickr/fullsizeImage.rhtml -->
2  <!-- fullsizeImage view of Flickr Photo Viewer. -->
3  <%= image_tag( @currentURL, :class => "image" ) %>
```

Fig. 20.55 | `fullsizeImage` view of Flickr Photo Viewer.

20.8 Web Resources

www.deitel.com/Ruby/
www.deitel.com/RubyOnRails/

The Deitel Ruby and Ruby on Rails Resource Centers contain links to some of the best Ruby and Rails resources on the web. There you'll find categorized links to forums, conferences, blogs, books, open source projects, videos, podcasts, webcasts and more. Also check out the tutorials for all skill levels, from introductory to advanced.

21

ASP.NET 2.0 and ASP.NET Ajax

OBJECTIVES

In this chapter you will learn:

- Web application development using Active Server Pages .NET (ASP.NET).

- To create Web Forms.

- To create ASP.NET applications consisting of multiple Web Forms.

- To maintain state information about a user with session tracking and cookies.

- To use the **Web Site Administration Tool** to modify web application configuration settings.

- To control user access to web applications using forms authentication and ASP.NET login controls.

- To use databases in ASP.NET applications.

- To design a master page and content pages to create a uniform look-and-feel for a website.

21.1 Introduction

This chapter introduces *web application development* with Microsoft's *Active Server Pages .NET (ASP.NET) 2.0* technology. Web-based applications create web content for web-browser clients. This web content includes Extensible HyperText Markup Language (XHTML), client-side scripting, images and binary data. If you are not familiar with XHTML, you should read Chapter 2 before studying this chapter. [*Note:* This chapter assumes that you know Visual Basic and are familiar with the .NET platform version 2.0. To learn more about Visual Basic, check out *Visual Basic 2005 How to Program, Third Edition*, or visit our Visual Basic Resource Center at www.deitel.com/visualbasic.]

We present several examples that demonstrate web application development using *Web Forms*, *web controls* (also called *ASP.NET server controls*) and Visual Basic programming. We also introduce ASP.NET Ajax and use it to enhance one of the earlier examples. Web Form files have the filename extension *.aspx* and contain the web page's GUI. You customize Web Forms by adding web controls including labels, text boxes, images, buttons and other GUI components. The Web Form file generates the web page that is sent to the client browser. From this point onward, we refer to Web Form files as *ASPX files*.

An ASPX file created in Visual Studio is implemented as a class written in a .NET language, such as Visual Basic. This class contains event handlers, initialization code, utility methods and other supporting code. The file that contains this class is called the *code-behind file* and provides the ASPX file's programmatic implementation.

To develop the code and GUIs in this chapter, we used Microsoft Visual Web Developer 2005 Express—an IDE designed for developing ASP.NET web applications. Visual Web Developer and Visual Basic 2005 Express share many common features and visual programming tools that simplify building complex applications, such as those that access a database (Sections 21.5–21.6). The full version of Visual Studio 2005 includes the functionality of Visual Web Developer, so the instructions we present for Visual Web Developer also apply to Visual Studio 2005. Note that you must install either Visual Web Developer 2005 Express (available from msdn.microsoft.com/vstudio/express/vwd/default.aspx) or a complete version of Visual Studio 2005 to implement the programs in this chapter.

21.2 Creating and Running a Simple Web Form Example

Our first example displays the web server's time of day in a browser window. When run, this program displays the text A Simple Web Form Example, followed by the web server's time. As mentioned previously, the program consists of two related files—an ASPX file (Fig. 21.1) and a Visual Basic code-behind file (Fig. 21.2), which we'll discuss in Section 21.2.5. We first display the markup, code and output, then we carefully guide you through the step-by-step process of creating this program. [*Note:* The markup in Fig. 21.1 and other ASPX file listings in this chapter is the same as the markup that appears in Visual Web Developer, but we've reformatted it for presentation purposes to make the code more readable.]

Visual Web Developer generates all the markup shown in Fig. 21.1 when you set the web page's title, type text in the Web Form, drag a Label onto the Web Form and set the properties of the page's text and the Label. We discuss these steps in Section 21.2.6.

```
 1   <%-- Fig. 21.1: WebTime.aspx --%>
 2   <%-- A page that displays the current time in a Label. --%>
 3   <%@ Page Language="VB" AutoEventWireup="false" CodeFile="WebTime.aspx.vb"
 4      Inherits="WebTime" EnableSessionState="False" %>
 5
 6   <!DOCTYPE html PUBLIC "-//W3C//DTD XHTML 1.0 Transitional//EN"
 7      "http://www.w3.org/TR/xhtml1/DTD/xhtml1-transitional.dtd">
 8
 9   <html xmlns="http://www.w3.org/1999/xhtml" >
10   <head runat="server">
11      <title>A Simple Web Form Example</title>
12   </head>
13   <body>
14      <form id="form1" runat="server">
15      <div>
16         <h2>
17         Current time on the Web server:</h2>
```

Fig. 21.1 | ASPX file that displays the web server's time. (Part 1 of 2.)

```
18          <p>
19              <asp:Label ID="timeLabel" runat="server" BackColor="Black"
20                  EnableViewState="False" Font-Size="XX-Large"
21                  ForeColor="Yellow"></asp:Label>
22          </p>
23      </div>
24      </form>
25  </body>
26  </html>
```

Fig. 21.1 | ASPX file that displays the web server's time. (Part 2 of 2.)

21.2.1 Examining an ASPX File

The ASPX file contains other information in addition to XHTML. Lines 1–2 are *ASP.NET comments* that indicate the figure number, the filename and the purpose of the file. ASP.NET comments begin with **<%--** and terminate with **--%>**. We added these comments to the file. ASP.NET comments are not output as part of the XHTML sent to the client. Lines 3–4 use a *Page* directive (in an ASPX file a *directive* is delimited by **<%@** and **%>**) to specify information needed by ASP.NET to process this file. The *Language* attribute of the Page directive specifies the language of the code-behind file as Visual Basic ("VB"); the code-behind file (i.e., the *CodeFile*) is WebTime.aspx.vb. A code-behind file-name usually consists of the full ASPX filename (e.g., WebTime.aspx) followed by a file-name extension indicating the programming language (.vb in this chapter's examples).

The *AutoEventWireup* attribute (line 3) determines how Web Form events are handled. When AutoEventWireup is set to true, ASP.NET determines which methods in the class are called in response to events generated in the Page. For example, ASP.NET will call methods Page_Init and Page_Load in the code-behind file to handle the Page's Init and Load events, respectively. AutoEventWireup requires the event-handling methods to follow specific naming copnventions. (We discuss these events later in the chapter.)

The *Inherits* attribute (line 4) specifies the page's class name—in this case, WebTime. We say more about Inherits momentarily. [*Note:* We explicitly set the *EnableSession-State* attribute (line 4) to False. We explain the significance of this attribute later in the chapter. The IDE sometimes generates attribute values (e.g., true and false) and control names (as you will see later in the chapter) that do not adhere to our standard code capitalization conventions (i.e., True and False). Like Visual Basic, ASP.NET markup is not case sensitive, so using a different case is not problematic. To remain consistent with the code generated by the IDE, we do not modify these values in our code listings or in our accompanying discussions.]

For this first ASPX file, we provide a brief discussion of the XHTML markup. For more information on XHTML, see Chapter 2. Lines 6–7 contain the document type declaration, which specifies the document element name (HTML) and the PUBLIC Uniform Resource Identifier (URI) for the DTD that defines the XHTML vocabulary.

Lines 9–10 contain the <html> and <head> start tags, respectively. XHTML documents have the root element html and mark up information about the document in the head element. Also note that the html element specifies the XML namespace of the document using the xmlns attribute (see Section 12.4).

Notice the *runat* attribute in line 10, which is set to *"server"*. This attribute indicates that when a client requests this ASPX file, ASP.NET processes the head element and its nested elements on the server and generates the corresponding XHTML, which is then sent to the client. In this case, the XHTML sent to the client will be identical to the markup in the ASPX file. However, as you will see, ASP.NET can generate complex XHTML markup from simple elements in an ASPX file.

Line 11 sets the title of this web page. We demonstrate how to set the title through a property in the IDE shortly. Line 13 contains the <body> start tag, which begins the body of the XHTML document; the body contains the main content that the browser displays. The form that contains our XHTML text and controls is defined in lines 14–24. Again, the runat attribute in the form element indicates that this element executes on the server, which generates equivalent XHTML and sends it to the client. Lines 15–23 contain a div element that groups the elements of the form in a block of markup.

Software Engineering Observation 21.1

Most ASP.NET controls must be placed in a form element in which the <form> tag has the runat="server" attribute.

Lines 16–17 are an XHTML h2 heading element. As we demonstrate shortly, the IDE generates this element in response to typing text directly in the Web Form and selecting the text as a second-level heading.

Lines 18–22 contain a p element to mark up a paragraph of content in the browser. Lines 19–21 mark up a Label web control. The properties that we set in the **Properties** window, such as Font-Size and BackColor (i.e., background color), are attributes here. The *ID* attribute (line 19) assigns a name to the control so that it can be manipulated programmatically in the code-behind file. We set the control's *EnableViewState* attribute (line 20) to False. We explain the significance of this attribute later in the chapter.

The *asp: tag prefix* in the declaration of the *Label* tag (line 19) indicates that the label is an ASP.NET web control, not an XHTML element. Each web control maps to a corresponding XHTML element (or group of elements)—when processing a web control on the server, ASP.NET generates XHTML markup that will be sent to the client to represent that control in a web browser.

Portability Tip 21.1

The same web control can map to different XHTML elements, depending on the client browser and the web control's property settings.

In this example, the asp:Label control maps to the XHTML *span* element (i.e., ASP.NET creates a span element to represent this control in the client's web browser). A span element particular element is used because span elements allow formatting styles to be applied to text. Several of the property values that were applied to our label are represented as part of the style attribute of the span element. You will soon see what the generated span element's markup looks like.

The web control in this example contains the runat="server" attribute–value pair (line 19), because this control must be processed on the server so that the server can translate the control into XHTML that can be rendered in the client browser. If this attribute pair is not present, the asp:Label element is written as text to the client (i.e., the control is not converted into a span element and does not render properly).

21.2.2 Examining a Code-Behind File

Figure 21.2 presents the code-behind file. Recall that the ASPX file in Fig. 21.1 references WebTime.aspx.vb in line 3.

Line 3 (Fig. 21.2) begins the declaration of class WebTime. A class declaration can span multiple source-code files, and the separate portions of the class declaration in each file are known as partial classes. The Partial modifier in line 3 indicates that the code-behind file is a partial class. We discuss the remainder of this class shortly.

Line 4 indicates that WebTime inherits from class *Page* in namespace *System.Web.UI*. This namespace contains classes and controls that assist in building web-based applications. Class Page provides events and objects necessary for creating web-based applications. In addition to class Page, System.Web.UI also includes class *Control*—the base class that provides common functionality for all web controls.

Lines 7–11 define method *Page_Init*, which handles the page's *Init* event. This event indicates that all the controls on the page have been created and initialized and additional application-specific initialization can now be performed. The only initialization required for this page is setting timeLabel's Text property to the time on the server (i.e., the computer on which this code executes). The statement in line 10 retrieves the current time and formats it as *hh*:*mm*:*ss*. For example, 9 AM is formatted as 09:00:00, and 2:30 PM is formatted as 14:30:00. Notice that the code-behind file can access timeLabel (the ID of the Label in the ASPX file) programmatically, even though the file does not contain a declaration for a variable named timeLabel. You will learn why momentarily.

```
1   ' Fig. 21.5: WebTime.aspx.vb
2   ' Code-behind file for a page that displays the current time.
3   Partial Class WebTime
4      Inherits System.Web.UI.Page
5
6      ' initializes the contents of the page
7      Protected Sub Page_Init(ByVal sender As Object, _
8         ByVal e As System.EventArgs) Handles Me.Init
9         ' display the server's current time in timeLabel
10        timeLabel.Text = DateTime.Now.ToString("hh:mm:ss")
11     End Sub ' Page_Init
12  End Class ' WebTime
```

Fig. 21.2 | Code-behind file for a page that displays the web server's time.

21.2.3 Relationship Between an ASPX File and a Code-Behind File

How are the ASPX and code-behind files used to create the web page that is sent to the client? First, recall that class WebTime is the base class specified in line 4 of the ASPX file (Fig. 21.1). This class (partially declared in the code-behind file) inherits from Page, which defines general web page functionality. Partial class WebTime inherits this functionality and defines some of its own (i.e., displaying the current time). The code in the code-behind file displays the time, whereas the code in the ASPX file defines the GUI.

When a client requests an ASPX file, ASP.NET creates two partial classes behind the scenes. The code-behind file contains one partial class named WebTime and ASP.NET generate another partial class containing the remainder of class WebTime, based on the markup in the ASPX file. For example, WebTime.aspx contains a *Label* web control with ID time-Label, so the generated partial class would contain a declaration for a variable named timeLabel of type System.Web.UI.WebControls.Label. Class Label represents a web control for displaying text. It is defined in namespace *System.Web.UI.WebControls*, which contains web controls for designing a page's user interface. Web controls in this namespace derive from class *WebControl*. When compiled, the partial class that declares timeLabel combines with the code-behind file's partial class declaration to form the complete WebTime class. This explains why line 10 in Fig. 21.2 can access timeLabel, which is created in lines 19–21 of WebTime.aspx (Fig. 21.1)—method Page_Init and control timeLabel are actually members of the same class, but defined in separate partial classes.

The partial class generated by ASP.NET is based on the ASPX file that defines the page's visual representation. This partial class is combined with the one in Fig. 21.2, which defines the page's logic. The first time the web page is requested, this class is compiled and an instance is created. This instance represents the page and creates the XHTML that is sent to the client. The assembly created from the compiled partial classes is placed in a subdirectory of

```
C:\WINDOWS\Microsoft.NET\Framework\VersionNumber\
   Temporary ASP.NET Files\WebTime
```

where *VersionNumber* is the version number of the .NET Framework (e.g., v2.0.50727) installed on your computer.

Once the web page has been compiled, no recompilation is required on subsequent requeses. New instances of the web page class will be created to serve each request. The project will be recompiled only when you modify the application; changes are detected by the runtime environment, and the application is recompiled to reflect the altered content.

21.2.4 How the Code in an ASP.NET Web Page Executes

Let's look briefly at how the code for our web page executes. When an instance of the page is created, the *PreInit* event occurs first, invoking method *Page_PreInit*, which can be used to set a page's theme and look-and-feel (and perform other tasks that are beyond this chapter's scope). The Init event occurs next, invoking method Page_Init. Method Page_Init is used to initialize objects and other aspects of the page. After Page_Init executes, the *Load* event occurs, and the *Page_Load* event handler executes. Although not present in this example, the PreInit and Load events are inherited from class Page. You will see examples of the Page_Load event handler later in the chapter. After the Load event handler finishes executing, the page processes events that are generated by the page's controls, such as user interactions with the GUI. When the user's request is considered fully processed, an *Unload* event occurs, which calls the *Page_Unload* event handler. This event, too, is inherited from class Page. Page_Unload typically contains code that releases resources used by the page. Other events occur as well, but are typically used only by ASP.NET controls to generate XHTML to render client-side controls. You can learn more about a Page's event life cycle at msdn2.microsoft.com/en-US/library/ms178472.aspx.

21.2.5 Examining the XHTML Generated by an ASP.NET Application

Figure 21.3 shows the XHTML generated by ASP.NET when a client browser requests WebTime.aspx (Fig. 21.1). To view this code, select **View > Source** in Internet Explorer. We added the comments in lines 1–2 and reformatted the XHTML for readability.

The markup in this page is similar to the ASPX file. Lines 7–9 define a document header comparable to that in Fig. 21.1. Lines 10–25 define the document's body. Line 11 begins the form, a mechanism for collecting user information and sending it to the web server. In this particular program, the user does not submit data to the web server for processing; however, processing user data is a crucial part of many applications that is facilitated by forms. We demonstrate how to submit form data to the server in later examples.

XHTML forms can contain visual and nonvisual components. Visual components include buttons and other GUI components with which users interact. Nonvisual components, called *hidden inputs*, store data, such as e-mail addresses, that the document author specifies. A hidden input is defined in lines 13–14. We discuss the precise meaning of this

```
1   <!-- Fig. 21.3: WebTime.html -->
2   <!-- The XHTML generated when WebTime.aspx is loaded. -->
3   <!DOCTYPE html PUBLIC "-//W3C//DTD XHTML 1.1//EN"
4      "http://www.w3.org/TR/xhtml11/DTD/xhtml11.dtd">
5
6   <html xmlns="http://www.w3.org/1999/xhtml" >
7   <head>
8      <title>A Simple Web Form Example</title>
9   </head>
10  <body>
11     <form name="form1" method="post" action="WebTime.aspx" id="form1">
12        <div>
13           <input type="hidden" name="__VIEWSTATE" id="__VIEWSTATE" value=
14              "/wEPDwUJODExMDE5NzY5ZGSzVbs789nqEeoNueQCnCJQEUgykw==" />
15        </div>
16
17        <div>
18           <h2>Current time on the Web server:</h2>
19           <p>
20              <span id="timeLabel" style="color:Yellow;
21                 background-color:Black;font-size:XX-Large;">13:51:12</span>
22           </p>
23        </div>
24     </form>
25  </body>
26  </html>
```

Fig. 21.3 | XHTML response when the browser requests WebTime.aspx.

hidden input later in the chapter. Attribute *method* of the form element (line 11) specifies the method by which the web browser submits the form to the server. The *action* attribute identifies the name and location of the resource that will be requested when this form is submitted—in this case, WebTime.aspx. Recall that the ASPX file's form element contained the runat="server" attribute–value pair (line 14 of Fig. 21.1). When the form is processed on the server, the runat attribute is removed. The method and action attributes are added, and the resulting XHTML form is sent to the client browser.

In the ASPX file, the form's Label (i.e., timeLabel) is a web control. Here, we are viewing the XHTML created by our application, so the form contains a span element (lines 20–21 of Fig. 21.3) to represent the text in the label. In this particular case, ASP.NET maps the Label web control to an XHTML span element. The formatting options that were specified as properties of timeLabel, such as the font size and color of the text in the Label, are now specified in the style attribute of the span element.

Notice that only those elements in the ASPX file marked with the runat="server" attribute–value pair or specified as web controls are modified or replaced when the file is processed by the server. The pure XHTML elements, such as the h2 in line 18, are sent to the browser as they appear in the ASPX file.

21.2.6 Building an ASP.NET Web Application

Now that we have presented the ASPX file, the code-behind file and the resulting web page sent to the web browser, we show the steps we used to create this application in Visual Web Developer.

Step 1: Creating the Website

In Visual Web Developer, select **File > New Web Site...** to display the **New Web Site** dialog (Fig. 21.4). In this dialog, select *ASP.NET Web Site* in the **Templates** pane. Below this pane, there are two fields in which you can specify the type and location of the web appli-

Fig. 21.4 | Creating an **ASP.NET Web Site** in Visual Web Developer.

cation you are creating. If it is not already selected, select **HTTP** from the drop-down list closest to **Location**. This indicates that the web application should be configured to run as an IIS application using HTTP (either on your computer or on a remote computer). We want our project to be located in `http://localhost`, which is the URL for IIS's root directory (this URL normally corresponds to the `C:\InetPub\wwwroot` directory on your machine). The name *`localhost`* indicates that the server resides on local computer. If the web server were located on a different computer, `localhost` would be replaced with the appropriate IP address or hostname. By default, Visual Web Developer sets the location where the website will be created to `http://localhost/WebSite`, which we change to `http://localhost/WebTime`.

If you do not have IIS on your computer or do not have permission to access it, you can select **File System** from the drop-down list next to **Location** to create the web application in a folder on your computer. You will be able to test the application using Visual Web Developer's internal ASP.NET Development Server, but you will not be able to access the application remotely over the Internet.

The **Language** drop-down list in the **New Web Site** dialog allows you to specify the language (i.e., Visual Basic, Visual C# or Visual J#) in which you will write the code-behind file(s) for the web application. Change the setting to Visual Basic. Click **OK** to create the website. This creates the directory `C:\Inetpub\wwwroot\WebTime` (in IIS) and makes it accessible through the URL `http://localhost/WebTime`. This action also creates a `WebTime` directory in the directory `My Documents\Visual Studio 2005\Projects` in which the project's solution files (e.g., `WebTime.sln`) are stored.

Step 2: Examining the Solution Explorer of the Newly Created Project

The next several figures describe the new project's content, beginning with the **Solution Explorer** shown in Fig. 21.5. Like Visual Basic 2005 Express, Visual Web Developer creates several files when you create a new project. It creates an ASPX file (i.e., Web Form) named `Default.aspx` for each new **ASP.NET Web Site** project. This file is open by default in the Web Forms Designer in **Source** mode when the project first loads (we discuss this momentarily). As mentioned previously, a code-behind file is included as part of the project. Visual Web Developer creates a code-behind file named `Default.aspx.vb`. To open the ASPX file's code-behind file, right click the ASPX file and select **View Code** or click the **View Code** button ( ) at the top of the **Solution Explorer**. Alternatively, you can

Fig. 21.5 | **Solution Explorer** window for project `WebTime`.

expand the node for the ASPX file to reveal the node for the code-behind file (see Fig. 21.5). You can also choose to list all the files in the project individually (instead of nested) by clicking the **Nest Related Files** button—this option is turned on by default, so clicking the button toggles the option off.

The **Properties** and **Refresh** buttons in Visual Web Developer's **Solution Explorer** behave like those in Visual Basic 2005 Express. Visual Web Developer's **Solution Explorer** also contains the buttons **View Designer, Copy Web Site** and **ASP.NET Configuration**. The **View Designer** button allows you to open the Web Form in **Design** mode, which we discuss shortly. The **Copy Web Site** button opens a dialog that allows you to move the files in this project to another location, such as a remote web server. This is useful if you are developing the application on your local computer, but want to make it available to the public from a different location. Finally, the **ASP.NET Configuration** button takes you to a web page called the **Web Site Administration Tool**, where you can manipulate various settings and security options for your application. We discuss this tool in greater detail in Section 21.6.

Step 3: Examining the Toolbox in Visual Web Developer

Figure 21.6 shows the **Toolbox** displayed in the IDE when the project loads. Figure 21.6(a) displays the beginning of the **Standard** list of web controls, and Fig. 21.6(b) displays the remaining web controls, and the list of **Data** controls used in ASP.NET. We discuss specific controls in Fig. 21.6 as they are used throughout the chapter. Notice that some controls in the **Toolbox** are similar to Windows controls.

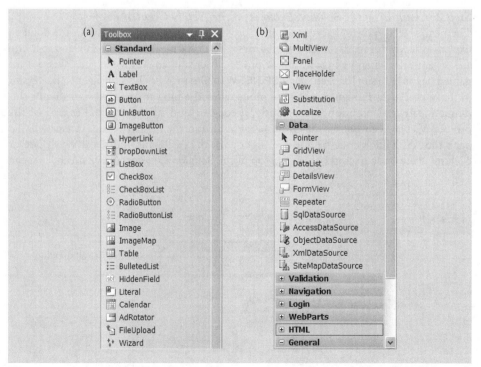

Fig. 21.6 | Toolbox in Visual Web Developer.

Step 4: Examining the Web Forms Designer

Figure 21.7 shows the Web Forms Designer in **Source** mode, which appears in the center of the IDE. When the project loads for the first time, the Web Forms Designer displays the autogenerated ASPX file (i.e., Default.aspx) in **Source** mode, which allows you to view and edit the markup that comprises the web page. The markup listed in Fig. 21.7 was created by the IDE and serves as a template that we'll modify shortly. Clicking the **Design** button in the lower-left corner of the Web Forms Designer switches to **Design** mode (Fig. 21.8), which allows you to drag and drop controls from the **Toolbox** onto the Web Form and see the controls. You can also type at the current cursor location to add text to the web page. We demonstrate this shortly. In response to such actions, the IDE generates the appropriate markup in the ASPX file. Notice that **Design** mode indicates the XHTML element where the cursor is currently located. Clicking the **Source** button returns the Web Forms Designer to **Source** mode, where you can see the generated markup.

Fig. 21.7 │ **Source** mode of the Web Forms Designer.

Fig. 21.8 │ **Design** mode of the Web Forms Designer.

Step 5: Examining the Code-Behind File in the IDE

The next figure (Fig. 21.9) displays `Default.aspx.vb`—the code-behind file generated by Visual Web Developer for `Default.aspx`. Right click the ASPX file in the **Solution Explorer** and select **View Code** to open the code-behind file. When it is first created, this file contains nothing more than a partial class declaration. We'll add the `Page_Init` event handler to this code momentarily.

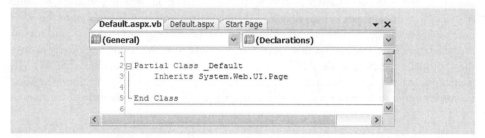

Fig. 21.9 | Code-behind file for `Default.aspx` generated by Visual Web Developer.

Step 6: Renaming the ASPX File

Now that you've seen the contents of the default ASPX and code-behind files, let's rename these files. Right click the ASPX file in the **Solution Explorer** and select **Rename**. Enter the new filename `WebTime.aspx` and press *Enter*. This updates the name of both the ASPX file and the code-behind file. The IDE also updates the `Page` directive's `CodeFile` attribute in `WebTime.aspx`.

Step 7: Renaming the Class in the Code-Behind File and Updating the ASPX File

Although renaming the ASPX file causes the name of the code-behind file to change, this action does not affect the name of the partial class declared in the code-behind file. Open the code-behind file and change the class name from `_Default` (line 2 in Fig. 21.9) to `WebTime`, so the partial class declaration appears as in line 3 of Fig. 21.2. Recall that this class is also referenced by the `Page` directive in the ASPX file. Using the Web Forms Designer's **Source** mode, modify the `Inherits` attribute of the `Page` directive in `WebTime.aspx`, so it appears as in line 4 of Fig. 21.1. The value of the `Inherits` attribute and the class name in the code-behind file must be identical; otherwise, you'll get errors when you build the web application.

Step 8: Changing the Title of the Page

Before designing the content of the Web Form, we change its title from the default `Untitled Page` (line 9 of Fig. 21.7) to `A Simple Web Form Example`. To do so, open the ASPX file in **Source** mode and modify the text in the `title` element—i.e., the text between the tags `<title>` and `</title>`. Alternatively, you can open the ASPX file in **Design** mode and modify the Web Form's *Title* property in the **Properties** window. To view the Web Form's properties, select DOCUMENT from the drop-down list in the **Properties** window; *DOCUMENT* represents the Web Form in the **Properties** window.

Step 9: Designing the Page

Designing a Web Form is as simple as designing a Windows Form. To add controls to the page, drag-and-drop them from the **Toolbox** onto the Web Form in **Design** mode. Like the

Web Form itself, each control is an object that has properties, methods and events. You can set these properties and events visually using the **Properties** window or programmatically in the code-behind file. However, unlike working with a Windows Form, you can type text directly on a Web Form at the cursor location or insert XHTML elements from the **Toolbox**.

Controls and other elements are placed sequentially on a Web Form, much as text and images are placed in a document using word-processing software like Microsoft Word. Controls are placed one after another in the order in which you drag-and-drop them onto the Web Form. The cursor indicates the point at which text and XHTML elements will be inserted. If you want to position a control between existing text or controls, you can drop the control at a specific position within the existing elements. You can also rearrange existing controls using drag-and-drop actions. By default, controls flow based on the width of the page. An alternate type of layout is known as *absolute positioning*, in which controls are located exactly where they are dropped on the Web Form. You can enable absolute positioning in **Design** mode by selecting **Layout > Position > Auto-position Options....**, clicking the first checkbox in the **Positioning options** pane of the **Options** dialog that appears, then selecting the appropriate positioning option from the drop-down menu.

Portability Tip 21.2

Absolute positioning is discouraged, because pages designed in this manner may not render correctly on computers with different screen resolutions and font sizes. This could cause absolutely positioned elements to overlap each other or display off-screen, requiring the client to scroll to see the full page content.

In this example, we use one piece of text and one `Label`. To add the text to the Web Form, click the blank Web Form in **Design** mode and type `Current time on the Web server:`. Visual Web Developer is a *WYSIWYG* (*What You See Is What You Get*) editor—whenever you make a change to a Web Form in **Design** mode, the IDE creates the markup (visible in **Source** mode) necessary to achieve the desired visual effects seen in **Design** mode. After adding the text to the Web Form, switch to **Source** mode. You should see that the IDE added this text to the `div` element that appears in the ASPX file by default. Back in **Design** mode, highlight the text you added. From the **Block Format** drop-down list (see Fig. 21.10), choose **Heading 2** to format this text as a heading that will appear bold in a font slightly larger than the default. This action encloses the text in an `h2` element. Finally, click to the right of the text and press the *Enter* key to start a new paragraph. This action generates a `p` (paragraph) element in the ASPX file's markup. The IDE should now look like Fig. 21.10.

You can place a `Label` on a Web Form either by dragging-and-dropping or by double clicking the **Toolbox**'s **Label** control. Ensure that the cursor is in the new paragraph, then add a `Label` that will be used to display the time. Using the **Properties** window, set the `(ID)` property of the `Label` to `timeLabel`. In the `Text` property, delete `timeLabel`'s text—this text will be set programmatically in the code-behind file. When a `Label` does not contain text, its name is displayed in square brackets in the Web Forms Designer (Fig. 21.11) as a placeholder for design and layout purposes. This text is not displayed at execution time. We set `timeLabel`'s `BackColor`, `ForeColor` and `Font-Size` properties to `Black`, `Yellow` and `XX-Large`, respectively. To change the `Label`'s font properties, select the `Label`, expand the `Font` node in the **Properties** window and change each relevant property.

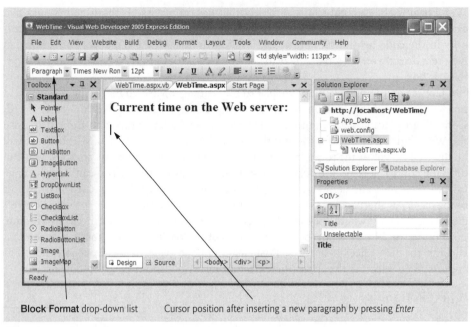

Block Format drop-down list   Cursor position after inserting a new paragraph by pressing *Enter*

Fig. 21.10 | `WebTime.aspx` after inserting text and a new paragraph.

As the `Label`'s properties are set, Visual Web Developer updates the ASPX file's contents. Figure 21.11 shows the IDE after setting these properties.

Next, set the `Label`'s `EnableViewState` property to `False`. Finally, select `DOCUMENT` from the drop-down list in the **Properties** window and set the Web Form's `EnableSessionState` property to `False`. We discuss both of these properties later in the chapter.

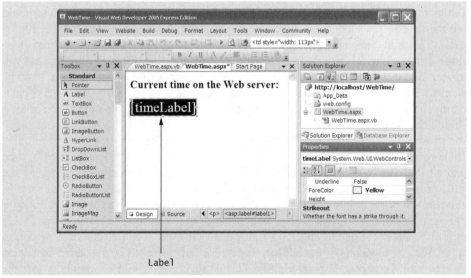

Label

Fig. 21.11 | `WebTime.aspx` after adding a `Label` and setting its properties.

Step 10: Adding Page Logic

Now that you've designed the user interface, you'll add Visual Basic code to the code-behind file to obtain the server's time. Open `WebTime.aspx.vb` by double clicking its node in the **Solution Explorer**. In this example, we add a `Page_Init` event handler (lines 7–11 of Fig. 21.2) to the code-behind file. Recall that `Page_Init` handles the `Init` event and contains code to initialize the page. The statement in line 10 of Fig. 21.2 sets `timeLabel`'s text to the server's current time.

Step 11: Running the Program

After creating the Web Form, you can view it several ways. First, you can select **Debug > Start Without Debugging**, which runs the application by opening it in a browser window. If you created the application on your local IIS server (as we did in this example), the URL shown in the browser will be `http://localhost/WebTime/WebTime.aspx` (Fig. 21.2), indicating that the web page (the ASPX file) is located within the virtual directory `WebTime` on the local IIS web server. IIS must be running to test the website in a browser. IIS can be started by executing `inetmgr.exe` from **Start > Run...**, right clicking **Default Web Site** and selecting **Start**. [*Note:* You might need to expand the node representing your computer to display the **Default Web Site**.]

If you created the ASP.NET application on the local file system, the URL shown in the browser will be `http://localhost:`*PortNumber*`/WebTime/WebTime.aspx`, where *PortNumber* is the number of the randomly assigned port on which Visual Web Developer's built-in test server runs. The IDE assigns the port number on a per-solution basis. This URL indicates that the `WebTime` project folder is being accessed through the root directory of the test server running at `localhost:`*PortNumber*. When you select **Debug > Start Without Debugging**, a tray icon appears near the bottom-right of your screen next to the computer's date and time to show that the **ASP.NET Development Server** is running. The test server stops when you exit Visual Web Developer.

To debug your application, you can select **Debug > Start Debugging** to view the web page in a web browser with debugging enabled. You cannot debug a web application unless debugging is explicitly enabled by the ***Web.config*** file—a file that stores configuration settings for an ASP.NET web application. You will rarely need to manually create or modify `Web.config`. The first time you select **Debug > Start Debugging** in a project, a dialog appears and asks whether you want the IDE to modify the `Web.config` file to enable debugging. After you click **OK**, the IDE enters **Running** mode. You can exit **Running** mode by selecting **Debug > Stop Debugging** in Visual Web Developer or by closing the browser window in which the ASPX file is displayed.

To view a specific ASPX file, you can right click either the Web Forms Designer or the ASPX filename (in the **Solution Explorer**) and select ***View In Browser*** to load the page in a web browser. Right clicking the ASPX file in the **Solution Explorer** and selecting **Browse With...** also opens the page in a browser, but first allows you to specify the web browser that should display the page and its screen resolution.

Finally, you can run your application by opening a browser window and typing the web page's URL in the **Address** field. When testing an ASP.NET application on the same computer running IIS, type `http://localhost/`*ProjectFolder*`/`*PageName*`.aspx`, where *ProjectFolder* is the folder in which the page resides (usually the name of the project), and *PageName* is the name of the ASP.NET page. If your application resides on the local file system, you must first start the **ASP.NET Development Server** by running the application using one of the methods described above. Then you can type the URL (including the *PortNumber* found in the test server's tray icon) in the browser to execute the application.

Note that all of these methods of running the application compile the project for you. In fact, ASP.NET compiles your web page whenever it changes between HTTP requests. For example, suppose you browse the page, then modify the ASPX file or add code to the code-behind file. When you reload the page, ASP.NET recompiles the page on the server before returning the HTTP response to the browser. This important new behavior of ASP.NET 2.0 ensures that clients always see the latest version of the page. You can manually compile a web page or an entire website by selecting **Build Page** or **Build Site**, respectively, from the **Build** menu in Visual Web Developer.

Windows Firewall Settings

If you would like to test your web application over a network, you may need to change your Windows Firewall settings. For security reasons, Windows Firewall does not allow remote access to a web server on your local computer by default. To change this, open the Windows Firewall utility in the Windows Control Panel. In Windows XP, Click the **Advanced** tab and select your network connection from the **Network Connection Settings** list, then click **Settings....** On the **Services** tab of the **Advanced Settings** dialog, ensure that **Web Server (HTTP)** is checked. In Windows Vista click the **Change settings** link, then click **Continue** in dialog that appears. Select the **Exceptions** tab and place a check next to **World Wide Web Services (HTTP)**.

21.3 Web Controls

This section introduces some of the web controls located in the **Standard** section of the **Toolbox** (Fig. 21.6). Figure 21.12 summarizes some of the web controls used in the chapter examples.

Web control	Description
Label	Displays text that the user cannot edit.
TextBox	Gathers user input and displays text.
Button	Triggers an event when clicked.
HyperLink	Displays a hyperlink.
DropDownList	Displays a drop-down list of choices from which you can select an item.
RadioButtonList	Groups radio buttons.
Image	Displays images (e.g., GIF and JPG).

Fig. 21.12 | Commonly used web controls.

21.3.1 Text and Graphics Controls

Figure 21.13 depicts a simple form for gathering user input. This example uses all the controls listed in Fig. 21.12, except Label, which you used in Section 21.2. The code in

Fig. 21.13 was generated by Visual Web Developer in response to dragging controls onto the page in **Design** mode. To begin, create an ASP.NET website named WebControls. [*Note:* This example does not contain any functionality—i.e., no action occurs when the user clicks **Register**. In subsequent examples, we demonstrate how to add functionality to many of these web controls.]

```
1   <%-- Fig. 21.13: WebControls.aspx --%>
2   <%-- Registration form that demonstrates Web controls. --%>
3   <%@ Page Language="VB" AutoEventWireup="false"
4      CodeFile="WebControls.aspx.vb" Inherits="WebControls" %>
5
6   <!DOCTYPE html PUBLIC "-//W3C//DTD XHTML 1.0 Transitional//EN"
7      "http://www.w3.org/TR/xhtml1/DTD/xhtml1-transitional.dtd">
8
9   <html xmlns="http://www.w3.org/1999/xhtml">
10  <head runat="server">
11     <title>Web Controls Demonstration</title>
12  </head>
13  <body>
14     <form id="form1" runat="server">
15     <div>
16        <h3>This is a sample registration form.</h3>
17        <p>
18           <em>Please fill in all fields and click Register.</em></p>
19        <p>
20           <asp:Image ID="userInformationImage" runat="server"
21              EnableViewState="False" ImageUrl="~/Images/user.png" />  
22        <span style="color: teal">
23           Please fill out the fields below.</span>
24        </p>
25        <table id="TABLE1">
26           <tr>
27              <td style="width: 230px; height: 21px" valign="top">
28                 <asp:Image ID="firstNameImage" runat="server"
29                    EnableViewState="False" ImageUrl="~/Images/fname.png" />
30                 <asp:TextBox ID="firstNameTextBox" runat="server"
31                    EnableViewState="False"></asp:TextBox>
32              </td>
33              <td style="width: 231px; height: 21px" valign="top">
34                 <asp:Image ID="lastNameImage" runat="server"
35                    EnableViewState="False" ImageUrl="~/Images/lname.png" />
36                 <asp:TextBox ID="lastNameTextBox" runat="server"
37                    EnableViewState="False"></asp:TextBox>
38              </td>
39           </tr>
40           <tr>
41              <td style="width: 230px" valign="top">
42                 <asp:Image ID="emailImage" runat="server"
43                    EnableViewState="False" ImageUrl="~/Images/email.png" />
44                 <asp:TextBox ID="emailTextBox" runat="server"
45                    EnableViewState="False"></asp:TextBox>
46              </td>
```

Fig. 21.13 | Web Form that demonstrates web controls. (Part 1 of 3.)

```
47              <td style="width: 231px" valign="top">
48                 <asp:Image ID="phoneImage" runat="server"
49                    EnableViewState="False" ImageUrl="~/Images/phone.png" />
50                 <asp:TextBox ID="phoneTextBox" runat="server"
51                    EnableViewState="False"></asp:TextBox>
52                 Must be in the form (555) 555-5555.
53              </td>
54           </tr>
55        </table>
56        <p>
57           <asp:Image ID="publicationsImage" runat="server"
58              EnableViewState="False"
59              ImageUrl="~/Images/publications.png" />  
60           <span style="color: teal">
61              Which book would you like information about?</span>
62        </p>
63        <p>
64           <asp:DropDownList ID="booksDropDownList" runat="server"
65              EnableViewState="False">
66              <asp:ListItem>Visual Basic 2005 How to Program 3e
67                 </asp:ListItem>
68              <asp:ListItem>Visual C# 2005 How to Program 2e
69                 </asp:ListItem>
70              <asp:ListItem>Java How to Program 6e</asp:ListItem>
71              <asp:ListItem>C++ How to Program 5e</asp:ListItem>
72              <asp:ListItem>XML How to Program 1e</asp:ListItem>
73           </asp:DropDownList>
74        </p>
75        <p>
76           <asp:HyperLink ID="booksHyperLink" runat="server"
77              EnableViewState="False" NavigateUrl="http://www.deitel.com"
78              Target="_blank">
79              Click here to view more information about our books
80           </asp:HyperLink>
81        </p>
82        <p>
83           <asp:Image ID="osImage" runat="server" EnableViewState="False"
84              ImageUrl="~/Images/os.png" />  
85           <span style="color: teal">
86              Which operating system are you using?</span>
87        </p>
88        <p>
89           <asp:RadioButtonList ID="operatingSystemRadioButtonList"
90              runat="server" EnableViewState="False">
91              <asp:ListItem>Windows XP</asp:ListItem>
92              <asp:ListItem>Windows 2000</asp:ListItem>
93              <asp:ListItem>Windows NT</asp:ListItem>
94              <asp:ListItem>Linux</asp:ListItem>
95              <asp:ListItem>Other</asp:ListItem>
96           </asp:RadioButtonList>
97        </p>
98        <p>
```

Fig. 21.13 | Web Form that demonstrates web controls. (Part 2 of 3.)

```
99          <asp:Button ID="registerButton" runat="server"
100            EnableViewState="False" Text="Register" />
101      </p>
102    </div>
103    </form>
104  </body>
105  </html>
```

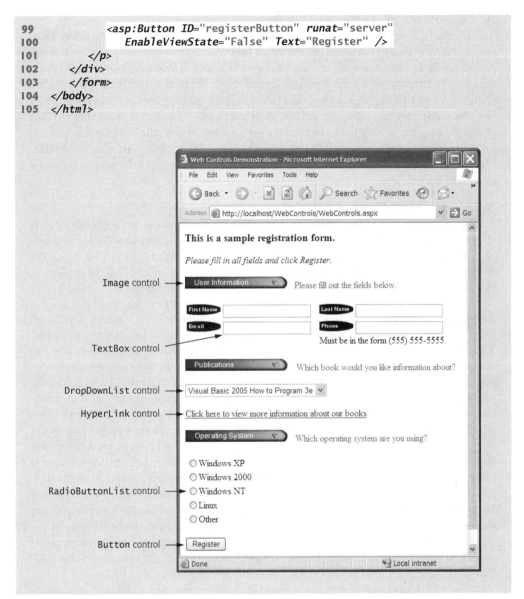

Fig. 21.13 | Web Form that demonstrates web controls. (Part 3 of 3.)

Before discussing the web controls used in this ASPX file, we explain the XHTML that creates the layout seen in Fig. 21.13. The page contains an h3 heading element (line 16), followed by a series of additional XHTML blocks. We place most of the web controls inside p elements (i.e., paragraphs), but we use an XHTML table element (lines 25–55) to organize the Image and TextBox controls in the user information section of the page. In the preceding section, we described how to add heading elements and paragraphs visually without manipulating any XHTML in the ASPX file directly. Visual Web Developer allows you to add a table in a similar manner.

Adding an XHTML Table to a Web Form

To create a table with two rows and two columns in **Design** mode, select the **Insert Table** command from the **Layout** menu. In the **Insert Table** dialog that appears, select the **Custom** radio button. In the **Layout** group box, change the values of **Rows** and **Columns** to 2. By default, the contents of a table cell are aligned vertically in the middle of the cell. We changed the vertical alignment of all cells in the table by clicking the **Cell Properties...** button, then selecting **top** from the **Vertical align** combo box in the resulting dialog. This causes the content of each table cell to align with the top of the cell. Click **OK** to close the **Cell Properties** dialog, then click **OK** to close the **Insert Table** dialog and create the table. Once a table is created, controls and text can be added to particular cells to create a neatly organized layout.

Setting the Color of Text on a Web Form

Notice that some of the instructions to the user on the form appear in a teal color. To set the color of a specific piece of text, highlight the text and select **Format > Foreground color...**. In the **Color Picker** dialog, click the **Named Colors** tab and choose a color. Click **OK** to apply the color. Note that the IDE places the colored text in an XHTML span element (e.g., lines 22–23) and applies the color using the span's style attribute.

Examining Web Controls on a Sample Registration Form

Lines 20–21 of Fig. 21.13 define an ***Image*** control, which inserts an image into a web page. The images used in this example are located in the chapter's examples directory. You can download the examples from www.deitel.com/books/ajaxfp. Before an image can be displayed on a web page using an Image web control, the image must first be added to the project. We added an Images folder to this project (and to each example project in the chapter that uses images) by right clicking the location of the project in the **Solution Explorer**, selecting **New Folder** and entering the folder name Images. We then added each of the images used in the example to this folder by right clicking the folder, selecting **Add Existing Item...** and browsing for the files to add. You can also drag a folder full of images onto the project's location in the **Solution Explorer** to add the folder and all the images to the project.

The ***ImageUrl*** property (line 21) specifies the location of the image to display in the Image control. To select an image, click the ellipsis next to the ImageUrl property in the **Properties** window and use the **Select Image** dialog to browse for the desired image in the project's Images folder. When the IDE fills in the ImageUrl property based on your selection, it includes a tilde and forward slash (~/) at the beginning of the ImageUrl—this indicates that the Images folder is in the root directory of the project.

Lines 25–55 contain the table element created by the steps discussed previously. Each td element contains an Image control and a ***TextBox*** control, which allows you to obtain text from the user and display text to the user. For example, lines 30–31 define a TextBox control used to collect the user's first name.

Lines 64–73 define a ***DropDownList***. This control is similar to the XHTML select control. When a user clicks the drop-down list, it expands and displays a list from which the user can make a selection. Each item in the drop-down list is defined by a ***ListItem*** element (lines 66–72). After dragging a DropDownList control onto a Web Form, you can add items to it using the **ListItem Collection Editor**. This process is similar to customizing a ListBox in a Windows application. In Visual Web Developer, you can access the **ListItem Collection Editor** by clicking the ellipsis next to the Items property of the DropDownList, or by using the **DropDownList Tasks** menu. You can open this menu by clicking the small arrowhead that appears in the upper-right corner of the control in **Design** mode (Fig. 21.14). This menu is called a *smart tag menu*. Visual Web Developer displays smart tag menus for many ASP.NET controls to facilitate common tasks. Clicking **Edit Items...** in the **DropDownList Tasks** menu opens the **ListItem Collection Editor**, which allows you to add ListItem elements to the DropDownList.

The ***HyperLink*** control (lines 76–80 of Fig. 21.13) adds a hyperlink to a web page. The ***NavigateUrl*** property (line 77) of this control specifies the resource (i.e., http:// www.deitel.com) that is requested when a user clicks the hyperlink. Setting the ***Target*** property to _blank specifies that the requested web page should open in a new browser window. By default, HyperLink controls cause pages to open in the same browser window.

Lines 89–96 define a ***RadioButtonList*** control, which provides a series of radio buttons from which the user can select only one. Like options in a DropDownList, individual radio buttons are defined by ListItem elements. Note that, like the **DropDownList Tasks** smart tag menu, the **RadioButtonList Tasks** smart tag menu also provides an **Edit Items...** link to open the **ListItem Collection Editor**.

The final web control in Fig. 21.13 is a ***Button*** (lines 99–100). A Button web control represents a button that triggers an action when clicked. This control typically maps to an XHTML input element with attribute type set to "submit". As stated earlier, clicking the **Register** button in this example does not do anything.

Fig. 21.14 | **DropDownList Tasks** smart tag menu.

21.3.2 AdRotator Control

Web pages often contain product or service advertisements, which usually consist of images. Although website authors want to include as many sponsors as possible, web pages can display only a limited number of advertisements. To address this problem, ASP.NET provides the ***AdRotator*** web control for displaying advertisements. Using advertisement data located in an XML file, an AdRotator randomly selects an image to display and generates a hyperlink to the web page associated with that image. Browsers that do not support images display alternate text that is specified in the XML document. If a user clicks the image or substituted text, the browser loads the web page associated with that image.

Demonstrating the AdRotator Web Control
Figure 21.15 demonstrates the AdRotator web control. In this example, the "advertisements" that we rotate are the flags of 10 countries. When a user clicks the displayed flag image, the browser is redirected to a web page containing information about the country that the flag represents. If a user refreshes the browser or requests the page again, one of the 10 flags is again chosen at random and displayed.

The ASPX file in Fig. 21.15 is similar to that in Fig. 21.1. However, instead of XHTML text and a Label, this page contains XHTML text (the h3 element in line 16) and an AdRotator control named countryRotator (lines 18–19). This page also contains an XmlDataSource control (lines 20–22), which supplies the data to the AdRotator control. The background attribute of the page's body element (line 13) is set to the image background.png, located in the project's Images folder. To specify this file, click the ellipsis provided next to the Background property of DOCUMENT in the **Properties** window and use the resulting dialog to select background.png from the Images folder. The images and XML file used in this example are both located in the chapter's examples directory.

You do not need to add any code to the code-behind file, because the AdRotator control "does all the work." The output depicts two different requests. Figure 21.15(a) shows

```
 1    <%-- Fig. 21.15: FlagRotator.aspx --%>
 2    <%-- A Web Form that displays flags using an AdRotator control. --%>
 3    <%@ Page Language="VB" AutoEventWireup="false"
 4       CodeFile="FlagRotator.aspx.vb" Inherits="FlagRotator" %>
 5
 6    <!DOCTYPE html PUBLIC "-//W3C//DTD XHTML 1.0 Transitional//EN"
 7       "http://www.w3.org/TR/xhtml1/DTD/xhtml1-transitional.dtd">
 8
 9    <html xmlns="http://www.w3.org/1999/xhtml" >
10    <head runat="server">
11       <title>Flag Rotator</title>
12    </head>
13    <body background="Images/background.png">
14       <form id="form1" runat="server">
15       <div>
16          <h3>AdRotator Example</h3>
17          <p>
18             <asp:AdRotator ID="countryRotator" runat="server"
19                DataSourceID="adXmlDataSource" />
20             <asp:XmlDataSource ID="adXmlDataSource" runat="server"
21                DataFile="~/App_Data/AdRotatorInformation.xml">
22             </asp:XmlDataSource>
23          </p>
24       </div>
25       </form>
26    </body>
27    </html>
```

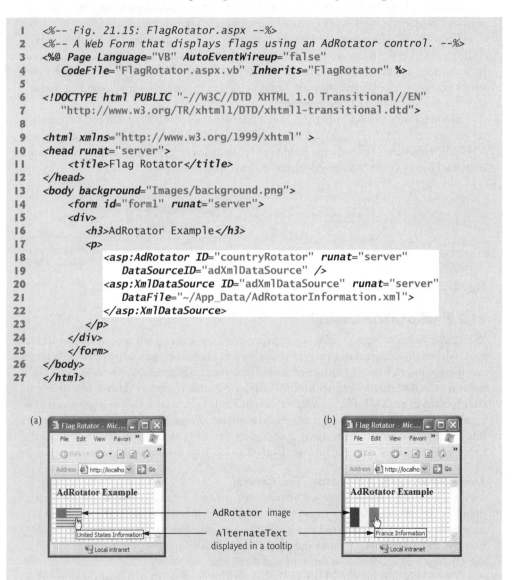

AdRotator image

AlternateText displayed in a tooltip

Fig. 21.15 | Web Form that demonstrates the AdRotator web control. (Part 1 of 2.)

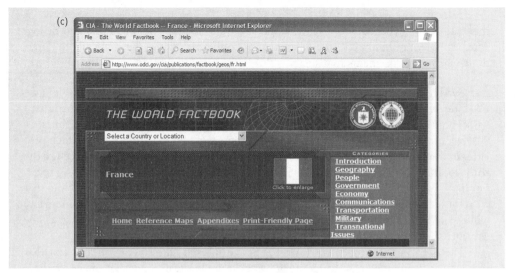

Fig. 21.15 | Web Form that demonstrates the `AdRotator` web control. (Part 2 of 2.)

the first time the page is requested, when the American flag is shown. In the second request, as shown in Fig. 21.15(b), the French flag is displayed. Figure 21.15(c) depicts the web page that loads when the French flag is clicked.

Connecting Data to an AdRotator Control

An `AdRotator` control accesses an XML file (presented shortly) to determine what advertisement (i.e., flag) image, hyperlink URL and alternate text to display and include in the page. To connect the `AdRotator` control to the XML file, we create an *XmlDataSource* control—one of several ASP.NET data controls (found in the **Data** section of the **Toolbox**) that encapsulate data sources and make such data available for web controls. An XmlData-Source references an XML file containing data that will be used in an ASP.NET application. Later in the chapter, you will learn more about data-bound web controls, as well as the `SqlDataSource` control, which retrieves data from a SQL Server database, and the `ObjectDataSource` control, which encapsulates an object that makes data available.

To build this example, we first add the XML file `AdRotatorInformation.xml` to the project. Each project created in Visual Web Developer contains an `App_Data` folder, which is intended to store all the data used by the project. Right click this folder in the **Solution Explorer** and select **Add Existing Item...**, then browse for `AdRotatorInformation.xml` on your computer. We provide this file in the chapter's examples directory in the subdirectory named `exampleXMLFiles`.

After adding the XML file to the project, drag an `AdRotator` control from the **Toolbox** to the Web Form. The **AdRotator Tasks** smart tag menu will open automatically. From this menu, select **<New Data Source...>** from the **Choose Data Source** drop-down list to start the **Data Source Configuration Wizard**. Select **XML File** as the data-source type. This causes the wizard to create an XmlDataSource with the ID specified in the bottom half of the wizard dialog. We set the ID of the control to adXmlDataSource. Click **OK** in the **Data Source Configuration Wizard** dialog. The **Configure Data Source - adXmlDataSource** dialog appears next. In this dialog's **Data File** section, click **Browse...** and, in the **Select XML File** dialog, locate and select the XML file you added to the App_Data folder. Click **OK** to exit this dialog, then click **OK** to exit the **Configure Data Source - adXmlDataSource** dialog. After completing these steps, the AdRotator is configured to use the XML file to determine which advertisements to display.

Examining an XML File Containing Advertisement Information

XML document AdRotatorInformation.xml (Fig. 21.16)—or any XML document used with an AdRotator control—must contain one ***Advertisements*** root element (lines 4–94). Within that element can be several ***Ad*** elements (e.g., lines 5–12), each of which provides information about a different advertisement. Element ***ImageUrl*** (line 6) specifies the path (location) of the advertisement's image, and element ***NavigateUrl*** (lines 7–9) specifies the URL for the web page that loads when a user clicks the advertisement. Note that we reformatted this file for presentation purposes. The actual XML file cannot contain any whitespace before or after the URL in the NavigateUrl element, or the whitespace will be considered part of the URL, and the page will not load properly.

The ***AlternateText*** element (line 10) nested in each Ad element contains text that displays in place of the image when the browser cannot locate or render the image for some reason (i.e., the file is missing, or the browser is not capable of displaying it), or to assist the visually impaired. The AlternateText element's text is also a tooltip that Internet Explorer displays when a user places the mouse pointer over the image (Fig. 21.15). The ***Impressions*** element (line 11) specifies how often a particular image appears, relative to the other images. An advertisement that has a higher Impressions value displays more frequently than an advertisement with a lower value. In our example, the advertisements display with equal probability, because the value of each Impressions element is set to 1.

```
1    <?xml version="1.0" encoding="utf-8"?>
2    <!-- Fig. 21.16: AdRotatorInformation.xml -->
3    <!-- XML file containing advertisement information. -->
4    <Advertisements>
5       <Ad>
6          <ImageUrl>Images/france.png</ImageUrl>
7          <NavigateUrl>http://www.cia.gov/library/publications/
8             the-world-factbook/geos/fr.html
9          </NavigateUrl>
10         <AlternateText>France Information</AlternateText>
11         <Impressions>1</Impressions>
12      </Ad>
13
14      <Ad>
15         <ImageUrl>Images/germany.png</ImageUrl>
16         <NavigateUrl>http://www.cia.gov/library/publications/
17            the-world-factbook/geos/gm.html
18         </NavigateUrl>
19         <AlternateText>Germany Information</AlternateText>
20         <Impressions>1</Impressions>
21      </Ad>
22
```

Fig. 21.16 | XML file containing advertisement information used in AdRotator example. (Part 1 of 3.)

```
23    <Ad>
24       <ImageUrl>Images/italy.png</ImageUrl>
25       <NavigateUrl>http://www.cia.gov/library/publications/
26          the-world-factbook/geos/it.html
27       </NavigateUrl>
28       <AlternateText>Italy Information</AlternateText>
29       <Impressions>1</Impressions>
30    </Ad>
31
32    <Ad>
33       <ImageUrl>Images/spain.png</ImageUrl>
34       <NavigateUrl>http://www.cia.gov/library/publications/
35          the-world-factbook/geos/sp.html
36       </NavigateUrl>
37       <AlternateText>Spain Information</AlternateText>
38       <Impressions>1</Impressions>
39    </Ad>
40
41    <Ad>
42       <ImageUrl>Images/latvia.png</ImageUrl>
43       <NavigateUrl>http://www.cia.gov/library/publications/
44          the-world-factbook/geos/lg.html
45       </NavigateUrl>
46       <AlternateText>Latvia Information</AlternateText>
47       <Impressions>1</Impressions>
48    </Ad>
49
50    <Ad>
51       <ImageUrl>Images/peru.png</ImageUrl>
52       <NavigateUrl>http://www.cia.gov/library/publications/
53          the-world-factbook/geos/pe.html
54       </NavigateUrl>
55       <AlternateText>Peru Information</AlternateText>
56       <Impressions>1</Impressions>
57    </Ad>
58
59    <Ad>
60       <ImageUrl>Images/senegal.png</ImageUrl>
61       <NavigateUrl>http://www.cia.gov/library/publications/
62          the-world-factbook/geos/sg.html
63       </NavigateUrl>
64       <AlternateText>Senegal Information</AlternateText>
65       <Impressions>1</Impressions>
66    </Ad>
67
68    <Ad>
69       <ImageUrl>Images/sweden.png</ImageUrl>
70       <NavigateUrl>http://www.cia.gov/library/publications/
71          the-world-factbook/geos/sw.html
72       </NavigateUrl>
73       <AlternateText>Sweden Information</AlternateText>
```

Fig. 21.16 | XML file containing advertisement information used in `AdRotator` example. (Part 2 of 3.)

```
74          <Impressions>1</Impressions>
75      </Ad>
76
77      <Ad>
78          <ImageUrl>Images/thailand.png</ImageUrl>
79          <NavigateUrl>http://www.cia.gov/library/publications/
80              the-world-factbook/geos/th.html
81          </NavigateUrl>
82          <AlternateText>Thailand Information</AlternateText>
83          <Impressions>1</Impressions>
84      </Ad>
85
86      <Ad>
87          <ImageUrl>Images/unitedstates.png</ImageUrl>
88          <NavigateUrl>http://www.cia.gov/library/publications/
89              the-world-factbook/geos/us.html
90          </NavigateUrl>
91          <AlternateText>United States Information</AlternateText>
92          <Impressions>1</Impressions>
93      </Ad>
94  </Advertisements>
```

Fig. 21.16 | XML file containing advertisement information used in `AdRotator` example. (Part 3 of 3.)

21.3.3 Validation Controls

This section introduces a different type of web control, called a *validation control* (or *validator*), which determines whether the data in another web control is in the proper format. For example, validators could determine whether a user has provided information in a required field or whether a zip-code field contains exactly five digits. Validators provide a mechanism for validating user input on the client. When the XHTML for our page is created, the validator is converted into JavaScript that performs the validation. However, some clients do not support scripting or disable scripting. So, for security reasons, validation is always performed on the server too—whether or not scripting is enabled on the client. For this example, we assume the client has JavaScript enabled.

Validating Input in a Web Form

The example in this section prompts the user to enter a name, e-mail address and phone number. A website could use a form like this to collect contact information from site visitors. After the user enters any data, but before the data is sent to the web server, validators ensure that the user entered a value in each field and that the e-mail address and phone number values are in an acceptable format. In this example, (555) 123-4567, 555-123-4567 and 123-4567 are all considered valid phone numbers. Once the data is submitted, the web server responds by displaying an appropriate message and an XHTML table repeating the submitted information. Note that a real business application would typically store the submitted data in a database or in a file on the server. We simply send the data back to the form to demonstrate that the server received the data.

Figure 21.17 presents the ASPX file. Like the Web Form in Fig. 21.13, this Web Form uses a `table` to organize the page's contents. Lines 24–25, 36–37 and 58–59 define

TextBoxes for retrieving the user's name, e-mail address and phone number, respectively, and line 78 defines a **Submit** button. Lines 80–82 create a Label named outputLabel that displays the response from the server when the user successfully submits the form. Notice that outputLabel's *Visible* property is initially set to False (line 81), so the Label does not appear in the client's browser when the page loads for the first time.

Using RequiredFieldValidator Controls

In this example, we use three *RequiredFieldValidator* controls (found in the **Validation** section of the **Toolbox**) to ensure that the name, e-mail address and phone number Text-Boxes are not empty when the form is submitted. A RequiredFieldValidator makes an input control a required field. If such a field is empty, validation fails. For example, lines 26–30 define RequiredFieldValidator nameInputValidator, which confirms that nameTextBox is not empty. Line 28 associates nameTextBox with nameInputValidator by setting the validator's *ControlToValidate* property to nameTextBox. This indicates that nameInputValidator verifies the nameTextBox's contents. We set the value of this property (and the validator's other properties) by selecting the validator in **Design** mode and using the **Properties** window to specify property values. Property *ErrorMessage*'s text (line 29) is displayed on the Web Form if the validation fails. If the user does not input any data in nameTextBox and attempts to submit the form, the ErrorMessage text is displayed in red. Because we set the validator's *Display* property to Dynamic (line 28), the validator is displayed on the Web Form only when validation fails. Space is allocated dynamically when validation fails, causing the controls below the validator to shift downward to accommodate the ErrorMessage, as seen in Fig. 21.17(a)–(c).

Using RegularExpressionValidator Controls

This example also uses *RegularExpressionValidator* controls to match the e-mail address and phone number entered by the user against regular expressions. These controls determine whether the e-mail address and phone number were each entered in a valid format. For example, lines 44–51 create a RegularExpressionValidator named emailFormat-Validator. Line 46 sets property ControlToValidate to emailTextBox to indicate that emailFormatValidator verifies the emailTextBox's contents.

```
 1    <%-- Fig. 21.17: Validation.aspx --%>
 2    <%-- Form that demonstrates using validators to validate user input. --%>
 3    <%@ Page Language="VB" AutoEventWireup="false"
 4       CodeFile="Validation.aspx.vb" Inherits="Validation" %>
 5
 6    <!DOCTYPE html PUBLIC "-//W3C//DTD XHTML 1.0 Transitional//EN"
 7       "http://www.w3.org/TR/xhtml1/DTD/xhtml1-transitional.dtd">
 8
 9    <html xmlns="http://www.w3.org/1999/xhtml" >
10    <head runat="server">
11       <title>Demonstrating Validation Controls</title>
12    </head>
13    <body>
14       <form id="form1" runat="server">
15       <div>
```

Fig. 21.17 | Form that demonstrates using validators to validate user input. (Part 1 of 4.)

```
16          Please fill out the following form.<br /><em>All fields are
17          required and must contain valid information.</em><br />
18          <br />
19          <table>
20             <tr>
21                <td style="width: 100px" valign="top">
22                   Name:</td>
23                <td style="width: 450px" valign="top">
24                   <asp:TextBox ID="nameTextBox" runat="server">
25                   </asp:TextBox><br />
26                   <asp:RequiredFieldValidator
27                      ID="nameInputValidator" runat="server"
28                      ControlToValidate="nameTextBox" Display="Dynamic"
29                      ErrorMessage="Please enter your name.">
30                   </asp:RequiredFieldValidator>
31                </td>
32             </tr>
33             <tr>
34                <td style="width: 100px" valign="top">E-mail address:</td>
35                <td style="width: 450px" valign="top">
36                   <asp:TextBox ID="emailTextBox" runat="server">
37                   </asp:TextBox>
38                    e.g., user@domain.com<br />
39                   <asp:RequiredFieldValidator
40                      ID="emailInputValidator" runat="server"
41                      ControlToValidate="emailTextBox" Display="Dynamic"
42                      ErrorMessage="Please enter your e-mail address.">
43                   </asp:RequiredFieldValidator>
44                   <asp:RegularExpressionValidator
45                      ID="emailFormatValidator" runat="server"
46                      ControlToValidate="emailTextBox" Display="Dynamic"
47                      ErrorMessage=
48                         "Please enter an e-mail address in a valid format."
49                      ValidationExpression=
50                         "\w+([-+.']\w+)*@\w+([-.]\w+)*\.\w+([-.]\w+)*">
51                   </asp:RegularExpressionValidator>
52                </td>
53             </tr>
54             <tr>
55                <td style="width: 100px; height: 21px" valign="top">
56                   Phone number:</td>
57                <td style="width: 450px; height: 21px" valign="top">
58                   <asp:TextBox ID="phoneTextBox" runat="server">
59                   </asp:TextBox>
60                    e.g., (555) 555-1234<br />
61                   <asp:RequiredFieldValidator
62                      ID="phoneInputValidator" runat="server"
63                      ControlToValidate="phoneTextBox" Display="Dynamic"
64                      ErrorMessage="Please enter your phone number.">
65                   </asp:RequiredFieldValidator>
66                   <asp:RegularExpressionValidator
67                      ID="phoneFormatValidator" runat="server"
68                      ControlToValidate="phoneTextBox" Display="Dynamic"
```

Fig. 21.17 | Form that demonstrates using validators to validate user input. (Part 2 of 4.)

```
69                        ErrorMessage=
70                           "Please enter a phone number in a valid format."
71                        ValidationExpression=
72                           "((\(\d{3}\) ?)|(\d{3}-))?\d{3}-\d{4}">
73                     </asp:RegularExpressionValidator>
74                  </td>
75               </tr>
76            </table>
77            <br />
78            <asp:Button ID="submitButton" runat="server" Text="Submit" /><br />
79            <br />
80            <asp:Label ID="outputLabel" runat="server"
81               Text="Thank you for your submission." Visible="False">
82            </asp:Label>
83         </div>
84         </form>
85      </body>
86   </html>
```

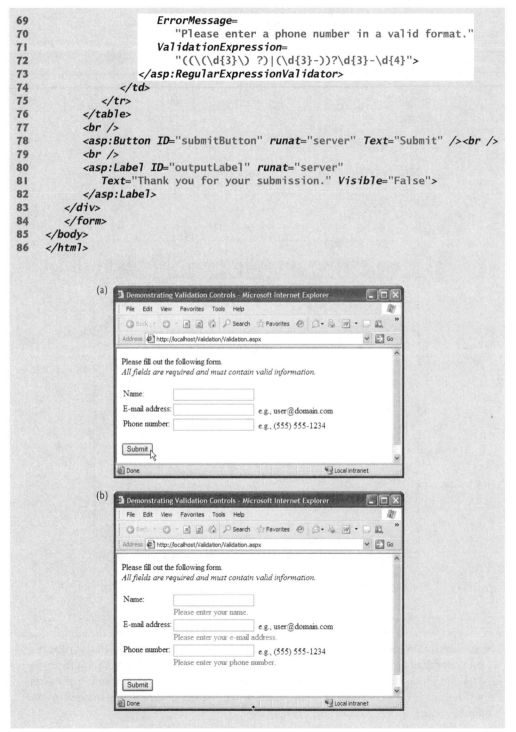

Fig. 21.17 | Form that demonstrates using validators to validate user input. (Part 3 of 4.)

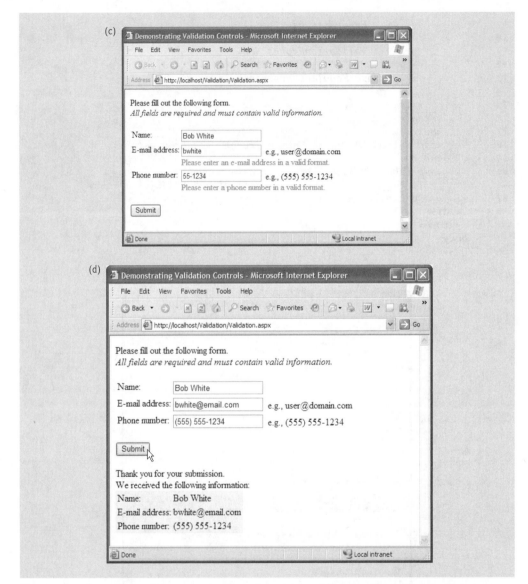

Fig. 21.17 | Form that demonstrates using validators to validate user input. (Part 4 of 4.)

A RegularExpressionValidator's ***ValidationExpression*** property specifies the regular expression that validates the ControlToValidate's contents. Clicking the ellipsis next to property ValidationExpression in the **Properties** window displays the **Regular Expression Editor** dialog, which contains a list of **Standard expressions** for phone numbers, zip codes and other formatted information. You can also write your own custom expression. For the emailFormatValidator, we selected the standard expression **Internet e-mail address**, which uses the validation expression

```
\w+([-+.']\w+)*@\w+([-.]\w+)*\.\w+([-.]\w+)*
```

This regular expression indicates that an e-mail address is valid if the part of the address before the @ symbol contains one or more word characters (i.e., alphanumeric characters or underscores), followed by zero or more strings comprised of a hyphen, plus sign, period or apostrophe and additional word characters. After the @ symbol, a valid e-mail address must contain one or more groups of word characters potentially separated by hyphens or periods, followed by a required period and another group of one or more word characters potentially separated by hyphens or periods. For example, bob.white@email.com, bob-white@my-email.com and bob's-personal.email@white.email.com are all valid e-mail addresses. If the user enters text in the emailTextBox that does not have the correct format and either clicks in a different text box or attempts to submit the form, the ErrorMessage text is displayed in red. You can learn more about regular expressions at the website www.regular-expressions.info.

We also use RegularExpressionValidator phoneFormatValidator (lines 66–73) to ensure that the phoneTextBox contains a valid phone number before the form is submitted. In the **Regular Expression Editor** dialog, we select **U.S. phone number**, which assigns

$$((\(\d{3}\) \ ?)|(\d{3}-))?\d{3}-\d{4}$$

to the ValidationExpression property. This expression indicates that a phone number can contain a three-digit area code either in parentheses and followed by an optional space or without parentheses and followed by required hyphen. After an optional area code, a phone number must contain three digits, a hyphen and another four digits. For example, (555) 123-4567, 555-123-4567 and 123-4567 are all valid phone numbers.

If all five validators are successful (i.e., each TextBox is filled in, and the e-mail address and phone number provided are valid), clicking the **Submit** button sends the form's data to the server. As shown in Fig. 21.17(d), the server then responds by displaying the submitted data in the outputLabel (lines 80–82).

Examining the Code-Behind File for a Web Form That Receives User Input
Figure 21.18 depicts the code-behind file for the ASPX file in Fig. 21.17. Notice that this code-behind file does not contain any implementation related to the validators. We say more about this soon.

```
1   ' Fig. 21.18: Validation.aspx.vb
2   ' Code-behind file for the form demonstrating validation controls.
3   Partial Class Validation
4      Inherits System.Web.UI.Page
5
6      ' Page_Load event handler executes when the page is loaded
7      Protected Sub Page_Load(ByVal sender As Object, _
8         ByVal e As System.EventArgs) Handles Me.Load
9         ' if this is not the first time the page is loading
10        ' (i.e., the user has already submitted form data)
11        If IsPostBack Then
12           ' retrieve the values submitted by the user
13           Dim name As String = nameTextBox.Text
14           Dim email As String = emailTextBox.Text
```

Fig. 21.18 | Code-behind file for the form demonstrating validation controls. (Part 1 of 2.)

```
15                  Dim phone As String = phoneTextBox.Text
16
17              ' create a table indicating the submitted values
18              outputLabel.Text &= _
19                "<br />We received the following information:" & _
20                "<table style=""background-color: yellow"">" & _
21                "<tr><td>Name: </td><td>" & name & "</td></tr>" & _
22                "<tr><td>E-mail address: </td><td>" & email & "</td></tr>" & _
23                "<tr><td>Phone number: </td><td>" & phone & "</td></tr>" & _
24                "<table>"
25              outputLabel.Visible = True ' display the output message
26          End If
27      End Sub ' Page_Load
28  End Class ' Validation
```

Fig. 21.18 | Code-behind file for the form demonstrating validation controls. (Part 2 of 2.)

Web programmers using ASP.NET often design their web pages so that the current page reloads when the user submits the form; this enables the program to receive input, process it as necessary and display the results in the same page when it is loaded the second time. These pages usually contain a form that, when submitted, sends the values of all the controls to the server and causes the current page to be requested again. This event is known as a *postback*. Line 11 uses the **IsPostBack** property of class Page to determine whether the page is being loaded due to a postback. The first time that the web page is requested, IsPostBack is False, and the page displays only the form for user input. When the postback occurs (from the user clicking **Submit**), IsPostBack is True.

Lines 13–15 retrieve the values of nameTextBox, emailTextBox and phoneTextBox. When data is posted to the web server, the XHTML form's data is accessible to the web application through the properties of the ASP.NET controls. Lines 18–24 append to outputLabel's Text a line break, an additional message and an XHTML table containing the submitted data, so the user knows that the server received the data correctly. In a real business application, the data would be stored in a database or file at this point in the application. Line 25 sets the outputLabel's Visible property to True, so the user can see the thank you message and submitted data.

Examining the Client-Side XHTML for a Web Form with Validation

Figure 21.19 shows the XHTML and ECMAScript sent to the client browser when Validation.aspx loads after the postback. (We added the comments in lines 1–2.) To view this code, select **View > Source** in Internet Explorer. Lines 27–55, lines 126–190 and lines 196–212 contain the ECMAScript that provides the implementation for the validation controls and for performing the postback. ASP.NET generates this ECMAScript. You do not need to be able to create or even understand ECMAScript—the functionality defined for the controls in our application is converted to working ECMAScript for us.

The EnableViewState attribute determines whether a web control's value is retained when a postback occurs. Previously, we explicitly set this attribute to False. The default value, True, indicates that the control's value is retained. In Fig. 21.17(d), notice that the user input is retained after the postback occurs. A hidden input in the XHTML document (lines 17–25 of Fig. 21.19) contains the data of the controls on this page. This element is always named **__VIEWSTATE** and stores the controls' data as an encoded string.

```
 1   <!-- Fig. 21.19 -->
 2   <!-- The XHTML and ECMAScript generated for Validation.aspx -->
 3   <!DOCTYPE html PUBLIC "-//W3C//DTD XHTML 1.0 Transitional//EN"
 4      "http://www.w3.org/TR/xhtml1/DTD/xhtml1-transitional.dtd">
 5   <html xmlns="http://www.w3.org/1999/xhtml" >
 6   <head>
 7   <title>Demonstrating Validation Controls</title>
 8   </head>
 9   <body>
10   <form name="form1" method="post" action="Validation.aspx"
11      onsubmit="javascript:return WebForm_OnSubmit();" id="form1">
12      <div>
13         <input type="hidden" name="__EVENTTARGET" id="__EVENTTARGET"
14            value="" />
15         <input type="hidden" name="__EVENTARGUMENT" id="__EVENTARGUMENT"
16            value="" />
17         <input type="hidden" name="__VIEWSTATE" id="__VIEWSTATE"
18            value="/wEPDwUJMzg4NDI1NzgzD2QWAgIDD2QWAgITDw8WBB4EVGV4dAWVA1RoY
19            W5rIH1vdSBmb3IgeW91ciBzdWJtaXNzaW9uLjxiciciAvP1d1IHJlY2VpdmVkIHRoZ
20            SBmb2xsb3dpbmcgaW5mb3JtYXRpb246PHRhYmxlIHN0eWxlPSJiYWNrZ3JvdW5kL
21            WNvbG9yOiB5ZWxsb3ciPjx0cj48dGQ+TmFtZTogPC90ZD48dGQ+Qm9iIEFdoaXRlP
22            C90ZD48L3RyPjx0cj48dGQ+RS1tYW1sIGFkZHJlc3M6IDwvdGQ+PHRkPmJ3aG10Z
23            ZUB1bWFpbC5jb208L3RkPjwvdHI+PHRyPjx0ZD5QaG9uZSBudW1iZXI6IDwvdGQ+
24            PHRkPig1NTUpIDU1NS0xMjM0PC90ZD48L3RyPjx0YWJsZT4eB1Zpc2libGVnZGRk
25            qbjgKg1/1LZfogqihtkd1C7nmSk=" />
26      </div>
27      <script type="text/javascript">
28      <!--
29      var theForm = document.forms['form1'];
30      if (!theForm) {
31         theForm = document.form1;
32      }
33      function __doPostBack(eventTarget, eventArgument) {
34         if (!theForm.onsubmit || (theForm.onsubmit() != false)) {
35            theForm.__EVENTTARGET.value = eventTarget;
36            theForm.__EVENTARGUMENT.value = eventArgument;
37            theForm.submit();
38         }
39      }
40      // -->
41      </script>
42      <script src="/Validation/WebResource.axd?d=g4BXOwpt2-0jwFwNi7BCNQ2
43         &amp;t=632670465355304640" type="text/javascript"></script>
44      <script src="/Validation/WebResource.axd?d=Z1FGPYdcOpaOPqraRf9s2PN8QeuH
45         PzQxnkR5mPVtAVc1&amp;t=632670465355304640"
46         type="text/javascript"></script>
47      <script type="text/javascript">
48      <!--
49      function WebForm_OnSubmit() {
50         if (typeof(ValidatorOnSubmit) == "function" &&
51            ValidatorOnSubmit() == false) return false;
```

Fig. 21.19 | XHTML and ECMAScript generated by ASP.NET and sent to the browser when
`Validation.aspx` is requested. (Part 1 of 5.)

```
52          return true;
53      }
54      // -->
55      </script>
56      <div>
57          Please fill out the following form.<br />
58          <em>All fields are required and must contain valid information.
59          </em><br />
60          <br />
61          <table>
62              <tr>
63                  <td style="width: 100px" valign="top"> Name:</td>
64                  <td style="width: 450px" valign="top">
65                      <input name="nameTextBox" type="text" value="Bob White"
66                          id="nameTextBox" />
67                      <br />
68                      <span id="nameInputValidator"
69                          style="color:Red;display:none;">
70                          Please enter your name.</span> </td>
71              </tr>
72              <tr>
73                  <td style="width: 100px" valign="top">E-mail address:</td>
74                  <td style="width: 450px" valign="top">
75                      <input name="emailTextBox" type="text"
76                          value="bwhite@email.com" id="emailTextBox" />
77                       e.g., user@domain.com<br />
78                      <span id="emailInputValidator"
79                          style="color:Red;display:none;">
80                          Please enter your e-mail address.</span>
81                      <span id="emailFormatValidator"
82                          style="color:Red;display:none;">Please enter an e-mail
83                          address in a valid format.</span> </td>
84              </tr>
85              <tr>
86                  <td style="width: 100px; height: 21px" valign="top">
87                      Phone number:</td>
88                  <td style="width: 450px; height: 21px" valign="top">
89                      <input name="phoneTextBox" type="text"
90                          value="(555) 555-1234" id="phoneTextBox" />
91                       e.g., (555) 555-1234<br />
92                      <span id="phoneInputValidator"
93                          style="color:Red;display:none;">
94                          Please enter your phone number.</span>
95                      <span id="phoneFormatValidator"
96                          style="color:Red;display:none;">Please enter a phone
97                          number in a valid format.</span> </td>
98              </tr>
99          </table>
100         <br />
101         <input type="submit" name="submitButton" value="Submit"
102             onclick="javascript:WebForm_DoPostBackWithOptions(
```

Fig. 21.19 | XHTML and ECMAScript generated by ASP.NET and sent to the browser when Validation.aspx is requested. (Part 2 of 5.)

```
103              new WebForm_PostBackOptions(&quot;submitButton&quot;,
104                &quot;&quot;, true, &quot;&quot;, &quot;&quot;, false,
105                false))" id="submitButton" />
106        <br />
107        <br />
108        <span id="outputLabel">Thank you for your submission.<br />
109           We received the following information:
110           <table style="background-color: yellow">
111              <tr>
112                 <td>Name: </td>
113                 <td>Bob White</td>
114              </tr>
115              <tr>
116                 <td>E-mail address: </td>
117                 <td>bwhite@email.com</td>
118              </tr>
119              <tr>
120                 <td>Phone number: </td>
121                 <td>(555) 555-1234</td>
122              </tr>
123           <table>
124        </span>
125     </div>
126     <script type="text/javascript">
127     <!--
128        var Page_Validators = new Array(
129           document.getElementById("nameInputValidator"),
130           document.getElementById("emailInputValidator"),
131           document.getElementById("emailFormatValidator"),
132           document.getElementById("phoneInputValidator"),
133           document.getElementById("phoneFormatValidator"));
134     // -->
135     </script>
136     <script type="text/javascript">
137     <!--
138        var nameInputValidator = document.all ?
139           document.all["nameInputValidator"] :
140           document.getElementById("nameInputValidator");
141        nameInputValidator.controltovalidate = "nameTextBox";
142        nameInputValidator.errormessage = "Please enter your name.";
143        nameInputValidator.display = "Dynamic";
144        nameInputValidator.evaluationfunction =
145           "RequiredFieldValidatorEvaluateIsValid";
146        nameInputValidator.initialvalue = "";
147        var emailInputValidator = document.all ?
148           document.all["emailInputValidator"] :
149           document.getElementById("emailInputValidator");
150        emailInputValidator.controltovalidate = "emailTextBox";
151        emailInputValidator.errormessage =
152           "Please enter your e-mail address.";
153        emailInputValidator.display = "Dynamic";
```

Fig. 21.19 | XHTML and ECMAScript generated by ASP.NET and sent to the browser when Validation.aspx is requested. (Part 3 of 5.)

```
154        emailInputValidator.evaluationfunction =
155           "RequiredFieldValidatorEvaluateIsValid";
156        emailInputValidator.initialvalue = "";
157        var emailFormatValidator = document.all ?
158           document.all["emailFormatValidator"] :
159           document.getElementById("emailFormatValidator");
160        emailFormatValidator.controltovalidate = "emailTextBox";
161        emailFormatValidator.errormessage =
162           "Please enter an e-mail address in a valid format.";
163        emailFormatValidator.display = "Dynamic";
164        emailFormatValidator.evaluationfunction =
165           "RegularExpressionValidatorEvaluateIsValid";
166        emailFormatValidator.validationexpression =
167           "\\w+([-+.\']\\w+)*@\\w+([-.]\\w+)*\\.\\w+([-.]\\w+)*";
168        var phoneInputValidator = document.all ?
169           document.all["phoneInputValidator"] :
170           document.getElementById("phoneInputValidator");
171        phoneInputValidator.controltovalidate = "phoneTextBox";
172        phoneInputValidator.errormessage =
173           "Please enter your phone number.";
174        phoneInputValidator.display = "Dynamic";
175        phoneInputValidator.evaluationfunction =
176           "RequiredFieldValidatorEvaluateIsValid";
177        phoneInputValidator.initialvalue = "";
178        var phoneFormatValidator = document.all ?
179           document.all["phoneFormatValidator"] :
180           document.getElementById("phoneFormatValidator");
181        phoneFormatValidator.controltovalidate = "phoneTextBox";
182        phoneFormatValidator.errormessage =
183           "Please enter a phone number in a valid format.";
184        phoneFormatValidator.display = "Dynamic";
185        phoneFormatValidator.evaluationfunction =
186           "RegularExpressionValidatorEvaluateIsValid";
187        phoneFormatValidator.validationexpression =
188           "((\\(\\d{3}\\) ?)|(\\d{3}-))?\\d{3}-\\d{4}";
189     // -->
190     </script>
191     <div>
192        <input type="hidden" name="__EVENTVALIDATION" id="__EVENTVALIDATION"
193           value="/wEWBQL6jZCbCAKLsYSOBwKCkfPgDAKE8IO1CQKSuuDUC0eN037OTaQqZQ
194           0WPApDOKktGC5N" />
195     </div>
196     <script type="text/javascript">
197     <!--
198        var Page_ValidationActive = false;
199        if (typeof(ValidatorOnLoad) == "function") {
200           ValidatorOnLoad();
201        }
202
203        function ValidatorOnSubmit() {
204           if (Page_ValidationActive) {
```

Fig. 21.19 | XHTML and ECMAScript generated by ASP.NET and sent to the browser when Validation.aspx is requested. (Part 4 of 5.)

```
205                 return ValidatorCommonOnSubmit();
206             }
207             else {
208                 return true;
209             }
210         }
211     // -->
212     </script>
213 </form>
214 </body>
215 </html>
```

Fig. 21.19 | XHTML and ECMAScript generated by ASP.NET and sent to the browser when `Validation.aspx` is requested. (Part 5 of 5.)

Performance Tip 21.1

Setting `EnableViewState` to `False` reduces the amount of data passed to the web server with each request.

Software Engineering Observation 21.2

Client-side validation cannot be trusted by the server because there are too many ways to circumvent client-side validation. For this reason, all important validation should be peformed on the server.

21.4 Session Tracking

Originally, critics accused the Internet and e-businesses of failing to provide the kind of customized service typically experienced in "brick-and-mortar" stores. To address this problem, e-businesses began to establish mechanisms by which they could personalize users' browsing experiences, tailoring content to individual users while enabling them to bypass irrelevant information. Businesses achieve this level of service by tracking each customer's movement through the Internet and combining the collected data with information provided by the consumer, including billing information, personal preferences, interests and hobbies.

Personalization

Personalization makes it possible for e-businesses to communicate effectively with their customers and also improves users' ability to locate desired products and services. Companies that provide content of particular interest to users can establish relationships with customers and build on those relationships over time. Furthermore, by targeting consumers with personal offers, recommendations, advertisements, promotions and services, e-businesses create customer loyalty. Websites can use sophisticated technology to allow visitors to customize home pages to suit their individual needs and preferences. Similarly, online shopping sites often store personal information for customers, tailoring notifications and special offers to their interests. Such services encourage customers to visit sites more frequently and make purchases more regularly.

Privacy

A trade-off exists, however, between personalized e-business service and protection of privacy. Some consumers embrace the idea of tailored content, but others fear the possible adverse consequences if the info they provide to e-businesses is released or collected by tracking technologies. Consumers and privacy advocates ask: What if the e-business to which we give personal data sells or gives that information to another organization without our knowledge? What if we do not want our actions on the Internet—a supposedly anonymous medium—to be tracked and recorded by unknown parties? What if unauthorized parties gain access to sensitive private data, such as credit card numbers or medical history? All of these are questions that must be debated and addressed by programmers, consumers, e-businesses and lawmakers alike.

Recognizing Clients

To provide personalized services to consumers, e-businesses must be able to recognize clients when they request information from a site. As we have discussed, the request/response system on which the web operates is facilitated by HTTP. Unfortunately, HTTP is a stateless protocol. This means that web servers cannot determine whether a request comes from a particular client or whether the same or different clients generate a series of requests.

To circumvent this problem, sites can use the concept of a "session" to identify individual clients. A session represents a unique client on a website. If the client leaves a site and then returns later, the client will still be recognized as the same user. To help the server distinguish among clients, each client must identify itself to the server. Tracking individual clients, known as *session tracking*, can be achieved in a number of ways. One popular technique uses cookies (Section 21.4.1); another uses ASP.NET's HttpSessionState object (Section 21.4.2). Additional session-tracking techniques include the use of input form elements of type "hidden" and URL rewriting. Using "hidden" form elements, a Web Form can write session-tracking data into a form in the web page that it returns to the client in response to a prior request. When the user submits the form in the new web page, all the form data, including the "hidden" fields, is sent to the form handler on the web server. When a website performs URL rewriting, the Web Form embeds session-tracking information directly in the URLs of hyperlinks that the user clicks to send subsequent requests to the web server.

Note that our previous examples set the Web Form's EnableSessionState property to False. However, because we wish to use session tracking in the following examples, we keep this property's default setting—True.

21.4.1 Cookies

Cookies provide web developers with a tool for identifying and tracking web users. A cookie is a piece of data stored in a small text file on the user's computer. A cookie maintains information about the client during and between browser sessions. The first time a user visits the website, the user's computer might receive a cookie; this cookie is then retrieved each time the user revisits that site. The collected information is intended to be an anonymous record containing data that is used to personalize the user's future visits to the site. For example, cookies in a shopping application might store unique identifiers for users. When a user adds items to an online shopping cart or performs another task resulting in a request to the web server, the server receives a cookie containing the user's unique identifier. The server then uses the unique identifier to locate the shopping cart and perform any necessary processing.

In addition to identifying users, cookies also can indicate users' shopping preferences. When a web server receives a request from a client, the server can examine the cookie(s) it sent to the client during previous communications, identify the users's preferences and immediately return products of interest to the client.

Every HTTP-based interaction between a client and a server includes a header containing information either about the request (when the communication is from the client to the server) or about the response (when the communication is from the server to the client). When a web server receives a request, the header includes information such as the request type (e.g., Get) and any cookies that have been sent previously from the server to be stored on the client machine. When the server formulates its response, the header information contains any cookies the server wants to store on the client computer and other information, such as the MIME type of the response.

The *expiration date* of a cookie determines how long the cookie remains on the client's computer. If you do not set an expiration date for a cookie, the web browser maintains the cookie for the duration of the browsing session. Otherwise, the Web browser maintains the cookie until the expiration date occurs. When the browser requests a resource from a web server, cookies previously sent to the client by that Web server are returned to the web server as part of the request formulated by the browser. Cookies are deleted when they *expire*.

Portability Tip 21.3

Users may disable cookies in their browsers to ensure that their privacy is protected. Such users will experience difficulty using sites that depend on cookies to maintain state information.

Using Cookies to Provide Book Recommendations

The next web application demonstrates the use of cookies. The example contains two pages. In the first page (Figs. 21.20–21.21), users select a favorite programming language from a group of radio buttons and submit the XHTML form to the web server for processing. The web server responds by creating a cookie that stores a record of the chosen language, as well as the ISBN number for a book on that topic. The server then returns an XHTML document to the browser, allowing the user either to select another favorite programming language or to view the second page in our application (Figs. 21.22–21.23), which lists recommended books pertaining to the programming language that the user selected previously. When the user clicks the hyperlink, the cookies previously stored on the client are read and used to form the list of book recommendations.

The ASPX file in Fig. 21.20 contains five radio buttons (lines 20–26) with the values **Visual Basic 2005**, **Visual C# 2005**, **C**, **C++**, and **Java**. Recall that you can set the values of radio buttons via the **ListItem Collection Editor**, which you open either by clicking the RadioButtonList's **Items** property in the **Properties** window or by clicking the **Edit Items...** link in the **RadioButtonList Tasks** smart tag menu. The user selects a programming language by clicking one of the radio buttons. When the user clicks **Submit**, we'll create a cookie containing the selected language. Then, we'll add this cookie to the HTTP response header, so the cookie will be stored on the user's computer. Each time the user chooses a language and clicks **Submit**, a cookie is written to the client. Each time the client requests information from our web application, the cookies are sent back to the server.

When the postback occurs, certain controls are hidden and others are displayed. The Label, RadioButtonList and Button used to select a language are hidden. Toward the bottom of the page, a Label and two HyperLinks are displayed. One link requests this page (lines 32–35), and the other requests Recommendations.aspx (lines 37–40). Clicking the first hyperlink (the one that requests the current page) does not cause a postback to occur. The file Options.aspx is specified in the NavigateUrl property of the hyperlink. When the hyperlink is clicked, a new request for this page occurs. Recall that earlier in the chapter, we set NavigateUrl to a remote website (http://www.deitel.com). To set this property to a page within the same ASP.NET application, click the ellipsis button next to the NavigateUrl property in the **Properties** window to open the **Select URL** dialog. Use this dialog to select a page within your project as the destination for the HyperLink.

```
1    <%-- Fig. 21.20: Options.aspx --%>
2    <%-- Allows client to select programming languages and access --%>
3    <%-- book recommendations. --%>
4    <%@ Page Language="VB" AutoEventWireup="false"
5        CodeFile="Options.aspx.vb" Inherits="Options" %>
6
7    <!DOCTYPE html PUBLIC "-//W3C//DTD XHTML 1.0 Transitional//EN"
8        "http://www.w3.org/TR/xhtml1/DTD/xhtml1-transitional.dtd">
9
10   <html xmlns="http://www.w3.org/1999/xhtml" >
11   <head runat="server">
12       <title>Cookies</title>
13   </head>
14   <body>
15       <form id="form1" runat="server">
16       <div>
17           <asp:Label ID="promptLabel" runat="server" Font-Bold="True"
18               Font-Size="Large" Text="Select a programming language:">
19           </asp:Label>
20           <asp:RadioButtonList ID="languageList" runat="server">
21               <asp:ListItem>Visual Basic 2005</asp:ListItem>
22               <asp:ListItem>Visual C# 2005</asp:ListItem>
23               <asp:ListItem>C</asp:ListItem>
24               <asp:ListItem>C++</asp:ListItem>
25               <asp:ListItem>Java</asp:ListItem>
26           </asp:RadioButtonList>
27           <asp:Button ID="submitButton" runat="server" Text="Submit" />
28           <asp:Label ID="responseLabel" runat="server" Font-Bold="True"
29               Font-Size="Large" Text="Welcome to cookies!" Visible="False">
30           </asp:Label><br />
31           <br />
32           <asp:HyperLink ID="languageLink" runat="server"
33               NavigateUrl="~/Options.aspx" Visible="False">
34               Click here to choose another language
35           </asp:HyperLink><br />
36           <br />
37           <asp:HyperLink ID="recommendationsLink" runat="server"
38               NavigateUrl="~/Recommendations.aspx" Visible="False">
```

Fig. 21.20 | ASPX file that presents a list of programming languages. (Part 1 of 2.)

```
39                    Click here to get book recommendations
40           </asp:HyperLink>
41       </div>
42       </form>
43   </body>
44   </html>
```

Fig. 21.20 | ASPX file that presents a list of programming languages. (Part 2 of 2.)

Adding and Linking to a New Web Form

Setting the NavigateUrl property to a page in the current application requires that the destination page exist already. Thus, to set the NavigateUrl property of the second link (the one that requests the page with book recommendations) to Recommendations.aspx, you must first create this file by right clicking the project location in the **Solution Explorer** and selecting **Add New Item...** from the menu that appears. In the **Add New Item** dialog, select **Web Form** from the **Templates** pane and change the name of the file to Recommendations.aspx. Finally, check the box labeled **Place code in separate file** to indicate that the IDE should create a code-behind file for this ASPX file. Click **Add** to create the file. (We discuss the contents of this ASPX file and code-behind file shortly.) Once the Recommendations.aspx file exists, you can select it as the NavigateUrl value for a HyperLink in the **Select URL** dialog.

Writing Cookies in a Code-Behind File

Figure 21.21 presents the code-behind file for Options.aspx (Fig. 21.20). This file contains the code that writes a cookie to the client machine when the user selects a programming language. The code-behind file also modifies the appearance of the page in response to a postback.

```vb
 1  ' Fig. 21.21: Options.aspx.vb
 2  ' Processes user's selection of a programming language
 3  ' by displaying links and writing a cookie to the user's machine.
 4  Partial Class Options
 5     Inherits System.Web.UI.Page
 6     ' stores values to represent books as cookies
 7     Private books As New System.Collections.Hashtable()
 8
 9     ' initializes the Hashtable of values to be stored as cookies
10     Protected Sub Page_Init(ByVal sender As Object, _
11        ByVal e As System.EventArgs) Handles Me.Init
12        books.Add("Visual Basic 2005", "0-13-186900-0")
13        books.Add("Visual C# 2005", "0-13-152523-9")
14        books.Add("C", "0-13-142644-3")
15        books.Add("C++", "0-13-185757-6")
16        books.Add("Java", "0-13-148398-6")
17     End Sub ' Page_Init
18
19     ' if postback, hide form and display links to make additional
20     ' selections or view recommendations
21     Protected Sub Page_Load(ByVal sender As Object, _
22        ByVal e As System.EventArgs) Handles Me.Load
23
24        If IsPostBack Then
25           ' user has submitted information, so display message
26           ' and appropriate hyperlinks
27           responseLabel.Visible = True
28           languageLink.Visible = True
29           recommendationsLink.Visible = True
30
31           ' hide other controls used to make language selection
32           promptLabel.Visible = False
33           languageList.Visible = False
34           submitButton.Visible = False
35
36           ' if the user made a selection, display it in responseLabel
37           If languageList.SelectedItem IsNot Nothing Then
38              responseLabel.Text &= " You selected " & _
39                 languageList.SelectedItem.Text.ToString()
40           Else
41              responseLabel.Text &= " You did not select a language."
42           End If
43        End If
44     End Sub ' Page_Load
45
```

Fig. 21.21 | Code-behind file that writes a cookie to the client. (Part 1 of 2.)

```
46        ' write a cookie to record the user's selection
47        Protected Sub submitButton_Click(ByVal sender As Object, _
48           ByVal e As System.EventArgs) Handles submitButton.Click
49           ' if the user made a selection
50           If languageList.SelectedItem IsNot Nothing Then
51              Dim language As String = languageList.SelectedItem.ToString()
52
53              ' get ISBN number of book for the given language
54              Dim ISBN As String = books(language).ToString()
55
56              ' create cookie using language-ISBN name-value pair
57              Dim cookie As New HttpCookie(language, ISBN)
58
59              ' add cookie to response to place it on the user's machine
60              Response.Cookies.Add(cookie)
61           End If
62        End Sub ' submitButton_Click
63     End Class ' Options
```

Fig. 21.21 | Code-behind file that writes a cookie to the client. (Part 2 of 2.)

Line 7 creates variable books as a *Hashtable* (namespace System.Collections)—a data structure that stores *key–value pairs*. A program uses the key to store and retrieve the associated value in the Hashtable. In this example, the keys are strings containing the programming languages' names, and the values are strings containing the ISBN numbers for the recommended books. Class Hashtable provides method *Add*, which takes as arguments a key and a value. A value that is added via method Add is placed in the Hashtable at a location determined by the key. The value for a specific Hashtable entry can be determined by indexing the Hashtable with that value's key. The expression

HashtableName(keyName)

returns the value in the key–value pair in which *keyName* is the key. For example, the expression books(language) in line 54 returns the value that corresponds to the key contained in language.

Clicking the **Submit** button creates a cookie if a language is selected and causes a postback to occur. In the submitButton_Click event handler (lines 47–62), a new cookie object (of type *HttpCookie*) is created to store the language and its corresponding ISBN number (line 57). This cookie is then Added to the *Cookies* collection sent as part of the HTTP response header (line 60). The postback causes the condition in the If statement of Page_Load (line 24) to evaluate to True, and lines 27–42 execute. Lines 27–29 reveal the initially hidden controls responseLabel, languageLink and recommendationsLink. Lines 32–34 hide the controls used to obtain the user's language selection. Line 37 determines whether the user selected a language. If so, that language is displayed in responseLabel (lines 38–39). Otherwise, text indicating that a language was not selected is displayed in responseLabel (line 41).

Displaying Book Recommendations Based on Cookie Values
After the postback of Options.aspx, the user may request a book recommendation. The book recommendation hyperlink forwards the user to Recommendations.aspx (Fig. 21.22) to display the recommendations based on the user's language selections.

```
 1   <%-- Fig. 21.22: Recommendations.aspx --%>
 2   <%-- Displays book recommendations using cookies. --%>
 3   <%@ Page Language="VB" AutoEventWireup="false"
 4      CodeFile="Recommendations.aspx.vb" Inherits="Recommendations" %>
 5
 6   <!DOCTYPE html PUBLIC "-//W3C//DTD XHTML 1.0 Transitional//EN"
 7      "http://www.w3.org/TR/xhtml1/DTD/xhtml1-transitional.dtd">
 8
 9   <html xmlns="http://www.w3.org/1999/xhtml" >
10   <head runat="server">
11      <title>Book Recommendations</title>
12   </head>
13   <body>
14      <form id="form1" runat="server">
15      <div>
16         <asp:Label ID="recommendationsLabel" runat="server"
17            Font-Bold="True" Font-Size="X-Large" Text="Recommendations">
18         </asp:Label><br />
19         <br />
20         <asp:ListBox ID="booksListBox" runat="server" Height="125px"
21            Width="450px"></asp:ListBox><br />
22         <br />
23         <asp:HyperLink ID="languageLink" runat="server"
24            NavigateUrl="~/Options.aspx">
25            Click here to choose another language
26         </asp:HyperLink> </div>
27      </form>
28   </body>
29   </html>
```

Fig. 21.22 | ASPX file that displays book recommendations based on cookies.

Recommendations.aspx contains a Label (lines 16–18), a ListBox (lines 20–21) and a HyperLink (lines 23–26). The Label displays the text **Recommendations** if the user selects one or more languages; otherwise, it displays **No Recommendations**. The ListBox displays the recommendations specified by the code-behind file (Fig. 21.23). The Hyper-Link allows the user to return to Options.aspx to select additional languages.

Code-Behind File That Creates Book Recommendations from Cookies

In the code-behind file (Fig. 21.23), method Page_Init (lines 7–28) retrieves the cookies from the client, using the Request object's **Cookies** property (line 10). This returns a collection of type **HttpCookieCollection**, containing cookies that have previously been written to the client. Cookies can be read by an application only if they were created in the domain in which the application is running—a web server can never access cookies created outside the domain associated with that server. For example, a cookie created by a web server in the deitel.com domain cannot be read by a web server in any other domain. [*Note*: Depending on the settings in web.config and whether other pages store cookies, other cookie values may be displayed by this web application.]

Line 13 determines whether at least one cookie exists. Lines 14–17 add the information in the cookie(s) to the booksListBox. The loop retrieves the name and value of each cookie using i, the loop's control variable, to determine the current value in the cookie collection. The **Name** and **Value** properties of class HttpCookie, which contain the language and corresponding ISBN, respectively, are concatenated with " How to Program.

```
 1    ' Fig. 21.23: Recommendations.aspx.vb
 2    ' Creates book recommendations based on cookies.
 3    Partial Class Recommendations
 4       Inherits System.Web.UI.Page
 5
 6       ' read cookies and populate ListBox with any book recommendations
 7       Protected Sub Page_Init(ByVal sender As Object, _
 8          ByVal e As System.EventArgs) Handles Me.Init
 9          ' retrieve client's cookies
10          Dim cookies As HttpCookieCollection = Request.Cookies
11
12          ' if there are cookies, list the appropriate books and ISBN numbers
13          If cookies.Count <> 0 Then
14             For i As Integer = 0 To cookies.Count - 1
15                booksListBox.Items.Add(cookies(i).Name & _
16                   " How to Program. ISBN#: " & cookies(i).Value)
17             Next
18          Else
19             ' if there are no cookies, then no language was chosen, so
20             ' display appropriate message and clear and hide booksListBox
21             recommendationsLabel.Text = "No Recommendations"
22             booksListBox.Items.Clear()
23             booksListBox.Visible = False
24
25             ' modify languageLink because no language was selected
26             languageLink.Text = "Click here to choose a language"
27          End If
28       End Sub ' Page_Init
29    End Class ' Recommendations
```

Fig. 21.23 | Reading cookies from a client to determine book recommendations.

ISBN# " and added to the ListBox. Lines 21–26 execute if no language was selected. We summarize some commonly used HttpCookie properties in Fig. 21.24.

Properties	Description
Domain	Returns a String containing the cookie's domain (i.e., the domain of the web server running the application that wrote the cookie). This determines which web servers can receive the cookie. By default, cookies are sent to the web server that originally sent the cookie to the client. Changing the Domain property causes the cookie to be returned to a web server other than the one that originally wrote it.
Expires	Returns a DateTime object indicating when the browser can delete the cookie.
Name	Returns a String containing the cookie's name.
Path	Returns a String containing the path to a directory on the server (i.e., the Domain) to which the cookie applies. Cookies can be "targeted" to specific directories on the web server. By default, a cookie is returned only to applications operating in the same directory as the application that sent the cookie or a subdirectory of that directory. Changing the Path property causes the cookie to be returned to a directory other than the one from which it was originally written.
Secure	Returns a Boolean value indicating whether the cookie should be transmitted through a secure protocol. The value True causes a secure protocol to be used.
Value	Returns a String containing the cookie's value.

Fig. 21.24 | HttpCookie properties.

21.4.2 Session Tracking with HttpSessionState

Session-tracking capabilities are provided by the FCL class ***HttpSessionState***. To demonstrate basic session-tracking techniques, we modified the example of Figs. 21.20–21.23 to use HttpSessionState objects. Figures 21.25–21.26 present the ASPX file and code-behind file for Options.aspx. Figures 21.28–21.29 present the ASPX file and code-behind file for Recommendations.aspx. Options.aspx is similar to the version presented in Fig. 21.20, but Fig. 21.25 contains two additional Labels (lines 32–33 and lines 35–36), which we discuss shortly.

Every Web Form includes an HttpSessionState object, which is accessible through property ***Session*** of class Page. Throughout this section, we use property Session to manipulate our page's HttpSessionState object. When the web page is requested, an HttpSessionState object is created and assigned to the Page's Session property. As a result, we often refer to property Session as the Session object.

Adding Session Items

When the user presses Submit on the Web Form, submitButton_Click is invoked in the code-behind file (Fig. 21.26, lines 55–66). Method submitButton_Click responds by adding a key–value pair to our Session object, specifying the language chosen and the ISBN number for a book on that language. These key–value pairs are often referred to as *session items.* Next, a postback occurs. Each time the user clicks **Submit**, submitButton_Click adds a new session item to the HttpSessionState object. Because much of this example is identical to the last example, we concentrate on the new features.

```
1   <%-- Fig. 21.25: Options.aspx --%>
2   <%-- Allows client to select programming languages and access --%>
3   <%-- book recommendations. --%>
4   <%@ Page Language="VB" AutoEventWireup="false"
5      CodeFile="Options.aspx.vb" Inherits="Options" %>
6
7   <!DOCTYPE html PUBLIC "-//W3C//DTD XHTML 1.0 Transitional//EN"
8      "http://www.w3.org/TR/xhtml1/DTD/xhtml1-transitional.dtd">
9
10  <html xmlns="http://www.w3.org/1999/xhtml" >
11  <head id="Head1" runat="server">
12     <title>Sessions</title>
13  </head>
14  <body>
15     <form id="form1" runat="server">
16     <div>
17        <asp:Label ID="promptLabel" runat="server" Font-Bold="True"
18           Font-Size="Large" Text="Select a programming language:">
19        </asp:Label>
20        <asp:RadioButtonList ID="languageList" runat="server">
21           <asp:ListItem>Visual Basic 2005</asp:ListItem>
22           <asp:ListItem>Visual C# 2005</asp:ListItem>
23           <asp:ListItem>C</asp:ListItem>
24           <asp:ListItem>C++</asp:ListItem>
25           <asp:ListItem>Java</asp:ListItem>
26        </asp:RadioButtonList>
27        <asp:Button ID="submitButton" runat="server" Text="Submit" />
28        <asp:Label ID="responseLabel" runat="server" Font-Bold="True"
29           Font-Size="Large" Text="Welcome to sessions!" Visible="False">
30        </asp:Label><br />
31        <br />
32        <asp:Label ID="idLabel" runat="server" Visible="False">
33        </asp:Label><br />
34        <br />
35        <asp:Label ID="timeoutLabel" runat="server" Visible="False">
36        </asp:Label><br />
37        <br />
38        <asp:HyperLink ID="languageLink" runat="server"
39           NavigateUrl="~/Options.aspx" Visible="False">
40           Click here to choose another language
41        </asp:HyperLink><br />
42        <br />
43        <asp:HyperLink ID="recommendationsLink" runat="server"
44           NavigateUrl="~/Recommendations.aspx" Visible="False">
45           Click here to get book recommendations
46        </asp:HyperLink>
47     </div>
48     </form>
```

Fig. 21.25 | ASPX file that presents a list of programming languages. (Part 1 of 2.)

```
49    </body>
50    </html>
```

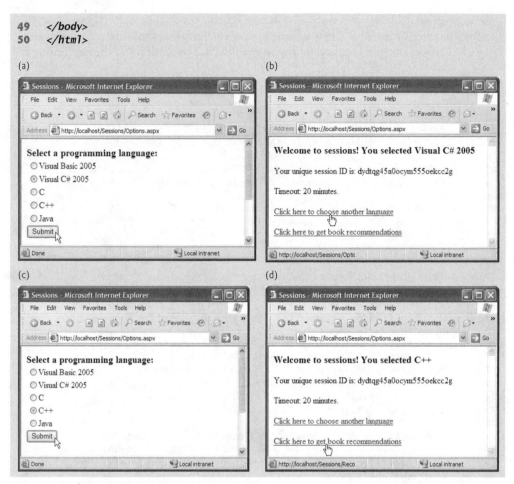

Fig. 21.25 | ASPX file that presents a list of programming languages. (Part 2 of 2.)

Software Engineering Observation 21.3

A Web Form should not use instance variables to maintain client state information, because each new request or postback is handled by a new instance of the page. Instead, maintain client state information in HttpSessionState objects, because such objects are specific to each client.

Like a cookie, an HttpSessionState object can store name–value pairs. These session items are placed in an HttpSessionState object by calling method **Add**. Line 64 calls Add to place the language and its corresponding recommended book's ISBN number in the HttpSessionState object. If the application calls method Add to add an attribute that has the same name as an attribute previously stored in a session, the object associated with that attribute is replaced.

Software Engineering Observation 21.4

A benefit of using HttpSessionState objects (rather than cookies) is that HttpSessionState objects can store any type of object (not just Strings) as attribute values. This provides you with increased flexibility in determining the type of state information to maintain for clients.

```vb
1   ' Fig. 21.26: Options.aspx.vb
2   ' Processes user's selection of a programming language
3   ' by displaying links and writing information in a Session object.
4   Partial Class Options
5      Inherits System.Web.UI.Page
6      ' stores values to represent books
7      Private books As New System.Collections.Hashtable()
8
9      ' initializes the Hashtable of values to be stored in a Session
10     Protected Sub Page_Init(ByVal sender As Object, _
11        ByVal e As System.EventArgs) Handles Me.Init
12        books.Add("Visual Basic 2005", "0-13-186900-0")
13        books.Add("Visual C# 2005", "0-13-152523-9")
14        books.Add("C", "0-13-142644-3")
15        books.Add("C++", "0-13-185757-6")
16        books.Add("Java", "0-13-148398-6")
17     End Sub ' Page_Init
18
19     ' if postback, hide form and display links to make additional
20     ' selections or view recommendations
21     Protected Sub Page_Load(ByVal sender As Object, _
22        ByVal e As System.EventArgs) Handles Me.Load
23
24        If IsPostBack Then
25           ' user has submitted information, so display message
26           ' and appropriate hyperlinks
27           responseLabel.Visible = True
28           idLabel.Visible = True
29           timeoutLabel.Visible = True
30           languageLink.Visible = True
31           recommendationsLink.Visible = True
32
33           ' hide other controls used to make language selection
34           promptLabel.Visible = False
35           languageList.Visible = False
36           submitButton.Visible = False
37
38           ' if the user made a selection, display it in responseLabel
39           If languageList.SelectedItem IsNot Nothing Then
40              responseLabel.Text &= " You selected " & _
41                 languageList.SelectedItem.Text.ToString()
42           Else
43              responseLabel.Text &= " You did not select a language."
44           End If
45
46           ' display session ID
47           idLabel.Text = "Your unique session ID is: " & Session.SessionID
48
49           ' display the timeout
50           timeoutLabel.Text = "Timeout: " & Session.Timeout & " minutes."
51        End If
52     End Sub ' Page_Load
```

Fig. 21.26 | Processes user's selection of a programming language by displaying links and writing information in a Session object. (Part 1 of 2.)

```
53
54        ' record the user's selection in the Session
55     Protected Sub submitButton_Click(ByVal sender As Object, _
56        ByVal e As System.EventArgs) Handles submitButton.Click
57        ' if the user made a selection
58        If languageList.SelectedItem IsNot Nothing Then
59           Dim language As String = languageList.SelectedItem.ToString()
60
61           ' get ISBN number of book for the given language
62           Dim ISBN As String = books(language).ToString()
63
64           Session.Add(language, ISBN) ' add name/value pair to Session
65        End If
66     End Sub ' submitButton_Click
67  End Class ' Options
```

Fig. 21.26 | Processes user's selection of a programming language by displaying links and writing information in a Session object. (Part 2 of 2.)

The application handles the postback event (lines 24–51) in method Page_Load. Here, we retrieve information about the current client's session from the Session object's properties and display this information in the web page. The ASP.NET application contains information about the HttpSessionState object for the current client. Property **SessionID** (line 47) contains the *unique session ID*—a sequence of random letters and numbers. The first time a client connects to the web server, a unique session ID is created for that client and a temporary cookie is written to the client so the server can identify the client on subsequent requests. When the client makes additional requests, the client's session ID from that temporary cookie is compared with the session IDs stored in the web server's memory to retrieve the client's HttpSessionState object. Recall that clients may disable cookies in their web browsers to ensure that their privacy is protected. Such clients will experience difficulty using web applications that depend on HttpSessionState objects and cookies to maintain state information. The HttpSessionStrate property IsCookieless indicates whether URL rewriting or cookies are used for session tracking. Property **Timeout** (line 50) specifies the maximum amount of time that an HttpSessionState object can be inactive before it is discarded. Figure 21.27 lists some common HttpSessionState properties.

Properties	Description
Count	Specifies the number of key–value pairs in the Session object.
IsNewSession	Indicates whether this is a new session (i.e., whether the session was created during loading of this page).
IsReadOnly	Indicates whether the Session object is read-only.

Fig. 21.27 | HttpSessionState properties. (Part 1 of 2.)

Properties	Description
Keys	Returns a collection containing the Session object's keys.
SessionID	Returns the session's unique ID.
Timeout	Specifies the maximum number of minutes during which a session can be inactive (i.e., no requests are made) before the session expires. By default, this property is set to 20 minutes.

Fig. 21.27 | HttpSessionState properties. (Part 2 of 2.)

Displaying Recommendations Based on Session Values

As in the cookies example, this application provides a link to Recommendations.aspx (Fig. 21.28), which displays a list of book recommendations based on the user's language selections. Lines 20–21 define a ListBox web control that is used to present the recommendations to the user.

```
1   <%-- Fig. 21.28: Recommendations.aspx --%>
2   <%-- Displays book recommendations using a Session object. --%>
3   <%@ Page Language="VB" AutoEventWireup="false"
4      CodeFile="Recommendations.aspx.vb" Inherits="Recommendations" %>
5
6   <!DOCTYPE html PUBLIC "-//W3C//DTD XHTML 1.0 Transitional//EN"
7      "http://www.w3.org/TR/xhtml1/DTD/xhtml1-transitional.dtd">
8
9   <html xmlns="http://www.w3.org/1999/xhtml" >
10  <head id="Head1" runat="server">
11      <title>Book Recommendations</title>
12  </head>
13  <body>
14      <form id="form1" runat="server">
15      <div>
16         <asp:Label ID="recommendationsLabel" runat="server"
17            Font-Bold="True" Font-Size="X-Large" Text="Recommendations">
18         </asp:Label><br />
19         <br />
20         <asp:ListBox ID="booksListBox" runat="server" Height="125px"
21            Width="450px"></asp:ListBox><br />
22         <br />
23         <asp:HyperLink ID="languageLink" runat="server"
24            NavigateUrl="~/Options.aspx">
25            Click here to choose another language
26         </asp:HyperLink> </div>
27      </form>
28  </body>
29  </html>
```

Fig. 21.28 | Session-based book recommendations displayed in a ListBox. (Part 1 of 2.)

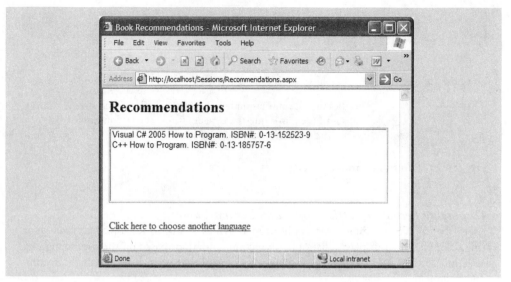

Fig. 21.28 | Session-based book recommendations displayed in a ListBox. (Part 2 of 2.)

Code-Behind File That Creates Book Recommendations from a Session

Figure 21.29 presents the code-behind file for Recommendations.aspx. Event handler Page_Init (lines 7–30) retrieves the session information. If a user has not selected a language on Options.aspx, our Session object's **Count** property will be 0. This property provides the number of session items contained in a Session object. If Session object's Count property is 0 (i.e., no language was selected), then we display the text **No Recommendations** and update the Text of the HyperLink back to Options.aspx.

```
1    ' Fig. 21.29: Recommendations.aspx.vb
2    ' Creates book recommendations based on a Session object.
3    Partial Class Recommendations
4       Inherits System.Web.UI.Page
5
6       ' read Session items and populate ListBox with any book recommendations
7       Protected Sub Page_Init(ByVal sender As Object, _
8          ByVal e As System.EventArgs) Handles Me.Init
9          ' determine whether Session contains any information
10         If Session.Count <> 0 Then
11            For i As Integer = 0 To Session.Count - 1
12               ' get current key name from Session object
13               Dim keyName As String = Session.Keys(i)
14
15               ' use keyName to display one of Session's name-value pairs
16               booksListBox.Items.Add(keyName & _
17                  " How to Program. ISBN#: " & _
18                  Session(keyName).ToString())
19            Next
20         Else
```

Fig. 21.29 | Session data used to provide book recommendations to the user. (Part 1 of 2.)

```
21          ' if there are no session items, no language was chosen, so
22          ' display appropriate message and clear and hide booksListBox
23          recommendationsLabel.Text = "No Recommendations"
24          booksListBox.Items.Clear()
25          booksListBox.Visible = False
26
27          ' modify languageLink because no language was selected
28          languageLink.Text = "Click here to choose a language"
29       End If
30    End Sub ' Page_Init
31 End Class ' Recommendations
```

Fig. 21.29 | Session data used to provide book recommendations to the user. (Part 2 of 2.)

If the user has chosen a language, the loop in lines 11–19 iterates through our Session object's session items, temporarily storing each key name (line 13). The value in a key–value pair is retrieved from the Session object by indexing the Session object with the key name, using the same process by which we retrieved a value from our Hashtable in the preceding section.

Line 13 accesses the **Keys** property of class HttpSessionState, which returns a collection containing all the keys in the session. Line 13 indexes this collection to retrieve the current key. Lines 16–18 concatenate keyName's value to the String " How to Program. ISBN#: " and the value from the Session object for which keyName is the key. This String is the recommendation that appears in the ListBox.

21.5 Case Study: Connecting to a Database in ASP.NET

Many websites allow users to provide feedback about the website in a *guestbook*. Typically, users click a link on the website's home page to request the guestbook page. This page usually consists of an XHTML form that contains fields for the user's name, e-mail address, message/feedback and so on. Data submitted on the guestbook form is then stored in a database located on the web server's machine.

In this section, we create a guestbook Web Form application. This example's GUI is slightly more complex than that of earlier examples. It contains a **GridView** ASP.NET data control, as shown in Fig. 21.30, which displays all the entries in the guestbook in tabular format. We explain how to create and configure this data control shortly. Note that the GridView displays **abc** in **Design** mode to indicate string data that will be retrieved from a data source at runtime.

The XHTML form presented to the user consists of a name field, an e-mail address field and a message field. The form also contains a **Submit** button to send the data to the server and a **Clear** button to reset each of the fields on the form. The application stores the guestbook information in a SQL Server database called Guestbook.mdf located on the web server. (We provide this database in the examples directory for this chapter. You can download the examples from www.deitel.com/books/ajaxfp.) Below the XHTML form, the GridView displays the data (i.e., guestbook entries) in the database's Messages table.

Fig. 21.30 | Guestbook application GUI in **Design** mode.

21.5.1 Building a Web Form That Displays Data from a Database

We now explain how to build this GUI and set up the data binding between the GridView control and the database. We present the ASPX file generated from the GUI later in the section, and we discuss the related code-behind file in the next section. To build the guestbook application, perform the following steps:

Step 1: Creating the Project

Create an **ASP.NET Web Site** named Guestbook and name the ASPX file Guestbook.aspx. Rename the class in the code-behind file Guestbook, and update the Page directive in the ASPX file accordingly.

Step 2: Creating the Form for User Input

In **Design** mode for the ASPX file, add the text Please leave a message in our guestbook: formatted as an h2 header. As discussed in Section 21.3.1, insert an XHTML table with two columns and four rows, configured so that the text in each cell aligns with the top of the cell. Place the appropriate text (see Fig. 21.30) in the top three cells in the table's left column. Then place TextBoxes named nameTextBox, emailTextBox and messageTextBox in the top three table cells in the right column. Set messageTextBox to be a multiline TextBox. Finally, add Buttons named submitButton and clearButton to the bottom-right table cell. Set the buttons' Text properties to Submit and Clear, respectively. We discuss the buttons' event handlers when we present the code-behind file.

Step 3: Adding a GridView Control to the Web Form

Add a GridView named messagesGridView that will display the guestbook entries. This control appears in the **Data** section of the **Toolbox**. The colors for the GridView are specified through the **Auto Format...** link in the **GridView Tasks** smart tag menu that opens when you place the GridView on the page. Clicking this link causes an **Auto Format** dialog to open with several choices. In this example, we chose **Simple**. We soon show how to set the GridView's data source (i.e., where it gets the data to display in its rows and columns).

Step 4: Adding a Database to an ASP.NET Web Application
To use a SQL Server 2005 Express database in an ASP.NET web application, it is easiest to first add it to the project's App_Data folder. Right click this folder in the **Solution Explorer** and select **Add Existing Item…**. Locate the Guestbook.mdf file in the exampleDatabases subdirectory of the chapter's examples directory, then click **Add**.

Step 5: Binding the GridView to the Messages Table of the Guestbook Database
Now that the database is part of the project, we can configure the GridView to display its data. Open the **GridView Tasks** smart tag menu, then select **<New data source…>** from the **Choose Data Source** drop-down list. In the **Data Source Configuration Wizard** that appears, select **Database**. In this example, we use a *SqlDataSource* control that allows the application to interact with the Guestbook database. Set the ID of the data source to messagesSqlDataSource and click **OK** to begin the **Configure Data Source** wizard. In the **Choose Your Data Connection** screen, select Guestbook.mdf from the drop-down list (Fig. 21.31), then click **Next >** twice to continue to the **Configure the Select Statement** screen.

The **Configure the Select Statement** screen (Fig. 21.32) allows you to specify which data the SqlDataSource should retrieve from the database. Your choices on this page design a SELECT statement, shown in the bottom pane of the dialog. The **Name** drop-down list identifies a table in the database. The Guestbook database contains only one table named Messages, which is selected by default. In the **Columns** pane, click the checkbox marked with an asterisk (*) to indicate that you want to retrieve the data from all the columns in the **Message** table. Click the **Advanced** button, then check the box next to **Gen-**

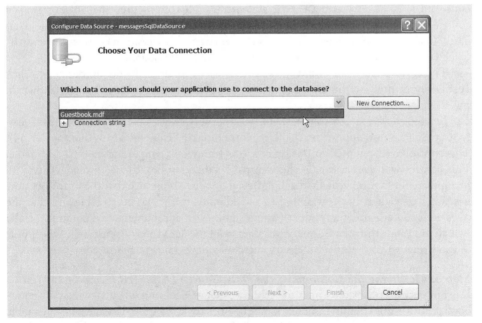

Fig. 21.31 | Configure **Data Source** dialog in Visual Web Developer.

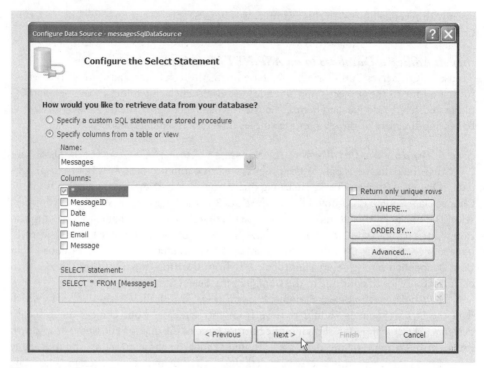

Fig. 21.32 | Configuring the SELECT statement used by the SqlDataSource to retrieve data.

erate **UPDATE, INSERT and DELETE statements**. This configures the SqlDataSource control to allow us to change data in, insert new data into and delete data from the database. We discuss inserting new guestbook entries based on users' form submissions shortly. Click **OK**, then click **Next >** to continue the **Configure Data Source** wizard.

The next screen of the wizard allows you to test the query that you just designed. Click **Test Query** to preview the data that will be retrieved by the SqlDataSource (shown in Fig. 21.33).

Finally, click **Finish** to complete the wizard. Notice that a control named messagesSqlDataSource now appears on the Web Form directly below the GridView (Fig. 21.34). This control is represented in **Design** mode as a gray box containing its type and name. This control will *not* appear on the web page—the gray box simply provides a way to manipulate the control visually through **Design** mode. Also notice that the GridView now has column headers that correspond to the columns in the Messages table and that the rows each contain either a number (which signifies an autoincremented column) or **abc** (which indicates string data). The actual data from the Guestbook database file will appear in these rows when the ASPX file is executed and viewed in a web browser.

Step 6: Modifying the Columns of the Data Source Displayed in the GridView

It is not necessary for site visitors to see the MessageID column when viewing past guestbook entries—this column is merely a unique primary key required by the Messages table within the database. Thus, we modify the GridView so that this column does not display

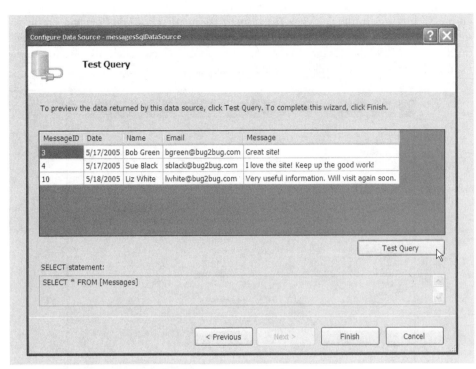

Fig. 21.33 | Previewing the data retrieved by the SqlDataSource.

Fig. 21.34 | **Design** mode displaying SqlDataSource control for a GridView.

on the Web Form. In the **GridView Tasks** smart tag menu, click **Edit Columns**. In the resulting **Fields** dialog (Fig. 21.35), select **MessageID** in the **Selected fields** pane, then click the **X**. This removes the `MessageID` column from the `GridView`. Click **OK** to return to the main IDE window. The `GridView` should now appear as in Fig. 21.30.

Fig. 21.35 | Removing the `MessageID` column from the `GridView`.

Step 7: Modifying the Way the SqlDataSource Control Inserts Data
When you create a `SqlDataSource` in the manner described here, it is configured to permit `INSERT` SQL operations against the database table from which it gathers data. You must specify the values to insert either programmatically or through other controls on the Web Form. In this example, we wish to insert the data entered by the user in the `nameTextBox`, `emailTextBox` and `messageTextBox` controls. We also want to insert the current date—we'll specify the date to insert programmatically in the code-behind file, which we present shortly.

To configure the `SqlDataSource` to allow such an insertion, select the `messagesSql-DataSource` control then click the ellipsis button next to the control's *InsertQuery* property of the `messagesSqlDataSource` control in the **Properties** window. The **Command and Parameter Editor** (Fig. 21.36) that appears displays the `INSERT` command used by the `Sql-DataSource` control. This command contains parameters `@Date`, `@Name`, `@Email` and `@Message`. You must provide values for these parameters before they are inserted into the database. Each parameter is listed in the **Parameters** section of the **Command and Parameter Editor**. Because we'll set the **Date** parameter programmatically, we do not modify it here. For each of the remaining three parameters, select the parameter, then select **Control** from the **Parameter source** drop-down list. This indicates that the value of the parameter should be taken from a control. The **ControlID** drop-down list contains all the controls on the Web Form. Select the appropriate control for each parameter, then click **OK**. Now the `SqlDataSource` is configured to insert the user's name, e-mail address and message in the

Fig. 21.36 | Setting up INSERT parameters based on control values.

Messages table of the Guestbook database. We show how to set the date parameter and initiate the insert operation when the user clicks **Submit** shortly.

ASPX File for a Web Form That Interacts with a Database

The ASPX file generated by the guestbook GUI (and messagesSqlDataSource control) is shown in Fig. 21.37. This file contains a large amount of generated markup. We discuss only those parts that are new or noteworthy for the current example. Lines 19–58 contain the XHTML and ASP.NET elements that comprise the form that gathers user input. The GridView control appears in lines 60–85. The <asp:GridView> start tag (lines 60–63) contains properties that set various aspects of the GridView's appearance and behavior, such as whether grid lines should be displayed between rows and columns. The **DataSourceID** property identifies the data source that is used to fill the GridView with data at runtime.

Lines 66–75 define the Columns that appear in the GridView. Each column is represented as a **BoundField**, because the values in the columns are bound to values retrieved from the data source (i.e., the Messages table of the Guestbook database). The DataField property of each BoundField identifies the column in the data source to which the column in the GridView is bound. The HeaderText property indicates the text that appears as the column header. By default, this is the name of the column in the data source, but you can change this property as desired. Lines 76–84 contain nested elements that define the styles used to format the GridView's rows. The IDE configured these styles based on your selection of the **Simple** style in the **Auto Format** dialog for the GridView.

The messagesSqlDataSource is defined by the markup in lines 86–115 in Fig. 21.37. Line 87 contains a **ConnectionString** property, which indicates the connection through which the SqlDataSource control interacts with the database. The value of this property uses an *ASP.NET expression*, delimited by **<%\$** and **%>**, to access the Guestbook-ConnectionString stored in the ConnectionStrings section of the application's Web.config configuration file. Recall that we created this connection string earlier in this section using the **Configure Data Source** wizard. Lines 88–95 define the *DeleteCommand*, *InsertCommand*, *SelectCommand* and *UpdateCommand* properties, which contain the DELETE, INSERT, SELECT and UPDATE SQL statements, respectively. These were generated by the **Configure Data Source** wizard. In this example, we use only the InsertCommand. We discuss invoking this command shortly.

```
1    <%-- Fig. 21.37: Guestbook.aspx --%>
2    <%-- Guestbook Web application with a form for users to submit --%>
3    <%-- guestbook entries and a GridView to view existing entries. --%>
4    <%@ Page Language="VB" AutoEventWireup="false"
5       CodeFile="Guestbook.aspx.vb" Inherits="Guestbook" %>
6
7    <!DOCTYPE html PUBLIC "-//W3C//DTD XHTML 1.0 Transitional//EN"
8       "http://www.w3.org/TR/xhtml1/DTD/xhtml1-transitional.dtd">
9
10   <html xmlns="http://www.w3.org/1999/xhtml" >
11   <head runat="server">
12      <title>Guestbook</title>
13   </head>
14   <body>
15      <form id="form1" runat="server">
16      <div>
17         <h2>
18            Please leave a message in our guestbook:</h2>
19         <table>
20            <tr>
21               <td style="width: 130px; height: 21px" valign="top">
22                  Your name:<br />
23               </td>
24               <td style="width: 300px; height: 21px" valign="top">
25                  <asp:TextBox ID="nameTextBox" runat="server"
26                     Width="300px"></asp:TextBox>
27               </td>
28            </tr>
29            <tr>
30               <td style="width: 130px" valign="top">
31                  Your e-mail address:<br />
32               </td>
33               <td style="width: 300px" valign="top">
34                  <asp:TextBox ID="emailTextBox" runat="server"
35                     Width="300px"></asp:TextBox>
36               </td>
37            </tr>
38            <tr>
39               <td style="width: 130px" valign="top">
40                  Tell the world:<br />
41               </td>
```

Fig. 21.37 | ASPX file for the guestbook application. (Part 1 of 4.)

```
42              <td style="width: 300px" valign="top">
43                  <asp:TextBox ID="messageTextBox" runat="server"
44                      Height="100px" Rows="8" Width="300px">
45                  </asp:TextBox>
46              </td>
47          </tr>
48          <tr>
49              <td style="width: 130px" valign="top">
50              </td>
51              <td style="width: 300px" valign="top">
52                  <asp:Button ID="submitButton" runat="server"
53                      Text="Submit" />
54                  <asp:Button ID="clearButton" runat="server"
55                      Text="Clear" />
56              </td>
57          </tr>
58      </table>
59      <br />
60      <asp:GridView ID="messagesGridView" runat="server"
61          AutoGenerateColumns="False" CellPadding="4"
62          DataKeyNames="MessageID" DataSourceID="messagesSqlDataSource"
63          ForeColor="#333333" GridLines="None" Width="600px">
64          <FooterStyle BackColor="#1C5E55" Font-Bold="True"
65              ForeColor="White" />
66          <Columns>
67              <asp:BoundField DataField="Date" HeaderText="Date"
68                  SortExpression="Date" />
69              <asp:BoundField DataField="Name" HeaderText="Name"
70                  SortExpression="Name" />
71              <asp:BoundField DataField="Email" HeaderText="Email"
72                  SortExpression="Email" />
73              <asp:BoundField DataField="Message" HeaderText="Message"
74                  SortExpression="Message" />
75          </Columns>
76          <RowStyle BackColor="#E3EAEB" />
77          <EditRowStyle BackColor="#7C6F57" />
78          <SelectedRowStyle BackColor="#C5BBAF" Font-Bold="True"
79              ForeColor="#333333" />
80          <PagerStyle BackColor="#666666" ForeColor="White"
81              HorizontalAlign="Center" />
82          <HeaderStyle BackColor="#1C5E55" Font-Bold="True"
83              ForeColor="White" />
84          <AlternatingRowStyle BackColor="White" />
85      </asp:GridView>
86      <asp:SqlDataSource ID="messagesSqlDataSource" runat="server"
87          ConnectionString="<%$ ConnectionStrings:ConnectionString %>"
88          DeleteCommand="DELETE FROM [Messages] WHERE [MessageID] =
89              @MessageID" InsertCommand="INSERT INTO [Messages]
90              ([Date], [Name], [Email], [Message])
91              VALUES (@Date, @Name, @Email, @Message)"
92          SelectCommand="SELECT * FROM [Messages]" UpdateCommand=
93              "UPDATE [Messages] SET [Date] = @Date, [Name] = @Name,
94              [Email] = @Email, [Message] = @Message
```

Fig. 21.37 | ASPX file for the guestbook application. (Part 2 of 4.)

```
95                    WHERE [MessageID] = @MessageID">
96                <DeleteParameters>
97                    <asp:Parameter Name="MessageID" Type="Int32" />
98                </DeleteParameters>
99                <UpdateParameters>
100                   <asp:Parameter Name="Date" Type="String" />
101                   <asp:Parameter Name="Name" Type="String" />
102                   <asp:Parameter Name="Email" Type="String" />
103                   <asp:Parameter Name="Message" Type="String" />
104                   <asp:Parameter Name="MessageID" Type="Int32" />
105                </UpdateParameters>
106                <InsertParameters>
107                   <asp:Parameter Name="Date" Type="String" />
108                   <asp:ControlParameter ControlID="nameTextBox" Name="Name"
109                       PropertyName="Text" Type="String" />
110                   <asp:ControlParameter ControlID="emailTextBox" Name="Email"
111                       PropertyName="Text" Type="String" />
112                   <asp:ControlParameter ControlID="messageTextBox"
113                       Name="Message" PropertyName="Text" Type="String" />
114                </InsertParameters>
115            </asp:SqlDataSource>
116        </div>
117        </form>
118  </body>
119  </html>
```

(a)

Fig. 21.37 | ASPX file for the guestbook application. (Part 3 of 4.)

Fig. 21.37 | ASPX file for the guestbook application. (Part 4 of 4.)

Notice that the SQL commands used by the SqlDataSource contain several parameters (prefixed with @). Lines 96–114 contain elements that define the name, the type and, for some parameters, the source of the parameter. Parameters that are set programmatically are defined by *Parameter* elements containing Name and Type properties. For example, line 107 defines the Date parameter of Type String. This corresponds to the @Date parameter in the InsertCommand (line 91). Parameters that obtain their values from controls are defined by *ControlParameter* elements. Lines 108–113 contain markup that sets up the relationships between the INSERT parameters and the Web Form's TextBoxes. We established these relationships in the **Command and Parameter Editor** (Fig. 21.36). Each ControlParameter contains a ControlID property indicating the control from which the parameter gets its value. The PropertyName specifies the property that contains the actual value to be used as the parameter value. The IDE sets the PropertyName based on the type of control specified by the ControlID (indirectly via the **Command and Parameter Editor**). In this case, we use only TextBoxes, so the PropertyName of each ControlParameter is Text (e.g., the value of parameter @Name comes from nameTextBox.Text). However, if we were using a DropDownList, for example, the PropertyName would be SelectedValue.

21.5.2 Modifying the Code-Behind File for the Guestbook Application

After building the Web Form and configuring the data controls used in this example, double click the **Submit** and **Clear** buttons in **Design** view to create their corresponding Click event handlers in the Guestbook.aspx.vb code-behind file (Fig. 21.38). The IDE generates empty event handlers, so we must add the appropriate code to make these but-

```
 1    ' Fig. 21.38: Guestbook.aspx.vb
 2    ' Code-behind file that defines event handlers for the guestbook.
 3    Partial Class Guestbook
 4       Inherits System.Web.UI.Page
 5
 6       ' Submit Button adds a new guestbook entry to the database,
 7       ' clears the form and displays the updated list of guestbook entries
 8       Protected Sub submitButton_Click(ByVal sender As Object, _
 9          ByVal e As System.EventArgs) Handles submitButton.Click
10          ' create a date parameter to store the current date
11          Dim currentDate As New System.Web.UI.WebControls.Parameter( _
12             "Date", TypeCode.String, DateTime.Now.ToShortDateString())
13
14          ' set the @Date parameter to the date parameter
15          messagesSqlDataSource.InsertParameters.RemoveAt(0)
16          messagesSqlDataSource.InsertParameters.Add(currentDate)
17
18          ' execute an INSERT SQL statement to add a new row to the
19          ' Messages table in the Guestbook database that contains the
20          ' current date and the user's name, e-mail address and message
21          messagesSqlDataSource.Insert()
22
23          ' clear the TextBoxes
24          nameTextBox.Text = ""
25          emailTextBox.Text = ""
26          messageTextBox.Text = ""
27
28          ' update the GridView with the new database table contents
29          messagesGridView.DataBind()
30       End Sub ' submitButton_Click
31
32       ' Clear Button clears the Web Form's TextBoxes
33       Protected Sub clearButton_Click(ByVal sender As Object, _
34          ByVal e As System.EventArgs) Handles clearButton.Click
35          nameTextBox.Text = ""
36          emailTextBox.Text = ""
37          messageTextBox.Text = ""
38       End Sub ' clearButton_Click
39    End Class ' Guestbook
```

Fig. 21.38 | Code-behind file for the guestbook application.

tons work properly. The event handler for clearButton (lines 33–38) clears each TextBox by setting its Text property to an empty string. This resets the form for a new guestbook submission.

Lines 8–30 contain the event-handling code for submitButton, which adds the user's information to the Messages table of the Guestbook database. Recall that we configured messagesSqlDataSource's INSERT command to use the values of the TextBoxes on the Web Form as the parameter values inserted into the database. We have not yet specified the date value to be inserted, though. Lines 11–12 assign a String representation of the current date (e.g., "3/27/06") to a new object of type Parameter. This Parameter object is identified as "Date" and is given the current date as a default value. The SqlData-

Source's `InsertParameters` collection contains an item named `Date` (at position 0), which we `Remove` in line 15 and replace in line 16 by `Add`ing our `currentDate` parameter. Invoking `SqlDataSource` method `Insert` in line 21 executes the `INSERT` command against the database, thus adding a row to the `Messages` table. After the data is inserted into the database, lines 24–26 clear the `TextBox`es, and line 29 invokes `messagesGridView`'s `Data-Bind` method to refresh the data that the `GridView` displays. This causes `messagesSql-DataSource` (the data source of the `GridView`) to execute its `SELECT` command to obtain the `Messages` table's newly updated data.

21.6 Case Study: Secure Books Database Application

This case study presents a web application in which a user logs into a secure website to view a list of publications by an author of the user's choosing. The application consists of several ASPX files. Section 21.6.1 presents the application and explains the purpose of each of its web pages. Section 21.6.2 provides step-by-step instructions to guide you through building the application and presents the markup in the ASPX files.

21.6.1 Examining the Completed Secure Books Database Application

This example uses a technique known as *forms authentication* to protect a page so that only users known to the website can access it. Such users are known as the site's members. Authentication is a crucial tool for sites that allow only members to enter the site or a portion of the site. In this application, website visitors must log in before they are allowed to view the publications in the `Books` database. The first page that a user would typically request is `Login.aspx` (Fig. 21.39). You will soon learn to create this page using a `Login` control, one of several *ASP.NET login controls* that help create secure applications using authentication. These controls are found in the **Login** section of the **Toolbox**.

The `Login.aspx` page allows a site visitor to enter an existing user name and password to log into the website. A first-time visitor must click the link below the **Log In** button to create a new user before logging in. Doing so redirects the visitor to `CreateNewUser.aspx`

Fig. 21.39 | `Login.aspx` page of the secure books database application.

(Fig. 21.40), which contains a `CreateUserWizard` control that presents the visitor with a user registration form. We discuss the `CreateUserWizard` control in detail in Section 21.6.2. In Fig. 21.40, we use the password pa$$word for testing purposes—as you will learn, the `CreateUserWizard` requires that the password contain special characters for security purposes. Clicking **Create User** establishes a new user account. After creating the account, the user is automatically logged in and shown a success message (Fig. 21.41).

Fig. 21.40 | `CreateNewUser.aspx` page of the secure books database application.

Fig. 21.41 | Message displayed to indicate that a user account was created successfully.

Clicking the **Continue** button on the confirmation page sends the user to Books.aspx (Fig. 21.42), which provides a drop-down list of authors and a table containing the ISBNs, titles, edition numbers and copyright years of books in the database. By default, all the books by Harvey Deitel are displayed. Links appear at the bottom of the table that allow you to access additional pages of data. When the user chooses an author, a postback occurs, and the page is updated to display information about books written by the selected author (Fig. 21.43).

Fig. 21.42 | Books.aspx displaying books by Harvey Deitel (by default).

Fig. 21.43 | Books.aspx displaying books by Andrew Goldberg.

Note that once the user creates an account and is logged in, `Books.aspx` displays a welcome message customized for the particular logged-in user. As you will soon see, a `LoginName` control provides this functionality. After you add this control to the page, ASP.NET handles the details of determining the user name.

Clicking the **Click here to log out** link logs the user out, then sends the user back to `Login.aspx` (Fig. 21.44). This link is created by a `LoginStatus` control, which handles the log out details. After logging out, the user would need to log in through `Login.aspx` to view the book listing again. The `Login` control on this page receives the user name and password entered by a visitor. ASP.NET compares these values with user names and passwords stored in a database on the server. If there is a match, the visitor is *authenticated* (i.e., the user's identity is confirmed). We explain the authentication process in detail in Section 21.6.2. When an existing user is successfully authenticated, `Login.aspx` redirects the user to `Books.aspx` (Fig. 21.42). If the user's login attempt fails, an appropriate error message is displayed (Fig. 21.45).

Fig. 21.44 | Logging in using the `Login` control.

Fig. 21.45 | Error message displayed for an unsuccessful login attempt.

Notice that `Login.aspx`, `CreateNewUser.aspx` and `Books.aspx` share the same page header containing the logo image from the fictional company Bug2Bug. Instead of placing this image at the top of each page, we use a *master page* to achieve this. As we demonstrate shortly, a master page defines common GUI elements that are inherited by each page in a set of *content pages*. Just as Visual Basic classes can inherit instance variables and methods from existing classes, content pages inherit elements from master pages—this is known as *visual inheritance*.

21.6.2 Creating the Secure Books Database Application

Now that you are familiar with how this application behaves, you'll learn how to create it from scratch. Thanks to the rich set of login and data controls provided by ASP.NET, you will not have to write *any* code to create this application. In fact, the application does not contain any code-behind files. All of the functionality is specified through properties of controls, many of which are set through wizards and other visual programming tools. ASP.NET hides the details of authenticating users against a database of user names and passwords, displaying appropriate success or error messages and redirecting the user to the correct page based on the authentication results. We now discuss the steps you must perform to create the secure books database application.

Step 1: Creating the Website
Create a new **ASP.NET Web Site** at `http://localhost/Bug2Bug` as described previously. We'll explicitly create each of the ASPX files that we need in this application, so delete the IDE-generated `Default.aspx` file (and its corresponding code-behind file) by selecting `Default.aspx` in the **Solution Explorer** and pressing the *Delete* key. Click **OK** in the confirmation dialog to delete these files.

Step 2: Setting Up the Website's Folders
Before building the pages in the website, we create folders to organize its contents. First, create an `Images` folder by right clicking the location of the website in the **Solution Explorer** and selecting **New Folder**, then add the `bug2bug.png` file to it. This image can be found in the examples directory for this chapter. Next, add the `Books.mdf` database file (located in the `exampleDatabases` subdirectory of the chapter's examples directory) to the project's `App_Data` folder. We show how to retrieve data from this database later in the section.

Step 3: Configuring the Application's Security Settings
In this application, we want to ensure that only authenticated users are allowed to access `Books.aspx` (created in *Step 9* and *Step 10*) to view the information in the database. Previously, we created all of our ASPX pages in the web application's root directory (e.g., `http://localhost/ProjectName`). By default, any website visitor (regardless of whether the visitor is authenticated) can view pages in the root directory. ASP.NET allows you to restrict access to particular folders of a website. We do not want to restrict access to the root of the website, however, because all users must be able to view `Login.aspx` and `CreateNewUser.aspx` to log in and create user accounts, respectively. Thus, if we want to restrict access to `Books.aspx`, it must reside in a directory other than the root directory. Create a folder named `Secure`. Later in the section, we'll create `Books.aspx` in this folder. First, let's enable forms authentication in our application and configure the `Secure` folder to restrict access to authenticated users only.

Select **Website > ASP.NET Configuration** to open the ***Web Site Administration Tool*** in a web browser (Fig. 21.46). This tool allows you to configure various options that determine how your application behaves. Click either the **Security** link or the **Security** tab to open a web page in which you can set security options (Fig. 21.47), such as the type of authentication the application should use. In the **Users** column, click **Select authentication type**. On the resulting page (Fig. 21.48), select the radio button next to **From the internet** to indicate that users will log in via a form on the website in which the user can enter a username and password (i.e., the application will use forms authentication). The default setting—**From a local network**—relies on users' Windows user names and passwords for authentication purposes. Click the **Done** button to save this change.

Now that forms authentication is enabled, the **Users** column on the main page of the **Web Site Administration Tool** (Fig. 21.49) provides links to create and manage users. As you saw in Section 21.6.1, our application provides the CreateNewUser.aspx page in which users can create their own accounts. Thus, while it is possible to create users through the **Web Site Administration Tool**, we do not do so here.

Even though no users exist at the moment, we configure the Secure folder to grant access only to authenticated users (i.e., deny access to all unauthenticated users). Click the **Create access rules** link in the **Access Rules** column of the **Web Site Administration Tool** (Fig. 21.49) to view the **Add New Access Rule** page (Fig. 21.50). This page is used to create an *access rule*—a rule that grants or denies access to a particular web application directory for a specific user or group of users. Click the Secure directory in the left column of the page to identify the directory to which our access rule applies. In the middle column, select the radio button marked **Anonymous users** to specify that the rule applies to users who

Fig. 21.46 | Web Site Administration Tool for configuring a web application.

Fig. 21.47 | **Security** page of the **Web Site Administration Tool**.

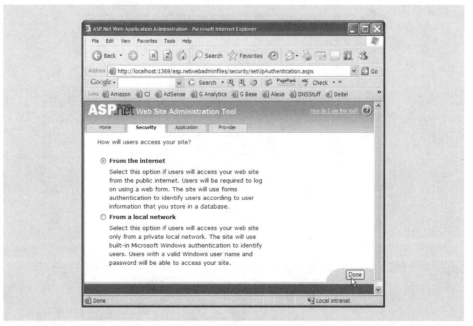

Fig. 21.48 | Choosing the type of authentication used by an ASP.NET web application.

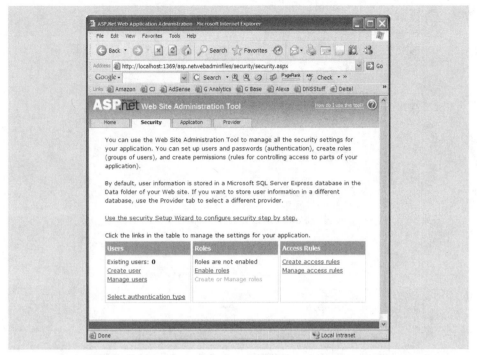

Fig. 21.49 | Main page of the **Web Site Administration Tool** after enabling forms authentication.

Fig. 21.50 | **Add New Access Rule** page used to configure directory access.

have not been authenticated. Finally, select **Deny** in the right column, labeled **Permission**, then click **OK**. This rule indicates that *anonymous users* (i.e., users who have not identified themselves by logging in) should be denied access to any pages in the Secure directory (e.g., Books.aspx). By default, anonymous users who attempt to load a page in the Secure directory are redirected to the Login.aspx page so that they can identify themselves. Note that because we did not set up any access rules for the Bug2Bug root directory, anonymous users may still access pages there (e.g., Login.aspx, CreateNewUser.aspx). We create these pages momentarily.

Step 4: Examining the Autogenerated Web.config Files

We have now configured the application to use forms authentication and created an access rule to ensure that only authenticated users can access the Secure folder. Before creating the website's content, we examine how the changes made through the **Web Site Administration Tool** appear in the IDE. Recall that Web.config is an XML file used for application configuration, such as enabling debugging or storing database connection strings. Visual Web Developer generates two Web.config files in response to our actions using the **Web Site Administration Tool**—one in the application's root directory and one in the Secure folder. [*Note:* You may need to click the **Refresh** button in the **Solution Explorer** to see these files.] In an ASP.NET application, a page's configuration settings are determined by the current directory's Web.config file. The settings in this file take precedence over the settings in the root directory's Web.config file.

After setting the authentication type for the web application, the IDE generates a Web.config file at http://localhost/Bug2Bug/Web.config, which contains an *authentication* element

```
<authentication mode="Forms" />
```

This element appears in the root directory's Web.config file, so the setting applies to the entire website. The value "Forms" of the *mode* attribute specifies that we want to use forms authentication. Had we left the authentication type set to **From a local network** in the **Web Site Administration Tool**, the mode attribute would be set to "Windows".

After creating the access rule for the Secure folder, the IDE generates a second Web.config file in that folder. This file contains an *authorization* element that indicates who is, and who is not, authorized to access this folder over the web. In this application, we want to allow only authenticated users to access the contents of the Secure folder, so the authorization element appears as

```
<authorization>
    <deny users="?" />
</authorization>
```

Rather than grant permission to each individual authenticated user, we deny access to those who are not authenticated (i.e., those who have not logged in). The *deny* element inside the authorization element specifies the users to whom we wish to deny access. When the users attribute's value is set to "?", all anonymous (i.e., unauthenticated) users are denied access to the folder. Thus, an unauthenticated user will not be able to load http://localhost/Bug2Bug/Secure/Books.aspx. Instead, such a user will be redirected to the Login.aspx page—when a user is denied access to a part of a site, ASP.NET by default sends the user to a page named Login.aspx in the application's root directory.

Step 5: Creating a Master Page

Now that you have established the application's security settings, you can create the application's web pages. We begin with the master page, which defines the elements we want to appear on each page. A master page is like a base class in a visual inheritance hierarchy, and content pages are like derived classes. The master page contains placeholders for custom content created in each content page. The content pages visually inherit the master page's content, then add content in place of the master page's placeholders.

For example, you might want to include a ***navigation bar*** (i.e., a series of buttons for navigating a website) on every page of a site. If the site encompasses a large number of pages, adding markup to create the navigation bar for each page can be time consuming. Moreover, if you subsequently modify the navigation bar, every page on the site that uses it must be updated. By creating a master page, you can specify the navigation bar markup in one file and have it appear on all the content pages, with only a few lines of markup. If the navigation bar changes, only the master page changes—any content pages that use it are updated the next time the page is requested.

In this example, we want the Bug2Bug logo to appear as a header at the top of every page, so we'll place an Image control in the master page. Each subsequent page we create will be a content page based on this master page and thus will include the header. To create a master page, right click the location of the website in the **Solution Explorer** and select **Add New Item....** In the **Add New Item** dialog, select **Master Page** from the template list and specify Bug2Bug.master as the filename. Master pages have the filename extension **.master** and, like Web Forms, can optionally use a code-behind file to define additional functionality. In this example, we do not need to specify any code for the master page, so leave the box labeled **Place code in a separate file** unchecked. Click **Add** to create the page.

The IDE opens the master page in **Source** mode (Fig. 21.51) when the file is first created. [*Note:* We added a line break in the DOCTYPE element for presentation purposes.] The

Fig. 21.51 | Master page in **Source** mode.

markup for a master page is almost identical to that of a Web Form. One difference is that a master page contains a *Master* directive (line 1 in Fig. 21.51), which specifies that this file defines a master page using the indicated Language for any code. Because we chose not to use a code-behind file, the master page also contains a *script* element (lines 6–8). Code that would usually be placed in a code-behind file can be placed in a script element. However, we remove the script element from this page, because we do not need to write any additional code. After deleting this block of markup, set the title of the page to Bug2Bug. Finally, notice that the master page contains a *ContentPlaceHolder* control (lines 17–18 of Fig. 21.51). This control serves as a placeholder for content that will be defined by a content page. You will see how to define content to replace the Content-PlaceHolder shortly.

At this point, you can edit the master page in **Design** mode (Fig. 21.52) as if it were an ASPX file. Notice that the ContentPlaceHolder control appears as a large rectangle with a gray bar indicating the control's type and ID. Using the **Properties** window, change the ID of this control to bodyContent.

To create a header in the master page that will appear at the top of each content page, we insert a table into the master page. Place the cursor to the left of the ContentPlace-Holder and select **Layout > Insert Table**. In the **Insert Table** dialog, click the **Template** radio button, then select **Header** from the drop-down list of available table templates. Click **OK** to create a table that fills the page and contains two rows. Drag and drop the Content-PlaceHolder into the bottom table cell. Change the valign property of this cell to top, so the ContentPlaceHolder vertically aligns with the top of the cell. Next, set the Height of the top table cell to 130. Add to this cell an Image control named headerImage with its ImageUrl property set to the bug2bug.png file in the project's Images folder. Figure 21.53 shows the markup and **Design** view of the completed master page. As you will see in *Step*

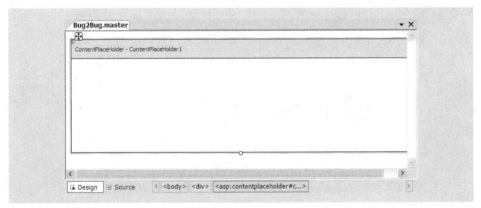

Fig. 21.52 | Master page in **Design** mode.

```
1    <%-- Fig. 21.53: Bug2bug.master --%>
2    <%-- Master page that defines common features of all pages in the --%>
3    <%-- secure book database application. --%>
```

Fig. 21.53 | Bug2Bug.master page that defines a logo image header for all pages in the secure book database application. (Part 1 of 2.)

```
4   <%@ Master Language="VB" %>
5
6   <!DOCTYPE html PUBLIC "-//W3C//DTD XHTML 1.0 Transitional//EN"
7       "http://www.w3.org/TR/xhtml1/DTD/xhtml1-transitional.dtd">
8
9   <html xmlns="http://www.w3.org/1999/xhtml" >
10  <head runat="server">
11      <title>Bug2Bug</title>
12  </head>
13  <body>
14      <form id="form1" runat="server">
15      <div>
16          <table border="0" cellpadding="0" cellspacing="0"
17              style="width: 100%; height: 100%">
18              <tr>
19                  <td height="130" style="width: 887px">
20                      <asp:Image ID="headerImage" runat="server"
21                          ImageUrl="~/Images/bug2bug.png" />
22                  </td>
23              </tr>
24              <tr>
25                  <td style="width: 887px" valign="top">
26                      <asp:contentplaceholder id="bodyContent" runat="server">
27                      </asp:contentplaceholder>
28                  </td>
29              </tr>
30          </table>
31           
32      </div>
33      </form>
34  </body>
35  </html>
```

Fig. 21.53 | Bug2Bug.master page that defines a logo image header for all pages in the secure book database application. (Part 2 of 2.)

6, a content page based on this master page displays the logo image defined here, as well as the content designed for that specific page (in place of the ContentPlaceHolder).

Step 6: Creating a Content Page

We now create a content page based on Bug2Bug.master. We begin by building Create-NewUser.aspx. To create this file, right click the master page in the **Solution Explorer** and select **Add Content Page**. This action causes a Default.aspx file, configured to use the master page, to be added to the project. Rename this file CreateNewUser.aspx, then open it in **Source** mode (Fig. 21.54). Note that this file contains a Page directive with a Language property, a MasterPageFile property and a Title property. The Page directive indicates the *MasterPageFile* that is used as a starting point for this new page's design. In this case, the MasterPageFile property is set to "~/Bug2Bug.master" to indicate that the current file is based on the master page we just created. The *Title* property specifies the title that will be displayed in the web browser's title bar when the content page is loaded. This value, which we set to Create a New User, replaces the value (i.e., Bug2Bug) set in the title element of the master page.

Fig. 21.54 | Content page CreateNewUser.aspx in **Source** mode.

Because CreateNewUser.aspx's Page directive specifies Bug2Bug.master as the page's MasterPageFile, the content page implicitly contains the contents of the master page, such as the DOCTYPE, html and body elements. The content page file does not duplicate the XHTML elements found in the master page. Instead, the content page contains a *Content* control (lines 3–5 in Fig. 21.54), in which we'll place page-specific content that will replace the master page's ContentPlaceHolder when the content page is requested. The ContentPlaceHolderID property of the Content control identifies the ContentPlace-Holder in the master page that the control should replace—in this case, bodyContent.

The relationship between a content page and its master page is more evident in **Design** mode (Fig. 21.55). The gray shaded region contains the contents of the master page Bug2Bug.master as they will appear in CreateNewUser.aspx when rendered in a web browser. The only editable part of this page is the Content control, which appears in place of the master page's ContentPlaceHolder.

Step 7: Adding a CreateUserWizard Control to a Content Page

Recall from Section 21.6.1 that CreateNewUser.aspx is the page in our website that allows first-time visitors to create user accounts. To provide this functionality, we use a *CreateUserWizard* control. Place the cursor inside the Content control in **Design** mode and double click CreateUserWizard in the **Login** section of the **Toolbox** to add it to the

Fig. 21.55 | Content page CreateNewUser.aspx in **Design** mode.

page at the current cursor position. You can also drag-and-drop the control onto the page. To change the CreateUserWizard's appearance, open the **CreateUserWizard Tasks** smart tag menu, and click **Auto Format**. Select the **Professional** color scheme.

As discussed previously, a CreateUserWizard provides a registration form that site visitors can use to create a user account. ASP.NET creates a SQL Server database (named ASPNETDB.MDF and located in the App_Data folder) to store the user names, passwords and other account information of the application's users. ASP.NET also enforces a default set of requirements for filling out the form. Each field on the form is required, the password must contain at least seven characters (including at least one nonalphanumeric character) and the two passwords entered must match. The form also asks for a security question and answer that can be used to identify a user in case the user needs to reset or recover the account's password.

After the user fills in the form's fields and clicks the **Create User** button to submit the account information, ASP.NET verifies that all the form's requirements were fulfilled and attempts to create the user account. If an error occurs (e.g., the user name already exists), the CreateUserWizard displays a message below the form. If the account is created successfully, the form is replaced by a confirmation message and a button that allows the user to continue. You can view this confirmation message in **Design** mode by selecting **Complete** from the **Step** drop-down list in the **CreateUserWizard Tasks** smart tag menu.

When a user account is created, ASP.NET automatically logs the user into the site (we say more about the login process shortly). At this point, the user is authenticated and allowed to access the Secure folder. After we create Books.aspx later in this section, we set the CreateUserWizard's ContinueDestinationPageUrl property to ~/Secure/Books.aspx to indicate that the user should be redirected to Books.aspx after clicking the **Continue** button on the confirmation page.

Figure 21.56 presents the completed CreateNewUser.aspx file (reformatted for readability). Inside the Content control, the CreateUserWizard control is defined by the markup in lines 7–36. The start tag (lines 7–10) contains several properties that specify formatting styles for the control, as well as the `ContinueDestinationPageUrl` property, which you will set later in the chapter. Lines 11–16 specify the wizard's two steps—`CreateUserWizardStep` and `CompleteWizardStep`—in a `WizardSteps` element. `Create-UserWizardStep` and `CompleteWizardStep` are classes that encapsulate the details of creating a user and issuing a confirmation message. Finally, lines 17–35 contain elements that define additional styles used to format specific parts of the control.

The sample outputs in Fig. 21.56(a) and Fig. 21.56(b) demonstrate successfully creating a user account with `CreateNewUser.aspx`. We use the password pa$$word for testing purposes. This password satisfies the minimum length and special character requirement imposed by ASP.NET, but in a real application, you should use a password that is more difficult for someone to guess. Figure 21.56(c) illustrates the error message that appears when you attempt to create a second user account with the same user name—ASP.NET requires that each user name be unique.

```
1   <%-- Fig. 21.56: CreateNewUser.aspx --%>
2   <%-- Content page using a CreateUserWizard control to register users. --%>
3   <%@ Page Language="VB" MasterPageFile="~/Bug2Bug.master"
4      Title="Create a New User" %>
5   <asp:Content ID="Content1" ContentPlaceHolderID="bodyContent"
6      Runat="Server">
7      <asp:CreateUserWizard ID="CreateUserWizard1" runat="server"
8         BackColor="#F7F6F3" BorderColor="#E6E2D8" BorderStyle="Solid"
9         BorderWidth="1px" Font-Names="Verdana" Font-Size="0.8em"
10        ContinueDestinationPageUrl="~/Secure/Books.aspx">
11        <WizardSteps>
12           <asp:CreateUserWizardStep runat="server">
13           </asp:CreateUserWizardStep>
14           <asp:CompleteWizardStep runat="server">
15           </asp:CompleteWizardStep>
16        </WizardSteps>
17        <SideBarStyle BackColor="#5D7B9D" BorderWidth="0px"
18           Font-Size="0.9em" VerticalAlign="Top" />
19        <TitleTextStyle BackColor="#5D7B9D" Font-Bold="True"
20           ForeColor="White" />
21        <SideBarButtonStyle BorderWidth="0px" Font-Names="Verdana"
22           ForeColor="White" />
23        <NavigationButtonStyle BackColor="#FFFBFF" BorderColor="#CCCCCC"
24           BorderStyle="Solid" BorderWidth="1px" Font-Names="Verdana"
25           ForeColor="#284775" />
26        <HeaderStyle BackColor="#5D7B9D" BorderStyle="Solid"
27           Font-Bold="True" Font-Size="0.9em"
28           ForeColor="White" HorizontalAlign="Center" />
29        <CreateUserButtonStyle BackColor="#FFFBFF" BorderColor="#CCCCCC"
30           BorderStyle="Solid" BorderWidth="1px" Font-Names="Verdana"
31           ForeColor="#284775" />
32        <ContinueButtonStyle BackColor="#FFFBFF" BorderColor="#CCCCCC"
33           BorderStyle="Solid" BorderWidth="1px" Font-Names="Verdana"
34           ForeColor="#284775" />
```

Fig. 21.56 | `CreateNewUser.aspx` content page that provides a user registration form. (Part 1 of 2.)

```
35              <StepStyle BorderWidth="0px" />
36          </asp:CreateUserWizard>
37      </asp:Content>
```

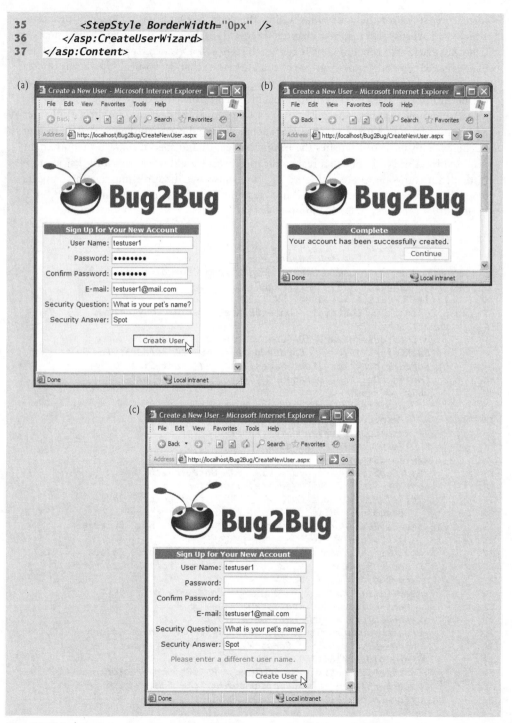

Fig. 21.56 | `CreateNewUser.aspx` content page that provides a user registration form. (Part 2 of 2.)

Step 8: Creating a Login Page

Recall from Section 21.6.1 that Login.aspx is the page in our website that allows returning visitors to log into their user accounts. To create this functionality, add another content page named Login.aspx and set its title to Login. In **Design** mode, drag a *Login* control (located in the **Login** section of the **Toolbox**) to the page's Content control. Open the **Auto Format** dialog from the **Login Tasks** smart tag menu and set the control's color scheme to **Professional**.

Next, configure the Login control to display a link to the page for creating new users. Set the Login control's CreateUserUrl property to CreateNewUser.aspx by clicking the ellipsis button to the property's right in the **Properties** window and selecting the Create-NewUser.aspx file in the dialog. Then set the CreateUserText property to Click here to create a new user. These property values cause a link to appear in the Login control.

Finally, change the value of the Login control's DisplayRememberMe property to False. By default, the control displays a checkbox and the text Remember me next time. This can be used to allow a user to remain authenticated beyond a single browser session on the user's current computer. However, we want to require that users log in each time they visit the site, so we disable this option.

The Login control encapsulates the details of logging a user into a web application (i.e., authenticating a user). When a user enters a user name and password, then clicks the **Log In** button, ASP.NET determines whether the items provided match those of an account in the membership database (i.e., ASPNETDB.MDF created by ASP.NET). If they match, the user is authenticated (i.e., the user's identity is confirmed), and the browser is redirected to the page specified by the Login control's DestinationPageUrl property. We set this property to the Books.aspx page after creating it in the next section. If the user's identity cannot be confirmed (i.e., the user is not authenticated), the Login control displays an error message (see Fig. 21.57), and the user can attempt to log in again.

```
1   <%-- Fig. 21.57: Login.aspx --%>
2   <%-- Content page using a Login control that authenticates users. --%>
3   <%@ Page Language="VB" MasterPageFile="~/Bug2Bug.master" Title="Login" %>
4   <asp:Content ID="Content1" ContentPlaceHolderID="bodyContent"
5      Runat="Server">
6      <asp:Login ID="Login1" runat="server" BackColor="#F7F6F3"
7         BorderColor="#E6E2D8" BorderPadding="4" BorderStyle="Solid"
8         BorderWidth="1px" CreateUserText="Click here to create a new user"
9         CreateUserUrl="~/CreateNewUser.aspx" DisplayRememberMe="False"
10        Font-Names="Verdana" Font-Size="0.8em" ForeColor="#333333"
11        DestinationPageUrl="~/Secure/Books.aspx">
12        <TitleTextStyle BackColor="#5D7B9D" Font-Bold="True"
13           Font-Size="0.9em" ForeColor="White" />
14        <InstructionTextStyle Font-Italic="True" ForeColor="Black" />
15        <TextBoxStyle Font-Size="0.8em" />
16        <LoginButtonStyle BackColor="#FFFBFF" BorderColor="#CCCCCC"
17           BorderStyle="Solid" BorderWidth="1px" Font-Names="Verdana"
18           Font-Size="0.8em" ForeColor="#284775" />
19     </asp:Login>
20  </asp:Content>
```

Fig. 21.57 | Login.aspx content page using a Login control. (Part 1 of 2.)

Fig. 21.57 | `Login.aspx` content page using a `Login` control. (Part 2 of 2.)

Figure 21.57 presents the completed `Login.aspx` file. Note that, as in `CreateNew-User.aspx`, the `Page` directive indicates that this content page inherits content from `Bug2Bug.master`. In the `Content` control that replaces the master page's `ContentPlace-Holder` with ID `bodyContent`, lines 6–19 create a `Login` control. Note the `CreateUser-Text` and `CreateUserUrl` properties (lines 8–9) that we set using the **Properties** window. Line 11 in the start tag for the `Login` control contains the `DestinationPageUrl` (you will set this property in the next step). The elements in lines 12–18 define various formatting styles applied to parts of the control. Note that all of the functionality related to actually logging the user in or displaying error messages is completely hidden from you.

When a user enters the user name and password of an existing user account, ASP.NET authenticates the user and writes to the client an *encrypted* cookie containing information about the authenticated user. Encrypted data is data translated into a code that only the sender and receiver can understand—thereby keeping it private. The encrypted cookie contains a `String` user name and a `Boolean` value that specifies whether this cookie should persist (i.e., remain on the client's computer) beyond the current session. Our application authenticates the user only for the current session.

Step 9: Creating a Content Page That Only Authenticated Users Can Access
A user who has been authenticated will be redirected to `Books.aspx`. We now create the `Books.aspx` file in the `Secure` folder—the folder for which we set an access rule denying access to anonymous users. If an unauthenticated user requests this file, the user will be redirected to `Login.aspx`. From there, the user can either log in or a create a new account, both of which will authenticate the user, thus allowing the user to return to `Books.aspx`.

To create `Books.aspx`, right click the `Secure` folder in the **Solution Explorer** and select **Add New Item...**. In the resulting dialog, select **Web Form** and specify the filename `Books.aspx`. Check the box **Select Master Page** to indicate that this Web Form should be created as a content page that references a master page, then click **Add**. In the **Select a Master Page** dialog, select `Bug2Bug.master` and click **OK**. The IDE creates the file and opens it in **Source** mode. Change the `Title` property of the `Page` directive to Book Information.

Step 10: Customizing the Secure Page

To customize the `Books.aspx` page for a particular user, we add a welcome message containing a *LoginName* control, which displays the current authenticated user name. Open `Books.aspx` in **Design** mode. In the `Content` control, type `Welcome` followed by a comma and a space. Then drag a `LoginName` control from the **Toolbox** onto the page. When this page executes on the server, the text `[UserName]` that appears in this control in **Design** mode will be replaced by the current user name. In **Source** mode, type an exclamation point (!) directly after the `LoginName` control (with no spaces in between). [*Note:* If you add the exclamation point in **Design** mode, the IDE may insert extra spaces or a line break between this character and the preceding control. Entering the ! in **Source** mode ensures that it appears adjacent to the user's name.]

Next, add a `LoginStatus` control, which will allow the user to log out of the website when finished viewing the listing of books in the database. A *LoginStatus* control renders on a web page in one of two ways—by default, if the user is not authenticated, the control displays a hyperlink with the text `Login`; if the user is authenticated, the control displays a hyperlink with the text `Logout`. Each link performs the stated action. Add a `LoginStatus` control to the page by dragging it from the **Toolbox** onto the page. In this example, any user who reaches this page must already be authenticated, so the control will always render as a `Logout` link. The **LoginStatus Tasks** smart tag menu allows you switch between the control's **Views**. Select the **Logged In** view to see the `Logout` link. To change the actual text of this link, modify the control's `LogoutText` property to `Click here to log out`. Next, set the `LogoutAction` property to `RedirectToLoginPage`.

Step 11: Connecting the CreateUserWizard and Login Controls to the Secure Page

Now that we have created `Books.aspx`, we can specify that this is the page to which the `CreateUserWizard` and `Login` controls redirect users after they are authenticated. Open `CreateNewUser.aspx` in **Design** mode and set the `CreateUserWizard` control's `ContinueDestinationPageUrl` property to `Books.aspx`. Next, open `Login.aspx` and select `Books.aspx` as the `DestinationPageUrl` of the `Login` control.

At this point, you can run the web application by selecting **Debug > Start Without Debugging**. First, create a user account on `CreateNewUser.aspx`, then notice how the `LoginName` and `LoginStatus` controls appear on `Books.aspx`. Next, log out of the site and log back in using `Login.aspx`.

Step 12: Generating a DataSet Based on the Books.mdf Database

Now, let's add the content (i.e., book information) to the secure page `Books.aspx`. This page will provide a `DropDownList` containing authors' names and a `GridView` displaying information about books written by the author selected in the `DropDownList`. A user will select an author from the `DropDownList` to cause the `GridView` to display information about only the books written by the selected author. As you will see, we create this functionality entirely in **Design** mode without writing any code.

To work with the `Books` database, we use an approach slightly different than in the preceding case study, in which we accessed the `Guestbook` database using a `SqlDataSource` control. Here we use an *ObjectDataSource* control, which encapsulates an object that provides access to a data source. An `ObjectDataSource` can encapsulate a `TableAdapter` and use its methods to access the data in the database. This helps separate the data-access logic from the presentation logic. As you will see shortly, the SQL statements used to retrieve data do not appear in the ASPX page when using an `ObjectDataSource`.

The first step in accessing data using an `ObjectDataSource` is to create a `DataSet` that contains the data from the `Books` database required by the application. In Visual Basic 2005 Express, this occurs automatically when you add a data source to a project. In Visual Web Developer, however, you must explicitly generate the `DataSet`. Right click the project's location in the **Solution Explorer** and select **Add New Item...**. In the resulting dialog, select **DataSet** and specify `BooksDataSet.xsd` as the filename, then click **Add**. A dialog will appear that asks you whether the `DataSet` should be placed in an **App_Code** folder—a folder whose contents are compiled and made available to all parts of the project. Click **Yes** for the IDE to create this folder to store `BooksDataSet.xsd`.

Step 13: Creating and Configuring an AuthorsTableAdapter

Once the `DataSet` is added, the **Dataset Designer** will appear, and the **TableAdapter Configuration Wizard** will open. This wizard allows you to configure a `TableAdapter` for filling a `DataTable` in a `DataSet` with data from a database. The `Books.aspx` page requires two sets of data—a list of authors that will be displayed in the page's `DropDownList` (created shortly) and a list of books written by a specific author. We focus on the first set of data here—the authors. Thus, we use the **TableAdapter Configuration Wizard** first to configure an `AuthorsTableAdapter`. In the next step, we'll configure a `TitlesTableAdapter`.

In the **TableAdapter Configuration Wizard**, select `Books.mdf` from the drop-down list. Then click **Next >** twice to save the connection string in the application's `Web.config` file and move to the **Choose a Command Type** screen.

In the wizard's **Choose a Command Type** screen, select **Use SQL statements** and click **Next >**. The next screen allows you to enter a `SELECT` statement for retrieving data from the database, which will then be placed in an `Authors` `DataTable` within the `BooksDataSet`. Enter the SQL statement

      SELECT AuthorID, FirstName + ' ' + LastName *AS* Name *FROM* Authors

in the text box on the **Enter a SQL Statement** screen. This query selects the `AuthorID` of each row. This query's result will also contain the column `Name` that is created by concatenating each row's `FirstName` and `LastName`, separated by a space. The *AS* SQL keyword allows you to generate a column in a query result—called an *alias*—that contains a SQL expression's result (e.g., `FirstName + ' ' + LastName`). You'll soon see how we use this query's result to populate the `DropDownList` with items containing the authors' full names.

After entering the SQL statement, click the **Advanced Options...** button and uncheck **Generate Insert, Update and Delete statements**, since this application does not need to modify the database's contents. Click **OK** to close the **Advanced Options** dialog. Click **Next >** to advance to the **Choose Methods to Generate** screen. Leave the default names and click **Finish**. Notice that the **DataSet Designer** (Fig. 21.58) now displays a `DataTable` named `Authors` with `AuthorID` and `Name` members, and `Fill` and `GetData` methods.

Step 14: Creating and Configuring a TitlesTableAdapter

`Books.aspx` needs to access a list of books by a specific author and a list of authors. Thus we must create a `TitlesTableAdapter` that will retrieve the desired information from the

Fig. 21.58 | Authors DataTable in the **Dataset Designer**.

database's Titles table. Right click the **Dataset Designer** and from the menu that appears, select **Add > TableAdapter...** to launch the **TableAdapter Configuration Wizard**. Make sure the BooksConnectionString is selected as the connection in the wizard's first screen, then click **Next >**. Choose **Use SQL statements** and click **Next >**.

In the **Enter a SQL Statement** screen, open the **Advanced Options** dialog and uncheck **Generate Insert, Update and Delete statements**, then click **OK**. Our application allows users to filter the books displayed by the author's name, so we need to build a query that takes an AuthorID as a parameter and returns the rows in the Titles table for books written by that author. To build this complex query, click the **Query Builder...** button.

In the **Add Table** dialog that appears, select **AuthorISBN** and click **Add**. Then **Add** the **Titles** table, too. Our query requires access to data in both of these tables. Click **Close** to exit the **Add Table** dialog. In the **Query Builder** window's top pane (Fig. 21.59), check the box marked *** (All Columns)** in the **Titles** table. Next, in the middle pane, add a row with **Column** set to AuthorISBN.AuthorID. Uncheck the **Output** box, because we do not want

Fig. 21.59 | **Query Builder** for designing a query that selects books written by a particular author.

the **AuthorID** to appear in our query result. Add an `@authorID` parameter in this row's **Filter** column. The SQL statement generated by these actions retrieves information about all books written by the author specified by parameter `@authorID`. The statement first merges the data from the `AuthorISBN` and `Titles` tables. The `INNER JOIN` clause specifies that the `ISBN` columns of each table are compared to determine which rows are merged. The `INNER JOIN` results in a temporary table containing the columns of both tables. The `WHERE` clause of the SQL statement restricts the book information from this temporary table to a specific author (i.e., all rows in which the `AuthorID` column is equal to `@authorID`).

Click **OK** to exit the **Query Builder**, then in the **TableAdapter Configuration Wizard**, click **Next >**. On the **Choose Methods to Generate** screen, enter `FillByAuthorID` and `GetDataByAuthorID` as the names of the two methods to be generated for the `TitlesTableAdapter`. Click **Finish** to exit the wizard. You should now see a `Titles DataTable` in the **Dataset Designer** (Fig. 21.60).

Fig. 21.60 | **Dataset Designer** after adding the `TitlesTableAdapter`.

Step 15: Adding a DropDownList Containing Authors' First and Last Names

Now that we have created a `BooksDataSet` and configured the necessary `TableAdapters`, we add controls to `Books.aspx` that will display the data on the web page. We first add the `DropDownList` from which users can select an author. Open `Books.aspx` in **Design** mode, then add the text `Author:` and a `DropDownList` control named `authorsDropDownList` in the page's `Content` control, below the existing content. The `DropDownList` initially displays the text `[Unbound]`. We now bind the list to a data source, so the list displays the author information placed in the `BooksDataSet` by the `AuthorsTableAdapter`. In the **DropDownList Tasks** smart tag menu, click **Choose Data Source...** to start the **Data Source Configuration Wizard**. Select **<New data source...>** from the **Select a data source** dropdown list in the first screen of the wizard. Doing so opens the **Choose a Data Source Type** screen. Select **Object** and set the ID to `authorsObjectDataSource`, then click **OK**.

An `ObjectDataSource` accesses data through another object, often called a *business object*. Recall that the middle tier of a three-tier application contains business logic that controls the way an application's top-tier user interface (in this case, `Books.aspx`) accesses the bottom tier's data (in this case, the `Books.mdf` database file). Thus, a business object represents the middle tier of an application and mediates interactions between the other two tiers. In an ASP.NET web application, a `TableAdapter` typically serves as the business object that retrieves the data from the bottom-tier database and makes it available to the top-tier user interface through a `DataSet`. In the **Choose a Business Object** screen of the **Configure Data Source** wizard (Fig. 21.61), select `BooksDataSetTableAdapters.AuthorsTableAdapter`. [*Note:* You may need to save the project to see the `AuthorsTableAdapter`.]

BooksDataSetTableAdapters is a namespace declared by the IDE when you create Books-DataSet. Click **Next >** to continue.

The **Define Data Methods** screen (Fig. 21.62) allows you to specify which of the business object's methods (in this case, AuthorsTableAdapter) should be used to obtain the data accessed through the ObjectDataSource. You can choose only methods that return data, so the only choice is method GetData, which returns an AuthorsDataTable. Click **Finish** to close the **Configure Data Source** wizard and return to the **Data Source Configuration Wizard** for the DropDownList (Fig. 21.63). The new data source (i.e., authorsObject-

Fig. 21.61 | Choosing a business object for an ObjectDataSource.

Fig. 21.62 | Choosing a data method of a business object for use with an ObjectDataSource.

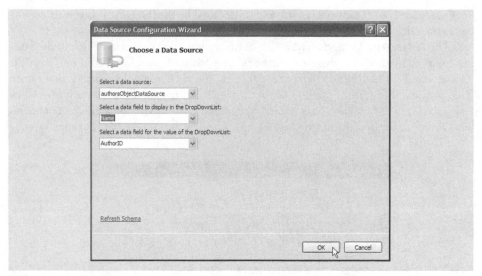

Fig. 21.63 | Choosing a data source for a `DropDownList`.

`DataSource`) should be selected in the top drop-down list. The other two drop-down lists on this screen allow you to configure how the `DropDownList` control uses the data from the data source. Set `Name` as the data field to display and `AuthorID` as the data field to use as the value. Thus, when `authorsDropDownList` is rendered in a web browser, the list items display the author names, but the underlying values associated with each item are the author `AuthorID`s. Finally, click **OK** to bind the `DropDownList` to the specified data.

The last step in configuring the `DropDownList` on `Books.aspx` is to set the control's **_AutoPostBack_** property to `True`. This property indicates that a postback occurs each time the user selects an item in the `DropDownList`. As you will see shortly, this causes the page's `GridView` (created in the next step) to display new data.

Step 16: Creating a GridView to Display the Selected Author's Books

We now add a `GridView` to `Books.aspx` for displaying the book information by the author selected in the `authorsDropDownList`. Add a `GridView` named `titlesGridView` below the other controls in the page's `Content` control.

To bind the `GridView` to data from the `Books` database, select **<New data source...>** from the **Choose Data Source** drop-down list in the **GridView Tasks** smart tag menu. When the **Data Source Configuration Wizard** opens, select **Object** and set the `ID` of the data source to `titlesObjectDataSource`, then click **OK**. In the **Choose a Business Object** screen, select the `BooksDataSetTableAdapters.TitlesTableAdapter` from the drop-down list to indicate the object that will be used to access the data. Click **Next >**. In the **Define Data Methods** screen, leave the default selection of `GetDataByAuthorID` as the method that will be invoked to obtain the data for display in the `GridView`. Click **Next >**.

Recall that `TitlesTableAdapter` method `GetDataByAuthorID` requires a parameter to indicate the `AuthorID` for which data should be retrieved. The **Define Parameters** screen (Fig. 21.64) allows you to specify where to obtain the value of the `@authorID` parameter in the SQL statement executed by `GetDataByAuthorID`. Select **Control** from the **Parameter source** drop-down list. Select `authorsDropDownList` as the **ControlID** (i.e., the ID of the

Fig. 21.64 | Choosing the data source for a parameter in a business object's data method.

parameter source control). Next, enter 1 as the **DefaultValue**, so books by Harvey Deitel (who has AuthorID 1 in the database) display when the page first loads (i.e., before the user has made any selections using the authorsDropDownList). Finally, click **Finish** to exit the wizard. The GridView is now configured to display the data retrieved by TitlesTableAdapter.GetDataByAuthorID, using the value of the current selection in authorsDropDownList as the parameter. Thus, when the user selects a new author and a postback occurs, the GridView displays a new set of data.

Now that the GridView is tied to a data source, we modify several of the control's properties to adjust its appearance and behavior. Set the GridView's CellPadding property to 5, set the BackColor of the AlternatingRowStyle to LightYellow, and set the BackColor of the HeaderStyle to LightGreen. Change the Width of the control to 600px to accommodate long data values.

Next, in the **GridView Tasks** smart tag menu, check **Enable Sorting**. This causes the column headings in the GridView to turn into hyperlinks that allow users to sort the data in the GridView. For example, clicking the Titles heading in the web browser will cause the displayed data to appear sorted in alphabetical order. Clicking this heading a second time will cause the data to be sorted in reverse alphabetical order. ASP.NET hides the details required to achieve this functionality.

Finally, in the **GridView Tasks** smart tag menu, check **Enable Paging**. This causes the GridView to split across multiple pages. The user can click the numbered links at the bottom of the GridView control to display a different page of data. GridView's **PageSize** property determines the number of entries per page. Set the PageSize property to 4 using the **Properties** window so that the GridView displays only four books per page. This technique for displaying data makes the site more readable and enables pages to load more quickly (because less data is displayed at one time). Note that, as with sorting data in a GridView, you do not need to add any code to achieve paging functionality. Figure 21.65 displays the completed Books.aspx file in **Design** mode.

Fig. 21.65 | Completed Books.aspx in **Design** mode.

Step 17: Examining the Markup in Books.aspx

Figure 21.66 presents the markup in Books.aspx (reformatted for readability). Aside from the exclamation point in line 8, which we added manually in **Source** mode, all the remaining markup was generated by the IDE in response to the actions we performed in **Design** mode. The Content control (lines 5–53) defines page-specific content that will replace the ContentPlaceHolder named bodyContent. Recall that this control is located in the master page specified in line 3. Line 8 creates the LoginName control, which displays the authenticated user's name when the page is requested and viewed in a browser. Lines 9–11 create the LoginStatus control. Recall that this control is configured to redirect the user to the login page after logging out (i.e., clicking the hyperlink with the LogoutText).

Lines 15–18 define the DropDownList that displays the names of the authors in the Books database. Line 16 contains the control's AutoPostBack property, which indicates that changing the selected item in the list causes a postback to occur. The DataSourceID property in line 16 specifies that the DropDownList's items are created based on the data obtained through the authorsObjectDataSource (defined in lines 19–23). Line 21 specifies that this ObjectDataSource accesses the Books database by calling method GetData of the BooksDataSet's AuthorsTableAdapter (line 22).

Lines 26–42 create the GridView that displays information about the books written by the selected author. The start tag (lines 26–29) indicates that paging (with a page size of 4) and sorting are enabled in the GridView. The AutoGenerateColumns property indicates whether the columns in the GridView are generated at runtime based on the fields in the data source. This property is set to False, because the IDE-generated Columns element

```
 I   <%-- Fig. 21.66: Books.aspx --%>
 2   <%-- Displays information from the Books database. --%>
 3   <%@ Page Language="VB" MasterPageFile="~/Bug2Bug.master"
 4      Title="Book Information" %>
 5   <asp:Content ID="Content1" ContentPlaceHolderID="bodyContent"
 6      Runat="Server">
 7      Welcome,
 8      <asp:LoginName ID="LoginName1" runat="server" />!
 9      <asp:LoginStatus ID="LoginStatus1" runat="server"
10         LogoutAction="RedirectToLoginPage"
11         LogoutText="Click here to log out" />
12      <br />
13      <br />
14      Author:
15      <asp:DropDownList ID="authorsDropDownList" runat="server"
16         AutoPostBack="True" DataSourceID="authorsObjectDataSource"
17         DataTextField="Name" DataValueField="AuthorID">
18      </asp:DropDownList>
19      <asp:ObjectDataSource ID="authorsObjectDataSource"
20         runat="server" OldValuesParameterFormatString="original_{0}"
21         SelectMethod="GetData"
22         TypeName="BooksDataSetTableAdapters.AuthorsTableAdapter">
23      </asp:ObjectDataSource>
24      <br />
25      <br />
26      <asp:GridView ID="titlesGridView" runat="server" AllowPaging="True"
27         AllowSorting="True" AutoGenerateColumns="False" CellPadding="5"
28         DataKeyNames="ISBN" DataSourceID="titlesObjectDataSource"
29         PageSize="4" Width="600px">
30         <Columns>
31            <asp:BoundField DataField="ISBN" HeaderText="ISBN"
32               ReadOnly="True" SortExpression="ISBN" />
33            <asp:BoundField DataField="Title" HeaderText="Title"
34               SortExpression="Title" />
35            <asp:BoundField DataField="EditionNumber"
36               HeaderText="EditionNumber" SortExpression="EditionNumber" />
37            <asp:BoundField DataField="Copyright" HeaderText="Copyright"
38               SortExpression="Copyright" />
39         </Columns>
40         <HeaderStyle BackColor="LightGreen" />
41         <AlternatingRowStyle BackColor="LightYellow" />
42      </asp:GridView>
43      <asp:ObjectDataSource ID="titlesObjectDataSource" runat="server"
44         OldValuesParameterFormatString="original_{0}"
45         SelectMethod="GetDataByAuthorID"
46         TypeName="BooksDataSetTableAdapters.TitlesTableAdapter">
47         <SelectParameters>
48            <asp:ControlParameter ControlID="authorsDropDownList"
49               DefaultValue="1" Name="authorID"
50               PropertyName="SelectedValue" Type="Int32" />
51         </SelectParameters>
52      </asp:ObjectDataSource>
53   </asp:Content>
```

Fig. 21.66 | Markup for the completed Books.aspx file. (Part 1 of 2.)

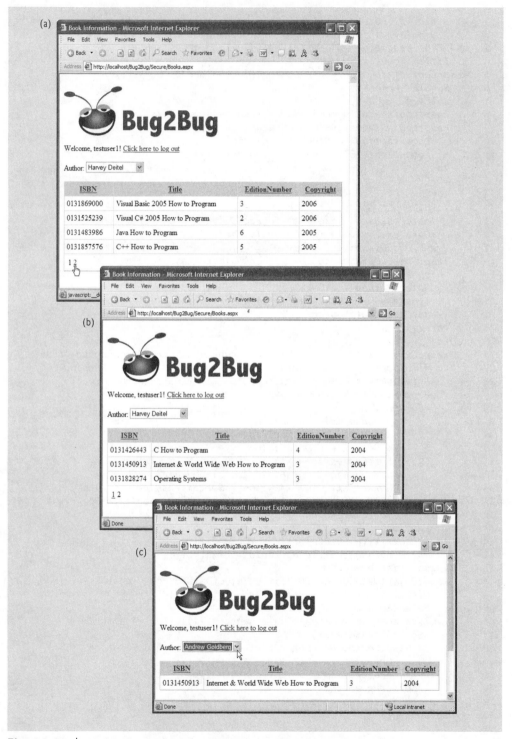

Fig. 21.66 | Markup for the completed Books.aspx file. (Part 2 of 2.)

(lines 30–39) already specifies the columns for the GridView using BoundFields. Lines 43–52 define the ObjectDataSource used to fill the GridView with data. Recall that we configured titlesObjectDataSource to use method GetDataByAuthorID of the Books-DataSet's TitlesTableAdapter for this purpose. The ControlParameter in lines 48–50 specifies that the value of method GetDataByAuthorID's parameter comes from the SelectedValue property of the authorsDropDownList.

Figure 21.66(a) depicts the default appearance of Books.aspx in a web browser. Because the DefaultValue property (line 49) of the ControlParameter for the titles-ObjectDataSource is set to 1, books by the author with AuthorID 1 (i.e., Harvey Deitel) are displayed when the page first loads. Note that the GridView displays paging links below the data, because the number of rows of data returned by GetDataByAuthorID is greater than the page size. Figure 21.66(b) shows the GridView after clicking the 2 link to view the second page of data. Figure 21.66(c) presents Books.aspx after the user selects a different author from the authorsDropDownList. The data fits on one page, so the GridView does not display paging links.

21.7 ASP.NET Ajax

In this section, we introduce how you can use *ASP.NET Ajax* to quickly and easily add Ajax functionality to existing ASP.NET web applications. You can download the latest version of ASP.NET Ajax from www.asp.net/ajax/downloads. Run the .msi installer you downloaded and follow the on-screen instructions to install the *Ajax Extensions package*.

The Ajax Extensions package implements basic Ajax functionality. Microsoft also provides the *ASP.NET Ajax Control Toolkit*, which contains rich, Ajax-enabled GUI controls. There is also a link to the download the latest version of the Ajax Control Toolkit from the ASP.NET Ajax download page listed above. The toolkit does not come with an installer, so you must extract the contents of the toolkit's ZIP file to your hard drive.

To make using the ASP.NET Ajax Control Toolkit more convenient, you'll want to add its controls to the **Toolbox** in Visual Web Developer (or in Visual Studio) so you can drag and drop controls onto your Web Forms. To do so, right click the **Toolbox** and choose **Add Tab.** Type Ajax Toolkit in the new tab. Then right click the tab and select **Choose Items.** Navigate to the folder in which you extracted the Ajax Control Toolkit and select AjaxControlToolkit.dll from the SampleWebSite\Bin folder. A list of available Ajax controls will appear under the **Ajax Toolkit** tab when you are in **Design** mode.

To demonstrate ASP.NET Ajax capabilities we'll enhance the Validation application from Fig. 21.17. The only modifications to this application will appear in its .aspx file. This application was not initially set up to support Ajax functionality, so we must first modify the web.config file. First, in Visual Web Developer select **File > New Website...** to display the **New Website** dialog. Then, create an empty **ASP.NET Ajax-Enabled Website.** Open the web.config file in this new application and copy its contents. Next, open the Validation application and replace the contents of its web.config file with the contents of the web.config file you just copied. The new web.config file adds the system.web.extensions, httpHandlers and httpModules sections, which specify the settings for running scripts that enable Ajax functionality. If you'd like to learn more about the details of these web.config modifications, please visit the site www.asp.net/ajax/documentation/live/configuringASPNETAJAX.aspx.

We'll now use Ajax-enabled controls to add Ajax features to this application. Figure 21.67 is a modified validation.aspx file that enhances the application by using the ToolkitScriptManager, UpdatePanel and ValidatorCalloutExtender controls.

```
 1   <%-- Fig. 21.67: Validation.aspx --%>
 2   <%-- Validation application enhanced by ASP.NET Ajax. --%>
 3   <%@ Page Language="VB" AutoEventWireup="false"
 4      CodeFile="Validation.aspx.vb" Inherits="Validation" %>
 5   <%@ Register Assembly="AjaxControlToolkit" Namespace="AjaxControlToolkit"
 6      TagPrefix="ajax" %>
 7
 8   <!DOCTYPE html PUBLIC "-//W3C//DTD XHTML 1.0 Transitional//EN"
 9      "http://www.w3.org/TR/xhtml1/DTD/xhtml1-transitional.dtd">
10
11   <html xmlns="http://www.w3.org/1999/xhtml" >
12   <head runat="server">
13      <title>Demonstrating Validation Controls</title>
14   </head>
15   <body>
16      <form id="form1" runat="server">
17      <div>
18         <ajax:ToolkitScriptManager ID="ToolkitScriptManager1"
19            runat="server">
20         </ajax:ToolkitScriptManager>
21          Please fill out the following form. <br /><em>All fields are
22         required and must contain valid information.</em><br /><br />
23         <table>
24            <tr>
25               <td style="width: 100px" valign="top">
26                  Name:</td>
27               <td style="width: 450px" valign="top">
28                  <asp:TextBox ID="nameTextBox" runat="server">
29                  </asp:TextBox>
30                  <br />
31                  <asp:RequiredFieldValidator
32                     ID="nameInputValidator" runat="server"
33                     ControlToValidate="nameTextBox" Display="None"
34                     ErrorMessage="Please enter your name.">
35                  </asp:RequiredFieldValidator>
36                  <ajax:ValidatorCalloutExtender ID="nameInputCallout"
37                     runat="server" TargetControlID="nameInputValidator"/>
38               </td>
39            </tr>
40            <tr>
41               <td style="width: 100px" valign="top">E-mail address:</td>
42               <td style="width: 450px" valign="top">
43                  <asp:TextBox ID="emailTextBox" runat="server">
44                  </asp:TextBox>
45                   e.g., user@domain.com<br />
46                  <asp:RequiredFieldValidator
47                     ID="emailInputValidator" runat="server"
```

Fig. 21.67 | Validation application enhanced by ASP.NET Ajax. (Part 1 of 3.)

```
48              ControlToValidate="emailTextBox" Display="None"
49              ErrorMessage="Please enter your e-mail address.">
50          </asp:RequiredFieldValidator>
51          <ajax:ValidatorCalloutExtender ID="emailInputCallout"
52              runat="server" TargetControlID="emailInputValidator"/>
53          <asp:RegularExpressionValidator
54              ID="emailFormatValidator" runat="server"
55              ControlToValidate="emailTextBox" Display="None"
56              ErrorMessage=
57                  "Please enter an e-mail address in a valid format."
58              ValidationExpression=
59                  "\w+([-+.']\w+)*@\w+([-.]\w+)*\.\w+([-.]\w+)*">
60          </asp:RegularExpressionValidator>
61          <ajax:ValidatorCalloutExtender ID="emailFormatCallout"
62              runat="server"
63              TargetControlID="emailFormatValidator"/>
64      </td>
65  </tr>
66  <tr>
67      <td style="width: 100px; height: 21px" valign="top">
68          Phone number:</td>
69      <td style="width: 450px; height: 21px" valign="top">
70          <asp:TextBox ID="phoneTextBox" runat="server">
71          </asp:TextBox>
72           e.g., (555) 555-1234<br />
73          <asp:RequiredFieldValidator
74              ID="phoneInputValidator" runat="server"
75              ControlToValidate="phoneTextBox" Display="None"
76              ErrorMessage="Please enter your phone number.">
77          </asp:RequiredFieldValidator>
78          <ajax:ValidatorCalloutExtender ID="phoneInputCallout"
79              runat="server" TargetControlID="phoneInputValidator"/>
80          <asp:RegularExpressionValidator
81              ID="phoneFormatValidator" runat="server"
82              ControlToValidate="phoneTextBox" Display="None"
83              ErrorMessage=
84                  "Please enter a phone number in a valid format."
85              ValidationExpression=
86                  "((\(\(\d{3}\) ?)|(\d{3}-))?\d{3}-\d{4}">
87          </asp:RegularExpressionValidator>
88          <ajax:ValidatorCalloutExtender ID="PhoneFormatCallout"
89              runat="server"
90              TargetControlID="phoneFormatValidator"/>
91      </td>
92  </tr>
93  </table>
94  <asp:UpdatePanel ID="UpdatePanel1" runat="server">
95      <ContentTemplate>
96          <asp:Button ID="submitButton" runat="server" Text="Submit" />
97          <br /><br /><br /> 
98          <asp:Label ID="outputLabel" runat="server"
99              Text="Thank you for your submission." Visible="False">
100         </asp:Label>
```

Fig. 21.67 | Validation application enhanced by ASP.NET Ajax. (Part 2 of 3.)

```
101          </ContentTemplate>
102        </asp:UpdatePanel>
103    </div>
104    </form>
105  </body>
106  </html>
```

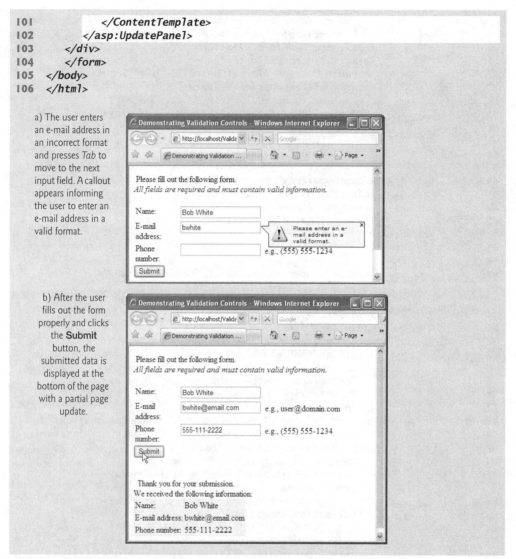

a) The user enters an e-mail address in an incorrect format and presses *Tab* to move to the next input field. A callout appears informing the user to enter an e-mail address in a valid format.

b) After the user fills out the form properly and clicks the **Submit** button, the submitted data is displayed at the bottom of the page with a partial page update.

Fig. 21.67 | Validation application enhanced by ASP.NET Ajax. (Part 3 of 3.)

ScriptManager Control

The key control in every ASP.NET Ajax-enabled application is the ***ScriptManager***, which manages the client-side scripts that enable asynchronous Ajax functionality. There can be only one ScriptManager per page. To incorporate controls from the Ajax Control Toolkit you should use the ***ToolkitScriptManager*** that comes with the toolkit contorls, rather than the ScriptManager from the ASP.NET Ajax Extensions. The ToolkitScriptManager bundles all the scripts associated with ASP. NET Ajax Toolkit controls to optimize the application's performance. Drag the ToolkitScriptManager from the **Ajax Toolkit** tab in the toolbox to the top of the page—a script manager must appear before any controls that use the scripts it manages. This generates lines 5–6 and lines 18–20. Lines 5–6 associate the

AjaxControlToolkit assembly with the tag prefix ajax, allowing us to put Ajax Control Toolkit elements on the page. Lines 18–20 load the ToolkitScriptManager on the page.

Common Programming Error 21.1

Putting more than one instance of the ScriptManager control on a Web Form causes the application to throw an InvalidOperationException when the page is initialized.

Partial Page Updates Using the UpdatePanel Control

The **UpdatePanel** *control* eliminates full-page refreshes by isolating a section of a page for a partial-page update. To implement a partial-page update, drag the UpdatePanel control from the **Ajax Extensions** tab in the **Toolbox** to your form. Then, drag into the UpdatePanel the control to update and the control that triggers the update. For this example, drag the outputLabel and submitButton elements into the UpdatePanel. The components that are managed by the UpdatePanel are placed in the ContentTemplate element (lines 95–101) of the UpdatePanel (lines 94–102). When the user clicks the **Submit** button, the UpdatePanel intercepts the request and makes an asynchronous request to the server instead. Then the response is inserted in the outputLabel element, and the UpdatePanel reloads the label to display the new text without refreshing the entire page.

Adding Ajax Functionality to ASP.NET Validation Controls Using Ajax Extenders

Several controls in the Ajax Control Toolkit are *extenders*—components that enhance regular ASP.NET controls. Lines 36–37, 51–52, 61–63, 78–79 and 88–90 define **ValidatorCalloutExtender** *controls* that display error messages in small yellow callouts next to the input fields. Line 37 sets the targetControlID property, which indicates the validator control from which the ValidatorCalloutExtender should obtain the error message to display. The ValidatorCalloutExtenders display error messages with a nicer look and feel, so we no longer need the validator controls to display these messages on their own. For this reason, line 33 sets the Display property of the first validator to None. The remaining control extenders and validator controls are configured similarly.

Additional ASP.NET Information

The Ajax Control Toolkit contains many other extenders and independent controls. You can check them out using the sample website included with the toolkit. The live version of the sample website can be found at www.asp.net/ajax/control-toolkit/live/. For more information on ASP.NET Ajax, check out our ASP.NET Ajax Resource Center at www.deitel.com/aspdotnetajax.

21.8 Web Resources

www.deitel.com/aspdotnet/
The Deitel ASP.NET Resource Center focuses on the vast amount of free ASP.NET content available online, plus some for-sale items. Start your search here for tools, downloads, text and video tutorials, webcasts, podcasts, wikis, documentation, reference manuals, conferences, FAQs, books, e-books, sample chapters, articles, newsgroups, forums, downloads from CNET's download.com, jobs and contract opportunities, and more that will help you develop ASP.NET-based applications. Keep track of ASP.NET blogs for the latest news and developments, or sign up for RSS feeds to be notified promptly of each new development. Also, download free open-source ASP.NET projects.

22

JavaServer™ Faces (JSF) Web Applications

OBJECTIVES

In this chapter you will learn:

- Web application development using Java Technologies and Netbeans.
- To create JavaServer Pages with JavaServer Faces components.
- To create web applications consisting of multiple pages.
- To validate user input on a web page.
- To maintain state information about a user with session tracking and cookies.

If any man will draw up his case, and put his name at the foot of the first page, I will give him an immediate reply. Where he compels me to turn over the sheet, he must wait my leisure.
—Lord Sandwich

Rule One: Our client is always right.
Rule Two: If you think our client is wrong, see Rule One.
—Anonymous

A fair question should be followed by a deed in silence.
—Dante Alighieri

You will come here and get books that will open your eyes, and your ears, and your curiosity, and turn you inside out or outside in.
—Ralph Waldo Emerson

22.1 Introduction

In this chapter, we introduce web application development with Java-based technology. Web-based applications create web content for web browser clients. This web content includes Extensible HyperText Markup Language (XHTML), client-side scripting, images and binary data. If you are not familiar with XHTML, you should read Chapter 2 before studying this chapter. [*Note:* This chapter assumes that you know Java. To learn more about Java, check out *Java How to Program, Seventh Edition*, or visit our Java Resource Centers at `www.deitel.com/ResourceCenters.html`.]

This chapter begins with an overview of multitier application architecture and Java's web technologies for implementing multitier applications. We then present several examples that demonstrate web application development. The first example introduces you to Java web development. In the second example, we build a web application that simply shows the look-and-feel of several web application GUI components. Next, we demonstrate how to use validation components and custom validation methods to ensure that user input is valid before it is submitted for processing on the server. The chapter finishes with two examples of customizing a user's experience with session tracking.

In Chapter 23, we continue our discussion of Java web application development with more advanced concepts, including the AJAX-enabled components from Sun's Java BluePrints. AJAX helps web-based applications provide the interactivity and responsiveness that users typically expect of desktop applications.

Throughout this chapter and Chapter 23, we use the *Netbeans 5.5.1* IDE, its *Visual Web Pack* and the *Sun Java System Application Server (SJSAS)*. The Visual Web Pack helps you build web applications using Java technologies such as JavaServer Pages and JavaServer Faces. To implement the examples presented in this chapter, you must install all three software products. A bundle of Netbeans 5.5.1 and SJSAS is available at

```
www.netbeans.info/downloads/index.php?rs=22&p=3
```

The Visual Web Pack is available at

```
www.netbeans.org/products/visualweb/
```

22.2 Java Web Technologies

Java web technologies continually evolve to provide developers with higher levels of abstraction and greater separation of the application's tiers. This separation makes web applications more maintainable and extensible. It also allows for an effective division of labor. A graphic designer can build the application's user interface without concern for the underlying page logic, which will be handled by a programmer. Meanwhile, you are free to focus on the application's business logic, leaving the details of building an attractive and easy-to-use application to the designer. Netbeans is the latest step in this evolution, allowing you to develop a web application's GUI in a drag-and-drop design tool, while handling the business logic in separate Java classes.

Java multitier applications are typically implemented using the features of Java Enterprise Edition (Java EE). The technologies we use to develop web applications in Chapters 22–23 are part of Java EE 5 (java.sun.com/javaee).

22.2.1 Servlets

Servlets are the lowest-level view of web development technologies in Java that we'll discuss in this chapter. They use the HTTP request/response model of communication between client and server.

Servlets extend a server's functionality by allowing it to generate dynamic content. For instance, servlets can dynamically generate custom XHTML documents, help provide secure access to a website, interact with databases on behalf of a client and maintain unique session information for each client. A web server component called the *servlet container* executes and interacts with servlets. Packages *javax.servlet* and *javax.servlet.http* provide the classes and interfaces to define servlets. The servlet container receives HTTP requests from a client and directs each request to the appropriate servlet. The servlet processes the request and returns an appropriate response to the client—usually in the form of an XHTML or XML (Extensible Markup Language) document to display in the browser. XML is a language used to exchange structured data on the web.

Architecturally, all servlets must implement the **Servlet** interface of package javax.servlet, which ensures that each servlet can execute in the framework provided by the servlet container. Interface Servlet declares methods used by the servlet container to manage the servlet's life cycle. A servlet's life cycle begins when the servlet container loads it into memory—usually in response to the first request for the servlet. Before the servlet can handle that request, the container invokes the servlet's init method, which is called only once during a servlet's life cycle to initialize the servlet. After init completes execution, the servlet is ready to respond to its first request. All requests are handled by a servlet's *service method*, which is the key method in defining a servlet's functionality. The service method receives the request, processes it and sends a response to the client. During a servlet's life cycle, `service` is called once per request. Each new request is typically handled in a separate thread of execution (managed by the servlet container), so each servlet must be thread safe. When the servlet container terminates the servlet (e.g. when the servlet container needs more memory or when it is shut down), the servlet's `destroy` method is called to release any resources held by the servlet.

22.2.2 JavaServer Pages

JavaServer Pages (*JSP*) technology is an extension of servlet technology. Each JSP is translated by the JSP container into a servlet. Unlike servlets, JSPs help you separate presentation from content. JavaServer Pages enable web application programmers to create dynamic content by reusing predefined components and by interacting with components using server-side scripting. JSP programmers can use special software components called JavaBeans and custom tag libraries that encapsulate complex, dynamic functionality. A *JavaBean* is a reusable component that follows certain conventions for class design. For example, JavaBeans classes that allow reading and writing of instance variables must provide appropriate *get* and *set* methods. The complete set of class design conventions is discussed in the JavaBeans specification (`java.sun.com/products/javabeans/glasgow/index.html`).

Custom Tag Libraries
Custom tag libraries are a powerful feature of JSP that allows Java developers to hide code for database access and other complex operations in *custom tags*. To use such capabilities, you simply add the custom tags to the page. This simplicity enables web-page designers who are not familiar with Java to enhance web pages with powerful dynamic content and dynamic processing capabilities. The JSP classes and interfaces are located in the packages `javax.servlet.jsp` and `javax.servlet.jsp.tagext`.

JSP Components
There are four key components to JSPs—directives, actions, scripting elements and tag libraries. *Directives* are messages to the *JSP container*—the web server component that executes JSPs. Directives enable you to specify page settings, to include content from other resources and to specify custom tag libraries for use in JSPs. *Actions* encapsulate functionality in predefined tags that programmers can embed in JSPs. Actions often are performed based on the information sent to the server as part of a particular client request. They also can create Java objects for use in JSPs. *Scripting elements* enable you to insert Java code that interacts with components in a JSP (and possibly other web application components) to perform request processing. *Tag libraries* are part of the *tag extension mechanism* that enables programmers to create custom tags. Such tags enable web-page designers to manipulate JSP content without prior Java knowledge. The *JavaServer Pages Standard Tag Library* (*JSTL*) provides the functionality for many common web application tasks, such as iterating over a collection of objects and executing SQL statements.

Static Content
JSPs can contain other static content. For example, JSPs normally include XHTML or XML markup. Such markup is known as *fixed-template data* or *fixed-template text*. Any literal text or XHTML markup in a JSP is translated to a `String` literal in the servlet representation of the JSP.

Processing a JSP Request

When a JSP-enabled server receives the first request for a JSP, the JSP container translates the JSP into a servlet that handles the current request and future requests to the JSP. JSPs thus rely on the same request/response mechanism as servlets to process requests from and send responses to clients.

> **Performance Tip 22.1**
>
> *Some JSP containers translate JSPs into servlets at the JSP's deployment time (i.e., when the application is placed on a web server). This eliminates the translation overhead for the first client that requests each JSP, as the JSP will be translated before it is ever requested by a client.*

22.2.3 JavaServer Faces

JavaServer Faces (JSF) is a web application framework (similar to ASP.NET) that simplifies the design of an application's user interface and further separates a web application's presentation from its business logic. A *framework* simplifies application development by providing libraries and sometimes software tools to help you organize and build your applications. Though the JSF framework can use many technologies to define the pages in web applications, this chapter focuses on JSF applications that use JavaServer Pages. JSF provides a set of user interface components, or *JSF components*, that simplify web-page design. These components are similar to the Swing components used to build GUI applications. JSF provides two JSP custom tag libraries for adding these components to a JSP page. JSF also includes APIs for handling component events (such as processing component state changes and validating user input), navigating between web application pages and more. You design the look-and-feel of a page with JSF by adding tags to a JSP file and manipulating their attributes. You define the page's behavior separately in a related Java source-code file.

Though the standard JSF components are sufficient for most basic web applications, you can also write custom component libraries. Additional component libraries are available through the *Java BluePrints* project—which shows best practices for developing Java applications. Many other vendors provide JSF component libraries. For example, Oracle provides almost 100 components in its ADF Faces library. In the next chapter, we discuss one such component library, the BluePrints AJAX components library, which can be found at `blueprints.dev.java.net/ajaxcomponents.html`.

22.2.4 Web Technologies in Netbeans

Netbeans web applications consist of one or more JSP web pages built in the JavaServer Faces framework. These JSP files have the filename extension `.jsp` and contain the web pages' GUI elements. The JSPs can also contain JavaScript to add functionality to the page. JSPs can be customized in Netbeans by adding JSF components, including labels, text fields, images, buttons and other GUI components. The IDE allows you to design pages visually by dragging and dropping these components onto a page; you can also customize a web page by editing the `.jsp` file manually.

Every JSP file created in Netbeans represents a web page and has a corresponding JavaBean class called the *page bean*. A JavaBean class must have a default (or no-argument) constructor, and *get* and *set* methods for all of the bean's properties (i.e., instance variables). The page bean defines properties for each of the page's elements. The page bean also contains event handlers and page life-cycle methods for managing tasks such as page initialization and rendering, and other supporting code for the web application.

Every Netbeans web application has three other JavaBeans. The **RequestBean** object is maintained in *request scope*—this object exists only for an HTTP request's duration. A **SessionBean** object has *session scope*—the object exists throughout a user's browsing session or until the session times out. There is a unique SessionBean object for each user. Finally, the **ApplicationBean** object has *application scope*—this object is shared by all instances of an application and exists as long as the application remains deployed on a web server. This object is used for application-wide data storage or processing; only one instance exists for the application, regardless of the number of open sessions.

22.3 Creating and Running a Simple Application in Netbeans

Our first example displays the web server's time of day in a browser window. When run, this program displays the text "Current Time on the Web Server", followed by the web server's time. The application contains a single web page and, as mentioned previously, consists of two related files—a JSP file (Fig. 22.1) and a supporting page bean file (Fig. 22.3). The application also has the three scoped data beans for request, session, and application scopes. Since this application does not store data, these beans are not used in this example. We first discuss the markup in the JSP file, the code in the page bean file and the application output, then we provide step-by-step instructions for creating the program. [*Note:* The markup in Fig. 22.1 and other JSP file listings in this chapter is the same as the markup that appears in Netbeans, but we have reformatted these listings for presentation purposes to make the code more readable.]

```
 1    <?xml version = "1.0" encoding = "UTF-8"?>
 2
 3    <!-- Fig. 22.1: Time.jsp -->
 4    <!-- JSP file generated by Netbeans that displays -->
 5    <!-- the current time on the web server -->
 6    <jsp:root version = "1.2"
 7        xmlns:f = "http://java.sun.com/jsf/core"
 8        xmlns:h = "http://java.sun.com/jsf/html"
 9        xmlns:jsp = "http://java.sun.com/JSP/Page"
10        xmlns:webuijsf = "http://www.sun.com/webui/webuijsf">
11        <jsp:directive.page contentType = "text/html;charset=UTF-8"
12            pageEncoding = "UTF-8" />
13        <f:view>
14            <webuijsf:page binding = "#{Time.page1}" id = "page1">
15                <webuijsf:html binding = "#{Time.html1}" id = "html1">
```

Fig. 22.1 | JSP file generated by Netbeans that displays the current time on the web server. (Part 1 of 2.)

```
16        <webuijsf:head binding = "#{Time.head1}" id = "head1"
17           title = "Web Time: A Simple Example">
18           <webuijsf:link binding = "#{Time.link1}" id = "link1"
19              url = "/resources/stylesheet.css"/>
20           <webuijsf:meta content = "60" httpEquiv = "refresh" />
21        </webuijsf:head>
22        <webuijsf:body binding = "#{Time.body1}" id = "body1"
23           style = "-rave-layout: grid">
24           <webuijsf:form binding = "#{Time.form1}" id = "form1">
25              <webuijsf:staticText binding = "#{Time.timeHeader}"
26                 id = "timeHeader" style = "font-size: 18px;
27                    left: 24px; top: 24px; position: absolute"
28                 text = "Current time on the web server:" />
29              <webuijsf:staticText binding = "#{Time.clockText}"
30                 id = "clockText" style = "background-color: black;
31                    color: yellow; font-size: 18px; left: 24px;
32                    top: 48px; position: absolute" />
33           </webuijsf:form>
34        </webuijsf:body>
35     </webuijsf:html>
36  </webuijsf:page>
37  </f:view>
38 </jsp:root>
```

Fig. 22.1 | JSP file generated by Netbeans that displays the current time on the web server. (Part 2 of 2.)

Netbeans generates all the markup shown in Fig. 22.1 when you set the web page's title, drag two **Static Text** components onto the page and set the properties of the **Static Text** components. **Static Text** components display text that cannot be edited by the user. We show these steps shortly.

22.3.1 Examining a JSP File

The JSP files used in this and the following examples are generated almost entirely by Netbeans, which provides a Visual Editor that allows you to build a page's GUI by dragging and dropping components onto a design area. The IDE generates a JSP file in response to your interactions. Line 1 of Fig. 22.1 is the XML declaration, indicating the fact that the JSP is expressed in XML syntax and the version of XML that is used. Lines 3–5 are comments that we added to the JSP to indicate its figure number, filename and purpose.

Line 6 begins the JSP's root element. All JSPs must have this **jsp:root** element, which has a version attribute to indicate the JSP version being used (line 6) and one or more xmlns attributes (lines 7–10). Each **xmlns attribute** specifies a prefix and a URL for a tag library, allowing the page to use tags from that library. For example, line 9 allows the page to use the standard JSP elements. To use these elements, each element's tag must be preceded by the jsp prefix. All JSPs generated by Netbeans include the tag libraries specified in lines 7–10 (the JSF core components library, the JSF HTML components library, the JSP standard components library and the JSF user interface components library).

Lines 11–12 are the **jsp:directive.page** element. Its contentType attribute specifies the MIME type (text/html) and the character set (UTF-8) the page uses. The page-

Encoding attribute specifies the character encoding used by the page source. These attributes help the client (typically a web browser) determine how to render the content.

All pages containing JSF components are represented in a ***component tree*** (Fig. 22.2) with the root JSF element ***f:view***, which is of type ***UIViewRoot***. This component tree structure is represented in a JSP by enclosing all JSF component tags inside the f:view element (lines 13–37).

Lines 14–21 begin the JSP's definition with the ***webuijsf:page***, ***webuijsf:html*** and ***webuijsf::head*** tags, all from the webuijsf (JSF user interface components) tag library. These and many other webuijsf page elements have a binding attribute. For example, the webuijsf:head element (line 16) has the attribute binding = "#{Time.head1}." This attribute uses ***JSF Expression Language*** notation (i.e., #{Time.head1}) to reference the head1 property in the Time class that represents the page bean (you'll see this class in Fig. 22.3). You can bind an attribute of a JSP element to a property in any of the web application's JavaBeans. For instance, the text attribute of a ***webuijsf:label*** component can be bound to a String property in the application's SessionBean (shown in Section 22.5.2).

The webuijsf:head element (lines 16–21) has a title attribute that specifies the page's title. This element also contains a ***webuijsf:link*** element (lines 18–19) that specifies the CSS stylesheet used by the page, and a ***webuijsf:meta*** element (line 20) that specifies the page's refresh rate. The ***webuijsf:body*** element (lines 22–34) contains a ***webuijsf:form*** element (lines 24–33), which contains two ***webuijsf:staticText*** components (lines 25–28 and 29–32) that display the page's text. The timeHeader component (lines 25–28) has a text attribute (line 28) that specifies the text to display (i.e., "Current time on the web server"). The clockText component (lines 29–32) does not specify a text attribute because this component's text will be set programmatically.

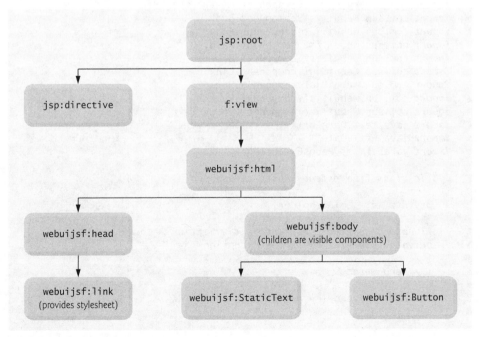

Fig. 22.2 | Sample JSF component tree.

For the markup in this file to be displayed in a browser, all the JSP's elements are automatically mapped to XHTML elements that the browser recognizes. The same web component can map to different XHTML elements, depending on the client browser and the component's property settings. In this example, the `webuijsf:staticText` components (lines 25–28, 29–32) map to XHTML *span* elements. A span element contains text that is displayed on a web page and is typically used to control the formatting of the text. The `style` attributes of a JSP's `webuijsf:staticText` element will be represented as part of the corresponding span element's `style` attribute when the browser renders the page. We show momentarily the XHTML document that results when `Time.jsp` is requested by a browser.

22.3.2 Examining a Page Bean File

Figure 22.3 presents the page bean file. Line 3 indicates that this class belongs to package `webtime`. This line is autogenerated and specifies the project's name as the package name. Line 18 begins class `Time`'s declaration and indicates that it inherits from class **Abstract-PageBean** (from package **com.sun.rave.web.ui.appbase**). All page bean classes that support JSP files with JSF components must inherit from the abstract class `AbstractPageBean`, which provides page life-cycle methods. Note that the IDE makes the class name match the page name. Package **com.sun.webui.jsf.component** includes classes for many of the basic JSF components (see the `import` statements at lines 6–13).

```java
1  // Fig. 22.3: Time.java
2  // Page bean file that sets clockText to the time on the Web server.
3  package webtime;
4
5  import com.sun.rave.web.ui.appbase.AbstractPageBean;
6  import com.sun.webui.jsf.component.Body;
7  import com.sun.webui.jsf.component.Form;
8  import com.sun.webui.jsf.component.Head;
9  import com.sun.webui.jsf.component.Html;
10 import com.sun.webui.jsf.component.Link;
11 import com.sun.webui.jsf.component.Meta;
12 import com.sun.webui.jsf.component.Page;
13 import com.sun.webui.jsf.component.StaticText;
14 import java.text.DateFormat;
15 import java.util.Date;
16 import javax.faces.FacesException;
17
18 public class Time extends AbstractPageBean
19 {
20    private int __placeholder;
21
22    // auto-generated component initialization method.
23    private void _init() throws Exception
24    {
25    } // end method _init
26
27    private Page page1 = new Page();
28
```

Fig. 22.3 | Page bean file that sets `clockText` to the time on the web server. (Part 1 of 5.)

```
29        public Page getPage1()
30        {
31           return page1;
32        } // end method getPage1
33
34        public void setPage1( Page p )
35        {
36           this.page1 = p;
37        } // end method setPage1
38
39        private Html html1 = new Html();
40
41        public Html getHtml1()
42        {
43           return html1;
44        } // end method getHtml1
45
46        public void setHtml1( Html h )
47        {
48           this.html1 = h;
49        } // end method setHtml1
50
51        private Head head1 = new Head();
52
53        public Head getHead1()
54        {
55           return head1;
56        } // end method getHead1
57
58        public void setHead1( Head h )
59        {
60           this.head1 = h;
61        } // end method setHead1
62
63        private Link link1 = new Link();
64
65        public Link getLink1()
66        {
67           return link1;
68        } // end method getLink1
69
70        public void setLink1( Link l )
71        {
72           this.link1 = l;
73        } // end method setLink1
74
75        private Body body1 = new Body();
76
77        public Body getBody1()
78        {
79           return body1;
80        } // end method getBody1
81
```

Fig. 22.3 | Page bean file that sets clockText to the time on the web server. (Part 2 of 5.)

```
82      public void setBody1( Body b )
83      {
84         this.body1 = b;
85      } // end method setBody1
86
87      private Form form1 = new Form();
88
89      public Form getForm1()
90      {
91         return form1;
92      } // end method getForm1
93
94      public void setForm1( Form f )
95      {
96         this.form1 = f;
97      } // end method setForm1
98
99      private StaticText timeHeader = new StaticText();
100
101     public StaticText getTimeHeader()
102     {
103        return timeHeader;
104     } // end method getTimeHeader
105
106     public void setTimeHeader( StaticText st )
107     {
108        this.timeHeader = st;
109     } // end method setTimeHeader
110
111     private StaticText clockText = new StaticText();
112
113     public StaticText getClockText()
114     {
115        return clockText;
116     } // end method getClockText
117
118     public void setClockText( StaticText st )
119     {
120        this.clockText = st;
121     } // end method setClockText
122
123     private Meta meta1 = new Meta();
124
125     public Meta getMeta1()
126     {
127        return meta1;
128     } // end method getMeta1
129
130     public void setMeta1( Meta m )
131     {
132        this.meta1 = m;
133     } // end method setMeta1
134
```

Fig. 22.3 | Page bean file that sets clockText to the time on the web server. (Part 3 of 5.)

```
135       public Time()
136       {
137       } // end Time constructor
138
139       // initializes page content
140       public void init()
141       {
142          super.init();
143
144          try
145          {
146             _init();
147          } // end try
148          catch ( Exception e )
149          {
150             log( "Time Initialization Failure", e );
151             throw e instanceof FacesException ? ( FacesException ) e :
152                new FacesException( e );
153          } // end catch
154       } // end method init
155
156       // method called when postback occurs
157       public void preprocess()
158       {
159       } // end method preprocess
160
161       // method called before the page is rendered
162       public void prerender()
163       {
164          clockText.setValue( DateFormat.getTimeInstance(
165             DateFormat.LONG ).format( new Date() ) );
166       } // end method prerender
167
168       // method called after rendering completes, if init was called
169       public void destroy()
170       {
171       } // end method destroy
172
173       // return a reference to the scoped data bean
174       protected SessionBean1 getSessionBean1()
175       {
176          return ( SessionBean1 ) getBean( "SessionBean1" );
177       } // end method getSessionBean1
178
179       // return a reference to the scoped data bean
180       protected ApplicationBean1 getApplicationBean1()
181       {
182          return ( ApplicationBean1 ) getBean( "ApplicationBean1" );
183       } // end method getApplicationBean1
184
185       // return a reference to the scoped data bean
186       protected RequestBean1 getRequestBean1()
187       {
```

Fig. 22.3 | Page bean file that sets clockText to the time on the web server. (Part 4 of 5.)

```
188          return ( RequestBean1 ) getBean( "RequestBean1" );
189      } // end method getRequestBean1
190  } // end class Time
```

Fig. 22.3 | Page bean file that sets clockText to the time on the web server. (Part 5 of 5.)

This page bean file provides *get* and *set* methods for every element of the JSP file of Fig. 22.1. These methods are generated automatically by the IDE. We included the complete page bean file in this first example, but in future examples these properties and their *get* and *set* methods will be omitted to save space. Lines 99–109 and 111–121 of the page bean file define the two **Static Text** components that we dropped onto the page and their *get* and *set* methods. These components are objects of class StaticText in package com.sun.webui.jsf.component.

The only logic required in this page is to set the clockText component's text to read the current time on the server. We do this in the prerender method (lines 162–166). The meaning of this and other page bean methods will be discussed shortly. Lines 164–165 fetch and format the time on the server and set the value of clockText to that time.

22.3.3 Event-Processing Life Cycle

Netbeans's application model places several methods in the page bean that tie into the JSF *event-processing life cycle*. These methods represent four major stages—initialization, preprocessing, prerendering and destruction. Each corresponds to a method in the page bean class—init, preprocess, prerender and destroy, respectively. Netbeans automatically creates these methods, but you can customize them to handle life-cycle processing tasks, such as rendering an element on a page only if a user clicks a button.

The *init method* (Fig. 22.3, lines 140–154) is called by the JSP container the first time the page is requested and on postbacks. A *postback* occurs when form data is submitted, and the page and its contents are sent to the server to be processed. Method init invokes its superclass version (line 142) then tries to call the method _init (declared in lines 23–25). The _init method is also automatically generated and handles component initialization tasks (if there are any), such as setting the options for a group of radio buttons.

The *preprocess method* (lines 157–159) is called after init, but only if the page is processing a postback. The *prerender method* (lines 162–166) is called just before a page is rendered (i.e., displayed) by the browser. This method should be used to set component properties; properties that are set sooner (such as in method init) may be overwritten before the page is actually rendered by the browser. For this reason, we set the value of clockText in the prerender method.

Finally, the ***destroy method*** (lines 169–171) is called after the page has been rendered, but only if the `init` method was called. This method handles tasks such as freeing resources used to render the page.

22.3.4 Relationship Between the JSP and Page Bean Files

The page bean has a property for every element that appears in the JSP file of Fig. 22.1, from the `html` element to the two `Static Text` components. Recall that the elements in the JSP file were explicitly bound to these properties by each element's `binding` attribute using a JSF Expression Language statement. Because this is a JavaBean class, *get* and *set* methods for each of these properties are also included (lines 27–133). This code is automatically generated by the IDE for every web application project.

22.3.5 Examining the XHTML Generated by a Java Web Application

Figure 22.4 shows the XHTML generated when `Time.jsp` (Fig. 22.1) is requested by a client web browser. To view this XHTML, select **View > Source** in Internet Explorer or **View > Page Source** in Firefox. [*Note:* We reformatted the XHTML to conform to our coding conventions.]

```
 1  <!DOCTYPE html PUBLIC "-//W3C//DTD XHTML 1.0 Transitional//EN"
 2     "http://www.w3.org/TR/xhtml1/DTD/xhtml1-transitional.dtd">
 3  <html xmlns = "http://www.w3.org/1999/xhtml"
 4     xmlns:wairole = "http://www.w3.org/2005/01/wai-rdf/GUIRoleTaxonomy#"
 5     xmlns:waistate = "http://www.w3.org/2005/07/aaa">
 6     <head>
 7        <meta content = "no-cache" http-equiv = "Pragma" />
 8        <meta content = "no-cache" http-equiv = "Cache-Control" />
 9        <meta content = "no-store" http-equiv = "Cache-Control" />
10        <meta content = "max-age=0" http-equiv = "Cache-Control" />
11        <meta content = "1" http-equiv = "Expires" />
12        <title>Web Time: A Simple Example</title>
13        <link rel = "stylesheet" type = "text/css" href = "/WebTime/theme/
14           com/sun/webui/jsf/suntheme/css/css_master.css" />
15        <link rel = "stylesheet" type = "text/css" href = "/WebTime/theme/
16           com/sun/webui/jsf/suntheme/css/ie7.css" />
17        <script type = "text/javascript">
18           djConfig = {
19              "isDebug": false,
20              "parseWidgets": false,
21              "debugAtAllCosts": false
22           };
23        </script>
24        <script type = "text/javascript"
25           src = "/WebTime/theme/META-INF/dojo/dojo.js"></script>
26        <script type = "text/javascript"
27           src = "/WebTime/theme/META-INF/json/json.js"></script>
28        <script type = "text/javascript"
29           src = "/WebTime/theme/META-INF/prototype/prototype.js"></script>
30        <script type = "text/javascript"
31           src = "/WebTime/theme/META-INF/com_sun_faces_ajax.js"></script>
```

Fig. 22.4 | XHTML response generated when the browser requests `Time.jsp`. (Part 1 of 2.)

```
32        <script type = "text/javascript">
33           dojo.hostenv.setModulePrefix( "webui.suntheme",
34              "/WebTime/theme/com/sun/webui/jsf/suntheme/javascript" );
35           dojo.require( 'webui.suntheme.*' );
36        </script>
37        <link id = "link1" rel = "stylesheet" type = "text/css"
38           href = "/WebTime/resources/stylesheet.css" />
39        <meta id = "j_id_id7" http-equiv = "refresh" content = "60" />
40     </head>
41     <body id = "body1" style = "-rave-layout:grid" onload="" onunload="">
42        <form id = "form1" class = "form" method = "post"
43           action = "/WebTime/faces/Time.jsp"
44           enctype = "application/x-www-form-urlencoded">
45        <span id = "form1:timeHeader" style = "font-size: 18px; left: 24px;
46           top: 24px; position: absolute">Current time on the web server:
47        </span>
48        <span id = "form1:clockText" style = "background-color: black;
49           color: yellow; font-size: 18px; left: 24px; top: 48px;
50           position: absolute">12:30:49 PM EDT</span>
51        <input id = "form1_hidden" name = "form1_hidden"
52           value = "form1_hidden" type = "hidden" />
53        <input type = "hidden" name = "javax.faces.ViewState"
54           id = "javax.faces.ViewState" value = "j_id173:j_id174" />
55        </form>
56        <script type = "text/javascript">
57           webui.suntheme.common.body = new webui.suntheme.body(
58              '/Time.jsp', '/WebTime/faces/Time.jsp', null, null,
59              'com_sun_webui_util_FocusManager_focusElementId');</script>
60     </body>
61  </html>
```

Fig. 22.4 | XHTML response generated when the browser requests `Time.jsp`. (Part 2 of 2.)

The XHTML document in Fig. 22.4 is similar in structure to the JSP file of Fig. 22.1. Lines 1–2 are the document type declaration, which declares this document to be an XHTML 1.0 Transitional document. The XHTML meta tags in lines 7–11 are equivalent to HTTP headers and are used to control browser behavior.

Lines 41–60 define the body of the document. Lines 42–55 define an XHTML form. In this particular program, the user does not submit data to the web server for processing. We demonstrate how to submit data to the server in later examples. Attribute method of the form element (line 42) specifies the method by which the web browser submits the form to the server. By default, JSPs use the post method. The form's action attribute (line 43) identifies the resource that will be requested when this form is submitted—in this case, /WebTime/faces/Time.jsp.

Note that the two **Static Text** components (i.e., timeHeader and clockText) are represented by two span elements in the XHTML document (lines 45–47, 48–50) as previously discussed. The formatting options that were specified as properties of timeHeader and clockText, such as the font size and text color in the components, are now specified in each span element's style attribute.

22.3.6 Building a Web Application in Netbeans

Now that we have presented the JSP file, the page bean file and the resulting XHTML web page sent to the web browser, we discuss the steps to create this application. To build the WebTime application, perform the following steps in Netbeans:

Step 1: Creating the Web Application Project
Select **File > New Project...** to display the **New Project** dialog. In this dialog, select **Web** in the **Categories** pane, **Visual Web Application** in the **Projects** pane and click **Next**. Change the project name to WebTime. In the **Project Location** field, specify where you'd like to store the project. These settings will create a WebTime directory to store the project's files in the parent directory you specified. Keep the other default settings and click **Finish** to create the web application project.

Step 2: Examining the Visual Editor Window of the New Project
The next several figures describe important features of the IDE, beginning with the *Visual Editor* window (Fig. 22.5). Netbeans creates a single web page named Page1 when a new project is created. This page is open by default in the Visual Editor in **Design** *mode* when the project first loads. As you drag and drop new components onto the page, **Design** mode allows you to see how your page will be rendered in the browser. The JSP file for this page, named Page1.jsp, can be viewed by clicking the **JSP** button at the top of the visual editor or by right clicking anywhere in the Visual Editor and selecting **Edit JSP Source**. As mentioned previously, each web page is supported by a page bean file. Netbeans creates a file named Page1.java when a new project is created. To open this file, click the **Java** button at the top of the Visual Editor or right click anywhere in the Visual Editor and select **Edit Java Source**.

The **Preview in Browser** button at the top of the Visual Editor window allows you to view your pages in a browser without having to build and run the application. The **Refresh** button redraws the page in the Visual Editor. The **Show Virtual Forms** button allows you to see which form elements are participating in virtual forms (we discuss this concept in Chapter 23). The **Target Browser Size** drop-down list lets you specify the optimal browser

Fig. 22.5 | Visual Editor window in **Design** mode.

resolution for viewing the page and lets you see what the page will look like in different screen resolutions.

Step 3: Examining the Palette in Netbeans

Figure 22.6 shows the **Palette** displayed in the IDE when the project loads. Part (a) displays the beginning of the **Basic** list of web components, and part (b) displays the remaining **Basic** components, as well as the list of **Layout** components. We discuss specific components in Fig. 22.6 as they are used throughout the chapter.

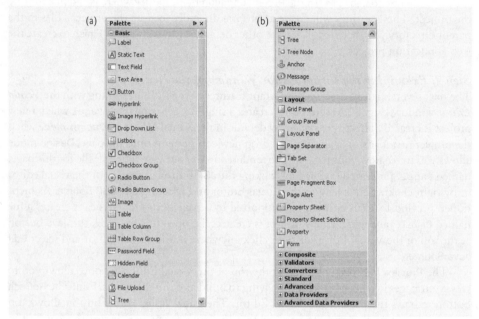

Fig. 22.6 | Palette in Netbeans.

Step 4: Examining the Projects Window

Figure 22.7 displays the **Projects** window, which appears in the upper-left corner of the IDE. This window displays the hierarchy of all files included in the project. The JSP files for each page are listed under the **Web Pages** node. This node also includes the **resources** folder, which contains the CSS stylesheet for the project and any other files the pages may need to display properly, such as image files. All of the Java source code, including the page bean file for each web page and the application, session and request scope beans, can be found under the **Source Packages** node. Another useful file displayed in the project window is the **Page Navigation** file, which defines rules for navigating the project's pages based on the outcome of some user-initiated event, such as clicking a button or a link. The **Page Navigation** file can also be accessed by right clicking in the Visual Editor while in **Design** mode and selecting **Page Navigation**.

Step 5: Examining the JSP and Java Files in the IDE

Figure 22.8 displays `Page1.jsp`—the JSP file generated by Netbeans for `Page1`. [*Note:* We reformatted the code to match our coding conventions.] Click the **JSP** button at the top

CSS stylesheet, images and other page resources

JSP file

Page Navigation definition file

Java page bean file

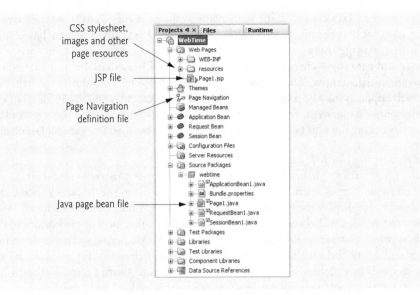

Fig. 22.7 | **Projects** window for the WebTime project.

Fig. 22.8 | JSP file generated for Page1 by Netbeans.

of the Visual Editor to open the JSP file. When it is first created, this file contains some tags for setting up the page, including linking to the page's style sheet and defining the necessary JSF libraries. Otherwise, the JSP file's tags are empty, as no components have been added to the page yet.

Figure 22.9 displays part of Page1.java—the page bean file generated by Netbeans for Page1. Click the **Java** button at the top of the Visual Editor to open the page bean file.

This file contains a Java class with the same name as the page (i.e., `Page1`), which extends the class `AbstractPageBean`. As previously mentioned, `AbstractPageBean` has several methods that manage the page's life cycle. Four of these methods—`init`, `preprocess`, `prerender` and `destroy`—are overridden by `Page1.java`. Other than method `init`, these methods are initially empty. They serve as placeholders for you to customize the behavior of your web application. The page bean file also includes *get* and *set* methods for all of the page's elements—page, `html`, `head`, `body` and `link` to start. You can view these *get* and *set* methods by clicking the plus (+) sign on the line that says **Managed Component Definition**.

Step 6: Renaming the JSP and JSF Files

Typically, you'll want to rename the JSP and Java files in your project, so that their names are relevant to your application. Right click the `Page1.jsp` file in the **Projects Window** and select **Rename...** to display the **Rename Class Page1** dialog. Enter the new filename `Time`. If **Preview All Changes** is checked, the **Refactoring Window** will appear at the bottom of the IDE when you click **Next >**. *Refactoring* is the process of modifying source code to improve its readability and reusability without changing its behavior—for example, by renaming methods or variables, or breaking long methods into shorter ones. Netbeans has built-in refactoring tools that automate some refactoring tasks. Using these tools to rename the project files updates the name of both the JSP file and the page bean file. The refactoring tool also changes the class name in the page bean file and all of the attribute bindings in the JSP file to reflect the new class name. Note that none of these changes will be made until you click **Do Refactoring** in the **Refactoring Window**. If you do not preview the changes, refactoring occurs when you click **Next >** in the **Rename Class Page1** dialog.

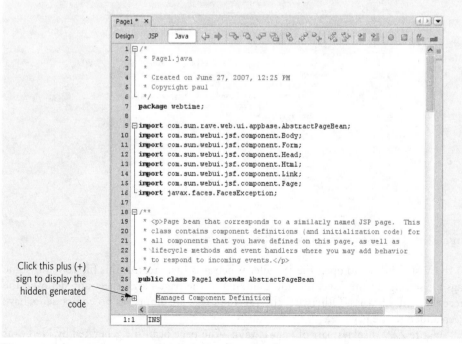

Fig. 22.9 | Page bean file for `Page1.jsp` generated by Netbeans.

Step 7: Changing the Title of the Page

Before designing the content of the web page, we give it the title "Web Time: A Simple Example". By default, the page does not have a title when it is generated by the IDE. To add a title, open the JSP file in **Design** mode. In the **Properties** window, enter the new title next to the **Title** property and press *Enter*. View the JSP to see that the attribute title = "Web Time: A Simple Example" was automatically added to the webuijsf:head tag.

Step 8: Designing the Page

Designing a web page is simple in Netbeans. To add components to the page, you can drag and drop them from the **Palette** onto the page in **Design** mode. Like the web page itself, each component is an object that has properties, methods and events. You can set these properties and events visually using the **Properties** window or programmatically in the page bean file. *Get* and *set* methods are automatically added to the page bean file for each component you add to the page.

The IDE generates the JSP tags for the components you drag and drop using a grid layout, as specified in the webuijsf:body tag. The components are rendered using *absolute positioning*—they appear exactly where they are dropped on the page. As you add components, the style attribute in each component's JSP element will include the number of pixels from the top and left margins of the page at which the component is positioned.

This example uses two **Static Text** components. To add the first one to the page, drag and drop it from the **Palette**'s **Basic** components list to the page in **Design** mode. Edit the component's text by typing "Current time on the web server:" directly into the component. The text can also be edited by changing the component's text property in the **Properties** window. Netbeans is a WYSIWYG (What You See Is What You Get) editor—whenever you make a change to a web page in **Design** mode, the IDE creates the markup (visible in **JSP** mode) necessary to achieve the desired visual effects seen in **Design** mode. After adding the text to the web page, switch to **JSP** mode. You should see that the IDE added a webuijsf:staticText element to the page body, which is bound to the object staticText1, in the page bean file and whose text attribute matches the text you just entered. Back in **Design** mode, click the **Static Text** component to select it. In the **Properties** window, click the ellipsis button next to the style property to open a dialog box to edit the text's style. Select 18 px for the font size and click **OK**. Again in the **Properties** window, change the id property to timeHeader. Setting the id property also changes the name of the component's corresponding property in the page bean and updates its binding attribute in the JSP accordingly. Notice that font-size: 18 px has been added to the style attribute and the id attribute has been changed to timeHeader in the component's tag in the JSP file. The IDE should now appear as in Fig. 22.10.

Drop a second **Static Text** component onto the page and set its id to clockText. Edit its style property so that the font size is 18 px, the text color is yellow, and the background color is black. Do not edit the component's text, as this will be set programmatically in the page bean file. The component will display with the text *Static Text* in the IDE, but will not display any text at runtime unless the text is set programmatically. Figure 22.11 shows the IDE after the second component is added.

Step 9: Adding Page Logic

After designing the user interface, you can modify the page bean file to set the text of the clockText element. In this example, we add a statement to method prerender (lines 170–

Fig. 22.10 | `Time.jsp` after inserting the first **Static Text** component.

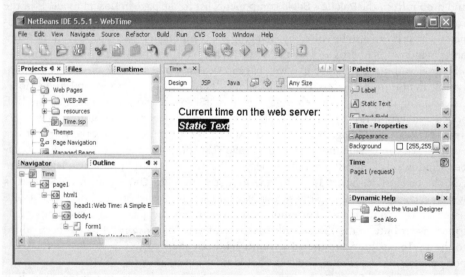

Fig. 22.11 | `Time.jsp` after adding the second `StaticText` component.

174 of Fig. 22.3). Recall that we use method `prerender` to ensure that `clockText` will be updated each time the page is refreshed. Lines 164–165 of Fig. 22.3 programmatically set the text of `clockText` to the current time on the server. For this statement to work, you'll also need the two imports shown in lines 14–15 of Fig. 22.3.

We would like this page to refresh automatically to display an up-to-date time. To accomplish this, add `<webuijsf:meta content = "60" httpEquiv = "refresh" />` to the JSP file, before the end of the `webuijsf:head` tag. This tag tells the browser to reload the page automatically every 60 seconds. You can also add this tag by dragging a **Meta** component from the **Advanced** section of the **Palette** to your page, then setting the component's content attribute to 60 and its httpEquiv attribute to refresh. If you do this, the **Meta** component will show up in the **Outline** window.

Step 10: Examining the Outline Window

Figure 22.12 displays the **Outline** *window* in Netbeans. The **Time** node representing the page bean file is expanded and shows the contents of the component tree. The request, session and application scope beans are collapsed by default, as we have not added any properties to these beans in this example. Clicking an item in the page's component tree selects the item in the Visual Editor.

Fig. 22.12 | **Outline** window in Netbeans.

Step 11: Running the Application

After creating the web page, you can view it several ways. First, you can select **Build > Build Main Project**, and after the build completes, select **Run > Run Main Project**, to run the application in a browser window. You can run a project that has already been built by pressing the **Run Main Project** icon ( ) in the toolbar at the top of the IDE. Note that if changes are made to a project, the project must be rebuilt before they will be reflected when the application is viewed in a browser. Because this application was built on the local file system, the URL displayed in the address bar of the browser when the application is run will be http://localhost:8080/WebTime/ (Fig. 22.3), where 8080 is the port number on which the test server—*Sun Java System Application Server (SJSAS)*—runs by default. [*Note:* The port number will depend on the server to which you deploy your web application.]

Alternatively, you can press *F5* to build the application, then run it in debug mode—the Netbeans built-in debugger can help you troubleshoot applications. If you type *F6*, the program executes without debugging enabled.

Error-Prevention Tip 22.1

*If you have trouble building your project due to errors in the Netbeans-generated XML files used for building, try cleaning the project and building again. You can do this by selecting **Build > Clean and Build Main Project** or by pressing Shift + F11.*

Finally, you can run your built application by opening a browser window and typing the web page's URL in the **Address** field. Since your application resides on the local file system, you must first start the Sun Java System Application Server. If you have previously run the application using one of the methods above, the server will already be started. Otherwise, you can start the server from the IDE by opening the **Runtime** tab (located in the same panel as the **Projects**), expanding the **Servers** node, right clicking **Sun Java System Application Server 9** and selecting **Start**. Then you can type the URL (including the port number for the application server, 8080) in the browser to execute the application. For this example it is not necessary to type the entire URL, `http://localhost:8080/WebTime/faces/Time.jsp`. The path to the file `Time.jsp` (i.e., `faces/Time.jsp`) can be omitted, because this file was set by default as the project's start page. For projects with multiple pages, you can change the start page by right clicking the desired page in the **Projects** window and selecting **Set As Start Page**. The start page is indicated by a green arrow next to the page's name in the **Projects** window.

22.4 JSF Components

This section introduces some of the JSF components featured in the **Palette** (Fig. 22.6). Figure 22.13 summarizes some of the JSF components used in the chapter examples.

JSF component	Description
Label	Displays text that can be associated with an input element.
Static Text	Displays text that the user cannot edit.
Text Field	Gathers user input and displays text.
Button	Triggers an event when clicked.
Hyperlink	Displays a hyperlink.
Drop Down List	Displays a drop-down list of choices.
Radio Button Group	Groups radio buttons.
Image	Displays images (e.g., GIF and JPG).

Fig. 22.13 | Commonly used JSF components.

22.4.1 Text and Graphics Components

Figure 22.14 displays a simple form for gathering user input. This example uses all the components listed in Fig. 22.13, except `Label`, which you will see in later examples. All the code in Fig. 22.14 was generated by Netbeans in response to actions performed in **Design** mode. This example does not perform any tasks when the user clicks **Register**. In successive examples, we demonstrate how to add functionality to many of these JSF components.

Before discussing the JSF components used in this JSP file, we explain the XHTML that creates the layout in Fig. 22.14. As discussed previously, Netbeans uses absolute positioning, so components are rendered wherever they were dropped in the Visual Editor. In this example, in addition to absolute positioning, we use a ***Grid Panel*** component (lines 37–61) from the **Palette's Layout** component group. The `h:` prefix indicates that it can be found in the JSF HTML tag library. This component, an object of class `HtmlPanelGrid` in package `javax.faces.component.html`, controls the positioning of the components it contains. The **Grid Panel** component allows the designer to specify the number of columns the grid should contain. Components may then be dropped anywhere inside the panel, and they will automatically be repositioned into evenly spaced columns in the order in which they are dropped. When the number of components exceeds the number of columns, the panel moves the additional components to a new row. In this way, the **Grid Panel** behaves like an XHTML table, and is in fact rendered to the browser as an XHTML table. In this example, we use the **Grid Panel** to control the positions of the **Image** and **Text Field** components in the user information section of the page.

```
1    <?xml version = "1.0" encoding = "UTF-8" ?>
2
3    <!-- Fig. 22.14: WebComponents.jsp -->
4    <!-- Registration form that demonstrates JSF components -->
5    <jsp:root version = "1.2"
6       xmlns:f = "http://java.sun.com/jsf/core"
7       xmlns:h = "http://java.sun.com/jsf/html"
8       xmlns:jsp = "http://java.sun.com/JSP/Page"
9       xmlns:webuijsf = "http://www.sun.com/webui/webuijsf">
10      <jsp:directive.page contentType = "text/html;charset=UTF-8"
11         pageEncoding = "UTF-8" />
12      <f:view>
13         <webuijsf:page binding = "#{WebComponents.page1}" id = "page1">
14            <webuijsf:html binding = "#{WebComponents.html1}" id = "html1">
15               <webuijsf:head binding = "#{WebComponents.head1}" id = "head1"
16                  title = "Sample Registration Form">
17                  <webuijsf:link binding = "#{WebComponents.link1}"
18                     id = "link1" url = "/resources/stylesheet.css" />
19               </webuijsf:head>
20               <webuijsf:body binding = "#{WebComponents.body1}" id = "body1"
21                  style = "-rave-layout: grid">
22                  <webuijsf:form binding = "#{WebComponents.form1}"
23                     id = "form1">
24                     <webuijsf:staticText binding = "#{WebComponents.header}"
25                        id = "header" style = "font-size: 18px; left: 24px;
26                        top: 24px; position: absolute; width: 264px"
27                        text = "This is a sample registration form" />
28                     <webuijsf:staticText
29                        binding = "#{WebComponents.instructions}"
30                        id = "instructions" style = "font-size: 12px;
31                        font-style: italic; left: 24px; top: 48px;
32                        position: absolute"
33                        text = "Please fill in all fields and click Register"/>
34                     <webuijsf:image binding = "#{WebComponents.userImage}"
35                        id = "userImage" style = "left: 24px; top: 72px;
36                        position: absolute" url = "/resources/user.JPG" />
37                     <h:panelGrid binding = "#{WebComponents.gridPanel}"
38                        columns = "4" id = "gridPanel" style = "height: 96px;
39                        left: 24px; top: 96px; position: absolute"
40                        width = "576">
41                        <webuijsf:image binding = "#{WebComponents.image1}"
42                           id = "image1" url = "/resources/fname.JPG" />
```

Fig. 22.14 | Registration form that demonstrates JSF components. (Part 1 of 3.)

```
43              <webuijsf:textField
44                 binding = "#{WebComponents.firstNameTextField}"
45                 id = "firstNameTextField" />
46              <webuijsf:image binding = "#{WebComponents.image2}"
47                 id = "image2" url = "/resources/lname.JPG" />
48              <webuijsf:textField
49                 binding = "#{WebComponents.lastNameTextField}"
50                 id = "lastNameTextField" />
51              <webuijsf:image binding = "#{WebComponents.image4}"
52                 id = "image4" url = "/resources/email.JPG" />
53              <webuijsf:textField
54                 binding = "#{WebComponents.emailTextField}"
55                 id = "emailTextField" />
56              <webuijsf:image binding = "#{WebComponents.image3}"
57                 id = "image3" url = "/resources/phone.JPG" />
58              <webuijsf:textField
59                 binding = "#{WebComponents.phoneTextField}"
60                 id = "phoneTextField" />
61           </h:panelGrid>
62           <webuijsf:image binding = "#{WebComponents.image5}"
63              id = "image5" style = "left: 24px; top: 216px;
64              position: absolute"
65              url = "/resources/publications.JPG" />
66           <webuijsf:staticText
67              binding = "#{WebComponents.publicationLabel}"
68              id = "publicationLabel" style = "font-size: 12px;
69              left: 216px; top: 216px; position: absolute"
70              text = "Which book would you like information about?"/>
71        <webuijsf:dropDown
72              binding = "#{WebComponents.booksDropDown}"
73              id = "booksDropDown" items =
74              "#{WebComponents.booksDropDownDefaultOptions.options}"
75              selected= "#{WebComponents.booksDropDownDefaultOptions.
76              selectedValue}" style = "left: 24px; top: 240px;
77              position: absolute" />
78        <webuijsf:radioButtonGroup
79              binding = "#{WebComponents.osRadioGroup}"
80              id = "osRadioGroup" items =
81              "#{WebComponents.osRadioGroupDefaultOptions.options}"
82              selected = "#{WebComponents.osRadioGroupDefaultOptions.
83              selectedValue}" style = "left: 24px; top: 336px;
84              position: absolute" />
85        <webuijsf:button binding =
86              "#{WebComponents.registerButton}" id = "registerButton"
87              style = "left: 23px; top: 480px; position: absolute;
88              width: 100px" text = "Register" />
89           <webuijsf:image binding = "#{WebComponents.image6}"
90              id = "image6" style = "left: 24px; top: 312px;
91              position: absolute" url = "/resources/os.JPG" />
92           <webuijsf:staticText binding = "#{WebComponents.osLabel}"
93              id = "osLabel" style = "font-size: 12px; left: 216px;
94              top: 312px; position: absolute"
95              text = "What operating system are you using?" />
```

Fig. 22.14 | Registration form that demonstrates JSF components. (Part 2 of 3.)

```
 96                              <webuijsf:hyperlink
 97                                  binding = "#{WebComponents.deitelHyperlink}"
 98                                  id = "deitelHyperlink" style = "left: 24px; top: 264px;
 99                                  position: absolute" target = "_blank"
100                                  text = "Click here to learn more about our books"
101                                  url = "http://www.deitel.com" />
102                          </webuijsf:form>
103                      </webuijsf:body>
104                  </webuijsf:html>
105              </webuijsf:page>
106          </f:view>
107     </jsp:root>
```

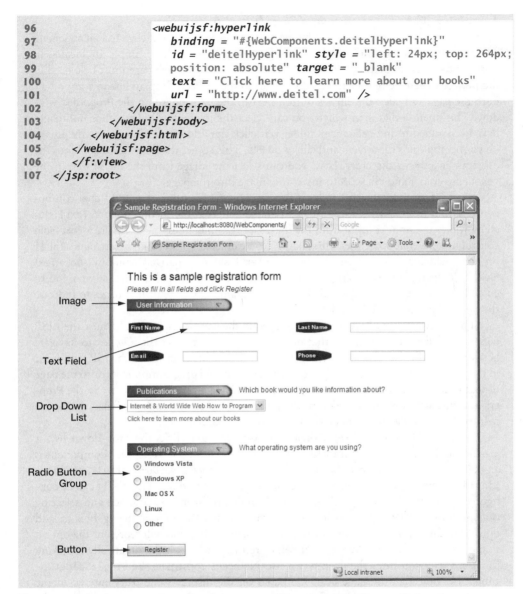

Fig. 22.14 | Registration form that demonstrates JSF components. (Part 3 of 3.)

Adding a Formatting Component to a Web Page

To create the layout for the **User Information** section of the form shown in Fig. 22.14, drag a **Grid Panel** component onto the page. In the **Properties** window, change the component's id to gridPanel and set the component's columns property to 4. The component also has properties to control the cell padding, cell spacing and other elements of the component's appearance. In this case, accept the defaults for these properties. Now you can simply drag the **Image**s and **Text Field**s for user information into the **Grid Panel**. The **Grid Panel** will manage their spacing and their organization into rows and columns.

Examining Web Components on a Sample Registration Form

Lines 34–36 of Fig. 22.14 define an **Image** component, an object of class ImageComponent which inserts an image into a web page. The images used in this example are located in this chapter's examples directory. Images to be displayed on a web page must be placed in the project's resources folder. To add images to the project, drop an **Image** component onto the page and click the ellipsis button next to the **url** property in the **Properties** window. This opens a dialog in which you can select the image to display. Since no images have been added to the resources folder yet, click the **Add File** button, locate the image on your computer's file system and click **Add File**. This copies the file you selected into the project's resources directory. Now you can select the image from the list of files in the resources folder and click **OK** to insert the image into the page.

Lines 37–61 contain an h:panelGrid element representing the **Grid Panel** component. Within this element, there are eight **Image** and **Text Field** components. **Text Field**s allow you to obtain text input from the user. For example, lines 43–45 define a **Text Field** control used to collect the user's first name. You can label a **Text Field** by setting its label property, which places text directly above the **Text Field**. Alternatively, you can label a **Text Field** by dragging and dropping a **Label** component onto the page, which allows you to customize the **Label**'s position and style. In this example, we are using images to indicate the purpose of each **Text Field**.

The order in which **Text Fields** are dragged to the page is important, because their JSP tags are added to the JSP file in that order. When a user presses the *Tab* key to navigate between input fields, they will navigate the fields in the order in which the JSP tags occur in the JSP file. To specify the navigation order, you should drag components onto the page in that order. Alternatively, you can set each input field's tabIndex property in the **Properties** window to control the order in which the user will tab through the fields. A component with a tab index of 1 will be the first in the tab sequence.

Lines 71–77 define a **Drop Down List**. When a user clicks the drop-down list, it expands and displays a list from which the user can make a selection. This component is an object of class DropDown and is bound to the object booksDropDownDefaultOptions, a SingleSelectOptionsList object that controls the list of options. This object can be configured automatically by right clicking the drop-down list in **Design** mode and selecting **Configure Default Options...**, which opens the **Options Customizer** dialog box to add options to the list. Each option consists of a display String that will represent the option in the browser and a value String that will be returned when programmatically retrieving the user's selection from the drop-down list. Netbeans constructs the SingleSelectOptionsList object in the page bean file based on the display-value pairs entered in the **Options Customizer** dialog box. To view the code that constructs the object, close the dialog box by clicking **OK**, open the page bean file, and expand the **Creator-managed Component Definition** node near the top of the file. The object is constructed in the _init method, which is called from method init the first time the page loads.

Lines 78–84 define a **Radio Button Group** component of class RadioButtonGroup, which provides a series of radio buttons from which the user can select only one. Like **Drop Down List**, a **Radio Button Group** is bound to a SingleSelectOptionList object. The options can be edited by right clicking the component and selecting **Configure Default Options....** Also like the drop-down list, the SingleSelectOptionsList is automatically generated by the IDE and placed in the _init method of the page bean class.

Lines 85–88 define a ***Button*** component of class Button that triggers an action when clicked. A **Button** component typically maps to an input XHTML element with attribute type set to submit. As stated earlier, clicking the **Register** button in this example does not do anything.

The ***Hyperlink*** component (lines 96–101) of class Hyperlink adds a link to a web page. The url property of this component specifies the resource (http://www.deitel.com in this case) that is requested when a user clicks the hyperlink. Setting the target property to _blank specifies that the requested web page should open in a new browser window. By default, **Hyperlink** components cause pages to open in the same browser window.

22.4.2 Validation Using Validator Components and Custom Validators

This section introduces form *validation*. Validating user input is an important step in collecting information from users. Validation helps prevent processing errors due to incomplete or improperly formatted user input. For example, you may perform validation to ensure that all required fields have been filled out or that a zip-code field contains exactly five digits. Netbeans provides three validator components. A ***Length Validator*** determines whether a field contains an acceptable number of characters. ***Double Range Validators*** and ***Long Range Validators*** determine whether numeric input falls within acceptable ranges. Package ***javax.faces.validators*** contains the classes for these validators. Netbeans also allows custom validation with validator methods in the page bean file. The following example demonstrates validation using both a validator component and custom validation.

Validating Form Data in a Web Application
The example in this section prompts the user to enter a name, e-mail address and phone number. After the user enters any data, but before the data is sent to the web server, validation ensures that the user entered a value in each field, that the entered name does not exceed 30 characters, and that the e-mail address and phone number values are in an acceptable format. If the client does not have JavaScript enabled, then the validation would be performed on the server. In this example, (555) 123-4567, 555-123-4567 and 123-4567 are all considered valid phone numbers. Once the data is submitted, the web server responds by displaying an appropriate message and a **Grid Panel** component repeating the submitted information. Note that a real business application would typically store the submitted data in a database or in a file on the server. We simply send the data back to the page to demonstrate that the server received the data.

Building the Web Page
This web application introduces two additional JSF components—**Label** and **Message** from the **Basic** section of the **Palette**. Each of the page's three text fields should have its own label and message. ***Label*** components describe other components and can be associated with user input fields by setting their for property. ***Message*** components display error messages when validation fails. This page requires three **Text Fields**, three **Labels** and three **Messages**, as well as a submit **Button**. To associate the **Label** components and **Message** components with their corresponding **Text Field** components, hold the *Ctrl* and *Shift* keys, then drag the label or message to the appropriate **Text Field**. In the **Properties** window, notice that each **Label** and **Message** component's for property is set to the appropriate **Text Field**.

You should also add a **Static Text** component to display a validation success message at the bottom of the page. Set the text to "Thank you for your submission.
We received the following information:" and change the component's id to resultText. In the **Properties** window, unset the component's rendered and escaped properties. The *rendered* property controls whether the component will be displayed the first time the page loads. Setting *escaped* to false enables the browser to recognize the <br/> tag so it can start a new line of text rather than display the characters "<br/>" in the web page.

Finally, add a **Grid Panel** component below the resultText component. The panel should have two columns, one for displaying **Static Text** components that label the user's validated data, and one for displaying **Static Text** components that echo back that data. The panel's rendered property should be set to false so that it is not initialially displayed.

The JSP file for this page is displayed in Fig. 22.15. Lines 34–40, 48–52 and 60–64 define webuijsf:textFields for retrieving the user's name, e-mail address and phone number, respectively. Lines 31–33, 45–47 and 57–59 define webuijsf:labels for each of these text fields. Lines 41–44, 53–56 and 65–68 define the text fields' *webuijsf:message* elements. Lines 69–73 define a **Submit** webuijsf:button. Lines 74–78 create a webuijsf:staticText named resultText that displays the response from the server when the user successfully submits the form, and lines 79–99 define a webuijsf:panelGrid that contains components for echoing validated user input to the browser.

```
1   <?xml version = "1.0" encoding = "UTF-8"?>
2
3   <!-- Fig. 22.15: Validation.jsp -->
4   <!-- JSP that demonstrates validation of user input. -->
5   <jsp:root version = "1.2"
6      xmlns:f = "http://java.sun.com/jsf/core"
7      xmlns:h = "http://java.sun.com/jsf/html"
8      xmlns:jsp = "http://java.sun.com/JSP/Page"
9      xmlns:webuijsf = "http://www.sun.com/webui/webuijsf">
10     <jsp:directive.page contentType = "text/html;charset=UTF-8"
11        pageEncoding = "UTF-8"/>
12     <f:view>
13     <webuijsf:page binding = "#{Validation.page1}" id = "page1">
14        <webuijsf:html binding = "#{Validation.html1}" id = "html1">
15           <webuijsf:head binding = "#{Validation.head1}" id = "head1">
16              <webuijsf:link binding = "#{Validation.link1}" id = "link1"
17                 url = "/resources/stylesheet.css"/>
18           </webuijsf:head>
19           <webuijsf:body binding = "#{Validation.body1}" id = "body1"
20              style = "-rave-layout: grid">
21              <webuijsf:form binding = "#{Validation.form1}" id = "form1">
22                 <webuijsf:staticText binding = "#{Validation.headerText}"
23                    id = "headerText" style = "font-size: 14px; font-weight:
24                    bold; left: 24px; top: 24px; position: absolute"
25                    text = "Please fill out the following form:"/>
26                 <webuijsf:staticText binding =
27                    "#{Validation.instructionText}" id = "instructionText"
28                    style = "font-size: 12px; font-style: italic; left:
```

Fig. 22.15 | JSP that demonstrates validation of user input. (Part 1 of 4.)

```
29        24px; top: 48px; position: absolute" text = "All fields
30        are required and must contain valid information."/>
31    <webuijsf:label binding = "#{Validation.nameLabel}" for =
32        "nameTextField" id = "nameLabel" style = "left: 24px;
33        top: 75px; position: absolute" text = "Name:"/>
34    <webuijsf:textField binding = "#{Validation.nameTextField}"
35        id = "nameTextField" required = "true" style = "left:
36        96px; top: 72px; position: absolute; width: 216px"
37        validatorExpression =
38        "#{Validation.nameLengthValidator.validate}"
39        valueChangeListenerExpression =
40        "#{Validation.nameTextField_processValueChange}"/>
41    <webuijsf:message binding = "#{Validation.nameMessage}"
42        for = "nameTextField" id = "nameMessage" showDetail =
43        "false" showSummary = "true"
44        style = "left: 336px; top: 74px; position: absolute"/>
45    <webuijsf:label binding = "#{Validation.emailLabel}" for =
46        "emailTextField" id = "emailLabel" style = "left: 24px;
47        top: 109px; position: absolute" text = "E-Mail:"/>
48    <webuijsf:textField binding =
49        "#{Validation.emailTextField}" id = "emailTextField"
50        required = "true" style = "left: 96px; top: 106px;
51        position: absolute; width: 216px" validatorExpression =
52        "#{Validation.emailTextField_validate}"/>
53    <webuijsf:message binding = "#{Validation.emailMessage}"
54        for = "emailTextField" id = "emailMessage" showDetail =
55        "false" showSummary = "true" style = "left: 336px; top:
56        108px; position: absolute"/>
57    <webuijsf:label binding = "#{Validation.phoneLabel}" for =
58        "phoneTextField" id = "phoneLabel" style = "left: 24px;
59        top: 143px; position: absolute" text = "Phone:"/>
60    <webuijsf:textField binding =
61        "#{Validation.phoneTextField}" id = "phoneTextField"
62        required = "true" style = "left: 96px; top: 140px;
63        position: absolute; width: 216px" validatorExpression =
64        "#{Validation.phoneTextField_validate}"/>
65    <webuijsf:message binding = "#{Validation.phoneMessage}"
66        for = "phoneTextField" id = "phoneMessage" showDetail =
67        "false" showSummary = "true" style = "left: 336px; top:
68        142px; position: absolute"/>
69    <webuijsf:button actionExpression =
70        "#{Validation.submitButton_action}" binding =
71        "#{Validation.submitButton}" id = "submitButton" style =
72        "left: 23px; top: 192px; position: absolute; width:
73        100px" text = "Submit"/>
74    <webuijsf:staticText binding = "#{Validation.resultText}"
75        escape = "false" id = "resultText" rendered = "false"
76        style = "left: 24px; top: 216px; position: absolute"
77        text = "Thank you for your submission.&lt;br/&gt;We
78        received the following information:"/>
79    <h:panelGrid binding = "#{Validation.resultGridPanel}"
80        columns = "2" id = "resultGridPanel" rendered = "false"
81        style = "border-width: 1px; border-style: solid;
```

Fig. 22.15 | JSP that demonstrates validation of user input. (Part 2 of 4.)

```
82                          background-color: #ffff99; height: 96px; left: 24px;
83                          top: 264px; position: absolute" width = "288">
84                          <webuijsf:staticText binding =
85                              "#{Validation.nameResultLabel}"
86                              id = "nameResultLabel" text = "Name:"/>
87                          <webuijsf:staticText binding =
88                              "#{Validation.nameResult}" id = "nameResult"/>
89                          <webuijsf:staticText binding =
90                              "#{Validation.emailResultLabel}"
91                              id = "emailResultLabel" text = "E-Mail:"/>
92                          <webuijsf:staticText binding =
93                              "#{Validation.emailResult}" id = "emailResult"/>
94                          <webuijsf:staticText binding =
95                              "#{Validation.phoneResultLabel}"
96                              id = "phoneResultLabel" text = "Phone:"/>
97                          <webuijsf:staticText binding =
98                              "#{Validation.phoneResult}" id = "phoneResult"/>
99                      </h:panelGrid>
100                  </webuijsf:form>
101              </webuijsf:body>
102          </webuijsf:html>
103      </webuijsf:page>
104    </f:view>
105  </jsp:root>
```

Fig. 22.15 | JSP that demonstrates validation of user input. (Part 3 of 4.)

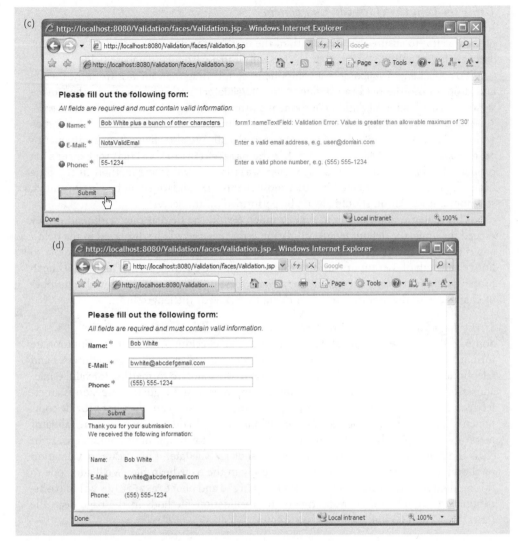

Fig. 22.15 | JSP that demonstrates validation of user input. (Part 4 of 4.)

Setting the Required Property of an Input Component

Ensuring that the user has made a selection or entered some text in a required input element is a basic type of validation. This is accomplished by checking the *required* box in the element's **Properties** window. If you add a validator component or custom validator method to an input field, the field's `required` property must be set to `true` for validation to occur. Notice that each of the three input `webuijsf:textFields` in this example has its `required` property set to `true`. Also note in the Visual Editor that the label for a required field is automatically marked by a red asterisk. If a user submits this form with empty text fields, the default error message for a required field will be displayed in the empty field's associated `webuijsf:message` component. To customize the error message, you must provide a custom validator.

Using the LengthValidator Component

In this example, we use the **Length Validator** component (found in the **Validators** section of the **Palette**) to ensure that the length of the user's name does not exceed 30 characters. This might be useful to ensure that a value will fit in a particular database field.

To add a **Length Validator** to a component, simply drag the validator from the **Palette** and drop it onto the field to validate. A **lengthValidator1** node will appear in the **Outline** window. To edit the validation component's properties, click this node and set the `max-imum` and `minimum` properties to the desired number of characters in the **Properties** window. Here, we set only the `maximum` property to 30. We also changed the component's `id` to `nameLengthValidator`. Notice that the `nameTextField`'s `validationExpression` property has been bound to the `nameLengthValidator`'s `validate` method in the page bean file (lines 37–38). Remember that most client-side validation can be circumvented, so important validation should always be performed on the server.

This validator allows users to type as much text in the field as they wish, and if they exceed the limit, the default length validation error message will be displayed in the field's `webuijsf:message` component after the user clicks the **Submit** button. It is possible to limit the length of user input without using validation. By setting a **Text Field**'s `maxLength` property, the **Text Field**'s cursor will not advance beyond the maximum allowable number of characters, so the user cannot submit data that exceeds the length limit.

Using Regular Expressions to Perform Custom Validation

Some of the most common validation tasks involve checking user input for appropriate formatting. For instance, it may be necessary to check user-entered e-mail addresses and telephone numbers to ensure that they conform to the standard formatting for valid e-mail addresses and phone numbers. Matching user input against a regular expression is an effective way to ensure that the input is properly formatted. Netbeans does not provide components for validation using regular expressions, so we'll add our own custom validator methods to the page bean file. To add a custom validator to an input component, right click the component and select **Edit Event Handler > validate**. This creates a validation method for the component with an empty body in the page bean file. We'll add code to this method shortly. Note that both `emailTextField` and `phoneTextField`'s `validate` attributes are bound to their respective custom validation methods in the page bean file (lines 51–52 and 63–64).

Examining the Page Bean File for a Form That Receives User Input

Figure 22.16 contains the page bean file for the JSP file in Fig. 22.15. Line 31 sets the maximum length for the `nameLengthValidator`, which is a property of this page bean. Recall that the name text field was bound to this property in the JSP file. Method `emailTextField_validate` (lines 410–422) and `phoneTextField_validate` (lines 426–438) are the custom validator methods that verify the user-entered e-mail address and phone number, respectively. The `submitButton_action` method (lines 441–452) echoes the data back to the user if validation succeeds. The validator methods are called before the event handler, so if validation fails, `submitButton_action` will not be called and the user input will not be echoed.

The two custom validator methods in this page bean file validate a text field's contents against a regular expression using the `String` method `match`, which takes a regular expression as an argument and returns `true` if the `String` conforms to the specified format.

```
1    // Fig. 22.16: Validation.java
2    // Validating user input.
3    package validation;
4
5    import com.sun.rave.web.ui.appbase.AbstractPageBean;
6    import com.sun.webui.jsf.component.Body;
7    import com.sun.webui.jsf.component.Button;
8    import com.sun.webui.jsf.component.Form;
9    import com.sun.webui.jsf.component.Head;
10   import com.sun.webui.jsf.component.Html;
11   import com.sun.webui.jsf.component.Label;
12   import com.sun.webui.jsf.component.Link;
13   import com.sun.webui.jsf.component.Message;
14   import com.sun.webui.jsf.component.Page;
15   import com.sun.webui.jsf.component.StaticText;
16   import com.sun.webui.jsf.component.TextField;
17   import javax.faces.FacesException;
18   import javax.faces.application.FacesMessage;
19   import javax.faces.component.UIComponent;
20   import javax.faces.component.html.HtmlPanelGrid;
21   import javax.faces.context.FacesContext;
22   import javax.faces.validator.LengthValidator;
23   import javax.faces.validator.ValidatorException;
24
25   public class Validation extends AbstractPageBean
26   {
27      private int __placeholder;
28
29      private void _init() throws Exception
30      {
31         nameLengthValidator.setMaximum( 30 );
32      } // end method _init
33
34      // To save space, we omitted the code in lines 34-407. The complete
35      // source code is provided with this chapter's examples.
36
408     // validates entered email address against the regular expression
409     // that represents the form of a valid email address.
410     public void emailTextField_validate( FacesContext context,
411        UIComponent component, Object value )
412     {
413        String email = String.valueOf( value );
414
415        // if entered email address is not in a valid format
416        if ( !email.matches(
417           "\\w+([-+.']\\w+)*@\\w+([-.]\\w+)*\\.\\w+([-.]\\w+)*" ) )
418        {
419           throw new ValidatorException( new FacesMessage(
420              "Enter a valid email address, e.g. user@domain.com" ) );
421        } // end if
422     } // end method emailTextField_validate
423
```

Fig. 22.16 | Page bean for validating user input and redisplaying that input if valid. (Part 1 of 2.)

```
424     // validates entered phone number against the regular expression
425     // that represents the form of a valid phone number.
426     public void phoneTextField_validate( FacesContext context,
427        UIComponent component, Object value )
428     {
429        String phone = String.valueOf( value );
430
431        // if entered phone number is not in a valid format
432        if ( !phone.matches(
433           "((\\(\\d{3}\\) ?)|(\\d{3}-))?\\d{3}-\\d{4}" ) )
434        {
435           throw new ValidatorException( new FacesMessage(
436              "Enter a valid phone number, e.g. (555) 555-1234" ) );
437        } // end if
438     } // end method phoneTextField_validate
439
440     // displays the values the user entered
441     public String submitButton_action()
442     {
443        String name = String.valueOf( nameTextField.getValue() );
444        String email = String.valueOf( emailTextField.getValue() );
445        String phone = String.valueOf( phoneTextField.getValue() );
446        nameResult.setValue( name );
447        emailResult.setValue( email );
448        phoneResult.setValue( phone );
449        resultGridPanel.setRendered( true );
450        resultText.setRendered( true );
451        return null;
452     } // end method submitButton_action
453  } // end class Validation
```

Fig. 22.16 | Page bean for validating user input and redisplaying that input if valid. (Part 2 of 2.)

For the emailTextField_validate method, we use the validation expression

```
\w+([-+.']\w+)*@\w+([-.]\w+)*\.\w+([-.]\w+)*
```

Note that each backslash in the regular expression String (line 417) must be escaped with another backslash (as in \\), because the backslash character normally represents the beginning of an escape sequence in Java. This regular expression indicates that an e-mail address is valid if the part before the @ symbol contains one or more word characters (i.e., alphanumeric characters or underscores), followed by zero or more Strings comprised of a hyphen, plus sign, period or apostrophe and additional word characters. After the @ symbol, a valid e-mail address must contain one or more groups of word characters potentially separated by hyphens or periods, followed by a required period and another group of one or more word characters potentially separated by hyphens or periods. For example, the e-mail addresses bob's-personal.email@white.email.com, bob-white@my-email.com and bob.white@email.com are all valid. If the user enters text in emailTextField that does not have the correct format and attempts to submit the form, lines 419–420 throw a ValidatorException. The Message component catches this exception and displays the message in red.

The regular expression in phoneTextField_validate ensures that the phoneTextBox contains a valid phone number before the form is submitted. The user input is matched against the regular expression

$$((\(\(\backslash d\{3\}\backslash)\ ?)|(\backslash d\{3\}-))?\backslash d\{3\}-\backslash d\{4\}$$

(Again, each backslash is escaped in the regular expression String in line 433.) This expression indicates that a phone number can contain a three-digit area code either in parentheses and followed by an optional space or without parentheses and followed by a required hyphen. After an optional area code, a phone number must contain three digits, a hyphen and another four digits. For example, (555) 123-4567, 555-123-4567 and 123-4567 are all valid phone numbers. If a user enters an invalid phone number, lines 435–436 throw a ValidatorException The Message component catches this exception and displays the error message in red.

If all six validators are successful (i.e., each TextField contains data, the name is less than 30 characters and the e-mail address and phone number are valid), clicking the **Submit** button sends the form's data to the server. As shown in Fig. 22.15(d), the submitButton_action method displays the submitted data in a gridPanel (lines 446–449) and a success message in resultsText (line 450).

22.5 Session Tracking

In the early days of the Internet, e-businesses could not provide the kind of customized service typically experienced in "brick-and-mortar" stores. To address this problem, e-businesses began to establish mechanisms by which they could personalize users' browsing experiences, tailoring content to individual users while enabling them to bypass irrelevant information. Businesses achieve this level of service by tracking each customer's movement through their websites and combining the collected data with information provided by the consumer, including billing information, personal preferences, interests and hobbies.

Personalization

Personalization makes it possible for e-businesses to communicate effectively with their customers and also improves the user's ability to locate desired products and services. Companies that provide content of particular interest to users can establish relationships with customers and build on those relationships over time. Furthermore, by targeting consumers with personal offers, recommendations, advertisements, promotions and services, e-businesses create customer loyalty. Websites can use sophisticated technology to allow visitors to customize home pages to suit their individual needs and preferences. Similarly, online shopping sites often store personal information for customers, tailoring notifications and special offers to their interests. Such services encourage customers to visit sites and make purchases more frequently.

Privacy

A trade-off exists, however, between personalized e-business service and protection of privacy. Some consumers embrace the idea of tailored content, but others fear the possible adverse consequences if the info they provide to e-businesses is released or collected by tracking technologies. Consumers and privacy advocates ask: What if the e-business to which we give personal data sells or gives that information to another organization without our knowledge? What if we do not want our actions on the Internet—a supposedly anonymous medium—to be tracked and recorded by unknown parties? What if unauthorized parties gain access to sensitive private data, such as credit card numbers or medical history? All of these are questions that must be debated and addressed by programmers, consumers, e-businesses and lawmakers alike.

Recognizing Clients

To provide personalized services to consumers, e-businesses must be able to recognize clients when they request information from a site. As we have discussed, the request/response system on which the web operates is facilitated by HTTP. Unfortunately, HTTP is a stateless protocol—it does not support persistent connections that would enable web servers to maintain state information regarding particular clients. So, web servers cannot determine whether a request comes from a particular client or whether a series of requests comes from one or several clients. To circumvent this problem, sites can provide mechanisms to identify individual clients. A session represents a unique client on a website. If the client leaves a site and then returns later, the client will still be recognized as the same user. To help the server distinguish among clients, each client must identify itself to the server.

Tracking individual clients, known as *session tracking*, can be achieved in a number of ways in JSPs. One popular technique uses cookies (Section 22.5.1); another uses the `SessionBean` object (Section 22.5.2). Additional session-tracking techniques include using `input form` elements of type `"hidden"` and URL rewriting. With `"hidden"` form elements, a Web Form can write session-tracking data into a `form` in the web page that it returns to the client in response to a prior request. When the user submits the form in the new web page, all the form data, including the `"hidden"` fields, is sent to the form handler on the web server. With URL rewriting, the web server embeds session-tracking information directly in the URLs of hyperlinks that the user clicks to send subsequent requests to the web server.

22.5.1 Cookies

Cookies provide web developers with a tool for personalizing web pages. A cookie is a piece of data typically stored in a text file on the user's computer. A cookie maintains information about the client during and between browser sessions. The first time a user visits the website, the user's computer might receive a cookie; this cookie is then reactivated each time the user revisits that site. The aim is to create an anonymous record containing data that is used to personalize the user's future visits to the site. For example, cookies in a shopping application might store unique identifiers for users. When a user adds items to an online shopping cart or performs another task resulting in a request to the web server, the server receives a cookie from the client containing the user's unique identifier. The server then uses the unique identifier to locate the shopping cart and perform any necessary processing.

In addition to identifying users, cookies also can indicate clients' shopping preferences. When a web server receives a request from a client, the server can examine the cookie(s) it sent to the client during previous communications, identify the client's preferences and immediately display products of interest to the client.

Every HTTP-based interaction between a client and a server includes a header containing information either about the request (when the communication is from the client to the server) or about the response (when the communication is from the server to the client). When a page receives a request, the header includes information such as the request type (e.g., GET or POST) and any cookies that have been sent previously from the server to be stored on the client machine. When the server formulates its response, the header information contains any cookies the server wants to store on the client computer and other information, such as the MIME type of the response.

The *expiration date* of a cookie determines how long the cookie remains on the client's computer. If you do not set an expiration date for a cookie, the web browser maintains the cookie for the duration of the browsing session. Otherwise, the web browser maintains the cookie until the expiration date occurs. When the browser requests a resource from a web server, cookies previously sent to the client by that web server are returned to the web server as part of the request formulated by the browser. Cookies are deleted when they *expire*.

Portability Tip 22.1

Clients may disable cookies in their web browsers for more privacy. When such clients use web applications that depend on cookies to maintain state information, the applications will not execute correctly.

Using Cookies to Provide Book Recommendations

The next web application shows how to use cookies. The example contains two pages. In the first page (Figs. 22.17 and 22.19), users select a favorite programming language from a group of radio buttons and submit the form to the web server for processing. The web server responds by creating a cookie that stores the selected language and the ISBN number for a recommended book on that topic. The server then renders new components in the browser that allow the user either to select another favorite programming language or to view the second page in our application (Figs. 22.20–22.21), which lists recommended books pertaining to the programming language(s) that the user selected. When the user clicks the hyperlink, the cookies previously stored on the client are read and used to form the list of book recommendations.

The JSP file in Fig. 22.17 contains a **Radio Button Group** (lines 26–30) with the options **Java**, **C++**, **Visual Basic 2005**, **Visual C# 2005** and **Internet & Web** (set in the page bean). Recall that you can set the display and value Strings of radio buttons by right clicking the **Radio Button Group** and selecting **Configure Default Options....** The user selects a programming language by clicking a radio button. When the user presses **Submit**, the web application creates a cookie containing the selected language. This cookie is added to the HTTP response header and sent to the client as part of the response.

```
I    <?xml version = "1.0" encoding = "UTF-8"?>
2
3    <!-- Fig. 22.17: Options.jsp -->
4    <!-- JSP file that allows the user to select a programming language -->
5    <jsp:root version = "1.2"
6       xmlns:f = "http://java.sun.com/jsf/core"
```

Fig. 22.17 | JSP file that allows the user to select a programming language. (Part 1 of 4.)

```
7        xmlns:h = "http://java.sun.com/jsf/html"
8        xmlns:jsp = "http://java.sun.com/JSP/Page"
9        xmlns:webuijsf = "http://www.sun.com/webui/webuijsf">
10       <jsp:directive.page contentType = "text/html;charset=UTF-8"
11          pageEncoding = "UTF-8"/>
12       <f:view>
13       <webuijsf:page binding = "#{Options.page1}" id = "page1">
14          <webuijsf:html binding = "#{Options.html1}" id = "html1">
15             <webuijsf:head binding = "#{Options.head1}" id = "head1">
16                <webuijsf:link binding = "#{Options.link1}" id = "link1"
17                   url = "/resources/stylesheet.css"/>
18             </webuijsf:head>
19             <webuijsf:body binding = "#{Options.body1}" id = "body1"
20                style = "-rave-layout: grid">
21                <webuijsf:form binding = "#{Options.form1}" id = "form1">
22                   <webuijsf:staticText binding = "#{Options.instructionText}"
23                      id = "instructionText" style = "font-size: 18px;
24                      left: 24px; top: 24px; position: absolute"
25                      text = "Select a programming language:"/>
26                   <webuijsf:radioButtonGroup binding =
27                      "#{Options.languageRadioGroup}" id =
28                      "languageRadioGroup" items =
29                      "#{Options.languageRadioGroupDefaultOptions.options}"
30                      style = "left: 24px; top: 48px; position: absolute"/>
31                   <webuijsf:button actionExpression =
32                      "#{Options.submitButton_action}" binding =
33                      "#{Options.submitButton}" id = "submitButton" style =
34                      "left: 23px; top: 192px; position: absolute;
35                      width: 100px" text = "Submit"/>
36                   <webuijsf:staticText binding = "#{Options.responseText}"
37                      id = "responseText" rendered = "false" style =
38                      "font-size: 18px; left: 24px; top: 24px;
39                      position: absolute"/>
40                   <webuijsf:hyperlink actionExpression =
41                      "#{Options.languagesLink_action}" binding =
42                      "#{Options.languagesLink}" id = "languagesLink"
43                      rendered = "false" style = "left: 24px; top: 72px;
44                      position: absolute" text =
45                      "Click here to choose another language."/>
46                   <webuijsf:hyperlink actionExpression =
47                      "#{Options.recommendationsLink_action}" binding =
48                      "#{Options.recommendationsLink}" id =
49                      "recommendationsLink" rendered = "false" style =
50                      "left: 24px; top: 96px; position: absolute"
51                      text = "Click here to get book recommendations."
52                      url = "/faces/Recommendations.jsp"/>
53                </webuijsf:form>
54             </webuijsf:body>
55          </webuijsf:html>
56       </webuijsf:page>
57       </f:view>
58    </jsp:root>
```

Fig. 22.17 | JSP file that allows the user to select a programming language. (Part 2 of 4.)

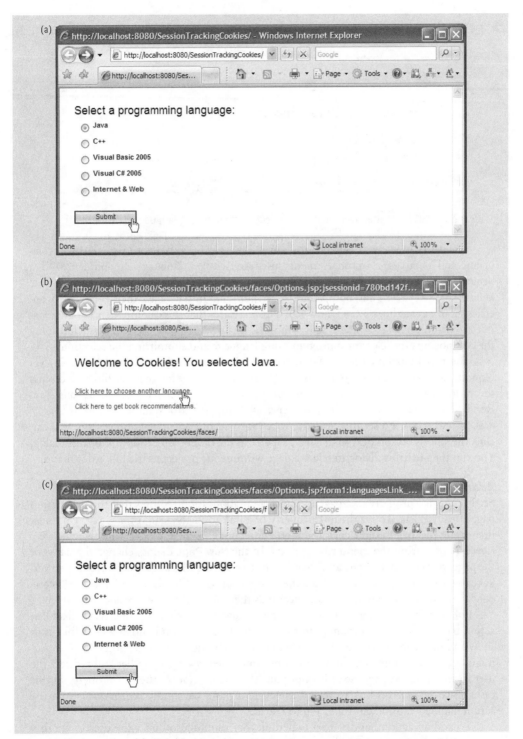

Fig. 22.17 | JSP file that allows the user to select a programming language. (Part 3 of 4.)

Fig. 22.17 | JSP file that allows the user to select a programming language. (Part 4 of 4.)

When the user clicks **Submit**, the webuijsf:staticText, webuijsf:radioButton-Group and webuijsf:button elements used to select a language are hidden, and a webuijsf:staticText and two webuijsf:hyperlink elements are displayed. One webuijsf:staticText and both webuijsf:hyperlinks initially have their rendered properties set to false (lines 37, 43, and 49). This indicates that these components are not visible the first time the page loads, as we want the user's first view of the page to include only the components for selecting a programming language and submitting the selection.

The first hyperlink (lines 40–45) requests this page, and the second (lines 46–52) requests Recommendations.jsp. The url property is not set for the first link; we discuss this momentarily. The second link's url property is set to /faces/Recommendations.jsp. Recall that earlier in the chapter, we set a url property to a remote website (http://www.deitel.com). To set this property to a page within the current application, you can click the ellipsis button next to the url property in the **Properties** window to open a dialog. You can then use this dialog to select a page within your project as the link's destination.

Adding and Linking to a New Web Page

Setting the url property to a page in the current application requires that the destination page already exists. To set the url property of a link to Recommendations.jsp, you must first create this page. Right click the **Web Pages** node in the **Projects** window and select **New > Page...** from the menu that appears. In the **New Page** dialog, change the name of the page to Recommendations and click **Finish** to create the files Recommendations.jsp and Recommendations.java. (We discuss the contents of these files shortly.) Once the Recommendations.jsp file exists, you can select it as the url value for recommendationsLink.

For Options.jsp, rather than setting the languagesLink's url property, we'll add an action handler for this component to the page bean. The action handler will enable us to show and hide components of the page without redirecting the user to another page. Specifying a destination url would override the component's action handler and redirect the user to the specified page, so it is important that we do not set the url property in this case. Since we use this link to reload the current page, we simply return null from the action handler, causing Options.jsp to reload.

To add an action handler to a hyperlink that should also direct the user to another page, you must add a rule to the **Page Navigation** file (Fig. 22.18). To edit this file, right

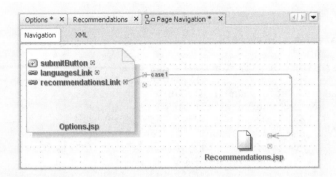

Fig. 22.18 | Editing the **Page Navigation** file.

click anywhere in the Visual Designer and select **Page Navigation**. Click Options.jsp in the navigation designer to display its components that might cause the page to request another page. Locate the link whose navigation rule you would like to set (recommendationsLink in this case) and drag it to the destination page. Now the link can direct the user to a new page (Recommendations.jsp) without overriding its action handler. Editing the **Page Navigation** file is also useful when you would like action elements that cannot specify a url property, such as buttons, to direct users to another page. You'll configure a link from Recommendations.asp to Options.jsp later in this section.

Figure 22.19 contains the code that writes a cookie to the client machine when the user selects a programming language. The file also determines which components appear on the page, displaying either the components for choosing a language or the links for navigating the application, depending on the user's actions.

```
 I   // Fig. 22.19: Options.java
 2   // Page bean that stores user's language selection as a client cookie.
 3   package sessiontrackingcookies;
 4
 5   import com.sun.rave.web.ui.appbase.AbstractPageBean;
 6   import com.sun.webui.jsf.component.Body;
 7   import com.sun.webui.jsf.component.Button;
 8   import com.sun.webui.jsf.component.Form;
 9   import com.sun.webui.jsf.component.Head;
10   import com.sun.webui.jsf.component.Html;
11   import com.sun.webui.jsf.component.Hyperlink;
12   import com.sun.webui.jsf.component.Link;
13   import com.sun.webui.jsf.component.Page;
14   import com.sun.webui.jsf.component.RadioButtonGroup;
15   import com.sun.webui.jsf.component.StaticText;
16   import com.sun.webui.jsf.model.SingleSelectOptionsList;
17   import java.util.Properties;
18   import javax.faces.FacesException;
19   import javax.servlet.http.Cookie;
20   import javax.servlet.http.HttpServletResponse;
21
```

Fig. 22.19 | Page bean that stores the user's language selection in a client cookie. (Part 1 of 3.)

```
22    public class Options extends AbstractPageBean
23    {
24       private int __placeholder;
25
26       private void _init() throws Exception
27       {
28          languageRadioGroupDefaultOptions.setOptions(
29             new com.sun.webui.jsf.model.Option[] {
30                new com.sun.webui.jsf.model.Option( "Java", "Java" ),
31                new com.sun.webui.jsf.model.Option( "C++", "C++" ),
32                new com.sun.webui.jsf.model.Option( "Visual-Basic-2005",
33                   "Visual Basic 2005" ),
34                new com.sun.webui.jsf.model.Option( "Visual-C#-2005",
35                   "Visual C# 2005" ),
36                new com.sun.webui.jsf.model.Option( "Internet-&-Web",
37                   "Internet & Web" )
38             } // end array initializer
39          ); // end call to setOptions
40       } // end method _init
41
42       // To save space, we omitted the code in lines 42-199. The complete
43       // source code is provided with this chapter's examples.
44
200      private Properties books = new Properties();
201
202      // Construct a new page bean instance and initialize the properties
203      // that map languages to ISBN numbers of recommended books.
204      public Options()
205      {
206         // initialize the Properties object of values to be stored as
207         // cookies.
208         books.setProperty( "Java", "0132222205" );
209         books.setProperty( "C++", "0136152503" );
210         books.setProperty( "Visual Basic 2005", "0131869000" );
211         books.setProperty( "Visual C# 2005", "0131525239" );
212         books.setProperty( "Internet & Web", "0131752421" );
213      } // end Options constructor
214
215      // To save space, we omitted the code in lines 215-257. The complete
216      // source code is provided with this chapter's examples.
217
258      // Action handler for the Submit button. Checks whether a language
259      // was selected and, if so, registers a cookie for that language and
260      // sets the responseText to indicate the chosen language.
261      public String submitButton_action()
262      {
263         String msg = "Welcome to Cookies! You ";
264
265         // if the user made a selection
266         if ( languageRadioGroup.getSelected() != null )
267         {
268            String language = languageRadioGroup.getSelected().toString();
269            msg += "selected " + language.replace( '-', ' ' ) + ".";
```

Fig. 22.19 | Page bean that stores the user's language selection in a client cookie. (Part 2 of 3.)

```
270
271            // get ISBN number of book for the given language
272            String ISBN = books.getProperty( language );
273
274            // create cookie using language-ISBN name-value pair
275            Cookie cookie = new Cookie( language, ISBN );
276
277            // add cookie to response header to place it on user's machine
278            HttpServletResponse response =
279               ( HttpServletResponse ) getExternalContext().getResponse();
280            response.addCookie( cookie );
281         } // end if
282         else
283            msg += "did not select a language.";
284
285         responseText.setValue( msg );
286         languageRadioGroup.setRendered( false );
287         instructionText.setRendered( false );
288         submitButton.setRendered( false );
289         responseText.setRendered( true );
290         languagesLink.setRendered( true );
291         recommendationsLink.setRendered( true );
292         return null; // reloads the page
293      } // end method submitButton_action
294
295      // redisplay the components for selecting a language
296      public String languagesLink_action()
297      {
298         responseText.setRendered( false );
299         languagesLink.setRendered( false );
300         recommendationsLink.setRendered( false );
301         languageRadioGroup.setRendered( true );
302         instructionText.setRendered( true );
303         submitButton.setRendered( true );
304         return null;
305      } // end method languagesLink_action
306 } // end class Options
```

Fig. 22.19 | Page bean that stores the user's language selection in a client cookie. (Part 3 of 3.)

As mentioned previously, the _init method handles component initialization. Since this page contains a RadioButtonGroup object that requires initialization, method _init (lines 26–40) constructs an array of Option objects to be displayed by the buttons.

Lines 208–212 in the constructor initialize a Properties object—a data structure that stores String key/value pairs. The application uses the key to store and retrieve the associated value in the Properties object. In this example, the keys are Strings containing the programming language names, and the values are Strings containing the ISBN numbers for the recommended books. Class Properties provides method set-Property, which takes as arguments a key and a value. A value that is added via method setProperty is placed in the Properties at a location determined by the key. The value for a specific Properties entry can be determined by invoking the method getProperty on the Properties object with that value's key as an argument.

Software Engineering Observation 22.1

Netbeans can automatically import any missing packages your Java file needs. For example, after adding the Properties *object to* Options.java, *you can right click in the Java editor window and select* **Fix Imports** *to automatically import* java.util.Properties.

Clicking **Submit** invokes the event handler submitButton_action (lines 261–293), which displays a message indicating the selected language in the responseText element and adds a new cookie to the response. If a language was selected (line 266), the selected item is retrieved (line 268). Line 269 adds the selected language to the results message.

Line 272 retrieves the ISBN for the selected language from the books Properties objectc. Then line 275 creates a new Cookie object (in package javax.servlet.http), using the selected language as the cookie's name and a corresponding ISBN as the cookie's value. This cookie is added to the HTTP response header in lines 278–280. An object of class HttpServletResponse (from package javax.servlet.http) represents the response. This object can be accessed by invoking the method getExternalContext on the page bean, then invoking getResponse on the resulting object. If a language was not selected, line 283 sets the results message to indicate that no selection was made.

Lines 285–291 control the appearance of the page after the user clicks **Submit**. Line 285 sets the responseText to display the String msg. Since the user has just submitted a language selection, the components used to collect the selection are hidden (lines 286–288) and responseText and the links used to navigate the application are displayed (lines 289–291). The action handler returns null at line 292, which reloads Options.jsp.

Lines 296–305 contain the languagesLink's event handler. When the user clicks this link, responseText and the two links are hidden (lines 298–300), and the components that allow the user to select a language are redisplayed (lines 301–303). The method returns null at line 304, causing Options.jsp to reload.

Displaying Book Recommendations Based on Cookie Values
After clicking **Submit**, the user may request a book recommendation. The book recommendations hyperlink forwards the user to Recommendations.jsp (Fig. 22.20) to display recommendations based on the user's language selections.

```
1    <?xml version = "1.0" encoding = "UTF-8"?>
2
3    <!-- Fig. 22.20: Recommendations.jsp -->
4    <!-- Displays book recommendations using cookies -->
5    <jsp:root version = "1.2"
6       xmlns:f = "http://java.sun.com/jsf/core"
7       xmlns:h = "http://java.sun.com/jsf/html"
8       xmlns:jsp = "http://java.sun.com/JSP/Page"
9       xmlns:webuijsf = "http://www.sun.com/webui/webuijsf">
10      <jsp:directive.page contentType = "text/html;charset=UTF-8"
11         pageEncoding = "UTF-8"/>
12      <f:view>
13      <webuijsf:page binding = "#{Recommendations.page1}" id = "page1">
14         <webuijsf:html binding = "#{Recommendations.html1}" id = "html1">
15            <webuijsf:head binding = "#{Recommendations.head1}" id = "head1">
```

Fig. 22.20 | JSP file that displays book recommendations based on cookies. (Part 1 of 2.)

```
16          <webuijsf:link binding = "#{Recommendations.link1}"
17             id = "link1" url = "/resources/stylesheet.css"/>
18          </webuijsf:head>
19          <webuijsf:body binding = "#{Recommendations.body1}"
20             id = "body1" style = "-rave-layout: grid">
21             <webuijsf:form binding = "#{Recommendations.form1}"
22                id = "form1">
23                <webuijsf:label binding =
24                   "#{Recommendations.recommendationsLabel}" for =
25                   "recommendationsListbox" id = "recommendationsLabel"
26                   style = "font-size: 18px; left: 24px; top: 24px;
27                   position: absolute" text = "Recommendations"/>
28                <webuijsf:listbox binding =
29                   "#{Recommendations.recommendationsListbox}" id =
30                   "recommendationsListbox" items = "#{Recommendations.
31                   recommendationsListboxDefaultOptions.options}"
32                   style = "height: 96px; left: 24px; top: 48px;
33                   position: absolute; width: 360px"/>
34                <webuijsf:hyperlink actionExpression =
35                   "#{Recommendations.optionsLink_action}" binding =
36                   "#{Recommendations.optionsLink}" id = "optionsLink"
37                   style = "left: 24px; top: 168px; position: absolute"
38                   text = "Click here to choose another language."/>
39             </webuijsf:form>
40          </webuijsf:body>
41       </webuijsf:html>
42    </webuijsf:page>
43    </f:view>
44 </jsp:root>
```

Fig. 22.20 | JSP file that displays book recommendations based on cookies. (Part 2 of 2.)

Recommendations.jsp contains a **Label** (lines 23–27), a **Listbox** (lines 28–33) and a **Hyperlink** (lines 34–38). The **Label** displays the text Recommendations at the top of the page. A ***Listbox*** component displays a list of options from which a user can make multiple selections. The **Listbox** in this example displays the recommendations created by the Recommendations.java page bean (Fig. 22.21), or the text "No Recommendations. Please select a language." The **Hyperlink** allows the user to return to Options.jsp to select additional languages. You can configure this hyperlink using the **Page Navigation** file as described earlier in this section.

Page Bean That Creates Book Recommendations from Cookies

In Recommendations.java (Fig. 22.21), method prerender (lines 180–210) retrieves the cookies from the client, using the request object's getCookies method (lines 183–185). An object of class HttpServletRequest (from package javax.servlet.http) represents the request. This object can be obtained by invoking method getExternalContext on the page bean, then invoking getRequest on the resulting object. The call to getCookies returns an array of the cookies previously written to the client. Cookies can be read by an application only if they were created by a server in the domain in which the application is running—a web server cannot access cookies created by servers in other domains. For example, a cookie created by a web server in the deitel.com domain cannot be read by a web server in any other domain.

```
1    // Fig. 22.21: Recommendations.java
2    // Displays book recommendations based on cookies storing user's selected
3    // programming languages.
4    package sessiontrackingcookies;
5
6    import com.sun.rave.web.ui.appbase.AbstractPageBean;
7    import com.sun.webui.jsf.component.Body;
8    import com.sun.webui.jsf.component.Form;
9    import com.sun.webui.jsf.component.Head;
10   import com.sun.webui.jsf.component.Html;
11   import com.sun.webui.jsf.component.Hyperlink;
12   import com.sun.webui.jsf.component.Label;
13   import com.sun.webui.jsf.component.Link;
14   import com.sun.webui.jsf.component.Listbox;
15   import com.sun.webui.jsf.component.Page;
16   import com.sun.webui.jsf.component.StaticText;
17   import com.sun.webui.jsf.model.DefaultOptionsList;
18   import com.sun.webui.jsf.model.Option;
19   import javax.faces.FacesException;
20   import javax.servlet.http.Cookie;
21   import javax.servlet.http.HttpServletRequest;
22
23   public class Recommendations extends AbstractPageBean
24   {
25      private int __placeholder;
26
27      private void _init() throws Exception
28      {
29         recommendationsListboxDefaultOptions.setOptions(
30            new com.sun.webui.jsf.model.Option[] {} );
31      }
32
```

Fig. 22.21 | Page bean that displays book recommendations based on cookies storing user's selected languages. (Part 1 of 2.)

```
33     // To save space, we omitted the code in lines 33-178. The complete
34     // source code is provided with this chapter's examples.
35
179    // displays the book recommendations in the Listbox
180    public void prerender()
181    {
182        // retrieve client's cookies
183        HttpServletRequest request =
184            ( HttpServletRequest ) getExternalContext().getRequest();
185        Cookie [] cookies = request.getCookies();
186
187        // if there are cookies, store the corresponding books and ISBN
188        // numbers in an array of Options
189        Option [] recommendations;
190
191        if ( cookies.length > 1 )
192        {
193            recommendations = new Option[ cookies.length - 1 ];
194
195            for ( int i = 0; i < cookies.length - 1; i++ )
196            {
197                String language = cookies[ i ].getName().replace( '-', ' ' );
198                recommendations[ i ] = new Option( language +
199                    " How to Program.  ISBN#: " + cookies[ i ].getValue() );
200            } // end for
201        } // end if
202        else
203        {
204            recommendations = new Option[ 1 ];
205            recommendations[ 0 ] = new Option(
206                "No recommendations. Please select a language." ) ;
207        } // end else
208
209        recommendationsListbox.setItems( recommendations );
210    } // end method prerender
211
212    // To save space, we omitted the code in lines 212-230. The complete
213    // source code is provided with this chapter's examples.
214
231    // redirects user to Options.jsp
232    public String optionsLink_action()
233    {
234        return "case1"; // returns to Options.jsp
235    } // end method optionsLink_action
236 } // end class Recommendations
```

Fig. 22.21 | Page bean that displays book recommendations based on cookies storing user's selected languages. (Part 2 of 2.)

Line 191 determines whether at least one cookie exists. Lines 195–200 add the information in the cookie(s) to an Option array. Arrays of Option objects can be displayed as a list of items in a **Listbox** component. The loop retrieves the name and value of each cookie, using the control variable to determine the current value in the cookie array. If no language was selected, lines 204–206 add to an Options array a message instructing the user to select a language. Line 209 sets recommendationsListBox to display the resulting Options array. We summarize commonly used Cookie methods in Fig. 22.22.

Method	Description
getDomain	Returns a String containing the cookie's domain (i.e., the domain from which the cookie was written). This determines which web servers can receive the cookie. By default, cookies are sent to the web server that originally sent the cookie to the client. Changing the Domain property causes the cookie to be returned to a web server other than the one that originally wrote it.
getMaxAge	Returns an int indicating how many seconds the cookie will persist on the browser. This is –1 by default, meaning the cookie will persist until the browser is shut down.
getName	Returns a String containing the cookie's name.
getPath	Returns a String containing the path to a directory on the server to which the cookie applies. Cookies can be "targeted" to specific directories on the web server. By default, a cookie is returned only to applications operating in the same directory as the application that sent the cookie or a subdirectory of that directory. Changing the Path property causes the cookie to be returned to a directory other than the one from which it was originally written.
getSecure	Returns a bool value indicating whether the cookie should be transmitted through a secure protocol. The value true causes a secure protocol to be used.
getValue	Returns a String containing the cookie's value.

Fig. 22.22 | `javax.servlet.http.Cookie` methods.

22.5.2 Session Tracking with the SessionBean Object

You can also perform session tracking with the SessionBean class that is provided in each web application created with Netbeans. When a web page in the project is requested, a SessionBean object is created. Properties of this object can be accessed throughout a browser session by invoking the method getSessionBean on the page bean. To demonstrate session-tracking techniques using the SessionBean, we modified the page bean files in Figs. 22.19 and 22.21 so that they use the SessionBean to store the user's selected languages. We begin with the updated Options.jsp file (Fig. 22.23). Figure 22.26 presents the SessionBean.java file, and Fig. 22.27 presents the modified page bean file for Options.jsp.

The Options.jsp file in Fig. 22.23 is similar to that presented in Fig. 22.17 for the cookies example. Lines 40–48 define two webuijsf:staticText elements that were not present in the cookies example. The first element displays the text "Number of selections so far:". The second element's text attribute is bound to property numSelections in the SessionBean (line 48). We discuss how to bind the text attribute to a SessionBean property momentarily.

```
 1   <?xml version = "1.0" encoding = "UTF-8"?>
 2
 3   <!-- Fig. 22.23: Options.jsp -->
 4   <!-- JSP file that allows the user to select a programming language -->
 5   <jsp:root version = "1.2"
 6      xmlns:f = "http://java.sun.com/jsf/core"
 7      xmlns:h = "http://java.sun.com/jsf/html"
 8      xmlns:jsp = "http://java.sun.com/JSP/Page"
 9      xmlns:webuijsf = "http://www.sun.com/webui/webuijsf">
10      <jsp:directive.page contentType = "text/html;charset=UTF-8"
11         pageEncoding = "UTF-8"/>
12      <f:view>
13         <webuijsf:page binding = "#{Options.page1}" id = "page1">
14            <webuijsf:html binding = "#{Options.html1}" id = "html1">
15               <webuijsf:head binding = "#{Options.head1}" id = "head1">
16                  <webuijsf:link binding = "#{Options.link1}" id = "link1"
17                     url = "/resources/stylesheet.css"/>
18               </webuijsf:head>
19               <webuijsf:body binding = "#{Options.body1}" id = "body1"
20                  style = "-rave-layout: grid">
21                  <webuijsf:form binding = "#{Options.form1}" id = "form1">
22                     <webuijsf:staticText binding = "#{Options.instructionText}"
23                        id = "instructionText" style = "font-size: 18px;
24                        left: 24px; top: 24px; position: absolute"
25                        text = "Select a programming language:"/>
26                     <webuijsf:radioButtonGroup binding =
27                        "#{Options.languageRadioGroup}" id =
28                        "languageRadioGroup" items =
29                        "#{Options.languageRadioGroupDefaultOptions.options}"
30                        style = "left: 24px; top: 48px; position: absolute"/>
31                     <webuijsf:button actionExpression =
32                        "#{Options.submitButton_action}" binding =
33                        "#{Options.submitButton}" id = "submitButton" style =
34                        "left: 23px; top: 192px; position: absolute;
35                        width: 100px" text = "Submit"/>
36                     <webuijsf:staticText binding = "#{Options.responseText}"
37                        id = "responseText" rendered = "false" style =
38                        "font-size: 18px; left: 24px; top: 24px;
39                        position: absolute"/>
40                     <webuijsf:staticText binding = "#{Options.selectionsText}"
41                        id = "selectionsText" rendered = "false" style =
42                        "position: absolute; left: 24px; top: 72px" text =
43                        "Number of selections so far:"/>
44                     <webuijsf:staticText binding =
45                        "#{Options.selectionsValueText}" id =
46                        "selectionsValueText" rendered = "false" style =
47                        "left: 168px; top: 72px; position: absolute"
48                        text = "#{SessionBean1.numSelections}"/>
49                     <webuijsf:hyperlink actionExpression =
50                        "#{Options.languagesLink_action}" binding =
51                        "#{Options.languagesLink}" id = "languagesLink"
52                        rendered = "false" style = "left: 24px; top: 120px;
```

Fig. 22.23 | JSP file that allows the user to select a programming language. (Part 1 of 3.)

```
53                         position: absolute"
54                     text = "Click here to choose another language."/>
55                 <webuijsf:hyperlink actionExpression =
56                     "#{Options.recommendationsLink_action}" binding =
57                     "#{Options.recommendationsLink}" id =
58                     "recommendationsLink" rendered = "false" style =
59                     "left: 24px; top: 144px; position: absolute"
60                     text = "Click here to get book recommendations."
61                     url = "/faces/Recommendations.jsp"/>
62             </webuijsf:form>
63         </webuijsf:body>
64      </webuijsf:html>
65   </webuijsf:page>
66   </f:view>
67 </jsp:root>
```

Fig. 22.23 | JSP file that allows the user to select a programming language. (Part 2 of 3.)

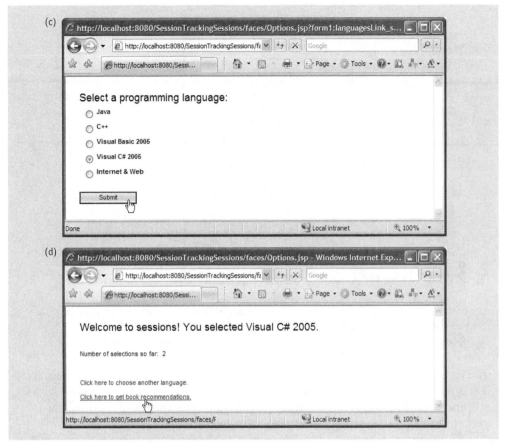

Fig. 22.23 | JSP file that allows the user to select a programming language. (Part 3 of 3.)

Adding Properties to the SessionBean

In this example, we use session tracking to store not only the user's selected languages, but also the number of selections made. To store this information in the SessionBean, we add properties to the SessionBean class.

To add a property that will store the number of selections so far, right click the SessionBean1 node in the **Outline** window and select **Add > Property** to display the **New Property Pattern** dialog (Fig. 22.24). This dialog allows you to add primitive, String or primitive type-wrapper (e.g., Integer, Double) properties to the SessionBean. Add an int property named numSelections and click **OK** to accept the default settings for this property. Open the SessionBean file, and at the bottom of the source code you'll see a new property definition, a *get* method and *set* method for numSelections.

Property numSelections is manipulated in the page bean file to store the number of languages the user selected. To display the value of this property in the selectionsValue-Text element in the JSP file, right click the element in the **Outline** window and select **Bind to Data....** In the **Bind to Data** dialog (Fig. 22.25), select the **Bind to an Object** tab, locate property numSelections under the SessionBean1 node and click **OK**. The **Static Text** element will now always display the value of SessionBean1's numSelections property. If the

Fig. 22.24 | **New Property** dialog for adding a property to the `SessionBean`.

property's value changes, the text changes as well, so that you need not programmatically set the text in the page bean file.

Now that we've added a property to store the number of selections in the `SessionBean1`, we must add a second property to store the selections themselves. We'd like to store selections as key/value pairs of the selected language and the ISBN number of a related book, similar to the way selections were stored using cookies. To do this, we add a `Properties` object named `selectedLanguages` to the `SessionBean`. We manually added this property to the `SessionBean` file, but you can add it using the **New Property** dialog in Fig. 22.24. Simply type `java.util.Properties` in the **Type** drop-down list's field, configure the property and click **OK**. The modified `SessionBean` file (after the two properties have been added) is displayed in Fig. 22.26.

Fig. 22.25 | Bind to Data dialog.

```java
 1   // Fig. 22.26: SessionBean.java
 2   // SessionBean file for storing language selections.
 3   package sessiontrackingsessions;
 4
 5   import com.sun.rave.web.ui.appbase.AbstractSessionBean;
 6   import javax.faces.FacesException;
 7
 8   public class SessionBean1 extends AbstractSessionBean
 9   {
10      // To save space, we omitted the code in lines 10-52. The complete
11      // source code is provided with this chapter's examples.
12
53      // holds value of property numSelections
54      private int numSelections;
55
56      // returns value of numSelections
57      public int getNumSelections()
58      {
59         return this.numSelections;
60      } // end method getNumSelections
61
62      // sets new value of numSelections
63      public void setNumSelections(int numSelections)
64      {
65         this.numSelections = numSelections;
66      } // end method setNumSelections
67
68      // holds value of property selectedLanguages
69      private java.util.Properties selectedLanguages =
70         new java.util.Properties();
71
72      // returns selectedLanguages
73      public java.util.Properties getSelectedLanguages()
74      {
75         return this.selectedLanguages;
76      } // end method getSelectedLanguages
77
78      // sets new value of property selectedLanguages
79      public void setSelectedLanguages(
80         java.util.Properties selectedLanguages )
81      {
82         this.selectedLanguages = selectedLanguages;
83      } // end method setSelectedLanguages
84   } // end class SessionBean1
```

Fig. 22.26 | SessionBean file for storing language selections.

Line 54 declares the numSelections property, and lines 57–60 and 63–66 declare its *get* and *set* methods, respectively. This portion of the code was generated automatically when we used the **New Property** dialog. Lines 69–70 define the Properties object selectedLanguages that will store user selections. Lines 73–76 and 79–83 are the *get* and *set* methods for this property.

Manipulating SessionBean Properties in a Page Bean File

The page bean file for the Options.jsp page is displayed in Fig. 22.27. Because much of this example is identical to the preceding one, we concentrate on the new features.

```java
1    // Fig. 22.27: Options.java
2    // Page bean that stores language selections in a SessionBean property.
3    package sessiontrackingsessions;
4
5    import com.sun.rave.web.ui.appbase.AbstractPageBean;
6    import com.sun.webui.jsf.component.Body;
7    import com.sun.webui.jsf.component.Button;
8    import com.sun.webui.jsf.component.Form;
9    import com.sun.webui.jsf.component.Head;
10   import com.sun.webui.jsf.component.Html;
11   import com.sun.webui.jsf.component.Hyperlink;
12   import com.sun.webui.jsf.component.Link;
13   import com.sun.webui.jsf.component.Page;
14   import com.sun.webui.jsf.component.RadioButtonGroup;
15   import com.sun.webui.jsf.component.StaticText;
16   import com.sun.webui.jsf.model.SingleSelectOptionsList;
17   import java.util.Properties;
18   import javax.faces.FacesException;
19   import javax.servlet.http.Cookie;
20   import javax.servlet.http.HttpServletResponse;
21
22   public class Options extends AbstractPageBean
23   {
24      private int __placeholder;
25
26      private void _init() throws Exception
27      {
28         languageRadioGroupDefaultOptions.setOptions(
29            new com.sun.webui.jsf.model.Option[] {
30               new com.sun.webui.jsf.model.Option( "Java", "Java" ),
31               new com.sun.webui.jsf.model.Option( "C++", "C++" ),
32               new com.sun.webui.jsf.model.Option( "Visual Basic 2005",
33                  "Visual Basic 2005" ),
34               new com.sun.webui.jsf.model.Option( "Visual C# 2005",
35                  "Visual C# 2005" ),
36               new com.sun.webui.jsf.model.Option( "Internet & Web",
37                  "Internet & Web")
38            } // end array initializer
39         ); // end call to setOptions
40      } // end method _init
41
42      // To save space, we omitted the code in lines 42-225. The complete
43      // source code is provided with this chapter's examples.
44
226      // Construct a new page bean instance and initialize the properties
227      // that map languages to ISBN numbers of recommended books.
228      public Options()
229      {
```

Fig. 22.27 | Page bean that stores language selections in a SessionBean property. (Part 1 of 3.)

```
230            // initialize the Properties object of values to be stored
231            // in the session
232            books.setProperty( "Java", "0132222205" );
233            books.setProperty( "C++", "0136152503" );
234            books.setProperty( "Visual Basic 2005", "0131869000" );
235            books.setProperty( "Visual C# 2005", "0131525239" );
236            books.setProperty( "Internet & Web", "0131752421" );
237      } // end Options constructor
238
239      // To save space, we omitted the code in lines 239-281. The complet
240      // source code is provided with this chapter's examples.
241
282      // Action handler for the Submit button. Checks whether a language
283      // was selected and, if so, registers a cookie for that language and
284      // sets the responseText to indicate the chosen language.
285      public String submitButton_action()
286      {
287            String msg = "Welcome to sessions!  You ";
288
289            // if the user made a selection
290            if ( getLanguageRadioGroup().getSelected() != null )
291            {
292                String language = languageRadioGroup.getSelected().toString();
293                msg += "selected " + language + ".";
294
295                // get ISBN number of book for the given language.
296                String ISBN = books.getProperty( language );
297
298                // add the selection to the SessionBean's Properties object
299                Properties selections = getSessionBean1().getSelectedLanguages();
300                Object result = selections.setProperty( language, ISBN );
301
302                // increment numSelections in the SessionBean and update
303                // selectedLanguages if user has not made this selection before
304                if ( result == null )
305                {
306                    int numSelected = getSessionBean1().getNumSelections();
307                    getSessionBean1().setNumSelections( ++numSelected );
308                } // end if
309            } // end if
310            else
311                msg += "did not select a language.";
312
313            responseText.setValue( msg );
314            languageRadioGroup.setRendered( false );
315            instructionText.setRendered( false );
316            submitButton.setRendered( false );
317            responseText.setRendered( true );
318            selectionsText.setRendered( true );
319            selectionsValueText.setRendered( true );
320            languagesLink.setRendered( true );
321            recommendationsLink.setRendered( true );
```

Fig. 22.27 | Page bean that stores language selections in a `SessionBean` property. (Part 2 of 3.)

```
322        return null; // reloads the page
323    } // end method submitButton_action
324
325    // redisplay the components for selecting a language
326    public String languagesLink_action()
327    {
328        responseText.setRendered( false );
329        selectionsText.setRendered( false );
330        selectionsValueText.setRendered( false );
331        languagesLink.setRendered( false );
332        recommendationsLink.setRendered( false );
333        languageRadioGroup.setRendered( true );
334        instructionText.setRendered( true );
335        submitButton.setRendered( true );
336        return null;
337    } // end method languagesLink_action
338
339    // forwards user to Recommendations.jsp
340    public String recommendationsLink_action()
341    {
342        return "case1";
343    } // end method recommendationsLink_action
344 } // end class Options
```

Fig. 22.27 | Page bean that stores language selections in a `SessionBean` property. (Part 3 of 3.)

The `submitButton`'s action handler (lines 285–323) stores the user's selections in the `SessionBean` and increments the number of selections made, if necessary. Line 299 retrieves from the `SessionBean` the `Properties` object that contains the user's selections. Line 300 adds the current selection to the `Properties` object. Method `setProperty` returns the value previously associated with the new key, or `null` if this key was not already stored in the `Properties` object. If adding the new property returns `null`, then the user has made a new selection. In this case, lines 306–307 increment the `numSelections` property in the `SessionBean`. Lines 313–321 and the `languaguesLink` action handler (lines 326–337) control the components that are displayed, just as in the cookies examples.

Software Engineering Observation 22.2

A benefit of using `SessionBean` *properties (rather than cookies) is that they can store any type of object (not just* `Strings`*) as attribute values. This provides you with increased flexibility in maintaining client-state information.*

Displaying Recommendations Based on Session Values

As in the cookies example, this application provides a link to `Recommendations.jsp`, which displays a list of book recommendations based on the user's language selections. Since this JSP is identical to the version in Fig. 22.20, we show only the sample output of this page in Fig. 22.28.

Page Bean That Creates Book Recommendations from a SessionBean Property

Figure 22.29 presents the page bean for `Recommendations.jsp`. Again, much of it is similar to the page bean used in the cookies example. We discuss only the new features.

Fig. 22.28 | JSP file that displays book recommendations based on language selections stored in session scope.

```
1   // Fig. 22.29: Recommendations.java
2   // Page bean that displays book recommendations based on a SessionBean
3   // property.
4   package sessiontrackingsessions;
5
6   import com.sun.rave.web.ui.appbase.AbstractPageBean;
7   import com.sun.webui.jsf.component.Body;
8   import com.sun.webui.jsf.component.Form;
9   import com.sun.webui.jsf.component.Head;
10  import com.sun.webui.jsf.component.Html;
11  import com.sun.webui.jsf.component.Hyperlink;
12  import com.sun.webui.jsf.component.Label;
13  import com.sun.webui.jsf.component.Link;
14  import com.sun.webui.jsf.component.Listbox;
15  import com.sun.webui.jsf.component.Page;
16  import com.sun.webui.jsf.model.DefaultOptionsList;
17  import com.sun.webui.jsf.model.Option;
18  import java.util.Enumeration;
19  import java.util.Properties;
20  import javax.faces.FacesException;
21
22  public class Recommendations extends AbstractPageBean
23  {
24     // To save space, we omitted the code in lines 24-177. The complete
25     // source code is provided with this chapter's examples.
26
178    // displays the book recommendations in the Listbox
179    public void prerender()
180    {
181       // retrieve user's selections and number of selections made
182       Properties languages = getSessionBean1().getSelectedLanguages();
183       Enumeration selectionsEnum = languages.propertyNames();
```

Fig. 22.29 | Displays book recommendations based on a SessionBean property. (Part 1 of 2.)

```
184        int numSelected = getSessionBean1().getNumSelections();
185
186        Option [] recommendations;
187
188        // if at least one selection was made
189        if ( numSelected > 0 )
190        {
191           recommendations = new Option[ numSelected ];
192
193           for ( int i = 0; i < numSelected; i++ )
194           {
195              String language = (String) selectionsEnum.nextElement();
196              recommendations[ i ] = new Option( language +
197                 " How to Program.  ISBN#: " +
198                 languages.getProperty( language ) );
199           } // end for
200        } // end if
201        else
202        {
203           recommendations = new Option[ 1 ];
204           recommendations[ 0 ] = new Option(
205              "No recommendations. Please select a language." );
206        } // end else
207
208        recommendationsListbox.setItems( recommendations );
209     } // end method prerender
210
211     // To save space, we omitted the code in lines 211-229. The complete
212     // source code is provided with this chapter's examples.
213
230     // redirects user to Options.jsp
231     public String optionsLink_action()
232     {
233        return "case1"; // returns to Options.jsp
234     } // end method optionsLink_action
235  } // end class Recommendations
```

Fig. 22.29 | Displays book recommendations based on a `SessionBean` property. (Part 2 of 2.)

Line 182 retrieves the `Properties` object containing the user's selections from the `SessionBean`, and line 183 gets an enumeration of all of the keys in that `Properties` object. Line 184 retrieves the number of selections made from the `SessionBean`. If any selections were made, line 191 constructs an appropriately sized `Option` array to display the selections in the `webuijsf:listBox` element of `Recommendations.jsp`. Lines 193–199 add each of the user's selections to this `Option` array. Line 195 gets the next key from the enumeration of keys, and lines 196–198 add a recommendation to the `Option` array.

22.6 Web Resources

Our Java Resource Centers focus on the enormous amount of free Java content available online. We currently provide six Java-related Resource Centers:

```
www.deitel.com/java/
www.deitel.com/JavaCertification/
www.deitel.com/JavaDesignPatterns/
www.deitel.com/JavaEE5/
www.deitel.com/JavaFX/
www.deitel.com/JavaSE6Mustang/
```

You can view our complete list of Resource Centers at

```
www.deitel.com/ResourceCenters.html
```

23

Ajax-Enabled JavaServer™ Faces Web Applications

OBJECTIVES

In this chapter you will learn:

- To use data providers to access databases from web applications built in Netbeans.
- To include Ajax-enabled JSF components in a Netbeans web application project.
- To configure virtual forms that enable subsets of a form's input components to be submitted to the server.

*Whatever is in any way
beautiful hath its source of
beauty in itself, and is
complete in itself; praise
forms no part of it.*
—Marcus Aurelius Antoninus

*There is something in a face,
An air, and a peculiar grace,
Which boldest painters
cannot trace.*
—William Somerville

*Cato said the best way to
keep good acts in memory
was to refresh them with
new.*
—Francis Bacon

*I never forget a face, but in
your case I'll make an
exception.*
—Groucho Marx

*Painting is only a bridge
linking the painter's mind
with that of the viewer.*
—Eugéne Delacroix

23.1 Introduction

This chapter continues our discussion of web application development with several advanced concepts. We discuss accessing, updating and searching databases in a web application, adding virtual forms to web pages to enable subsets of a form's input components to be submitted to the server, and using Ajax-enabled component libraries to improve application performance and component responsiveness. [*Note:* This chapter assumes that you know Java. To learn more about Java, check out *Java How to Program, Seventh Edition,* or visit our Java Resource Centers at www.deitel.com/ResourceCenters.html.]

We present a single address book application developed in three stages to illustrate these concepts. The application is backed by a Java DB database for storing the contact names and their addresses.

The address book application presents a form that allows the user to enter a new name and address to store in the address book and displays the contents of the address book in table format. It also provides a search form that allows the user to search for a contact and, if found, display the contact's address on a map. The first version of this application demonstrates how to add contacts to the database and how to display the list of contacts in a JSF **Table** component. In the second version, we add an Ajax-enabled **AutoComplete Text Field** component and enable it to suggest a list of contact names as the user types. The last version allows you to search the address book for a contact and display the corresponding address on a map using the Ajax-enabled **Map Viewer** component that is powered by Google Maps (maps.google.com).

As in Chapter 22, this chapter's examples were developed in Netbeans. We installed a supplementary component library—the *Java BluePrints Ajax component library*—which provides the Ajax-enabled components used in the address book application.

Instructions for installing this library are included in Section 23.3. These Ajax-enabled components use the Dojo Toolkit (which we introduced in Chapter 13) on the client side.

23.2 Accessing Databases in Web Applications

Many web applications access databases to store and retrieve persistent data. In this section, we build a web application that uses a Java DB database to store contacts in the address book and display contacts from the address book on a web page.

The web page enables the user to enter new contacts in a form. This form consists of **Text Field** components for the contact's first name, last name, street address, city, state and zip code. The form also has a **Submit** button to send the data to the server and a **Clear** button to reset the form's fields. The application stores the address book information in a database named `AddressBook`, which has a single table named `Addresses`. (We provide this database in the examples directory for this chapter. You can download the examples from www.deitel.com/books/ajaxfp/). This example also introduces the **_Table_** JSF component, which displays the addresses from the database in tabular format. We show how to configure the **Table** component shortly.

23.2.1 Building a Web Application That Displays Data from a Database

We now explain how to build the `AddressBook` application's GUI and set up a data binding that allows the **Table** component to display information from the database. We present the generated JSP file later in the section, and we discuss the related page bean file in Section 23.2.2. To build the `AddressBook` application, perform the following steps:

Step 1: Creating the Project

In Netbeans, create a **Visual Web Application** project named `AddressBook`. Rename the JSP and page bean files to `AddressBook` using the refactoring tools.

Step 2: Creating the Form for User Input

In **Design** mode, add a **Static Text** component to the top of the page that reads "Add a contact to the address book:" and use the component's `style` property to set the font size to 18px. Add six **Text Field** components to the page and rename them `fnameTextField`, `lnameTextField`, `streetTextField`, `cityTextField`, `stateTextField` and `zipText-Field`. Set each **Text Field**'s `required` property to `true` by selecting the **Text Field**, then clicking the `required` property's checkbox. Label each **Text Field** with a **Label** component and associate the **Label** with its corresponding **Text Field**. Finally, add a **Submit** and a **Clear** button. Set the **Submit** button's **_primary_** property to `true` to make it stand out more on the page than the **Clear** button and to allow the user to submit a new contact by pressing *Enter* rather than by clicking the **Submit** button. Set the **Clear** button's **_reset_** property to `true` to prevent validation when the user clicks the **Clear** button. Since we are clearing the fields, we don't need to ensure that they contain information. We discuss the action handler for the **Submit** button after we present the page bean file. The **Clear** button does not need an action-handler method, because setting the `reset` property to `true` automatically configures the button to reset all of the page's input fields. When you have finished these steps, your form should look like Fig. 23.1.

Fig. 23.1 | AddressBook application form for adding a contact.

Step 3: Adding a Table Component to the Page

Drag a **Table** component from the **Basic** section of the **Palette** to the page and place it just below the two **Button** components. Name it addressesTable. The **Table** component formats and displays data from database tables. In the **Properties** window, change the **Table**'s title property to Contacts. We show how to configure the **Table** to interact with the AddressBook database shortly.

Step 4: Creating a Java DB Database

This example uses a database called AddressBook to store the address information. To create this database, perform the following steps:

1. Select **Tools > Java DB Database > Create Java DB Database....**

2. Enter the name of the database to create (AddressBook), a username (iw3htp4) and a password (iw3htp4), then click **OK** to create the database.

In the Netbeans **Runtime** tab (to the right of the **Projects** and **Files** tabs), the preceding steps create a new entry in the **Databases** node showing the URL of the database (jdbc:derby://localhost:1527/AddressBook). This URL indicates that the database resides on the local machine and accepts connections on port 1527.

Step 5: Adding a Table and Data to the AddressBook Database

You can use the **Runtime** tab to create tables and to execute SQL statements that populate the database with data:

1. Click the **Runtime** tab and expand the **Databases** node.

2. Netbeans must be connected to the database to execute SQL statements. If Netbeans is already connected, proceed to *Step 3*. If Netbeans is not connected to the database, the icon 🔌 appears next to the database's URL (jdbc:derby://localhost:1527/AddressBook). In this case, right click the icon and click **Connect....** Once connected, the icon changes to 🔲.

3. Expand the node for the AddressBook database, right click the **Tables** node and select **Execute Command...** to open a **SQL Command** editor in Netbeans. We provided the file AddressBook.sql in this chapter's examples folder. Open that file in a text editor, copy the SQL statements and paste them into the **SQL Command** editor in Netbeans. Then, highlight all the SQL commands, right click inside the **SQL Command** editor and select **Run Selection**. This will create the Addresses table with the sample data shown in Fig. 23.2. You may need to refresh the **Tables** node of the **Runtime** tab to see the new table.

FirstName	LastName	Street	City	State	Zip
Bob	Green	5 Bay St.	San Francisco	CA	94133
Liz	White	100 5th Ave.	New York	NY	10011
Mike	Brown	3600 Delmar Blvd.	St. Louis	MO	63108
Mary	Green	300 Massachusetts Ave.	Boston	MA	02115
John	Gray	500 South St.	Philadelphia	PA	19147
Meg	Gold	1200 Stout St.	Denver	CO	80204
James	Blue	1000 Harbor Ave.	Seattle	WA	98116
Sue	Black	1000 Michigan Ave.	Chicago	IL	60605

Fig. 23.2 | Addresses table data.

Step 6: Binding the Table *Component to the* Addresses *Table of the* AddressBook *Database*

Now that we've configured a data source for the Addresses database table, we can configure the Table component to display the AddressBook data. Simply drag the database table from the Servers tab and drop it on the Table component to create the binding.

To select specific columns to display, right click the Table component and select Bind to Data to display the Bind to Data dialog containing the list of the columns in the Addresses database table (Fig. 23.3). The items under the Selected heading will be displayed in the Table. To remove a column, select it and click the < button. We'd like to display all the columns in this example, so you should simply click OK to exit the dialog.

By default, the Table uses the database table's column names in all uppercase letters as headings. To change these headings, select a column and edit its headerText property in the Properties window. To select a column, click the column's name in the Design mode. We also changed the id property of each column to make the variable names in the code more readable. In Design mode, your Table's column heads should appear as in Fig. 23.4.

Fig. 23.3 | Dialog for binding to the Addresses table.

Fig. 23.4 | `Table` component after binding it to a database table and editing its column names for display purposes.

An address book might contain many contacts, so we'd like to display only a few at a time. Clicking the checkbox next to the table's `paginationControls` property in the **Properties** window configures this **Table** for automatic pagination. This adds buttons to the bottom of the **Table** for moving forward and backward between groups of contacts. You may use the **Table Layout** dialog's **Options** tab to select the number of rows to display at a time. To view this tab, right click the **Table**, select **Table Layout...**, then click the **Options** tab. For this example, we set the **Page Size** property to 5.

Next, set the `addressesTable`'s `internalVirtualForm` property. Virtual forms allow subsets of a form's input components to be submitted to the server. Setting this property prevents the pagination control buttons on the **Table** from submitting the **Text Field**s on the form every time the user wishes to view the next group of contacts. Virtual forms are discussed in Section 23.4.1.

Binding the **Table** to a data provider added a new `addressesDataProvider` object (an instance of class ***CachedRowSetDataProvider***) to the **AddressBook** node in the **Outline** window. A `CachedRowSetDataProvider` provides a scrollable `RowSet` that can be bound to a **Table** component to display the `RowSet`'s data. This data provider is a wrapper for a `CachedRowSet` object. If you click the **addressesDataProvider** element in the **Outline** window, you'll see in the **Properties** window that its `CachedRowSet` property is set to `addressesRowSet`, an object (in the session bean) that implements interface `CachedRowSet`.

Step 7: Modifying addressesRowSet's SQL Statement
The `CachedRowSet` object wrapped by our `addressesDataProvider` is configured by default to execute a SQL query that selects all the data in the `Addresses` table of the `AddressBook` database. You can edit this SQL query by expanding the `SessionBean` node in the **Outline** window and double clicking the `addressesRowSet` element to open the query editor window (Fig. 23.5). We'd like to edit the SQL statement so that records with duplicate last names are sorted by last name, then by first name. To do this, click in the **Sort Type** column next to the **LASTNAME** row and select **Ascending**. Then, repeat this for the **FIRSTNAME** row. Notice that the expression

```
ORDER BY IW3HTP4.ADDRESSES.LASTNAME ASC,
         IW3HTP4.ADDRESSES.FIRSTNAME ASC
```

was added to the SQL statement at the bottom of the editor.

Step 8: Adding Validation
It is important to validate the form data on this page to ensure that the data can be successfully inserted into the `AddressBook` database. All of the database's columns are of type `varchar` (except the ID column) and have length restrictions. For this reason, you should

Fig. 23.5 | Editing addressesRowSet's SQL statement.

either add a **Length Validator** to each **Text Field** component or set each **Text Field** component's maxLength property. We chose to set the maxLength property of each. The first name, last name, street, city, state and zip code **Text Field** components may not exceed 30, 30, 150, 30, 2 and 5 characters, respectively.

Finally, drag a ***Message Group*** component onto your page to the right of the **Text Fields**. A **Message Group** component displays system messages. We use this component to display an error message when an attempt to add a contact to the database fails. Set the **Message Group**'s showGlobalOnly property to true to prevent component-level validation error messages from being displayed here.

JSP File for a Web Page That Interacts with a Database
The JSP file for the application is shown in Fig. 23.6. This file contains a large amount of generated markup for components you learned in Chapter 22. We discuss the markup for only the components that are new in this example.

```
1   <?xml version="1.0" encoding="UTF-8"?>
2   <!-- Fig. 23.6: AddressBook.jsp -->
3   <!-- AddressBook JSP with an add form and a Table JSF component. -->
4   <jsp:root version="1.2"
5      xmlns:f="http://java.sun.com/jsf/core"
6      xmlns:h="http://java.sun.com/jsf/html"
7      xmlns:jsp="http://java.sun.com/JSP/Page"
8      xmlns:webuijsf="http://www.sun.com/webui/webuijsf">
9      <jsp:directive.page contentType="text/html;charset=UTF-8"
10        pageEncoding="UTF-8"/>
```

Fig. 23.6 | AddressBook JSP with an add form and a **Table** JSF component (Part 1 of 5.)

```
11      <f:view>
12      <webuijsf:page binding="#{AddressBook.page1}" id="page1">
13        <webuijsf:html binding="#{AddressBook.html1}" id="html1">
14          <webuijsf:head binding="#{AddressBook.head1}" id="head1">
15            <webuijsf:link binding="#{AddressBook.link1}" id="link1"
16              url="/resources/stylesheet.css"/>
17          </webuijsf:head>
18          <webuijsf:body binding="#{AddressBook.body1}" id="body1"
19            style="-rave-layout: grid">
20            <webuijsf:form binding="#{AddressBook.form1}" id="form1">
21              <webuijsf:staticText binding="#{AddressBook.staticText1}"
22                id="staticText1" style="font-size: 18px; left: 24px;
23                top: 24px; position: absolute"
24                text="Add a contact to the address book:"/>
25              <webuijsf:label binding="#{AddressBook.fnameLabel}"
26                for="fnameTextField" id="fnameLabel" style=
27                "position: absolute; left: 24px; top: 72px"
28                text="First name:"/>
29              <webuijsf:textField binding="#{AddressBook.fnameTextField}"
30                id="fnameTextField" maxLength="30" required="true"
31                style="left: 100px; top: 72px; position: absolute;
32                width: 192px"/>
33              <webuijsf:label binding="#{AddressBook.lnameLabel}"
34                for="lnameTextField" id="lnameLabel" style="left: 312px;
35                top: 72px; position: absolute" text="Last name:"/>
36              <webuijsf:textField binding="#{AddressBook.lnameTextField}"
37                id="lnameTextField" maxLength="30" required="true"
38                style="left: 390px; top: 72px; position: absolute;
39                width: 214px"/>
40              <webuijsf:label binding="#{AddressBook.streetLabel}"
41                for="streetTextField" id="streetLabel" style="position:
42                absolute; left: 24px; top: 96px" text="Street:"/>
43              <webuijsf:textField binding=
44                "#{AddressBook.streetTextField}" id="streetTextField"
45                maxLength="150" required="true" style="left: 100px;
46                top: 96px; position: absolute; width: 504px"/>
47              <webuijsf:label binding="#{AddressBook.cityLabel}"
48                for="cityTextField" id="cityLabel" style="left: 24px;
49                top: 120px; position: absolute" text="City:"/>
50              <webuijsf:textField binding="#{AddressBook.cityTextField}"
51                id="cityTextField" maxLength="30" required="true"
52                style="left: 100px; top: 120px; position: absolute;
53                width: 240px"/>
54              <webuijsf:label binding="#{AddressBook.stateLabel}"
55                for="stateTextField" id="stateLabel" style="left: 360px;
56                top: 120px; position: absolute" text="State:"/>
57              <webuijsf:textField binding="#{AddressBook.stateTextField}"
58                id="stateTextField" maxLength="2" required="true"
59                style="left: 412px; top: 120px; position: absolute;
60                width: 48px"/>
61              <webuijsf:label binding="#{AddressBook.zipLabel}"
62                for="zipTextField" id="zipLabel" style="left: 490px;
63                top: 120px; position: absolute" text=" Zip:"/>
```

Fig. 23.6 | AddressBook JSP with an add form and a **Table** JSF component (Part 2 of 5.)

```
64          <webuijsf:textField binding="#{AddressBook.zipTextField}"
65              id="zipTextField" maxLength="5" required="true"
66              style="left: 534px; top: 120px; position: absolute;
67              width: 70px"/>
68          <webuijsf:button actionExpression=
69              "#{AddressBook.submitButton_action}" binding=
70              "#{AddressBook.submitButton}" id="submitButton"
71              primary="true" style="left: 100px; top: 168px;
72              position: absolute; width: 100px" text="Submit"/>
73          <webuijsf:button binding="#{AddressBook.clearButton}"
74              id="clearButton" reset="true" style="left: 215px; top:
75              168px; position: absolute; width: 100px" text="Clear"/>
76          <webuijsf:messageGroup binding=
77              "#{AddressBook.messageGroup1}" id="messageGroup1"
78              showGlobalOnly="true" style="left: 624px; top: 72px;
79              position: absolute"/>
80          <webuijsf:table augmentTitle="false" binding=
81              "#{AddressBook.addressesTable}" id="addressesTable"
82              paginateButton="true" paginationControls="true"
83              style="left: 24px; top: 216px; position: absolute"
84              title="Contacts" width="816">
85              <webuijsf:tableRowGroup binding=
86                  "#{AddressBook.tableRowGroup1}" id="tableRowGroup1"
87                  rows="5"
88                  sourceData="#{AddressBook.addressesDataProvider}"
89                  sourceVar="currentRow">
90                  <webuijsf:tableColumn binding=
91                      "#{AddressBook.fnameColumn}" headerText=
92                      "First Name" id="fnameColumn"
93                      sort="ADDRESSES.FIRSTNAME">
94                      <webuijsf:staticText binding=
95                          "#{AddressBook.staticText2}" id="staticText2"
96                          text="#{currentRow.value[
97                          'ADDRESSES.FIRSTNAME']}"/>
98                  </webuijsf:tableColumn>
99                  <webuijsf:tableColumn binding=
100                     "#{AddressBook.lnameColumn}"
101                     headerText="Last Name" id="lnameColumn"
102                     sort="ADDRESSES.LASTNAME">
103                     <webuijsf:staticText binding=
104                         "#{AddressBook.staticText3}" id="staticText3"
105                         text="#{currentRow.value[
106                         'ADDRESSES.LASTNAME']}"/>
107                 </webuijsf:tableColumn>
108                 <webuijsf:tableColumn binding=
109                     "#{AddressBook.streetColumn}" headerText="Street"
110                     id="streetColumn" sort="ADDRESSES.STREET">
111                     <webuijsf:staticText binding=
112                         "#{AddressBook.staticText4}" id="staticText4"
113                         text="#{currentRow.value[
114                         'ADDRESSES.STREET']}"/>
115                 </webuijsf:tableColumn>
```

Fig. 23.6 | AddressBook JSP with an add form and a **Table** JSF component (Part 3 of 5.)

```
116                          <webuijsf:tableColumn binding=
117                             "#{AddressBook.cityColumn}" headerText="City"
118                             id="cityColumn" sort="ADDRESSES.CITY">
119                             <webuijsf:staticText binding=
120                                "#{AddressBook.staticText5}" id="staticText5"
121                                text="#{currentRow.value['ADDRESSES.CITY']}"/>
122                          </webuijsf:tableColumn>
123                          <webuijsf:tableColumn binding=
124                             "#{AddressBook.stateColumn}" headerText="State"
125                             id="stateColumn" sort="ADDRESSES.STATE">
126                             <webuijsf:staticText binding=
127                                "#{AddressBook.staticText6}" id="staticText6"
128                                text="#{currentRow.value['ADDRESSES.STATE']}"/>
129                          </webuijsf:tableColumn>
130                          <webuijsf:tableColumn binding=
131                             "#{AddressBook.zipColumn}" headerText="Zip"
132                             id="zipColumn" sort="ADDRESSES.ZIP" width="106">
133                             <webuijsf:staticText binding=
134                                "#{AddressBook.staticText7}" id="staticText7"
135                                text="#{currentRow.value['ADDRESSES.ZIP']}"/>
136                          </webuijsf:tableColumn>
137                       </webuijsf:tableRowGroup>
138                    </webuijsf:table>
139                 </webuijsf:form>
140              </webuijsf:body>
141           </webuijsf:html>
142        </webuijsf:page>
143     </f:view>
144  </jsp:root>
```

a)

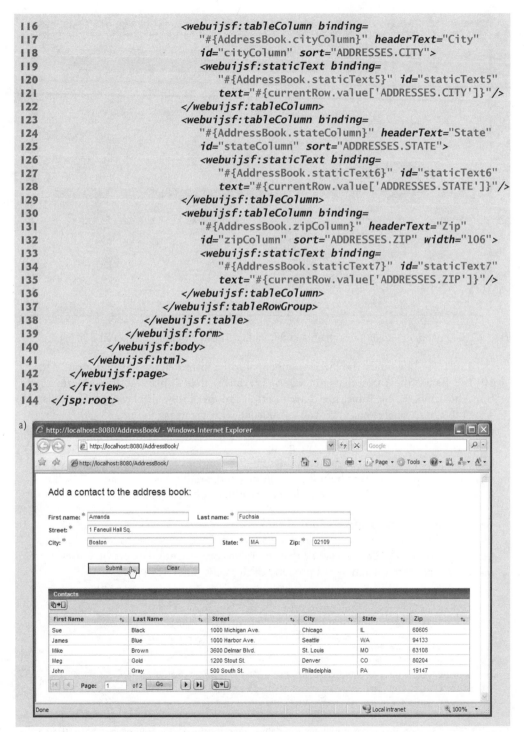

Fig. 23.6 | `AddressBook` JSP with an add form and a **Table** JSF component (Part 4 of 5.)

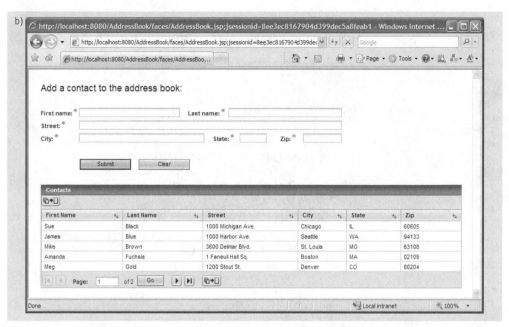

Fig. 23.6 | AddressBook JSP with an add form and a **Table** JSF component (Part 5 of 5.)

Lines 21–75 contain the JSF components for the form that gathers user input. Lines 80–138 define the **Table** element (webuijsf:table) that displays address information from the database. JSF **Table**s may have multiple groups of rows displaying different data. This **Table** has a single webuijsf:tableRowGroup with a start tag in lines 85–89. The row group's sourceData attribute is bound to our addressesDataProvider and given the variable name currentRow. The row group also defines the **Table**'s columns. Each webuijsf:tableColumn element (e.g., lines 90–98) contains a webuijsf:staticText element with its text attribute bound to a column in the data provider currentRow. These webuijsf:staticText elements enable the **Table** to display each row's data.

Session Bean for the AddressBook Application
Figure 23.7 displays the SessionBean1.java file generated by Netbeans for the AddressBook application. The CachedRowSet that the **Table** component's data provider uses to access the AddressBook database is a property of this class (lines 31–41).

```
1   // Fig. 23.7: SessionBean1.java
2   // Session bean that initializes the data source for the
3   // AddressBook database.
4   package addressbook;
5
6   import com.sun.rave.web.ui.appbase.AbstractSessionBean;
7   import com.sun.sql.rowset.CachedRowSetXImpl;
8   import javax.faces.FacesException;
```

Fig. 23.7 | Session Bean that initializes the data source for the AddressBook database. (Part 1 of 2.)

```
9
10   public class SessionBean1 extends AbstractSessionBean
11   {
12      private int __placeholder;
13
14      private void _init() throws Exception
15      {
16         addressesRowSet.setDataSourceName(
17            "java:comp/env/jdbc/dataSource" );
18         addressesRowSet.setCommand(
19            "SELECT ALL IW3HTP4.ADDRESSES.FIRSTNAME, \n" +
20            "IW3HTP4.ADDRESSES.LASTNAME, \n" +
21            "IW3HTP4.ADDRESSES.STREET, \n" +
22            "IW3HTP4.ADDRESSES.CITY, \n" +
23            "IW3HTP4.ADDRESSES.STATE, \n" +
24            "IW3HTP4.ADDRESSES.ZIP \n" +
25            "FROM IW3HTP4.ADDRESSES\n" +
26            "ORDER BY IW3HTP4.ADDRESSES.LASTNAME ASC, \n" +
27            "IW3HTP4.ADDRESSES.FIRSTNAME ASC " );
28         addressesRowSet.setTableName( "ADDRESSES" );
29      } // end method _init
30
31      private CachedRowSetXImpl addressesRowSet = new CachedRowSetXImpl();
32
33      public CachedRowSetXImpl getAddressesRowSet()
34      {
35         return addressesRowSet;
36      }
37
38      public void setAddressesRowSet( CachedRowSetXImpl crsxi )
39      {
40         this.addressesRowSet = crsxi;
41      }
42
43      // To save space, we omitted the code in lines 42-78. The complete
44      // source code is provided with this chapter's examples.
79   } // end class SessionBean1
```

Fig. 23.7 | Session Bean that initializes the data source for the `AddressBook` database. (Part 2 of 2.)

The `_init` method (lines 14–29) configures `addressesRowSet` to interact with the `AddressBook` database (lines 16–28). Lines 16–17 connect the row set to the database. Lines 18–27 set `addressesRowSet`'s SQL command to the query configured in Fig. 23.5. Line 28 sets the `RowSet`'s table name.

23.2.2 Modifying the Page Bean File for the AddressBook Application

After building the web page and configuring the components used in this example, double click the **Submit** button to create an action event handler for this button in the page bean file. The code to insert a contact into the database will be placed in this method. The page bean with the completed event handler is shown in Fig. 23.8 below.

```
 1    // Fig. 23.8: AddressBook.java
 2    // Page bean for AddressBook.jsp.
 3    package addressbook;
 4
 5    import com.sun.data.provider.RowKey;
 6    import com.sun.data.provider.impl.CachedRowSetDataProvider;
 7    import com.sun.rave.web.ui.appbase.AbstractPageBean;
 8    import com.sun.webui.jsf.component.Body;
 9    import com.sun.webui.jsf.component.Button;
10    import com.sun.webui.jsf.component.Form;
11    import com.sun.webui.jsf.component.Head;
12    import com.sun.webui.jsf.component.Html;
13    import com.sun.webui.jsf.component.Label;
14    import com.sun.webui.jsf.component.Link;
15    import com.sun.webui.jsf.component.MessageGroup;
16    import com.sun.webui.jsf.component.Page;
17    import com.sun.webui.jsf.component.StaticText;
18    import com.sun.webui.jsf.component.Table;
19    import com.sun.webui.jsf.component.TableColumn;
20    import com.sun.webui.jsf.component.TableRowGroup;
21    import com.sun.webui.jsf.component.TextField;
22    import com.sun.webui.jsf.model.DefaultTableDataProvider;
23    import javax.faces.FacesException;
24
25    public class AddressBook extends AbstractPageBean
26    {
27       private int __placeholder;
28
29       private void _init() throws Exception
30       {
31          addressesDataProvider.setCachedRowSet(
32             ( javax.sql.rowset.CachedRowSet ) getValue(
33                "#{SessionBean1.addressesRowSet}" ) );
34          addressesTable.setInternalVirtualForm( true );
35       } // end method _init
36
37       // To save space, we omitted the code in lines 37-505. The complete
38       // source code is provided with this chapter's examples.
39
506       public void prerender()
507       {
508          addressesDataProvider.refresh();
509       } // end method prerender
510
511       public void destroy()
512       {
513          addressesDataProvider.close();
514       } // end method destroy
515
516       // To save space, we omitted the code in lines 516-530. The complete
517       // source code is provided with this chapter's examples.
518
```

Fig. 23.8 | Page bean for adding a contact to the address book. (Part I of 2.)

```
531        // action handler that adds a contact to the AddressBook database
532        // when the user clicks Submit
533        public String submitButton_action()
534        {
535           if ( addressesDataProvider.canAppendRow() )
536           {
537              try
538              {
539                 RowKey rk = addressesDataProvider.appendRow();
540                 addressesDataProvider.setCursorRow( rk );
541
542                 addressesDataProvider.setValue( "ADDRESSES.FIRSTNAME",
543                    fnameTextField.getValue() );
544                 addressesDataProvider.setValue( "ADDRESSES.LASTNAME",
545                    lnameTextField.getValue() );
546                 addressesDataProvider.setValue( "ADDRESSES.STREET",
547                    streetTextField.getValue() );
548                 addressesDataProvider.setValue( "ADDRESSES.CITY",
549                    cityTextField.getValue() );
550                 addressesDataProvider.setValue( "ADDRESSES.STATE",
551                    stateTextField.getValue() );
552                 addressesDataProvider.setValue( "ADDRESSES.ZIP",
553                    zipTextField.getValue() );
554                 addressesDataProvider.commitChanges();
555
556                 // reset text fields
557                 lnameTextField.setValue( "" );
558                 fnameTextField.setValue( "" );
559                 streetTextField.setValue( "" );
560                 cityTextField.setValue( "" );
561                 stateTextField.setValue( "" );
562                 zipTextField.setValue( "" );
563              } // end try
564              catch ( Exception ex )
565              {
566                 error( "The address book was not updated.  " +
567                    ex.getMessage() );
568              } // end catch
569           } // end if
570
571           return null;
572        } // end method submitButton_action
573     } // end class AddressBook
```

Fig. 23.8 | Page bean for adding a contact to the address book. (Part 2 of 2.)

Lines 533–572 contain the event-handling code for the **Submit** button. Line 535 determines whether a new row can be appended to the data provider. If so, a new row is appended at line 539. Every row in a CachedRowSetDataProvider has its own key; method **appendRow** returns the key for the new row. Line 540 sets the data provider's cursor to the new row, so that any changes we make to the data provider affect that row. Lines 542–553 set each of the row's columns to the values entered by the user in the corresponding **Text Field**s. Line 554 stores the new contact by calling method *commitChanges* of class CachedRowSetDataProvider to insert the new row into the AddressBook database.

Lines 557–562 clear the form's **Text Field**s. If these lines are omitted, the fields will retain their current values after the database is updated and the page reloads. Also, the **Clear** button will not work properly if the **Text Field**s are not cleared. Rather than emptying the **Text Field**s, it resets them to the values they held the last time the form was submitted.

Lines 564–568 catch any exceptions that might occur while updating the Address-Book database. Lines 566–567 display a message indicating that the database was not updated as well as the exception's error message in the page's MessageGroup component.

In method prerender, line 508 calls CachedRowSetDataProvider method *refresh*. This re-executes the wrapped CachedRowSet's SQL statement and re-sorts the **Table**'s rows so that the new row is displayed in the proper order. If you do not call refresh, the new address is displayed at the end of the **Table** (since we appended the new row to the end of the data provider). The IDE automatically generated code to free resources used by the data provider (line 513) in the destroy method.

23.3 Ajax-Enabled JSF Components

The *Java BluePrints Ajax component library* provides *Ajax-enabled JSF components*. These components rely on Ajax technology to deliver the feel and responsiveness of a desktop application over the web. Figure 23.9 summarizes the current set of components that you can download and use with Netbeans. We demonstrate the **AutoComplete Text Field** and **Map Viewer** components in the next two sections.

Component	Description
AutoComplete Text Field	Makes Ajax requests to display a list of suggestions as the user types in the text field.
Buy Now Button	Initiates a transaction through the PayPal website.
Map Viewer	Uses the Google Maps API to display a map that pans, zooms, and can display markers for locations of interest.
Popup Calendar	Provides a calendar that enables a user to scroll between months and years. Fills a **Text Field** with a formatted date when the user selects a day.
Progress Bar	Visually displays the progress of a long-running operation. Uses a programmer-supplied calculation to determine the progress percentage.
Rating	Provides a customizable five-star rating bar that can display messages as the user moves the mouse over the ratings.
Rich Textarea Editor	Provides an editable text area that allows the user to format text with fonts, colors, hyperlinks and backgrounds.
Select Value Text Field	Displays a list of suggestions in a drop-down list as the user types, similar to the **AutoComplete Text Field**.

Fig. 23.9 | Java BluePrints component library's Ajax-enabled components.

Downloading the Java BluePrints Ajax-Enabled Components

To use the Java BluePrints Ajax-enabled components in Netbeans, you must download and import them. The IDE provides a wizard for installing this group of components (Internet access is required). To access it, choose **Tools > Update Center** to display the **Update Center Wizard** dialog. Click **Next >** to search for available updates. In the **Available Updates and New Modules** area of the dialog, locate and select **BluePrints AJAX Components** then click the **Add >** button to add them to the list of items you'd like to install. Click **Next >** and follow the prompts to accept the terms of use and download the components. When the download completes, click **Next >** then click **Finish**. Click **OK** to restart the IDE.

Importing the Java BluePrints Ajax-Enabled Components into the Netbeans Palette

Next, you must import the components into the **Palette**. Select **Tools > Component Library Manager**, then click **Import...**. Click **Browse...** in the **Component Library Manager** dialog that appears. Select the `ui.complib` file and click **Open**. Click **OK** to import both the **BluePrints AJAX Components** and the **BluePrints AJAX Support Beans**. Close the **Component Library Manager** to return to the IDE.

To see the new components in the **Palette**, you must add the **BluePrints AJAX Components** library to your visual web application. To do so, make sure your application's node is expanded in the **Projects** tab. Right click the **Component Libraries** node and select **Add Component Library**. In the **Add Component Library** dialog box, select the **BluePrints AJAX Components library** and click **Add Component Library**. You should now see two new nodes in the **Palette**. The first, **BluePrints AJAX Components**, provides the eight components listed in Fig. 23.9. The second, **BluePrints AJAX Support Beans**, includes components that support the Ajax components. You can now build high-performance Ajax web applications by dragging, dropping and configuring the component's properties, just as you do with other components in the **Palette**.

23.4 AutoComplete Text Field and Virtual Forms

We demonstrate the **AutoComplete Text Field** component from the BluePrints catalog by modifying the form in our `AddressBook` application. The *AutoComplete Text Field* provides a list of suggestions as the user types. It obtains the suggestions from a data source, such as a database or web service. Eventually, the new form will allow users to search the address book by last name, then first name. If the user selects a contact, the application will display the contact's name and address on a map of the neighborhood. We build this form in two stages. First, we'll add the **AutoComplete Text Field** that will display suggestions as the user types a contact's last name. Then we'll add the search functionality and map display in the next step.

Adding Search Components to the AddressBook.jsp Page

Using the `AddressBook` application from Section 23.2, drop a **Static Text** component named `searchHeader` below `addressesTable`. Change its text to `"Search the address book by last name:"` and change its font size to 18px. Now drag an **AutoComplete Text Field** component to the page and name it `nameAutoComplete`. Set this field's `required` property to `true`. Add a **Label** named `nameSearchLabel` containing the text `"Last name:"` to the left of the **AutoComplete Text Field**. Finally, add a button called `lookUpButton` with the text `Look Up` to the right of the **AutoComplete Text Field**.

23.4.1 Configuring Virtual Forms

Virtual forms are used when you would like a button to submit a subset of the page's input fields to the server. Recall that the **Table**'s internal virtual forms were enabled so that clicking the pagination buttons would not submit any of the data in the **Text Field**s used to add a contact to the AddressBook database. Virtual forms are particularly useful for displaying multiple forms on the same page. They allow you to specify a *submitter* component and one or more *participant* components for a form. When the virtual form's submitter component is clicked, only the values of its participant components will be submitted to the server. We use virtual forms in our AddressBook application to separate the form for adding a contact to the AddressBook database from the form for searching the database.

To add virtual forms to the page, right click the **Submit** button on the upper form and choose **Configure Virtual Forms...** from the popup menu to display the **Configure Virtual Forms** dialog. Click **New** to add a virtual form, then click in the **Name** column and change the new form's name to addForm. Double click the **Submit** column and change the option to **Yes** to indicate that this button should be used to submit the addForm virtual form. Click **OK** to exit the dialog. Next, select all the **Text Field**s used to enter a contact's information in the upper form. You can do this by holding the *Ctrl* key while you click each **Text Field**. Right click one of the selected **Text Field**s and choose **Configure Virtual Forms...**. In the **Participate** column of the addForm, change the option to **Yes** to indicate that the values in these **Text Field**s should be submitted to the server when the form is submitted. Click **OK** to exit.

Repeat the process described above to create a second virtual form named searchForm for the lower form. Figure 23.10 shows the **Configure Virtual Forms** dialog after both virtual forms have been added. The **Look Up** Button should submit the searchForm, and nameAutoComplete should participate in the searchForm. Next, return to **Design** mode and click the **Show Virtual Forms** button ( ) at the top of the Visual Designer panel to display a legend of the virtual forms on the page. Your virtual forms should be configured as in Fig. 23.11. The **Text Field**s outlined in blue participate in the virtual form addForm. Those outlined in green participate in the virtual form searchForm. The components outlined with a dashed line submit their respective forms. A color key is provided at the bottom right of the **Design** area so that you know which components belong to each virtual form.

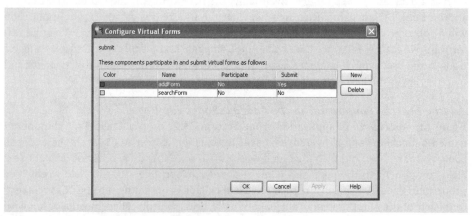

Fig. 23.10 | **Configure Virtual Forms** dialog.

Fig. 23.11 | Virtual forms legend.

23.4.2 JSP File with Virtual Forms and an AutoComplete Text Field

Figure 23.12 presents the JSP file generated by Netbeans for this stage of the AddressBook application. A new tag library is specified in the root element (xmlns:bp="http://java.sun.com/blueprints/ui/14"; line 5). This is the BluePrints catalog library that provides Ajax-enabled components such as the **AutoComplete Text Field** component. We focus only on the new features of this JSP.

Lines 22–25 configure the virtual forms for this page. Lines 147–151 define the **Auto-Complete Text Field** component. This component's completionMethod attribute is bound to the page bean's nameAutoComplete_complete method (discussed in Section 23.4.3), which provides the list of options the **AutoComplete Text Field** component should suggest. To create this method, right click the nameAutoComplete component in **Design** view and select **Edit Event Handler > complete**. Notice that the **Look Up** button (lines 155–157) does not specify an action-handler method binding; we'll add this in Section 23.5.

```
1   <?xml version="1.0" encoding="UTF-8"?>
2   <!-- Fig. 23.12: AddressBook.jsp -->
3   <!-- AddressBook JSP with an add form and a Table JSF component. -->
4   <jsp:root version="1.2"
5     xmlns:bp="http://java.sun.com/blueprints/ui/14"
6     xmlns:f="http://java.sun.com/jsf/core"
7     xmlns:h="http://java.sun.com/jsf/html"
8     xmlns:jsp="http://java.sun.com/JSP/Page"
9     xmlns:webuijsf="http://www.sun.com/webui/webuijsf">
```

Fig. 23.12 | AddressBook JSP with an **AutoComplete Text Field** component. (Part 1 of 5.)

```
10    <jsp:directive.page contentType="text/html;charset=UTF-8"
11      pageEncoding="UTF-8"/>
12    <f:view>
13    <webuijsf:page binding="#{AddressBook.page1}" id="page1">
14      <webuijsf:html binding="#{AddressBook.html1}" id="html1">
15        <webuijsf:head binding="#{AddressBook.head1}" id="head1">
16          <webuijsf:link binding="#{AddressBook.link1}" id="link1"
17            url="/resources/stylesheet.css"/>
18        </webuijsf:head>
19        <webuijsf:body binding="#{AddressBook.body1}" id="body1"
20          style="-rave-layout: grid">
21          <webuijsf:form binding="#{AddressBook.form1}" id="form1"
22            virtualFormsConfig="addForm | zipTextField lnameTextField
23              fnameTextField streetTextField cityTextField
24              stateTextField | submitButton , searchForm |
25              nameAutoComplete | lookUpButton">
26            <webuijsf:staticText binding="#{AddressBook.staticText1}"
27              id="staticText1" style="font-size: 18px; left: 24px;
28              top: 24px; position: absolute"
29              text="Add a contact to the address book:"/>
30            <webuijsf:label binding="#{AddressBook.fnameLabel}"
31              for="fnameTextField" id="fnameLabel" style="position:
32              absolute; left: 24px; top: 72px" text="First name:"/>
33            <webuijsf:textField binding="#{AddressBook.fnameTextField}"
34              id="fnameTextField" maxLength="30" required="true"
35              style="left: 100px; top: 72px; position: absolute;
36              width: 192px"/>
37            <webuijsf:label binding="#{AddressBook.lnameLabel}"
38              for="lnameTextField" id="lnameLabel" style="left: 312px;
39              top: 72px; position: absolute" text="Last name:"/>
40            <webuijsf:textField binding="#{AddressBook.lnameTextField}"
41              id="lnameTextField" maxLength="30" required="true"
42              style="left: 390px; top: 72px; position: absolute;
43              width: 214px"/>
44            <webuijsf:label binding="#{AddressBook.streetLabel}"
45              for="streetTextField" id="streetLabel" style="position:
46              absolute; left: 24px; top: 96px" text="Street:"/>
47            <webuijsf:textField binding=
48              "#{AddressBook.streetTextField}" id="streetTextField"
49              maxLength="150" required="true" style="left: 100px;
50              top: 96px; position: absolute; width: 504px"/>
51            <webuijsf:label binding="#{AddressBook.cityLabel}"
52              for="cityTextField" id="cityLabel" style="left: 24px;
53              top: 120px; position: absolute" text="City:"/>
54            <webuijsf:textField binding="#{AddressBook.cityTextField}"
55              id="cityTextField" maxLength="30" required="true"
56              style="left: 100px; top: 120px; position: absolute;
57              width: 240px"/>
58            <webuijsf:label binding="#{AddressBook.stateLabel}"
59              for="stateTextField" id="stateLabel" style="left: 360px;
60              top: 120px; position: absolute" text="State:"/>
```

Fig. 23.12 | AddressBook JSP with an **AutoComplete Text Field** component. (Part 2 of 5.)

```
61    <webuijsf:textField binding="#{AddressBook.stateTextField}"
62       id="stateTextField" maxLength="2" required="true"
63       style="left: 412px; top: 120px; position: absolute;
64       width: 48px"/>
65    <webuijsf:label binding="#{AddressBook.zipLabel}"
66       for="zipTextField" id="zipLabel" style="left: 490px;
67       top: 120px; position: absolute" text="Zip:"/>
68    <webuijsf:textField binding="#{AddressBook.zipTextField}"
69       id="zipTextField" maxLength="5" required="true"
70       style="left: 534px; top: 120px; position: absolute;
71       width: 70px"/>
72    <webuijsf:button actionExpression=
73       "#{AddressBook.submitButton_action}" binding=
74       "#{AddressBook.submitButton}" id="submitButton" primary=
75       "true" style="left: 100px; top: 168px; position:
76       absolute; width: 100px" text="Submit"/>
77    <webuijsf:button binding="#{AddressBook.clearButton}"
78       id="clearButton" reset="true" style="left: 215px; top:
79       168px; position: absolute; width: 100px" text="Clear"/>
80    <webuijsf:messageGroup binding=
81       "#{AddressBook.messageGroup1}" id="messageGroup1"
82       showGlobalOnly="true" style="left: 624px; top: 72px;
83       position: absolute"/>
84    <webuijsf:table augmentTitle="false" binding=
85       "#{AddressBook.addressesTable}" id="addressesTable"
86       paginateButton="true" paginationControls="true"
87       style="left: 24px; top: 216px; position: absolute"
88       title="Contacts" width="816">
89       <webuijsf:tableRowGroup binding=
90          "#{AddressBook.tableRowGroup1}" id="tableRowGroup1"
91          rows="5" sourceData=
92          "#{AddressBook.addressesDataProvider}"
93          sourceVar="currentRow">
94          <webuijsf:tableColumn binding=
95             "#{AddressBook.fnameColumn}" headerText=
96             "First Name" id="fnameColumn"
97             sort="ADDRESSES.FIRSTNAME">
98             <webuijsf:staticText binding=
99                "#{AddressBook.staticText2}" id="staticText2"
100               text="#{currentRow.value[
101               'ADDRESSES.FIRSTNAME']}"/>
102         </webuijsf:tableColumn>
103         <webuijsf:tableColumn binding=
104            "#{AddressBook.lnameColumn}"
105            headerText="Last Name" id="lnameColumn"
106            sort="ADDRESSES.LASTNAME">
107            <webuijsf:staticText binding=
108               "#{AddressBook.staticText3}" id="staticText3"
109               text="#{currentRow.value[
110               'ADDRESSES.LASTNAME']}"/>
111         </webuijsf:tableColumn>
```

Fig. 23.12 | AddressBook JSP with an **AutoComplete Text Field** component. (Part 3 of 5.)

```
112                       <webuijsf:tableColumn binding=
113                           "#{AddressBook.streetColumn}" headerText="Street"
114                           id="streetColumn" sort="ADDRESSES.STREET">
115                           <webuijsf:staticText binding=
116                               "#{AddressBook.staticText4}" id="staticText4"
117                               text="#{currentRow.value[
118                               'ADDRESSES.STREET']}"/>
119                       </webuijsf:tableColumn>
120                       <webuijsf:tableColumn binding=
121                           "#{AddressBook.cityColumn}" headerText="City"
122                           id="cityColumn" sort="ADDRESSES.CITY">
123                           <webuijsf:staticText binding=
124                               "#{AddressBook.staticText5}" id="staticText5"
125                               text="#{currentRow.value['ADDRESSES.CITY']}"/>
126                       </webuijsf:tableColumn>
127                       <webuijsf:tableColumn binding=
128                           "#{AddressBook.stateColumn}" headerText="State"
129                           id="stateColumn" sort="ADDRESSES.STATE">
130                           <webuijsf:staticText binding=
131                               "#{AddressBook.staticText6}" id="staticText6"
132                               text="#{currentRow.value['ADDRESSES.STATE']}"/>
133                       </webuijsf:tableColumn>
134                       <webuijsf:tableColumn binding=
135                           "#{AddressBook.zipColumn}" headerText="Zip"
136                           id="zipColumn" sort="ADDRESSES.ZIP" width="106">
137                           <webuijsf:staticText binding=
138                               "#{AddressBook.staticText7}" id="staticText7"
139                               text="#{currentRow.value['ADDRESSES.ZIP']}"/>
140                       </webuijsf:tableColumn>
141                   </webuijsf:tableRowGroup>
142               </webuijsf:table>
143               <webuijsf:staticText binding="#{AddressBook.searchHeader}"
144                   id="searchHeader" style="font-size: 18px; left: 24px;
145                   top: 420px; position: absolute"
146                   text="Search the address book by last name:"/>
147        <bp:autoComplete binding="#{AddressBook.nameAutoComplete}"
148            completionMethod=
149            "#{AddressBook.nameAutoComplete_complete}"
150            id="nameAutoComplete"
151            style="left: 96px; top: 444px; position: absolute"/>
152               <webuijsf:label binding="#{AddressBook.label1}"
153                   for="nameAutoComplete" id="label1" style="left: 24px;
154                   top: 447px; position: absolute" text="Last name:"/>
155               <webuijsf:button binding="#{AddressBook.lookUpButton}"
156                   id="lookUpButton" style="left: 288px; top: 446px;
157                   position: absolute; width: 100px" text="Look Up"/>
158           </webuijsf:form>
159       </webuijsf:body>
160     </webuijsf:html>
161   </webuijsf:page>
162   </f:view>
163 </jsp:root>
```

Fig. 23.12 | AddressBook JSP with an **AutoComplete Text Field** component. (Part 4 of 5.)

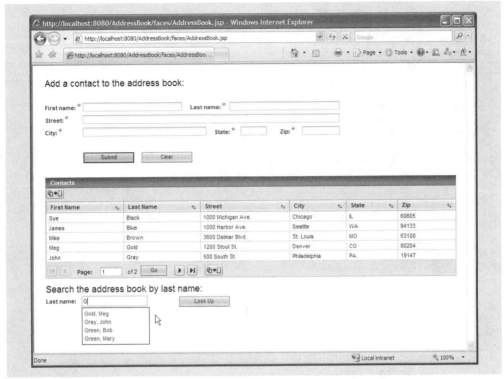

Fig. 23.12 | AddressBook JSP with an **AutoComplete Text Field** component. (Part 5 of 5.)

23.4.3 Providing Suggestions for an AutoComplete Text Field

Figure 23.13 displays the page bean file for the JSP in Fig. 23.12. It includes the method nameAutoComplete_complete, which provides the functionality for the **AutoComplete Text Field**. Otherwise, this page bean is identical to the one in Fig. 23.8.

```
1   // Fig. 23.13: AddressBook.java
2   // Page bean for AddressBook.jsp.
3   package addressbook;
4
5   import com.sun.data.provider.RowKey;
6   import com.sun.data.provider.impl.CachedRowSetDataProvider;
7   import com.sun.j2ee.blueprints.ui.autocomplete.AutoCompleteComponent;
8   import com.sun.j2ee.blueprints.ui.autocomplete.CompletionResult;
9   import com.sun.rave.web.ui.appbase.AbstractPageBean;
10  import com.sun.webui.jsf.component.Body;
11  import com.sun.webui.jsf.component.Button;
12  import com.sun.webui.jsf.component.Form;
13  import com.sun.webui.jsf.component.Head;
14  import com.sun.webui.jsf.component.Html;
15  import com.sun.webui.jsf.component.Label;
```

Fig. 23.13 | Page bean that suggests names in the **AutoComplete Text Field**. (Part 1 of 3.)

```
16  import com.sun.webui.jsf.component.Link;
17  import com.sun.webui.jsf.component.MessageGroup;
18  import com.sun.webui.jsf.component.Page;
19  import com.sun.webui.jsf.component.StaticText;
20  import com.sun.webui.jsf.component.Table;
21  import com.sun.webui.jsf.component.TableColumn;
22  import com.sun.webui.jsf.component.TableRowGroup;
23  import com.sun.webui.jsf.component.TextField;
24  import com.sun.webui.jsf.model.DefaultTableDataProvider;
25  import javax.faces.FacesException;
26  import javax.faces.context.FacesContext;
27
28  public class AddressBook extends AbstractPageBean
29  {
30     // To save space, we omitted the code in lines 30-625. The complete
31     // source code is provided with this chapter's examples.
32
626    // action handler for the autocomplete box that fetches names
627    // from the address book whose prefixes match the letters typed so far
628    // and displays them in a suggestion list.
629    public void nameAutoComplete_complete(
630       FacesContext context, String prefix, CompletionResult result )
631    {
632       try
633       {
634          boolean hasNext = addressesDataProvider.cursorFirst();
635
636          while ( hasNext )
637          {
638             // get a name from the database
639             String name =
640                (String) addressesDataProvider.getValue(
641                "ADDRESSES.LASTNAME" ) + ", " +
642                (String) addressesDataProvider.getValue(
643                "ADDRESSES.FIRSTNAME" ) ;
644
645             // if the name in the database starts with the prefix,
646             // add it to the list of suggestions
647             if ( name.toLowerCase().startsWith( prefix.toLowerCase() ) )
648             {
649                result.addItem( name );
650             } // end if
651             else
652             {
653                // terminate the loop if the rest of the names are
654                // alphabetically less than the prefix
655                if ( prefix.compareTo( name ) < 0 )
656                {
657                   break;
658                } // end if
659             } // end else
660
```

Fig. 23.13 | Page bean that suggests names in the **AutoComplete Text Field**. (Part 2 of 3.)

```
661              // move cursor to next row of database
662              hasNext = addressesDataProvider.cursorNext();
663           } // end while
664        } // end try
665        catch ( Exception ex )
666        {
667           result.addItem( "Exception getting matching names." );
668        } // end catch
669     } // end method nameAutoComplete_complete
670  } // end class AddressBook
```

Fig. 23.13 | Page bean that suggests names in the **AutoComplete Text Field**. (Part 3 of 3.)

Method `nameAutoComplete_complete` (lines 629–669) is invoked after every keystroke in the **AutoComplete Text Field** to update the list of suggestions based on the text the user has typed so far. The method receives a string (`prefix`) containing the text the user has entered and a `CompletionResult` object (`result`) that is used to display suggestions to the user. The method loops through the rows of the `addressesDataProvider`, retrieves the name from each row, checks whether the name begins with the letters typed so far and, if so, adds the name to `result`. Line 634 sets the cursor to the first row in the data provider. Line 636 determines whether there are more rows in the data provider. If so, lines 639–643 retrieve the last name and first name from the current row and create a `String` in the format *last name, first name*. Line 647 compares the lowercase versions of `name` and `prefix` to determine whether the `name` starts with the characters typed so far. If so, the name is a match and line 649 adds it to `result`.

Recall that the data provider wraps a `CachedRowSet` object that contains a SQL query which returns the rows in the database sorted by last name, then first name. This allows us to stop iterating through the data provider once we reach a row whose name comes alphabetically after the text entered by the user—names in the rows beyond this will all be alphabetically greater and thus are not potential matches. If the `name` does not match the text entered so far, line 655 tests whether the current name is alphabetically greater than the `prefix`. If so, line 657 terminates the loop.

Performance Tip 23.1

*When using database columns to provide suggestions in an **AutoComplete Text Field**, sorting the columns eliminates the need to check every row in the database for potential matches. This significantly improves performance when dealing with a large database.*

If the name is neither a match nor alphabetically greater than `prefix`, then line 662 moves the cursor to the next row in the data provider. If there is another row, the loop iterates again, checking whether the name in the next row matches the `prefix` and should be added to `results`.

Lines 665–668 catch any exceptions generated while searching the database. Line 667 adds text to the suggestion box indicating the error to the user.

23.5 Google Maps **Map Viewer** Component

We now complete the `AddressBook` application by adding functionality to the **Look Up Button**. When the user clicks this **Button**, the name in the **AutoComplete Text Field** is used to search the `AddressBook` database. We also add a ***Map Viewer*** Ajax-enabled JSF component to the page to display a map of the area for the address. A **Map Viewer** uses the *Google Maps API* web service to find and display maps. (The details of web services are covered in Chapter 24.) In this example, using the Google Maps API is analogous to making ordinary method calls on a **Map Viewer** object and its supporting bean in the page bean file. When a contact is found, we display a map of the neighborhood with a ***Map Marker*** that points to the location and indicates the contact's name and address.

23.5.1 Obtaining a Google Maps API Key

To use the **Map Viewer** component, you must have an account with Google. Visit the site `https://www.google.com/accounts/ManageAccount` to register for a free account if you do not have one. Once you have logged in to your account, you must obtain a key to use the Google Maps API from `www.google.com/apis/maps`. The key you receive will be specific to this web application and will limit the number of maps the application can display per day. When you sign up for the key, you will be asked to enter the URL for the application that will be using the Google Maps API. If you are deploying the application only on Sun Java System Application Server, enter `http://localhost:8080/` as the URL.

After you accept Google's terms and conditions, you'll be redirected to a page containing your new Google Maps API key. Save this key in a text file in a convenient location for future reference.

23.5.2 Adding a Map Viewer Component to a Page

Now that you have a key to use the Google Maps API, you are ready to complete the AddressBook application. With `AddressBook.jsp` open in **Design** mode, add a **Map Viewer** component named `mapViewer` below the `nameAutoComplete`. In the **Properties** window, set the **Map Viewer**'s key property to the key you obtained for accessing the Google Maps API. Set the `rendered` property to `false` so that the map will not be displayed when the user has not yet searched for an address. Set the `zoomLevel` property to `1` (In) so the user can see the street names on the map.

Drop a **Map Marker** (named `mapMarker`) from the **BluePrints AJAX Support Beans** section of the **Palette** anywhere on the page. This component (which is not visible in **Design** view) marks the contact's location on the map. You must bind the marker to the map so that the marker will display on the map. To do so, right click the **Map Viewer** in the **Outline** tab and choose **Property Bindings...** to display the **Property Bindings** dialog. Select `info` from the **Select bindable property** column of the dialog, then select `mapMarker` from the **Select binding target** column. Click **Apply**, then **Close**.

Finally, drop a ***Geocoding Service Object*** (named `geoCoder`) from the **BluePrints AJAX Support Beans** section of the **Palette** anywhere on the page. This object (which is not visible in **Design** view) converts street addresses into latitudes and longitudes that the **Map Viewer** component uses to display an appropriate map.

Adding a Data Provider to the Page

To complete this application, you need a second data provider to search the `AddressBook` database based on the first and last name entered in the **AutoComplete Text Field**. We want to create a new data source rather than reuse the existing one, because the query to search for contacts is different from the query to display all the contacts. On the **Runtime** tab, expand the **Databases** node, the **AddressBook** database's node and its **Tables** node to reveal the **Addresses** table. Drag the **Addresses** table onto the page to create the new data provider. Select the new data provider in the **Navigator** tab and change its id to addresses-SearchDataProvider. In the **Outline** tab, a new node named addressesRowSet1 has been added to the SessionBean1 node. Change the id of addressesRowSet1 to addresses-SearchRowSet.

Double click the addressesSearchRowSet node to edit the SQL statement for this RowSet. Since we'll use this row set to search the database for a given last and first name, we need to add search parameters to the SELECT statement the RowSet will execute. To do this, enter the text "= ?" in the **Criteria** column of both the first and last name rows in the SQL statement editor table. The number 1 should appear in the **Order** column for first name and 2 should appear for last name. Notice that the lines

```
WHERE JHTP7.ADDRESSES.FIRSTNAME = ?
  AND JHTP7.ADDRESSES.LASTNAME = ?
```

have been added to the SQL statement. This indicates that the RowSet now executes a parameterized SQL statement. The parameters can be set programmatically, with the first name as the first parameter and the last name as the second.

23.5.3 JSP File with a Map Viewer Component

Figure 23.14 presents the JSP file for the completed address-book application. It is nearly identical to the JSP for the previous two versions of this application. The new feature is the **Map Viewer** component (and its supporting components) used to display a map with the contact's location. We discuss only the new elements of this file. [*Note:* This code will not run until you have specified your own Google Maps key in lines 165–166. You can paste your key into the **Map Viewer** component's key property in the **Properties** window.]

Lines 162–168 define the mapViewer component that displays a map of the area surrounding the address. The component's center attribute is bound to the page bean property mapViewer_center. This property is manipulated in the page bean file to center the map on the desired address.

```
1   <?xml version="1.0" encoding="UTF-8"?>
2   <!-- Fig. 23.14: AddressBook.jsp -->
3   <!-- AddressBook JSP with an add form and a Table JSF component. -->
4
5   <jsp:root version="1.2"
6      xmlns:bp="http://java.sun.com/blueprints/ui/14"
7      xmlns:f="http://java.sun.com/jsf/core"
8      xmlns:h="http://java.sun.com/jsf/html"
9      xmlns:jsp="http://java.sun.com/JSP/Page"
10     xmlns:webuijsf="http://www.sun.com/webui/webuijsf">
11     <jsp:directive.page contentType="text/html;charset=UTF-8"
12        pageEncoding="UTF-8"/>
13     <f:view>
14     <webuijsf:page binding="#{AddressBook.page1}" id="page1">
15        <webuijsf:html binding="#{AddressBook.html1}" id="html1">
```

Fig. 23.14 | AddressBook JSP with a **Map Viewer** component. (Part 1 of 5.)

```
16          <webuijsf:head binding="#{AddressBook.head1}" id="head1">
17            <webuijsf:link binding="#{AddressBook.link1}" id="link1"
18              url="/resources/stylesheet.css"/>
19          </webuijsf:head>
20          <webuijsf:body binding="#{AddressBook.body1}" id="body1"
21            style="-rave-layout: grid">
22            <webuijsf:form binding="#{AddressBook.form1}" id="form1"
23              virtualFormsConfig="addForm | zipTextField lnameTextField
24              fnameTextField streetTextField cityTextField stateTextField
25              | submitButton , searchForm | nameAutoComplete |
26              lookUpButton">
27              <webuijsf:staticText binding=
28                "#{AddressBook.staticText1}" id="staticText1" style=
29                "font-size: 18px; left: 24px; top: 24px; position:
30                absolute" text="Add a contact to the address book:"/>
31              <webuijsf:label binding="#{AddressBook.fnameLabel}"
32                for="fnameTextField" id="fnameLabel" style="position:
33                absolute; left: 24px; top: 72px" text="First name:"/>
34              <webuijsf:textField binding="#{AddressBook.fnameTextField}"
35                id="fnameTextField" maxLength="30" required="true"
36                style="left: 100px; top: 72px; position: absolute;
37                width: 192px"/>
38              <webuijsf:label binding="#{AddressBook.lnameLabel}"
39                for="lnameTextField" id="lnameLabel" style="left: 312px;
40                top: 72px; position: absolute" text="Last name:"/>
41              <webuijsf:textField binding="#{AddressBook.lnameTextField}"
42                id="lnameTextField" maxLength="30" required="true"
43                style="left: 390px; top: 72px; position: absolute;
44                width: 214px"/>
45              <webuijsf:label binding="#{AddressBook.streetLabel}"
46                for="streetTextField" id="streetLabel" style="position:
47                absolute; left: 24px; top: 96px" text="Street:"/>
48              <webuijsf:textField binding=
49                "#{AddressBook.streetTextField}" id="streetTextField"
50                maxLength="150" required="true" style="left: 100px;
51                top: 96px; position: absolute; width: 504px"/>
52              <webuijsf:label binding="#{AddressBook.cityLabel}"
53                for="cityTextField" id="cityLabel" style="left: 24px;
54                top: 120px; position: absolute" text="City:"/>
55              <webuijsf:textField binding="#{AddressBook.cityTextField}"
56                id="cityTextField" maxLength="30" required="true"
57                style="left: 100px; top: 120px; position: absolute;
58                width: 240px"/>
59              <webuijsf:label binding="#{AddressBook.stateLabel}"
60                for="stateTextField" id="stateLabel"
61                style="left: 360px; top: 120px; position: absolute"
62                text="State:"/>
63              <webuijsf:textField binding="#{AddressBook.stateTextField}"
64                id="stateTextField" maxLength="2" required="true"
65                style="left: 412px; top: 120px; position: absolute;
66                width: 48px"/>
67              <webuijsf:label binding="#{AddressBook.zipLabel}"
68                for="zipTextField" id="zipLabel" style="left: 490px;
```

Fig. 23.14 | AddressBook JSP with a **Map Viewer** component. (Part 2 of 5.)

```
69              top: 120px; position: absolute" text="Zip:"/>
70          <webuijsf:textField binding="#{AddressBook.zipTextField}"
71              id="zipTextField" maxLength="5" required="true"
72              style="left: 534px; top: 120px; position: absolute;
73              width: 70px"/>
74          <webuijsf:button actionExpression=
75              "#{AddressBook.submitButton_action}" binding=
76              "#{AddressBook.submitButton}" id="submitButton"
77              primary="true" style="left: 100px; top: 168px; position:
78              absolute; width: 100px" text="Submit"/>
79          <webuijsf:button binding="#{AddressBook.clearButton}"
80              id="clearButton" reset="true" style="left: 215px; top:
81              168px; position: absolute; width: 100px" text="Clear"/>
82          <webuijsf:messageGroup binding=
83              "#{AddressBook.messageGroup1}" id="messageGroup1"
84              showGlobalOnly="true" style="left: 624px; top: 72px;
85              position: absolute"/>
86          <webuijsf:table augmentTitle="false" binding=
87              "#{AddressBook.addressesTable}" id="addressesTable"
88              paginateButton="true" paginationControls="true"
89              style="left: 24px; top: 216px; position: absolute"
90              title="Contacts" width="816">
91              <webuijsf:tableRowGroup binding=
92                  "#{AddressBook.tableRowGroup1}" id="tableRowGroup1"
93                  rows="5" sourceData=
94                  "#{AddressBook.addressesDataProvider}"
95                  sourceVar="currentRow">
96                  <webuijsf:tableColumn binding=
97                      "#{AddressBook.fnameColumn}"
98                      headerText="First Name" id="fnameColumn"
99                      sort="ADDRESSES.FIRSTNAME">
100                     <webuijsf:staticText binding=
101                         "#{AddressBook.staticText2}" id="staticText2"
102                         text="#{currentRow.value[
103                         'ADDRESSES.FIRSTNAME']}"/>
104                 </webuijsf:tableColumn>
105                 <webuijsf:tableColumn binding=
106                     "#{AddressBook.lnameColumn}"
107                     headerText="Last Name" id="lnameColumn"
108                     sort="ADDRESSES.LASTNAME">
109                     <webuijsf:staticText binding=
110                         "#{AddressBook.staticText3}" id="staticText3"
111                         text="#{currentRow.value[
112                         'ADDRESSES.LASTNAME']}"/>
113                 </webuijsf:tableColumn>
114                 <webuijsf:tableColumn binding=
115                     "#{AddressBook.streetColumn}" headerText="Street"
116                     id="streetColumn" sort="ADDRESSES.STREET">
117                     <webuijsf:staticText binding=
118                         "#{AddressBook.staticText4}" id="staticText4"
119                         text="#{currentRow.value[
120                         'ADDRESSES.STREET']}"/>
121                 </webuijsf:tableColumn>
```

Fig. 23.14 | AddressBook JSP with a **Map Viewer** component. (Part 3 of 5.)

```
122                            <webuijsf:tableColumn binding=
123                               "#{AddressBook.cityColumn}" headerText="City"
124                               id="cityColumn" sort="ADDRESSES.CITY">
125                               <webuijsf:staticText binding=
126                                  "#{AddressBook.staticText5}" id="staticText5"
127                                  text="#{currentRow.value['ADDRESSES.CITY']}"/>
128                            </webuijsf:tableColumn>
129                            <webuijsf:tableColumn binding=
130                               "#{AddressBook.stateColumn}" headerText="State"
131                               id="stateColumn" sort="ADDRESSES.STATE">
132                               <webuijsf:staticText binding=
133                                  "#{AddressBook.staticText6}" id="staticText6"
134                                  text="#{currentRow.value['ADDRESSES.STATE']}"/>
135                            </webuijsf:tableColumn>
136                            <webuijsf:tableColumn binding=
137                               "#{AddressBook.zipColumn}" headerText="Zip"
138                               id="zipColumn" sort="ADDRESSES.ZIP" width="106">
139                               <webuijsf:staticText binding=
140                                  "#{AddressBook.staticText7}" id="staticText7"
141                                  text="#{currentRow.value['ADDRESSES.ZIP']}"/>
142                            </webuijsf:tableColumn>
143                         </webuijsf:tableRowGroup>
144                      </webuijsf:table>
145                      <webuijsf:staticText binding="#{AddressBook.searchHeader}"
146                         id="searchHeader" style="font-size: 18px; left: 24px;
147                         top: 420px; position: absolute"
148                         text="Search the address book by last name:"/>
149                      <bp:autoComplete binding=
150                         "#{AddressBook.nameAutoComplete}" completionMethod=
151                         "#{AddressBook.nameAutoComplete_complete}"
152                         id="nameAutoComplete"
153                         style="left: 96px; top: 444px; position: absolute"/>
154                      <webuijsf:label binding="#{AddressBook.label1}"
155                         for="nameAutoComplete" id="label1" style="left: 24px;
156                         top: 447px; position: absolute" text="Last name:"/>
157                      <webuijsf:button actionExpression=
158                         "#{AddressBook.lookUpButton_action}"
159                         binding="#{AddressBook.lookUpButton}" id="lookUpButton"
160                         style="left: 288px; top: 446px; position: absolute;
161                         width: 100px" text="Look Up"/>
162                      <bp:mapViewer binding="#{AddressBook.mapViewer}"
163                         center="#{AddressBook.mapViewer_center}"
164                         id="mapViewer" info="#{AddressBook.mapMarker}"
165                         key="XXXXXXXXXXXXXXXXXXXXXXXXXXXXXXXXXXXXXXXXXXXXXXXXXXXXXX
166                         XXXXXXXXXXXXXXXXXXXXXXXXXXXXXXXXXXXXX"
167                         style="height: 550px; left: 24px; top: 480px;
168                         position: absolute; width: 814px" zoomLevel="4"/>
169                   </webuijsf:form>
170                </webuijsf:body>
171             </webuijsf:html>
172          </webuijsf:page>
173       </f:view>
174    </jsp:root>
```

Fig. 23.14 | AddressBook JSP with a **Map Viewer** component. (Part 4 of 5.)

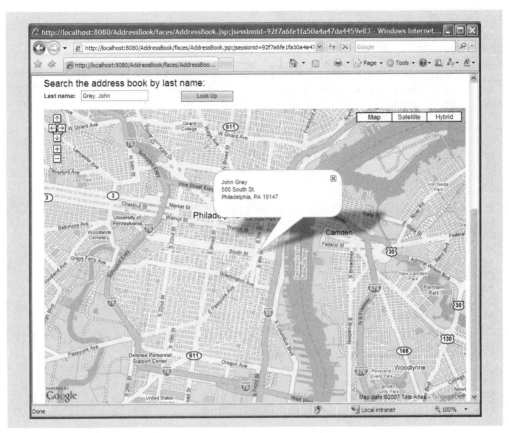

Fig. 23.14 | AddressBook JSP with a **Map Viewer** component. (Part 5 of 5.)

The **Look Up** Button's action attribute is now bound to method lookUpButton_action in the page bean (lines 157–158). This action handler searches the AddressBook database for the name entered in the **AutoComplete Text Field** and displays the contact's name and address on a map of the contact's location. We discuss this method in Section 23.5.4.

23.5.4 Page Bean That Displays a Map in the Map Viewer Component

Figure 23.15 presents the page bean for the completed AddressBook application. Most of this file is identical to the page beans for the first two versions of this application. We discuss only the new action-handler method, lookUpButton_action.

```
1   // Fig. 23.15: AddressBook.java
2   // Page bean for AddressBook.jsp.
3   package addressbook;
4
5   import com.sun.data.provider.RowKey;
6   import com.sun.data.provider.impl.CachedRowSetDataProvider;
```

Fig. 23.15 | Page bean that gets a map to display in the **Map Viewer** component. (Part 1 of 3.)

```
 7    import com.sun.j2ee.blueprints.ui.autocomplete.AutoCompleteComponent;
 8    import com.sun.j2ee.blueprints.ui.autocomplete.CompletionResult;
 9    import com.sun.j2ee.blueprints.ui.geocoder.GeoCoder;
10    import com.sun.j2ee.blueprints.ui.geocoder.GeoPoint;
11    import com.sun.j2ee.blueprints.ui.mapviewer.MapComponent;
12    import com.sun.j2ee.blueprints.ui.mapviewer.MapMarker;
13    import com.sun.j2ee.blueprints.ui.mapviewer.MapPoint;
14    import com.sun.rave.web.ui.appbase.AbstractPageBean;
15    import com.sun.webui.jsf.component.Body;
16    import com.sun.webui.jsf.component.Button;
17    import com.sun.webui.jsf.component.Form;
18    import com.sun.webui.jsf.component.Head;
19    import com.sun.webui.jsf.component.Html;
20    import com.sun.webui.jsf.component.Label;
21    import com.sun.webui.jsf.component.Link;
22    import com.sun.webui.jsf.component.MessageGroup;
23    import com.sun.webui.jsf.component.Page;
24    import com.sun.webui.jsf.component.StaticText;
25    import com.sun.webui.jsf.component.Table;
26    import com.sun.webui.jsf.component.TableColumn;
27    import com.sun.webui.jsf.component.TableRowGroup;
28    import com.sun.webui.jsf.component.TextField;
29    import javax.faces.FacesException;
30    import javax.faces.context.FacesContext;
31
32    public class AddressBook extends AbstractPageBean
33    {
34       private int __placeholder;
35
36       private void _init() throws Exception
37       {
38          addressesDataProvider.setCachedRowSet(
39             ( javax.sql.rowset.CachedRowSet ) getValue(
40             "#{SessionBean1.addressesRowSet}" ) );
41          addressesTable.setInternalVirtualForm( true );
42          mapViewer.setRendered( false );
43          addressesSearchDataProvider.setCachedRowSet(
44             ( javax.sql.rowset.CachedRowSet ) getValue(
45             "#{SessionBean1.addressesSearchRowSet}" ) );
46       } // end method _init
47
48       // To save space, we omitted the code in lines 48-741. The complete
49       // source code is provided with this chapter's examples.
50
742       // action handler for the lookUpButton that searches the address book
743       // database and displays the requested address on a corresponding map.
744       public String lookUpButton_action()
745       {
746          // split text in autocomplete field into first and last name
747          String name = String.valueOf( nameAutoComplete.getValue() );
748          int splitIndex = name.indexOf( "," );
749          String lname = name.substring( 0, splitIndex );
750          String fname = name.substring( splitIndex + 2 );
```

Fig. 23.15 | Page bean that gets a map to display in the **Map Viewer** component. (Part 2 of 3.)

```
751
752         try
753         {
754            // set the parameters for the addressesSearchDataProvider
755            addressesSearchDataProvider.getCachedRowSet().setObject(
756               1, fname );
757            addressesSearchDataProvider.getCachedRowSet().setObject(
758               2, lname );
759            addressesSearchDataProvider.refresh();
760            String street = (String) addressesSearchDataProvider.getValue(
761               "ADDRESSES.STREET" );
762            String city = (String) addressesSearchDataProvider.getValue(
763               "ADDRESSES.CITY" );
764            String state = (String) addressesSearchDataProvider.getValue(
765               "ADDRESSES.STATE" );
766            String zip =  (String) addressesSearchDataProvider.getValue(
767               "ADDRESSES.ZIP" );
768
769            // format the address for Google Maps
770            String googleAddress = street + ", " + city + ", " + state +
771               " " + zip;
772
773            // get the geopoints for the address
774            GeoPoint points[] = geoCoder.geoCode( googleAddress );
775
776            // if Google Maps cannot find the address
777            if ( points == null )
778            {
779               error( "Map for " + googleAddress + " could not be found" );
780               mapViewer.setRendered( false ); // hide map
781               return null;
782            } // end if
783
784            // center the map for the given address
785            mapViewer_center.setLatitude( points[0].getLatitude() );
786            mapViewer_center.setLongitude( points[0].getLongitude() );
787
788            // create a marker for the address and set its display text
789            mapMarker.setLatitude( points[0].getLatitude() );
790            mapMarker.setLongitude( points[0].getLongitude() );
791            mapMarker.setMarkup(  fname + " " + lname + "<br/>" + street +
792               "<br/>" + city + ", " + state + " " + zip );
793
794            mapViewer.setRendered( true ); // show map
795         } // end try
796         catch ( Exception e )
797         {
798            error( "Error processing search. " + e.getMessage() );
799         } // end catch
800
801         return null;
802      } // end method lookUpButton_action
803   } // end class AddressBook
```

Fig. 23.15 | Page bean that gets a map to display in the **Map Viewer** component. (Part 3 of 3.)

Method lookUpButton_action (lines 744–802) is invoked when the user clicks the **Look Up** button in the lower form on the page. Lines 747–750 retrieve the name from the **AutoComplete Text Field** and split it into Strings for the first and last name. Lines 755–758 obtain the addressesSearchDataProvider's CachedRowSet, then use its method setObject to set the parameters for the query to the first and last name. The setObject method replaces a parameter in the SQL query with a specified string. Line 759 refreshes the data provider, which executes the wrapped RowSet's query with the new parameters. The result set now contains only rows that match the first and last name from the **Auto-Complete Text Field**. Lines 760–767 fetch the street address, city, state and zip code for this contact from the database. Note that in this example, we assume there are not multiple entries in the address book for the same first and last name, as we fetch only the address information for the first row in the data provider. Any additional rows that match the first and last name are ignored.

Lines 770–771 format the address as a String for use with the Google Maps API. Line 774 calls the **Geocoding Service Object**'s geoCode method with the address as an argument. This method returns an array of GeoPoint objects representing locations that match the address parameter. GeoPoint objects provide the latitude and longitude of a given location. We supply a complete address with a street, city, state and zip code as an argument to geoCode, so the returned array will contain just one GeoPoint object. Line 777 determines whether the array of GeoPoint objects is null. If so, the address could not be found, and lines 779–781 display a message in the **Message Group** informing the user of the search error, hide the **Map Viewer** and return null to terminate the processing.

Lines 785–786 set the latitude and longitude of the **Map Viewer**'s center to those of the GeoPoint that represents the selected address. Lines 789–792 set the **Map Marker**'s latitude and longitude, and set the text to display on the marker. Line 794 displays the recentered map containing the **Map Marker** that indicates the contact's location.

Lines 796–799 catch any exceptions generated throughout the method body and display an error message in the **Message Group**. If the user has simply selected a name from the list of selections in the **AutoComplete Text Field**, there will be no errors in searching the database, as the name is guaranteed to be in the proper *last name, first name* format and included in the AddressBook database. We did not include any special error-handling code for cases in which the user types a name that cannot be found in the AddressBook or for improperly formatted names.

23.6 Web Resources

Our Java Resource Centers focus on the enormous amount of free Java content available online. We currently provide six Java-related Resource Centers:

```
www.deitel.com/java/
www.deitel.com/JavaCertification/
www.deitel.com/JavaDesignPatterns/
www.deitel.com/JavaEE5/
www.deitel.com/JavaFX/
www.deitel.com/JavaSE6Mustang/
```

You can view our complete list of Resource Centers at

```
www.deitel.com/ResourceCenters.html
```

Web Services

> *A client is to me a mere unit,*
> *a factor in a problem.*
> —Sir Arthur Conan Doyle

> *They also serve who only*
> *stand and wait.*
> —John Milton

> *...if the simplest things of*
> *nature have a message that*
> *you understand, rejoice, for*
> *your soul is alive.*
> —Eleonora Duse

> *Protocol is everything.*
> —Francoise Giuliani

OBJECTIVES

In this chapter you will learn:

- What a web service is.
- How to publish and consume Java web services in Netbeans.
- The elements that comprise web services, such as service descriptions and classes that implement web services.
- How to create client desktop and web applications that invoke web service methods.
- The important part that XML and the Simple Object Access Protocol (SOAP) play in enabling web services.
- How to use session tracking in web services to maintain client state information.
- How to connect to databases from web services.
- How to pass objects of user-defined types to and return them from a web service.
- How to build a REST-based web service in ASP.NET.

24.1 Introduction

This chapter introduces web services, which promote software portability and reusability in applications that operate over the Internet. A *web service* is a software component stored on one computer that can be accessed via method calls by an application (or other software component) on another computer over a network. Web services communicate using such technologies as XML and HTTP. Several Java APIs facilitate web services. In this chapter, we'll be dealing with Java APIs that are based on the *Simple Object Access Protocol (SOAP)*—an XML-based protocol that allows web services and clients to communicate, even if the client and the web service are written in different languages. There are other web services technologies, such as Representational State Transfer (REST), which we cover in the contect of ASP.NET web services in Section 24.9. For information on web services, see the web resources in Section 24.10 and visit our Web Services Resource Center at www.deitel.com/WebServices. The Web Services Resource Center includes information on designing and implementing web services in many languages, and information about web services offered by companies such as Google, Amazon and eBay. You'll also find many additional tools for publishing and consuming web services. [*Note:* This chapter assumes that you know Java for Sections 24.2–24.8. To learn more about Java, check out our book *Java How to ProgramSeventh Edition* (www.deitel.com/books/ jhtp7/), or visit our Java Resource Centers at www.deitel.com/ResourceCenters.html. For Section 24.9, the chapter assumes you know Visual Basic and ASP.NET. To learn more about Visual Basic and ASP.NET, check out our book *Visual Basic 2005 How to Program, Third Edition* or visit our Visual Basic Resource Center (www.deitel.com/visual-basic/) and our ASP.NET Resource Center (www.deitel.com/aspdotnet/).]

Web services have important implications for *business-to-business (B2B) transactions*. They enable businesses to conduct transactions via standardized, widely available web services rather than relying on proprietary applications. Web services and SOAP are platform and language independent, so companies can collaborate via web services without worrying about the compatibility of their hardware, software and communications technologies. Companies such as Amazon, Google, eBay, PayPal and many others are using web services to their advantage by making their server-side applications available to partners via web services.

By purchasing web services and using extensive free web services that are relevant to their businesses, companies can spend less time developing new applications and can create innovative new applications. E-businesses can use web services to provide their customers with enhanced shopping experiences. Consider an online music store. The store's website links to information about various CDs, enabling users to purchase the CDs, to learn about the artists, to find more titles by those artists, to find other artists' music they may enjoy, and more. Another company that sells concert tickets provides a web service that displays upcoming concert dates for various artists and allows users to buy tickets. By consuming the concert-ticket web service on its site, the online music store can provide an additional service to its customers, increase its site traffic and perhaps earn a commission on concert-ticket sales. The company that sells concert tickets also benefits from the business relationship by selling more tickets and possibly by receiving revenue from the online music store for the use of the web service.

Any Java programmer with a knowledge of web services can write applications that can "consume" web services. The resulting applications would call web service methods of objects running on servers that could be thousands of miles away. To learn more about Java web services read the Java Technology and Web Services Overview at java.sun.com/ webservices/overview.html.

Netbeans
Netbeans—developed by Sun—is one of the many tools that enable programmers to "publish" and/or "consume" web services. We demonstrate how to use Netbeans to implement web services and invoke them from client applications. For each example, we provide the web service's code, then present a client application that uses the web service. Our first examples build web services and client applications in Netbeans. Then we demonstrate web services that use more sophisticated features, such as manipulating databases with JDBC and manipulating class objects. For information on downloading and installing the Netbeans 5.5.1 IDE, its Visual Web Pack and the Sun Java System Application Server (SJSAS), see Section 22.1.

24.2 Java Web Services Basics

A web service normally resides on a *server*. The application (i.e., the client) that accesses the web service sends a method call over a network to the remote machine, which processes the call and returns a response over the network to the application. This kind of distributed computing is beneficial in many applications. For example, a client application without direct access to a database on a remote server might be able to retrieve the data via a web service. Similarly, an application lacking the processing power to perform specific computations could use a web service to take advantage of another system's superior resources.

In Java, a web service is implemented as a class. In previous chapters, all the pieces of an application resided on one machine. The class that represents the web service resides on a server—it's not part of the client application.

Making a web service available to receive client requests is known as *publishing a web service*; using a web service from a client application is known as *consuming a web service*. An application that consumes a web service consists of two parts—an object of a *proxy class* for interacting with the web service and a client application that consumes the web service by invoking methods on the object of the proxy class. The client code invokes methods on the proxy object, which handles the details of communicating with the web service (such as passing method arguments to the web service and receiving return values from the web service) on the client's behalf. This communication can occur over a local network, over the Internet or even with a web service on the same computer. The web service performs the corresponding task and returns the results to the proxy object, which then returns the results to the client code. Figure 24.1 depicts the interactions among the client code, the proxy class and the web service. As you'll soon see, Netbeans creates these proxy classes for you in your client applications.

Requests to and responses from web services created with *JAX-WS 2.0* (one of many different web service frameworks) are typically transmitted via SOAP. Any client capable of generating and processing SOAP messages can interact with a web service, regardless of the language in which the web service is written. We discuss SOAP in Section 24.5.

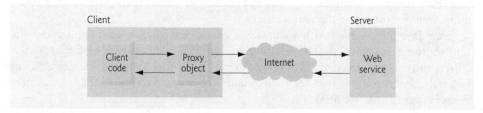

Fig. 24.1 | Interaction between a web service client and a web service.

24.3 Creating, Publishing, Testing and Describing a Web Service

The following subsections demonstrate how to create, publish and test a HugeInteger web service that performs calculations with positive integers up to 100 digits long (maintained as arrays of digits). Such integers are much larger than Java's integral primitive types can represent. The HugeInteger web service provides methods that take two "huge integers" (represented as Strings) and determine their sum, their difference, which is larger, which is smaller or whether the two numbers are equal. These methods will be services available to other applications via the web—hence the term web services.

24.3.1 Creating a Web Application Project and Adding a Web Service Class in Netbeans

When you create a web service in Netbeans, you focus on the web service's logic and let the IDE handle the web service's infrastructure. To create a web service in Netbeans, you first create a **Web Application** project. Netbeans uses this project type for web services that are invoked by other applications.

Creating a Web Application Project in Netbeans
To create a web application, perform the following steps:

1. Select **File > New Project** to open the **New Project** dialog.
2. Select **Web** from the dialog's **Categories** list, then select **Web Application** from the **Projects** list. Click **Next >**.
3. Specify the name of your project (HugeInteger) in the **Project Name** field and specify where you'd like to store the project in the **Project Location** field. You can click the **Browse** button to select the location.
4. Select **Sun Java System Application Server 9** from the **Server** drop-down list.
5. Select **Java EE 5** from the **J2EE Version** drop-down list.
6. Click **Finish** to dismiss the **New Project** dialog.

This creates a web application that will run in a web browser, similar to the **Visual Web Application** projects used in Chapters 22 and 23. Netbeans generates additional files to support the web application. This chapter discusses only the web-service-specific files.

Adding a Web Service Class to a Web Application Project
Perform the following steps to add a web service class to the project:

1. In the **Projects** tab in Netbeans, right click the **HugeInteger** project's node and select **New > Web Service...** to open the **New Web Service** dialog.
2. Specify HugeInteger in the **Web Service Name** field.
3. Specify com.deitel.iw3htp4.ch28.hugeinteger in the **Package** field.
4. Click **Finish** to dismiss the **New Web Service** dialog.

The IDE generates a sample web service class with the name you specified in *Step 2*. You can find this class in the **Projects** tab under the **Web Services** node. In this class, you'll define the methods that your web service makes available to client applications. When you eventually build your application, the IDE will generate other supporting files (which we'll discuss shortly) for your web service.

24.3.2 Defining the HugeInteger Web Service in Netbeans

Figure 24.2 contains the HugeInteger web service's code. You can implement this code yourself in the HugeInteger.java file created in Section 24.3.1, or you can simply replace the code in HugeInteger.java with a copy of our code from this example's folder. You can find this file in the project's `src\java\com\deitel\iw3htp4\ch28\hugeinteger` folder. The book's examples can be downloaded from www.deitel.com/books/ajaxfp/.

```java
1   // Fig. 24.2: HugeInteger.java
2   // HugeInteger web service that performs operations on large integers.
3   package com.deitel.iw3htp4.ch28.hugeinteger;
4
5   import javax.jws.WebService; // program uses the annotation @WebService
6   import javax.jws.WebMethod; // program uses the annotation @WebMethod
7   import javax.jws.WebParam; // program uses the annotation @WebParam
8
9   @WebService( // annotates the class as a web service
10     name = "HugeInteger", // sets class name
11     serviceName = "HugeIntegerService" ) // sets the service name
12  public class HugeInteger
13  {
14     private final static int MAXIMUM = 100; // maximum number of digits
15     public int[] number = new int[ MAXIMUM ]; // stores the huge integer
16
17     // returns a String representation of a HugeInteger
18     public String toString()
19     {
20        String value = "";
21
22        // convert HugeInteger to a String
23        for ( int digit : number )
24           value = digit + value; // places next digit at beginning of value
25
26        // locate position of first non-zero digit
27        int length = value.length();
28        int position = -1;
29
30        for ( int i = 0; i < length; i++ )
31        {
32           if ( value.charAt( i ) != '0' )
33           {
34              position = i; // first non-zero digit
35              break;
36           }
37        } // end for
38
39        return ( position != -1 ? value.substring( position ) : "0" );
40     } // end method toString
41
42     // creates a HugeInteger from a String
43     public static HugeInteger parseHugeInteger( String s )
44     {
45        HugeInteger temp = new HugeInteger();
46        int size = s.length();
47
48        for ( int i = 0; i < size; i++ )
49           temp.number[ i ] = s.charAt( size - i - 1 ) - '0';
```

Fig. 24.2 | HugeInteger web service that performs operations on large integers. (Part 1 of 3.)

```
50
51        return temp;
52     } // end method parseHugeInteger
53
54     // WebMethod that adds huge integers represented by String arguments
55     @WebMethod( operationName = "add" )
56     public String add( @WebParam( name = "first" ) String first,
57        @WebParam( name = "second" ) String second )
58     {
59        int carry = 0; // the value to be carried
60        HugeInteger operand1 = HugeInteger.parseHugeInteger( first );
61        HugeInteger operand2 = HugeInteger.parseHugeInteger( second );
62        HugeInteger result = new HugeInteger(); // stores addition result
63
64        // perform addition on each digit
65        for ( int i = 0; i < MAXIMUM; i++ )
66        {
67           // add corresponding digits in each number and the carried value;
68           // store result in the corresponding column of HugeInteger result
69           result.number[ i ] =
70              ( operand1.number[ i ] + operand2.number[ i ] + carry ) % 10;
71
72           // set carry for next column
73           carry =
74              ( operand1.number[ i ] + operand2.number[ i ] + carry ) / 10;
75        } // end for
76
77        return result.toString();
78     } // end WebMethod add
79
80     // WebMethod that subtracts integers represented by String arguments
81     @WebMethod( operationName = "subtract" )
82     public String subtract( @WebParam( name = "first" ) String first,
83        @WebParam( name = "second" ) String second )
84     {
85        HugeInteger operand1 = HugeInteger.parseHugeInteger( first );
86        HugeInteger operand2 = HugeInteger.parseHugeInteger( second );
87        HugeInteger result = new HugeInteger(); // stores difference
88
89        // subtract bottom digit from top digit
90        for ( int i = 0; i < MAXIMUM; i++ )
91        {
92           // if the digit in operand1 is smaller than the corresponding
93           // digit in operand2, borrow from the next digit
94           if ( operand1.number[ i ] < operand2.number[ i ] )
95              operand1.borrow( i );
96
97           // subtract digits
98           result.number[ i ] = operand1.number[ i ] - operand2.number[ i ];
99        } // end for
100
101        return result.toString();
102     } // end WebMethod subtract
```

Fig. 24.2 | HugeInteger web service that performs operations on large integers. (Part 2 of 3.)

```
103
104     // borrow 1 from next digit
105     private void borrow( int place )
106     {
107        if ( place >= MAXIMUM )
108           throw new IndexOutOfBoundsException();
109        else if ( number[ place + 1 ] == 0 ) // if next digit is zero
110           borrow( place + 1 ); // borrow from next digit
111
112        number[ place ] += 10; // add 10 to the borrowing digit
113        --number[ place + 1 ]; // subtract one from the digit to the left
114     } // end method borrow
115
116     // WebMethod that returns true if first integer is greater than second
117     @WebMethod( operationName = "bigger" )
118     public boolean bigger( @WebParam( name = "first" ) String first,
119        @WebParam( name = "second" ) String second )
120     {
121        try // try subtracting first from second
122        {
123           String difference = subtract( first, second );
124           return !difference.matches( "^[0]+$" );
125        } // end try
126        catch ( IndexOutOfBoundsException e ) // first is less than second
127        {
128           return false;
129        } // end catch
130     } // end WebMethod bigger
131
132     // WebMethod that returns true if the first integer is less than second
133     @WebMethod( operationName = "smaller" )
134     public boolean smaller( @WebParam( name = "first" ) String first,
135        @WebParam( name = "second" ) String second )
136     {
137        return bigger( second, first );
138     } // end WebMethod smaller
139
140     // WebMethod that returns true if the first integer equals the second
141     @WebMethod( operationName = "equals" )
142     public boolean equals( @WebParam( name = "first" ) String first,
143        @WebParam( name = "second" ) String second )
144     {
145        return !( bigger( first, second ) || smaller( first, second ) );
146     } // end WebMethod equals
147  } // end class HugeInteger
```

Fig. 24.2 | `HugeInteger` web service that performs operations on large integers. (Part 3 of 3.)

Lines 5–7 import the annotations used in this example. By default, each new web service class created with the JAX-WS APIs is a *POJO (plain old Java object)*, meaning that—unlike prior Java web service APIs—you do not need to extend a class or implement an interface to create a web service. When you compile a class that uses these JAX-WS 2.0 annotations, the compiler creates all the *server-side artifacts* that support the web service—that is, the compiled code framework that allows the web service to wait for client requests and respond to those requests once the service is deployed on an application server. Popular application servers that support Java web services include the Sun Java System Application Server (www.sun.com/software/products/appsrvr/index.xml), GlassFish (glassfish.dev.java.net), Apache Tomcat (tomcat.apache.org), BEA Weblogic Server (www.bea.com) and JBoss Application Server (www.jboss.org/products/jbossas). We use Sun Java System Application Server in this chapter.

Lines 9–11 contain a @WebService annotation (imported at line 5) with properties name and serviceName. The *@WebService annotation* indicates that class HugeInteger implements a web service. The annotation is followed by a set of parentheses containing optional elements. The annotation's *name element* (line 10) specifies the name of the proxy class that will be generated for the client. The annotation's *serviceName element* (line 11) specifies the name of the class that the client uses to obtain an object of the proxy class. [*Note:* If the serviceName element is not specified, the web service's name is assumed to be the class name followed by the word Service.] Netbeans places the @WebService annotation at the beginning of each new web service class you create. You can then add the name and serviceName properties in the parentheses following the annotation.

Line 14 declares the constant MAXIMUM that specifies the maximum number of digits for a HugeInteger (i.e., 100 in this example). Line 15 creates the array that stores the digits in a huge integer. Lines 18–40 declare method toString, which returns a String representation of a HugeInteger without any leading 0s. Lines 43–52 declare static method parseHugeInteger, which converts a String into a HugeInteger. The web service's methods add, subtract, bigger, smaller and equals use parseHugeInteger to convert their String arguments to HugeIntegers for processing.

HugeInteger methods add, subtract, bigger, smaller and equals are tagged with the *@WebMethod annotation* (lines 55, 81, 117, 133 and 141) to indicate that they can be called remotely. Any methods that are not tagged with @WebMethod are not accessible to clients that consume the web service. Such methods are typically utility methods within the web service class. Note that the @WebMethod annotations each use the *operationName* element to specify the method name that is exposed to the web service's client.

Common Programming Error 24.1

Failing to expose a method as a web method by declaring it with the @WebMethod annotation prevents clients of the web service from accessing the method.

Common Programming Error 24.2

Methods with the @WebMethod annotation cannot be static. An object of the web service class must exist for a client to access the service's web methods.

Each web method in class HugeInteger specifies parameters that are annotated with the *@WebParam annotation* (e.g., lines 56–57 of method add). The optional @WebParam element *name* indicates the parameter name that is exposed to the web service's clients.

Lines 55–78 and 81–102 declare HugeInteger web methods add and subtract. We assume for simplicity that add does not result in overflow (i.e., the result will be 100 digits or fewer) and that subtract's first argument will always be larger than the second. The subtract method calls method borrow (lines 105–114) when it is necessary to borrow 1 from the next digit to the left in the first argument—that is, when a particular digit in the left operand is smaller than the corresponding digit in the right operand. Method `borrow` adds 10 to the appropriate digit and subtracts 1 from the next digit to the left. This utility method is not intended to be called remotely, so it is not tagged with `@WebMethod`.

Lines 117–130 declare `HugeInteger` web method `bigger`. Line 123 invokes method `subtract` to calculate the difference between the numbers. If the first number is less than the second, this results in an exception. In this case, `bigger` returns `false`. If `subtract` does not throw an exception, then line 124 returns the result of the expression

```
!difference.matches( "^[0]+$" )
```

This expression calls `String` method `matches` to determine whether the `String` difference matches the regular expression `"^[0]+$"`, which determines if the `String` consists only of one or more 0s. The symbols ^ and $ indicate that `matches` should return `true` only if the entire `String` `difference` matches the regular expression. We then use the logical negation operator (`!`) to return the opposite `boolean` value. Thus, if the numbers are equal (i.e., their difference is 0), the preceding expression returns `false`—the first number is not greater than the second. Otherwise, the expression returns `true`.

Lines 133–146 declare methods `smaller` and `equals`. Method `smaller` returns the result of invoking method `bigger` (line 137) with the arguments reversed—if `first` is less than `second`, then `second` is greater than `first`. Method `equals` invokes methods `bigger` and `smaller` (line 145). If either `bigger` or `smaller` returns `true`, line 145 returns `false`, because the numbers are not equal. If both methods return `false`, the numbers are equal and line 145 returns `true`.

24.3.3 Publishing the `HugeInteger` Web Service from Netbeans

Now that we've created the `HugeInteger` web service class, we'll use Netbeans to build and publish (i.e., deploy) the web service so that clients can consume its services. Netbeans handles all the details of building and deploying a web service for you. This includes creating the framework required to support the web service. Right click the project name (`HugeInteger`) in the Netbeans **Projects** tab to display the pop-up menu shown in Fig. 24.3. To determine if there are any compilation errors in your project, select the **Build Project** option. When the project compiles successfully, you can select **Deploy Project** to deploy the project to the server you selected when you set up the web application in Section 24.3.1. If the code in the project has changed since the last build, selecting **Deploy Project** also builds the project. Selecting **Run Project** executes the web application. If the web application was not previously built or deployed, this option performs these tasks first. Note that both the **Deploy Project** and **Run Project** options also start the application server (in our case Sun Java System Application Server) if it is not already running. To ensure that all source-code files in a project are recompiled during the next build operation, you can use the **Clean Project** or **Clean and Build Project** options. If you have not already done so, select **Deploy Project** now.

24.3.4 Testing the `HugeInteger` Web Service with Sun Java System Application Server's Tester Web page

The next step is to test the `HugeInteger` web service. We previously selected the Sun Java System Application Server to execute this web application. This server can dynamically

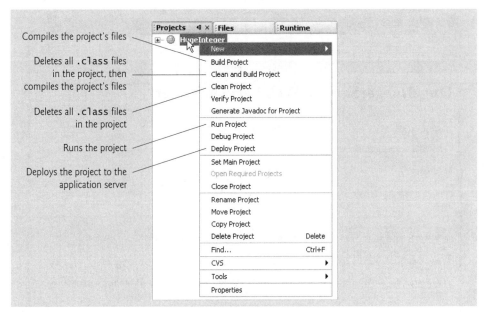

Compiles the project's files

Deletes all .class files in the project, then compiles the project's files

Deletes all .class files in the project

Runs the project

Deploys the project to the application server

Fig. 24.3 | Pop-up menu that appears when you right click a project name in the Netbeans **Projects** tab.

create a web page for testing a web service's methods from a web browser. To enable this capability:

1. Right click the project name (HugeInteger) in the Netbeans **Projects** tab and select **Properties** from the pop-up menu to display the **Project Properties** dialog.

2. Click **Run** under **Categories** to display the options for running the project.

3. In the **Relative URL** field, type /HugeIntegerService?Tester.

4. Click **OK** to dismiss the **Project Properties** dialog.

The **Relative URL** field specifies what should happen when the web application executes. If this field is empty, then the web application's default JSP displays when you run the project. When you specify /HugeIntegerService?Tester in this field, then run the project, Sun Java System Application Server builds the Tester web page and loads it into your web browser. Figure 24.4 shows the Tester web page for the HugeInteger web service. Once you've deployed the web service, you can also type the URL

```
http://localhost:8080/HugeInteger/HugeIntegerService?Tester
```

in your web browser to view the Tester web page. Note that HugeIntegerService is the name (specified in line 11 of Fig. 24.2) that clients, including the Tester web page, use to access the web service.

To test HugeInteger's web methods, type two positive integers into the text fields to the right of a particular method's button, then click the button to invoke the web method and see the result. Figure 24.5 shows the results of invoking HugeInteger's add method with the values 9999999999999999 and 1. Note that the number 9999999999999999 is larger than primitive type long can represent.

Fig. 24.4 | `Tester` web page created by Sun Java System Application Server for the `HugeInteger` web service.

Note that you can access the web service only when the application server is running. If Netbeans launches the application server for you, it will automatically shut it down when you close Netbeans. To keep the application server up and running, you can launch it independently of Netbeans before you deploy or run web applications in Netbeans. For Sun Java System Application Server running on Windows, you can do this by selecting

Fig. 24.5 | Testing `HugeInteger`'s add method. (Part I of 2.)

b) Results of calling the `HugeInteger` web service's **add** method with `"99999999999999999"` and `"1"`

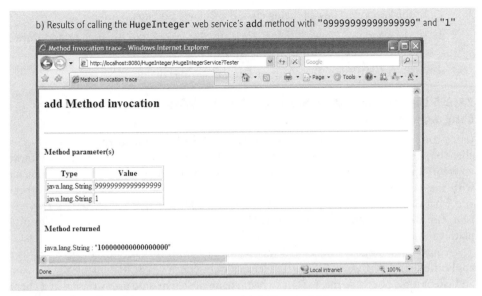

Fig. 24.5 | Testing `HugeInteger`'s `add` method. (Part 2 of 2.)

Start > All Programs > Sun Microsystems > Application Server PE 9 > Start Default Server. To shut down the application server, you can select the **Stop Default Server** option from the same location.

Testing the `HugeInteger` Web Service from Another Computer

If your computer is connected to a network and allows HTTP requests, then you can test the web service from another computer on the network by typing the following URL (where *host* is the hostname or IP address of the computer on which the web service is deployed) into a browser on another computer:

```
http://host:8080/HugeInteger/HugeIntegerService?Tester
```

Note to Windows XP Service Pack 2 and Windows Vista Users

For security reasons, computers running Windows XP Service Pack 2 or Windows Vista do not allow HTTP requests from other computers by default. If you wish to allow other computers to connect to your computer using HTTP, perform the following steps on Windows XP SP2:

1. Select **Start > Control Panel** to open your system's **Control Panel** window, then double click **Windows Firewall** to view the **Windows Firewall** settings dialog.

2. In the **Windows Firewall** dialog, click the **Exceptions** tab, then click **Add Port...** and add port 8080 with the name SJSAS.

3. Click **OK** to dismiss the **Windows Firewall** settings dialog.

To allow other computers to connect to your Windows Vista computer using HTTP, perform the following steps:

1. Open the **Control Panel**, switch to **Classic View** and double click **Windows Firewall** to open the **Windows Firewall** dialog.

2. In the **Windows Firewall** dialog click the **Change Settings...** link.

3. In the **Windows Firewall** dialog, click the **Exceptions** tab, then click **Add Port...** and add port 8080 with the name SJSAS.

4. Click **OK** to dismiss the **Windows Firewall** settings dialog.

24.3.5 Describing a Web Service with the Web Service Description Language (WSDL)

Once you implement a web service, compile it and deploy it on an application server, a client application can consume the web service. To do so, however, the client must know where to find the web service and must be provided with a description of how to interact with the web service—that is, what methods are available, what parameters they expect and what each method returns. For this purpose, JAX-WS uses the *Web Service Description Language (WSDL)*—a standard XML vocabulary for describing web services in a platform-independent manner.

You do not need to understand the details of WSDL to take advantage of it—the application server software (SJSAS) generates a web service's WSDL dynamically for you, and client tools can parse the WSDL to help create the client-side proxy class that a client uses to access the web service. Since the WSDL is created dynamically, clients always receive a deployed web service's most up-to-date description. To view the WSDL for the HugeInteger web service (Fig. 24.6), enter the following URL in your browser:

```
http://localhost:8080/HugeInteger/HugeIntegerService?WSDL
```

or click the **WSDL File** link in the Tester web page (shown in Fig. 24.4).

Fig. 24.6 | A portion of the .wsdl file for the HugeInteger web service.

Accessing the HugeInteger Web Service's WSDL from Another Computer
Eventually, you'll want clients on other computers to use your web service. Such clients need access to the web service's WSDL, which they would access with the following URL:

```
http://host:8080/HugeInteger/HugeIntegerService?WSDL
```

where *host* is the hostname or IP address of the computer on which the web service is deployed. As we discussed in Section 24.3.4, this will work only if your computer allows HTTP connections from other computers—as is the case for publicly accessible web and application servers.

24.4 Consuming a Web Service

Now that we've defined and deployed our web service, we can consume it from a client application. A web service client can be any type of application or even another web service. You enable a client application to consume a web service by *adding a web service reference* to the application. This process defines the proxy class that allows the client to access the web service.

24.4.1 Creating a Client in Netbeans to Consume the HugeInteger Web Service

In this section, you'll use Netbeans to create a client Java desktop GUI application, then you'll add a web service reference to the project so the client can access the web service. When you add the web service reference, the IDE creates and compiles the *client-side artifacts*—the framework of Java code that supports the client-side proxy class. The client then calls methods on an object of the proxy class, which uses the rest of the artifacts to interact with the web service.

Creating a Desktop Application Project in Netbeans
Before performing the steps in this section, ensure that the HugeInteger web service has been deployed and that the Sun Java System Application Server is running (see Section 24.3.3). Perform the following steps to create a client Java desktop application in Netbeans:

1. Select **File > New Project...** to open the **New Project** dialog.

2. Select **General** from the **Categories** list and **Java Application** from the **Projects** list, then click **Next >**.

3. Specify the name UsingHugeInteger in the **Project Name** field and uncheck the **Create Main Class** checkbox. In a moment, you'll add a subclass of JFrame that contains a main method.

4. Click **Finish** to create the project.

Adding a Web Service Reference to an Application
Next, you'll add a web service reference to your application so that it can interact with the HugeInteger web service. To add a web service reference, perform the following steps.

1. Right click the project name (UsingHugeInteger) in the Netbeans **Projects** tab.

2. Select **New > Web Service Client...** from the pop-up menu to display the **New Web Service Client** dialog (Fig. 24.7).

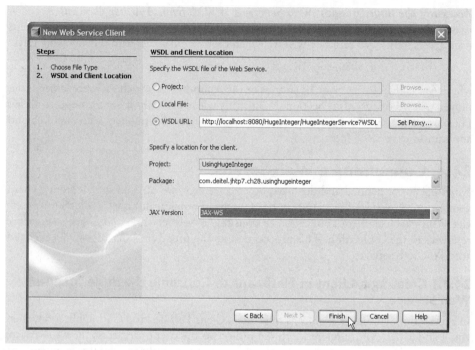

Fig. 24.7 | New Web Service Client dialog.

3. In the **WSDL URL** field, specify the URL `http://localhost:8080/HugeInteger/HugeIntegerService?WSDL` (Fig. 24.7). This URL tells the IDE where to find the web service's WSDL description. [*Note:* If the Sun Java System Application Server is located on a different computer, replace `localhost` with the hostname or IP address of that computer.] The IDE uses this WSDL description to generate the client-side artifacts that compose and support the proxy. Note that the **New Web Service Client** dialog enables you to search for web services in several locations. Many companies simply distribute the exact WSDL URLs for their web services, which you can place in the **WSDL URL** field.

4. In the **Package** field, specify `com.deitel.iw3htp4.ch28.usinghugeinteger` as the package name.

5. Click **Finish** to dismiss the **New Web Service Client** dialog.

In the Netbeans **Projects** tab, the `UsingHugeInteger` project now contains a `Web Service References` folder with the `HugeInteger` web service's proxy (Fig. 24.8). Note that the proxy's name is listed as `HugeIntegerService`, as we specified in line 11 of Fig. 24.2.

When you specify the web service you want to consume, Netbeans accesses the web service's WSDL information and copies it into a file in your project (named `HugeIntegerService.wsdl` in this example). You can view this file from the Netbeans **Files** tab by expanding the nodes in the `UsingHugeInteger` project's `xml-resources` folder as shown in Fig. 24.9. If the web service changes, the client-side artifacts and the client's copy of the WSDL file can be regenerated by right clicking the `HugeIntegerService` node shown in Fig. 24.8 and selecting **Refresh Client**.

Fig. 24.8 | Netbeans **Project** tab after adding a web service reference to the project.

Fig. 24.9 | Locating the `HugeIntegerService.wsdl` file in the Netbeans **Files** tab.

You can view the IDE-generated client-side artifacts by selecting the Netbeans **Files** tab and expanding the `UsingHugeInteger` project's **build** folder as shown in Fig. 24.10.

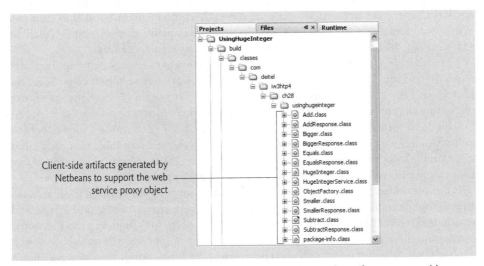

Fig. 24.10 | Viewing the `HugeInteger` web service's client-side artifacts generated by Netbeans.

24.4.2 Consuming the HugeInteger Web Service

For this example, we use a GUI application to interact with the web service `HugeInteger`
web service. To build the client application's GUI, you must first add a subclass of `JFrame`
to the project. To do so, perform the following steps:

1. Right click the project name in the Netbeans **Project** tab.

2. Select **New > JFrame Form...** to display the **New JFrame Form** dialog.

3. Specify `UsingHugeIntegerJFrame` in the **Class Name** field.

4. Specify `com.deitel.iw3htp4.ch28.hugeintegerclient` in the **Package** field.

5. Click **Finish** to close the **New JFrame Form** dialog.

Next, use the Netbeans GUI design tools to build the GUI shown in the sample screen
captures at the end of Fig. 24.11.

The application in Fig. 24.11 uses the `HugeInteger` web service to perform computations with positive integers up to 100 digits long. To save space, we do not show the Netbeans autogenerated `initComponents` method, which contains the code that builds the
GUI components, positions them and registers their event handlers. To view the complete
source code, open the `UsingHugeIntegerJFrame.java` file in this example's folder under
`src\java\com\deitel\iw3htp4\ch28\hugeintegerclient`. Netbeans places the GUI
component instance-variable declarations at the end of the class (lines 326–335). Java
allows instance variables to be declared anywhere in a class's body as long as they are placed
outside the class's methods. We continue to declare our own instance variables at the top
of the class.

Lines 6–7 import the classes `HugeInteger` and `HugeIntegerService` that enable the
client application to interact with the web service. We include these `import` declarations
only for documentation purposes here. These classes are in the same package as `Usin-
gHugeIntegerJFrame`, so these `import` declarations are not necessary. Notice that we do
not have `import` declarations for most of the GUI components used in this example.
When you create a GUI in Netbeans, it uses fully qualified class names (such as
`javax.swing.JFrame` in line 11), so `import` declarations are unnecessary.

Lines 13–14 declare the variables of type `HugeIntegerService` and `HugeInteger`,
respectively. Line 24 in the constructor creates an object of type `HugeIntegerService`.
Line 25 uses this object's `getHugeIntegerPort` method to obtain the `HugeInteger` proxy
object that the application uses to invoke the web service's method.

Lines 165–166, 189–190, 213–214, 240–241 and 267–268 in the various `JButton`
event handlers invoke the `HugeInteger` web service's web methods. Note that each call is
made on the local proxy object that is referenced by `hugeIntegerProxy`. The proxy object
then communicates with the web service on the client's behalf.

The user enters two integers, each up to 100 digits long. Clicking any of the five `JBut-
tons` causes the application to invoke a web method to perform the corresponding task and
return the result. Our client application cannot process 100-digit numbers directly.
Instead the client passes `String` representations of these numbers to the web service's web
methods, which perform tasks for the client. The client application then uses the return
value of each operation to display an appropriate message.

```
 1    // Fig. 24.11: UsingHugeIntegerJFrame.java
 2    // Client desktop application for the HugeInteger web service.
 3    package com.deitel.iw3htp4.ch28.hugeintegerclient;
 4
 5    // import classes for accessing HugeInteger web service's proxy
 6    import com.deitel.iw3htp4.ch28.hugeintegerclient.HugeInteger;
 7    import com.deitel.iw3htp4.ch28.hugeintegerclient.HugeIntegerServic
 8
 9    import javax.swing.JOptionPane; // used to display errors to the user
10
11    public class UsingHugeIntegerJFrame extends javax.swing.JFrame
12    {
13       private HugeIntegerService hugeIntegerService; // used to obtain proxy
14       private HugeInteger hugeIntegerProxy; // used to access the web service
15
16       // no-argument constructor
17       public UsingHugeIntegerJFrame()
18       {
19          initComponents();
20
21          try
22          {
23             // create the objects for accessing the HugeInteger web service
24             hugeIntegerService = new HugeIntegerService();
25             hugeIntegerProxy = hugeIntegerService.getHugeIntegerPort();
26          }
27          catch ( Exception exception )
28          {
29             exception.printStackTrace();
30          }
31       } // end UsingHugeIntegerJFrame constructor
32
33       // The initComponents method is autogenerated by Netbeans and is called
34       // from the constructor to initialize the GUI. This method is not shown
35       // here to save space. Open UsingHugeIntegerJFrame.java in this
36       // example's folder to view the complete generated code (lines 37-153).
37
154      // invokes HugeInteger web service's add method to add HugeIntegers
155      private void addJButtonActionPerformed(
156         java.awt.event.ActionEvent evt )
157      {
158         String firstNumber = firstJTextField.getText();
159         String secondNumber = secondJTextField.getText();
160
161         if ( isValid( firstNumber ) && isValid( secondNumber ) )
162         {
163            try
164            {
165               resultsJTextArea.setText(
166                  hugeIntegerProxy.add( firstNumber, secondNumber ) );
167            } // end try
168            catch ( Exception e )
169            {
```

Fig. 24.11 | Client desktop application for the HugeInteger web service. (Part 1 of 6.)

```
170                 JOptionPane.showMessageDialog( this, e.toString(),
171                     "Add method failed", JOptionPane.ERROR_MESSAGE );
172                 e.printStackTrace();
173             } // end catch
174         } // end if
175     } // end method addJButtonActionPerformed
176
177     // invokes HugeInteger web service's subtract method to subtract the
178     // second HugeInteger from the first
179     private void subtractJButtonActionPerformed(
180         java.awt.event.ActionEvent evt )
181     {
182         String firstNumber = firstJTextField.getText();
183         String secondNumber = secondJTextField.getText();
184
185         if ( isValid( firstNumber ) && isValid( secondNumber ) )
186         {
187             try
188             {
189                 resultsJTextArea.setText(
190                     hugeIntegerProxy.subtract( firstNumber, secondNumber ) );
191             } // end try
192             catch ( Exception e )
193             {
194                 JOptionPane.showMessageDialog( this, e.toString(),
195                     "Subtract method failed", JOptionPane.ERROR_MESSAGE );
196                 e.printStackTrace();
197             } // end catch
198         } // end if
199     } // end method subtractJButtonActionPerformed
200
201     // invokes HugeInteger web service's bigger method to determine whether
202     // the first HugeInteger is greater than the second
203     private void biggerJButtonActionPerformed(
204         java.awt.event.ActionEvent evt )
205     {
206         String firstNumber = firstJTextField.getText();
207         String secondNumber = secondJTextField.getText();
208
209         if ( isValid( firstNumber ) && isValid( secondNumber ) )
210         {
211             try
212             {
213                 boolean result =
214                     hugeIntegerProxy.bigger( firstNumber, secondNumber );
215                 resultsJTextArea.setText( String.format( "%s %s %s %s",
216                     firstNumber, ( result ? "is" : "is not" ), "greater than",
217                     secondNumber ) );
218             } // end try
219             catch ( Exception e )
220             {
221                 JOptionPane.showMessageDialog( this, e.toString(),
222                     "Bigger method failed", JOptionPane.ERROR_MESSAGE );
```

Fig. 24.11 | Client desktop application for the HugeInteger web service. (Part 2 of 6.)

```
223            e.printStackTrace();
224         } // end catch
225      } // end if
226   } // end method biggerJButtonActionPerformed
227
228   // invokes HugeInteger web service's smaller method to determine
229   // whether the first HugeInteger is less than the second
230   private void smallerJButtonActionPerformed(
231      java.awt.event.ActionEvent evt )
232   {
233      String firstNumber = firstJTextField.getText();
234      String secondNumber = secondJTextField.getText();
235
236      if ( isValid( firstNumber ) && isValid( secondNumber ) )
237      {
238         try
239         {
240            boolean result =
241               hugeIntegerProxy.smaller( firstNumber, secondNumber );
242            resultsJTextArea.setText( String.format( "%s %s %s %s",
243               firstNumber, ( result ? "is" : "is not" ), "less than",
244               secondNumber ) );
245         } // end try
246         catch ( Exception e )
247         {
248            JOptionPane.showMessageDialog( this, e.toString(),
249               "Smaller method failed", JOptionPane.ERROR_MESSAGE );
250            e.printStackTrace();
251         } // end catch
252      } // end if
253   } // end method smallerJButtonActionPerformed
254
255   // invokes HugeInteger web service's equals method to determine whether
256   // the first HugeInteger is equal to the second
257   private void equalsJButtonActionPerformed(
258      java.awt.event.ActionEvent evt )
259   {
260      String firstNumber = firstJTextField.getText();
261      String secondNumber = secondJTextField.getText();
262
263      if ( isValid( firstNumber ) && isValid( secondNumber ) )
264      {
265         try
266         {
267            boolean result =
268               hugeIntegerProxy.equals( firstNumber, secondNumber );
269            resultsJTextArea.setText( String.format( "%s %s %s %s",
270               firstNumber, ( result ? "is" : "is not" ), "equal to",
271               secondNumber ) );
272         } // end try
273         catch ( Exception e )
274         {
```

Fig. 24.11 | Client desktop application for the HugeInteger web service. (Part 3 of 6.)

```
275              JOptionPane.showMessageDialog( this, e.toString(),
276                 "Equals method failed", JOptionPane.ERROR_MESSAGE );
277              e.printStackTrace();
278           } // end catch
279        } // end if
280     } // end method equalsJButtonActionPerformed
281
282     // checks the size of a String to ensure that it is not too big
283     // to be used as a HugeInteger; ensure only digits in String
284     private boolean isValid( String number )
285     {
286        // check String's length
287        if ( number.length() > 100 )
288        {
289           JOptionPane.showMessageDialog( this,
290              "HugeIntegers must be <= 100 digits.", "HugeInteger Overflow",
291              JOptionPane.ERROR_MESSAGE );
292           return false;
293        } // end if
294
295        // look for nondigit characters in String
296        for ( char c : number.toCharArray() )
297        {
298           if ( !Character.isDigit( c ) )
299           {
300              JOptionPane.showMessageDialog( this,
301                 "There are nondigits in the String",
302                 "HugeInteger Contains Nondigit Characters",
303                 JOptionPane.ERROR_MESSAGE );
304              return false;
305           } // end if
306        } // end for
307
308        return true; // number can be used as a HugeInteger
309     } // end method validate
310
311     // main method begins execution
312     public static void main( String args[] )
313     {
314        java.awt.EventQueue.invokeLater(
315           new Runnable()
316           {
317              public void run()
318              {
319                 new UsingHugeIntegerJFrame().setVisible( true );
320              } // end method run
321           } // end anonymous inner class
322        ); // end call to java.awt.EventQueue.invokeLater
323     } // end method main
324
325     // Variables declaration - do not modify
326     private javax.swing.JButton addJButton;'
```

Fig. 24.11 | Client desktop application for the HugeInteger web service. (Part 4 of 6.)

```
327     private javax.swing.JButton biggerJButton;
328     private javax.swing.JLabel directionsJLabel;
329     private javax.swing.JButton equalsJButton;
330     private javax.swing.JTextField firstJTextField;
331     private javax.swing.JScrollPane resultsJScrollPane;
332     private javax.swing.JTextArea resultsJTextArea;
333     private javax.swing.JTextField secondJTextField;
334     private javax.swing.JButton smallerJButton;
335     private javax.swing.JButton subtractJButton;
336     // End of variables declaration
337 } // end class UsingHugeIntegerJFrame
```

Fig. 24.11 | Client desktop application for the HugeInteger web service. (Part 5 of 6.)

Fig. 24.11 | Client desktop application for the `HugeInteger` web service. (Part 6 of 6.)

24.5 SOAP

SOAP (Simple Object Access Protocol) is a platform-independent protocol that uses XML to facilitate remote procedure calls, typically over HTTP. SOAP is one common protocol for passing information between web service clients and web services. The protocol that transmits request-and-response messages is also known as the web service's *wire format* or *wire protocol*, because it defines how information is sent "along the wire."

Each request and response is packaged in a *SOAP message* (also known as a *SOAP envelope*)—an XML "wrapper" containing the information that a web service requires to process the message. SOAP messages are written in XML so that they are platform independent. Many *firewalls*—security barriers that restrict communication among networks—are configured to allow HTTP traffic to pass through so that clients can browse websites on web servers behind firewalls. Thus, XML and HTTP enable computers on different platforms to send and receive SOAP messages with few limitations.

The wire format used to transmit requests and responses must support all data types passed between the applications. Web services also use SOAP for the many data types it supports. SOAP supports primitive types (e.g., `int`) and their wrapper types (e.g., `Integer`), as well as `Date`, `Time` and others. SOAP can also transmit arrays and objects of user-defined types (as you'll see in Section 24.8). For more SOAP information, visit `www.w3.org/TR/soap/`.

When a program invokes a web method, the request and all relevant information are packaged in a SOAP message and sent to the server on which the web service resides. The web service processes the SOAP message's contents (contained in a SOAP envelope), which specify the method that the client wishes to invoke and the method's arguments. This process of interpreting a SOAP message's contents is known as *parsing a SOAP message*. After the web service receives and parses a request, the proper method is called with any specified arguments, and the response is sent back to the client in another SOAP message. The client-side proxy parses the response, which contains the result of the method call, and returns the result to the client application.

Figure 24.5 used the `HugeInteger` web service's `Tester` web page to show the result of invoking `HugeInteger`'s add method with the values 99999999999999999 and 1. The `Tester` web page also shows the SOAP request and response messages (which were not previously shown). Figure 24.12 shows the SOAP messages in the `Tester` web page from Fig. 24.5 after the calculation. In the request message from Fig. 24.12, the text

```
<ns1:add>
<first>99999999999999999</first>
```

```
<second>1</second>
</ns1:add>
```

specifies the method to call (add), the method's arguments (first and second) and the arguments' values (9999999999999999 and 1). Similarly, the text

```
<ns1:addResponse>
<return>10000000000000000</return>
</ns1:addResponse>
```

from the response message in Fig. 24.12 specifies the return value of method add.

As with the WSDL for a web service, the SOAP messages are generated for you automatically, so you don't need to understand the details of SOAP or XML to take advantage of it when publishing and consuming web services.

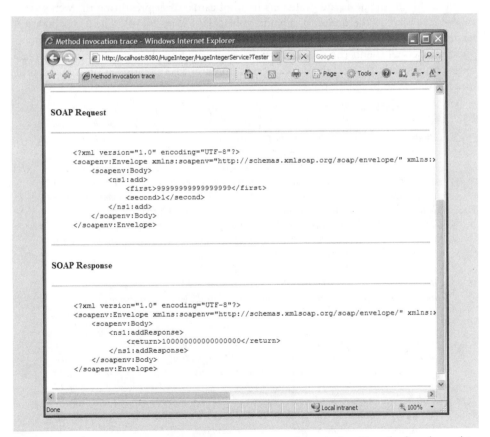

Fig. 24.12 | SOAP messages for the HugeInteger web service's add method as shown by the Sun Java System Application Server's Tester web page.

24.6 Session Tracking in Web Services

Section 22.5 described the advantages of using session tracking to maintain client state information so you can personalize the users' browsing experiences. Now we'll incorporate session tracking into a web service. Suppose a client application needs to call several methods from the same web service, possibly several times each. In such a case, it can be beneficial for the web service to maintain state information for the client, thus eliminating the need for client information to be passed between the client and the web service multiple times. For example, a web service that provides local restaurant reviews could store the client user's street address during the initial request, then use it to return personalized, localized results in subsequent requests. Storing session information also enables a web service to distinguish between clients.

24.6.1 Creating a Blackjack Web Service

Our next example is a web service that assists you in developing a blackjack card game. The Blackjack web service (Fig. 24.13) provides web methods to shuffle a deck of cards, deal a card from the deck and evaluate a hand of cards. After presenting the web service, we use it to serve as the dealer for a game of blackjack (Fig. 24.14). The Blackjack web service uses an HttpSession object to maintain a unique deck of cards for each client application. Several clients can use the service at the same time, but web method calls made by a specific client use only the deck of cards stored in that client's session. Our example uses the following blackjack rules:

> Two cards each are dealt to the dealer and the player. The player's cards are dealt face up. Only the first of the dealer's cards is dealt face up. Each card has a value. A card numbered 2 through 10 is worth its face value. Jacks, queens and kings each count as 10. Aces can count as 1 or 11—whichever value is more beneficial to the player (as we'll soon see). If the sum of the player's two initial cards is 21 (i.e., the player was dealt a card valued at 10 and an ace, which counts as 11 in this situation), the player has "blackjack" and immediately wins the game—if the dealer does not also have blackjack (which would result in a "push"—i.e., a tie). Otherwise, the player can begin taking additional cards one at a time. These cards are dealt face up, and the player decides when to stop taking cards. If the player "busts" (i.e., the sum of the player's cards exceeds 21), the game is over, and the player loses. When the player is satisfied with the current set of cards, the player "stands" (i.e., stops taking cards), and the dealer's hidden card is revealed. If the dealer's total is 16 or less, the dealer must take another card; otherwise, the dealer must stand. The dealer must continue taking cards until the sum of the dealer's cards is greater than or equal to 17. If the dealer exceeds 21, the player wins. Otherwise, the hand with the higher point total wins. If the dealer and the player have the same point total, the game is a "push," and no one wins. Note that the value of an ace for a dealer depends on the dealer's other card(s) and the casino's house rules. A dealer typically must hit for totals of 16 or less and must stand for totals of 17 or more. However, for a "soft 17"—a hand with a total of 17 with one ace counted as 11—some casinos require the dealer to hit and some require the dealer to stand (we require the dealer to stand). Such a hand is known as a "soft 17" because taking another card cannot bust the hand.

The web service (Fig. 24.13) stores each card as a String consisting of a number, 1–13, representing the card's face (ace through king, respectively), followed by a space and a digit, 0–3, representing the card's suit (hearts, diamonds, clubs or spades, respectively). For example, the jack of clubs is represented as "11 2", and the two of hearts is represented as "2 0". To create and deploy this web service, follow the steps presented in Sections 24.3.2–24.3.3 for the HugeInteger service.

```
1    // Fig. 24.13: Blackjack.java
2    // Blackjack web service that deals cards and evaluates hands
3    package com.deitel.iw3htp4.ch28.blackjack;
4
5    import java.util.ArrayList;
6    import java.util.Random;
7    import javax.annotation.Resource;
8    import javax.jws.WebService;
9    import javax.jws.WebMethod;
10   import javax.jws.WebParam;
11   import javax.servlet.http.HttpSession;
12   import javax.servlet.http.HttpServletRequest;
13   import javax.xml.ws.WebServiceContext;
14   import javax.xml.ws.handler.MessageContext;
15
16   @WebService( name = "Blackjack", serviceName = "BlackjackService" )
17   public class Blackjack
18   {
19      // use @Resource to create a WebServiceContext for session tracking
20      private @Resource WebServiceContext webServiceContext;
21      private MessageContext messageContext; // used in session tracking
22      private HttpSession session; // stores attributes of the session
23
24      // deal one card
25      @WebMethod( operationName = "dealCard" )
26      public String dealCard()
27      {
28         String card = "";
29
30         ArrayList< String > deck =
31            ( ArrayList< String > ) session.getAttribute( "deck" );
32
33         card = deck.get( 0 ); // get top card of deck
34         deck.remove( 0 ); // remove top card of deck
35
36         return card;
37      } // end WebMethod dealCard
38
39      // shuffle the deck
40      @WebMethod( operationName = "shuffle" )
41      public void shuffle()
42      {
43         // obtain the HttpSession object to store deck for current client
44         messageContext = webServiceContext.getMessageContext();
45         session = ( ( HttpServletRequest ) messageContext.get(
46            MessageContext.SERVLET_REQUEST ) ).getSession();
47
48         // populate deck of cards
49         ArrayList< String > deck = new ArrayList< String >();
50
51         for ( int face = 1; face <= 13; face++ ) // loop through faces
52            for ( int suit = 0; suit <= 3; suit++ ) // loop through suits
53               deck.add( face + " " + suit ); // add each card to deck
```

Fig. 24.13 | Blackjack web service that deals cards and evaluates hands. (Part 1 of 3.)

```
54
55        String tempCard; // holds card temporarily during swapping
56        Random randomObject = new Random(); // generates random numbers
57        int index; // index of randomly selected card
58
59        for ( int i = 0; i < deck.size() ; i++ ) // shuffle
60        {
61           index = randomObject.nextInt( deck.size() - 1 );
62
63           // swap card at position i with randomly selected card
64           tempCard = deck.get( i );
65           deck.set( i, deck.get( index ) );
66           deck.set( index, tempCard );
67        } // end for
68
69        // add this deck to user's session
70        session.setAttribute( "deck", deck );
71     } // end WebMethod shuffle
72
73     // determine a hand's value
74     @WebMethod( operationName = "getHandValue" )
75     public int getHandValue( @WebParam( name = "hand" ) String hand )
76     {
77        // split hand into cards
78        String[] cards = hand.split( "\t" );
79        int total = 0; // total value of cards in hand
80        int face; // face of current card
81        int aceCount = 0; // number of aces in hand
82
83        for ( int i = 0; i < cards.length; i++ )
84        {
85           // parse string and get first int in String
86           face = Integer.parseInt(
87              cards[ i ].substring( 0, cards[ i ].indexOf( " " ) ) );
88
89           switch ( face )
90           {
91              case 1: // if ace, increment aceCount
92                 ++aceCount;
93                 break;
94              case 11: // jack
95              case 12: // queen
96              case 13: // king
97                 total += 10;
98                 break;
99              default: // otherwise, add face
100                total += face;
101                break;
102           } // end switch
103        } // end for
104
```

Fig. 24.13 | Blackjack web service that deals cards and evaluates hands. (Part 2 of 3.)

```
105           // calculate optimal use of aces
106           if ( aceCount > 0 )
107           {
108               // if possible, count one ace as 11
109               if ( total + 11 + aceCount - 1 <= 21 )
110                   total += 11 + aceCount - 1;
111               else // otherwise, count all aces as 1
112                   total += aceCount;
113           } // end if
114
115           return total;
116       } // end WebMethod getHandValue
117   } // end class Blackjack
```

Fig. 24.13 | Blackjack web service that deals cards and evaluates hands. (Part 3 of 3.)

Session Tracking in Web Services

The Blackjack web service client first calls method shuffle (lines 40–71) to shuffle the deck of cards. This method also places the deck of cards into an HttpSession object that is specific to the client that called shuffle. To use session tracking in a Web service, you must include code for the resources that maintain the session state information. In the past, you had to write the sometimes tedious code to create these resources. JAX-WS, however, handles this for you via the **@Resource annotation**. This annotation enables tools like Netbeans to "inject" complex support code into your class, thus allowing you to focus on your business logic rather than the support code. The concept of using annotations to add code that supports your classes is known as **dependency injection**. Annotations like @Web-Service, @WebMethod and @WebParam also perform dependency injection.

Line 20 injects a WebServiceContext object into your class. A **WebServiceContext** object enables a web service to access and maintain information for a specific request, such as session state. As you look through the code in Fig. 24.13, you'll notice that we never create the WebServiceContext object. All of the code necessary to create it is injected into the class by the @Resource annotation. Line 21 declares a variable of interface type **MessageContext** that the web service will use to obtain an HttpSession object for the current client. Line 22 declares the HttpSession variable that the web service will use to manipulate the session state information.

Line 44 in method shuffle uses the WebServiceContext object that was injected in line 20 to obtain a MessageContext object. Lines 45–46 then use the MessageContext object's get method to obtain the HttpSession object for the current client. Method get receives a constant indicating what to get from the MessageContext. In this case, the constant MessageContext.SERVLET_REQUEST indicates that we'd like to get the HttpServlet-Request object for the current client. We then call method getSession to get the HttpSession object from the HttpServletRequest object.

Lines 49–70 generate an ArrayList representing a deck of cards, shuffle the deck and store the deck in the client's session object. Lines 51–53 use nested loops to generate Strings in the form "*face suit*" to represent each possible card in the deck. Lines 59–67 shuffle the deck by swapping each card with another card selected at random. Line 70 inserts the ArrayList in the session object to maintain the deck between method calls from a particular client.

Lines 25–37 define method dealCard as a web method. Lines 30–31 use the session object to obtain the "deck" session attribute that was stored in line 70 of method shuffle. Method getAttribute takes as a parameter a String that identifies the Object to obtain from the session state. The HttpSession can store many Objects, provided that each has a unique identifier. Note that method shuffle must be called before method dealCard is called the first time for a client—otherwise, an exception occurs at line 33 because get-Attribute returns null at lines 30–31. After obtaining the user's deck, dealCard gets the top card from the deck (line 33), removes it from the deck (line 34) and returns the card's value as a String (line 36). Without using session tracking, the deck of cards would need to be passed back and forth with each method call. Session tracking makes the dealCard method easy to call (it requires no arguments) and eliminates the overhead of sending the deck over the network multiple times.

Method getHandValue (lines 74–116) determines the total value of the cards in a hand by trying to attain the highest score possible without going over 21. Recall that an ace can be counted as either 1 or 11, and all face cards count as 10. This method does not use the session object because the deck of cards is not used in this method.

As you'll soon see, the client application maintains a hand of cards as a String in which each card is separated by a tab character. Line 78 tokenizes the hand of cards (represented by hand) into individual cards by calling String method split and passing to it a String containing the delimiter characters (in this case, just a tab). Method split uses the delimiter characters to separate tokens in the String. Lines 83–103 count the value of each card. Lines 86–87 retrieve the first integer—the face—and use that value in the switch statement (lines 89–102). If the card is an ace, the method increments variable aceCount. We discuss how this variable is used shortly. If the card is an 11, 12 or 13 (jack, queen or king), the method adds 10 to the total value of the hand (line 97). If the card is anything else, the method increases the total by that value (line 100).

Because an ace can have either of two values, additional logic is required to process aces. Lines 106–113 of method getHandValue process the aces after all the other cards. If a hand contains several aces, only one ace can be counted as 11. The condition in line 109 determines whether counting one ace as 11 and the rest as 1 will result in a total that does not exceed 21. If this is possible, line 110 adjusts the total accordingly. Otherwise, line 112 adjusts the total, counting each ace as 1.

Method getHandValue maximizes the value of the current cards without exceeding 21. Imagine, for example, that the dealer has a 7 and receives an ace. The new total could be either 8 or 18. However, getHandValue always maximizes the value of the cards without going over 21, so the new total is 18.

24.6.2 Consuming the Blackjack Web Service

The blackjack application in Fig. 24.14 keeps track of the player's and dealer's cards, and the web service tracks the cards that have been dealt. The constructor (lines 34–83) sets up the GUI (line 36), changes the window's background color (line 40) and creates the Blackjack web service's proxy object (lines 46–47). In the GUI, each player has 11 JLabels—the maximum number of cards that can be dealt without automatically exceeding 21 (i.e., four aces, four twos and three threes). These JLabels are placed in an ArrayList of JLabels, (lines 59–82), so we can index the ArrayList during the game to determine the JLabel that will display a particular card image.

With JAX-WS 2.0, the client application must indicate whether it wants to allow the web service to maintain session information. Lines 50–51 in the constructor perform this task. We first cast the proxy object to interface type BindingProvider. A **BindingProvider** enables the client to manipulate the request information that will be sent to the server. This information is stored in an object that implements interface **RequestContext**. The BindingProvider and RequestContext are part of the framework that is created by the IDE when you add a web service client to the application. Next, lines 50–51 invoke the BindingProvider's **getRequestContext** *method* to obtain the RequestContext object. Then the RequestContext's **put** *method* is called to set the property BindingProvider.SESSION_MAINTAIN_PROPERTY to true, which enables session tracking from the client side so that the web service knows which client is invoking the service's web methods.

```
1    // Fig. 24.14: BlackjackGameJFrame.java
2    // Blackjack game that uses the Blackjack Web Service
3    package com.deitel.iw3htp4.ch28.blackjackclient;
4
5    import java.awt.Color;
6    import java.util.ArrayList;
7    import javax.swing.ImageIcon;
8    import javax.swing.JLabel;
9    import javax.swing.JOptionPane;
10   import javax.xml.ws.BindingProvider;
11   import com.deitel.iw3htp4.ch28.blackjackclient.Blackjack;
12   import com.deitel.iw3htp4.ch28.blackjackclient.BlackjackService;
13
14   public class BlackjackGameJFrame extends javax.swing.JFrame
15   {
16      private String playerCards;
17      private String dealerCards;
18      private ArrayList< JLabel > cardboxes; // list of card image JLabels
19      private int currentPlayerCard; // player's current card number
20      private int currentDealerCard; // blackjackProxy's current card number
21      private BlackjackService blackjackService; // used to obtain proxy
22      private Blackjack blackjackProxy; // used to access the web service
23
24      // enumeration of game states
25      private enum GameStatus
26      {
27         PUSH, // game ends in a tie
28         LOSE, // player loses
29         WIN, // player wins
30         BLACKJACK // player has blackjack
31      } // end enum GameStatus
32
33      // no-argument constructor
34      public BlackjackGameJFrame()
35      {
36         initComponents();
37
```

Fig. 24.14 | Blackjack game that uses the Blackjack web service. (Part 1 of 10.)

```
38          // due to a bug in Netbeans, we must change the JFrame's background
39          // color here rather than in the designer
40          getContentPane().setBackground( new Color( 0, 180, 0 ) );
41
42          // initialize the blackjack proxy
43          try
44          {
45             // create the objects for accessing the Blackjack web service
46             blackjackService = new BlackjackService();
47             blackjackProxy = blackjackService.getBlackjackPort();
48
49             // enable session tracking
50             ( ( BindingProvider ) blackjackProxy ).getRequestContext().put(
51                BindingProvider.SESSION_MAINTAIN_PROPERTY, true );
52          } // end try
53          catch ( Exception e )
54          {
55             e.printStackTrace();
56          } // end catch
57
58          // add JLabels to cardBoxes ArrayList for programmatic manipulation
59          cardboxes = new ArrayList< JLabel >();
60
61          cardboxes.add( 0, dealerCard1JLabel );
62          cardboxes.add( dealerCard2JLabel );
63          cardboxes.add( dealerCard3JLabel );
64          cardboxes.add( dealerCard4JLabel );
65          cardboxes.add( dealerCard5JLabel );
66          cardboxes.add( dealerCard6JLabel );
67          cardboxes.add( dealerCard7JLabel );
68          cardboxes.add( dealerCard8JLabel );
69          cardboxes.add( dealerCard9JLabel );
70          cardboxes.add( dealerCard10JLabel );
71          cardboxes.add( dealerCard11JLabel );
72          cardboxes.add( playerCard1JLabel );
73          cardboxes.add( playerCard2JLabel );
74          cardboxes.add( playerCard3JLabel );
75          cardboxes.add( playerCard4JLabel );
76          cardboxes.add( playerCard5JLabel );
77          cardboxes.add( playerCard6JLabel );
78          cardboxes.add( playerCard7JLabel );
79          cardboxes.add( playerCard8JLabel );
80          cardboxes.add( playerCard9JLabel );
81          cardboxes.add( playerCard10JLabel );
82          cardboxes.add( playerCard11JLabel );
83       } // end no-argument constructor
84
85       // play the dealer's hand
86       private void dealerPlay()
87       {
88          try
89          {
```

Fig. 24.14 | Blackjack game that uses the Blackjack web service. (Part 2 of 10.)

```
90         // while the value of the dealer's hand is below 17
91         // the dealer must continue to take cards
92         String[] cards = dealerCards.split( "\t" );
93
94         // display dealer's cards
95         for ( int i = 0; i < cards.length; i++ )
96            displayCard( i, cards[ i ] );
97
98         while ( blackjackProxy.getHandValue( dealerCards ) < 17 )
99         {
100           String newCard = blackjackProxy.dealCard();
101           dealerCards += "\t" + newCard; // deal new card
102           displayCard( currentDealerCard, newCard );
103           ++currentDealerCard;
104           JOptionPane.showMessageDialog( this, "Dealer takes a card",
105              "Dealer's turn", JOptionPane.PLAIN_MESSAGE );
106        } // end while
107
108        int dealersTotal = blackjackProxy.getHandValue( dealerCards );
109        int playersTotal = blackjackProxy.getHandValue( playerCards );
110
111        // if dealer busted, player wins
112        if ( dealersTotal > 21 )
113        {
114           gameOver( GameStatus.WIN );
115           return;
116        } // end if
117
118        // if dealer and player are below 21
119        // higher score wins, equal scores is a push
120        if ( dealersTotal > playersTotal )
121           gameOver( GameStatus.LOSE );
122        else if ( dealersTotal < playersTotal )
123           gameOver( GameStatus.WIN );
124        else
125           gameOver( GameStatus.PUSH );
126     } // end try
127     catch ( Exception e )
128     {
129        e.printStackTrace();
130     } // end catch
131  } // end method dealerPlay
132
133  // displays the card represented by cardValue in specified JLabel
134  public void displayCard( int card, String cardValue )
135  {
136     try
137     {
138        // retrieve correct JLabel from cardBoxes
139        JLabel displayLabel = cardboxes.get( card );
140
```

Fig. 24.14 | Blackjack game that uses the Blackjack web service. (Part 3 of 10.)

```
141         // if string representing card is empty, display back of card
142         if ( cardValue.equals( "" ) )
143         {
144             displayLabel.setIcon( new ImageIcon( getClass().getResource(
145                 "/com/deitel/iw3htp4/ch28/blackjackclient/" +
146                 "blackjack_images/cardback.png" ) ) ) ;
147             return;
148         } // end if
149
150         // retrieve the face value of the card
151         String face = cardValue.substring( 0, cardValue.indexOf( " " ) );
152
153         // retrieve the suit of the card
154         String suit =
155             cardValue.substring( cardValue. indexOf( " " ) + 1 );
156
157         char suitLetter; // suit letter used to form image file
158
159         switch ( Integer.parseInt( suit ) )
160         {
161             case 0: // hearts
162                 suitLetter = 'h';
163                 break;
164             case 1: // diamonds
165                 suitLetter = 'd';
166                 break;
167             case 2: // clubs
168                 suitLetter = 'c';
169                 break;
170             default: // spades
171                 suitLetter = 's';
172                 break;
173         } // end switch
174
175         // set image for displayLabel
176         displayLabel.setIcon( new ImageIcon( getClass().getResource(
177             "/com/deitel/iw3htp4/ch28/blackjackclient/blackjack_images/" +
178             face + suitLetter + ".png" ) ) );
179     } // end try
180     catch ( Exception e )
181     {
182         e.printStackTrace();
183     } // end catch
184 } // end method displayCard
185
186 // displays all player cards and shows appropriate message
187 public void gameOver( GameStatus winner )
188 {
189     String[] cards = dealerCards.split( "\t" );
190
191     // display blackjackProxy's cards
192     for ( int i = 0; i < cards.length; i++ )
193         displayCard( i, cards[ i ]);
```

Fig. 24.14 | Blackjack game that uses the Blackjack web service. (Part 4 of 10.)

```
194
195        // display appropriate status image
196        if ( winner == GameStatus.WIN )
197           statusJLabel.setText( "You win!" );
198        else if ( winner == GameStatus.LOSE )
199           statusJLabel.setText( "You lose." );
200        else if ( winner == GameStatus.PUSH )
201           statusJLabel.setText( "It's a push." );
202        else // blackjack
203           statusJLabel.setText( "Blackjack!" );
204
205        // display final scores
206        int dealersTotal = blackjackProxy.getHandValue( dealerCards );
207        int playersTotal = blackjackProxy.getHandValue( playerCards );
208        dealerTotalJLabel.setText( "Dealer: " + dealersTotal );
209        playerTotalJLabel.setText( "Player: " + playersTotal );
210
211        // reset for new game
212        standJButton.setEnabled( false );
213        hitJButton.setEnabled( false );
214        dealJButton.setEnabled( true );
215     } // end method gameOver
216
217     // The initComponents method is autogenerated by Netbeans and is called
218     // from the constructor to initialize the GUI. This method is not shown
219     // here to save space. Open BlackjackGameJFrame.java in this
220     // example's folder to view the complete generated code (lines 221-531)
221
532     // handles standJButton click
533     private void standJButtonActionPerformed(
534        java.awt.event.ActionEvent evt )
535     {
536        standJButton.setEnabled( false );
537        hitJButton.setEnabled( false );
538        dealJButton.setEnabled( true );
539        dealerPlay();
540     } // end method standJButtonActionPerformed
541
542     // handles hitJButton click
543     private void hitJButtonActionPerformed(
544        java.awt.event.ActionEvent evt )
545     {
546        // get player another card
547        String card = blackjackProxy.dealCard(); // deal new card
548        playerCards += "\t" + card; // add card to hand
549
550        // update GUI to display new card
551        displayCard( currentPlayerCard, card );
552        ++currentPlayerCard;
553
554        // determine new value of player's hand
555        int total = blackjackProxy.getHandValue( playerCards );
556
```

Fig. 24.14 | Blackjack game that uses the Blackjack web service. (Part 5 of 10.)

```
557        if ( total > 21 ) // player busts
558            gameOver( GameStatus.LOSE );
559        if ( total == 21 ) // player cannot take any more cards
560        {
561            hitJButton.setEnabled( false );
562            dealerPlay();
563        } // end if
564    } // end method hitJButtonActionPerformed
565
566    // handles dealJButton click
567    private void dealJButtonActionPerformed(
568        java.awt.event.ActionEvent evt )
569    {
570        String card; // stores a card temporarily until it's added to a hand
571
572        // clear card images
573        for ( int i = 0; i < cardboxes.size(); i++ )
574            cardboxes.get( i ).setIcon( null );
575
576        statusJLabel.setText( "" );
577        dealerTotalJLabel.setText( "" );
578        playerTotalJLabel.setText( "" );
579
580        // create a new, shuffled deck on remote machine
581        blackjackProxy.shuffle();
582
583        // deal two cards to player
584        playerCards = blackjackProxy.dealCard(); // add first card to hand
585        displayCard( 11, playerCards ); // display first card
586        card = blackjackProxy.dealCard(); // deal second card
587        displayCard( 12, card ); // display second card
588        playerCards += "\t" + card; // add second card to hand
589
590        // deal two cards to blackjackProxy, but only show first
591        dealerCards = blackjackProxy.dealCard(); // add first card to hand
592        displayCard( 0, dealerCards ); // display first card
593        card = blackjackProxy.dealCard(); // deal second card
594        displayCard( 1, "" ); // display back of card
595        dealerCards += "\t" + card; // add second card to hand
596
597        standJButton.setEnabled( true );
598        hitJButton.setEnabled( true );
599        dealJButton.setEnabled( false );
600
601        // determine the value of the two hands
602        int dealersTotal = blackjackProxy.getHandValue( dealerCards );
603        int playersTotal = blackjackProxy.getHandValue( playerCards );
604
605        // if hands both equal 21, it is a push
606        if ( playersTotal == dealersTotal && playersTotal == 21 )
607            gameOver( GameStatus.PUSH );
608        else if ( dealersTotal == 21 ) // blackjackProxy has blackjack
609            gameOver( GameStatus.LOSE );
```

Fig. 24.14 | Blackjack game that uses the Blackjack web service. (Part 6 of 10.)

```
610        else if ( playersTotal == 21 ) // blackjack
611           gameOver( GameStatus.BLACKJACK );
612
613        // next card for blackjackProxy has index 2
614        currentDealerCard = 2;
615
616        // next card for player has index 13
617        currentPlayerCard = 13;
618     } // end method dealJButtonActionPerformed
619
620     // begins application execution
621     public static void main( String args[] )
622     {
623        java.awt.EventQueue.invokeLater(
624           new Runnable()
625           {
626              public void run()
627              {
628                 new BlackjackGameJFrame().setVisible(true);
629              }
630           }
631        ); // end call to java.awt.EventQueue.invokeLater
632     } // end method main
633
634     // Variables declaration - do not modify
635     private javax.swing.JButton dealJButton;
636     private javax.swing.JLabel dealerCard10JLabel;
637     private javax.swing.JLabel dealerCard11JLabel;
638     private javax.swing.JLabel dealerCard1JLabel;
639     private javax.swing.JLabel dealerCard2JLabel;
640     private javax.swing.JLabel dealerCard3JLabel;
641     private javax.swing.JLabel dealerCard4JLabel;
642     private javax.swing.JLabel dealerCard5JLabel;
643     private javax.swing.JLabel dealerCard6JLabel;
644     private javax.swing.JLabel dealerCard7JLabel;
645     private javax.swing.JLabel dealerCard8JLabel;
646     private javax.swing.JLabel dealerCard9JLabel;
647     private javax.swing.JLabel dealerJLabel;
648     private javax.swing.JLabel dealerTotalJLabel;
649     private javax.swing.JButton hitJButton;
650     private javax.swing.JLabel playerCard10JLabel;
651     private javax.swing.JLabel playerCard11JLabel;
652     private javax.swing.JLabel playerCard1JLabel;
653     private javax.swing.JLabel playerCard2JLabel;
654     private javax.swing.JLabel playerCard3JLabel;
655     private javax.swing.JLabel playerCard4JLabel;
656     private javax.swing.JLabel playerCard5JLabel;
657     private javax.swing.JLabel playerCard6JLabel;
658     private javax.swing.JLabel playerCard7JLabel;
659     private javax.swing.JLabel playerCard8JLabel;
660     private javax.swing.JLabel playerCard9JLabel;
661     private javax.swing.JLabel playerJLabel;
662     private javax.swing.JLabel playerTotalJLabel;
```

Fig. 24.14 | Blackjack game that uses the Blackjack web service. (Part 7 of 10.)

```
663    private javax.swing.JButton standJButton;
664    private javax.swing.JLabel statusJLabel;
665    // End of variables declaration
666 } // end class BlackjackGameJFrame
```

a) Dealer and player hands after the user clicks the **Deal** JButton.

b) Dealer and player hands after the user clicks **Hit** twice, then clicks **Stand**. In this case, the player wins.

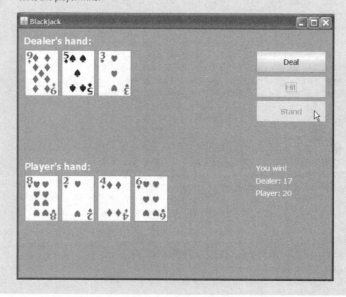

Fig. 24.14 | Blackjack game that uses the Blackjack web service. (Part 8 of 10.)

c) Dealer and player hands after the user clicks **Stand** based on the initial hand. In this case, the player loses.

d) Dealer and player hands after the user is dealt blackjack.

Fig. 24.14 | Blackjack game that uses the `Blackjack` web service. (Part 9 of 10.)

e) Dealer and player hands after the dealer is dealt blackjack.

Fig. 24.14 | Blackjack game that uses the `Blackjack` web service. (Part 10 of 10.)

Method `gameOver` (lines 187–215) displays all the dealer's cards, shows the appropriate message in `statusJLabel` and displays the final point totals of both the dealer and the player. Method `gameOver` receives as an argument a member of the `GameStatus` enumeration (defined in lines 25–31). The enumeration represents whether the player tied, lost or won the game; its four members are PUSH, LOSE, WIN and BLACKJACK.

When the player clicks the **Deal** `JButton`, method `dealJButtonActionPerformed` (lines 567–618) clears all of the `JLabels` that display cards or game status information. Next, the deck is shuffled (line 581), and the player and dealer receive two cards each (lines 584–595). Lines 602–603 then total each hand. If the player and the dealer both obtain scores of 21, the program calls method `gameOver`, passing `GameStatus.PUSH` (line 607). If only the dealer has 21, the program passes `GameStatus.LOSE` to method `gameOver` (line 609). If only the player has 21 after the first two cards are dealt, the program passes `GameStatus.BLACKJACK` to method `gameOver` (line 611).

If `dealJButtonActionPerformed` does not call `gameOver`, the player can take more cards by clicking the **Hit** `JButton`, which calls `hitJButtonActionPerformed` in lines 543–564. Each time a player clicks **Hit**, the program deals the player one more card and displays it in the GUI. If the player exceeds 21, the game is over and the player loses. If the player has exactly 21, the player is not allowed to take any more cards, and method `dealerPlay` (lines 86–131) is called, causing the dealer to take cards until the dealer's hand has a value of 17 or more (lines 98–106). If the dealer exceeds 21, the player wins (line 114); otherwise, the values of the hands are compared, and `gameOver` is called with the appropriate argument (lines 120–125).

Clicking the **Stand** `JButton` indicates that a player does not want to be dealt another card. Method `standJButtonActionPerformed` (lines 533–540) disables the **Hit** and **Stand** buttons, enables the **Deal** button, then calls method `dealerPlay`.

Method displayCard (lines 134–184) updates the GUI to display a newly dealt card. The method takes as arguments an integer index for the JLabel in the ArrayList that must have its image set and a String representing the card. An empty String indicates that we wish to display the card face down. If method displayCard receives a String that's not empty, the program extracts the face and suit from the String and uses this information to display the correct image. The switch statement (lines 159–173) converts the number representing the suit to an integer and assigns the appropriate character to suit-Letter (h for hearts, d for diamonds, c for clubs and s for spades). The character in suit-Letter is used to complete the image's filename (lines 176–178).

In this example, you learned how to set up a web service to support session handling so that you could keep track of each client's session state. You also learned how to indicate from a desktop client application that it wishes to take part in session tracking. You'll now learn how to access a database from a web service and how to consume a web service from a client web application.

24.7 Consuming a Database-Driven Web Service from a Web Application

Our prior examples accessed web services from desktop applications created in Netbeans. However, we can just as easily use them in web applications created with Netbeans. In fact, because web-based businesses are becoming increasingly prevalent, it is common for web applications to consume web services. In this section, we present an airline reservation web service that receives information regarding the type of seat a customer wishes to reserve and makes a reservation if such a seat is available. Later in the section, we present a web application that allows a customer to specify a reservation request, then uses the airline reservation web service to attempt to execute the request.

24.7.1 Configuring Java DB in Netbeans and Creating the Reservation Database

In this example, our web service uses a Reservation database containing a single table named Seats to locate a seat matching a client's request. To build the Reservation database, review the steps presented in Section 23.2.1 for building the AddressBook database. This chapter's examples directory contains a SQL script to build the Seats table and populate it with sample data. The sample data is shown in Fig. 24.15.

Number	Location	Class	Taken
1	Aisle	Economy	0
2	Aisle	Economy	0
3	Aisle	First	0
4	Middle	Economy	0
5	Middle	Economy	0

Fig. 24.15 | Seats table's data. (Part I of 2.)

Number	Location	Class	Taken
6	Middle	First	0
7	Window	Economy	0
8	Window	Economy	0
9	Window	First	0
10	Window	First	0

Fig. 24.15 | Seats table's data. (Part 2 of 2.)

Creating the Reservation Web Service

You can now create a web service that uses the Reservation database (Fig. 24.16). The airline reservation web service has a single web method—reserve (lines 26–78)—which searches the Seats table to locate a seat matching a user's request. The method takes two arguments—a String representing the desired seat type (i.e., "Window", "Middle" or "Aisle") and a String representing the desired class type (i.e., "Economy" or "First"). If it finds an appropriate seat, method reserve updates the database to make the reservation and returns true; otherwise, no reservation is made, and the method returns false. Note that the statements at lines 34–39 and lines 44–48 that query and update the database use objects of JDBC types ResultSet and PreparedStatement.

Software Engineering Observation 24.1

Using PreparedStatements to create SQL statements is highly recommended to secure against so-called SQL injection attacks in which executable code is inserted SQL code. The site www.owasp.org/index.php/Preventing_SQL_Injection_in_Java provides a summary of SQL injection attacks and ways to mitigate against them..

Our database contains four columns—the seat number (i.e., 1–10), the seat type (i.e., Window, Middle or Aisle), the class type (i.e., Economy or First) and a column containing either 1 (true) or 0 (false) to indicate whether the seat is taken. Lines 34–39 retrieve the seat numbers of any available seats matching the requested seat and class type. This statement fills the resultSet with the results of the query

```
SELECT "NUMBER"
FROM "SEATS"
WHERE ("TAKEN" = 0) AND ("TYPE" = type) AND ("CLASS" = class)
```

The parameters *type* and *class* in the query are replaced with values of method reserve's seatType and classType parameters. When you use the Netbeans tools to create a database table and its columns, the Netbeans tools automatically place the table and column names in double quotes. For this reason, you must place the table and column names in double quotes in the SQL statements that interact with the Reservation database.

If resultSet is not empty (i.e., at least one seat is available that matches the selected criteria), the condition in line 42 is true and the web service reserves the first matching seat number. Recall that ResultSet method next returns true if a nonempty row exists, and positions the cursor on that row. We obtain the seat number (line 44) by accessing resultSet's first column (i.e., resultSet.getInt(1)—the first column in the row). Then lines 45–48 configure a PreparedStatement and execute the SQL:

UPDATE "SEATS"
SET "TAKEN" = 1
WHERE ("NUMBER" = *number*)

which marks the seat as taken in the database. The parameter *number* is replaced with the value of seat. Method reserve returns true (line 49) to indicate that the reservation was successful. If there are no matching seats, or if an exception occurred, method reserve returns false (lines 52, 57, 62 and 75) to indicate that no seats matched the user's request.

```java
1   // Fig. 24.16: Reservation.java
2   // Airline reservation web service.
3   package com.deitel.iw3htp4.ch28.reservation;
4
5   import java.sql.Connection;
6   import java.sql.PreparedStatement;
7   import java.sql.DriverManager;
8   import java.sql.ResultSet;
9   import java.sql.SQLException;
10  import javax.jws.WebService;
11  import javax.jws.WebMethod;
12  import javax.jws.WebParam;
13
14  @WebService( name = "Reservation", serviceName = "ReservationService" )
15  public class Reservation
16  {
17     private static final String DATABASE_URL =
18        "jdbc:derby://localhost:1527/Reservation";
19     private static final String USERNAME = "iw3htp4";
20     private static final String PASSWORD = "iw3htp4";
21     private Connection connection;
22     private PreparedStatement lookupSeat;
23     private PreparedStatement reserveSeat;
24
25     // a WebMethod that can reserve a seat
26     @WebMethod( operationName = "reserve" )
27     public boolean reserve( @WebParam( name = "seatType" ) String seatType,
28        @WebParam( name = "classType" ) String classType )
29     {
30        try
31        {
32           connection = DriverManager.getConnection(
33              DATABASE_URL, USERNAME, PASSWORD );
34           lookupSeat = connection.prepareStatement(
35              "SELECT \"NUMBER\" FROM \"SEATS\" WHERE (\"TAKEN\" = 0) " +
36              "AND (\"LOCATION\" = ?) AND (\"CLASS\" = ?)" );
37           lookupSeat.setString( 1, seatType );
38           lookupSeat.setString( 2, classType );
39           ResultSet resultSet = lookupSeat.executeQuery();
```

Fig. 24.16 | Airline reservation web service. (Part I of 2.)

```
40
41          // if requested seat is available, reserve it
42          if ( resultSet.next() )
43          {
44              int seat = resultSet.getInt( 1 );
45              reserveSeat = connection.prepareStatement(
46                  "UPDATE \"SEATS\" SET \"TAKEN\"=1 WHERE \"NUMBER\"=?" );
47              reserveSeat.setInt( 1, seat );
48              reserveSeat.executeUpdate();
49              return true;
50          } // end if
51
52          return false;
53      } // end try
54      catch ( SQLException e )
55      {
56          e.printStackTrace();
57          return false;
58      } // end catch
59      catch ( Exception e )
60      {
61          e.printStackTrace();
62          return false;
63      } // end catch
64      finally
65      {
66          try
67          {
68              lookupSeat.close();
69              reserveSeat.close();
70              connection.close();
71          } // end try
72          catch ( Exception e )
73          {
74              e.printStackTrace();
75              return false;
76          } // end catch
77      } // end finally
78   } // end WebMethod reserve
79 } // end class Reservation
```

Fig. 24.16 | Airline reservation web service. (Part 2 of 2.)

24.7.2 Creating a Web Application to Interact with the Reservation Web Service

This section presents a ReservationClient web application that consumes the Reservation web service. The application allows users to select seats based on class ("Economy" or "First") and location ("Aisle", "Middle" or "Window"), then submit their requests to the airline reservation web service. If the database request is not successful, the application instructs the user to modify the request and try again. The application presented here was built using the techniques presented in Chapters 22–23. We assume that you've already read those chapters, and thus know how to build a web application's GUI, create event handlers and add properties to a web application's session bean (Section 23.2.1).

Reserve.jsp

Reserve.jsp (Fig. 24.17) defines two DropDownLists and a Button. The seatTypeDrop-Down (lines 26–31) displays all the seat types from which users can select. The classType-DropDownList (lines 32–37) provides choices for the class type. Users click the reserveButton (lines 38–42) to submit requests after making selections from the Drop-DownLists. The page also defines three Labels—instructionLabel (lines 22–25) to display instructions, errorLabel (lines 43–47) to display an appropriate message if no seat matching the user's selection is available and successLabel (lines 48–51) to indicate a successful reservation. The page bean file (Fig. 24.18) attaches event handlers to seatType-DropDown, classTypeDropDown and reserveButton.

```
 1   <?xml version="1.0" encoding="UTF-8"?>
 2
 3   <!-- Fig. 24.17 Reserve.jsp -->
 4   <!-- JSP that allows a user to select a seat -->
 5   <jsp:root version="1.2"
 6      xmlns:f="http://java.sun.com/jsf/core"
 7      xmlns:h="http://java.sun.com/jsf/html"
 8      xmlns:jsp="http://java.sun.com/JSP/Page"
 9      xmlns:webuijsf="http://www.sun.com/webui/webuijsf">
10      <jsp:directive.page contentType="text/html;charset=UTF-8"
11         pageEncoding="UTF-8"/>
12      <f:view>
13      <webuijsf:page binding="#{Reserve.page1}" id="page1">
14         <webuijsf:html binding="#{Reserve.html1}" id="html1">
15            <webuijsf:head binding="#{Reserve.head1}" id="head1">
16               <webuijsf:link binding="#{Reserve.link1}" id="link1"
17                  url="/resources/stylesheet.css"/>
18            </webuijsf:head>
19            <webuijsf:body binding="#{Reserve.body1}" id="body1"
20               style="-rave-layout: grid">
21               <webuijsf:form binding="#{Reserve.form1}" id="form1">
22                  <webuijsf:label binding="#{Reserve.instructionLabel}"
23                     id="instructionLabel" style="left: 24px; top: 24px;
24                     position: absolute" text="Please select the seat type
25                     and class to reserve:"/>
26                  <webuijsf:dropDown binding="#{Reserve.seatTypeDropDown}"
27                     id="seatTypeDropDown" items=
28                     "#{Reserve.seatTypeDropDownDefaultOptions.options}"
29                     style="left: 310px; top: 21px; position: absolute"
30                     valueChangeListenerExpression=
31                     "#{Reserve.seatTypeDropDown_processValueChange}"/>
32                  <webuijsf:dropDown binding="#{Reserve.classTypeDropDown}"
33                     id="classTypeDropDown" items=
34                     "#{Reserve.classTypeDropDownDefaultOptions.options}"
35                     style="left: 385px; top: 21px; position: absolute"
36                     valueChangeListenerExpression=
37                     "#{Reserve.classTypeDropDown_processValueChange}"/>
```

Fig. 24.17 | JSP that allows a user to select a seat. (Part 1 of 3.)

```
38                   <webuijsf:button actionExpression=
39                      "#{Reserve.reserveButton_action}" binding=
40                      "#{Reserve.reserveButton}" id="reserveButton" style=
41                      "height: 20px; left: 460px; top: 21px; position:
42                      absolute; width: 100px" text="Reserve"/>
43                   <webuijsf:label binding="#{Reserve.errorLabel}"
44                      id="errorLabel" rendered="false" style="color: red;
45                      left: 24px; top: 48px; position: absolute" text="This
46                      type of seat is not available. Please modify your
47                      request and try again."/>
48                   <webuijsf:label binding="#{Reserve.successLabel}"
49                      id="successLabel" rendered="false" style="left: 24px;
50                      top: 24px; position: absolute"
51                      text="Your reservation has been made. Thank you!"/>
52                </webuijsf:form>
53             </webuijsf:body>
54          </webuijsf:html>
55       </webuijsf:page>
56       </f:view>
57  </jsp:root>
```

a) Selecting a seat:

b) Seat reserved successfully:

c) Attempting to reserve another window seat in economy when there are no such seats available:

Fig. 24.17 | JSP that allows a user to select a seat. (Part 2 of 3.)

d) No seats match the requested seat type and class:

Fig. 24.17 | JSP that allows a user to select a seat. (Part 3 of 3.)

Reserve.java

Figure 24.18 contains the page bean code that provides the logic for Reserve.jsp. As discussed in Section 22.5.2, the class that represents the page's bean extends AbstractPage-Bean. When the user selects a value in one of the DropDownLists, the corresponding event handler—classTypeDropDown_processValueChange (lines 262–267) or seatTypeDropDown_processValueChange (lines 270–275)—is called to set the session properties seatType and classType, which we added to the web application's session bean. The values of these properties are used as the arguments in the call to the web service's reserve method. When the user clicks **Reserve** in the JSP, the event handler reserveButton_action (lines 278–311) executes. Lines 282–284 use the proxy object (created in lines 38–39) to invoke the web service's reserve method, passing the selected seat type and class type as arguments. If reserve returns true, lines 288–293 hide the GUI components in the JSP and display the successLabel (line 292) to thank the user for making a reservation; otherwise, lines 297–302 ensure that the GUI components remain displayed and display the errorLabel (line 302) to notify the user that the requested seat type is not available and instruct the user to try again.

```
 1   // Fig. 24.18: Reserve.java
 2   // Page scope backing bean class for seat reservation client
 3   package com.deitel.iw3htp4.ch28.reservationclient;
 4
 5   import com.sun.rave.web.ui.appbase.AbstractPageBean;
 6   import com.sun.webui.jsf.component.Body;
 7   import com.sun.webui.jsf.component.Button;
 8   import com.sun.webui.jsf.component.DropDown;
 9   import com.sun.webui.jsf.component.Form;
10   import com.sun.webui.jsf.component.Head;
11   import com.sun.webui.jsf.component.Html;
12   import com.sun.webui.jsf.component.Label;
13   import com.sun.webui.jsf.component.Link;
14   import com.sun.webui.jsf.component.Page;
15   import com.sun.webui.jsf.model.SingleSelectOptionsList;
16   import javax.faces.FacesException;
17   import javax.faces.event.ValueChangeEvent;
```

Fig. 24.18 | Page scope backing bean class for seat reservation client. (Part 1 of 3.)

```
18   import reservationservice.ReservationService;
19   import reservationservice.Reservation;
20
21   public class Reserve extends AbstractPageBean
22   {
23      private int __placeholder;
24      private ReservationService reservationService; // reference to service
25      private Reservation reservationServiceProxy; // reference to proxy
26
27      private void _init() throws Exception
28      {
29         seatTypeDropDownDefaultOptions.setOptions(
30            new com.sun.webui.jsf.model.Option[] {
31               new com.sun.webui.jsf.model.Option( "Aisle", "Aisle" ),
32               new com.sun.webui.jsf.model.Option( "Middle", "Middle" ),
33               new com.sun.webui.jsf.model.Option( "Window", "Window" ) } );
34         classTypeDropDownDefaultOptions.setOptions(
35            new com.sun.webui.jsf.model.Option[] {
36               new com.sun.webui.jsf.model.Option( "Economy", "Economy" ),
37               new com.sun.webui.jsf.model.Option( "First", "First" ) } );
38         reservationService = new ReservationService();
39         reservationServiceProxy = reservationService.getReservationPort();
40      } // end method
41
42      // Lines 42-260 of the autogenerated code have been removed to save
43      // space. The complete code is available in this example's folder.
44
261     // store selected class in session bean
262     public void classTypeDropDown_processValueChange(
263        ValueChangeEvent event )
264     {
265        getSessionBean1().setClassType(
266           ( String ) classTypeDropDown.getSelected() );
267     } // end method classTypeDropDown_processValueChange
268
269     // store selected seat type in session bean
270     public void seatTypeDropDown_processValueChange(
271        ValueChangeEvent event )
272     {
273        getSessionBean1().setSeatType(
274           ( String ) seatTypeDropDown.getSelected() );
275     } // end method seatTypeDropDown_processValueChange
276
277     // invoke the web service when the user clicks Reserve button
278     public String reserveButton_action()
279     {
280        try
281        {
282           boolean reserved = reservationServiceProxy.reserve(
283              getSessionBean1().getSeatType(),
284              getSessionBean1().getClassType() );
285
```

Fig. 24.18 | Page scope backing bean class for seat reservation client. (Part 2 of 3.)

```
286            if ( reserved ) // display successLabel; hide all others
287            {
288               instructionLabel.setRendered( false );
289               seatTypeDropDown.setRendered( false );
290               classTypeDropDown.setRendered( false );
291               reserveButton.setRendered( false );
292               successLabel.setRendered( true );
293               errorLabel.setRendered( false );
294            } // end if
295            else // display all but successLabel
296            {
297               instructionLabel.setRendered( true );
298               seatTypeDropDown.setRendered( true );
299               classTypeDropDown.setRendered( true );
300               reserveButton.setRendered( true );
301               successLabel.setRendered( false );
302               errorLabel.setRendered( true );
303            } // end else
304         } // end try
305         catch ( Exception e )
306         {
307            e.printStackTrace();
308         } // end catch
309
310         return null;
311      } // end method reserveButton_action
312   } // end class Reserve
```

Fig. 24.18 | Page scope backing bean class for seat reservation client. (Part 3 of 3.)

24.8 Passing an Object of a User-Defined Type to a Web Service

The web methods we've demonstrated so far each receive and return only primitive values or Strings. Web services also can receive and return objects of user-defined types—known as *custom types*. This section presents an EquationGenerator web service that generates random arithmetic questions of type Equation. The client is a math-tutoring desktop application in which the user selects the type of mathematical question to attempt (addition, subtraction or multiplication) and the skill level of the user—level 1 uses one-digit numbers in each question, level 2 uses two-digit numbers and level 3 uses three-digit numbers. The client passes this information to the web service, which then generates an Equation consisting of random numbers with the proper number of digits. The client application receives the Equation, displays the sample question to the user in a Java application, allows the user to provide an answer and checks the answer to determine whether it is correct.

Serialization of User-Defined Types

We mentioned earlier that all types passed to and from SOAP web services must be supported by SOAP. How, then, can SOAP support a type that is not even created yet? Custom types that are sent to or from a web service are serialized into XML format. This process is referred to as *XML serialization*. The process of serializing objects to XML and deserializing objects from XML is handled for you automatically.

Requirements for User-Defined Types Used with Web Methods

A class that is used to specify parameter or return types in web methods must meet several requirements:

1. It must provide a `public` default or no-argument constructor. When a web service or web service consumer receives an XML serialized object, the JAX-WS 2.0 Framework must be able to call this constructor when deserializing the object (i.e., converting it from XML back to a Java object).

2. Instance variables that should be serialized in XML format must have `public` *set* and *get* methods to access the `private` instance variables (recommended), or the instance variables must be declared `public` (not recommended).

3. Non-public instance variables that should be serialized must provide both *set* and *get* methods (even if they have empty bodies); otherwise, they are not serialized.

Any instance variable that is not serialized simply receives its default value (or the value provided by the no-argument constructor) when an object of the class is deserialized.

Common Programming Error 24.3

A runtime error occurs if an attempt is made to deserialize an object of a class that does not have a default or no-argument constructor.

Defining Class Equation

Figure 24.19 defines class `Equation`. Lines 18–31 define a constructor that takes three arguments—two `int`s representing the left and right operands and a `String` that represents the arithmetic operation to perform. The constructor sets the `leftOperand`, `rightOperand` and `operationType` instance variables, then calculates the appropriate result. The no-argument constructor (lines 13–16) calls the three-argument constructor (lines 18–31) and passes default values. We do not use the no-argument constructor explicitly, but the XML serialization mechanism uses it when objects of this class are deserialized. Because we provide a constructor with parameters, we must explicitly define the no-argument constructor in this class so that objects of the class can be passed to or returned from web methods.

```
1   // Fig. 24.19: Equation.java
2   // Class Equation that contains information about an equation
3   package com.deitel.iw3htp4.generator;
4
5   public class Equation
6   {
7      private int leftOperand;
8      private int rightOperand;
9      private int resultValue;
10     private String operationType;
11
12     // required no-argument constructor
13     public Equation()
14     {
```

Fig. 24.19 | Class `Equation` that stores information about an equation. (Part 1 of 3.)

```
15          this( 0, 0, "+" );
16      } // end no-argument constructor
17
18      public Equation( int leftValue, int rightValue, String type )
19      {
20          leftOperand = leftValue;
21          rightOperand = rightValue;
22          operationType = type;
23
24          //determine resultValue
25          if ( operationType.equals( "+" ) ) // addition
26              resultValue = leftOperand + rightOperand;
27          else if ( operationType.equals( "-" ) ) // subtraction
28              resultValue = leftOperand - rightOperand;
29          else // multiplication
30              resultValue = leftOperand * rightOperand;
31      } // end three argument constructor
32
33      // method that overrides Object.toString()
34      public String toString()
35      {
36          return leftOperand + " " + operationType + " " +
37              rightOperand + " = " + resultValue;
38      } // end method toString
39
40      // returns the left hand side of the equation as a String
41      public String getLeftHandSide()
42      {
43          return leftOperand + " " + operationType + " " + rightOperand;
44      } // end method getLeftHandSide
45
46      // returns the right hand side of the equation as a String
47      public String getRightHandSide()
48      {
49          return "" + resultValue;
50      } // end method getRightHandSide
51
52      // gets the leftOperand
53      public int getLeftOperand()
54      {
55          return leftOperand;
56      } // end method getLeftOperand
57
58      // gets the rightOperand
59      public int getRightOperand()
60      {
61          return rightOperand;
62      } // end method getRightOperand
63
64      // gets the resultValue
65      public int getReturnValue()
66      {
```

Fig. 24.19 | Class Equation that stores information about an equation. (Part 2 of 3.)

```
67        return resultValue;
68     } // end method getResultValue
69
70     // gets the operationType
71     public String getOperationType()
72     {
73        return operationType;
74     } // end method getOperationType
75
76     // required setter
77     public void setLeftHandSide( String value )
78     {
79        // empty body
80     } // end setLeftHandSide
81
82     // required setter
83     public void setRightHandSide( String value )
84     {
85        // empty body
86     } // end setRightHandSide
87
88     // required setter
89     public void setLeftOperand( int value )
90     {
91        // empty body
92     } // end method setLeftOperand
93
94     // required setter
95     public void setRightOperand( int value )
96     {
97        // empty body
98     } // end method setRightOperand
99
100    // required setter
101    public void setReturnValue( int value )
102    {
103       // empty body
104    } // end method setResultOperand
105
106    // required setter
107    public void setOperationType( String value )
108    {
109       // empty body
110    } // end method setOperationType
111 } // end class Equation
```

Fig. 24.19 | Class Equation that stores information about an equation. (Part 3 of 3.)

Class Equation defines methods getLeftHandSide and setLeftHandSide (lines 41–44 and 77–80); getRightHandSide and setRightHandSide (lines 47–50 and 83–86); getLeftOperand and setLeftOperand (lines 53–56 and 89–92); getRightOperand and setRightOperand (lines 59–62 and 95–98); getReturnValue and setReturnValue (lines 65–68 and 101–104); and getOperationType and setOperationType (lines 71–74 and

107–110). The client of the web service does not need to modify the values of the instance variables. However, recall that a property can be serialized only if it has both a *get* and a *set* accessor, or if it is public. So we provided *set* methods with empty bodies for each of the class's instance variables. Method getLeftHandSide (lines 41–44) returns a String representing everything to the left of the equals (=) sign in the equation, and getRightHandSide (lines 47–50) returns a String representing everything to the right of the equals (=) sign. Method getLeftOperand (lines 53–56) returns the integer to the left of the operator, and getRightOperand (lines 59–62) returns the integer to the right of the operator. Method getResultValue (lines 65–68) returns the solution to the equation, and getOperationType (lines 71–74) returns the operator in the equation. The client in this example does not use the rightHandSide property, but we included it so future clients can use it.

Creating the EquationGenerator Web Service
Figure 24.20 presents the EquationGenerator web service, which creates random, customized Equations. This web service contains only method generateEquation (lines 18–31), which takes two parameters—the mathematical operation (one of "+", "-" or "*") and an int representing the difficulty level (1–3).

```java
1   // Fig. 24.20: Generator.java
2   // Web service that generates random equations
3   package com.deitel.iw3htp4.ch28.equationgenerator;
4
5   import java.util.Random;
6   import javax.jws.WebService;
7   import javax.jws.WebMethod;
8   import javax.jws.WebParam;
9
10  @WebService( name = "EquationGenerator",
11     serviceName = "EquationGeneratorService" )
12  public class EquationGenerator
13  {
14     private int minimum;
15     private int maximum;
16
17     // generates a math equation and returns it as an Equation object
18     @WebMethod( operationName = "generateEquation" )
19     public Equation generateEquation(
20        @WebParam( name = "operation" ) String operation,
21        @WebParam( name = "difficulty" ) int difficulty )
22     {
23        minimum = ( int ) Math.pow( 10, difficulty - 1 );
24        maximum = ( int ) Math.pow( 10, difficulty );
25
26        Random randomObject = new Random();
27
28        return new Equation(
29           randomObject.nextInt( maximum - minimum ) + minimum,
30           randomObject.nextInt( maximum - minimum ) + minimum, operation );
31     } // end method generateEquation
32  } // end class EquationGenerator
```

Fig. 24.20 | Web service that generates random equations.

Testing the EquationGenerator Web Service

Figure 24.21 shows the result of testing the EquationGenerator service with the Tester web page. In *Part b* of the figure, note that the web method's return value is XML encoded. However, this example differs from previous ones in that the XML specifies the values for all the data of the returned XML serialized object returned. The proxy class receives this return value and deserializes it into an object of class Equation, then passes it to the client.

Note that an Equation object is *not* being passed between the web service and the client. Rather, the information in the object is being sent as XML-encoded data. Clients created using Java will take the information and create a new Equation object. Clients created on other platforms, however, may use the information differently. Readers creating clients on other platforms should check the web services documentation for the specific platform they are using, to see how their clients may process custom types.

Details of the EquationGenerator Web Service

Let's examine web method generateEquation more closely. Lines 23–24 of Fig. 24.20 define the upper and lower bounds of the random numbers that the method uses to generate an Equation. To set these limits, the program first calls static method pow of class Math— this method raises its first argument to the power of its second argument. Variable minimum's value is determined by raising 10 to a power one less than difficulty (line 23). This calculates the smallest number with difficulty digits. If difficulty is 1, minimum is 1; if difficulty is 2, minimum is 10; and if difficulty is 3, minimum is 100. To calculate the value of maximum (the upper bound for numbers used to form an Equation), the program raises 10 to the power of the specified difficulty argument (line 24). If difficulty is 1, maximum is 10; if difficulty is 2, maximum is 100; and if difficulty is 3, maximum is 1000.

Lines 28–30 create and return a new Equation object consisting of two random numbers and the String operation received by generateEquation. Random method nextInt returns an int that is less than the specified upper bound. generateEquation generates operand values that are greater than or equal to minimum but less than maximum (i.e., a number with difficulty number of digits).

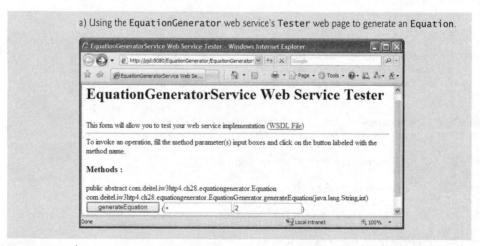

Fig. 24.21 | Testing a web method that returns an XML serialized Equation object. (Part 1 of 2.)

b) Result of generating an `Equation`.

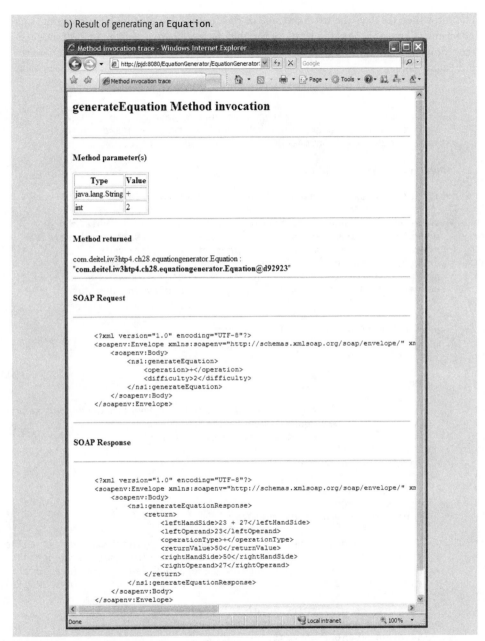

Fig. 24.21 | Testing a web method that returns an XML serialized `Equation` object. (Part 2 of 2.)

Consuming the EquationGenerator Web Service

The **Math Tutor** application (Fig. 24.22) uses the EquationGenerator web service. The application calls the web service's generateEquation method to create an Equation object.

The tutor then displays the left-hand side of the Equation and waits for user input. Line 9 declares a GeneratorService instance variable that we use to obtain an EquationGenerator proxy object. Lines 10–11 declare instance variables of types EquationGenerator and Equation.

```
1    // Fig. 24.22: EquationGeneratorClientJFrame.java
2    // Math tutoring program using web services to generate equations
3    package com.deitel.iw3htp4.ch28.equationgeneratorclient;
4
5    import javax.swing.JOptionPane;
6
7    public class EquationGeneratorClientJFrame extends javax.swing.JFrame
8    {
9       private EquationGeneratorService service; // used to obtain proxy
10      private EquationGenerator proxy; // used to access the web service
11      private Equation equation; // represents an equation
12      private int answer; // the user's answer to the question
13      private String operation = "+"; // mathematical operation +, - or *
14      private int difficulty = 1; // 1, 2 or 3 digits in each number
15
16      // no-argument constructor
17      public EquationGeneratorClientJFrame()
18      {
19         initComponents();
20
21         try
22         {
23            // create the objects for accessing the EquationGenerator service
24            service = new EquationGeneratorService();
25            proxy = service.getEquationGeneratorPort();
26         } // end try
27         catch ( Exception ex )
28         {
29            ex.printStackTrace();
30         } // end catch
31      } // end no-argument constructors
32
33      // The initComponents method is autogenerated by Netbeans and is called
34      // from the constructor to initialize the GUI. This method is not shown
35      // here to save space. Open EquationGeneratorClientJFrame.java in this
36      // example's folder to view the complete generated code (lines 37-156).
37
38      // obtains the difficulty level selected by the user
39      private void levelJComboBoxItemStateChanged(
40         java.awt.event.ItemEvent evt )
41      {
42         // indices start at 0, so add 1 to get the difficulty level
43         difficulty = levelJComboBox.getSelectedIndex() + 1;
44      } // end method levelJComboBoxItemStateChanged
45
```

Fig. 24.22 | Math tutoring application. (Part I of 4.)

```
46    // obtains the mathematical operation selected by the user
47    private void operationJComboBoxItemStateChanged(
48       java.awt.event.ItemEvent evt )
49    {
50       String item = ( String ) operationJComboBox.getSelectedItem();
51
52       if ( item.equals( "Addition" ) )
53          operation = "+"; // user selected addition
54       else if ( item.equals( "Subtraction" ) )
55          operation = "-"; // user selected subtraction
56       else
57          operation = "*"; // user selected multiplication
58    } // end method operationJComboBoxItemStateChanged
59
60    // checks the user's answer
61    private void checkAnswerJButtonActionPerformed(
62       java.awt.event.ActionEvent evt )
63    {
64       if ( answerJTextField.getText().equals( "" ) )
65       {
66          JOptionPane.showMessageDialog(
67             this, "Please enter your answer." );
68       } // end if
69
70       int userAnswer = Integer.parseInt( answerJTextField.getText() );
71
72       if ( userAnswer == answer )
73       {
74          equationJLabel.setText( "" );
75          answerJTextField.setText( "" );
76          checkAnswerJButton.setEnabled( false );
77          JOptionPane.showMessageDialog( this, "Correct! Good Job!",
78             "Correct", JOptionPane.PLAIN_MESSAGE );
79       } // end if
80       else
81       {
82          JOptionPane.showMessageDialog( this, "Incorrect. Try again.",
83             "Incorrect", JOptionPane.PLAIN_MESSAGE );
84       } // end else
85    } // end method checkAnswerJButtonActionPerformed
86
87    // generates a new Equation based on user's selections
88    private void generateJButtonActionPerformed(
89       java.awt.event.ActionEvent evt )
90    {
91       try
92       {
93          equation = proxy.generateEquation( operation, difficulty );
94          answer = equation.getReturnValue();
95          equationJLabel.setText( equation.getLeftHandSide() + " =" );
96          checkAnswerJButton.setEnabled( true );
97       } // end try
```

Fig. 24.22 | Math tutoring application. (Part 2 of 4.)

```
 98          catch ( Exception e )
 99          {
100             e.printStackTrace();
101          } // end catch
102       } // end method generateJButtonActionPerformed
103
104       // begins program execution
105       public static void main( String args[] )
106       {
107          java.awt.EventQueue.invokeLater(
108             new Runnable()
109             {
110                public void run()
111                {
112                   new EquationGeneratorClientJFrame().setVisible( true );
113                } // end method run
114             } // end anonymous inner class
115          ); // end call to java.awt.EventQueue.invokeLater
116       } // end method main
117
118       // Variables declaration - do not modify
119       private javax.swing.JLabel answerJLabel;
120       private javax.swing.JTextField answerJTextField;
121       private javax.swing.JButton checkAnswerJButton;
122       private javax.swing.JLabel equationJLabel;
123       private javax.swing.JButton generateJButton;
124       private javax.swing.JComboBox levelJComboBox;
125       private javax.swing.JLabel levelJLabel;
126       private javax.swing.JComboBox operationJComboBox;
127       private javax.swing.JLabel operationJLabel;
128       private javax.swing.JLabel questionJLabel;
129       // End of variables declaration
130  } // end class EquationGeneratorClientJFrame
```

Fig. 24.22 | Math tutoring application. (Part 3 of 4.)

Fig. 24.22 | Math tutoring application. (Part 4 of 4.)

After displaying an equation, the application waits for the user to enter an answer. The default setting for the difficulty level is **One-digit numbers,** but the user can change this by choosing a level from the **Choose level** JComboBox. Clicking any of the levels invokes levelJComboBoxItemStateChanged (lines 158–163), which sets the variable difficulty to the level selected by the user. Although the default setting for the question type is **Addition,** the user also can change this by selecting an operation from the **Choose operation** JComboBox. Doing so invokes operationJComboBoxItemStateChanged (lines 166–177), which sets the String operation to the appropriate mathematical symbol.

When the user clicks the **Generate Equation** JButton, method generateButtonActionPerformed (lines 207–221) invokes the EquationGenerator web service's generateEquation (line 212) method. After receiving an Equation object from the web service, the handler displays the left-hand side of the equation in equationJLabel (line 214) and enables the checkAnswerJButton so that the user can submit an answer. When the user clicks the **Check Answer** JButton, method checkAnswerJButtonActionPerformed (lines 180–204) determines whether the user provided the correct answer.

24.9 REST-Based Web Services in ASP.NET

[*Note:* This section assumes you already know ASP.NET (Chapter 21).] In this section, we discuss how to build ASP.NET REST-based web services. *Representational State Transfer (REST)* (originally proposed in Roy Thomas Fielding's doctoral dissertation[1]) refers to an architectural style for implementing web services. Though REST is not a standard, RESTful web services are implemented using web standards, such as HTTP, XML and JSON. Each operation in a RESTful web service is easily identified by a unique URL. So, when the server receives a request, it immediately knows what operation to perform. Such web services can be invoked from a program or directly from a web browser by entering the URL in the browser's address field. In some cases, the results of a particular operation may be cached locally by the browser. This can make subsequent requests for the same operation faster by loading the result directly from the browser's cache.[2] Many Web 2.0 web services provide RESTful interfaces.[3]

1. Fielding, R. T. "Architectural Styles and the Design of Network-based Software Architectures." <http://www.ics.uci.edu/~fielding/pubs/dissertation/top.htm>.
2. Costello, R. "REST Tutorial." *xFront*, 26 June 2002 <http://www.xfront.com/REST.html>.
3. Richardson, L. and S. Ruby. *RESTful Web Services*. O'Reilly, 2007.

We use ASP.NET here because it provides a simple way to build REST-based web services. We take advantage of the tools provided in Microsoft's Visual Web Developer 2005 Express, which you can download from msdn.microsoft.com/vstudio/express. The example in this section is the web service that we consumed in our Calendar application from Fig. 13.11 in the Ajax chapter.

24.9.1 REST-Based Web Service Functionality

Figure 24.23 presents the code-behind file for the CalendarSevice web service that you'll build in Section 24.9.2. When creating a web service in Visual Web Developer, you work almost exclusively in the code-behind file. This web service is designed to give the client access to a database of events. A client can access all events that occur on a specific day using the getItemsByDate method or request a specific event using the getItemById method. In addition, the client can modify an event by calling the Save method.

```
 1   ' Fig. 24.23 CalendarService.vb
 2   ' REST-based event web service.
 3   Imports System.Web
 4   Imports System.Web.Services
 5   Imports System.Web.Services.Protocols
 6   Imports System.Data ' Used to access a database
 7   Imports System.Web.Script.Serialization ' Used to return JSON
 8
 9   <WebService(Namespace:="http://www.deitel.com/")> _
10   <WebServiceBinding(ConformsTo:=WsiProfiles.BasicProfile1_1)> _
11   <Global.Microsoft.VisualBasic.CompilerServices.DesignerGenerated()> _
12   Public Class CalendarService
13      Inherits System.Web.Services.WebService
14
15      ' variables used to access the database
16      Private calendarDataSet As New CalendarDataSet()
17      Private eventsTableAdapter As _
18         New CalendarDataSetTableAdapters.EventsTableAdapter()
19
20      ' retrieve the event from the database given an id
21      <WebMethod(Description:="Gets a list of events for a given id.")> _
22      Public Sub getItemById(ByVal id As Integer)
23         ' set up the data set
24         eventsTableAdapter.FillById(calendarDataSet.Events, id)
25
26         ' insert the data into an Item object.
27         Dim identification As String = calendarDataSet.Events(0).ID
28         Dim description As String = calendarDataSet.Events(0).Description
29         Dim itemObject As New Item(identification, description)
30
31         ' convert the data to JSON and send it back to the client
32         Dim serializer As JavaScriptSerializer = New JavaScriptSerializer()
33         Dim response As String = serializer.Serialize(itemObject)
34         HttpContext.Current.Response.Write(response) ' send to client
35      End Sub ' getItemById
36
```

Fig. 24.23 | REST-based event web service. (Part 1 of 2.)

```
37      ' retrieve the list of events that occur on a specific date
38      <WebMethod(Description:="Gets a list of events for a given date.")> _
39      Public Sub getItemsByDate(ByVal eventDate As String)
40          eventsTableAdapter.FillByDate(calendarDataSet.Events, eventDate)
41          Dim identification As String ' string used to store the id
42          Dim description As String ' string used to store the description
43          Dim eventRow As DataRow ' used to iterate over the DataSet
44          Dim length As Integer = calendarDataSet.Events.Rows.Count
45          Dim itemObject As = New Item(0 To length - 1) {} ' initialize array
46          Dim count As Integer = 0
47
48          ' insert the data into an array of Item objects
49          For Each eventRow In calendarDataSet.Events.Rows
50              identification = eventRow.Item("ID")
51              description = eventRow.Item("Description")
52              itemObject(count) = New Item(identification, description)
53              count += 1
54          Next
55
56          ' convert the data to JSON and send it back to the client
57          Dim serializer As New JavaScriptSerializer()
58          Dim response As String = serializer.Serialize(itemObject)
59          HttpContext.Current.Response.Write(response)
60      End Sub ' getItemsByDate
61
62      ' modify the description of the event with the given id
63      <WebMethod(Description:="Updates an event's description.")> _
64      Public Sub Save(ByVal id As String, ByVal descr As String)
65          eventsTableAdapter.UpdateDescription(descr, id)
66          getItemById(id)
67      End Sub ' Save
68  End Class ' CalendarService
```

Fig. 24.23 | REST-based event web service. (Part 2 of 2.)

Lines 3–7 import all the necessary libraries for b. Lines 3–5 are generated by Visual Web Developer for every web service. Line 6 enables us to use capabilities for interacting with databases. Line 7 imports the System.Web.Script.Serialization namespace, which provides tools to convert .NET objects into JSON strings.

Line 9 contains a **WebService** attribute. Attaching this attribute to a web service class indicates that the class implements a web service and allows you to specify the web service's namespace. We specify http://www.deitel.com as the web service's namespace using the WebService attribute's **Namespace** property.

Visual Web Developer places line 10 in all newly created web services. This line indicates that the web service conforms to the *Basic Profile 1.1* (*BP 1.1*) developed by the *Web Services Interoperability Organization* (*WS-I*), a group dedicated to promoting interoperability among web services developed on different platforms with different programming languages. BP 1.1 is a document that defines best practices for various aspects of web service creation and consumption (www.WS-I.org). Setting the **WebServiceBinding** attribute's **ConformsTo** property to **WsiProfiles.BasicProfile1_1** instructs Visual Web Developer to perform its "behind-the-scenes" work, such as generating WSDL file and the ASMX file (which provides access to the web service) in conformance with the guidelines laid out in BP 1.1. For more information on web services interoperability and the Basic Profile 1.1, visit the WS-I web site at www.ws-i.org.

By default, each new web service class created in Visual Web Developer inherits from class System.Web.Services.WebService (line 13). Although a web service need not do this, class WebService provides members that are useful in determining information about the client and the web service itself. All methods in class CalendarService are tagged with the **WebMethod** *attribute* (lines 21, 38 and 63), which exposes a method so that it can be called remotely (similar to Java's @WebMethod annotation that you learned earlier in this chapter).

Accessing the Database

Lines 16–18 create the calendarDataSet and eventsTableAdapter objects that are used to access the database. The classes CalendarDataSet and CalendarDataSetTableAdapter.EventsTableAdapter are created for you when you use Visual Web Developer's **DataSet Designer** to add a DataSet to a project. Section 24.9.3 discusses the steps for this.

Our database has one table called Events containing three columns—the numeric ID of an event, the Date on which the event occurs and the event's Description. Line 24 calls the method FillById, which fills the calendarDataSet with results of the query

```
SELECT      ID, Description
FROM        Events
WHERE       (ID = @id)
```

The parameter @id is replaced with the id that was passed from the client, which we pass as an argument to the FillById method. Lines 27–29 store the results of the query in the variable of class Item, which will be defined shortly. An Item object stores the id and the description of an event. The id and description are obtained by accessing the ID and Description values of the first row of the calendarDataSet.

Line 40 calls the method FillByDate which fills the CalendarDataSet with results of the query

```
SELECT      ID, Description
FROM        Events
WHERE       (Date = @date)
```

The parameter @date is replaced with the eventDate that was passed from the client, which we pass as an argument to the FillByDate method. Lines 49–54 iterate over the rows in the calendarDataSet and store the ID and Description values in an array of Items.

Line 65 calls method UpdateDescription which modifies the database with the UPDATE statement.

```
UPDATE      Events
SET         Description = @descr
WHERE       (ID = @id)
```

The parameters @descr and @id are replaced with arguments passed from the client to the updateDescription method.

Responses Formatted as JSON

The web service uses JSON (discussed in Fig. 13.7) to pass data to the client. To return JSON data, we must first create a class to define objects which will be converted into JSON format. Figure 24.24 defines a simple Item class that contains Description and ID members, and two constructors. The Description and ID are declared as Public members so that Item objects can be properly converted to JSON.

Common Programming Error 24.4

Properties and instance variables that are not public will not be serialized as part of an object's JSON representation.

After the Item objects have been created and initialized with data from the database, lines 33 and 58 in Fig. 24.23 use the JavaScriptSerializer's Serialize method to con-

```vb
1   ' Fig. 24.24 Item.vb
2   ' A simple class to create objects to be converted into JSON format.
3   Imports Microsoft.VisualBasic
4   Public Class Item
5      Private descriptionValue As String ' the item's description
6      Private idValue As String ' the item's id
7
8      ' Default constructor
9      Public Sub New()
10     End Sub 'New
11
12     ' constructor that initializes id and description
13     Public Sub New(ByVal ident As String, ByVal descr As String)
14        id = ident
15        description = descr
16     End Sub 'New
17
18     ' property that encapsulates the description
19     Public Property description() As String
20        Get
21           Return descriptionValue
22        End Get
23        Set(ByVal value As String)
24           descriptionValue = value
25        End Set
26     End Property ' description
27
28     ' Property that encapsulates the id
29     Public Property id() As String
30        Get
31           Return idValue
32        End Get
33        Set(ByVal value As String)
34           idValue = value
35        End Set
36     End Property ' id.
37  End Class ' Item
```

Fig. 24.24 | A simple class to create objects to be converted into JSON format.

vert the objects into JSON strings. Then, lines 34 and 59 obtain a response object for the current client, using the `Current` property of the `HttpContext` object. Then we use this object to write the newly constructed JSON string as part of the response attribute, initiating the server response to the Ajax application in Fig. 13.11. To learn more about JSON visit our JSON Resource Center at www.deitel.com/JSON.

24.9.2 Creating an ASP.NET REST-Based Web Service

We now show you how to create the `CalendarService` web service in Visual Web Developer. In the following steps, you'll create an **ASP.NET Web Service** project that executes on your computer's local IIS web server. Note that when you run this web service on your local computer the Ajax application from Fig. 13.11 can interact with the service only if it is served from your local computer. We discuss this at the end of this section. To create the `CalendarService` web service in Visual Web Developer, perform the following steps:

Step 1: Creating the Project
To begin, use Visual Web Developer create a project of type **ASP.NET Web Service**. Select **File > New Web Site...** to display the **New Web Site** dialog (Fig. 24.25). Select **ASP.NET Web Service** in the **Templates** pane. Select **HTTP** from the **Location** drop-down list to indicate that the files should be placed on a web server. By default, Visual Web Developer indicates that it will place the files on the local machine's IIS web server in a virtual directory named `WebSite` (`http://localhost/WebSite`). Replace the name `WebSite` with `CalendarService` for this example. Next, select **Visual Basic** from the **Language** drop-down list to indicate that you will use Visual Basic to build this web service.

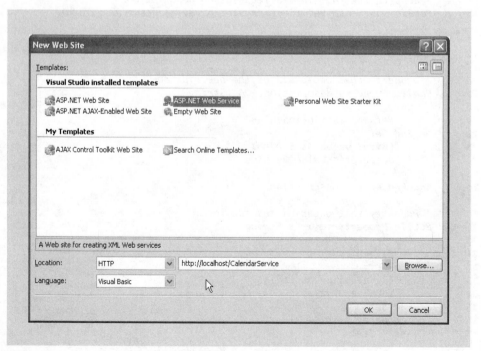

Fig. 24.25 | Creating an **ASP.NET Web Service** in Visual Web Developer

Step 2: Examining the Newly Created Project

After you create the project, you should see the code-behind file `Service.vb`, which contains code for a simple web service (Fig. 24.26). If the code-behind file is not open, it can be opened by double clicking the file in the **App_Code** directory from the **Solution Explorer**. Visual Web Developer includes three `Imports` statements that are helpful for developing web services (lines 1–3). By default, a new code-behind file defines a class named `Service` that is marked with the `WebService` and `WebServiceBinding` attributes (lines 5–6). The class contains a sample web method named `HelloWorld` (lines 11–14). This method is a placeholder that you will replace with your own method(s).

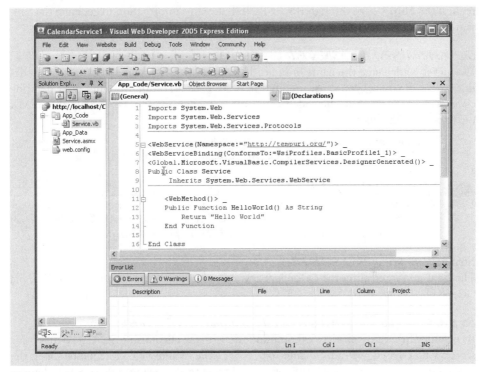

Fig. 24.26 | Code view of a web service.

Step 3: Modifying and Renaming the Code-Behind File

To create the `CalendarService` web service developed in this section, modify `Service.vb` by replacing the sample code provided by Visual Web Developer with the code from the `CalendarService` code-behind file (Fig. 24.23). Then rename the file `CalendarService.vb` (by right clicking the file in the **Solution Explorer** and choosing **Rename**). This code is provided in the examples directory for this chapter. You can download the examples from www.deitel.com/books/ajaxfp/.

Step 4 Creating an Item Class

Select **File > New File...** to display the **Add New Item** dialog. Select **Class** in the **Templates** pane and change the name of the file to `Item.vb`. Then paste the code for `Item.vb` (Fig. 24.24) into the file.

Step 5: Examining the ASMX File

The **Solution Explorer** lists a `Service.asmx` file in addition to the code-behind file. A web service's ASMX page, when accessed through a web browser, displays information about the web service's methods and provides access to the web service's WSDL information. However, if you open the ASMX file on disk, you will see that it actually contains only

```
<%@ WebService Language="vb" CodeBehind="~/App_Code/Service.vb"
Class="Service" %>
```

to indicate the programming language in which the web service's code-behind file is written, the code-behind file's location and the class that defines the web service. When you request the ASMX page through IIS, ASP.NET uses this information to generate the content displayed in the web browser (i.e., the list of web methods and their descriptions).

Step 6: Modifying the ASMX File

Whenever you change the name of the code-behind file or the name of the class that defines the web service, you must modify the ASMX file accordingly. Thus, after defining class `CalendarService` in the code-behind file `CalendarService.vb`, modify the ASMX file to contain the lines

```
<%@ WebService Language="vb" CodeBehind=
"~/App_Code/CalendarService.vb" Class="CalendarService" %>
```

Error-Prevention Tip 24.1

Update the web service's ASMX file appropriately whenever the name of a web service's code-behind file or the class name changes. Visual Web Developer creates the ASMX file, but does not automatically update it when you make changes to other files in the project.

Step 7: Renaming the ASMX File

The final step in creating the `CalendarService` web service is to rename the ASMX file `CalendarService.asmx`.

Step 8: Changing the `Web.Config` File to allow REST requests.

By default ASP.NET web services communicate with the client using SOAP. To make this service REST-based, we must change `web.config` file to allow REST requests. Open the `web.config` file from the **Solution Explorer** and paste the following code as a new element in the `system.web` element.

```
<webServices>
   <protocols>
      <add name="HttpGet"/>
      <add name="HttpPost"/>
   </protocols>
</webServices>
```

Step 9: Adding the `System.Web.Extensions` Reference

The `JavaScriptSerializer` class that we use to generate JSON strings, is part of the Ajax Extensions package. You can find information on installing and downloading ASP.NET Ajax in Section 21.7. After you have installed ASP.NET Ajax, right click the project name in the solution explorer and select **Add Reference...** to display the **Add Reference** window. Select `System.Web.Extensions` from the **.NET** tab and click **OK**.

24.9.3 Adding Data Components to a Web Service

Next, you'll use Visual Web Developer's tools to configure a DataSet that allows our Web service to interact with the Calendar.mdf SQL Server 2005 Express database file. You can download Calendar.mdf with the rest of the code for this example at www.deitel.com/books/ajaxfp. You'll add a new DataSet to the project, then configure the DataSet's TableAdapter using the **TableAdapter Configuration Wizard**. The wizard allows you to select the data source (Calendar.mdf) and to create the SQL statements necessary to support the database operations discussed in Fig. 24.23's description.

Step 1: Adding a DataSet to the Project
Add a DataSet named CalendarDataSet to the project. Right click the **App_Code** folder in the **Solution Explorer** and select **Add New Item...** from the pop-up menu. In the **Add New Item** dialog, select **DataSet**, specify CalendarDataSet.xsd in the **Name** field and click **Add**. This displays the CalendarDataSet in design view and opens the **TableAdapter Configuration Wizard**. When you add a DataSet to a project, the IDE creates appropriate TableAdapter classes for interacting with the database tables.

Step 2: Selecting the Data Source and Creating a Connection
You'll use the **TableAdapter Configuration Wizard** in the next several steps to configure a TableAdapter for manipulating the Events table in the Calendar.mdf database. Now, you must select the database. In the **TableAdapter Configuration Wizard**, click the **New Connection...** button to display the **Add Connection** dialog. In this dialog, specify **Microsoft SQL Server Database File** as the **Data source**, then click the **Browse...** button to display the **Select SQL Server Database File** dialog. Locate Calendar.mdf on your computer, select it and click the **Open** button to return to the **Add Connection** dialog. Click the **Test Connection** button to test the database connection, then click **OK** to return to the **TableAdapter Configuration Wizard**. Click **Next >**, then click **Yes** when you are asked whether you would like to add the file to your project and modify the connection. Click **Next >** to save the connection string in the application configuration file.

Step 3: Opening the Query Builder and Adding the Events Table from Calendar.mdf
You must specify how the TableAdapter will access the database. In this example, you'll use SQL statements, so choose **Use SQL Statements**, then click **Next >**. Click **Query Builder...** to display the **Query Builder** and **Add Table** dialogs. Before building a SQL query, you must specify the table(s) to use in the query. The Calendar.mdf database contains only one table, named Events. Select this table from the **Tables** tab and click **Add**. Click **Close** to close the **Add Table** dialog.

Step 4: Configuring a SELECT Query to Obtain a Specific Event
Now let's create a query which selects an event with a particular ID. Select **ID** and **Description** from the **Events** table at the top of the **Query Builder** dialog. Next, specify the criteria for selecting seats. In the **Filter** column of the **ID** row specify =@id to indicate that this filter value also will be specified as a method argument. The **Query Builder** dialog should now appear as shown in Fig. 24.27. Click **OK** to close the **Query Builder** dialog. Click **Next >** to choose the names of the methods to generate. Name the Fill method FillById. Click the **Finish** button to generate this method.

Fig. 24.27 | **QueryBuilder** dialog specifying a SELECT query that selects an event with a specific ID.

Step 5: Adding Another Query to the EventsTableAdapter for the CalendarDataSet

Now, you'll create an UPDATE query that modifies a description of a specific event. In the design area for the CalendarDataSet, click **EventsTableAdapter** to select it, then right click it and select **Add Query...** to display the **TableAdapter Query Configuration Wizard**. Select **Use SQL Statements** and click **Next >**. Select **Update** as the query type and click **Next >**. Clear the text field and click **Query Builder...** to display the **Query Builder** and **Add Table** dialogs. Then add the Events table as you did in *Step 3* and click **Close** to return to the **Query Builder** dialog.

Step 6: Configuring an UPDATE Statement to Modify a Description of a Specific Event

In the **Query Builder** dialog, select the **Description** column from the **Events** table at the top of the dialog. In the middle of the dialog, place the @descr in the **New Value** column for the **Description** row to indicate that the new description will be specified as an argument to the method that implements this query. In the row below **Description**, select **ID** and specify @id as the **Filter** value to indicate that the ID will be specified as an argument to the method that implements this query. The **Query Builder** dialog should now appear as shown in Fig. 24.28. Click **OK** to return to the **TableAdapter Query Configuration Wizard**. Then click **Next >** to choose the name of the update method. Name the method UpdateDescription, then click **Finish** to close the **TableAdapter Query Configuration Wizard**.

Step 7: Adding a getItemsByDate Query

Using similar techniques to *Steps 5–6*, add a query that selects all events that have a specified date. Name the query FillByDate.

Fig. 24.28 | **QueryBuilder** specifying an UPDATE statement used to modify a description.

Step 8: Testing the Web Service

At this point, you can use the CalendarService.asmx page to test the web service's methods. To do so, select **Start Without Debugging** from the **Debug** menu. Figure 24.29 shows the test page that is displayed for this web service when you run the web service application.

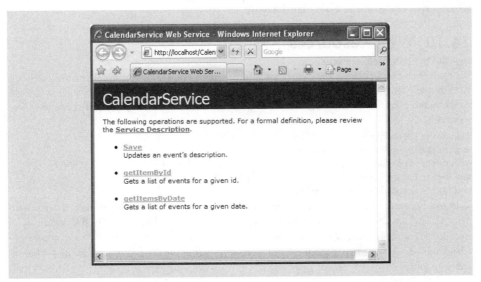

Fig. 24.29 | The test page for the CalendarService web service. (Part 1 of 2.)

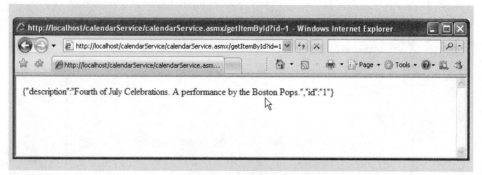

Fig. 24.29 | The test page for the CalendarService web service. (Part 2 of 2.)

Calling a REST-based web service is simpler than calling SOAP web services demonstrated earlier. Fig. 24.29 shows that you can invoke the web service directly from your browser. For example, if you type the URL http://localhost/calendarService/calendarService.asmx/getItemById?id=1 the browser will invoke the method getItemById and retrieve the event with the id value 1.

The client side interface for this application is implemented in the Ajax chapter, in Fig. 13.11. Because our Calendar application uses the Dojo Toolkit, you must have Dojo installed on your computer. Download Dojo 0.4.3 from dojotoolkit.org/downloads, extract the Dojo directory sand rename it to dojo043. Then place the CalendarService folder that contains your web service, the dojo043 folder that contains the Dojo toolkit and the Calendar.html file in the same directory in the root directory of your web server.

Run the web service and direct your browser to the location of the Calendar.html file. We populated the database only with events for July 2007, so the calendar is coded to always display July 2007 when the application is loaded. To test whether the web service works click a few dates like the fourth of July, the sixth of July or the twentieth of July for which events exist in the Calendar database

24.10 Web Resources

www.deitel.com/WebServices/
Visit our Web Services Resource Center for information on designing and implementing web services in many languages, and information about web services offered by companies such as Google, Amazon and eBay. You'll also find many additional Java tools for publishing and consuming web services.

www.deitel.com/java/
www.deitel.com/JavaSE6Mustang/
www.deitel.com/JavaEE5/
www.deitel.com/JavaCertification/
www.deitel.com/JavaDesignPatterns/
Our Java Resource Centers provide Java-specific information, such as books, papers, articles, journals, websites and blogs that cover a broad range of Java topics (including Java web services).

www.deitel.com/ResourceCenters.html
Check out our growing list of Resource Centers on programming, Web 2.0, software and other interesting topics.

`java.sun.com/webservices/jaxws/index.jsp`
The official site for the Sun Java API for XML Web Services (JAX-WS). Includes the API, documentation, tutorials and other useful links.

`www.webservices.org`
Provides industry-related news, articles and resources for web services.

`www-130.ibm.com/developerworks/webservices`
IBM's site for service-oriented architecture (SOA) and web services includes articles, downloads, demos and discussion forums regarding web services technology.

`www.w3.org/TR/wsdl`
Provides extensive documentation on WSDL, including a thorough discussion of web services and related technologies such as XML, SOAP, HTTP and MIME types in the context of WSDL.

`www.w3.org/TR/soap`
Provides extensive documentation on SOAP messages, using SOAP with HTTP and SOAP security issues.

`www.ws-i.org`
The Web Services Interoperability Organization's website provides detailed information regarding building web services based on standards that promote interoperability and true platform independence.

`webservices.xml.com/security`
Articles about web services security and standard security protocols.

REST-Based Web Services

`en.wikipedia.org/wiki/REST`
Wikipedia resource explaining Representational State Transfer (REST).

`www.xfront.com/REST-Web-Services.html`
Article entitled "Building Web Services the REST Way."

`www.ics.uci.edu/~fielding/pubs/dissertation/rest_arch_style.htm`
The dissertation that originally proposed the concept of REST-based services.

`rest.blueoxen.net/cgi-bin/wiki.pl?ShortSummaryOfRest`
A short introduction to REST.

`www.prescod.net/rest`
Links to many REST resources.

Index